37TH CONGRESS, 3d Session. | SENATE. | REP. COM. No. 108.

REPORT

OF

THE JOINT COMMITTEE

ON THE

CONDUCT OF THE WAR.

IN THREE PARTS.

WASHINGTON:
GOVERNMENT PRINTING OFFICE.
1863.

IN THE SENATE OF THE UNITED STATES, *March* 2, 1863.

Resolved, by the Senate of the United States, (the House of Representatives concurring,) That in order to enable the "Joint Committee on the Conduct of the War" to complete their investigations of certain important matters now before them, and which they have not been able to complete, by reason of inability to obtain important witnesses, be authorized to continue their sessions for thirty days after the close of the present Congress, and to place their testimony and reports in the hands of the Secretary of the Senate.

Resolved, further, That the Secretary of the Senate is hereby directed to cause to be printed, of the reports and accompanying testimony of the Committee on the Conduct of the War, 5,000 copies for the use of the Senate, and 10,000 copies for the use of the House of Representatives.

Attest: J. W. FORNEY, *Secretary.*

IN THE HOUSE OF REPRESENTATIVES, *March* 2, 1863.

Resolved, That the House concur in the foregoing resolutions of the Senate to continue the sessions of the "Joint Committee on the Conduct of the War" for thirty days, and to direct the Secretary of the Senate to cause the printing of the reports, &c., with the following amendment: insert at the end the words: "of the present Congress."

Attest: EM. ETHERIDGE, *Clerk.*

IN THE SENATE OF THE UNITED STATES, *March* 2, 1863.

Resolved, That the Senate concur in the foregoing amendment of the House of Representatives to said resolution.

Attest: J. W. FORNEY, *Secretary.*

APRIL 6, 1863.

Mr. WADE, from the Joint Committee on the Conduct of the War, in accordance with the preceding resolution, placed in the hands of the Secretary of the Senate the following report in three parts.

PART 1.—ARMY OF THE POTOMAC.

PART 2.—BULL RUN—BALL'S BLUFF.

PART 3.—WESTERN DEPARTMENT, OR MISSOURI—MISCELLANEOUS.

REPORT

OF THE

JOINT COMMITTEE ON THE CONDUCT OF THE WAR.

PART III.—DEPARTMENT OF THE WEST.

The joint committee on the conduct of the war submit the following report, with the accompanying testimony in relation to the department of the west.

Your committee have been unable to take all the testimony necessary to enable them to present a comprehensive report in relation to the administration of affairs in the department of the west, more particularly while under the command of General John C. Frémont. Compelled to remain in attendance upon Congress during its sessions, they were unable to visit the department in order to take the testimony of witnesses there. And they did not feel willing to call from so great a distance the witnesses whose testimony was necessary to fully elucidate all the facts, as their services were constantly required in the field. Throughout their investigations your committee have strictly adhered to the rule adopted by them from the first, to ask the attendance of those in the military service only when no detriment to the public interests would result from a temporary absence from their commands. When Congress closed its session last summer, many of those who had been most actively engaged in the operations to which your committee desired to direct their attention had been ordered to other parts of the country; some were in Tennessee and Mississippi, some in Arkansas, some in the army of the Potomac, and others in the department of the south under General Hunter. Such testimony as was within reach your committee have taken. But they are fully aware that their investigation upon that subject has been far from complete; and they, therefore, present but a brief report, together with such testimony as they have obtained.

When the rebellion commenced Missouri was one of the most turbulent among those States which the rebel leaders sought to gain over to their cause by the connivance and treachery of the State authorities, and by the presence of armed forces to operate upon the fears of the people. The number of federal troops in that region was very small; a great portion of our troops, stationed in the Territories and at our military posts upon the western frontier, had been basely surrendered by Twiggs to the rebels in Texas. St. Louis, the great commercial emporium of the State, was preserved from falling under rebel control only by the prompt and fearless course pursued by General, then Captain, Lyon, who, not waiting for orders or authority, occupied the United States arsenal, when threatened by the traitor governor of the State, and dispersed the rebel troops who were collected under the specious name of State guards, in a camp of instruction near St. Louis.

The difficulty under which our commanders there labored in obtaining supplies of arms, clothing, &c., for volunteers, was far greater than was felt in any other part of the country. Distant from all the principal depots, at a time when the ability of the government was taxed to the utmost to arm and equip the large number of volunteers called into the field, those who were, from time to time, placed in charge of that department were compelled to act under the greatest disadvantages.

Just previous to the appointment of General Frémont to the command of that department, the state of affairs in Missouri had become very alarming. In every portion of the State the rebel forces had appeared and assumed the offensive; all through the State they were committing their depredations, and Jackson, the governor, had appeared with a large force of troops, furnished by the rebel authorities from Arkansas and Texas, in addition to those he had been able to collect in Missouri. Pillow and other rebel generals had collected a large force from Tennessee, Kentucky, &c., and were threatening the southwestern portion of the State, and Cairo, at the mouth of the Ohio. General Lyon, who was the highest officer in command, after the removal of General Harney, had, with his limited means, been most active, and had taken the field for the purpose of preventing Jackson, with his superior forces, from getting possession of the northern portion of the State.

In July General Frémont was assigned to that command. He proceeded to New York city, where he spent some days, endeavoring to arrange for supplying his department with the arms, &c., which were absolutely requisite. He reached St. Louis on the 25th of July. General Pope, who had been assigned the command in northern Missouri, was calling for troops to enable him to take the field; General Lyon, in the southwestern portion of the State, had been calling for re-enforcements for some time; General Prentiss, at Cairo, was also asking for re-enforcements. General Frémont first re-enforced Cairo, as being the most important point, situated, as it was, at the junction of the Ohio and the Mississippi, and controlling the navigation of those two rivers. The number of troops that he could obtain for that purpose was small; but the enemy were led to believe, by the large number of steamboats that went down from St. Louis, that the re-enforcement was far greater than it really was; and Pillow, who had a force estimated at 12,000 men, was deterred from making the attack he had contemplated.

Cairo being re-enforced, General Frémont at once took steps to send troops to the assistance of General Lyon. The number of the enemy opposed to General Lyon was almost overwhelming. It was supposed by many that he would retire before them until he should meet supports. He himself seems to have contemplated such a movement, for after the affair of Dug Springs he retired to Springfield; and General Sturgis testifies that, at that time, General Lyon expressed his convictions that re-enforcements could not be sent to him.

Upon reaching Springfield, General Lyon halted his forces, and after waiting there some four or five days announced his intention to march out and attack the enemy. What reasons influenced him in forming that determination are not well established by the testimony. Some of the officers have expressed their conviction that he apprehended that the enemy, should he retire further from them, would fall upon his rear and cripple him, or force him to fight a battle under great disadvantages. His brave spirit, doubtless, led him to meet the enemy he had gone so far to reach, and endeavor to inflict such a blow as would lead them not to press very closely upon him. Whatever his reasons may have been, he determined upon the attack. The battle was fought at Wilson's creek, on the 10th of August, and, though the enemy outnumbered our forces four to one, our army was eminently successful.

General Lyon fell, leading on a regiment to the attack. His loss at that time was most deeply felt. Dying as a brave soldier would wish to die, fighting for the cause of his country against those who were seeking its destruction, his example has exercised its influence upon those who have since won the glorious victories which have made our armies in the west so illustrious.

After that battle our forces retired to Rolla, the enemy being so severely punished that they followed only at a distance. At Rolla they were joined by the troops that had been started to their relief, but had been delayed for want of transportation.

In September, Colonel Mulligan, who had been upon an expedition in the northern part of the State, was obliged to fall back before the forces of the enemy advancing against him under General Price. Colonel Mulligan made a stand at Lexington, and prepared to resist them, sending for re-enforcements. General Frémont, upon hearing of Colonel Mulligan's situation, made arrangements to send troops to his assistance; but from various causes they were unable to reach him, and the enemy succeeding in cutting off his supply of water he was compelled to surrender.

Shortly after this, General Frémont determined to take the field in person, with all the forces he could collect together. He was deficient in transportation, so much so that the adjutant general of the army reported to the Secretary of War that General Frémont would be unable to move. He did move, however, and, by the first of November, succeeded in reaching Springfield. The enemy, some 2,000 strong, had been driven from that place by Major Zagoni, who, with barely 100 cavalry, made the most brilliant charge of the war.

Preparations were made to engage the enemy, who were understood to be in force in the immediate neighborhood of Springfield. The day was fixed and the order of the attack determined upon. Just then General Frémont was removed from the command and General Hunter appointed as his successor.

General Hunter testifies that he became satisfied that the enemy were not so near as General Frémont had supposed. He determined, therefore, to withdraw to St. Louis, which was done, and active operations in the State were suspended for some time.

In relation to the administration of General Frémont much has been said about the high prices paid by him for arms and other supplies; the unnecessary fortification of St. Louis; delay in re-enforcing points threatened by the enemy; undue assumption of authority, &c. Your committee can but briefly notice those different points, on account of their inability to obtain full evidence in relation to them.

This much, at least, appears to be established: General Frémont, upon taking the command, was clothed with the most ample authority, and the exigencies of the department were such that much should be pardoned in one compelled to act so promptly, and with so little at his command. Whether that authority was exercised, in all respects, as it should have been—whether General Frémont was justified in all that he did by the circumstances under which he was called upon to act—your committee do not undertake to express a positive opinion.

In relation to the purchase of arms, &c., it appears that the department was very destitute of supplies of all kinds; the demand was most pressing, and the government was unable to supply it. Some of the arms engaged by General Frémont, for the soldiers in his department, were diverted to the army of the Potomac, the primary object of the government then being to collect and equip an army at Washington, as soon as could possibly be done. This rendered it the more important that other arms should be obtained; yet with all that General Frémont deemed it proper to do his department long felt the want of adequate supplies.

In reference to the fortifications about St. Louis, General Frémont but carried out what General Lyon, before him, had deemed necessary. In reference to the manner in which it was done—as the government has had its agents to examine the contracts for that work, as well as other contracts—your committee forbear expressing an opinion.

In regard to re-enforcing promptly those points threatened by the enemy, so far as your committee have the evidence before them, they believe that General Frémont acted with energy and promptness. He was peculiarly situated. The first call—that of General Lyon—was pressed upon him so soon after he took command of the department, and he was compelled to act so hastily, without time for fully surveying the field before him, and ascertaining the extent of the resources at his command, that even if he failed to do all that one under other circumstances might have done, still your committee can discover no cause of censure against him. But in regard to both General Lyon and Colonel Mulligan your committee have discovered no evidence of any disregard for the public interest, or want of energy or inclination upon the part of General Frémont. Troops were collected by him as soon as could be done, and they were promptly sent where the exigencies of the service demanded. Some of them were diverted to other purposes than those for which General Frémont designed them. The government called upon him for troops to be sent to the east at a time when he was most earnestly engaged in procuring forces for the assistance of Colonel Mulligan. Those that were left were sent promptly, and only failed to render the assistance needed from causes over which General Frémont had no control.

General Frémont early turned his attention to the building of gunboats for our western rivers. Whoever is entitled to the credit of originating the idea of employing such means of warfare in that section of country, it is not to be denied that General Frémont perceived the advantage to result from them. Our brilliant victories in the west will bear enduring testimony to the correctness of his judgment in that respect.

But that feature of General Frémont's administration which attracted the most attention at the time, and which will ever be most prominent among the many points of interest connected with the history of that department, is his proclamation of emancipation. Whatever opinion may be entertained in reference to the time when the policy of emancipation should have been inaugurated, or by whose authority it should have been promulgated, there can be no doubt that General Frémont at that early day rightly judged in regard to the most effective means of subduing this rebellion. In proof of that it is only necessary to refer to the fact that his successor, when transferred to another department, issued a proclamation embodying the same principle. And the President, as commander-in-chief of the army and navy, has applied the same principle to all the rebellious States, and few will deny that it must be adhered to until the last vestige of treason and rebellion is destroyed.

The administration of General Frémont was eminently characterized by earnestness, ability, and the most unquestionable loyalty. In the exercise of the almost unlimited power delegated to him, there was no evidence of any tenderness towards treason, or any failure to fully assert the dignity and power of the government of which he was the representative. The manner in which that power was exercised was to be judged by the results, and the policy of continuing him in command was a matter for the authorities above him to determine.

In order to pronounce a final judgment upon all the affairs in the western department, much more information is necessary than is in the possession of your committee. They have undertaken merely to state what seems to be borne out by such testimony as they have been able to obtain.

B. F. WADE, *Chairman.*
Z. CHANDLER.
JOHN COVODE.
GEO. W. JULIAN.

As the testimony which the committee submit in relation to the western department is so incomplete, the testimony of so many witnesses deemed material by the whole committee being wanting, the undersigned decline to concur in the above report, and for themselves prefer to submit the testimony without comment.

D. W. GOOCH.
M. F. ODELL.

TESTIMONY.

WESTERN DEPARTMENT.

WAR DEPARTMENT,
Washington City, D. C., March 12, 1862.

SIR: I have the honor, in compliance with your request of the 28th ultimo, to transmit herewith copies of the following papers, viz:

Report of Adjutant General Thomas upon the Western Department, and

The order discharging the body guard under Major Zagoni.

Very respectfully, your obedient servant,

EDWIN M. STANTON,
Secretary of War.

Hon. B. F. WADE,
Chairman Joint Committee on the conduct of the present war.

HARRISBURG, PA., *October* 19, 1861.

GENERAL: When I did myself the honor to ask you to accompany me on my western tour, it was with the view of availing myself of your experience as adjutant general of the army. Finding that the result of my investigations might (as I at first apprehended) have an important effect not only upon the army of the west, but upon the interests of the whole country, I requested you to take full notes upon all points connected with the object of my visit.

As you inform me that you have carefully complied with my wish, I now respectfully request you to submit your report as early as practicable, in order that the President may be correctly advised as to the administration of affairs connected with the army of the west.

Very respectfully, your obedient servant,

SIMON CAMERON, *Secretary of War.*

Brigadier General L. THOMAS,
Adjutant General of the United States Army.

WASHINGTON, D. C., *October* 21, 1861.

SIR: I have the honor to submit the report requested in your letter of the 19th instant:

We arrived at St. Louis, as you are aware, at 2½ a. m. October 11th. After breakfast, rode to Benton Barracks, above the city. On the street leading to the camp, passed a small fieldwork in course of construction. Found the camp of great extent, with extensive quarters, constructed of rough boards. Much has been said of the large sums expended in their erection; but some one mentioned that General McKinstry, principal quartermaster, who made the disbursements, gave the cost at $15,000. If so, it was judicious. The actual cost should be ascertained. General Curtis was in command. Force present 140 officers, 3,338 men; principally detachments, except the 1st Iowa cavalry, 34 officers, 904 men, having horses, but without equipments.

General Curtis said of General Frémont that he found no difficulty in having access to him, and when he presented business connected with his command it was attended to. General Frémont never consulted him on military matters, nor informed him of his plans. General Curtis remarked that while he would go with freedom to General Scott and express his opinions, he would not dare do so to General Frémont. He deemed General Frémont unequal to the command of an army, and said that he was no more bound by law than by the winds.

After dinner, rode to the arsenal below the city, Captain Callender in charge. The garrison for its protection is under Major Granger, 3d cavalry. But very few arms in hand; a number of heavy guns, designed for gunboats and mortar-boats. The captain is engaged in making ammunition. He said he heard that some person had a contract for making the carriages for these guns; that if so he knew nothing of it; and that it was entirely irregular, he being the proper officer to attend to the case. This, in my opinion, requires investigation. He expected soon to receive funds, and desired them for current purposes. Was fearful, however, that they might be diverted for other payments.

Visited a large hospital not distant from the arsenal, in charge of Assistant Surgeon Bailey, United States army. It was filled with patients, mostly doing well. In fine order and a credit to the service. The doctor had an efficient corps of assistants from the volunteer service, and in addition a number of sisters of charity as nurses. God bless these pure and disinterested women!

Colonel Andrews, chief paymaster, called, and represented irregularities in the pay department, and desired instructions from the Secretary for his government, stating that he was required to make payments and transfers of money contrary to law and regulations. Once, upon objecting to what he conceived an improper payment, he was threatened with confinement by a file of soldiers. He exhibited an order for the transfer of $100,000 to the quartermaster's department, which was irregular. Exhibited abstract of payments by one paymaster (Major Febiger) to 42 persons, appointed by General Frémont, viz: 1 colonel, 3 majors, 8 captains, 15 first lieutenants, 11 second lieutenants, 1 surgeon, 3 assistant surgeons; total, 42. Nineteen of these have appointments as engineers, and entitled to cavalry pay.—(See paper No. 1.) A second abstract of payments was furnished, but not vouched for as reliable, as the paymaster was sick, and is only given to show the excess of officers of rank appointed to the major general's body guard of only 300 men: the commander being a colonel, &c.—(See paper No. 2.) The whole number of irregular appointments made by General Frémont was said by Colonel Andrews to be nearly two hundred.

The following is a copy of one of these appointments:

"HEADQUARTERS WESTERN DEPARTMENT,
"*St. Louis, August* 28, 1861.

"SIR: You are hereby appointed captain of cavalry, to be employed in the land transportation department, and will report for duty at these headquarters.

"J. C. FRÉMONT,
"*Major General Commanding.*

"To Capt. FELIX VOGELE, *Present.*"

(See paper No. 3.)

I also saw a similar appointment given to an individual on General Frémont's staff, as director of music, with the rank and commission of *captain of engineers*. This person was a musician in a theatre in St. Louis. Colonel Andrews was verbally instructed by me not to pay him, the person having presented the two papers and demanded pay. Colonel Andrews also stated that these appointments bore one date, but directed payment, in some cases, a month or more anterior thereto. He was then without funds, except a small amount.

The principal commissary, Captain Haines, had no outstanding debts, and expected funds soon. Major Allen, principal quartermaster, had recently taken charge at St. Louis, but reported great irregularities in his department, and requested special instructions. These he deemed important, as orders were communicated by a variety of persons, in a very irregular manner, requiring disbursements of money. These orders are often verbally given.—(See paper No. 4, asking for instructions.) He was sending, under General Frémont's orders, large amounts of forage from St. Louis to the army at Tipton, where corn was abundant and very cheap. The distance was 160 miles. He gave the indebtedness of the quartermaster's department in St. Louis to be $4,506,309 73.—(See paper No. 5.)

In regard to contracts, without an examination of the accounts it would be difficult to arrive at the facts. It is the expressed belief of many persons that General Frémont has around him, in his staff, persons directly and indirectly concerned in furnishing supplies. The following is a copy of a letter signed by Leonidas Haskell, captain and aide-de-camp. He, though on General Frémont's staff, is said to be a contractor for hay and forage and mules; the person named in his note, Colonel Degraf, being his partner.

"HEADQUARTERS WESTERN DEPARTMENT,
"*Camp Lillis, October* 2, 1861.

"SIR: I am requested by the commanding general to authorize Colonel Degraf to take any hay that has been contracted for by the government, his receipt for the same being all the voucher you require.

"Respectfully yours,

"LEONIDAS HASKELL,
"*Captain and A. D. C.*"

(See Exhibit No. 6.)

What does this mean? Contractors deliver forage *direct* to quartermasters, who issue the same; but here another party steps in, and, if a contractor, or the partner of one, to fill his own contract. This double transaction, it is difficult to suppose, is done without a consideration. The accounts should be examined, and the price paid to Degraf compared with that paid to the contractors whose forage was seized.

This same Captain Haskell, aide-de-camp, was a contractor for mules. He desired Captain Turnley to receive his animals, good, bad, and indifferent, as Captain Turnley said. This he would not do, and stated his prices for different classes, wheel, lead, &c. Besides, he had more mules than he could possibly send to the army. Notwithstanding all this, he received an order to inspect and receive Mr. Haskell's mules as rapidly as possible. Captain Turnley very soon received orders from General Frémont to leave St. Louis and proceed to the interior.—(See paper No. 7, showing his great labor and heavy responsibility.)

By direction of General Meigs, advertisements were made to furnish grain and hay, and contracts made for specific sums—28 cents per bushel for corn, 30 cents for oats, and $17 95 per ton for hay. In face of this, another party at St. Louis, Baird, or Baird & Palmer, (Palmer being of the old firm in California of Palmer, Cook & Co.,) were directed to send to Jefferson City, (where hay and corn abound,) as fast as possible, 100,000 bushels of oats, with a corresponding amount of hay, at 33 cents per bushel for grain, and $19 per ton for hay.—(See paper No. 7—Captain Turnley's letter.)

Captain Edward M. Davis, a member of his staff, received a contract, by the direct order of General Frēmont, for blankets. They were examined by a board of army officers, consisting of Captain Hendershott, 4th artillery, Captain Harris, commissary of subsistence, and Captain Turnley, assistant quartermaster. The blankets were found to be made of cotton, and to be rotten and worthless. Notwithstanding this decision, they were purchased, and given to the sick and wounded soldiers in hospital. These facts can be ascertained from the report of the board or the officers themselves, and the bill of purchase.

Amongst the supplies sent by General Frēmont to the army now in the field may be enumerated 500 half barrels, to carry water, in a country of abundant supply, and 500 tons of ice.

We examined the barracks in course of construction in St. Louis, near and around the private house occupied by him as quarters—the Brant House, rented at $6,000 per annum. These barracks have brick foundations and brick outer walls, weatherboarded, and are sufficient as quarters and stables for 1,000 men. Like those of Camp Benton, these barracks were not built by contract or proposals; they are certainly more expensive and more permanent than the quarters of a temporary army would require; and the exact expense, though perhaps difficult to ascertain, should be discovered.

A pontoon bridge has been thrown across the Ohio river at Paducah. A ferry boat, in a region where such boats are readily procured, would be just as efficient and much less expensive.

Contracts, it will be seen, were given to individuals without resorting to advertisements for bids, as required by law and regulations.

Having received an intimation from another quarter of an impropriety, I called on Captain McKeever, assistant adjutant general, for the facts, which he gave me as follows: One week after the receipt of the President's order modifying General Frémont's proclamation relative to the emancipation of slaves, General Frēmont, by note to Captain McKeever, required him to have 200 copies of the original proclamation and address to the army of same date printed and sent immediately to Ironton, for the use of Major Gavitt, Indiana cavalry, for distribution through the country. Captain McKeever had the copies printed and delivered. The order is as follows:

"Adjutant general will have 200 copies of proclamation of commanding general, dated 30th August, together with address to the army of same date, sent immediately to Ironton for the use of Major Gavitt, Indiana cavalry. Major Gavitt will distribute it through the country.

"J. C. F., *Commanding General.*

"SEPTEMBER 23, 1861.

"A true copy:

"CHAUNCEY McKEEVER,
"*Ass't Adj't Gen'l.*"

We left St. Louis, October 12, for General Frémont's headquarters, at Tipton, 160 miles distant, passing the night at Jefferson City, the capital of Missouri, 125 miles from St. Louis; General Price was in command of the place with a force of 12,000 men. The 8th Iowa was there *en route* for Tipton. At this place there were accumulated a large quantity of forage landed from steamboats, and some wagons and mules for transportation; also the half barrels for carrying water, and a number of mules, which Captain Turnley said he could not get forward, having no control over the transportation by railroad.

Leaving Jefferson City on the 13th, we arrived at Tipton at 9 o'clock a. m. The Secretary of War was called upon by General Frémont, and upon the general's invitation accompanied him to Syracuse, five miles distant, to review the division under General McKinstry, nearly eight thousand strong. This body of troops is said to be the best equipped and best supplied of the whole army. They certainly are, so far as means of transportation are concerned. At Tipton, besides General Frémont and staff, his body-guard, &c., I found part of General Hunter's 1st division, and General Asboth's 4th division.

The force designed to act against Price consists of five divisions, as follows:

First division, Hunter's, at Tipton	9,750
Second division, Pope's, at Georgetown	9,220
Third division, Sigel's, at Sedalia	7,980
Fifth division, Asboth's, at Tipton	6,451
Sixth division, McKinstry's, at Syracuse	5,388
Total	38,789

As soon as I obtained a view of the several encampments at Tipton, I expressed the opinion that the forces there assembled could not be moved, as scarcely any means of transportation were visible. I saw General Hunter, second in command, and conversed freely with him. He stated that there was great confusion, and that Frémont was utterly incompetent; that his own division was greatly scattered, and the force then present defective in many respects; that he required one hundred wagons, yet he was ordered to march that day, and some of his troops were already drawn out on the road. His cavalry regiment (Ellis's) had horses, arms, (indifferent,) but no equipments; had to carry their cartridges in their pockets; consequently, on their first day's march from Jefferson City, in a heavy rain, the cartridges carried about their persons were destroyed. This march to Tipton (thirty-five miles) was made on a miry, heavy earth road parallel to the railroad and but a little distance from it. The troops were directed by General Frémont to march without provisions, knapsacks, and without transportation. A violent rain storm came up, and the troops were exposed to it all night; were without food for twenty-four hours, and when food was received the beef was found to be spoiled.

General Hunter stated that he had just received a written report from one of his colonels, informing him that but twenty out of one hundred of his guns would go off. These were the guns procured by General Frémont in Europe. I may here state that General Sherman, at Louisville, made a similar complaint of the great inferiority of these European arms. He had given the men orders to file down the nipples. In conversation with Colonel Swords, assistant quartermaster general, at Louisville, just from California, he stated that Mr. Selover, who was in Europe with General Frémont, wrote to some friend in San Francisco that his share of the profits of the purchase of these arms was $30,000.

When General Hunter, at Jefferson City, received orders to march to Tipton, he was directed to take forty-one wagons with him, when he had only forty mules, which fact had been duly reported to headquarters. At this time, Colonel Stevenson's 7th Missouri regiment was, without General Hunter's knowledge, taken from him, leaving him, when under marching orders, with only one regiment at Jefferson City fit to take the field.—(See paper No. 9.) General Hunter showed me the order for marching, dated October 10, which he only received the 12th.—(See paper No. 10. See Hunter's reply, showing the great wants of his command, marked No. 11.) The same day the order was changed to one day's march.—(See paper No. 12.)

When General Pope, at Georgetown, twenty-five miles distant, received this order of march, he wrote a private letter to Hunter, which I read. It set forth the utter impossibility of his moving for the want of supplies and transportation, and asked whether General Frémont could mean what he said.

All of the foregoing goes to show the want of military foresight and soldierly judgment on the part of General Frémont, in directing the necessary means for putting and maintaining in the field the forces under his command.

General Hunter stated that, though second in command, he never was consulted by General Frémont, and knew nothing whatever of his intentions. Such a parallel, I venture to assert, cannot be found in the annals of military warfare. I have also been informed that there is not a Missourian on his staff—not a man acquainted, personally, with the topography and physical characteristics of the country or its people.

The failure of General Frémont to re-enforce General Lyon demands brief notice. General Frémont arrived at St. Louis July 26, called thither from New York by telegraph, stating that General Lyon was threatened by 30,000 rebels. At this time General Pope had nine regiments in north Missouri, where the rebels had no embodied force, the confederate forces in the State being those under Price and McCulloch, near Springfield, southwest Missouri, and those under Pillow, Jeff. Thompson and Hardee, in southeast Missouri; two regiments held Rolla, the terminus of the southwestern branch of the Pacific railroad, whilst Jefferson City, Boonesville, Lexington and Kansas City had each a garrison of three or four hundred men, behind intrenchments. Cairo and Bird's Point were fortified and defended with heavy artillery. (Pilot Knob and Cape Girardeau were fortified after General Frémont's arrival.) All these places could be re-enforced by railroad and river from St. Louis and the northwestern States, and could hold out until re-enforced, even if attacked by superior forces. On his arrival in St. Louis, General Frémont was met by Captain Cavender, 1st Missouri, and Major Farrar, aide-de-camp to General Lyon, with statements from the latter, and asking for re-enforcements. Major Phelps, member of Congress from Springfield, Doctor Miller, of Omaha, and many other citizens, having ample means of information, made the same representations and urged the sending of re-enforcements. To Governor Gamble he said: "General Lyon is as strong as any other officer on this line." He failed to strengthen Lyon, and the result, as is well known, was the defeat of that most gallant officer. The two regiments at Rolla should have been pushed forward, and the whole of Pope's nine regiments brought by rail to St. Louis and Rolla, and thence sent to Lyon's force. Any other general, in such an emergency, would have pursued this obvious course.

The battle of Springfield, (or more strictly Wilson's creek,) one of the most desperate ever fought on this continent, took place August 10, when the brave Lyon fell, and the troops, borne down by greatly superior numbers, were obliged to fall back, but unpursued by a badly beaten foe.

General Frémont called four regiments from North Missouri and went with them to Cairo. It is evident that he had no intention of re-enforcing General Lyon, for the two regiments at Rolla, 125 miles only from Springfield, received no orders to march, and were not supplied with transportation, and thirty or forty hired wagons, just returned from Springfield, were discharged at Rolla August 4, seven days before the battle, and returned to St. Louis.

After the news of the battle reached St. Louis, four other regiments were drawn from Pope in North Missouri and sent to Rolla. Better to have called in these troops before the battle, as after the battle the whole revolutionary elements were called forth. The six regiments accomplished nothing, and were not ordered to advance and cover the retreat of Lyon's army, although it was supposed in St. Louis that Price and McCulloch were following it, and that Hardee had moved up to cut off its retreat on the Gasconade.

An advance of these regiments would have enabled the army to retrace its steps, and to beat the forces of Price and McCulloch so badly that they would have been unable to follow our forces in their retreat. It is said that every officer in Lyon's army expected to meet re-enforcements, and to return with them and drive Price and McCulloch from the southwest.

General Hunter arrived at St. Louis from Chicago, called thither on a suggestion from Washington as an adviser. General Frémont submitted to him, for consideration and advice, a paper called "Disposition for retaking Springfield." It sets out out with a statement that Springfield is the strong strategical point of that wide elevation which separates the waters of the Osage from those of the Arkansas; the key to the whole southwestern Missouri, commanding an area of nearly 60,000 miles. Why did not this enter the brain of the major general before the fall of Lyon, and he strain every nerve to hold that important key when in his possession?

General Hunter, in answer to the paper, replied: "Why march on Springfield, where there is no enemy and nothing to take? Let me take the troops and proceed to Lexington," in which direction Price was marching, and where he expected to be joined by 40,000 rebels. Instead of this he was sent to Rolla, without instructions, and remained there until ordered to Jefferson City, still without instructions, and thence to Tipton, where we found him.—(See Exhibit No. 13.)

No steps having been taken by General Frémont to meet Price in the field, he moved forward his line of march, plainly indicating his intention of proceeding to Lexington. When within some thirty-five miles of the place, he remained ten or more days, evidently expecting that some movement would be made against him. None being made, he advanced and, with his much superior force, laid siege to Lexington, defeated by Mulligan with 2,700 men September 12, and captured it the 21st, nine days thereafter.

Now for the facts to show that this catastrophe could have been prevented, and Price's army destroyed before or after that disastrous affair.

Before Price got to Lexington the forces to resist him were as follows: Jefferson City, 5,500; at Rolla, 4,000; along the Hannibal and St. Joseph railroad, about 5,000; western line of Missouri, under Lane, down near Fort Scott, 2,300; Mulligan's force at Lexington, 2,700; a large force in Illinois, along the Mississippi river, and on the Iowa line; outside of St. Louis, some 17,000; in St. Louis, 18,000, but say 10,000.

Hunter's plan, up to Sunday, 22d September, was to concentrate from St. Louis, Jefferson city, and Rolla; also from the Hannibal and St. Joseph railroad, 20,000 men, and relieve Mulligan. He said that if Price was a soldier, Lexington had then fallen, but he could, with energy, be captured with all his baggage and plunder.

The objection that there was no transportation is idle. The railroads and river were at command, and the march from Sedalia was only forty-five miles. The force could, General Hunter supposed, be thrown into Lexington by Thursday, as it appears, before it was taken.

General Frémont ordered Sturgis, in North Missouri, to Lexington, and by crossing the river to re-enforce Mulligan. Sturgis had only 1,100 men, and, on reaching the river opposite the town, found it commanded by Price, and, of course, was compelled to fall back. Hunter's plan of moving these troops was to strike the river at a point below Lexington in our control, cross, and march up to the place. In the interview with General Frémont the question was asked whether any orders had been given to re-enforce Mulligan, and the reply being in the negative, General Hunter suggested orders to Sturgis, and had the order then been given by telegraph, he would have reached the river before Price had taken possession of the north bank and could have crossed. The order was not given until three days after the interview. This loss of time was fatal.

Mulligan was ordered from Jefferson City, then garrisoned with 5,000 troops, with only one regiment, to hold Lexington until he could be relieved. When Lexington fell, Price had 20,000 men, his force receiving daily augmentation from the disaffected in the State. He was permitted to gather much plunder and fall back towards Arkansas unmolested, until we were at Tipton, the 13th October, when the accounts were that he was crossing the Osage. Frémont's order of march was issued to an army of nearly 40,000, many of the regiments badly equipped, with inadequate supplies of ammunition, clothing and transportation. With what prospect, it must be inquired, can General Frémont, under such circumstances, expect to overtake a retreating army, some one hundred miles ahead, with a deep river between?

General Hunter expressed to the Secretary of War his decided opinion that General Frémont was incompetent and unfit for his extensive and important command. This opinion he gave reluctantly, owing to his position as second in command.

The opinion entertained by gentlemen who have approached and observed him is, that he is more fond of the pomp than the stern realities of war; that his mind is incapable of fixed attention or strong concentration; that by his mismanagement of affairs since his arrival in Missouri the State has almost been lost, and that, if he is continued in command, the worst results may be anticipated.

This is the concurrent testimony of a very large number of the most intelligent men in Missouri.

Leaving Tipton on the 13th, we arrived at St. Louis late in the evening, and on the 14th the Secretary of War directed me to issue the following instructions to General Frémont:

"St. Louis, Mo., *October* 14, 1861.

"General: The Secretary of War directs me to communicate the following as his instructions for your government:

"In view of the heavy sums due, especially in the quartermaster's department in this city, amounting to some $4,500,000, it is important that the money which may now be in the hands of the disbursing officers, or be received by them, be applied to the current expenses of your army in Missouri, and these debts to remain unpaid until they can be properly examined and sent to Washington for settlement; the disbursing officers of the army to disburse the funds and not transfer them to irresponsible agents; in other words, those who do not hold commissions from the President, and are not under bonds. All contracts necessary to be made to be made by the disbursing officers. The senior quartermaster here has been verbally instructed by the secretary as above.

"It is deemed unnecessary to erect fieldworks around this city, and you will direct their discontinuance; also those, if any, in course of construction at Jefferson City. In this connexion it is seen that a number of commissions have been given by you. No payments will be made to such officers, except to those whose appointments have been approved by the President. This of course does not apply to the officers with volunteer troops. Colonel

Andrews has been verbally so instructed by the Secretary; also, not to make transfers of funds, except for the purpose of paying the troops.

"The erection of barracks near your quarters in this city to be at once discontinued.

"The Secretary has been informed that the troops of General Lane's command are committing depredations on our friends in western Missouri. Your attention is directed to this, in the expectation that you will apply the corrective.

"Major Allen desires the services of Captain Turnley for a short time, and the Secretary hopes you may find it proper to accede thereto.

"I have the honor to be, very respectfully, your obedient servant,

"L. THOMAS, *Adjutant General.*

"Major General J. C. FRÉMONT,

"*Commanding Department of the West, Tipton, Mo.*"

Instructions were previously given (October 12) to the Hon. James Craig to raise a regiment at St. Joseph, Missouri.

We left St. Louis October 14, and arrived at Indianapolis in the evening. I remained at Indianapolis October 15, and conversed freely with Governor Morton. We found that the State of Indiana had come nobly up to the work of suppressing the rebellion. Fifty-five regiments, with several batteries of artillery, had been raised and equipped; a larger number of troops, in proportion to population, than any other State had sent into the field. The best spirit prevailed, and it was manifest that additional troops could easily be raised.

The governor had established an arsenal, and furnished all the Indiana troops with full supplies of ammunition, including fixed ammunition for their batteries of artillery. This arsenal was visited, and found to be in full operation. It was under the charge of a competent pyrotechnist. Quite a number of females were employed in making cartridges, and I venture to assert that the ammunition is equal to that which is manufactured anywhere else. Governor Morton stated that his funds for this purpose were exhausted; but the Secretary desired him to continue his operations, informing him that the government would pay for what had been furnished to the troops in the field. It is suggested that an officer of ordnance be sent to Indianapolis to inspect the arsenal and ascertain the amount expended in the manufacture of ammunition, with a view to reimbursing the State.

Left Indianapolis October 16 for Louisville, Kentucky, where we arrived at 12½ o'clock p. m., and had an interview with General Sherman, commanding the department of the cumberland. He gave a gloomy picture of affairs in Kentucky, stating that the young men were generally secessionists, and had joined the confederates; while the Union men, the aged, and conservatives, would not enrol themselves to engage in conflict with their relations on the other side. But few regiments could be raised. He said that Buckner was in advance of Green river with a heavy force on the road to Louisville, and an attack might be daily expected, which, with the then force, he would not be able to resist, but that he would fight them. He, as well as citizens of the State, said that the border State of Kentucky must furnish the troops to drive the rebels from the State. His force then consisted of 10,000 troops in advance of Louisville, in camp at Nolin river, and on the Louisville and Nashville railroad, at various points; at Camp Dick Robinson, or acting in conjunction with General Thomas, 9,000; and two regiments at Henderson, on the Ohio, at the mouth of Green river.—(See paper No. 14.) On being asked the question, what force he deemed necessary, he promptly replied, 200,000 men. This conversation occurred in the presence of Mr. Guthrie and General Woods. The Secretary replied that he supposed that the Kentuckians would not, in any number, take up arms to operate against the rebels, but he thought General Sherman over estimated the number and power of the rebel forces; that the government would furnish troops to Kentucky to accomplish the work; that he (the Secretary) was tired of this defensive war, and that the troops must assume the offensive, and carry the war to the firesides of the enemy; that the season for operations in Western Virginia was about over, and that he would take the troops from there and send them to Kentucky; but he begged of General Sherman to assume the offensive, and to keep the rebels hereafter on the defensive. The Secretary desired that the Cumberland Ford and Gap should be siezed, and the East Tennessee and Virginia railroad taken possession of, and the artery that supplied the rebellion east. Complaint was made of the want of arms, and on the question being asked, "What became of the arms we sent to Kentucky?" we were informed by General Sherman that they had passed into the hands of the Home Guards, and could not be recovered; that many were already in the hands of the rebels, and others refused to surrender those in their possession, alleging the desire to use them in defence of their individual homes if invaded. In the hands of individuals, and scattered over the State, these arms are lost to the army in Kentucky. Having ascertained that 6,200 arms had arrived from Europe at Philadelphia, 3,000 were ordered to Governor Morton, who promised to place them immediately in the hands of troops for Kentucky. The remaining 3,200 were sent to General Sherman, at Louisville. Negley's brigade at Pittsburg, 2,800 strong, two companies of the 19th infantry from Indianapolis, the 8th Wisconsin at St. Louis, the 2d regiment of Minnesota volunteers at Pittsburg, and two regiments from Wisconsin, were then ordered to Kentucky, making in all a re-enforcement of about ten thousand men. We left Louisville at 3 o'clock p. m. for Lexington, accompanied by General Sherman and Mr. Guthrie. Remained there a few hours, and proceeded to Cincinnati, arriving at 8 o'clock p. m. At Lexington, also, we found that the opinion existed that the young men of Kentucky had joined the rebels; that no large bodies of troops could be raised in Kentucky, and that the defence of the State must necessarily devolve upon the free States of the west and northwest.

Having accomplished the object of our visit to the west, we left Cincinnati on the 18th and reached Washington on the 21st, having spent the 19th and 20th at Harrisburg.

Respectfully submitted.

L. THOMAS, *Adjutant General.*

Hon. SIMON CAMERON, *Secretary of War.*

[Paper No. 3.]

HEADQUARTERS WESTERN DEPARTMENT,
St. Louis, August 28, 1861.

SIR: You are hereby appointed captain of cavalry, to be employed in the land transport department, and will report for duty at these headquarters.

J. C. FRÉMONT,
Major General Commanding.

To Captain FELIX VOGELI, *Present.*

A true copy:

C. McKEEVER,
Assistant Adjutant General.

[Exhibit No. 6.]

HEADQUARTERS WESTERN DEPARTMENT,
Camp Siller, October 2, 1861.

SIR: I am requested by the commanding general to authorize Colonel Degraf to take any hay that has been contracted for by the government, his receipt for the same being all the voucher you require.

Respectfully, yours,

LEONIDAS HASKILL,
Captain and Aide-de-Camp.

[Paper No. 9.]

HEADQUARTERS FIRST DIVISION,
Jefferson City, Missouri, October 4, 1861.

COLONEL: Your letter of yesterday, ordering me to march this morning, was only received this morning at ten minutes after two. You will see by my report of transportation, sent you on the 2d instant, that for the forty-one wagons in possession of my quartermaster he has only forty mules. It will therefore be impossible for him to take the forty or more wagons agreeably to your order.

Colonel Stevenson, of the 7th Missouri regiment, informs me that he is attached to Colonel Totten's brigade of the fifth division. I must protest, in the strongest terms, against this very unmilitary proceeding of depriving me of the most important part of my command, when under marching orders, without giving me an official notice of the change. Detaching Colonel Stevenson from my division will leave me but one regiment here fit to take the field.

I have the honor to be, very respectfully, your obedient servant,

D. HUNTER,
Major General Commanding 1st Division.

Colonel J. H. EATON,
Acting Assistant Adjutant General,
Headquarters Western Department, Jefferson City.

[Paper No. 10.]

HEADQUARTERS WESTERN DEPARTMENT,
Camp Asboth, Tipton, Mo., October 10, 1861.

GENERAL: The following movements of the several divisions of the army of Western Missouri, under my command, have been decided upon:

Acting Major General Pope, with the forces under his immediate command, will march, by way of Otterville, to Sedalia, and from there by the most direct route to Leesville.

Acting Brigadier General Jefferson C. Davis will start on the 13th of October from Georgetown, by Sedalia, with the troops belonging to General Pope's division, and pursue the same direct road to Leesville, reaching his destination on the 15th instant.

Acting Major General Sigel will start from Sedalia on the 13th, and proceed in three marches by Spring Rock and Cole Camp to Warsaw, which place he will occupy; commence preparations immediately to cross the river the next day, supported by Acting Major General McKinstry's forces, and cross on the 16th at all hazards, if a position can be taken on the right bank under the protection of which a bridge may be built.

Acting Major General McKinstry will start on the 13th, and proceed in four marches, by Florence, How creek and Cole Camp, to Warsaw, where he will co-operate with General Sigel.

Major General Hunter will also start on the 13th instant, and proceed in four marches, by way of Versailles and Minerva, (Hibernia,) to Duroc Ferry.

Acting Major General Asboth will start with his division on the 14th, and march in three days to Cole Camp creek, by way of Wheatland and Hibernia.

Generals Sturgis and Lane are expected to be at the same time in Clinton on our extreme right. You are therefore instructed to commence your march on the day appointed for your troops to move, and proceed according to the directions above laid down.

The state of the roads is such that trains may not unfrequently be delayed, which renders it more than usually necessary that the troops should in all cases have at least one day's rations in their haversacks. The commanders of divisions will also in all cases where possible send forward, in advance of the march, a company of pioneers, protected by cavalry, to repair the bridges and roads wherever impassable.

J. C. FRÈMONT,
Major General Commanding.

Major General HUNTER,
Commanding First Division.

[Paper No. 4.]

QUARTERMASTER'S OFFICE,
St. Louis, Missouri, October 11, 1861.

GENERAL: I take the occasion of the presence of the honorable Secretary of War and yourself to make certain inquiries.

Is it competent for every member of the staff of Major General John C. Frémont to issue orders in the name of the general, directed to me, and involving an expenditure of money?

Am I bound to recognize any other signature than that of Captain McKeever, the regularly-constituted assistant adjutant general of the western department?

I desire to be instructed whether the simple approval of an account by the commanding general carries with it the weight of an *order*.

There are heavy accounts, involving hundreds of thousands of dollars, that have come under my observation, which are approved by Major General John C. Frémont, but in direct terms are not ordered. It is doubtless the intention of the general to order the payment. But as I understand the army regulations and the laws of Congress, an approval is not an order. If I am mistaken in this, I desire to be corrected.

Great latitude is taken in verbal orders. And the general being in the field, I cannot stop to question the authenticity of these orders, and feel it to be my duty to see them executed, although I have not the authority on paper necessary to carry these expenditures through the treasury.

Accounts involving hundreds of thousand of dollars have been presented to me within the few days I have been here, informal, irregular, and not authorized by law or regulations.

No quartermaster who understands his duty can pay this class of accounts without involving himself in irretrievable ruin. I do not mean to say that these accounts are not just, or should not be paid; but as they are outside of the regulations—in other words, extraordinary—they can be adjusted only by *extraordinary* authority.

Some three days ago I telegraphed the quartermaster general, M. C. Meigs, a message; and I give you an extract, from memory: "If the reckless expenditures in this department are not arrested by a stronger arm than mine, the quartermaster's department will be wrecked in Missouri alone."

I have the honor to be, very respectfully, your obedient servant,

ROB'T ALLEN, *Major and Quartermaster.*

General LORENZO THOMAS,
Adjutant General United States Army.

JEFFERSON CITY, MISSOURI, *October* 11, 1861.

GENERAL: In June, 1855, I left St. Louis with seven steamboats, with stores and troops for the Upper Missouri river. I remained there on duty until 1857. I joined General Johnston, and went to Utah. I returned from Utah last winter, on *the first and only* leave of absence I have had in twelve years. While on my way to Washington, in April, I stopped at Harrisburg; and, at the request of Governor Curtin, I remained there to assist in organizing the troops there assembling into camps, and to put their commissariat into order. From there I was on duty constantly, day and night, at various posts—York, Cockeysville, Baltimore, Perrysville, and Annapolis. Finally, about the 20th of July, I was ordered to report to General Frémont. I did so at New York. I was ordered on duty at St. Louis, where I resumed similar labors to those I had been at in the east, and have been on my feet night and day since. A few days ago I received orders to report at this place for duty in the field.

I left all my public accounts open, in an incomplete and exposed condition, on my office table in St. Louis, besides a vast deal of property not turned over. My health is so broken down that *I am not able* longer to stand up. I desire, as an act of simple justice to me, I be allowed to resume the leave of absence I surrendered in April, (it would have expired 15th June,) or else that I be ordered permanently to a post where I can get some rest, and be able to make up and forward to the Treasury Department my public accounts.

Your early reply to this is respectfully requested.

Respectfully,

P. T. TURNLEY, *Assistant Quartermaster.*

General L. THOMAS,
Adjutant General United States.

NOTE.—My unsettled and unadjusted accounts will reach over one million and a half dollars.

[Paper No. 11.]

HEADQUARTERS 1ST DIVISION, WESTERN DEPARTMENT,
Tipton, Missouri, October 12, 1861.

COLONEL: I have received the general's order directing my division to move in the morning. Not one-half of my division has yet reported. Colonel Ellis's cavalry are without ammunition, cartridge-boxes, swords, pistols, and great coats, and many of them are greatly in want of clothing.

The men of the Indiana batteries are in want of great coats, clothing, and ammunition.

Requisitions have been sent in for ambulances, but they have not been furnished. Some of our mules are unshod, and we shall have them lame and unservicable, unless we can be furnished with portable forges and blacksmith's tools. About fifty tents are needed for the division. As we shall have to send our teams back for provisions after four days' march, we should not leave here with less than sixty thousand rations, as we cannot calculate on their return in less than fifteen days to our camp, even if we should remain stationary at the end of our four days' march.

The cavalry regiment has not a wagon; and Colonel Palmer's and Colonel Bland's have neither of them sufficient for their baggage.

To enable us to move efficiently we need at least one hundred wagons, and the ambulances already ordered to be supplied to the division by the general commanding.

I have the honor to be, very respectfully your obedient servant.

D. HUNTER, *Major General Commanding.*

Colonel J. H. EATON,
Acting Assistant Adjutant General,
General Frémont's Headquarters.

[Paper No. 12.]

HEADQUARTERS WESTERN DEPARTMENT,
Camp Asboth near Tipton, Missouri, October 12, 1861.

GENERAL: In complying with the letter of instructions of yesterday, General Frémont directs that you proceed from Tipton for the present, only so far as the first convenient camp ground, for the purpose of bringing your immediate command together and to enable you to organize the better, your means of transportation. Colonel Woods, director of transportation, will confer with you to supply, at the earliest moment practicable, what is deficient. At a distance of two, three, or five miles, your wagons can return to Tipton for what is needed.

Respectfully, your obedient servant,

J. H. EATON, *A. A. A. G.*

Major General D. HUNTER,
Commanding 1st division, Tipton, Missouri.

[Paper No. 7.]

JEFFERSON CITY, *October* 13, 1861.

GENERAL: On the 25th September ultimo, I opened the bids, in my office at St. Louis, made under General Meigs's advertisement for furnishing grain and hay. I made contracts in accordance therewith, and gave notice to contractors of the amount I supposed would be required weekly. A day or two after, another party (a Mr. Baird or Baird & Palmer) in St. Louis informed me they had received an order (per telegraph) from Colonel Woods, or General McKinstry, then at Jefferson City with headquarters, to forward as fast a possible to Jefferson City, one hundred thousand bushels of oats, and a like or corresponding amount of hay. The *contractors* under advertisement objected to this order, because they said *Baird* got 33 cents for grain, and $19 per ton for hay, while contractors got 28 cents for corn, 30 cents for oats, and $17 95 per ton for hay. I then told contractors they *need not* send any forage up the river; or if they did they would be paid the same that Bird was.

About 29th or 30th September, after the headquarters, western department, had left St. Louis, (I being left there highest in *rank* in *my* department but no orders or instructions except the single remark of General Frémont that he wished no delay or obstacle whatever in the forwarding of supplies, &c.,) I was daily and almost hourly called upon by different persons and asked to have their mules inspected. All stated they were turning in mules on Mr. Haskell's account. I called for the contract or order under which Haskell furnished them, but never received any until I received a line from General McKinstry, quartermaster, stating that General Frémont desired me to inspect and receive Mr. Haskell's mules as rapidly as possible. I received mules from Mr. Haskell *only* as they were required to ship off for field service. I received some from other parties in like manner.

I have *good grounds* for believing that *in not* receiving all Mr. Haskell's mules, I gave much offence to him and to his friends. But I believed then, and do yet, that my action was for the best interest of the government.

Respectfully, P. T. TURNLEY,
Assistant Quartermaster.

General L. THOMAS, *Adjutant General United States.*

[Paper No. —.]

DISPOSITION FOR RETAKING SPRINGFIELD.

Springfield, the strategical point of that wide elevation which separates the waters of the Osage from those of the Arkansas river, is the key to the whole southwestern part of Missouri, commanding an area of nearly 60,000 square miles.

Around it is clustered a true and loyal population, large numbers of whom, driven from their homes and firesides, and burning with a desire to revenge their sufferings and recapture their homesteads, are eagerly awaiting the opportunity to join an advancing army.

Not only, therefore, military strategy, but a wise and humane policy, demands the reoccupation of that place.

To effect this in the shortest and speediest way, a combined movement of our troops should be made from Rolla and Jefferson City.

The column from the latter place, moving first, will cross, after two days' marching, the Osage river at Tuscumbia. To prevent delay in crossing, anchors, ropes, pulleys, and other portable necessaries for the construction of raft bridges, should be taken along from Jefferson City.

Upon an appointed day after the passage of the river has been accomplished, the column from Rolla will commence its march, and that place and Tuscumbia being each about one hundred miles from Springfield, in six days the two forces will be able to unite at their destination.

As the lines of march converge upon their approach to Springfield, it will be practicable at Lebanon and Cross Blain (ten miles north of Buffalo) to open communication between the columns. Strong scouting parties will best effect this object, and each body will thus support and assist the other.

The Cole county home guards should occupy Tuscumbia. After the column from Jefferson City had passed that place, a reserve should be left at Linn Creek to cover the rear provision train, while Warsaw, the most important point on the Osage, should be immediately occupied by the home guards of Johnson, Pettis and Benton county, re-enforced by a volunteer regiment and two pieces of artillery.

Rolla, Wanesville, and Lebanon can be occupied upon the withdrawal of the other troops, by regiments of the United States reserve corps from St. Louis, while Jefferson City can be placed in charge of an adequate force of General Sigel's brigade, now under re-organization.

To co-operate with this combined movement, General Lane will be directed to march from Fort Scott, in Kansas, to Springfield, by way of Lamar and Greenville, re-enforced if possible.

The successful execution of this plan puts us in possession of the entire southwesten portion of this State, forces the enemy to retire into Arkansas, and enables us, immediately after the concentration at Springfield, to assume the offensive against that State.

The exhausted condition of the country through which our troops are to pass, renders necessary the most particular attention to the organization and protection of the provision trains; the commencement of cool weather demands additional clothing for the men, and the sad experience of the past warns us to make every necessary preparation to meet their wants.

[Paper No. 14.]

In camp at Nolin river and on the Louisville and Nashville railroad at various points.

6th Indiana, Colonel Crittenden, Nolin river.
29th Indiana, Colonel Miller, Nolin river.
30th Indiana, Colonel Bass, Nolin river.
38th Indiana, Colonel Scribner, Nolin river.
39th Indiana, Colonel Harrison, Nolin river.
32d Indiana, Colonel Willich, New Han.
10th Indiana, Colonel Mansie, Bardstown.
19th Illinois, Colonel Turchin, Lib. Junction.
24th Illinois, Colonel Hecker, Colesburg.
34th Illinois, Colonel Kirk, Nolin river.
15th Ohio, Colonel Dickie, Nolin river.
49th Ohio, Colonel Gibson, Nolin river.
3d Kentucky, Colonel Rousseau, Nolin river.
4th Kentucky, (cavalry,) Colonel Board, Nolin river.
Stone's Kentucky light battery, four pieces, Nolin river.
Cotter's (Ohio) six rifled pieces will be in camp in two or three days at Nolin river.

At Camp Dick Robinson, or acting in conjunction with General Thomas's command.

Two Tennessee regiments, nearly full and nearly ready for service.

Four Kentucky regiments, in same condition as Tennessee regiments; one regiment cavalry.

14th Ohio, Colonel Stedman, Nicholasville.
37th Ohio, Colonel Connell, Nicholasville.
33d Indiana, Colonel Coburne, Camp Dick Robinson.
38th and 35th Ohio, Camp Robinson.
Three batteries of artillery, Ohio.

Four Ohio regiments on line of Covington and Lexington railroad, acting with General Thomas.

37th Indiana, Colonel Crufts, Owensboro'.

Also, three or four Kentucky regiments at Owensboro', under General Crittenden, not full nor ready for the field, but probably 1,500 men could turn out under arms.

HEADQUARTERS DEPARTMENT OF MISSOURI,
St. Louis, November 27, 1861.

Special Orders No. 13.]

* * * * * * * * *

6. Brigadier General Sturgis is hereby directed to muster out of service, to-morrow, the squadron of cavalry known as the Frémont Body-Guard. The chief quartermaster and ordnance officer will direct proper officers to receive and receipt for all property belonging to their respective departments now in possession of the commander of the squadron.

* * * * * * * * *

By order of Major General Halleck.

J. C. KELTON,
Assistant Adjutant General.

ADJUTANT GENERAL'S OFFICE, *March* 4, 1862.

Official.

E. D. TOWNSEND,
Assistant Adjutant General.

[Paper No. —.]

Name.	Rank.	Corps.
Emavic Meizaras	Captain	Frémont Hussars.
——— Kalmanuezze	do	Do.
James Waring	1st lieut. and q. m	Do.
G. W. Ebbert	1st lieutenant	Do.
Thomas W. Cooper	2d lieutenant	Do.
Randolph Blome	Major	Do.
C. Schaffer	Captain	Do.
Charles Casselman	do	Do.
G. E. Waring	Major	Frémont Body-Guard.
Hy. Chas. DeAlma	Colonel	Do.
Charles Zagonge	Captain	Do.
H. S. Newall	2d lieutenant	Do.
Napoleon Westerburg	do	Do.
Louis Vanstein Kiste	Captain	Do.
Daniel Abby	Major	Frémont Rangers.
D. Addone	1st lieutenant	General Frémont's staff.
A. Sacche	Captain	Do.
A. E. Kroger	2d lieutenant	Infantry.
G. Maggner	Chief of	United States artillery.
A. Asboth	Brigadier general	Volunteers.
F. J. White	Capt. and aide-de-camp	General Frémont.
E. W. Davis	Capt. and asst. q. m	Volunteer engineer pioneers.
Anton Geister	Captain	Engineer corps.
Hugh C. Long	do	Independent company vols.
Alex. Silverpare	2d lieutenant	Artillery.
Frank Kappner	Major	Engineers.

[Paper No. 5.]

Turnley	$456, 309 73
Rankin	950, 000 00
McKinstry	2, 500, 000 00
	3, 906, 309 73
Davis	100, 000 00
	4, 006, 309 73
Gunboats, 40 mortar boats	500, 000 00
	4, 506, 309 73

Abstract of payments made by P. M. Febiger, paymaster United States army, for the months of ——.

No. of vouchers.	Date of payment.	To whom paid.	Rank or grade.	Corps.
	From Sept. 23 to Oct. 12, 1861.	John Keis.	1st lieutenant	Missouri sappers and miners, 2d voucher, engineers.
		Chas. Lambecker	2d lieutenant	Engineers.
		Jas. W. Savage	Captain.	A. D. C. to General Frémont.
		George D. Friedlein	1st lieutenant	Engineers.
		Leonard Zwanziger	do.	Do.
		Hans A. De Werthern	do.	Do.
		John Cooper	Assistant surgeon	General Frémont's staff.
		C. S. Verdi	2d lieutenant	Do. do.
		Luigi Viria	do.	Engineers.
		Alfred Davenport	Captain.	General Frémont's staff.
		Charles S. Shelton	Surgeon.	Engineers.
		J. C. Woods	Major	A. D. C. to General Frémont.
		John D. Abey	2d lieutenant	Engineers.
		Joseph Weydenuycr	Captain	Artillery.
		John T. Fiala	Colonel.	General Frémont's staff.
		Edward Linderman	1st lieutenant	Do. do.
		Sebastian Volkner.	do.	Artillery.
		Adolph E. Kroeger.	2d lieutenant	Infantry.
		George Gordan DeLuna Byron.	Captain	Cavalry.
		Richard Flack	1st lieutenant	Pioneers.
		Antony Kilp	do.	Engineers.
		William H. C. Reinke	2d lieutenant	Do.
		Thomas F. Haskell	do.	Do.
		John A. Veith.	do.	Do.
		Charles Zagonyi	Major.	General Frémont's Body-Guard.
		Anton Guster	Captain	Engineers.
		Eben B. Sike	do.	Do.
		Bernhardt Kroeger	2d lieutenant	Infantry.
		John Matthan	do.	Artillery.
		Frederick Brandt	1st lieutenant	Engineers.
		H. C. Long	do.	Do.
		J. R. Muhleman.	2d lieutenant	Missouri sappers and miners.
		Isadore Paulin	1st lieutenant	General Frémont's staff, 1st voucher, Kukel's command.
		Cornelius Fornet	Major.	General Frémont's staff.
		Arden R. Smith	1st lieutenant	Infantry.
		William Hoelke.	do.	Engineers.
		Reinhold Pfenninghausen	Captain	Independent field battery, No. 4.
		E. L. Jones	1st lieutenant	Engineers.
		Arnold Hoeppner	do.	Do.
		Charles Gerick	Assistant surgeon	Independent field battery, No. 4.
		Felix Vogeli	Captain	Cavalry.
		Edmund Boerner	Assistant surgeon	3d regiment United States reserved corps, continued by Gen. Frémont.

WASHINGTON, *January* 9, 1862.

Colonel JOHN B. PLUMMER sworn and examined.

By the chairman:

Question. What is your rank in the army?

Answer. My rank in the old army is that of captain. I am colonel of the 11th regiment of Missouri volunteers.

Question. Where have you served during the present war?

Answer. In Missouri entirely.

Question. Under whose command?

Answer. Under the general command of General Frémont for a portion of the time, and subsequently under the general command of General Halleck; under the immediate command of General Lyon, and also of General Grant, who now commands the district in which my present post is situated.

By Mr. Chandler:

Question. You were in the battle at Springfield?

Answer. Yes, sir.

Question. At what time did you join General Lyon's column; or did you go under his command at that time?

Answer. We arrived in the neighborhood of Springfield—12 miles from Springfield—on the 13th J..ly. I joined General Lyon on Grand river about a week before that time.

Question. You joined him early in July?

Answer. Yes, sir.

Question. You then marched with General Lyon's column to Springfield?

Answer. Yes, sir; after joining him. The column I was with was Major Sturgis's column, that left Kansas City on the 23d of June, and joined General Lyon early in July on Grand river. We proceeded from there to Springfield in pursuit of Price's army. We arrived 12 miles from Springfield on the 23d of July. I remember that date, but not all the others.

Question. Will you give us, as briefiy as may be, the movements of General Lyon's column until the battle of Springfield was fought?

Answer. We lay there from the 13th of July until the 1st of August, waiting for re-enforcements.

Question. What was the strength of your army at that time?

Answer. It was about 5,500, as was stated by General Lyon in a council of war in which I was present. It was about that in round numbers—it fell a little short of that. General Lyon was satisfied that the enemy was too strong to pursue with the force he had, and he waited there for re-enforcements and supplies. He was short of supplies. We commanded the mills for some ten or fifteen miles about, and got flour in that way. The last two weeks of the time before the first of August we were without sugar and coffee, and what we call in the army "small rations," such as beans, rice, &c. We had fresh beef, and salt beef, and bread. On the 1st day of August the army moved in pursuit of Rains, leaving a force in Springfield to guard the train and town. We marched between twenty-five and thirty miles south of Springfield. We had a little skirmish with the enemy the second day out, at a place called Dug Springs, gave them a few shots, and there was a charge of cavalry there. On the morning of the 4th of August General Lyon called a council of war, at which I was present; all the commanding officers of battalions, regiments, and corps were present. I was at the time in command of a battalion of regulars. He stated to the council our force; that we had no rations—we knew before that we were out of small rations; that we had only about one day's ration of bread; that we would necessarily lose the command of the mills where we had obtained supplies of bread if we moved on; we would be reduced to salt and fresh beef, of which we could get a sufficient quantity; and that Rains had been retreating before us, apparently luring us on. The question he proposed to the council was whether we would pursue further, or fall back upon Springfield and wait for re-enforcements and supplies, or after we got back to Springfield act according to circumstances. The unanimous vote of the council was that we should fall back; that as we had no supplies it would be folly for us to pursue Rains further, who was retreating before us constantly. General Lyon stated the force of the enemy to be about 15,000 men, as near as he could ascertain from his spies, which, I would remark here, fell far short of their actual numbers.

Question. Was this council of war at Dug Springs?

Answer. It was beyond Dug Springs. We went one day's march beyond Dug Springs. We commenced the march back, and I think we arrived at

Springfield either on the morning of the fifth or the sixth. We commenced the march back on the fourth. I have been trying to recall whether we were two days or three days in making our march back, but I will not be positive. The enemy, at the same time, were moving on a different road south of us towards Springfield.. I commanded the rear guard of six companies the day of our starting back, and I could see the dust raised by the enemy's troops three or four miles on our left. They were evidently moving up towards Springfield on another road. I think it was the morning of the fifth that we reached Springfield. The question then arose, that morning, whether we would remain at Springfield and defend ourselves until we received re-enforcements, or whether we would continue our retreat right on towards Rolla or towards Fort Scott. Arriving at Springfield tolerably early—about 10 o'clock in the morning—we could have made some ten or fifteen miles further that day. General Lyon consulted several officers in regard to that—among the number was myself. Those whom he had known intimately he consulted. There were a great many prominent citizens of the neighborhood came around him, good Union people, urging him to remain. My own opinion was that we ought to remain a few days. We could defend ourselves; or, at least, we did not anticipate an immediate attack, probably not in four or five days. But my opinion was that we should wait at least two or three days for re-enforcements. He stated that he had repeatedly written for re-enforcements and was not expecting any. That he stated in the first council. He made the remark to me—on one occasion in private conversation—that he had written and telegraphed for re-enforcements; that he was aware that regiments had been sent out of Missouri after he had applied for re-enforcements, for what reason he did not know. And he did not know why he had not received any re-enforcements. Whether that be the case or not, I cannot say. I merely state what he said in conversation with me.

By the chairman:

Question. Did he say where they had been sent?

Answer. No, sir. Only they had been sent out of Missouri. The day we returned to Springfield our troops remained under arms, and waited some three or four hours while this matter was being considered. After the consultation was concluded in regard to our movements, General Lyon ordered the troops into camp; a decision which I believe was approved by all the officers. We lay there until the evening of the 9th, making one or two lit-excursions out during the time in pursuit of detached parties of the enemy. I think about that time we received a few wagon loads of supplies from Rolla, which gave us some five or six days rations. On the afternoon of the 9th we received marching orders.

In the conversations of General Lyon with his officers the only questions that arose were, whether we should intrench ourselves at Springfield and wait for re-enforcements, or retreat upon Rolla; or rather, if we retreated, whether we would retreat upon Rolla or upon Fort Scott, the distance to each place being about the same. Fort Scott lay just on the other side of the Missouri line, in Kansas: Rolla was at the end of a railroad. The determination to fight the battle of Springfield was his own—at least he did not consult me. I do not know whether he consulted other officers or not. But I would remark here, that I was afterwards notified that General Lyon adopted the wisest course. We had a valuable train, estimated at over half a million of dollars. There was aboard that train between $200,000 and $250,000 in specie. Had we retreated at once upon Rolla we would probably have had to fight every day on our retreat. It was a bad road of 110 miles, and being encumbered with a very large train our retreat might have resulted in the loss of a large portion of that train. To have intrenched ourselves in Springfield, being in doubt whether or not we should get any re-enforcements, and being in want of provisions, was a matter of perhaps rather doubtful policy.

On the afternoon of the 9th of August we marched out to fight the enemy. I do not think that General Lyon was aware of their real strength. He estimated them at 15,000 men. Our force with which we left Springfield was about 4,800 men. We had about 5,500 men there; but we had to leave a guard for the train in town, and then there were many of the men sick, and on extra duty, &c., which reduced our marching force to about 4,800. Of that number General Sigel had about 1,500: the two German regiments, one battery of artillery, and a squadron of cavalry. And in the consideration of the battle itself, General Sigel's force should be thrown out entirely, because his whole force was dispersed and his battery captured within a half an hour after the fight commenced. So that the battle itself was fought with about from 3,300 to 3,500 men against 23,000; for we ascertained afterward that to have been their numbers. Of our forces there were seven companies of regular infantry, and two batteries of artillery—I suppose altogether not over 600 regulars—and the rest were volunteers: the two Kansas regiments, the 1st Missouri, and the 2d Iowa, whose time had expired at that time.

I have but little more to say in regard to the battle, except that we whipped them. I was with my battalion in the advance that morning; we marched out the night before, and just laid down in the bushes about 12 or 1 o'clock. It rained upon us, and we had nothing to eat the next morning. I think very few of us had anything to eat that day—at least I did not. The battle commenced about 5 o'clock in the morning. It was a complete surprise; we surprised their camps. I drove in one of their pickets not more than a half a mile from their camp, and they had not even time to give the alarm in the camp before our guns opened upon them. The battle lasted from 5 o'clock until about half-past 11. They came up four distinct times to attack us, bringing up fresh troops each time.

By Mr. Chandler:

Question. Each time in force?

Answer. Yes, sir; each time in force, bringing up fresh troops.

By the chairman:

Question. Why did General Lyon pursue Rains when you first started if he had not a force sufficient?

Answer. McCulloch and Rains had not united, and the object was to prevent their doing so.

By Mr. Chandler:

Question. Will you give us the particulars of that fight?

Answer. I cannot particularize it. I was on the left myself, and carried forward the left attack. I was separated, with my battalion, from the main portion of the army by a creek. I was a quarter or a half a mile from the main portion of our army. I fought, for upwards of an hour, with 250 regulars, over 2,000 of the enemy, and was forced to retreat. I was severely wounded, and in the course of an hour and a half was myself in an ambulance.

Question. You did not see the latter part of the action?

Answer. No, sir. I can only state what officers have told me. My battalion was saved by Dubois's battery on that occasion. I found that I had overwhelming forces against me, and that my left flank was going to be turned. I had a creek behind me, with a dense chapparal bordering it on both sides, which was almost impenetrable except in one or two places. I came to the conclusion to fall back. I lost 49 men, in the course of an hour, out of 250.

Question Can yon state the casualties in our army?

Answer. I have Major Sturgis's official report. The casualties I can state to be over 1,200—I think over 1,300 killed and wounded. There were not certainly over 3,500 men of ours in action in the first place.

Question. Can you give a description of those four charges of the enemy from hearsay; that is, from the accounts of the officers engaged; particularly the last one?

Answer. I do not know that I could give you a description of it. I have heard officers speak of it; but in ordinary conversation each one describes the particular part of the field where he was himself; and it requires considerable reflection to put those different things together—to connect properly the different incidents in the different parts of the field.

Question. I will say that Major Schofield stated to me that after the last repulse it was a perfect rout; that the enemy fled in the wildest confusion.

Answer. Yes, sir; everybody says that.

Question. And he also stated that in attempting to ride forward to reconnoitre and see where the enemy were, their dead was piled up so thick that he could not ride over them, but had to make a considerable detour.

Answer. There was a flag of truce sent out after our return to Springfield, as I heard. A young doctor of the army went out with it, with a few men and some wagons, to obtain the body of General Lyon, and to look for our wounded left on the field. He told me that General McCulloch remarked to a non-commissioned officer—a sergeant—who attended the party, "Your loss was very great, but ours was four times yours;" and I think it but a fair estimate to put their loss at least as high as four thousand men killed and wounded.

Question. After this battle you retired?

Answer. Yes, sir.

Question. Can you give us the particulars of that retreat?

Answer. No, sir; except from hearsay.

Question. It was conducted in good order, and you were not pursued?

Answer. Yes, sir; we were not pursued. The fact was the enemy was completely crippled. We gained everything that General Lyon proposed to gain.

Question. How many additional troops, in your estimation, would have given you a victory and enabled you to have driven the enemy out of Missouri?

Answer. My opinion is that our victory would have been perfect and complete with two additional regiments. They were running at the time. They burned their trains—we saw them burning—so that they should not fall into our hands. They did not burn the whole, but what they could conveniently. If we had known it, we could have held the field as it was, for afterwards we heard that they were out of ammunition; that is, they had but a few rounds left.

By the chairman:

Question. How long did General Lyon wait at Springfield before he undertook his expedition against Rains?

Answer. He waited from the 13th of July till the 1st of August.

Question. Still his army was inferior to that of the enemy?

Answer. Constantly inferior.

Question. Vastly inferior?

Answer. Yes, sir; vastly inferior.

Question. Why did he advance upon a foe so much his superior?

Answer. The object of his advance I suppose was this: he had whipped the enemy at Boonville and pursued Jackson. Following him up, he was joined by the force at Kansas City and Leavenworth, with which detachment I was. His object was to overtake this force, whip them, and capture them or crush them out. But they, in retreating towards the Arkansas line, were constantly being re-enforced. When he commenced his pursuit they were not so far superior to his forces as they were afterwards. If he could have overtaken them on the Osage or the Grand river, he could have whipped them and captured them. That was his object. The reason why he did not do that was on account of the high water. The enemy burned the bridges as they fled, and it had rained incessantly for several days, and the whole country was flooded. We had to lay by two or three days at a time to get across the streams. In the mean time the enemy was re-enforced with Arkansas, Tennessee, Mississippi, Louisiana, and Texas troops. They had troops from all those States.

Question. How long after you joined him at Springfield did he start on this expedition?

Answer. I joined him about a week before we reached Springfield.

Question. If I understand you, at the time he started upon that expedition the enemy's force was not so much superior to his own?

Answer. No, sir; he was pursuing the same force that he whipped at Boonville. Then there was a force that lay near Kansas City that joined Price afterwards.

Question. Why did he wait so long for re-enforcements before he started on this expedition?

Answer. He did not wait for re-enforcements at that time. He was delayed some three or four days getting transportation for his troops.

Question. He was not waiting for re-enforcements?

Answer. No, sir; not at all. He only waited for re-enforcements after he reached Springfield, and found out what their strength was. Then, instead of advancing upon them, he waited for re-enforcements. The little advance that he made on the 1st of August was because he had an idea that he could divide their forces and whip them in detail. They had not united then. Rains had a separate column, Price had another, and McCulloch was coming up with re-enforcements. But at that time they were superior, very much superior, to our forces. I mean when we reached Springfield.

Question. They were much your superior then?

Answer. Yes, sir.

Question. Then why did he pursue from Springfield a force so much his superior?

Answer. He pursued there to attack a separate column. He was going to adopt the idea of Napoleon to whip his enemy in detail, thinking he could overtake Rains and whip his forces, and thus cripple them. But they were all united at the battle of Springfield—Rains, Price, and McCulloch.

Question. Did I understand you that he did not wait for re-enforcements at Springfield; and if not, where did he wait for them?

Answer. He waited at Springfield for them.

Question. I asked you, first, why, when the enemy had a superior force, he started on this expedition, for I understood you to say, just before that, that the force of the enemy was vastly superior to that of General Lyon. I understood you to say that the force was not so much superior when he started on the expedition, but it accumulated on the way.

Answer. I misunderstood you. When you referred to the starting of the expedition, I thought you referred to his starting from Boonville.

Question. I was trying to get at this. He had been waiting for re-enforcements at Springfield which he did not get. I wanted to know why, with an inferior force, he set out on the expedition from Springfield against the enemy?

Answer. I will explain that as I understand it. General Lyon was aware that the combined forces of the enemy were vastly superior to ours. He stated in the council of war that they had 15,000 men—about three to our one. But he had his spies out, who gave him an idea where each column of the enemy was. There were re-enforcements for the enemy coming up which were within striking distance of there. When General Lyon marched from Springfield he marched out in pursuit of Rains and his one detachment of the enemy's forces, thinking he could overtake him and whip him before the others could come up. But Rains retreated, drawing us on, and as they were pursuing the road which led them towards Springfield, we fell back upon Springfield, because we could not abandon that place and our baggage trains and supplies. I am speaking now of the expedition from Springfield of the 1st of August. We returned, I think, on the morning of the 5th of August.

Question. How far is Springfield from St. Louis?

Answer. It is one hundred and ten miles from Rolla, and I believe Rolla is about the same distance from St. Louis. Springfield is about two hundred and twenty miles from St. Louis.

Question. You made a stand at Springfield. Were you under the necessity of fighting a battle there, or could you have retreated still further from the enemy? You say your forces at Springfield were vastly inferior to those of the enemy.

Answer. I will give you what I believe was General Lyon's idea at the time.

Question. Could he retreat before them, and if so would it have been prudent to have done it?

Answer. My opinion is that the wisest course was to fight in the way he did fight. General Lyon was mistaken in the strength of the enemy. He did not think they were over 15,000 men, when in fact they were over 20,000. But the attacking force always has the advantage, in the moral effort upon the troops and in everything. If you move forward troops even a hundred yards in time of action it gives them courage. If you fall back that distance it intimidates them. General Lyon's idea was to surprise their camp as we did; to make a bold dash on them when our men were full of courage and animation, and whip them or cripple them, which in fact was accomplished with the loss of his own life.

By Mr. Chandler:

Question. So that they could not pursue?

Answer. Yes, sir. If we had retreated without that fight our forces would have been intimidated, and we would have had to fight every day, and perhaps lost a valuable train.

By the chirman:

Question. You say that General Lyon got no re-enforcements, and yet re-enforcements were sent out of the State. You understood General Lyon to say so.

Answer. I understood General Lyon to say that regiments were sent out of Missouri. He did not state where, and I do not know.

By Mr. Chandler:

Question. Do you know what forces were at St. Louis at that time?

Answer. I do not.

Question. And you do not know why re-enforcements were not sent to General Lyon?

Answer. No, sir.

Question. Had re-enforcements been sent when General Lyon first called for them would they have reached him in time for this battle?

Answer. Undoubtedly. He sent for them three or four weeks before. He arrived at Springfield on the 13th of July, and the call for re-enforcements was made a few days after. The battle was fought on the 10th of August. In a conversation with Colonel Wyman, he made the statement to me that one regiment was ordered forward from Rolla, and the colonel refused to march for want of transportation. That was stated to me by Colonel Wyman.

By Mr. Odell:

Question. How long would it have taken troops to have gone from St. Louis to Springfield by railroad and march?

Answer. Well, sir, in ordinary marching through the country it would have taken seven or eight days. But I want to qualify that by stating that on an emergency, forced marches could have been made. The distance, allowing one day from St. Louis to Rolla, on the railroad, and one hundred and ten miles of marching from Rolla to Springfield, could have been easily made in four days, if the men expected a battle. But if they did not expect anything at the end of their journey, they might have taken six or seven days. I would say they could have reached Springfield from St. Louis in six days at the outside.

By Mr. Gooch:

Question. You do not know whether it was in General Frémont's power to have re-enforced General Lyon or not?

Answer. I did not.

By Mr. Covode:

Question. Did General Lyon ever tell you upon whom he called for re enforcements?

Answer. It is my impression that he did remark to me that he had telegraphed to Washington for re-enforcements; that he not only had written to the headquarters of the department, but had sent telegraphic despatches through to Washington.

Question. Did he not tell you that he had first telegraphed to the War Department, and afterwards to Colonel Blair, to urge them to send on re-enforcements or he would be overpowered?

Answer. I could not state that. He may have said so. I had conversations with him several times. He was a classmate of mine, and I had rather frequent conversations with him, and the conversations I had with him at different times left the impression upon my mind that he had repeatedly written and telegraphed to St. Louis and Washington.

Question. Did he not tell you that he had repeatedly written and telegraphed to the War Department and got no reply, and then he telegraphed to Colonel Blair to urge it?

Answer. The last part of your remark I do not remember about: that he had telegraphed to the War Department and received no reply, I think he did say. There was no telegraph in operation at that time from Springfield to St. Louis. But he had sent telegraphic despatches through to be sent over the wires from St. Louis or the first telegraphic station.

By Mr. Chandler:

Question. Do you remember at what time General Frémont took command at St. Louis—on what day he arrived?

Answer. No, sir; I cannot recall it.

By the chairman:

Question. If General Lyon had not pursued the enemy at Springfield, but had waited there and intrenched himself, could he have defended himself?

Answer. That is a matter of opinion. In my opinion it would have been more difficult for him to have defended himself at Springfield against the attacks of the enemy, than it was to whip them in the open field.

Question. Then you do not believe much in intrenchments?

Answer. No, sir; I do not.

By Mr. Johnson:

Question. You think the stand you made was more effective than to have waited for re-enforcements?

Answer. Yes, sir; a thousand times.

WASHINGTON, *January* 10, 1862.

General JOHN C. FRÉMONT sworn and examined.

By the chairman:

Question. What is your rank, and what was your position in the army where you have commanded?

Answer. My rank is that of major general in the regular army.

Question. What department did you command?

Answer. I commanded what is called the western department.

Question. About what time did you assume the command?

Answer. I assumed the command in the department on the 25th day of last July.

Question. Please give a narration to the committee, in your own way, of the conduct of the department while under your command?

Answer. I have prepared no statement in relation to that subject. I have here all the principal orders, communications, letters and despatches concerning the most important events and acts of the period referred to. And I am ready to answer any questions which any member of the committee may desire to ask me.

After some time passed in consultation by the committee,

The chairman: I perceive that you have a large number of documents here which it will take some time to examine. The committee are of the opinion that the better way would be for you to prepare a statement, as brief as may be practicable, of such matters as you may deem important, connected with your administration of the western department, and submit it to the committee. If they should then desire to ask you any further questions relating to the subject, they can do so

The witness: I will do so.

[Examination accordingly suspended for the present.]

WASHINGTON, *January* 17, 1862.

General JOHN C. FRÉMONT—examination resumed.

The witness proceeded as follows:

Agreeably to a suggestion from the committee, I make the following statement concerning my administration of the western department:

Notwithstanding my unwillingness to engross the time of the committee, I shall have to ask that they will take the trouble to look over the documents which I have appended to this statement, and which comprehend the most important letters, orders, and telegraphic communications, concerning some of the most important events and acts of the period referred to. The magnitude of the department and its interests, the amount of business required to be done, the inadequacy of means, and the short space into which many events were crowded, together with the many accusations and the strained and rigorous account to which the western department has been held, make it quite impossible to present the subject with fairness in a brief paper.

In my desire not to cumber this statement, and having respect to my character of witness before your committee, I have omitted facts and considerations in vindication of myself on points where I have been attacked, but into which I shall ask the committee to examine. This paper is only directed to leading points, leaving their details and what is more directly personal to myself to the testimony of witnesses I have asked to have summoned, and to the accompanying papers.

When, in July last, I was assigned to the command of the western department, it comprehended, with Illinois, all the States and Territories west of the Mississippi river to the Rocky mountains, including New Mexico.

No special object was given me in charge to do, nor was I furnished with any particular plan of a campaign. The general discussions at Washington resulted in the understanding that the great object in view was the descent of the Mississippi, and for its accomplishment I was to raise and organize an army, and when I was ready to descend the river I was to let the President know. My command was then to be extended over Kentucky and down the left bank of the Mississippi. For military reasons it was judged inexpedient to do so in the beginning.

Full discretionary powers of the amplest kind were conferred on me. Not a line of written instructions was given me.

This leading object of the campaign being settled, the details of its accomplishment and the management of my department were left to my own judgment.

While at Washington I informed myself fully of the unprepared condition of the west, and its want of arms, from the governor of Illinois. Of the Illinois contingent, seven thousand men were unarmed. Their cavalry was without horses or sabres, their artillery companies had hardly any guns, and were wholly without equipment. Upon this information I procured an order for seven thousand stands of arms, which, upon my arrival in New York two days after, I found had been countermanded. Upon my complaint to Washington, and upon the direct interposition of the President, Major Hagner was sent to aid me in procuring what I judged immediately necessary for the department. With him I arranged for getting together from various arsenals, and forwarding to St. Louis, arms and equipments sufficient for the complete equipment of an army corps of twenty-three thousand men.

In the meantime the rebellion in the west was daily assuming a more threatening aspect; in the northwest aggravated disorders had broken out; General Pope was urgently requesting to take the field with the remainder of the Illinois contingent; General Harding was asking reinforcements for Cairo and the southeast; and General Lyon, for Springfield and the southwest.

Urged by this serious condition of affairs, I applied to General Scott for permission to take the field immediately, with any instructions he might have to give me. Having received this permission, and being informed there were no instructions for me, I left New York on the day following the battle of Manassas, and reached my command, at St. Louis, on the 25th day of July.

At this time the State of Missouri was throughout rebellious. A rebel faction in every county, at least equal to the loyal population in numbers, and excelling it in vindictiveness and energy. The local government was in confusion and unable to aid. St. Louis itself was a rebel city, and, as a rule, the influential and wealthy citizens were friendly to secession.

Of the new levies of the federal troops few were in the field—the term of enlistment of the three months men was just expiring—the troops in service had not been paid, were badly equipped and badly supplied, and, in addition to the rebel parties which swarmed throughout the State, a confederate army of nearly fifty thousand men was already on its southern frontier.

General Pope was in North Missouri with nearly all my disposable force; General Lyon was at Springfield, with about seven thousand eight hundred men; and General Prentiss was holding Cairo with seven regiments. General Lyon's troops was, in greater part, three months men, whose term of service was ending, and all of General Prentiss's force was in the same condition.

The arms collected for me in New York had been diverted to Virginia, and I had neither money nor credit. Want of arms and want of money were the chief difficulties to be met, while the necessity to meet the enemy on three sides at once was urgent and imminent. There was no lack of men. The loyal population of the west, and among them the Germans, with a noble unanimity, were willing to come in mass to the standard of the Union.

The saving of time, demanded by these most urgent circumstances, made me especially anxious to retain the services of the Home Guard regiments and three months men, whose term of service was just expiring. These were themselves anxious to remain in service, but the destitution of their families, made so by their absence and failure to receive the pay due them, rendered this impossible. In this necessity I directed the use of part of an unappropriated sum lying in the United States treasury, and reported the reason and fact of my conduct to the President, in the following letter:

[Unofficial.]

HEADQUARTERS WESTERN DEPARTMENT,
St. Louis, July 30, 1861.

MY DEAR SIR: You were kind enough to say that as occasions of sufficient gravity arose I might send you a private note.

I have found this command in disorder, nearly every county in an insurrectionary condition, and the enemy advancing in force by different points of the southern frontier. Within a circle of fifty miles around General Prentiss, there are about 12,000 of the confederate forces, and 5,000 Tennesseeans and Arkansas men, under Hardee, well armed with rifles, are advancing upon Ironton. Of these, 2,000 are cavalry, which yesterday morning were within twenty-four hours' march of Ironton. Colonel Bland, who had been seduced from this post, is falling back upon it. I have already re-enforced it with one regiment; sent on another this morning and fortified it. I am holding the railroad to Ironton, and that to Rolla, so securing our connexions with the south. Other measures which I am taking I will not trust to a letter, and I write this only to inform you as to our true condition, and to say that if I can obtain the material aid I am expecting, you may feel secure that the enemy will be driven out and the State reduced to order. I have ordered General Pope back to North Missouri, of which he is now in command. I am sorely pressed for want of arms. I have arranged with Adams Express Company to bring me everything with speed, and will buy arms to-day in New York. Our troops have not been paid, and some regiments are in a state of mutiny, and the men whose term of service is expired generally refuse to enlist. I lost a fine regiment last night from inability to pay them a portion of the money due. This regiment had been intended to move on a critical post last night. The Treasurer of the United States has here $300,000 entirely unappropriated. I applied to him yesterday for $100,000 for my paymaster, General Andrews, but was refused. We have not an hour for delay. There are three courses open to me. One, to let the enemy possess himself of some of the strongest points in the State, and threaten St. Louis, which is insurrectionary. Second: To force a loan from secession banks here. Third: To use the money belonging to the government, which is in the treasury here. Of course, I will neither loose the State nor permit the enemy a foot of advantage. I have infused energy and activity into the department, and there is a thorough good spirit in officers and men. This morning I will order the treasurer to deliver the money in his possession to General Andrews, and will send a force to the treasury to take the money, and will direct such payments as the exigency requires. I will hazard everything for the defence of the department you have confided to me, and I trust to you for support.

With respect and regard, I am yours truly,

J. C. FRÉMONT,
Major General Commanding.

The PRESIDENT *of the United States.*

I respectfully ask the attention of your committee to this letter, because the investigating committee, in their report, have made this act a serious charge against me, holding me up to the reprobation of the country, as having acted in a manner "arbitrary and illegal," dangerous to "constitutional liberty, and in defiance of law and superior authority."—(Pages 78 and 116.) They further say that this act was "alarming, unjustifiable, and deserving severest censure, especially as there was no pretence of any military or other necessity to justify this outrage."

That no reply was made to the above-quoted letter, or objection made to the act, will be sufficient to satisfy the committee that I was expected to do any act which in my judgment the public service might require, or, to use the words of a cabinet minister in the confidence of the administration—

WASHINGTON, *July* 26, 1861.

DEAR GENERAL: I have two telegrams from you, but find it impossible now to get any attention to Missouri or western matters from the authorities here. You will have to do the best you can, and take all needful responsibility to defend and protect the people over whom you are specially set.

* * * * * *

Yours truly, and in haste,

M. BLAIR.

I ask the committee to couple the facts set out in these letters, and the distress of General Lyon for want of money with which to retain his troops, with the censure of the committee.

With what has been said concerning the situation of affairs in Missouri, a glance at the map will make it apparent that Cairo was the point which first demanded immediate attention. The force under General Lyon could retreat, but the position at Cairo could not be abandoned; the question of holding Cairo was one which involved the safety of the whole northwest. Had the taking of St. Louis followed the defeat of Manassas, the disaster might have been irretrievable, while the loss of Springfield, should our army be compelled to fall back upon Rolla, would only carry with it the loss of a part of Missouri—a loss greatly to be regretted, but not irretrievable.

Having re-enforced Cape Girardeau and Ironton, by the utmost exertions I succeeded in getting together and embarking with a force of 3,800 men five days after my arrival in St. Louis.

From St. Louis to Cairo was an easy day's journey by water, and transportation abundant. To Springfield was a week's march, and before I could have reached it Cairo would have been taken, and with it, I believe, St. Louis.

On my arrival at Cairo I found the force under General Prentiss reduced to 1,200 men; consisting mainly of a regiment which had agreed to await my arrival. A few miles below, at New Madrid, General Pillow had landed a force estimated at 20,000, which subsequent events showed was not exaggerated Our force, greatly increased to the enemy by rumor, drove him to a hasty retreat, and permanently secured the position. To these facts the accompanying papers, and the testimony of General Prentiss and other officers, are offered to the committee.

I returned to St. Louis on the 4th, having, in the meantime, ordered Colonel Stephenson's regiment from Boonesville, and Colonel Montgomery from Kansas, to march to the relief of General Lyon.

Immediately upon my return from Cairo I set myself at work, amidst incessant demands upon my time from every quarter, principally to provide re-enforcements for General Lyon.

I do not accept Springfield as a disaster belonging to my administration. Causes, wholly out of my jurisdiction, had already prepared the defeat of General Lyon before my arrival at St. Louis. His letter to me of the 9th August, with other papers annexed, will show that I was already in communication with him, and that he knew his wants were being provided for. It will be seen that I had all reasonable expectations of being able to relieve him in time, and had he been able to adhere to the course indicated in this letter, a very short time would have found him efficiently sustained.

SPRINGFIELD, *Missouri, August* 9, 1861.

GENERAL: I have just received your note of the 6th instant by special messenger.

I retired to this place, as I have before informed you, reaching here on the 5th. The enemy followed within ten miles of here. He has taken a strong position, and is recruiting his supplies of horses, mules, and provisions, by forages into the surrounding country; his large force of mounted men enabling him to do this without much annoyance from me.

I find my position extremely embarrassing, and am at present unable to determine whether I shall be able to maintain my ground or forced to retire. I can resist any attack from the front, but if the enemy move to surround me I must retire. I shall hold my ground as long as possible, though I may, without knowing how far, endanger the safety of my entire force with its valuable material, being induced, by the important considerations involved, to take this step. The enemy yesterday made a show of force about five miles distant, and has doubtless a full purpose of making an attack upon me.

Very respectfully, your obedient servant,

N. LYON,
Brigadier General of Volunteers, Commanding.

Major General J. C. FRÉMONT,
Commanding Western Department, St. Louis, Missouri.

Upon the 10th of August General Lyon was killed in battle.

The charge that General Lyon had in any way suffered from any neglect was a surprise upon me. I heard nothing of it at the time, and believe it to have been an after-thought. Further to disprove it, in connexion with what has been said above, I refer to the statements of Adjutants General Harding and Kelton, through whose hands the business of the department at that time passed. Colonel Harding was General Lyon's adjutant general, charged with the management of affairs in Missouri during his absence. In the letter referred to he says:

General Frémont *was not* inattentive to the situation of General Lyon's column, and went so far as to remove the garrison of Booneville, in order to send him aid. During the first days of August troops arrived in the city in large numbers. Nearly all of them were unarmed; all were without transportation. Regiment after regiment laid for days in the city without any equipments, for the reason that the arsenal was exhausted, and arms and accoutrements had to be brought from the east. From these men General Lyon would have had re-enforcements, although they were wholly unpracticed in the use of the musket and knew nothing of movements in the field, but in the meantime the battle of the 10th of August was fought.

CHESTER HARDING, Jr.,
Late Assistant Adjutant General upon the Staff of Brigadier General Lyon.

It was under this great necessity—a greater than which is not likely to occur during this war—and to provide, among other demands, relief for General Lyon, that on the 6th of August I made the purchase of Austrian guns, for which I am censured by a committee charged to "investigate frauds."—(Page 40.)

This committee will be enabled to judge whether the purchase of these arms at this time can be appropriately called "a manifest improvidence."

I abstain from pursuing this subject further than to say that, although the arm itself was not a matter of choice, as this telegram will show—

St. Louis, *July* 29, 1861.

The agent of Adams's Express Company here has offered to bring me, by passenger train, any arms directed to me. Send everything you have for me by passenger trains, for which the express company will provide. Your letter of 24th received. There were no arms at the arsenal here to meet the order given for the 5,000. We must have arms—any arms, no matter what.

J. C. FRÉMONT,
Major General Commanding Western Department.

Major Hagner,
Fifth Avenue Hotel, New York.

it was still a good arm. Twelve thousand had been in service; thirteen thousand were new. They were percussion muskets, solid and strong; pronounced by Austrian officers to be considered in that service a good weapon; preferred by General Asboth for his division in their unaltered condition, and were in the hands of some of my best regiments, at Springfield, and scattered over the country in various corps, although the committee say "they were not in use." I think it due to myself to say that this committee came to St. Louis during my absence in the field, and no notice was at any time given me that my military acts were to be brought under examination, nor has any copy of the testimony collected during their proceedings been furnished me, of which I might avail myself in reply.

On the 13th August intelligence of the battle of Wilson's creek reached me at St. Louis. In expectation of an immediate advance by the enemy, I informed the President and governors of the neighboring States, requesting that all the disposable force that could be spared should be sent at once to Missouri. Fortunately, dissension in the camp of the enemy prevented them from using their success, and gave time, which I used to carry on as rapidly as possible the plan I had adopted for the defence of the State. This was to fortify Girardeau, Ironton, Rolla, and Jefferson City, with St. Louis as a base, holding these places with sufficient garrisons, and leaving the army free for operations in the field. It certainly seems superfluous to speak of the importance of St. Louis; but as the expediency of fortifying it has been questioned, it may be well to remind the committee that it was the first military position in the western department. Many of the things I am required to prove are as self-evident as this. St. Louis, then, is situated on the great highway of the Mississippi river, at a point where it is crossed by all the principal roads from the east, having itself seven different lines of communication to the interior and opposite ends of the State; that it is the great centre of politics and trade, and the object to which the efforts of the enemy were constantly directed and invited by the powerful and wealthy rebel portions of the citizens. It was certainly prudent to render permanently secure, beyond the reach of contingency, this great depot for supplies and reserves, and safe retreat for an army in the possible event of a disaster.

The importance of fortifying St. Louis had early occupied the attention of General Lyon, who had decided upon a plan much the same as that now adopted, and under the advice of the same officer by whom the present sites were selected, but which he was unable to carry out.

The necessity of these fortifications was concurred in by officers of unimpeachable loyalty and capacity; and such, also, was the judgment of the loyal inhabitants, to whom they gave, for the first time, a sense of protection and security. They were laid out with a view to command the city itself, as well as the approaches to it. The defences which rest upon St. Louis constitute the dike which separates the south from the northwest. It is easy, after a precaution has been successful, to say that it was not needed. I did not choose to expose myself to the chances of a neglect, either at St. Louis or Paducah, for both of which I have been censured, and with equal ignorance in either case. The unfairness of this attack consists in judging what was necessary for St. Louis then by its condition when I left the department.

I ask the committee to bear in mind that the plan for the defence of the State, and my operations generally, were all conducted in reference to the descent of the Mississippi, to which all preparations tended. To complete the defence of St. Louis, after the withdrawal of the army, five regiments of infantry, with one battalion of cavalry, and two batteries of field artillery, were considered amply sufficient.

It has been objected that I did not employ the troops under my command, instead of hired labor for this work. I did this in the exercise of my judgment. I did not consider it expedient to employ the volunteer troops in a work of this magnitude, involving so much labor and exposure. The hot suns and heavy dews of the unhealthy months of August and September need to be avoided in that climate. The troops were so little acquainted with arms that all their time was needed to fit them for the field, while, on the other hand, the employment of hired labor was of great service in tranquilizing the city, and relieving the wide-spread distress the war had entailed on it, and which private charity had exhausted itself in endeavoring to relieve.

Concerning the contract for this work, the committee of investigation say that it was made under the "special order and direction of General Frémont;" and concerning the payments, that they were made upon his "personal order." The following extract will show that not only was I recognized to have this power, but that I was, so late as the 3d of September, counselled to exercise it by the quartermaster general, General Meigs:

[Extract from letter of Hon. M. Blair, P. M. G]

WASHINGTON, *September* 3, 1861.

Meigs begged me this afternoon to get you to order 15-inch guns from Pittsburg for your gunboats. He says that the boats can empty any battery the enemy can make with such guns. He advises that you contract for them directly yourself, telling the contractor you will direct your ordnance officer to pay for them.

* * * * * * * * * *

Concerning the contractor, the committee say that he is "a Californian who followed Frémont to St. Louis."

I left California for Europe on the 1st of January. On the 1st of August, I think, Mr. Beard left there, coming overland to St. Louis. I never wrote to him, or in any way communicated with him, or knew of his intended coming. His arrival was equally a surprise and pleasure to me. I knew him to be a man of unusual energy and capacity, accustomed to the management of men on large works, and immediately applied to him to undertake the building of the fortifications. I sent an officer with him to make his examinations, and he began his work, I think, on the second day after his arrival. I assigned him one of my ablest officers to lay out and superintend the work, and to remain constantly with him, gave him every facility he asked, and drove him to the extent of his capacity. Six thousand men were employed upon it, working night and day, and it was finished rapidly in a workmanlike and durable manner. Extra pay was allowed to the laborers, forty cents per day, I think, and extra expenses incurred under the pressure authorized. I was satisfied with him and the work done by him. I asked no bonds from him, because he was a stranger and could have given none. He began his work before the contract was made, and accident delayed its execution by General McKinstry. When the prices for his work were under discussion, and were referred to me by General McKinstry, I directed this officer to reduce them to what was just and reasonable to both parties, having reference to the circumstances under which the work was done, and the extra prices that had been paid, so as to leave the contractor what might be strictly a fair profit on his labor; and his decision, whatever it was, was approved by me. For costs of construction, and other details with which I am not acquainted, I respectfully refer the committee to the testimony of the quartermaster and the contractor, whom I have asked to have summoned.

To show their nature and value the report and testimony of the engineers who planned and were superintending the work will be furnished the committee. The object aimed at was the completion of the city defences in the shortest possible time. The works were thoroughly and well built, covering and comprehending the city itself and the surrounding country on a length of about ten miles, and the total cost is, I think, less than $300,000!

In my judgment, having in view the time and manner in which they were built, the money was well applied, and as a measure of expediency and policy it was fully worth to the government what it cost.

And while examining into the conduct and events of the war, I think it right to call the attention of your committee to the fact, that a committee charged to "investigate fraud" came into a department which was under martial law, in the midst of civil dissensions, encouraging insubordination, discrediting and weakening the authority of the commanding general then absent in the field; and I offer testimony to show that their conduct, whilst at St. Louis, created a public opinion that their special object was to make out a case against myself, which should justify my removal from that department.—(See page 79 of their report.) And I offer testimony to show that they avoided and declined to receive, and have suppressed, testimony which militated against this object, and, further, to show that there are in their report many inaccuracies and perversions and some positive falsehoods.

The labors of the investigating committee appear to have resulted in a single resolution, in which the purchase of certain arms by myself is made a prominent subject. With respect to the sale of these arms by the government I have nothing to say. They were new, and I am told were sold without being condemned. The contract price at which they were bought by the government was, I believe, $17 50. The price at which they are set down in the ordnance manual is $21. After they had been rifled and otherwise improved, I purchased them at $22. Taking into consideration the advance in price of arms caused by the war, I submit that the purchase is not deserving of special censure.

I have digressed from the rule laid down at the outset in this paper, but as the passage of the resolution which is soon to be before the House would be a vote of censure, and as the report itself, together with other official accusations, have been broadly spread over the country, I respectfully ask that the committee will cause this statement, together with the accompanying documents, to have equal and immediate publicity given to them, in order that Congress may act understandingly, and the censure asked for go where it properly belongs.

The turbulent condition of the State at the end of August rendered it, in my judgment, necessary to issue a proclamation, extending martial law to the State of Missouri, and enforcing some penalties for rebellion.

As explanatory of some of the difficulties of my position, and of my ideas concerning the conduct of the war in my department, I refer the committee to the annexed correspondence with the President in this connexion.

So late as the 6th to the 10th September, as accompanying papers under this date show, no immediate danger was apprehended for Jefferson City or Lexington.

Price was still on the upper Osage, and I was organizing as rapidly as possible a force to march from Rolla and from Jefferson City upon Springfield, with the intention of forcing him to retreat, or cutting off his communications with Arkansas. Want of transportation, arms, and money was delaying this movement. We had just effected lodgments at Paducah and Fort Holt, and were occupied in contesting with the rebels western Kentucky, for which re-enforcements were constantly required. The condition of North Missouri required a vigorous effort to suppress rebellion in that quarter, and an expedition which occupied a considerable part of our real force was sent there under Generals Pope and Sturgis.

These three points, on which we were actively engaged, fully taxed our resources. At this time I sent for General Hunter, to give him command of the movement upon Springfield. On the 11th it will be seen that General Pope, with all the force under his command, was fully occupied in North Missouri. On the same day I received the rumor—and only as a rumor—of General Price's arrival at Clinton, more than 300 miles from St. Louis. Upon the 12th a despatch from General Davis informed me of Colonel Mulligan's arrival at Lexington. Colonel Mulligan reports a portion of his command, Colonel Marshall's regiment of cavalry, as scouring the country. The same day another despatch from him informs me that Price is reported near Warrensburg, with a force variously estimated at from 5,000 to 15,000 men. He informs me measures were being taken to begin fortifying Lexington. Finally, it appears that General Davis was giving his attention vigilantly to that section of the country. It will be seen from the telegrams of this day that Cairo was also requiring more troops.

On the 13th the regiments were ordered from St. Louis to Jefferson City, and two others from Jefferson City to the relief of Lexington, (Lexington is 240 miles from St. Louis, and 115 miles from Jefferson City,) if, in the opinion of General Davis, who occupied that place, it was deemed expedient. And generally it will be seen that all possible activity and promptitude was used in sending forward troops to the points threatened along the Missouri river, and meeting with all our disposable force the movements of General Price. It will be seen that up to the 13th Boonesville, and not Lexington, was considered the threatened point. On the 14th General Sturgis was directed to move with all practicable speed upon Lexington. General Pope's despatch of the 16th gave me every reason to believe as he did—that a re-enforcement of 4,000 men, with artillery, would be there in abundant time; and, if the committee will take the time to read the accompanying papers, it will be seen that from every quarter where there were disposable troops the promptest efforts were made to concentrate them on Lexington, but chance defeated these efforts. Also on the 14th, in the midst of this demand for troops, I was ordered by the Secretary of War and General Scott to "send 5,000 well armed infantry to Washington without a moment's delay."

It will in some degree explain my condition to insert the following telegram:

[Vol. 2, page 96.]

HEADQUARTERS WESTERN DEPARTMENT,
St. Louis, September 15, 1861.

Reliable information from the vicinity of Price's column shows his present force to be 11,000 at Warrensburg and 4,000 at Georgetown, with pickets extending towards Syracuse. Green is making for Boonesville with probable force of 3,000. Withdrawal of force from this part of the Missouri risks the State; from Paducah, loses western Kentucky. At the best, I have ordered two regiments from this city, two from Kentucky, and will make up the remainder from the new force being raised by the governor of Illinois.

J. C. FRÉMONT,
Major General Commanding.

Colonel E. D. TOWNSEND,
Ass't Adj't Gen'l, Headquarters of the Army, Washington, D. C.

It is well to recall the fact that the State of which I had the task to obtain possession, and which was in active rebellion, contained a white population of over a million—equal to that of Virginia, and 150,000 greater than that of Kentucky—and that the difficulties were increased by the fact that the several important points needed to be occupied for that purpose were very distant from the centre of operations at St. Louis, with long lines of communication to be kept open, in the midst of a brave and enterprising enemy.

To St. Joseph, 330 miles; to Sedalia, 189 miles; to Jefferson City, 125 miles; to Rolla, 118 miles; to Ironton, about 80 miles; to Cairo and Paducah, 200 miles.

HEADQUARTERS WESTERN DEPARTMENT,
September 14, 1861.

Subjoined is a list of our total force, with its distribution:

St. Louis, (including Home Guard)	6, 899
Under Brigadier General Pope, (including Home Guard)	5, 488
Lexington, (including Home Guard)	2, 400
Jefferson City, (one quarter Home Guard)	9, 677
Rolla	4, 700
Ironton	3, 057
Cape Girardeau	650
Bird's Point and Norfolk	3, 510
Cairo, (including McClernand's brigade)	4, 826

Fort Holt, opposite Cairo, Kentucky shore	3,595
Paducah	7,791
Under General Lane	2,200
Mound City, near Cairo	900
Total of present and absent on detached duty	55,693

J. C. FRÉMONT,
Major General Commanding.

Hon. SIMON CAMERON,
Secretary of War, Washington, D. C.

To these difficulties began now to be added the loss of consideration and credit, which the apparent withdrawal of the confidence of the government caused. The visit of high officers charged with inquiring into the affairs of my department, and the simultaneous and sustained attacks of leading journals, accumulated obstructions to my movements until I was openly removed from the command of the department. Except the victory, little advantage resulted to Price from the capture of Lexington, exposed and resting upon a broad river, which there was no chance for a large army to cross in case of defeat. As a military position, its occupation had no value for him. On the contrary, had I possessed the means of transportation to move forward my troops rapidly, I should have been well content to give up Lexington for the certainty of being able to compel Price to give me battle on the north side of the Osage; as he could not cross the Missouri without exposing himself to certain defeat, no other course would have remained open to him. In fact, when I did go forward, the appearance of my advance at Sedalia was the signal for his precipitate retreat. I ask the attention of the committee to the unreasonableness of expecting a general to be always successful. Admitting even that the western department had been thoroughly well supplied with men and arms, it could scarcely have been expected that no single casualty could have been met with in the course of the campaign. And it would seem more reasonable to judge of the capacity of the commander by the general results of his operations. From this statement, and the accompanying papers, the committee will form some idea of the condition of the department when I assumed command at the end of July. At the end of October, when I had succeeded in organizing and equipping an army, and was beginning to handle it in the field, we were everywhere, and uniformly along the whole extent of our lines, successful against the enemy. At Springfield one of the most brilliant actions, and at Fredericktown one of the most admirably conducted battles of the war had been fought. Isolated railroads had all been connected at St. Louis, and were in full and continuous operation over their whole extent. Additional cars had been provided, and at twenty-four hours' notice 10,000 men could be moved upon them from any one point to the opposite side of the State. All our posts, so far as the railroad went, had been fortified and connected by telegraphs, which were everywhere in full operation, and the daily mails were running to Springfield, from which place an officer, alone and in uniform, could ride through with safety to St. Louis. Quiet and comparative peace had been restored to the State, and the enemy was in full retreat before us to its southern boundary. A compact had been entered into with him, under which the authority of the State and federal courts was acknowledged, liberty of opinion and security of person were guarantied to both sides, all guerilla parties suppressed, and the war strictly confined to responsible officers and the armies in the field.

The State was in reality reclaimed, and in condition to leave the army free for the especial object of descending the Mississippi. The rebels already acknowledged the inutility of resistance to the federal authority; the doubtful came to the side of power, and the loyal who had borne the brunt of war, when to stand by the Union involved danger and losses, were everywhere encouraged to new efforts, and rewarded for their past aid.

The fall rains were over; the fine weather of the Indian summer had come; the hay was gathered and corn hardening, and we were about to carry out the great object of our campaign, under the most favorable auspices, with fewer hardships from exposure, and impediments from transportation, than at any other season. The spirit of the army was high. It was mainly composed of western men, whose interest as well as whose patriotism was involved in the opening of the Mississippi river, for the preparations to which they had contributed every possible effort, and we had every reason to believe that the campaign would open with a signal victory in the defeat or dispersion of the rebel army, with a move on Memphis as the immediate result.

These were the circumstances under which, without reason assigned, I was relieved of my command.

It is not grateful to me to have been myself compelled to set out the merits of my administration; but it was necessary in order to bring attention to points which otherwise might not have been presented, and which are necessary to a clear understanding of the subjects inquired into. Many acts which have been censured were, I think, for the public good. I know they were with that intention. I do not feel that in any case I overstepped the authority intended to be confided to me. Myself and the officers and men acting with me were actuated solely by a desire to serve the country. And I feel assured that this is realized by the people of the west, among whom we were acting.

After consultation by the committee Mr. Gooch was instructed to take the statement and papers submitted by General Frémont and examine them, with a view to determine what further inquiries it might be deemed necessary to make.

The witness was informed that when Mr. Gooch should have prepared himself for the further examination the committee would call him before them.

The witness: I shall be ready at any time to answer any questions the committee may desire to propound to me.

[Examination consequently suspended for the present.]

WASHINGTON, *January* 30, 1862.

General JOHN C. FRÉMONT—examination resumed.

By Mr. Gooch:

Question. Will you state concisely what powers were given you when you were assigned to the command of the western department?

Answer. No specific powers were given to me. But no restriction whatever was placed upon me in taking command of the department.

Question. Did you understand that you had the right, or were expected, to exercise any powers other than those which you held by virtue of your commission as major general?

Answer. I understood and expected to exercise any and whatever power was necessary to carry out the work I was sent to accomplish.

Question. Whether strictly within the limits of the power conferred by your commission or not?

Answer. Yes, sir.

Question. From whom did you derive your power in that respect?

Answer. From the President, and from conversations with the Secretary of

War and Mr. Blair, the Postmaster General; neither of whom used any expression which implied a restriction of power. On the contrary, the drift of the conversation was to the effect that I should exercise any power required. I have heard that the President said to the Illinois delegation—to Mr. Trumbull, perhaps—that he had given me more power than he had himself. I would like to remark, in passing, that I do not think it was clearly understood what was the nature of the power which a general commanding a department had.

By the chairman:

Question. All the powers incident and necessary to carry out the object to be obtained were given?

Answer. That is precisely the point.

By Mr. Gooch:

Question. Did you appoint military officers to act under you; and if so, why, and by virtue of what authority?

Answer. I did appoint such officers, and because they were necessary to the proper organization of the army, and the carrying out of the military operations. I did it under the authority of the Secretary of War and of the President of the United States, and under the general authority given to me.

Question. Do I understand that it was expected that, when you left Washington to assume the command of your department, you would exercise that power?

Answer. If I thought of it at all, I did. The governor of Missouri hesitated to appoint officers for the force raised in Missouri. A despatch was sent to the President—or through a cabinet officer to the President—asking him if he would confirm the officers appointed by me; to that effect, I think. At all events, the President replied that he would do so. And in all cases when I appointed officers they were appointed subject to the confirmation of the President; to be commissioned by him; so the commissions ran that I gave them. If the President approved the appointments, then they were to receive their commissions. Their appointment was necessary to the organization of the force in that department. We had to take officers wherever we could find them throughout the country.

Question. When you left Washington for your department you knew, of course, that you would find a great deficiency of arms in the department.

Answer. Yes, sir.

Question. And you had an order for 7,000 stand of arms in New York?

Answer. I had procured the order here.

Question. Will you state the facts in relation to that order?

Answer. I learned from the governor of Illinois that 7,000 of the Illinois contingent were unarmed. I went to the War Department and applied for arms for them. General Thomas went with me to Colonel Ripley, and he agreed to let me have 7,000 out of the number on hand, which, I think, was 25,000. He was to send them to three different points, named by me, on the Illinois river. I went on to New York, and the second day after reaching there I received a letter from Colonel Ripley to the effect that he thought the governor of Illinois was mistaken, and that those arms were not required, and, therefore, the order had not been issued for them. I sent that letter to Washington, and in reply I received a despatch informing me that the President would, himself, go to the War Department and arrange the matter for me. And in pursuance of that Major Hagner was sent to New York to endeavor to procure arms for the western department. I subsequently received an order for 5,000 muskets, to be delivered to me from the St. Louis arsenal, but they were not there. I think, when I got to St. Louis, the arms of all descriptions in the arsenal then did not exceed 1,200 or 1,300.

Question. What force did you find subject to your control upon your arrival at St. Louis?

Answer. I found a nominal force of perhaps 25,000 men, but a real force not exceeding 15,000 men; what I mean by that is, that of the three months men, whose terms of service were just expiring, so that you could not count upon them at all; there were about 10,000 men; while of the three years' men who were either in Missouri or going to it, there were, perhaps, 15,000 men. The two would make about 25,000 men.

Question. How was the force armed?

Answer. It was armed with all kinds of arms; some with rifled guns, and some with smooth bores. A small body of cavalry, of regular cavalry, I think, were armed with sabres.

Question. Was the whole of this force in possession of arms that could be used in the field?

Answer. I suppose they were, all except 7,000, for which, as I have before stated, I had no arms at all.

Question. When you were in New York was your attention called to what has since been known as the Austrian muskets?

Answer. Yes, sir.

Question. Did you examine them?

Answer. I looked at them. How far I examined them I do not recollect.

Question. Did you form an opinion of them at the time?

Answer. I probably did.

Question. Can you state what that opinion was?

Answer. I cannot state the opinion from recollection. I can state what I suppose the opinion must have been. I probably did not take the muskets then, because they differed somewhat from the arm in regular use in our service.

Question. Were those arms subsequently purchased?

Answer. Yes, sir; probably the same arms.

Question. Purchased in pursuance of your order?

Answer. By my direct order.

Question. To whom was your order given for the purchase of those arms?

Answer. I purchased them by telegraph from St. Louis, addressed to a firm in New York, Kruse, Drexel & Schmidt, the firm that held them. They offered me the arms, and after some interchange of despatches I purchased them.

Question. What was the price agreed to be paid for them?

Answer. I think it was $6 50.

Question. Will you state the reason for purchasing those arms after having seen them and considering that there were some objections to them?

Answer. Because I was in very pressing need of arms. We had no arms to furnish the regiments. We had plenty of men, but no arms. We were endeavoring to send re-enforcements to different points to meet the enemy in the field. We wanted arms for the troops to send to General Lyon, and for all our military operations.

Question. There were 25,000 of those arms?

Answer. Yes, sir. 13,000 new and 12,000 that had been in service.

Question. Was not your first proposition to purchase a part of them only?

Answer. Yes, sir.

Question. What was the reason that that was not done?

Answer. Because they would not sell to me without selling the whole of them; and I was afraid to wait long, because I supposed they would go to some other quarter to sell them.

Question. At that time was there not a great competition in the market for arms?

Answer. There was; at least I could get none. And in my judgment there could not have been—probably would not occur during the war—a greater necessity for arms than there was then. We were pressed in the State of Missouri, and about there, by the enemy. We had men, but no arms to give them. The troops sent there by the States came there unarmed.

Question. What proved to be the character and quality of these arms, as you learned after receiving them?

Answer. They proved to be a good, substantial arm. The German troops, a number of whom had been accustomed to use that particular arm, preferred them—were well satisfied with them. When the question of altering them came up, General Asboth asked me to let him have them unaltered for his division, as he preferred them in that way. They were strong; the barrels were thick, so that they could be easily rifled, and those that were altered were rifled. The only difference between that arm and our arm consisted in this: that instead of having a nipple upon which to put a percussion cap, there was a primer to be put in, something like three-quarters of an inch long. A cover was opened, the primer put in, and the cover shut down, precisely as in the old flint-lock musket you threw back the battery, poured in the powder for priming, and shut down the battery or pan again. I have seen it stated that the ammunition was different. The cartridge was exactly the same as for our musket. The only difference was, that instead of putting on a percussion cap, you put in a primer of the same material as the percussion cap.

Question. Then it is not true that the ammunition used must be different?

Answer. Not at all, except in using a primer instead of a cap.

By the chairman:

Question. Which could be handled in the shortest time, our gun or that kind?

Answer. I should think there was very little difference between them in that respect. The primer was long, and the cap is short and small. I should think that when a man's fingers were cold he could more readily handle the primer, three-quarters of an inch long, than to handle the cap. There were no more motions to go through with in the one case than in the other. There was one advantage: this cover shut down with a spring over the primer, so that it protected it from getting wet.

By Mr. Gooch:

Question. So that after the primer was put in, it remained protected and fit for use for almost any length of time?

Answer. Yes, sir.

Question. And the hammer struck on the primer cover?

Answer. Yes, sir.

By Mr. Chandler:

Question. The hammer came down upon the cover of the primer as it used to strike the steel in the old-fashioned flint-lock musket?

Answer. Yes, sir.

By Mr. Gooch:

Question. And the compression ignited the powder, as in the case of the percussion cap?

Answer. Yes, sir; a regular percussion hammer came right square down on the cover of the primer. I had with me an excellent officer, Colonel Albert, who had been for years in the Austrian service. He said that in that service they considered it a good weapon. I think he used a stronger expression than that, but I will stop with that.

Question. Did you have with them the primer, so that they could be used?

Answer. Yes, sir. When the muskets first got out there the primers did not come with them. Two boxes of primers were sent out first, but, in consequence of careless handling, they exploded somewhere near Pittsburg, and killed some two or three men, and that caused some delay.

Question. How long after you received the guns before you received the primers?

Answer. I do not know. Perhaps some ten days.

Question. Were any of those guns put in use in your army without any alteration being made in them?

Answer. Yes, sir.

Question. How many of them?

Answer. I think it was so arranged that probably 15,000 of them were distributed or subject to distribution, I think, were distributed, and 10,000 of them were set aside for alteration. The understanding was, that as fast as they were altered they should be distributed to the troops, and those that were unaltered recalled, so as to gradually get them all altered.

Question. Were they all altered?

Answer. I think not. I think the house in Cincinnati that had contracted to alter them refused to alter any more after my removal, from fear they would not get their pay. They had made arrangements to alter them at first at the rate of 200 a day, and then to increase it to 500 a day; and I was informed they had reached the point of 500 a day at the time of my removal, when they stopped work upon them.

Question. So that, previously to the alteration, you considered them an efficient arm?

Answer. Yes, sir.

Question. What was the cost of the alteration.

Answer. Between four and five dollars; four dollars and a half, I think.

Question. The gun having been altered, and having then cost the government eleven dollars, what was the value of the weapon then?

Answer. It would cost the government eleven dollars.

Question. Would it be a good arm at that price?

Answer. I should call it a thoroughly good arm at that price. It became then a rifled percussion musket of our pattern.

Question. Do you know the previous history of these muskets?

Answer. No, sir. All that I have seen about that is in the published report of the investigating committee of the House of Representatives. In respect to these muskets, I have a letter here, written to one of my staff from St. Louis, under date of January 21, 1862. The letter is written by Captain Hoskin, and this is what he says about these muskets: "Apropos of the long stories concerning the Austrian muskets, &c., which were so freely circulated in the newspapers, it is a very curious commentary on their alleged want of value, that I was last week ordered to go to Benton barracks, on the suggestion of Colonel Callender, to prove some of those very muskets, which had been issued to the troops. I need not say to you that the trial was a very conclusive one, and that two regiments, armed with them, marched next day for Cairo. The men had heard enough against those arms to make them feel very unwilling to take them; but, after the proving and trial, I judge they were very much better satisfied, Indeed, if it were not for these same despised weapons many of the regiments would have still remained unarmed; for the department of Missouri has been much neglected in that respect, as well as the department of the west, with a fair opportunity to solve the old task-work riddle of making bricks without straw."

By Mr. Odell:

Question. How many of these 25,000 Austrian muskets are now in use?

Answer. I presume all of them, probably, except those being altered. I tried in two places, Philadelphia and Cincinnati, to get these guns rifled and the locks altered. The Philadelphia house estimated the cost of alteration at something over five dollars, and I would have preferred their being altered as proposed by the Philadelphia house, even at the higher price; but I submitted the question to Captain Callender, the ordnance officer having charge of the arsenal there, and his judgment was that it would make a very good gun altered as the Cincinnati house proposed to alter it, and as they proposed to do it for a lower price, I contracted to have them altered there; but I think it would have been made a much better weapon to have been altered in Philadelphia, even at the greater price.

By Mr. Gooch:

Question. I desire now to call your attention to the Hall carbines, as they are called. Some of them were purchased in New York in pursuance of your order, were they not?

Answer. All of them, I think.

Question. Will you state the particulars of that transaction?

Answer. In brief, I received a despatch from Mr. Simon Stevens offering me carbines, and I purchased them at once.

Question. Did you know the character of that weapon at the time you purchased it, or the history of it?

Answer. I supposed it to be the usual Hall carbine which I had used in a journey overland on one occasion.

Question. You were familiar with it?

Answer. Yes, sir.

Question. What was the price paid for them?

Answer. I think it was $22.

Question. How did the gun prove itself—to be a good arm?

Answer. It proved to be a good arm. It was proved at the arsenal, and I think they had Captain Hoskin's report in regard to it, and he said it fired with reasonable accuracy. It proved to be, I supposed, an ordinarily good weapon. Further than that I do not know, It is a weapon for cavalry, and of course for close quarters. I have here an ordnance manual in which the regulation price is stated.

Question. What is the regulation price?

Answer. It is $21, (turning to the price as fixed in the manual.)

Question. Is that the price of the weapon after it was altered, or the original price?

Answer. The original price is $21. The alteration cost something over a dollar, as I have understood; I do not know.

Question. Was the alteration an improvement?

Answer. Yes, sir. It was rifled, so far as you may consider that an improvement of a short arm; and I think there was some contrivance put on for opening it more readily; and then the chamber was enlarged.

Question. Were you in need of these arms for immediate use at the time they were purchased?

Answer. Very much, indeed. I had cavalry in the field, and no arms whatever for them.

Question. Was Stevens an agent of the government at that time, or did he hold any appointment under you?

Answer. Not at that time.

Question. Not at the time of the purchase?

Answer. No, sir.

Question. Was he subsequently an aide-de-camp to you?

Answer. Yes, sir.

Question. Did he make any purchase in behalf of the government after he was appointed on your staff?

Answer. He was instructed to make some contracts—I think a contract with Mr. Wiard for some artillery. But I am not clear as to whether he made any purchase or not after his appointment.

By Mr. Odell:

Question. What was his rank on your staff?
Answer. That of Major.

By Mr. Gooch:

Question. Do you know anything in relation to the sale of those arms by the government—of their being condemned and sold?
Answer. Nothing whatever.
Question. You purchased them as carbines in the market?
Answer. Yes, sir.
Question. And, of course, as of good quality?
Answer. Yes, sir. I supposed they were about what such arms usually are. I am not very familiar with them.
Question. They proved to be so?
Answer. I think so.
Question. Did you confer with Major Hagner about the purchase of arms in New York?
Answer. After I had been some little time in the west I did not; first, because he permitted the arms which had been collected by him for me, under the arrangement I had with him, to be diverted to Virginia, the greater part of them—I do not remember that all were; secondly, because I could not get my wants attended to by him. I therefore left him entirely alone, and set to work to get what I wanted myself. I was entirely unsatisfied with Major Hagner's conduct in relation to my needs in the west, and on that account ceased to employ him, and sent him a message to that effect. This fact is to be considered in connexion with this question of obtaining arms. We had very few of them indeed. When I came to Washington and got the order for 7,000 muskets, I went from General Ripley over to Mr. Cameron, and said to him, "You have only 25,000 stand of arms altogether in your armories." He said, "You must be mistaken." I told him I was not, and asked him to send for General Ripley. He sent for General Ripley, and asked him if it was true that there were only 25,000 stand of arms in the government armories. General Ripley said that such was the case. General Cameron then turned to me and said, "I have learned more from you, General Frémont, in respect to our arms than I have been able to learn before since I have been in office here."
Question. Will you state the reasons which led you to erect fortifications around St. Louis?
Answer. The necessity for them consisted, first, in the fact that St. Louis was the base and centre of my department. It was to be my depot for supplies—the place for my reserves, from which all my operations were to be made. I wished to make St. Louis secure for a double reason. First, I considered it a rebel city, and that it was necessary to defend it from rebels inside as well as from attacks from without. It was constantly the object of the enemy to obtain possession of that city. For these reasons it was necessary to make it secure. Such was my opinion, and such was the opinion of officers whom I consulted in regard to our operations there. They considered it as a necessity about which there could possibly exist no doubt. My second reason was, that I was preparing to go down the Mississippi river, in which case I should take with me all my available force. My plan had been to fortify St. Louis, Cape Girardeau, Ironton, Rolla, and Jefferson City, provisioning them and holding them by garrisons during my absence; of course, thereby requiring a comparatively small force to hold the State tranquil after it had once been reduced to order. The

fortification of St. Louis was the centre of the whole plan. To make that place strongly secure by fortifications was a necessity, because it was the centre of all our operations. Really, the difficulty under which I seem to labor in many cases like that is, that I seem to be required to prove what is self-evident, what was merely an ordinary measure of precaution. The cost, in the first place, being in fact less for holding St. Louis by garrison with fortifications—very much less—that appeared to me to be a measure of ordinary necessity. The right wing of our entire force was resting on that point. From there we were going down the Mississippi, leaving that point in the midst of a State so actively rebellious as that one is. The plan was to fortify St. Louis, and hold it with a moderate force, and fortify some of the other positions about the State, and garrison and provision them, in order to keep the State secure. Those points commanded the railroads, occupied and defended the various lines of communications in the State. Just before I left the State I had succeeded in making the system of communication perfect. I had so arranged it that each railroad and each bridge on the line of the road were protected. I had had little barracks built at each important bridge, in which the men were to winter. St. Louis was the central support, the base upon which everything rested; not only St. Louis, but down the river.

Question. Was there the same necessity for fortifications there that there would be in any rebel territory where it was desirable to take and hold important strategical points?

Answer. Exactly and undoubtedly so.

Question. Did you consult with any officers connected with the engineer department of the government in relation to those fortifications?

Answer. I do not think I did. I doubt if there were any in the department, and I had full confidence in those officers who were with me. I had with me men who had seen many years' service in actual field operations; who in the line as well as in the capacity of engineers had done work with armies in the field. Therefore if I had had engineers of the regular army with me I should, probably, have given preference to these experienced officers.

Question. You considered them more competent to judge?

Answer. I did; because they had had the benefit of experience in absolutely practical operations.

Question. They had both the theory and the practice, instead of the theory only?

Answer. Yes, sir; and therefore naturally I would like to have the benefit of their experience.

Question. At most other points—and I do not know but at all—fortifications have been erected by the soldiers themselves. Why was not that done at St. Louis?

Answer. For several reasons. One was that, as a matter of judgment, I preferred to employ hired labor. It was with difficulty that the men could be induced to labor on fortifications, and in places where they did do it the work went on very slowly indeed; and my judgment was that it was better to employ the men in what they considered more particularly a soldier's duty, in preparing and instructing them for the field, rather than in that kind of hard labor, for which many of them considered they had not enlisted; and I wished to have the good will of the army, to put them in a good disposition to fight the enemy, that they should go into the field with all the feelings of patriotism and zeal with which they had enlisted. Practically that was one of the principal reasons. The condition of my department was such that the men were wanted as immediately as they could be armed. Another reason was, that it was much better for the health of the men not to expose them to the heat of the day and the dew of the night at that season of the year. And another reason having considerable force with me at the time was, that in the city was a large unemployed population of men whose families were in great want; and by the employment of that hired labor I conciliated a large body of men by giving them occupation, and, I think, produced a tone of feeling very favorable to the government in a class which in cities are generally inclined to be turbulent, and likely to be the first to be engaged in any difficulty.

Question. Was the condition of things in St. Louis at that time such that you felt that to be a desirable object to be sécured on the part of the government?

Answer. Decidedly so; and in that opinion I know I have the concurrence of the most respectable citizens of St. Louis.

Question. State concisely what arrangements you made for the construction of the forts. I do not mean the form and number of the forts, but the arrangements for building them.

Answer. When the work was first commenced it was placed under the superintendence and direction of Colonel Hassendenbel; subsequently under the direction of Major Kappner, whose operations, I think, were confined to the five southern forts. Afterwards Mr. Beard—a gentleman whom I had known as a contractor of large experience, and a man of uncommon energy and activity—arrived at St. Louis at a time when I was dissatisfied with the progress of the work, which did not go on as I desired it. I addressed myself to him to take charge of the fortifications and urge them forward with as much speed as was in any way possible.

By Mr. Julian:

Question. This Mr. Beard was from Indiana, was he not?

Answer. Yes, sir; he had been a contractor on the Wabash and Erie canal. He has been on quite a number of works. He is really very remarkable for his ability to control large bodies of men in work of that sort. He is a man of unusual force in that respect, and when he came to St. Louis I regarded it as quite a favorable accident to me, and put him on these works.

By Mr. Gooch:

Question. How were your forts designated—by numbers 1, 2, 3, &c.?

Answer. Yes, sir, I think so.

Question. The first five were built by Major Kappner?

Answer. He was one of the principal engineers on them; the latter part of the time he superintended them.

Question. Did he have the whole direction of the work, the hiring of the men, &c.?

Answer. Entirely. He had the direction of the work, the hiring of the men, having them attended to and paid, so that I know nothing of the building of the works as regards details.

Question. How did the five forts built by Major Kappner compare in size and cost of construction with those built by Mr. Beard?

Answer. As I have learned the forts built by Beard exceeded very much in price those built by Kappner. That would be the natural result of the manner in which they were built. Mr. Beard was directed to finish them forthwith.

Question. Were the five forts built by Major Kappner as large and extensive as those built by Mr. Beard, and would they have been as expensive if constructed in the same manner?

Answer. What was the relation of the different forts to each other, as to size, I am not certain. They were built of different sizes, according to locality, &c. I have asked for and endeavored to get a report on here, so as to be able to show the committee the character and size of the works, but I have not yet received it.

Question. Do you know the cost of the five forts built by Major Kappner?

Answer. I have seen it stated at about $60,000 in the report of the investigating committee.

Question. You do not know it otherwise?

Answer. I do not. I had no report made to me about the cost of those forts before I left the department.

Question. It has been stated that the forts built by Mr. Beard were no better or larger than those built by Major Kappner, though costing four or five times as much.

Answer. That, I think, is not true. I have no doubt they cost a great deal more, but not to that extent.

Question. Can you state the difference in their cost?

Answer. I cannot. I have seen a statement of Major Kappner, in which he said I did not know, and could not have known, the prices he was paying, for he never made any statement or report to me in connexion with the matter; and so it was with Mr. Beard. I never had a report from either of them as to the cost of their works. I will state the difference in regard to the manner in which those forts were built. Mr. Beard built five forts and seven outworks. In the contract with him I caused a stipulation to be inserted that each fort should be finished within five days after the engineers had laid it out, because it was a great point with me to have the city garrisoned when I should leave. Finally, when I was about to take the field at the head of the army, I sent for General Asboth, who was the chief of my staff, and told him that those forts must be finished; that I would give Mr. Beard five days to finish his forts, and I would give Major Kappner fifteen days to finish those he was constructing. I told him to send for them and inform them what I had determined upon. He sent for Mr. Beard, and he agreed to finish the forts in that time. They were to be finished, guns mounted, magazines stored, and colors flying, in five days. Major Kappner informed me that he could not undertake to finish his works in fifteen days, but he would do it in twenty days. I then directed the order to be made out to him to that effect; that within twenty days from that date those five forts were to be finished, guns mounted, magazines stored, and colors flying. I told Major Kappner that if he failed to comply with that order I would dismiss him from the service; that if he took that order, he took it subject to that condition. He agreed to take it. I mention this to show the different manner in which these forts were built. I did not wish to disturb Major Kappner and the engineers on the works he had in charge, and I gave the time he desired.

Question. Was the reason for the difference in the cost of the forts that in the one case the forts were built without any great pressure for time, and in the other they were built in the shortest possible time?

Answer. Yes, sir.

Question. That is your explanation of the difference of cost, so far as there was a difference of cost, in the building of those forts?

Answer. That is all the explanation I know of—that of hurry and press of time—the point with me being one of time, and the cost became greater.

Question. Did Mr. Beard commence the work before any contract was made with him?

Answer. He commenced it before any contract was drawn out. I put him immediately on the work, as soon as he agreed to do it, and left the contract to be made afterwards between him and General McKinstry, supposing, of course, that everything would be done correctly.

Question. And that contract was subsequently made out and signed by the parties?

Answer. Yes, sir.

Question. In relation to the payments, can you state in what sums, and at what times, the money was paid to Beard on his contract?

Answer. I cannot from memory. I can give a general statement in regard to the matter. The payments were made something in this way: there was a great scarcity of money, and each contractor and each man to whom money was due endeavored to obtain a portion for himself out of whatever happened to be on hand : and in Mr. Beard's case, as I judge from what I have seen there, money was given to him when it could be had, in order that he might have some on hand to meet the demands upon him when they should arise. He would get an order for the money, and if he could not get the money of the quartermaster he would go and negotiate in the city for it. General McKinstry might obtain money from some of the banks, and would apportion it out to meet the demands for it. We had very little money, and what we could get we divided out over the whole department. Of course the man who could get the most did the best for himself. In Beard's case, having a large number of men employed, his point was to have on hand as much money as he could for his men, because the next time he applied for money there might be none for him. For a long time all the money we got there we obtained from the banks by borrowing, taking and using their currency, such as it was.

Question. Was money paid to Beard in advance of the amount due him?

Answer. I have no doubt it was, in order that he might have a provision made to meet the demands on him when they should arise. I have seen printed what purported to be orders written by me for money to be paid to Mr. Beard. I never wrote out any order. Beard would come with a statement of the reasons why he wanted the money, and those statements were probably copied into the orders made out for him which I signed. For myself, when I ordered anything, I gave no reasons why I wanted it to any of my subordinate officers. But I can easily understand how some of these orders which I signed came to be made out as they were. Mr. Beard would present his reasons for the money, and the secretary in writing out the order would transfer the reasons into the order as an explanation to General McKinstry or whoever had the money to give, and he would regard it as a reason for giving more than he otherwise would.

Question. You did not write the order, but you signed it?

Answer. Yes, sir; I do not think there are any orders in my own handwriting.

Question. Before those payments were made, were there any estimates made or accounts rendered of the amount of work done by Mr. Beard?

Answer. No, sir; I do not think I ever received a statement of the amount of work done by Mr. Beard; nothing except information that such and such a fortification was in such a condition, when he would ask me to go out and inspect it, which I did. While I was in town I used to visit the fortifications, and see the progress of the works. In neither case, either of Major Kappner or Mr. Beard, was a statement ever made to me of that nature during the progress of the works.

Question. Were you at any time ordered to discontinue the field-works around the city of St. Louis?

Answer. I was.

Question. And not to pay any more money on account of them?

Answer. I was.

Question. From whom did that order issue?

Answer. From the Secretary of War, through General Thomas.

Question. Was that order complied with?

Answer. By me, no sir. Perhaps I better state the circumstances under which I received that order. I was at Warsaw, at the head of my army, on the way to Springfield, when I learned by report, somewhere, I suppose, about the 16th of October—thereabouts, I will not be certain as to date—that such an order had been issued. I wrote to Captain McKeever, my adjutant general, to protest against such an order as that, if any such had been issued, for the reason that St. Louis, as I have already stated, was the base of all my operations, upon the safety of which might depend the safety of my entire army, and the success of all my operations in the department. I considered the issuing of such an order as something extraordinary, unjustifiable, and not sustainable, as regards myself. I considered that the Secretary of War might as well have come to me in the field, when I was in face of the enemy and engaged in battle, and order me to discontinue the march of one column here, and another there, as to have made that order while I was in the field, as it struck at the base of my operations. Having directed my adjutant general to protest against that order, and to state to him that I would do so formally if I received any such written order, I let the matter stand. I think that on or about the 19th or 20th of October a letter came to me, not in the usual form or manner, through my adjutant general, but directly to me, from General Thomas. That letter I have not been able to find. It was directed, I think, to two points—the discontinuance of the fortifications, and, I think, the payment of the money. Having already stated my views by protesting against such an order, I simply neglected the matter, and let it stand as it was. I acted, I thought, in my right as commanding general of that department, carrying on military operations. I considered the stoppage of these fortifications as inexpedient, and possibly dangerous for the army in the field, and all my other positions; and having protested against it, as I have said, I let the matter rest there.

Question. You say you received a letter. Did that letter contain a peremptory order to discontinue those works?

Answer. I am not clear as to the form of the letter, whether it directed me to issue an order discontinuing those operations, or whether it informed me that the Secretary of War had issued such an order. At all events, my operations had been so much interfered with in my department; my remaining in command was so doubtful at that time; and my position as commanding general had been so much discredited and weakened, that I simply neglected acting further in the matter, and left it to the Secretary who had issued the order to have it carried out, if he saw fit to do so after my protest.

Question. If such an order was directed to you from the Secretary, would it not have been your duty to have promulgated an order to discontinue those works?

Answer. Under ordinary circumstances it might. But, as a matter of judgment, I am doubtful about it without consultation.

Question. You say you directed your adjutant general to protest against the order?

Answer. I wrote him a letter to that effect; but in what form I am not now certain, because I have not since conversed with him in relation to it.

Question. Do I understand that you directed Captain McKeever to notify the Secretary of War that you thought it not advisable?

Answer. That was the effect of my letter, in which case I should have been justifiable, and, in any case, to wait until I heard further from the Secretary. In the same way as General Lyon, being at Springfield, protested against the withdrawal from him by the Secretary of War of the little regular force which he had there, telling the Secretary that it was dangerous to do it, and until he heard further from him he would not obey the order, but would retain the troops.

Question. Did you receive any further order from the Secretary of War?

Answer. Nothing further.

Question. The order which you did receive is said to have directed the discontinuance of those works, and also to abstain from any further payment of money on account of those works.

Answer. I have seen it stated that it was so. I do not clearly recollect the purport of the letter I received. On the contrary, as regards the impression upon my mind of the purport of the letter, it was not that the Secretary of War directed me to order the discontinuance of the work, but rather it informed me that the Secretary had directed it to be discontinued. I have been trying to find that letter in order to ascertain what was the character of it, but I have not been able to do it.

Question. Your impression is that the communication which you received informed you of the fact that the Secretary of War had directed the discontinuance of those works?

Answer. That has been my impression. I must say it is not so clearly my impression now as it has been up to the time when I saw this statement in regard to it.

Question. How could he direct it? Could he make such a direction to any one but yourself?

Answer. Not properly to any one else.

Question. Do you know whether any money was paid after this time on account of those works?

Answer. I do not know anything about that.

Question. It has been stated that after this order you gave a peremptory order to Major Allen to pay over $66,000 to Mr. Beard; that he declined to do so, and communicated the fact to the department at Washington, and was told not to pay the money. Do you know whether that is so or not?

Answer. I do not know anything about that.

Question. Did you, in the contract made with Mr. Beard, fix the prices that he was to receive?

Answer. Not in detail. It was arranged and the price was determined upon between General McKinstry and Mr. Beard. Further than that I do not know.

Question. Was it left to General McKinstry to determine what would be a fair price for doing the work?

Answer. Yes, sir.

Question. General McKinstry was assistant quartermaster there, was he not?

Answer. He was quartermaster, at the head of the quartermaster's department, in that department.

Question. By whom appointed?

Answer. By the government. He was a quartermaster in the regular army, and had been there nearly two years before he was removed. I had him removed from the office. I applied to the President—knowing him to be a good soldier, and one who had really distinguished himself in Mexico—I applied to the President to give him a commission as brigadier general, which he did. I told the President he would be much more serviceable in the field at the head of a brigade than as a quartermaster.

Question. It was not at your solicitation that he was appointed quartermaster?

Answer. No, sir; not at all. I found him there as quartermaster. He had been there, I suppose, eighteen months when I got there.

Question. So that you were in nowise responsible for the acts which he did legitimately within his jurisdiction as quartermaster?

Answer. Certainly not. He was responsible to the government.

Question. He fixed the prices at which this labor was to be done?

Answer. Yes, sir; and I approved them.

Question. He agreed upon the price?

Answer. Yes; so I understood it.

Question. You did not fix the price, but simply approved it after the rest had been fixed by the quartermaster?

Answer. General McKinstry was, in the first instance, ordered by me to make the contract with Mr. Beard. When this contract, with the conditions desired by Mr. Beard, was presented to him, he referred the question of prices to me. I told him I would approve whatever he determined to be right, and I did so.

He told me the prices claimed by Mr. Beard had been too high, and I told him to put them at what he thought proper, having regard to the nature of the work and the peculiar circumstances under which it was done.

Question. Then it is not true that you fixed the prices between the quartermaster and the contractor?

Answer. Not true at all.

Question. They were approved by you after they had been fixed by Quartermaster McKinstry at what he deemed fair rates?

Answer. Yes, sir; so I understand. That is my recollection.

Question. Is it within the duties of the quartermaster to make contracts for the erection of fortifications?

Answer. Perhaps not strictly. I suppose it should come more under the direction of the engineer department, if there were such there. It would come under the direction strictly of the quartermaster's department to build barracks, and, under circumstances, fortifications. Certainly, under the circumstances, then, I think it might be considered that he was the proper officer to do that work. I am not familiar enough with the customs of our service to say who should properly attend to that work. Such works as barracks—quarters for the troops, of any kind—come under the direction of the quartermaster. I do not know but that strictly the whole of this may be considered to be within his department.

Question. Did you regard it at the time as within his department?

Answer. Yes, entirely so.

Question. Did he accept the service, and perform the duty as a part of the duty of the department?

Answer. I have no recollection of his having made any opposition to undertaking the work. If he did so I overruled it, certainly; but I have no recollection of it. I do not think he would have made any after having been directed by me to attend to it. I gave him positive orders to do so, and left him without any alternative.

Question. What position did Captain Turnley hold?

Answer. He was a quartermaster under General McKinstry, and succeeded him upon his appointment as brigadier general. He ranked next to General McKinstry, I think.

Question. In relation to the fund from which the money was to be taken to pay for these fortifications: from what source did you understand that that money was to be obtained?

Answer. From any source that it could be obtained from, whether quartermaster, or commissary, or anything else.

Question. You deemed you had the right to take money from the quartermaster's department to pay for the construction of these fortifications?

Answer. Certainly; and in that connexion I want to call the attention of the committee to the fact which renders that suggestion of no force, as it might have if the different departments had been supplied with money by the government; but, on the contrary, we ourselves a greater part of the time had to provide money by borrowing it, and then I directed it to be delivered to the quartermaster, the commissary, or other officer who most needed it. The money came from a general source, that is, from our credit and ability to borrow it. The government supplied us with very little money, in no way adequate to our necessities; all distinctions were lost; none existed, none were regarded. The money, wherever it was, was taken by me to pay any and the most pressing demands in any branch of the service, where I thought it was necessary.

Question. And obtaining the money as you did, you did not feel under obligations to confine it to the expenses of any particular department?

Answer. Not the slightest?

Question. In relation to the purchase of horses and mules for your department: by whom were those purchases made?

Answer. Made mainly by the quartermaster—some under special contracts; some were bought in Ohio, I think, under special contracts; some were intended to have been bought in Canada, or wherever they could be had. The quartermaster's business is to provide the horses.

Question. Did you have any immediate personal knowledge of those contracts?

Answer. Some of them not much personal knowledge, but some knowledge. Of some I had direct personal knowledge.

Question. Please state in regard to those contracts of which you had knowledge.

Answer. That of which I had the most particular knowledge is a contract with a man named Gustavus A. Sacchi, of New York. With the others I had so little to do, I do not think I had any information that would be of service to you.

Question. Did you order the purchase of a thousand Canadian cavalry horses by Augustus A. Sacchi, of New York; and if so, will you state the particulars of that transaction?

Answer. I did. Mr. Sacchi came to St. Louis and procured an interview with me for the purpose of offering to make that contract. It struck me as a good thing to be done. I knew that Canadian horses were valuable, for I had used them in the field. I knew them to be an unusually tough horse, easy to be got along with on the prairie where food was scarce; and I directed a contract to be made with him for the purchase of a thousand of them.

Question. Do you remember the price?

Answer. It was $120, I think.

Question. Were those horses delivered?

Answer. No, sir; I think two were.

Question. Only two?

Answer. That was all, I think. More were offered but only two were accepted.

Question. Are there any further particulars in relation to that transaction that you desire to state?

Answer. It has been stated that Mr. Woods intervened between the contractor and myself. I will state in regard to that that Mr. Woods had no power of intervention any further than this: after Mr. Sacchi had come to see me, which he did through another person—I think he was introduced to me by General Asboth—I sent for Mr. Woods, after the contract was decided upon, and told him to send for Captain Turnley and to say that that contract had been made. That was all that Captain Woods had to do with the matter in any connexion. It is also stated that Mr. Sacchi had difficulty in speaking English, so much so that Captain Turnley had to speak with him in Spanish. The fact is, that Mr. Sacchi speaks English correctly, and about as fluently as foreigners get to speak our language, and, as I am informed, he cannot speak Spanish at all, and knows very little about it. I spoke English with him without the least difficulty whatever.

Question. Did this Mr. Sacchi ever receive an appointment upon your staff?

Answer. No, sir; he never was on my staff. There was a Captain Sacchi on my staff at Springfield, who came from Italy for the purpose of serving with us. He was an officer who had been distinguished under Garibaldi, and decorated for gallantry; but he was not the man with whom I made the contract for horses.

Question. Did you have any reason to suppose that there was any collusion between Colonel Woods, of your staff, and Mr. Sacchi?

Answer. Not the slightest at all. I do not think there ever was the slightest. I have here a statement from Mr. Sacchi, who had seen those statements, and if the committee will examine they will perceive that they are without the slightest foundation whatever.

(Statement handed to the committee.)

Question. Did you order Colonel T. P. Andrews to make a payment to Captain Schwartz?

Annswer. I did.

Question. Please state the circumstances and the reasons for requiring Colonel Andrews to make that payment?

Answer. I had directed Captain Schwartz to recruit men for a battery, of which he was to have the command. I will state in this connexion that he was an artillery officer who had seen service. He is mentioned with distinction on account of his behavior at the battle of Belmont. I had directed him to recruit men for his battery. He brought me in a bill which he required to be paid of something over $200; I do not remember now how much it was. I sent him to the paymaster whom I directed to pay it, following out my general course of ordering money to be paid wherever it could be found. The paymaster sent back the paper with an indorsement on the back of it, that he had been in the service forty years and had never received such an order before, and refused to pay it. Before that came to me Captain Schwartz had left the house. I sent for him, and the next day sent him with another order to the paymaster directing him to pay that money; and I sent Captain Zagoni with a file of men, and gave him written instructions to the effect that if Colonel Andrews did not obey that order to arrest him and place him in confinement; to deliver him to Colonel McKinley, and have him confined in the town hall—that is to say, at the city garrison. Captain Zagoni went with Captain Schwartz; the order was presented, and Colonel Andrews again refused to pay it, and Captain Zagoni arrested him. After being arrested in that way Colonel Andrews paid the order.

Question. Was the money in Colonel Andrews's hands at that time money that had been obtained by you in the same manner as the sums to which you have before referred?

Answer. I do not know. I intended the order to be against any money he might have on hand, from whatever source it might have been obtained.

Question. Intending to be governed in your department according to the necessities of the case, without regard to restrictions?

Answer. Exactly.

Question. Did you at any time order or demand money of the assistant treasurer of the United States at St. Louis?

Answer. I did.

Question. Under what circumstances, and for what reasons?

Answer. Shortly after I went to the department, there being no money at all, the troops being about to disband and refusing to re-enlist because they were not paid, and there being an immediate demand for troops, I applied to the treasurer, who I understood to have about $300,000 then on hand, for $100,000. He declined to do so. I sent for him and had a conversation with him, in which I urged upon him the expediency and necessity of using that money, or a portion of it, in that way. He, however, after reflection, decided that he could not do it. I then ordered my adjutant general to take with him as much force as might be necessary and go and take the money, and deliver it to the paymaster, to be used as circumstances might require. I did that in the exercise of the power I understood myself to have, and which I believed I did have. I informed the President that I was about to do it, and should do it.

Question. Did you ever receive any reply in answer to that communication?

Answer. No, sir.

Question. In relation to orders for ice to be sent from St. Louis to Jefferson City. Will you state what order was given in relation to that matter, the necessity for the order, and what was done in pursuance of it?

Answer. A requisition was made upon me for ice by Doctor Tellekamp, who was my first medical officer, and I approved the requisition, of course, in the confidence that his judgment was correct as to the quantity of ice that would probably be required in the events that were then expected to take place. He made the requisition in anticipation of a battle between Sedalia and Lexington, in which 70,000 men would be engaged—that being about the number to which the forces on both sides amounted. In that event, there would be many killed and wounded, and that would necessitate the use of a large quantity of ice; and in order to be certain to have enough, he made a requisition for 500 tons so as to secure it at St. Louis. I believe that only a small quantity of ice was sent up, and only what the service actually required. I have no doubt myself that the order, though a large one, was a reasonable requisition on his part under the circumstances. At all events, I was guided by the opinion of the medical officer who made the requisition. I think it is clear, however, that when 70,000 men are engaged in battle, as was his expectation would be the case, there will be some use for ice on such an occasion. It is hardly necessary for me to say that that was the purpose for which it was ordered, and the only purpose for which it was ordered—for the use of the wounded and sick.

Question. Did Mr. Lamon, sometimes called General Lamon, make any application to you for any force to be sent under him into Western Virginia at any time during your administration of the western department?

Answer. He did.

Question. Will you state the circumstances in relation to that?

Answer. General Lamon overtook me on horseback on the road somewhere south of Warsaw. He brought with him a letter from the governor of Illinois, informing me of the purpose for which he came, which was to get the Yates Phalanx, a regiment which had recently come to St. Louis from Illinois. As nearly as I can now recollect the letter, it was an urgent one from Governor Yates, requesting me to let General Lamon have that regiment, stating that it would please him; would please the regiment, and would also please the President. The governor of Illinois had furnished a large body of troops for Missouri, and had always been very solicitous to aid our operations there in every way. And it did not occur to me to hesitate to agree at once to his request, and order the regiment to be turned over to General Lamon. It may be as well for me to remark here in this connexion, also, that at that time I was in expectation of being removed from the department; and, as you may have noticed, things were done a little loosely; I mean, referring in all cases to myself, not done with all the strictness that generally pervades a department like that. And I, probably, acceded to a request of that kind the more readily, and without as much formality as if I had been expecting to remain in command. At all events, I looked upon the presence of General Lamon there, with the letter from Governor Yates, much the same as a request from the President; knowing, as I did, the relations General Lamon bore to the President.

Question. Do I understand you that you considered the request of General Lamon, knowing the relations between him and the President, as having the sanction of the President?

Answer. I did.

Question. And that was the reason you complied with it?

Answer. That was one of the reasons, though General Lamon did not say anything about his relations with the President.

By Mr. Odell:

Question. What was Lamon's rank at that time?

Answer. I supposed his rank to be a brigadier general. He had on the uniform of a brigadier general. I understood from the governor's etter that he was to command a brigade.

Question. Do you know what became of that regiment?

Answer. I do not know. When I reached St. Louis again I was not in command, and it did not occur to me to inquire.

Question. At that time did you have an excess of troops, so that you could well spare this regiment?

Answer. No, sir. There never was an occasion when I could spare any troops. I remarked to General Lamon at the time that of course he could have the regiment, but that I need not say to him that it was not an agreeable thing to me to let any of my regiments go.

Question. Was there not a military necessity why you should not have let that regiment go?

Answer. Not strictly, I think. If there was not a military necessity for continuing the fortifications at St. Louis, there was not certainly a military necessity to keep one regiment, more or less, there.

Question. That regiment was at St. Louis at that time.

Answer. Yes, sir. There were other regiments to replace them. Very probably the governor suggested in his letter that other regiments would replace that one.

By Mr. Gooch:

Question. In complying with that request, did you feel that you took the responsibility of ordering that regiment from St. Louis to Western Virginia?

Answer. No, sir, I did not. The question of responsibility did not occur to me. I supposed, from the manner in which the thing was presented to me, that I was doing a thing of course. Business in our service is not done with the strictness which that would imply. If you remember, there was a great deal done in the western department which was not consistent with strict military propriety; a great deal. And in my condition, then, going south with my army, and not expecting to be retained in command long, it was not a matter to me of very great importance whether that regiment was retained or not, if others thought it best to send it somewhere else. So far as I can now recollect, I thought, when General Lamon overtook me and brought me that letter, that it was a thing I was expected to do, and I did it. And to take the opposite view of it, it would not have been very agreeable to me to refuse to do what I had reason to suppose would be agreeable to the President, and which the governor of Illinois told me would be agreeable to the President.

By Mr. Odell:

Question. It could not be done without a great expenditure of money, could it?

Answer. That was not for me to consider at all. If it was agreeable to the President, and pleased him, that was all that concerned me. I knew that a fine regiment had been ordered from me at St. Louis a short time before that to go to Washington. And consequently that would not probably have been considered by me to be a matter of importance.

By Mr. Gooch:

Question. As you have alluded to those five regiments, will you state what became of them? Did they come through to Washington?

Answer. No, sir. On their way from the point where they had been stationed—which was Fort Holt, in Kentucky, on the Mississippi river—before they reached Cincinnati, a bridge gave way, and there were some 140, more or less, of the men belonging to those regiments killed and wounded. They then went on to Camp Dennison and stopped there. I, in the meantime, had applied to the government, and urged the government not to take those regiments; not to take any more; and suggested that they should take two regiments of cavalry, which I could not arm, and leave me the other regiments. And, upon my representations, the result finally was that the government did not press for the five regiments, and permitted these regiments to remain. And seeing that General Anderson had need at the time of forces in Kentucky, as they had gone that far, I ordered them to join General Anderson.

Question. Did the five regiments leave you at that time?

Answer. Only these two.

Question. Was that at a time when you could spare the troops?

Answer. Not at all.

By Mr. Odell:

Question. From whom did you receive the order to send those five regiments on here?

Answer. From General Scott, and from the Secretary of War, both.

By Mr. Gooch:

Question. You constructed railroads and equipped them, purchased cars, &c. Will you state to the committee the reasons which led you to construct those railroads, and whether or not any advantages were derived from that work?

Answer. I ordered our superintendent of roads to examine the rolling stock of all the railroads, and ascertain what amount there was, in order to know what force could be moved at any time upon those roads. His report showed that the quantity of rolling stock was not at all equal to what our requirements demanded. I applied to the president of the Pacific railroad to ascertain if any, and what, arrangements could be made to provide more stock. It was found upon examination that it could not well be done through him, mainly because we had no money to give him to enable him to provide additional stock, even if that would have answered the purpose. I therefore had the matter further inquired into, and after some examination I ordered a contract for cars to be made, which was given to a Mr. Murray, of Cincinnati, who had founderies both at Cincinnati and St. Louis. And growing out of the same investigation, I suppose, it became apparent that great advantages would be derived if all those roads could be connected. At the extremities of the roads were our posts. The roads led through portions of country, or to points, which we supposed to be threatened by the enemy at any time, and a junction of the roads, with a sufficient quantity of rolling stock, would enable us to throw from any one or more points to any other point a force to meet any emergency. I therefore ordered a junction to be made which connected the road running from Ironton to St. Louis, the Pacific road, the road that runs to Rolla, and the road that runs through the northern part of the State, so that all the roads were connected; and the result of the whole arrangement was that with twenty-four hours' notice 20,000 troops could be moved from St. Louis to any point which might be threatened. It had this further advantage, the railroad was brought right along the river bank at St. Louis, so that upon the arrival of troops from Illinois, or any other State east, they could be brought over in the steamer always kept in readiness there and transferred directly to the railroad—they and their equipments and their supplies—and sent off immediately to any one of our posts, or to the interior of the State. Formerly the quartermaster's department had to hire wagons, sometimes hauling equipments and supplies two and two and a half miles through the city to the different depots, and troops arriving there had to move from one point to another with all their supplies. In this case, as we often had occasion to employ it, a regiment embarked at Ironton, for instance, and passed right through St. Louis, with all their equipments, &c., and proceeded directly to Jefferson City, or any other point where they were needed; or a regiment from any one of the posts would come to St. Louis and pass right through on the cars, without stopping at all in the city, and go to any other place where they were needed. And so with regiments arriving by the river boats.

By Mr. Covode:

Question. Where did you connect these roads?

Answer. In the city of St. Louis. They were all brought to a common landing place on the river. As an instance in point: the rebels tore up about 100 miles of track, more or less, on the North Missouri railroad, which runs to St. Joseph. Probably a part of the rolling stock of that road was on one side of that break and a part on the other. The military authorities went to the Pacific railroad and took 35 of these very cars which I had made as the best cars to be used, and transferred them to the North Missouri road, and no doubt that single operation was worth more to the government than the entire cost of all those cars.

Question. By this connexion you made the stock on all the roads available for any one road?

Answer. Yes, sir. I first sent across the river, before I ordered any cars to be made, to see if stock could be secured from the Illinois roads. But I found they would not answer, as the gauge was different, and I was obliged to have cars constructed. It gives this advantage to Missouri: that at any time, with 24 hours' notice, you can transport as large a body of troops as 20,000 men from one part of the State to any other part.

By Mr. Gooch:

Question. You say the government has availed itself, and is still availing itself, of the advantages of this connexion?

Answer. Unquestionably it is. It is an important advantage to the entire State and to the government in its operations there. It is but recently that the instance occurred to which I have referred, when 35 cars were taken from the Pacific road and used on another road.

Question. How many cars did you order to be made?

Answer. Fifty, I think.

By Mr. Odell:

Question. Do you remember the price?

Answer. I think somewhere near $800 a car. But I do not know exactly. I would not like to be positive.

By Mr. Gooch:

Question. Can you tell me how many regiments were stationed in Northern Missouri, under General Pope, at the time you took charge of the western department?

Answer. Not exactly; probably from five to seven regiments. I do not now remember the number. I had just reached the State then. The disposable force, whatever it was—all our Illinois disposable force—was ordered into Northern Missouri at General Pope's request.

Question. Do you know where those troops were stationed—at what points?

Answer. Along the line of the Hannibal and St. Joseph railroad, north of the road—scattered about the interior there.

Question. How many troops did you find at St. Louis at that time?

Answer. Few, if any; a regiment or two, possibly, and some home guard regiments.

Question. On what day did you arrive at St. Louis and take command?

Answer. On the 25th of July.

Question. And the battle of Wilson's Creek was on the 10th of August?

Answer. Yes, sir.

Question. When did you first learn that General Lyon was threatened by a superior force of the enemy?

Answer. While in New York city, I think.

Question. In what manner?

Answer. By a telegraphic despatch to the effect that he needed re-enforcements. That, I think, was about the 18th of July. A large part of the disposable force was then with him.

Question. Was it in your power at that time to have ordered any troops to the assistance of General Lyon?

Answer. No, sir; not under the circumstances.

Question. Did you at any time order any troops to his assistance?

Answer. About the 3d of August, I think, I ordered the regiment under Colonel Stephenson—one of our best regiments—and Colonel Montgomery, with his mounted command, from Kansas, both to march to the relief of General Lyon. And on my arrival at St. Louis I also ordered Colonel Wyman to march with his regiment from Rolla. Colonel Stephenson, who was at Boonville, got as far as Rolla on his way to General Lyon; and there were three regiments under marching orders to join General Lyon when he was defeated.

Question. Did those regiments have sufficient means of transportation to enable them to go to the relief of General Lyon?

Answer. That depends upon what would be considered sufficient. Colonel Stephenson did move from Boonville to Rolla. I received a letter from him informing me that he did not consider the transportation at Rolla sufficient; that he thought it inexpedient, or dangerous, to march from that point to the relief of General Lyon, because of the force of the enemy which he apprehended would be between him and the Mississippi river, and which would expose his force to great danger; and he and Colonel Wyman did not march from Rolla. I ordered Colonel Stephenson from Rolla to St. Louis, upon receiving his letter stating the reasons for his not having marched to the relief of General Lyon, intending to place him under arrest; but I admitted his reasons so far as not to do that. Colonel Wyman was already at Rolla with his regiment; and after Colonel Stephenson's regiment had arrived there, there were two regiments at that point which I had ordered to go to General Lyon.

Question. Was there sufficient transportation at Rolla, or transportation with which it would have been possible for those two regiments to have moved to the relief of General Lyon?

Answer. I should certainly consider it possible for those two regiments to have moved; that is to say, I would have moved those two regiments myself, if I had been there. I consider it would have been possible—not convenient, probably. The men would have been exposed to some suffering, no doubt. But that is a matter for the judgment of the officer there.

By Mr. Odell:

Question. What is the distance from Rolla to Springfield?

Answer. I think it is 118 miles.

By Mr. Gooch:

Question. There is no railroad from Rolla to Springfield?

Answer. No, sir.

Question. Had any of the transportation been ordered from Rolla to St. Louis prior to that time?

Answer. No, sir. The difficulty about transportation there was in this, as I remember it: General Lyon had retained the transportation at Springfield—had not sent back the supply train to Rolla. With that supply train there would have been abundant transportation, because the transportation afterwards gathered there amounted probably to between three hundred and four hundred wagons, large and small. There was abundant transportation if they could have had it there at that time.

Question. The transportation was with General Lyon at Springfield instead of at Rolla?

Answer. Yes, sir.

Question. And no transportation was ordered from Rolla to St. Louis?

Answer. I have no recollection of any such thing, and know no reason why any should have been so ordered.

Question. Either from Rolla or from any other point from which it might have gone to Rolla to have aided those two regiments to have moved to the support of General Lyon?

Answer. I have no recollection of that. Bear in mind the transportation was very deficient at that time. We had very little in the department compared with our requirements.

Question. Were you fully advised in relation to the situation of General Lyon for some days prior to the battle of Wilson's Creek?

Answer. I was advised as to his condition, I think; perhaps fully—I cannot say how fully. I knew generally of his condition; and you will see from his letter of the 9th of August what his condition was. And I had understood his condition to be about as he states it there. I knew he was in need of supplies and in need of re-enforcements, and we were doing everything it was possible to do to send him both. Bear in mind, in going along over this subject, that the first necessity had been to re-enforce Cairo. In the interim between arriving at St. Louis and the defeat of General Lyon I had gathered a force and taken it to Cairo to relieve General Prentiss.

Question. Did you deem it more advisable that Cairo should be strengthened than that General Lyon should be re-enforced?

Answer. Clearly so.

Question. State your reasons for that.

Answer. Cairo, as you are aware, is a permanent post, necessary to be held for the safety of St. Louis. It was occupied by General Prentiss with a force that was being disbanded, and was threatened by a largely superior force of the enemy. The danger to Cairo, therefore, was exceedingly imminent. General Lyon had something near 7,000 men with him, as I then estimated his force; and it was supposed that in case of extreme difficulty he would fall back. The whole point, in my mind, was whether General Lyon would choose to remain at Springfield or to retreat. General Prentiss could not retreat, and therefore I took the first relief to Cairo; went down with it myself. General Prentiss told me I was just in time. He said he had felled trees and barricaded the roads, and was hourly expecting an attack. In fact he said, I remember, that General Pillow was just forty-eight hours too late. Why he used the expression "forty-eight hours" I do not know. That was the expression he and his officers used. At all events, he had but 1,200 men under arms there, and informed me then, and has since told me, that the place would have been taken if I had not arrived in time. I considered the first necessity was to re-enforce Cairo. That was done, although with a very inadequate force. Still it was sufficient, as it proved. About 3,000 men was all I could take there.

By Mr. Odell:

Question. At what time did you re-enforce General Prentiss?

Answer. I left St. Louis on the 1st day of August, and was back again on the 4th of August, having before I got back sent orders to re-enforce General Lyon with the two regiments of Stephenson and Montgomery. As soon as I reached St. Louis I went to work to get what force I could in order to send it to General Lyon. I think it is very clear that if General Lyon had decided to fall back upon Rolla, instead of engaging the enemy, there would have been no disaster, except losing that part of the State.

By Mr. Gooch:

Question. You considered it in the power of General Lyon to have fallen back to Rolla?

Answer. General Lyon so says in his letter of August 9. It is always supposable that an officer will not allow himself, if he can avoid it, to get in a situation where he cannot fall back.

Question. Did you receive any despatch or communication, or intelligence in any way, that led you to suppose that it was not in General Lyon's power to fall back upon Rolla?

Answer. No, sir: on the contrary, our information was to the effect that General Lyon had had a successful skirmish with the enemy. General Lyon undoubtedly acted as he judged was best under the circumstances.

Question. Did you send any men to Cape Girardeau?

Answer. Yes, sir; I re-enforced Cape Girardeau at that time.

Question. Do you recollect how many men you sent there?

Answer. A regiment, I think. I am not clear, however, when I re-enforced that place.

Question. You say you regarded the obstacles in the way of Colonel Stephenson were so great as to excuse him in not going to the relief of General Lyon, although you think if you had been in command yourself there you would have pursued a different course?

Answer. Yes, sir; I think I might have done so.

By Mr. Odell:

Question. Does that apply to both regiments at Rolla?

Answer. Yes, sir; to the entire force there.

Question. The regiments were not both from the same point?

Answer. No, sir; Stephenson's and Wyman's regiments were at Rolla; that is, after Stephenson had arrived there from Boonville, Wyman had for some time previously been at Rolla, and I ordered him to go to General Lyon after I reached St. Louis. Colonel Montgomery I had previously ordered from Kansas.

Question. You only refer to Colonel Stephenson as disobeying orders?

Answer. Colonel Wyman joined with Colonel Stephenson in that matter.

Question. How about Colonel Montgomery?

Answer. Colonel Montgomery did not succeed in getting to General Lyon.

Question. Was he on his way there?

Question. I suppose so. The order was directed to be communicated to him. But the distance was considerable between St. Louis and Montgomery's position in Kansas; and the 10th of August came very quickly. I think you will find in the documents I have submitted all the circumstances under which Cape Girardeau was re-enforced. It seemed to be especially the object of attack of Jeff. Thompson, who was near there with 5,000 men, and Hardee was between there and Cairo with 7,000 or 8,000 men. You will see by that the exigency under which Prentiss and Marsh, commanding at Girardeau, supposed themselves to be. You will find all these matters fully set forth in the papers I have submitted.

By Mr. Gooch :

Question. Did you re-enforce Pilot Knob about this time—the 1st of August

Answer. Yes, sir.

Question. With what force ?

Answer. I think with a regiment.

Question. Will you state your reasons for strengthening Girardeau and Pilot Knob at that time?

Answer. They were the outposts of St. Louis. Cape Girardeau was one of the few high lands on the river—one of the points considered necessary to be held. It was a point which the enemy had endeavored to gain possession of; they directed their special attention to that object. And if the enemy had obtained the possession of that point upon the river they could have interrupted communication, by river, between St. Louis and Cairo.

Question. Did you send re-enforcements to Rolla, after the news of Lyon's defeat reached you?

Answer. Yes, sir.

Question. How soon?

Answer. As soon as I could get them there

Question. Could that force have been sent before and in season to have re-enforced General Lyon?

Answer. No, sir; we had sent before all we could.

Question. Did you order Colonel Mulligan to occupy and hold Lexington; if not, what order did you give him in relation to his movements?

Answer. It is difficult for me to recollect the orders I did give, without my order-book, which has been retained by General Halleck at St. Louis, contrary to my request.

Question. Those orders will not appear in the documents you have submitted to the committee?

Answer. No, sir. If any order of that kind was given to Colonel Mulligan—which I cannot now recollect—it will be in my order-book. Colonel Mulligan was more especially under the command of General Davis, who was acting brigadier general, and holding Jefferson City with a large body of our force, and controlling that part of the State. Colonel Mulligan was subject to the command of General Davis, and the command of General Pope. The county in which Lexington lies belonged to General Pope's command. General Pope had been assigned to the command of North Missouri, including the counties on both sides of the Missouri river, except St. Louis. General Davis had been sent to Jefferson City with a considerable body of troops, increased to 9,000 men, when Lexington fell. Colonel Mulligan would be more immediately under his order. General Davis was also in direct communication with him, General Pope being actively employed in the northwestern part of the State. That was the condition of affairs when Colonel Mulligan was at Lexington. Colonel Mulligan had been sent, I think, to some of the Osage towns to take the money from the banks at those places, to prevent it falling into the hands of the secessionists, and he was then returning from that expedition, when Price followed him up so closely and so rapidly that I think he reached Lexington nearly as quickly as Mulligan did—not much difference of time between them.

Question. Then you cannot state now, from recollection, whether you gave any order, either through General Davis or General Pope, or directly to Colonel Mulligan, for Colonel Mulligan to take and hold Lexington until he should receive re-enforcements?

Answer. Not any more clearly than you will see set forth in the telegraphic despatches and communications which I have laid before you. They comprise all the orders and all the despatches relating to that subject which I have in my possession. Whatever others there may be will be found in the order-book which General Halleck has. I think you will find these despatches here will carry on the account very connectedly and very clearly.

Question. Can you state how many troops you had under your command, and where they were stationed at the time that Colonel Mulligan was at Lexington?

Answer. No further than I have already given it in the statement I have submitted to the committee.

Question. Have you in that statement given the reasons for not re-enforcing Colonel Mulligan?

Answer. I have stated there that Davis was supporting him, and that re-enforcements were sent to him, but part of them failed to reach him.

Question. You have stated there all that was done towards re-enforcing Colonel Mulligan, and that the re-enforments sent failed to reach him?

Answer. I have stated the efforts made to re-enforce him, and what the result was.

Question. Were all the efforts made that could be made?

Answer. Yes, sir; all that were deemed necessary to make were made.

Question. Had you made any preparations at the time Price was at Lexington to cut off his retreat?

Answer. I was organizing a force to move south with the intention of occupying Springfield, and at the same time cutting off his line of retreat, when his sudden advance upon Lexington rendered different arrangements necessary. As I have said we were there in a state of preparation all the time. The case would have been vastly different if I had had a disposable force there. If I could have found on my arrival there a disposable force of 30,000, there would have been a very different account rendered of the condition of affairs there. When I reached St. Louis, 30,000 men would have enabled me to re-enforce Lyon, sustained Prentiss, and taken New Madrid and Memphis. But the whole difficulty consisted in the fact that while we were talking about re-enforcing we had nothing to do it with. It was impossible to do anything more towards re-enforcing General Lyon than was done. I do not think it was possible, except by means that I did not then see, and which nobody there saw, to re-enforce Lyon, sustain Cairo, or assist Mulligan. A great deal must depend upon the officer himself who is to be re-enforced. When an officer is two hundred miles in advance of his supports, he must do a great deal for himself. Fully as much depends upon his judgment and upon his action as upon those who are to re-enforce him. That was our case. Had General Lyon been able to retire—had Colonel Mulligan been able to preserve his boats, we could, of course, have re-enforced him. Had Colonel Mulligan retired towards Sedalia instead of entering Lexington, we could have re-enforced him. But nothing could possibly have enabled re-enforcements to have reached him any sooner under the circumstances than they did, from the time it was known to us that that was the point of attack, and that that was the place to be re-enforced. General Davis telegraphed to me several points that he said were threatened. And up to a very late hour, I think, several days after Price's march down towards Lexington, General Davis telegraphed to me that Boonville appeared to be the point threatened, and not Lexington. And he was a great deal nearer than I was.

Question. Was Colonel Mulligan acting under any instructions from you that rendered it imperative upon him to take and hold Lexington?

Answer. He may have been. I do not bear in mind whether he was or not. I have not seen my order-book since that date.

Question. Was any order given by you at any time to General Lane to fall back from Kansas City to Leavenworth and destroy his baggage trains, stores, &c.?

Answer. Destroy his baggagge trains? No, sir.

Question. Or to destroy his stores?

Answer. No, sir; I perceive to what transaction your inquiry refers. It became at one time a matter of expediency, so it was thought, to retire our force, which was cut off from our main body, and throw it around to St. Joseph, and on the railroad to Chillicothe, which formed a part of our line. I wished to withdraw the force at Kansas City and throw it on the north side of the Missouri river, on the line of the railroad to Chillicothe, where it could be connected with our army. Our army was stretching, and intended to stretch, at that time from the Osage river across the State to Chillicothe. We were occupying a sort of crescent-shaped line, intended to enclose General Price; and we were separated from these small forces by the Missouri river. Such as General Sturgis's command. The intention was to throw General Sturgis and his force from his position at Kansas City around to Chillicothe, and bring him upon the extreme right of our line, and connected with the rest of our force, so that there might be no more of these surrenders of small detached bodies of troops. It was doubtful whether or not they had any stores at Kansas City; the result of the best inquiries we could make was that there were none; but in directing General Sturgis to fall back and come around to Chillicothe I directed him, if he had any stores there to destroy them, rather than have them fall into the hands of the enemy. It was considered better, after a great deal of deliberation, to throw General Sturgis around, and have him in connexion with us, than to leave him there. General Lane I did not succeed in having much communication with. He was very difficult to communicate with. I never gave him any orders to destroy his baggage or provisions; and I think I gave none to him in regard to Kansas City.

By Mr. Odell:

Question. You do not remember to have authorized him to destroy the city?

Answer. To destroy the city! no, sir; I do not think I communicated with him, for General Sturgis was his superior officer. No order was given to destroy the city, but only any stores which might belong to us which were there. As I have already stated, it was very doubtful whether there were any stores there, but if there were any such General Sturgis was directed to destroy them rather than they should fall into the hands of the enemy. The order was not obeyed, however, because it did not reach General Sturgis. Our force was so scattered at that time that I frequently took the trouble and precaution to duplicate, and even triplicate the orders, to send different despatches, as they were very frequently intercepted by the enemy. Sometimes despatches reached General Lane, and sometimes they did not.

By Mr. Gooch:

Question. Were these orders given to destroy stores at any other point, or to burn any place on the retirement of our troops?

Answer. No, sir. It was after a great deal of discussion that this order to General Sturgis was determined upon. It was one of those cases in regard to which doubt existed. It was doubtful whether we should risk General Sturgis there, instead of ordering him to move around to the other position. But finally, as one disaster, as it was considered, had been suffered, it was decided to move him around.

Question. In regard to the suppression of newspapers in your department, will you state to the committee what was done in that respect?

Answer. I think there were three or four suppressions.

Question. For what reasons?

Answer. Because they were considered detrimental to the service there. We had but little of that to do. The most of that that was done was upon the declaration of martial law. It was generally acceded to, generally considered to be right. We gained over some papers. We treated the St. Louis Republican, having a large circulation, with a great deal of consideration, and it finally became, earnestly and emphatically, one of the supporters of the administration. I have always considered that one of the most important papers in Missouri. It was a hostile paper when I got there, but afterwards became a friendly paper.

Question. That paper was not suppressed?

Answer. No, sir. The object was to make it a friendly paper. Although it had been an opposing paper, it had never used violent language, or done anything with an obvious design and purpose to stir up the people against us. It had always taken a fair political stand. During the latter part of my administration there was nothing of the kind done there.

Question. There have been frequent rumors and statements that persons who came to you as messengers from officers in the field, and other persons having important communications relative to the conduct of the war in the western department, found it impossible to gain access to you while you were in command there.

Answer. I do not believe that such was the case at all. I think that all officers having reason to see me, having business with me, could readily find access to me, taking their turn. I always occupied from very early in the morning until very late at night with those things which were most pressing and necessary to be attended to.

By Mr. Odell:

Question. When you say, "taking their turn," do you mean that we should infer that it was a matter of two or three days for a man to get to see you?

Answer. No, sir; not any one having business in reference to the department, when I knew of it. I dare say there were men who waited two or three days, or even a week, to see me there; that may have been. But there was a standing order that an officer coming to see me, no matter what his business was, should come up without any hindrance. The business pertaining to the department I attended to first, and all other business as I could find time to dispose of it. The orders issued to the commanding officer of the guard were of such a nature that they could be easily ascertained by applying to him at any time.

By Mr. Gooch:

Question. It has been stated that the house occupied as your headquarters was unnecessarily expensive to the government. Will you state the facts in relation to that?

Answer. I do not think the quarters occupied were unusually expensive. They were comfortable and commodious, but I do not think that the resulting expense to the government was greater than would have been for any number of smaller houses which the department might have required. It was pretty well occupied by officers. The fact of that particular house having been taken happened in this way: On our arrival at St. Louis, and even before our arrival there, we were invited by Mrs. Brandt, who was Mrs. Frémont's cousin, to occupy her house. It was then vacant, she being absent from the city, and about to start for Europe. We occupied the house for some time without paying any rent, and then decided that it was so commodious and so suitable for headquarters that it should be hired. And it accordingly was hired. How the price paid for it would compare with other houses in other parts of the town I do not know.

By Mr. Odell:

Question. Do you remember the price paid?

Answer. It was $6,000. In it were accommodated all my working staff officers with myself; quite a number of them. It was made the central headquarters. The telegraph wires were brought there; and it was about such a house, and had about such accommodations, as a department of that size would require. At all events, it never occurred to me that we were incurring any unusual expense until I saw it afterwards questioned.

By Mr. Gooch:

Question. Will you state to the committee the reasons which induced you to make the proclamation which has been so much talked of since, and all the facts connected with that proclamation, so far as you remember them?

Answer. I judged it expedient to make the proclamation because I began to find myself pressed to meet what I considered serious dangers. Our means there were all the time very inadequate, and I thought that the time had come when it was necessary to strike some decided blow against the enemy, and I judged that the measures proposed by the proclamation were such as would give us a great and important advantage over our enemv. Without going into detail, I judged that the condition of the country, the activity and the universality of the rebellion, and the strength of the force against us, rendered it necessary that I should take the best measures I could to suppress the rebellion there.

By the chairman:

Question. How did it operate while it was in force?

Answer. It operated admirably while it was in force. The effect it produced fully satisfied me that it was a good measure.

By Mr. Julian:

Question. What was the effect of the modification of it?

Answer. It was, in my judgment, injurious, so far as my observation went. I made the proclamation as a war measure, judging that its effect would be immediate and beneficial; and it proved so, so far as I had an opportunity to judge; and, except in one of the clauses, I think the terms of that proclamation have been carried out since I left the department. The reasons for issuing that proclamation may be generally embraced in the statement that I then thought the condition of the department had become critical, and that decided measures and effective, such as I judged those to be, which would strike home, ought to be adopted at once. I came to the determination of issuing that proclamation, and immediately notified the President of the United States of its issue. For his answer, and the terms in which he modified that proclamation, I refer to the papers accompanying my statement. It will be there seen that the President modified the proclamation in two particulars: first, as regards freeing the slaves of rebels; and, secondly, as regards shooting rebels who should be taken in arms within our lines. His letter to that effect, and mine in answer, are among the papers I have submitted. That was the first act which met the disapprobation of the Executive in any way; and the President himself, in his letter suggesting or directing modifications, states that he does not imply any censure. About that time, however, as these papers will show, the confidence of the administration was withdrawn. The first committee of investigation came to my department shortly afterwards. I believe the committee—Mr. Blair and General Meigs—left Washington about the 6th of September. Up to that time I had the confidence of the administration, so far as indications were given to me. At least there was nothing to lead me to suppose that there had been any withdrawal of the confidence of the administration.

By Mr. Julian:

Answer You never heard of any dissatisfaction until the publication of that proclamation?

Answer. No, sir; and I think the papers I have submitted to the committee will show that up to that time no dissatisfaction on the part of the administration had been shown, and between the publication of that proclamation and the arrival of the first committee of investigation there had been no act of any marked importance in the department to call for any expression of opinion.

Colonel Blair's letter was dated the first day of September. The third day of September Montgomery Blair wrote me the letter which I have submitted. It was through him that I usually communicated with the administration here. Consequently, up to the third day of September, there would appear to have been nothing against my administration of affairs there.

Question. When the congressional committee came out there, had you any knowledge of its coming, or any opportunity to present facts before it?

Answer. I had no knowledge whatever of its coming, and no opportunity was afforded to me to present anything before it.

Question. You were in the field at that time?

Answer. I was in the field then. I never had any communication whatever of any kind with the committee. As to the proclamation I will remark that I issued it, having consideration to the exigencies of the department at that time, and considering it within the powers of a general commanding.

By the chairman:

Question. It is said that you organized a body guard that was in some military sense objectionable or unusual. Will you explain that?

Answer. It is altogether wrong to say that it was unusual, because every general has a body guard, or may have it, and ought to have it in the field, and this was organized as something necessary to a general. At first it consisted of one company only, and in nowise differing from ordinary body guards assigned to generals, that I am aware of. There was nothing unusual in the manner of their enlistment. They were enlisted like other troops for three years, and in precisely the same way. It has been said that their uniforms were something extraordinary, showy, and magnificent. Their uniform was as modest a one and as plain as well could be. As to their duties, they were important and arduous. They were liable to be called out at any hour of the day or night for any service. One among other reasons for forming this body guard was that we wished to have cavalry officers instructed, and this guard was considered a good school for cavalry officers. They were regularly instructed in all the duties of cavalry officers. Gradually, when we found that it was a success, it was increased to four companies. But the captain commanding the corps did not obtain the appointment of major until we were going to take the field. We never had, as has been stated, a greater number of officers for that corps than such a body of men were entitled to. There was a smaller number of officers, in fact. Results have shown how good a body of men they were; how successful they were in the field.

Question. It proved to be a success, did it?

Answer. It proved to be a thorough success. It was held by all officers, volunteers and regulars, that it was the best cavalry in the service. That was the opinion of Colonel Eaton, and other officers there, who resisted its being disbanded, and endeavored to have it retained in the service after the order for disbanding it had been issued. To show the class of men of which it was composed, a sergeant of that cavalry is now a lieutenant colonel, and other men are captains, scattered around the country.

By Mr. Odell:

Question. Made captains by your creation?

Answer. No, sir; have become so since I left.

By the chairman:

Question. How came it that such a body of men, who had so distinguished themselves, was disbanded?

Answer. They were disbanded, as I was informed by General McClellan, because they had expressed sentiments at Springfield which made it of doubt.

ful expediency whether or not they should be retained in the service. Although I had been removed from that department, I expected, of course, to go into the service again. I applied to General McClellan to allow me to retain that guard. I knew that a better body of men than that I could not find; and that in the field it is very important to have a body of men who would do what they were told to do, and do it thoroughly. In reply to my request he gave me that answer, and asked me to reply to it. I replied to him, and stated that I was not informed of any expression used by the guard at Springfield which made it of doubtful expediency whether or not they should be retained in the service of the country; but, on the contrary, that the gallantry of their conduct at Springfield had entitled them to the favorable consideration of the government; and I asked him, if any harsh measures had been directed against them, that he would reconsider the case, in view of these facts. To that the general never returned any answer, and they were disbanded. I am told that General Sturgis, when he went out to disband them, after the order had been issued, and they had been paraded for that purpose, when he saw them drawn up before him said that he would not disband them, but would go back to General Halleck and endeavor to get the order rescinded. He did go to him, but the order was carried out. It must be said that the men by that time had got into a very disorganized condition. They considered that they had been insulted and degraded. When they got back to St. Louis they could obtain no pay, and were allowed no food for their horses or rations for themselves. It was a severe shock to them. They had thought that on account of their conduct they had a right to be well considered. They thought, probably, that they would be promoted, or rewarded in some way; and when they met the order to disband, as though they had done something injurious to the country, they naturally were angry, and they refused to stay any longer. Those men were enlisted for three years, and enlisted regularly. They and their officers were mustered into the service by an officer of the regular army. They certainly did their duty. No application was ever made to me to know whether they had done their duty, or whether they had been guilty of any misconduct.

By Mr. Chandler:

Question. How many of those men made that charge at Springfield; three companies?

Answer. There were three companies of cavalry there belonging to what was called "the prairie scouts," Irish dragoons. They went with this guard down the lane. There were 149 or 150 of the guard, and then three companies of the others. At the head of the lane, where they emerged from the wood, they met so heavy a fire that it disorganized the three companies, but a portion of one of the three companies continued on with the guard; and some of the officers of one of those three companies jumped their horses over a very high fence that was there. I think some eight or ten men fell at that place. The three companies wheeled and took the road around another way. But the guards, when they failed to get through the fence—Major Zagoni found it was too severe there—charged down the lane some 150 or 200 yards, took the fence down, formed inside, and charged up the hill where the enemy was drawn up in line. About 149 of the guard made that charge, and there the principal fight took place. The enemy had some 500 cavalry, and the rest were foot.

By the chairman:

Question. And they routed the whole of them?

Answer. Yes, sir; they broke them up and dispersed them; they drove them into the woods, and charged upon them and fought them there; they drove them into the town, and charged upon them there and fought them through the town.

Question. Were you informed what those expressions were for which they were disbanded?

Answer. No, sir; I never have been informed. The correspondence between General McClellan and myself terminated at that point. He telegraphed to me to this effect: "I am officially informed that the body of cavalry known as your body guard expressed sentiments at Springfield which renders it of doubtful expediency whether or not they should be retained in the service. In consequence of that, I had, before receiving your request, already directed that they should be dismissed the public service." I think that is the substance of his communication. I telegraphed back, and informed him that I had not been informed of the expression of any sentiments by my guard at Springfield which would make it of doubtful expediency whether or not they should be retained in the service. But I stated that, on the contrary, I thought the gallantry of their conduct at Springfield entitled them to the favorable consideration of the government.

Question. To which he made no reply?

Answer. He made no reply at all. I asked him to reconsider the case, leav-it open to him, if he should reconsider it, to apply to me, as they were my guard, under my command, to learn what they had done to justify measures so harsh. I asked him, in view of these facts, to reconsider the case, in the event of any harsh measures having been directed against them.

By Mr. Odell:

Question. Where were these men from?

Answer. From Kentucky, mainly; some were from Ohio, and some from Missouri. There were 100 picked men from Kentucky, who came in a body. They certainly were as fine looking a body of men as you could meet anywhere. They were really a remarkable body of men.

By the chairman:

Question. Were they offered any court-martial, or court of inquiry, to ascertain what they had done to merit this treatment?

Answer. Nothing more than I have told you.

By Mr. Julian:

Question. Did they know anything about what they were charged with?

Answer. Nothing; nobody knows more than I have told you now. Major Zagoni is really a soldier, and a thorough one. For a man of his age he is really distinguished. He rose in the Hungarian army from a lieutenant to a captain; he fought his way up, and did good service there. He was an officer in a corps about the size of this guard, of about 300 or 400 men, and when Bem was surrounded they cut their way through two Austrian regiments that blocked up the road and carried Bem off. They lost nearly all their command, but they succeeded in carrying him off.

By the chairman:

Question. I want to inquire of you how far you had advanced with your army, what you expected to accomplish, and where was the enemy when you were superseded by General Hunter?

Answer. I was at Springfield when the order superseding me reached me on the 2d day of November. I was within nine miles of General Price's advance guard.

Question. What was the strength and condition of your army at that time?

Answer. It was in good fighting condition—in thoroughly good fighting condition. I should have gone into action on the morning of the 4th with 21,000 effective men. The other division, which had not then got up, would not have joined in that action. General Hunter would not have been in that action.

Question. What was the strength of the enemy, so far as you understood, at that time?

Answer. The reports sent in to me by General Sigel and General Asboth on the afternoon of the 3d stated the enemy to be 40,000 men, according to their best information. The report of General Asboth, late in the afternoon of the 3d, was that the enemy had advanced 7,000 men to Wilson's creek, which was nine miles from Springfield, and that all the roads and paths were filled with moving troops, and the whole number of the enemy was estimated at 40,000 men. I had turned over my command then; but the generals of division wrote me a letter, which I have, asking me not to give up the command of the army until after the battle should have been fought, but to hold command of the army and go on and fight the battle. In consequence of their address to me, and the request of many officers, I told them that if General Hunter did not arrive before the next morning I would take the army to battle. Accordingly, that evening I called a council of generals of divisions and brigades, and some of the colonels, at my headquarters, and we there decided upon the plan of the action to take place the next morning. General Sigel was to march at 6 o'clock; General McKinstry was to march at 6 o'clock; General Asboth was to march at 7 or 7½ o'clock, I forget now which, and General Pope was to have command of the reserve. The positions to which they were to march were assigned to them—the positions they were to occupy at Wilson's creek, where we supposed the enemy's whole force would be when we arrived. Eleven o'clock the next morning was designated as the hour at which that action was expected to take place.

About 10 o'clock that night General Hunter came into my headquarters. The officers were all present. I handed him the order to march and the plan drawn up for the battle of the next day, gave him all the information I could, and left the matter in his hands. Most of the officers supposed that, in the condition of things, General Hunter would not take the command at that time, but leave it to me until after the battle had been fought. He did take the command, and I left the next day.

At 12 o'clock General Hunter called a council of war, on which occasion he read a letter from the President suggesting the expediency of retiring and falling back upon St. Louis; but the President went on to say that at that distance he could not tell what ought to be done. General Hunter proposed to the officers to say whether they would retire or go forward and fight. They unanimously expressed themselves in favor of going forward. They knew the army was in good condition to fight; that it was in sufficient force; and that they would, in all probability, gain a signal victory. The council separated, all the officers under the impression that the battle would take place; but the next morning they had orders to retire.

Question. Was there any doubt about your coming up with the enemy and having a fight the next day?

Answer. I do not think there was any.

Question. Were your troops in high spirits?

Answer. They were in admirable spirits, and had been all the way along. A battle had been fought at Fredericktown with great success; an action had taken place at Wet Glaze, in which sixty of the enemy had been killed; Lexington had been entered by Major White, and the prisoners there liberated; and the brilliant action of Major Zagoni at Springfield had been fought, all in the same week. The troops were all in high spirits, and desirous of emulating what had already been done. To show the spirit of the troops, the officers of three or four regiments came to me and said that their men did not want to go into action with more than three or four rounds of ammunition; they preferred to use the bayonet. I do not think Price could have stood against them a half an hour.

Question. What was your intention if you had fought that battle and gained a victory?

Answer. It was understood that if Price was defeated he would probably go off down into Arkansas with the remainder of his force. Price and myself had just then made an agreement by which we each agreed that the fighting should be confined to the armies in the field; that is, that all guerilla parties should be suppressed; and both he and I agreed to lend our aid to suppress them. He and I invited the people to return to their homes, under our joint guarantee that no man should be arrested or considered subject to arrest for mere political opinions, or the private expression of political opinions, but should be left to the ordinary course of the legal tribunals if he did anything wrong. I think that was considered to be preparatory to his leaving the State. It was understood that the 15,000 Missourians he had with him would return home.

I had directed Commodore Foote to prepare for an attack upon Columbus, Belmont, and New Madrid. I was to move, after the battle which we expected, according to instructions to be then forwarded to them, so as to effect a junction with them at Bird's Point, and together attack those positions going on down to Memphis, or they were to go on and make the attack while the army under me proceeded directly to Memphis. General Prentiss had come to my camp by my order, after I had started on the road to Springfield, and it was arranged that he should go back and raise a brigade to replace his own troops at Cairo, and to have that much additional strength to make this movement. The movement was in that way a concerted one, to attack and carry Belmont, New Madrid, and Columbus, and go on to Memphis. And it was the opinion of all of us that that could be done.

Question. In the course of your command did you meet with any particular check or reverse?

Answer. I never met with one myself. The reverses at Springfield and Lexington I considered as accidents, coming up in the combination of which I had not then fully obtained the control. There was never anything which stopped the onward movement which we had commenced.

Question. Do you know why you were superseded, and your army placed under the command of another just on the eve of battle?

Answer. I am not clear in my own mind as to the reasons. I think that several causes operated to bring that about. I believe the excuse or reason, by means of which the movement against me was originated, was in the suggestions from Colonel Blair. I believe the dissatisfaction with me commenced there.

Question. About what?

Answer. Well sir, in brief, I believe I never should have had any difficulty *in that quarter*, if I had been willing to have allowed the moneyed and political power of the department to be used for individual benefit. That I refused to do. I believe the first split came up on a contract for the supply of 40,000 men, which two gentlemen, introduced to me by Colonel Blair, demanded to have. I discussed that with them for a couple of days, refused to give them the contract in full, but finally consented to allow a contract to be made for one-third that number of men, provided one-half of the work should be done in St. Louis. The restriction to one-third was made on the estimate of supplies to be furnished, on its margin. I agreed to that extent to indorse the contract over to General McKinstry, to whom I referred it, and recommended that such a contract be made. General McKinstry refused, and thereupon the contest began.

By Mr. Odell:

Question. What was the contract for?

Answer. They asked for a contract to furnish equipments, clothing, &c., for 40,000 men. Though I expected to need that much in time, I did not like to order so large an amount at that time, and of any one party. And then, probably following that, the proclamation was brought up as a reason why I should be removed. But as a matter simply of judgment and belief, I think that would not have been used but for suggestions growing out of the contract movement. In other words, I think if I had been willing to have made the contracts asked I should have had no difficulty. That is as near a statement of the reasons as they appear to my own mind as I am now able to give.

By the chairman:

Question. You agreed that they might have a contract for furnishing one-third of 40,000 men?

Answer. Yes, sir.

Question. And you say that General McKinstry vetoed that?

Answer. Yes, sir.

Question. Was it within his province to supersede you in a matter of that kind?

Answer. No, sir, not if I had made the order. I recommended it to him, and I think that in addition to other reasons that he may have had for his action, he felt that I had been annoyed by the pressure upon me for this contract, and thought that if he refused it would not be disagreeable to me. And I judge too, that General McKinstry supposed that if he had more time in which to make contracts they could be made to better advantage. We already had contracts out for a certain number of men. I recollect that was one of the objections I urged to making such a contract as that asked for; that a contract once ordered was a committal to that extent for that amount. I wished to have, and probably General McKinstry had that idea also, the power to buy in smaller quantities.

By Mr. Odell:

Question. Then you refused the contract, and used McKinstry to do it with?

Answer. I certainly did not contemplate that.

Question. It seems to me that that will be the inference drawn from your statement of the transaction?

Answer. I certainly do not want any such inference as that to be drawn from anything I have said.

The chairman: It seems to me that the statement made by General Frémont will not bear any such construction as that.

Mr. Odell called for the reading of what had been stated in reference to the matter.

It was accordingly read.

Mr. Odell: It is a matter with General Frémont entirely. If he is willing to have such a statement upon record, I shall not object. I thought it but right to call his attention to it, for I certainly should not like, if I was in his place, to make up such a record as that against myself.

The witness: I am much obliged to you for calling my attention to the matter. If any member of the committee thinks that any such construction can be or will be placed by any one upon what I have said, I certainly do not want it to stand. I was willing to let them have a contract for that amount. There was no positive order for the contract; I only made a recommendation to General McKinstry to make it. There is a great deal of difference between a positive order to him to make the contract, and merely recommending him to make it, leaving it to his discretion to make it or not, as he pleased. So far as I was myself concerned, I was willing to consent to a contract for one-third of the amount they asked, for I knew we were then requiring, or would soon require, supplies to an amount which might render such a contract to some extent expedient. I did not give a positive order to General McKinstry to make the contract, but so far as I was concerned, I recommended a contract to be made for one-third the amount originally asked. It was then General McKinstry's province to refuse it or make it, as he considered best. If he had considered that I had given an imperative order, he would no doubt have made the contract; but I gave no order.

By the chairman:

Question. You speak of General McKinstry. We have heard that he has been imprisoned for a long time. Do you know the cause of his imprisonment, or anything about it?

Answer. I do not know the reason. No reason for his arrest has been communicated to me. I have not heard from any source entitled to credit why he was arrested. I have, of course, heard many surmises, but I know of no reason for his arrest; certainly none in his conduct there, so far as I am acquainted with it.

By Mr. Odell:

Question. How came General McKinstry to know it would be agreeable to you if he would refuse this contract?

Answer. I suppose he had heard me say, while we were arguing it for those two days, that I did not want to make that contract. He knew, of course, that it had been pressed upon me for two days, before I consented to it.

Question. After you had consented that this contract should be made for one-third of the amount asked, did you have any communication with General McKinstry upon the subject, before he decided the matter?

Answer. None at all; they went directly to him.

Question. You mean to say that the contract for the one-third was not declined by General McKinstry at your instance?

Answer. Certainly; I said nothing to him about it.

By Mr. Covode:

Question. Would Mr. Blair's friends, in your opinion, have been satisfied with the one-third contract, or did they want the whole?

Answer. I think they wanted the whole. They wanted, I think, an uninterrupted dictation in the matter of contracts.

Question. Was there any interference with you here, on the part of Mr. Montgomery Blair, previous to the failure to get this contract?

Answer. No, sir. Up to the 3d of September, the date of the last letter from Mr. Montgomery Blair, our relations were of the friendliest kind.

Question. Can you explain so sudden a change in the correspondence between you and Mr. Blair? Was it produced altogether by the failure to get that contract?

Answer. That was one of the reasons, I think.

By Mr. Odell:

Question. Who were the parties who came to you with Colonel Frank Blair for the contract?

Answer. I think they were Mr. Gurney and Mr. Howe.

Question. Were they practical mechanics in St. Louis?

Answer. I think Mr. Howe resided in St. Louis and Mr. Gurney in Chicago.

Question. Had they the means of complying with what they proposed to do?

Answer. I think so, fully—I presume so.

Question. And so far as you know, they were all proper and right in their prices?

Answer. So far as I know. I estimated that one-third of 40,000 men was about what it would be expedient to make a contract for at that time.

The following telegrams, military reports, and despatches, letters, orders and other authentic papers are submitted by General Frémont, in connexion with his testimony, as explanatory of the conduct of affairs in the department of the west while under his command.

[By telegraph from Cairo, June 13, 1861.]

ST. LOUIS ARSENAL, *June* 13, 1861.

If you wish more troops from Illinois inform me at Cincinnati. Don't telegraph direct to any of my subordinates unless danger is imminent.

G. B. McCLELLAN, *Major General U. S. Army.*

Brigadier General N. LYON.

[By telegraph from Cincinnati, June 17, 1861.]

ST. LOUIS ARSENAL, *June* 17, 1861.

Colonel B. F. Smith, now at Quincy, has beenordered to re-enforce Colonel Curtis, on the Hannibal and St. Joseph railroad, with the companies of his regiment now at Quincy. No other assistance can be offered by me at present.

GEO. B. McCLELLAN,
Major General Commanding.

Captain CHESTER HARDING,
Assistant Adjutant General.

HEADQUARTERS ON WALNUT STREET,
St. Louis, June 17, 1861.

DEAR SIR: I enclose you despatch from Colonel Brown, which he sent me this morning. We should have tents enough to keep our guns dry at least, and utensils for cooking for the men. It is impossible to march any great distance without. Our men are in fine spirits and anxious for duty. There is a memorandum on the back of the despatch of the items needed. Colonel Sigel moved on this morning.

Very respectfully, yours,

J. B. SHAW,
Major 4th Regiment U. S. Reserve Corps.

Brigadier General SWEENY.

[Colonel Brown's report, enclosed.]

HEADQUARTERS 4TH REGIMENT U. S. RESERVE CORPS, AT ROLLA.

SIR: I have to report that, in obedience to orders, I marched with ten companies of my regiment, (825 men and officers,) leaving St. Louis at 2 o'clock, and reaching this place at 12 o'clock at night. I find here neither provisions, water, tents, cartridge-boxes, nor any other material. It will be absolutely necessary that they be provided for, and I send back one of my officers to try and urge forward the necessary supplies.

I remain, sir, yours, respectfully,

B. GRATZ BROWN,
Colonel 4th Regiment U. S. Reserve Corps.

Brigadier General T. W. SWEENY,
Commanding U. S. Reserve Corps.

Tents and cooking utensils; cartridge-boxes, belts, and bayonet scabbards; 500 blankets; 50 canteens, to replace others that leak; ropes and forage for five horses.

BOONVILLE, MISSOURI, *June* 18, 1862.

DR. HARDING: You have heard of us and our leaving Jefferson City on the 16th. We debarked next morning a little above Rockport, and had not proceeded more than two miles before we met their advanced pickets, and soon after their whole force. At first the secessionists made a weak effort, which doubtless was intended to lead us on to their stronghold, where they held on with considerable resolution, and gave us a check for a short time and made some havock. On moving forward, however, a straggling fire from the right and left made it necessary to move on with caution and slowness, and we reached the city about 2 o'clock p. m., where we were met by many people, under consternation from the erroneous impression that great violence would be perpetrated upon persons and property. I have been engaged more or less in removing this impression. I regret much that my proclamation was not published promptly, so that I could have had it here for distribution. I get no news of what is going on around us, but much fear the movement from Texas, and hope the subject will engage the attention of the general government. Keep McClellan advised upon the matter. I had hoped some of our Iowa troops would have been in this region by this time, but hear nothing of them. My suspense just now is painful.

Yours, truly,

N. LYON, *Commanding.*

HEADQUARTERS DEPARTMENT OF OHIO,
Cincinnati, June 18.

Have received order placing Missouri under my command. Will leave for St. Louis to-morrow. If more troops are needed telegraph me details of case.

G. B. McCLELLAN, *Major General.*

CHESTER HARDING, Jr.,
Assistant Adjutant General.

JEFFERSON CITY, *June* 21, 1861.

Please telegraph General McClellan as follows:

"BOONVILLE, MISSOURI, *June* 20, 1861.

"GENERAL McCLELLAN: I have notice that Missouri is assigned to your command. This Boonville is an important point, and should have at least a whole regiment, with an advance post at Warsaw, which is a nest of rebels, who have massacred at Cole Camp Union men. These will permit the 2d Missouri volunteer regiment to concentrate at Jefferson City. I would have you send a regiment here with a large supply of stores.

"N. LYON."

Colonel CHESTER HARDING,
Assistant Adjutant General.

[By telegraph from Boonville—24, 1861.]

ST. LOUIS ARSENAL, *June* 24, 1861.

Hope to get off on the 26th. Think provisions now coming up will be enough for some time. About four companies more should be here. A force can go to Cape Girardeau; but an expedition to Pocahontas should be made with care. It might be cut off.

N. LYON, *Commanding.*

Colonel HARDING.

[By telegraph from Boonville—26, 1861.]

ST. LOUIS ARSENAL, *June* 27, 1861.

The interests of the government require that no boats ply along the river between this and Kansas City for the present, and you will notify the collector that no boats will be allowed to pass above here until further orders. Much confusion attends my train arrangements, and delay is unavoidable. Shall try to get off to-morrow, but am not certain. I want Colonel Stevenson to come here and take command with some of his companies. Schofield arrived this afternoon.

N. LYON, *Commanding.*

Colonel HARDING.

[By telegraph from Grafton, Virginia—27, 1861.]

ST. LOUIS ARSENAL, *June* 27, 1861.

How many troops have you in St. Louis, and how many do you consider necessary for its defence? Answer at once.

G. B. McCLELLAN.

CHESTER HARDING, Jr., *Adjutant General.*

[By telegraph from Grafton, Virginia—28, 1861.]

ST. LOUIS, *June* 28, 1861.

Have ordered three Illinois regiments to move to Cairo whenever called for by General Prentiss, who will look out for the southeast, and also telegraphs "No rebels at Bloomfield." Will not a movement from Bird's Point do the best?

GEO. B. McCLELLAN,
Major General U. S. Army.

CHESTER HARDING, Jr.

[By telegraph from Boonville—27, 1861.]

ST. LOUIS ARSENAL, *June* 27, 1861.

Colonel Stiefel's command and four companies 7th regiment arrived. Provisions wanted. Send at once to Hermann, by first train 400 barrels hard bread, 90 bushels beans, 3,350 pounds rice, 2,000 pounds sugar, and 600 pounds coffee. The rains are terrible. I cannot get off. Steamer goes down to meet provisions. Answer.

N. LYON, *Commanding.*

Colonel HARDING.

[By telegraph from Boonville, July 1, 1861.]

ST. LOUIS ARSENAL, *July* 1, 1861.

What is going on in the southeast? You sent me word that McClellan would attend to that quarter. He says I may have one regiment from Quincy and one from Caseyville, and Prentiss is authorized to call for four more regiments if he wants them. Cannot all these be put in movement to meet the danger threatened? See what Prentiss says and send word to McClellan.

N. LYON, *Commanding.*

Colonel HARDING.

BOONVILLE, *Missouri, July* 2, 1861.

DEAR COLONEL: I hope to move to-morrow, and think it more important just now to go to Springfield. My force in moving from here will be about 2,400 men. Major Sturgis will have about 2,200 men, and you know what force has gone to Springfield from St. Louis, so that you see what amount of provisions we shall want supplied at that point. Please attend to us as effectually as possible. Our line should be kept open by all means. I must be governed by circumstances at Springfield. You will, of course, have due attention to the southeast. *The State Journal* is outrageous and must be stopped; you will take such measures as you think best to effect this. Our cause is suffering from too much indulgence, and you must so advise our friends in St. Louis. Colonel Stevenson must have pretty strong garrisons at the points he occupies on the river, and he must have support from other States as occasion seems to require. Colonel Curtis is, I suppose, on the Hannibal and St. Joseph road; rigorous measures should be shown the disorderly in that region. Our operations are becoming extensive, and our staff officers must keep up with our emergencies. We need here a regular quartermaster and commissary. Cannot something be done for us from Washington?

Yours, truly,

N. LYON, *Commanding.*

Colonel HARDING, *St. Louis Arsenal.*

P. S.—I cannot spare more than 300 stand of arms for home guards at Jefferson. I shall not be able to supply other portions of the State with the same proportion.

N. L.

CAMP CAMERON, *July* 2, 1861.

DEAR COLONEL: Please forward to Washington the enclosed return, or incorporate it in a department return to be sent there. Also, it would be well to make a report to the adjutant general of movements of troops in the State.

Yours, very truly,

J. M. SCHOFIELD.

Colonel CHESTER HARDING.

HEADQUARTERS MISSOURI VOLUNTEERS,
Camp Cameron, July 2, 1861.

General Orders No. 4.]

The following troops, under command of Brigadier General N. Lyon, will take up the line of march for the south at 7 o'clock a. m. to-morrow, viz:

	Officers.	Men.
Brigadier general and staff	4	..
Company B, second infantry	..	61
Company F, second artillery	1	60
Recruits, United States army	1	134
First regiment Missouri volunteers	29	866
Two companies second regiment Missouri volunteers	6	205
Pioneer detachment	1	46
Artillery	1	13
First regiment Iowa volunteers	34	892
Total	77	2, 277
Aggregate		2, 354

The following troops will remain for the present at this place:

	Comp's.	Officers.	Men.
Second regiment Missouri volunteers	4	10	381
Seventh regiment Missouri volunteers	4	13	349
Fifth regiment reserve corps	8	30	558
Total		53	1,288
Left behind sick			44

The troops which take the field under General Lyon will be joined by a force of 2,200 regulars and Kansas volunteers, under command of Major Sturgis, United States army, at Osceola, Missouri. The united command will then proceed toward Springfield, Missouri. Colonel Chester Harding, adjutant general Missouri volunteers, will forward to Springfield the commissary supplies necessary for this command, in addition to that already in the field in that portion of the State. Colonel Harding is also charged with the duty of forwarding supplies for the troops that remain at this and other points on the river.

Special orders No. 1, dated June 29, 1861, from these headquarters, are so far modified as to authorize Colonel John D. Stevenson to retain at this post, or at Jefferson City, such companies of the 2d regiment as may wish to remain in the service for three years, but not necessarily in the regiment to which they now belong.

Such companies will be reorganized at once, and incorporated into regiments as soon as may be.

By order of General Lyon.

J. M. SCHOFIELD,
Assistant Adjutant General.

HEADQUARTERS DEPARTMENT OF OHIO,
Buckhannon, July 5, 1861.

Communicate freely with Prentiss. If he does not need Wyman, you can take him. Telegraph to General Pope, at Alton, to give you a regiment; and to Hurlbut, at Quincy, to give you another.

Do not lose sight of importance of Cairo, and of its operations in Southeastern Missouri. Write to me fully.

G. B. McCLELLAN, *Major General, U. S. A.*

CHESTER HARDING,
Assistant Adjutant General.

ST. LOUIS ARSENAL, *July* 5, 1861.

General Lyon is moving down from Boonville toward Springfield, Greene county, Missouri, with 2,400 troops. Major Sturgis is on the way from Fort Leavenworth with 2,200. There are 3,500 on the southwest branch of Pacific railroad and the line thence to Mount Vernon, beyond Springfield. In a day or two another regiment will be moved down. There is a depot for supplies at Rolla, the terminus of the southwest branch; another must be established at Springfield. All the supplies for, say 10,000 troops, must take that direction. From Rolla on for 60 miles the country is mountainous and barren. Teams have to take their own forage. It is absolutely necessary that a large amount of wagon transportation should be immediately provided. Will you see that the necessary orders are given by the quartermaster general, by telegraph, to Major McKinstry, early in the morning?

General Lyon urges that regular quartermasters and commissaries be sent him at once.

CHESTER HARDING, Jr.,
A. A. G. Missouri Volunteers.

General Thomas,
Adjutant General, Washington.

St. Louis Arsenal, *July* 5, 1861.

Order Schittner's regiment home. A boat will be there to-day to take them.

CHESTER HARDING, Jr.,
A. A. G. Missouri Volunteers.

General Prentiss, *Cairo.*

St. Louis Arsenal, *July* 5, 1861.

Just received despatch from McClellan, which may change order for Schittner's return. Will telegraph again.

C. HARDING.

General Prentiss, *Cairo.*

St. Louis Arsenal, *July* 6, 1861.

General Lyon has sent Wyman's regiment to southwest. This, with the 700 troops now there, will be enough for the present. Colonel Wyman is in command, with instructions to keep open the line of communication, on which all supplies will be sent hereafter. General Lyon has moved down towards Springfield with 2,400 men, and Major Sturgis with 2,200 on the frontier. Sweeny is there, and at Mt. Vernon, beyond there, with 2,500, besides guards at posts on line. Marsh's Alton regiment is here. I will equip them. They will go to Cape Girardeau and be subject to General Prentiss's call in case of necessity. The Quincy regiment will go to Ironton, and thence to Greenfield. I will write particulars to-night. Think the force sufficient, and will not order more unless necessary.

CHESTER HARDING, Jr.,
A. A. G. Missouri Volunteers.

General McClellan, *Buckhannon, Virginia.*

St. Louis Arsenal, *July* 9, 1861.

Schittner's enlistment expires about the 22d instant. I want them for reorganization. The City of Alton goes down to day to carry Marsh to Cape Girardeau. He was delayed by want of mules, now furnished. Will you let Schittner come up by same boat after reorganization? I can send you a full three-year regiment made up of Schittner's and others, under good officers.

C. HARDING, Jr.,
A. A. G. Missouri Volunteers.

General Prentiss, *Cairo.*

St. Louis Arsenal, *July* 9, 1861.

Buell's battery, raised under order of General Lyon, needs equipment for immediate service. Will you authorize the muster? Very efficient company.

CHESTER HARDING,
A. A. G. Missouri Volunteers.

General McClellan, *Buckhannon, Virginia.*

St. Louis Arsenal, *July* 11, 1861.

I hope Grant's regiment will be allowed to come. He and Marsh can aid Cairo and Bird's Point effectually by operations in Cape Girardeau, Scott, Stoddard, Wayne, and Butler counties. Bland's regiment (6th Missouri) will be with them. Wyman is at and below Rolla; Buell's battery was wanted for Grant. Department has not answered in regard to it.

CHESTER HARDING, Jr.,
A. A. G. Missouri Volunteers.

Major S. Williams, *A. A. G., Buckhannon.*

St. Louis Arsenal, *July* 13, 1861.

With cavalry on our prairies we could crush secession in our State within two months. The want of it has not only embarrassed us, but lost us the fruits of hard-earned victories. The rebel General Harris would now be a prisoner if we had mounted forces. Two regiments are needed. What may we do? Colonel F. P. Blair can explain. We hope to catch Harris in any event.

CHESTER HARDING, Jr.,
A. A. G. Missouri Volunteers.

Hon. Simon Cameron,
Secretary of War, Washington.

Headquarters Southwest Expedition,
Springfield, Missouri, July 13, 1861.

Sir: I arrived at this place early this evening two or three hours in advance of my troops, who are encamped a few miles back. I have about 5,000 men to be provided for, and have expected to find stores here, as I have ordered. The failure of stores reaching here seems likely to cause serious embarrassment, which must be aggravated by continued delay, and in proportion to the time I am forced to wait for supplies. * * * I shall endeavor to take every due precaution to meet existing emergencies, and hope to be able to sustain the cause of the government in this part of the State. But there must be no loss of time in furnishing me the resources I have herein mentioned. I have lost in reaching this place about four days' time, by the high waters in Grand and Osage rivers, which made it necessary to ferry them. The same difficulty prevented Sturgis from co-operating with Sigel in time to afford any aid. Please telegraph to McClellan and to Washington anything in this letter you deem of importance to these headquarters. Shoes, shirts, blouses, &c., are much wanted, and I would have you furnish them, if possible, in considerable quantities.

Yours, truly,

N. LYON, *Brigadier General Commanding.*

Colonel Chester Harding, *St. Louis Arsenal.*

St. Louis Arsenal, *July* 15, 1861.

We have here Captain Buell, an old artillery soldier, who was authorized by General Lyon to raise a full battery—six pieces. He has 130 experienced men, and wants 20 more, with 110 horses. It is absolutely necessary that he should be equipped. There will be hot work here before the end of the month, and our three batteries (four pieces each) are now in the southwest. Send order to equip Buell and to raise his force to full complement. You are needed here. About 2,500 men, in three columns, are now on an expedition to kill secession in Northeast Missouri. Our operations are becoming large.

CHESTER HARDING, Jr.,
A. A. G. Missouri Volunteers.

Major General Frémont, *New York.*

Copy of the following was sent to assistant adjutant general at Washington, to General Frémont, New York, and to Colonel Blair, Washington:

Springfield, *Missouri, July* 13, 1861.

My effective force will soon be reduced by discharge of three months volunteers to about 4,000 men, including the Illinois regiment now on the march from Rolla. Governor Jackson will soon have in this vicinity not less than 30,000. I must have at once an additional force of 10,000 men, or abandon my position. All must have supplies and clothing.

N. LYON, *Brigadier General Commanding.*

St. Louis Arsenal, *July* 15, 1861.

Have you received General McClellan's despatch of to-day? If so, what's your plan? Will aid you in any way, but think best aid is to operate as before indicated. Have you official notice that General Frémont is our department commander?

CHESTER HARDING, Jr.,
A. A. G. Missouri Volunteers.

General Prentiss, *Cairo.*

[By telegraph from Chicago, July 15, 1861.]

St. Louis Arsenal, *July* 15, 1861.

Have despatched condition of affairs to General Frémont, and asked authority to take the field in Northern Missouri with five more regiments. Expect answer to-night. Will go down and confer with you as soon as I hear. How did you succeed with Harris?

JOHN POPE, *Brigadier General.*

Chester Harding, Jr.

[By telegraph from Cairo, July 15, 1861.]

St. Louis Arsenal, *July* 15, 1861.

I have received McClellan's despatch. My plan would be to start a strong column across Missouri from this point, leaving it well guarded; at the same time, advance from Cape Girardeau and Greenville, concentrating with Lyon, or Missouri forces, and drive them back. It would be better first to break up rebel encampment at Union City, in Tennessee, to prevent their crossing at Hickman or Madrid to get in our rear. All of which I could do if ordered by major general commanding. I must await orders. I have not been officially informed that Frémont commands us.

B. M. PRENTISS, *Brigadier General.*

Chester Harding, Jr.

Headquarters Army of the West,
Springfield, Missouri, July 15, 1861.

Colonel: General Lyon is now here with about 7,000 men. Of these fully one-half are three months volunteers, whose term of service has nearly expired—the latest expiring on the 14th August. Governor Jackson is concentrating his forces in the southwestern part of the State, and is receiving large re-enforcements from Arkansas, Tennessee, Louisiana, and Texas.

His effective force will soon be certainly not less than 30,000 men—probably much larger. All idea of any further advance movement, or of even maintaining our present position, must soon be abandoned unless the government furnish us promptly with large re-enforcements and supplies. Our troops are badly clothed, poorly fed, and imperfectly supplied with tents; none of them have yet been paid; and the three months volunteers have become disheartened to such extent that very few of them are willing to renew their enlistment. The blank pay-rolls are not here; and the long time required to get them here, fill them up, send them to Washington, have the payment ordered, and the paymaster reach us, leaves us no hope that our troops can be paid for five or six weeks to come. Under these circumstances, there remains no other course but to urgently press upon the attention of the government the absolute necessity of sending us fresh troops at once, with ample supplies for them and for those now here. At least 10,000 men should be sent, and that promptly. You will send the enclosed despatch by telegraph to General McClellan, and also to the War Department, and forward by mail a copy of this letter. Lose no time in fitting for the field the three years volunteers now at the arsenal, and send them here as soon as possible. Call for Colonel McNeil's regiment of home guards to garrison at the arsenal; and allow him to organize, if for the regular three years service, if he desires to do so. It is believed that the remaining home guards will be sufficient for the city. Should it be necessary, their term of service can be renewed for a short period, for the purpose of a city garrison. The general is not aware whether Colonel Smith's regiment has yet taken the field. If not, he presumes that both his and Colonel Bland's regiments may be sent here without delay. You may doubtless leave the care of the southeast part of the State to General Prentiss. Should St. Louis be in danger from that direction, troops could easily be called from Illinois and Indiana for its defence. Moreover, a force moving on St. Louis from the south would be exposed to attack in rear from Cairo. Hence there seems little or no danger from that direction. Unless we are speedily re-enforced here, we will soon lose all we have gained. Our troops have made long marches, done much effective service, and suffered no small privations. They have received no pay nor clothing from the government, and the small stock furnished by private contribution is now exhausted; so that unless the government gives us relief speedily, our thus far successful campaign will prove a failure.

I am, sir, very respectfully, your obedient servant,

J. M. SCHOFIELD,
Captain 11th Infantry, Assistant Adjutant General.

Colonel CHESTER HARDING,
Adjutant General Missouri Volunteers, St. Louis Arsenal, Missouri.

P. S.—Cannot Colonel Curtis's regiment be spared from St. Joseph? And if so, send it forward.

N. LYON, *Commanding.*

WASHINGTON, *July* 15, 1861.

The President is going in person to the War Department to arrange matters for you.

M. BLAIR.

Major General FRÉMONT, *Astor House.*

[By telegraph from New York, July 16.]

ST. LOUIS ARSENAL, *July* 16, 1861.

Have Captain Buell's force raised to full complement and equipped. General Pope will go to Alton to-morrow. Keep me fully advised by telegraph.

J. C. FRÉMONT,
Major General Commanding.

Assistant Adjutant General CHESTER HARDING.

WASHINGTON, *July* 16, 1861.

The arms will be sent immediately to Illinois. Major Hagner will call on you with authority to supply your wants. War Department will advise you particularly.

LYMAN TRUMBULL.

General JOHN C. FRÉMONT.

HEADQUARTERS ARMY OF THE WEST,
Springfield, Missouri, July 16, 1861.

Special Orders No. 18.]

Colonel Brown's regiment (4th) United States reserve corps will proceed to the city of St. Louis, where it will, at the expiration of its three months term, be mustered out of service.

By order of General Lyon.

J. M. SCHOFIELD,
Assistant Adjutant General.

DEAR MISS ——: I have not heard from you yet, but make free to trust this to your care:

HEADQUARTERS RIPLEY COUNTY BATTALION,
Camp Burrows, July 16, 1861.

DEAR SIR: If there is any way to communicate with the governor through any person in St. Louis, please let me know it. I am advancing, and General Yell will follow me in a few days with 5,000 men. He will take position between Rolla and Ironton, and act as circumstances dictate. General Watkins will move up, sustained by General Pillow, and if proper energy is exercised we can drive the enemy north of the Missouri and into St. Louis in thirty days. You will please let me hear from you, verbally or not, through the person through whom this passes; and please send *The Daily Journal* for a short time to Doniphan, as it will be sent to me by my couriers.

Yours, respectfully,

M. JEFF. THOMPSON,
Commanding Ripley County Battalion.

JOSEPH TUCKER, Esq.,
Editor of The State Journal, St. Louis.

SPRINGFIELD, *Missouri, July* 17, 1861.

SIR: I enclose you a copy of a letter to Colonel Townsend on the subject of an order from General Scott, which calls for five companies of the 2d infantry to be withdrawn from the west and sent to Washington. A previous order withdraws the mounted troops, as I am informed, and were it not that some of them were *en route* to this place they would now be in Washington. This order carried out would not now leave at Fort Leavenworth a single company. I have companies B and E, 2d infantry, now under orders for Washington; and if all these troops leave me, I can do nothing, and must retire in the absence of other troops to supply their places. In fact, I am badly enough off at the best, and must utterly fail if my regulars all go. At Washington troops from all the northern, middle, and eastern States are available for the support of the army in Virginia, and more are understood to be already there than are wanted; and it seems strange that so many troops must go on from the west and strip us of the means of defence. But if it is the intention to give up the west, let it be so; it can only be the victim of imbecility or malice. Scott will cripple us if he can. Cannot you stir up this matter and secure us relief. See Frémont, if he has arrived. The want of supplies has crippled me so that I cannot move, and I do not know when I can. Everything seems to combine against me at this point. Stir up Blair.

Yours, truly,

N. LYON, *Commanding.*

Colonel HARDING, *St. Louis Arsenal, Mo.*

[By telegraph from Chicago, dated July 16, 1861.—Received July 17, 1861.]

I am again urgently solicited by adjutant general in St. Louis to take command in North Missouri. What shall I do? The forces are gradually closing around Harris. I think a vigorous campaign of a week will settle secession in North Missouri, and leave the troops at your disposal for other service. Please answer to Alton. We need arms much.

JOHN POPE, *Brigadier General.*

Major General FRÉMONT, *New York.*

[By telegraph from Quincy, dated July 17.—Received July 17, 1861.]

I am ordered to hold the Hannibal and St. Joseph railroad. I have three regiments posted along the road, in communication at the west with Iowa troops, for detached service and breaking up camps of rebels. I need better arms than the smooth musket. I have one regiment wholly unarmed in camp here, and can get no arms in St. Louis or Springfield. Can you send me Minies and ammunition?

S. A. HURLBUT, *Brigadier General.*

Major General FRÉMONT, *New York.*

[By telegraph from Chicago, dated July 17.—Received July 17, 1861.]

We need specially, to fit out one or two regiments of cavalry, sabres and revolvers. There are absolutely none in this part of the country.

JOHN POPE, *Brigadier General.*

Major General FRÉMONT, *U. S. A., New York.*

HEADQUARTERS ARMY OF THE WEST,
Springfield, Missouri, July 17, 1861.

SIR: I have the honor to acknowledge the receipt of Special Order No. 112, from headquarters, under date of July 5, directing the removal from the department of the west of companies B, C, F, G, and H, 2d infantry, and of Captain Sweeny, now acting brigadier general by election of volunteers. The communication reached me yesterday at this place.

I have been drawn to this point by the movements of the rebel forces in this State, and have accumulated such troops as I could make available, including those in Kansas. My aggregate is between 7,000 and 8,000 men, more than half of whom are three months volunteers, some of whose term of enlistment has just expired; others will claim a discharge within a week or two, and the dissolution of my forces from this necessity, already commenced, will leave me less than 4,000 men, including companies B and E, 2d infantry, now with me. In my immediate vicinity it is currently reported there are 30,000 troops and upward, whose number is constantly augmenting, and who are diligently accumulating arms and stores. They are making frequent lawless and hostile demonstrations, and threaten me with attack. The evils consequent upon the withdrawal of any portion of my force will be apparent; loyal citizens will be unprotected, repressed treason will assume alarming boldness, and possible defeat of my troops in battle will peril the continued ascendency of the federal power itself, not only in the State, but in the whole west. If the interests of the government are to be sustained here, and in fact the whole valley of the Mississippi, large bodies of troops should be sent forward to this State, instead of being withdrawn from it, till by concentration there may be ability to overpower any force that can be gathered in the west to act against the government. Troops properly belonging to the valley of the Mississippi from Wisconsin, Michigan, Indiana, and Ohio, have already been withdrawn to the east. The moral effect of the presence of the few regulars in my command is doubtless the main consideration that holds the enemy in check, and with them I may be able to retain what has already been achieved until I am strengthened; but any diminution will be imminently hazardous.

The volunteers with me have yet had no pay for their services, and their duties have been arduous. Their clothing has become dilapidated, and as a body they are dispirited. But for these facts they would probably nearly all have re-enlisted. I have no regular officers of the pay department, nor the commissary and quartermaster; the affairs of both the last are, consequently, indifferently administered, from want of experience. Nothing but the immense interests at stake could have ever induced me to undertake the great work in which I am engaged, under such discouraging circumstances. In this state of affairs, presumed to have been unknown when the order was issued, I have felt justified in delaying its execution for further instruction, so far as the companies with me are concerned.

Very respectfully, your obedient servant,

N. LYON, *Brigadier General Commanding.*

Lieutenant Colonel TOWNSEND,
Assistant Adjutant General, &c.

[Received July 18, 1861.]

SPRINGFIELD, *Illinois, July* 18, 1861.

All the Illinois forces are in Missouri, excepting the Irish regiment and three companies of cavalry at Quincy, and three regiments of infantry, two companies of cavalry, and battery of artillery at Alton. Shall assume command at once. Moving with the force from Alton to St. Charles to-night, and that at Quincy, will take position on line of Hannibal and St. Joseph railroad to-day, and will put the entire force in North Missouri into action immediately.

JOHN POPE, *Brigadier General Commanding.*

Major General JOHN C. FREMONT, *New York.*

ASTOR HOUSE, *New York, July* 18, 1861.

North Missouri railroad torn up and obstructed by State forces. Mails cannot be transported. Tracks torn up behind the United States troops.

Some fighting between these and State forces. I have ordered General Pope to take the command in North Missouri with three regiments from Alton. He moves this morning. General Lyon calls for re-enforcements.

J. C. FREMONT, *Major General Commanding.*

Colonel TOWNSEND,
Assistant Adjutant General, Washington, D. C.

[Received at the Astor House, 4.30 p. m.]

WAR DEPARTMENT, *Washington, July* 18, 1861.

Your letter of 16th and telegram of 18th received. The general-in-chief says please proceed to your command without coming here. He has no particular instructions for you at present. He adds, for your information, the term of service of three months volunteers began with date of reception and muster into service.

E. D. TOWNSEND, *Assistant Adjutant General.*

General FREMONT, *United States Army.*

[Received July 18, 1861.]

SPRINGFIELD, *Illinois, July* 18, 1861.

No force at St. Louis except necessary guard for arsenal and city. I leave for Missouri in a few minutes.

JOHN POPE, *Brigadier General.*

Major General FREMONT, *New York.*

ST. LOUIS, *July* 19, 1861.

Governor Yates has referred your despatch to me. The fourteen guns need caissons, harness and equipments. Only available regiment for immediate service is Mulligan's, at Quincy, but it has no arms; will get them here. I open North Missouri road to-morrow. Three Alton regiments landed there to-night. Several regiments will be available in three days.

JOHN POPE, *Brigadier General.*

Major General FREMONT, *United States Army.*

ST. LOUIS, *July* 19, 1861.

It was the design to occupy Southwest Missouri, cutting off all approaches from Arkansas by way of Pocahontas, to occupy Poplar Bluffs, Bloomfield, Greenville, and the line of the Cairo and Fulton railroad. Accordingly one regiment is at Ironton, ready to advance when re-enforced. Grant was under orders, but his orders were countermanded. Marsh is at Cape Girardeau, instructed to keep open communication with Bloomfield, where Grant was to be. General Prentiss has eight regiments at Cairo, and could spare five of them to go into that country. If we once lose possession of the swamps of that region, a large army will be required to clear them, while if we get possession first and hold the causeway, a smaller force will do. General McClellan telegraphed that he had authentic intelligence of a large army gathering at Pocahontas, according with what I have advised for weeks. Expecting you here daily, I have not telegraphed before; but if you do not come at once, will you take into consideration the importance to Cairo that the southeast should be held by us?

CHESTER HARDING, JR.,
Assistant Adjutant General.

Major General FRÉMONT.

HEADQUARTERS ARMY OF THE WEST,
Springfield, Missouri, July 19, 1861.

SIR: The 4th and 5th regiments of Iowa volunteers are reported to me as available for service. They are at present at Burlington, in that State, and it is desirable to have them actively at work. If they are not otherwise needed, I wish you to order them forward to join my column, with all possible despatch.

Very respectfully, your obedient servant,

N. LYON, *Brigadier General Commanding.*

Colonel CHESTER HARDING, Jr,
Assistant Adjutant General, St. Louis Arsenal.

[By telegraph from Washington, July 20, 1861.]

ST. LOUIS ARSENAL, *July* 20, 1861.

General Thomas authorized me to say that you can accept as many three years regiments as shall offer, until further notice.

F. P. BLAIR, *Colonel 1st Regiment.*

Colonel CHESTER HARDING,
Assistant Adjutant General.

[By telegraph from New York, July 20, 1861.]

ST. LOUIS ARSENAL, *July* 20, 1861.

Have you later reliable intelligence from General Lyon?

J. C. FRÉMONT,
Major General Commanding.

Colonel HARDING, *Assistant Adjutant General.*

ST. LOUIS ARSENAL, *July* 20, 1861.

Nothing later from General Lyon, but I have obtained authority to accept regiments as fast as offered. Can soon re-enforce him. Will begin next week. When will you start?

CHESTER HARDING,
Assistant Adjutant General.

Major General FRÉMONT, *New York.*

[By telegraph from Cincinnati, July 20, 1861.]

ST. LOUIS ARSENAL, *July* 20, 1861.

In case of attack on Cairo, have none but Illinois troops to re-enforce, and only 11,000 arms in Illinois. Will direct two regiments to be ready at Caseyville, but you will only use them for defence of St. Louis and in case of absolute necessity. Telegraph me from time to time.

G. B. McCLELLAN, *Major General U. S. Army.*

CHESTER HARDING, Jr., *Assistant Adjutant General.*

[By telegraph from New York, July 20, 1861.]

ST. LOUIS ARSENAL, *July* 20, 1861.

Can clothing, camp equipage, and other ordinary supplies be had in St. Louis? I come on immediately.

J. C. FRÉMONT, *Major General Commanding.*

Colonel HARDING, *Assistant Adjutant General.*

St. Louis Arsenal, *July* 21, 1861.

General: Before referring to your recent communications, allow me to explain the state of affairs in other parts of Missouri outside of your line of operations.

Before you left Boonville I had the honor to advise you that large forces were gathering at Pocahontas. In accordance with your instructions, I communicated freely by telegraph with General McClellan, and, as I supposed, succeeded in having placed at your disposal sufficient troops from Illinois to hold the swamp counties of the southeast. Accordingly, I commenced by sending Brand's regiment to Ironton, with directions to proceed as far as he could, with entire safety, in the direction of Greenville. At the same time Colonel Grant's regiment was ordered here, to proceed to Bloomfield, and Colonel Marsh to Cape Girardeau, where he could have easy communication with either Cairo or Bloomfield. I armed 800 home guards in Cape Girardeau and Scott counties, to act as skirmishers, scouts, and guides in the marshes, and obtained authority from the Secretary of War to raise a force of mounted scouts. With these forces, and with arms for home guards in Wayne, Stoddard, and Butler, I expected to keep down local rebellion in that region, encourage Union men, hold the causeway through the swamps, and prevent the approach of an army from Pocahontas until the commanding generals and the authorities at Washington became convinced that it was the design of the enemy to march upon Bird's Point and St. Louis as soon as sufficient strength was gathered.

General McClellan countermanded his order to Grant. I could get no answer in regard to equipping Buell's battery, (though now the authority is here and a portion of the battery in service on the Missouri river,) and Bland and Marsh are at the points which they were sent to, without the force to accomplish the object named. General McClellan's reason for countermanding the order to Grant was that Cairo was threatened. Therefore, instead of occupying the country through which the enemy must come, eight regiments are lying in that sickly hole, Cairo, where General Prentiss can see the whole of them at once. He also has cavalry and two light batteries.

A week since General McClellan telegraphed that he had the same definite information of troops crossing from Tennessee and coming up from all parts of Arkansas to Pocahontas, which I had learned from our scouts and spies (one of them a pilot on a Memphis boat which had conveyed some of the troops over,) and had sent to him.

Now, in the southeast we stand thus: two regiments, not in communication with each other; no artillery, and a few home guards, against, what they expect to be, 20,000 men, (regular troops, well provided,) who design marching upon St. Louis.

I have explained all this to General Frémont, who will be here Tuesday, and who (as does General Pope) understands the threatened movement, and will take vigorous measures to meet it.

So much for the southeast. Meanwhile, your departure from Boonville, and the necessity of having 1,800 troops to garrison Jefferson City, Boonville, and Lexington, encouraged the rebels in Northeast Missouri. Brigadier General Tom Harris gathered a force below Monroe Station, in camp. I took the liberty of *ordering* Colonel Smith, of Illinois, who was lying eighteen miles from him, to break up the camp. He waited a day or two until Harris had got together 1,600 men, proceeded part way, shut himself up in a seminary, and sent back for re-enforcements, as his men had been marched off in such a hurry that they forgot to fill their cartridge-boxes and had only four rounds apiece. He was relieved, and Harris marched southwestwardly, on his way through Calloway county, to make a combined attack upon Jefferson City, with forces from Pettis, Osage, and Linn counties.

To check this I ordered up Schüttner's regiment from Cairo. As soon as the boat arrived I gave Colonel Schüttner his marching orders, and immediately went to work to equip his regiment. McKinstry helped, and both of us worked all night. The field officers, except Hammer, and nearly all the company officers went up town, and McKinstry and I were colonels, captains, adjutants, and quartermasters, as occasion required. I finally got them off, to go to Jefferson City, to cross there. As the regiment was in the worst possible state of discipline, and as Hammer is no soldier, (Schüttner and the balance I put in arrest as soon as they appeared at the gate at reveille,) I couldn't trust him, and ordered McNeil to take seven of his companies and follow him and take command. Hammer had with him forty-two mounted orderlies. The two commands united were to proceed from Jefferson City, *via* Fulton, to Mexico, between which two places last named Harris was.

At the same time Colonel M. L. Smith, 8th regiment, with two companies, and four companies of the 2d, under Schaeffer, were sent up to Mexico by rail, where it was arranged with Hurlbut that either Palmer's or Grant's regiment should join them and scour the country down toward Jefferson. After fully entering into the plan, and after I had sent off our forces, Hurlbut sent Palmer on to guard the Chariton Bridge *with his entire regiment*, and left Smith to do the best he could. I, of course, immediately re-enforced him. Meanwhile the enemy burned the bridge above Mexico.

Hammer telegraphed from Hermann that he concluded to leave the river there, as transportation was easily procured, and that he had made arrangements to effect a junction with McNeil. The next I heard of him he was at *New Florence, on the railroad*, and McNeil, with 460 men, was near Fulton, where I then knew he would meet Harris. You can imagine my anxiety, and afterward my relief, when I heard from that brave fellow McNeil that he had fought and routed the rebels.

The next day after this affair General Pope sent me word that he would go into Northeast Missouri with a large force. He has done so. He expects to have 7,000 men there, two batteries, and four companies of cavalry. McNeil still lies at Fulton. Hammer came down from the railroad, and McNeil has ordered him here. Everything quiet in Calloway. The northeast may be considered secure.

From Jefferson I have had nothing but trouble. It being impossible to supply the places of Boernstein's six companies, I have left him there, and—but I won't stop to mention his performances.

At home our friends are alarmed, and the city is uneasy. I receive about five deputations per diem, warning me that I ought not to send away so many troops, (2,200 United States reserve corps left,) and sometimes hinting that I will be overhauled by higher powers for doing so. The only danger is in case of an advance from Arkansas. But the first demonstration will result in clearing St. Louis of its secession element.

As far as your command is concerned, I fear that you think I have been neglectful of my duties, but I cannot admit the fact. Every order that you have sent I have immediately put into execution, and have seen it executed, so far as I could give my personal supervision to it. Mismanagement of transportation at Rolla, to which place 110 wagons had been sent before Brown moved, and probably the inferior kind of transportation furnished, accounts for the delay in getting supplies forward. Arms, ammunition, and provisions were lying for weeks at Rolla, while I supposed they were going forward, and I was not informed of the fact. When I did learn it I telegraphed to Washington, and had instructions sent to McKinstry to buy everything I required. McKinstry has also had sent to Rolla, at my request, one of Van Vliet's experienced clerks, Thomas O'Brien, to whom I have given the entire control of quartermaster's affairs from Rolla onward. A large number of army wagons, with mules, have been bought and sent down, and I trust that there will be no more trouble there. 250,000 rations were ordered on the 6th; 4,000 shoes and clothing to match were ordered on receipt of your letter of the 13th, and I presume are all on the way. I know that part have been shipped.

The line of communication from Rolla to Springfield is kept open by Wyman and Bayles. Wyman's is a splendid regiment, and I am trying to get other troops to supply his place and send him forward; but I am embarrassed by conduct which I scarcely think meets your approval, although I am informed that you gave your consent to it. Lieutenant Colonel Hassendeubel, who arrived here yesterday, but has not reported himself, brought up with him one of Bayles's companies, (company L, rifles, 4th regiment formerly, but since organized with others as a battalion,) and has ordered company M up, also, for the purpose of forming a three years regiment, of which he is to take the command.

I have been strengthening Bayles all I could. There are three companies here now, mustered and ready to go down as soon as armed, (by Tuesday at furthest,) and the other two companies will be ready during the week, in all probability. The ten companies were to be commanded by Saxton. He is said to be on his way here at this time, and Saxton would be invaluable, either in command on the line or with you. When Lieutenant Colonel Hassendeubel reports I shall send that company back, unless I am satisfied that he had good authority for his action.

As to re-enforcements I shall reorganize the 2d and 4th under their captains, and put the first ten companies formed into one regiment, without regard to the preferences of individuals. This can be done during the week, as Boernstein, Schaeffer, and Hammer are all to come here to-morrow.

The surplus can be organized under a temporary battalion organization, sent to the field, and afterwards filled up.

Smith's 8th can go down during the week, and a splendid regiment it is.

Last night the adjutant general gave me authority to accept any regiment that offered. Two are formed in the country. Both will be ready in two weeks. Others will come. I have caused the notice of the authority to be published. Bland can't be spared; nor can Curtis's men. St. Jo and the surrounding country are reported to be ready to rise. In fact, the whole State is.

McNeil can doubtless raise a regiment without difficulty. He is ordered home as soon as Pope relieves him.

The 9th and 10th are filling up fast, and can be ready in two weeks, probably. These statements are made upon the supposition that arms and equipments will be here as ordered.

Mulligan's regiment of Illinois volunteers, I forgot to say, arrived here yesterday for arms. I sent some companies to Jefferson to-day, and the remainder will go up Tuesday.

But, better than all, General Frémont telegraphed me last night that he would start for St. Louis immediately, and when I can have the opportunity of going over the map with him I trust that he will use his power to fill this State with troops. A few weeks' delay would make the whole State a battle-field.

And now, general, I can say that to be relieved of the responsibility which I have had upon me since you left, without the authority, after the change in the department command, to do what I saw was necessary, with my representations to the department generally unnoticed, and without even a competent clerk to aid me in the ordinary routine of business, is truly a relief; and no one can be so glad that Frémont is coming as I am. I have never before had the time to write you fully, and I presume that now the office is full of people, who are waiting upon the same errands with which you were formerly so much annoyed.

I shall always feel proud of the confidence which you have placed in me, and I hope you will think that I have endeavored to justify it.

Very respectfully and truly,

CHESTER HARDING, Jr.

Brigadier General Lyon, *Commanding.*

[By telegraph from Coshocton, Ohio, July 23, 1861.]

July 23, 1861.

Telegram received, and will be attended to. Will be in St. Louis Thursday morning.

J. C. FRÉMONT, *Major General.*

Chester Harding,
Assistant Adjutant General.

[By telegraph from Cairo, July 23, 1861.]

St. Louis Arsenal, *July* 23, 1861.

Have but eight (8) regiments here. Six (6) of them are three (3) months men. Their time expires this week; are reorganizing now. I have neither tents nor wagons, and must hold Cairo and Bird's Point. The latter is threatened. I have but two guns equipped for moving. Thus you see I cannot comply with request. Again, news of this morning changes policy of rebels in Kentucky. They are organizing opposite. Watkins is encamped with 2,000, seven miles from Bloomfield. He has no cannon, and poorly armed. This may be the force you have heard from.

B. M. PRENTISS, *Brigadier General.*

Chester Harding.

Headquarters Army of the West,
Springfield, Missouri, July 26, 1861.

Your order relative to the State Journal meets with the general's approbation. The general would like you to join him as soon as you can be spared by General Frémont. No doubt General F. will need you for a while, till he becomes familiar with the details of affairs in the State; but he will have a full staff of regular officers, and must be able to spare you soon. You are much needed here, and will be more so soon. It will soon be very necessary for me to be with my regiment, and officers fit for staff duties are very scarce here. We have heard of the defeat of our troops in Virginia, though hardly enough to judge of its extent. I fear this will prevent our getting re-enforcements. If so, the next news will be of our defeat also.

Re-enforcements should be sent on at once. Our men are very much in need of clothing, particularly shoes. Many of the men are entirely barefooted, and hence unable to march. I hope something can be done for us soon.

Yours, very truly,

J. M. SCHOFIELD.

Colonel Chester Harding,
Adjutant General Missouri Volunteers, St. Louis Arsenal.

WASHINGTON, *July* 26, 1861.

DEAR GENERAL: I have two telegrams from you, but find it impossible now to get any attention to Missouri or western matters from the authorities here. You will have to do the best you can, and take all needful responsibility to defend and protect the people over whom you are specially set. * * *

Yours, truly, and in haste,

M. BLAIR.

CAIRO, *July* 26, 1861.

Five steamers were to leave Memphis last night to take troops from Randolph to New Madrid. Union city troops are under orders to cross Mississippi. If they fail to assail us, Ironton and Cape Girardeau will need re-enforcements. Colonel Marsh has no battery. I have none to spare and no transportation to intercept rebels. I am of opinion that Bird's Point is their destination.

B. M. PRENTISS, *Brigadier General.*

Colonel HARDING, Jr.,
Assistant Adjutant General.

SPRINGFIELD, *Missouri, July* 27, 1861.

DEAR SIR: I have your notes about matters in St. Louis, &c., and your proceeding seems to me perfectly correct. Now that matters north seem more quiet, cannot you manage to get a few regiments this way? I am in the deepest concern on this subject, and you must urge this matter upon Frémont, as of vital importance. These three months volunteers would re-enlist if they could be paid, but they are now dissatisfied, and if troops do not replace them, all that is gained may be lost. I have not been able to move for want of supplies, and this delay will exhaust the term of the three months men. Cannot something be done to have our men and officers paid as well as our purchases paid for? If the government cannot give due attention to the west, her interests must have a corresponding disparagement.

Yours, truly,

N. LYON, *Brigadier General Commanding.*

Colonel C. HARDING, *St. Louis Arsenal, Mo.*

Memorandum by Colonel Phelps, from General Lyon, to General Frémont, July 27.

See General Frémont about troops and stores for the place. Our men have not been paid, and are rather dispirited; they are badly off for clothing, and the want of shoes unfits them for marching. Some staff officers are badly needed, and the interests of the government suffer for the want of them. The time of the three months volunteers is nearly out, and on returning home, as most of them are disposed to, my command will be reduced too low for effective operations. Troops must at once be forwarded to supply their place. The safety of the State is hazarded; orders from General Scott strip the entire west of regular forces, and increase the chances of sacrificing it. The public press is full of reports that troops from other States are moving toward the northern border of Arkansas for the purpose of invading Missouri.

JEFFERSON CITY, *Missouri, July* 27, 1861.

Surgeon Boemer, of 3d regiment reserve corps, left at Fulton by Colonel McNeil, reports this morning that, by the evacuation of that place by Colonel McNeil, the rebels are again gathering, and threatening Union men with vengeance. Either a battalion of General Pope's brigade, or some other force, should immediately occupy the town. I am also advised of a gathering of a large force at Warsaw, estimated at 10,000 and increasing. Also, an encampment, eight miles from Glasgow, of 2,000. With an additional regiment, so as to leave a garrison force of 500 men at Boonville, I will be able to disperse both forces. If they are promptly met they can be easily dispersed with the force indicated.

JOHN B. STEVENSON, *Col. Com. Missouri River.*

Maj Gen. JOHN C. FRÉMONT.

WASHINGTON, *July* 27, 1861

What disposition was made by you of the arms which you purchased in Europe? We are without information on that point, which is very desirable. Please answer at once by telegraph and by letter. Send an invoice of the articles.

WILLIAM H. SEWARD.

JOHN C. FRÉMONT.

ST. LOUIS, *July* 28, 1861.

I ordered the arms shipped to New York to my order, expecting to forward, on the arrival, to my department. I trust you will confirm this disposition of them. The rebels are advancing in force from the south upon these lines. We have plenty of men but absolutely no arms, and the condition of the State critical.

J. C. FRÉMONT, *Major General Commanding.*

Hon. W. H. SEWARD, *Washington.*

CAIRO, *July* 28, 1861.

Rebels from Tennessee are concentrating at New Madrid, Missouri, with the avowed intention of assaulting Bird's Point. They may intend going to Cape Girardeau. Colonel Marsh has no battery. I have none to spare. My command is merging from three months to three years service on half recess. Mustering in yesterday and to-day. I have but two 6-pounders prepared to move. I can hold Cairo and Bird's Point, but cannot move to intercept a large force going to Cape Girardeau. I suggest that Colonel Marsh, if not re-enforced, be sent to Bird's Point. Entire force at Cairo and Bird's Point, 6,350.

B. M. PRENTISS, *Brigadier General.*

Major General FRÉMONT.

CAIRO, *July* 28, 1861. (Received ST. LOUIS, *July* 29, 1861.)

On yesterday 3,000 rebels, west of Bird's Point 40 miles; 300 at Madrid and three regiments from Union City ordered there; also troops from Randolph and Corinth. The number of organized rebels within 50 miles of me will exceed 12,000—that is including Randolph troops ordered and not including several companies opposite, in Kentucky.

B. M. PRENTISS, *Brigadier General.*

Major General FRÉMONT.

ST. LOUIS, *July* 29, 1861.

The agent of Adams's Express Company here has offered to bring me by passenger train any arms directed to me. Send everything you have for me by passenger trains, for which the Express Company will provide. Your letter of 24th received. There were no arms at the arsenal here to meet the order given for the 5,000. We must have arms—any arms, no matter what.

J. C. FRÉMONT, *Maj. Gen. Com'g W. D.*

Major HAGNER, *Fifth Avenue Hotel, New York.*

[Unofficial.]

HEADQUARTERS WESTERN DEPARTMENT,
St. Louis, July 30, 1861.

MY DEAR SIR: You were kind enough to say that as occasions of sufficient gravity arose, I might send you a private note.

I have found this command in disorder, nearly every county in an insurrectionary condition, and the enemy advancing in force by different points of the southern frontier. Within a circle of fifty miles around General Prentiss, there are about 12,000 of the confederate forces, and 5,000 Tennesseeans and Arkansas men, under Hardee, well armed with rifles, are advancing upon Ironton. Of these, 2,000 are cavalry, which yesterday morning were within 24 hours march of Ironton. Colonel Bland, who had been seduced from this post, is falling back upon it. I have already re-enforced it with one regiment; sent on another this morning, and fortified it. I am holding the railroad to Ironton and that to Rolla, so securing our connexions with the south. Other measures, which I am taking, I will not trust to a letter, and I write this only to inform you as to our true condition, and to say that if I can obtain the material aid I am expecting you may feel secure that the enemy will be driven out and the State reduced to order. I have ordered General Pope back to North Missouri, of which he is now in command. I am sorely pressed for want of arms. I have arranged with Adams's Express Company to bring me everything with speed, and will buy arms to-day in New York. Our troops have not been paid, and some regiments are in a state of mutiny, and the men whose term of service is expired generally refuse to enlist. I lost a fine regiment last night from inability to pay them a portion of the money due. This regiment had been intended to move on a critical post last night. The Treasurer of the United States has here $300,000 entirely unappropriated. I applied to him yesterday for $100,000 for my paymaster general, Andrews, but was refused. We have not an hour for delay. There are three courses open to me. One, to let the enemy possess himself of some of the strongest points in the State, and threaten St. Louis, which is insurrectionary. Second, to force a loan from secession banks here. Third, to use the money belonging to the government, which is in the treasury here. Of course I will neither lose the State or permit the enemy a foot of advantage. I have infused energy and activity into the department, and there is a thorough good spirit in officers and men. This morning I will order the treasurer to deliver the money in his possession to General Andrews, and will send a force to the treasury to take the money, and will direct such payments as the exigency requires. I will hazard everything for the defence of the department you have confided to me, and I trust to you for support.

With respect and regard, I am yours truly,

JOHN C. FRÉMONT, *Major General Commanding.*

The PRESIDENT *of the United States.*

HEADQUARTERS OF THE WESTERN DEPARTMENT,
St. Louis, July 31, 1861.

At Camp Monroe, near Cincinnati, there is company C, 4th artillery, (regulars,) under 1st Lieutenant R. V. W. Howard; aggregate 76 men. Also, another company at Cincinnati in charge of Captain Kingsbruy, 6 rifled Parrott guns. I have asked Adjutant General Thomas if these can be ordered to me.

J. C. FRÉMONT, *Major General.*

Hon. MONTGOMERY BLAIR,
President's Square, Washington City.

HEADQUARTERS OF THE WESTERN DEPARTMENT,
St. Louis July 31, 1861.

At camp Monroe, near Cincinnati, there is company C, 4th artillery, (regulars,) under 1st Lieutenant R. V. W. Howard, aggregate 76 men. Also, another company at Cincinnati, in charge of Captain Kingsbury—six rifled Parrott guns. Can these be ordered here?

J. C. FRÉMONT,
Major General Commanding.

Adjutant General THOMAS,
War Department, Washington.

[By telegraph from Cairo, August 1, 1861.]

The following just received from Colonel Marsh, with request to send to you by telegraph. A scout of his from Pillow's camp brought the information; also a proclamation of Pillow's, who says no quarters to be given those in arms against him.

B. M. PRENTISS,
Brigadier General.

Major General FRÉMONT, *St. Louis.*

[By telegraph from Cairo, August 1, 1861.]

The following information just received is, I believe, reliable. General Pillow was at New Madrid on the morning of the 31st, with 11,000 troops well armed and well drilled; two regiments of cavalry splendidly equipped; one battery of flying artillery, 10-pounders, and ten guns, manned and officered by foreigners; several mountain Howitzers, and other artillery, amounting in all to 100. 9,000 more moving to re-enforce. He has promised Governor Jackson to place 20,000 men in Missouri at once. I have a copy of his proclamation and also one of his written passes.

C. C. MARSH,
Colonel Commanding Camp Frémont.

Major General FRÉMONT, *St. Louis.*

Upon this day, August 1, General Frémont went in person to re-enforce Cairo, with what troops he could gather, and with as much display as possible, in order to increase the apparent size of his small force.

[By telegraph from St. Louis, August 2, 1861.]

General Scott has telegraphed that two batteries of artillery have been sent from Cincinnati. Shall I forward them to you when they arrive? General Lyon wants soldiers—soldiers—soldiers! So says General Hammer, who has just arrived from Springfield.

J. C. KELTON,
Assistant Adjutant General.

General FRÉMONT, *Cairo.*

[By telegraph from Washington, August 2, 1861.]

This despatch was sent yesterday to commanding officer, Department Ohio, Cincinnati. Order two (2) companies fourth artillery, with their batteries, under Howard and Kingsbury, to St. Louis, without delay.

WINFIELD SCOTT.
M. BLAIR,
Post Master General.

Major General J. C. FRÉMONT, *Cairo.*

WAR DEPARTMENT,
Washington, August 2, 1861

Since ordering the two batteries for you yesterday, it appears one company has no guns and the other is in Western Virginia; neither can be withdrawn The order is countermanded.

WINFIELD SCOTT.

HEADQUARTERS,
Fort Leavenworth, Kansas, August 3, 1861.

SIR: From a communication this day received from Lieutenant Colonel O. E. Learned, I am informed that General Lyon relies upon the 3d regiment Kansas volunteers, under your command, to take charge of at Fort Scott and conduct to his (the general's) headquarters, the supply train now en route to Fort Scott, under the command of Colonel William Weer, 4th regiment Kansas volunteers. This is an important supply train, and the operations of General Lyon are, in a great measure, dependent upon an early reception of it. You will, therefore, please perfect, at the earliest possible moment, your arrangements to move with your command upon Fort Scott, with a view to carry out the intentions and orders of General Lyon. I shall direct the commissary at this post to turn over to you two months' supplies for your regiment, which, with the other supplies intended for your command, will be placed under your orders and directed to proceed to Fort Scott, *via* Lawrence, Kansas. To more fully understand the terms of the contract entered into by the War Department and Messrs. Irwin, Jackman & Co., respecting the transportation of army supplies, I enclose a copy of paragraph viii of that contract, for your information.

Please report to me the name of the officer selected by you as the commissary of your regiment, in order that the supplies may be duly invoiced to him.

Respectfully, your obedient servant,

W. E. PRINCE, *Captain 1st Infantry.*

Colonel MONTGOMERY,
3d Regiment Kansas Volunteers.

Copy respectfully submitted for information of General Frémont.

W. E. PRINCE, *Captain, &c.*

The following despatch was sent to General Frémont, at Cairo, the messenger having arrived at St. Louis, from General Lyon, in General Frémont's absence. The original despatch is in cipher:

ST. LOUIS, *August* 3, 1861.

General Lyon has sent a special messenger, Colonel Hammer, to say that he needs re-enforcements; that Jackson's army is in Jasper and adjacent counties, with not less than 20,000 men; that Lyon's force is not much more than one-fourth; that the inhabitants are moving this way as fast as their teams will carry them, leaving homes and crops desolated; that to insure a continuous and safe transport of provisions and supplies, the road from Rolla should be well protected. I have referred him to Captain Kelton.

E. M. D.

Captain DAVIS, *of the staff of General Frémont.*

(August 4, Frémont returned to St. Louis.)

CAIRO, *August* 4, 1861.

Information last night of a large force at Bloomfield, reported from eight (8) to ten thousand (10,00;) at Garrison Mills, on Picket road, five hundred (500;) at Castor Mills, five hundred (500;) at Strong's Mills, on Castor river, five hundred (500;) about five miles above Strong's Mills they are herding beef cattle. On 1st and 2d August they had orders to cook four days' rations of bread.

C. C. MARSH,
Colonel 20th Illinois Volunteers, Commanding.

Major General J. C. FRÉMONT.

INDIANAPOLIS, *August* 4, 1861.

Can send five regiments, if leave is granted by the department, as I am ordered to send them east as fast as ready. They are mostly river men, and are well adapted to your expedition. They have been promised rifles by the department which have not arrived as yet. What kind of guns will you give them, and where are they at? Will telegraph the department.

O. P. MORTON.

Major General FRÉMONT.

HEADQUARTRS WESTERN DEPARTMENT,
St. Louis, August 4, 1861.

The governor of Indiana, in answer to my urgent request for troops, informed me by telegraph, that he has five regiments ready, chiefly made up of river boatmen, but they are under orders for the east. He will ask for them to be kept on western duty. They cannot be more urgently needed at any place than here, and I ask for them as immediately as the order can be given. Answer by telegraph.

J. C. FRÉMONT,
Major Genrral Commanding.

Honorable MONTGOMERY BLAIR, *Washington City.*

HEADQUARTERS WESTERN DEPARTMENT,
St. Louis, August 4, 1861.

Seeing that the Secretary at War is absent from Washington, I telegraphed to you to ask that the five Indiana regiments, now under orders for the east, may be sent at once to me for immediate duty in this State. Governor Morton joins me in this request. Nowhere can they be more urgently needed, and nowhere can the river boatmen, from whom they are largely recruited, be so useful to the cause.

J. C. FRÉMONT,
Major General Commanding.

Honorable JAMES A. SCOTT,
Acting Secretary at War, Washington City.

HEADQUARTERS WESTERN DEPARTMENT,
St. Louis, August 4, 1861.

The general commanding desires me to say to you that an urgent application goes to-morrow to the War Department, for 3,000 California troops, to be placed as speedily as possible at El Paso, to keep Texas troops from aiding Arkansas. See the Postmaster General and Secretary of War, and answer by telegraph.

I. C. WOODS.

Honorable M. S. LATHAM,
United States Senate, Washington City.

[Received St Louis, 5th.]

CAPE GIRARDEAU,
August 4—11 *a. m., via Jonesborough.*

Thompson is advancing within sixteen miles of me. Am fortifying the hill in rear of Mills. Send me re-enforcements and ammunition. Express waiting for reply.

C. C. MARSH,
Colonel 20th Illinois Volunteers, Commanding.

Major General FRÉMONT.

CAPE GIRARDEAU,
August 5—9 *p. m., via Jonesborough.*

Enemy close on me, over 5,000 strong. Will be attacked before morning; send me aid.

C. C. MARSH, *Colonel.*

Major General FRÉMONT.

CAIRO, *August* 5, 1861.

The following despatch was just received :

"*Cape Girardeau, August* 4—11 *p. m.*

"GENERAL PRENTISS : Enemy advancing within sixteen miles of me. Help me if you can.

"C. C. MARSH."

B. M. PRENTISS,
Major General.

Major General FRÉMONT.

BY TELEGRAPH FROM THE ARSENAL,
August 5, 1861.

There are now in the arsenal 2,933 men, besides Smith's 630 at the barracks. Smith's and Coler's men don't know the facings and marchings. Ought not Coler to go to the barracks, and should not the officers of the 13th regulars be instructed to drill both regiments?

CHESTER HARDING, JR.

General FRÉMONT, *St. Louis*

HEADQUARTERS WESTERN DEPARTMENT,
St. Louis, August 5, 1861.

1. The commanding officer directs that Colonel Montgomery's force joins General Lyon's command, át Springfield, Missouri, immediately.

2. The force under Colonel Dodge, at Council Bluff, is ordered to St. Joseph forthwith. On its arrival at that point the commanding officer of the regiment will report to these headquarters for orders.

J. C. KELTON, *A. A. G.*

Forward these orders with the utmost despatch.

J. C. KELTON, *A. A. G.*

Captain PRINCE, *Fort Leavenworth, Kansas.*

[By telegraph from Washington, August 5, 1861.]

The President desires to know briefly the situation of affairs in the region of Cairo. Please answer.

JOHN G. NICHOLAY, *Private Secretary.*

Major General FRÉMONT.

HEADQUARTERS WESTERN DEPARTMENT,
St. Louis, August 6, 1861.

I re-enforce you this morning with a heavy battery of 24s and one regiment. General Prentiss re-enforces you from below. Keep me posted.

J. C. FRÉMONT,
Major General Commanding.

Colonel C. C. MARSH, *Cape Girardeau.*

WASHINGTON, *August* 6, 1861.

All the troops are ordered out of New Mexico. The first detachment will leave about the 15th. Volunteers received in New Mexico are reported unreliable in defending the large amount of United States property there. Those stores cannot be moved east. There is danger of their falling into the hands of the Texans. Nevertheless, the regulars must come away as ordered. At least two regiments of volunteers, say from Kansas, should be sent without delay to New Mexico, with a competent officer for the immediate command of all the troops there. Confer with the governor of Kansas, and arrange for the safety of New Mexico as soon as possible.

WINFIELD SCOTT.

Major General FRÉMONT.

HEADQUARTERS WESTERN DEPARTMENT,
St. Louis, August 6, 1861.

COLONEL: I send by special engine Mr. Edward H. Castle for any information you may have of General Lyon's position. Mr. Castle will inform you what progress Colonel Stevenson has made, who, with his regiment, is on his way to General Lyon's camp. Communicate to me through Mr. C., who is instructed to return with any information you may have—all of which you may safely intrust to him.

Enclosed letters to be forwarded as immediately as possible to General Lyon.

J. C. FRÉMONT,
Major General Commanding.

Colonel WYMAN, *Rolla.*

[By telegraph from Cairo]

ARSENAL, *August* 6, 1861.

I have just ordered four companies, with two 6-pounders on board steamer, to send. They are, no doubt, fighting now. See general. If not countermanded, will hurry them forward. Marsh has called for help again. Enemy, 5,000 and over. Citizens have left Cape Girardeau. Answer if I must send them.

B. M. PRENTISS, *Brigadier General.*

CHESTER HARDING.

ARSENAL, *August* 6, 1861.

Prentiss telegraphs that hot fighting is no doubt going on at Cape Girardeau, and that he has on board, ready to start, four companies and two 6-pounders to go to his aid. He asks if he shall send them. Please answer him. Ought he not to increase the re-enforcements. Enemy 5,000 strong.

CHESTER HARDING, JR.

Major General FRÉMONT.

CAIRO, *August* 6, 1861.

Colonel McArthur, with six companies and four field-pieces, left for Cape Girardeau 7½ a. m. Will hurry intrenchments at Bird's Point.

R. M. PRENTISS, *General Commanding.*

Major General FRÉMONT.

WASHINGTON, *August* 6, 1861.

Orders have been sent Governor Morton to forward five regiments to your department. Hoffman's battery of artillery, from Cincinnati, have been ordered to report to you for orders.

THO'S A. SCOTT,
Acting Secretary of War.

Major General FRÉMONT.

HEADQUARTERS, *August* 6, 1861.

Heavy battery of six 24-pounders and 1,000 men left at midnight for Girardeau under an experienced officer.

J. C. FRÉMONT,
Major General Commanding.

Brigadier General B. M. PRENTISS, *Cairo.*

DECATUR, *August* 7, 1861.

Six companies of rebels (three from Williamson, two from Franklin, and one from Jackson county, in this State,) are reported as ready to join Thompson at Cape Girardeau to invade Illinois. They are drilled and uniformed, and pretend to be Union men. They ought to be looked after by you. They are armed. You may, if you desire, reach me until to-morrow morning at Centralia, Illinois.

R. S. PHILLIPS,
United States Marshal.

General FRÉMONT.

HEADQUARTERS FORT LEAVENWORTH,
Kansas, August 7, 1861.

COLONEL: I herewith enclose you a copy of the telegram received and shown you last night, to wit:

"HEADQUARTERS OF THE WESTERN DEPARTMENT,
"*St. Louis, August* 5, 1861.

"CAPTAIN PRINCE: The commanding officer directs that Montgomery's force join General Lyon's command at Springfield immediately."

Independent of the reasons set forth in my communication to you of the 3d instant, you will see the necessity for adopting at once the most active measures to unite your forces with those of General Lyon. The train is now loading, and the mule wagons intended for your regiment have, I believe, been turned over to you. I would therefore suggest that these mule wagons be loaded with arms and ammunition intended for the home guards at Fort Scott, with the rations of Colonel Weer's command, and such rations for your own command as will fill them up. By this arrangement you will be able to detach, if necessary, the mule teams for a more rapid march. I would also suggest the propriety of proceeding in advance of your command, with Lieutenant Hollister, United States army, the officer detailed to complete the muster of your regiment. This officer will leave this morning, and will move with rapidity, and I do not wish his labors delayed, upon his arrival at Mound City. This officer is charged also with the mustering in of home guards at Fort Scott, and is directed to apply to you for the arms received by you from the governor of the State, which will be turned over to the guards. Please respond to his requisition, and aid him in the performance, if necessary, of this duty.

To carry out with the utmost promptitude, twenty mule wagons will be turned over to you for the transportation of these supplies. This will enable you to take ten days' rations for eight hundred men, besides the supply ordered for Colonel Weer's command, and the arms and ammunition for the home guard.

I understand you have camp women to transport; if so, and such is your intention, they should be transported in ox teams, so as not to encumber the mule wagons.

Respectfully,

W. E. PRINCE, *Captain 1st Infantry.*

Colonel MONTGOMERY,
3d Regiment Kansas Volunteers.

HEADQUARTERS OF FORT LEAVENWORTH, *August* 8, 1861.

Copy respectfully submitted for the information of the commanding general.

W. E. PRINCE, *Captain 1st Infantry.*

HEADQUARTERS OF THE WESTERN DEPARTMENT,
St. Louis, August 8, 1861.

In consequence of unfounded rumors, I send you the following despatch:

Intelligence just received of a battle fought, Friday, at Dug Springs, nineteen miles south of Springfield, between Lyon's forces, eight thousand strong, and troops of McCulloch, estimated at fifteen thousand. Lyon's loss, eight killed, thirty wounded; McCulloch's, forty killed and forty-four wounded. Lyon seized eighty stand of arms, fifteen horses and wagons of provisions. Twenty-seven United States cavalry came suddenly on the enemy's infantry, estimated four thousand, rode on them, created a stampede among the infantry, cut their way through, and came back with the loss of five men. Cavalry charge most brave. Enemy found with their heads cloven entirely through by force of sabre strokes. Enemy retreated during the night to McCulloch's store, a few miles south. Lyon took possession of the battle-field. Pickets fired on Saturday morning. Fight momentarily expected. Reports Sunday morning of a battle going on; not authentic. Rumors of a large force of rebels west of Springfield. Attack expected.

J. C. FRÉMONT,
Major General Commanding.

ABRAHAM LINCOLN,
President of the United States, Washington.

BIRD'S POINT, *August* 8, 1861.

The men want to go home, and if detained much longer the worst consequences may be feared. Their time of service expired yesterday. Provide for their return. They are of little use in their present spirit. I wait your answer

ROBT. ROMBAUER.

Major General FRÉMONT.

HEADQUARTERS OF THE WESTERN DEPARTMENT,
St. Louis, August 9, 1861.

General Lyon not defeated; had a brilliant and successful skirmish. Sent telegram to Major Sidell.

J. C. FRÉMONT,
Major General Commanding.

LOVELL H. ROSSEAU,
Camp Joseph Holt, Jeffersonville.

[By telegraph from Cairo, August 9, 1861.]

ST. LOUIS ARSENAL, *August* 9, 1861.

Full statement forwarded by mail.

B. M. PRENTISS,
Brigadier General.

Colonel CHESTER HARDING, jr.

SPINGFIELD, *Missouri, August* 9, 1861.

GENERAL: I have just received your note of the 6th instant by special messenger.

I retired to this place, as I have before informed you, reaching here on the 5th. The enemy followed to within ten miles of here. He has taken a strong position, and is recruiting his supplies of horses, mules, and provisions by forages into the surrounding country; his large force of mounted men enabling him to do this without much annoyance from me.

I find my position extremely embarrassing, and am at present unable to determine whether I shall be able to maintain my ground or be forced to retire. I can resist any attack from the front, but if the enemy move to surround me I must retire. I shall hold my ground as long as possible, though I may, without knowing how far, endanger the safety of my entire force, with its valuable material, being induced, by the important considerations involved, to take this step. The enemy yesterday made a show of force about five miles distant, and has doubtless a full purpose of making an attack upon me.

Very respectfully, your obedient servant,

N. LYON,
Brigadier General of Volunteers Commanding.

Major General J. C. FRÉMONT,
Commanding Western Department, St. Louis, Mo.

Upon the 10th of August General Lyon was killed in battle.

The Assistant Adjutant General's official statement of General Lyon's command:

First brigade, Major Sturgis:	
Four companies cavalry, one company dragoons	250
Four companies first infantry	350
Two companies Missouri volunteers	200
One battery	84
Total	884
Second Brigade, General Sigel:	
Third Missouri	700
Fifth Missouri	600
Two batteries	120
Total	1, 420
Third brigade, Colonel Andrews:	
First Missouri	900
Four companies infantry (regulars)	300
One battery	64
Total	1, 264
Fourth brigade, Colonel Deitzler:	
Two Kansas regiments	1, 400
First Iowa regiment	900
Total	2, 300

RECAPITULATION.

First brigade	884
Second brigade	1, 420
Third brigade	1, 264
Fourth brigade	2, 300
Total	5, 868

J. C. KELTON, *Assistant Adjutant General.*

General FRÉMONT, *Commanding Department.*

CAIRO, *August* 10, 1861.

The rebels are concentrating at Madrid. The least number reported me 10,000. They are procuring wagons, mules, and horses, by seizure from inhabitants, and are intrenching at Madrid. I have a man with them who will return on Sunday night. The force that was near Charleston is reported now to be at Madrid. They seem to await our coming.

B. M. PRENTISS, *Brigadier General.*

Major General FRÉMONT.

CAIRO, *August* 12, 1861.

A scout sent out several days ago from here has just returned. He left New Madrid on Saturday evening at six o'clock. He reports that the forces there are embarking to return to Memphis. Two steamers had left for below, loaded with troops, and some others were loading with troops and munitions. All the field artillery, some twenty or thirty pieces, were shipped. I think the information reliable. Scout came up through the country. Saw no indications of troops after leaving New Madrid. Other of our scouts were in Charleston this morning and report that there are no troops there or in that vicinity. The reason assigned for this movement, according to his statement, is that the confederate officers had information that General Fremont was preparing a move on Tennessee by way of Columbus and the railroad to Union city.

W. H. L. WALLACE, *Colonel Commanding.*

Major General FRÉMONT.

HEADQUARTERS WESTERN DEPARTMENT,
August 12, 1861.

Will you ask the Secretary of War to send me Captain A. Baird with Captain Fry, as assistant adjutant generals. Work is heavy and aid of experienced officers is necessary.

J. C. FRÉMONT,
Major General Commanding.

Hon. MONTGOMERY BLAIR,
Washington, D. C.

HEADQUARTERS WESTERN DEPARTMENT,
August 12, 1861.

Will you order the Groesbeck regiment, 39th Ohio, now at Camp Dennison, to be transferred to me? The regiment is willing to come.

J. C. FRÉMONT,
Major General Commanding.

Hon. Mr. CAMERON,
Secretary of War, Washington City.

HEADQUARTERS WESTERN DEPARTMENT,
St. Louis, August 13, 1861.

Despatch received. Our soldiers are not promptly paid, partly from the small force of paymasters, more from want of money, which fatally embarrasses every branch of the public service here. I require this week three millions for quartermaster's department.

J. C. FRÉMONT,
Major General Commanding.

Hon. THOMAS A. SCOTT,
Assistant Secretary of War.

HEADQUARTERS WESTERN DEPARTMENT,
St. Louis, August 13, 1861.

Let the governor of Ohio be ordered forthwith to send me what disposable force he has. Also governors of Indiana, Illinois, and Wisconsin. Order the utmost promptitude. The German Groesbeck, 39th Ohio, regiment, at Camp Dennison, might be telegraphed directly here. We are badly in want of field artillery, and up to this time very few of our small arms have arrived.

J. C. FRÉMONT,
Major General Commanding.

The SECRETARY OF WAR, *Washington City.*

HEADQUARTERS WESTERN DEPARTMENT,
August 13, 1861.

Will the President read my urgent despatch to the Secretary of War?

J. C. FRÉMONT,
Major General Commanding.

The PRESIDENT *of the United States.*

HEADQUARTERS WESTERN DEPARTMENT,
August 13, 1861.

See instantly my despatch to the Secretary of War. My judgment is that some regiments with arms in their hands, and some field artillery ready for use, with arms and ammunition, ought to be expressed to this point. The report of the action comes from General Lyon's aid, Major Farrar. If true, you have no time to lose.

J. C. FRÉMONT,
Major General Commanding.

Hon. MONTGOMERY BLAIR, *Washington City.*

HEADQUARTERS WESTERN DEPARTMENT,
St. Louis, August 13, 1861.

Will you order company of regular artillery at Cincinnati to report to me forthwith, together with the battery at Bellair?

J. C. FRÉMONT,
Major General Commanding.

Hon. THOMAS A. SCOTT,
Assistant Secretary of War.

HEADQUARTERS WESTERN DEPARTMENT,
St. Louis, August 13, 1861.

Severe engagement near Springfield on 10th. Our force 8,000; enemy 23,000 strong. Our loss 800 killed and wounded. General Lyon killed. Enemy's loss 1,500, including McCulloch and Price killed. Sigel retreated to Springfield, whence next morning continued retreat toward Rolla, bringing with him his baggage-trains and $250,000 in gold from Springfield Bank. I am sending re-enforcements to Rolla.

J. C. FRÉMONT,
Major General Commanding.

Brigadier General B. M. PRENTISS, *Quincy, Illinois.*

BIRD'S POINT, *August* 13, 1861.

Three more secessionists, two of them belonging to a Missouri company and one to a Mississippi company, all mounted and armed, were captured this morning at daylight, two miles south of Charleston, by Sergeant Canon and two men belonging to Captain Burns's cavalry of my command. One of them says he left New Madrid Sunday p. m.; that six steamboats had arrived from below with some 5,000 of the same troops that left on Saturday evening. The cavalry had also returned. Rumors from other sources say that the confederate forces all landed at New Madrid last night. Rumor that Jeff. Thompson's force is advancing on Cape Girardeau.

W. H. L. WALLACE,
Colonel Commanding.

Major General FRÉMONT.

JEFFERSON CITY, *August* 13, 1861.

Rumor here from across the country of fight at Springfield, with great loss on both sides. If State forces are in possession of Springfield we ought to have 20,000 men here in two days. Answer.

THOS. L. PRICE.

Major General FRÉMONT.

HEADQUARTERS WESTERN DEPARTMENT,
St. Louis, August 13, 1861.

General Lyon, in three columns, under himself, Sigel and Sturgis, attacked the enemy at half past 6 o'clock on the morning of the 10th, nine miles south-east of Springfield; engagement severe. Our loss about 800 killed and wounded. General Lyon killed in charge at head of his column. Our force 8,000, including 2,000 home guards. Muster-roll reported taken from the enemy, 23,000, including regiments from Louisiana, Tennessee, Mississippi, with Texas Rangers and Cherokee half-breeds. This statement corroborated by prisoners. Their loss reported heavy, including Generals McCulloch and Price. Their tents and wagons destroyed in the action. Sigel left one gun on the field, and retreated to Springfield; whence, at 3 o'clock on the morning of the 11th, continued his retreat upon Rolla, bringing off his baggage trains and $250,000 in specie from Springfield Bank. I am doing what is possible to support him, but need aid of some organized force to repel the enemy, reported advancing on other points in considerable strength.

J. C. FRÉMONT, *Maj. Gen. Commanding.*

Colonel E. D. TOWNSEND,
Assistant Adjutant General, Washington City.

HEADQUARTERS WESTERN DEPARTMENT,
St. Louis, August 13, 1861.

Severe engagement near Springfield reported; General Lyon killed; Sigel retreating in good order on Rolla. Send forthwith all disposable force you have, arming as you best can for the moment. Use utmost despatch.

J. C. FRÉMONT, *Maj. Gen. Commanding.*

Gov. YATES, *Springfield, Ill.*

HEADQUARTERS WESTERN DEPARTMENT,
St. Louis, August 13, 1861.

Severe engagement near Springfield reported; General Lyon killed; Sigel retreating in good order on Rolla. Send forthwith all disposable force you have, arming them as you best can for the moment. Use utmost despatch.

J. C. FRÉMONT, *Maj. Gen. Commanding.*

Gov. MORTON, *Indianapolis.*

HEADQUARTERS WESTERN DEPARTMENT,
St. Louis, August 13, 1861.

A severe engagement near Springfield reported; heavy loss on both sides; General Lyon killed; Sigel retreating on Rolla. Get the Grœsbeck regiment ordered here forthwith; get it from the governor.

J. C. FRÉMONT, *Maj. Gen. Commanding.*

Hon. J. A. GURLEY, *Cincinnati, Ohio.*

HEADQUARTERS WESTERN DEPARTMENT,
August 13, 1861.

Severe engagement reported near Springfield; General Lyon killed; Sigel retreating in good order on Rolla. Send forthwith all disposable force you have, arming as you best can for the moment. Order Warren's cavalry here at once. Use utmost despatch.

J. C. FRÉMONT, *Maj. Gen. Commanding.*

Adjt. Gen. BAKER, *Burlington, Iowa.*

Also telegraph to the same effect to Governor Dennison, Columbus, Ohio.

Subsequent despatches show how unsatisfactory was the *actual* response (not *verbal*) to these demands for aid.

The following despatch was sent to Mr. J. T. Howard, of New York, who, at General Frémont's request, was endeavoring to procure certain arms from the Union Defence Committee of that city:

ST. LOUIS, *August* 13, 1861.

Despatch received; send the arms without further bargaining, and also send your address. Ship per Adams & Co.'s fast freight, who collect here on delivery. Good men are loosing their lives while the men whom they defend are debating terms. Answer.

J. C. FRÉMONT,
Major General Commanding.

J. T. HOWARD.

Disposition for the protection of St. Louis.

AUGUST 13, 1861.

In Lafayette Park a camp is to be established for a regiment.

The heavy guns to be put in position and a regiment encamped under the reservoir.

On the height south of the arsenal, called Jacques's Garden, two guns with a howitzer to be planted.

The 3d and 4th home guard regiments to be paid off and reorganized immediately. After the arrival of the combined regiment under Lieutenant Colonel Rombauer from Bird's Point, the 1st and 2d home guard regiments, and also the 5th, under Colonel Stifel, to be paid and reorganized.

Martial law to be proclaimed at once. The secret police increased and systematically organized. A provost marshal shall be appointed with a staff. The reserve home guard, under Filley and Hill, to be organized in accordance with suggestions contained in the orders to the different colonels.

Captain Kowald's artillery company, 100 men strong, to be fitted out immediately, and the company from Belleville to be ordered in. Captains Vœrster's and Genter's pioneer companies to be completed and set at work on the fortifications. Laborers also to be employed.

J. C. FRÉMONT,
Major General Commanding,

Disposition for the State.

AUGUST 13. 1863.

Rolla, the receiving point of the southwestern army, must be occupied with a large force, in order that the retiring army of Springfield can find a place of rest; and from this place the offensive can be assumed in case that Springfield is to be retaken. The communication from Rolla to Sigel's troops must be kept open, scouting parties sent out as far as Salem, in Dent county, to ascertain if any attack is intended from the centre column of the enemy on Rolla. The protection of the bridge and road of the S. W. B. P. railroad to be kept constantly in view.

Warsaw, on the Osage river. Under the present circumstances it is of great importance to have the Osage river line protected, because this is the natural defence line and secures us all the counties lying between the Missouri and Osage rivers. If we give up or lose this line then all cities and towns of the Missouri river, of which many are of great importance, will be endangered. *and the enemy can open the communication with the country north of that river.*

Warsaw is the most important crossing place on the Osage river, and should be occupied by troops. Kansas City, Lexington, Boonville, and Jefferson City are to be occupied by volunteer troops, who are to act in concert with the home guards, in order that the secessionists may not gather in larger forces, and to secure uninterrupted communication on the river.

The home guards between the Osage and Missonri rivers should be concentrated at Cole Camp. A second camp should be formed in Georgetown as reserve position of the troops in Warsaw, and the places along the river. From these camps the Union men can be protected from the assaults of secessionists.

Tuscumbia, on the Osage river. This is the second (to Warsaw) importan position, a commanding place, and protecting Jefferson City. It is situated on high ground and commands the river.

Linn creek, county seat of Linn county. There should be situated an observation force at this place. It is not probable that the enemy will try to effect a crossing, on account of the broken, hilly, steep country of the neighborhood.

The fortifications of *Ironton,* and the placing of the guns therein, should be pushed forward to completion as quickly as possible. One or two artillery companies should be sent out to manage the cannons, and to have the light and heavy batteries thoroughly organized. Centreville and Frederickstown should be occupied by our forces, for the protection of the flanks of our troops at Pilot Knob, and one moving column sent out on the road to Greenville to make reconnoissances of the enemy's intentions, strength, &c.

Caledonia and Potosi.—The home guards of these places to send out frequent patrols to Fourche-à-Courtois mines.

Cape Girardeau.—Scouting parties to be sent to Jackson and Dallas, to watch the secessionists and their movements. There is no doubt that the enemy intends to reach the Missouri river and take possession of Lexington, Boonville, or Jefferson City—most probably the latter place. This can only be avoided by strengthening our forces at Rolla, and all along the Osage line; therefore all our available force should be sent to those points.

HEADQUARTERS WESTERN DEPARTMENT,
St. Louis, August 14, 1861.

General Grant, commanding at Ironton, attacked yesterday at 6 by a force reported at 13,000. Railroad seized by the enemy at Big River Bridge, on this side of Ironton. The governor of Ohio postponed my urgent request for aid until ordered by you. Will you issue peremptory orders to him and other governors to send me instantly any disposable troops and arms? An artillery company of regulars at Cincinnati, which has been there three months. I have applied for it repeatedly. The enemy is in overpowering force, and we are very weak in men and arms. We have neglected nothing, and will do all that is possible, but not one moment should be lost in giving us any possible aid in fixed artillery, and men with arms in their hands. A little immediate relief in good material might prevent great sacrifices.

J. C. FRÉMONT,
Major General Commanding.

The PRESIDENT *of the United States.*

ST. LOUIS, *August* 4, 1861.

Yours of the 4th received to-day. See despatch to President. I have made a loan from the banks here. Send money. It is a moment for the government to put forth its power.

J. C. FRÉMONT,
Major General Commanding.

Hon. MONTGOMERY BLAIR, *Washington City.*

HEADQUARTERS WESTERN DEPARTMENT,
August 14, 1861.

Your letter of the 4th received this day. All your suggestions will be fully attended to. But this department should be largely supplied with funds to prevent a recurrence of what you speak of.

J. C. FRÉMONT,
Major General Commanding.

Hon. S. P. CHASE, *Secretary of the Treasury.*

WASHINGTON, *August* 14, 1861.

Your message to President read. Positive orders were given yesterday to Governor Dennison, and to governors of Indiana, Illinois, and Michigan, to send all their organized forces, with full supply of artillery and small arms. Governor Dennison replies that Groesbeck's regiment will be promptly forwarded.

SIMON CAMERON.

General J. C. FRÉMONT.

WASHINGTON, *August* 14, 1861.

All the governors designated in your message were immediately advised to forward regiments and arms. Governor Dennison was instructed to send the Groesbeck regiment without a moment's delay.

THOS. A. SCOTT,
Assistant Secretary of War.

General J. C. FRÉMONT.

WASHINGTON, *August* 14, 1861.

Mr. Leslie tells me orders have been issued to Ohio, Indiana, Illinois, and Michigan to forward all available forces to you.

M. BLAIR, *Postmaster General.*

General J. C. FRÉMONT.

WASHINGTON, *August* 5, 1861.

Been answering your messages ever since day before yesterday. Do you receive the answers? The War Department has notified all the governors you designate to forward all available force. So telegraphed you. Have you received these messages? Answer immediately.

A. LINCOLN.

Major General FRÉMONT.

WAR DEPARTMENT, *August* 14, 1861.

SIR: Your letter of the 9th instant, to the Hon. Montgomery Blair, has been submitted to me by him.

With a view to place the raw troops under your command in a state of efficiency for active service in the shortest possible time, you are authorized to carry into effect your suggestion of accepting the services of instructed officers and men who have seen service, to form the skeleton or framework for the organization of your forces.

Let the captains of companies thus begun procure transportation from the railroad companies, and give their receipts to the road as vouchers.

Very respectfully, your obedient servant,

SIMON CAMERON,
Secretary of War.

Major General JOHN C. FRÉMONT,
Commanding Department of the West, St. Louis, Mo.

CINCINNATI, *August* 6, 1861.

War Department has despatched Adjutant McLean, that they cannot let Hoffman have guns, and suggests that the company had better be retained here until further orders. This will not do, if you can supply them with guns. They want to come to St. Louis as soon as mustered. What shall I do? Answer quickly.

R. M. CORWINE.

Major General FRÉMONT.

WASHINGTON, *August* 16, 1861.

Every available man and all the money in the public chest have been sent. We will send more money immediately, our financial arrangements at New York having been perfected. Let our fellows cheer up—all will be well.

M. BLAIR, *Postmaster General.*

Colonel BLAIR.

CINCINNATI, *August* 16, 1861.

E. D. Townsend despatches me the following in reply to your telegram to the President: General Scott says the battery of company E, fourth artillery, cannot be spared from the department of the Ohio.

R. M. CORWINE.

Major General FRÉMONT.

WASHINGTON, *August* 16, 1861.

General Scott says: Take steps to replace two companies of fourth artillery, at Fort Randall, by a sufficient number of volunteer companies from Kansas and Iowa, and bring the regulars to Cincinnati, to be subject to General Robert Anderson's order. Arrange so that least time possible shall be lost. Benham is with Rosecrans. C. F. Smith is not brigadier general.

E. D. TOWNSEND.

Major General FRÉMONT.

ST. LOUIS, *August* 19, 1861.

It is necessary, in order to facilitate the organization here, that Major General Frémont have power to commission officers, as Governor Gamble has neglected to accede to a request to do it, much to the detriment of the public service.

If the President telegraphs that he will appoint the officers General Frémont commissions, it will remove a great stumbling-block from our path.

FRANK P. BLAIR, JR.

Hon. MONTGOMERY BLAIR,
Washington, D. C.

In answer to this, Mr. Montgomery Blair telegraphed that if Governor Gamble would not commission officers the President would; but some mistake rendering the despatch incomprehensible, the President repeated it himself, as follows:

[By telegraph from Washington, 21st, 1861.]

I repeat I will commission the officers of Missouri volunteers.

A. LINCOLN.

Colonel BLAIR.

HEADQUARTERS WESTERN DEPARTMENT,
August 21, 1861.

DEAR MR. BLAIR: Quartermaster Turnley brought me this morning a despatch to himself, from General Meigs, informing him that the Secretary of War disapproved a purchase of horses ordered by me; and, still further, going to impute to me a disposition to extravagance in my expenditures here. If there should be here any act of mine wrong enough to merit the censure of the administration, and grave enough to justify them in making it, I think that it should be made to me directly, and not through the medium of an inferior, to one of his subordinates, who is under my command. Such a course is intolerable, not because it is derogatory and humiliating, but also because it seriously impairs my efficiency, by lessening the respect in which my conduct is to be held by the officers of my command, and also by the discouragement it inflicts on myself. To give full efficiency to my acts no one here should be able to suppose a possibility of my ordinary administrative acts, or, indeed, of any other, being questioned. I have not written to General Meigs, judging it better to ask the attention of the President to this want of official courtesy. I am not only willing, but I am happy to devote my best energies to the service of the country and the President. But I trust that he will at once put his foot upon any attempt to impair my usefulness, or cause me mortification in the discharge of my duties here. I trouble you often; will you allow me to ask that you acquaint the President with this occurrence, and oblige,

Yours, very truly,
J. C. FRÉMONT.

Hon. MONTGOMERY BLAIR, *Washington City.*

WASHINGTON, *August* 24, 1861.

DEAR GENERAL: Don't suppose that I don't attend to your matters, and do all that I can to forward them because I do not write frequently. I am to be interrupted, if I take up a pen, by people that have the run of my office or house, and so I keep out of both, and go after your business in person, and effect it if I can.

I write now, to-day, in reply to your letter about Meigs, that you must not suppose that he intended by his telegram to Turnley to reflect upon you. Far from it. I happened in his office when he opened Turnley's requisition, and remarked to me, substantially, what he telegraphed to Turnley. But he did not know that Turnley had any instructions from you to get horses of any superior quality. No such suggestion accompanied the requisition, and I will guarantee that if Turnley makes any explanation, which puts the responsibility on you, it will be satisfactory to Meigs.

I say this without having seen him at all since the receipt of yours on the subject; but, I think, I understand him fully. I heard him say to General Scott, some time ago, that if he would name a day when he must have horses they should be ready. "If next week, they would cost $150; if the week after, $125. The price was nothing. A horse might be worth the price many times to the government if ready when wanted, and of course of no value if not." This is the style of man he is, and you will have, and I believe have not had any delay or difficulty from him. The trouble is elsewhere. Chase has more horror of seeing treasury notes below par than of seeing soldiers killed, and, therefore, has held back too much, I think. I don't believe at all in that style of managing the treasury. It depends on the war, and it is better to get ready and beat the enemy by selling stocks at fifty per cent. discount than wait to negotiate and lose a battle. I have got you a splendid officer for your navy department and guns. He will be *en route* for you in a day or two, when he will be posted up and call for what you want. You will have credit at the Navy Department when you get him under you.

I showed the President Billings's letter, and read him yours about Adams. He said that you were right in saying that Adams was devoted to his money-bags.

Schuyler had already gone to Europe about arms when I wrote and telegraphed you, and your letter in reply was handed to Mr. Seward, to be forwarded to him. I suppose it would put him in relation with Billings, which would bring about your wishes. If I had known when you were here what you communicated to my father, I think from my knowledge of Meigs, with your indorsement, I could have turned the whole matter over to him. At the same time you must not expect too much of me in the cabinet. I have, as you know, very little influence, and even now, when the policy I have advocated from the first is being inaugurated, it does not seem to bring me any greater power over the administration. This, I can see, is partly my own fault. I have been too obstreperous, perhaps, in my opposition, and men do not like those who have exposed their mistakes beforehand, and taunt them with them afterwards. The main difficulty is, however, with Lincoln himself. He is of the whig school, and that brings him naturally not only to incline to the feeble policy of whigs, but to give his confidence to such advisers. It costs me a great deal of labor to get anything done, because of the inclination of mind on the part of the President or leading members of the cabinet, including Chase, who never voted a democratic ticket in his life. But you have the people at your back, and I am doing all I can to cut red tape and get things done. I will be more civil and patient than heretofore, and see if that won't work.

Yours, truly, M. BLAIR.

HEADQUARTERS WESTERN DEPARTMENT,
St. Louis, August 25, 1861.

Jefferson C. Davis, a lieutenant in the United States army, was sent here by the governor of Indiana in command of a regiment. He is informed by Adjutant General Thomas that he cannot retain his command.

Will you ask if he, and a few army officers I have found, may be allowed to retain command of their regiments?

J. C. FRÉMONT,
Major General Commanding.

Hon. MONTGOMERY BLAIR,
Postmaster General, Washington City, D. C.

CINCINNATI, *August* 26, 1861.

In answer to a despatch directing the Gibson regiment to go to St. Louis by the northern route, our governor sends the following: We can spare at present only Colonel Paschner's regiment for General Frémont's command, in addition to the force already sent. Gibson's will be sent to Western Virginia.

JOHN A. GURLEY.

Major General FRÉMONT.

LOUISVILLE, *August* 24, 1861.

It is earnestly requested by the Union men to permit Colonel Rousseau's brigade to remain where they are twenty or thirty days.

G. D. PRENTICE.
J. H. HARNEY.

General J. C. FRÉMONT.

General Frémont refused this request through Major Corwine, and represented to these gentlemen the imperative necessity for the movement of these troops.

CINCINNATI, *August* 26, 1861.

Colonel Rousseau despatches me that he will leave between 3 and 4 o'clock p. m.

R. M. CORWINE.

Major General FRÉMONT.

WASHINGTON, *August* 26, 1861.

Intelligent gentlemen at Louisville say the presence of Rousseau's regiment is needed there. Pardon us for countermanding your order to him to join your department.

A. LINCOLN.

General FRÉMONT.

CINCINNATI, *August* 28, 1861.

General Rosecrans ordered the Poschun regiment to Virginia. Reason, Tyler's defeat. Governor Dennison sends them to-day.

JNO. A. GURLEY.

Major General FRÉMONT.

WASHINGTON, *August* 27, 1861.

Greenleaf discharged when appointment in volunteers sent here. Jefferson C. Davis can remain.

M. BLAIR.

To Colonel BLAIR.

General Frémont was furnished with only a copy of the following letter, and was not shown the original:

QUARTERMASTER GENERAL'S OFFICE,
Washington, August 28, 1861.

DEAR COLONEL: Your brother, the Postmaster General, has handed me your letter of the 21st August. I asked him to let me have it that I might, by a few words, strengthen your hands and General Frémont's, and disabuse both him and you of some errors which may give trouble.

If there is any deficiency in the quartermaster's department of Missouri, the blame does not rest here. All requisitions have been promptly met here, and the officers have been instructed to spare no effort and no means of this department in aiding, to the extent of their power, General Lyon's movements. There may be reasons of time, of quality, which induce a general to order a purchase at a higher rate; and while I communicated to the quartermaster as to the ruling prices of horses, the market rates, I called upon the treasury to send all the money he asked for.

Tell General Frémont that no man more than myself desires to sustain him, no one is more ready to take the responsibility to assist him, and that he has, in my opinion, already the power which you say ought to be conferred upon him by the President. Whatever a general commanding orders, the subordinates of his staff are, by regulations, compelled to do if possible.

The general is charged with saving the country. The country will be very careful to approve his measures, and will judge his mistakes, if any, very tenderly if successful. Success crowns the work, and let him spare no responsibility, no effort to secure it.

All the requisitions for money in Missouri have been promptly passed through this office. The delay, if any has occurred, is at the Treasury Department, which has allowed the department to fall in debt in Cincinnati and Philadelphia, each about a million of dollars for clothing and camp equipage.

There are wagons making in Cincinnati, which Captain Dickinson will send to St. Louis, if wanted. Those made at Milwaukie I ordered to St. Louis long ago.

A number of wagons are ordered to be made in St. Louis, and authority given to Major McKinstry to provide all that might be required for moving the armies of that department.

In regard to advertising and delivery, the law of 1861 and the regulations expressly provide that in case of public exigencies, supplies are to be bought in open market or between individuals. Exercise this power. Moreover, advertisements or public notice does not require postponing, opening of bids for a month, or a week, or two days. If forage-wagons, horses, are wanted, the law, the necessity, are fully met by putting a notice in the papers, and purchasing as fast as offers come in. The next day, or the same day, take the then lowest bidder, or the then most advantageous offer. The day after you will have a still better offer; take that for a portion of your supplies, and so on till you have all you need. By this system I have brought down the price of horses from $128 to $120, of wagons from $111 to $108 since I came here, and have got abundant supplies.

These explanations will, I hope, remove many difficulties from the way of our armies in Missouri. Count upon me as ready to aid in what I believe the right, cheap, strategic, statesmanlike mode of conducting the war—that which I am sure the people desire, and the want of which they censure—the most rapid possible concentration of overwhelming forces by the United States.

Yours, very truly,

M. C. MEIGS.

Hon. F. P. BLAIR, *St. Louis, Missouri.*

WASHINGTON *August* 30, 1861.

The President hesitates about Smith, but if you say so, he will appoint him a brigadier general.

M. BLAIR.

General FRÉMONT.

[Rough draft of a letter to Montgomery Blair.]

AUGUST 9, 1861.

[The letter as sent does not differ from this in any material point. No copy of it is in General Frémont's possession.]

The greater part of the old troops, especially the foreign element, is going out of service. The new levies are literally the rawest ever got together. They are reported by the officers to be literally, entirely, unacquainted with the rudiments of military exercises. To bring them face before the enemy, in their present condition, would be a mere unmanageable mob. I can remedy this if I can be authorized by the President and Secretary of War to collect throughout the States instructed men who have seen service. With them I could make a skeleton—meagre—but still a framework on which to form the army. This authority ought to be allowed and the cost of transportation. Don't lose time, but get it quick. I assure you it will require all we can do, and do it in the best manner, to meet the enemy. I ought to be supplied here with four or five millions of dollars in treasury notes, and the disbursing officers allowed to sell them at the ruling discount.

All such equipments as I can procure abroad in much less time than I could get them here I ought to be allowed to send for.

These are my suggestions. They are valuable. Pray act upon them, and what you do, do quickly. It would subserve the public interest if an officer were directed to report to me, to have command of the operations on the Mississippi. Show this to the President. The contest in the Mississippi valley will be a severe one. We had best meet it in the face at once, and by so doing we can rout them. Who now serves the country quickly serves it twice.

JOHN C. FRÉMONT.

HEADQUARTERS WESTERN DEPARTMENT,
St. Louis, September 17, 1861.

CAPTAIN: The general directs me to say to you that Major Farrar, late of General Lyon's staff, states publicly in the city that he came to these headquarters and applied for re-enforcements for General Lyon; that the re-enforcements were refused, and that from the *manner* of refusal the intention was to leave General Lyon to his fate. What are the facts in the case?

Respectfully,

J. H. EATON,
Major U. S. Army and M. S.

Captain J. C. KELTON, *A. A. G.*

To which Captain Kelton replied as follows:

SEPTEMBER 21, 1861.

MAJOR: Your note was not read till this moment. I have no recollection of Major Farrar bringing application for re-enforcements to General Lyon. That every effort was made to send General Lyon additional troops, after the arrival of General Frémont, I do know. It was found impossible to do so and keep open the railroad communication extending toward Springfield, and at the same time to meet the threatened advance up the Mississippi. I do not know anything of the manner in which the refusal to send re-enforcements was made. I can only recall, now, Major Farrar in connexion with his application to me for a pass over the Pacific railroad for his horses, which I declined, after the quartermaster had informed me it could not be authorized. If I had any conversation with Major Farrar on the subject to which your note alludes, it has escaped me entirely.

Very respectfully,

JNO. C. KELTON,
Late A. A. G., Colonel 9th Reg. M. V.

The following is an extract from a statement voluntarily drawn up and offered to General Frémont by Colonel Chester Harding, assistant adjutant general to General Lyon:

PACIFIC, *October* 5, 1861.

* * * * Looking, then, to the position of affairs in this State on the 26th July, 1861, it will be found that General Lyon was in the southwest in need of re-enforcements. There was trouble in the northwest, requiring more troops than were there. In the northeast there were no more troops than were required to perform the task allotted to them, while in the south and southeast there was a rebel army of sufficient force to endanger Bird's Point, Cape Girardeau, Ironton, Rolla, and St. Louis, and no adequate preparation was made to meet it.

General Frémont sent the 8th Missouri to Cape Girardeau, and the 4th United States reserve corps (whose term of service was to expire on the 8th of August,) to re-enforce Bland at Ironton. He took some of General Pope's force from him, added to it two battalions of the 1st and 2d United States reserve corps, (whose term of service was to expire on the 7th of August,) equipped Buel's light battery, and started about the 1st of August for Bird's Point with the troops thus collected, being something less than 3,800 men, and being also all the available troops in this region, expecting to find an enemy not less than 20,000 strong.

Subsequent events showed that the rebel force was not overestimated, and nothing but the re-enforcements sent to the points above named, and the expeditions down the river, prevented its advance upon them. Common report greatly magnified these re-enforcements; and it was generally believed in the city, and no doubt so reported to the rebel leaders, that Frémont had moved some 10,000 or 12,000 troops to the southeast, while in fact he did not have over 5,500 to move, and was not strong enough at any point to take the field and commence offensive operations.

General Frémont *was not* inattentive to the situation of General Lyon's column, and went so far as to remove the garrison of Boonville, in order to send him aid. During the first days of August troops arrived in the city in large numbers. Nearly all of them were unarmed; all were without transportation. Regiment after regiment laid for days in the city without any equipments, for the reason that the arsenal was exhausted, and arms and accoutrements had to be brought from the east. From these men General Lyon would have had re-enforcements, although they were wholly unpracticed in the use of the musket, and knew nothing of movements in the field; but in the meantime the battle of the 10th of August was fought.

CHESTER HARDING, JR.,
Late Ass't Adj't General upon the Staff of Brig. Gen Lyon.

[This series of papers embraces the time between September 1 and September 23, having especial reference to the affair at Lexington, and the contemporaneous complications in the department of the west.]

[Personal.]

HEADQUARTERS WESTERN DEPARTMENT, *September* 4, 1861.

MY DEAR SIR: Your note of the 19th was handed me by Judge Evans, who was here with me at the same time with Judge Watts, of New Mexico. Agreeably to your desire I conferred fully with them, and made such arrangements for co-operation and communication as is just now possible. They are undoubtedly both able to render efficient service, and both seem to understand well the necessities of their respective States. Judge Watts I retained here for one day, which did not, however, in any way retard his arrival in New Mexico.

Judge Evans is so well known that it would be scarcely possible for him to reach Texas through the Missouri country. I endeavored to find a way for him through New Mexico, but his journey that way would be very laborious and almost equally unsafe. I therefore advised him to go by way of Tampico, whence he would have a good road of only 500 miles, and would have an opportunity to ascertain what supplies and war munitions are being carried by that route to the confederates.

In this Judge Evans agreed with me, and accordingly left yesterday for Washington. All accounts from the south show great activity, and their recent movements indicate that the confederates are now giving great attention to the Mississippi valley. Their recent operations show that better officers have recently been sent to the Memphis district.

I would be glad to benefit sometimes by your leisure moments, if you can find any sometimes for a few lines, and am, meantime,

Yours, truly,

J. C. FRÉMONT.

Hon. Mr. SEWARD, *Washington, D. C.*

[Translation.]

ST. LOUIS, *September* 5, 1861.

The Kentucky side opposite Cairo should be fortified, and at once. Steps should be taken forthwith. From Cape Girardeau, Cairo and Bird's Point six infantry regiments, cavalry, and a section of artillery will be sent at once. The requisitions of Captain Brintz for ammunition will be attended to immediately.

Paducah is to be occupied, if possible. If not on the opposite shore, facing the mouth of the Tennessee, to be very closely watched.

In a fortnight four regiments will be sent there. I advise you to watch, with the greatest care, Belmont, Charleston, Sykeston, and New Madrid.

[To Washington, for the President, through a Hungarian gentleman.]

ST. LOUIS, *September* 5.

You will communicate to the President that the enemy's gunboats are covered with sheet iron, and equipped with cannon in the best way, and a great deal lighter draught and swifter than ours. Their officers are all from our navy, and ours are inexperienced, including the artillery. The consequence will be, that when they meet, ours will be captured. In Cairo we need immediately heavy artillery. I send Rodgers to the President, that he shall see to having the artillery hurried up.

The enemy begins to occupy, on the Kentucky side, every good place between Paducah and Hickman. I think the time has come to extend my command.

J. C. FRÉMONT,
Major General Commanding.

HEADQUARTERS JEFFERSON CITY, MISSOURI,
September 5, 1861.

GENERAL: The steamers which transported Colonel Worthington's command up the river returned yesterday, bringing considerable property, which they had taken, and some prisoners. Harris is in that section, beyond doubt, and I hope Worthington may find him.

I have despatches from Colonel Marshall, at Lexington. This place is for the present perfectly safe.

Colonel Mulligan's command is progressing well, and nothing is to be apprehended from him—other than success.

News from the country south and west of this confirm my reports of yesterday.

I am, general, very respectfully, your obedient servant,

JEFF. C. DAVIS,
Colonel 22d Indiana, Commanding.

Major General J. C. FRÉMONT, *St. Louis, Mo.*

HEADQUARTERS JEFFERSON CITY, MISSOURI,
September 6, 1861.

GENERAL: The news since yesterday is still more convincing that Price, Parsons, and Rains are directing their movements up the Osage, with the view eventually, I think, of taking position somewhere on the river above here—probably just below Lexington.

Their movements certainly threaten Fort Scott, and they may attack it; but their intention is, in my judgment, to take a strong position on the river and cut us off from the forces above. This is necessary for them to do, in order to get the forces and supplies now raised in Northeast Missouri across the river.

In my communications to General Pope, some days ago, I ventured to suggest the propriety of sending a reliable force to occupy Warsaw, or some point in that vicinity. A well-managed force at this point would in a great measure prevent recruits and supplies being raised there for McCulloch's forces.

It would render Price's movements very insecure, as he would be nearly if not quite cut off from McCulloch, and might, if he moves further north, be easily captured by a concentrated movement of troops upon him from this place, Fort Scott, Warsaw, and Lexington.

The plan submitted to you by Major Kraut for the defence of this place meets with my approval. A few well selected sites for field-works, flanked and supported by a series of block-houses, abatis, &c., seem to be the best I could recommend. The material for building here is abundant, and sites which would secure them from the range of the enemy's artillery can generally be found. Should you think proper to order these works to be commenced it would do much to allay the fears of the citizens of this place. There seems to be no grounds of fear from immediate danger; but they think so.

The home guards give me much trouble on account of not being clothed and equipped. When called upon for duty they make this a complaint.

Reports (not very reliable) last night state that Colonel Worthington had taken possession of Columbia. The rebels evacuated it at his approach, but had made a stand, some four miles from there, in such force that he was doubtful about attacking them. I have a regiment and boats in readiness to succor him at once should it be necessary.

I am, general, very respectfully, your obedient servant,

JEFF. C. DAVIS,
Colonel 22d Indiana Volunteers.

Major General J. C. FRÉMONT,
St. Louis, Missouri.

HEADQUARTERS, MEXICO, MO., *September* 9, 1861.

SIR: I have the honor to inform you of my arrival at this place to-day at 10 o'clock a. m., with my entire command, except the cavalry and baggage wagons, none of which have arrived, nor will it before to-morrow.

The supply of engines and cars was not sufficient to reach this point earlier or to bring it all. The consequence is that we may not be able to move as soon as might be hoped. From all I can learn Green's band is some place in the vicinity of Florida. Nothing has reached me yet from General Pope. Considering the raw character of the troops under my command, I would respectfully suggest that if a few companies of regular infantry could be spared from Rolla they would add greatly to our hopes of success in case we should fall in with the whole rebel force. The rebels, furthermore, are all, or nearly so, mounted; and should they feel disposed to scatter (which they are sure to do if we are too strong for them) it will be impossible to overtake them with infantry, and therefore more cavalry (particularly regular) is very desirable.

I am, sir, very respectfully, your obedient servant,

S. D. STURGIS,
Brigadier General Commanding.

Captain J. C. KELTON,
Assistant Adjutant General, Western Department.

NEW ALBANY, *September* 9, 1861.

Pillow is marching upon Paducah, Ky., with about 7,000 men and artillery. Look out for him. I have this from a Tennessee officer in Louisville. The Tennesseans are going to make a forward movement to-night, or to-morrow, to Kentucky, per Louisville and Nashville railroad. This news is reliable. * *

——— ———,
A secret agent of the government.

Major General FÉRMONT.

ST. LOUIS, *September* 6, 1861.

SIR: According to the report received at these headquarters, Colonel Williams, with his command of 800 men, has been forced to retreat from Shelbina to Macon City, (Hudson,) by a band of rebels, under Green, numbering about 3,000, where he is now cut off from all lines of communication east of his position.

In order to arrest the constant depredations of the rebels in Marion, Monroe, Shelby, Macon and adjoining counties, and to visit on them the whole rigor of martial law, I have resolved upon a combined attack on Green's men, and their total annihilation.

To effect this object you will be re-enforced by the first Kansas regiment and the twenty-third Indiana regiment.

Brigadier General Sturgis will advance on Macon City (Hudson) with the seventh Ohio regiment; Colonel Groesbeck's thirty-ninth Ohio regiment; one squadron Frémont Hussars, under Captain Von Blume, and Captain Schwartz's full battery, under command of the first lieutenant.

You will leave a comparative reserve at Palmyra, and then advance west towards Salt river, and you will, under any circumstances, endeavor to put yourself in communication with the command of Brigadier General Sturgis, who will operate towards the east against Shelbina.

It will be your object not only to disperse the enemy, but to follow him into his hiding places and annihilate him.

After having put yourself in communication with Brigadier General Sturgis, by means of a reliable messenger, and after General Sturgis has advanced east towards Shelbina, you will force the passage of Salt river, (should the bridge be destroyed, you will find a suitable bridge towards the north or south,) and thus make a combined attack on the rebels.

After the junction of the forces has been accomplished, Brigadier General Sturgis will be under your command.

As communication between you and General Sturgis will be subject to the constant hazard of interruption, you will report by telegraph as often as necessary, to these headquarters, whence despatches may be sent to him.

I enclose a copy of the order addressed to Brigadier General Sturgis.

J. C. FRÉMONT, *Major General Commanding.*

Brigadier General POPE.

ST. LOUIS, *September* 6, 1861.

SIR: In order to put a stop to the robberies and violences committed by the rebel hordes under Green, who are now assembled at Shelbina to the number of about 3,000, and who have cut off Colonel Williams from his eastern communication lines, I have resolved upon a combined attack on the rebels and their annihilation.

General Pope will endeavor, with his disposable force, re-enforced by the 1st Kansas and the 23d Indiana regiment, to force a passage across Salt river, or to gain a crossing by some other means. Further details concerning the general plan and the junction of the forces General Pope will endeavor to transmit to you by a reliable messenger.

To carry out this combined attack you will assume command of the following forces:

The 27th Ohio regiment, Colonel Foster.

The 39th Ohio regiment, Colonel Groesbeck.

One squadron of Frémont hussars, Captain M. Blume.

Captain Schwartz's full battery, under command of the first lieutenant.

Your main endeavor will be to cut off the enemy from the road leading to Shelbyville, and generally to render impossible the dispersion of his forces by squads, and to annihilate the gang of rebels as a whole.

As the communication between you and General Pope will be subject to the constant hazard of interruption, you will report as often as necessary by telegraph to headquarters, whence despatches can be sent to him.

I enclose a copy of the order addressed to Brigadier General Pope.

J. C. FRÉMONT, *Major General Commanding.*

Brigadier General STURGIS, *Commanding at Arsenal.*

HEADQUARTERS, ST. CHARLES,
September 7, 1861—11½ *p. m.*

SIR: Your letter is just received. We have been delayed here, which my previous letter will explain. Green is evidently fallen down to Mexico with the view to destroy the bridge at that point. The 2d regiment will start at daylight. In view of the present condition I will order them to take position in the advance at the bridge, and hold it until we can get the cars and artillery. They have not reached this point.

Respectfully, S. D. STURGIS,
Brigadier General Missouri Volunteers.

Major I. C. WOODS, *Department Headquarters.*

HEADQUARTERS, *September* 8, 1861.

GENERAL: I have just received despatches from Boonville. Affairs there are progressing very satisfactorily.

I have also despatches from the command (Colonel Golden) I sent in the direction of Linn creek. I have some hope that the party who confiscated Colonel McClurg's property are nearly overtaken, as they are being closely pursued.

I have sent five companies of Illinois volunteers to make a scout on the east side of the river, opposite Portland, and there to take post on the bridge until relieved.

Your obedient servant, JEFF. C. DAVIS.

Major General FRÉMONT.

KANSAS CITY, *September* 9, 1861.

In accordance with Colonel Peabody's order, I forward to you the following information, which was received 7 o'clock p. m. yesterday evening: Colonel Peabody marched from Lexington towards Warrensburg on Sunday, intending to camp at said point last night, where the Irish brigade awaits them. When the junction is formed the strength of combined forces will be 4,000. Colonel Peabody, acting under the impression that General Lane is retreating on this point before Price, says that he will form a junction with General Lane twenty-five or thirty miles south of this point; also that I must move from here to keep the communication open between him, General Lane, and Colonel Marshal, in command at Lexington. Should the forces leave here at this time, we give the town up to pillage. West of Warrensburg, thirty miles, the enemy is gathering around in parties from 200 to 300. Rains's advance is at Barinsville. I forwarded a copy of Colonel Peabody's command to General Lane. Have been on the road twelve hours.

M. T. BERRY,
Major Commanding.

Captain W. E. PRINCE.

HEADQUARTERS WESTERN DEPARTMENT,
September 9, 1861.

Has General Smith gone to Paducah? I am credibly informed from Louisville that Pillow, with 7,000 men and artillery, is marching on Paducah; also that the Tennesseeans are going to make a forward movement to-night or to-morrow to Kentucky. Has the re-enforcement from St. Louis reached Cairo? Inform General Smith, at Paducah, that I direct him to place a battery at the marine hospital immediately, and the other on the heights near Cross creek, and prepare for forward movements towards Mayfield, as soon as re-enforcements arrive.

J. C. FRÉMONT,
Major General Commanding.

Brigadier General U. S. GRANT.

ST. LOUIS, *September* 9, 1861.

COLONEL: I am instructed by Colonel Jefferson C. Davis, commanding at Jefferson City, to ask two additional regiments of infantry, (Indiana,) two batteries 8th artillery, (Indiana,) and some heavy guns for the field-work now under construction at that place. Colonel Davis instructed me to say that this force will be necessary to the execution of his plans touching Warsaw and other places in that direction. He would like to have the Indiana cavalry, if ready for service.

Respectfully,

GORDON TAVENER,
Major 22d Indiana Volunteers.

Colonel J. H. EATON,
Military Secretary, St. Louis.

HEADQUARTERS KANSAS BRIGADE,
Fort Lane, Barinsville, September 10, 1861.

SIR: I am thus far on my march eastward. I propose to march east as far as Papinsville, if possible, clearing out the valley of the Osage. I will from there turn north, clearing out the valleys of the Marie-de-Cygnes, Butler, Harrisonville, Osceola and Clinton, and proceed in that direction until I hear from the column under Peabody. If attacked by an overwhelming superior force I will, of course, fall back on Kansas.

I am moving with a column of about 1,200 infantry, 800 cavalry, and two pieces of artillery. I will leave at Fort Scott about 200 cavalry, at Fort Lincoln 300 infantry and cavalry, at Barinsville, Fort Lane, 200 infantry and cavalry, which I think sufficient to protect these points.

I will camp in the neighborhood of Ball's Mill to-night, and in the neighborhood of Papinsville to-morrow.

J. H. LANE,
Commanding Kansas Brigade.

Captain W. E. PRINCE,
Commanding Post, Fort Leavenworth.

HEADQUARTERS IRISH BRIGADE,
Lexington, September 10, 1861.

COLONEL: I enclose you a copy of a letter this morning received by Colonel Marshall. If true, and Colonel M., who is acquainted with the writer, feels confidence in this statement, stores, both ordnance and provision, cannot be too rapidly pushed to this point. If Colonel M.'s command and also Colonel Peabody's, now in Warrensburg, reunite with us, as I have no doubt they will, our force would reach 2,700 men. We have about 35 rounds to a man. This morning I commence marching. We will hold out to the last.

Truly yours,

JAMES A. MULLIGAN.

Colonel JEFF. C. DAVIS,
Commanding Jefferson City.

JEFFERSON CITY, *September* 10, 1861.

My mail for you to-day, I have just learned, was left. It was not very important. A detachment I sent up the river two days ago has returned without firing a shot. Thought they heard the enemy move ahead of them. I have ordered them back peremptorily.

JEFF. C. DAVIS, *Colonel Commanding.*

Major General J. C. FRÉMONT.

HEADQUARTERS WESTERN DEPARTMENT,
September 10, 1861.

Despatch received. Your promptitude is approved.

J. C. FRÉMONT,
Major General Commanding.

Colonel JEFF. C. DAVIS, *Jefferson City.*

HEADQUARTERS WESTERN DEPARTMENT,
September 10, 1861.

Despatch received. Push forward actively on the Missouri side. Move the gunboats cautiously in concert with the troops on shore, and confine yourself to holding the positions we have taken in Kentucky. Gratified to know that Fort Holt is progressing well. Inform General Smith that the 11th Indiana regiment, with three companies of regular cavalry and one of volunteer cavalry, left for Paducah this morning at four.

J. C. FRÉMONT,
Major General Commanding.

Brigadier General GRANT, *Cairo.*

HEADQUARTERS WESTERN DEPARTMENT,
September 10, 1861.

Report from General Grant, at Cairo, says that "gunboats engaged batteries at Lucas Bend all day. Found sixteen guns on Missouri shore. Rebel batteries all silenced. One man on the Conestoga wounded. The gunboat Yankee was disabled, and would have been taken but for land batteries near Columbus.

J. C. FRÉMONT,
Major General Commanding.

Adjutant General THOMAS,
War Department, Washington City.

HEADQUARTERS WESTERN DEPARTMENT,
St. Louis, September 10, 1861.

Will your health permit you to come here within a few days? There is service required which I would like you to undertake.

J. C. FRÉMONT,
Major General Commanding.

Major General HUNTER, *Chicago, Illinois.*

HEADQUARTERS WESTERN DEPARTMENT,
St. Louis, September 11, 1861.

Report of General Pope to-day from Hunnewell. Made night marches on Green, Sunday night, who, however, got notice of his approach, but was successful in causing the dispersion of Green's 3,000 rebel force, leaving behind them much baggage, provisions, and forage, and the public property captured by Green at Shelbina. Pope's infantry too much fatigued to pursue; the horsemen followed in pursuit ten or fifteen miles until the enemy scattered; he starts west with 16th Illinois; was to continue pursuit immediately; but as Green's force is mounted, infantry cannot do much in overtaking them. Railroad east of Brookfield is open, and no more secession camps will be made within twenty miles.

General Grant telegraphs from Cairo that the first gun is in position at Fort Holt, Kentucky.

J. C. FRÉMONT,
Major General Commanding.

Col. E. D. TOWNSEND, *Ass't Adjutant General,*
Headquarters of the Army, Washington, D. C.

HEADQUARTERS WESTERN DEPARTMENT,
St. Louis, September 11, 1861.

Is it impossible for you to get me some sabres and dragoon revolvers?

J. C. FRÉMONT,
Major General Commanding.

Hon. MONTGOMERY BLAIR, *Washington, D. C.*

HEADQUARTERS WESTERN DEPARTMENT,
St. Louis, September 11, 1861.

Can you spare for a time T. J. Rodman, captain ordnance department, for duty here? I think it would be very much to the advantage of the service here if it could be done.

J. C. FRÉMONT,
Major General Commanding.

Hon. SIMON CAMERON,
Secretary of War, Washington.

[This request was not granted.]

JEFFERSON CITY, *September* 11, 1861.

It is rumored that General Price has arrived with 5,000 men at Clinton. Whether true or not I shall find out at once.

JEFF. C. DAVIS, *Colonel Commanding.*

Major General J. C. FRÉMONT.

HEADQUARTERS WESTERN DEPARTMENT,
St. Louis, September 12, 1861.

Despatch received and will have attention.

J. C. FRÉMONT,
Major General Commanding.

Colonel J. C. DAVIS, *Jefferson City.*

HEADQUARTERS WESTERN DEPARTMENT,
St. Louis, September 12, 1861.

The following information, received here from General Pope, at Hudson, to-day: Illinois 16th and Kansas 2d, 1,100 strong, with two pieces of artillery, go this morning to St. Joseph. Green and Bevere are aiming to cross the Missouri at Glasgow, in three columns, from Hudson, Brookfield, and Sturgeon. I shall march upon Glasgow when Platte River bridge is repaired; small squads from Green's command at Florida.

J. C. FRÉMONT,
Major General Commanding.

Colonel JEFF. C. DAVIS, *Jefferson City.*

JEFFERSON CITY, *September* 12, 1861.

Received despatch last night from Lexington, by the hands of Lieutenant Pease, dated 9th. Colonel Mulligan had arrived all safe, and Colonel Marshall was scouring the country. Despatches from Warrensburg leave no doubt but that Price is there in strong force, and is moving on towards Lexington; some of his cavalry took possession of Georgetown Tuesday, causing great consternation among the people. Boonville is menaced by a small force, but if the troops I sent yesterday do their duty they have landed there by this time.

JEFF. C. DAVIS, *Colonel Commanding.*

Major General J. C. FRÉMONT.

HEADQUARTERS WESTERN DEPARTMENT,
St. Louis, September 12, 1861.

What is your effective force, and how located?

J. C. FRÉMONT,
Major General Commanding.

Colonel JEFF. C. DAVIS, *Jefferson City.*

JEFFERSON CITY, *September* 12, 1861.

Two Indiana regiments, 1,986; 25th Illinois, 860; 5th Iowa, 850; Davidson's battery, 4 pieces, 4 horses each and 99 men; Home Guards, 1,362, not efficient; want of organization and equipments. Some ammunition wanted for all. Will present requisition.

JEFF. C. DAVIS.

Major General J. C. FRÉMONT.

JEFFERSON CITY, *September* 12, 1861.

I have just received the following, latest from Colonel Mulligan at Lexington: "Ten or fifteen thousand men, under Price, Jackson & Co., are reported near Warrensburg, moving on to this post. We will hold out. Strengthen us; we will require it." The expressmen had his horse taken from him, but saved his despatches.

JEFF. C. DAVIS, *Colonel Commanding.*

Major General J. C. FRÉMONT.

JEFFERSON CITY, *September* 12, 1861.

GENERAL: I have been in hourly receipt of despatches from above. Much confusion exists in the different accounts, but that Price is at Warrensburg with considerable force, and moving in the direction of Lexington is now beyond doubt. Many persons are coming in hourly from that vicinity, confirming the fact.

His force is variously estimated at from 5,000 to 15,000. His cavalry took possession of Georgetown on Tuesday. The commander at Boonville sent me two despatches last night, asking for re-enforcements, as that place was also threatened by 600 men. I had, however, anticipated this, and sent a detachment up the river yesterday, sufficient to drive them off if they do their duty.

Lieutenant Pease, a very intelligent officer, arrived last night with despatches from Colonel Mullegan, at Lexington, and reports all quiet there. They had not heard of Price's advance, but the colonel informed me that he had secured the money in the bank at that place, and was taking steps to secure that of other banks, in obedience to my orders. I also ordered him, immediately after his arrival, to commence fortifying Lexington, which he informs me he is doing. No troops from Kansas, except about 300, had arrived. Nothing was known there of General Pope's movements. Affairs south of this, and in Calloway county, are being vigorously straightened out by some detachments I sent out some days ago.

The mail closes.

I am, very respectfully, your obedient servant,

JEFF. C. DAVIS,
Colonel Commanding.

Major General J. C. FRÉMONT,
St. Louis, Missouri.

HEADQUARTERS WESTERN DEPARTMENT,
St. Louis, September 12, 1861.

I will send you more troops; keep me informed minutely.

J. C. FRÉMOFT,
Major General Commanding.

Brigadier General U. S. GRANT, *Cairo.*

HEADQUARTERS, *Washington, D. C., Sept.* 12, 1861.

Your telegram to Secretary of War received. The Utah troops cannot be deviated from their destination. Given in Specials 143, of August 28.

WINFIELD SCOTT.

Major General J. C. FRÉMONT.

JEFFERSON CITY, *September* 12, 1861.

Cannot re-enforcements be sent by the Hannibal and St. Joseph road, to march from Utica? I shall to-night put 300 men to work on Lamine bridge.

JEFF. C. DAVIS.

Major General FRÉMONT.

JEFFERSON CITY, *September* 12, 1861.

When General Pope arrives at Glasgow how will he cross the river, the boats having been withdrawn recently? Shall I send one? Do you not mean Lexington, instead of Glasgow, that you intend to march upon? Telegraph confused.

JEFF. C. DAVIS,
Colonel Commanding.

Major General FRÉMONT.

HEADQUARTERS WESTERN DEPARTMENT,
St. Louis, September 13, 1861,

In my despatch to you I was quoting General Pope's words; refer to it. Pope did not say when Battle Bridge would be finished. I send you to-day two regiments to remain at Jefferson City. In the mean time, send forward immediately two regiments to the relief of Lexington, provided nothing has occurred since your last despatch to render it inexpedient. Perhaps they may aid General Pope at Glasgow. Nothing heard from General Sturgis for several days. Move promptly. Inform me minutely.

J. C. FRÉMONT,
Major General Commanding.

Colonel JEFF. C. DAVIS, *Jefferson City.*

HEADQUARTERS WESTERN DEPARTMENT,
St. Louis, September 13, 1861.

The general commanding desires to say that two Indiana regiments leave for Jefferson City to-night or to-morrow early; a third regiment leaves to-morrow, and probably two batteries of artillery. Brigadier General Sturgis will be ordered from Mexico to move on. Have you forwarded the two regiments to Lexington? What other news?

I. C. WOODS,
Major and Aide-de-Camp,

Colonel JEFF. C. DAVIS, *Jefferson City.*

HEADQUARTERS WESTERN DEPARTMENT,
St. Louis, September 13, 1861.

SIR: Information having been received at these headquarters of an intended attack on Boonville, you are hereby ordered to move at once by the shortest possible route, and with all practicable speed, direct to that place with your force of infantry and artillery.

J. C. FRÉMONT,
Major General Commanding.

Brigadier General STURGIS, *Mexico.*

General Pope having gone on to Macon City after the sending of the above, rendered a change of orders necessary for the 14th.

JEFFERSON CITY, *September* 13, 1861.

Received a courier from Lexington to-day; Union troops burning the bridges ahead of Price; his force still estimated 10,000 to 15,000; shall send a regiment on the War Eagle, with some cannon, to Arrow Rock and Glasgow; hope to prevent Green's crossing.

JEFF. C. DAVIS, *Colonel Commanding.*

Major General FRÉMONT.

JEFFERSON CITY, *September* 13, 1861.

Express from Colonel Eads, commanding at Syracuse, says that about 3,000 from Price's column are advancing to Boonville, and later information indicates that as the most threatened point. Large re-enforcements for future operations from this point can no longer be delayed. A force of sufficient strength to give the enemy a successful battle in his rear would settle all trouble about here.

JEFF. C. DAVIS.

Major General FRÉMONT.

HEADQUARTERS WESTERN DEPARTMENT,
St. Louis, September 13, 1861.

Despatch received. Have you sent off the two regiments as directed?

J. F. FRÉMONT,
Major General Commanding.

Colonel JEFF. C. DAVIS, *Jefferson City.*

JEFFERSON CITY, *September* 13, 1861.

Despatch from Boonville since 6 o'clock this morning; the home guards were still defending their intrenchments; enemy 600 or 800 strong. I shall re-enforce Boonville to-morrow, but think it probable that that point is Price's aim; all day goes to confirm it.

JEFF. C. DAVIS.

Major General FRÉMONT.

JEFFERSON CITY, *September* 13, 1861.

SIR: I left Boonville this morning at half-past 6 o'clock; at that time the federal troops, numbering 150, were attacked by about 800 or 1,000 secessionists. The firing continued until I was out of hearing of the place. What the result, I know not, but I fear our troops have been taken.

Respectfully yours,

J. O. REAVERPLA, *Captain.*

Major General FRÉMONT.

JEFFERSON CITY, *September* 13, 1861.

Green has crossed at Arrow Rock, and is marching on to Boonville. The Iowa fifth leaves early to-morrow morning, on the War Eagle, to that place The Indiana regiments I shall send to Syracuse, and make a forced march to-morrow night, so as to get in Green's rear, with a view to capture him. Send me the troops and I will take care of this place and Boonville. Let General Sturgis operate higher up the river and support Lexington. Let Sturgis send a courier to me when he leaves the Hannibal and St. Joseph road, informing me where he will strike the river.

JEFF. C. DAVIS, *Colonel Commanding.*

Major General FRÉMONT.

HEADQUARTERS WESTERN DEPARTMENT,
St. Louis, September 14, 1861.

COLONEL: You are hereby ordered to leave immediately with your regiment, per railroad, to Jefferson City, and report yourself to Colonel Jeff. C. Davis commanding.

By order of Major General Frémont.

ASBOTH.

Colonel FRIED. SCHAEFFER.

HEADQUARTERS WESTERN DEPARTMENT,
St. Louis, September 14, 1861.

SIR: As a column of the enemy's forces is moving upon Lexington, you are hereby directed immediately to order two of the regiments under your command to the re-enforcement of that place. Orders have already been issued to two regiments in this city to proceed to Jefferson City, and re-enforce your command.

Brigadier General Sturgis, now at Mexico, will also repair to Jefferson City with his entire force of infantry and a battery of artillery. On his arrival he will assume command of all the troops at that place.

J. C. FREMONT,
Major General Commanding.

Colonel JEFF. C. DAVIS,
Colonel Commanding at Jefferson City.

HEADQUARTERS WESTERN DEPARTMENT,
St. Louis, September 14, 1861.

SIR: You are hereby directed to move, *via* Utica, with all practicable speed to Lexington, on the Missouri river, with your force of infantry and artillery. You will send back the three companies of the Frémont Hussars, under Captain Blume, to St. Louis.

The most practicable route from Utica to Lexington for you will be by Austinville, Finney's Grove, and Morton.

J. C. FRÉMONT, *Maj. Gen. Commanding.*

Brig. Gen. STURGIS, *Mexico.*

JEFFERSON CITY, *September* 14, 1861.

Rumor states that the troops at Boonville have surrendered; the War Eagle is off for there; I shall have 1,200 men ready to march from Syracuse to-night. The heavy rains of the last thirty-six hours have caused some delay; push forward re-enforcements.

JEFF. C. DAVIS, *Colonel Commanding.*

Major General FREMONT.

HEADQUARTERS WESTERN DEPARTMENT,
September 14, 1861.

Despatch received. Colonel Veetch, 25th Indiana, and Colonel Schaeffer, 2d Missouri, are now at depot, to leave to-night for Jefferson City. Battery goes to-morrow.

I. C. WOODS, *Major and Aide-de-Camp.*

JEFFERSON C. DAVIS, *Jefferson City.*

JEFFERSON CITY, *September* 14, 1861.

Major Eppstein has held his position at Boonville. The rebels had given up the fight and waiting for Green. All right to-night if my troops get in his rear. The detachment I ordered back a few days ago to retrieve their conduct, gave battle to Green's forces while crossing the river at Glasgow. They exchanged fire half an hour, when a battery opened upon them and they retreated here to-day. Green had captured the steamer Clara Bell. Probable rebel loss at Boonville, 12 killed and 40 wounded. Eppstein's, one killed and four wounded; the rebels lost some at Glasgow, we hear.

JEFF. C. DAVIS, *Colonel Commanding.*

Major General FREMONT.

HEADQUARTERS WESTERN DEPARTMENT,
September 14, 1861.

Send forward at once to junction of North Missouri road the necessary transportation to move Brigadier General Sturgis, with his command of 1,700 infantry and a section of horse artillery, to Utica on your road. Answer by telegraph.

J. C. FRÉMONT, *Major General Commanding.*

T. R. HARDWOOD,
Superintendent Hannibal and St. Joseph Railroad, Hannibal.

HEADQUARTERS WESTERN DEPARTMENT,
September 14, 1861.

COLONEL VEETCH: 25th Indiana regiment, under marching orders, reports no transportation arrived at camp at half past ten o'clock.

I. C. WOODS, *Major and Aide-de-Camp.*

Brigadier General J. MCKINSTRY,
Quartermaster, United States Army.

HEADQUARTERS, *September* 14, 1861.

I have just come in from Camp Benton; find your orders for battery to go to Jefferson City; what train takes it? Where is Castle?

TURNLEY.

Captain KELTON.

HEADQUARTERS WESTERN DEPARTMENT,
St. Louis, September 14, 1861.

Re-enforcements will be sent you to-day; the 8th Indiana left at six a. m. this morning for Jefferson City; other regiments will follow to-day. Sturgis will move forward. We will telegraph you further respecting his movement. General Pope, with some force, is at or near St. Joseph.

J. C. FREMONT, *Maj. Gen. Com'g.*

Colonel JEFFERSON C. DAVIS, *Jefferson City.*

WASHINGTON, *September* 14, 1861.

On consultation with the President and head of department, it was determined to call upon you for five thousand well-armed infantry, to be sent here without a moment's delay. Give them three days' cooked rations. This draft from your forces to be replaced by you from the States of Illinois, Iowa, Kansas, &c. How many men have you under arms in your district? Please answer fully and immediately.

SIMON CAMERON, *Secretary of War.*

Major General FRÉMONT.

WASHINGTON, *September* 14, 1861.

Detach five thousand infantry from your department, to come here without delay, and report the number of the troops that will be left with you. The President dictates.

WINFIELD SCOTT.

Major General FRÉMONT.

HEADQUARTERS WESTERN DEPARTMENT,
St. Louis, September 14, 1861.

I am preparing to obey the orders received this evening for the five regiments.

J. C. FREMONT, *Maj. Gen. Com'g.*

Colonel E. D. TOWNSEND,
Assistant Adjutant General, Washington City.

HEADQUARTERS WESTERN DEPARTMENT,
St. Louis, September 14, 1861.

I am preparing to obey the orders received this evening from the Secretary at War for the five regiments. I also send messenger.

J. C. FREMONT, *Maj. Gen. Com'g.*

General THOMAS, *Adjutant General, Washington City.*

The following despatches were answers to inquiries addressed thereupon to the governors of various States:

INDIANAPOLIS, *September* 14, 1861.

We have received orders to send all available forces to Washington.

O. P. MORTON, *Governor of Indiana.*

COLUMBUS, *September* 15, 1861.

No troops are ordered to Eastern Virginia. All our troops are ordered to Western Virginia. Dennison is in Washington.

W. T. COGGESALL.

HEADQUARTERS WESTERN DEPARTMENT,
September 14, 1861.

Subjoined is a list of our total force, with its distribution:

St. Louis (including home-guard)	6,899
Under Brigadier General Pope (including home-guard)	5,488
Lexington (including home-guard)	2,400
Jefferson City (¼ home-guard)	9,677
Rolla	4,700
Trenton	3,057
Cape Girardeau	650
Bird's Point and Norfolk	3,510
Cairo (including McClernand's brigade)	4,826
Fort Holt, opposite Cairo, Kentucky shore	3,595
Paducah	7,791
Under General Lane	2,200
Monroe city, near Cairo	900
Total of present and absent on detached duty	55,693

J. C. FRÉMONT,
Major General Commanding.

Hon. SIMON CAMERON,
Secretary of War, Washington, D. C.

HEADQUARTERS, *September* 15, 1861.

Embark with as little delay as possible on the Illinois railroad, at Cairo, for Sandoval, the regiments of Colonel Hecker, twenty-fourth Illinois; Colonel Turchin, nineteenth Illinois. Transportation will await them there. By order of the President.

Answer on receipt of this; telegraph when they will be there.

J. C. FRÉMONT,
Major General Commanding.

Brigadier General U. S. GRANT, *Cairo.*

CAIRO, *September* 15, 1861.

Your despatch just received. Colonel Hecker's twenty-fourth is at Fort Holt, the nineteenth regiment at Fort Jefferson. They will be despatched at once.

U. S. GRANT,

General J. C. FRÉMONT.

WASHINGTON, *September* 15, 1861.

Your message received. When does force leave for Washington? Please answer.

SIMON CAMERON, *Secretary of War.*

General FRÉMONT.

HEADQUARTERS, *September* 15, 1861.

Colonel Schaffer's regiment left here at daylight this morning for Jefferson City. Telegraph me calibre of guns and amount ammunition requisite. What movements do you make to-day? What intelligence have you from Lexington and Boonville?

J. C. FRÉMONT,
Major General Commanding.

JEFFERSON C. DAVIS, *Jefferson City.*

HEADQUARTERS, *September* 15, 1861.

What is the strength of Price, according to latest accounts?

J. C. FRÉMONT,
Major General Commanding.

JEFFERSON C. DAVIS, *Jefferson City.*

JEFFERSON CITY, *September* 15, 1861.

Information, reliable, just received shows Price at Warrensburg with 11,000; Parsons at Georgetown with 4,000. Green had not probably crossed the Lamine near Boonville last night, so I ordered my troops not to make the march from Syracuse until to-night, as soon as he has crossed. I have ordered the bridge destroyed. Two Indiana regiments have arrived.

JEFF. C. DAVIS.

Major General FRÉMONT.

JEFFERSON CITY, *September* 15, 1861.

Reliable information from the vicinity of Price's column shows his force to be 11,000 at Warrensburg and 4,000 at George h pickets extending in the direction of Syracuse. Green is making fo e

JEFF. C. DAVIS

Major General FRÉMONT.

HEADQUARTERS WESTERN DEPARTMENT,
St. Louis, September 15, 1861.

Reliable information from the vicinity of Price's column shows his present force to be 11,000 at Warrensburg and 4,000 at Georgetown, with pickets extending toward Syracuse. Green is making for Boonville with probable force of 3,000. Withdrawal of force from this part of the Missouri risks the State; from Paducah, loses Western Kentucky. As the best, I have ordered two regiments from this city, two from Kentucky, and will make up the remainder from the new force being raised by the governor of Illinois.

J. C. FRÉMONT,
Major General Commanding.

Colonel E. D. TOWNSEND,
Asst. Adj. Gen. Headquarters of the Army, Washington, D. C.

HEADQUARTERS, *September* 15, 1861.

What is the strength of the regiment at Centralia? Are they armed and clothed?

J. C. FRÉMONT,
Major General Commanding.

Hon. RICHARD YATES, *Springfield.*

HEADQUARTERS WESTERN DEPARTMENT,
St. Louis, September 15, 1861.

Information of such positive character has come to my knowledge implicating Colonel F. P. Blair, jr., 1st Missouri volunteers, in insidious and dishonorable efforts to bring my authority into contempt with the government, and to undermine my influence as an officer, that I have ordered him in arrest, and shall submit charges to you for his trial.

J. C. FRÉMONT,
Major General Commanding.

Colonel E. D. TOWNSEND,
Ass't Adj't General, Headquarters of the Army, Washington, D. C.

HEADQUARTERS WESTERN DEPARTMENT,
St. Louis, September 15, 1861.

Captain Kean's Indiana battery, six 6-pounders, left per Pacific railroad at 2 p. m. to-day.

I. C. WOODS, *Major and Aide-de-Camp.*

JEFF. C. DAVIS, *Jefferson City.*

[Memorandum.]

General Frémont desires Colonel Eaton to draw up a letter to the War Department at Washington, based upon the within letter. Making points of the facts that this department is deficient in artillery officers, and that Major Schoepf is experienced and likely to be efficient in that arm of the service; requesting his appointment.

J. R. HOWARD.

SEPTEMBER 16, 1861.

(Request not granted.)

HEADQUARTERS WESTERN DEPARTMENT,
Jefferson City, September 16, 1861.

Colonel Hovey left by Pacific railroad to-day. Colonel Wheatley left on two steamers for Lexington to report to General Sturgis; each steamer has two ship guns complete. Colonel Wheatley is to be ordered to recapture steamers seized by Green.

J. C. FRÉMONT,
Major General Commanding.

JEFF. C. DAVIS.

JEFFERSON CITY, *September* 16, 1861.

Boonville tranquil. Indiana troops marched across the country last night from Syracuse. No intelligence from Lexington to-day. Green is augmenting his forces from the other side of the river. Secession feeling increasing and people rising, particularly in Howard county. Rains have been excessive for the last four days, but we are persevering in our works.

JEFF. C. DAVIS.

General J. C. FRÉMONT.

JEFFERSON CITY, *September* 16, 1861.

Have just received despatches from Glasgow, Arrow Rock, and Boonville, by the hand of a man who escaped from the steamer Sunshine. This proves to be the boat captured and used by Green at Glasgow, and not the Clara Bell, as reported. Green has not crossed the bridge. This boatman helped to cross Green, and reports the numbers at 3,000, and 1,200 more ready to cross—all horsemen, with two pieces of artillery. He reports Lexington as having been attacked with 10,000 men on Thursday, but held the work. Subsequently it was reported as having surrendered. This is improbable.

JEFF. C. DAVIS, *Colonel Commanding.*

Major General J. C. FRÉMONT.

HUDSON, *September* 16, 1861.

Just arrived here on my way to Keokuk. —— Ohio regiments on their way to Utica. If you can send Tindall's regiment to Chilicothe immediately, the sixteenth Illinois and third Iowa can also be forwarded to Lexington. There will be no more considerable trouble in north Missouri.

JNO. POPE, *Brigadier General.*

General FRÉMONT.

PALMYRA, *September* 16, 1861.

From paper just handed me I learn, for first time, that important matters are occurring at Lexington. The troops I sent to Lexington will be there the day after to-morrow, and consist of two full regiments of infantry, four pieces of artillery, and 150 irregular horse. These, with the two Ohio regiments, which will reach there on Thursday, will make a re-enforcement of 4,000 men and four pieces of artillery. Do you wish me to come down to St. Louis or go to Canton and Keokuk to finish matters in this section? The following force along this road at Hannibal: at Kansas, 480; at Palmyra, 320 of twentieth Illinois; at Hudson, 450 of Taster's men; at Brookfield, 650 of Morgan's regiment; at St. Joseph, coming east, 3,000 Iowa and Missouri irregular troops. Please answer to Quincy.

JNO. POPE, *Brigadier General.*

Major General FRÉMONT.

JEFFERSON CITY, *September* 16, 1861.

My spy has just returned from Pryor Camp, not far from Lexington. He left Warrensburg yesterday, and says they report their number at 14,000. The fight at Lexington was a sortię made by Mulligan on Thursday. A regular attack had not been made until Saturday.

JEFF. C. DAVIS, *Colonel.*

General J. C. FRÉMONT.

JEFFERSON CITY, *September* 16, 1861.

Send forward teams; have not enough for camp purposes. Forward thirty sets of harness, and I can organize that many teams at once. See Major Neville at Everett House for particulars.

JEFF. C. DAVIS, *Colonel Commanding.*

Captain JAS. BRADSHAW, *Assistant Quartermaster.*

HEADQUARTERS, *September* 16, 1861.

Send back our engines and cars as soon as possible. Answer by telegraph.

J. C. FRÉMONT,
Major General Commanding.

Colonel JEFF. C. DAVIS, *Jefferson City.*

The engine and cars will be sent back promptly. Later intelligence reports Colonel Mulligan as having repulsed a vigorous attack of Thursday, and the fight renewed on Friday. This news comes through secession channels.

JEFF. C. DAVIS,

Major General FRÉMONT.

JEFFERSON CITY, *September* 17, 1861.

I yesterday ordered the troops at Boonville to make an expedition against Green, and sent the Iatan as an additional transport. This was done just before your despatch was received.

J. C. DAVIS.

General FRÉMONT.

JEFFERSON CITY, *September* 17, 1861.

Send forward troops and supplies, and let me move forward to Georgetown and get in rear of enemy. If General Pope sustains Lexington, a move of this kind is all that is now required. I am determined to move in four days. I have this place so intrenched that a small force will suffice to hold it.

J. C. DAVIS, *Colonel.*

General J. C. FRÉMONT.

HEADQUARTERS, *September* 16, 1861.

We were at this moment giving you the order to move forward and attack Georgetown. Do so, and do not delay at all with a view to re-enforce Lexington. Exercise your own judgment. Send despatches frequently.

J. C. FRÉMONT,
Major General Commanding.

Colonel JEFF. C. DAVIS, *Jefferson City.*

HEADQUARTERS WESTERN DEPARTMENT,
St. Louis, September 17, 1861.

I have detached the 19th and 24th Illinois regiments under your requisition. They are in Cincinnati to-day. Information of the most reliable character reaches me that General Johnston has arrived at Columbus, Kentucky, and taken command. He is threatening our lines with superior forces. At the same time the enemy, in separate bodies, numbering upward of 20,000, is hovering between Lexington and Boonville. I need all the troops now here and expected. I ask the department most urgently to permit me to retain the remainder of the 5,000 infantry called for, and to substitute these for two regiments of Illinois cavalry, accepted by the War Department, and which I am unable to arm. The other troops will take away just so many arms from me, which I cannot for some time replace.

J. C. FRÉMONT,
Major General Commanding.

Colonel E. D. TOWNSEND, *A. A. G.*,
Headquarters of the Army, Washington, D. C.

JEFFERSON CITY, *September* 17, 1861.

Have sent forward Hovey's regiment to Lamine. Shall forward more as fast as possible, and forward supplies. Send Superintendent McKissock up at once. He is entirely too slow.

J. C. DAVIS, *Colonel Commanding.*

General J. C. FRÉMONT.

HEADQUARTERS WESTERN DEPARTMENT,
St. Louis, September 17, 1861.

Where are the 1st and 2d Kansas? Can the 3,000 men referred to in your despatches as coming from St. Joseph go also to Lexington?

J. C. FRÉMONT,
Major General Commanding.

Brigadier General JOHN POPE,
Palmyra, (to follow him if not there.)

CAIRO, *September* 17, 1861.

The taking of two regiments from this command makes me deem it prudent to withdraw troops from vicinity of Fort Jefferson to Fort Holt. The order is given.

U. S. GRANT, *Brigadier General.*

Major General FRÉMONT.

HEADQUARTERS, *September* 17, 1861.

Brigadier General Pope says a portion of his force from Utica will be at Lexington to-morrow, the 18th; balance on the 19th—4,000 men in all.

I. C. WOODS,
Major and Aide-de-Camp.

Colonel JEFF. C. DAVIS, *Jefferson City.*

WASHINGTON, *September* 18, 1861.

General Scott acquiesces to your wishes in your proposition to retain troops not already forwarded. He has telegraphed order to retain the two regiments which have left to Cincinnati to wait orders for a few days, if they have not passed beyond that city.

E. D. TOWNSEND.

Major General FRÉMONT.

JEFFERSON CITY, *September* 18, 1861.

Positive news from Lexington Sunday evening. Main attack had not been made. I have sent two regiments to Arrow Rock, with orders to take part, in a day or two, opposite Glasgow. Sent a regiment to Syracuse last evening. Will send more to Boonville. Forward harness and wagons; can't do anything with mules without them.

J. C. DAVIS, *Colonel Commanding.*

Major General FRÉMONT.

HEADQUARTERS, *September* 18, 1861.

We have positive information that the "Sunshine" was at Cambridge the 16th, disabled. The rebels have carried off cylinder head, and throttle valves thrown in the river.

I. C. WOODS,
Major and Aide-de-Camp.

Colonel JEFFERSON C. DAVIS, *Jefferson City.*

[Received at St. Louis September 18, 1861.]

FORT LEAVENWORTH,
September 7, 1861, *via Omaha and Burlington.*

The communication by railroad and wire entirely cut off on the Hannibal and St. Joseph. Lane reports enemy's column marching on Lexington. Can a force attack from Jefferson City while Lane attacks from the west?

W. E. PRINCE.

Major General FRÉMONT.

HEADQUARTERS WESTERN DEPARTMENT,
St. Louis, September 18, 1861.

SIR: You are hereby directed to increase your forces at the crossing of the Pacific railroad over Lamine creek to the number of 5,000, adding artillery and cavalry according to your judgment, and march upon the enemy stationed at Georgetown.

All the information received at these headquarters leads to the conclusion that the force of the rebels at that place does not amount to more than 3,000 to 4,000 men, of whom most are poorly armed, and over whom a victory may be certainly anticipated. After putting them to flight, take, with your main body, the road toward Lexington, directing your cavalry to pursue the enemy some miles on their line of retreat toward Warrensburg, and to unite again by the first cross-road. Brigadier General Sturgis, commanding at Lexington, will be informed of this order and directed to co-operate with you in such a manner as, if possible, to make with you a combined attack upon the enemy that now surrounds Lexington.

It is confidently expected that, even if you should fail to defeat the enemy, you will be at least strong enough to break through his lines and effect a junction with our forces at Lexington, which, by your aid and that of other re-enforcements ordered to that point, will then be strong enough not only to defend that place successfully but to assume the offensive.

It is expected that General Lane, who will be kept fully informed of these movements, will be able to act in concert with you from Kansas City; but should the rebel forces change their line of operations and attack that place you will unite with him and General Sturgis in its defence.

J. C. FRÉMONT,
Major General Commanding.

Colonel JEFFERSON C. DAVIS,
Commanding at Jefferson City.

HEADQUARTERS WESTERN DEPARTMEMT,
St. Louis, September 18, 1861.

SIR: Colonel Jefferson C. Davis, commanding at Jefferson City, has been this day ordered to increase his forces at the crossing of the Pacific railroad over Lamine creek to 5,000 men, adding, according to his judgment, artillery and cavalry, attack the rebels at Georgetown, and after defeating them take the road to Lexington.

Should he fail to defeat the enemy it is still confidently expected that he will be able to break through his lines, and, in co-operation with you, make a combined attack upon the forces now surrounding Lexington.

It is expected that General Lane, who will be kept fully informed of these movements, will be able to act in concert with you from Kansas City.

J. C. FRÉMONT,
Major General Commanding.

Brigadier General STURGIS,
Commanding U. S. forces at Lexington.

HEADQUARTERS WESTERN DEPARTMENT,
St. Louis, September 18, 1861.

SIR: Colonel Jefferson C. Davis, commanding at Jefferson City, has been ordered to increase his forces at the crossing of the Pacific railroad over Lamine creek to 5,000 men, adding, according to his judgment, artillery and cavalry, attack the rebels at Georgetown, and after defeating them take the road to Lexington.

Should he fail to defeat the enemy, it is still confidently expected that he will be able to break through their lines, and, in co-operation with the forces stationed at Lexington, make a combined attack upon the rebel forces now menacing that place.

You are therefore directed to march with your forces on the State line road to Kansas City, put yourself immediately in communication with Brigadier General Sturgis, commanding at Lexington, and co-operate with him to defeat the enemy.

If the rebel forces should change their line of attack, and advance upon Kansas City, the above-mentioned commanders will co-operate with you in the defense of that place.

J. C. FRÉMONT,
Major General Commanding.

General J. LANE,
Commanding Kansas Brigade.

JEFFERSON CITY, *September* 18, 1861.

News just received from Lexington—probably reliable. The fight commenced on Monday; was very severe all day. Price assaulted the works and was repulsed with heavy [loss] on yesterday morning. The fighting was very feeble when courier left. Lane was marching for Lexington, and was at Johnstown on Monday morning. The rebel loss is reported at 4,000—ours at 800. This is evidently exaggerated.

JEFF. C. DAVIS.

Major General FRÉMONT.

HEADQUARTERS WESTERN DEPARTMENT,
St. Louis, September 19, 1861.

Colonel J. C. Davis, at Jefferson City, telegraphs to me on 18th as follows:—(See above telegram.)

From Cincinnati telegram as follows: "Colonels Hecker and Turchin's commands in Camp Dennison; wounded all in Marine Hospital; dead buried in Spring Grove to-day."

J. C. FRÉMONT,
Major General Commanding.

Colonel E. D. TOWNSEND,
Adjutant General, Headquarters, Washington, D. C.

JEFFERSON CITY, *September* 19, 1861.

No further news from Lexington. McKissock, railroad superintendant, informs me that the bridge will be brought forward to-day. Means of transportation is all required to move forward. I have a number of mules but no harness.

JEFF. C. DAVIS,

Major General FRÉMONT.

JEFFERSON CITY, *September* 19, 1861.

News just come in says Lexington is taken. I hardly think it reliable. I have received your order directing me to take Georgetown. This place is and has been, except a few hours some days ago, in my possession. There are no rebel troops now threatening. I have and am sending forward troops, but I cannot take permanent position with any considerable force until I get means, either by rail or wagons, to get forward supplies. I wrote you on the subject of McKissock's conduct in regard to the bridge, also on the subject of mules and wagons and harness. My troops will all be in advance of the means of transportation. Let it be furnished at once.

JEFF. C. DAVIS, *Colonel Commanding.*

Major General FREMONT.

JEFFERSON CITY, *September* 19, 1861.

The rumored surrender at Lexington is this evening discredited.

JEFF. C. DAVIS.

Major General FRÉMONT.

HEADQUARTERS, JEFFERSON CITY,
September 19, 1861.

GENERAL: The news last night from Lexington I telegraphed you. Nothing since has been received. I shall continue to throw forward troops so as to concentrate them in a few hours at Georgetown. I have a small detachment there now of cavalry. I hope you will send me more cavalry.

If the rebels have been defeated at Lexington, they will, in my opinion, retire to the Osage, in order to be supported by McCulloch.

That would be difficult if Warsaw were occupied, and I cannot get there without transportation. I am exerting every effort to get teams organized to make a move in that direction. If I were now at Georgetown I could cut off his retreat. The bridge across the Lamine is now the great obstacle to progress in that direction to Sedalia. I shall overcome that as soon as possible.

I am, very truly, your obedient servant,

JEFF. C. DAVIS.

General J. C. FRÉMONT, *St. Louis, Missouri.*

SEPTEMBER 20, 1861.

Mr. King left Lexington last Wednesday night, after the attack by Price, and Mulligan was still in possession of his fortifications; he is well fortified on a high bluff. Price made an attempt to get possession of ferry-boats and small steamer, but with large loss. Mulligan's intrenchments are good, and he can hold out against any force if his ammunition is not exhausted. Major Sturgis expected to re-enforce Mulligan on Wednesday night, Jim Lane on Thursday night. Mulligan's batteries could not defend the river well, where the boats lay; that was the reason that Price obtained possession of them. Messenger saw a large number of Price's men wounded that were being conveyed up the river.

CHAS. NOYES, *Secret Agent.*

Major General FRÉMONT, *Headquarters, Western Department.*

JEFFERSON CITY, *September* 20, 1861.

No expedition has gone from Georgetown, except a home guard as scouts.

JEFF. C. DAVIS, *Colonel Commanding.*

General J. C. FRÉMONT.

HEADQUARTERS, *September* 20, 1861.

Can you break through the rebel lines and effect a junction with Mulligan?

ASBOTH.

Colonel JEFF. C. DAVIS, *Jefferson City.*

JEFFERSON CITY, *September* 20, 1861.

I can drive the rebels to the Osage if I can get to them, but I have no means of transportation here. My boats are up the river with troops. I have no teams.

JEFF. C. DAVIS.

General ASBOTH.

JEFFERSON CITY, *September* 20, 1861.

Send me all the cavalry you can spare. I can furnish them with carbines and ammunition.

JEFF. C. DAVIS,
Acting Brigadier General.

Major General FRÉMONT.

HEADQUARTERS, ST. LOUIS, *September* 20, 1861.

How many carbines and how much ammunition can you furnish?

J. C. FRÉMONT,
Major General Commanding.

Colonel JEFF. C. DAVIS, *Jefferson City.*

JEFFERSON CITY, *September* 20, 1861.

The guns I have are those issued to Colonel Nugent's Missouri cavalry. I don't know the number, but I can arm a regiment some way or other. The colonel, when he left, told me there was a full supply of ammunition.

JEFF. C. DAVIS,
Acting Brigadier General.

Major General J. C. FRÉMONT.

HEADQUARTERS OF THE WESTERN DEPARTMENT,
St. Louis, September 20, 1861.

Concentrate a force strong enough, in your judgment, at Georgetown, and push forward to relieve Mulligan. I trust that you can take provisions for two days with the means of transportation which you have. Order back your boats to Jefferson City, and send provisions and troops by them to Lexington. Two hundred wagons will be sent from here to-night to Syracuse, which will follow you. Troops are going from here. Answer.

J. C. FRÉMONT,
Major General Commanding.

Colonel JEFF. C. DAVIS, *Jefferson City.*

JEFFERSON CITY, *September* 20, 1861.

I will send on the troops as fast as possible. Two days' provisions from Syracuse won't answer to reach Lexington and engage an enemy. I will attempt it, however.

JEFF. C. DAVIS, *Acting Brigadier General.*

Major General FRÉMONT.

HEADQUARTERS, *September* 20, 1861.

Despatch received. Take as much provisions as will answer. Never let the men go into action without food. We, on our part, intend to move promptly from here. Use your judgment for details.

J. C. FRÉMONT,
Major General Commanding.

Acting Brigadier General JEFF. C. DAVIS,
Jefferson City.

HEADQUARTERS WESTERN DEPARTMENT,
St. Louis, September 20, 1861.

Fort Leavenworth despatch received. Will send instructions as to Delawares. Where is the 2d Kansas by to-day? Where is General Lane?

J. H. EATON, *Major U. S. A. and M. S.*

Captain W. E. PRINCE.

HEADQUARTERS WESTERN DEPARTMENT,
St. Louis, September 20, 1861.

SIR: It is reported that Lexington is surrounded by an overwhelming rebel force of 16,000, and that our re-enforcements from Utica and Liberty, under command of Brigadier General Sturgis, are opposite Lexington, and prevented from crossing the river by two rebel batteries. To assist Colonel Mulligan and his brave little band of two thousand, General Lane will harass the enemy by sudden attacks upon exposed posts upon his flank and rear; and you will act according to the order of the 18th, and will endeavor to break through the enemy's lines. Should you not succeed in effecting a junction with Colonel Mulligan, at Lexington, you are to retreat, and take such a position as your own strength and the movements and force of the enemy may render advisable.

Should the whole force of the enemy be concentrated around Lexington, it may be sufficient to retreat to Davis's creek, or, at furthest, to Dunkburg, in either of which cases a junction with the forces of General Lane (consisting of 2,200 volunteers, with a large home guard force) may be effected.

Should the rebels hold Warrensburg with a larger force than yours, or if reliable information should reach you that McCulloch is also operating towards Lexington, you will take position at Georgetown or Sedalia.

Should McCulloch operate towards Jefferson City, but not be able to reach that place before I can re-enforce it, (and I will start on Monday,) it should not detain your forward movements from Georgetown to Lexington.

You will keep me constantly informed of your own movements and those of the enemy, and will watch constantly the re-enforcements pouring in on the Pacific railroad, so that you may direct them immediately to their destination, and avoid confusion.

A corps of observation will be left at Rolla; all other troops now stationed at that place will also be drawn to Jefferson City, to operate with the main body of the corps of army.

J. C. FRÉMONT,
Major General Commanding.

Acting Brig. General JEFFERSON C. DAVIS,
Commanding at Jefferson City.

HEADQUARTERS WESTERN DEPARTMENT,
St. Louis, September 20, 1861.

SIR: It is reported that Lexington is surrounded by an overwhelming rebel force of 16,000, and that our re-enforcements from Utica and Liberty, under command of Brigadier General Sturgis, are opposite Lexington, and prevented from crossing the river by two rebel batteries. To assist Colonel Mulligan and his brave little band of 2,000, you will harass the enemy as much as possible by sudden attacks upon his flank and rear.

Should Acting Brigadier General Jefferson C. Davis not succeed in effecting a junction with Colonel Mulligan at Lexington, he will retreat, and take such a position as his own strength and the movements and force of the enemy may render advisable.

In case the whole rebel force is concentrated around Lexington, he will probably retreat to Davis's creek, or, at furthest, to Dunkburg, at either of which places a junction with your forces may be effected.

Should the rebels hold Warrensburg with a larger force than that of Acting Brigadier General Davis, or should he ascertain that McCulloch is also operating towards Lexington, he will take position at Georgetown or Sedalia.

You will keep me constantly informed of your own movements and those of the enemy.

J. C. FRÉMONT, *Major General Commanding.*

General J. LANE, *in the field.*

(Sent through Captain Prince, Fort Leavenworth.)

SEPTEMBER 20, 1861.

How many horses, wagons, harnesses, and mules have you? Give me the order, and I will make every effort to hire teams for you, if not on hand.

I. C. WOODS,
Colonel, A. D. C., and Director of Transportation.

Colonel J. C. DAVIS, *Jefferson City.*

JEFFERSON CITY, *September* 20, 1861.

I can to-morrow start 50 teams on the road. The 8th Indiana leaves to-night for Syracuse; a battery to-morow.

JEFF. C. DAVIS.

Colonel I. C. WOODS.

HEADQUARTERS, *September* 20, 1861.

We have news of Lexington being burned. Rebels with guns planted at ferry; our troops intrenched on College Hill and surrounded. Have you thrown forward a column for their relief. Telegraph particulars.

J. H. EATON, *Major U. S. Army and M. S.*

Colonel JEFFERSON C. DAVIS, *Jefferson City.*

SEPTEMBER 20, 1861.

Mr. E. Farmer, clerk of the quartermaster's department at Springfield, Illinois, reports to me his arrival in the city of St. Louis at 9.20 o'clock last evening, (Thursday.) Left Jefferson City at 12 o'clock same day. Messenger at Jefferson City just arrived from Lexington as he left. Reports Colonel Mulligan's command strongly intrenched, with the assistance of 2,000 home guards and the Iowa 5th regiment, the latter having one 64-pounder howitzer, besides several small pieces of ordnance.

Colonel Mulligan had repelled Price and his command, estimated at 14,000 to 20,000 strong, and believed he could hold and strengthen himself in the intrenchments until re-enforced. Major General Sturgis was expected to arrive with from 6,000 to 8,000 by Thursday last. General Lane reported approaching from the southeast, forty miles distant, with 5,000 troops, to Colonel Mulligan's assistance. It was believed that Price and Rains would be surrounded and cut off from a retreat. Nothing known of McCulloch's movement that is now reported at Jefferson City.

Yours, &c., CHARLES NOYES,
A Secret Agent.

Major General J. C. FRÉMONT,
Commanding Western Department.

JEFFERSON CITY, *September* 20, 1861.

I shall leave about 3,000 home guards and Iowa 6th to take care of this place. I would recommend some one of energy be appointed to command them. General Thomas Price, who is now in St. Louis, would be an excellent man. They must be kept at work on these field-works, &c.

JEFFERSON C. DAVIS,
Acting Brigadier General Commanding.

General J. C. FRÉMONT.

HEADQUARTERS WESTERN DEPARTMENT,
St. Louis, September 21, 1861.

GENERAL: By a telegram of to-day, sent to Captain W. E. Prince, of Fort Leavenworth, the officer in command of the 2d Kansas regiment has been directed to take the steamer West Wind, or any other steamer, and proceed at once carefully down the river to join you.

You will, therefore, send a messenger up the river to communicate to the commander of the 2d Kansas regiment such orders as you may deem proper to secure a safe landing of the boat, and then make every effort to cross the river and effect a junction with Colonel Mulligan. Acting Brigadier General Jefferson C. Davis, of Jefferson City, will also endeavor, with his force, to join Colonel Mulligan from Georgetown by land, and from Glasgow by steamer. Every effort, therefore, should be made to retain the post of Lexington.

J. C. FRÉMONT,
Major General Commanding.

Brigadier General S. D. STURGIS,
Opposite Lexington.

HEADQUARTERS WESTERN DEPARTMENT,
St. Louis, September 21, 1861.

Carlin's battery, six pieces, to remain in Jefferson City; and Bissell's command, (300 mechanics,) for Lamine bridge, left here 2 p. m.

I. C. WOODS,
Colonel, and Director of Transportation.

Acting Brigadier General JEFFERSON C. DAVIS,
Jefferson City.

JEFFERSON CITY, *September* 21, 1861.

The War Eagle and Iatan have just returned. The three Indiana regiments took possession of all points as far as Glasgow, but unfortunately for their reputation as soldiers, their scouts fired into each other, severely wounding Major Tanner and several others, and killing three. They retook the steamer Sunshine, ten miles above Glasgow. The 26th Indiana proceeded on for Lexington.

JEFFERSON C. DAVIS,
Acting Brigadier General Commanding.

General J. C. FRÉMONT.

HEADQUARTERS WESTERN DEPARTMENT,
St. Louis, September 22, 1861.

Hold yourself in readiness to move forward to Kentucky when telegraphed for by General Anderson.

J. C. FRÉMONT,
Major General Commanding.

Colonel HECKER,
Camp Dennison, near Cincinnati.

HEADQUARTERS, *September* 22, 1861.

I have placed the two Illinois regiments, commanded by Colonels Hecker and Turchin, under your orders. They are now at Camp Dennison, Cincinnati. Answer.

J. C. FRÉMONT,
Major General Commanding.

Brigadier General ROBERT ANDERSON,
Louisville, Kentucky.

LOUISVILLE, KY., *September* 22, 1861.

Accept my thanks for the two regiments placed subject to my order.

ROBERT ANDERSON, *Brigadier General.*

Major General FRÉMONT, *St. Louis*

ST. LOUIS, *September* 22, 1861.
INDIANAPOLIS, *September* 22, 1861.

I much regret that subsequent events have prevented me from sending you the troops. Reliable advisers on Friday show an advance on Louisville by a force of not less than 10,000 men, and Anderson had not more than 3,000. Anderson begged for troops. Our own safety required that they should be furnished. We have sent him four regiments, and one to Evansville. We are out of arms. Can you not lend us 5,000 for the time? Louisville is considered in great danger this morning, and many doubt whether it can be saved. Please send us arms by special train.

O. P. MARTIN, *Governor of Indiana.*

Major General J. C. FRÉMONT.

ST. LOUIS, *September* 22, 1861.

You did not state how many men you send in this direction or when they leave. General Frémont says you make a mistake in sending men in the direction of Kentucky from your place, and urges all the men to be sent here that you can raise. Please keep him posted.

D. G. ROSE.

Governor MORTON.

CHICAGO, *September* 22, 1861.

Great anxiety here to know the fate of the Irish brigade and Tom Marshall's cavalry. Have they surrendered?

CHICAGO TRIBUNE.

Major General FRÉMONT.

JEFFERSON CITY, *September* 22, 1861.

Your communication of the 20th, directing me to move forward, just received. I am throwing forward troops to Arrow Rock, Boonville, and Syracuse as fast as possible. This I have been doing since the 18th. Troops cannot reach Lexington without some teams. The harness for these arrived in part only night before last. Yesterday all that could be possibly gotten together were sent forward to these different points. More is leaving to-day and will continue to leave until I can move on Lexington.

JEFF. C. DAVIS,
Acting Brigadier General.

Major General FRÉMONT.

CHICAGO, *September* 22, 1861.

Intense excitement here to know the fate of Colonel Mulligan. If consistent, may I know if he has surrendered?

OWEN LOVEJOY.

General J. C. FRÉMONT.

HEADQUARTERS WESTERN DEPARTMENT,
St. Louis, September 22, 1861.

Colonel Mulligan has not surrendered by latest reports. It is believed he is sustaining himself in his position. Re-enforcements are moving from four points of the compass—from all directions.

J. C. FRÉMONT.

Colonel OWEN LOVEJOY, *Chicago, Illinois.*

HEADQUARTERS WESTERN DEPARTMENT,
St. Louis, September 22, 1861.

Your despatch received. I am informed by the President that the rebels have seized Owensboro'. Direct Captain Foote to use gunboats to drive the rebels from there and to protect the Ohio river. Have Noble's cavalry reached Fort Massac? Direct him to report for orders to General Smith.

Send forward three heavy guns to General Smith, to be placed at Smithland.

J. C. FRÉMONT,
Major General Commandiyg.

Brigadier General U. GRANT, *Cairo.*

WASHINGTON, *September* 22, 1861.

Governor Morton telegraphs as follows: Colonel Lane, just arrived by special train, represents Owensboro', 40 miles above Evansville, in possession of secessionists. Green river is navigable. Owensboro' must be seized. We want a gunboat sent up from Paducah for that purpose. Send up the gunboat if, in your discretion, you think it right. Perhaps you had better order those in charge of the Ohio river to guard it vigilantly at all points.

A. LINCOLN.

Major General FRÉMONT.

HEADQUARTERS WESTERN DEPARTMENT,
St. Louis, September 22, 1861.

Your despatch received. I have immediately ordered Captain Foote with gunboat to dislodge the rebels from Owensboro', and will take measures to guard the Ohio.

Have placed my two Illinois regiments at Camp Dennison, near Cincinnati, at the disposal of General Anderson, and so informed him by telegraph.

J. C. FRÉMONT,
Major General Commanding.

A. LINCOLN, *President, Washington.*

JEFFERSOF CITY, *September* 22, 1861.

Price has arrived, and I have turned over the home guards and the fortifications to his charge. This will enable me to move forward myself to-night or to-morrow. If you are coming on to-morrow I will proceed to Arrow Root, and start from there to Marshall. If you do not come, it will be better for me to start from Syracuse on the march. Please answer at once.

JEFF. C. DAVIS,
Acting Brigadier General Commanding.

Major General FRÉMONT.

JEFFERSON CITY, *September* 22, 1861.

I am informed that the Lamine bridge will be finished on Tuesday. News from Lexington this evening states that place not taken up to Friday.

JEFF. C. DAVIS,
Acting Brigadier General Commanding.

Major General J. C. FRÉMONT.

JEFFERSON CITY, *September* 22, 1861.

Reliable. U. D. Fields, of Lexington, released prisoner from Price's army, here to-night, reports fighting at Lexington Thursday noon. Mulligan not taken; thinks if water holds out he is safe for some days yet. If efficient and prompt movements be made he may be saved. Everything depends on what we can do in the next few days. McCulloch last Monday in Barton county, moving on Lexington. He must be drawing close on by this time. Price's force estimated at nearly 20,000.

THOS. L. PRICE.

Major General J. C. FRÉMONT.

BROOKFIELD, *September* 22, 1861.

I have just arrived here from Quincy, and have 100 of our men that were in the battle at Lexington; 2,000 more are at Hamilton, fifty miles west of this. Colonel Mulligan surrendered at 4 p. m. Friday. Water cut off. The entire command, after surrendering, were disarmed; non-commissioned officers and privates sworn and released; commissioned officers are held as prisoners. Federal loss, 39 killed and 120 wounded; rebels, 1,400 killed and wounded. I send provisions forward to our gallant soldiers that have not been fed for two days. They were not re-enforced.

B. M. PRENTISS.

Major General J. C. FRÉMONT.

HEADQUARTERS WESTERN DEPARTMENT,
St. Louis, September 23, 1861.

GENERAL: Your despatch received. The surgeons of my staff and the sanitary commission are directed to communicate with you in regard to the wounded. Keep me fully informed of facts in relation to them, so that their wants may be provided for as promptly as possible.

J. C. FRÉMONT, *Major General.*

Brigadier General B. M. PRENTISS, *Quincy, Illinois.*

HEADQUARTERS WESTERN DEPARTMENT,
St. Louis, September 22, 1861.

GENERAL: As Lexington surrendered on Friday, and a combined attack on the rebel force will be made without delay by my command, you are hereby directed to prevent, by all means, the enemy crossing the Missouri river; to co-operate with me upon my approach, and to keep me, as I advance, constantly informed, by frequent reports, of the strength and movements of the enemy.

J. C. FRÉMONT, *Major General Commanding.*

Brigadier General STURGIS.

HEADQUARTERS WESTERN DEPARTMENT,
St. Louis, September 22, 1861.

GENERAL: Lexington having surrendered, a combined attack upon the rebels infesting the country between Springfield and Lexington will be made by the troops under my command without delay. You are directed to watch the enemy as narrowly as possible, to hold Kansas City at all hazards, and to keep me constantly informed of his and your movements.

J. C. FRÉMONT, *Major General Commanding.*

General J. LANE, *Commanding Kansas City.*

HEADQUARTERS, *September* 22, 1861.

Lexington surrendered on Friday afternoon for want of water. Hold Georgetown and Glasgow. Sturgis will prevent the enemy's crossing the river. Lane will watch Kansas City and defend it if attacked.

J. C. FRÉMONT, *Major General Commanding.*

Acting Brigadier General JEFF. C. DAVIS, *Jefferson City.*

HEADQUARTERS WESTERN DEPARTMENT,
St. Louis, September 23, 1861.

I have telegram from Brookfield that Lexington has fallen into Price's hands, he having cut off Mulligan's supply of water. Re-enforcements, four thousand strong, under Sturgis, by capture of ferry-boats, had no means of crossing the river in time. Lane's force from the southwest, and Davis's from southeast, upwards of eleven thousand in all, could not get there in time. I am taking the field myself, and hope to destroy the enemy either before or after the junction of forces under McCulloch.

Please notify the President immediately.

J. C. FRÉMONT, *Major General Commanding.*

Colonel E. D. TOWNSEND, *A. A. G.*,
Headquarters of the Army, Washington, D. C.

WASHINGTON, *September* 23, 1861.

What further news have you from Lexington? Can you give us results?

SIMON CAMERON *Secretary of War.*

Major General FRÉMONT.

HEADQUARTERS WESTERN DEPARTMENT,
St. Louis September 23, 1861.

Nothing since my despatch of this morning; our loss, thirty-nine killed and one hundred and twenty wounded; loss of enemy, one thousand four hundred killed and wounded. Our non-commissioned officers and privates sworn and released; commissioned officers held as prisoners. Our troops are gathering around the enemy. I will send you, from the field, more details in a few days.

J. C. FRÉMONT, *Major General Commanding.*

Hon. SIMON CAMERON,
Secretary of War, Washington City.

HEADQUARTERS OF THE ARMY,
Washington, D. C., September 13, 1861.

Your despatch of this day is received. The President is glad you are hastening to the scene of action. His words are, he expects you to repair the disaster at Lexington without loss of time.

WINFIELD SCOTT.

Major General FRÊMONT, *Headquarters.*

[Private.]

WASHINGTON, D. C., *September* 2, 1861.

MY DEAR SIR: Two points in your proclamation of August 30 give me some anxiety.

First. Should you shoot a man, according to the proclamation, the confederates would very certainly shoot our best men in their hands, in retaliation; and so, man for man, indefinitely. It is, therefore, my order that you allow no man to be shot, under the proclamation, without first having my approbation or consent.

Second. I think there is great danger that the closing paragraph, in relation to the confiscation of property, and the liberating slaves of traitorous owners, will alarm our southern Union friends, and turn them against us; perhaps ruin our rather fair prospect for Kentucky. Allow me, therefore, to ask that you will, as of your own motion, modify that paragraph so as to conform to the *first* and *fourth* sections of the act of Congress entitled "An act to confiscate property used for insurrectionary purposes," approved August 6, 1861, and a copy of which act I herewith send you. This letter is written in a spirit of caution, and not of censure. I send it by a special messenger, in order that it may certainly and speedily reach you.

Yours, very truly,

A. LINCOLN.

Major General FRÉMONT.

HEADQUARTERS WESTERN DEPARTMENT,
St. Louis, September 3, 1861.

MY DEAR SIR: Your letter of the 2d, by special messenger, I know to have been written before you had received my letter, and before my telegraphic despatches and the rapid development of critical conditions here had informed you of affairs in this quarter. I had not written to you fully and frequently; first, because in the incessant change of affairs I would be exposed to give you contradictory accounts; and, secondly, because the amount of the subjects to be laid before you would demand too much of your time.

Trusting to have your confidence, I have been leaving it to events themselves to show you whether or not I was shaping affairs here according to your ideas. The shortest communication between Washington and St. Louis generally involves two days, and the employment of two days in time of war goes largely towards success or disaster. I therefore went along according to my own judgment, leaving the result of my movements to justify me with you. And so in regard to my proclamation of the 30th. Between the rebel armies, the provisional government, and home traitors, I felt the position bad and saw danger. In the night I decided upon the proclamation and the form of it. I wrote it the next morning and printed it the same day. I did it without consultation or advice with any one, acting solely with my best judgment to serve the country and yourself, and perfectly willing to receive the amount of censure which should be thought due, if I had made a false movement. This is as much a movement in the war as a battle, and in going into these I shall have to act according to my judgment of the ground before me, as I did on this occasion. If, upon reflection, your better judgment still decides that I am wrong in the article respecting the liberation of slaves, I have to ask that you will openly direct me to make the correction. The implied censure will be received as a soldier always should the reprimand of his chief. If I were to retract of my own accord it would imply that I myself thought it wrong, and that I had acted without the reflection which the gravity of the point demanded. But I did not. I acted with full deliberation, and upon the certain conviction that it was a measure right and necessary, and I think so still.

In regard to the other point of the proclamation to which you refer, I desire to say that I do not think the enemy can either misconstrue or urge anything against it, or undertake to make unusual retaliation. The shooting of men who shall rise in arms against an army in the military occupation of a country is merely a necessary measure of defence, and entirely according to the usages of civilized warfare. The article does not at all refer to prisoners of war, and certainly our enemies have no ground for requiring that we should waive in their benefit any of the ordinary advantages which the usages of war allow to us. As promptitude is itself an advantage in war, I have also to ask that you will permit me to carry out upon the spot the provisions of the proclamation in this respect. Looking at affairs from this point of view, I am satisfied that strong and vigorous measures have now become necessary to the success of our arms; and hoping that my views may have the honor to meet your approval,

I am, with respect and regard, very truly yours,

J. C. FRÉMONT.

The PRESIDENT.

[Private.]

HEADQUARTERS WESTERN DEPARTMENT,
September 8, 1861.

MY DEAR SIR: I send by another hand what I ask you to consider in respect to the subject of the note by your special messenger.

In this I desire to ask your attention to the position of affairs in Kentucky. As the rebel troops, driven out from Missouri, had invaded Kentucky in considerable force, and by occupying Union City, Hickman, and Columbus, were preparing to seize Paducah and attack Cairo, I judged it impossible, without losing important advantages, to defer any longer a forward movement. For this purpose I have drawn from the Missouri side a part of the force which had been stationed at Bird's Point, Cairo and Cape Girardeau, to Fort Holt and Paducah, of which places we have taken possession. As the rebel forces outnumber ours, and the counties of Kentucky between the Mississippi and Tennessee rivers, as well as those along the latter and the Cumberland, are strongly secessionist, it becomes imperatively necessary to have the co-operation of the loyal Union forces under Generals Anderson and Nelson, as well as of those already encamped opposite Louisville, under Colonel Rousseau. I have re-enforced, yesterday, Paducah, with two regiments, and will continue to strengthen the position with men and artillery. As soon as General Smith, who commands there, is re-enforced sufficiently to enable him to spread his forces, he will have to take and hold Mayfield and Lovelaceville, to be in the rear and flank of Columbus, and to occupy Smithland, controlling in this way the mouths of both the Tennessee and the Cumberland rivers. At the same time Colonel Rosseau should bring his force, increased, if possible, by two Ohio regiments, in boats to Henderson, and taking the Henderson and Nashville railroad, occupy Hopkinsville, while General Nelson should go with a force of 5,000 by railroad to Louisville, and from there to Bowling Green. As the population in all the counties through which the above railroads pass are loyal, this movement could be made without delay or molestation to the troops. Meanwhile General Grant would take possession of the entire Cairo and Fulton railroad, Piketon, New-Madrid and the shore of the Mississippi opposite Hickman and Columbus. The foregoing disposition having been effected, a combined attack will be made upon Columbus, and if successful in that, upon Hickman, while Rousseau and Nelson will move in concert, by railroad, to Nashville, Tennessee, occupying the State capital, and, with an adequate force, New Providence. The conclusion of this movement would be a combined advance toward Memphis, on the Mississippi, as well as the Memphis and Ohio railroad, and I trust the result would be a glorious one to the country. In a reply to a letter from General Sherman, by the hand of Judge Williams, in relation to the vast importance of securing possession in advance of the country lying between the Ohio, Tennessee and Mississippi, I have to-day suggested the first part of the preceding plan. By extending my command to Indiana, Tennessee and Kentucky, you would enable me to attempt the accomplishment of this all-important result; and in order to secure the secrecy necessary to its success, I shall not extend the communication which I have made to General Sherman, or repeat it to any one else.

With high respect and regard, I am, very truly, yours,

J. C. FRÉMONT.

The PRESIDENT.

[Extracts from letters of Hon. M. Blair, Postmaster General.]

WASHINGTON, *September* 3, 1861.

"Meigs begged me this afternoon to get you to order 15-inch guns from Pittsburg for your gunboats. He says that the boats can empty any battery the enemy can make with such guns. He advises that you contract for them directly yourself, telling the contractor you will direct your ordnance officer to pay for them."

* * * * * * * *

"I think you will find General Hunter an able, and at the same time an agreeable, co-operator. He has considerable energy and much good sense, and his influence with the President may be useful to secure you support here."

* * * * * * * *

WASHINGTON, *February* 5, 1862.

Honorable MONTGOMERY BLAIR sworn and examined.

By the chairman:

Question. We have been ordered to inquire as to the war in the western department. It is a very general subject, but we know that you are very fully acquainted with it, and you will please, therefore, tell us, in your own way, what you may consider pertinent to the inquiry.

Answer. I have taken special interest in the western department. I resided in Missouri many years. This and my brother's position there created this interest, and for that reason I became active in reference to military affairs there even before the change of administration. Having learned from my brother the design of the conspirators to seize the arsenal, I induced General Scott to order General (then Captain) Lyon from Fort Scott to St. Louis, knowing Lyon's determination of character. I acted here in concert with the tried men in St. Louis, and none have ever been more thoroughly tried. They spoke to me generally through my brother, who has had their confidence more than any other person for many years. But I had many other correspondents in the State. I obtained, at my brother's instance, and wrote the orders for arming the troops there, for superseding Harney because he disobeyed it or put obstacles in the way of executing it, for the capture of Camp Jackson, and under which he was about to capture Governor Jackson and his legislature at Jefferson, when Harney was permitted, without my knowledge, to reappear on the scene, supersede Lyon, and suspend his operations for about a month, and till Harney could be again got rid of. Harney, on being superseded the first time, came on to Washington and wrote and published a letter protesting his loyalty. I did not believe and do not now believe he was disloyal, but his associations were with a class whose sympathies or *fears* enabled the conspirators to dupe them into the belief that Lyon and those who were not so deceived were *the* dangerous men to the peace of the country. It was most unfortunate that just after Lyon struck his first blow, and before he could finish the work by the capture of the conspirators at Jefferson City, that Harney was sent back to supersede him by Mr. Cameron, without the knowledge of the President. After it was notorious that Price was organizing a military force, under a law which Harney himself had pronounced unconstitutional, he was influenced by the class of persons I have mentioned to treat with Price, who was Jackson's major general, under it. And even after Harney was again superseded for this and other mistakes, and Lyon had fought their organized army at Boonville, many sincere Union men of that class, here and in Missouri, continued to oppose his policy and his being retained in the command of the department; and it was by such influences Missouri was put in McClellan's department, although McClellan was, at the time occupied in Western Virginia, and Lyon was operating in Western Missouri, and was an older soldier and more experienced commander in the field than McClellan. I made many efforts but failed, even though seconded warmly by Governor Chase, to get the general-in-chief to revoke this order. It was necessary to have a general in the department, and as this prejudice against Lyon prevented his having the place, and as General Frémont had a reputation sufficiently great to secure it, I and all the advocates of Lyon's policy were gratified in having it assigned to him. I believed that he would not only sustain Lyon's vigorous policy, but give fresh impulse to it. The sequel proved that those of us who were most solicitous for his promotion overestimated his qualifications for military command.

As soon as he was appointed I urged him to go to his department. I did so both on my own judgment and because the President expressed to me, every day he delayed, a growing solicitude for Lyon's command. Frémont, however, after his appointment, went to the city of New York and remained some time—I forget how long. It seemed to me a very long and most unaccountable delay. The President questioned me every day about his movements. I told him so often that Frémont was off or was going next day, according to my information, that I felt mortified when allusion was made to it, and dreaded a reference to the subject. Finally, on the receipt of a despatch from Lyon by my brother, describing the condition of his command, I felt justified in telegraphing General Frémont that he must go at once. But he remained till after Bull Run, and even then, when he should have known the inspiration that would give the rebels, he travelled leisurely to St. Louis. He stopped, as I learned, for the night on the mountains and passed a day at Columbus. And after all, when he reached St. Louis, he did not even attempt to succor Lyon, the object which was nearest the heart of the President and the whole country, and the most obvious necessity to all observers. In urging him to go at once, I told him I would attend to everything for him here, and from my greater familiarity with the bureaus and departments, I thought I could do better for him than he could do for himself. I kept this promise. I spent the greater part of my time, from the date of his appointment till September, in forwarding his wishes in that respect. I did not succeed always to my satisfaction, but my whole heart was in the work, so much so that I scolded or growled, as General Cameron called it, unreasonably at delays and obstacles. That the administration did everything it could in fact to sustain Frémont, the committee may judge by the fact that on one occasion the Secretary of the Treasury sent Frémont a considerable sum of money, being every dollar there was at the time in the treasury. We did not meet his demands, it is true, as I wanted them to be met at the time; nevertheless he obtained actually an immense force and means, but made no effective use of them for the public service, as I soon began to discover. With the news of the death of Lyon, and thence on till about the end of August, information came from the most reliable men in Missouri, showing this. The retreat of Lyon's command from Springfield produced the result which he had foretold in a paper laid before Frémont about the 26th of July, by Colonel Phelps. Price advanced; his adherents rose; and the State was "devastated." Finally, on the 1st September, my brother wrote the letter to me which has been published, showing that he, too, was forced to concur in the general opinion of the well-informed men of the State, that Frémont was making no use of the means put into his hands by the people, the banks, the States, and general government, to repress the rebellion. I laid this letter, and the letters previously received from other gentlemen, before the President. He directed General Meigs and myself to proceed to St. Louis. We arrived there on the 12th September. Meigs made some inquiries in regard to the quartermaster's department. I waited on General Frémont and stated the anxiety felt by the President at the condition of his department, and inquired of him what orders he had given to meet the movement of Price on Lexington, the extent of his force, and what he proposed to do. As respected the orders already given, he said he had instructed Colonel Jefferson C. Davis, commanding at Jefferson City, to take care of the Upper Missouri. To the question whether he had given any specific instructions in view of Price's advance, he replied he had not. I then asked whether Davis had reported to him what he intended to do. He replied that he had not. He stated in detail the number and position of his troops. He had, according to my recollection, more than 20,000 men in Missouri at his disposal, for the protection of Lexington, and means to put them there in less than a week. To the question what he proposed to do, he replied by sending for General Asboth, who brought in a brief paper addressed to General Hunter, entitled "dispositions for the reoccupation of Springfield." Having learned that General Hunter was to command, I proposed that the general, who was seated in the passage at the time I came to the house, should be called in to take part in the conversation. He acceded to this, and General Hunter came in. I expressed the opinion that Price was at that moment before Lexington, and probably bombarding it. He was announced as at Warrensburg, only 40 miles off, before I left Washington. I thought that a movement on Springfield was not the proper way to meet the emergency. That all his disposable force should be sent at once to Lexington. General Hunter concurred in this, thought the disposable force, if so applied, ample, and wanted the command. It was a far greater force, and much better armed than Price's army, and was four times greater than the force with which Lyon had defeated a larger army under Price at Springfield, than he had at Lexington. General Frémont made no reply. He seemed to be bewildered. Afterwards he seemed to adopt the suggestion made to him by General Hunter and myself, but did not move with promptitude, and not at all until he had got an army of near 40,000 men, which was certainly three times greater than there was the least necessity for, and than has been since deemed necessary by General Halleck. It must have been known at St. Louis that Price was moving on Lexington for a week before this conversation, which was on the 13th of September, I think, and he was there for nineteen days afterwards. Being convinced that General Frémont was unequal to so great a command, I joined in recommending his removal from the western department. But after stating the facts and giving my opinion, I have deemed it proper on all accounts there to leave the matter, and have since forborne to mention the subject to the President.

By Mr. Odell:

Question. What do you know about the expenditure of money in Missouri by General Frémont?

Answer. No particulars. I knew before Frémont went to St. Louis that he was not a capable man in money transactions, and never supposed that he would interfere in that business in Missouri.

WASHINGTON, *February* 7, 1862.

Hon. FRANK P. BLAIR sworn and examined.

By the chairman:

Question. Will you state, in your own way, what you know concerning the administration of the military department of the west?

Answer. I was, as is well known to the committee, living in that department, at St. Louis, at the beginning of the outbreak of this rebellion. As soon as Mr. Lincoln was elected, and the demonstrations were made at the south to break up the government—seizing the forts, arsenals, armories, and the treasure everywhere that belonged to the country—I knew very well that it was the design of the secessionists in Missouri to seize the arms and munitions of war in St Louis belonging to the government, and also the treasure belonging to the government, of which there was a considerable amount there. I made representations at once to persons here in Washington in regard to it.

In addition to that, having no sort of confidence in Mr. Buchanan's administration, and believing from what had transpired that he was rather conniving at these seizures than otherwise, I felt that it was necessary that we should take some steps for our own protection. And the Union men in St. Louis raised a considerable force of men, and put them under regular drill. As the winter progressed both parties commenced arming in St. Louis, one with the purpose of seizing the arsenal, where there were 60,000 stand of arms and munitions of war of more than a million of dollars in value. We raised, principally among the Germans, a large force—probably nearly equal to four regiments.

About the middle of January, I think, Captain Nathaniel Lyon was ordered to St. Louis from Kansas with his company. I believe my brother was the means of having him ordered there. He was ordered there because Major Bell, who was then in command of the arsenal, was not regarded as a safe man. In fact, he had avowed his intention, if an overwhelmning force demanded the surrender of the arsenal, to surrender it. He afterwards resigned his commission in the army, and went probably over to the secessionists. I never have heard of him since.

Captain Lyon came down there, and we immediately communicated with him. We received the assurance from him that, whether the government ordered him to give arms to the citizens or not, if we had such an organization as I assured him we had, if the arsenal was attacked he would consider it his duty to deliver arms to the citizens and receive their assistance to repel any attack that might be made. I took him to see our regiments and to review them. He agreed to take command of them, without any authority from the government, and to arm them.

This state of affairs went on. The secessionists in my State called a convention, and the Union men determined to contend for the mastery in that convention. These troops that we raised in the city were raised not only with the view of defending the arsenal, but also to protect the Union men, in their privilege of voting, from the violence which was threatened. The city of St. Louis gave, I think, 5,000 or 6,000 majority for the unconditional Union ticket against the pretended conditional Union ticket, but which was, in fact, a secession ticket. The decisive result in St. Louis, with the unexpected Union majorities throughout the State for the convention, checked for a moment the tide of secession in the State, and no doubt delayed their determination to seize the arsenal, which was their primary object, so as to arm themselves and deprive the northwest of arms.

I mention these matters more particularly, because I want to do justice to General Lyon, to whose efforts I think the government owes the salvation of our State. I think the State of Missouri would now be in the condition of Georgia if he had not come there. The stand which he took came to be understood by the secessionists in our midst. He was regarded as the great obstacle in their way, and efforts were made to have him superseded and sent away from there. These efforts were insidiously made, and he was at one time, actually after Mr. Lincoln came into the government, ordered away upon the pretence of a court of inquiry in Kansas. I think it was in some remote place out there. It was upon some old affair which had occurred six months before, and of which no notice was taken at all until it got to be known that he was an obstacle in the way of the secessionists. As soon as the matter was represented to the government, however, the order was instantly countermanded, and he was allowed to remain in command there.

When Fort Sumter fell, the governor of our State refused to respond to the call of the President for volunteers, and sent him an insulting despatch of refusal. I was here at the time of the fall of Fort Sumter. I returned home and immediately sent a despatch to the Secretary of War, informing him that if he would receive volunteers, we would raise the quota from Missouri, notwithstanding the governor had refused to furnish them. A despatch immediately came from the Secretary of War—the response was almost instantaneous—saying that volunteeres would be accepted and mustered into service. We brought our men up to be mustered in, and General Harney, who was then in command of that department, refused to have them mustered in or armed. The riot in Baltimore having at that time broken up railroad and telegraph communication between Washington and the north, by way of Baltimore, I telegraphed the fact of the refusal of General Harney to Governor Curtin, of Pennsylvania, then at Harrisburg, and requested him to send it through to Washington by an express. He did so, and returned an answer that the government relieved General Harney from the command there, and directed the men to be taken into service. In one week we mustered in four regiments, which was the quota of Missouri. I had sent on a memorial asking the government to give us five other regiments as home guards, which was granted; and in a week more we mustered them all in.

In the meantime the secessionists in the State were making every preparation for carrying out their schemes. The legislature had been called together in extra session, and were sitting with closed doors, passing acts all looking to the secession of the State and preparations for that event. Their troops were being marshalled in what they called camps of instruction throughout the State. At St. Louis they had one of those camps, called Camp Jackson, which was situated within the city limits. They called together a body of men, among others, men they had been mustering in during the winter, called minute men, and such of the old volunteer State militia as they could induce to go into their organization, after weeding out the Union men. They were receiving arms from the south. They received a large assortment, a cargo of arms from the Baton Rouge arsenal, which had been seized by the secessionists. I think they sent up 9 cannon, 600 or 700 stand of arms, and other descriptions of arms, such as sabres and pistols. This cargo of arms was landed on the levee at St. Louis, I think, on Thursday, the 9th day of May. They had passed Cairo safely; they did not appear to make very strict examination there, but let these packages of arms pass, as they were marked "marble." They were landed on our levee, and carried by the city police out to Camp Jackson and deposited there, and they raised a grand shout of jubilee over it.

Captain Lyon was then in command of the department, there being no officer senior to him in the department, Harney having been relieved of his command and called to Washington. As soon as this landing of arms from the south was made known to Captain Lyon, he determined to take this camp, take those there prisoners and take their arms from them. The arms were landed on the 9th of the month. The next day Captain Lyon ordered out his command, marched them to Camp Jackson, and gave the rebels there 15 minutes to surrender unconditionally. They surrendered, and he marched them to the arsenal and took away from them all their arms of every kind and description—both those which they had had brought up from Baton Rouge, and those they had obtained in other ways. There was immediately an effort made to have Captain Lyon superseded in his command; and another effort was made on the part of some of us to have the government acknowledge his services by promotion. General Harney, by some unexpected means, returned the next day to the city of St. Louis, and assumed the command of the department. It was Lyon's intention to have seized the legislature on the next day. They had got an inkling of the fact, and had burned the railroad bridges. But Lyon's determination was to have taken steamboats and gone up and seized the legislature and the governor of the State, because we had absolute knowledge of the fact that they were contriving all sorts of treasonable schemes. Harney, however, got back the next day, and although I have always believed, and still believe, he was a Union man, yet he did not think there was any necessity for doing this to save the Union; thought it was not best to make any body mad by interfering with the schemes of these secessionists. The truth was, that General Harney, whilst a loyal man himself as I believe, and always shall believe, unless I have other evidence, had friends and connexions who were men that, whilst professing to be Union men, sympathized silently with this movement against the government; and they probably imposed upon his better judgment, and led him to believe that these men did not mean anything by all this business they were carrying on, but would agree to some compromise, lay down their arms, and become good citizens again if we did not do anything to irritate them. In accordance with these views Harney attempted to pacify the State by an agreement with the governor, who was represented in the conference by General Price. They entered into an agreement, the exact terms of which I do not now remember, not having the agreement before me. I was familiar with it. It was understood that the government would make no further attempt to put down this spirit in Missouri by force. On the other hand, the secessionists through General Price, agreed that the State government would cease its preparations. It was notorious, however, to all of us who had any observation of events there, that they did not cease at all. They went on organizing with great rapidity throughout the State under a secret act of the legislature, which compelled them to swear allegiance to the State government alone, without any reference to the general government; they selected and appointed their officers, all of a stripe they could rely upon. Union men were constantly being driven from their homes, and came down to make their complaints. General Harney was told of all this, but he thought it was incredible that there was any such bad faith on the part of these people. He would refer the complaints to General Price, who made plausible excuses, &c., &c., and this thing went on until the government here at Washington found that the policy of General Harney would not suit them, and they relieved him again from his command there.

They had previously made Captain Lyon a brigadier general of volunteers. When Harney was relieved, General Lyon immediately set to work to forward the preparation of Union troops as far as he could. And it was so evident that it was his design to maintain the supremacy of the general government at all hazards, that there was another overture made from Jackson, the governor of the State, through General Price, and both of them, at the request of their friends, came down under a safeguard from General Lyon to make another attempt at negotiation with him, having been so successful with General Harney. I was present on the occasion. General Lyon told them they need not be apprehensive of any man being molested in any way so long as he made no effort against the government and the country. He told them that he believed in the supremacy of the general government, and that it was his duty to maintain that supremacy, and he would do it, and would allow nothing to stand in his way of doing it. They broke off upon that, and said that unless he would agree that the federal troops should not be moved through the State without their consent, and many other things of that kind, they would have to prepare to defend themselves. He told them that if they had any designs against the government they had better prepare. They left, burning down the railroad bridges again to prevent his following them.

The day afterwards General Lyon embarked his troops on boats and followed them to Jefferson City, where they had a considerable force. They dispersed, however, before we reached there, and went to Boonville, some fifty-odd miles further up the river. There they collected troops, and gave out that they were going to make a stand. General Lyon pursued them immediately, as soon as he could make disposition of his troops to hold Jefferson City, leaving a portion of his troops there, and reached Boonville with about 1,700 men on the 17th of June, having left St. Louis on the 12th. We found the enemy drawn up a few miles below Boonville. We landed, pitched into them, and cleaned them out in about two and a half hours. There were three thousand of them. We killed a great many of them, took a great many with their arms, and scattered them in every direction.

General Lyon's plan was this: Before he left St. Louis he had sent General Sigel with about two regiments out by what is known as the southwestern branch of the Pacific railroad. He intended that force to move down towards Springfield, to cut off re-enforcements and arms which we knew were being sent into the State from Arkansas. Having failed to get them sent in by way of St. Louis, they sent them in in that way. While this force under Sigel was to go down there, General Lyon intended to pursue with his force and strike the enemy in the rear.

At the same time he sent orders to our troops at Fort Leavenworth. I do not know exactly who was the commanding officer at Fort Leavenworth at that time; but I know that subsequently Major Sturgis—now General Sturgis—was in command, and led the troops, under orders from Lyon, in the first place, down to Kansas City to attack a body of men who were known to have been collected in Jackson county, which is the county in which Kansas City is situated. A large force was also collected at Lexington, which is in the county below. The force at Fort Leavenworth was ordered to Kansas City to strike at these men; but they never waited for the attack, but fled towards the south, Jackson and his men having fled in that direction.

The order was to pursue them. General Lyon made as rapid preparations as possible to pursue with his own body of men, to unite with the rest at or near Springfield. I believe that the committee all know that in the flight of this body of men, Sigel, who had penetrated the southwestern part of the State, fought a battle with them at Carthage, but they were too large in number for his force; in fact they were in overwhelming numbers; they joined all their commands there; they had those there that had been beaten by General Lyon at Boonville, those who had fled from Lexington and from Jackson county, and parties which had fled from the north side of the river, which had been occupied about that time, under orders from General Lyon, by some Iowa regiments. Colonel Curtis, now General Curtis, of the 2d Iowa regiment, Colonel Bates, and I think a portion of the Illinois regiments, occupied the northern part of the State. The whole of the rebels who had been gathered in these camps of instruction fled off towards the south; they were met there at Carthage by Sigel, and he had an engagement which lasted the greater portion of the day. He killed a great number of them, and succeeded in drawing off his force, with a loss of not more than two or three men, in the face of a very overwhelming force of the enemy. Even as early as at that time McCulloch had penetrated into Missouri, and had captured one company of Sigel's men who were posted at a small town below Carthage, near Arkansas.

General Lyon in making this movement talked it all over with me before he made the plan of the campaign. He expected to strike a decisive blow before these men could mass themselves together anywhere, or overrun the State while they were in scattered bodies. He expected that even with the small force that he had and was able to spare he could drive them out of the State; and he had no doubt but what he should succeed, because the President having called for a large body of troops, and having the whole northwest to draw upon, he had very little doubt of being sufficiently re-enforced so as to be enabled to hold his position in the southwest. After having cleared the State of secessionists, before they could raise any great army in the southwest to attack him there, he had no doubt of being re-enforced in overwhelming numbers from the northwestern States. He calculated with confidence upon being supported. That was his plan, and so far as he was concerned, I believe everybody knows his plan was executed with vigor, promptitude, and success. That he was not supported was not his fault, for he ceased to be the commander of the department, even before the appointment of Frémont. There was, among a class of our Union people, great distrust and great apprehension felt of him, on account of his vigor and earnestness, and they protested against his having the command of the department.

By Mr. Odell:

Question. The Union people had a distrust of General Lyon?

Answer. Yes, sir; it comes from a class of people, of men who liked the Union very much, but did not see the necessity of fighting for it, who thought the best way to put down the rebellion was to make a show of force, but not to use it at all.

By Mr. Johnson.

Question. Carrying on war without fighting?

Answer. There were a great many who fell into that error, who were as good Union men as anybody. I do not make any charges against them. But that was not General Lyon's plan, and he was obnoxious to that kind of criticism. Many said he was alienating the people, making enemies to the nation, by the rigor of his movement, and the promptitude with which he drove these people before him. The State of Missouri was, by an order from the War Department, attached to General McClellan's command, he being at that time in Cincinnati, and soon afterwards he took the field in person in the mountains of Western Virginia. It was impossible for General Lyon to communicate with him. It was impossible for General McClellan to know what General Lyon wanted, and to give him a proper support. My brother and myself had conceived a very different opinion of General Lyon from that which was held by the persons of whom I have spoken. We thought he was the right man in the right place. We had very strongly urged upon the President his appointment as brigadier general. We thought he was the best man to command that department, and insisted upon his being allowed to command it. But when we were overborne by representations made by others to the President, and it was determined that he should not command it, we thought it best to have some one appointed to the command who would carry out the same policy, and who would take the field in person. Hence, we both urged the appointment of General Frémont. I do not know whether anything we said had any influence at all upon that appointment. I am inclined, however, to think that it did. We not only wanted him appointed, but we wanted him there. He went to New York, however, and remained there for some time. I had left Boonville; had left the column under General Lyon to come here to Congress. I received a despatch from General Lyon, dated either the 17th or 19th of July. I am inclined to think it was the 17th. The despatch stated that he was threatened by a force of 30,000 men, and he must be overwhelmed unless he was supported. I got my brother—who was a member of the cabinet, and I thought would speak with more authority—to send that despatch verbatim to General Frémont in New York, with an additional message, urging him to go to Missouri. I believe he started almost immediately after receiving that despatch. At any rate he reached St. Louis on the 26th of July. There were rumors then of an attack to be made upon Cairo by General Pillow; and it was also rumored that General Hardee, in the southeastern part of the State, would make an attack upon Pilot Knob, where we had a military station and a small force. But General Frémont was met by messengers from General Lyon, reiterating exactly what he had stated in his despatch to me. There were several messengers from General Lyon to General Frémont, urging the sending him re-enforcements and sustaining him at Springfield, predicting that if he was not supported he could not hold his ground there successfully against such odds.

By Mr. Julian:

Question. What date was that?
Answer. The 26th of July.

By Mr. Odell:

Question Was Frémont there then?
Answer. He was there then; he got there on that day, I think. As a matter of course, I state now what I have heard of other men. I can give their names: Captain Cavender, who was a captain in my regiment, which was at Boonville, had accompanied Lyon down to Springfield. He came up and was in St. Louis at the time General Frémont reached there. He bore a message to Frémont, as he himself told me, stating the condition of affairs at Springfield; that General Lyon had but 6,000 effective men with him, and that the enemy had over 20,000 men, as there was no doubt about it, the fact having been well ascertained. Colonel Farrar, who was then on General Lyon's staff, as an aide-de-camp, was also in St. Louis, having started from Springfield a few days later than Captain Cavender. He was charged by General Lyon to state his condition to General Frémont, and he told the same story, and urged the same state of facts. Hon. John S. Phelps, a member of the House of Representatives, whose home was at Springfield, and who had taken up arms for the government, and was the colonel of a regiment—he came up to St. Louis, on his way to Jefferson city, to attend a meeting of the convention which met there early in August, and also coming on to Washington to take his seat here, which he afterwards did. He came from General Lyon's camp and went to General Frémont and told the same story. And there were other persons, not, I believe, directly from General Lyon, but men who, living in the city of St. Louis, some of them were greatly interested in our affairs there, and having heard the statement of facts as they existed in the southwest, thought it their duty to call upon General Frémont and tell him of it. I understood from Captain Cavender that General Frémont promised to support General Lyon. But he seems to have thought that the greatest peril to his command was in the direction of the southeast, at Cairo. And he went down to Cairo himself, taking with him, I think, four regiments of infantry; and he sent another regiment, Colonel Baylies's regiment, to Cape Girardeau, which is sixty miles above Cairo. He had abundant force under his command to have relieved General Lyon. There were nine regiments at that time in northern Missouri, where there were no secessionists embodied in the northern part of the State on the line of the railroads.
Question. What do you mean by northern Missouri?
Answer. I mean that part of the State north of the Missouri river. There were no forces of the secessionists embodied at that time in any of that part of the State. Or if there was, they were too insignificant to attract any attention or do any harm.

By Mr. Johnson:

Question. Were there regiments where they could be ordered to General Lyon's relief?
Answer. Yes, sir; there were nine of them there. And there was also one regiment, at the time he arrived in St. Louis, at Rolla, which is 120 miles from Springfield, on the direct road to Springfield.

By Mr. Odell:

Question. Who was in command of that regiment?

Answer. Colonel Wyman. I think it was the 12th or 13th Illinois regiment. At the time General Frémont reached St. Louis that regiment was then at Rolla. Another regiment, the 7th Missouri, Colonel Stevenson, was subsequently sent to Rolla. It was stationed at Boonville when General Frémont reached St. Louis, and he ordered it to Rolla, with a view, it is supposed, of ordering it down to support Lyon. It would have gone from Boonville direct, and reached Springfield just as soon as from Rolla. And there was no enemy intervening between Boonville and Springfield. And there was a great deal better road there, a little further from Springfield than Rolla was. I have heard it stated that he gave an order to Stevenson to repair to Rolla from Boonville Stevenson said that he was a great deal delayed in getting there by not having transportation; and when he got to Rolla there was no transportation to take him on. He got there on the 6th of August, as I have understood from Colonel Stevenson. There was transportation which came into Rolla from the southwest. Wagons had been hired by the quartermaster's department to take provisions down to Springfield, as I have understood, and as I have no doubt is the fact, having seen the paper discharging one of these wagons from service. The quartermaster discharged the wagon from service after it came in. There were thirty or forty wagons came into Rolla on or about the 4th of August, and they were discharged from service and sent down to St. Louis—transportation enough to have taken both regiments off.

Question. Were they discharged after General Frémont had given orders to those regiments to go to the relief of General Lyon?

Answer. I do not know that he ever gave any such order. Colonel Stevenson told me that he never got such an order, and I never heard it alleged that Colonel Wyman was so ordered. Colonel Stevenson was ordered to Rolla, as he said, he supposed with a view of being ordered on to Springfield. But I have never heard that he was ordered to Springfield; but, on the contrary, I heard from Stevenson that he was not ordered on to Springfield after he reached Rolla, and he had no transportation of any kind to take him forward.

Question. You say that Stevenson said he had no transportation to take him forward?

Answer. Yes, sir.

Question. Who ordered the transportation back to St. Louis from Rolla?

Answer. The quartermaster. I know the fact to be that that transportation was discharged from service. It was transportation that, under General Lyon's orders, was hired. He was not able to avail himself of the purchase of wagons to obtain transportation, and in the great hurry in which he sent Sigel and the rest of that command out to the southwest he ordered wagons to be hired in the city by Quartermaster Saxton and Quartermaster Carey Gratz. He ordered, in my hearing, that they should employ this transportation for that purpose, and it was employed. And I knew the fact to be that some 30 or 40 wagons reached Rolla, returning from Springfield, on the 4th of August, and they were discharged and sent down to St. Louis, although the owners of the transportation were very anxious that it should be kept in the service.

By Mr. Gooch:

Question. Had General Frémont any knowledge of the fact that that transportation was there and had been discharged?

Answer. I do not know. I do not think he knew anything about it. My impression is, that he does not know anything about it, and did not know anything about it.

By Mr. Odell:

Question. Who was responsible for that discharge?

Answer. I think he ought to have known it, and ought to have seen not only that troops were sent down to re-enforce General Lyon, but that they should have the means of doing it. I think that he had ample notice of Lyon's danger, enough troops to have relieved him, and plenty of time to do it in. But he failed to do it by not ordering the troops there, for if he did order any troops at all, I have never heard it alleged that he ordered more than one regiment, and that was Stevenson's.

By Mr. Johnson:

Question. And this transportation which was discharged there could have been used to take these regiments on?

Answer. Undoubtedly. They got there on the 4th of August, and there were six days between that and the 10th when the battle was fought. It could have been used for that purpose.

By Mr. Odell:

Question. The distance from Rolla to Springfield was 120 miles?

Answer. Yes, sir.

Question. Any railroad?

Answer. No, sir; it was a bad road. The battle need not have been fought on the 10th, and it would not have been fought on the 10th if they had had any assurance of re-enforcements. It was fought in utter desperation of any relief from any quarter, and in order to save himself and save his army. I have understood from surviving officers, who were present there, that he made his determination to strike a blow so desperate that, if he failed to drive them before him, they could not follow his army if he was obliged to retreat.

Question. I asked you the distance with reference to whether there was sufficient time, after General Frémont knew of General Lyon's condition, for those regiments to have reached him?

Answer. I have a letter here from John M. Palmer. I will state, before I read this letter, that after reaching St. Louis General Frémont drew off one of these regiments from North Missouri, as I understand, to go down with him to Cairo. I think one of those regiments were a portion of the force under General Pope's command in North Missouri. I do not know whether all of them were; and I do not know exactly what regiment they were; I cannot recall them. But my opinion is—I think I have heard it so stated, certainly that has been my impression about it—that one of those nine regiments were taken by Frémont to Cairo. He drew them from Pope's command, and shipped them on eight steamboats, and took them down to Cairo. They were infantry regiments.

By the chairman:

Question. Then he left five regiments. Where were they?

Answer. They were stationed on the railroads up there; all communicating by river and railroad with St. Louis. They could all have been brought to St. Louis in 24 hours. There was, in addition to that, Colonel Mulligan's regiment at Jefferson City. There were, also, in St. Louis or near St. Louis, five regiments that were called Home Guards, men who had been mustered into service by General Lyon under the order of which I have previously spoken.

By Mr. Odell:

Question. Were they disposable to be sent out of St. Louis?

Answer. Yes, sir; they had been sent out of St. Louis frequently by General Lyon to occupy different points in the State, and could have been made use of for that purpose. If it had been intended to send Stevenson's regiment to Springfield it need not have been brought to Rolla, but could have been sent more expeditiously and securely from Boonville, where it was stationed. The road from there was much better than from Rolla to Springfield, and the distance was not much greater. Instead of that it was carried down the river by steamboat. There were a great many delays in getting steamboat transportation, and then it was taken by railroad to Rolla, where it got on the 6th of August.

Question. Were there any means of transportation at Boonville, to have taken the regiment from Boonville to Springfield?

Answer. The country is of such a character, it being a wealthy country and highly improved, that there would have been no difficulty in an emergency in impressing teams enough or in marching through the country without any teams, because you could always calculate upon getting subsistence through that country, which is one of the best cultivated portions of Missouri. In fact, Lyon got all his transportation there, I think, with which he marched south. The country surrounding Boonville is about the wealthiest and best cultivated in the State. I have already mentioned that there was a regiment in St. Louis, Colonel Baylies's regiment of rifles, which was sent down on the 6th of August to Cape Girardeau; that regiment was available to have been sent to Rolla and to Springfield; and what makes the thing perfectly conclusive is that, as soon as the news of the battle reached St. Louis, four regiments from Illinois that were in North Missouri were instantly sent to Rolla. They could just as well have been sent before and better; because, after that battle, the secession element in the State—throughout the State—was in a perfect ferment, and the troops could better have been spared before the battle than after it. The secessionists commenced organizing in every part of the State as soon as the result of the battle was known.

By the chairman:

Question. What necessity was there for General Lyon to fight the battle there against such odds, and what objection, under the circumstances, to his retreating; what obstacle in the way of his retreat?

Answer. This is the state of facts: He had no cavalry at all, except a few companies of regular cavalry, while the enemy had 5,000 cavalry, and the rest infantry. A very large proportion of their force was mounted. It would have been impossible for him to have retreated before such a force. They could have cut him off and destroyed him on the retreat by the nature of the country through which he had to pass. It is a broken country, cut up by streams, some rapid and large streams, such as the Gasconade river. The country is very broken, hilly, and wooded; and General Hardee was to have cut him off at the Gasconade, and would have done so if Price had been able to pursue.

Question. I should have supposed that would have made against their cavalry.

Answer. Yes, sir; but it would have compelled Lyon to have marched his troops in a long line extending over seven miles. It would have been easy enough for their cavalry to have come up with them and held them in that disordered condition until the balance of the infantry regiments could have pursued and engaged them whenever they saw proper to engage them, on any spot of ground they chose. They would have been encumbered, also, with the women and children of the Union people of Springfield and the southwest, and their baggage, as they were in their march encumbered with these people. Thousands of them fled, while the secessionists remained there. That was General Lyon's judgment about it, and I adduce these facts in justification of his judgment. And there is another thing to be said about it: he had a great reluctance to do any retreating at all.

The chairman: I like him for that, certainly.

The witness: And he believed, I expect, (in fact, I have no doubt about it,) that he could vanquish them on that field; and if he had lived I do not believe our army would ever have moved from the field, which was fairly won. One or two more regiments would have been all that he would have asked.

The chairman: I guess he would have whipped them as it was if he had lived.

The witness: He did whip them; they were driven from the field; our army remained masters of the field. As much as I have read about battles in this country, from the accounts I have received of that fight at Springfield, I do not believe there ever was such another fight on the continent of America. There were 23,000 men of the enemy. Our men attacked them about daylight, and they fought until 11 o'clock. At 11 o'clock there was not an enemy to be seen. They were repulsed by our troops three several times. When they had brought up fresh troops, they were repulsed and driven out of sight each time; and on the third and last assault, which was a desperate one, and almost a hand-to-hand encounter, our men succeeded in driving them out of sight, until they could not see where they were; and the victory was ours, and belongs to our army. There was lost in killed and wounded pretty nearly one-third of our forces. My regiment, the first Missouri regiment, went into the battle with about 700 men, and there were 315 of them killed and wounded. One of the Kansas regiments suffered about an equal loss. The killed and wounded of the enemy is only conjectural, because the reports which they have made about it are absolutely false. They must have lost 4,000 or 5,000 men in killed and wounded. I have since seen published in the newspapers a string of their officers killed and wounded at that fight. I saw it published in the New York Herald; and there were over fifty officers that were killed and wounded that were named in that list, a great many of whom I knew well. I know the fact to be that they were killed. It was a very destructive fight to them, and also to our own people, who had to withstand attack after attack from fresh troops.

By Mr. Odell:

Question. What do you make our force to have been?

Answer. The force we had then in the field and in the fight was, I think, about 5,000 men. There were, I think, about 1,200 or 1,400 men under Sigel, and about 3,800 men under Lyon. They attacked in two columns. The enemy succeeded in defeating Sigel's column.

By Mr. Chandler:

Question. Do you know whether Sigel's column ever rallied and came into action again?

Answer. No, sir; it was scattered and driven off. The camp which the enemy occupied on Wilson's creek extended, they tell me, from four to five miles in length; and the attack was made at the two opposite ends of the camp; Lyon at one end and Sigel at the other. At first Sigel's attack was successful; he drove off the enemy and occupied their camp, which he set on fire. The enemy rallied and scattered him with overwhelming numbers, and his men were considerably scattered, I am told. The enemy succeeded in capturing five of his six cannon, scattered his men and drove them off, taking a great many prisoners; I think two hundred or three hundred prisoners;

and then the whole fight was maintained by the column under Lyon. I am told that Lyon was killed about 9 o'clock in the day. He had been wounded twice before, once in the head and once in the leg, a ball cutting him through the scalp, and one passing through his leg. He was shot down at the head, I think, of one of the Iowa regiments, or one of the Kansas regiments, I am not certain which, leading an attack; he was shot through the breast. His death was not known for some time, except to a few officers. Finally, when the enemy were driven clear off the field, Major Sturgis was the senior officer in command, the lieutenant colonel of my regiment having been wounded, and the colonel and lieutenant colonel of each of the Kansas regiments having been wounded and shot down. The colonel of the Iowa regiment never went into the field; I think he was sick. Major Sturgis was the commanding officer. A council of war was called, and it was determined, as the ammunition of the men was pretty nearly exhausted, there being left not more than two or three rounds to a man, that they should at least fall back until they ascertained what had become of Sigel's column. They fell back upon a more commanding position, from which, after looking over the whole ground, ascertaining that Sigel's men were really driven back entirely, and that they could expect no support from him, they determined to fall back upon Springfield, which they reached about midnight, having left it a little after dusk the night before. The distance was twelve miles. The enemy never made the least attempt to follow them. The officers say that if they had been re-enforced upon their return from Springfield—the transportation of Ben McCulloch's and Price's army having been destroyed in the battle and their army being so cut up—it was their determination to have turned back and renewed the fight. But they reached Rolla without being re-enforced by a single man. They found six regiments at Rolla, four of which had been sent there after the battle, and two of which, Wyman's and Stevenson's, were there before the battle; Wyman's having been there probably a month; a great while at any rate. It is my opinion, formed from conversation with many persons in the service out there, that no effort of any kind was made to re-enforce Lyon; certainly none which deserved to be called an effort. Yet the means were ample, the time was sufficient, and the notice was ample. I doubt very much whether the general commanding there had any appreciation of the importance of the matter, even after he had all the information that everybody else had upon the subject. Cairo was fortified, had heavy artillery, heavy ordnance—the kind of ordnance mounted usually in such works—and was defended by six or eight regiments. It was within reach by railroad and river of re-enforcements from the entire northwest, and could have been re-enforced from Philadelphia before Pillow could have moved up from New Madrid against it, and before he could have waded the Mississippi or the Ohio to have attacked those fortifications there. It was a simple absurdity to have considered that the point of danger. If those four regiments had been all that he had the disposition of, it was a simple absurdity to relieve Cairo, fortified and defended as it was, by its natural position at the junction of the Ohio and Mississippi rivers, with the immense armament it had there, sufficient to have defended it against all the river craft the rebels had on the river and on the ocean. It was a simple piece of absurdity to send four regiments of infantry down there, if they had been all that we had in the city, or in his department, instead of sending them to Lyon.

By Mr. Odell:

Question. You stated that he went himself with these four regiments to Cairo?

Answer. He did go with them.

Question. Do you know what time he went

Answer. I think he started on the 1st of August; that is my impression.

Question. And he was notified of Lyon's condition on the 26th of July?

Answer. Yes, sir; previous to that. He was notified of it before he left New York. He was notified by a despatch from Lyon to me, which my brother sent to him. He had full notice of that before he left New York. And what shows that he had the regiments to send to him was that these same regiments, which were in North Missouri before the battle, he sent to Rolla after the news of the battle reached him, and they reached Rolla a week afterwards. They could have been just as well sent before, and better spared.

Question. As a military man, it is clearly your opinion that the regiments he himself took to Cairo should have been sent to Lyon's relief?

Answer. Undoubtedly; that is my opinion. I do not know whether it is worth anything or not, but I give my reasons for it.

By the chairman:

Question. This idea occurs to me. The enemy were over 20,000 strong, and Lyon had only 5,000 men. Now, all the re-enforcements General Frémont could have sent to him would have still left Lyon vastly inferior to the enemy?

Answer. There is a doubt about that. It would have left him inferior in numbers, perhaps, and yet he might have been very superior, for he managed to beat them with 5,000.

Question. Would not that be a difficulty with military men; would it not be considered rash to re-enforce him with an amount of men that would leave him still weaker than the enemy?

By Mr. Johnson:

Question. If that had been the determination upon the part of the commander-in-chief, should he not have notified General Lyon of that?

Answer. He said he would re-enforce him.

By the chairman:

Question. I should say that a military man should have said, "I cannot re-enforce you; you must retreat." That is what I think. I do not know anything about that, however.

Answer. In reply to that, I would say this, that if he had four regiments that were disposable they should have been sent where they were wanted rather than where they were not wanted. Now, it must be a pretty clear case, I think, that those four regiments of infantry could not have been any great addition to the fortifications at Cairo, where they had mounted such heavy ordnance, and where they had such strong works, and where the natural position was so strong that it was almost impossible to take it.

By Mr. Chandler:

Question. Do you know what the force was there at Cairo at that time?

Answer. My general idea about it is that there were six or eight regiments there at Cairo. I have a letter here from General Palmer, to which I have already referred. I will read it:

"St. Louis, Missouri, *November* 22, 1861.

"Dear Sir: On the 5th July, 1861, the 14th regiment of Illinois volunteers (900 strong) crossed the Mississippi river, and on the 13th moved from Hannibal to Macon City, and remained there and at Revick and Sturgeon, on the North Missouri railroad, until the 9th of August, and on the 10th reached Jefferson barracks. When this regiment left Hannibal, the

3d Iowa and the 16th Illinois were on the line of the Hannibal and St. Joseph railroad. On the 13th July Colonel Turchin's Illinois regiment came into the State of Missouri. On the 14th Colonel Grove's 21st Illinois was at Palmyra, at which place Colonel Turchin was stationed. On the 31st of July I found at Mexico Colonel Marshall's 1st Illinois cavalry, and one battalion of the 15th Illinois, Colonel Hecker's regiment having left the same place a few days before. During the month of July the following regiments were in North Missouri, and within twenty-four hours of St. Louis:

"14th Illinois volunteers, Palmer	900	strong.
"16th Illinois volunteers, Smith	800	"
"19th Illinois volunteers, Turchin	800	"
"15th Illinois volunteers, Turner	800	"
"21st Illinois volunteers, Grant	800	"
"1st Illinois cavalry, Marshall	600	"
"24th Illinois, Hecker	900	"
"3d Iowa, Williams	700	"
"Total	6,300	men.

"All these regiments were then full, and the estimate of their actual strength is low.

"Very truly, yours,

"J. M. PALMER.

Colonel F. P. Blair.

"P. S.—If it be inquired what all these regiments were doing, the answer is, eating their rations and holding railroads.

"J. M. PALMER."

There was, in addition to these regiments, a battalion under Major Hunt, at Hannibal, of three companies. There was a battalion of four companies at St. Joseph's, under Colonel Peabody, and all available at that time. If we had succeeded in completely driving and routing the enemy under Price at Springfield, I do not believe there would have been any occasion for another regiment in North Missouri.

Question. Do you know which of these regiments went to Cairo?

Answer. I know that some of them went, but I do not now know which they were. This force was in North Missouri, that I know of. Then there were Baylies's regiment in St. Louis; Stevenson's regiment at Boonville; Wyman's regiment at Rolla; Mulligan's regiment at Jefferson City; and five regiments of Home Guards in St. Louis, or about St. Louis. Some of them might have been a little distance off. Those regiments were available without weakening the force either at Pilob Knob, Cape Girardeau, Bird's Point, or Cairo; and I think, if he had been disposed to help Lyon, to re-enforce him, and had told the governors of Illinois and Indiana of the fact, he c6uld have got twenty regiments in time. I know very well that in a week or two afterwards—a week, I think—certainly not more than ten days after this battle was fought—they sent eight regiments and two batteries from Indiana to him. If the condition of Lyon had been made known to the governor of Illinois and the governor of Indiana, and a demand made for troops, either to go to Cairo, so that he could have gone with what he had in Missouri to the aid of Lyon, or to have sent them directly from those States to the aid of Lyon, I believe he could have got anywhere from twenty to thirty regiments from those two States in time.

By Mr. Odell:

Question. Were these regiments you have referred to as being at these different localities armed at that time?

Answer. Yes, sir. I heard of this disaster to our arms on my way to St. Louis; and I think it will be easily understood by those who know my relations to General Frémont previously, that I was very loth to attribute any blame to him; and it was not until I had ascertained to my own satisfaction, from information which came to me, in many instances unsolicited, that he had troops at his disposal, that the truth forced itself upon my mind that he was responsible for that; that my opinions of him, which were favorable previously, were shaken and changed; and then I confess that what I observed of General Frémont in the after conduct of the war was anything but reassuring.

He surrounded himself by the worst men that probably any man ever had the misfortune to be surrounded by—men whose whole history, I believe, as far as I have heard anything said about them, go to show that they did not have the public interest at heart at all, but were seeking their private ends at the expense of the government; and a very singular circumstance occurred there, which probably is worthy of mention; I do not recollect when it was, but it was some time after the disaster at Springfield. It was rumored that Jeff. Thompson was cutting up some of his antics down in the southeastern part of the State. General Frémont ordered a concerted movement from Cairo, under General Grant, and from Pilot Knob, under General Prentiss, to go down and catch him. The order to General Prentiss was sent down, as a matter of course, by the Iron Mountain railroad, and the order to General Grant was sent down by his chief of staff, in the same way; and these orders would necessarily have been compelled to go through the enemy's lines to have reached General Grant, instead of sending the order around by the Illinois railroad, or down the river, so as to insure General Grant getting his orders about as early as General Prentiss got his orders at Pilot Knob. As a matter of course, General Grant did not get his order, and the movement was not executed, growing out of the ignorance of the chief of staff of the mere geography of the country.

It was very well understood in Missouri, after this fight at Springfield, that the secessionists had taken heart, were encouraged, and were rising up in every part of the State. In fact, they were so emboldened that very soon afterwards they began to attack our people at the different positions that had been assigned them, where they had been perfectly secure before. There was an attempt made upon the force at Boonville, or in the intrenchments near there, which was beaten off by the Home Guards. There was an attack made at Lexington that was beaten off by the three or four companies then inside the intrenchments there, and Colonel Marshall, with his Illinois cavalry regiment, was sent up to the relief of Lexington. Mulligan's regiment was sent up there, Mulligan commanding the post; and, as I have understood—and I believe such was the case—Mulligan was instructed to hold Lexington. It was then understood that Lexington was to be invested by Price. Mulligan went there and took possession, probably a week or so—I do not recollect the dates, nor is it material—before Price appeared before Lexington. It was understood that he was working his way around there by the head of the Osage, to get into that country which was so rich, and in which supplies were so abundant. Mulligan was instructed, as I have understood, and as I believe, to hold Lexington until he was relieved. He had ample means of escape, even when Price was within ten miles of the place. He had steamboats at his command, and could have moved across the river and saved his whole command, if he had not obeyed orders; but instead of that he obeyed orders, and remained there. Price's army was so large that he soon succeeded in getting between Mulligan and the river, and destroying the boats. Mulligan was then regularly invested and cut off from water, and remained there so invested and fighting for nine days, when he surrendered, from sheer starvation and exhaustion.

General Frémont had troops enough in St. Louis, at Rolla, at Jefferson City, and all along the line of road, and in North Missouri, to have relieved him. In fact, he either intended to relieve him when he ordered him to hold Lexington until he was relieved, and believed that he was strong enough to do it, or he did not intend to relieve him, but intended that he should be taken One or the other horn of the dilemma he must take. I understand that General Frémont says that about the time he was going to move to relieve him, five regiments were ordered here. But it is a matter of history that he did not move a single regiment out of Missouri to fill that order; and the order was not received by Frémont till three or four days after Price had invested Lexington.

By Mr. Odell :

Question. The order that came from here to send on five regiments?

Answer. Yes, sir ; he sent two regiments from Cairo or Paducah, I think, and the other three were regiments which had just then completed their organization at or near Chicago, or somewhere in the interior of Illinois, but he did not weaken his command in Missouri one man—not one. That is a matter of history, and clears up that excuse. The order was soon countermanded, and only two regiments left the department, those from Paducah and Cairo, and those only got to Cincinnati and were sent to Buell's department in Kentucky.

I do not know the number of men Frémont had in Missouri at that time. I simply know that he had a large force there I think he had 5,000 or 6,000 men at least at Rolla, which was on the railroad, and who could have been sent up to Jefferson City and above that by railroad. I know there must have been at least 8,000 or 10,000 in St. Louis, because he inaugurated Benton barracks the Wednesday before the Friday on which Mulligan surrendered. That inauguration was to have taken place on Monday, but it rained on Monday and the ceremonies were postponed. It rained on Tuesday, and the pageant was again put off; but on Wednesday the ceremony came off. General Frémont was there and reviewed what the newspapers stated were from 8,000 to 10,000 men ; and there were several regiments in the city which were not included—that were not there at all. My regiment, what was left of it, was within two miles of this ceremony, and although they were willing to have participated in it, they were not there. I mention this simply to show that the whole force was not at this ceremony.

Question. You say that this took place on the Wednesday before Mulligan's surrender, on Friday?

Answer. Yes, sir ; and the fight went on for nine days before he surrendered. I know it lasted that long, and no troops were moved, as far as I know or have ever been able to ascertain, until the surrender was made, unless they were troops on the north side of the river which came down under Sturgis and found no means of crossing. I have been informed by a gentleman, whose name is Shaffer, now on General Hunter's staff, that after the surrender occurred he left Rolla with General Hunter and went to Jefferson City, and there had to wait a few hours to get Colonel Jeff. C. Davis's quarters, who was reported by General Frémont on the same day to have moved, and to have with Lane 11,000 men south of the river and below Price's army. Yet Price remained in Lexington ten days and moved off unmolested by anybody, and St. Louis by river and railroad is not four days from Lexington ; a swift boat could make it in two days.

Question. You can get from St. Louis to Lexington in two days?

Answer. You can go within sixty miles of it by railroad, and then be so far south of it that an army there would have to make very good time to get south of you; or you can go directly to Lexington by steamboat. The very slowest boats go there in four days from St. Louis. The reviewing of the troops at Benton barracks was intended for Monday, but postponed until Wednesday on account of the rain. Now, if he had started troops from St. Louis on Monday they could have got there in time.

Question. Did General Frémont know anything about General Mulligan's condition?

Answer. He knew a great deal about it, and could have known more if he had not refused to see people who did know. I have a paper in my pocket which is a curiosity. A man, commanding the steamboat Sunshine, a government transport, came down with despatches from Mulligan to Jefferson C. Davis, at Jefferson City, giving a statement of his condition. He had a guard of ten or twelve men with him. The boat was seized at Glasgow by a party of secessionists under Martin Green, brother of ex-senator Green, and another fellow, who made a great deal of noise there, whose name I have forgotten. They had some 5,000 men, and seized the boat and made it ferry them across the river to Glasgow. They were going to re-enforce Price's army. They kept the boat, but the captain made his escape and came down to St. Louis. He sent up this paper to General Frémont when he got to St. Louis:

"Captain George W. Willard, of steamboat Sunshine, taken by State troops at Glasgow, has despatches from Colonel Mulligan to Colonel Jefferson C. Davis, at Jefferson City, sent by his guard, and secreted by me when the guard were taken prisoners."

The reply on the same piece of paper is: "Captain, a train leaves to-morrow for Jefferson City, by which you can forward the despatches or go. If you are not of the army you can leave the despatches here. Should be pleased to see you to-morrow."

This is signed by the secretary. He refused to see him then, but said he would see him to-morrow.

Question. This Jefferson Davis is one of our men?

Answer. Yes, sir. This is Jefferson C. Davis, of Indiana, colonel commanding at Jefferson City. I will state this further: that if General Frémont did not know the condition of Colonel Mulligan, he was ignorant of what every man in St. Louis knew, and what the newspapers published every morning about the condition of that command. It was well known there. It was known two weeks previous that Price's army was advancing. It was known exactly when he reached Warrensburg; it was known exactly when he invested the town of Lexington; it was known that they had large numbers, &c. All this was well understood in St. Louis, and known to everybody, if it was not known to the general commanding.

There is one thing very certain upon this point, without being any military authority myself, or pretending to any military knowledge. Mulligan and Marshall and others were in the trenches at Lexington with 2,300 men, and they had orders to hold it until they were re-enforced or relieved, and the general who gave that order without knowing that he could relieve them is responsible for what occurred, because Mulligan could have gone across the river and escaped with his whole command, and with his entire property that he had there, even after the advance guard of Price appeared in town. Nothing could have stopped him. He had the boats at his command, and could have taken off his troops without difficulty, had he not obeyed orders to hold the place until re-enforced or relieved.

General Frémont despatched to the President—that is, I saw the despatch published—as soon as the news of the surrender of Lexington reached the city, that he had 4,000 men on the north side of the river moving down on Price, and 11,000 under Lane and Davis south of the river, and he was about taking the field himself, and hoped to cut Price off. Yet Price actually remained in Lexington ten days after the surrender, and was not cut off. Now, the fact is that Davis had not moved; the fact is that Lane had not moved, and they were not south of Price at all with 11,000 men. The fact is that Sturgis had only 1,200 men, and no means of crossing the river. It might have occurred to anybody that such would have been the case; that it was impossible to cross such a river as the Missouri in the face of a superior enemy. And instead of taking the field, as he said when he sent that despatch, General Frémont remained in St. Louis several days afterwards. He then went to Jefferson City, and stayed there over a week. He went to Tipton, and stopped there another week. And he remained some time at Warsaw, building a bridge, and finally got down to Springfield, I think, in about a month from the time that he left St. Louis.

By Mr. Johnson:

Question. Where was Price then, when he got to Springfield?

Answer. Price was between seventy and eighty miles south and west of him. He never gained a foot on him.

Question. As the two armies marched, Price rather increased the distance between them, did he? How is that?

Answer. I do not know whether he did or not. He increased it when he wanted to increase it; he stopped whenever he had occasion to stop anywhere for anything; he did not seem to be in much of a hurry. Yet when Frémont got down to Springfield he seemed to think, he imagined, he had the hallucination, that the enemy were about to attack him, and he sent messenger after messenger back to Hunter to come up, and Hunter did make forced marches and came up and found Frémont in a perfect panic about fighting a battle with Price, who was seventy miles off from him. The most remarkable characteristic of the man seeming to be an insensibility to fear when others were in danger; he seemed to have no appreciation of the danger in which Lyon was and Mulligan was; when others were exposed to great and imminent danger, he thought they could do well enough; but was in a perfect panic of fear when he himself was in the field, and the enemy seventy miles off, and he himself surrounded by 35,000 or 40,000 men, well armed and equipped, and with eighty cannon. I don't mean by this that he was in "bodily fear," but that he was paralyzed by his incapacity to deal with great affairs, overwhelmed by a responsibility to which he was unequal.

As a matter of course, I state these things upon what I have heard from officers who were there. So far as the report or rumor about his expecting a battle the next day is concerned—which rumor is a matter of history and perfectly notorious in Missouri—it is a fact just as well known that the enemy were nowhere within three days' march of him. I have heard, and I think it can be substantiated, that he was very reluctant to give up his command. He knew the President had given that order, yet he was present at a mutinous meeting of his officers, in which those officers, those personally attached to him and around him, were shouting "Hurra for Frémont, and down with Hunter;" and he was bowing to them with approbation while these expressions of mutiny were going on; and the newspapers in his interest in Missouri, German and English, were every day fulminating threats that the army would resist and would not accept any other general; whereas he had suppressed several newspapers, one at least, that had been a stanch supporter of the Union; suppressed it for a mild criticism upon the fall of Lexington; stopped its publication and imprisoned its editors. He allowed those newspapers in his own interest to threaten the government that the army would revolt and mutiny if he was superseded; permitted it to be done, and is responsible for it, because he did not prevent it.

By Mr. Odell:

Question. What paper do you refer to?

Answer. The St. Louis Republican, the St. Louis Democrat and the Anzieger des Westers, &c.

Question. I mean the paper suppressed because it criticised the matter of Lexington.

Answer. The Evening News, a stanch Union paper in the very darkest hours of our trouble. He suppressed it and imprisoned its editor for a respectful criticism upon his military ability.

Question. When did he receive the order to give up his command?

Answer. That was about the first of November; I think about that time.

Question. Just at that time how far was the enemy from his position?

Answer. Well, sir, it was from sixty to seventy miles; that is as well known as it was known that he was at Springfield at the head of our army.

Question. At what point was the enemy?

Answer. Somewhere near Carsville, in one of those southwestern counties.

By Mr. Gooch:

Question. Was there any considerable portion of the enemy's forces in his immediate vicinity?

Answer. No, sir; there is no pretence that there was by anybody that I have ever heard of, and I have conversed with a great many officers that was there at the time. I have seen large numbers of them, some of the most intelligent and the best informed. His paroxysms there were the subject of universal ridicule among intelligent men. A great many thought he wanted to retain the command, and as it was published in the newspapers that he was not to be relieved if he was in the presence of the enemy, he made this pretence. My own opinion is that he did not know any better. General Hunter told me that on the night he arrived there, after getting information of his appointment to the command, he reached the town and asked for General Frémont, and found him at his headquarters surrounded by his brigadier generals and generals of divisions, with a plan all marked out for a battle to occur the next day at Wilson's creek. It was a beautiful plan of battle, and he says he had no doubt if he had not arrived there that night and taken the command the army would have marched the next morning to Wilson's creek to battle, the only enemies there being the dead bodies of the secessionists left there by Lyon.

By Mr. Johnson:

Question. Was it in the direction of the enemy?

Answer. Yes, sir; it was in the direction, I think.

By Mr. Odell:

Question. How far was it from where they were to Wilson's creek?

Answer. Well, sir, I suppose it was twelve miles from Springfield.

By Mr. Johnson:

Question. And in the direction of the enemy, who were some sixty or seventy miles off?

Answer. Yes, sir, according to my understanding of it. I made a remark about General Frémont now that may be considered rather harsh and unjustifiable. I do not mean to impute to him any personal apprehension by what I have said. I do not want it taken in that sense. I said that he showed great insensibility to fear when other people were exposed to danger, as in the case of Lyon and in the case of Mulligan, and made no effort to relieve them; but that he was in a perfect paroxysm of apprehension at being threatened with his own command; urging Hunter to come up by forced marches, when in fact he was in no danger. He had an army there capable of coping with all the secessionists on the west bank of the Mississippi. What I mean is that he was conscious of his own incapacity, and overwhelmed by apprehension growing out of this consciousness.

His disregard of danger threatening others is illustrated by what occurred at Fredericktown. He was then some 25 miles south of Tipton, off the railroad line and off the telegraph line, when, on the 15th of October, news was received in St. Louis that Jeff. Thompson had burned the Big River bridge on the Iron Mountain railroad, the largest bridge on that road, cutting off a detachment of our troops, some 1,500, then at Pilot Knob. Immediately Captain McKeever, who was his adjutant general, sent a despatch on the same day to Grant to send troops up from Cape Girardeau to cut off Thompson. Colonel Carlin, who was in command at Pilot Knob, telegraphed for re-enforcements. General Curtis and McKeever, together, made great efforts, and got off the 8th Wisconsin and Boyd's Missouri regiment, and a battery from my regiment under Major Schofield, to go down this road and pass around this burned bridge, and thus proceed to Pilot Knob to the aid of Colonel Carlin.

In the House, the other day, two columns of despatches, purporting to give an account of that affair, were read by Colonel Shanks, or caused to be read by him. But there was a singular omission. They purported to be extracted from General Frémont's register of despatches, and to give a full and complete account of the affair. There was an omission of one despatch which General Curtis received from General Frémont on the 21st of October, as soon as he could reasonably be expected to hear of this affair of the burning of this bridge and the threatening attack of Jeff. Thompson on Colonel Carlin, and of the movement of troops under the orders of McKeever for their relief, given without Frémont's knowledge. That despatch ordered back the re-enforcements and upbraided Carlin for not himself having taken care of all the bridges between St. Louis and Pilot Knob, some ninety miles to be guarded by 1,500 men, and at the same time cope with Jeff. Thompson, who had some 3,000 or 4,000 men. Re-enforcements were sent by McKeever, Grant, and Curtis; but the order to withdraw the re-enforcements came from Frémont, and that order was omitted from the list of despatches. General Curtis gave me the despatch which is so singularly omitted from General Frémont's narrative of events. I have the despatches here. One is a despatch from Carlin asking for re-enforcements; the second is a despatch from Brigadier General McKinstry to Captain McKeever, by which it appears that General Frémont was not in a position on the 15th of October to hear of the occurrence, there being no telegraph from Syracuse, or from any part of this railroad line south to where Frémont had gone, 25 miles south. As will be seen by these despatches, McKeever and Curtis co-operated in sending down the troops from St. Louis to the assistance of Carlin. McKeever on that day, when Frémont was 25 miles south of Syracuse, ordered Grant to send up re-enforcements from Cape Girardeau, and they did go under Colonel Plummer and cut off Jeff. Thompson.

By the chairman:

Question. Where were you during this period?

Answer. I was in St. Louis. On the 21st this order came from Frémont:

"Order all the troops you have sent on the Iron Mountain road back to Benton barracks. The whole affair has been grossly exaggerated. Colonel Carlin should have kept the road open without any additional force.

"By order of—

"GENERAL FRÉMONT."

And signed by Captain McKeever, as assistant adjutant general. This despatch was not sent by McKeever and could not have been because he had co-operated in sending down these very troops.

The battle was fought the next day at Fredericktown, against at least 3,000 of Jeff. Thompson's men, and he was completely routed by an equal force of our people; and it was then convenient for General Frémont to claim that victory, which happened to be the only one for the federal troops during his time there.

I had made up my mind before the fall of Lexington that the command was too large for General Frémont, and I communicated that fact to my brother, expressing the hope that he would communicate the fact to the government, so that they could act upon it. I did not have any unkind feelings to General Frémont; I did not make the communication in that sense. But I had some interest in my own State, and some in the government. And I had come to that conclusion from my observation of things, and facts that had come to my knowledge, some of which are named in the letter, and some of which I did not name in the letter at all. I came to the conclusion that he was unfit for that command, and I stated that fact to my brother, and Mrs. Frémont came on here and went to see the President, and subsequently went to see my father and asked him about it. And he communicated the fact to Mrs. Frémont that I had written such a letter, and immediately upon her return to St. Louis I was arrested. That, as well as I can recollect, was about the middle of September. The charges were not preferred for some time afterwards. The charges he preferred were that I had written this letter and had communicated with the President and had shaken the confidence of the President in the general commanding out there; I was charged with insubordination. Upon the charges being sent forward here, General Scott dismissed them as being frivolous and untenable. Prior to that, however, General Frémont wrote me a letter, stating that I had made unfounded accusations against him to the government, but he released me from arrest at the request of my brother.

I then wrote to the adjutant general and sent the communication through him, stating that I felt myself called upon to make good these accusations, which General Frémont pronounced unfounded. I wrote that I would prefer charges as soon as I could get them in form. Whereupon I was re-arrested for doing what every well informed person knows I had a perfect right to do, to prefer charges against him or anybody else in the army.

By Mr. Odell:

Question. Did you prefer charges against him?

Answer. I did.

Question. What became of them?

Answer. They are on file in the War Department. I have held myself ready to make them good whenever General Frémont asks for a trial, or the government chooses to order one, whenever the government is in condition to supply officers high enough in rank to be ordered on the trial. If the charges are ever brought to trial I hold myself in readiness to make them good. I will simply state here at this point that I did not make any charges in the letter which I wrote, and which has been published, affecting General Frémont's private character at all. I said nothing that could have been construed as growing out of any unkind spirit towards him, which I did not have at that time. I have not sought to make this controversy—never given a turn to this matter to make it a personal affair between General Frémont and myself. The whole of that grew out of his arrest of me, which was converted into, or had the aspect of, a personal affair between himself and myself, by reason of the arrest and the subsequent proceedings under that arrest, upon charges which, when preferred, were pronounced frivolous by the general-in-chief. I had on disposition to quarrel with him. Certainly it was a very great humiliation to me to have come to the conclusions which I did about it. It could not have been a matter of any congratulation to me to make a breach with a man whose friend I had been, and although I am under no obligations of any kind to him, and never was, yet, with whose family—Colonel Benton's family—I had, ever since I can recollect, maintained the warmest relations. Both of the families, not only myself, but my own family and my father's family, all of us maintained the warmest and kindest relations, personally and politically, with General Frémont's and Colonel Benton's families.

Question. Do you remember the date of that letter which you sent here?

Answer. I think it was dated the 1st of September—about that time. The letter has been published, and it states what I thought proper to lay before the government. There was a great deal said about the frauds in contracts at that time, by those people who were surrounding him there. Those Californians had come and settled down there like obscene birds of prey. It was notorious that they enjoyed his special confidence and favor; that is, they had them at his instance; that was well known. But I did not at that time wish to disparage him in any way that affected him personally, because I did not wish to speak about anything from which any unkind or personal feeling can be argued. The grounds I alleged as to his incompetency were public grounds, and all the rancor and all the littleness that has grown out of this controversy, has arisen by his own act in treating charges of a public nature as a private feud, and acting upon it in that way. I never had any private grief against General Frémont up to that time.

Question. Had you any difference with him?

Answer. None.

Question. Not upon any subject?

Answer. None.

Question. Business relations?

Answer. Not upon any earthly subject. At the time I wrote that letter, and for long afterwards—many days, weeks afterwards—I never had asked him a favor that he hesitated to grant for one instant. I was compelled, as the representative of the district, and as a citizen, and from the supposed relations between us—I was applied to again and again by persons to recommend them to him for contracts. I never asked him to give anybody a contract that he did not give it without the slightest hesitation—never. I did not ask him for many. I asked him for some when I understood that he was disposing of them; when I understood that they were not going through the quartermaster's department; that, as a matter of favor, he was giving them to the men from California, men from New York, and from those distant cities, where the people had not felt the slightest effect in their business, or very little, from the devastations of the war. And when people whom I represented in Congress had lost nearly everything, whose business had been all destroyed and they were reduced to poverty; when these men came to me and asked me to represent the facts of what they were, what they had suffered, what they had done for the Union cause, and that they had as good right to have these government contracts if they were given out of favor, or a right to compete for them if given out in the usual way, then I could not refuse to ask for them. And those were the only grounds upon which I did ask for them. And I take occasion to say again that he never refused them. I never asked him to appoint anybody to office that he did not appoint him.

Question. Do you speak now of all the time?

Answer. I mean up to the time of my arrest. I never asked him for anything subsequent to that. I of course never had any communication with him other than official communication subsequent to that.

Question. I do not mean, of course, by my question that you asked him for contracts personally, but in behalf of friends.

Answer. I understand that. I went to him and made these representations to him, and recommended persons to him as officers that I knew would be serviceable to the country and to him, most of which recommendations he adopted. If he did refuse any, it was such a small affair that it has left no trace upon my memory. After this breach occurred, these newspapers in the city attacked me, imputed personal motives to me for my conduct, said that I was disappointed in not controlling everything—asserted it over and over again. And I knew perfectly well that these accusations had his sanction. And I knew at the same time that if he did not absolutely dictate those things—I knew from the style of the articles in the newspapers, with which style I was perfectly familiar; I knew from the nature of the accusations themselves, and from other circumstances—that he or some of his immediate staff or surroundings were instigating those attacks upon me. I knew at the same time that they were all false, and that he knew it. One of those accusations was that I wanted to be a brigadier general, or wanted to be a general in his place. Well, I had in the first place been offered it by the government—by those who had a right to confer such a place. I had been offered the position of general, and declined it. It was when General Lyon was made a general. They offered to make me a general instead of him. I knew he could do more service to the country and was better fitted for it, and I recommended him. And General Frémont wrote a letter to my brother—I think it was dated on the 8th of September, long after the letter that I wrote here to Washington—in which he stated to my brother that he had frequently urged me to receive high position in the army, and that I had declined it. So that he knew the accusation was not true.

Question. Do you remember any application of yours, in behalf of friends, for a large contract of clothing, &c., which was not granted?

Answer. I recollect the only large contract that I ever asked him for for clothing. It must have been that one, for I never asked him for any other. I recollect that so far from not granting it, he approved it. And I can refer you now to the very application in the report of the committee of the other house, with "I approve" indorsed on it. It was refused by McKinstry. You will find in that report the only contract I ever asked for. I went to him subsequently, after McKinstry refused to give this contract, and there was some modification of it. The contract was at the prices paid others at the eastern cities here. I asked him for that. I went and saw him; and so far from refusing it, he indorsed his approval upon it instantly. And I gave it to my friend, John Howe, who went up and gave it to McKinstry. Mr. Howe had had a quarrel with McKinstry—he thought McKinstry was not loyal—and McKinstry would not then give him anything. I then went to General Frémont about it. McKinstry then made a publication about it—made a blow over it in all the telegraphic despatches to the east, to get a little reputation as being a man who had stipulated for only the prices given at the eastern depots.

Question. Do you recollect how many suits of clothing it was for?

Answer. I do not. It was for a large amount. The application was made on behalf of one gentleman residing in St. Louis and another gentleman residing in Chicago; and it was thought that it was but reasonable that those two cities should have a lot of clothing to be made up, and thus furnish employment for the families of our absent soldiers who were in the field against the enemy.

By Mr. Julian:

Question. Did General Frémont give you all that you asked?

Answer. Everything.

Question. Without any hesitation?

Answer. Without any hesitation, not only in the matter of this contract, but in every other.

By Mr. Odell:

Question. Did these parties get this contract?

Answer. They did not. It was modified, and only a portion of it was given to Mr. Howe.

Question A portion was given to Mr. Howe?

Answer. Yes, sir; he was satisfied with it. I insisted upon it after McKinstry's refusal and publication. I was determined he should have it. He did modify it in this shape and give it.

Question. Modified it as to quantity or as to price?

Answer. As to quantity.

Question. Was that before or after you had written your letter to your brother?

Answer. It was before.

Question. In the first place, it was granted for the whole?

Answer. Yes, sir; and subsequently granted as to a part to Mr. Howe.

Question. And Mr. Howe executed the contract?

Answer. Yes, sir; and I believe got paid for it.

By Mr. Gooch:

Question. The limitation of the amount was made by McKinstry and not by Frémont?

Answer. Made by McKinstry. The whole resistance to the contract, to their obtaining it to the full amount, was made by McKinstry. Frémont signed the original contract as originally asked for; approved it without any sort of hesitation.

By Mr. Johnson:

Question. Which was granting all that you asked in the aggregate?

Answer. Yes, sir; and the contract, I expect, can be shown with his signature upon it, in his own handwriting, because I saw him put it there myself

By Mr. Odell:

Question. What do you know about the difficulty of access to General Frémont?

Answer. I never had any myself. He gave a special order that I should be admitted to see him whenever I came. But I know that it was almost impossible for any one to see him who was not so accredited; and the sort of people that did have access to him were of such a class that I was very much ashamed after a while to exercise the privilege that was accorded to me in their company. The first day that I went to see him after I arrived there he gave orders to his guard to admit me whenever I called. It was a very onerous duty for me. Almost everybody would come to me and say they could not get access to him, and that they knew I could. Many of the best men in the country would go there and be denied admittance—be denied an interview. Men came there proffering to raise regiments—men that I know were fully able to do it, and were good men, and they could not get to see him. Governors of States, congressmen, colonels of regiments, men bearing information from the disturbed portions of the State, right from the hostile part of our State, would come with information to him, and could not get a glimpse of him. I know several instances of that kind.

Question. Was not the pressure upon him, natural to his official position, such as to justify the difficulty in getting to see him?

Answer. I do not know. He assumed to do duties that he had no business to do; that he was not charged to do by the government. He assumed to do all the contracting—to give out all the contracts. He assumed the duties of the commissary, quartermaster, and all the other departments, and, of course, was occupied by these contractors, when they ought to have been turned over to other officers.

Question. Was that the general course of his business, or only occasional?

Answer. He seemed to be chiefly so engaged.

Question. Do you mean to say that as a general thing the men who obtained contracts for supplies for the army of any description would have to go to him rather than to the quartermaster or the commissary?

Answer. Yes, sir; I mean to say so; that that was the general fact. I know I was urged again and again, by men that I refused to do it for, to go to him for those matters. In some cases I would write to the quartermaster and ask him to give them a contract, if he could do so, to the advantage of the public service. There is a fact that I want to place upon record in my testimony. I want to state this for the information of the committee. I have seen a statement of the receipts and disbursements made in St. Louis from January, 1861, to January, 1862, an authenticated statement of that kind, and up to August the disbursements of this year were less than of the year previous. I make this statement in this shape as affecting General Lyon. Whilst he may have been said to run in debt, and did run in debt, (because the troops were not paid at all; my regiment was not paid until October; never got a cent; never got any clothes from the government; never got anything from the government,) this only goes to show how a man who was in earnest to work for the government could work and did work for the government. Whilst General Lyon was there the expenditures made by the government were less than in the year previous. Since that time the expenditures have amounted up enormously.

Question. Do you know the aggregate amount of that statement?

Answer. I do not.

Question. You said you had seen the statement, and I did not know but what you remembered the figures.

Answer. I know that in the years 1860–61, the expenditures were $7,000,000, and this year they are over $25,000,000, and the greater portion of it has been expended there since August—the great bulk of it; that is, up to August it was not so large as it was in the year previous. It only goes to show this: I know that General Frémont's friends had made the complaint that he had no money and could not do anything, and could not be expected to do anything; that the government had neglected him. I understand that he has shown a letter in his statement—I do not get this from any member of the committee—written by Lyon, heaping coals of fire on General Scott's head for not supporting him, throwing the blame on

Scott for his overthrow there, and saying that Scott did nothing to support him; and it is argued from this that Frémont would have supported him if he had had the means. Now the fact is that Frémont had large means to supply him, and of his large means in men and money, so far from doing anything to compare in brilliancy with what was done by Lyon, he undid everything that was done by Lyon; had even to exchange the prisoners that Lyon had taken at Camp Jackson for the men taken prisoners at Lexington under his command. He undid all that was done by Lyon; at the same time Lyon had no sort of aid in money rendered him by the government, while the other man had an abundance of everything, so much so that he used it very profligately in dispensing it to unworthy people; that contract which he made with Beard, dated on the 25th day of September, for building fortifications around St. Louis which were nearly completed, one-half of which had been built by the officers, under their superintendance, and upon which Beard had never hired a man to strike a lick; it was all covered by his contract, and charged for at prices four times what it cost to build them. That has been testified to by those who know the facts in the case—that this contract was made by McKinstry, under the special orders of General Frémont; the prices paid for the different species of work having been fixed by Frémont himself, and incorporated by McKinstry under his orders. The work done by officers of the army, and to some extent by the soldiers, or which had been completed by them, this man's contract covered, and he charged at least four times the prices paid for it.

By Mr. Odell:

Question. Do you mean to say that General Frémont himself fixed the prices?

Answer. I mean to say that the testimony shows that. I do not know the fact myself from my own knowledge.

Question. You mean that the prices fixed were fixed by General Frémont, and not by the quartermaster—that that is the testimony generally?

Answer. I mean to say that.

By the chairman:

Question. You do not mean to say that from your own knowledge?

Answer. I mean to say it from the knowledge of those who have testified to it, and who know the facts.

The chairman: That testimony we must get otherwhere.

The witness: I can get the testimony for you here if you want it.

By Mr. Odell:

Question. All my question implied was simply this: I understand you to say that McKinstry was furnished by Frémont with the figures at which this was paid?

Answer. Yes, sir.

Question. I wanted to know if you did mean to say that?

Answer. I meant to say that; and if you want the parties who can testify to that fact, of their own knowledge, I will give you the names of the men.

The chairman: Give us the names of the men.

The witness: I will send their names to you. Mr. Clements, the clerk of McKinstry, has stated the fact on oath before the Van Wyck committee.

By Mr. Gooch:

Question Do you know whether there was any necessity for building the last five forts in a very short time, such as would justify the building them at the prices paid?

Answer. I know there was no necessity for building the forts there at any time. St. Louis never was threatened by anybody after General Lyon caged all those fellows at Camp Jackson. There is one point about that testimony. I have understood that it has been alleged that General Lyon would, if he had had the means, have fortified the city, and that he selected those sites for fortifications. I do not know the fact to be that he would not have done it; but I will state what I believe is pretty well known: that I was as constantly and as confidentially with General Lyon as any other man throughout the whole period covering his command there, and I never heard him once utter a single, solitary word about fortifying the city of St. Louis. He did talk about fortifying the hill immediately above the arsenal, for the protection of the arsenal. The arsenal was in very low ground, and commanded by these elevations. He intended to seize those elevations, which was the key to the possession of the arsenal, and hold them. I know that to be true. But as for fortifying any other part of the city, I do not believe it to be true; for I think it very improbable that he would contemplate anything of the sort without speaking to me about it. And the only time the city was ever in danger from anybody, as far as my judgment is worth anything, was when General Lyon was there. The whole expenditure was useless—a mere job, and intended for that.

By Mr. Johnson:

Question. What has been the amount expended in that way, estimated at?
Answer. $360,000.

By Mr. Julian:

Question. Who were these bad men that General Frémont surrounded himself by?
Answer. There were five or six from California—I do not remember the number exactly—men who are in the worst possible repute in California, and whose names figure pretty largely in the public prints: Palmer, Beard, Haskell, and others who were on his staff, some of whom were connected with him officially, and at the same time had contracts under him—men of no repute, or very bad repute, in California, for their peculations.

By the chairman:

Question. On his staff and had contracts? Name them.
Answer. Haskell was on his staff; he was director of police, when he ought to have been in the hands of the police, instead of being director of the police. Leonidas Haskell, he was captain on his staff, in an office created for him, that did not exist in the military service at all.

By Mr. Julian:

Question. Any others that you think of?
Answer. There were a number of men from eastern cities who were on his staff, connected with him, and had contracts.
Question. Was Woods one of them?
Answer. Yes, sir; Isaac Woods. He was on his staff. I never heard of his having any contracts.

By Mr. Odell:

Question. Was he on his staff?
Answer. Yes, sir; he was on his staff. He is said to have been recommended by my brother. I was present when my brother recommended him to Frémont verbally. I heard him talk about him. He told Frémont that Woods had proved very serviceable to him in the post office department as a sort of spy, or rather as an agent for organizing a spy corps; and by his energy in getting the mails

through Baltimore at the time of the interruption; and also in putting the custom-house and post office officers into their places from which they had been excluded by fear of the mob; he showed courage and tact in this service. He thought he would be serviceable to Frémont in the same capacity. He never recommended him for anything else than his qualifications in that respect. He did not at that interview; I do not know about any other time; I would not speak of anything more than I know. He recommended him for the qualities he had exhibited in that way. Frémont said he knew Woods well, in Calfornia, and coincided in my brother's judgment of his activity and sagacity; and I should suppose he would be very useful to him in that capacity myself. The capacity in which he was placed by Frémont was a sort of principal man. He regulated all the admissions of persons to Frémont's presence; he had the general superintendence of that sort of thing. I never discovered that he was very serviceable in that particular. I will say here that in all the testimony I have seen and heard in regard to Woods, although I know he had a very bad name, and have heard since that his name in California was not very good, I have never heard of anything that has been brought home to him of a criminal character in regard to contracts.

By Mr. Julian:

Question. Is General McKinstry one of the men you would classify with these others?

Answer. General McKinstry was a regular army officer, the quartermaster at that post. In regard to General McKinstry, I think he was about the worst man at that post. I am very sorry to say that I was somewhat instrumental myself in having him there. I will state this: that there were such representations made to me about McKinstry that I interfered to have him restored to that position after he had been relieved from it. I never had seen the man myself, then; but relying upon the statements made by Union men, whom I knew to be such, I interfered in his behalf at their solicitation. But I think after surveying the whole field that he was the worst man that Frémont had about him; worse in morals and every other way. I think that he, by his flattery and by pandering to Frémont's love of show and parade, and obtained an ascendency over his weak mind that was very controlling, and that was exercised for the very worst purposes possible.

Exhibits to accompany the testimony of Frank P. Blair, Jr.

Since delivering my testimony I have found among my papers several letters bearing upon portions of it which I desire to incorporate in my testimony.

First. A copy of a letter from honorable Montgomery Blair to honorable Edward Bates.

Second. A copy of extract from letter from General Frémont to honorable M. Blair, dated Astor House, July 13, 1861.

Third. A copy of extract from letter from General Frémont to honorable M. Blair, dated September 8, 1861, and a copy of a proposal for contract from John How and W. S. Gurnee to General Frémont, dated August 19, 1861, indorsed and recommended to Quartermaster McKinstry, by General Frémont, which will be found in the testimony of H. W. G. Clements, clerk to Quartermaster McKinstry, at page 977 of the report of the House committee on contracts, of which Mr. Van Wyck is chairman. This is the only contract for clothing that I ever asked General Frémont to give to any one, and it is the same that, I understand, he says he refused to give. His own indorsement on the paper shows the contrary, and proves that I could have had no dissatisfaction with him on that account. McKinstry did refuse to give the contract, and published his refusal in a flaming letter, intended to affect a virtue he did not possess. Subsequently, he gave a contract to Mr. How, at my instance, for about one-half the amount.

WASHINGTON, *June* 19, 1861.

DEAR SIR: At my solicitation Governor Chase yesterday called on General Scott in reference to relieving our friends in Missouri from the annoyance of being subjected to an officer whose attention must necessarily be, to a great extent, directed to another field of operations; showing him General McClellan's letter, in which he confesses that he does not understand the course of policy proper to be pursued in Missouri, and says that he is embarrassed in the matters in his more immediate charge by having Missouri added to his division.

General Scott declined to detach Missouri from McClellan's division on the ground of your objection to it.

I conjure you to withdraw that objection. Lyon is an older officer than McClellan. He has seen much more service in the field, and has in his conduct of affairs in Missouri exhibited good judgment as a commanding officer. There is, indeed, so far as I can discover, no sufficient reason for subjecting his operations in Missouri to any intermediate supervision. When the differences in Missouri shall have been disposed of, and it becomes necessary to combine the movement of the forces of the west upon the south—for which purpose alone I understood you to desire to have Missouri added to the Ohio division—it may then be restored to it. But while the operations are so distinct as at present, McClellan's attention being limited almost exclusively to one field, and Lyon's entirely to another, it is surely unnecessary to place the older officer under the younger.

Hoping that you will concede this to men who are your tried friends, and that you will not co-operate with those whose evident design is to embarrass them, to deprive them of the credit of their success, whilst subjecting them to all the discredit of defeat, if they meet it.

I remain yours, truly,

M. BLAIR.

HON. EDWARD BATES.

Proposition of J. How and W. S. Gurnee for furnishing clothing, &c.

ST. LOUIS, *August* 19, 1861.

SIR: Referring to the conversation had with you some three weeks ago, by one of the undersigned, (Mr. Gurnee,) in relation to army supplies, and to what extent such supplies could be furnished at Chicago with the promptitude required for the fitting out of an army, we have to say that Mr. Gurnee, having conferred with the principal manufacturers of Chicago, returned to this city prepared to give satisfactory answers, but learning here that St. Louis claimed a portion of the work, he proposed to her associate in these communications, (Mr. John How,) to unite in this proposition with the understanding that the goods, as far as practicable, be manufactured in Chicago and St. Louis and in equal proportions.

They now make out and submit to the commanding general the following propositions:

First. They will furnish and deliver at any depot or office in Chicago or St. Louis, the goods manufactured in the respective cities, as follows:

20,000 coats or jackets, at rate of 1,500 per week.
20,000 pairs of pants, at rate of 1,500 per week.

20,000 pairs of drawers, at rate of 1,500 per week.
40,000 flannel shirts, at rate of 3,000 per week.
70,000 pairs of socks, at rate of 5,000 per week.
15,000 overcoats, at rate of 1,000 per week.
35,000 boots or shoes for infantry, at rate of 1,000 per week.
5,000 cavalry boots, at rate of 400 per week.
17,000 caps or felt hats, at rate of 2,000 per week.
15,000 knapsacks, at rate of 2,000 per week.
15,000 haversacks, at rate of 2,000 per week.
15,000 canteens, at rate of 2,000 per week.
2,000 horse equipments, at rate of 200 per week.

All the supplies furnished shall correspond to the patterns and samples now being made for government service, unless changed by your order; and the price to be the same at which contracts are now being filled in the principal of the quartermaster's departments for the United States, with allowance to us when superior articles are required, and deduction if inferior are delivered, we to be notified at the time if deductions are claimed. We will commence the delivery of the goods within twenty days after the signing of the contract, and will, as far as practicable, increase the deliveries, and even the amount of goods when required by your department.

An early answer is respectfully requested, as the time is short within which to supply the army of the West, and have them prepared for the coming winter.

JOHN HOW.
W. S. GURNEE.

Major General JOHN C. FRÉMONT,
Commanding Department of the West.

I recommend this proposal for contract to Major McKinstry.

J. C. FRÉMONT,
Major General Commanding.

A true copy.

H. W. G. CLEMENTS.

Extract from a letter from General Frémont to Hon. M. Blair.

ASTOR HOUSE, *July* 13, 1861.

* * * * * * * * * *

My idea is to have as much as possible the advantage of the particular abilities which Woods and Davis can bring to the service. I. C. Woods in the quartermaster's department, and Ed. M. Davis in the commissary department—both, of course, under the regular army. I wish to have both of these near me, and will consider them part of my staff. Pray have the appointments made out for them immediately—their brigade duties won't interfere with greater usefulness. * * * * *

Yours, truly,

J. C. FRÉMONT.

Hon. M. BLAIR, *&c., &c., &c., Washington.*

Extract from a private letter from Major General Frémont to Hon. Montgomery Blair, dated September 8, 1861.

* * * * * * * *

"Frank's regiment will be a brigade, and a fit command for a general of artillery. I *urged* him several times to accept high rank and go into the war, but he does not like to lose his position in Congress. I think he is wrong, but we all set different values on the same thing."

* * * * * * *

Upon this extract I make this remark: that General Frémont does not appear to have understood the motive which led me to decline "high rank." It was from no indisposition to "go into the war," but because I thought others more competent to render service to the country. I had gone into the war long before he entered the service, and under circumstances far more trying than any that surrounded him. The extract, and the contract to which his recommendation is attached, and which is set out in this testimony, are quoted for the purpose of disposing of the charges made by him and his hangers-on to impugn my motives in asking for his removal from the western department. It is a curious coincidence that every imputation of this kind against me is shown to be untrue by his own handwriting and signature.

WASHINGTON, *February* 24, 1862.

Major CHARLES ZAGONYI sworn and examined.

By the chairman:

Question. What rank did you hold in the army of the northwest under General Frémont?

Answer. I first entered the army as a captain; later I was appointed major.

Question. How long were you with General Frémont?

Answer. From the 12th of July till the 6th of November, when we came back from Springfield.

Question. You accompanied him on his expedition down to Springfield?

Answer. Yes, sir; I did.

Question. In what capacity?

Answer. As major, commanding my command of cavalry, three companies. A fourth company remained behind.

Question. What was your command called?

Answer. The body-guard.

Question. Proceed in your own way to give an account of what you observed about the army in its progress to Springfield.

Answer. I think it would be well for me to state how this command was formed, and for what purpose.

Question. Very well; please do that.

Answer. On the 2d of August, as we were returning to St. Louis from Cairo, I had a conversation with General Frémont, and suggested to him that it would be well for him to have a separate company of infantry or cavalry—I advised him to have cavalry—for a body-guard. It is customary in Europe, and also here, as I saw in the newspapers before we left, for the different generals to have body guards. In Europe a body guard for the general is used in this way: whenever a guard is wanted at headquarters, instead of detailing them from the different companies of soldiers, they are taken from this body guard; and when the general goes into the field he has a company of cavalry upon which he can rely in case of necessity. I told General Frémont that if he would allow me to form such a company, I would make every man in it fit to be an officer in a cavalry regiment, of which we were then in great need in the west. The general agreed to the proposition, and I commenced to raise the company; but before I had completed organizing one company I had men enough for three companies. I reported that fact to him, and at last he agreed that I should take all that came, with the idea that eventually they should be formed into a regiment. During this time this cavalry, as far as it was raised, did every kind of duty in

St. Louis. I have been ordered out many times in the middle of the night, when any trouble was apprehended by the provost marshal, or if there was any confusion or disobedience anywhere. We did regular duty; and when we started to enter the field, I can say that all the rest of the cavalry there did not do as much duty as the three companies under my command. We were everywhere scouting, reconnoitring, performing night-guard duty. Everything of that kind was done by my three companies, so that we never had twelve hours' rest at any time—no man of us.

Question. How were they dressed and equipped?

Answer. Just the same as other cavalry, only more simply, because there was not a bit of cord on their uniforms, which was the plain cloth of the uniforms, with the buttons.

Question. Just like other cavalry, only the uniform was more simple?

Answer. Yes, sir. The uniform was made by the order of the quartermaster, General McKinstry. No one had anything to do with it but him; he equipped the whole force.

Question. How were you armed?

Answer. Each man had a revolver, and generally a sabre, and about two-thirds had carbines.

Question. I have heard it said that that body-guard was equipped and dressed very extravagantly and expensively. How was that?

Answer. I cannot account in any way why that should be said. I knew that, before we started, we had been abused in every way by everybody; so I heard. When I was trying to equip my troops, I was refused, and troubled, and kept back in everything I undertook to do.

Question. You have stated all you know about their dress?

Answer. Yes, sir; just as it was.

Question. You accompanied the expedition to Springfield?

Answer. Yes, sir.

Question. What was the particular duty of this body-guard on the march?

Answer. Just as the rest, we marched ahead; except that it was my duty generally to keep a guard at the general's headquarters, to send out pickets and patrols, and do every duty like that. There was no particular duty. I went out several times on expeditions. At Warsaw a rumor came that the enemy had a force lately recruited of about 150 men. I was sent out to see about it. We went out in the night, going about twenty miles between 7 o'clock and 10 o'clock; but the enemy had fled. However, I was fortunate enough to capture about 40 mules and horses, and 170 bushels of wheat, which we found in a mill, belonging to Price's army.

Question. Had you seen military service in Europe?

Answer. Yes, sir; I was in active service in 1848 and 1849 in the Hungarian war against the Austrian and Russian army.

Question. What do you say in regard to General Frémont's skill in handling the army on this expedition?

Answer. I had only the rank of major; but I had experience. I served in 1848 and 1849 under the best of generals, (General Bem,) and I never had a warmer attachment or higher esteem for any man than for General Frémont as a military man, as a commander, and as a general.

Question. Will you tell us about your charge at Springfield?

Answer. On the 24th of October news came that some 300 or 400 men of the rebel army from Price's command were in Springfield. The man who brought the news told it to me, and I immediately reported it to General Frémont, and asked his permission to go and attack them. The general answered that he would let me go the next day, but not that day. After some further remonstrances that it would probably be too late the next day, he consented to let me go that evening. I had intended to go with my own force alone; but the general did not wish to risk my force alone, and gave me an order for 150 men from another command.

From that evening till the next morning about 11 o'clock I made fifty miles, stopping only one single hour on the road to rest. I had a scout with me that I sent forward to learn about the enemy's strength, and I found that the enemy, instead of having only 300 or 400, had 1,800 or 1,900. I inquired how they were armed, and what kind of soldiers they were. I asked if they were well drilled, and the scout said they were. I thought it over in my mind as to what I should do. It was a little risky for me to try the experiment, but we had been so shamefully abused I could not do anything else, and I thank God we did not turn back, but went forward. If I had not gone forward and won that battle, I think I should have left this country for shame. I made up my mind I would go forward and see the enemy, and then do what I should think best. I did not know whether I would attack them. Before I started I sent a despatch to the general, which was worded something like this:

"GENERAL: From reliable assurances I report that the enemy is 1,800 or 1,900 strong. I would ask you, general, to send me a re-enforcement, that in case I am defeated I may fall back upon them, or if I am successful I may be able to hold the place."

From that the general could see my mind was made up to attack the enemy. I went forward. In a short time I met a Union man, who told me the enemy would hardly stop to receive me, but would retreat. I inquired about the place, how it lay, for I did not know anything about it, and what way they would be likely to retreat. I made a detour around of about seven miles on the prairie, so that, in case they should retreat, I should be able to catch them. That brought me, about half-past 4 o'clock, near Springfield. I learned, upon inquiring from Union people and from foreigners, that it was true that there were 1,800 or 1,900 of the enemy, and one man told me there was not less than 2,200; and after the battle was over I found out there was indeed 2,200. I thought the enemy were on the other side of Springfield, which would give me about two miles ride yet. I ordered my command forward; and on coming from a little wooded space out in front of my command about twenty or twenty-five yards, all at once the bullets were whistling around me. I looked around and saw the enemy drawn up in line of battle. I heard another round of firing, and saw another force of about 300 men. The bullets, by fifties and sixties, were whistling around me. I had nothing to do but to retreat or go forward. A look showed me there was hardly any place to get at them but down a lane. I ordered my cavalry forward in quick trot down the lane. Before I had got 200 yards down the lane, I had lost about forty men, not killed or wounded, but mostly disabled by their horses being shot down. I then stopped my command, opened a fence, and went into a field about 150 yards from the enemy's camp. I formed my command, which at the time was hardly more than a hundred men, and with them I attacked the enemy, and in less than five seconds the enemy were completely broken to pieces and running in every direction. My men were so much excited that ten or fifteen of them would attack hundreds of the enemy; and in that single attack I lost fifteen men killed—that was all I lost in dead; and the enemy's dead men on the ground were 106.

Question. How did you kill them—with sabres or with revolvers?

Answer. Mostly with the sabre. We Hungarian cavalrymen teach our soldiers never to use the revolver, as they are of very little use. The sabre is the only arm the cavalry need if they are well drilled. There were no swords of my men that were not bloody; and I saw swords from which the blood was running down on the hand. The men were drilled very well. I had only six weeks from the time I had the first man sworn in the service to the time we started for the field; but in those six weeks I brought them forward so far as I ever thought I should be able to do. They were mostly Americans—about one-fourth Germans.

Question. Were they raw men when you took them?

Answer. Not a single one ever served before.

Question. Can you teach men the use of the sabre in that time?

Answer. Yes, sir; but we worked from the time the sun was up till the sun went down; and in the evening I gave extra hours to my officers and non-commissioned officers, so that I had hardly four or five hours to myself nights; and I never saw that the general slept more. He beat me in work every day.

By Mr. Chandler:

Question. How many did you have wounded besides the fifteen killed?

Answer. I had twenty-eight wounded, but only two dangerously; that is, neither of them died, but they were badly wounded. One was an officer, and another a non-commissioned officer.

Question. This battle was outside of Springfield?

Answer. Yes, sir.

Question. Did your force charge into the town of Springfield?

Answer. Yes, sir; through every street, and all around wherever we could see an enemy, until night came upon us.

Question. Do you know the number of wounded of the enemy?

Answer. No, sir; I do not, but I heard that it was a great many; and that a great many of them would die, because they had mostly received heavy cuts on the head. All the dead were cut in the head. Some of the enemy behaved themselves very bravely indeed, but they were not able to hold up against this tremendous charge. To show the spirit of my men, about half an hour before I made the charge I halted my command, as my men had made twenty hours' ride without eating any thing or feeding their horses; I thought that, being young men, they would be worn out; I asked if any of them were broken down, or sick, or tired out, to step forward from the command, and I would leave them behind, and employ them on extra duty. I stated to them that when I started I expected to find about 300 or 400 of the enemy; but, instead of that, the probability was that there were 1,900 of the enemy. I told them I had made up my mind to attack the enemy, and I promised victory; but, I said, that I did not want to throw away any lives; and I asked those who felt tired to step forward two steps, and I would put them on extra duty; but not one single man showed any tired or sickness; and every one of them, I saw their eyes grow big like your fist—every one.

By the chairman:

Question. What have become of your men?

Answer. They have been discharged; dismissed with disgrace, really, not discharged. They were dismissed with disgrace. I saw a telegraphic despatch from Washington, which stated that we used some expressions at Springfield for which our further service in the United States army is of doubtful expediency. So there was a reason why we should be dismissed from the service of the United States.

By Mr. Chandler:

Question. What were those expressions?

Answer. I did not know. I have been brought up a soldier, and have been an officer for years long, and understand my duty. I did my duty towards every superior officer, and to every officer, and I taught my men to do their duty. There never came to me a single complaint from the beginning to the last hour against my men that they were disrespectful in any way. But I know one thing—I found out later what was that expression—it was nothing more than this: When I was leading my men on to that charge, to excite them a little, I said that our war-cry would be, "the Union," and "Frémont" our general. It is customary in Europe, when attacking the enemy, to have a war-cry—"Liberty!" "the Union!" And, as a general thing, if we like and respect the general, it is customary to use the name of the general in the war-cry. In Hungary, where we were fighting for liberty, my government and the ministers did not feel offended because when we charged the enemy, we used the name of General Bem.

By the chairman:

Question. That had been your custom in Europe, and you thought it right to do so here?

Answer. Yes, sir. That must be the only crime that we have committed against the country, or against our superior officers.

Question. Was there in your command, or in any other part of General Frémont's army, any intention to set General Frémont up above other officers, or against the government?

Answer. No, sir. I never heard anything of the kind, except one time one of my officers received a letter from Iowa. He was a countryman of mine—the only countryman I had in the body-guard. He was a finely educated man; his father was a count at home, but, at present, is a farmer in Iowa. His father wrote him a letter in which there was something said of a public meeting in Davenport, Iowa, to set up a western republic, or something of the kind. I ridiculed the idea. I told him I did not believe General Frémont, as a citizen, a patriot, a soldier, ever would think of such a thing; and as a soldier in the United States army, I told him I would not even follow General Frémont, or any general, no matter how much I liked him.

Question. Was that ever communicated to General Frémont?

Answer. No, sir.

By Mr. Gooch:

Question. Was there any manifestation of such feeling at any time among the body-guard?

Answer. No, sir; no, sir. I took service in the United States army only for the reason that I wanted to see this great country united again, and put down the rebellion, and not to divide it more and more. I am not a fortune hunter. I had no idea of begging anything. I had made up my mind that I would fight for no country but my own. But later, being called to serve under General Frémont whom I had never seen in my life, but for whom I had high esteem, I offered my services, and was accepted.

By the chairman:

Question. Were you present with the army at the time General Frémont was superseded?

Answer. Yes, sir; I was present.

Question. Will you tell us what was the situation of General Frémont's army and that of the enemy at that time; where were they?

Answer. Just the day the order came to supersede him, we got information of the enemy in this way. The scout which the general gave me when I went forward to Springfield, I had kept in my own employment until that time. On the first day of November I asked him to go forward towards Wilson's creek, &c., until he could see the enemy and find out where was his advance-guard, which I expected would be cavalry, and how strong they were, and bring me the news. I told him if he did not bring me the truth his life would be in peril, for I should take him along with me. He came back on the 2d of November, and informed me that at Wilson's creek were six hundred picked men, of the very best cavalry of the enemy, and about nine or ten miles beyond were the rest of the army at two or three different places, the names of which I cannot remember. I at once gave orders to my officers to call their companies together, and inspect their arms, and to pick out the best men and the best horses, and have about one hundred and fifty men ready to start in the evening; to put them perfectly in order in arms, equipment, and everything. I intended to go up to the general and ask for permission to capture the enemy. I did not mean to drive them off, but I was going to surround them, get behind on the left and right, and capture or annihilate them, if possible. Before I was ready to go to the general my adjutant came to me and said that there was some news circulating around the camp and at headquarters that the general was superseded. I found out in a short time that that was true. I was myself so disheartened that I gave up every idea of going forward; and it was not only I, but the whole army felt so. I can say, without exception, that I do not believe that a single regiment in that whole army was not disheartened.

Question. What number of troops had General Frémont at that time?

Answer. Indeed I cannot tell; may be 22,000 or 23,000. I think over 20,000 at any rate.

Question. Did you go far enough to ascertain the position of the enemy on that occasion?

Answer. Yes, sir; I did from my scout perfectly. He could not tell me what was the whole force, but he mentioned one or two places where the army was standing—I do not remember the places—and told me there were not less than 25,000 or 30,000 men.

Question. Where were they about that time?

Answer. About nine or ten miles beyond Wilson's creek. The advance guard of the enemy was at Wilson's creek, but the main body about nine or ten miles beyond, or about twenty miles from Springfield. My scout could go no further than where the advance-guard was; he could not penetrate beyond with safety. But he ascertained from citizens who were fleeing from their homes where the enemy was. On that same day I met General Asboth for the first time since he had got to Springfield. He congratulated me that I was so successful at Springfield, but at the same time told me that may be it would bring the greatest trouble on the whole army, because the enemy would find out that our whole army had not arrived at Springfield. General McKinstry was not up there yet. General Hunter we could not hear from, and General Asboth was very much afraid they would attack us, and that we would be obliged to retreat. He told me, indeed, that there was nothing left but to retreat. I answered to him that I would make sure about it, and I would start and bring him news.

Question. Who were the scouts that had gone out and seen the enemy?

Answer. They were sent out from different divisions of cavalry. They intended to send me out that day, but I asked permission to rest my men and horses, because they were very much tired. I did not tell my reason for not wanting to go out, but it was that I wanted to go out in the night. There is no doubt about the enemy. The men were very enthusiastic to go forward, and I am perfectly confident that, if Price had had 50,000 men, we would have been victorious; we would have driven him completely away, and perfectly annihilated his army.

Question. There has been some doubt expressed that the enemy were so near as you seem to apprehend they were at that time.

Answer. There was no doubt about it; we could not doubt it. We had been out with the general, too, and had met, I cannot tell how many, twenty or thirty families who brought news besides our own scouts. There were General Sigel's scouts, and General Asboth's scouts, and scouts from various quarters and from different regiments, and every one of them told the same story. And these Union families running away told us the same story, and that they were hardly able to escape. And I perfectly know it from my own scout, upon whom I felt assured to rely, because he had brought me the best news from Springfield before—that the advance guard of the enemy was at Wilson's creek.

Question. How long, in your judgment, would it have taken General Frémont to have overtaken the army of Price, if he had not been superseded?

Answer. Had not the enemy attacked us, we would have overtaken him before forty-eight hours, certain. I do not know as I could tell exactly, for I never heard about it much, but I know an arrangement was made already, or talked over with the generals. One or two persons knew it besides the generals. The intention was to send out most all the cavalry force, which was about 3,000, and a couple of batteries of artillery, have them go forward in double quick time and overtake the enemy, and keep them from retreating, so that there was no possibility that they would be able to run away from us; and in using this cavalry to go forward, and hold the enemy until the main body of the army could come up, the design was to go to the right and left and encircle the enemy, and in case of retreat or disorder to annihilate the whole army.

By Mr. Julian:

Question. At the time General Frémont was superseded, were there any signs of mutiny in his army, and did he countenance any insubordination?

Answer. Mutiny I did not see. There was great attachment to General Frémont; there was a disappointment of nearly all the army at his removal. Only one general in my life have I seen before, to whom his army was so much attached as to General Frémont, and that was General Bem, under whom I served in Hungary; and he was loved so much by his army that every soldier called him his father. The second instance was that of General Frémont. They were so much disappointed after he was superseded that I believe, and I express it perfectly confident that, had not the enemy been so near, one-half of the army would have laid down their arms.

Question. What did General Frémont say to that? Did he encourage it?

Answer. No, sir; he quieted them in the very best way. I spoke with the generals; I was upon good terms with them, as my position was; they were kind towards me. General McKinstry, General Pope, General Asboth, General Sigel—I conversed with them, but mostly with General McKinstry and General Sigel—I conversed with them a long time, and I heard their ideas. They told me the general's wishes, which I heard from the general also, that he obeyed orders, and he advised them all to do their duty as soldiers and citizens. Nothing of encouragement at all, but there was a feeling of disappointment there. There came up a body of officers, from 100 to 150, all the colonels came up, and asked General Frémont to retain his command and lead them against the enemy. He spoke to them a few kind words, and told them he must obey his superiors and they must obey theirs, and that they must go forward and beat the enemy. They cheered him then. And in the evening before he left he told them that if General Hunter did not come up and the enemy showed signs of coming forward, he would lead them against the enemy, and they should tell all the soldiers the same. Well, in the evening in every camp the fires were blazing, bon-fires, and cheering and cheering until midnight, from regiment to regiment all around Springfield in every camp. The general was serenaded by different bands that evening; there were fifty or sixty musicians playing at once, all together, feeling happy that he would lead them against the enemy.

Question. When General Hunter came up was he resolved to fight?

Answer. I did not see General Hunter; he came up towards midnight. I heard that he had come up, and hearing that, I was perfectly assured that all was over with us, and that General Frémont would go home the next morning. So I felt no more interest about it. I was only afraid that in case the enemy should attack them very quickly, the soldiers were so disheartened that it was a critical affair. That was the only thing that troubled me—nothing more.

Question. You did not know anything about General Hunter holding a council?

Answer. No, sir; I heard it later; but I did not know it personally at the time.

By the chairman:

Question. Do you think of anything more that you would like to state?

Answer. Nothing more; except that I would like to say a few words about our being disbanded. When we got to St. Louis I was refused rations for my men and forage for my horses. My horses for thirty-six hours had not anything. I went to the quartermaster and asked him why he refused; he told me he had the order. He said we were not regularly in the service. I asked him how he could say that? I asked him if he had not before given me everything I needed, as he had to every one else? I asked him if he did not know that my men were sworn in for three years, or as long as the war lasts? I told him I would turn the horses loose, because I could not see them starve. At last he consented to give us forage, with the condition that he wrote on my requisition that no matter what was done with the body-guard the horses must be supplied, because they belonged to the government. I asked him why he put that in; I told him that it was an insult to my command. I told him he was an old United States officer, and I would like to have him show me as good a command, so well trained, so well drilled as my young soldiers. But he said nothing.

Question. Have you received your pay?

Answer. Yes, sir; I received it after much trouble; but we have been hunted down.

Question. Who was this quartermaster?

Answer. Captain Turnley. I was refused rations for my men; but after General Halleck came up he ordered that I should have everything. But with him we had a great deal of trouble in the last days; we could not get any pay for the men. My men were ragged, had no overcoats, the weather was bad, and the snow falling; they had no accommodations at all; they had been promised their pay from day to day, and were put off day after day, and then they said they could not pay us because we did not give up everything. We did give up everything, and I went to the paymaster, and he said that he had received a letter from the commanding general that the quartermaster said I had not returned everything. I went to the quartermaster and asked him if he considered that there was so much as a pin from the government that I had not returned. He looked over the accounts and found everything complete and perfect, and our pay was ordered. But there was taken from the men's pay all the clothing to the last penny that the government had given us; I protested against it; I said that at least one suit of the clothes should be allowed for this four months' service. But it was all taken out; we paid for everything the government had given us. My men were ragged; their pants and boots were torn to pieces; in the whole army was no such ragged command as mine.

After my command was paid off I reported myself to the commanding general, and requested him to do something with my officers. I recommended them in the highest terms, that they were young men, that I had drilled them, that they were good for service, and the whole western department had not such good officers as they were. He paid no attention to it; said he could do nothing with them. I made as a complaint that they did not make one half with all their pay, as what they had spent for their uniforms and horses if they were turned off now. But that did not matter; their services were not needed, and they were dismissed.

Even here, in Washington, I was hunted. I went to the paymaster general to get travelling expenses for three of my officers and myself—two of us from Philadelphia, and two from New York; they would not pay me, and really insulted me, by telling me that General Frémont had no right to appoint officers all over the country. I showed him an extract I had cut from one of the New York papers, which showed that General Frémont had the right to appoint me; then they said that he had no right to write for his California friends and appoint them to office. Then seeing that we were hunted and insulted, I could not longer bear it, I just told him in plain words, right out before his secretary, that it was a lie. After that, he picked up the papers and ordered me to be paid off. It showed that if I had not taken the hard step against him he had the feeling to keep it back from us.

WASHINGTON, *February* 24, 1862.

Major JAMES M. SAVAGE sworn and examined.

By the chairman:

Question. Were you with General Frémont in the western department?

Answer. Yes, sir.

Question. What was your rank and position?

Answer. At first I was captain; after the 20th of September last I was a major on his staff.

Question. Go on and state what appears to you material touching the conduct of the war in that department.

Answer. During the whole of the time I was in St. Louis, and a portion of the time we were in the field, I was assigned by General Frémont to General Asboth, who was his chief of staff, and I did duty under him. My duties under General Ashboth, in St. Louis, were confined to the reducing to writing of the orders and the dispositions and reports which General Asboth made. Although he was an accomplished scholar he found it difficult to write the English language. Besides that, I had to examine a great many little matters which came up in the course of the administration of such a department. I knew nothing of contracts, with the exception of one that I desire to speak about. That was a contract made with Mr. Sacchi, for horses, and known as the "Sacchi contract." I have known Mr. Sacchi, in New York city, for twelve years. During the whole of that time he has occupied an office in William street, and during a portion of that time, and at present, he resides in Twenty-sixth street, near Fifth avenue. He is a man of family, and generally reputed to be a man of property. His knowledge of the English language is as perfectly good as I have ever known a foreigner to acquire. I wish to say, also, that he enjoys a perfectly good reputation among those who know him in the city of New York. Mr. Sacchi visited St. Louis on the application and at the invitation of General Asboth, and was induced by him to make an offer for a contract to purchase and supply horses. He never, to my knowledge, had more than one or two interviews with General Frémont, and never held any position on his staff, or any office whatever under him. And it may be proper for me to say, as certain charges have been made in the papers, very freely, with regard to the ostentation shown by General Frémont, and his inaccessibility, that during the whole of the time I was there in St. Louis I was at the headquarters every day, and all day, and usually until ten and eleven o'clock at night, and sometimes until midnight, and during the whole of that time I never saw General Frémont in a carriage but twice; and I believe he could hardly have been in a carriage during that time without my knowing it.

The only sign of ostentation or display I ever saw was when the re-enforcements left St. Louis for Cairo. I then understood, and it was generally understood by the staff, that a certain degree of display was then used; that more steamers were taken than were absolutely necessary to carry the troops to Cairo, in order to give the enemy the idea that the re-enforcements were larger than they in fact were. I know also that during the passage down the Mississippi to Cairo, whenever the faster steamers got ahead of the others, we were obliged to tie up to the bank until the others came up, with the intention of going into Cairo with a very full show of force, and as large a display as was possible.

There never was any difficulty in the way of any person who had any military business with General Frémont, which was of the slightest importance to the army, procuring an interview with him. Delays of hours and possibly days might occur in some instances. But where persons came with pressing business, and disclosed it specifically, either to me or to General Asboth, they were always sent up to General Frémont, and had an interview with him. I never heard any specific instance of a person being refused admission, except in the case of one man, who, I am told, stated that he waited three days for admission to General Frémont, and that it was five hours before he could get into the ante-room. By the ante-room he undoubtedly meant the room in which I was stationed. I did not credit the report at all, from the fact that I know the last portion of it could not be true. No person ever had the slightest difficulty in getting into the room in which I was stationed and making known his business to the officers there.

Question. Who was this man?

Answer. I was told by a captain in Colonel Mulligan's regiment that he was a man who came with information of the state of the force at Lexington. Now, if he disclosed the nature of his business, or represented that it related to the armies in the field, I know that he could have met with no delay or difficulty.

Question. Did you accompany General Frémont on his expedition to Springfield?

Answer. Yes, sir. I was assigned to duty at Springfield with General Asboth, and was encamped about a half a mile from General Frémont's headquarters. On the 2d of November, I think, I received reports from Major Clark Wright, an accomplished officer then in command of a battalion there, who had fought at Wilson's Creek on the 10th of August, and who was thoroughly familiar with the country about there, that the enemy had appeared at Wilson's Creek in considerable numbers—I do not now recollect the numbers—and that a much larger force, and, as he concluded from the reports of his scouts, the whole force of General Price was within a few miles of Wilson's Creek. This report was confirmed by other officers of his; by scouts sent out by Major Waring, commanding a regiment of cavalry called the Frémont Hussars; and by several other officers and privates in the regiments of Colonel Rombaner and Colonel Kalmann, and others whose names I do not now recollect. I prepared a report from the statement of Major Wright, which was signed by General Asboth, and transmitted to General Frémont. On the 3d of November I rode out with General Frémont and visited the outposts about Springfield. At several of the outposts we found long trains of wagons drawn by oxen, containing Union families, or families who represented themselves to be such, coming in from Wilson's Creek and vicinity, as they stated, all terrified at the near approach of the enemy, representing in many instances that the men belonging to the family had waited behind until the enemy appeared in sight, and had only escaped by having a few minutes the start.

Question. Were you with the army at the time General Frémont was superseded by General Hunter?

Answer. I was; yes, sir.

Question. Were there any signs of mutiny at the time the troops became aware that General Frémont was superseded?

Answer. The men were very much excited, and I think they could easily have been started up to a mutiny by careless or wicked officers. But I saw nothing on the part of any man that approached a mutiny. The officers themselves, the Germans particularly, were very much excited, and very loud in the expression of their disappointment; one or two of them, in particular, in their denunciation of the conduct of the government in thus acting towards General Frémont. But during the course of the day they seemed to become reconciled to the order, and to make up their minds to obey whatever commander should be placed over them.

Question. What was the bearing and conduct of General Frémont on the occasion when they manifested this dissatisfaction? Was it calculated to increase the dissatisfaction, or to allay it?

Answer. One officer called upon General Frémont and made him a short address, in the presence of several other officers, and in the hearing of many outside of his headquarters, to the effect that his men would fight for General Frémont and under General Frémont, and for nobody else. The reply of General Frémont was less loud, and more difficult for those outside to hear. But I heard enough to show me that General Frémont reproved him for his remarks, and repeated, in substance, the recommendations of his farewell address to the soldiers, to the effect that every man must do his duty, notwithstanding the action of the authorities. I am confident that he did not, in a single instance, countenance or advise a single man leaving the army, but that he would have put down by force, if necessary, any attempt at mutiny.

Question. Do you know anything about his ability to have relieved General Lyon? Were you in a condition to know that?

Answer. No, sir; neither in relation to the Springfield matter, nor the Lexington matter. My mind has been made up from the orders sent and the reports made, and those, I understand, have been furnished to this committee.

Question. Did you accompany General Frémont to Cairo when he re-enforced that place?

Answer. Yes, sir.

Question. What was the condition of things there? What was the amount of force there?

Answer. The force at Cairo, when we reached there, was represented to be 1,200 men, besides a large number of men—whether one, or two, or three regiments, I do not know—whose time had expired, and who were demoralized and disorganized to such a degree that they were without arms, and were waiting there only for their pay.

Question. How many effective, reliable men were there at that time?

Answer. I can only answer from hearsay, that at the time there were only 1,200.

Question. Was the place threatened?

Answer. A large force of the enemy were threatening it, as we learned from all the scouts and spies sent out, at New Madrid; a force, I believe, amounting to about 20,000 men, and an attack was daily and almost hourly anticipated.

Question. So that the place was under the greatest necessity for succor?

Answer. Yes, sir; and the re-enforcements were received with the greatest outbursts of joy and satisfaction, both on the part of the soldiers and officers at Cairo and at Bird's Point; and I would state here that one of the regiments taken by General Frémont to Cairo, at that time, was composed from two regiments whose time was just expiring, and who had been appealed to by General Frémont to serve for the few days that it was supposed would be necessary before they could be replaced by another regiment. They did, in fact, serve for several weeks from the time when they should have been discharged.

Question. What amount of re-enforcement did he take down there at that time?

Answer. About 4,000.

Question. Do you know how it was at Pilot Knob?

Answer. I do not know how it was at Pilot Knob. I know that Cape Girardeau was threatened both at that time and subsequently; and it was regarded generally by officers, and is an undoubted fact, that Cape Girardeau was one of the most important points along the line of the river.

Question. You are acquainted with the condition of General Frémont's forces at that time. Do you think, as a military man, that it was proper under the circumstances, or that he could have relieved General Lyon at that time?

Answer. I think it absolutely impossible for the general to have done more than he did at the time. I never heard, either from General Sigel, or any of the other officers who were present at Wilson's Creek when that battle was fought, with many of whom I have conversed, the slightest hint that General Frémont could, or should, have re-enforced them.

Question. Do you know how it was about Colonel Mulligan?

Answer. I know hardly anything about that Lexington matter?

Question. Is there anything else you know in regard to that department that you deem useful or important for the government to know?

Answer. There is only this one thing that occurs to me at this moment. In a letter of Mr. Thurlow Weed to the Albany Evening Journal, there is this charge made, that the army of General Frémont was guilty, in many cases, of depredations upon the property of Union men; that the divisions of General Sigel and General Asboth, on their march from Tipton to Warsaw, utterly despoiled a Union man by taking his corn, grain, cattle, and everything from his farm. Now, I was with the division of General Asboth on that march, and know, in the first place, that nothing of the kind could have taken place; and in the second place, the division of General Sigel never marched over that line of road from Tipton to Warsaw; but it marched from Sedalia, a point some 30 or 40 miles further up the railroad.

Question. What were General Frémont's orders about that?

Answer. They were very strict upon the officers to restrain their men from any plundering, and I think the army passed through the whole march with as little theft as possible. You cannot always keep soldiers from stealing apples, and chickens, too.

By Mr. Covode:

Question. Did you understand what was the immediate cause of difficulty between General Frémont and Mr. Blair?

Answer. I have never understood it. All that I know is, that Colonel Blair, from being a frequent, almost daily visitor at headquarters, ceased entirely to show himself there; and I knew and heard nothing about the matter, except certain charges that appeared in the newspapers.

By the chairman:

Question. Do you know anything about the contracts about which so much has been said?

Answer. No, sir; except the Sacchi contract, of which I have spoken.

WASHINGTON, *February* 24, 1862.

Colonel I. C. WOODS sworn and examined.

By the chairman:

Question. Were you in the army of the west, under General Frémont?

Answer. I was.

Question. What was your rank and position there?

Answer. I was, in the first place, a major upon the general's staff. I then held a commission as captain in the commissary department from the Secretary of War, the duties of which I never performed, as I was ordered by General Frémont to remain upon his staff. I was promoted by him to a colonelcy, and placed in charge of the transportation.

Question. Did you accompany the army on its way to Springfield?

Answer. I did.

Question. Will you state, in your own way, what you think it material to state in relation to the army there, the administration of the department, anything about contracts, contractors, any misconduct or frauds upon the part of anybody, or anything else you know which you think the public should know?

Answer. I have made a memorandum of a few things, about which there has been some talk, with a few notes in the margin to assist my memory in stating what I have myself observed.

Question. You can use your notes to refresh your memory. The rule of law is, that notes may be used to refresh the memory; but you must state what you know outside of your notes.

Answer. The first memorandum I have is about some Austrian muskets, about which a great deal has been said officially and unofficially. I know those muskets were a kind that had been used for a long time in the Austrian army. That information I obtained from Colonel Albert, who was upon General Frémont's staff. When he first saw the muskets in St. Louis he remarked that they were an old friend of his. I know when the muskets were first offered to General Frémont in New York, at which place I joined him, they were refused upon the ground that the primer, which was used in place of the percussion cap, was not to be had in this country. The battle of Bull Run had not been fought then, and it was supposed that there were a plenty of other arms in the country.

After General Frémont had arrived in St. Louis, and the government had issued orders to have all the arms procurable forwarded from New York to Washington, it became impossible to get other arms. These Austrian arms were then bought; but upon the condition that the importers should manufacture, in New York, this percussion primer (which was used on them instead of a percussion cap,) in sufficient quantities to answer the purpose for these arms. And as quite a large portion of the army of the west were foreign soldiers, and a great many of the officers were familiar with the arm, and a great many of the soldiers had before used it, although it took one more motion to prime it than it did to put the cap on our muskets, still as it took the same bullet—the Minnie bullet—that our muskets did, it was decided that it was absolutely necessary to have them.

There were at that time many companies of home guards who were wanting arms to guard railroad bridges, &c., and it was considered that these arms would answer their purpose.

The facts in relation to the character of these arms have been very carefully and particularly set forth by Captain Callender on another occasion. He is an ordnance officer, and had charge of the St. Louis arsenal for some time. I know that after the arms arrived in St. Louis, Captain Callender took two of them, took out the breech-pin and rifled them, and brought them to headquarters to show how well they rifled. He stated to me then that the breech of these arms was a little thicker in metal than our own muskets, and rifled better than our own muskets did.

One of them was sent to Cincinnati and one to Philadelphia as a sample to be altered by way of experiment. When they were altered they were returned and examined; and Captain Callender made an official report, recommending that they should be altered, and I am pretty sure that he recommended that they should be altered by the Cincinnati manufacturer, as being cheaper than the other, and at the same time answering the purpose.

The reason he did not alter them himself, which he was as competent to do as the person in Cincinnati, and which he has been doing since—for from the time that General Frémont left, up to the middle or last of December, no other arms were sent to the west, but Captain Callender was engaged in rifling these very arms—the reason he did not do it when they were received by General Fremont, and while General Frémont was there, was, that he was engaged in rifling Springfield muskets, of which there were several thousands to be rifled. He had but one rifling machine, which would rifle about 60 a day; and by computation he found that he could not rifle more than enough for two regiments in a month. These Austrian muskets, therefore, were sent to Cincinnati.

Previous to that quite a number of regiments of home guards were supplied with them. I remember that one regiment, which was about 15 miles out from Sedalia on the road to Springfield, learning that a car-load of these altered arms had arrived, marched in to get these arms, and marched back again the same day. Other regiments had them unaltered, all with the understanding that they were to be exchanged for the altered ones when they should be received.

At headquarters in St. Louis, taking into consideration that we had a great many foreign soldiers who were used to these arms, we looked upon that purchase even at first as being a very excellent one; and when it was found that they could be altered and made a very good weapon, it was looked upon as a very economical purchase in every point of view. As they cost but about $11 50 each when ready to be put finally into the hands of our soldiers, it was looked upon as a better and far more economical arm than we could otherwise get.

Now, with reference to the Hall carbines, about which so much has been said. I know nothing about their purchase, but I know a great deal about their issue. I know that when they came there we had no other arms for our cavalry. The 2d Illinois cavalry regiment were supplied entirely with Hall's carbines; four companies of Kansas cavalry were supplied with them, as were other regiments; and 500 of them were sent to General Pope, in North Missouri, to be issued to home guards there. They were issued very quickly after their receipt, and we had no other arms for cavalry to take their place.

There has been something said in regard to a matter of $200 which was wanted by Captain Schwartz, who was recruiting a battery, for recruiting purposes. He came to me for it, and I told him we had no money at headquarters. I sent him, with either a verbal message or a note, to the proper officer who was the mustering officer at the arsenal. He, by the regulations of the department, was the recipient and distributor of the funds for recruiting purposes appropriated by Congress. But he had no funds. In the absence of funds in the hands of the mustering officer it was the business of the quartermaster's department to advance the money. But the quartermaster had no funds, and there were no funds in the department except the funds in the hands of the paymaster.

Captain Schwartz was an educated artillery officer from Baden; had served all through the revolution there, and had served all through the war in Nicaragua. His first officer was a Swede, his second officer a Dane, both of whom had been decorated for gallantry in the Schlesswig-Holstein war; and the battery they were raising promised to be a very efficient one. This was early in August—about the 13th, I think—and the general was very anxious to have the battery perfected, and the only way was to order the paymaster to advance the $200.

I am told by officers who were in the Mexican war that it was a very common thing there, in the exigencies of the war, for one department to turn over funds to another department, to be replaced afterwards when the other department should be in funds again, although it was contrary to regulations. The exigencies of the service in Missouri were, I presume, what induced the general to make that order.

In relation to contracts, I know a great deal about them. We found a beef contract in the Missouri department which had been made with some parties there, which the government had a right to discontinue at any time. General Frémont directed the captain who had charge of the commissary department to advertise the ordinary time for proposals, and then to make a new contract with the lowest bidder, with certain stringent provisions, among which was one for driving beef-cattle along with the army, so that we might have less weight to transport in our wagons. The contract was advertised and let, and it was done wholly and entirely by the officer in charge of the commissary department. Of course the general directed him as to the fact that he should advertise, and it was let regularly to the lowest bidder. Captain Hague said it was a very good contract. So far as that department was concerned, this was the only transaction in the way of contracts that was ever executed in the department, I think, while General Frémont was there.

I think that in the ordnance department there were no contracts whatever issued during the time the general was there, either by his order or by Captain Callender. There were a great many propositions for contracts for furnishing shot and shell. I remember very distinctly that quite a number were placed in my hands for presentation; but the general gave orders after the first was received to send them all to Captain Callender, which was done.

In the matter of guns, field artillery, of which the department had very little, it became necessary to order some made. There was no contract, but Greenwood, of Cincinnati, had made guns for the State of Indiana, and the general ordered him to make some guns for him. He appointed an officer to examine them, to see that they were well bored, &c. The prices were to be the same as charged to the State of Indiana, of which no complaint had been made. Then some parties in St. Louis offered to cast some bronze guns. Their propositions were all referred to Captain Callender. I do not think he made a contract with them, but he gave them an order to furnish some bronze guns.

In the matter of small arms, pistols, sabres, muskets, carbines, and those smaller weapons that come under the supervision of the ordnance department, there was no contract made for them, because, of course, it could not be filled; but orders were made direct to parties in New York and Philadelphia to purchase them. This was to save time, for to have made requisitions would have necessitated the going around by way of Washington, and would have taken a long time. They were, accordingly, ordered direct from the parties by telegraph. That I believe is about the state of facts in reference to the ordnance department.

In reference to the quartermaster's department, I know positively that there never was but one contract made at headquarters, and that was made by Captain Turnley, who had been assigned to the general as quartermaster upon his staff. We were overrun with proposals to buy horses; every one seemed to want us to buy horses. We made a computation one day and found that we had had offers in a very short time for 50,000 horses. There was a proposition came to General Frémont, through General Asboth, for some parties to furnish a thousand horses from Canada. The proposition was first made in New York, as I subsequently learned. But I first heard of it in St. Louis when General Asboth introduced Mr. Sacchi to me. He had previously introduced him to the general. Mr. Sacchi's proposition was to furnish 3,000 horses from Canada. It was very clear that he could not furnish Canadian horses up to the government standard of height. His proposition was to furnish them at $150 each. Finally, as General Asboth was very anxious to have some Canadian horses, the general directed that Mr. Sacchi should be allowed to furnish 1,000 horses, at $130 each, at the government standard. It was very evident to General Asboth and myself, who discussed this matter the very day the contract was executed, that Mr. Sacchi never could execute that contract; that the price was too low, the standard too high, and the time was too short. Subsequently he asked for an extension of time, which General Frémont, upon my recommendation, refused. He then asked permission to furnish the horses from somewhere else, which the general refused. Finally, Mr. Burling, or Betting, the purchaser of the contract, from New York, brought fifty horses there. Captain Turnley requested Mr. Reeside to inspect them, and he passed two only. It is fair to say that only two horses were delivered under contract. The fifty horses were taken by Captain Turnley, there being no horses in St. Louis, and General Smith, at Paducah, being in want of horses; but the other 48 were purchased in open market after being rejected under the contract. That was the only contract for horses executed by the direct order of General Frémont.

There were several memoranda for horses made by Captain Turnley, but they were not made into contracts. The government was at liberty to take five, fifty, or one hundred horses, as it pleased. The Frémont Hussars were buying horses under the command of Major Waring. Their officers were all foreign officers. Two were Austrian cavalry officers, and had served at Solferino. The captains and nearly all the lieutenants were foreign officers. They recruited their ranks very quickly, principally from the foreign population of St. Louis. They were very anxious for horses—good horses. They came to General Asboth and made strong representations for good horses, which they could not get at the quartermaster's department. They brought there two or three horse contractors, and by direction of General Frémont, through General Frémont and the officers of the hussars, Captain Turnley made a few memoranda for horses, the horses to be inspected by Colonel Morrill, an officer of the United States army. These memoranda were the only memoranda of horses made at headquarters, and I think that perhaps 500 or 600 horses were delivered under these memoranda. The great bulk of the horses bought in the western department were bought in open market. According to a report that has been made of the number of horses bought by General McKinstry, made by his chief clerk, a few of which were bought before General Frémont went there, there were some 6,000 horses bought, of which only some 200 or 300 were bought under contract. The rest were all bought in open market. Of these 6,000 horses we never heard anything connected with them at headquarters. Major McKinstry bought them in open market as he pleased, and two-thirds of them he bought from persons recommended by Colonel Blair. And I will state in this connexion that we were very careful in St. Louis always. We found the city full of secessionists, and it was with great difficulty that we could get our baggage carried through the streets up to headquarters, the secession feeling was so strong. We exercised a great deal of caution in order to learn who to deal with. We required some sort of certificate about every man we dealt with. And that was the case in regard to the 6,000 horses bought by Major McKinstry. But those were not all the horses bought there. When Captain Turnley first came there he made an estimate of the number of horses and mules wanted. As I had had something to do with horses and mules for several years, and expected to have something to do with the transportation there, I submitted to the general a written statement, objecting to the use of horses for transportation purposes, and urging the use of mules. I objected to horses being bought in St. Louis, for, though St. Louis is a good mule mart, government had stripped Missouri of all good horses. Captain Turnley made an estimate for some three-quarters of a million of dollars, sent it on here, and it was approved and the money placed to his credit in New York.

At the time we went down to Cairo I talked with the general about buying stock, and made some representations to him about the difficulty of getting good stock, the possibility of getting it good if he dealt promiscuously with any and every man who had stock to sell, and the total folly of endeavoring to get good horses by contract. I urged the general to select some person, as an inspector of horses, to inspect all that were wanted for the western department. I recommended Mr. John E. Reeside, of this city, for that purpose. I had had a great deal to do with stock, and I had found Mr. Reeside the best judge of horses I ever saw; and, as I wanted to favor the interests of the western department, I recommended this man, though he was no friend of mine. The general sent for him, and gave him a commission to inspect horses. I also urged the general to buy all his horses in Ohio and not in St. Louis. Mr. Reeside went to Ohio, where I knew he could get good horses, and from there shipped horses to St. Louis, and all the best horses we had in St. Louis came from Ohio. Two-thirds of the horses used by the body-guard were Ohio horses, and they performed remarkably well. Their march from the time they left camp in the morning, on one occasion, fought their battle, and returned to camp, was ninety-two miles, without hardly loosing a girth, and not a horse was hurt. The battle of Fredericktown was an artillery battle, and the horses there were Ohio horses, and so on through the department; wherever you found good cavalry horses perform good service they were almost generally Ohio horses. The State of Massachusetts bought all her horses, as we bought Ohio horses. In reference to other contracts in the quartermaster's department, General Frémont stated he would have as little to do with contracts as possible; and when people sent in propositions they were almost universally sent to the quartermaster's department without their being shown to General Frémont, unless there was something special about them. There were a great many propositions for all sorts of articles. There was one particular proposition that was presented at headquarters for a long time. Mr. Gurney, of Chicago, recommended by a great many of the first men of Chicago and Illinois, and Mr. How, an ex-mayor of St. Louis, made a proposition to furnish a large quantity of supplies for the army, amounting in the aggregate to three-quarters of a million of dollars. They were around the headquarters for three or four weeks. That was about the only one that was pressed there. The rest were generally satisfied when they were refused, and went away. I think this one was pressed for two or three weeks. Mr. Gurney saw the general two or three times about it; and it was urged by Colonel Blair that this contract should be made, so as to give employment to the Union citizens of St. Louis. The proposition was sent to me after the general had first approved it, and I indorsed upon the proposition a recommendation to General McKinstry to make the contract if the prices and quality were equal to those he generally made. General McKinstry refused to make the contract, stating that so large a contract for so much money should not be made without advertisement; but it is a significant fact that some six or seven days General McKinstry did give an order to Mr. How for about one-third of this very order, amounting to about $225,000. I doubt if there was anything wrong about it. General McKinstry had a memorandum from the general to furnish supplies for fifteen or twenty regiments; he could not get any supplies from Washington, and this was among various orders that he gave to get these supplies. I believe that is about all the details I have to state in regard to contracts, except that it was not the policy of General Frémont at headquarters to have anything to do with contracts.

There was a contract made for the manufacture of cars; that was made by General McKinstry, General Frémont directing him to make it. Then there was a contract made by General McKinstry with Mr. Beard for fortifications; but the prices and everything connected with that contract were regulated by General McKinstry. I recollect very distinctly having written a letter in which General McKinstry was directed to make the contract, the prices being left to him. The reason for making that contract with Mr. Beard was that the officers in charge of the fortifications were getting along very slowly, and it was necessary to get some one else who would carry the work along night and day, as the city was then very disturbed, and it was deemed necessary to have some fortifications and mount them with guns to control the city. I believe I have now referred to all the material contracts.

By the chairman:

Question. It has been said that the prices paid for these fortifications were very extravagant. What do you know about that?

Answer. I know nothing about that; I only know that General Frémont also knew nothing about the prices. I do know that in the order which I wrote myself, and which I took a great deal of pains with, because I wanted to be sure and protect the general in every possible way, I threw upon General McKinstry the responsibility of fixing the prices. But as to the prices themselves, whether they were high or low, I am no judge.

Question. What else do you know, connected with that department, that would be of interest?

Answer. I would like to mention one fact here which came to my knowledge while I was in St. Louis. During the time the St. Louis arsenal was being threatened by the secessionists, when there were 30,000 of the best Springfield muskets stored there, which the secessionists were determined to get, at that very time this arsenal was busily engaged, under the contract of Major Hagner, in rifling muskets for General Buckner, of Kentucky, for the Kentucky State guards; and those arms, after being altered, were sent to Kentucky and supplied to the State guard. That information I received from Captain Tracy, 10th infantry, who was on the general's staff in Missouri.

When we went to St. Louis the government had no credit, and it was with some little difficulty that anybody could be found willing to trust them. The merchants had expected that the secessionists would take the city, and they were timid and afraid to trust the government. That will account, perhaps, for large orders given by General McKinstry on particular firms he may have dealt with. I know that was the fact, so much so that officers of the army were unwilling to appear alone in the streets with their uniforms on.

In reference to Cairo, I would say that the question was agitated at headquarters whether the general would go himself with the force he could muster, and try to protect the place, or whether he would send out all the force he had on the road to Springfield. He could not do both; that was the opinion at headquarters. Jeff. Thompson, the rebel, was in below Cape Girardeau, in the swamps; and Hardee had come up to Pocahontas, in Arkansas, with quite a force and well armed. General Pillow had landed at New Madrid with a large force, estimated at from 12,000 to 15,000 men. And the three were threatening Cairo. We received information that they intended to cross the river at Commerce, burn the bridges on the Illinois Central railroad, and then attack Bird's Point, and so go on and attack Cairo. General Frémont persuaded some of the German troops whose time had expired—one regiment of them—to embark in these steamers for Cairo. When we got down there we found that there was only one regiment at Cairo, and those were three months men, whose times were expiring, and they were about being paid off. Other three months regiments were paid off, and were about reorganizing. I was informed by Colonel Wagner, at Cairo, at the time we landed there, that there were only some 600 men under arms there. Others had been allowed a parole to go home before joining for the war. I doubt if it is known to the public at all, the fact I have stated about there being but 600 men under arms at Cairo then. Of course we did not allow that to get out at that time.

Question. What was the force of the enemy then threatening the points along there?

Answer. We never could ascertain exactly. Jeff. Thompson, as near as we could understand, had about 3,500 men. He was in a secession portion of the country, and there was a railroad from Bird's Point out to where he was. Then Hardee's force we could never fully ascertain; as near as we could learn he had some 6,000 or 7,000 men, and was moving up from Arkansas; and we could never fairly determine where he intended to operate. But if he and Jeff. Thompson had united their forces upon Bird's Point they could have captured that place and Cairo when General Frémont went down there. Then at the same time that General Frémont took this force to Cairo, on the very day he returned to St. Louis, he had ordered three regiments to re-enforce General Lyon, one from Rolla, one from Jefferson City, and one from some other place. They would not have reached him in season, as the result showed. But there were three regiments ordered to his assistance.

Question. It has been stated that there were seven thousand or eight thousand men in North Missouri at that time which could have been disposed of for the assistance of General Lyon.

Answer. I think there were four regiments in North Missouri, a portion of them guarding the North Missouri railroad, and a portion guarding the Hannibal and St. Joseph railroad, under command of General Pope. General Pope telegraphed from Quincy to General Frémont as early as the 18th of July for permission to take these regiments in Illinois and go up the North Missouri railroad and take possession of that and the Hannibal and St. Joseph railroad. He did go there and fight one or two small battles. The rebels had burned one or two bridges of the Hannibal and St. Joseph railroad. It was deemed of great consequence to keep open that road, as it was the only reliable means of communication with Fort Leavenworth and Kansas. General Frémont could have withdrawn those troops from North Missouri, but it was believed that if he did so the whole country there would have risen in arms at once.

Question. How many troops could have been withdrawn from there at the sacrifice of that portion of the State?

Answer. I suppose he could have withdrawn three regiments. I think he did withdraw three regiments after the battle of Springfield, and send one or two of them to Rolla. But he would have left these roads unguarded and permitted the enemy to rise there.

Question. If he had sent those regiments to the aid of General Lyon, would they have increased his force so as to have made him strong enough to stand against Price?

Answer. It was not supposed at headquarters that General Lyon, with the force he had, the time of three or four of his regiments having nearly expired, would fight the enemy at all, but that he would retire, in front of the enemy and let Sigel take command of the rear guard and retire as Sigel did from Carthage. The so-called battle of Carthage was but a retreat, the enemy having been kept at bay with artillery. General Lyon had all the transportation at his end of the line—one hundred and seventy-five six-mule teams, and, I think, one hundred and twenty-five two-horse teams. His force was small, and he could not spare any of his troops to escort this transportation back again. He kept them all there, and that prevented the other regiments from having the transportation they required, and which they would have otherwise had if he could have spared an escort to take it back. Knowing these facts, it was supposed at headquarters that he would retire before Price until General Frémont could have the opportunity of sending him re-enforcements, and then take the field offensively again as soon as the re-enforcements reached him.

Question. What have you to say about General Frémont's ostentatious display and exclusiveness?

Answer. So far as the matter of exclusiveness is concerned, I suppose I know more about it than anybody else. When he went there he had not a thorough and efficient staff, and he was obliged to attend to everything that came up with such materials as he had. The three months men going out and the three years men coming in made an enormous amount of work at headquarters. For a period of several weeks I was the channel of communication between outsiders and General Frémont. The guard were stationed below at the stairs leading up to his office. We were in the habit of rising about daylight and breakfasting after we had done considerable work. I remember one day in particular I came down about half past ten o'clock, after getting my breakfast. My office was about twenty feet off. I did not reach it until half past two in the afternoon; there were so many there who had to be disposed of. So far as the charge of exclusiveness is concerned, it was absolutely necessary and essential that he should put some guard between himself and the public, to discriminate what business should go to him and what should go to the other officers. Nine-tenths of all the business went to other officers. But volunteers and others, not understanding where they were to go, assumed that everything was done at headquarters. Soldiers who wanted passes over railroads, or who wanted to get into the hospital—in fact, every form of business came to headquarters.

Question. Was he unreasonably exclusive for a commanding general having such a department under him?

Answer. My opinion is that he was not exclusive enough. That was my opinion at the time, and I have never changed it. I considered that he was too anxious to accommodate those who called to see him. So far as ostentation was concerned, I was a member of his family during the entire time he was in St. Louis. We occupied a very fine residence in St. Louis, but it was simply because a relative of his wife offered it to him for his occupation; and doing the business he did, it was absolutely necessary that he should eat, and sleep, and do his work all under one roof, and that necessitated the taking a large house, where he could have all his officers at work together. For a period of five weeks, while I was there, he never went further from his door than on to the sidewalk, where he went to review some troops that had arrived and wished to be reviewed there in front of the house. The house was a very fine house, and he took some pains to take care of it. Zagoni's horse, which was intended as a school for officers, and given out as such, in which were a great many gentlemen of education and fine attainments who had enlisted in the ranks, ten or eleven physicians, graduates, or many of them—a portion of their duties was to attend about headquarters. That was as much for the good of the men as to take care of the property. At the same time, when we first went there, it was necessary to have some secure and safe place for the arms of the guard, for we were afraid the city would rise and break out in rebellion. Indeed, General McKinstry, the provost marshal, reported once or twice that they intended to rise. The arms of the guard were put in a room in the basement that had iron shutters, and it was necessary they should be there to guard that. I never saw anything in the way of ostentation.

Question. Do you know any reason why he was superseded at the time he was?

Answer. I think I do. We all had a conviction on that subject at headquarters. Not that I ever talked with the general about it; but we on the staff all had the conviction that the primary cause of his being recalled was his proclamation.

Question. Were you present at the time he was superseded at Springfield?

Answer. In one sense I was present, and in one I was not. My tent was near that of the general, and when the civilian came with this letter from General Curtis I was in the yard, but not in the room where the general was.

Question. What do you know about the situation of the enemy at that time, whether there was any enemy there, and how near the enemy was?

Answer. We had no doubt in our minds that the enemy were near, and we subsequently had positive testimony that the enemy was near us. The day the general was superseded—I think it was Saturday, the 2d of November—I rode out with the general to the outer pickets, and we there found on one of the roads a refugee family that had come in from Wilson's Creek. We talked with one of them, a very intelligent man, who stated that he had left home in consequence of the Texas ranger cavalry coming there. Four or five of them came to his house, and there were some 400 of them close by. Colonel Richardson, who had charge of the recruits, told me positively, several times over, that he was satisfied, from what his scouts and spies represented to him, that the enemy were marching from Cassville to Springfield towards us—his spies had seen them.

Question. How far is Cassville from Springfield?

Answer. I do not now remember; I have forgotten. The day that he was superseded, Lieutenant Max Tosk and Mr. Thompson went to Price's army with the convention between General Frémont and General Price for the pacification of the State. We looked upon that as one of the most important measures that had come up during the war. General Price had offered to confine the war to the regular armies in the field, and do away with the guerilla fighting entirely, and that no man should be disturbed for any opinion he entertained, if he did not express them and force them upon the public. Documents were drawn up, and Mr. Thompson and Lieutenant Tosk went with them to Price's army; and when they came back they stated emphatically that it was the intention of the enemy to fight us. Lieutenant Tosk said he overheard conversations between staff-officers of General McCulloch, in which they expressed their intention to give us battle, and that they were on their way to do so; and when they heard that General Frémont was superseded, they received it as very gratifying intelligence. They represented their army as being very large—from 40,000 to 50,000 strong. There was no doubt upon the mind of any member of General Frémont's staff, or of any officer in the army that I conversed with, that the enemy were close at hand and intended to give us battle.

Question. Had General Frémont made any disposition for a battle?

Answer. When General Frémont was superseded he was waiting for General Pope to come up with his troops, the most pressing orders having been sent back to them to hurry forward, in order that we could go forward and meet the enemy. The most pressing orders were sent to General Hunter to come up with his division. But General Frémont would not wait for him after General Pope came up. When he was superseded on Saturday his first intention was to leave on Sunday morning, and go back to St. Louis, but he was persuaded by his officers to remain. There was a written request presented to him, signed by the principal generals, requesting him to remain until General Hunter came up, and, I believe, involved in that request was one that he should give battle to the enemy. He decided to remain until General Hunter came up. On Sunday, when it was supposed the enemy was close at hand, he called a conference of the leading officers in his command, and in that conference all the dispositions in reference to a battle the ensuing morning were made. General Hunter came up while the conference was in session, and the plan agreed upon was submitted to him, and, upon the supposition that the enemy were close at hand, it was believed that a battle would ensue the next morning. General Frémont had insisted to lead the army if General Hunter had not come up.

Question. Did the army show any mutinous disposition when it was ascertained that General Frémont had been superseded?

Answer. There was no mutinous manifestation on the part of the soldiers at all. A great many of the German officers, who were very much attached to General Frémont, came to headquarters and expressed their sympathy for him, and stated that they were very sorry to part with him, and one or two made speeches, and there were cheers for the general. But I saw nothing on the part of the officers or men of what I would call a mutinous disposition.

Question. What was the bearing of General Frémont in regard to any demonstrations that were made? What was his course of conduct on being superseded?

Answer. He seemed very much relieved; was much more pleasant and cheerful than he had been for weeks before. He issued an order, through Colonel Eaton, relinquishing the command of the army to General Hunter. He then wrote his farewell address to the army, and both of them were printed. We had taken a little printing press along with us, and had got a detail of printers from the various regiments to work it, and had found some type and printing paper in Springfield, and were doing the printing for the army. That order relinquishing the command and the farewell address were printed and circulated. General Frémont was much more cheerful than I had seen him for weeks before.

Question. It has been said that they cheered him, and made very strong demonstrations in his favor, and perhaps against the government, and he bowed assent to it.

Answer. There was no demonstration of soldiers made at all until we started out of Springfield on Monday morning. I rode out with the general then, riding just in rear of him. The only military demonstration was made by the Benton Cadets, an infantry corps he had raised, intending to make it a school for infantry officers, as the body-guard was for cavalry officers. The Benton Cadets were drawn up in the road and presented arms as the general passed. That was the only military demonstration that was made. We did not pass through the different camps, but as we passed the cadets and through the town the soldiers would run out from their camps, come up to the fence, and those who knew the general would cheer him. So far as regards any mutinous conduct on the part of the army, I never saw anything at all of it. There were some few of the officers who felt very much aggrieved, who felt they had lost everything, and who, in a private way, may have felt for the moment that they would be willing to do almost anything. But it was one of those momentary feelings which they did not give expression to as a general thing, and I doubt if any of that came to the ears of General Frémont. If it did, I am perfectly certain that he did not listen to it for an instant, but promptly rebuked it.

Question. Are there any other matters of importance you desire to mention?

Answer. Our great want in the western department was the want of money. There was very little money ever sent there. A great many things could have been bought cheaper than they were if the government had furnished us money to pay for them. The quartermaster's department particularly could have dealt to much better advantage if they had had money. But not having it, they were under the necessity of dealing with those who had money or credit. In regard to extravagance, I am of opinion, and I have not hesitated to express that opinion publicly, that the western department during General Frémont's administration will be found to have been more cheaply administered, so far as regards dollars and cents, than any other department of the army. Our provisions cost less than anywhere else; our horses cost no more; the transportation of the men cost no more; the arms for the department cost no more than they did anywhere else; our purchase of Austrian muskets was a very economical one. the clothing and equipments for the men only cost the additional freight from the east; our army did not cost half as much as any other army of the same size in the country, for the reason that they did not have the clothing—they never were properly clothed. I have here copies of requisitions made from every division in October for overcoats and blankets. Not one-half of our army had overcoats, but used blankets instead. The Benton Cadets went all the way to Springfield without overcoats, and so did the body-guard; the army did not have them.

The provisions that we consumed between the terminus of the railroad and Springfield, the forage and hay for the horses, cost next to nothing. When we got it from secessionists we paid nothing for it. When we got it from Union men we gave them printed certificates of the market prices, with the statement that they would be paid if they proved their continued loyalty. The army lived on about half rations during the entire march from Sedalia to Springfield. Every mill anywhere near the line of our march we took possession of. We gathered the wheat in wagons. We had millers with us who ground the wheat, and the army was fed in that way. In Springfield General Asboth's division was fed almost entirely on corn-meal and beef. The rations were reduced from 2,200 and odd pounds to the thousand rations down to 800 and odd pounds, so that feeding the army with beef at 3½ cents per pound, and corn at 25 cents a bushel, made it very cheap supporting the army.

In the matter of transportation we had the most motley assemblage of wagons that ever any army had. We had ox wagons, two, four, and six yokes, horse and mule wagons of every kind. We had government transportation, our own transportation, and pressed transportation. However, that relates rather to the question of speed in getting over the road, than to economy.

A great deal has been said about musical directors, adlatus, &c. General Frémont had no staff of any kind allowed him by the government. As is well known, previous to this rebellion there never was much necessity for a staff. A major general by the law of July, 1829, was allowed three aids, to be selected from the army. The War Department construed that "army" meant line of the army, and they would not give him aids out of the various departments that had been charged with staff duties. I was a captain in the commissary department: they would not allow General Frémont to select me as one of his aids. When General Frémont ordered me to leave St. Louis to accompany him, General Halleck threatened me with arrest if I went, and I had to remain. The law of August 5, 1861, allowing major generals to nominate to the President for appointment, gave as many aids as a major general wanted. Under that law General Frémont appointed a great many people to assist him; but he did not appoint them in the sense understood by the public. His appointments were especially and particularly contingent upon the confirmation of the President. He complied strictly with the law. And having selected fifteen or eighteen, whatever the number was that he had, it became necessary to assign to them certain duties. He assigned Colonel Albert, who was an officer of fourteen years' experience in the Austrian army—who had fought, I believe, in twenty-eight pitched battles—he assigned him to General Asboth, who called him an adlatus, which means an aid to the chief of staff. Of course General Frémont let him call him whatever he pleased. Colonel Albert was thoroughly familiar with all the routine of a soldier's duty. Major Darsheimer was assigned to postal duties. Captain Tracy was assigned to commissary's duties. He did not receive any commissary stores; he made no contracts; but he carried the orders to those who did provide those stores. I never held a dollar's worth of public property in my hands while there. As a staff-officer I avoided that, although a captain in the commissary department. I was simply a channel of communication for the general's orders to those who provided the articles wanted. I never made any contracts; I never was ordered to do so. Captain Waldaner, on the staff, was called the musical director. Congress had provided for the enlistment of twenty-four musicians for each infantry regiment, and sixteen musicians for each cavalry regiment. But Congress had provided no way to obtain the instruments for these musicians, and there were continued applications for them. Captain Waldaner was directed to arrange for the ordering of these instruments, and to arrange with the adjutants of the regiments to take charge of the matter. And so on with the different officers throughout the staff. They were appointed under the act of August 5, and were assigned to this, that, or the other duty, so as to subdivide the duty, and thus give greater efficiency to the staff. It is stated in General Thomas's report, and elsewhere, that members of General Frémont's staff were interested as speculators. As I was with the general from the time he started from New York to the time he left St. Louis to return east, and as I knew every staff officer he had, I am as conversant with the facts connected with them as any one can be. And I state, confidently, that, in my opinion, no member of his staff ever had a dollar's interest in any contract, purchase, or sale; no interest, directly or indirectly, in anything connected with the furnishing of supplies. Captain Haskell was not a contractor, but a seller of mules to the government before he went on the staff. I know he did not want to go upon the staff, and did not know he had been appointed until he saw it announced publicly. And he then immediately assigned away all interest he had in those matters. I saw him every day, as he was on the staff, and I know he tried to do his duty to the general and to the country, as far as he was able. I had no interest in contracts at all. On the contrary, I probably sacrificed as much as any man ever did sacrifice who ever went upon any general's staff in this country, for I had a large interest in Texas before the war commenced, and there was a great deal of that still left; and I sacrificed the whole of it that I might have something to do with putting down this rebellion—not particularly in going upon General Frémont's staff. No one knows, perhaps, as well as myself, except General Frémont himself, of the economy and management of that department. Let me refer here to one matter I think of in relation to the Lexington affair. It has been said that General Frémont did not receive a man who brought news that Colonel Mulligan was in great stress and danger. I know more about that than any one else. When General Frémont retired at night we were very careful to allow no one to disturb him. If anything special came it was brought to me. About twelve or one o'clock at night the guard came up and awoke me, and said there was a communication from captain so and so. I looked it over and saw that it was something in reference to Lexington, and that we had received the same information that day by telegraph. I said, "Tell him to call in the morning." He was very pertinacious to see General Frémont; but I sent him away, as we had already received the same information. Now, in reference to sending succor to Lexington, I had the copies of the orders in my hand; I wrote a great many of the telegraphic despatches. I know that Colonel Jefferson C. Davis was ordered to take his troops, with three days' rations in their knapsacks, and break through the enemy's lines and relieve Colonel Mulligan. Orders were sent to Sturgis, and Lane, and Davis to make a combined movement for the relief of Lexington. The reason why those orders did not succeed was because Colonel Mulligan, according to our views at headquarters, had no business on that side of the river. He ought to have put the river between him and the enemy before they took his steamers. While he had the control of the steamers he should have put his men upon them and have taken them to the other side of the river, where he could have united with Sturgis, and then with him he could have again crossed the river and joined General Lane. General Sturgis arrived upon the river bank, but had no means of crossing, and had to leave.

By Mr. Gooch:

Question. Did Colonel Mulligan's orders permit him to do that, or were they peremptory—in such terms as to exclude him from doing that?

Answer. No, sir; he had no orders in reference to those matters at all. The movement across the river is one of those things about which an officer must exercise his own judgment. That is never provided for, except when an officer is ordered to hold a post at all hazards. Colonel Mulligan was never so ordered.

Question. Do you know the order to Colonel Mulligan about Lexington?

Answer. Yes, sir, because I was familiar with the order that directed him to occupy Lexington. He was simply directed to move to Lexington and occupy it. It was one of those points which it was not considered necessary to hold at all hazards. I did not see that order, but I understood it.

Question. Do you know that, by the terms of the order, he was authorized to cross the river if he had thought best?

Answer. I know that as well as any man can know it who has never seen the order. I know that, according to his instructions, he should have crossed the river. He had general instructions to occupy Lexington.

Question. Had he any orders, do you know, to hold Lexington at all hazards?

Answer. No, sir.

Question. His instructions were general, and in your judgment it was his duty to have taken the other side of the river?

Answer. I do not put it upon my judgment, because I am not a military man. But my own judgment corroborates the judgment of military men on the staff, that in the absence of positive instructions to hold the place at all hazards, it was his duty to put the river between the enemy and himself. For instance, Fort Leavenworth was to be held at all hazards and at all costs, as essential for the protection of that section of country there. But Lexington was not a place of that importance. There is no dispute about the bravery with which the the troops fought at Lexington. But Colonel Mulligan had within his intrenchments a regiment of cavalry, and no officer in defence of a post wants any cavalry inside intrenchments for they are positively an incumbrance and not a benefit.

By Mr. Covode:

Question. I discover that you are familiar with all the transactions there; can you tell at what time the first difficulties took place between General Frémont and the administration here, or the parties representing it?

Answer. I think I can pretty closely. As I remarked before, the general issued his proclamation; then the President requested him to modify it. He telegraphed word back to the President that he would modify it if ordered to do so. The President ordered the modification. Then about that time came this difficulty about the Howe & Gurney contract. There was a great pressure made at headquarters to have that contract executed.

Question. Did Colonel Blair want this contract for these men?

Answer. They were indorsed by Colonel Blair. He introduced them to General Frémont. He was their channel of communication.

Question. Do you know the date of that contract? As far as I can ascertain the relations between General Frémont and Colonel Blair were good up to the 24th of August, judging from letters. Now, I want to see how soon after that contract was refused?

Answer. The contract was not refused by General Frémont; but General McKinstry was recommended to make it if the prices and qualities were the same as under other contracts. But General McKinstry refused to make that contract.

Question. What time was the contract refused by General McKinstry?

Answer. I think it was the 25th of August that General McKinstry refused to make the contract; and then, singularly enough, on the 6th of September, General McKinstry gave this Mr. Howe a memorandum to furnish 10,000 infantry overcoats; 25,000 pairs army sewed shoes; 5,000 uniform coats; 10,000 trousers; 15,000 drawers; 15,000 flannel shirts; 20,000 pairs stockings; 5,000 blankets; 5,000 haversacks; 5,000 canteens, cork and strap; 50 sergeant's sabres; 5,000 fatigue overalls; 5,000 infantry hats, trimmed; and 5,000 blue flannel sackcoats. After he had refused to make the contract with

Howe & Gurney, he then gave Howe this memorandum. You could not say that it was for any particular number of men. But the value of the contract asked for was about three-quarters of a million of dollars.

Question. Were the relations between General Frémont and Colonel Blair good up to the time that contract was refused?

Answer. Yes, sir.

By Mr. Julian:

Question. Did Blair himself apply in person to General Frémont for the whole of this contract?

Answer. Yes, sir. Colonel Blair was one of the very few men who was allowed access to General Frémont at all hours. The sentinel on the stairs below had a list of persons who could pass up at all times. Colonel Blair could walk up at any time to see General Frémont, or any of the family, and he could take others up with him. I never at any time introduced either Mr. Gurney or Mr. Howe. They came there by direction of Colonel Blair.

Question. The relations between General Frémont and Colonel Blair were good up to the time that large contract was rejected?

Answer. That is what we understood at headquarters.

Question. Did you discover any immediate change after that was rejected?

Answer. Yes, sir. The first we heard were rumors from outside that Mr. Blair was speaking against General Frémont among the citizens and people there.

Question. Did you hear anything of that before this claim was rejected?

Answer. I cannot fix the exact date in my mind. But Mr. Blair did not come to General Frémont from about that time. I think he was getting dissatisfied previous to that time, but it culminated in that.

Question. In what way did General Frémont indicate his refusal of two-thirds of the contract? Did he do it by enclosing in brackets a portion of the offer?

Answer. The offer was an offer to furnish so and so. General Frémont had made some lines, or scores, or marks upon it, and passed it over to me, and told me to send that to General McKinstry. I wrote across the back of it an indorsement in my own handwriting, and wrote it as I did all other indorsements. I was opposed to contracts coming to headquarters; I was opposed to people speculating and making money out of the government. I wrote on it that General McKinstry was recommended to make the within contract, and then named the qualifications.

Question. Did you sign General Frémont's name to it?

Answer. No, sir. I carried it to General Frémont and he wrote his name on it.

By Mr. Gooch:

Question. That was an offer to furnish so many goods?

Answer. Yes, sir.

Question. Do I understand you that it was to be accepted with General McKinstry's approval for a portion of it?

Answer. For one-third.

Question. It was not approved generally by General Frémont for the whole amount?

Answer. No, sir; not all for the whole amount, but recommended for about one-third.

Question. How was the one-third indicated?

Answer. He made some marks upon it. He made some marks upon the margin, and indicated that one-third of that was the amount that he would recommend; except some articles which he erased. I think the proposition contained wagons; I know it contained harness. General McKinstry had ordered all the wagons that were wanted; or if it did not contain wagons it was some article that General McKinstry had enough of before. General Frémont then indicated upon the margin one-third of what was left. And the recommendation which I wrote and which he signed was for what he had indicated.

Question. What did General Frémont put upon that document to indicate that he was willing to give one-third of it?

Answer. They wrote a proposition to do so and so. I think it was written upon foolscap paper, and it came to General Frémont folded so that it would go into a large envelope. He drew his pen through certain articles which he had enough of already. He then indicated one-third upon the margin of the rest of the articles. I do not now remember the exact form in which he indicated that.

Question. The writing which he put upon the paper conveyed to General McKinstry the intelligence that he was willing a contract should be made for one-third, but not for the whole?

Answer. That is my recollection. Then the indorsement I wrote upon the paper covered it as it then existed.

Question. With the limitations General Frémont had then put upon it?

Answer. Yes, sir.

By Mr. Julian:

Question. You do not remember whether General Frémont indicated the one-third on the inside by writing on the margin or by marks around the articles?

Answer. My impression is that he drew a line around the articles and then wrote upon the side some words to indicate that he was willing to let a contract for one-third be made. Mr. Blair was near run down with applications; everybody wanted his recommendation. And for the first three weeks when Mr. Blair was friendly to General Frémont I sent to him a dozen times to know whether such and such a man were good men. For example, a refugee by the name of Morse came there and wanted to be a government inspector, and wanted government to buy horses of refugees from southwestern Missouri. I required him to get a recommendation from Colonel Blair, which he did. And General Frémont decided that he would discriminate in favor of refugees who were driven from their homes and had horses and mules to sell. He did that as a matter of policy to create good feeling in the State.

By Mr. Covode:

Question. Did Blair continue to recommend anything after the failure to get this large contract?

Answer. I cannot fix the exact date, but about that time friendly relations between them were broken off.

Question. Who recommended you to General Frémont?

Answer. Montgomery Blair. I had been doing business for his department for three years.

By Mr. Julian:

Question. He knew you well?

Answer. Yes, sir; I was in Charleston on my way to Texas when Fort Sumter was bombarded. I immediately came north and volunteered to Judge Blair to do anything he wanted me to do. I went over to Baltimore, when communication was interrupted, and did what he wanted done there, and then I looked around for further opportunity of doing something, and he recommended me to General Frémont, who did not know me at that time. The following from my official report as directior of transportation, made to General Frémont in November last, gives the facts in reference to many important matters connected with the western department:

CONNEXION OF PACIFIC AND IRON MOUNTAIN RAILROADS, AND ITS ADVANTAGES AS A MILITARY MEASURE.

Some time prior to the date of my appointment, the rails had, by your order, been laid down, which joined the Pacific and Iron Mountain railroads, and this connexion being made to pass along the city levee, both roads had, in common, an excellent landing on the Mississippi river.

The connexion of these two roads, completed September 12th, placed at your control, for use upon either, the entire rolling stock of both.

For moving troops up the Pacific road, which is the longer of the two, only a limited number of cars or engines could be borrowed for any length of time from the Iron Mountain road; but if, on the other hand, there had arisen a necessity for concentrating troops upon Ironton, it could have been done with great rapidity. You could have placed several regiments upon cars at Rolla, at Syracuse, or Jefferson City, (points on the Pacific road,) taking upon the same train troops from Benton barracks, and the arsenal in the city; while steamers from points up the Mississippi could have landed their forces at the railroad junction on the levee, and the whole have been moved over the Iron Mountain railroad to their destination, without change of cars, even to those regiments passing through the streets of this city. Trains have been taken by us from the arsenal, along the levee, through the streets, and thence over the Pacific road to Jefferson City.

On the 24th of September two Illinois regiments were disembarked from steamers at the levee, placed on board the cars at the railroad junction, with all their equipage, and without delay from the want of wagon transportation, were taken by rail to their destination at Ironton. From Ironton, the 1st Nebraska regiment, Colonel Thayer, with all its camp and garrison equipage, was placed upon the same trains, and taken to Syracuse, on the Pacific railroad, halting, as it passed through the streets of St. Louis, only long enough for the citizens and soldiers to exchange congratulations. Syracuse was the rendezvous for General McKinstry's division, to which Colonel Thayer's regiment belonged, and it was, at the date I refer to, the western terminus of the Pacific railroad, as Colonel Bissell had not, at that time, finished repairing the railroad bridge over the Lamine river—destroyed by order of Governor Jackson.

TELEGRAPH LINES.

At the time of your arrival in St. Louis there was no telegraphic communication between St. Louis and Ironton, or along the line of the Iron Mountain railroad; none from St. Louis along the line of the North Missouri railroad to the Hannibal & St. Joseph railroad; none along the line of the southwest branch of the Pacific railroad to Rolla, and none west of Jefferson City on the main stem of the Pacific road. The telegraphic corps, organized under your orders, consisting of two companies, completed the telegraph line to Ironton, which included an office established at Jefferson Barracks; they also completed the line to Rolla. Two days after your arrival in Jefferson City, the telegraph corps reached headquarters by steamer; and when you camped at "Camp Lily" they opened telegraphic communication with St. Louis in two hours from the time Captain Smith received your orders to connect the camp by telegraph with the railroad depot. The communication was made by means of an insulated copper wire, carried upon a reel, the reel mounted on two wheels, and drawn by one horse. The wire was attached to the line at the depot, and uncoiled upon the ground as the horse was driven toward camp, a distance of nearly two miles from the main telegraph line. At first the wire was allowed to remain upon the top of the ground; afterward a trench was dug and the wire buried. Immediately upon your leaving Jefferson City the telegraphic company, by your orders, commenced repairing the line between Jefferson City and Syracuse; they also erected so much new line as was necessary to complete telegraphic connexion with Sedalia. Then, by your order, they commenced repairing the old telegraph line from Syracuse to Fort Smith, Arkansas, which had been partially destroyed by the rebels. This line passes through Warsaw, Bolivar, and Springfield. Upon your return from Springfield we met the telegraph corps at the town of Warsaw, which place was then in telegraphic communication with the headquarters of the army at Washington. As the poles were all standing, and but little of the wire removed between Warsaw and Springfield, the captain of the telegraph corps informed us that he expected to place Springfield in telegraphic communication with St. Louis in the course of the following week or ten days.

POST OFFICES AND COMMUNICATION BY LINE OF STAGES.

Immediately upon our occupation of Warsaw, the post office in that town was reopened by your orders, and a loyal citizen selected to take charge of it as postmaster, under the general supervision of Major William Dorsheimer, of your staff, postal director. Under your specific instructions, I re-established, in wagons, the semi-weekly mail line between Warsaw and the Pacific railroad at Tipton, which line, after a few days, was found to be so useful to every department of the army that you ordered it increased to a daily. As a mode of rapid, regular, and frequent communication between an army in the field and the base of its operations, the advantage of a daily line of wagons are so self-evident that I need not comment upon the establishment of this line. Under your instructions this mail communication in wagons was extended southward as the army progressed. On our arrival in Springfield we reopened the post office there, as had been done in Warsaw, and we carried to the people in that town the first mail they had received for four months. During your stay in Springfield the mail communication with Tipton, by way of Warsaw, and over the line herein referred to was regular and frequent.

All the facts connected with the reopening of the post offices, the selection of postmasters, and re-establishment of the mail line, were communicated from time to time to the Post Office Department in Washington as they occurred.

HEADQUARTERS WESTERN DEPARTMENT, IN THE FIELD,
Office of Director of Transportation, Warsaw, October 20, 1861.

The prescribed blank forms (H) are now ready for delivery, to be given in every case to the people of the country for property impressed for the uses of the army. Officers in charge of parties impressing are directed to take only wagons, horses, animals, and forage. When necessary, they will impress either horse, mule, or cattle teams, as the emergency demands; but will not take loose animals for the purpose of mounting men not entitled by the regulations of the service to ride. They will prevent all depredations upon private property by the men while in the execution of their duty. They will avoid stripping a family entirely of their wagons or animals, unless there exists imperative necessity for so doing. They will have all property carefully examined, in order to take none but what is in good order and suited to the uses of the army, and everything must be carefully appraised at its lowest cash value by two competent commissioned or non-commissioned officers, experts, if possible, whose names shall be entered in the body of the receipt. The owner will sign the prescribed form of oath of allegiance on the back of the receipt before its issue. Every officer will keep correct memoranda of the name and address of the parties from whom he takes property, its description, value, and to whom each receipt was issued, reporting the details to the director of transportation. Any officer or soldier of the army having in his possession any animal or property belonging to the people of the country will report the same to the quartermaster of the regiment, who will report to the brigade quartermaster, for the action of the proper officers.

I. C. WOODS, *Colonel aud D. O. T.*

Official.

J. H. EATON,
Acting Assistant Adjutant General.

(H)

No. ——.]

HEADQUARTERS WESTERN DEPARTMENT,
Office of Director of Transportation, Camp near ——, ——, 186 .

Received this day ———, for which the government agrees to pay ———.
Total to be paid by the United States to Mr. ———.

Property valued by —————————, appraisers.

This appraised value to be paid to the owner of the above property by the government of the United States, subject to the conditions indorsed on the back of this receipt.

Indorsement.—This receipt is only intended to be binding upon the government when given to true and loyal citizens of the United States, whose property we have been compelled to take by the exigences of the service.

The property of all those who have in any way aided or abetted the rebels is forfeited to the use of the government by the act of Congress; and before this claim can be paid satisfactory evidence must be produced of a continued obedience of Mr. ——— to the Constitution and laws.

(Signed) ———.

WAGONS AND HARNESSES.

Late in the month of August General McKinstry ordered quite a large number of wagons and harnesses; 200 from manufacturers in St. Louis; 200 from manufacturers in Cincinnati; 450 from D. G. Wilson, J. Childs & Co., Philadelphia; 200 from J. S. & A. Abbott, Concord, New Hampshire, and the governor of Massachuseits was requested to send 200 of the same pattern as furnished to the Massachusetts troops.

The wagons from Philadelphia commenced arriving about the middle of September, as they were on hand at the manufactury when ordered; but the wagons and harnesses to fill the other orders had to be made after receipt of the telegrams from General McKinstry, and, with every desire on the part of the manufacturers to urge them forward, could not, with a few exceptions, commence arriving at St. Louis until after your departure from the city. The greatest difficulty encountered in providing transportation was to procure the requisite number of harnesses. The shops at St. Louis were engaged in making cavalry equipment and artillery harness as well as team harness, but their capacity is comparatively limited. The facilities in Chicago and Cincinnati were also limited, and, besides, both cities had large orders to fill for infantry equipments for their State troops. New York and Philadelphia have been the only places where we could procure any large amount of team harness. In those cities we were fortunate enough to arrange with Betts, Nichols & Co., of New York, and Lacy & Phillips, of Philadelphia, large army contractors, to execute orders for this department upon the same terms as executed for the department at Washington.

These orders have been filled as to time of delivery, and very faithfully as to the quality of work.

The first army wagons received here for the use of this department were manufactured in Indiana, and contracted for by the authorities in Washington. These wagons proved to be made of inferior material; the poles, perches, and hounds were easily broken on the road; none of which complaints, I would state, can be made against any other wagons sent to this department. Those made in St. Louis, Cincinnati, and Philadelphia were good; while those from Boston and Concord, New Hampshire, were very superior in every respect. No harnesses were ordered to be made to accompany the wagons from Indiana, a very serious omission, which left the quartermaster's department in St. Louis so short of transportation, though having a plenty of wagons, that up to the time of your departure from St. Louis for Jefferson City, September 27, the post duty connected with moving the baggage of new regiments arriving here was nearly all performed by hired teams, because the quartermaster had not the organized transportation at his command.

AMBULANCES.

Doctor Buell, of the sanitary commission, reported to you in September that he was unable to find more than one ambulance in this department. A requisition was made upon the quartermaster's department in Washington for quite a number of both two and four horse ambulances, with harnesses complete, but none ever came forward. All that were procurable in St. Louis were purchased, but as a whole, the entire army under your command, which moved from Jefferson City to Springfield, was never furnished with an average of one ambulance to two regiments, because they could not be had. In returning from Springfield we had only a few sick, nearly all who were ill from fever and ague, contracted along the line of the Pacific railroad, having recovered in the clear mountain air of the Ozark ranges, in which you campaigned. We made an excellent substitute for an ambulance, putting a frame of light plank upon four buggy springs in a common wagon, the springs were floored over, and then two inclined planes were raised upon this floor at an angle of about thirty degrees each, which enabled six persons to ride comfortably in the wagon. This substitute worked extremely well on the return road from Springfield to Sedalia.

OX TEAMS FOR SUPPLY TRAINS.

During our stay at Warsaw I was enabled, under your orders, to make an arrangement with Jones & Cartwright, of Fort Leavenworth, to sell to the quartermaster's department two hundred wagons, one thousand or more yoke of cattle, who were to be broken to draught, with yokes, bows, chains, and wagon fixtures complete, being the same transportation they had used in the Pike's Peak trade. I also secured the services and experience of that firm to superintend the hiring of competent wagonmasters and teamsters, while all the details of this purchase of ox teams, the prices, the terms, &c., were left to be arranged by Major Robert Allen, quartermaster, St. Louis. In view of the approach of winter and bad roads, the want of enough organized mule teams in your department, and the fact that ox teams can haul heavier loads at much less expense, both of original outlay and cost of maintenance, I considered this arrangement with Jones & Cartwright to have been of great value to the public service in this department.

FORWARDING SHARPSHOOTERS IN WAGONS FROM BOLIVAR TO SPRINGFIELD.

At Bolivar, on the evening of the 26th of October, you directed me to prepare a number of wagons immediately, and to have the sharpshooters, under command of Major Holman, sent forward in them to Springfield with every possible despatch.

In compliance with this order I prepared nine of the regular army wagons, by placing narrow seats for the men between the bows of the wagons, the latter being left standing to hold on by. The wagon covers were removed. Knapsacks and haversacks were packed in the bottom of the wagon.

One hundred and fifty men were thus placed in the nine wagons, being the whole number of Major Holman's command.

The little party started from Bolivar at 7 p. m. of the 26th, and reached Springfield, a distance of thirty miles, at daylight the next morning, Sunday where they found and relieved the garrison of twenty-six men.

PURCHASE OF WAGON KEGS FROM WARDEN OF STATE PRISON.

The warden of the State Prison at Jefferson City manufactures barrels, half barrels, and kegs for the St. Louis market.

I directed the post quartermaster to accept an offer he made, to furnish for the use of the army five hundred of the five, ten, or fifteen gallon kegs, which we needed for the teamsters, one to each wagon. These kegs were to be paid for by our transporting to St. Louis a quantity of empty barrels and half barrels, which we could and did easily carry in the hold of any of the chartered steamers. This contract gave the kegs to the government free of cost.

SUPPLIES OF HAY AND GRAIN AT JEFFERSON CITY AND TIPTON.

As a consequence of the large number of animals which had been collected at Jefferson City, amounting to several hundreds, the surrounding country not being well stocked with oats and hay, and the fodder being yet unfit for food, the forage had become well nigh exhausted even before our arrival. A few days after we reached there, the forage contractor at the post was unable to fill the increased requisitions upon him. The new crop of corn at that date, October 1st, was too green to be fed to our animals, and the cavalry horses were, as a consequence, put upon half or quarter rations. In view of these facts, and after numerous complaints from the officers of the different regiments, Brigadier General McKinstry gave a large order, October 1st, for oats and hay, to be forwarded at once from St. Louis to Jefferson City. Under his directions I sent the following telegram:

CAMP LILY, JEFFERSON CITY,
October 1, 1861.

Brigadier General McKinstry directs me to order you to send at once one hundred thousand (100,000) bushels of oats, with a proportional amount of hay, some part of both to come to-night by railroad, the other by boat.

You will call on E. H. Castle for railroad transportation, and on B. Able for steam transportation.

I. C. WOODS, *Colonel and D. O. T.*

E. L. BEARD, *St. Louis*, 223 *Main street.*

The railroad trains of October 3 brought a little oats and hay, shipped in compliance with the telegram, and it continued to arrive there daily until the 10th of October, at which date, being then in Tipton myself, I ordered further shipments discontinued.

The army commenced leaving Jefferson City on the 4th of October. Your headquarters were moved forward on the 7th of October, and reached Tipton on the 9th, by a three days' march. On our arrival, I ordered the surrounding country to be thoroughly examined by our forage master and his assistants, in order to ascertain what was the supply of oats and hay among the farmers. The quantity of oats and of old corn proved to be inadequate to the feeding of our stock, as was the case in Jefferson City; but in the elapsed time between October 1, the date of General McKinstry's order for oats, and the 9th of October, the date of our arrival at Tipton, and owing to the change of locality, we found the new crop of corn was fit to be fed to our animals. Upon the 10th of October, the day following our arrival at Tipton, by your order, I telegraphed as follows to Major Allen, quartermaster at Saint Louis:

No. 13.

TIPTON, *October* 10, 1861.

We are able at present to supply ourselves with hay here; no more should be sent to Jefferson City until their stock is reduced, as they lack storage for it.

I. C. WOODS, *Colonel and D. O. T.*

Major ROBERT ALLEN, *Quartermaster, St. Louis.*

No oats or hay were ordered from St. Louis to Tipton, or from St. Louis to points beyond Tipton. The following telegram shows why a limited amount of forage was ordered from Jefferson City to Tipton.

No. 160.

TIPTON, *October* 16, 1861.

Your surplus mules and horses will come forward here. I have ordered the shipment of forage from St. Louis to be discontinued. The animals will be collected here. You can send us any surplus oats or corn you may have.

I. C. WOODS, *Colonel and D. O. T.*

J. G. KLINCK, *Quartermaster, Jefferson City.*

The horses and mules were ordered moved from Jefferson City to Tipton, because the latter place had been made the depot for all army supplies. The shipment of forage from St. Louis west had been ordered discontinued on the 10th of October, but the surplus which had accumulated at Jefferson City had to be ordered away from there, or it would have been spoiled by the weather. By this time, October 16, a fortnight having elapsed, the new corn at Jefferson City had also become fit for feeding to animals, if used sparingly.

USE OF THE PRISON MECHANICS AT JEFFERSON CITY.

At Jefferson City we were unable to procure citizen mechanics for the needed repairs of wagons and harnesses, or for the shoeing of our animals.

There were few public shops, fewer workmen, and a large amount of work had to be done before the army could move forward.

In this condition of things, by your order, I directed that a contract be made between J. J. Neville, post quartermaster, Jefferson City, and the warden of the State prison, by which contract the army were enabled to have the benefit at once of shops and mechanics. Blacksmiths, horseshoers, carpenters, wheelwrights, and harness makers were provided by the contract from among the convicts at the prison.

The work done at the prison was placed under the superintendence of Mr. E. Morgan Davis, of Indiana, whose report I have annexed, (Exhibit K.)

After the departure of the army from Tipton, and the removal of the stock from Jefferson City, the post quartermaster, Captain Klinck, by proper notice, as provided in the contract, discontinued the use of the prison labor.

ST. LOUIS, *November* 12, 1861.

COLONEL: Under orders from you I went to Jefferson City and established workshops for the use of government. These consisted of blacksmith, wagon-makers', and harness shops, in which were employed 24 blacksmiths, 10 wagon-makers, and 5 saddlers, all of whom were convicts from the State penitentiary at Jefferson City.

These workshops were constantly employed from the time they were started (October 2) until Friday, November 8, 1861.

The contract for the labor was made by Quartermaster Neville, under your orders, at the following rates per diem: Blacksmiths, $1 50; wagon-makers, $1 25; saddlers, $1; and there was of their time consumed in government service the following: 24 blacksmiths, 717 days in all; 10 wagon-makers, 312 days in all; 5 or 6 saddlers, 161 days in all.

From the above is to be deducted for short hours worked the following: 24 blacksmiths, 1 hour each day from October 9 to November 8, 79½ days; 10 wagon-makers, 1 hour each day from October 9 to November 8, 29 days; 5 saddlers, 1 hour each day from October 9 to November 8, 14½ days.

The property remaining on hand I have turned over to the post quartermaster at Jefferson City, Captain J. G. Klinck, to whom a complete inventory was given, but who refuses to receipt to me for the reason that I have hitherto acted without any recognized order from the government.

During the few days preceding the closing up of the works the labor was employed upon the manufacture of the parts of wagons, harnesses, &c., which could be sent forward to any train in motion, and would be sufficient, in every case of merely partial injury, to completely repair and set right whatever may have been damaged.

Most of the portions prepared for repairs of wagons, &c., have been handed over to trains, and have been consumed in the service of the army.

All which is respectfully submitted.

Your obedient servant,

E. MORGAN DAVIS,
Superintendent at Government Workshops.

Colonel I. C. WOODS.

In Warsaw, October 18, I had the honor of reporting the condition of the army transportation to be as follows:

First division—Major General Hunter.

13th Illinois, Colonel Wyman	26	government teams.
14th Illinois, Colonel Palmer	15	do.
15th Illinois, Colonel Turner	19	do.
24th Indiana, Colonel Hovey	11	do.
26th Indiana, Colonel Wheatley	16	do.
6th Missouri, Colonel Bland	7	do.
Staff teams	8	do.
1st Missouri cavalry, Colonel Ellis	18	do.
At Tipton, from Rolla	35	do.
En route from Rolla, subsistence trains with General Wyman	50	do.
	205	

Prior to the 17th October, the day of my leaving Tipton for Warsaw, the old mules came by railroad from Rolla to supply thirty-five wagons referred to in my report as "at Tipton from Rolla," belonging to General Hunter's division. Subsequent to that date, and prior to the 23d, the Douglas brigade regiment arrived at Tipton, having, in addition to their own wagons, twenty-five for General Asboth, to whose division they belonged. They joined General Hunter's column, en route, and I lost sight of them after that date.

General Hunter also procured quite a number of wagons, harness, and mules from the quartermaster at Tipton, prior to 23d October, the account of which was never forwarded to me, but which, in my opinion, must have increased his means of transportation enough to compensate for the fifty wagons which Colonel Wyman was to have brought by land from Rolla, and which never reached General Hunter's division. The division of General Asboth, as shown by the statement enclosed, was not supplied with enough transportation for both regimental purposes and field train; but this deficiency was compensated for in the facilities offered by the country through which we passed.

FORAGE FOR THE ARMY WHILE EN ROUTE FROM TIPTON TO SPRINGFIELD.

During the march of the army from Jefferson City to Springfield, the animals were fed with oats, corn, or hay obtained from the farmers along the line of our march. When this forage was taken from active secessionists, who had abandoned their property either to join Price's army or upon our approach, no receipt or form of acknowledgment was given them for the property, but when taken from Union men, or from citizens who claimed to be law abiding, then a printed form of receipt was given to each person, after an appraisement of the property, and an agreement of allegiance signed upon the reverse side, that being the form instituted at Tipton, for issue to loyal owners of property, impressed into the service for hire or for permanent use.

WANT OF TRANSPORTATION AS AFFECTING THE RATIONS OF THE ARMY.

In consequence of the scarcity of transportation, the advance divisions of the army were very short of flour, bread, coffee, sugar, and some minor articles. I was unable to respond to the requisitions of the acting chief commissary, Colonel Tracy, for means of transportation for the rations which were in abundance at the depots in Tipton, Jefferson City, and Sedalia.

To remedy this want as far as possible, I aided him at Warsaw and at Yost's Station in his endeavor to procure mechanics to work the various mills he found near the line of our march. I furnished also means of transportation to gather in the wheat and old corn procured by thoroughly examining the farm houses and out-buildings as we passed along.

At Springfield, for the first time, the new corn was considered in a fit state to be ground into meal for the use of the troops. Large quantities were gathered and so ground at the steam mill in the town, which, with fresh beef and salt found in Warsaw and Springfield, formed the principal food of the soldiers.

At Warsaw the regiment of Colonel Carr was supplied with flour and corn-meal by the colonel using a small donkey mill near their camp. Salt was found in Warsaw in quite large quantities, and taken possession of by Colonel Tracy, acting chief commissary of subsistence on your staff, and some considerable molasses was also found at the same place, and taken. The steam mill in the town of Warsaw was worked by order of Colonel Tracy, with millers and engineers taken from the regiments. Post bread, of unbolted flour, was baked in an oven made or found in the town, and supplied to the troops.

By a concert of action with Colonel Tracy, acting commissary of subsistence of your staff, I succeeded in getting the weight of our rations very much reduced. By your approval he changed the proportion, making them much better adapted to our wants. By the new army regulations, 1861, the 1,000 rations are in weight as follows:

Bacon	750.00	pounds.
Bread	1,000.00	pounds.
Beans	155.00	pounds.
Rice	100.00	pounds.
Coffee	100.00	pounds.
Sugar	150.00	pounds.
Vinegar	92.50	pounds.
Candles	15.00	pounds.
Soap	40.00	pounds.
Salt	33.75	pounds.
	2,436¼	pounds to 1,000 rations.

In the last requisitions from Colonel Tracy, made upon me at Springfield, and which I transmitted to my agents in Sedalia, this ration was, as to number, reduced and altered to the following proportions:

Bacon, 2-7	214 2-7	pounds to	1,000 rations.
Bread, 2-7	285 5-7	"	"
Coffee, 10-7	142 6-7	"	"
Sugar, 10-7	214 2-7	"	"
Candles, 7-7	17.50	"	"
Soap, 3-7	17 1-7	"	"
	891 5½-7	"	"

Regulation allowance	2, 436¼
Reduced as above	891 5½-7

A reduction of nearly two-thirds; an immense saving in transportation, and, in the same proportion, an addition to the mobility of your army.

I ceased to act officially after the publication of your farewell address of Saturday, November 2, and since that date have taken no cognizance of the army transportation.

In conclusion, I beg leave to express the opinion that the army you left at Springfield was capable of great efforts in celerity of movement. The divisions of General Sigel and General Asboth have earned particular distinction in this respect. They had become habituated to marching with little baggage, scanty transportation, and short rations; they were getting familiar with camp life generally; rain and bad roads were no strangers to them. The division of General Asboth, more particularly, had learned to live on fresh beef, salt, and corn meal.

SOME CAUSES OF WANT OF TRANSPORTATION.

There were great and serious delays in our transportation getting forward from the railroad.

When once the wagons, animals, and harness were at Tipton there was but little energy or knowledge of the business shown by the quartermaster's department there in organizing teams and sending them forward to the army. My orders to the quartermaster were frequent and urgent, but yet the delay continued. A train of pack-mules, for one item, was delayed at Tipton a fortnight, waiting for some trifling article from Saint Louis. These pack animals were intended to accompany the advance of the army, as a means of transportation for the baggage of any cavalry scouting party moving across the country where no roads existed.

This comparatively small matter of the pack animals is referred to by me as an illustration. The packs were furnished in Saint Louis before you left; the packers and mules reached Tipton the day after I left that place for Warsaw, on the 17th of October; yet the train was met by us at the Osage river on the 6th of November, on our return from Springfield.

HEADQUARTERS WESTERN DEPARTMENT,
St. Louis, September 24, 1861.

Allow me respectfully to recommend to the attention of the general commanding that the quartermaster here should be ordered to buy no more horses in Missouri. The number on hand is large and embarrassing, and, besides, they can be bought at any time when wanted. I would state that I believe nearly or quite enough horses have already been bought and contracted for in Ohio, to mount the cavalry and supply the artillery, while for transportation purposes mules are preferable.

I would also respectfully recommend that the quartermaster adopt the system of advertising, the quartermaster reserving to himself the right of rejecting any or all bids offered. Wagons, harness, and all articles needed in the transportation department should be bought at the discretion of the quartermaster, whether to be purchased in open market of responsible men, or from the manufactories at regular prices, or obtained by advertising in the same manner as proposed to be done in the purchase of mules. The system, as adopted by General Meigs, is to open the bids when a day is fixed. On that day he buys from the lowest bidder, takes any number he pleases; on the following day the same way from other bids, and so on, thus securing his animals at reasonable prices and keeping entire control of the market.

Very respectfully, your obedient servant,

I. C. WOODS, *Colonel and D. of T.*

Major General J. C. FRÉMONT.

Indorsed as follows:

Approved and Quartermaster P. T. Turnly ordered to comply.
By order of Major General Frémont,

J. H. EATON,
Colonel, A. D. C., and Military Secretary.

HEADQUARTERS WESTERN DEPARTMENT,
St. Louis, September 25, 1861.

Requisition signed acting regimental quartermaster twelfth Missouri volunteers, was approved by you, and Captain Bradshaw ordered to issue it.

Other requisitions have passed through my hands, and been approved by me, and ordered to be issued. Other requisitions have been sent direct from commanding officer to Captain Bradshaw to issue. The complications which must necessarily result from a divided responsibility, I would respectfully suggest that the good of the public service requires that all requisitions for transportation should pass through my hands before being ordered to be issued by Captain Bradshaw. Some system must be arranged between us.

Respectfully,

I. C. WOODS, *Colonel and D. of T.*

Captain P. T. TURNLY,
Assistant Quartermaster, United States Army.

SEPTEMBER 26, 1861.

This arrangement is right.

Colonel Woods will control the issue or management of all transportation wagons, ambulances, steamers, cars, &c., and pack mules. Captain Bradshaw will take note hereof.

P. T. TURNLY, *Assistant Quartermaster.*

LOSS IN PURCHASES FROM WANT OF FUNDS.

It may not be inappropriate here to state that, in my opinion, based upon observation and experience, where the cost to the government for any supplies furnished to the army of the western department has been increased one dollar by the combination of parties in interest wishing to obtain contracts, it has been increased ten dollars by the want of funds with which to make the purchases. In the department of transportation this want of funds has been a heavy drawback. Losses have arisen from a want of proper corrals, from improper feeding, and from incompetent attendance upon the draught animals in St. Louis. There has been a want felt of proper shops in St. Louis for shoeing and wagon work. The public property, in many cases, has been exposed to damage from the elements; with the inefficient guard maintained, stampedes of the animals, and losses therefrom, were not uncommon.

In my opinion, too much stress cannot be laid upon the evils which the withholding of money from your department has caused you. Money lies at the basis of the most simple wants of the soldier, and withholding that money from the executive officers here, who had charge of supplying those wants, has compelled them, as a first step, to use the credit of the government or to do without them. Instantly, when they attempt to use credit, the control over all supplies passes from the government into the hands of those who do have money, or into the hands of merchants, speculators, banks and capitalists, who form the intermediate link between the producer and the government. Money must be used to procure goods or products from first hands, and when any department of the government ceases to have money, it must lose connexion with the producers, must make use of the middle men as a substitute, and must pay dearly for its want of money and for its experience. In any department without money, there is no course left to choose between high prices or ceasing to move the machinery of the department.

WASHINGTON, *February* 14, 1862.

GENERAL: Since my official report to you, on the 20th of November last, I have seen the report of the Van Wyck investigating committee of the House of Representatives, in which the members of that committee, O. H. Van Wyck, E. B. Washburne, W. S. Holman, R. E. Fenton, H. L. Dawes, and W. G. Steele, have put their names to the following statement, on page 96 of their report: "That I was one of the gang of California patriots who hovered like sharks about the headquarters of the commanding general;" and on page 93, referring to a horse contract, they say: "Your committee believe, from the testimony of Captain Turnly, that this was a scheme by which the said Colonel Woods (who was denominated on the staff of General Frémont 'director of transportation,') intended to defraud the government, and that he found in this man Sacchi, in the language of Captain Turnly, 'a good person through whom to work.'"

The facts are, general, that I never had any interest, presently or remotely, pecuniarily, politically, or otherwise, in any purchase or sale, made to or for your "department," whether made by contract or otherwise; never from any of these personal considerations did I recommend any man or men to you for any place or position, civil or military, during my connexion with the "department of the west," which connexion, I am proud to say, commenced with its existence and continued to its close.

I remain, sir, very respectfully, your obedient servant,

I. C. WOODS.

Major General J. C. FRÉMONT, *United States Army.*

WASHINGTON, *February* 27, 1862.

General S. D. STURGIS sworn and examined.

By the chairman:

Question. What is your rank and position in the army?

Answer. I am a major of the 4th regular cavalry, and a brigadier general of volunteers.

Question. Did you serve in the western army under General Frémont; and if so, in what capacity?

Answer. I served under him last summer as a major of cavalry, and subsequently, from the early part of September until his recall, as a brigadier general.

Question. Will you state in your own way your connexion with that army, about what time you joined it, how long you were with it, and whatever you deem material relating to it?

Answer. I served under General Frémont from the time he took command of that department until he was relieved from it. I went from Kansas City, in June, with a force of about two thousand three hundred men, and marched to Springfield, and joined General Lyon there. After General Lyon was killed I took command of the army and marched it to Rolla. From there I went to St. Louis to look after the interest of the command, and was put in command of the St. Louis arsenal.

Question. You were at the battle of Wilson's creek, at the time General Lyon was killed.

Answer. Yes, sir.

Question. What amount of force did General Lyon have there?

Answer. He had about five thousand men, including Colonel Sigel's column. That column, however, took but a small part in the fight. The fight really was conducted with about three thousand seven hundred men.

Question. What was the strength of the enemy at that time?

Answer. The estimate I gave in my report was twenty-three thousand men. I took the lowest estimate that was made of their force, but found a consolidated morning report placing it at that number.

Question. Do you know what was the condition of General Frémont's command at that time in regard to his ability to re-enforce General Lyon?

Answer. No, sir, I cannot say. I know there were two fine regiments at Rolla, because I saw them there as I returned from Springfield. Without attempting to go into the whole analysis of the matter, I should think that for that emergency they might have gone to Springfield. And I think if they had been there the tables would have been turned against the enemy, because, although we held the field, we were unable only from weakness, want of ammunition, and a general want of numbers, to pursue Price and his army.

Question. Do you know of any other force that could have been sent to the relief of General Lyon?

Answer. No, sir, I cannot say that I do.

Question. Do you know what disposition General Frémont did make of those two regiments at Rolla?

Answer. They remained at Rolla, and, as far as I know, they are at Rolla yet. I found them there after the battle, and I know they remained there a long time.

Question. How far is Rolla from Springfield?

Answer. We were some six days marching from Springfield to Rolla. It must be some ninety or one hundred miles.

Question. Now, in your opinion as a military man, considering that the dis parity of forces was so great, would it have been good generalship for General Frémont to have sent those two regiments on from Rolla, or should General Lyon have retreated before so immensely superior a force?

Answer. I think General Lyon should have retreated without a fight. I said so myself repeatedly. I voted for that. I told General Lyon that we were too weak to pretend to cope with the enemy. I told him that even if we encountered them and whipped them, it would lead us to ruin merely, for every time we encountered them we would become more and more weakened, and at last we would have to surrender. I told him that we were too weak to hold the country, and I held that we should retreat.

Question. Is it your opinion that it was the duty of General Frémont to have endeavored to re-enforce General Lyon?

Answer. I think so, as long as he did not withdraw him.

Question. Had General Lyon any orders that compelled him to remain there and fight?

Answer. I think not. He never showed any.

Question. You still adhere to your opinion, as a military man, that it was General Lyon's duty to have retreated, and not to have fought?

Answer. Yes, sir.

Question. Do you know what was the condition of things at that time at Cairo and Pilot Knob?

Answer. No, sir. I had come up from Texas to Missouri, and had never been at St. Louis.

Question. Did you accompany the army afterwards to Springfield under General Frémont?

Answer. Yes, sir; that is, I marched by one road converging towards his line, and joined him at Springfield.

Question. What was the condition of his army when you joined him at Springfield, and before he was superseded?

Answer. I went over myself to visit him before we arrived at Springfield, and, so far as I could judge of the army as it marched, I should judge it was in good condition.

Question. While he was there at Springfield, and before he was superseded, what was the position of the enemy?

Answer. That is very difficult to say. For fear I might be asked that question I have brought with me here my order-book, which I brought to this city with me for another purpose. I will read a letter which I wrote to General Frémont on the same day that I joined him at Springfield. On the 30th of October I was stationed at Greenfield, some 35 miles from Springfield. On the evening of the 30th I received an order from General Frémont to repair to Springfield with as great haste as possible, and not to regard provisions; that if I expected to be in the battle at all, I must make haste. I marched all night, and got to Springfield the next day. This is the letter that I wrote that morning to General Frémont:

"HEADQUARTERS,
"*Greenfield, Missouri, October* 30, 1861.

"SIR: I have the honor to report the arrival of my command at this place yesterday at half past 2 o'clock p. m. We found a rebel flag flying near the court-house, and took it down to-day. It will be replaced by a United States flag presented by the ladies of Greenfield.

"I have read General Lane's despatch to General Frémont, and have to say that all the information I receive goes to confirm what he says in regard to the rebel army (combined) being prepared to receive us at or near Neosho.

"I remain at this place until further orders."

This letter I addressed to Colonel J. H. Eaton, General Frémont's assistant adjutant general.

Question. How far is Neosho from Springfield?

Answer. I take it to be 80 or 100 miles.

Question. That is where you supposed they would make their stand?

Answer. Yes, sir. We got to Springfield late in the afternoon of the next day, the 31st of October, a distance of 35 miles; we marched pretty nearly all night. The next day after I got there, I think, (though I may not be accurate as to dates, and may mistake as to a day or so,) General Frémont called us together—on the 2d November, I think. He stated in council that the enemy was at Wilson's Creek, at the old battle-ground, and proposed his plan of battle. After we got through, General Hunter, who was to replace General Frémont, arrived there. General Frémont stated to General Hunter his plans. General Hunter, without saying much—I do not know as he said anything—walked out, and in the morning he countermanded the orders to move. And the next day after that he took an escort and went down to Wilson's Creek, as a matter of curiosity, to see the battle-field. I did not go myself, but the general impression created upon my mind, and the minds of all of us, by the officers who did go along, was that the enemy had not been there at Wilson's Creek. If that impression was correct, then the scouts must have imposed upon General Frémont.

Question. Did you understand that General Frémont had sent out scouts there who had ascertained the position of the enemy?

Answer. No, sir; but I took it for granted, as we always had our scouts out.

Question. Who did you say went down to Wilson's Creek the next day but one after General Frémont was superseded?

Answer. General Hunter, with an escort, and many officers who had been in the battle there under General Lyon, and wanted to go out there as a matter of curiosity.

Question. What day of the month did they go out there?

Answer. About the 4th or 5th of November; somewhere about that date.

By Mr. Julian:

Question. What day was General Frémont superseded?

Answer. He was superseded on the night of the 2d or 3d of November. General Hunter lay over one day, and then went down to the old battle-field.

By the chairman:

Question. How long was it after General Hunter commenced his retreat before Price commenced to advance?

Answer. That would be difficult for me to say. I am not sure, from anything I know, that he ever did advance.

Question. You do not know that he ever advanced at all?

Answer. No, sir; because I withdrew with the army to Sedalia, and was then ordered to St. Louis.

Question. Is there any other fact that is connected with General Frémont's administration of that department that you desire to make any statement about?

Answer. No, sir; not that I know of. I am not as well posted in regard to matters as one might think I ought to be, coming from Missouri, for I was all the time in the field; and people not there might very likely obtain from newspaper reports more actual knowledge than we in the field had. I am very badly posted, indeed, in regard to matters there.

By Mr. Gooch :

Question. Could General Lyon have retreated from Springfield without great danger of being cut off by the enemy?

Answer. Yes, sir; without any danger whatever; that is, if he had retreated in time. At the time he had his council at Dug Spring, he could have retreated without danger, if he had kept right on in his retreat from Dug Spring.

Question. How long after he left Dug Spring before the battle of Wilson's Creek?

Answer. The battle was on the 10th of August. He left Dug Spring, I think, some two weeks before. He had gone beyond Springfield in pursuit of the enemy, and had pursued them as far as Dug Spring, where we became satisfied that they were too strong for us to attack them. That was some 30 or 40 miles from Springfield. We there determined to retreat until we fell in with re-enforcements. I told General Lyon that we could not hold the country, and that we should retreat as soon as we could. He said that there was no hope of re-enforcements, because there were no re-enforcements to send. I told him that we should then retreat as soon as we could. We then started for Springfield, and could have kept right on to Rolla. But after sitting on our horses for three or four hours, something, I do not know what, seemed to change the opinion of the general, and he ordered us to encamp there. And after a day or two had passed the enemy came up in strong numbers to Wilson's Creek and near to Springfield, and then it was too late to retreat.

Question. It then became necessary to fight?

Answer. Yes, sir. I do not think that General Frémont should be held responsible for General Lyon not retreating; I think that was optional with General Lyon. In his council of advisers General Lyon laid before us the substance of every document he had in regard to his re-enforcements. And I think it was altogether optional with him whether he should retreat or not.

Question. Then, if I understand you, you give it as your opinion that General Frémont had a right to suppose that General Lyon would retreat if he found himself unable to meet the enemy?

Answer. Yes, sir; I think so. Without knowing anything more of the facts in the case, I should take that for granted. If I had been in General Lyon's place, from all that I know of his instructions, I should have considered that it was discretionary with me to remain or not. I might say, in pursuance of the same idea, that General Lyon said he had called again and again for re-enforcements, had stated that the enemy were collecting in large numbers, and that re-enforcements were necessary; and I think that if General Frémont did not recall him under these circumstances, when he could not re-enforce him, it then must be considered that it was discretionary with him to withdraw or not as he thought best. General Lyon said that he had been informed from headquarters that re-enforcements that had been intended for him had, of necessity, been diverted to other points, and therefore General Lyon said he had now no hope of re-enforcements.

Question. When did General Lyon have that information?

Answer. That I cannot exactly say.

Question. Was it before he came back to Springfield from Dug Spring?

Answer. Yes, sir.

Question. While he had it in his power to retreat?

Answer. Yes, sir. This information he gave us in council at Dug Spring.

By Mr. Odell:

Question. Did General Lyon send to General Frémont for re-enforcements in time for them to have been sent to him before the battle of Wilson's Creek.

Answer. Yes, sir; I take it so. From having heard so often of his having asked for re-enforcements, I take it that they were asked for in time for them to have been sent, if there had been any to send.

Question. Do you know whether General Lyon had sent to General Frémont an account of his exposed condition, his danger, and his necessities?

Answer. General Lyon stated that he had done so repeatedly.

By Mr. Julian:

Question. Do you know whether General Frémont had any re-enforcements to spare?

Answer. No, sir. I do not know. I had not been in that part of the State since the war broke out.

By Mr. Covode:

Question. How many composed the council at Dug Spring?

Answer. I should think about fifteen officers.

Question. What was the general opinion there? Were there any others than yourself that advised a retreat?

Answer. Yes, sir; it was unanimous. The only question of difference was as to which way we should retreat. Some wanted to fall back towards Kansas—Fort Scott; and others wanted to fall back to Rolla. Colonel Sigel said (and many agreed with him afterwards) that we should fall back to Rolla, or until we should meet with re-enforcements.

By Mr. Gooch:

Question. Were you ordered to relieve Colonel Mulligan, or to re-enforce him while he was at Lexington?

Answer. Yes, sir.

Question. From whom did you receive that order, and what did you do in pursuance of it?

Answer. I was ordered by General Frémont, while I was at Hudson, on the Hannibal and St. Joseph railroad, to repair to Lexington by way of Utica, with all the infantry and artillery I had. He ordered me to send back all the cavalry I had, and to advance with my infantry and artillery. I had no artillery, for it had been ordered away by General Pope, under whose immediate command I was. I started at once with all the infantry I could get together—some 1,100 men. We left the railroad when we got to Utica, and we marched night and day, I think, until we got to the river bottom. We had heard firing the day before, but having no cavalry, I was unable to cut off the enemy's scouts, who ran ahead with information of our approach. The consequence was that before we arrived there, the enemy made a desperate effort, and got possession of the boats, and threw a large force of infantry, 3,000 strong, over into the timber before I got there. I saw then that I could not get across the river, and I accordingly diverged from there towards Kansas City.

Question. Why were you instructed to march without your cavalry?

Answer. That I do not know.

Question. Would your force have been more efficient for the purpose for which you were sent if you had taken your cavalry along with you?

Answer. If I had had a little cavalry—enough to have cut off these scouts that we saw going ahead with the news—ten or fifteen men would probably have changed the whole matter.

By Mr. Odell:

Question. How much cavalry had you when you received your orders?

Answer. I had had three companies, but my cavalry had been reduced to half a company by orders from General Pope. But General Frémont did not know that; his order was to send back the three companies.

By Mr. Gooch:

Question. It would have been of no service to you to have taken a large body of cavalry—say three companies?

Answer. No, sir.

Question. But a small squad of cavalry might have been of great service to you?

Answer. Yes, sir. I do not think General Frémont knew the exact condition of my command at that time. General Pope, under whose immediate command I was, had taken away a part of my force before, and had taken away the last piece of artillery I had. General Frêmont was not aware of that, and could not have been expected to be aware of it.

By Mr. Odell:

Question. Where were you at that time?

Answer. I was at Hudson, on the Hannibal and St. Joseph railroad. I went by railroad to Utica, and then marched to Lexington, which, I think, took us two days and two nights.

By Mr. Julian:

Question. Were there any signs of mutiny in the army at Springfield, immediately after General Frémont was superseded?

Answer. No, sir; not at all; not the slightest.

Question. Were there any indications of a disposition to refuse any longer to serve the country?

Answer. Not that I saw; there was none in my division. I heard of nothing of the kind, except that I did hear that one officer (a German) broke his sword.

Question. Do you know the conduct of General Frémont in relation to that demonstration you have mentioned?

Answer. No, sir; I do not; I do not even know that the demonstration took place.

Question. You merely heard of it?

Answer. I heard of it. If it was done it was done so quietly that I knew nothing of it. I saw it stated in the papers, but I saw nothing in the camp.

By Mr. Gooch:

Question. At the night of the council—the night that General Hunter arrived, when the battle for the next day was being planned—did you suppose the enemy to be at Wilson's Creek, or in that vicinity?

Answer. At that time I supposed the enemy to be at Wilson's Creek; I had no doubt of it all, upon the simple principle that I supposed the commanding officer knew. I had just arrived, but my letter from Greenfield to General Frémont showed what my opinion then was, based upon my information from my scouts, and what I could gather up.

By Mr. Julian:

Question. Do you know what was the belief of other generals and officers at that time?

Answer. I do not know that the matter was discussed at the council. I am pretty sure that it was not discussed. But I know what the officers said the next day; they were divided in opinion: Some said the enemy were there, and some said they were not there at all.

Question. But at the time of the council?

Answer. I took it for granted that the enemy were there. I did not doubt that at all.

Question. Was that the conviction of the other officers?

Answer. I had no conversation with them upon the subject, but I took it, from the tone of the council, that the most of them thought as I did in that respect.

By Mr. Odell:

Question. Would not that follow from the statement made by the general calling the council of the necessity for it? Would he not give a reason for calling a council of war?

Answer. I do not recollect his explanation exactly; but it was to the effect that he had information that the enemy was there. I had no reason to doubt it, and whether he was there or not it would be very difficult for me to say even now, but I think the sequel showed that he was not there. But that is a mere matter of opinion.

Question. What force would have been sufficient to have saved you at Wilson's Creek?

Answer. I think if General Lyon could have had 2,500 or 3,000 fresh re-enforcements, we could have driven the enemy out of the country entirely. They were staggered when we left them, and when we withdrew from the field there was not a gun fired at all. But we had no means of advancing. The artillery horses were scattered or killed and wounded. There were large ravines in front of us, and our ammunition was exhausted. If we had advanced, and the enemy had found that our ammunition was exhausted, they could have rallied and destroyed us.

Question. Do you know of any force that could have been sent to you?

Answer. There was no force, except the two regiments of Colonel Wyman and Colonel Stephenson at Rolla, that could have been sent to us.

Question. Was there anything in the way of those regiments having been sent to you?

Answer. No, sir, not that I know of; but I am not posted in regard to that matter. If they had been sent, I think, myself, it would have changed the fate of the day.

Question. Do you not think, as a military man, that they should have been sent to you, as you were situated?

Answer. I think either the whole army of General Lyon should have been withdrawn or he should have been re-enforced, even with the two regiments at Rolla. I know of no reason for their being at Rolla, except their being on their way to Springfield. But there may have been other reasons.

By Mr. Covode:

Question. Were there many rebels in your rear—between you and Rolla—at the time you fought at Wilson's Creek?

Answer. No armed bodies.

Question. Had you not, in your opinion, advanced too far without knowing whether you would have re-enforcements or support?

Answer. That I have already answered. My opinion for a long time before the fight was, that, unless we were re-enforced, we were too weak to hold that country.

WASHINGTON, *March* 3, 1862.

General S. D. STURGIS recalled.

The witness said: I forgot to state when I testified before, that the day after General Hunter assumed command at Springfield he sent a reconnoitring party out to Wilson's Creek, under Colonel Morrill, which established the fact that there was no enemy there; neither had there been any nearer than Cassville for a long time.

By Mr. Gooch:

Question. How far is Cassville from Springfield?

Answer. Some 60 or 80 miles. I desire to state that I received the order from General Frémont to join him at Springfield, on the 31st of October, the day after I wrote the letter which I have read in evidence here.

By Mr. Chandler:

Question. Where did you first meet General Sigel after the fight at Wilson's Creek was over?

Answer. At Springfield, where I called a council of war after dark that same evening.

Question. Was his force so utterly demoralized after their repulse as not to be able to render you any assistance?

Answer. Yes, sir; we never saw his force until we got within three miles of Springfield, when we met a part of it coming in from the west, under Lieutenant Farrand, of the regular service.

Question. Were Sigel's guns, after being captured by the enemy, brought to bear upon your force during the battle?

Answer. Yes, sir; they were. We recognized them the moment they were fired, by their ammunition.

By Mr. Gooch:

Question. How many men had General Sigel under his command that day, and what did they do on the field?

Answer. He had of all arms from 1,200 to 1,300. That included three companies of cavalry and a battery of artillery of six pieces. All I know in regard to their operations is what I gathered from the officers and men of the expedition afterwards. We surprised the enemy, according to programme, and drove them from their camp. Then, supposing that the enemy were routed, General Sigel's men went to the camp and took to pillaging, and to eating the half-cooked victuals on the fires, and some even went in bathing in the stream. And while they were disorganized in this manner, the enemy rallied and took their battery from, them and routed them.

Question. How did they get to Springfield?

Answer. All that I know about that matter is that General Sigel told me that he himself got into Springfield with ten men, and that his men had retreated by all the roads they could find—meaning by that that they had got scattered.

WASHINGTON, *March* 1, 1862.

HORACE A. CONANT sworn and examined.

By the chairman:

Question. What has been your rank in the army?

Answer. I have never been, legally speaking, in the army. I had an informal appointment, or an appointment from General Lyon, last May, on his staff.

Question. In the western army?
Answer. Yes, sir.
Question. Were you with the force under General Frémont at Springfield?
Answer. I was.
Question. At the time he was superseded by General Hunter?
Answer. Yes, sir.
Question. What was his proximity to General Price's army at that time, as you understood it?
Answer. As I understood it, we were near them. I have a little memorandum-book or journal here, which I made at that time during our trip. I went down from Rolla; the general went down from Sedalia. Some two or three days before General Frémont was relieved, [looking at his memorandum-book,] on October 30, I was at Wilson's Creek myself, and there were reported at that time to be some 2,000 rebels at Flat Creek, some 45 or 50 miles below Springfield.
Question. When was General Frémont superseded?
Answer. He received notice on the 2d of November; but General Hunter did not arrive until the evening of the 3d, after dark.
Question. Were you sent out with any scouts to ascertain the position of the enemy?
Answer. I was not. After General Hunter took command, Colonel Wyman, of the 13th Illinois regiment, was made provost marshal, and I acted as his deputy. I was actually provost marshal, for the colonel was sick, and I was obliged to act for him. The day that General Hunter took command he let Major Wright make a reconnoissance, and he scouted around some 24 hours, from 5 to 25 and 30 miles about Springfield. He found none of the enemy whatever, but heard of their being within 10, 15, or 20 miles of Springfield, burning haystacks, mills, &c., in numbers of from 100 to 300; those were the largest numbers we could hear of.
Question. Where was the main body of Price's army at that time?
Answer. We understood that it was at Cassville, and it was reported to Major Wright, by the parties with whom he came in contact in his scouting, that they were retreating from there.
Question. Do you know what the scouts reported whom General Frémont sent out?
Answer. I do not, from my own knowledge. But the general impression before General Frémont was relieved was that the enemy was in force in large numbers near Springfield. That, I think, was the general impression of the whole army.
Question. Was it the general impression that there was to be a fight there?
Answer. Yes, sir.
Question. But, in your judgment, that impression was erroneous?
Answer. I could form no judgment of it until after General Frémont was relieved, because none but scouts were allowed to leave the camp, and we were under orders to be ready to march at a moment's notice.
Question. Was it your opinion, up to that time, that a battle was imminent?
Answer. Having been in the battle before under General Lyon, I did not think that Price would give us battle where the forces were anything like equal; but at that time I had a belief, based upon the judgment of officers in command, that we were to have a battle. General McKinstry made an armed reconnoissance, or started to do it, on the first day of November, I think, with a brigade of 5,000 or 6,000 men, but he was ordered back; and I remember hearing, at the time, Colonel Eaton, the adjutant general of General Frémont, rather reprimand him for taking so large a force.
Question. Is there anything else connected with the administration of that

department that you deem it material to state? I do not know anything of what you do know, so that I am unable to direct you at all.

Answer. There are a great many things a man might give as matters of opinion, having been associated thoroughly with the campaign; but not having had access to the documents and orders, I should not be able to state them from positive knowledge. I could give my ideas from what was the general impression, from the time we left our posts at Rolla and Sedalia, until General Frémont was relieved.

Question. Are you a military man? Have you had a military education?

Answer. I never was in a military school. I have been in the volunteer militia of the State of Missouri for eight or nine years. I was unfortunately connected with the expedition under General Cross that went out after Montgomery some fifteen or eighteen months ago. That was my first active service.

Question. You do not pretend to have a knowledge of military science?

Answer. No, sir; I do not feel that I have any great military abilities. Still, I think there are a great many men outside of military schools whose good common sense teaches them what to do, as well as a West Point education.

Question. I do not think you are so far wrong in that opinion. Do you know anything about the force that General Lyon had at the battle of Wilson's Creek?

Answer. It was within a few hundred of 5,000. There were, I should judge, about 4,800 in the battle.

Question. What was the force of the enemy that he had to encounter there?

Answer. We know them to have been 19,000 a day or two before the battle, and we had every reason to believe that they were re-enforced by 3,000 or 4,000 that night, making their force something like 23,000.

Question. General Frémont was at St. Louis then?

Answer. Yes, sir.

Question. How long had he been there previous to the battle?

Answer. I do not know positively; I should judge about two weeks.

Question. What was the number and condition of his forces, at that time so far as you know?

Answer. I suppose he had something near 10,000 men, in and around St. Louis, that could have been ordered off. There were no troops in the State at that time that were what we would call, in military parlance, thoroughly equipped and ready for the field. A great many might have had equipments, but they had no transportation. There was one regiment (Colonel Stephenson's) which General Frémont ordered to join us, but they disobeyed orders, and plead, as a reason for doing so, that they did not have transportation.

By Mr. Odell:

Question. Colonel Stephenson disobeyed orders?

Answer. I said he disobeyed orders. I know we got a copy of the order from General Frémont, after General Lyon's death, in which he ordered Colonel Stephenson to move his regiment to join us, and Colonel Stephenson was put under arrest for disobedience of orders; but he was afterwards released.

By the chairman:

Question. Was there a necessity for General Lyon making a stand there at Springfield and fighting a battle at that time?

Answer. It was so decided, after a thorough consultation of all the officers having any command, however small, from a battalion to a regiment. The reason of that was this: we had gone down there and were out of provisions almost, and after the battle of Dug Spring we fell back upon Springfield, and were in no condition to retreat. There were narrow defiles in the Ozark mountains where it was almost impossible for one wagon to pass another. We could not withstand an attack there by their forces, and, in the judgment of the officers the only course left was to attack the enemy.

Question. You say you were out of provisions?

Answer. We had but few provisions. We had sent a train to Rolla for provisions, and were grinding corn in the mills in the neighborhood to sustain the army.

Question. Could you have sustained many re-enforcements there? How would you have got provisions for re-enforcements if they had come?

Answer. We had a train of over one hundred wagons at Rolla, which was detained there by negligence, I might say.

Question. By whose negligence?

Answer. It is hard for me to say. But we then supposed it was through the negligence of Major McKinstry; and I have seen no reason to change my opinion on that point since.

Question. In what capacity was he then acting?

Answer. He was quartermaster of the department of the west. I was acting as quartermaster there at Springfield, and my wagonmasters were to have been gone nine days, and they were gone twenty-two days. Wagons that had been hired were ordered to St. Louis and paid off, and in the place of them new wagons were ordered up, and fresh mules without shoes; but they could not travel over the rough roads of the mountains, and shoes were afterwards sent up to them, and eventually blacksmiths were sent to put them on. And finally, but sixty-five wagons came instead of nearly one hundred that were sent for provisions.

Question. What was the condition of Cairo at that time, in regard to the number of men there? Do you know?

Answer. I do not know positively. General Prentiss was in command there, and we were in communication with him; but there were no official reports that came to General Lyon in reference to the number of troops there.

WASHINGTON, *March* 5, 1862.

General DAVID HUNTER sworn and examined.

By the chairman:

Question. What is your rank and position in the army?

Answer. I am colonel of the 6th cavalry, and a major general of volunteers.

Question. Where is your station now?

Answer. I am commanding the department of Kansas at present.

Question. Were you in the army under General Frémont at any time?

Answer. Yes, sir.

Question. Please give us a narrative, in your own way, of all that you deem material, without questioning.

Answer. Unless you would question me I would hardly know what points you desire to arrive at.

Question. We want to know how that western department was administered; if there were any defects that came under your notice or observation, or anything that would require a military man to take notice of it. We desire to know all about it.

Answer. It struck me that there were a great many defects in the department as soon as I went into it. In the first place, the whole property of the government was in the hands of irresponsible agents, who had given no bonds and knew nothing about the administration of the different branches of the service.

Question. Give us a narrative of when you went into the army there, what you found, what was the condition of the department, the important events that took place, &c.

Answer. I was ordered by General Scott to go to Illinois.

Question. About what time?

Answer. The last of August. I arrived at Chicago about the first of September, and had orders to report to General Frémont, at St. Louis. I did so by letter from Chicago. A short time afterwards I received a telegram from St. Louis from General Frémont, stating that he wished me to go to St. Louis; that he had something for me to do as soon as I was well enough. I thought I was well enough to go down there at any rate, and I went down the next day and reported to General Frémont. A short time after I had been in his office General Asboth brought in a programme of what it was expected I would do. General Frémont handed it to me, and requested me to examine it carefully, and look at the maps, and tell him what I thought of it. It commenced by stating that Springfield was a great strategic point, in the midst of a large plateau of fertile country, &c., and stated that he wanted me to go to Rolla and advance with all the disposable force from there on Springfield. At the same time Colonel Jeff. C. Davis was to leave Jefferson City with all the force he had there, cross the Osage at Tuscumbia, join me near Springfield, and advance and take possession of Springfield. After looking it over I was very much surprised, because I knew, at the same time, that General Price was at Warrensburg, thirty-five miles south of Lexington, advancing on Lexington. I asked General Frémont why I should go and take possession of Springfield, where there was no enemy, and leave Price at Warrensburg, advancing on Lexington. I proposed to him to give me the command of all the available force at Rolla and St. Louis, and let me go out at once to Sedalia and attack Price before he could get to Lexington. Fortunately for me, Mr. Montgomery Blair was present during the whole of this interview. Mr. Blair said, "Certainly; why should you go to Springfield, where there is no enemy, and leave Price marching on Lexington?" General Frémont shrugged his shoulders, but made no reply about that, and some time afterwards Mr. Blair and myself left. I heard nothing more for three or four days, when I received orders to go to Rolla, but with no orders what to do there. I went there and remained a week, when I was ordered back to Jefferson City to join General Frémont in his advance to the south.

Question. What amount of troops did you have at Rolla and under your command in the expedition to Springfield?

Answer. I had about 3,700 men at Rolla. There was a large division assigned me on paper, but it was scattered all over the face of the earth.

Question. What amount had Price under him when he was going to Lexington?

Answer. He had about 21,000 men, and others joining him. Harris and Green were crossing the Missouri, at Glasgow and at Arrow Rock, for the purpose of forming a junction with him. I went to Jefferson City, where I remained some time. General Frémont finally came up.

Question. Did you propose to go and intercept Price's advance on Lexington with that amount of force?

Answer. No, sir; not at all. I proposed this: there were some 15,000 or 20,000 troops at St. Louis at the time, and there were those troops at Rolla, and those with Colonel Davis, which would have given me a column equal to Price's, or very nearly equal to it. I could give you a pretty good idea of what I thought of the state of affairs by reading you some of my telegrams and letters to General Frémont, which I have copied here in this book. And I can give you some letters from General Pope, which will show you what he thought of the state of affairs.

Question. Your telegrams and letters to General Frémont would be proper.

Answer. In the first place, I received notice of what my division was to be composed of. They were scattered in every direction, and I did not know where or when they would report. My first telegram to General Frémont, through his adjutant general, is from Jefferson City, dated September 26, 1861, and is as follows:

"I have just received your letter of the 22d instant, designating the regiments of my division. Have all these regiments been ordered to report to me, and at what place? Please send me six of the largest maps of Missouri."

Here is another of the same date:

"I have ordered, agreeably to the general's order of the 24th instant, Colonel Stephenson, 7th Missouri, to move, with his regiment and 4th Iowa, directly from Rolla to Linn Creek; after which to send the 4th Iowa to Tuscumbia. Please telegraph if this order meets with the approbation of General Frémont, that I may countermand it if necessary."

Still another telegram to General Frémont from the same place and of the same date:

"I believe McCulloch is near Mount Vernon, in Lawrence county. A force of 4,000 men is reported at Linn Creek. Colonel Wyman, in consequence of a railroad accident, has not yet left Rolla. If the general wishes, he could move on Linn Creek immediately with the four regiments of my division now at Rolla."

Here is a letter from Jefferson City to Colonel Eaton, the adjutant general of General Frémont, dated October 4, 1861:

"COLONEL: Your letter of yesterday, ordering me to march this morning, was only received this morning at ten minutes after two. You will see by my report of transportation sent you on the second instant that for the forty-one wagons in possession of my quartermaster he has only forty mules. It will therefore be impossible for him to take the forty or more wagons agreeably to your order. Colonel Stephenson, of the 7th Missouri regiment, informs me that he is attached to Colonel Totten's brigade, of the 5th division. I must protest in the strongest terms against this very unmilitary proceeding of depriving me of the most important part of my command, when under marching orders, without giving me official notice of the change. Detaching Colonel Stephenson from my division will leave me but one regiment here fit to take the field."

We marched in obedience to that order, and my next communication is from California, Missouri, on the 6th of October:

"COLONEL: I informed you yesterday, by telegram, that the command had been without rations for more than twenty-four hours, and the supply here is so small that we should be without to-day had it not been for this fast. The baggage is not yet all up, and our men were exposed the night before last to one of the violent storms of the season without shelter. I fear much all the ammunition is injured, particularly in Ellis's regiment, where they have neither greatcoats nor cartridge-boxes, and have been obliged to carry their ammunition in their pockets. Should these men remain without greatcoats at this season of the year, I fear great sickness and mortality among them. Colonel Ellis is in want of swords, pistols, cartridge-boxes, gun-slings, greatcoats, ammunition, and wagons and mules for transportation. Colonel Stephenson is also without wagons or mules for transportation. Colonel Marshall is also destitute of transportation, and so is Captain Stanley. Colonel Turner has but seven teams, and Colonel Bland but nine four-mule teams. Please send us transportation at once, and the supply of provisions. The fresh beef sent from Jefferson City was spoiled on the way up and thrown away."

Here is also a telegram of the 6th of October:

"I have received your telegram to Lieutenant H. W. Greiner, directing him to notify General Hunter to halt with his own division, until further orders, at

Tipton. We have not transportation sufficient to move the command as I reported this morning, and have no provisions. We cannot depend upon the railroad, as they are only now delivering the baggage due the day before yesterday. Some of it has not yet arrived. Volunteers without provisions, tents, greatcoats, or blankets, become perfectly demoralized. Shall I move to Tipton in the morning, leaving what baggage I cannot transport, and without provisions?"

From Tipton I telegraphed, on the 7th, as follows:

"I did not receive your telegram ordering me to move with all the troops from California to Tipton till after my arrival here. Consequently, I brought only my own division, agreeably to previous orders."

On the 12th I wrote as follows:

"I have received the general's orders directing my division to move in the morning. Not one-half of my division has yet reported. Colonel Ellis's cavalry are without ammunition, cartridge-boxes, swords, pistols, and greatcoats, and many of them are greatly in want of clothing. The men of the Indiana batteries are in want of greatcoats, clothing, and ammunition. Requisitions have been sent in for ambulances, but they have not been furnished. Some of our mules are unshod, and we shall have them lame and unserviceable unless we can be furnished with portable forges and blacksmiths' tools. About fifty tents are needed for the division. As we shall have to send our teams back for provisions after four days' march, we should not leave here with less than 60,000 rations, as we cannot calculate on their return in less than fifteen days to our camp, even if we should remain stationary at the end of our four days' march. The cavalry regiment has not a wagon, and Colonel Palmer's and Colonel Bland's have, neither of them, sufficient for their baggage. To enable them to move efficiently we need at least 100 wagons and the ambulances already ordered to be supplied to the division by the general commanding."

Here is a letter to Adjutant General Thomas in relation to the same affair:

"CAMP NEAR TIPTON, *October* 15.

"GENERAL: When I parted, day before yesterday, from General Cameron, he remarked to me: 'On you, sir, I place great dependence.' I hope you will consider it due to me to explain fully to the honorable Secretary of War how completely I have been ignored in the department of the west. On the 13th of September I reported to General Frémont, in St. Louis, and did not see him again while I remained in that city. Instead of being permitted to attack General Price, who was then at Warrensburg marching to attack Lexington, I was, on the 16th, ordered to Rolla. After remaining a week at Rolla I was ordered to Jefferson City. You will see by my letter of the 4th instant that instead of a division, I informed General Frémont that I marched from Jefferson with only one regiment fit to take the field, and this regiment was without the necessary transportation. This morning I have for duty only 2,684 men, the cavalry portion of the command being without swords, pistols, cartridge-boxes, and ammunition for their guns. We are here by order of General Frémont, waiting transportation. You can see plainly, by this simple state of facts, that no blame or praise can attach to me on account of any of the operations in this department."

On the 18th of October I wrote to General Frémont from Tipton a letter, from which I read the following:

"I have made every effort to obtain the necessary supplies, but without success. I shall move to Versailles to-morrow, but without the means to transport supplies. The division will soon be in a destitute condition. Please inform me at Versailles if the general commanding wishes me, under the circumstances in which we are placed, still to advance."

Dr. Barnes, my medical director, was ordered to report to General Frémont. In my reply to the order, I state to Colonel Eaton:

"I am very sorry to have received, this evening, the order detaching Surgeon Barnes from my command, as he was assigned to me by the President at my particular request. I, however, fully appreciate the necessity of Dr. Barnes being at headquarters, as I found the hospital at Warsaw with 300 sick in it, who had been absolutely without anything to eat for two days. I shall be at Mountview to-morrow with a part of my command, but without provisions, and with my transportation in a very crippled state, from the want of mules and horses."

[See letter of General Pope to General Hunter, hereto attached.]

That comprises pretty much all the information up to that time. I arrived at Springfield on the 3d day of November, just as tattoo was beating, about 9 o'clock. I was under the impression, from what I had heard on the way, that General Frémont had left for the east. I inquired where the quarters were that he had vacated, intending to take possession of them myself, and learned that he was still there. I found him, with all the generals of his command assembled, discussing a plan for attacking the enemy the next morning at Wilson's Creek—everything arranged for the attack. I said nothing on the subject at all; but I was fully convinced, from what I had heard, that there was no enemy at all. It is said that I countermanded General Frémont's order for the battle the next day. It is not so. I gave no order in the case whatever. General Frémont left the next morning for the east, and I assumed the command. I spent the day in examining the positions around Springfield and the different camps there. I sent out a couple of regiments of cavalry to reconnoitre and examine the ground about Wilson's Creek. They returned in the evening, and reported that no enemy had been there, and that they were sixty or seventy miles off, at Cassville. The next day after that I went out myself to Wilson's Creek, with a party to bury some dead that were said to have been left on the battle-field there. We found five bodies, and buried them.

By Mr. Julian:

Question. This was the 5th of November that you went out there?

Answer. I think it was the 5th, but I am not confident about that; it may have been the 6th. But that General Price was at Cassville at that time will appear from a letter of his own, (that is, one from his adjutant general,) enclosing a treaty that had been made by General Frémont with General Price. Here is a copy of that letter:

"HEADQUARTERS MISSOURI STATE GUARDS,
"*Cassville, Missouri, November* 5, 1861.

"GENERAL: I am instructed by Major General Price to acknowledge the receipt of Assistant Adjutant General Eaton's letter of November 2, enclosing a proclamation drawn up in accordance with the propositions submitted in my letter of the 26th of October. Major General Price directs me to say that he receives your assent to his propositions with much satisfaction, and the agreements and provisions set forth in the proposed mutual proclamation fully meet his approbation. He has filled up and signed both copies of said proclamation received from Assistant Adjutant General Eaton, one of which is retained for publication and distribution, and the other herewith enclosed to you for a like purpose. Major General Price also approves of the agreement entered into on his part by Messrs. Williams and Barclay, and herewith returns the original statement, retaining a copy of the same.

"I am, general, very respectfully, your obedient servant,

"HENRY LITTLE, *Adjutant General.*

"Major General J. C. Frémont,

"*Commanding United States Forces, Springfield, Missouri.*"

That is a letter from General Price's command at Cassville, of the 5th, the day after I took command.

By Mr. Odell:

Question. When was this battle to have been fought?

Answer. On the morning of the 4th, the morning I took command.

By Mr. Gooch:

Question. On what information did you come to the conclusion that there was no enemy at Wilson's Creek, or in that vicinity?

Answer. I came to that conclusion from conversations with various officers of my acquaintance there, who, notwithstanding the reports, did not believe anything of the kind.

Question. How did you find the belief of the officers generally on that point?

Answer. I asked them about what they thought of it, and I found that they did not believe it at all.

Question. Was that the general belief of the officers?

Answer. It was among those I met with.

Question. You saw and conversed with a great many of the officers?

Answer. Yes, sir.

Question. When you made the reconnoissance out in the vicinity of Wilson's Creek, were there any traces of the enemy having been there?

Answer. Not the least. I questioned people who lived there—a man who had a mill-right on the creek where the battle had been fought, and he said there had been no enemy there at all. There might have been a few scouts, but not any force at all.

Question. Were they Union people living out in that vicinity?

Answer. One man that we found at the mill professed to be a Union man. There were a great many Union people through that part of Missouri, about Springfield. I think Mrs. Phelps, who appeared to be better posted than anybody else there, told me that there was no enemy in the neighborhood there at all. She is the wife of Colonel Phelps, member of Congress from Missouri.

By the chairman:

Question. Did you continue the arrangement made by General Frémont with General Price?

Answer. No, sir; I annulled it at once. Here is the letter I wrote to headquarters:

"Headquarters Western Department,

"*Springfield, Missouri, November* 7, 1861.

"General: Enclosed you will find copies of certain negotiations carried on between Major General J. C. Frémont, of the first part, and Major General Sterling Price, of the second part, having for objects, first, to make arrangements for the exchange of prisoners; second, to prevent arrests or forcible interference in the future 'for the mere entertainment or expression of political opinions;' third, to insure that 'the war now progressing shall be confined exclusively to armies in the field;' and, fourth, the immediate disbandment of 'all bodies of armed men acting without the authority or recognition of the major general commanding, and not legitimately connected with the armies in the field.'

"You will also find enclosed a copy of my letter of this date, despatched under a flag of truce, to General Price, stating that 'I can in no manner recognize the agreement aforesaid, or any of its provisions, whether implied or direct, and I can neither issue nor allow to be issued the joint proclamation purporting to have been signed by Generals Price and Frémont on the 1st day of November, A. D. 1861.' It would be, in my judgment, impolitic in the highest degree to have ratified General Frémont's negotiations, for the following, amongst many other, obvious reasons: The second stipulation, if acceded to, would render the enforcement of martial law in Missouri, or any part of it, impossible, and would give absolute liberty to the propagandists of treason throughout the length and breadth of the State. The third stipulation, confining operations exclusively to armies in the field, would practically annul the confiscation act passed during the last session of Congress, and would furnish perfect immunity to those disbanded soldiers of Price's command who have now returned to their homes, but with the intention and under the pledge of rejoining the rebel forces whenever called upon; and, lastly, because the fourth stipulation would blot out the existence of loyal men of the Missouri home guards, who have not, it is alleged, been recognized by act of Congress, and who, it would be claimed, are therefore 'not legitimately connected with the armies in the field.'

"There are many other objections quite as powerful and obvious, which might be urged against ratifying this agreement. It is addressed 'to the peaceably disposed citizens of the State of Missouri,' fairly allowing the inference to be drawn that citizens of the United States (the loyal and true men of Missouri) are not included within its benefits. In fact, the agreement would seem to me, if ratified, a concession of all the principles for which the rebel leaders are contending, and a practical liberation for use in other and more immediately important localities of all their forces now kept employed in this portion of the State.

"I have the honor to be, general, most respectfully, your most obedient servant,

"D. HUNTER,

"*Major General Commanding.*

"Brigadier General THOMAS, *Adjutant General U. S. A.*"

By Mr. Covode:

Question. Did you hold a council of war after arriving at Springfield?

Answer. I did.

Question. At that council did you determine to retreat, fall back, or to advance? What was the decision of that council?

Answer. There was a difference of opinion in regard to what should be done. I had read to them a letter which I had received from the President on the subject of returning, and asked their opinion on it. General McKinstry recommended that we should go forward, not that he expected to meet Price at all. None of us believed he would allow us to overtake him, but he thought a demonstration should be made; that we should go forward. General Pope, I believe, did not at that time express any very decided opinion one way or the other; but he stated afterwards that he thought I was right in not going forward. The two Germans—Asboth and Sigel—chimed in with McKinstry.

Question. They wanted to go forward?

Answer. They thought a demonstration would have a better effect. None of them pretended that they thought we could catch Price at all. But they thought it would have a better effect on the country to make a move forward. General Turner was the other general of division, and he thought differently.

By the chairman:

Question. What were your orders from the President?

Answer. I have a copy of them here:

"WASHINGTON, *October* 24, 1861

"SIR: The command of the department of the west having devolved upon you, I propose to offer you a few *suggestions*, knowing how hazardous it is to bind down a distant commander in the field to specific lines of operations, as so much always depends on the knowledge of localities and passing events. It is intended, therefore, to leave considerable margin for the exercise of your judgment and discretion.

"The main rebel army (Prices) west of the Mississippi is believed to have passed Dade county in full retreat upon northwestern Arkansas, leaving Missouri almost free from the enemy, excepting in the southeast part of the State. Assuming this basis of fact, it seems desirable—as you are not likely to overtake Price, and are in danger of making too long a line from your own base of supplies and re-enforcements—that you should give up the pursuit, halt your main army, divide it into two corps of observation, one occupying Sedalia and the other Rolla, the present *termini* of railroads, then recruit the condition of both corps by re-establishing and improving their discipline and instruction, perfecting their clothing and equipments, and providing less uncomfortable quarters. Of course both railroads must be guarded and kept open, judiciously employing just so much force as is necessary for this. From these two points, Sedalia and Rolla, and especially in judicious co-operation with Lane on the Kansas border, it would be very easy to concentrate and repel any army of the enemy returning on Missouri on the southwest. As it is not probable any such attempt to return will be made before or during the approaching cold weather, before spring the people of Missouri will be in no favorable mood for renewing, for next year, the troubles which have so much afflicted and impoverished them during this.

"If you take this line of policy, and if as I anticipate you will see no enemy in great force approaching, you will have a surplus force which you can withdraw from those points and direct to others, as may be needed—the railroads furnishing ready means of re-enforcing those main points, if occasion requires.

"Doubtless local uprisings, for a time, will continue to occur, but those can be met by detachments, and local forces of our own, and will, ere long, tire out of themselves.

"While, as stated at the beginning of this letter, a large discretion must be, and is left with yourself, I feel sure that an indefinite pursuit of Price, or an attempt, by this long and circuitous route, to reach Memphis, will be exhaustive beyond endurance, and will end in the loss of the whole force engaged in it.

"Your obedient servant,

"A. LINCOLN.

"The COMMANDER *of the department of the west*."

By Mr. Gooch:

Question. Did your own judgment correspond with the instructions from the President?

Answer. Yes, sir.

By Mr. Covode:

Question. What time did you receive that letter? Before the council?

Answer. Yes, sir; I submitted it to the council.

By Mr. Gooch:

Question. On what day did you call your council?

Answer. My impression is that it was on the 7th of November.

Question. Composed of the same officers that General Frémont had in his council?

Answer. No, sir; I only called the generals commanding divisions—five of them.

Question. Those generals were also in General Frémont's council?

Answer. Yes, sir.

Question. There were others in his council?

Answer. Yes, sir; he had the brigade generals in his council.

Question. The same men you had in your council were also in his council?

Answer. Yes, sir; with the exception of General Turner, who took command of my division when I left it.

Question. Was there any question in your council as to where the enemy was?

Answer. I think not.

Question. Where did you believe him to be at that time?

Answer. At Cassville.

Question. Did the generals composing your council concur in that belief?

Answer. I think they did.

Question. Have you any doubt now that he was then at Cassville?

Answer. None whatever.

Question. Was there any considerable portion of his force at a nearer point—at Wilson's creek, or in its vicinity?

Answer. I do not believe there was any force at all at Wilson's creek. He had a guard in advance of Cassville, of course, and McCulloch was said to be about fifteen miles south of Cassville, with his command, still nearer the Arkansas line.

By Mr. Julian:

Question. You say that McKinstry, Asboth and Sigel, all believed there was no enemy near?

Answer. Yes, sir, that is my impression. In fact I have reports now from Sigel, whom I sent out to Wilson's creek, that there was no enemy in that neighborhood at all. I had reports every day from men in Price's camp. There was a certain Major Wright there, who had a battalion of spies—very efficient men, indeed—all young men from that portion of the country in southwestern Missouri. They would go off in their farmer clothes and stay two or three days in Price's camp; and every day, almost, Major Wright would receive a report from some of those men.

Question. Those generals were still for making an advance?

Answer. Yes, sir.

Question. What was General Frémont's opinion about the locality of Price's army at the time you took the command?

Answer. He notified me several times during the day I arrived there that Price was immediately on him; that an attack would take place the next day. He appeared to think, of course, that they were at Wilson's creek, or he would not have made dispositions to attack him the next morning.

By Mr. Gooch:

Question. Do you know on what information General Frémont came to the conclusion that the enemy was at Wilson's creek?

Answer. No, sir, I do not.

By Mr. Julian:

Question. Do you know whether he had sent out scouts to determine that fact?

Answer. I presumed he had, of course.

By Mr. Gooch:

Question. Is it not a remarkable fact that there should have been so much doubt in relation to that matter; that General Frémont, being there in command, should be under the impression that he was to attack the enemy the next morning, and you, upon assuming command, should be convinced that there was no enemy there?

Answer. Yes, sir, I think it is very remarkable indeed.

Question. Did you convey to General Frémont the order to supersede him?

Answer. No, sir; he had it two or three days before; he sent it to me.

Question. His relinquishing the command and your taking it was contingent upon your coming up and reaching that point at Springfield?

Answer. Yes, sir. He was to have left for St. Louis before I arrived, but he concluded to remain until I arrived. He had made all preparations to leave for St. Louis before I arrived. Here is an order I sent to the colonel commanding the Indiana brigade, on the first of November. I had left him behind, on account of not having transportation sufficient to come up:

"MOUNT VIEW, *November* 1, 1861.

"COLONEL HOREY: General Frémont informs me the enemy is marching on him at Sprnigfield. You will join me with the least delay with your command, leaving all your tents, and bringing with you only your mess-pans and camp kettles. I march at daylight in the morning, and hope you will join me during the night."

He was some ten or twelve miles in my rear. He did join me during the night, and we marched at daylight in the morning.

Question. Was the movement of General Frémont to Springfield from St. Louis, at the time it was made, a judicious movement, in a military point of view, considering the condition of the enemy and the position of Missouri at the time?

Answer. I did not so consider it. Price had gone up to Lexington and done all the damage he could there, and he retreated from Lexington when we had only about a couple of thousand of men at Sedalia, making seventy miles in two days. And when he was going at the rate of seventy miles in two days from a force of two thousand men at Sedalia, I had no idea he was going to allow General Frémont to catch him; and I thought those troops might be used to much greater advantage on the Mississippi and in Kentucky than to be following after General Price down to Arkansas.

Question. Was not the movement of General Frémont necessary to compel or induce Price to leave Missouri?

Answer. Certainly; I have no idea he would have gone out without that movement, but what was the object of making him go out compared with the using these thirty odd thousand troops in another direction?

Question. You think that object was accomplished, but more might have been accomplished by using the troops in another direction?

Answer. Yes, sir; no doubt that object was accomplished, because I had positive notice before I left Springfield that Price was in Arkansas. There had been so much talk about a battle there that I delayed marching for several days to see if there was any possibility of his coming to attack us, or any probability of his allowing us to attack him.

By Mr. Covode:

Question. What was the effect upon the country of your falling back at that time; was there not a considerable amount of mischief done?

Answer. Yes, sir; there always is.

Question. Had you remained at Springfield would it have been in your power to have prevented that?

Answer. Yes, sir.

Question. Had you advanced would the enemy have fled from you?

Answer. Yes, sir.

Question. Then it would have saved a great deal of Western Missouri from desolation if you had advanced from Springfield.

Answer. I do not know that we would have saved much. They had ravaged the whole country twice—in going up and coming down.

Question. Did you fall back without any other council of war?

Answer. Yes, sir.

Question. So that there was no council that determined to fall back?

Answer. No, sir; I called a council merely to get their views. In regard to General McKinstry, I had no confidence in him whatever. I considered him a traitor. And with respect to the two German generals, they are very good soldiers. Sigel is a very good soldier. They merely said, with General McKinstry, that we better make a demonstration—not that they believed we would catch Price at all, but they thought it would have a great deal better effect on the country to march out two or three days and come back again. An hour after the council was over my adjutant general came to me and said I had been betrayed; that he had heard the whole proceeding of this council repeated by a newspaper reporter. He told me what he had heard and asked me if such and such things had taken place in the council. I told him that was precisely what had taken place. He said "Somebody has betrayed you." I said "It is General McKinstry; you order him to leave here to-morrow morning and report at St. Louis." So I disposed of him at once. The day after I had a telegram from Washington ordering me to put him in close confinement, to be sent down to St. Louis. I forwarded that on to St. Louis and had it done.

Question. Do you know where that order originated?

Answer. I do not know about that; I assumed my command on the 4th, and had no communication with the government here before that.

By Mr. Julian:

Question. You think he disclosed the proceedings of that council?

Answer. I have no doubt about it at all. In regard to the opinion of those German generals, I think they just chimed in with McKinstry, because he stated his opinion in a very positive, dogmatical manner, and they had been so accustomed to defer to him that they simply assented to what he said. I took the whole responsibility of the retrograde movement on myself; that is, I had the approval of General Pope and General Turner.

Question. What was the condition of the troops when you took command?

Answer. They were in pretty good condition. We have heard a great deal of talk about their being in a state of mutiny, and very insubordinate, &c., but I noticed nothing of the kind. I did not notice the first act of insubordination.

Question. I mean their physical condition?

Answer. They were in pretty good physical condition. We fortunately had very fine weather, indeed, and the stopping at Springfield enabled the trains to come up.

Question. They were in good spirits?

Answer. Yes, sir.

By Mr. Odell:

Question. When did this mutinous spirit show itself?

Answer. I saw nothing of it at all.

By Mr. Gooch:

Question. Was there, as far as you could judge, any desire on the part of the troops to push forward?

Answer. I do not know that there was; I do not think that there was; I never knew them to express any feeling one way or the other.

By Mr. Odell:

Question. Was there any dissatisfaction manifested by the troops upon your taking command?

Answer. Not that I know of.

By Mr. Julian:

Question. Was there any feeling manifested by the officers or men on account of General Frémont being superseded?

Answer. No, sir; not so far as I witnessed. I was told that the German officers had called upon General Frémont, and he had made them speeches, and they had made him speeches, and some of the speeches made in the presence of General Frémont were insubordinate; but I saw nothing of the kind when I assumed command.

By Mr. Covode:

Question. What course did General Frémont take in regard to the insubordinate speeches?

Answer. He took no course whatever, according to the statement I heard. He did not reprove them at all for it, but I believe rather encouraged it.

By Mr. Julian:

Question. Did you see any act of insubordination?

Answer. No, sir; none at all.

Question. You do not know anything about it?

Answer. No, sir.

By Mr. Gooch:

Question. So that, of your own knowledge, you do not know that any insubordinate speeches were made?

Answer. No, sir.

By Mr. Covode:

Question. How did you learn that he rather encouraged them?

Answer. From the officers there.

Question. From whom?

Answer. I could not name any particular individual.

Question. We think it is important.

Answer. If the committee want a statement of that kind I can get a hundred officers who will make the statement.

Question. We only want one or two names.

Answer. My impression is that General Pope was one of them. I do not remember any other name now.

By Mr. Odell:

Question. Are there any other facts connected with this western department that you deem it important or essential to state?

Answer. I do not think of anything at present.

The following letters from General Pope to General Hunter were read :

HEADQUARTERS SECOND DIVISION,
Syracuse, October 12, 1861.

DEAR GENERAL: I received, at one o'clock last night, the extraordinary order of General Frémont for a forward movement of his whole force.

The wonderful manner in which the actual facts and condition of things here are ignored stupefies me. One would suppose from this order that divisions and brigades are organized, and are under immediate command of their officers; that transportation is in possession of all; that every arrangement of supply trains to follow the army has been made; in fact, that we are in a perfect state of preparation for a move.

You know, as well as I do, that the exact reverse is the fact; that neither brigades nor divisions have been brought together, and that if they were there is not transportation enough to move this army one hundred yards; that, in truth, not one solitary preparation of any kind has been made to enable this advance movement to be executed. I have never seen my division, nor do I suppose you have seen yours. I have no cavalry even for a personal escort, and yet this order requires me to send forward companies of pioneers protected by cavalry. Is it intended that this order be obeyed, or, rather, that we try to obey it, or is the order only designed for Washington and the papers? If such a movement is made without provision or camp equipage of any kind, of necessity the whole force must return ignominiously, the next day, to the railroad. Please explain to me all this, and let me know what you design doing.

I am here without a command. Only the other day I was ordered here with the force from Boonville. Now I am ordered to go back in the direction of Sedalia. I am here myself, as I happened to be in Georgetown when the order reached me; but Kelton has no transportation for his brigade at Boonville, and has for ten days been trying to press wagons for thirty miles in every direction around him. I suppose that he has met with little success, as that whole region has been stripped before he reached there.

I went to Jefferson City, the last time I saw you, for the express purpose of getting transportation for my division, and explained to General Frémont precisely what I have said above.

Now, in the face of the fact that he knew no transportation was furnished, and that Kelton has none, he should coolly order such a movement, and expect it to be made, I cannot understand on any reasonable or common-sense hypothesis. Please enlighten me, if you can, and at all events let me know what you intend to do, as I presume you to be in the same situation that I am.

I will be obliged to you for any late paper or news.

Very truly, yours,

JNO. POPE.

Major General HUNTER, *Tipton.*

CAMP THREE MILES WEST OF OTTERVILLE,
October 18, 1861.

DEAR GENERAL: I received your note yesterday morning, and I am really sorry I could not come down to see you before I left Syracuse. I am anxious to know the result of the Secretary's visit and its object. Upon his action on the subject, in my judgment, rests the safety of this command from great suffering. If we attempt to go south of the Osage without supplies for at least a month, and without much better preparation for everything than exists now, I do not believe one-half of these troops will ever return alive. The winter is coming on us. The men of this division are without overcoats, their clothes in rags, and only one blanket apiece; no provision trains or depots organized, and, so far as I can see, no object in view.

I shall, however, move from here and occupy the point designated with five regiments, being all I can get anything like transportation for. I can, perhaps, carry eight or ten days' rations for the five regiments by making very short marches. I have nearly a thousand sick men in the division—of course there is no sort of arrangement to take care of them. I have had buildings hired in Otterville, and shall establish a hospital there for the division, as far as I can do so, without hospital supplies of any kind.

Each division commander is left to himself. I don't know where to look for provisions short of St. Louis, or where for quartermaster or any other stores short of the same place, neither do I know to whom I can apply for anything this side of St. Louis. I have written and telegraphed for 300,000 rations, as I intend to establish at Otterville a depot of provisions and of such stores as I can get for my own command.

Altogether this is the most remarkable campaign I ever saw, heard of, or read of.

Do let me know all about the Secretary's visit and its results. Write me, if you have time, about your own movements and plans, what steps you have taken to get the means to move, and how soon you expect to go.

Give my regards to Shaffer, and believe me truly yours,

JNO. POPE.

Major General HUNTER,
Camp near Tipton.

I have not a single ambulance in the whole division.

CAMP NEAR QUINCY, *October* 26.

DEAR GENERAL: I reached here last evening, and intend to remain until my trains come up. I found that by going direct to Hazle creek I merely got into a pocket, to get out of which I would be compelled to return to the forks of the road. I am on the main road to Stockton, about eighteen miles from Warsaw.

Frémont left a point twelve miles beyond this yesterday, intending to be at Bolivar last night. Why he has gone so much further east I don't know, unless (as I suspect) he intends to return to St. Louis by way of Rolla, leaving us to get back as we best can.

I have no orders for any further movement; have you? I saw the expressman from Frémont with despatches for you, is my reason for asking.

I have a good camp, open prairie near the timber, good water, and forage enough for a few days.

I shall anxiously await orders from you.

Very truly, yours,

JNO. POPE.

Major General D. HUNTER, *Warsaw.*

CAMP OF SECOND DIVISION,
Near Quincy, October 26, 1861.

DEAR GENERAL: I received an hour ago, by the hands of Dr. Mack, "beef contractor," the order for a further movement to the south. Dr. Mack has the same order for you, but for fear of accident I send you a copy of mine.

Dr. Mack states that the troops in advance of us are living on quarter rations, and are pushing forward to "Neosho" at the rate of twenty miles a day. Within a few days they will be out of subsistence entirely. He says they talk of supply trains behind to be coming up, but none have passed me, nor do I know of any between here and Rolla. Even, however, if there were such trains they could not possibly overtake a command travelling at such a rate. The troops in advance seem to me doomed to destruction, or to such suffering as would make death grateful. I have few days' rations and cannot move until my trains reach here, which, I trust, will be in a couple of days. Of course, following in the rear of the armies of Frémont and Price no supplies can be expected from the country.

Price is doubtless in Arkansas, as he was at Neosho five days ago still moving south. When our forces have succeeded in reaching Neosho, or Arkansas itself, what is to be accomplished, or rather what does any sane man suppose will be the result? The prospect before us is appalling, and we seem to be led by mad men. Of course, General Frémont and the men around him, whose official existence depends upon his not being superseded, are desperate. But should they be permitted to drag to destruction, or at least to great and unnecessary suffering, the 30,000 men of this army, for no other purpose than to save, if possible, their own official lives? I shall obey the order and go on as soon as my supplies arrive here, but it will be with a heavy heart and grievous forbodings. If anything were to be accomplished it would, perhaps, be endurable. But no possible result will be or can be attained, except to allow Price to deprive the country of 30,000 troops for the entire winter. Let what will come these troops cannot be again put into the field before spring.

Please write me what you propose to do, that we may act in concert and save the force in advance of us from starvation, although we suffer great hardships ourselves in the attempt.

As soon as I receive my supply trains I will push on and share my rations with those who will be in the most need of them. My supplies, even under the most favorable circumstances, will go but a little way with so large a force as is in advance, but I will do the best I can.

I think Frémont crazy or worse.

Very truly your friend,

JNO. POPE.

Major General D. HUNTER, *in camp.*

Please send me any late papers you may have.

WASHINGTON, *March* 8, 1862.

Captain CHAUNCEY MCKEEVER sworn and examined.

By the chairman:

Question. What is your rank and position in the army?

Answer. I am a captain of the regular service in the adjutant general's department.

Question. Were you with General Frémont while in command of the western department?

Answer. Yes, sir.

Question. Please state in your own way what you deem material concerning the administration of that department.

Answer. I arrived at St. Louis the latter part of August—about the 30th of August—and remained on duty there until General Frémont was relieved. When I arrived there I found not a very large number of troops in the department that were organized; and the most of them appeared to be wanting either in instruction or in arms or clothing, for they were very badly armed and very poorly clothed. There was a great scarcity of everything. There seemed to be very little transportation; a great scarcity of wagons and animals. There seemed to be a great deficiency particularly of wagons and harness. There was a very small amount of money in the quartermaster's department. The constant complaint was that there was not money to buy anything with.

Question. What effective force do you suppose General Frémont had when you went there—what force well appointed and ready for the field?

Answer. There was a large number on the rolls, but I doubt whether he had an effective army of over 20,000 men at that time. There were a great many came in afterwards, but the most of them, as they arrived in St. Louis, received arms there, so they could not have had any before at all—had been in camp without arms. I saw very few regiments during the whole time I was there that I considered well armed. Their arms generally were of an inferior character.

Question. What was the condition of the department when you arrived there as regards the position and strength of the enemy, and what was necessary to be done?

Answer. At the time I arrived there very little seemed to be known at all about the position of Price and his army. I do not think it was known that he was so near Lexington, or that it was expected he would attack Lexington at all; and there were occasional reports that the enemy were advancing up along the Mississippi river in the direction of Ironton, Pilot Knob, and Cape Girardeau. The first I knew at all of Price's army being in so large a force was after we heard he had attacked Lexington. But I had then been but a very short time in the department, and had very little to do except with the rolls. I was not the senior adjutant general then. Captain Kelton was the senior adjutant general. I therefore knew very little of what was going on, or what were the plans. I knew very little about the military disposition of the enemy, or of our own force. I think Price's attack on Lexington was rather unexpected. I supposed at the time an effort would be made to relieve Lexington, and made from the northern side of the river, from General Pope's command; and my impression always was that the proper plan for Colonel Mulligan to pursue would have been to vacate his position in Lexington, because it was not a defensible one. I do not see how he could very well expect to get re-enforcements when he allowed the passage of the river to be obstructed by the enemy's seizing his steamers. He certainly knew the strength of the enemy for some days, and if they were as strong as he represents I do not think he should have remained there. I do not think that either courage or prudence required him to remain there. His position, if chosen in a military point of view, was certainly an indefensible one, for if he was cut off from water he certainly could not expect to hold out long. The river at that time of the year is low, and large steamboats cannot go up there. The railroad did not go near Lexington, and it was almost impossible for an army to march from the terminus of the railroad to Lexington for want of transportation; and at the time we heard of the attack upon Lexington there were very few troops in the city of St. Louis.

Question. What was the distance from the end of the railroad to Lexington?

Answer. I do not recollect exactly how far it was; I should suppose it was fifty or sixty miles. They had burned the Lamine River bridge, so that the road was not passable much beyond California. They had to repair the bridge afterwards.

Question. Were you with General Frémont when he was superseded by General Hunter?

Answer. No, sir; I was in St. Louis in charge of his headquarters there. All the papers and records were kept, and all the office duty was performed in St. Louis, under direction of General Frémont, in pursuance of special orders.

Question. What do you know about the construction of the fortifications about St. Louis, of which so much has been said?

Answer. My impression is that they were constructed on what is called the German plan, which the engineers in our army were not inclined to think was the best system by any means. I do not know that they cost any more; but I believe our engineers think that is not the best system. The German system is rather an old system, upon which a great many improvements have now been made.

Question. Under whose direction were they built?

Answer. Under the direction of Major Kappner and Colonel Hessendenbet. Major Kappner, who, I have understood, is an old Austrian officer, is rather an elderly man; I should think he is over sixty years of age. So far as my intercourse with him is concerned, I should think him a very honorable, upright man. I believe he built five forts at day labor. Those that I saw appeared to be thoroughly built, and capable of a pretty strong defence.

Question. Do you know whether they were economically built or otherwise?

Answer. The five built by Major Kappner were built as cheaply as they well could be built under the circumstances. The labor and the material used were paid for at a higher rate probably than otherwise would have been the case, because they did not know when they could get their money. The quartermaster's department, as they knew, was out of funds, and then, too, there were rumors afloat that General Frémont would be superseded, and they supposed his accounts would be suspended, and they might not get their pay at all. The five forts that were built by Major Kappner cost perhaps $60,000, as I have understood. That seemed to me to be a very reasonable sum to pay for them.

Question. What do you know about the other forts built there?

Answer. I have never read the whole of the contract; but I have seen either the original or a certified copy of it, which was in the hands of the congressional contract committee that went out there. It appeared to me that the prices were very high indeed. I think there were five other forts, or six at the outside; and if they were paid for entirely according to the terms of that contract, I think the contractor must have received $250,000 or $300,000, and must have made a good thing out of it if he was anything of a business man. I have never examined the forts, but I have heard the engineers who examined them say they were about the size of the others. The only ground I ever heard for paying so much more for these forts than the others was, that the contractor said that he worked on them day and night. But that does not seem to me to justify the difference between $60,000 and $250,000, unless the forts were very much larger; and Major Kappner says the plan and material used were about the same for all. And he is one who should know that, as I understand he laid them out, staked them off and all that, and was to inspect the work from time to time, as the building of the forts progressed, upon which money was to be advanced to the contractor. If the estimates were handed in, they never came to the office, but the money was paid over on the positive orders of General Frémont on the quartermaster's department. I should say if the contractor was paid at that rate, he must have made a very handsome sum of money if he understood his business at all.

Question. Did you observe, during your service there, any maladministration in that department; if so, who was to blame for it?

Answer. I never thought the quartermaster's department was well managed. The person who was acting as quartermaster when I arrived there, Major McKinstry, seemed to me to have too many duties to perform. He was quartermaster of the city, acting quartermaster general on General Frémont's staff, provost marshal of the city, and, afterwards, acting general of division. It seemed to me that those were more duties than any one man could well and promptly perform. And it struck me that there was not sufficient preparation made to take the field in the way of transportation. The quartermaster had not provided wagons or harness, and they had but just commenced purchasing animals when I arrived there. When General Frémont left St. Louis to take the field, about the 27th of September, I do not think there was transportation enough to have moved one division of his army as it should be moved, or, at any rate, not more than enough for one division. They were purchasing wagons and harness as late as the 25th of October or the 1st of November. Even at that time his army was not sufficiently supplied with transportation. They were all complaining of want of transportation.

Question. Was General Frémont deficient in exertions to get transportation?

Answer. No, sir; as soon as he made up his mind to take the field after Price, he made every exertion to get transportation. He ordered the quartermaster to purchase wherever he could get it without limiting the price or anything. I received orders several times to direct the quartermaster to purchase mules, wagons, harness, &c. Whether he knew before he started that the quartermaster had not then purchased the transportation I do not know. There was a great scarcity of transportation at the time. The fact is, at the time Lexington was attacked, there was scarcely any troops prepared to take the field. They were waiting for arms. I think some 10,000 Austrian muskets had been sent to Cincinnati to be altered and rifled. But I did not consider they were a good weapon even when improved. They did not seem to give satisfaction at all. Complaints were made that the locks were not good; that the guns would go off at half-cock; that the locks would break; that the hammers would break off. General Frémont had considerable cavalry there. The most of them had horses, but they did not have sabres, carbines, or pistols; and as late as the 1st of November there were several regiments there that had not arms at all. After General Frémont started he was continually urging me to send forward the 1st Iowa cavalry to join him; but I was unable to do so because they could not be supplied with arms. It was a regiment a thousand strong, and they had had horses for some months; but they had no arms, nor had General Frémont a sufficient number of field pieces to supply his artillery. There were companies in St. Louis when I left that had not been supplied with guns, and several others were down at Jefferson Barracks waiting for guns to come on from the east. There was a great deficiency in arms of all kinds there. I think General Frémont tried in all directions to get them. The reply from Washington was that they had no arms to give him; that the ordnance department could not supply them. The impression here seemed to be that there were more arms in Missouri than there really were. When the Secretary of War came out there, he asked what had become of some 10,000 arms sent out to General Lyon, but no one seemed to know anything about them. It was supposed that they had been distributed to the home guards, and not turned in. What arms were there were rusty, out of order, and not in condition to be used at all. Captain Callender, the ordnance officer there, certainly exerted himself to the utmost, and purchased wherever he could find weapons, and whenever he could get authority to do so. He seemed to make all the exertions in his power. And I think that the fact that so many reports came out to St. Louis, and the west, that General Frémont was to be removed interfered a great deal with the efficiency of his command. I do not think all his orders were as promptly obeyed, or that the same exertions were made by a great many of the officers, because they thought he was to be removed, and they could act as they pleased with impunity.

Question. They thought that General Frémont was in disfavor with the administration?

Answer. Yes, sir; I think so. General Curtis, I think, acted under that supposition. He undertook to take powers upon himself that certainly were not delegated to him by the army regulations, or any orders from Washington, that I am aware of. He undertook to send a flag of truce through our lines to Price, at Springfield, for an exchange of prisoners, for which he was reprimanded by General Frémont, and informed that if he, or any other officer, undertook to do a like act again he should be arrested. He seemed to think he had a right to send troops out of the city when and where he pleased, just because General Frémont was absent; that I could not act in General Frémont's name because he was not there, although I had written instructions from General Frémont what to do, and special instructions for special cases.

There were certain reports came to St. Louis that Jeff. Thompson, whom I was instructed to keep an eye upon, was advancing. I was instructed to watch Cape Girardeau and Ironton, and see that they were re-enforced in case of attack. On learning that Jeff. Thompson, or a part of his force, had burned the Big River bridge, I ordered General Grant, in the name of General Frémont, to send re-enforcements to Cape Girardeau, and ordered the command to start from there to intercept Thompson's retreat. I also re-enforced Ironton and Pilot Knob. I also sent a battery of the 1st Missouri light artillery, under the command of Major Schofield. I sent him in charge because I knew he was an officer of experience, and I felt a little solicitous about the place. He went at my special request. Of course I consulted him about it, and he agreed to go. All the orders were issued, of course, in the name of General Frémont, according to instructions. Major Schofield had been assistant adjutant general for General Lyon, and I knew he was thoroughly posted there. We agreed that that was all the re-enforcements that were necessary; that Colonel Carlin, with his own force and the additional force I had sent him, ought to be able to drive Jeff. Thompson back; and with Colonel Plummer coming up from Cape Girardeau, I was in hopes to cut off Thompson entirely. A despatch that was sent from Colonel Plummer to Colonel Carlin informing him what he was going to do, was intercepted by the enemy, and he immediately fell back off the main road to Fredericktown. Colonel Carlin and Colonel Plummer joined their forces, and attacked the enemy there, and whipped him. There was telegraphic communication opened between Pilot Knob and St. Louis, and I was kept fully informed of the condition of things there. General Curtis also received some telegrams from some parties who gave him wrong information, exaggerated Jeff. Thompson's forces, said that he had 10,000 or 15,000 men, and was advancing on St. Louis. And General Curtis acted as though he thought it was all true. He went out and inspected all the fortifications, and ordered the 1st Iowa cavalry down to Jefferson Barracks to scout out from there. Now, I had positive information that there was no enemy there. This Iowa cavalry had been under orders for some time to join General Frémont as soon as they were equipped. One squadron had been equipped the day previous, but, owing to pressing business and the re-enforcing Pilot Knob, I had not sent them off. And I then ordered this cavalry to proceed and join General Frémont at Tipton. General Curtis ordered also a part of one of the Missouri regiments down. I directed him, in the name of General Frémont, to withdraw those troops, as they were not needed down there. The battle was fought as I had expected, and as I had ordered. I ordered Colonel Carlin distinctly to attack Jeff. Thompson. He did so and defeated him. They pursued them but a short distance. I do not know why they did not pursue them further. They were successful, had an ample force, and there was no need of any more troops. To have sent more troops down there would have been an expense to the government that was not necessary. I think there was no necessity for General Curtis interfering in the matter at all. I reported to General Frémont, and he approved of what I had done.

Question. What is your opinion in regard to the failure to re-enforce Colonel Mulligan at Lexington?

Answer. I had been so short a time in the office that I knew but little of the general affairs of the department at that time. It was only after the surrender of Colonel Mulligan that I was appointed the principal adjutant general. I therefore knew very little about what could be done. I did not know exactly how General Frémont's troops were posted, or how many he had. I think he had only some 2,000 or 3,000 in the city. Regiments were arriving there every day, but they had no arms, and no baggage wagons, and no tents. There was a great scarcity of tents in the department. It appeared to me almost impossible for General Frémont to have sent troops to Lexington in sufficient numbers to save it before it fell. Of course, however, having arrived there so lately, I could not tell what might have been done to strengthen Lexington if it had been understood that Price was going there. After it was attacked it appeared to me too late to do anything to save it. I do not know what information General Frémont had in reference to Price's movements; whether he could have anticipated the attack on Lexington or not; and I did not know what orders Colonel Mulligan had. I know that General Frémont ordered troops from the northern part of Missouri to go to the relief of Lexington; but when they arrived at the river, they were scarcely in sufficient numbers to have been of much service, and they had no means to cross the river, the boats having all been seized by Price's army before they got there. I have no means of estimating the number of Price's force. I have always supposed it was very much exaggerated, because I do not think he could have brought that number there and subsisted them without more having been known about it. He had enough to take the place, and I suppose that was all that was necessary.

Question. How was General Frémont about being accessible to those who had important business with him?

Answer. It was very frequently difficult to get to see him; but I think that was because he had so much to do—because he was so busy. I think he devoted his whole time to business. He was in his office from very early in the morning until late at night.

Question. Had he any system by which persons having important business with him could be admitted to see him?

Answer. I think a great deal depended upon certain members of his staff. I think that they frequently did not tell the general that persons were there in waiting; that they took upon themselves to decide whether their business was of importance or not. There were a great many persons came there with what they considered important information, when they really had no information at all, as the general knew all about it beforehand. But they seemed to think that because they had just come from the country they had information of importance.

Question. I refer to those who came upon important business, or with information that it was necessary for the general to have.

Answer. I have heard persons talk about their not being able to see him; but I never knew of an instance where it was very necessary for a person to see the general that he did not see him. If he knew that they were there and had important business with him, they could generally see him. I heard the honorable Mr. Gurley say once that he had to wait two days to see him. I do not know that the general knew he was there, or, if he did, that there was anything particular the general had to say to him. Mr. Gurley went there as a member of General Frémont's staff some time before he took the field, and I suppose he had no particular orders to give him.

Question. Was there anything unusual about his accessibility as a person engaged in the business he was engaged in?

Answer. No, sir; I think not. It is always more or less difficult to see a commander of a department. General Halleck was so overrun with visitors he had a staff officer there who would sometimes take your card up, and sometimes not. General Frémont's officers were all at his headquarters, and he was always there, and it seemed to me that somebody was with him all the time. After I was the chief adjutant general I always walked into his room whenever I had matters of importance to communicate to him, and got through with the business as rapidly as possible, because the general always seemed to be busy.

WASHINGTON, *March* 14, 1862

Colonel CHESTER HARDING, Jr., sworn and examined.

By the chairman:

Question. Please state to us your rank and position in the army.

Answer. I am at present adjutant general of the State of Missouri.

Question. Were you there under the administration of the western department by General Frémont?

Answer. Yes, sir; during the whole time.

Question. Please give us a statement of all that you deem material in that administration that came under your notice.

Answer. On the 26th of July, when General Frémont arrived, I was stationed at the arsenal. I had been acting for General Lyon, under his orders, from the time of his departure. Here is that order:

HEADQUARTERS DEPARTMENT WEST,

Special order.] *St. Louis Arsenal, June* 13, 1861.

1. In the absence of the department commander, Lieutenant Colonel Chester Harding, jr., will give the necessary directions for carrying out the proper policy of the government as has been verbally expressed by the undersigned, and all orders given by him will be regarded as by authority.

N. LYON,

Brigadier General United States Volunteers, Commanding.

When General Frémont arrived, he ordered me to report to him for duty as assistant adjutant general upon his staff. I went with General Frémont to Cairo, as his adjutant general in the field, and returned with him.

Question. State what force you took there.

Answer. We took 3,800 men. That is not the exact number, but it was in the neighborhood of 3,800.

Question. How did you go there?

Answer. In seven steamboats, besides the one which General Frémont had himself—seven transports for troops.

Question. For what purpose did he charter a boat for himself to go there; what was the object of it?

Answer. He had considerable business to do, and I suppose it was for the purpose of being more private than he could have been had he been on the same boat with the troops.

Question. How was that boat furnished; was there anything extraordinary expensive, or ostentatious about it? Please state how that was.

Answer. The boat was always a very fine boat and magnificently furnished, and had been furnished by the Alton Packet Company. There were very few state-rooms in her. The saloon and cabin were supplied with sofas.

Question. Did General Frémont add anything to it?

Answer. I do not know of any change being made in and about her in consequence of General Frémont taking her—either extra furniture or any change at all.

Question. Please state whether there was on that expedition anything showy or ostentatious above the ordinary movement of armies.

Answer. Nothing that I discovered. I heard some talk about General Frémont coming down to the boat in a carriage drawn by four horses, but I did not see the carriage myself. I went on board the boat early in the morning before he arrived. She was lying in the stream then.

Question. Was he ostentatious in his bearing and deportment about St. Louis?

Answer. It never struck me so. He had a fine house, and he had plenty of orderlies around stationed at different passages. They were generally in the basement of the house, and they had plenty to do to keep people from rushing up stairs; but I never saw anything indicating a desire to be very magnificent.

Question. What do you say of his inaccessibility? It has been sometimes a matter of complaint that even a man of business could not get at him.

Answer. I presume it was very difficult for citizens who went there not upon business to see him; and perhaps it was difficult for those who went upon business and he was engaged and occupied with other matters. I have myself had to wait a day or two even after I had been ordered there, and get in the room. He would tell me he could not attend to me then and ask me to call again at such a time.

Question. Was he attentive to business there?

Answer. He was occupied all the time. I never saw him idle one moment.

Question. Was he unnecessarily exclusive in your judgment?

Answer. In my judgment he was not. If he had received all the visitors who wished to see him he never would have done any business at all.

Question. You have spoken of the visit to Cairo. What was the condition of affairs when you got there; what amount of troops were there?

Answer. General Prentiss made to me a brigade return when we arrived there, showing the forces which he had in Cairo and opposite to Bird's Point. My impression is, that, including the three months men, that report showed something like 5,600 men.

Question. Does that report include those that Frémont took along or not?

Answer. No, sir; exclusive of the re-enforcements.

Question. How were they armed and equipped?

Answer. I made no inspection, and saw none of the troops excepting two or three regiments that were on the west bank of the river at Bird's Point. These were very well armed; but I do not think that any regiment in the service in the western States at that time could be said to be well equipped with everything.

Question. Were those positions, Cairo and Bird's Point, or either of them, threatened in any way by the enemy?

Answer. Yes, sir; all the southeastern part of Missouri and the different points there were threatened.

Question. By what force, as near as you could ascertain?

Answer. We supposed from all the reports that we could gather, and from intelligence that General McClellan, General Prentiss, and General Pope received, that they could collect, including Missouri irregulars, something like 20,000 troops at Pocahontas and Pitman's Ferry, and would be joined by Watkins with his men from New Madrid, and by McBride, who was collecting forces, and had at one time 2,500 men in Oregon and Texas counties, on the borders.

Question. State the condition of things in the western department when General Frémont arrived there. What was the amount of the forces, and how were they armed, equipped, &c., when he took command?

Answer. On the 26th day of July, 1861, there were in St. Louis, four regiments of the United States reserve corps, who could not be ordered from the county of St. Louis without their own consent. They numbered very nearly four thousand men. The term of service of the first and second regiments was to expire on the 7th day of August, and of the 3d and 4th, on the 8th day of August. The 5th regiment of the United States reserve corps, whose time was to expire on the 11th of August, was part of it in Lexington and part of it in St. Louis. The 4th regiment of Missouri volunteers, Colonel Schittner, the 2d regiment, Colonel Boernstine, with the exception of two companies under (now) Colonel Austerhaus, and a portion of the 3d and 5th Missouri were in the arsenal or near it, their term of service having expired. They remained together simply to obtain their pay and to be re-organized. The 8th Missouri volunteers was not quite complete in its organization, but still could have taken the field, and was sent to Cape Girardeau in the course of a few days. They had no transportation. They numbered about 800 men at that time, or very nearly up to the minimum. A portion of Backhof's artillery battalion was in the arsenal for the purpose of being mustered out and paid off. Those were all the troops in or near the city, with the exception of skeleton companies of the 9th and 10th regiments of Missouri volunteers, which were then forming.

Question. Can you give in general terms the number of the troops available in his department at that time?

Answer. Here is a statement which shows the position of all our Missouri troops at the time when General Frémont arrived. The 1st regiment, Colonel Blair, was at Springfield. The 2d regiment was in the arsenal for mustering out and reorganization. The 3d regiment was in the field at Springfield, Missouri, with the exception of the three months' men, who had returned to be mustered out. The 4th regiment was in the arsenal to be mustered out and reorganized. The 5th regiment was in the field at Springfield, Missouri, with the exception of the three months' men, who had returned to be mustered out. The 6th regiment, Colonel Bland, was at Pilot Knob and Ironton. Of the 7th regiment, two companies were in Jefferson City and eight in Boonville. The 8th regiment was then at the Abbey Park, in St. Louis. The 9th regiment had but 226 men, distributed around among skeleton companies, and they were at the arsenal, not clothed or equipped. The 10th regiment was in the same condition, and with about the same number of troops. What afterwards became the engineer regiment of the west was then just started, and there were 76 mechanics in the arsenal. Buel's battery, 154 men, were in the arsenal, and we had just received authority to keep them and get them their guns and artillery accoutrements. There were 554 of Bayle's rifle battalion at Rolla. There were 307, that is, three companies, of the 23d Illinois in the arsenal, but under orders to go to Jefferson City, where the remaining seven companies were stationed. There were two companies of Backhof's artillery battalion in the field at Springfield; a portion of one company was at Jefferson City and another portion at Boonville. Of the pioneer company, 120 men, half of it was at Springfield; a section was in St. Charles, and a section at Pilot Knob. The first four regiments of the United States reserve corps were in St. Louis; and of the 5th, a part was at Lexington and a part at St. Louis. Besides these, there were 23 companies of home guards, who were guarding the railroad bridges and tracks in different parts of the State; making a total of 15,943 troops.

Question. How were they armed and equipped?

Answer. The regiments in the field were tolerably well armed and equipped. There had been great difficulty in procuring cartridge-boxes, knapsacks, &c., and the other accoutrements for the field when General Lyon started for Boonville, and Sigel's command went to the field insufficiently supplied with these. Subsequently, from the accoutrements which the government sent with ten thousand arms for distribution among the loyal inhabitants of the State of Missouri, we took enough to supply the troops in the field. None of the regiments had a proper supply of army wagons.

Question. Were you there at the time that General Lyon fought the battle of Springfield?

Answer. Yes, sir.

Question. It has been said that General Frémont was culpable for not granting aid or sending him re-enforcements. How was that?

Answer. My own opinion is that General Frémont had the choice of one of two things to do; to re-enforce General Lyon, which he might have done by neglecting the southeast, or let Lyon get along the best way he could with what force he had, and keep the southeast. He had not force enough in a condition to move to accomplish both purposes at that time.

Question. What do you mean by the southeast?

Answer. That whole country from Pocahontas up by Pitman's Ferry, including Ironton, Rolla, and Cairo.

Question. You have stated how that part was threatened at the time?

Answer. Yes, sir. Geueral Frémont's plan of operations there was not the plan that I would have followed if I had been in command.

Question. In what particular, in your judgment, did he err?

Answer. I thought all along, and so advised General McClellan and the other generals, that the proper way to prevent troops from coming up from Pocahontas was to occupy the heads of the only roads by which they could move, and to push down our forces by the way of Greenville towards the Arkansas line. In fact, that plan was agreed to at one time, and the forces were ordered over to me at the arsenal for the purpose of making a movement; but subsequently General McClellan countermanded the movement of some regiments that were intended to go in that direction.

Question. Where did he order them to when he countermanded the movement?

Answer. They were held in reserve in case Cairo should be attacked. It was upon the representations of General Prentiss and General Pope that the order was countermanded. That was all the force we wanted to keep the southeast, and if we could have had the five regiments General Lyon could have been re-enforced easy enough.

Question. And that, you say, was prevented by General McClellan's orders?

Answer. He countermanded the order which had been given in the first place for Grant's and some other regiments.

Question. So that five regiments had to be held in reserve instead of going on that expedition?

Answer. No, sir; not the five. Wyman's regiment was one of the regiments that was ordered off, and Marsh's 20th Illinois was another. Our stores at Rolla had accumulated so that there was a vast amount of government property there at risk, and McBride was not far off with forces varying from day to day, never having any permanent force, but varying from 1,500 to 2,500 men. Farmers would come out and join him and stay two or three days and go home again; but, at any time, he could collect a large force to make a dash upon an exposed point. It was necessary to protect that place, and I sent Wyman there. I sent Marsh to Cape Girardeau, because it was a very good base for operations through the southeastern portion of the State, with a good road back from there to Bloomfield and Greenville, and communication could be kept up with Ironton very easily; and because, also, there was so much talk about Cairo, and so much apprehension felt that it was in danger, I wanted him to be where General Prentiss could feel that, in case of an attack, he could call on Marsh to re-enforce him. Cape Girardeau is only fifty miles from Cairo.

Question. It has been thought that re-enforcements might have been spared from Rolla to go down and help Lyon?

Answer. It was through some of General Lyon's orders that the troops were not moved forward from Rolla. As I stated before, Wyman was at Rolla. I had been organizing, as fast as I could, the men for Bayles's rifle regiment, and had some 500 of them sent down and stationed at Rolla, with a design to move Wyman forward as soon as Bayles was strong enough to hold the place. Before the battle of Springfield, and after the three months' men began to be anxious about their pay, General Lyon sent some of them back. He sent back, among others, the 4th regiment United States reserve corps, which was at

Springfield with him; and he gave authority to the officers who were going to reorganize some of the three months regiments to pick up everybody they could find and bring them to the arsenal for reorganization. In that way nearly the whole of Bayles's command came up to the arsenal just about the time General Fremont arrived, and left nobody at Rolla but Wyman's force.

Question. Then, in your opinion, General Lyon could not be spared any troops from Rolla, for the reasons you have given?

Answer. No, sir.

Question. Was there any military necessity for Lyon fighting the battle there, or could he have retreated?

Answer. Of that I can only speak from what the regular officers and others have said since their return. There have been various opinions about it. Some think that the battle was fought in the best place; that it was necessary to fight it there. Others think there was another stronger place nearer Springfield which might have been held, and that our troops should have awaited the attack of Price there; it was known Price was about to attack us; but how much weight their opinion is entitled to I have no means of judging.

Question. It is a debatable question among military gentlemen?

Answer. Yes, sir.

Question. You know the amount of troops under Frémont; you know the condition of Cairo and other exposed parts of his department; and taking it all into consideration, under all the circumstances, what do you say as a military man of Frémont not re-enforcing Lyon?

Answer. I would think that, according to his own views about the necessities of the case, he acted in a proper manner; but the view which he took, and which the other generals took, of affairs in Missouri, was one that I never did agree to, and am not convinced yet.

Question. I am not now speaking of the original plan of the campaign; but, under the circumstances that he had planned it, was it in his power and ought he to have really re-enforced Lyon?

Answer. I do not think he could have done it and carried out his plans. The troops were not there to do it with; that is, to do it immediately. He ordered them as he came along, and they commenced coming rapidly to the State, and we were hard at work furnishing them after they arrived as rapidly as possible, trying to get them ready to take the field.

Question. Did you accompany Frémont to Springfield and were you present when he was superseded?

Answer. No, sir. On the 15th of August I left General Frémont's staff and took command of a regiment. He assigned me to the command of a district embracing the lines of the Pacific railroad and Southwest Branch; and from that time until he was removed I was in charge of that department, a brigade command.

Question. His commissary department and his contracts have been criticised; do you know anything about those things?

Answer. Nothing in the world. I was never in General Frémont's confidence in respect to his campaign or his operations in the city for supplying his troops.

Question. Do you know anything about the building of those fortifications in St. Louis?

Answer. Nothing at all, further than that I have seen them and been in them.

Question. But you do not know whether the prices for them were exorbitant or moderate?

Answer. No, sir.

Question. Now let me ask you as to the necessity of building those fortifications, or the military expediency of them?

Answer. I do not think they were necessary myself; but a great many persons, who ought to know better than I, did think so.

Question. Would they not enable our forces to defend the city with less force than to attempt it without fortifications?

Answer. I think that the battle that will defend St. Louis will have to be fought a good many miles away from it. They would not have assisted us in case of an attack by the river.

Question. What would be the difference, as to the propriety of it, between fortifying that city and this? Was it necessary that this city should have been defended by fortifications?

Answer. I certainly think so, with the enemy right at the door. They came as near as Arlington Heights, as I understand.

Question. Suppose then that they had come that near St. Louis, as they did approach pretty near sometimes?

Answer. If they ever got as far as St. Louis they would be in strength enough to pay very little attention to the forts.

Question. You do not believe much in fortifications?

Answer. Oh! yes, sir; but I think that our fight for St. Louis must necessarily have taken place at a long distance from the city.

By Mr. Gooch:

Question. I see that you differ greatly from General Frémont in regard to the amount of forces at Cairo at the time of your visit?

Answer. I saw in General Frémont's publication a statement that General Prentiss had about 1,200 men. That led me to reflect, and I think that that is a mistake. I think that among his adjutant general's papers in St. Louis will be found General Prentiss's report of the 3d of August.

By Mr. Chandler:

Question. May not the discharge of the three months men about that time explain it?

Answer. In making the statement I did of 5,500 men I included the three months men.

By Mr. Wade:

Question. The time of their enlistment was about expiring at that time?

Answer. Yes, sir.

Question. Might not that reconcile the discrepancy?

Answer. That will reconcile it. I do not think there were over 1,200 three years men.

By Mr. Gooch:

Question. Can you give us the whole force of the western department at the time General Frémont took command?

Answer. In addition to what I have already mentioned, there were two regiments of Illinois troops, and one of Iowa troops, the second Iowa, Colonel, now General, Curtis upon the line of the Hannibal and St. Joseph railroad. General Pope was in northeast Missouri with a portion of his division. I do not know what troops or regiments constituted his force. Colonel Mulligan was at Jefferson City. General Lyon's column consisted of the 1st Missouri rifle battalion, of the 2d Missouri, two companies, the 3d Missouri and the 5th Missouri, these last two regiments having been weakened by the loss of their three months men, the 1st Iowa, the 1st and 2d Kansas, five companies of regular infantry, and five companies, I think, of regular cavalry; I believe there were five. I have a post return at my room. He also had Totten's battery, regulars, two volunteer batteries, and Dubois's regular battery.

Question. Can you give us a statement of the whole force in the western department at the time General Frémont took command?

Answer. I can, with the exception of giving the numbers of General Pope's command in northwestern Missouri.

Question. Have you stated the aggregate amount, with the exception of the forces under General Pope?

Answer. No. I did not include General Lyon's column, nor did I include the three regiments that were stationed on the Hannibal and St. Joseph road in the statement which I gave.

Question. Adding those to those you have already referred to, and excepting the forces under General Pope, how many were there in all?

Answer. Besides the 15,000 I have spoken of, there were in the State when General Frémont arrived: Marsh's 20th Illinois regiment, about 900 strong, at Cape Girardeau; Wyman's regiment, about a thousand strong, at Rolla; the 2d Iowa, about 950 strong, at St. Joseph and along the line of the Hannibal and St. Joseph railroad; the 16th Illinois, Colonel Smith, about 900 strong, also guarding the line of that road; and another Illinois regiment, the number of which I have forgotten, about 900 strong. With General Lyon, besides the 1st, 2d, 3d, and 5th Missouri and an artillery battalion, which I have included in the list before given, there were two Kansas regiments and one Iowa regiment, making an aggregate of about 2,400 men, and the regular infantry and cavalry of which I have spoken. Besides these, General Pope had moved into northeast Missouri with a portion of his troops from Illinois. I do not know the strength of his command. I believe those were all the troops that were in Missouri on the 26th of July.

Question. What other troops were there in the western department, aside from those in Missouri?

Answer. I have no means of knowing what troops there were in the western department outside of Missouri.

Question. State what changes were made in the department, including the State of Missouri, from the 4th of March to the time when General Frémont took command?

Answer. On the 4th of March General Harney was in command of the department of the west. This department included the territory between the Mississippi river and the department of New Mexico. Captain Lyon, the senior line officer of the United States army, was subsequently placed in command of the troops, and General Harney, to that extent, relieved. General Harney was afterwards reinstated, and again relieved. Captain Lyon had been, in the meantime, promoted to a brigadier generalship and the command of the department devolved upon him by reason of seniority. While General Lyon was at Boonville, in June, an order was issued detaching Missouri from the department of the west and attaching it to the department of the Ohio, then commanded by General McClellan. This organization continued until the western department was created, and General Frémont assigned to the command of it.

Question. Will you state the effect which was produced upon Missouri by those changes?

Answer. The effect of attaching Missouri to a command already as large as that of the department of the Ohio was to deprive us of the supervision and action of a commanding general upon the spot. General McClellan was busy with his column in Western Virginia, and it was very difficult to advise with him, or apprise him of occurrences in the State, and he could not give us the attention which our situation required. I attribute our troubles, to a great extent, to the change in the department. There never was a time when we did not need the personal presence of the general who had the power to order what circumstances required.

Question. Do you know the instructions given to Colonel Mulligan in relation to holding Lexington, and the reasons why he was not re-enforced?

Answer. I have no knowledge on the subject.

Question. What force, in your judgment, should have been kept at Cairo?

Answer. Enough to garrison the forts and man the batteries. If a land attack was threatened it must necessarily come by the way of the roads through the swamp region in the southeast, and those roads would be easily held by a small number of troops.

Question. What is your estimate in numbers of the troops necessary to man the fortifications and hold the roads to which you have alluded?

Answer. I should suppose four thousand men plenty. If re-enforcements were required at any time they could very easily be sent by the Illinois Central railroad and by the river in time to meet any attack. I have made a concise statement of matters in Missouri, and I also have certain letters and telegraphic despatches which I offer to the committee as a part of my testimony.

PACIFIC, *October* 5, 1861.

On the 14th June, 1861, Brigadier General Lyon moved up the Missouri river, taking with him the 1st and 2d regiments Missouri volunteers, three small companies of regular infantry, Totten's battery, (four pieces,) and an eight-inch howitzer, with a few artillerists. On the day before a battalion of the 3d Missouri had been sent to the southwest, and was speedily followed by the remainder of that regiment, the 5th Missouri, two batteries (four pieces each) of light artillery, and a battalion of rifles. The last-named corps was to occupy the railroad to Rolla, until relieved by the Home Guard, and afterwards to garrison that place. Such of the troops as could be spared from Fort Leavenworth and two regiments of Kansas volunteers had been ordered to make their way to Springfield, where it was designed that the three columns should effect a junction. At the same time, the fourth Missouri occupied Bird's point, one Illinois and two Iowa regiments held the line of the Hannibal and St. Joseph railroad; the arsenal was garrisoned by the skeleton companies of the then unformed 6th, 7th, and 8th Missouri, numbering about eight hundred bayonets, all told; the powder magazine was held by Captain Tracy, with a half company of recruits, and St. Louis was left in charge of a small company of United States general service recruits and the United States reserve corps, who could not be moved from there without their consent. Excepting a few small outposts in Kansas and Nebraska there were no other troops subject to General Lyon's orders. The Home Guard, which afterwards did good service in protecting the railroads, had not been armed or equipped by the United States.

At Boonville General Lyon was joined by the 1st Iowa, and troops from Illinois were sent to fill their places on the Hannibal and St. Joseph railroad, the country along the line being in such a disturbed condition that a large force had to be maintained in that region.

While General Lyon was lying at Boonville, he received the official information that Missouri had been detached from the department of the west and attached to the department of the Ohio, under command of Major General McClellan. During the same interval, the 5th regiment United States reserve corps was sent up the river, and eventually became the garrison of Lexington; the 4th regiment of the same corps, with three companies of the 3d, and the small company of general service recruits above mentioned, were ordered to the southwest, to strengthen Sigel's column; a part, and, at a later period, the whole, of the 7th Missouri, were stationed at Boonville, which place they held on the 26th July, 1861, the date of Major General Frémont's arrival at St. Louis.

There now came intelligence of the gathering of a formidable army in the unprotected southeast. Tennessee and Arkansas troops were concentrating at Pocahontas and Pitman's Ferry; Missouri rebels were assembling under Watkins and McBride. There seemed little reason to doubt that the enemy could advance, threatening Bird's Point, Cairo, Ironton, Rolla, and even St. Louis, with a force exceeding twenty thousand men. So great appeared the danger that General Lyon hesitated for a time whether he would not give up his projected expedition to Springfield, and take the field in the southeast. Leaving that region, however, to the care of the then commanding general, he finally carried out his original plan, and took up his line of march from Boonville, starting about July 4. In the face of the information received, it would have been criminal neglect to leave Rolla or Ironton unprotected. The 13th Illinois was brought from Caseyville and sent to the former place; the 6th Missouri, still incomplete, went to the latter. The 20th Illinois embarked for Cape Girardeau, it being the intention that other Illinois troops should occupy the intervening country and points further south. They could not be obtained, however, and from the 7th July, until General Frémont's expedition down the Mississippi had reached Bird's Point, there never was a day when the rebels could not have overrun the southeast.

By the middle of July every bayonet that could be spared from the city had been sent into the field. The remaining seven companies of the 3d United States reserve corps, all the organized companies of the 8th Missouri, Lieutenant Colonel Schaeffer's battalion of the 2d, the 4th Missouri, then just returned from Bird's Point, were all actively employed in northeast Missouri in meeting the movement of Harris and others, supposed to be an advance upon the capital, while a similar advance was to take place from the southwest, thus dispersing or capturing the convention then about to meet. In fact, there remained scarcely enough men in the arsenal to perform the ordinary guard duty, and in the city proper so few of the reserve corps that daily visits were paid to headquarters by prominent citizens remonstrating against leaving the city defenceless.

This state of affairs lasted only a few days. The expedition into northeast Missouri returned in about a week. The 4th regiment United States reserve corps and the detachment of the 3d before mentioned returned to the city from the southwest. The rifle battalion, theretofore stationed at Rolla, and most of the three months men of the 3d and 5th Missouri, came back at about the same time. The battalion of the 2d, which had been stationed at Jefferson City, was relieved by Mulligan's Irish brigade, so that on the 26th July, 1861, General Frémont found, in the city and arsenal, the 1st and 2d regiments United States reserve corps, whose term of service would expire on the 7th August; the 3d and 4th regiments United States reserve corps, whose term would expire on the 8th August; the 2d Missouri, a part of the 3d and 5th, and the whole of the 4th and of the rifle battalion, together with a part of Backhof's artillery battalion, all of whose terms of service had then expired, and who kept together merely to be mustered out of service and paid. In other words, there were no troops except the 8th Missouri in or near the city at the time of General Frémont's arrival, who could be ordered upon any distant service. About the 20th of July General Pope, with a part of his brigade, took the field in northeast Missouri, in pursuance of orders from General Frémont. His force was the only increase that had been made in the number of troops on duty in this State, and he had enough work on his hands to give it employment in the region to which it was assigned.

Looking, then, to the position of affairs in this State on the 26th of July, 1861, it will be found that General Lyon was in the southwest, in need of re-enforcements. There was trouble in the northwest, requiring more troops than were there. In the northeast there were no more troops than were required to perform the task allotted to them; while in the south and southeast there was a rebel army of sufficient force to endanger Bird's Point, Cape Girardeau, Ironton, Rolla, and St. Louis, and no adequate preparation was made to meet it.

General Frémont sent the eighth Missouri to Cape Girardeau and the fourth United States reserve corps (whose term of service was to expire on the 8th of August) to re-enforce Bland at Ironton. He took some of General Pope's force from him, added to it two battalions of the first and second United States reserve corps, (whose term of service was to expire on the 7th of August,) equipped Buel's light battery, and started about the first of August for Bird's Point with the troops thus collected, being something less than 3,800 men, and being also all the available troops in this region, expecting to find an enemy not less than 20,000 strong. Subsequent events showed that the rebel force was not over-estimated, and nothing but the re-enforcements sent to the points above named, and the expedition down the river, prevented its advance upon them. Common report greatly magnified these re-enforcements, and it was generally believed in the city, and no doubt so reported to the rebel leaders, that Frémont had moved some ten or twelve thousand troops to the southeast; while, in fact, he did not have over fifty-five hundred to move, and was not strong enough at any point to take the field and commence offensive operations. General Frémont was not inattentive to the situation of General Lyon's column, and went so far as to remove the garrison of Boonville, in order to send him aid. During the first days of August troops arrived in the city in large numbers; nearly all of them were unarmed—all were without transportation; regiment after regiment laid for days in the city without any equipments, for the reason that the arsenal was exhausted, and arms and accoutrements had to be brought from the east. From these men General Lyon would have had re-enforcements, although they were wholly unpracticed in the use of the musket and knew nothing of movements in the field; but, in the meantime, the battle of the 10th of August was fought.

CHESTER HARDING, Jr.,
Late Ass't Adj't Gen'l upon the Staff of Brig. Gen. Lyon.

WASHINGTON, *March* 17, 1862.

Colonel ANSELM ALBERT sworn and examined.

By the chairman:

Question. What is your rank and position in the army?

Answer. I am a colonel, but not of any regiment. I was appointed by General Frémont on his staff, and so missed the opportunity to enter a regiment. I then commanded the second brigade in the fourth division as acting brigadier general, but have never been confirmed as colonel or general.

By Mr. Odell:

Question. Are you now in the army?

Answer. I am now on General Sigel's staff.

By the chairman:

Question. At whose instance have you appeared before the committee?

Answer. I understood I was to be summoned, and hurried up and came on and found the summons here.

Question. Were you with General Frémont during his command of the western department?

Answer. I was, from a little before he started from St. Louis for Springfield.

Question. About what time was that?

Answer. I was appointed on his staff on the 23d of August, but I did not enter upon active service until about the 23d of September. When General Frémont first came to St. Louis I was with the army at Springfield under General Lyon. I was wounded and made prisoner at the battle of Wilson's creek, when I was exchanged and came back. I was still unwell and could not enter immediately upon active service.

Question. What amount of force had General Frémont when he first took command of that department?

Answer. I think he had but a small force. I was in the field, and know that we had under General Lyon only some four thousand and some few hundred effective men. The most of them were three months men who had served out their time, and were only kept by the efforts of their officers, who told them it was absolutely necessary for them to remain until other troops could come and relieve them.

Question. Do you know anything about General Frémont fortifying St. Louis?

Answer. I found the city fortified when my health was re-established and I entered upon service again; the fortificatious were nearly completed then.

Question. You know nothing about the cost of those fortifications?

Answer. No, sir; my opinion is that the fortifications were absolutely necessary and that they helped a great deal.

Question. You were with General Lyon at the time he fought the battle at Wilson's creek?

Answer. Yes, sir; and I was wounded and captured there. At that time I was lieutenant colonel of the 3d Missouri three months volunteers.

Question. What induced General Lyon to fight that battle instead of retreating before so large an army?

Answer. There was a difference of opinion whether to retreat or to fight. It was thought that it might be more dangerous to retreat without fighting them than it was to fight them. We underrated the enemy and the enemy overrated us. I know General Lyon's views about it very well, because on a former occasion, about the first of August, we had advanced against the enemy as far as Dug Spring, and there General Lyon was not sure whether he should continue to advance and attack the enemy, or whether he should fall back to Springfield or still further back. He called a council of war there, at which I was present. His spies at the time reported that there were about 25,000 or 30,000 in the enemy's army. Still he thought we might be able to beat the enemy. But in case we were beaten we would be entirely lost. He asked the opinion of everybody there in the council of war, and, if I recollect rightly, there was nobody there but General Sigel who at all expressed the opinion that we should attack the enemy. General Lyon complained very bitterly at the time of how much his command had been neglected.

By Mr. Odell:

Question. What did he mean by being neglected?

Answer. It was neglected in every way. He was not re-enforced; the men had hardly any clothes to wear, and had not been paid.

By the chairman:

Question. Were the council, all but General Sigel, for retreating?

Answer. Yes, sir.

Question. What was the final decision of that council?

Answer. The decision of the council of war would very likely have been to retreat further than Springfield. But it was broken up by the report that our outposts had been attacked by the enemy, and as we had merely agreed to retreat, we left the council undecided how far we should retreat. We retreated only to Springfield.

Question. You say that General Lyon made great complaint of being neglected. Did he say who was to blame?

Answer. He said that instead of re-enforcing him they had at one time gone so far as to order him to send one of his regiments to the east.

Question. Who made that order?

Answer. The order must have been issued by the War Department, or by General Scott.

Question. What regiment was that?

Answer. The first Missouri, Colonel Blair.

Question. Where was it?

Answer. It was with us.

By Mr. Odell:

Question. Was it removed?

Answer. No, sir; the order was countermanded. General Lyon said the neglect towards him had gone so far that they had actually ordered away one of his regiments.

By the chairman:

Question. Do you know enough about the necessities of General Frémont's command at that time to give an opinion as to whether he could and ought to have re-enforced General Lyon?

Answer. I do not think that at the time he had any troops to spare in St. Louis, and every place in Missouri was threatened by attack of the enemy; and it was quite natural that some misfortune should happen at some one place. I think Bird's Point and Cairo were very important places to be taken care of.

By Mr. Odell:

Question. Did you not get re-enforcements after the battle?

Answer. After the battle I only know what I was told, for I was a prisoner.

Question. Were you not told that there were re-enforcements sent to Lyon's division after the battle?

Answer. I understood that Colonel Wyman, at Rolla, had orders to go to him, but he disobeyed them. I do not know whether for good reasons or for bad ones.

Question. Was not Colonel Stephenson also ordered to go to General Lyon's relief?

Answer. That I do not know.

Question. Was not your division re-enforced after the battle?

Answer. After the battle the whole force retreated to Rolla, and several regiments came there.

Question. How many?

Answer. I do not know, I was a prisoner for three or four weeks after the battle and was sick and did not know what was going on.

Question. Did not General Frémont send several regiments to re-enforce General Lyon's division after the battle of Springfield?

Answer. I do not know.

Question. You have an opinion about it, have you not?

Answer. I suppose several regiments were sent, because when I went through Rolla afterwards I saw several regiments there that I did not see before.

Question. Could not they have been sent to Springfield as well as to Rolla?

Answer. There is a railroad all the way to Rolla, but between Rolla and Springfield is about one hundred and twenty miles, and no railroad at all, and it would have been difficult to get the troops on.

Question. Armies should not stop for bad roads, should they?

Answer. We always marched, whether the roads were good or bad. But those troops could not have got to Springfield in time. Our regiment once marched three days to gain about eleven miles; still they marched.

Question. Did General Lyon make any complaint about not being re-enforced?

Answer. He made those complaints I have said.

Question. When?

Answer. Before the battle.

Question. How long before?

Answer. About nine days, at the council of war at Dug Spring. He never made any allusion to General Frémont. He made one allusion against Colonel Blair.

By Mr. Covode:

Question. What was that?

Answer. Because the 1st Missouri regiment of volunteers had been ordered east, and if it had been so ordered, it was through the influence of its commander, Colonel Blair.

By Mr. Odell:

Question. Do you know anything about the surrender of Lexington?

Answer. I can say very little about that. I know the general state of affairs, and that it was very difficult to move the army, because there was hardly any transportation or troops to move. And the cavalry had no arms; one regiment I know had to drill with stick swords, just the same principle as wooden cannon. A day or two before Colonel Mulligan surrendered, I went to the office, though I was hardly able to do any work; I recollect hearing some telegraphic correspondence with Colonel Jefferson C. Davis at Jefferson City. He was asked whether he thought he was strong enough to break through the enemy's lines and take some provisions to our troops. He said he was strong enough to break through the lines, but he had no transportation to take provisions. Of course it would be of no use to get through without they could take provisions with them.

By Mr. Gooch:

Question. Did you go with General Frémont on his march to Springfield?

Answer. Yes, sir.

Question. Were you present with General Frémont at Springfield the night before he was superseded?

Answer. I was.

Question. Were you present at his council of war?

Answer. Yes, sir.

Question. What can you tell us about the position of the enemy at that time?

Answer. The enemy were at different places on the road from Springfield to Cassville. The nearest part of their forces were at Wilson's creek, which is about ten miles from Springfield, and then they were at all the good camping places along the road, at Dug Spring and Crane creek. The reserves were at Springfield, where General Price had his headquarters.

Question. How many of the enemy were at Wilson's creek?

Answer. Only the advance guard, as you might call it, a couple of thousand of men, more or less.

Question. How near to them were the nearest forces?
Answer. Some five or six miles beyond Wilson's creek, and at different places along the road.

By Mr. Odell:

Question. The main body of the army was at Cassville?
Answer. The reserves; I did not say the main body.

By Mr. Gooch:

Question. Where was the main body?
Answer. It may have been at Dug Spring.
Question. How far is that from Springfield?
Answer. Perhaps eighteen or twenty miles.
Question. How do you know that Price's forces were located as you have represented?
Answer. I know that because General Frémont had entered into an agreement with General Price about the war in Missouri, that no guerillas should be employed, and he had sent Lieutenant Max Tosk with a flag of truce to the headquarters of General Price to have the agreement signed. I saw this officer going and when he came back, and as I was very much interested at the time to know everything about the position of the enemy I questioned him. The agreement was signed at Cassville, and the furthest troops we had were there; there could hardly be any doubt about that.

By Mr. Odell:

Question. How far is Cassville from Springfield?
Answer. It is sixty or seventy miles, I should think.
Question. That was where General Price's headquarters were?
Answer. Yes, sir. The agreement was signed there.
Question. Do you know the date of that agreement?
Answer. I think it was the 2d of November.
Question. What day was General Frémont superseded?
Answer. I think it was the 4th of November.
Question. Within two days of the time the agreement was signed?
Answer. Yes, sir.
Question. You say you questioned this officer?
Answer. Yes, sir.
Question. What information did you get from him?
Answer. Just as I have stated to you. He said he found the enemy's troops at all these different places; he told me the names of several of the officers whose acquaintance I had made when a prisoner—Lieutenant Tosk had been made prisoner also at the battle of Wilson's creek, and knew those men by sight, and personally, and so he knew when he saw them that certain regiments were there.
Question. Was this messenger one of General Frémont's messengers?
Answer. Yes, sir.
Question. Who had been to Cassville?
Answer. Yes, sir.
Question. And he returned directly to General Frémont and told you this?
Answer. He did not come back while General Frémont was there. He came back after General Hunter had taken the command.
Question. You say he told you the forces were thus stationed?
Answer. Yes, sir.
Question. How long after General Hunter had taken the command did he come back?
Answer. I think the next day, say the 5th of November.
Question. Is that the only means you have of knowing what the position of the enemy was?

Answer. No, sir; I was asked how I know now that the enemy was at those places, and I told what he said, but it was a part of my business then to send out spies and scouting parties to get all the information I could, and all the reports of the scouts and of the spies were to the effect that the main body of the enemy were very near us, only a few miles beyond Wilson's creek. But I regard the information got from Lieutenant Tosk as more valuable than any other, because he had a better chance to see the enemy, and he had no interest to make himself important, and he told me all he knew about it.

Question. You were present at that council of war?

Answer. Yes, sir.

Question. Did you expect to engage the enemy the next day?

Answer. We expected to march towards the enemy and engage him if we found him at or near Wilson's creek; if we had not found him at that place we would have found him somewhere else. On that march from Tipton the enemy had all the advantage in retreating quickly through an open country, while we lacked transportation, and our provisions were scarce; still we gained forty miles on him in about ten days. After reaching Springfield the enemy had to retreat over a narrow road to Arkansas, through timber and up the hills, while we could take the open road and gain twice the time; I know we should have caught him at Cassville, or at least have caught his main body there. It was calculated so that if we did not find him at this place we should find him at the second or third place.

By Mr. Gooch:

Question. From the information which your scouts brought to you at that time, did you believe that the enemy was in considerable force within twenty or thirty miles of Springfield?

Answer. We had every reason to believe so. Major Clark Wright, who had command of Missouri volunteers, made a report very nearly in these words: "My scouts report that, not only every road, but every footpath is alive with soldiers. They are swarming like bees in a hive, and advancing towards Wilson's creek."

Question. You supposed that the enemy were coming back to give you battle?

Answer. I supposed they were going to make a show of doing so, and I believe if we had not waited in Springfield afterwards, we should have had an opportunity of beating them; and if we had not beaten them the results would have been very important. At that time, if we had driven Price's men into Arkansas, the most of his Missouri troops would have left him, especially as the agreement between him and General Frémont would have been in force, which agreement General Hunter revoked.

Question. Did you, after that council of war, go forward from Springfield on any reconnoitering party?

Answer. I myself did not.

Question. So you have no personal knowledge from anything which you had seen before, or anything which you have seen since that council of war, of the position of the enemy, but you judge wholly from the reports of scouts and messengers sent out?

Answer. I have some other reasons for believing that the enemy were very near. While we were waiting there the enemy set fire to everything to prevent our marching after them, and the fires were as near as ten miles from Springfield. And I have been over that same country twice since, and have seen what had been done there, and have heard what the few people left there have told me. They said that the sun could not be seen distinctly for two or three days on account of the smoke.

By Mr. Odell:

Question. What force had the enemy?

Answer. Perhaps 25,000 or 30,000 men.

Question. What was your force?

Answer. About 32,000 effective men.

By Mr. Gooch:

Question. Did you retreat with the army under General Hunter?

Answer. Yes, sir.

By Mr. Odell:

Question. At what time did General Hunter take command?

Answer. The 4th of November, I think.

Question. When he took command you were in council?

Answer. We were in council when he arrived.

Question. Did you communicate to him that the enemy were advancing?

Answer. He heard the proceedings of the council of war.

Question. Did you tell him about it?

Answer. My functions on the staff ceased when General Hunter took command.

Question. Did any of the other officers tell him?

Answer. These reports to General Frémont were made in the presence of General Hunter. He did not say at the time that he would take command immediately.

By Mr. Gooch:

Question. Have you any doubt now that the forces of the enemy were stationed at the points you have indicated?

Answer. I have not the least doubt about it. I have been over that road twice since. I went to Arkansas on General Sigel's staff, under General Curtis, and have just returned from there. There are but few men left there who can tell anything about it.

Question. Did the information which you obtained as you passed over the road since that time satisfy you that Price's troops were there at that time?

Answer. I am perfectly satisfied of it.

Question. You say there were 2,000 men at Wilson's creek?

Answer. I cannot tell the exact number, but there was a large number, a large advance guard; that is, it would be an advance guard, supposing their army to be facing this way.

Question. Did you learn which way that force was moving at that time—whether towards Springfield or towards Arkansas?

Answer. They were just waiting there. They commenced their retreat several days afterwards—in fact, they did not retreat far. The Arkansas troops crossed over the line, and went into winter quarters about ten miles beyond the line, and the Missouri troops came back into Missouri right away after we left.

By Mr. Odell:

Question. Did not a reconnoissance go out with General Hunter?

Answer. I went with General Hunter one time, but we did not go more than a half a mile or a mile from town.

Question. Did not a reconnoissance go out the day after General Hunter took command?

Answer. I do not know.

By Mr. Gooch :

Question. Did you at any time make a reconnoissance with General Hunter ?

Answer. Yes, sir ; but only a half a mile or a mile outside of town.

Question. Do you know whether he sent a reconnoissance out as far as Wilson's creek ?

Answer. I do not know.

By Mr. Julian :

Question. Was there any difference of opinion in the council of war as regards the position of the enemy ?

Answer. There was not the least doubt expressed by anybody.

Question. It was agreed on all hands that there would be a fight soon ?

Answer. Yes, sir. The most would have gone out with the expectation to meet the enemy soon. My opinion was that the enemy would not have given us battle until we had got to Crane creek, which was about the centre of his lines, so that their forces, in advance, could fall back to that place, and the reserves could come up and concentrate there.

Question. You think the fortifications at St. Louis were necessary ?

Answer. Yes, sir.

Question. Why do you think so ?

Answer. The city of St. Louis, like most American cities, is built over a very large space of ground, and if you want to defend such a city you want an enormous number of men, and if you have not the necessary number of men, you must make it up of fortifications or something else. The population of the city itself, at that time, was troublesome enough. One of the most dangerous classes of population were the Irishmen. They were all gained to our side by being employed to build those fortifications, and now they flock to our regiments, though it was hardly possible to get one or two regiments before that time.

Question. You are acquainted with the subject of fortifications ?

Answer. Yes, sir.

Question. Are the fortifications there well constructed ?

Answer. Yes, sir, I think so. They are very well laid out. The general plan of the fortifications is very good. I only saw them when they were nearly done.

Question. You do not know anything about the contracts for building them ?

Answer. No, sir.

WASHINGTON, *March* 17, 1862.

E. L. BEARD sworn and examined.

By Mr. Julian :

Question. At what time did you enter into the employ of the government under General Frémont ?

Answer. About the last of August; I do not recollect the exact date.

Question. Where had you been residing previous to that time ?

Answer. For 13 years previous I had been residing in California.

Question. In what business was you engaged in California ?

Answer. In farming and in building mills for crushing quartz, but farming was my principal business.

Question. Are you acquainted with machinery?

Answer. Yes, sir, with the constructing of machinery, putting up mills, &c.

Question. Prior to your going to California, where was your residence, and what was your business?

Answer. I resided at Lafayette, Indiana, for some 13 years. My business was constructing the Wabash and Erie canal from 1834 to 1842. After that, I was engaged in milling, running freight boats on the canal, &c.

Question. How did you happen to come to St. Louis at the time you mentioned? At whose instance?

Answer. At my own instance.

Question. General Frémont employed you?

Answer. After my arrival there, yes, sir. He sent for me soon after my arrival; a day or two after.

Question Go on and state about your contract, its terms, &c.

Answer. Soon after my arrival in St. Louis General Frémont sent for me, and in an interview I had with him he said that the fortifications that were then being built by the government forces were progressing very slowly, and that he doubted whether they would be finished in six months at the rate at which they were then being prosecuted. He wished to know from me in what time I could build them, and for what amount. He requested me to go with the engineer and see the ground, and the fortifications then commenced, and report to him as soon as I could. I did so, and submitted a proposition to finish the works in thirty days, for the sum of $315,000. That proposition was made on the 4th of September, in writing, and it was indorsed on the back by General Frémont, requesting the quartermaster to make out a contract with me. It was not an order to make a contract as I had proposed, but it was left to the quartermaster to decide how to make it. I went to General McKinstry with the order, and he objected to making a contract for a gross sum. He stated that I must make a bid for each separate article, so much per yard for excavation and embankment, so much for lumber, &c. For one reason or other, during the press of business there, the signing of the contract was delayed until the 25th of September, and at that time the work was nearly finished.

Question. What time did the work begin?

Answer. About the first of September I commenced purchasing tools and breaking ground; but I did not really commence work until the 4th of September, about. I was collecting materials together, &c., but there was some delay on the part of the engineers in laying off the work. There were really some two or three errors in the first that were laid, in getting under way. The work was substantially completed and ready for mounting guns; the stock-houses completed about the 4th of October. I was at work until the 20th or 21st of October, sodding the embankments, fixing up the soldiers' quarters in the block-houses, and building drawbridges into the forts. They could not be finished until the guns were moved inside. There was some delay for the want of gun-carriages, I believe, and the guns were not mounted, though they were on hand. In the meantime, by the 10th or 15th of October, when the work was finished, the exigency at that time really to all appearance had vanished; St. Louis was then considered safe. But at the time I commenced the work the general impression was to the effect that it was doubtful whether St. Louis could be held or not; it was feared that Price would take it. After the fall of Lexington, there was really quite a panic and a feeling of doubt that St. Louis would follow.

Question. Was the contract drawn up according to the suggestions you mentioned, specifying the items, &c.?

Answer. Yes, sir; General McKinstry and myself fixed the prices.

Question. Was the contract made between you and General McKinstry?

Answer. Yes, sir.

Question. General Frémont left it to General McKinstry?

Answer. Yes, sir; altogether. The prices were arranged between General McKinstry and myself.

Question. Whose names were signed to the contract?

Answer. General McKinstry's and my own; no others. It was inserted by the clerk in the body of the contract that it was by order of Major General J. C. Frémont.

By Mr. Covode:

Answer. Did you not say that it was not made in accordance with the proposition you submitted to General Frémont, but in accordance with the suggestions of General McKinstry?

Answer. I made my proposition to the general, who submitted it or referred it to the quartermaster to make a contract; and the quartermaster and myself settled upon the prices, and we were disputing about the prices for some time before the contract was completed.

By Mr. Julian:

Question. General Frémont referred it all to General McKinstry?

Answer. Yes, sir; he did not go into the details at all; that was for the quartermaster to attend to.

Question. General Frémont was very busy, I suppose?

Answer. Not only that; he did not interfere in such matters. General McKinstry and I were discussing the prices for some time, but finally we agreed upon them.

Question. What do you say about those prices?

Answer. I say that if I had had sixty or ninety days to do the work in those prices would be extravagantly high. But to do it in the time I was compelled to do it in, they are not too high. The contract specifies that I am to do each particular portion of the work in five days. It has been stated that I was to do all the work in five days, which is not correct. The contract specified that I was to do each portion of the work within five days of the time when it should be laid off; and I complied with the contract in every instance in that particular; the block-houses, and all the work pertaining to the fortifications.

Question. In view of the limited time in which you were compelled to complete the works, were the prices fair prices, or were they exorbitant?

Answer. They were very fair prices; they gave a good profit. The work cost two or three times more, doing it in the time I did, than it would cost if I had had three or four times as much time to do it in.

Question. In what respect was the cost so much increased by the limited time?

Answer. I had to keep on hand a large number of men ready to cover the work as fast as it was laid off. Then I had to work men night and day; and the costs of lights for night work alone was over $3,000. The cost of the lumber was very much enhanced. Nearly all the mills in St. Louis were engaged in getting out lumber for mortarboats and gunboats then being built. I had to bring my saw-logs by railroad some forty miles, and could only get two or three mills to work for me.

Question. You say you made a good profit?

Answer. I cannot tell. I do not know what the work amounts to. I have been denied the measurement of the work. The work has been measured, but I cannot obtain a certified copy of it. I have applied to General Halleck for it, and to General Cullom, who is the chief of the topographical engineers at St. Louis, and to the parties who made the measurement. But the order of General Cullom to the engineers who made the measurement was that under no circumstances was I to be allowed any note or information by which I could ascertain the measurement of the work. All means of arriving at the cost of the work is denied me. I do not know anything about it. I cannot tell whether I have made anything or not. But my supposition was that I would make something. I have made application to the Secretary of War for an order to General Halleck to furnish me a certified copy of the measurement which he has in his office in St. Louis; but the Secretary of War declined to do so, on the ground that it would be exercising arbitrary authority over General Halleck's department.

Question. You were required, I understand, to complete the work in a very limited time?

Answer. Yes, sir; I agreed to finish it in thirty days, but that stipulation is not in the contract. The difficulty was in having the work laid off fast enough. I found that was the great obstacle to having the work finished in thirty days; and when I came to have the contract made out I bound myself to have each portion of the work finished within five days from the time it was laid off. I did that in order to protect myself. I might be bound to do everything in thirty days, and then, not having the work laid off, I would not be able to do it in that time, but would be left too much at the mercy of the engineers.

Question. You had the work completed within the time agreed upon?

Answer. Yes, sir; the work was all substantially finished on the 4th of October, ready for the guns to be mounted. The block-houses were completed. There was a little work, such as sodding, to be done. That was not all done until the 21st or the 22d of October.

By Mr. Covode:

Question. When General McKinstry told you that you would have to make your proposition in detail for the work did you speak to General Frémont about it?

Answer. I told General Frémont that General McKinstry refused to give a contract for the amount in gross, but required me to make it in detail. The general told me that it was very proper that it should be so done, and that General McKinstry and myself must arrange that between ourselves.

Question. He declined to interfere?

Answer. He did not interfere for me at all.

By Mr. Gooch:

Question. When were the rates agreed upon between you and McKinstry?

Answer. They were finally settled on the 25th day of September.

Question. They were not agreed upon until that time?

Answer. No, sir; there were some alterations made on that day.

Question. Then the larger part of the work was done before the rates were agreed upon?

Answer. Yes, sir.

Question. What more did it cost you to build those works in haste than they would have cost if built within a reasonable time?

Answer. I should say, perhaps, three times as much.

Question. What did you pay extra per day for your men?

Answer. For carpenters I paid half a dollar per day extra.

Question. What was the ordinary price for carpenters?

Answer. We paid a dollar and a half and a dollar and seventy-five cents apiece for carpenters, and for boss carpenters five dollars to seven dollars a day.

Question. What percentage above ordinary prices?

Answer. I did not pay over fifty per cent. extra on the labor.

Question. Did you pay fifty per cent. extra.

Answer. Yes, sir; about that on the labor.

Question. What would be a fair price for excavation at St. Louis per cubic yard?

Answer. In ordinary times, and to do it as it is ordinarily done, I would take it for twenty to twenty-five cents a yard.

Question. Would not that be a very liberal price?

Answer. Twenty-five cents would be; twenty cents would be a fair price.

Question. What for earth embankments?

Answer. About twenty-five or thirty cents in ordinary times.

Question. What would be a fair price for puddled earth?

Answer. From forty-five to fifty cents.

Question. Would not that be a very liberal price?

Answer. No, sir. On the Wabash and Erie canal I have had as high as sixty cents for puddled earth.

Question. What would ordinarily be a fair price for sodding?

Answer. About fifty cents a yard.

Question. What would be a fair price for paving yards and walks?

Answer. I think about a dollar a yard would be about right.

Question. You think you got about fairly paid for that?

Answer. I think I did not get enough.

Question. What would be about a fair price per gallon for building cisterns?

Answer. I think six cents a gallon would be a fair price. There was a large profit on the cisterns, but I did not make anything on the earthworks.

Question. What would be a fair price for lumber in St. Louis?

Answer. I paid as high as $23, $27, and $32 per M. I bought some for $15 per M. The ordinary price is from $12 to $15 per M, but I had to pay as high as $23, $27, and $32 per M.

Question. And got $100 per M?

Answer. Yes, sir; that is, measured in the work after it is all done.

Question. That includes the work and the lumber?

Answer. Yes, sir.

Question. What percentage of loss is there upon the lumber in measuring it in the work?

Answer. That I could not tell. I did not keep an account of it.

Question. I do not mean exactly, but what would be the probable amount?

Answer. I should think about fifteen per cent. of loss.

Question. What was the proportion of each kind of lumber used?

Answer. I could not state that, except from memory. But the most of it was squared timber that I had to pay big prices for.

Question. What is a fair price for roofing?

Answer. I think I paid $3 50 and I got $4 50 for it. I paid $3 50 or $4, I forget which.

Question. So you commenced the work and worked some twenty or twenty-five days, and then agreed upon the prices?

Answer. The prices were talked over all the time from the 4th of September until the contract was made. But they were not finally agreed upon until the 25th of September, when the contract was signed.

Question. Why did you go to work before you knew the rates at which you were to be paid for it?

Answer. Just on the assurance of the general and the necessities of the case. I trusted to the quartermaster for the prices. I thought we could make a bargain in some way.

Question. What is the whole amount of your claim for building those fortifications?

Answer. I could not tell that for the reason that I have not been able to settle all my bills yet; they are not all in. As soon as I can get the measurement of the work and a settlement with the quartermaster, I can tell.

By Mr. Odell:

Question. You have your own measurement?

Answer. No, sir.

By Mr. Gooch:

Question. Can you not get a measurement?

Answer. No, sir; I cannot get it.

Question. Did you not make any measurement or cause any to be made?

Answer. No, sir, only a rough guess at it. I am to settle with the quartermaster at the prices stipulated in my contract on the certificate of the engineer in charge of the work. But I cannot get that certificate.

Question. Were the moneys paid you all paid without a certificate?

Answer. Yes, sir; paid on account of the contract, without a certificate of the engineer of the amount of work done.

Question. When did you begin?

Answer. I began breaking ground about the first of September; but I did not get fairly at work before the 4th of September.

Question. When did you receive your first payment?

Answer. The general ordered $10,000 to be paid to me somewhere along the last of August; and then $15,000 more soon after.

Question. You received $25,000 before you had done anything?

Answer. I had commenced, but had not done much.

Question. How many dollars worth of work had been done on the 2d day of September?

Answer. Scarcely anything had been done except purchasing tools, making preparations, &c.

Question. You had $25,000 paid you in advance?

Answer. Yes, sir.

Question. How much work had been done on the 5th day of September?

Answer. I had some 3,000 or 4,000 men employed at work there.

Question. How much work had been done then?

Answer. I could not tell you how much work had been done.

Question. They had been at work two days?

Answer. Yes, sir; three or four days; but they had not done much until the 4th day of September. I had made large demonstrations, but they had not got at work.

Question. On September 5 you received $60,000?

Answer. Yes, sir.

Question. That made $85,000 in all that you had then received?

Answer. Yes, sir. The difficulty was in getting money; the quartermaster was short. I had made an estimate of how much money I would require to go on and finish the work. I made a requisition on the 4th, 5th or 6th of September for $135,000. The quartermaster had only $60,000, and the order was given for that. Then there was $66,000 in the hands of Mr. Turnley, and an order was given me for that to make up my requisition for $130,000.

Question. Then you had been paid $151,000 when you had been at work only two days?

Answer. Six or eight days only. I did not receive the $66,000 then, I think.

Question. You had $151,000 when you had been at work only two days?

Answer. Well, sir; when I had been at work, fairly at work, two days.

Question. Why was that?

Answer. Because I required that amount of money on hand to enable me to finish the work in time.

Question. Then you took your whole pay in advance?

Answer. To that extent, yes, sir.

Question. You had no contract?

Answer. I had merely made a proposition.

Question. You had been at work two days?

Answer. I had broken ground on the 1st of September, but had not done much until the 4th.

Question. Then you had really been at work two days when you had paid to you $151,000, and that without any bond, contract or agreement?

Answer. There was no contract, bond or agreement, except the proposition I made.

By Mr. Odell:

Question. Had your proposition been accepted?

Answer. No, sir; it was not accepted the way I had made it. I made a proposition, and General Frémont indorsed on the back of it an order to the quartermaster to make out a contract.

Question. What was your proposition?

Answer. To do all the earthwork and timberwork required by the engineers for the fortifications and defence of St. Louis from St. Malachi church to the bank of the Mississippi river, with all the fieldworks, block-houses, &c., and have it all completed within thirty days, and to do each portion within five days from the time it was laid off—to do all that was required of me for that purpose for the sum of $315,000.

By Mr. Gooch:

Question. When did you receive the next payment, after having received this $151,000?

Answer. I do not recollect.

Question. I have seen it somewhere stated that on the 19th of September you received an order for another sum of $35,000.

Answer. Yes, sir; but I did not get any money on that order for a long time afterwards.

Question. How much money had you expended up to the 19th of September?

Answer. I could not tell?

Question. Had you spent the half of what you had received?

Answer. I should suppose I had spent about that much.

Question. Then having on hand at that time some $75,000 of the government's money, you received another order for $35,000 more?

Answer. Yes, sir; $20,000 was paid on that order, that was all that was paid. Altogether I received $171,000.

Question. All this money was paid to you before this contract was completed?

Answer. Yes, sir.

Question. And you never had a survey made, but all the payments made to you were made without a survey?

Answer. Yes, sir. I never could get a measurement. I have been trying a long time to get one, but so far have failed.

Question. Are you familiar with the forts built by Major Kappner?

Answer. No, sir. I went in about the 1st of September to see the manner in which they were being built, the size of them, &c., and have never seen them since except in passing by.

Question. Do you know how the forts you built compare as to size and expense of building with those he built, provided the time of building was the same for all of them?

Answer. I think the forts I built are larger. But that is merely guess-work. I could not tell by merely passing them.

Question. Did you go to St. Louis for the purpose of taking this contract?

Answer. No, sir. I had no idea of taking any contract when I left California.

Question. Did you have any partner, or any one associated with you in this contract?

Answer. No, sir.

Question. What representations did you make to General Frémont which induced him to advance money to you?

Answer. That I should want the money to enable me to complete the work in time; that was all.

Question. What did you mean by that?

Answer. To finish the work.

Question. You do not mean that you wanted that much money to pay for the work as it was progressing?

Answer. No, sir; but to finish all that was to be done.

Question. Why did you get orders for the money in advance of the amounts due you?

Answer. The idea was this: It was very difficult to get money at St. Louis then; there was very great difficulty in getting it. I employed a very large number of men, and I wanted the means on hand to be sure of paying them.

Question. If there was great difficulty in the government getting money to carry on its business there at that time, and you were paid to this extent in advance, must not other persons working for the government have been very much embarrassed by it?

Answer. Yes, sir; all persons were. Every man that furnished forage, mules, or any credit to the government was very much embarrassed. The gunboats, mortarboats and fortifications were considered by the general, I suppose, a matter of primary necessity, and for that reason the means were provided for prosecuting those works, and paying for the labor on them as fast as it was done.

Question. Would it not have been more in accordance with custom to have paid you the amounts due you as the work progressed?

Answer. That is very likely. In most cases it would be so.

Question. Did you ever take any contract before where you had money advanced to you?

Answer. I have had money advanced to me before?

Question. To the same extent?

Answer. No, sir. I never did any work before in the same hurry.

Question. On the whole, it was a very unusual proceeding from beginning to end, was it not?

Answer. The whole war, and all matters connected with it, are very unusual proceedings.

By Mr. Odell:

Question. What do you understand the price of labor to be there?

Answer. Just what men are willing to work for, and men are willing to give. You can hire laborers there for 40 to 50 cents a day, I suppose. I believe they are paying 50 cents a day for city work there.

Question. How much did you pay a day?

Answer. I paid 80 cents and a dollar a day.

Question. Why did you pay some a dollar a day, and others only 80 cents a day?

Answer. I paid some a dollar for night work, and others 80 cents for day work.

Question. The city paid 50 cents, and you paid 80 cents?

Answer. I think the city was hiring some for 50 cents. I do not know that it was so.

Question. What did you pay the night men of the same grade?

Answer. At first 80 cents, and afterwards a dollar a night.

Question. What are the wages of carpenters there?

Answer. I cannot tell you.

Question. What did you pay?

Answer. From $1 50 to $1 75 a day.

Question. How much for night work?

Answer. The same.

By Mr. Gooch:

Question. Did your carpenters do any night work?

Answer. Certainly.

By Mr. Odell:

Question. You spoke of overseers that you paid higher prices.

Answer. Yes, sir.

Question. How much did you pay them?

Answer. From $3 to $3 50 a day.

Question. How many did you employ?

Answer. From 80 to 100 altogether. I could not tell exactly without the check roll. Perhaps more. It is all guess-work. But I should think about one hundred.

Question. How were your gangs divided between day and night?

Answer. About equally.

Question. Did you work your night gangs from the beginning to the close of the work?

Answer. Not all the time.

Question. What proportion of the time?

Answer. I think about three-fourths of the time I worked nights.

Question. You speak of its costing $3,000 for lights. How was what?

Answer. For torch baskets, rosin, coal, kindling, men to attend the fires, &c.

Question. What is your estimate of the indebtedness of the government to you?

Answer. I should think the work would amount to about $250,000 altogether; perhaps $260,000, or $270,000; I cannot tell exactly. I should think about $250,000 or $260,000. That is my own guess about it.

Question. You would have had a pretty good thing of it if you had got your proposition accepted in the lump?

Answer. Yes, sir; it was made at a guess. The fieldworks outside of the fortifications extended some six miles in length; the fortifications some three or four miles.

Question. Have you paid the laborers and mechanics?

Answer. I have paid all the day laborers. The boss mechanic, and the man who hired the carpenters under him, are unpaid. A great deal of the lumber is still not paid for.

Question. What amount is yet due the mechanics and those who furnished the materials?

Answer. I think somewhere between $22,000 and $28,000.

The following is a copy of the proposal submitted by Mr. Beard, and referred to in the foregoing testimony:

St. Louis, *September* 4, 1861.

The undersigned proposes to build all the fortifications, redoubts, bastions, and all else required of timber and earthwork for the defence of the city of St. Louis, from fortification No. 6, at St. Malachi church, to the northern limit of the city, all to be done according to and under the direction of the engineer or engineers in charge of the work, binding myself to complete the work in five (5) days after the same is laid out, for the sum of ($315,000) three hundred and fifteen thousand dollars.

E. L. BEARD.

J. C. Frémont, *Major General Commanding.*

The following is a copy of the indorsement by General Frémont:

Headquarters, *September* 4, 1861.

In order to place this city immediately in a state of, at least, partial defence, I recommend the execution of a contract with Mr. E. L. Beard, who makes this proposition.

J. C. FRÉMONT,
Major General Commanding.

Brigadier General J. McKinstry,
Quartermaster United States Army.

MISCELLANEOUS.

The joint committee on the conduct of the war submit the testimony taken upon the following subjects:

HATTERAS INLET EXPEDITION.
PORT ROYAL EXPEDITION.
BURNSIDE EXPEDITION.
FORT DONELSON, &c.
CAPTURE OF NEW ORLEANS.
INVASION OF NEW MEXICO.
ACCOMAC EXPEDITION.
BATTLE OF WINCHESTER, MARCH 23, 1862.
MONITOR AND MERRIMAC.
PROTECTING REBEL PROPERTY.
REBEL BARBARITIES.
WOUNDED FROM FRONT ROYAL, VIRGINIA
CONVALESCENT CAMP, ALEXANDRIA, VIRGINIA.
TRADE IN MILITARY DISTRICTS.
COMMUNICATING COUNTERSIGN.
PAYMASTERS, RETURNING SLAVES, &c.

B. F. WADE, *Chairman.*

HATTERAS INLET EXPEDITION.

WASHINGTON, *January* 15, 1862.

General BENJ. F. BUTLER sworn and examined.

By the chairman:

Question. What is your rank and position in the army?

Answer. I am a major general of volunteers; appointed on the 16th day of May last, and qualified, I think, on the 19th of May.

Question. In what department of the army have you been acting?

Answer. Immediately upon my appointment I was ordered to the then department of Virginia, headquarters at Fortress Monroe. I would like to say a word or two about the Little Bethel affair. Some time about the 8th of June—I speak from memory as to dates—I learned that there was a detachment of the enemy at a place known as Great Bethel, with an advanced guard at a place known as Little Bethel—the one being a large church, and the other being the headquarters of a camp-meeting—a grove. Each of them was used as a depot from which to make excursions among the Union men around Fortress Monroe, and carry off both the men and their negroes. I caused a reconnoissance to be made by means of two negro spies. They reported to me, as subsequent events have proved, the exact state of the works and of the men there, except the numbers. I directed two detachments to march; one to march from Newport News, consisting of about 700 men, and the other to march from Hampton, consisting of about 600 men. I ordered them to surround the detachment of the enemy at Little Bethel and capture them, and then, if they thought best, under the cover of that capture, to go to Great Bethel, which was about two miles beyond—Great Bethel being about eight miles from each starting place; and I ordered two regiments, with two pieces of cannon, to march two hours later, for the purpose of supporting these detachments, if necessary, in case any re-enforcements should be sent to the enemy. At daybreak, precisely, the two detachments first named were before Little Bethel, and were just at that moment about to make an attack, when the two rear detachments, which were to meet about three miles in the rear, met each other in the grey of the morning, and one of the detachments fired upon the other. The two detachments in front immediately retrograded, and returned about two miles, when the mistake was found out. General Pierce, then in command, acting upon his judgment, moved forward still upon Great Bethel—Little Bethel having been taken and destroyed. He then sent back word to me that he had so done, and that he thought he could get on without any re-enforcements. He made an attack upon Great Bethel. That attack was not successful principally from the reason that our men were frightened by reports of the great number of the enemy said to be there present. Word was sent back to me for re-enforcements, and I ordered up two further detachments, so that there were 3,000 of our troops before Great Bethel. The last detachment reached there at one o'clock in the day, having marched, at most, but eight miles. But upon consultation—it being believed that there were 4,000 men and twenty pieces of cannon behind the intrenchments, whereas I had sent them out to meet but 600 men and four pieces of cannon—they concluded that they were overmatched, and that it was best to withdraw in good order, which was not done, however, but in bad order; and when they got home that night seventeen officers sent in their resignation. I had a report from one of the colonels that he saw 1,200 men come out of the intrenchments, with four pieces of artillery, and attempt to outflank him; and that his regiment was fired upon by, at least, twenty pieces of artillery in position. That report of Colonel Allen is to be found printed in the Rebellion Record. Now, in truth and fact, the enemy never had more than 600 men engaged there. They sent to Yorktown and got a part of a Louisiana regiment, which marched eighteen miles on a pretty warm day, and when they reached Big Bethel they lay down and gasped and panted for breath. And it appears by the reports of the enemy that as soon as our troops let them alone they retreated immediately to Yorktown. That night Great Bethel was without an inhabitant, and the intrenchments were without a man there, except my two negro spies, whom I sent up there, and who came back to me and reported that fact; and the enemy did not return there for something like a week after. I attribute the defeat of Great Bethel, first, to the unfortunate collision in the morning, and secondly, to the fact that there was no vigorous attack made, owing to the fear of our people that they were to meet 4,000 men and twenty pieces of artillery, instead of 600 men and four pieces of artillery that I had supposed they would meet. I have never been inclined to attribute much blame to the officer in charge, because he was no more frightened with these reports than the rest were. Every one of them came back that night with reports variously estimating the enemy at 4,000 and 5,000 men, and that they were intrenched in a very strong position. Now the truth, as subsequently ascertained, was that the intrenchments were but three feet high, and they could not see exactly what there was there, because there was nothing to be seen. They took the reports of the women and negroes along the road as to the number of men there; and my experience has been that they always overate from four to six times. If our men had remained fifteen minutes longer they would have taken the works, for the enemy did not stop there fifteen minutes after our troops left. Both parties retreated from each other with equal celerity. It was a misfortune of which, if any share of the blame attaches to me, I am quite willing to bear it; but it was a misfortune that resulted from the use of raw troops.

Question. That is the second or third time in our investigation that we have found that misfortunes have befallen us from mistaking our own men for the enemy, or *vice versa*. How is that?

Answer. That must necessarily happen when the uniforms on both sides are exactly alike, the officers' uniforms especially being exactly alike, and the formation of the regiments and the drill are also exactly alike. There has been devised no means of distinguishing the two. Indeed, to the naked eye, at 300 yards, a good rebel flag cannot be distinguished from the American flag. The red and white blend together, and there is a blue field and stars on both.

Question. You were with the expedition to Hatteras, I believe?

Answer. Yes, sir.

Question. Will you give us a little account of that?

Answer. Some time in June I sent to the War Department a memorandum stating that there were works being built at Hatteras, and that it was being made a depot for the rebel privateers. I suggested that something should be done to break it up, and I thought a small expedition might achieve that purpose. That memorandum, I suspect, was turned over to the Navy Department, because about the 8th or 9th of August I heard from it from that department. General Wool had been appointed to that department, but had not then arrived. A memorandum came to me that the navy would take as much force as they chose and could get together, and attempt a bombardment of the forts at Hatteras. I was to take as much land force as was thought proper and could be spared, and co-operate with the navy, and when the rebels were driven out of the forts at Hatteras, we were then to take certain schooners loaded with stone and stop up by sinking them there. General Wool having in the meantime come down, I made a requisition on him for as much force as he could spare, and he spared me 860 men, to be joined by 100 marines from on board the ships. We took the Wabash, the Minnesota, the Susquehanna, and the Constellation frigates, and the troops on board three transports, and went down to Hatteras. When we arrived there we found a very heavy sea running on the beach. After a consultation we undertook to land, and did land 319 men of the land force, including one company of marines, when the surf stove every one of our boats. We then undertook to land with whale boats and ship boats, and a very deserving officer, trying to do it, was thrown on shore with his men, and the boat stove. In the meantime, leaving these men on shore, as it was impossible to reach them, the fleet bombarded one of the forts, known as Fort Clark—a strong square redoubt, mounting eight guns—and silenced it. But in consequence of the threatening aspect of the weather we were obliged to get an offing. The next morning we returned and commenced the bombardment of Fort Hatteras. After two hours of heavy bombarding I went to work to land the rest of the troops. In the meantime I had sent my aid on shore, with directions to the troops there to advance. While engaged in landing the rest a white flag was run up, and the place was surrendered to us. There were surrendered about 750 men, a thousand stand of arms, 25 cannon, and two strong forts. Though my orders were distinctly to sink vessels there and abandon the place, yet after learning the exact condition of things, upon consultation with Commodore Stringham, it appeared to me to be a very important situation to be held for our own purposes. It was the opening to a great inland sea, running up 90 miles to Newbern, and so giving water communication up to Norfolk. It seemed to me that if we ever intended to operate in North Carolina and southern Virginia, we should operate by way of that inland sea, and should not stop ourselves out. But it would be much better for us to take possession of the fort there and hold it. I had just about men enough with me for a garrison for that purpose; the enemy having had about 750 men and I having about 860. I could not pursue the advantage gained, because the inner bar, about two miles up from the opening, carried only about eight feet of water, while I had no gunboat that carried less than ten feet. It was, therefore, impossible for us to go inside. I had a canal boat there, the Fanny, which had a couple of field pieces mounted upon her, and which afterwards went inside and was captured. She was the only boat that could go inside, and she could not carry more than 100 men. Having come to that conclusion I garrisoned Fort Hatteras, and having disobeyed express and written orders, it was necessary for me to report in person here; and I came to be court-martialed, or to make such representations as I could to have my actions and doings sanctioned. Upon representing the matter to the government, to the commanding general, the War Department, and afterwards to the members of the cabinet, my action was approved, and the forts are now garrisoned; and I have reason to believe that there is at present an expedition going into Fort Hatteras, which never could have gone there had it been stopped up by this stone fleet which we took there with us for that purpose.

Question. Would it be easy to destroy the navigation there?

Answer. I do not believe it possible to destroy the navigation there, and for this reason: If you will look upon the map you will perceive that there is a sea there, or an arm of the ocean, 90 miles broad, and extending along for 400 miles of the coast; and it is only separated from the main ocean by a narrow belt of sand, about two miles wide at its widest, and in some narrow places not more than a half a mile wide, averaging about a mile in width. When the southeastern winds prevail the water inside is thrown up very high, so that for weeks together, after the storm abates, no matter what is the state of the tide, the water is continually running out into the ocean. Hatteras inlet is only about 12 years old. Ocracoke inlet, which is below, was the main inlet; but it is now filling up, and Hatteras inlet is widening. For that reason you cannot find Hatteras inlet upon most of the maps; it is a new creation. I have not believed at all in blocking up any large inlet by means of any artificial structure. You may change the channel, but the water going in there must come out somewhere. You can stop up some particular channel; but, in my judgment, you simply destroy a channel that we know, and open another we do not know of.

Question. Unless there is a rocky bottom all along there?

Answer. The whole coast is sand. This thing has been tried by the very nation that now complains of its barbarity. The English, in the time of Napoleon, tried to stop up the harbor of Boulogne by sinking ships in the same way, but they found it wholly ineffectual; and I think it will be found wholly ineffectual now.

Question. You have answered, what has been frequently asked, why that expedition did not pursue their advantages on the main land, perhaps as far as Beaufort or Newbern.

Answer. I meant to have stated at first that I had but 860 men, which was hardly enough to attack a large coast. I had to go into Pimlico Sound, and go ninety miles to reach that place. I had but one boat which drew less than ten feet of water, and the bar carried only eight feet. That boat had no armament, and no capacity to carry more than 100 men. It was simply a canal propeller, brought down from the Raritan canal, and was used simply as a tug and to run around in shallow waters, and to carry supplies. She was taken down there simply to act as a tender, if she could live down around the cape, which it was difficult for her to do, though it was fine weather. She was intended to carry supplies from the larger ships to the men on shore.

Question. Do you know whether the late storm has injured the fortifications there? I have seen some statement that it had.

Answer. I watched that matter with a great deal of interest. The storm has not injured the fortification at all. The point at Hatteras Inlet is almost square, like the corner of this table. The larger fort is on the point; the smaller one is above. What the storm has done has been to open a six-feet deep channel between the two forts; a channel six feet deep and something like sixty feet wide, all around Fort Hatteras, making a ditch there, and rendering it perfectly impervious to any land attack. The rebels understood this matter as well as we did, and a great deal better. The fort was made with a great deal of skill, under the direction of Major Andrews, who, I believe, was educated at West Point. The whole face of the fort had been sheathed by means of plank sheathing driven into the sand to prevent the washing of the surf from undermining it. And the glacis had been entirely covered by heavy turf of marsh grass, brought about three miles, to prevent the sand from washing out. The storm would not injure the fort. The only danger there is the unhealthy location, on account of the fog and damp there. Nothing is ever dry there, not even the powder. One reason they made no better fight against us was, that the magazine had not been properly aired, and the powder would hardly burn. After I took possession of the fort, I took enough of their powder to fire a national salute at the raising of our flag, and though the muzzles of the guns were from us, yet, standing as far back as across this room, the wind blowing towards us when the guns were fired, blew back upon us kernels of powder entirely unburned, until we were almost covered with them.

Question. Have we done anything to strengthen those fortifications since you captured them?

Answer. Nothing but to mount some heavy guns of long range. The only guns they had were 32-pounders, which came from Norfolk. One interesting fact that we learned by the capture of that fort was the official declaration that the 8, 9, and 10-inch guns which they had captured at Norfolk had given out, that is, they had used them all up, and could not supply any more. That statement was made in reply to a very urgent appeal for some heavy guns; and thereupon one 10-inch gun had been sent down from the Tredegar works at Richmond. The rebels, as usual, had got notice of our coming, and they had got that gun down the day before; but being a little dilatory with the shell, they did not get the shell down in season, and they had no gun that could reach us to do any harm.

By Mr. Gooch:

Question. Was it in contemplation at that time that your expedition was to be followed up by a military force to operate in the interior?

Answer. No, sir. On the contrary, we were to stop up the channel and leave; and it was owing to my disobedience of orders, and acting upon counsel with Commodore Stringham, who agreed with me in regard to the necessity of having a naval depot there, that it was not done. It will be seen by reference to the map that Cape Hatteras extends out here and makes a perfect lee for all northern winds. The winds that prevail all through the winter are the northeast and northwest winds, against which this cape affords a great shelter. Fortress Monroe, two days' sail from Hatteras, was the nearest point where our vessels could find a coal depot and get water and supplies, for all the harbors below there were then in possession of the enemy or stopped up, and it was that consideration which induced me to leave that there as a coaling station, or a place of refuge for light vessels and all the small steamers for the blockade.

By the chairman:

Question. What is your estimate of the enemy's forces across the river, now at Centreville and Manassas, the rebel army, generally called their army of the Potomac?

Answer. That is a matter upon which I suppose I have no business to have an opinion. I have never had anything to do with the army of the Potomac, and I have no sources of information but what are open to all of you.

Question. But we are not all shrewd enough, perhaps, to make the calculations.

Answer. Perhaps, if you will allow me, I will give the data upon which I form my opinion, and then you can form opinions for yourselves. I have never believed the strength of the rebel army to be anything like what it has been represented to be. I may be wrong, and probably should defer my opinion to others; but I will give you the grounds upon which I base my judgment. In the first place, I know the tendency of the human mind to exaggerate, and I know the certainty that there will be exaggeration in regard to numbers, and I can give you no better illustration than this: when I put on board at Hampton Roads, for the Hatteras expedition, the 860 men I had, I did so in four detachments, and a very respectable gentleman, a reporter, sent a despatch in good faith to the New York papers, that I had started with 4,000 men—in fact, I had but 860 all told. Now, I have known our strength, and I have known the efforts we have made to get a given number of troops for the army of the Potomac, and I have come to the conclusion that if, with the great expenditure of money and means, offering men more than enough, with our railroads, canals, and other means, we could only get so large an army, then the south, without that material, without that means, without those facilities—although they might have men enough—must have found it impossible to get so large an army as has been attributed to them.

I then look at another thing. I examined with some care the reports of the battle of Bull Run; and I believe that it is now agreed that Johnston brought to the rebel forces re-enforcements to the extent only of about 10,000 men, and I believe that it is now agreed that there was only about 25,000 on a side engaged there at first. It was said that there were 100,000 men in the rebel army at Manassas. Now, I cannot believe that the rebel general was so stupid as to risk a flank movement—a flank march all the way from Winchester—with an enemy on the rear if Patterson had followed him up, in order to re-enforce 25,000 men with 10,000 men, when he had at the same time 75,000 men lying idle within four miles behind them. I cannot conceive that to have been done. A flank movement is always one of the most dangerous movements that can be made. And I cannot conceive he would risk a flank march, with an enemy on his rear which they had no reason to believe, I trust, would not follow at once. I cannot believe he would run all that risk to bring 10,000 men so far to re-enforce 25,000 men, when he had 75,000 men lying idle, doing nothing, within so short a distance. And Beauregard says in his report, if I remember the words, that he was in despair until he was told that Johnston's re-enforcements were coming up. Now, why should a general be in despair for the want of a re-enforcement of 10,000 men, when he had 50,000, 60,000, or any other number of men lying so much nearer which he could use?

Again, it is well known among military men, and to everybody else, I suppose, that soldiers are very tenacious of the honor of being in a battle, and it would be more than a general's life is worth for him to omit in his report the names of regiments who took part in a battle, for that is a part of the history of those regiments. Then, General Beauregard, among our southern friends, who are considered especially tenacious about this matter, must have named every regiment in that battle. And if any gentleman has ever read Beauregard's report, he may number the regiments; and then, taking 750 men as the fighting strength of a regiment 1,000 strong, he can easily estimate the number of troops in the rebel army in that battle.

But to go further than that. You all understand that regiments in both armies, from any State, are numbered according to the number of regiments raised in that State. Now, how many do you find—how high is the number? You will not find that Beauregard talks about the 40th Georgia, or the 50th South Carolina, or the 60th Louisiana; but he will tell you of the 6th Georgia, the 7th South Carolina, or the 8th Louisiana, and so on. You will find that he seldom, except when speaking of militia regiments, ever gets into the teens. Then add to that the fact that on the 28th day of August I captured at Hatteras the last regiment of North Carolina volunteers that had been raised up to that time, and that was the 7th regiment, and the colonel had not been elected a week when he was taken. Therefore North Carolina had only seven regular regiments in the field on the 28th day of August, and it is hardly to be presumed that she had more than that on the 21st of July.

You will find, too, that when southern papers speak of their troops marching from place to place, they do not say that such a regiment has just marched through Tallahassee, or Columbus, or any other place; but it is such a company—the Lionine Braves, the Pulaski Guards, or some other company.

Therefore I have put all these things together, and reckoned a little as to the number of regiments they had. It was for my own amusement and edification, for it was nothing to me, and I had no particular business to know it. It is your business as much as mine, and probably more, for it is your business to look after the conduct of the war, while I only have to look after a division. I have no sources of information but what are open to anybody; yet I do not believe that their whole regular army has ever exceeded, or does to-day exceed, one hundred and fifty thousand—that is, all their force. And I never have believed, and I never shall believe, until it is made certain to me, that there has ever been more than seventy thousand men at the outside in and about Manassas. Now, I know I have no right to know about this matter, for I have no more means of information than anybody else has. I have given the grounds for my opinion. And I want to give another instance as bearing upon this question: When I lay at the Relay House, out here, just before I went to Baltimore, I was very much frightened about the number of the enemy at Harper's Ferry. I was told that there was a very large force at Harper's Ferry. I got all manner of reports, usually estimating the number at eight thousand or nine thousand, and some going as high as twelve thousand or fifteen thousand men there. I had occasion to send a spy up there. Now, I knew he could not tell about numbers any better than others could. I knew that no man, not accustomed to tell the number of men by their appearance, could get at the right number. Unless he knew about the organization, he would evidently think that a regiment was at least three thousand or four thousand men. I told my spy, therefore, to find out the number and shape of the tents, if they were in tents, and if they were in buildings, to give me the size and the number of the buildings. He brought me the number of tents, saying they were mostly encamped in tents. And from calculation, allowing to each tent all that it could possibly accommodate, I made out that there were from eighteen hundred to two thousand men up there. So that I felt perfectly safe, leaving a thousand men at the Relay House that I should not be troubled by those at Harper's Ferry if I went to Baltimore with the rest of my force. So that which appeared very rash to General Scott, who believed that there were eight thousand men at Harper's Ferry, and who scolded me very roundly for going away from the Relay House and leaving only a thousand men there, was not so very rash after all.

Take the case of Big Bethel. It is admitted now, on all hands, that there were only six hundred men in the intrenchments there, and four pieces of cannon. If you will send for the Rebellion Record I would like to have you read the report of the colonel, who says he himself saw twelve hundred men file out of that intrenchment with four pieces of cannon. Now, what he did see was this: in making the attack Colonel Tompkins got two companies of his men separated from him by a ravine which was fringed with bushes. As they marched up to the battery, these men who had become separated appeared, and he saw them. Not knowing that they were his own men, and supposing that he was being outflanked, he gave the order to retreat, and then these companies began to retreat also; and marching back, Colonel Allen saw these men, and took them to be twelve hundred men. It is a universal rule that no man can give the slightest judgment of numbers of men at any time or anywhere.

And I will make another observation; that is, that 5,000 men cannot stand, shoulder to shoulder, so close that they will touch, in double rank in less than a mile front. Each man will average at the least two feet width of space, which will give 5,000 feet for double rank of 5,000 men, which in round numbers may be called a mile. Now, battalions are drawn up with 22 paces—66 feet—between each two battalions; and more than that, artillery and cavalry treble space of infantry, at least for their front; so that, take a column of 5,000 men, with the proper proportion of the several arms of the service, and they cannot stand in line of battle short of two miles at least. Now, when you get 100,000 men ready to be deployed in line of battle, it is a very easy sum to calculate as to how much front there should be, provided there are no inequalities of surface in the ground where they are standing. I am calculating now for a perfectly level parade ground, like the Champs d'Elysés, or any other perfectly level piece of ground.

By Mr. Odell:

Question. You put your men in two ranks only?

Answer. That is our formation of a line of battle. It is a universal rule that you must not march in column with one company nearer to the next company than the front of the line in which that company should deploy into line of battle. They must march "company distance," as it is called, so that whether they are in line of battle, or in column, or encamped, it is all the same. The rule of encampment is that you must make each camp just as wide as would be required for the front of your division, brigade, or regiment, as the case may be, in line of battle, so that whatever may be the formation, you must have so much room. The formation of an army in attack is usually made in double rank and double lines—that is, a front line and a line of reserve; so that an army of 50,000 or 100,000 men should have a front of at least a mile, reckoning upon double lines, for each five miles, and that is allowing nothing for inequalities. Then there is another thing to be considered: human sight is finite. If any gentleman, when travelling on a railroad, will step upon the rear car and look back over a level, straight piece of track, the perspective of the two lines of rails will run together in less than three-quarters of a mile; that is the end of vision. Now, the space between the rails is four feet and six inches. Now, apply the rules of perspective to a body of men drawn up in line and see how soon the perspective will run out when looking down a line of men. It will run out as soon in the one case as in the other, and at the distance of a mile on a level you cannot see any soldiers; so that, standing on the ground on a level, no man ever yet saw 5,000 soldiers drawn up in line of battle.

I feel bound to give all the grounds upon which my judgment in this matter is based. I put these views forth with very great deference to the opinions of others, saying, simply, that it is only the result of reason, and that upon which I form my opinion. And I wish simply to add this: that in every other department of the great battle of life we have beaten these gentlemen of the south, and I do not believe they can beat us so easily in raising armies.

By Mr. Chandler:

Question. You came to Washington to report your success at Hatteras and to have your course sanctioned by the government. Did you then contemplate another and a further movement in that direction, and did you ask for troops for that purpose?

Answer. I did, but the exigencies of the army of the Potomac and of other branches of the service would not permit troops to be spared for me. I got back here and made my report about the first of September. General Sherman's command was expected to start on the seventh of September, and the exigencies of his command required all the troops that could be then spared. He did not start until the 28th of October, owing to various delays in getting troops, &c. I obtained authority on the 10th of September to raise some regiments for the service. I have now got those regiments, and hope to move soon.

Question. You state that you had 860 men upon your Hatteras expedition. I would like to inquire whether if you had had 10,000 or 15,000 men and sufficient transportation at that time, it is your opinion that you could have taken possession of the principal towns in North Carolina?

Answer. If I had had 10,000 men—yes, if I had had 5,000, or even 3,000 men—and boats of three guns each that could have got across the bar, I could have taken possession of all the principal towns of North Carolina then, or at least have troubled them a great deal. That might have been done with 3,000 men, for they were thoroughly frightened—in as great panic as they were at Charleston when Sherman's expedition landed at Port Royal. I captured the engineer and the commandant of the port there. They had relied upon their defences at Hatteras, and had expended their entire strength upon their preparations there, and when those preparations and defences gave way, they thought the whole thing was gone.

Question. And a panic seized them?

Answer. Yes, sir.

Question. So that with 10,000 men you could have captured Newbern itself?

Answer. I have no doubt we could have gone anywhere with 10,000 men—to Newbern, Wilmington, Raleigh—anywhere up to Norfolk. There were 8,000 men in and around Norfolk.

Question. And probably about that number now?

Answer. Not more than that, except it may be the militia. There never was up to the first of September, and I have not heard that there has been any increase of force until very lately perhaps. There never was over 8,000 men at Yorktown. And here I would like to say a word in regard to the number of men I was always credited with having at Fortress Monroe. The number on our side there has always been put at from 15,000 to 18,000 men, as I have no doubt all the members of this committee have heard time and again. Now the uttermost number of men at any one time, reckoning everything that was white at Fortress Monroe, never came up to 10,000 men; and 4,500 of those men, more than one-half of the fighting force of the entire effective strength there, was sent to Baltimore and Washington on the Wednesday after the disaster at Bull Run. And that will afford an illustration of the matter at Yorktown. The enemy was always credited with having 25,000 men there. Now, General Magruder, when he marched down to attack Newport News, took with him the whole available force at Yorktown, except two regiments. That I learned in this way: I captured the messenger who had the letter bag of the enemy's volunteers, and I examined the letters it contained. The soldiers were writing home to Richmond and other places, just as our soldiers write home, telling all the news of the camp, what was going to be done, who were to stay here, and who were to go there. It was stated that all were going to march but two regiments, and the regiments that were going to march were all named. Thus, by averaging the strength of their regiments at 700, I found that they marched down to Newport News with from 5,000 to 6,000 men, leaving about 1,500 men in Yorktown. The letters named the two regiments that were to be left, and those that were to go, and yet at that very time I observed a calculation in the New York Herald which put their forces at Yorktown at 25,000 men.

Question. Have you not found that, in every instance where you have been able to get accurate information, they have represented their forces at from three to four times what they actually were?

Answer. Yes, sir; not only their own forces but ours. For instance, I have seen three different paragraphs going the rounds of the southern papers, stating that I am now at Ship island with from 5,000 to 7,000 men; whereas General Phelps is there with 1,900 men all told, and of course I have not been there at all. A pretty intelligent Virginian once passed through my camp when we were drilling our men on each side of the road. He was saying something about the number of men there, and I asked him how many he thought there were there in camp. Said he, "You must have as many as 6,000 men, perhaps more." Now there were less than 1,800 men there all told.

By the chairman:

Question. I wish to ask you whether intoxicating liquors are used in the army, and to what extent, so far as it has come under your observation?

Answer. I can state to you that intoxicating liquor is used in the army to a most woful extent. There is nothing that a soldier will not do to get it, and officers, too, in many instances. To give you an illustration: We used to send a picket guard up a mile and a half from Fortress Monroe. The men would leave perfectly sober, yet every night when they came back we would have trouble with them on account of being drunk. Where they got their liquor we could not tell. Night after night we instituted a vigorous examination, but it was always the same. They were examined; their canteens were inspected, and yet we found nothing. At last it was observed that they seemed to hold the guns up very straight, and upon examination every gun barrel was found to be filled with whiskey. And it is not always the soldiers who do this. I ordered a search of the premises of the Adams Express Company, and examined the packages sent by friends to the soldiers; and in one day I have taken 150 different packages of liquor from the trunks, boxes, and packages sent to the soldiers by sympathizing friends at home. In one regiment I got hold of the pass-book of the sutler, containing the men's names and the names of every one of the officers, and every officer but four was down in the book for from $8 to $60 worth of liquor in the course of 22 days. Of course the officers would not drink that much themselves—those who got the lowest amount might have done it, perhaps—but they sold it to their men; that is to say, it was charged to them on orders they had given their men for it. One officer I had reason to believe was in partnership with the sutler. I instantly called him in—the one I supposed to be in partnership with the sutler selling to his own men—I called him in, made him resign, and sent him home; sent the sutler home, and stove in the heads of the liquor casks.

By Mr. Gooch:

Question. Is it not in the power of the principal officers to suppress this thing, if they are so disposed?

Answer. Entirely so. In the expedition I am getting up I have made it a condition in every charter of my transports that the carrying of any spirituous liquors outside of the surgeon's supplies shall work a forfeiture of all the money earned. When I have no men under me, when I am at home, I like my wines, &c., and I use it. But I have become satisfied from my experience that the moment that I or any officer goes into camp, we must not only not drink any liquor ourselves, but we must insist that no one under us shall drink any; otherwise, neither the officer nor the army is safe. Just so long as an officer takes his own wine, he must let his men have their whiskey. I have given very stringent orders to the sutler I have appointed for my present expedition. I said to him: "The moment I catch you selling liquor, that day you go home. I am going to deprive myself of anything like spirituous liquor, and you must aid me in this matter. I shall find you out if you do not." He agreed to it, and shortly afterwards brings to me a new trap. He brings to me a small flat bottle, marked somebody's hair oil, put up in Dey street, New York. At first sight it looked all right enough, but upon examination each one was found to contain about half a pint of whiskey with a few drops of olive oil on top, which probably did not harm the whiskey any. This was to be sold by the sutler at 25 cents a bottle. It could be put up for, say, about five cents a bottle, and they wanted to sell it to any sutler for eight cents a bottle. These men said to my sutler: "You can conceal this when you start; they will not examine these bottles at all." And one of them said: "I sold many thousands of these bottles at Fortress Monroe."

To show you how difficult a matter it is to stop this thing, I appointed a quartermaster for one of my regiments. The first thing I knew a man comes to me and says: "There are a couple of casks of vinegar on here, marked 'hospital stores,' are they to go on board the Constitution?" "Not hospital stores," said I, "but commissary stores." "No," he said, "they are marked 'hospital stores.'" I thought that a little singular, and concluded to examine into the matter. I found the two casks of "vinegar" were, in fact, two casks of whiskey. I traced them back to my quartermaster, and now there is another quartermaster in that regiment. Now, to give you another story about the way in which whiskey will get into camp. A woman will come in with her crinoline made, not of springs of steel, or whatever is generally used, but of gutta-percha tubes filled with whiskey. In regard to suttlers, you would be doing a good thing if you would prevent their selling anything to the soldiers that they can eat or drink without first cooking it. Preserved meats, dessicated vegetables, solidified milk; those things are all well enough, for the soldiers will not eat them without some preparation. They generally want something they can take in their hands and eat standing. If you restrict your sutlers in that way, they would be a good institution. It is true, a soldier may use tobacco to excess, but he will not buy too much thread, needles, pins, tape, buttons, &c. But if you let him, he will continue to buy too much to eat and drink. If you impose that restriction you will not have your sutlers make too much money out of the men. Take this matter of common whiskey, that is worth from 25 to 30 cents a gallon, and is sold to the men for $2 and $3 a gallon; indeed the men will give almost anything for it when they have got their money on pay-day.

By Mr. Odell:

Question. What has been your experience in regard to chaplains?

Answer. Well, sir, a good chaplain is a very good thing, but a poor chaplain is as much worse than none at all as you can well conceive. The chaplains, as a rule, in the forces I commanded were not worth their pay by any manner of means. I think there should not be more than one chaplain to a brigade, except in one particular case. I am bound to say that I have never seen a Roman Catholic chaplain that did not do his duty, because he was responsible to another power than that of the military. I would not ask for more than one chaplain to a brigade, except in the case of Roman Catholic regiments. In that case I think there should be a chaplain to a regiment, for they have a great many duties to perform, to write all the letters, &c. They have always been faithful, so far as my experience goes. They are able men, appointed by the bishop, and are responsible to the bishop for the proper discharge of their duties. That is not always the case with other chaplains. I remember running against one young man in one of my regiments who, from his dress and uniform, I saw must be a chaplain. I said to him: "You are the chaplain, are you?" "Yes, sir," he replied; yet the last time I had seen him before that he was a journeyman printer. In my judgment, no chaplain should be appointed who is under forty-five years of age. Young men may be very good men, but they do not have the respect of the soldiers. I never appointed but one chaplain, and he is a doctor of divinity—Dr. Cleveland. I appointed him because he was a man of genial temperament and will obtain the confidence of the soldiers, and I believe him to be a pious man.

By Mr. Gooch:

Question. You think it better to diminish the number and to elevate the character of chaplains?

Answer. Yes, sir; I do. I would have a chaplain to a brigade, and he should not be appointed unless there was some religious authority to which he would be responsible, or some religious body who would recommend him after having examined him. There was a chaplain who went out with the expedition to Big Bethel. He remained about three miles in the rear, and spent his time in consoling a secession widow in a house there. When he was called up, he gave as an excuse that she was very much frightened. I sent him home; he was not a catholic. Colonel Duryee had one chaplain at Fortress Monroe—Rev. Mr. Winslow—who had the respect of every man there, and did infinite good. One such chaplain as that was worth all the rest put together.

Question. You would not think well of reducing the pay of chaplains, but you would reduce the number?

Answer. My idea is that the better way is to reduce the number to one to a brigade, except in case of Roman Catholic regiments.

PORT ROYAL EXPEDITION.

WASHINGTON, *April* 15, 1862.

General T. W. SHERMAN sworn and examined.

By Mr. Gooch:

Question. What is your rank and position in the army?

Answer. I am a brigadier general of volunteers.

Question. Where have you served during the present war?

Answer. I have recently been in command of the expeditionary corps to the southern coast.

Question. Will you give to the committee as concisely as possible a history of the object of your expedition, and what has been done in the department of which you have had the command?

Answer. If I had been aware of the object of the inquiry the committee desired to make of me, I could have prepared myself much better by an examination of my papers upon the subject.

Question. Can you prepare yourself by to-morrow?

Answer. Yes, sir.

[Examination suspended till to-morrow.]

WASHINGTON, *April* 16, 1862.

General T. W. SHERMAN'S examination resumed.

By the chairman:

Question. Have you prepared yourself to make the statement asked of you yesterday?

Answer. I have.

Question. You will please proceed then to state, in your own way, what was the object of the expedition of which you have had the command, and what has been done by it.

Answer. Near the close of July last I was sent for by the Secretary of War who took me to a cabinet meeting in the President's House. I was there informed that there was an expedition on foot to the southern coast. The general object of that expedition was stated in that meeting, and I was asked to take charge of the land force to accompany it. The Secretary of War directed me to General Scott, and informed me that I was to confer with him and receive all my directions from him; that is, that I was to have nothing more to do with the Secretary of War upon the subject. General instructions were put into my hands, signed by the Secretary, and approved by the President of the United States, which were all the instructions I ever received from the Executive on the subject of this expedition, with the exception of some secondary matters. I have not these instructions with me, but I can repeat them almost word for word. They were as follows:

"You will organize an expedition, in connexion with Commodore DuPont, of 12,000 men, and will decide upon the points of assault after the expedition has sailed," (or something to that effect.) "The expedition should start at the earliest practicable moment."

These were all the written instructions I received. After having received these instructions, I was to confer with General Scott. I did so. General Scott assembled a council composed of himself, General Totten, Commodore DuPont, General Meigs, General Wright, and myself. I think these were all who were present. We had some four or five meetings on the subject of this expedition. It appeared that this expedition was got up in consequence of two reports made by a board of officers that had been assembled previously. These reports were read to the meeting or conference assembled by General Scott. One of the reports was dated July 5, 1861; the other was dated July 13, 1861. That board was composed of the following officers: Commodore DuPont, of the navy; Major Barnard, of the engineers; Professor Bache, superintendent of the coast survey, and Captain Davis, of the navy. These reports were read and discussed at these conferences.—[See Appendix.] This board recommended that certain points on the coast should be seized and occupied, as rendevouz for the blockading squadron. At that time there was not a single point on the coast below Old Point that could be occupied by the navy. This plan was for the purpose of rendering the blockade more efficient. Their report of July 5th designated that Fernandina, Florida, should be occupied by the navy, in connexion with a land force of 3,000 men. The report of July 13th discusses the propriety of holding three different points: one was Bull's bay, an important harbor just north of Charleston, St. Helena sound, and Port Royal sound. The board came to the conclusion that Bull's bay, of these three points, should be one point occupied. They also discussed the merits of St. Helena sound and Port Royal harbor, and gave strong reasons why Bull's bay should be the point occupied. Then if any other point should be deemed necessary to occupy, they thought St. Helena should be seized before Port Royal was. We took these reports into consideration, and discussed the matter generally. The council agreed that two points should be siezed. And although the commanders of the expedition were not limited to the occupying of any two particular points, the council recommended, and the expedition was got under way with the calculation that Bull's bay and Fernandina should be the two points seized and occupied. By the President's instructions we were authorized, as a matter of course, to go where we deemed it best. Still it was the decided understanding that the two points I have named should be the points occupied. It was also further agreed that 8,000 men should be sent to Bull's bay, and 4,000 men to Fernandina, in connexion with the fleet. I was directed to go to New York to fit out the expedition. The transports were divided into two divisions, one for Bull's bay, and the other for Fernandina. The armaments, commissary stores, and everything of the kind were distributed between the two divisions, according to the number of men of which those divisions were to be composed. In fact, it was the understanding then between Commodore DuPont and myself that these were the two points to be occupied.

But while the expedition was being fitted out it was somewhat enlarged. I had been directed, in the first place, to take eleven or twelve regiments; afterwards the force was increased to thirteen or fourteen regiments, with the addition of a battery of light artillery. Commodore DuPont's squadron, I believe, was somewhat extended; I think he had an additional number of gunboats. While engaged in fitting out this expedition, I found that the people of New York were very generally impressed with the belief that it was intended for something more than we were really going to do with it. Commodore DuPont and myself were enjoined to keep our business to ourselves; the object of the expedition was not to be made known to any one. We therefore could not undeceive the public in regard to the matter. I had a conversation on this very subject with Commodore DuPont, in the city of New York. I told him that the expedition would never come up to the public expectation, from what I could perceive; and I recommended that we should do something or other in the military line, in order to justify public opinion, or else endeavor to rectify it—one or the other. Of course, we could not well do the latter, as we were enjoined not to say a word about it. Nothing was done in that respect until we got to Old Point Comfort, where the expedition rendezvoused before finally sailing. Just prior to sailing we had a meeting on board the flag-ship in reference to the object of the expedition. The council was composed of Commodore DuPont; Captain Davis, his flag captain; General Stevens; General Wright; General Viele and myself. After full discussion we came to the conclusion that the capture of Bull's bay was rather too insignificant an operation for a force of the dimensions that we were to take with us; and we came to the conclusion that Port Royal ought to be the first point struck at, for the reason that Port Royal, although more strongly defended than Bull's bay, was a harbor of magnificent proportions, with deep water—indeed, the best harbor on the whole coast. We thought we had a sufficient force to carry it; accordingly, it was agreed upon, before leaving Old Point, that Port Royal should first be taken, and afterward we would take Fernandina.

I do not know as I have sufficiently explained the real object of the expedition. The object was to obtain two good harbors, the selection to be left to the discretion of Commodore DuPont and myself, that would give the naval blockading squadron facilities for shelter. In the council called by General Scott, in Washington, it was determined, after discussion, that no ulterior operations by land were to be considered in getting up this expedition; that is, any ulterior operations that would probably be demanded by circumstances, were not to be anticipated at that time; and therefore no preparations were to be made for anything of the sort. That was well understood. All the preparations to be made were simply with reference to the seizure and occupation of those two important harbors; the expedition was fitted out with that object alone. No land transportation was taken on this expedition, further than was necessary for provisioning the men, get them wood and water, &c., at certain localities; not to march into the interior at all.

With regard to light-water transportation, it was agreed upon between the quartermaster general of the army, Commodore DuPont, and myself, that Commodore DuPont would furnish all the means for debarking the land forces of the expedition. I had no responsibility in that respect. He was to put me and my force on shore; that was all well understood. Consequently Commodore DuPont had from forty to fifty surf-boats manufactured for the landing the troops, and he obtained two light draught steamboats and two steam-tugs for the same purpose. I think that is about the extent of the transportation that we started with. The surf-boats all arrived safely with the expedition. The small steamers did not arrive; they encountered a violent gale, and I think they all put back, and we did not get one of them.

I am particular to mention these circumstances; the importance of it will be seen hereafter. It will show how pinched we were for transportation of that sort, when I come to explain why we did not go into the interior.

It is not necessary for me to enlarge at all upon the manner in which Port Royal was captured; it is well known. It was captured by the navy. Immense preparations were made to assist in the capture of Port Royal, or any other place we should attack, by the army; but the army had little or no hand in the capture of Port Royal. We knew nothing about the place before we went there. We had no idea of the distance which it would be necessary to transport troops in boats; and it had to be agreed upon between Commodore DuPont and myself, that the land force of the expedition should remain quiescent upon the steamboats, while he captured Port Royal.

When it was captured, we found ourselves greatly deceived in our expectations. We had no idea, in preparing the expedition, of such immense success. We found, to our surprise, that instead of having difficult work to get one harbor, after one harbor was obtained we had a half a dozen important harbors at once. Such a panic was created among the enemy by the fall of Port Royal, that they deserted the whole coast from the North Edisto to Warsaw sound. This threw into our possession not only the harbor of Port Royal, but the magnificent harbor of St. Helena, and the harbors of North Edisto, South Edisto, Tybee roads, Warsaw sound, and Ossabaw sound. In fact, the real object of the expedition was already accomplished, although Fernandina had not yet been taken. To carry out the programme, of course, we should have gone immediately to Fernandina, although we had already taken all these harbors, sufficient for all the wants of the blockading squadron. The land force was all ready to proceed to Fernandina; our transports, as I have before stated, having been divided into two divisions. Had we been able to proceed right on to Fernandina, the troops of that division need not have been debarked at all. But that was not the case, and we landed the troops, while the transports remained in the harbor, ready to proceed the moment the navy was ready. It was necessary to land the troops, as they had then been on the transports nearly three weeks.

Commodore DuPont informed me that he would be unable to proceed to Fernandina at once, for the reason that he had used the bulk of his ammunition in capturing Port Royal. I think he said he had fired away three-fourths of it, or something to that effect; and he did not think it prudent or safe to go to Fernandina or anywhere else with the amount of ammunition that he had on hand. We were therefore compelled to wait while he sent north for a supply of ammunition. Port Royal was captured on the 7th or 8th of November, and Commodore DuPont received his new supply of ammunition about the last of November. The expedition, however, did not proceed to Fernandina, for the reason that the commodore in the meantime had received orders from the Navy Department to take charge of and sink what was termed the "stone fleet" that had been sent out there. This, of course, absorbed his gunboats, so as to make it entirely impossible to carry on both expeditions at the same time. The Fernandina expedition was, therefore, still further postponed.

Our transports had all this time been retained there at high cost to the government. Some of them were large steamers, costing the government an immense amount. Many of the provisions on board the transports were of a perishable nature, and it was absolutely necessary to proceed to Fernandina at once, or to unload them. I had an interview with Commodore DuPont upon that subject, the result of which was the conclusion that the expedition to Fernandina should be indefinitely postponed. It might be taken up again at some future time, but we would then indefinitely postpone it, and unload our vessels and send them back to New York. I am a little particular in stating this, because I consider it very important. It gave me a great deal of annoyance and uneasiness to have so many vessels, at high prices, laying there idle for nearly a month. I could not have anticipated that the commodore would have found himself unable to proceed; I do not see that he could have anticipated it himself. This stone fleet was sent there, and he had his orders to take charge of it and distribute and sink it where desired.

A month had elapsed, and in the meantime this country that had fallen into our hands had to be taken care of. I had received no instructions in regard to the internal operations of our expedition, but I had my own views upon the subject. I therefore laid out a plan, after having landed, for the capture of Savannah, Fort Pulaski, and the country in that vicinity. I could not see what else we could do that would be profitable. In the meantime I went to work and established a basis of operations at Hilton Head. Port Royal is the key of the whole system there. In order to retain that coast, Port Royal must be maintained because it was so well fortified, vessels of any size could ride safely in the harbor there, and there is such an immense system of waters around it. It is the key of the whole coast, and must be maintained. I therefore constructed one immense fieldwork around Hilton Head island, nearly a mile in extent—a pretty large work, mounted with heavy ordnance. The calculation was to have a system of defences there, so that the key of our position—Port Royal Harbor—could be held by 2,000 men, leaving the remainder available for other purposes.

I will state here that according to the reports of the commission which gave rise to this expedition, it was held that it would require 12,000 men to hold Port Royal. I suppose it would, if seriously attacked without defences. But my object was to have as many of my troops available for interior operations as possible; and for that reason I constructed these works. And I do not hesitate to say that Port Royal bay can now be held by 2,000 men against any force that can be brought against it.

St. Helena sound had also to be taken care of, and I had it thoroughly reconnoitred in connexion with the navy. It was found that the occupation of Otter island in that sound would subserve every purpose of its defence, and would prevent any communication by water between Savannah and Charleston. There is a network of waters, an inland water communication, running all the way from Charleston to Savannah, which had been used all the time by the rebels until we obtained possession there. Of course, the important point was to prevent the enemy from coming by water from Charleston and attacking us on our flank. I erected a fort on Otter island which entirely prevents that. No vessel can go through St. Helena sound in any direction without passing Otter island, which is now held by only 600 men.

By reconnoissance of the navy, Tybee was found to be deserted, and we took possession of it, and constructed a fort there for the purpose of covering Tybee roads. Although Fort Pulaski is at the mouth of the Savannah river, still outside of Pulaski is a fine harbor in which any vessel can ride. Not only that, the enemy can run the blockade there while it is in their possession. We constructed a fort there, and armed it with heavy cannon, to protect that channel.

After this had been done we felt ourselves secure from any attack from any quarter.

While this work was going on, I was looking about for something else to do. As early as the 15th of November, eight days after landing at Port Royal, I wrote to the War Department as follows:

"I have the honor to report that in consequence of the difficulty and great amount of labor in landing our stores, some delay must necessarily occur in continuing operations. This delay is as distasteful to us as it must be to the authorities at Washington.

"In the meanwhile a matter of the first importance is to erect proper defences at Hilton Head, as well as to strengthen the land side of the fort, to the end of securing these important points with the least number of men. This is being done, and a plan of the same will be furnished as soon as it can be prepared.

"In conducting operations here two modes suggest themselves, first, to hold Hilton Head and Phillip's island with a strong force, and proceed with a sufficient force, in connexion with the naval fleet, under Commodore DuPont, and open another harbor. This would be carrying out the original and actual object of the expedition, as I understand it, and for which object only our means have been provided; second, to occupy the points first mentioned, as well as Beaufort, as a base of operations, and act thence on a line of operations embracing Port Royal island and the road to Pocotaligo—the nearest point of the Savannah and Charleston railroad—into the southern counties of the State, threatening Savannah, &c., or to operate from the base of Hilton Head through the interior creeks and channels leading into the Savannah river below Savannah, near Fort Jackson, thus laying siege to Savannah, &c., and cutting off Fort Pulaski.

"For these last operations, the first will require more land transportation than we are provided with, and the last will require an outfit of boats that we are also insufficiently provided with. The former will also require a small cavalry force.

"The only course, therefore, at present is, notwithstanding the apparent opening for more brilliant operations, the first and original plan."

This was a mere preliminary letter, suggesting what I had discovered to be necessary for operations there. The whole country between Hilton Head and Savannah was a marshy country, where you could operate only by boats. All the transportation I was furnished with was forty-six surf boats; and in the occupation of St. Helena sound and Tybee island nearly all the boats I had had been absorbed. We had no wharves; all our transports had to lay out at a distance from the shore, and everything had to be landed by means of these surf-boats. Our light-draught steamers, with the exception of one, had put back to New York. There was one that we chartered ourselves that we had there. Our surf-boats had to be distributed about among these different ports, and we had nothing to operate with. I, therefore, informed the department of it in time—on the 15th of November—so that I might be furnished some means of transportation that would enable me to operate through those waters. At that time there was no opportunity for any operations under heaven, except to go and take Fernandina; and as I have explained, that was soon rendered impossible in consequence of the naval fleet being diverted to another purpose.

Two days afterwards, on the 17th of November, I again wrote to the War Department as follows:

"I have the honor to report that the position of the forces here necessitate the most active operations during the coming winter; the climate and localities of these islands rendering it impracticable to carry on operations upon them after April next.

"We have now possession of the valuable harbors of Port Royal and St. Helena; one more will probably be in our possession in a short time. A fort should be constructed on Hunting island to secure that important roadstead of St. Helena. After well securing these important points and establishing a firm base from which to operate inland, there will not be left a very large force disposable for internal operations. I would therefore recommend that an additional force of 10,000 men be sent to this point as early as practicable.

"We shall require three or four steamers drawing not over seven feet and capable of carrying 800 to 1,000 men each for operations in the rivers and creeks; and a couple of ferry-boats drawing not over five or six feet would be of the greatest advantage. We will require, also, about 100 row-boats, capable of carrying from forty to fifty men each, with kedges and oars. A few of them should be large enough and so constructed as to transport pieces of artillery, with their carriages, including siege guns."

I asked for that on the 17th of November. I did not intimate to the department the precise plan I desired to pursue, because at that time that affair of Fernandina was still in the way, and I did not know when it was to be carried out.

On the 27th of November I again wrote to the department, asking to be furnished with armament sufficient for the reduction of Fort Pulaski. I stated in my letter that I had examined Tybee island, and had ascertained that it would be practicable to bombard Fort Pulaski from that island. I had found out that their casemate guns were not effective on the island; that only their barbette guns were effective. And although the distance from the island to the fort gave a pretty long range artillery, still I had no doubt but what the fort could be crushed by 13-inch mortar shells.

My recommendation was approved by General McClellan, and the armament for the bombardment of Fort Pulaski was ordered to be furnished me. I believe, however, it had all to be cast at Pittsburg. It was but recently that any of it has arrived; it did not all get there until the latter part of last month.

On the 28th of November I wrote to General Meigs, quartermaster general, reiterating, to some extent, what I had written to the department in my letters of the 15th and 17th of November, stating my need of re-enforcements, increase of transportation, &c., and stating my anxiety at that time to go ahead and do something, knowing, as I did, that the season for operations in that region would be a short one. The delay in getting off to Fernandina caused me to feel very anxious, while at the same time I had no means to move anywhere else. After thinking the matter over thoroughly, I laid down in my own mind a plan which I thought could be carried out, and which I desired to pursue at once; and I accordingly wrote to the department, after having been at Port Royal a month and three days, as follows, on the 10th of December:

"I have the honor to submit the following to the consideration of the general-in-chief and to the War Department. The object of this expedition was to seize upon at least two important points of our southern coast, and hold the same for the protection of our blockading squadron when compelled to seek a harbor, as well as to create something of a diversion in favor of our armies in the field.

"After the taking of Port Royal it was intended to proceed to Fernandina and get possession of that harbor, but in consequence of circumstances unnecessary here to particularly relate, that part of the expedition has not yet been accomplished; and although I have been for some time prepared for it, a still further delay arises from the fact that the gunboats of the navy have first to be occupied in the work of disposing of the stone fleet just arrived from the north.

"But our operations resulting from the capture of Port Royal have become so developed as to lead to the occupation of St. Helena sound, the Tybee, and, in short, to the full possession of the coast from South Edisto to Tybee, and to which may be added Warsaw and Ossabaw sounds, which, if not yet occupied by us, have been deserted by the enemy.

"In the meantime there is a formidable strategic line formed and forming in our front, its right resting on Green island, in Vernon river, passing by Thunderbolt or Augustine creek, (at both of which places there are earthworks, mounted with heavy guns,) Fort Jackson, Savannah, and thence along the line of the Savannah and Charleston railroad, indefinitely, towards Charleston, the line having its principal bodies of troops between Vernon river and Savannah, at Savannah, Hardieville, Grahamville, Coosawatchie, Pocotaligo, Salt Ketchie, &c., and its most advanced posts at Pulaski, New River Bridge, Bluffton, &c.

"The object of this line appears to be to resist an invasion of the main land, and not to attack the occupied coast, which, from all that can be learned, the enemy have concluded they cannot maintain, and have given up all hope of doing so."

I now come to the point that I insisted so strongly upon, and I think it is a great pity I had not been listened to and allowed to go on.

"It may hence be inferred that the main object of the expedition has been already accomplished, and that the point of Fernandina is now of so secondary a character as to render it not only almost insignificant, but the operation of taking it actually prejudicial to the great work which the development of circumstances appears to have set before us. I am aware of the good effect that the capture of Fernandina would have upon the public mind, but the military is the only point of view that should be taken of it. It is no point from which to operate, and will probably fall of itself the moment Savannah is occupied by our forces, and therefore the resources of the navy and army here should be husbanded for a more important operation, viz, the attack of the enemy's line the moment preparations can be made."

I maintain this, that if we could have got Savannah and Pulaski the moment those places fell, that moment all these forts below St. Simon's, Brunswick, Fernandina, St. John's, St. Augustine—all those places below Savannah would have fallen without firing a gun. That was what I maintained at the time. Therefore, the great point was to occupy Savannah; that inasmuch as we had already delayed the attack upon Fernandina for more than a month, why should we think of it again until we had accomplished the work at Savannah? I gave my reasons for it, and I shall even insist that I was right about it. Indeed, it has turned out that a serious threat alone against Savannah caused the fall of all these places. To proceed with my letter:

"The precise point of the hostile line to be struck, and the mode of attack, cannot now be specifically set out without first knowing the means to be placed in our hands, and must therefore be left to time and circumstances.

"But in my judgment, with the necessary means, Savannah should be the point, and to be accomplished somewhat in this way: Pulaski to be vigorously shelled as already recommended in a former communication; at the same time the gunboats of the naval squadron to shell out the garrisons of the forts on Vernon and Augustine rivers, to be closely followed up by the landing of the land forces in the vicinity of Montgomery and Beaulieu, thus taking Augustine river, Fort Jackson, and Savannah in reverse; this operation to be connected at the same time with one from this point on Bluffton, New River Bridge, and Hardieville to get effectual possession of the railroad crossing the Savannah river, and prevent re-enforcements arriving at Savannah from the centre and left of their line. A small head of column shown at Port Royal ferry would have its effect in aiding this demonstration.

"I am firmly convinced that an operation of this sort would not only give us Savannah, but, if successful and strong enough to follow up the success, would shake the so-called southern confederacy to its very centre.

"Not knowing precisely what forces the enemy may have available, it is difficult to estimate for the men and means necessary to the success of the operation. But I must modify the terms of my letter of the 27th November, which did not look to this precise operation, and recommend that the 'one regiment of cavalry, one regiment of regular artillery, ten regiments of infantry, and one pontoon bridge,' be extended to one regiment of cavalry, one regiment of artillery, and twenty regiments of infantry, and as many pontoon bridges as can be sent here.

"An addition to our armament will also be required to enable us to carry on a siege, if necessary, for which the ordnance officer will make requisition.

"I do not say that the thing cannot be done with less troops, but it would be better to have too many than too few, particularly as any success should be followed up rapidly and with sufficient force."

That is the plan I laid before the department, and I am sorry we were not permitted to go on and carry it out.

I will state another plan by which Savannah might have been taken, without involving all this time and expense that the other plan required—something I did not know when this letter was written. About the 1st of January I had all this country reconnoitred—all these flats, marshes, creeks, &c.—with the object of ascertaining the best mode of getting into the Savannah river. I found out that the passage from Wright river into the Savannah river was not so deep as I had expected, and I therefore regarded it as rather impracticable to take my position at the head of Elbow island, which had been my intention. I sent a topographical engineer to reconnoitre the Savannah river further down; and in doing so he examined Wall's cut closely. He sounded the Savannah river in the night, passing around Cumberland Point, the south end of Jones's island. I was very agreeably disappointed in the result of his report. It was that if Wall's cut could be opened, vessels drawing from twelve to fifteen feet might be taken into the Savannah river at high water. That was about the 1st of January. From that time I went to work to open Wall's cut, and succeeded in finding a man who could invent a machine to saw off piles twenty feet under water. He invented the machine, and went down there, and we made out to get those piles sawed off, and to get an old hulk out of the way, so as to enable us to get vessels through into the Savannah river.

On the 14th of January Wall's cut was opened. Whilst being opened we took some prisoners from Savannah, who informed me of the state of the defences round the city of Savannah, the first information of a reliable character that I had been able to obtain from that quarter. I found that there were no defences about Savannah, excepting Fort Jackson, which had eleven guns mounted on its barbettes. They were building a fort on the south end of Hudson's island; and there was a little island, directly opposite Fort Jackson, upon which they were building a fort. But there was not a single gun mounted except at Fort Jackson; and at that time I suppose there were not over 10,000 men in and around Savannah. That I was sure of, because we had taken several prisoners, and they all agreed upon that.

I immediately wrote a communication to Commodore DuPont stating the facts, and recommending that we should both go to work, take advantage of Wall's cut which I had opened, and proceed to take Savannah by a *coup de main*. He replied to me that he thought it was an excellent thing, and that he would unite with me and do all that he could, and that he would set aside for what I proposed that which he was about going to do. He desired to have a conference upon the subject, which we did have the next day, I think, on board the flag-ship; at which was present Commodore DuPont, Captain Davis, Captain C. R. P. Rodgers, General Wright, Captain Gilmore, and myself. This matter I had proposed was discussed, and it was agreed upon as I understood it, and as all my officers understood it; it was agreed that we should by a combined army and naval force go right into the Savannah river and go up and take Fort Jackson and the city of Savannah. I think every officer present regarded the thing as very feasible, indeed. I told them that after garrisoning all my forts I would have an available force of 9,000 men. I did not care at all about Fort Jackson; all I wanted was to have my men landed there. I was so firmly convinced that the matter was agreed upon that the last thing I said to Commodore DuPont was, "the point is Savannah, and immediately?" He replied, "Yes." The council was dissolved that afternoon with the thorough understanding that this matter was to be carried out; and I went to work immediately to make preparations for it.

In one or two days I received a private note from Commodore DuPont in which he stated that he had given this subject more serious consideration, and had some suggestions to make to me that he thought would be satisfactory, and that he would send Captain Davis over to me the next day to explain it. I did not wait for Captain Davis to come, but jumped into a boat the next morning and went over to the flag-ship myself to see about it. I was there informed that in consequence of a discussion of this matter between officers on board the flag-ship, they had come to the conclusion that we could not take Fort Jackson. As I understood them, they stated that not more than two gunboats could act upon Fort Jackson at the same time, and that two gunboats could not take such a work as that. And not only that, but they represented that five rafts were being prepared by the enemy, which would make it difficult to take wooden vessels into the Savannah river. And that, as the going into the Savannah river was a new thing, they thought it was very hazardous. The commodore therefore came to the conclusion that he could not attempt it. I told them that I did not ask them to take Fort Jackson; that all I wanted was to be landed at the mouth of Augustine creek, and I would march on Fort Jackson—on the rear of it. However, that plan was given up. That was the reason why Savannah was not taken by *coup de main* when it might have been taken. Of course, a week or two afterwards the other forts for the protection of the river were completed.

The point with us then was, what was the next best thing to be done. Something had to be done, and we agreed upon this, that we would make a strong demonstration on Savannah, and take advantage of that demonstration to move off to Fernandina and take that place; frighten them at Savannah and then go and take Fernandina. But there were certain things to be done besides. This demonstration was to be made in a particular way, which I will relate in order that the whole thing may be properly understood.

Three gunboats were to enter the Savannah river on the north side. These three boats were to escort General Viele with a considerable force which I was to send with him, and a quantity of guns which we had already put on board flats—twelve or fifteen guns already mounted on carriages; they were to take these down there, and the gunboats were to cover the landing of them. This battery was to be erected on Venus Point, and afterwards another battery was to be erected on Bird island, directly opposite. The three gunboats were to be used so as to cause the people of Savannah to believe that we were going up the river. Captain Davis, with half a dozen gunboats, and General Wright, with a brigade of three regiments, were to enter Warnar sound, pass up Wilmington Narrows, and make a threat of going up to Savannah by way of Wilmington river—up Wilmington Narrows through Augustine creek. That was done on the 27th or 28th of January.

While this was being done, Commodore Tatnall of the rebel service came down with a fleet of several vessels, supposed to be loaded with provisions, and went down to Fort Pulaski. We fired on these boats from Wilmington Narrows on one side and Wright river on the other—a pretty wide range—and stopped a portion of them; the rest ran down to the fort. The object of the Savannah people undoubtedly was to provision Fort Pulaski. No doubt they thought that would be their last chance to do so, and that our gunboats were going up to Savannah.

We were two or three days about this. Then the force under Captain Davis and General Wright fell back into Warsaw sound, and there lay at anchor. The demonstration on the other side remained in *statu quo*. General Viele was there with his artillery, ready to land it on Venus Point whenever he could get it there. But the gunboats did not go around into the river as was agreed upon, and these people lay there from the 28th or 29th of January until the 10th day of February before that battery was put up.

By Mr. Wright:

Question. This force, under General Viele, then remained there some thirteen days?

Answer. Yes, sir; about that time. I think the battery was put up the 10th of February. And during all that time the enemy were provisioning Fort Pulaski; boats were running up and down the river nearly every day. I urged the matter on all I could. I went over to the flag-ship and had consultations with Commander DuPont very often, and, as I understood it, he ordered Captain Rodgers to go into the river. But he did not go in, occupying a great deal of his time in sounding the river. But in the meantime our men in charge of the engineer officer cut logs and made a corduroy road across the island, so that the artillery could be landed at another point and taken across there. The road was not constructed with that object at all, for I expected to have the artillery towed around on the flats on which they were, and landed on the point. But they could not do it without being supported, for Tatnall was watching us all the time. But I directed the engineer officer to construct a corduroy road across there, because, after the battery was erected, we wanted to keep up a communication with our base without being obliged to go around the point. I became so tired of the delay that I gave General Viele orders to go into the river, and land and erect that battery, whether the navy would assist him or not. I went down myself, intending to see that that was done. But when I got down there I found that the battery had been landed on the island at another place, and I therefore permitted them to go around the other way. They took the artillery across the island the next night, and the battery was erected without molestation. The enemy came down the next day to drive us off, but were themselves driven back. After this battery was constructed we constructed a similar battery on Bird island, which completely blocked the enemy there. Then three vessels took position in my rear. However, the thing all turned out well, with the exception that the delay of ten or twelve days enabled the enemy to put six or eight months' provisions into Fort Pulaski. When I found out the feasibility of getting into the Savannah river, as I have stated, I made up my mind that the slow, tedious, and expensive process of reducing Fort Pulaski by bombardment would be unnecessary, and calculated that the construction of batteries there, thus cutting the fort off from supplies from Savannah, would be all that would be required to reduce the work; and I think it would have been but for this delay, which enabled them to provision the fort from Savannah.

After I had constructed these forts, as I have related, I was unwilling to risk the reduction of Fort Pulaski by simply cutting it off, for the prisoners themselves told me that they had then some nine months' provisions in it. I therefore continued my work of erecting batteries on Tybee Island to bombard the fort. With regard to the other portion of that demonstration Commodore DuPont promised that the demonstration should not be more than five or six days in being made; that is, that the fleet and my brigade should not remain in Warsaw sound more than five or six days at the utmost. I told him that it would be utterly impossible to keep the troops long on the transports there without being sick; and it was only in consequence of that agreement on his part that I consented to the demonstration. But my brigade remained there under General Wright in Warsaw sound, exposed to the most stormy portion of the winter from the 27th of January until about the last of February. I looked upon that whole month as lost. I had to recall one of those regiments and send them back to Hilton Head on account of ship fever. It may, however, have redounded to our benefit by giving the enemy an opportunity to withdraw their guns from the southern forts, so that they could offer no resistance to us. After making this demonstration the expedition left for Fernandina about the first of March. In the meantime the Georgians evacuated St. Simon's and Brunswick, and took all their forces and artillery from there and carried them to Leavenworth, and when the expedition got to Fernandina it found the enemy in the process of evacuating that place. They had got off all their guns with, I think, the exception of about fifteen. Having taken Fernandina with so much ease the expedition kept on and took St. John's, which was also evacuated. They also took Jacksonville and St. John's Bluff, and they kept on around to St. Augustine, which was also evacuated, having been evacuated by the enemy the evening before our expedition arrived there. All these places down there fell without striking a blow, in consequence no doubt of the threats upon Savannah and our victories at the sametime in the west.

It will be observed that though I early made requisition for means to move my land forces, those means never reached me. The light-draught steamers that I asked for were obtained and sent to me, leaving New York the latter part of December. For some reason or other, probably on account of stress of weather, they put into Hatteras inlet, and I am informed that they were seized by the Burnside expedition. They never reached me. I was informed by the Assistant Secretary of War the other day that they were still with General Burnside. Of the 100 rowboats I asked for about 50 reached me, but not until about the 27th of March, some three days before I was relieved from that department.

I have dwelt at some length upon the two plans I formed for taking Savannah. Having formed one plan, I conceived another and a shorter one; that I have recounted at some length, that of taking Savannah by a *coup de main.* That last plan failing, of course I reverted back to the former plan. I supposed, of course, that we were to be allowed to pursue that plan, especially as the authorities at Washington had sent me a siege train which I had applied for, not knowing what were the character of the defences about Savannah; not that I thought I should be under the necessity of laying regular siege to Savannah, but simply that I desired to be upon the safe side, to be prepared for any event. Without answering my communication they sent me the siege train, which reached me in February.

When Commodore DuPont and myself agreed to the demonstration upon Savannah for the purpose of the more easily taking Fernandina, it was fully admitted by us both that it would be utterly impossible then to take Savannah by *coup de main,* as the opportunity for doing so had been allowed to pass, and the batteries and forts about Savannah were probably ready to fire upon us at any moment; that the guns would be mounted upon them the moment this demonstration was made. This was the case, as we learned from prisoners and contrabands. Savannah, also, receiving an accession of all the heavy artillery down at St. Simon's, and a portion of that at Fernandina.

The results of the expedition may be summed up as follows: The occupation of the whole coast from North Edisto, South Carolina, to St. Augustine, Florida, and so occupied as to be of permanent tenure; the return to the federal government of three of the permanent fortifications stolen by a reckless and unprincipled party; the holding of 50,000 rebel troops on the line from Brunswick to Charleston, thus far lightening the burden of the war on the northern borders of the rebel States.

It is safe for me to say that the object of the expedition has been thoroughly accomplished. But in consequence of our unlooked for success, had the means of transportation I early asked for been put into my hands, far more would have been easily accomplished. Savannah, a most important strategic point, would have been in our possession ere this, could my plans have been pursued; or, if I had been timely warned that I would not have been allowed to carry out those plans as far as the taking of Savannah, such other disposition of our troops would have been made in the meanwhile as to create consternation among the enemy in another quarter. For the country's sake, not my own, I deeply regret that I should have been stopped in my course on Savannah. The acquisition of Fort Pulaski was indispensable, it is true; but the acquisition of Savannah would have thrown the whole State of Georgia into our hands, and, supported by Burnside's victories in the north, would have rendered the capture of Charleston and the acquisition of all South Carolina an easy conquest.

On the 3d of March I received a sort of semi-official letter from General McClellan, written on the 14th of February by himself, not through his adjutant general. He writes thus in regard to my operations:

"After giving the subject all the consideration in my power, I am forced to the conclusion that, under the circumstances, the siege and capture of Savannah do not promise results commensurate with the sacrifices necessary. When I heard that it was possible for the gunboats to reach the Savannah river above Fort Pulaski, two operations suggested themselves to my mind as its inevitable result. First, the capture of Savannah by *coup de main*, the result of an instantaneous advance and attack by the army and navy. The time for this has passed, and your letter indicates that you are not accountable for the failure to seize the propitious moment, but that, on the contrary, you perceived its advantages. Second, to isolate Fort Pulaski, cut off its supplies, and at least facilitate its reduction by a bombardment.

"Although we have a long delay to deplore, the last course still remains to us, and I strongly advise the close blockade of Pulaski, as well as its bombardment so soon as the 13-inch mortars and heavy guns reach you. I am confident that you can thus reduce it. With Pulaski you gain all that is essential: you obtain complete control of the harbor; you relieve the blockading fleet, and render the main body of your force disposable for other operations. I do not consider the possession of Savannah worth a siege after Pulaski is in our hands; but the possession of Pulaski is of the first importance.

"The expedition to Fernandina is well, and I shall be glad to hear that it is ours. * * * * * * * * *

"In the meantime it is my advice and will that no further attempt be made on Savannah, unless it can be carried with certainty by a *coup de main*. Please concentrate your attention upon Pulaski and Fernandina."

He also informed me in that letter that he was not aware, until the day he wrote, that I had sent for a siege train. In a letter written the 8th of March I informed General McClellan that, agreeably to his instructions, no further preparations would be made for an attack on Savannah.

I desire to do General McClellan justice in regard to this matter. He considered that the taking of Fort Pulaski was the most important thing to be done. I agreed to that myself, that Fort Pulaski was more important than Savannah alone; but I could not see why we could not take them both.

In this same letter, too, General McClellan desired me to study the problem of Charleston. He thought it was much more desirable to take Charleston than Savannah, and informed me that measures would be very soon taken, after certain movements had been effected, for the capture of Charleston and the forts around it. I had already studied the problem of Charleston, and had communicated my views to him upon that subject. I also wrote him another letter on the same subject.

On the 21st of March I received, through Commodore DuPont, a letter, dated the 5th of March, more decidedly official in its character, through the Adjutant General's Office, directing me to continue my operations against Pulaski, and proceed no further against Savannah. I had already been directed by General McClellan to abstain from any further preparations for the siege of Savannah, and to confine myself to the siege of Pulaski and the taking of Fernandina. Both the Navy and the War Departments seemed to insist upon our taking Fernandina, showing the importance they attached to that place. It is seen that my views down there and the views of the authorities here were somewhat different. What I regarded as the most essential operations they did not seem to care much about. On the 26th of March I wrote, through the Adjutant General's Office, to the War Department, as follows:

"Your letter of the 5th recommends me to reduce Fort Pulaski in preference to attacking Savannah. In my letter of the 14th of December last, the department will perceive that my plan was to carry on both at once. The essential features of that plan I have not departed from, and have been very desirous of carrying out, particularly after the opportunity we discovered for taking Savannah by *coup de main* failed for want of co-operation of the navy, the particulars of which the department is already apprised of. I humbly bow to the decision of my superiors at Washington; but still, general, from the point here I can but regret that my plan could not have been carried out. I had every confidence in it, and believe it would have been executed with not so much sacrifice as the general seems to imagine."

I then go on and state that the preparations for the bombardment of Fort Pulaski are being made as rapidly as possible, and say:

"The work is of such a character, you are well aware, that we must be in a state of perfect preparation before opening fire. It is hoped that we shall be permitted to go through this job early enough in the season to afford a pretty large force in the direction of Charleston, the nucleus of which I have formed in the shape of two regiments on the North Edisto river."

There is something to be said in regard to the distribution of my forces. A great deal has been said in the country in regard to the occupation of Beaufort; because it was a fine city, I suppose. It was said that, two weeks after having occupied Port Royal, I had not occupied Beaufort, and that was considered an evidence of inactivity. Now, my plan at first was to not occupy Beaufort at all. The place is entirely untenable by the enemy; a single gun-boat up there can keep the enemy out of the place. The enemy never pretended to occupy that island. The only reason that we occupied it was that the enemy got to blockading the streams there by driving piles down in them. I concluded that they had some important object in doing that, and thought it necessary to occupy that island so as to stop that proceeding on their part. Had it been my object to have gone into the interior and occupied the railroad near that point, I should have wanted to have occupied Port Royal island. I could have gone up and occupied that railroad, but I had no idea of doing anything of that sort. I could have set myself down there with a force of the enemy on each side of me, but it would have required a force of 50,000 men to have maintained the position. But my object was to obtain possession of the Savannah end of the line. But the moment I committed myself to the other point I would be involved in an affair that would require the sending out of some 30,000 or 40,000 men to maintain the position, and we should never have been able to do anything upon Savannah or Charleston with these troops. For that reason I did not pay much attention to the occupation of Port Royal island when I went there. But afterwards I felt that it was necessary to occupy it, to prevent these people from coming down and blockading us. After we occupied Port Royal island, the enemy came down and undertook to build forts. They were said to have been mounted with heavy guns. General Stevens took a brigade over there and drove them off, and took the guns. I directed them to return after the object of the commission was accomplished; we had not pushed on to the railroad. My object, at that time, was Savannah, for which we wanted all our available troops. But if I had anticipated that we should not be allowed to make any operations against Savannah, I should have gone up to the railroad and occupied that. I am sorry I did not. After being forced to cease operations upon Savannah, then General Stevens and myself came to the conclusion that we would take possession of this country up there on the railroad, and preparations were being made for that purpose when I left. We thought it would be a healthy country; and I think it should be occupied this summer.

By Mr. Chandler:

Question. There is another railroad around to Charleston from Savannah?

Answer. Yes, sir; around through Augusta, Georgia, and but a few hours further than the direct road from Savannah.

Question. What is to prevent our troops from going up to Savannah, now that Fort Pulaski is taken?

Answer. They have now a great many fortifications there.

Question. The new fortifications you have referred to?

Answer. Yes, sir. They are very strongly fortified there. I do not think you could very well take Savannah by way of the river without a great fight at the mouth of Augustine creek. Charleston is much more assailable than Savannah at this time. If you want to go to Savannah on fast land, you must go by way of Wilmington river and Ossabaw sound. All the country below is one complete marsh, where men cannot walk.

Question. What force did you estimate the enemy had in front of you there?

Answer. There has been, since the first of December, from Savannah to Charleston, on the railroad, some 40,000 men, perhaps. The country there is divided into districts, and there are two or three brigades in each district. They have fortified all the streams, and have an extended system of earthworks for the protection of the railroad, which, however, can be carried.

Question. Could you, immediately after the capture of Port Royal, have taken Savannah and Charleston if you had marched on them at once?

Answer. No, sir. There was not the slightest opportunity to do anything of the sort. You will remember that, by the evidence I have already given, that even as late as the 20th of January, when we discovered that there were not more defences about Savannah than I have stated, it was utterly impossible, utterly impracticable, to get to the city to take it. I could have gone, and wanted to go; but the navy said it was impracticable for them to go there; and if it was impracticable in January it certainly was in November. Indeed, we knew a great deal more of the country in January than we did in November.

Question. Do you think your instructions or the conclusions of your council were ever communicated to the rebels in any way?

Answer. I have no reason to suppose they were, though I was very fearful before we left here that something of the kind might be done, but I have no reason to suppose that it was done. I think that perhaps it would be well for me to state more fully in regard to the impracticability of our taking Savannah and Charleston when we got there. All my staff officers and some other officers and myself were well occupied from the 1st to the 15th of January in ascertaining the practicability of moving over the low marshy country between Hilton Head and Savannah. Most of it had to be done at night. Of course, we could do nothing in the Savannah river at night. It was fifteen days before I could notify Commodore DuPont that I was ready to go to Savannah. So, even if the navy had thought it feasible for their gunboats to go into the Savannah river, it would not have been possible to have gone directly to Savannah at the time of the landing at Port Royal.

Question. How would it have been had you followed the retreating rebels and gone up by land?

Answer. We had no means of moving an army by land.

Question. No transportation?

Answer. No, sir; no land transportation. The country there is a network of marshes, swamps, creeks, and ravines. We were located on islands, and required a particular kind of transportation in order to move. With so large a force, you must be well prepared in order to move at all. This expedition contemplated combined operations of the fleet under Commodore DuPont and certain land forces under command of myself. Neither of us had command or control of the whole matter. It was a divided command. An officer of land forces cannot command a naval officer, nor can a naval officer command an officer of the army. Until I was furnished with the means I had asked for in my letters, it was utterly impossible for me to do anything without being in connexion with the naval fleet there. I was dependent entirely upon the navy for any movement I made, until I got means for acting independently, which I never did get.

Question. Was it necessary to detain for so long a time so large a number of transports as you had there?

Answer. That was rather the fault of circumstances. To carry out fully the object of the expedition required the taking of Fernandina. It was uncertain when the navy would be ready to go there, and I did not feel myself authorized to break up the expedition in that respect by ordering the vessels to be unloaded and to return north. It was understood that it would not require more than fifteen days to supply Commodore DuPont with the ammunition he desired before he could, in his estimation, proceed with safety.

Question. You retained the transports for the Fernandina movement?

Answer. Certainly; thinking that almost every day we would be prepared to start. But it was postponed from day to day, until finally, after the ammunition did come and everything was ready, Commodore DuPont got orders to attend to something else. I then took the responsibility, so far as I was concerned, of breaking up that part of the expedition, by ordering the vessels to be unloaded and sent north. By that time the vessels had been waiting there a month or more. As I have said before, for a long time I had believed that the second part of the expedition—that against Fernandina—had become unimportant. The great trouble was that there was no one there responsible for the whole command. If Commodore DuPont or myself had had the sole command I think we could have accomplished a great deal more.

Question. You say that the usage of this government is such that officers of one service cannot command those of another. What, in your opinion, is necessary to remedy that?

Answer. There should be some law giving the command of a combined naval and land expedition, say, to the senior officer.

Question. Cannot the President, as commander-in-chief of the army and navy, designate an officer of one service to command both?

Answer. He may have the power to do so; but as it has never yet been exercised, there is no precedent to govern in such cases.

WASHINGTON, *April* 17, 1862.

General T. W. SHERMAN—examination resumed.

By Mr. Chandler:

Question. What time was originally fixed for the sailing of your expedition?

Answer. When this expedition was first broached to me, when I was before the cabinet, it was stated that it was necessary for the expedition to be off by the first of September—the first week in September, I think, was the time mentioned.

Question. Can you state briefly the causes of the delay?

Answer. There were several causes of delay. The most prominent ones were raised in the council assembled by General Scott. In the minds of the members of that council the most important cause of delay was the climate. It appeared to be the general opinion that the climate would be too severe for our northern soldiers to land anywhere on that coast in the month of September. General Scott was very much in favor of having me go to the Secretary and have the expedition postponed. I told the council that the idea of the cabinet was to have the expedition start early in September, so that it could land there before cotton was picked. Commodore DuPont also raised objections to going at that time. He said he thought he should not be ready; that all his gunboats would not be in readiness then. It was therefore generally concluded that the expedition should be postponed to, at least, the first of October, unless there were some reasons of state—I think that was the expression used—why it should go in September. While one day in the office of the Secretary of State talking with the Secretary, Commodore DuPont came in and informed the Secretary that he was requested to ask him if there were any reasons of policy of state why this expedition should leave in the month of September. The Secretary replied that there were none that he knew of. The inference, of course, was that the Secretary was perfectly willing for the expedition to be postponed until October, if there were good reasons for doing so. It was therefore concluded, with the approval of the President and Secretary of War, I think, that the expedition should not start until October.

Question. What was the character of the force under you? Were they disciplined troops, troops taken from the army of the Potomac, or were they new troops raised for your expedition?

Answer. I was directed by the Secretary of War to visit the different New England States, and consult with the governors of those States on the subject of furnishing the troops for this expedition. I did so, and saw all of them except the governor of Vermont. I also saw the governor of New York. I consulted with these governors upon the subject of furnishing a certain quota of troops for this expedition. I had a circular drawn up by the Secretary of War to these governors, requesting them to furnish a stated number of troops, the whole number amounting to twelve regiments. These governors promised me the troops should be furnished as soon as they could be organized. I was not able to get any troops of any experience. None that I had had been drilled; some of them even came without arms. And not only that, but even the advantages we were expected to make use of, before the sailing of the expedition, were ignored in this way. I was originally required to concentrate all these troops on Long Island, and there form a camp of instruction and train them preparatory to sailing. I had concentrated three regiments there, when I was directed by telegraph to proceed immediately to Washington city with all the troops I had. I did so; I came promptly to Washington. After that the concentration of troops for this expedition was made at Washington city, and at Annapolis, Maryland, according as the troops came in. Those that came first came to Washington city; those that came last did not join us until we got to Annapolis. The consequence of this was that our troops were brigaded in different positions in this city, where they could not well be manœuvered; in fact, where circumstances would not permit much instruction to the men. I was very sorry for it, but I could not help it. I could not get more than three regiments together in any one place. I found a little vacant place out towards the Congressional burial ground, and some other little places in different parts of the city, where I collected my men together. They were scattered all around the city, and had little or no opportunity for instruction.

Question. Was there any delay in consequence of waiting for these troops to be raised for your expedition?

Answer. I cannot say there was any delay on that account. Still, if the original purpose had been adhered to of starting the expedition off in September, the troops would not have been forthcoming. In some of the States the troops that were raised for the expedition, instead of coming to me, were ordered to Washington. There was a panic here two or three times during the organization of this expedition, which caused all the troops to be sent to Washington.

Question. Were these troops, which were raised for you but sent to Washington, finally made over to you?

Answer. No, sir; not all of them. For instance, the State of Massachusetts had two or three regiments organized early in September, which I supposed I was to have. But I did not get one of them.

Question. They were absorbed in the army of the Potomac?

Answer. Yes, sir. I supposed, as a matter of course, that Colonel Wilson's regiment was to be given to me; but it was not, and that was the case with two or three other regiments. In consequence of an apparent threat upon the city of Washington, or what was supposed to be a threat, a great many of the troops intended for this expedition were ordered to Washington, and were finally absorbed in the army here. The three regiments I brought down here myself I succeeded in retaining, and others were added to my command afterwards.

Question. You took fresh regiments that arrived here, and not those that had been drilled here?

Answer. Yes, sir; those that General McClellan gave me to take the place of those absorbed in his army were raw troops. He did not give me a single regiment of experienced troops. When General Stevens joined me at Annapolis he was very anxious to get his old regiment of which he was once colonel. General McClellan refused to let him have them. After two or three days telegraphing, I finally telegraphed directly to the President, stating how important it was that we should have that regiment. At first he gave way to General McClellan, but finally I succeeded in getting his order for them. It was the 79th regiment, formerly under Colonel Cameron, then under Colonel Stevens. There had been a mutiny in the regiment, and a portion had been sent out to the Tortugas. The remainder I succeeded in getting, and those were all the experienced troops I was able to get.

I was sent for one night to a conference in the house of the Secretary of State upon the subject of this expedition. I thought it a fine opportunity to broach this subject, for I felt a little sore about the character of the troops assigned to me. The President was there, with several members of the cabinet, General McClellan, and Commodore DuPont. I broached the subject, and stated several reasons why a portion at least of my command should be troops of some experience. Commodore DuPont supported me in my argument. I suggested that inasmuch as General McClellan was not going to push forward any of his troops for some time, which was evident from the drift of the conversation that night—that he was not going to move forward for at least two months—I suggested that he should turn over to me a few of his old regiments, and take some of these raw troops off my hands. General McClellan replied that he thought I was asking too much of him; that he had given me my old battery. By the way, he had given me my old light battery; the one I had formerly commanded. I did prevail upon him to let me have that. He said, "You have your old battery, and I think you have done pretty well." I appealed to the President, thinking it was then just the time to speak, but the President coincided with General McClellan, and thought I was well enough off, and there the matter rested. It was after that that I got this 79th regiment—the Highland regiment.

Question. At what time did this conference take place?

Answer. It must have been somewhere between the 1st and 5th of November. I am positive it was on my last visit to Washington.

By Mr. Covode:

Question. Have you seen the law passed by Congress for the cultivation of cotton lands?

Answer. I have seen it, and examined it pretty carefully.

Question. What do you think of it? Will it answer the purpose?

Answer. In my opinion it is the exact sort of legislation the subject required. It not only covers the course being pursued down there at this time, but it goes further, and leaves it optional with the government to pursue this particular course, or change it into leasing the lands if it should find that plan would work best. It gives them a fair opportunity to carry out both experiments, which I am very glad to see. I think the course being pursued there now is the best that could be adopted, and this law sanctions and legalizes it, and gives also the option to pursue any other course that may be deemed best.

By Mr. Gooch:

Question. As I understand you, with ten or twelve additional regiments you could have taken Savannah?

Answer. I would have risked myself upon Savannah without any additional troops at all, if I had only been furnished with the means of transportation. I was not so much in want of troops as of transportation. We had altogether too many troops to lie still. What I wanted the most was means of moving the troops I had. From the time I landed there until I left I received an increase of force, consisting of five regiments of infantry, one of cavalry, and one battery of light artillery. When I left the command I left there upwards of 17,000 men. I landed there with about 12,000 men; so that we were pretty strong in troops there.

Question. Then you would have undertaken the capture of Savannah without any additional troops if you had had sufficient transportation?

Answer. Yes, sir; I would have done it. Whether it would have been wise or not the result must have determined.

Question. What additional force would you have wanted to have taken Charleston in addition to Savannah?

The witness: You suppose Savannah to be in our hands before going to Charleston?

Mr. Gooch: I mean for you to have a force to use in your own way, and at your own time, necessary to take both Savannah and Charleston. I do not mean you to move the same day on both.

The witness: That is, the expedition is to go out there to take both of those cities in the way we may please. We would have to take one place and hold it, and, as a matter of course, that would absorb a great many troops; and you mean to have the coast occupied as it is at present?

Mr. Gooch: Yes, sir; I mean to ask what additional troops you would require for that purpose?

Answer. I would have felt myself perfectly safe with 25,000 men in addition to what I had there.

Question. Now in relation to transportation: What additional transportation would you have needed to have taken those two points?

Answer. With regard to the taking of Savannah, there was no trouble about that; with regard to the taking of Charleston there is a great deal of guess-work, without visiting a great many of those localities. Indeed, the problem of the capture of Charleston would have to be determined before we could make a very accurate estimate of the amount of transportation required. It would depend upon the manner in which we calculated to capture it.

Question. Then what additional means of transportation would you have required to have taken Savannah?

Answer. Over and above what I had, I wanted one hundred row-boats, capable of carrying from 30 to 40 men each; at least five light-draught steamboats, capable of carrying from 800 to 1,000 men each, and not drawing over six or seven feet each. We wanted, also, at least two hundred more wagons and teams, requiring somewhere about 1,000 horses and mules. That was what would be really necessary. Of course, I would not have waited for all that transportation, but at a pinch I could have done with a portion of it, at the risk of some delay, and probably considerable suffering on the part of the troops. With regard to the amount of transportation it would require to take Charleston, I should want some little time to reflect upon that matter before I could give an understanding estimate upon that subject. I suppose that it is very likely that the same amount of transportation that we would use to take Savannah would be used to take Charleston, and perhaps would be all that would be necessary.

Question. You would probably require no additional transportation to take Charleston?

Answer. Probably none. At all events, I think I would have tried it. However, I will make another remark about that. The amount of transportation that I have mentioned as necessary to take Savannah is precisely what I asked for in November and December last. The calculation at that time—and I have not changed my opinion upon the subject since—was that that transportation would be sufficient to meet any demands that could have been required of the army during the whole winter, whether we went to Savannah or to Charleston, or to other places. It may have been deficient, but I think that with that amount of transportation I should have been ready to go anywhere where circumstances would require me to go. In regard to the number of troops required to take Savannah, I would say that 5,000 troops in addition to what is down there would be sufficient to take Savannah; and I should want some 20,000 more to take Charleston.

By Mr. Covode:

Question. Could you have taken Charleston with 12,000 or 15,000 troops in addition to the force you had when you landed?

Answer. I can hardly say. I should hardly have liked to have risked it. When I arrived at Port Royal I obtained information, statistics, &c., at Port Royal, that there were 10,000 troops at that time in Charleston, and I have no reason to suppose that the number has been diminished at any time since.

Question. What force, in your judgment, would have been necessary to have taken Charleston at that time?

Answer. I think we should have been perfectly safe in moving on Charleston with 20,000 men.

Question. If after taking Charleston you had destroyed the place, could you not with the same force have moved on and taken Savannah?

Answer. Destroyed Charleston.

Question. Yes, sir. Could you not then have taken Savannah with the same troops?

Answer. I suppose we could if we had chosen to abandon the harbor of Charleston. But I hardly know what object would have been gained by taking Charleston without holding it, even if you had destroyed it. We should have wanted to have held it, for the harbor there is an important one. There is a great deal to be done before you go to the cities; and therefore I think we could have hardly taken those two places without 25,000 additional troops?

Question. Has not the time gone by for taking and holding those places this summer?

Answer. I think the time is rapidly passing. I think Charleston may be taking during this month or the month of May; if we work briskly during the month of May I think we may take it. But if it is not taken then I should hardly advise any operations against it until fall, because Charleston is the most sickly portion of the coast.

By Mr. Odell:

Question. Did you not have a large amount of steamship tonnage in the employ of this expedition?

Answer. We had a large amount.

Question. Also of sailing vessels as transports?

Answer. We had very few sailing vessels during the latter part of the expedition; we had some. And the number of steam transports were diminished, finding they were so expensive, and cheap sailing vessels were substituted for them. During the latter part of the expedition the bulk of the business was done with sailing vessels.

Question. Have you any knowledge of the cost of the expedition for steamers and transports?

Answer. Do you mean the total cost?

Question. Yes, sir.

Answer. I can speak only from memory at this time. But from what I can recollect of the examination of the report of persons and articles hired by Captain Saxton for the month of March, I think it is something short of $2,000,000. But I am only speaking from memory.

Question. In your judgment have not these vessels been nearly paid for by these charters? That is, has not their equivalent of value been paid for by these charters? In other words, would it not have been cheaper for the government to have bought them?

Answer. I think it would have been very wise if some of the steamers had been purchased for the government at the outset of the expedition, and I so said at the time. Some of these vessels that have been in the employment of the expedition since its commencement, I think, have nearly eaten themselves up by the sums paid them by the government, which are about equal to their value.

Question. Have not the government furnished coal in some instances to these vessels?

Answer. Yes, sir; as a matter of necessity.

Question. Do you know at what cost it was furnished?

Answer. No, sir; I do not. I know nothing about it.

Question. In your judgment should not the government have made some arrangement with the owners of these vessels by which they could have furnished themselves with coal?

Answer. If anything of the kind could be done, it would have been very well. But I do not see how the government could have made any other arrangement to supply steamboats out there with coal than the one that was made.

Question. Should not the owners of these steamboats have paid the full value of the coal there rather than have paid merely New York prices?

Answer. I think so. But that is a matter of detail that I know nothing about. If they have been supplied at New York prices there, I think it is rather hard upon the government. My impression has been that there should have been a private coal-yard at Port Royal, before this time, as a matter of private enterprise, where the owners of steamboats could have supplied themselves with coal.

Question. Have you been satisfied with the manner in which the transportation has been managed there? I refer to the detention of the transports there for so long a time, &c.

Answer. It has been my habit to carry on the public service with the greatest amount of economy that I have been capable of. I never was aware before of so much expenditure in the way of transportation as there was in this expedition, I must confess. I have been somewhat aggrieved on several occasions this winter, that we should be such an expense to the government in the way of transportation. I have looked into the matter several times. I have investigated it to see how this expense could be reduced. I have consulted with my chief quartermaster, Captain Saxton, on this subject on several occasions. I do not think that we have been able to do much good, any further than to have employed a large number of sailing vessels, and used them wherever sailing vessels could be used. That thing had some effect in reducing the expenses. But I must confess that I have never felt completely satisfied in regard to this matter, even up to the last. My impression is, and has been, that these steam transports have been paid too high a price; a price that may have answered very well for a short time, when they were first chartered. But in the long run I think the price has been too high, and that has been my impression all the time. However, it is a matter of detail that belonged to the quartermaster's department with which I never could well interfere. If I had had time in New York to have looked into this matter, I think we could have got this expedition off much cheaper. But we were obliged to get up everything in a hurry; the the whole matter was arranged in great haste. But I am very sure that it was expected when these large steamers were first employed they would not be employed more than 20 or 30 days at the furthest.

There was another thing, in connexion with the transportation, which caused me some uneasiness, but for which I was not responsible. There were six steamers that lay in Wassaw sound upwards of thirty days, doing nothing in the world but holding a number of men upon them, when it was promised me that they should not lay there over five days, before they should be started off on this Fernandina expedition.

Question. In whose charge was that?

Answer. I was in charge of the land forces, and Commodore DuPont in charge of the sea forces. We combined an expedition against Savannah. The idea was that six gunboats and a brigade of soldiers, under General Wright, should make a demonstration on the south side of the river. When the demonstration was completed they were to fall back into Wassaw sound, and there to remain until the fleet at Port Royal was ready to join it and proceed to Fernandina. I agreed to that demonstration with the express understanding that this brigade should not remain in Wassaw sound more than five days. I insisted repeatedly that I could not afford to keep a brigade of troops and all the necessary transportation in Wassaw sound any length of time, but that the matter must be concluded in five days, or I could not agree to it. It was agreed that they should get out of the sound in five days at the furthest. Now, who is responsible for the delay I will not say, but it was thirty-two days before the expedition was got off, and these transports were lying there perfectly idle all that time.

Question. Did you ever learn any good reason why they were detained so long?

Answer. No full reason was ever given to me. I have been told unofficially that the navy was out of ammunition, and was waiting all this time for a supply from the north. I have already mentioned that when we first landed at Port Royal there was a delay of a month in reference to the same expedition to Fernandina.

Question. What was the cause of that first delay?

Answer. They were waiting for ammunition; and then, when the ammunition came, orders came to Commodore DuPont to distribute and sink the stone fleet all up and down the coast. That, of course, broke up the expedition at that time, and I unloaded the vessels and sent them back to New York.

Question. Your troops were debarked?

Answer. The troops had been on board three weeks when we got there, and I had them debarked; but the stores, ordnance, &c., intended for that particular locality were left on board the transports as long as there was any prospect that the expedition would proceed.

Question. Did the naval part of your expedition use an unusual quantity of ammunition at Port Royal?

Answer. I think Commodore DuPont told me that in the Port Royal affair he used about two-thirds of the ammunition he had brought with him, so that he did not consider it safe to start for Fernandina with the amount he had left, in which I think he was wise.

Appendix.

Copies of reports of a commission appointed by the Navy Department in reference to expeditions to the southern coast.

WASHINGTON, *July* 5, 1861.

SIR: We have the honor to inform you that the conference, in compliance with your wishes, communicated through Captain DuPont, has had under consideration that part of your letters of instructions of the 25th ultimo which relates to the necessity of occupying two or more points on the Atlantic coast, Fernandina being particularly mentioned as one of those points.

It seems to be indispensable that there should exist a convenient coal depot on the southern extremity of the line of Atlantic blockade, and it seems to the conference that if this coal depot was suitably selected, it might be used, not only as a depot for coal, but as a depot of provisions and common stores, as a harbor of refuge, and as a general rendezvous or headquarters for that part of the coast.

We separate in our minds the two enterprises of a purely military expedition, and an expedition the principal object of which is the establishment of a naval station for promoting the efficiency of the blockade. We shall have the honor to present plans for both expeditions; but we will begin with the latter, premising, however, that we think both of them should be conducted simultaneously.

Fernandina is, by its position, obviously the most suitable point for a place of deposit, answering at one end of the line to Hampton Roads at the other. In addition to its position in this respect, it enjoys several other advantages almost peculiar to itself and well suited to the object in view.

It has fourteen feet of water on the bar at low water, and twenty at high water, a convenient depth for all steam vessels of the navy, either propelled by screws or side-wheels, rated as "second class steamships," and under; for all of those rated as "first class steamships," which are propelled by screws; and by [for] most of the same class propelled by side-wheels, when light; and by [for] all the newly purchased and chartered steamers of every description, with the exception, perhaps, of one or two of the very largest mail-packet steamers when deeply loaded.

These depths are perfectly convenient for the new sloops and gunboats now on the stocks, and for the ordinary merchant vessels chartered for freight. The main ship channel, over St. Mary's bar into Fernandina harbor, though not direct, is by no means tortuous or difficult; it is easily defined by buoys, and a range by means of beacons renders the passage of the bar itself secure.

A steam-tug will always be at hand to take in sailing vessels when necessary

Inside of the bar there is an unlimited extent of deep water accommodation, and also the protection of smooth water before reaching the land-locked basins.

The anchorage in Amelia river possesses the quiet and safety of an enclosed dock. Repairs of all kinds may be carried on there without the fear of accidents arising from motion of the water.

The town of Fernandina and the wharves and depots of the Florida railroad company furnish conveniences the value of which need not be enlarged upon. If the seizure were conducted so suddenly as to prevent the destruction of property amd buildings, (which it would be difficult to replace,) the facilities for landing and storing coal and other materials will be found ready for use.

Another feature of the port, and one which has appeared to us of sufficient importance to engage your particular attention, is the isolated position of Fernandina, territorially and in population. Fernandina is on an island, bounded by the ocean on one side and having on the other an interior poor and uninteresting in all respects, sparse in population, remote from large cities or centres of military occupation, and not easily accessible by railroad or water communication.

By the census of 1850, the population of Fernandina was about 600; it is now 1,000; St. Mary's, 700; Darien, 550; Jacksonville, 1,145; St. Augustine, 1,934. The distance, by water, from Fernandina to St. Mary's is 9 miles; from Fernandina to Brunswick is 35 miles; from Fernandina to Darien is 51 miles; from Fernandina, by railroad, to Baldwin is 47 miles; from Baldwin, by railroad, to Jacksonville is 20 miles; from Fernandina, by water, to Savannah is 120 miles; from Fernandina, by water, to Charleston is 166 miles; from Fernandina, by railroad, to Cedar Keys is 154 miles; and from Fernandina, by railroad, to Tallahassee, by the railroad to the Baldwin Junction and Alligator, nearly two hundred miles, (192 miles.) With all the above mentioned places there is water communication, except Cedar Keys, Tallahassee, and the railroad stations between them.

But it is apparent that any military opposition of weight must come from Savannah and Charleston, principally through Cumberland sound; and the depth (less than ten feet in some places) of this line of interior navigation would require the transportation of the troops in the light steamers employed there. These steamers are so light and devoid of shelter, that an expedition would hardly be undertaken if Amelia island were properly garrisoned.

The environs of Fernandina form a natural protection against an attack by land. They consist of marsh and sand, which alone compose the shores of the rivers and bayous.

We are careful to avoid making this communication unnecessarily long by entering upon a comparison of Fernandina with other places in the same region of coast; such as Brunswick, for example, which is now connected by railroad with Savannah, and being more in the interior is less healthy; or St. John's entrance, which could be fortified against us, and has an insuperable objection in its bar. But we take pains to say that such comparisons have formed a large part of our study of the whole subject. We have not spoken of the *peculiar* advantages of Fernandina as a depot and naval station without attaching a meaning to the word.

Although an open and rapid communication with the Gulf of Mexico, by the Florida railroad to Cedar Keys, accomplished in eleven hours, would undoubtedly be desirable, still it has not entered into our project to recommend the maintenance of this communication. To do so would employ a force disproportioned to the possible benefits to be derived from it. The Central railroad to Tallahassee, which connects with this road at Baldwin, is completed as far as Alligator, and for a certain distance from Tallahassee east, about twenty miles. The country on the line of the road is thickly wooded, and has few inhabitants. A road of such length (154 miles) in an obscure and inhospitable district may be easily rendered impassable.

Fort Clinch is not thought to be defensible in its present condition; and the sand batteries on the shore can, probably, be easily turned.

The water is so smooth, in ordinary times, on the outer shore of Amelia island, that a landing can be effected there with facility, and will, in our opinion, be advisable at more than one point. This landing cannot be covered by large ships, especially such as the "screw frigates." Vessels of small draught must be selected for this duty, and when the points of landing are fixed upon, the lines of approach for the covering vessels must be distinctly traced out.

The Florida railroad, from the west shore of Amelia island across the river, is built on piles for the distance of about one mile, similar to the long bridges across the Bush and Gunpowder.

When the attack is made one or more small gunboats might take the back entrance, through Nassau inlet and sound, and prevent the destruction of this bridge by the rebels. Nassau entrance is, no doubt, unguarded. Nassau bar has only five feet of water on it, and even this depth is not to be relied upon; launches may therefore be employed. A rapid survey, immediately preceding the attack, will correct any misapprehension on this point. The preservation of this trestle bridge is worth an effort. The remainder of the road can be replaced with less cost, because it runs through a naturally level country.

It is estimated that three thousand men would take and hold the place, with the assistance of such force as could be furnished by the fleet. After the place was taken a portion of the defensive force would be found on board the vessels in port. Thus the number of troops to be added to the marines and seamen, employed in the attack and subsequent defence, would not, probably, at any time, exceed this number of three thousand.

The details of the expedition to Fernandina, if decided upon, will fall under the several bureaus of the War and Navy Departments, and the chiefs of the expedition, to whom the conference will be always ready to offer such information and make such suggestions as may result from their careful study of the ground.

The sailing directions for the port of Fernandina, the instructions for the disposition of the buoys and beacons, the outer and inner anchorage, the pilotage, and the meteorology of this section of coast will hereafter be furnished by the conference from the archives of the Coast Survey.

It is known that Fernandina is healthy, and that it can supply wood and water in abundance. Its market supplies remain to be developed.

Finally, we will repeat the remark made in the beginning of this report, that we think this expedition to Fernandina should be undertaken simultaneously with a similar expedition having a purely military character.

We are preparing a brief report on the latter, which we shall have the honor to submit in a few days.

We have the honor to be, most respectfully, your obedient servants,

S. F. DUPONT,
Captain United States Navy and President.
J. G. BARNARD,
Major United States Engineers, Member.
A. D. BACHE,
Superintendent United States Coast Survey, Member.
CHARLES PLINY DAVIS,
Commander United States Navy, Member and Secretary.

Hon. GIDEON WELLES,
Secretary of the Navy, Washington.

WASHINGTON, D. C., *July* 13, 1861.

SIR: We have the honor to inform you that, in further prosecution of the duties assigned us, we have made a careful study of three of the most important of the secondary bays or harbors on the southern coast, for the purpose of military occupation. These are Bull's bay, St. Helena sound, and Port Royal sound—all on the coast of South Carolina.

We shall describe each one of them separately, offering some suggestions as to their advantages and the best mode of occupying them; and we will endeavor to explain, by a comparison of their relative merits, the grounds for preferring the two former over the latter for immediate occupation. We have taken them up in the order of their situation, from north to south.

Bull's bay, which has been justly called a noble harbor of refuge, is fifteen miles southeast of Cape Romain, and twenty-two miles from the main bar of Charleston habor. The passage into it is direct, there being but one single course over the bar. The light-house is plainly in sight, being less than four miles distant from the outer curve of the bar, and its bearing, together with the soundings and buoys, when properly placed, makes the entrance easy. Twenty feet may be carried in at high water of common tides, and fifteen feet at low water. The channel-way is marked by breakers on either hand, and inside there is a snug, well-protected anchorage in deep water, with good holding ground.

Bull's bay is situated below the parallel at which the West India hurricanes leave the coast, which very much increases its value as a harbor of refuge.

Bull's island, from which the bay takes its name, is six and a half miles long, and about a mile and a half wide. The northeast bluff, at the entrance, is high and wooded, and admits of being strongly fortified without delay or great expense. But batteries erected to defend the entrance may be taken in the rear, by landing about three miles south of the northeast bluff, and keeping on the beach till within a mile of the light-house, where a wood road, near a fence, passes close in the rear of the entire range of sand hills commanding the entrance.

It is suggested, therefore, that the extremity of the island should be secured by an enclosed work on the point, and a line of intrenchments across the island, at a distance of two miles (more or less) from the light-house.

For defence, Bull's bay possesses this striking advantage, that it can be held at a single point. Excepting the small sand key, Bird island, there is no fast land from which it can be attacked; Bird island is two miles off, not easy of access, and insignificant.

It is not probable that any defensive works constructed by the rebels will oppose a very formidable obstacle to the occupation of the place; but it is to be considered that its proximity to Charleston subjects it to assault. This assault may be made by combined forces from both directions, for there is interior water communication with the Santee on the north as well as with Charleston on the south. Vessels drawing not more than four and a half feet can come out of the Santee, through Alligator creek at the "Horns," pass within Cape island and Raccoon keys, traverse Bull's bay, and keep inside all the way to Charleston. Very few white men know the whole route, but many negroes are familiar with it. There are six "divides," or places where the tides diverge, or converge, between Cape Romain and Charleston harbor. Four of these run dry at low water, and the other two are encumbered with mud and oyster banks. At this season of the year, however, the rice crops having been carried to market, there is but little intercourse with the Santee district by water. Taking these liabilities into account, it is thought that four thousand men, well intrenched, would hold the island; though without an exact knowledge of its topography it is impossible to speak with certainty.

The island affords good water, and timber for constructing wharves for coaling, or for other uses, if needed. In this respect, and as a harbor of refuge, there is no point north of Charleston that can be made so useful. It is so easy of access, and so perfectly healthy in the hot season, that the authorities of Charleston have recommended it for the seat of a quarantine during their stranger's (or yellow) fever months.

The military occupation of Bull's bay secures the easy command of the four inlets (Price's, Caper's, Dewee's, and Breach inlets) lying intermediate between it and Charleston harbor. Neither of these enjoy any trade now; but Dewee's inlet has seven feet at low water, or twelve feet at mean high water, and an excellent anchorage in four fathoms on the inside. It might prove a useful harbor to vessels of light draught. A deep creek, navigable for boats at low water even to Station Fuller, (see chart,) enters Dewee's inlet. From Fuller to Mount Pleasant is nine miles, and it is connected with Hocobaw Point, in rear of Fort Moultrie and Castle Pinckney, for the greater part of the distance by a well-travelled road in a fine forest. The high road from Charleston to Georgetown, through Christ Church parish, passes at an average distance of four miles from the shore. It is well-conditioned, the resort of a regular travel, and preserves a communication with the banks of the two Pedees that would suffer no interruption from our occupation of Bull's island.

St. Helena sound, situated nearly midway between Charleston and Savannah, is particularly well adapted to promote the efficiency of the blockading squadron. There are two anchorages, which are healthy throughout the year—one, near Otter island on the north, and one near Hunting island on the south; and the other bay is so wide that these two roadsteads may be considered wholly independent of each other. There are three channels of approach; the east, the southeast, and the south channels. The first has only eight feet on the bar at mean low water, and fourteen feet at high; the second, which is a little less direct, has ten and sixteen feet; and the third has seventeen feet at mean low, and twenty-three feet at mean high water. It should be remarked that the mouth of South Edisto river is embraced within the northern limits of this sound. The South Edisto is the Edisto proper, the North Edisto being the outlet of Wadmelaw sound and the Dawhoo, while the Edisto itself is a long river, from which large quantities of lumber are sent annually to Charleston. It is navigable for vessels drawing nine feet of water up to Governor Aiken's rice plantation at Ichassee, where it communicates with the North Edisto river through the Dawhoo. The Dawhoo is navigable for steamers drawing not more than six feet, at all times of tide, under the direction of a pilot. Thirteen feet of water at mean low, and nineteen feet at mean high water, can be carried into the South Edisto, and there is good anchorage inside, west of Big Bay island, in five fathoms; but the anchorage on the north side of the bay which we first mentioned, that under Otter island, is the better and healthier of the two. The continuous ranges of sand shoals which compose the bar at the several entrances of St. Helena sound extend, unfortunately, six miles to seaward, and the land is low and difficult to distinguish. The channels, therefore, if used, must be distinctly marked with buoys, the light-ship must be anchored in a suitable place, and the light-house which has been built on Hunting island, together with the beacon-light near it, must be maintained. Capable pilots must be at hand. The delta shoals in St. Helena sound are long and narrow; between them are deep and very regular channels, running in directions nearly parallel to each other, that may be called natural as regards the rivers of which they are the drains. Beyond these delta shoals a mass of irregular shoals extend out to the southward from Fenwick and Otter islands, (separating South Edisto from the sound,) which, by breaking the sea in easterly storms, preserve comparatively smooth water in the sound.

The Ashepoo, Combahee, Bull, Coosaw, Morgan Island and Hunting Island rivers empty into the sound. To complete our topographical description we must speak of them in order. The Ashepoo enters the sound at Otter island, and at its mouth, under the shelter of the island, is the safe and healthy anchorage we have twice mentioned—safe in all weathers and healthy in all seasons—requiring protection from no other point than Otter island. Near the anchorage, but separated from it by the delta of the Ashepoo and Combahee, is another equally healthy and safe anchorage in six fathoms of water, equidistant between Otter and Morgan islands, and nearly a mile and a half (nautical) from each, not easily molested therefore from the land if Otter island were in our possession. In crossing the bar and ascending the sound, to reach the anchorage, a vessel need not approach Hunting island so near as two miles or Otter island nearer than a mile and a half. The Ashepoo is navigable, for vessels drawing nine feet of water, twelve miles above the point of Otter island, where they can supply themselves with fresh water on the last of the ebb. Seven miles above is the mouth of Mosquito creek, which connects with South Edisto through Bull's cut. The light-draught steamers, plying on the inland passage from Charleston, south, go through this cut, descend the Ashepoo, cross the Combahee bank through a small channel, and thence ascend the Coosaw to Beaufort and Port Royal Ferry. This is only possible for steamers drawing five feet; those of larger draught must pass outside of Otter island. We have to penetrate to the depth of six miles into the sound of St. Helena to reach the point of junction of the Combahee and Coosaw rivers. The first of these rivers is navigable for vessels drawing ten feet of water some twenty miles up. Fresh water may be had on the ebb about ten miles up. There is a boat connexion with the Ashepoo about ten miles up. The Coosaw is broader and shoaler than the Combahee. It forms a part of the interior navigation from Charleston. Steamers drawing eight or nine feet will run outside from Charleston to St. Helena sound, and entering the latter by the most convenient channel, according to the tide, will proceed up the Coosaw to its junction with the Beaufort river at the brick-yard, and thence down to Beaufort on the inside way from Savannah and Florida, or the same steamer may continue up Coosaw river to its head, near Port Royal Ferry, and go thence through Whale Branch into Broad river and Port Royal bay. Vessels bound up the Coosaw may go by the way of Morgan river to Parrot creek, which connects the two rivers by a fifteen feet channel. All these connexions are readily traced on a map of a suitable scale. They are pointed out in detail, because you will perceive from them how large a tract of country, and how extensive, important, and complex a series of lines of interior trade and navigation will be threatened and commanded by the military possession of St. Helena sound.

Hitherto we have specified two anchorages as desirable; it remains for us to speak of the third and the best. The south channel, as we have said before, has seventeen feet at low water, and twenty-three feet at mean high water; it is, therefore, quite superior to the others. It leads to an anchorage in five fathoms of water, within half a mile of the northeast point of Hunting island, and near the new light-house. Both the anchorage and the adjacent shore are healthy throughout the year. The island is about six miles long, with an average width of little more than half a mile to Johnson's creek. It is wooded, and is stocked with deer, being used as a game preserve. A small creek, (Johnson's,) with a narrow channel fifteen feet deep near its mouth, runs close to the shore. This is a suitable place for a coaling depot. There is timber for constructing a wharf, for which there is a natural site near the mouth of a small creek. We have said that the two anchorages on the north and south sides of the sound are independent of each other. It is so; but the isolation of that which is protected by Hunting island is the most complete. Here, as in Bull's bay, and in these two places alone, the military occupation of a single point, remote and inaccessible to a large force, except by great expense of time, labor, and money, secures the roadstead, the depot, and the channel of approach;

and, moreover, this channel is the best of the three leading into St. Helena sound, from the broader space of which it is effectually separated by a natural barrier of banks, partially dry at low water. Neither shells nor solid shot could molest the shipping; nor, hardly, projectiles from rifled cannon. And the possession of this anchorage commands a considerable extent of inland navigation, though less than that on the north side. Vessels of heavy draught can pass into Morgan river by turning the spit of a shoal near Hunting Island point, and those of light draught by an inner channel between Oyster and Egg banks. Vessels drawing ten feet of water may take an inside passage from Hunting island to Port Royal bay, entering the latter through Station creek.

Three points of meeting of the tide occur. The channel is bold, in general, but intricate, requiring a pilot. Many wooded hammocks and one large house must be passed within pistol-shot. Between St. Helena sound and Port Royal bay are found four inlets—Tripp's, Skull, Pritchard's, and Trenchard's—of which the first and last only, having ten and thirteen feet respectively at high water, can be made available for the uses of commerce.

It is estimated that four thousand men, in addition to the co-operating naval force, would be sufficient to take and hold Hunting island, which would be defended like Bull's island, by an enclosed work on the point, and a line of entrenchments across from the sea to Johnson's creek, at some distance from the light. The entrenchments would be less extreme on account of the island being much narrower.

In order to fill out our notes on this vicinity, we shall observe that at the eastern end of St. Helena island, which forms the right bank of the outlet of Morgan river into St. Helena sound, stands the plantation of Mr. Coffin, at whose place commences a public road called the Sea-side road, that extends thirteen miles to Port Royal bay, at Land's End. Two miles from Mr. Coffin's a road diverges to the right, leading to Ladies' island and Beaufort, distant eleven miles. Both these roads are lined with the residences of gentlemen, and sea-island cotton plantations. Parrot creek, joining Morgan and Coosaw rivers, has been referred to; opposite to it is Village creek, leading to a village on a bluff, the summer resort of the St. Helena planters. Four fathoms may be carried up Morgan river to Dalthaw island, which is separated from St. Helena sound by a creek. This creek unites at its head with Cowan creek, while the latter separates St. Helena from Ladies' island. Boats pass by this route from Beaufort to St. Helena sound. The road to Beaufort from Ashton's, just mentioned, crosses the creek by a bridge, at the plantation of the late Mrs. General Eustis. Ladies' island, at the head of Morgan river, is a little more than a mile wide. The town of Beaufort is on the opposite shore of the river of that name. A road leads from Mr. McKee's plantation, at the head of Morgan river, across to the bluff opposite Beaufort.

The above description will enable you to form an idea of the interdependence and of the intercommunication by boat and carriage between the islands filling up the head of St. Helena sound and the waters emptying into it; of the advantages to be derived from its military occupation; and of the opposition, with its means and facilities of combination, which this occupation is likely to provoke.

Port Royal bay is the finest harbor south of Chesapeake bay, which it resembles in capacity and extent. It is approached by three channels, the least of which has seventeen feet of water, while the two others have nineteen feet at mean low, and twenty-five feet at mean high water. Several of our screw frigates of the first class can pass the bar, and when the entrance is once made a whole navy can ride at anchor in the bay in uninterrupted health and security. The bar, however, is badly situated; the narrowest and shoalest part is so far out from the headlands, which generally furnish natural beacons and sailing marks, that a conspicuous object is needed on the spot.

The light-ships should be replaced, and large buoys should be planted in proper places. (An open screw-pile basket-beacon, well braced, might be put down with great advantage in a well protected spot, under the the lee of Martin's Industry and the southeast breakers.) We are looking ahead a little in saying this. The absence of light-vessels, beacons, and buoys, will by no means prevent access to the bay. The ships of the expedition will pass through a lane of small vessels anchored on the borders of the natural channel.

It is probable that the entrance to the harbor has been fortified on both sides, and especially at Bay Point. This point may be approached in the rear by landing at Pritchard's inlet, next east of Trenchard's inlet, near high water, pulling through the creek connecting the two, down Trenchard's inlet to a point near Luce Station, and thence passing along the beach and through the woods to Bay Point. On the Hilton Head side it is more difficult to take the point in the rear.

The entrance is over two miles wide; there is fine achorage under Bay Point; on the shore is a number of rough houses, the summer resort of planters. Under the head of St. Helena we have entered into some details respecting the interior communications and navigation, that need not be repeated. The town of Beaufort, on Port Royal island, has no commercial importance. During the hot weather, when the planters are in their summer residences, the population numbers about two thousand; at other periods of the year it has but little more than five hundred inhabitants. A battery of eight guns, it is said, has been erected at the eastern end of the town.

Water may be had at the station Port Royal, Land's End, St. Helena sound, or by sinking wells from six to ten feet deep anywhere along shore, or casks at Bay Point. Near this point may be constructed a wharf for a coaling station, above the mouth of the little creek that appears on the coast survey chart. The piece of marsh between the fort land and deep water (on the chart) must be crossed by a bridge. Timber grows close by. The woods, directly in the rear of the sea-beach, consists chiefly of pine, interspersed with chinquapin and live oak. Portions of the island are clear and open. Near the beach there are many clumps of myrtle bushes matted together with jack vines and Cherokee roses. The island is healthy where exposed to the influence of the sea breeze. Perry island, which separates Beaufort and Broad rivers, is about five miles long, and is devoted to the culture of sea-island cotton. Broad river is navigable up to the Charleston and Savannah railroad station at Pocotaligo. Steamers and sailing vessels from St. Helena pass around Port Royal island and enter Broad river by way of Port Royal ferry and Whale Branch.

Port Royal is one of the wealthiest of the sea islands, and is devoted to the culture of sea-island cotton. Besides the passage of communication between Port Royal bay and St. Helena sound, through Whale Branch, there is a narrow passage, having nine feet at low water, between Lemon and Daw islands, going down the Chechesee river, and entering Skull creek. A depth of nineteen feet may be carried from Port Royal bay up Chechesee river to Foot Point, on the Colleton river. This range, a distance of —— miles, was surveyed in 1859, with reference to a naval depot and coaling station at Foot Point.

Hilton Head island, which is devoted to the culture of sea-island cotton, extends from Port Royal bay to Calibogue sound, and thirteen feet may be carried up the Chechesee through Skull creek to the sound, which constitutes the inland passage to Savannah. The outer shore of Hilton Head island is so effectually protected by Gaskin bank, and the shoals inside of it, that a landing is practicable in moderate weather. This is facilitated by an inshore channel within the outer breakers. It may be stated, as one general fact, true of the whole coast of South Carolina, that there are from one to two feet less water on the bars during and immediately after westerly gales, and as much more during and after northeast and southeast gales; the latter cause the heaviest sea. Another general fact is that those are the most healthy sites which are open to the direct action of the sea breeze. Sheltered points close to the sea shore will often be unhealthy, while others, with a southern exposure, six or eight miles inland, will be perfectly healthy during summer and autumn.

For the military occupation of Port Royal bay, it would be necessary, in order to escape molestation, to hold three points, and this would probably involve, as the easiest method of holding them, the occupation of the three islands of which these points form part; that is, Hilton Head island, Parry's island, and Philip's island. It is difficult to give any precise estimate of the exact number of troops required to hold these islands. At the present moment, when most of the southern troops are in Virginia or Tennessee, it is probable that, notwithstanding the contiguity of Savannah and Charleston, no very large bodies could be concentrated against us, but the operation would be likely to withdraw the troops from the north. This effect, almost certain as it is, will compensate us for the application of a considerable force at this point. Six thousand men might take possession of Port Royal, but to hold it permanently would probably require ten or twelve thousand men, in addition to the available navy contingent. Of these three places, Bull's bay, St. Helena sound, and Port Royal bay, we have no hesitation in recommending the immediate military occupation of the first, for the reasons already fully given in the preceding pages, viz: its accessibility, direct channel, safe anchorage; all of which make it a most convenient harbor of refuge, and its being securely held by the possession of a single point.

With regard to St. Helena sound and Port Royal bay there is more room for doubt. We have compared the two somewhat as follows: If Port Royal has the greater depth over the bar, twenty-three feet to twenty-five, yet the bar of the former is eight miles from the land, whilst that of the latter is only three and a half miles. St. Helena is held by the occupation of a single point. Port Royal requires that three points should be taken and fortified. The entrance of the former is six miles wide, and the west channel can only be molested from Hunting island. That of the latter is only two miles wide, and the attacking fleet will be subject to fire from both sides. The resources for wood and coal are about the same in each. St. Helena is more central between Charleston and Savannah; Port Royal commands a larger interior communication and trade. The whole bay of Port Royal comprises one large, open space, capable of containing any number of vessels anchored in one body. The anchorages of St. Helena are divided, and distinct from each other. It seems to us that St. Helena ought to be seized before Port Royal, because it will be so much more easily taken and held. The former is a comparatively obscure place, little known, and but little resorted to, while the latter is constantly talked of as the first point of attack, and is closely looked after. Stephen Elliott, jr., of Parry island, a nephew of George P. Elliott, has been employed in fortifying Port Royal, every foot of which he is familiar with, while not a planter knows St. Helena.

Finally, believing that the three points we have recommended will suffice for the purpose of coaling stations and harbors of refuge for the blockading squadrons, we are not disposed to recommend any immediate measures for the taking of Port Royal. The putting of twelve or fifteen thousand men thus in the immediate neighborhood of Charleston and Savannah, and the presence of a considerable fleet in this noble harbor, would, doubtless, be a sore annoyance to the rebels, and necessitate the constant maintenance of large forces in those cities and on those shores. Yet the same force, naval and military, organized as an expedition, and held in hand at New York for a blow anywhere, would threaten not only Savannah and Charleston, but the whole southern coast.

If, in the organization of such a force, its destination should be absolutely undefined, the threat would be equally against every important point of the southern coast, from Hatteras to the Rio Grande. The simple putting to sea of such a force, if it were only but to return again to its post, would cause general alarm, and the Gulf States could no longer permit their troops to swell the armies of Virginia.

The force thus organized, after having, by frequent embarcations and disembarcations, used as a means of threat, and thus perfectly drilled to its intended service, might, at last, be permitted to strike its blow, whether at New Orleans, or Mobile, or Pensacola, or Savannah, or Port Royal, or that focus of rebellion —the scene of the great indignity offered our flag—Charleston, might be decided at the last moment.

We have the honor to be, very respectfully, your obedient servants,

S. F. DUPONT,
Captain United States Navy, President.
A. D. BACHE,
Superintendent United States Coast Survey, Member.
J. G. BARNARD,
Major United States Engineers, Member.
CHARLES PLINY MILES,
Commander United States Navy, Secretary and Member.

Honorable GIDEON WELLES,
Secretary of the Navy.

WASHINGTON, *April* 15, 1862.

Captain RUFUS SAXTON sworn and examined.

By the chairman :

Question. What is your rank and position in the army?

Answer. I am a captain in the quartermaster's department—an assistant quartermaster.

Question. Where have you served during the present war?

Answer. My first service was with General Lyon, in Missouri; I was his chief quartermaster. I served with him during the siege at the St. Louis arsenal, and also at the attack on Jackson. I continued to serve with him until a short time before the battle of Springfield. I was then ordered to the department of Western Virginia, where I served with General McClellan during his campaign there as his chief quartermaster. When that campaign was over, I was sent to New York city to assist General Sherman in organizing his expedition to Port Royal. I organized that expedition and went with it to Port Royal, and served there until a week ago last Sunday.

Question. What force had General Sherman under him there?

Answer. When I left there were about 17,000 men there.

Question. What time did you arrive there?

Answer. Early in November last. We left New York in October. We met a very severe storm on the way down, which scattered our fleet. We thought at first that it would annihilate our expedition, but it did not. We collected it together again, and proceeded to our destination.

Question. What number of vessels had you in that expedition?

Answer. I do not recollect the exact number.

Question. You had the whole army on board?

Answer. Yes, sir; we had 15,000 men afloat, besides the naval force.

By Mr. Odell :

Question. Your vessels were all chartered?

Answer. Yes, sir.

Question. Were all the vessels chartered by you? Here is a list of vessels chartered, purporting to give the names of those chartering them. Did you charter all assigned you in this list?—(Senate Executive Document No. 37, 37th Congress, 2d session.)

Answer. [Examining the list.] Yes, sir; the list is correct.

Question. Are all you chartered contained in this list?

Answer. I do not recollect of any others than those mentioned here.

Question. There are some schooners mentioned here as being chartered by you?

Answer. Yes, sir; we chartered them down at Port Royal; we found it cheaper to do so than to keep the steamers there.

Question. Did you charter the steamers by the day?

Answer. Yes, sir, mostly; some few of them by the month. I think the most of them were chartered by the day.

Question. The Atlantic and Baltic were chartered by the day?

Answer. Yes, sir; at $1,500 each; the Vanderbilt and Ocean Queen were chartered at $2,000 a day each.

Question. The prices contained in this list are correct?

Answer. Yes, sir.

Question. For what time did you charter these steamers?

Answer. It was entirely indefinite—as long as the government might want them. Some few of them we had to agree to take for a certain length of time; but I avoided that whenever I could, and sought to keep it entirely optional with myself when they should be discharged. Some of the owners insisted that they should be retained in service a certain number of days, or they would not let me have their steamers at all.

When I went to New York to charter these vessels no one knew about the expedition, or that any such expedition was going, and I kept it secret; and in that way I got the vessels a great deal less than I should have done had I let it be known in New York that I was going to charter so many vessels. No two persons were allowed to know at that time that this expedition was to be fitted out.

Question. Did you charter the vessels directly from the owners themselves?

Answer. Yes, sir.

Question. Without the intervention of brokers or agents?

Answer. I consulted with two men who understood shipping as advisers. I had no agents at all.

Question. There were no agents between you and the parties owning the vessels?

Answer. No, sir; I was a stranger there, and I employed men who knew about ships to advise me; to see the owners of the ships and the vessels; but there was no one between me and the owners.

Question. So far as you know, were there any commissions paid by the owners of these vessels to any of these parties?

Answer. No, sir; not that I know of. If there had been, and I had known it, I would not have taken the ships. No commissions were paid, to my knowledge. If I had supposed that there had been any, that would have been a reason for my not taking the ships. I received nothing myself, and I did not allow anybody else to take anything, to my knowledge.

Question. It has been charged that these vessels have been detained at Port Royal at a very heavy expense.

Answer. There has been no vessel detained there that was not absolutely necessary.

Question. Take the steamer Marion; how long has she been there?

Answer. A very long time; I do not recollect how many days. We were operating all along the whole coast. We had possession of the coast from the harbor down to Augustine, and we kept vessels there for days and weeks, because we did not know how far we would have to go, or where.

Question. Did you use these vessels for that purpose?

Answer. Yes, sir; altogether. Sometimes we kept vessels there for weeks, and did not use them at all; but it was the understanding of General Sherman that they would be used. I sent the vessels home as soon as I could learn they would not be needed, and I did not keep them after we were through with them.

Question. How many did you keep there?

Answer. Sometimes more, and sometimes less. At first we had to land everything through the surf in small boats. There was no pier there, and sometimes it would be so windy for days that we could not do anything. We set to work immediately to build a pier, and finally finished it, when we could unload much faster. The vessels were then unloaded and sent home, except those that we considered it necessary to keep for our operations

Question. How many steamers did you have there for fifty days?

Answer. A great many, I should think. I cannot tell the number.

Question. Were they not idle most of the time?

Answer. Yes, sir; they were idle. They had loads on, however. There were cargoes on them that we could not get out. We used to work our men in the water night and day taking out the cargoes. We were waiting some weeks for the navy to move to operate down at San Augustine.

Question. But all this time the cost of these vessels was running on at the rate of from $1,000 to $2,000 a day?

Answer. Yes, sir; they were lying there idle all the time. It was a matter over which I had not the slightest control. I was merely an agent. No vessel could leave there without the order of the general commanding.

Question. Did you represent to the general commanding that there was an enormous expense going on?

Answer. Yes, sir; a great many times.

Question. Could you not get from him authority to send them home?

Answer. We could not spare them. It was not safe for the army there without these vessels. We did not know what force they had in front of us, and without these vessels we had nothing to fall back upon. It was supposed that there were some 60,000 or 70,000 of the enemy in front of us.

Question. You kept these vessels as a refuge—something to fall back upon, should it become necessary to do so?

Answer. Yes, sir; and to move troops also. We could do nothing there except by water.

By Mr. Chandler:

Question. How many men did you say you had in front of you?

Answer. We estimated that there were some 60,000 on the line, including those in Savannah, along the line of the railroad, and in Charleston.

By Mr. Odell:

Question. Have you any data with you which would enable you to tell how long you kept these steamers there?

Answer. I have in my office.

Question. In this city?

Answer. Yes, sir. I have given certificates for the time the vessels served there. It will all appear in the quartermaster's office.

Question. Can you furnish this committee with a list of steamers and other vessels that you chartered, and the time for which you gave them certificates?

Answer. Yes, sir; I will do that.

Question. Do these charters for the steamers in every instance cover all expenses?

Answer. The whole running expenses, coaling and all. I chartered the fleet that took down our force of 15,000 men, and we took them down there without losing a single vessel which I chartered, or losing a single life, and we passed through one of the severest storms ever seen on this coast. There were vessels lost, but none that were chartered by me.

Question. According to the terms of the charter-parties, the owners of the vessels that you chartered were to furnish coal?

Answer. Yes, sir; every one, except the Ben Deford, perhaps. For that, I think, I agreed to furnish the coal, but all the rest had to furnish coal for themselves. They received a great deal of coal from the government, but every pound of coal that they got from me I charged on their charter-party.

Question. Why did you furnish coal to them?

Answer. It was when they had none down there.

Question. Was it not rather their business to furnish the coal than yours?

Answer. Yes, sir; but the charter stipulated that in case the government furnished coal they should pay for it.

Question. How did you charge the cost of the coal?

Answer. At New York prices.

Question. Then you gave them the cost of transporting the coal down there?

Answer. They would not charter to pay for coal what it might be worth wherever they got it. They agreed to furnish coal and to run the ships; but if they used government coal they were to receive it at New York prices.

Question. Did you furnish coal to the whole of them?

Answer. No, sir; not to half of them. I furnished it only in cases of absolute necessity, when they were entirely out of it, and were ordered off somewhere and had no coal. Then I let them have government coal which had been sent down there.

Question. Sent by the government?

Answer. Mr. Tucker sent it.

Question. The government transported the coal down there, and then furnished it to the owners of these steamers at New York prices?

Answer. Yes, sir; that was in the charter; they would not make any other agreement.

By the chairman:

Question. What is the expense of running one of those steamers that you chartered, for instance, at $1,000 a day?

Answer. I cannot tell; I am not acquainted with the cost of running ships. I know that it would cost the government a great deal more than it would cost a private company. But I am not able to say what it would cost.

By Mr. Odell:

Question. Did you keep an account of the cotton shipped from there, or was that shipped under your superintendence?

Answer. It was shipped under my superintendence at first, but afterwards it was all turned over to Colonel Reynolds, the government agent. I commenced the collection of the cotton, and got it under way before Colonel Reynolds got down there, and when he came I furnished him transportation for it.

Question. Has the cotton exported by your expedition anything like compensated the demurrage of the ships there?

Answer. No, sir; it has not, if you reckon the steamers.

Question. I mean reckoning all.

Answer. No, sir; it has not.

Question. Has it half done it?

Answer. No, sir; I should think not. I do not imagine there has been more than $700,000 worth of cotton shipped; certainly not more than a million of dollars worth. I do not think the cotton has been sold for its full value. It was very fine cotton, and I think worth more than it was sold for.

Question. Are these vessels still there?

Answer. Very few of them are there now. I sent them off as fast as we thought we could spare them.

Question. There has been a large number of vessels chartered to take coal there, chartered either by yourself or others?

Answer. Yes, sir.

Question. It has been said that care has not been taken to clear these vessels out as soon as might be.

Answer. All I can say is, that any such charge as that is false. Every precaution was taken to get them off as soon as possible We worked our men night and day in the water to get the coal landed and the vessels sent off. We got piers erected as soon as possible, and had the coal landed as rapidly as possible. And even after we had done that, it was a question whether the greater length of time it took to coal the steamers from the docks was not enough to make up for all the demurrage in keeping the coals on the vessels and loading the ships directly from the coal transports. I know that I worked for the interest of the government as well as I could, and so did my assistants. I pronounce all such statements as that false.

Question. You refer to sending off the transports?

Answer. I refer to every vessel down there, so far as the unloading them is concerned. Every effort was made to unload those ships rapidly. I worked night and day at it, as did my agents—night and day, Sundays and all. Ships may have been detained there when it was not necessary. But I am not responsible for that. That comes under the commanding general. Every ship was sent off as quickly as I could get orders to send it; and I could not send it before.

By the chairman:

Question. What is the condition of the army there in regard to their health and efficiency?

Answer. They were very healthy when I left. There seemed to be very little sickness there. In the course of the winter it was otherwise; it was very sickly for a time; but that we attributed to working the men in the water night and day, carrying stores ashore—especially the working them in the water after night.

Question. Why did you not employ contrabands for that business?

Answer. We did employ a great many of them. We could not have got along without the assistance of the contrabands. They worked very cheerfully, and were of great assistance to us. But it is a very great undertaking to supply an army of 17,000 men on shore from vessels, without piers to land the stores upon.

Question. There seemed to be a time when the army might have advanced upon Charleston and Savannah, and have proceeded into the interior. Do you know any reason why that was not done?

Answer. No, sir; I do not. I suppose the officers in command were not aware of the panic that seized the people there after the taking of Port Royal. After we took the forts there, there was a complete panic throughout the whole southern country. We could have gone into Savannah at that time with 200 men, I believe. And the reason we did not, I suppose, was because the condition of the country was not known.

Question. Do you know what were the orders from headquarters to the commanding officers of the expedition?

Answer. Their orders were to open two harbors on the southern coast, in order that the blockading squadron should have some place to go into when necessary. They were to open two ports, if possible; one certainly.

Question. Were their orders such as to prohibit their making expeditions into the interior?

Answer. Not so far as I am aware.

Question. In brief, what was the condition of affairs that you found there? You have already said that there was such a panic created by your landing that Charleston and Savannah might have been taken easily. In regard to the white inhabitants there, did they leave the country?

Answer. They deserted the country, leaving everything behind. They tried to take their negroes with them, but they would not go. They shot down their negroes in many instances because they would not go with them. They tied them behind their wagons, and tried to drag them off; but the negroes would not go. The great majority of the negroes remained behind, and came into our lines.

Question. What is the condition of the negroes there now?

Answer. It is improving very much. There have been a great many articles sent down to them from the north. Ladies have gone down there, and are teaching them, and they are going to work on the plantations now; and I think their condition is very much improved.

By Mr. Odell:

Question. Has the culture of the soil been gone into to any great extent?

Answer. To quite a large extent.

Question. Enough to give employment to the contrabands?

Answer. Yes, sir. There is no trouble about employing them if they can receive the products of their labor. I have been told by many of the negroes that if they can be assured that they will receive the benefit of their own labor, they are ready to go to work. They can take care of themselves.

Question. What has been your hospital accommodations there?

Answer. At first they were very poor. But we have a very good hospital there now.

Question. The accommodations now are all that are necessary?

Answer. Yes, sir; we have a hospital there 1,300 feet long—a temporary hospital—raised up from the ground and well ventilated; as good a hospital as there is in the country anywhere.

Question. Well appointed?

Answer. Yes, sir; with good, skilful surgeons, and everything necessary to make the sick comfortable. I built it myself, and I know all about it. I think that in the course of the spring, and certainly if we go into the interior, there must be a great deal of sickness from the malaria that arises from the swamps, and which is very dangerous. But I think there will be no difficulty in remaining at Hilton Head all summer. Beaufort, too, I think is healthy, and also Tybee island and a great part of the Edisto. But the trouble is, that going into the interior will bring us into these malarious swamps.

By Mr. Gooch:

Question Could you not have used a large force there to good advantage?

Answer. Yes, sir; we needed a larger force. We could have used 50,000 men to great advantage, and ought to have had them.

By Mr. Odell:

Question. What could you have done with that force if you had had it?

Answer. We could have taken Savannah and Charleston, both.

Question. How early could you have done that?

Answer. Very soon after we received the force, I think.

By Mr. Gooch:

Question. Has there been any time when you could not have taken Charleston and Savannah with a force of 50,000 men?

Answer. No, sir; no time at all.

Question. You mean by 50,000, if your force had been increased to 50,000?

Answer. Yes, sir; we then could have taken both of those places at any time. We should have first marched to their railroad and cut off their communication, and then we could have moved from Pocotaligo, which was very near our line, to Savannah and Charleston.

Question. Do you know whether application was made for more force?

Answer. I do not know certainly about that. I know that application was made for horses and wagon trains, for I made the application myself, but they were not supplied. It is my impression that General Sherman applied for more troops; I am pretty sure he did.

Question. What did you want with horses and wagons?

Answer. To make these onward movements. We wanted to move on Savannah, and also on Charleston.

Question. You say "we wanted to."

Answer. By that I refer to the whole army.

Question. Including the general in command?

Answer. Yes, sir.

Question. Then why did you not move on Savannah?

Answer. There were two plans of action. The general's orders, I think, were to secure two harbors on the coast, to make a place for the blockading squadron to go into in case of bad weather. Having taken Port Royal, we found that a great deal more fell into our hands; indeed we got possession of the entire coast. The question then arose whether it would be better to take possession of all the harbors on the coast and hold them, or to keep the force inland and move directly on Savannah. And I think that upon consultation with the Navy Department the decision was that it was better to occupy the coast. And in consequence of that the movement upon Savannah was given up until re-enforcements should arrive.

Question. If your force had been increased to 50,000 men, you could then have occupied the coast, and taken Charleston and Savannah, too?

Answer. I think so; I know that if I had been in command I should have liked very much to have had an opportunity to have attempted it.

Question. In army operations, as a general thing, can a considerable portion of colored people be used without putting arms into their hands?

Answer. Yes, sir; they are ready to do anything for us.

By Mr. Covode:

Question. Could they not be made use of in fortifications in the sickly season?

Answer. Yes, sir; with very great advantage.

By Mr. Gooch:

Question. If our army should remain in the south, would it be possible to employ quite a large number of negroes to aid and assist the army?

Answer. Yes, sir. We have some five hundred now employed in the Port Royal department. They will do anything we tell them to do.

Question. As a general thing do you find them willing to work?

Answer. Yes, sir.

Question. Are they reasonably intelligent?

Answer. Some of them are very intelligent, while others are not. There is a wide distinction between them in that respect.

Question. In your opinion, what could you have accomplished if, within, say, sixty or ninety days after you landed there, you had been re-enforced to 75,000 men?

Answer. I think we could have taken military possession of the greater portion of South Carolina and Georgia. I think that there are a great many loyal men there who would have joined our cause the moment there was a show of force there to sustain the cause of the government. I think we could have taken possession of all their lines of railroads and all their principal towns. I have conversed with a great many prisoners whom we have taken there, and have frequently found men in the middle and lower conditions of life to whom this rebellion is exceedingly distasteful. They only serve in the rebel ranks because they are forced to do so.

By Mr. Odell:

Question. Is that the general verdict of the men you have taken prisoners?

Answer. Yes, sir; of that class.

Question. That they are in the rebel army because they are obliged to be there?

Answer. Yes, sir; and they have told me that if they could only be assured that they would not be forced to violate their oath of allegiance, they would take it and go back to their homes.

By Mr. Gooch:

Question. It is, then, your opinion that if we had taken military possession of South Carolina and Georgia, as we might have done, with an army of 75,000 men, we should have found a large portion of the people ready to give in their allegiance to the government as soon as they could have felt assured of protection?

Answer. Yes, sir; that is my opinion.

Question. And by not doing that before this time, has not the best season of the year for operations in that country been lost?

Answer. Yes, sir; I think it has.

Question. Have you had sufficient transportation to have taken such an army from Annapolis, or some other point in this vicinity, to the southern coast?

Answer. Yes, sir, by making several trips.

Question. How many trips would it have required to have taken 75,000 men down there?

Answer. Our fleet took down between 14,000 and 15,000 at one time. The best policy would have been to have employed some of those large steamers that could have gone down there in 60 hours. They would have taken the troops down very rapidly.

Question. How long would it have taken, with the means of transportation that you had, to have transferred 60,000 men from the Potomac to your scene of operations?

Answer. I should think it might all have been done in a month.

Question. And without any very great increase of expense to the government?

Answer. Yes, sir. I think a great portion of the army of the Potomac might have been taken down there, and have fought several battles, and come back here again before they were needed for operations here, and been all the better prepared to fight here from the experience they would have gained.

By Mr. Odell:

Question. Would it have been possible for the enemy, with the means of transportation at their command, to have concentrated an army down there in time to have met the force that we could have taken there?

Answer. I think not. We should have taken possession of the railroad lines at the very first, and could have retained all the advantages we had in the beginning.

By Mr. Gooch:

Question. Has this been a subject of discussion among military men where you were, that the seat of war should have been transferred to the cotton States?

Answer. Yes, sir. We have all along felt that that should have been done.

By Mr. Covode:

Question. In your judgment would it have been safe to have trusted arms in the hands of the colored men there?

Answer. Yes, sir, I think it would.

Question. They would have used them against the rebels?

Answer. Most undoubtedly. There can be no question about that.

By Mr. Gooch:

Question. Have the enemy in any instance armed their slaves?

Answer. We understood that they had one or two regiments of slaves in New Orleans. But I do not think they could rely upon them at all.

By Mr. Covode:

Question. You think they could be relied upon to fight for our side?

Answer. I am sure of that.

Question. Are the local attachments of these negroes very strong?

Answer. Yes, sir.

Question. Do you think that if slavery should be abolished that we of the north would be seriously troubled by their coming among us?

Answer. No, sir. I do not think they would leave their old homes willingly. It is my impression that if you would give each of these negroes a little strip of land to cultivate for themselves, enough to support themselves and their families, they would take care of themselves, and the remaining land would soon become worth more than all the land and all the negroes were worth before.

Question. In your opinion, has it not been a military mistake that we have not before this made use of the muscle of the blacks to aid us in putting down this rebellion?

Answer. Yes, sir; I think so.

List of vessels chartered by Captain Rufus Saxton, Assistant Quartermaster, Headquarters Expeditionary Corps, with the rate of pay, and time in service, &c.

No.	Name of vessel.	Class.	Term of service.		No. of days.	Rate of pay.	Per day or month.	Amount.	Remarks.
			From—	To—					
1	Atlantic	Steamship	Oct. 1, 1861	Mar. 31, 1862	182	$1,500 00	Day	$273,000 00	Transferred to Colonel J. W. Shaffer, A. Q. M., March 31, 1862.
2	Baltic	do	Oct. 4, 1861	Nov. 18, 1861	46	1,500 00	do	69,000 00	Transferred to Colonel D. D. Tompkins, A. Q. M. G., November 18, 1861.
3	Vanderbilt	do	do	Jan. 3, 1862	92	2,000 00	do	184,000 00	Transferred to Colonel D. D. Tompkins, A. Q. M. G., January 3, 1862.
4	Ocean Queen	do	Oct. 5, 1861	Nov. 27, 1861	54	2,000 00	do	108,000 00	Transferred to Colonel D. D. Tompkins, A. Q. M. G., November 27, 1861.
5	Ariel	do	do	Dec. 27, 1861	84	1,100 00	do	92,400 00	Transferred to Colonel D. D. Tompkins, A. Q. M. G., December 27, 1861.
6	Daniel Webster	do	do	Dec. 17, 1861	74	900 00	do	66,600 00	Transferred to Colonel D. D. Tompkins, A. Q. M. G., December 17, 1861.
7	Illinois	do	do	Nov. 25, 1861	52	1,500 00	do	78,000 00	Transferred to Colonel D. D. Tompkins, A. Q. M. G., November 25, 1861.
8	Empire City	do	do	Dec. 25, 1861	82	1,000 00	do	82,000 00	Transferred to Colonel D. D. Tompkins, A. Q. M. G., December 25, 1861.
9	Philadelphia	do	do	Dec. 17, 1861	74	1,000 00	do	74,000 00	Transferred to Colonel D. D. Tompkins, A. Q. M. G., December 17, 1861.
10	Coatzacoalcos	do	do	Nov. 12, 1861	39	1,300 00	do	50,700 00	Transferred to Colonel D. D. Tompkins, A. Q. M. G., November 12, 1861.
11	Roanoke	do	do	Dec. 30, 1861	87	750 00	do	65,250 00	Transferred to Colonel D. D. Tompkins, A. Q. M. G., December 30, 1861.
12	Star of the South	do	do	Dec. 18, 1861	75	750 00	do	56,250 00	Transferred to Colonel D. D. Tompkins, A. Q. M. G., December 18, 1861.
13	Marion	do	do	Dec. 21, 1861	78	1,000 00	do	78,000 00	Transferred to Colonel D. D. Tompkins, A. Q. M. G., December 21, 1861.
14	Cahawba	do	do	Dec. 30, 1861	87	1,300 00	do	113,100 00	Transferred to Colonel D. D. Tompkins, A. Q. M. G., December 30, 1861.
15	Ericsson	do	Oct. 7, 1861	Nov. 22, 1861	47	1,200 00	do	56,400 00	Transferred to Colonel D. D. Tompkins, A. Q. M. G., November 22, 1861.
16	Ben Deford	do	Oct. 15, 1861	Mar. 31, 1862	168	750 00	do	126,000 00	Transferred to Colonel Shaffer, A. Q. M., March 31, 1862.
17	Belvidere	do	Oct. 14, 1861	do	169	650 00	do	109,850 00	Do. do. do. do.
18	Parkersburg	do	Oct. 5, 1861	do	178	500 00	do	89,000 00	Do. do. do. do.
19	Potomac	do	Oct. 10, 1861	do	173	350 00	do	60,550 00	Do. do. do. do.
20	Locust Point	do	do	do	173	350 00	do	60,550 00	Do. do. do. do.
21	Honduras	do	Feb. 12, 1862	do	48	400 00	do	19,200 00	Do. do. do. do.
22	Mayflower	Steamboat	Oct. 14, 1861	Feb. 28, 1862	138	400 60	do	55,200 00	Purchased by the United States, March 1, 1862.
23	Great Republic	Ship	Oct. 3, 1861	Dec. 5, 1861	63½	500 00	do	31,750 00	Transferred to Colonel Tompkins, A. Q. M. G., Dec. 5, 1861.
24	Golden Eagle	Ship	Oct. 5, 1861	Feb. 14, 1862	133	250 00	do	33,250 00	Transferred to Colonel Tompkins, A. Q. M. G., Feb. 14, 1862.
25	Ocean Express	Ship	Oct. 9, 1861	Jan. 16, 1862	99½	350 00	do	34,825 00	Transferred to Colonel Tompkins, A. Q. M. G., Jan. 16, 1862.
26	Zenas Coffin	Ship	Oct. 26, 1861	Jan. 27, 1862	94	100 00	do	*2,080 00 9,400 00	Transferred to Colonel Tompkins, A. Q. M. G., Jan. 27, 1862.

List of vessels chartered by Captain Rufus Saxton, Assistant Quartermaster, &c.—Continued.

No.	Name of vessel.	Class.	Term of service. From—	Term of service. To—	No. of days.	Rate of pay.	Per day or month.	Amount.	Remarks.
27	Fanny Keating	Schooner	Dec. 25, 1861	Mar. 31, 1862	97	$40 00	Day	$3,880 00	Transferred to Colonel Shaffer, A. Q. M., March 31, 1862.
28	James M. Holmes	do	Jan. 27, 1862	do	64	30 00	do	1,920 00	Do. do. do. do.
29	R. J. Mercer	do	Jan. 29, 1862	Mar. 13, 1862	44	20 00	do	880 00	Transferred to Colonel Tompkins, A. Q. M. G., March 13, 1862.
30	N. Stowers	Brig	Jan. 27, 1862	Mar. 11, 1862	44	30 00	do	1,320 00	Transferred to Colonel Tompkins, A. Q. M. G., March 11, 1862.
31	John Guyant	Schooner	Jan. 25, 1862	Mar. 31, 1862	66	15 00	do	990 00	Transferred to Colonel Shaffer, A. Q. M., March 31, 1862.
32	J. P. Ellicott	Brig	Jan. 30, 1862	do	61	30 00	do	1,830 00	Do. do. do. do.
33	Alexander Young	Schooner	Feb. 4, 1862	Mar. 28, 1862	53	27 00	do	1,431 00	Transferred to Colonel Tompkins, A. Q. M. G., March 28, 1862.
34	Wm. G. Audenreid	do	Feb. 1, 1862	Mar. 26, 1862	54	25 60	do	1,382 40	Transferred to Colonel Tompkins, A. Q. M. G., March 26, 1862.
35	F. P. Simpson	do	do	Mar. 29, 1862	57	22 50	do	1,282 50	Transferred to Colonel Tompkins, A. Q. M. G., March 29, 1862.
36	Blackbird	do	Feb. 2, 1862	Mar. 19, 1862	46	20 00	do	920 00	Transferred to Colonel Tompkins, A. Q. M. G., March 19, 1862.
37	James G. Stille	do	Feb. 1, 1862	Mar. 31, 1862	59	17 00	do	1,003 00	Transferred to Colonel Shaffer, A. Q. M., March 31, 1862.
38	Virginia Price	do	Mar. 7, 1862	do	25	30 00	do	750 00	Do. do. do. do.
39	J. B. Myers	do	Mar. 13, 1862	do	19	32 00	do	608 00	Do. do. do. do.
40	Rachel S. Miller	do	Mar. 21, 1862	do	11	30 00	do	330 00	Do. do. do. do.
41	John Rose	do	Mar. 22, 1862	do	10	25 00	do	250 00	Do. do. do. do.
42	Azalia	do	Mar. 18, 1862	do	14	600 00	Month	270 97	Do. do. do. do.
43	Reindeer	do	Mar. 22, 1862	do	10	16 00	Day	160 00	Do. do. do. do.
	Total							2,097,562 87	

I certify that the foregoing is a true list of all the vessels chartered by me that were used on the expedition to Port Royal. Other vessels were chartered by Colonel D. D. Tompkins, assistant quartermaster general, and John Tucker, esq., general transport agent of the War Department, but, as copies of their charter-parties were not furnished me, I am unable to state all the particulars connected with them.

R. SAXTON, *Captain U. S. Army, Assistant Quartermaster.*

* Freight on 520 tons coal, at $4 per ton.

BURNSIDE EXPEDITION.

WASHINGTON, *March* 19, 1863.

Major General A. E. BURNSIDE recalled and examined.

By Mr. Gooch:

Question. Will you give the committee a statement of all matters of interest connected with the origin and operations of the coast division, commonly known as the Burnside expedition?

Answer. In the early part of September, 1861, I was in command of the provisional brigades in the city of Washington, which were formed from the new troops as they arrived. During that time I had several conversations with General McClellan with reference to the blockade of the Potomac, and movements of discontented people in the southern counties of Maryland on the boarders of the Patuxent river, as well as along the coast of the eastern shore counties of Virginia and Maryland. During one of those conversations I said to him that I thought it would be well to organize a division composed of men from the eastern States, and to equip vessels of proper draught and capacity to operate in those waters, with a view to taking possession of points on the rivers and coast occupied by the enemy, and prevent the occupation of other important points. He said that he had long felt the want of something of that kind, and he would be very glad if I would mature the plan of which I had been thinking, and submit a written proposition to him. I did so. The plan was about as follows:

To organize in the eastern States regiments near the sea-coast, composed as much as possible of men who knew more or less about steamers, sailing vessels, surf-boats, &c., and to arm and equip a sufficient number of vessels of light draught to carry this division of men, (which at that time it was intended should number about 10,000 men,) so that they could be moved quickly from one point on the coast to another. The object in arming these vessels with heavy guns was to enable them to overcome any slight opposition that they might meet with on the rivers or coast, without the necessity of waiting for assistance from the navy, which might not be at hand. All these vessels were to be well supplied with surf-boats, launches, and other means of landing troops. The vessels were to be of the lightest draught possible, in order to navigate all the bays, harbors and rivers of the waters of the Chesapeake bay and of North Carolina.

It was first contemplated to place this division at work in the waters of Chesapeake bay, and the rivers running into it, then to be transferred to the waters of North Carolina. This plan was approved by General McClellan, and I carried it to the Secretary of War, had it approved by him, and got the necessary orders issued for the fitting out of the command. I then repaired to New York, and from there to New England, where I succeeded in getting the troops, and in fitting out the best vessels that could be obtained; as soon as the expedition was fitted out it repaired to Annapolis. The three brigades of the division were commanded by Generals Reno, Parke, and Foster. In the meantime I had been informed by General McClellan that it had been decided to send the expedition into the waters of North Carolina. I was summoned to go to Washington, where, in the presence of the President, Secretary Seward, General McClellan and Commodore Goldsborough—to all of whom I explained the nature of my force—it was decided that I should sail at the earliest day possible to Hatteras inlet, cross into the sound in connexion with a naval fleet, to be under the command of Commodore Goldsborough, and take if possible, first, Roanoke island, and then such other points as it should appear necessary to hold on the coast and the sounds of that State. I returned to Annapolis, and at once made my arrangements for embarking. Having received my instructions from General McClellan, I sailed from there on the 8th of January, 1862. When the expedition was twenty miles out from Fortress Monroe, the commanders of the vessels having been furnished by me with sealed orders, opened them, and the whole fleet concentrated at Hatteras inlet, as had been contemplated. Upon leaving Fortress Monroe we were overtaken by a very severe storm, which continued almost incessantly for twenty-eight days. The history of that period is so well known that it is not worth while to go into a detail of it.

By Mr. Odell:

Question. How many vessels did you lose in that storm?

Answer. We lost three steamers and some half a dozen sailing vessels—sloops and schooners. There were but three lives lost by the storm. By the 6th of February we succeeded in getting all our vessels, with our troops on board, over the bulkhead at Hatteras inlet. We started at once for Roanoke island, where the fleet concentrated, and on the night of the 7th succeeded in landing our troops under cover of our own gunboat Picket and the naval gunboat Delaware; there were some 7,500 troops landed in all, the remainder of them having been left at Hatteras inlet. During the day of the 7th, and before landing the troops, the naval portion of the expedition, together with the armed troop vessels, engaged the shore batteries until the troops commenced landing.

On the morning of the 8th the command was moved forward. At a point one mile and a half from the landing we came upon an intrenched position of the enemy of which we had been informed by spies. After some four hours' fighting we succeeded in carrying that position. The troops were then pushed rapidly up to the head of the island, at which point the whole rebel garrison was captured before they had time to embark. Their vessels ran up the sound without them. We took about 2,700 prisoners and 44 guns.

The next day the naval part of the enemy's fleet was followed by our naval fleet, under Commodore Rowan, and overtaken at Elizabeth, where they were all either destroyed or captured.

Our vessels had suffered very much from the violence of the storm, so that it required a considerable time to repair them.

By the 8th of March we had everything in readiness for another movement. The troops were embarked, and, in accordance with the instructions given to us, we sailed for Newbern. We landed, under cover of Commodore Rowan's gunboats, at a point about eighteen miles from there, at the mouth of Slocum's creek, early on the morning of the 13th—getting about 7,500 on shore. From that point the troops marched up to within five miles of Newbern, where we came upon the enemy's intrenchments on the night of the 13th. Early on the morning of the 14th we engaged the enemy, in conjunction with the naval fleet, and in two and a half hours carried their intrenchments, capturing three batteries of field artillery and all their shore batteries—in all, about 69 guns—and took some 500 prisoners, and all their camps, quartermaster, commissary, and ordnance stores. Their army saved itself by retreating across the Trent river and destroying the two bridges over it, which prevented us from following them.

Within two or three days I started General Parke's division down across the country with a view to investing Fort Macon, which was the next point we were ordered to attack. The bridges between Newbern and Beaufort, which was opposite Fort Macon, were destroyed by the enemy. But General Parke succeeded in taking possession of Moorehead City and Beaufort in two days.

Within a week the bridges on the road were repaired, and hand-cars, which we had taken with us in the vessels, were placed upon the track, by means of which we were enabled to transport all the means necessary to besiege Fort Macon.

We labored under great difficulty in getting across Bogue sound on to the banks, in order to invest the fort, as there were no vessels or boats at Moorehead City or Beaufort, and Cove sound was guarded by the batteries of the enemy. The fort also protected the entrance to the harbor. General Parke, on the second or third day after he reached Moorehead City, discovered a small sailing vessel coming up Bogue sound, and at once sent out a launch (which we succeeded in carrying over the country on a hand-car) with some armed men and captured her. On it we found a mail of the enemy and some corn for the fort, of all of which we took possession. With this vessel General Parke succeeded in throwing across, during the forepart of the night, some 200 men who held their position on that bank until they were re-enforced the next night; and finding some scows on the opposite bank, they were brought over, and he succeeded within a week in getting his whole command of 3,500 men on to the banks. The channel across there was very intricate and shallow, and the transportation of the troops was attended with very great difficulties.

After getting the troops over, the heavy guns, mortars, and ammunition were then transported across, together with some horses to move them; at which time General Parke commenced the erection of batteries in the sand-hills outside of the fort; and by the morning of the 25th of April we were enabled to open our batteries upon the fort. That afternoon at 4 o'clock the enemy ran up a white flag. During the time of the siege we communicated with the vessels outside by means of surf-boats, and those vessels joined in the attack on the 25th.

Our batteries ceased firing as soon as the white flag was discovered, and I was placed in communication with the commanding officer of the fort, and arranged with him for a meeting the next morning at six o'clock, on board my vessel, which was lying just off Beaufort. At eight o'clock the articles of capitulation were signed. We then went on shore and General Parke received the fort with all its armament, and the arms of the garrison, from Colonel White, who had been in command of the fort.

An expedition was then sent to Washington to take possession of that place; and subsequently one was sent to Plymouth to take possession of that place, and our boats held Elizabeth City and Edenton, and points on the Chowan river up as high as Winton.

From that time up to the 4th of July nothing of great importance occurred in the department, excepting some demonstrations threatening the rear of Norfolk. During one of those demonstrations General Reno had a sharp engagement with the enemy at South Mills. After having accomplished the purpose of his expedition he returned with his force to Newbern.

We held so many points and so long a line of coast that it was not possible to spare from any one point any force for an important expedition; a great many unimportant scouts and skirmishes occurred in the mean time.

By Mr. Gooch:

Question. Will you state the strength of the several positions of the enemy at Roanoke island, Newbern, and Fort Macon, and the obstacles you had to overcome in taking those places?

Answer. At Roanoke island we were forced to land at a point below the shore batteries, on a very low and swampy shore. The men in leaping from the boats were at once more than knee-deep in mud and water. After going up a short distance from shore, a hundred yards or so, they came upon a causeway, some ten feet wide, which led up through a dense thicket and swamp for a mile and a half to where we found the enemy's battery. In front of the battery, for some 800 yards, the enemy had cleared away all the timber and undergrowth, so as to give full play to their guns over the ground in front as well as down the causeway.

General Foster led off with his brigade and occupied the enemy in front of the battery, just in the skirting of timber which bordered this cleared space. As soon as General Foster had got into position General Reno turned his brigade off to the left, and General Parker turned his brigade off to the right, with a view to flanking the battery. The moment the troops left the causeway they found themselves from knee to waist deep in mud and water in that dense thicket. They succeeded by extraordinary efforts in getting into positions which gave them a flanking fire upon the battery. As soon as the enemy became at all shaken by this fire the troops charged forward into the cleared space and carried the works. This was the first time the troops had been under fire, and in my estimation no troops ever behaved more gallantly. The enemy retreated in great confusion and were closely followed, as I have before said, by our forces, and all on the island captured.

At Newbern the enemy's intrenchments extended from the Neuse river to an impenetrable swamp, the borders of which run parallel to the river, and within a mile and a half of the river bank. Across this space of a mile and a half the enemy had a continuous line of intrenchments, rifle-pits, and redans for field-pieces. On the river bank there was a part of thirteen heavy guns commanding the river and protecting the line of intrenchments. In front of this line, as we had to approach it, the timber was cleared away as at Roanoke island, and our troops had to be deployed in the timber which skirted this clearing. The three brigades engaged the whole line of the enemy's works, until General Parke's brigade succeeded in breaking through the centre, when the line of works was charged by the brigades of General Foster and General Reno, and carried. Three batteries of light artillery behind the intrenchments and in the redans, as well as all the shore batteries, were captured. As at Roanoke, the troops in this action behaved as gallantly as any men could.

At the siege of Fort Macon the hardships and difficulties which the troops had to undergo in the transportation of the guns, mortars, ammunition, and provisions, through the intricate channels and over the sand-hills, exceeded anything that I have ever known in the way of land service. It was all performed by the men without a murmur.

It would be well to state here that I was most cordially supported in everything I attempted to do by Generals Foster, Reno, and Parke, and the navy never failed to co-operate.

On the 4th of July we heard of the retreat of General McClellan's army. I received a telegram from the President of the United States saying that I better send at once all the infantry possible to the support of General McClellan. The message was sent by telegraph as far as Fort Monroe, and from there sent through to me by way of the canal which we had just succeeded in opening, it having previously been obstructed by the enemy. I at once decided to go myself, with as much force as could possibly be spared, to Fort Monroe. The troops were at once embarked, and we arrived there, I think, on the 7th of July.

Question. What was the amount of the force under your command on the 4th of July, and at different periods previous to that time?

Answer. I cannot give the exact figures, but it was very nearly as follows: We reached Hatteras inlet with 11,500 men. We left a portion at Hatteras inlet, and succeeded in landing on Roanoke island from 7,000 to 7,500 men. A garrison was left at Roanoke island. Upon going to Newbern, I took a portion of the force that had been left at Hatteras inlet, landing at Newbern with about 7,500 men. At the siege of Fort Macon General Parke had about 3,000 or 3,500 men. In other words, our whole force, up to that period, was about 11,500 men. After the siege of Fort Macon we received re-enforcements, which made our force something over 15,000. Of that number I took to Fort Monroe a little over 7,000 men, and was joined there by a division from General Hunter, which increased my command to about 11,000 men.—(See testimony upon "Army of the Potomac.")

FORT DONELSON, ETC.

WASHINGTON, *July* 9, 1862.

General LEWIS WALLACE sworn and examined.

By Mr. Covode:

Question. Where do you reside?

Answer. In the State of Indiana.

Question. What is your position and rank in the army?

Answer. I am major general of volunteers.

Question. Will you please to give us as condensed a statement as you can conveniently of what you have witnessed about the conduct in the west that may be of interest and importance to this committee?

Answer. In the first place I would state that my knowledge of operations in the west extend only to the conduct of my own particular command. I do not think I ever had the honor to be present at a council of war except upon one occasion.

Question. What occasion was that?

Answer. That was the day before the troops marched from Fort Henry to the attack on Donelson. I was then a brigadier general, commanding a brigade. Upon notice from General Grant, I, with others commanding brigades, went on board his boat and attended a council of war. The question before us was whether the troops should immediately march upon Donelson or not. It was a very unceremonious council of war; no formal opinions were expressed at all. We all appeared to be of the same opinion, and that was that the troops should march upon Donelson. We being, as I said, quite unanimous on that point, of course there was no debate. Marching upon Donelson being agreed upon, the question was as to the time of marching. There were some who held to the opinion that we should march immediately. A few thought we better wait a day or two for re-enforcements. The result of it was that the main body of troops marched at once. I was left behind on that occasion, with my brigade, in command of Fort Henry. The rest of the troops were gone two days before I received an order to bring my command up. I immediately marched with my command and reached there on Friday. Of course I was ignorant of the position of our army, and knew nothing of the lines of the enemy. I arrived at Fort Donelson, and was put in command of a division. I had no time to organize my division, except as it marched past me, going to take its position. I had my position assigned to me, and went and took it. The battle opened on Saturday morning. My orders were simply to hold the position I occupied, which was in the centre of the line of attack. I was to hold it for the purpose of repelling any sally from the enemy's lines. I had no authority whatever given me to make an offensive movement, and I accordingly held my position. The battle commenced early Saturday morning on the extreme right. General McClernand's command was attacked, the object of the enemy being, if possible, to drive him from the right, that they might have a road by which to get out from the fort. I did not see it; I knew nothing about the particulars of the fight. I only knew that it was McClernand's command that was engaged.

I very soon, however, saw the results; I saw a large portion of his command coming back in confusion. I had in the meantime sent in a portion of my command to re-enforce him. The brigade I sent him reached him, but, like all the rest, it was compelled to fall back. I am glad to say, however, that it fell back in good order. The prospect looked very gloomy for a little while. I could find nobody who could give me an intelligent opinion or account of what was transpiring. It was a matter of great solicitude to me to know whether the enemy were pursuing. I finally saw an officer, now dead, and through information obtained from him, I obtained some knowledge which enabled me to take up a position with my remaining troops, and fortunately took it just in time to repel the enemy. They were following in rapid pursuit, but were repulsed. There was no fighting after that until about 3 o'clock in the day.

About 3 o'clock I was ordered to take my command over to the right and make an attack there, for the purpose of recovering the road that had been lost in the morning. I did so. My command immediately took the position and held it all that night. In the morning, while I was making dispositions to storm the works of the enemy, they sent out a flag of truce, and told me that they had surrendered, and that the place was ours. Of course, I marched in and took possession of that side of the fort.

Question. How many prisoners did you take there?

Answer. I never saw the official report of them. My opinion, however, formed from the statements of rebel officers, is, that between 13,000 and 15,000 prisoners were taken there. I went over the ground, and came to the conclusion that it was a matter of marvel, and must always remain a matter of marvel, that we took the place. I was not more rejoiced than astonished at our success.

Question. If it had not been for the decision of your council to move forward, and to do it promptly, is it not very probable that your campaign there might have been a failure?

Answer. To do General Grant justice, I will say that I became satisfied at the council that it was his determination to march in any event I am satisfied that he had determined in his own mind, no matter what the opinion of the council might have been, to march on Donelson. I am therefore satisfied that the result would have been the same, no matter what conclusion the council might have reached.

Question. Did you get your instructions from Washington how to proceed in those matters, or did they come from officers in the west? What do you know about that?

Answer. All I knew about orders was when I received them myself. I received them through the proper channel. I always understood, as a matter of course, that all orders for movements came from General Halleck. Those I received were passed down through the regular channels to me.

Question. Was there any time or opportunity, while operating at Donelson, for you to receive orders from Washington by telegraph?

Answer. I do not know.

Question. How far were you from the nearest telegraph station?

Answer. The nearest I think was at Paducah.

Question. How far off was that?

Answer. Probably some forty or fifty miles.

Question. Too far off to direct a battle, of course?

Answer. I think so. After the battle of Fort Henry the wires were brought up to Smithland, and then they were very promptly brought across to Fort Henry. That was after the battle of Donelson, however, whether the march upon Donelson was ordered by General Halleck, or whether it was undertaken by General Grant of his own accord, I do not know. I do not know who indicated that movement.

Question. Is it a common thing in battles for commanders of divisions and brigades to know so little about what is going on, about the position of the enemy, &c.? It would appear that there is a great deal of uncertainty as to what is going on.

Answer. I know nothing about other armies. But I have understood from what military reading I have had, that every army, whether on the march or in action, has its head, and that all movements come from that head, as a matter of course.

Question. From your statement it would appear that there was not much connexion between the heads of divisions in this battle of Donelson. Do not I so understand it?

Answer. Yes, sir; you do. I saw General Grant in the battle of Donelson on Saturday but once. I saw his adjutant general and one of his aids passing along the lines on different occasions. But I saw General Grant but once, and that was at three o'clock in the afternoon. He then ordered this attack on the night I have spoken of. He first gave the order to General McClernand; but General McClernand not having the troops in readiness at the time, requested me to make the attack. I sent two or three messages to General Grant on Saturday morning, while the disaster to McClernand was occurring, requesting or asking permission to send him re-enforcements. But my messengers did not get to him. He afterwards explained it by saying, that at that time he was on board the gunboats. I, however, assumed the responsibility of sending re-enforcements to General McClernand.

Question. You had to act on your own judgment?

Answer. In that particular, I did.

Question. And in doing so you saved the army, did you not?

Answer. I am satisfied my command repulsed the enemy; I know they did. They were not pursued.

Question. Please proceed and state in regard to your movements after that.

Answer. After the battle of Donelson, an hour after General Grant arrived and took possession of the town of Dover, and the enemy's works, and the prisoners, I received an order to proceed with my division back to Fort Henry. I immediately proceeded to execute the order, and what took place at Donelson afterwards I do not know. I marched back to Fort Henry, put my division in position there, and lay there for some days. I then received information that we were going up the river. The transports arrived and our troops were put on board. We moved up the river in a kind of column. General C. F. Smith was in command of that movement. That part of it, I think, was unquestionably conducted with most soldierly ability. There is no doubt of that; it was a very orderly proceeding. The embarking of so many troops on board the transports, always a matter of considerable difficulty, was done in good order and with celerity.

Question. To what place did you go?

Answer. We moved up the river to Savannah. I learned from General Smith what was the object of the movement. It had in contemplation an attack on Corinth. We arrived at Savannah, and lay there a day or two, while the general was obtaining information as to the nature of the country, the number of the enemy's forces, &c. He was very frank with me. For the first time, I may say, I was satisfied with the treatment I received. He told me what his designs were, and I frankly state my opinion that if General Smith had retained his health we would have had Corinth, and there would have been no battle at Pittsburg Landing. Without any delay he undertook his preliminary movements. One of them was conducted by General Sherman, an attack on, or an effort to break, the Memphis and Charleston railrosd east of Corinth. Owing to a rise of water there, the general failed, although he tried most gallantly to carry out his orders. I was sent with my division to break the road running from Jackson, Tennessee, to Corinth. Not having so far to march, I was more successful than General Sherman, and succeeded in burning the bridges and tearing up the track. From the information given me by General Smith, I considered these movements as preliminary. Those roads being broken, he intended to march right straight on Corinth. Unfortunately he was hurt, got sick, and had to turn the command over.

Question. To whom?

Answer. The command was turned over to General Grant. General Grant, as I understand, made a disposition of what forces we had there, the exact number of which I do not know. I think there were between 30,000 and 40,000 effective men. He put the main body of the troops at Pittsburg Landing. My division he put at Crump's Landing, six miles below Pittsburg Landing. The object of putting me there was to observe the road to Purdy, four miles beyond that point. That railroad offered the enemy a facility for sending troops and getting on our right flank. We lay there a considerable time, waiting for General Halleck, as I understood. That was merely my understanding, however.

One Sunday morning I heard cannonading in the direction of Pittsburg Landing. I heard it very early in the morning, and from its continuance I very soon became satisfied that a battle was going on. I commenced, as a matter of course, making what I considered the best disposition of my troops, because I had no doubt that the enemy would attack me.

As near as I can now recollect, about 8 o'clock, or 8.15 in the morning, General Grant passed up the river on a boat. He stopped and asked me a few questions, and directed me to hold myself in readiness for orders. What took place on Sunday morning at that battle I have no personal knowledge of. I only know from the remarks of others there is a great dispute as to whether General Grant was surprised or not. I do not undertake to say that the general was surprised. But from the statements of soldiers of some of the regiments, I am satisfied that some of his regiments were surprised. But on that point I will endeavor to do justice to General Grant. My opinion is that if there was a surprise, the responsibility does not properly attach to him. If any one could have gone to his headquarters and seen the immense mass of details that he had to attend to, he would readily have understood how absolutely impossible it was for him to go around the picket lines and see whether they were all right or not. From the very nature of his situation he had to confide much in the officers.

About eleven or half past eleven o'clock that forenoon I received an order in writing, unsigned, brought me, as I understood, by Quartermaster Baxter.

He at that time was on General Grant's staff. I was told that he had received the order verbally from some officer coming down the river, and had stopped on board a boat to write it out. It was brought to him verbally, and he put it in writing and brought it to me. The order directed me to move up with my division and take position on the extreme right of our lines, as they were on Sunday morning; and upon arriving at that point to form in line of battle at right angles with the river. As I understood it, the point to which I was to march was between three and four miles from the river.

I started exactly at 12 o'clock, giving my men time to eat their dinners. I marched in the direction indicated to me, and got within probably two and a half miles of the point at which I was to form a junction with our forces, when I was overtaken by an aid of General Grant, Captain Rowley, who told me that our lines had been beaten back from the point to which I was marching, and were then not far from the river. He gave me, in other words, quite a disastrous account of the fight. I received, however, no countermanding of my previous order. No directions were given to me; merely a statement of a fact. It was a very serious fact, however. It threw the responsibility of my movements upon myself. The question with me was, whether I should go on in pursuance of my order, or should I countermarch and take another road that would take me to Pittsburg Landing, and form a junction there. For reasons satisfactory to myself I concluded that I would endeavor to take the other road, called the river road, following the windings of the Tennessce bottom, crossing Snake creek—a place very difficult to pass at all times on account of its boggy bottom—crossing Snake creek about a mile from Pittsburg Landing. Subsequent events satisfied me that I did the best thing I could have done, for if I continued on as I started at first, I should have met Prentiss's fate, and been taken prisoner or destroyed

While I was marching to the other road I met two other officers of General Grant's staff, his adjutant general and Colonel McPherson, and they gave me, if anything, a still more gloomy picture of the condition of the fight. They informed me that our troops were gathered almost immediately around Pittsburg Landing, and that it was a very desperate struggle, and that I would, in all probability, have to fight my way to them. Again there were no orders or directions to me; and understanding nothing said to me to be in the nature of an order, I think I would have been justified in going back to Crumps Landing with my command for the purpose of saving it. I did not do that, however. I went on and met a great many fugitives escaping from the battle.

At dusk in the evening I crossed Sante creek. My foremost regiment went in in line of battle, and passed under the guns of the enemy. It was so dark, however, that they did not fire at us. Of course I reported to General Grant immediately upon forming the junction. The battle was then over for the night at least. He told me to occupy the road I had marched in on.

There was a council of war that night; at least I understood so. I did not attend it. It was my own fault, however. I went once to try to find it and could not, and then went back. I asked for a diagram showing me the enemy's lines and our own lines. It was promised me, but I never got it. I had to take a soldier and go myself in the night and ascertain as well as I could the position of the enemy relatively to my own position. Having obtained that knowledge, the best I could, I made the best disposition of my troops that I considered possible. I selected a position for my batteries at a point which I thought would enable me to command the enemy's batteries, or at least to fight them. Between one and two o'clock that night I laid down and tried to get some sleep. But it stormed all night, raining terribly, and the gunboats kept up a fire every five minutes, so that sleep was almost impossible.

The next morning, a little after daybreak, one of my batteries opened fire; the enemy replied, and the battle began. While this fight between the batteries was going on, General Grant rode down to where I was. He gave me the simple direction to march forward with my command, in a direction that was directly at right angles with the river. That was about all the order I received. I marched them forward accordingly, having dislodged the enemy's batteries. They had two batteries. Having driven them back, I pushed forward with my command. I had nobody to tell me the nature of the ground. I got on a hill opposite, where I had been, and rode forward and found out that if I persisted in going forward in the direction I was then going, I should find myself and my whole command in this almost impassable bottom of Snake creek. I was not disposed to go there. I saw a chance, as I thought, of turning the enemy's left flank. I accordingly changed the direction of my command by a left half wheel, and we pushed forward. The skirmishers were all the time engaged. The batteries changed their position two or three times, and their supports, as a matter of course, had to follow them. I did not see General Grant until about 4 o'clock that afternoon. I was left entirely to my own direction, except the simple direction which I had received at first. General Sherman was on my left, and I had some conversation with him. I told him I would endeavor to act in concert with him; that I would depend upon him to support my left flank, which he readily agreed to do, and which he did do. About 4 o'clock in the afternoon General Grant came down to where I was—I had driven the enemy back then—and told me to change my direction again. As from the original position I was marching in a left oblique direction. The new change of position would take me back almost in the original direction I started from. I obeyed his order, of course, and marched on. About that time the enemy broke, and after that I understand it became a rout. I followed them from that point probably a mile and three-quarters. I then halted and sent my cavalry out on my left, knowing there was nobody on my right, to find out who were supporting me. They brought up directly against the enemy's pickets, and then came back and reported. I sent them then in a direction left in my rear; but not finding anybody in that direction to support me, and finding the enemy on my left, I dropped back probably three-quarters of a mile and took up quarters for the night in the tents from which our troops had been driven on Sunday morning, and there I remained for the night. At 3 o'clock the next morning I formed line of battle, expecting an order to pursue the enemy; but no order came. We took up our position there and waited. The result of it all is, that so far as any orders in the battle were concerned, I did not know of any orders except the two I have mentioned. The result of the second day's battle was in our favor, and the enemy were routed.

Question. What turned the scale? What movement of the troops decided it in our favor on the second day of the battle?

Answer. It is very difficulty to say. I cannot sit in judgment on what was done, fcr I do not know what was being done. I could only tell how the battle was going by the sound of the cannon and musketry. That on the left sounded to me like a steady advance during the day. The troops to the centre repulsed our troops two or three times. I had to halt three times to wait until the support of my left came up. I turned their left flank; at least I thought I did. They were compelled to send strong columns from their centre to strengthen their left. On the enemy's right wing, I understood that General Nelson and the troops of Buell's command turned their right. So that the enemy were driven back in that way.

Question. With all your opportunities of knowing what was going on in the west, could you tell whether you were acting upon some general plan from Washington, or were you acting upon a plan inaugurated in the west? I refer now to all your movements in the west?

Answer. I can only speak for myself.

Question. Well, in all your movements did you know anything about any plans from Washington?

Answer. No, sir. That was a matter frequently discussed among us, but nobody knew. I could not see such a plan. I do not pretend to say there was not such a plan. I do not profess any knowledge about the matter. I confess to you I was profoundly ignorant in regard to the whole conduct of that campaign. I was profoundly ignorant of the intentions of it until they were shown to me by the movements of it. During the most of it I was a brigadier general of volunteers; and it is my opinion that there is not much importance attached to the opinions of such officers; and believing that to be the case I never thrust myself forward. I always believed it to be unmilitary to ask, when orders came, "what does it mean?"—"What is the object of it?"—"Is it a part of a system?" I never asked such questions. I ventured two or three times to make suggestions. I better not have done it.

Question. I gather from your remarks that so far as your own fighting was concerned, it was not done in accordance with any general plan from Washington?

Answer. Not that I know of. It was not done, as I understood it, in accordance with any plan from anywhere. You understand that it is the duty of an officer to obey his orders without questioning. Suppose I issue an order to a subordinate: it would be very improper for him to demand to know the reasons for it. In other words, that would result in having a general council of war consisting of all the officers and all the soldiers: a thing impossible in itself.

I was at General Halleck's headquarters once after he arrived at Pittsburg Landing. I remained there about five minutes. My business was to see about the reinstatement of an officer who had fought gallantly in my division at the battle of Pittsburg Landing, and who I thought had been unjustly dismissed the service. The reply of the general to my application was very unsatisfactory to me. I got on my horse and rode off, and never went near his headquarters after that. I remained in my own camp, and when he sent orders to me I executed them to the best of my ability.

After the battle of Pittsburg Landing, when the movement against Corinth was inaugurated, I found myself put in what was called the reserve, with General McClernand. Singularly enough, General McClernand and myself were both of us then major generals of volunteers. As to the operations against Corinth, it is but simple truth for me to say that of my personal knowledge I know nothing about it, except that I was there. My command policed the roads from Pittsburg Landing to Corinth. We built bridges and corduroyed the roads. My command was scattered from almost the advance to within about ten miles of Pittsburg Landing. It would have taken me a day, I think, at any time, to have concentrated my command, if I had been brought up to act as the reserve. I think I understood the motive. I have no part in the siege of Corinth—had no hand in it. I heard the guns, and two or three times I had my command in readiness to march, upon receiving orders—had them formed upon their color lines. That is as near as I got to the siege.

Question. Had you much difficulty in getting along on account of mud and the bad roads?

Answer. At the time the roads were almost impassable. I do not think I ever saw anything like it before.

Question. And yet you pushed through?

Answer. Yes, sir. At times the roads were almost literally impassable, and yet I got through.

Question. Could you account for the long delay in making the attack on Corinth, thus permitting the rebels to get away?

Answer. Of course I can account for it, by simply saying that I suppose that General Halleck, from the information he possessed, was satisfied that the enemy were there in force, and he thought it wiser to approach the place cautiously. He approached it systematically, I thought. And if the enemy were in superior numbers, or even equal to us in numbers, there is no question about the wisdom of his method of approach. It was slow, but it was very safe.

Question. What means had you of knowing the force of the enemy at that time?

Answer. Had I myself of knowing?

Question. Yes, sir; or any of you in the army. Had you any means of even approximately getting at the force of the enemy at the time you were approaching Corinth?

Answer. I had my scouts employed. But my scouts were generally sent out in the direction of Purdy. Their operations were confined to that direction, and never in front. From the citizens of Purdy, and from men who had deserted from the rebel army, we got all the items of information we received. Negroes once in a while would give us information.

Question. Would the negroes give you correct information?

Answer. I would to-day take the statement of a negro, whom I knew to have means of knowing, in preference to the statement of a white man there.

Question. They were, then, the most reliable source of information you had in that country?

Answer. I have no doubt of it.

Question. What was the practice, generally speaking, of the officers commanding our forces in regard to availing themselves of information to be obtained in that way?

Answer. That depends upon circumstances. When I was upon an expedition, having for the time being to act independently, I accepted their information, and acted upon it.

Question. And you found it safe to do so?

Answer. Certainly. I will illustrate: I come up to a house where I find a man or woman at home. I take dinner there, and ask them questions for the purpose of getting information of the enemy's movements, their position, and their numbers. Perhaps I pursue my questioning in regard to late visits on their part to that neighborhood. To these questions they give certain answers. My negro servant, a contraband, under my direction in all such cases, betakes himself to the kitchen, where he asks questions of the negroes. When we start off he comes to me and gives me information directly the opposite of that which I have received from the whites there.

Question. Which do you find out to be correct?

Answer. The chances are ten to one that the information I receive from the whites is false, while that which the negro brings me is correct. That is why I would give more credence to the statements of a negro than I would to those of a white person.

Question. What did you understand to be the force of the enemy at Corinth?

Answer. There was such a conflict in the statements that it was almost impossible to tell. My opinion was that the force there approximated to 100,000 or 110,000 in all; of which number from 20,000 to 25,000 were sick. I always supposed that their effective force was in the neighborhood of 90,000 men.

Question. At that time what was our effective force?

Answer It is impossible for me to tell. Nobody knew that except the commanding general and his assistant adjutant general.

Question. Was it, in your judgment, as large or larger than their force?

Answer. My judgment is that our force was larger than theirs; that it was larger than theirs by 10,000 or 15,000 men.

Question. How was it as to the equipment and armament of the two forces?

Answer. From the specimens of their arms which I saw there, I should say that they had quite as good arms as we had—I mean their small arms.

Question. How about their heavy artillery?

Answer. That I don't know anything about; they took them all away—left none behind.

Question. Did they lose any of their trains, and not succeed in getting them away, in consequence of the burning of a bridge?

Answer. I understood that they lost some trains by mistaking some order, and burning the wrong bridge. But what was taken then I never knew. I was informed that they burned some of their trains. It is proper for me to state here that, in answering many of these questions, I am simply giving my opinions. As a matter of course, there are in General Halleck's headquarters reports and documents which would answer these questions more correctly than I can. Of those reports I know nothing. I may be mistaken, hugely mistaken, in many opinions I have expressed. My means of information were very limited, and it is very probable that I may be mistaken in some things. Still, I have given you frankly my opinions.

Question. You say that at the time of the battle of Monday, at Pittsburg Landing, you pursued the enemy until you found you were not supported. Do you know why you were not supported?

Answer. I do not.

Question. Could not our army have driven the enemy from Corinth at that time, routed as they were, if we had pursued them?

Answer. There is no question about that, in my mind. I think we could have done it. I never knew the reason why we did not pursue the enemy. On the night after the battle at Pittsburg Landing I required my men to lie down in order of battle; in other words, on their arms. I had no more doubt that, when the morning came, I would be ordered with my division, co-operating with other divisions, to pursue the enemy, than that I was then a living man. I waited for those orders, and waited; but they never came. Why they did not, I do not know, nor did General Grant ever inform me. I have heard it stated that it was on account of orders that he had. Whether he had any orders I do not know.

Question. Orders from whom?

Answer. Said to have been from General Halleck; but General Halleck was not on the ground at that time. But I had no idea that General Halleck had any idea that there would be a battle fought, or that there had been one fought. I knew of no telegraphic communication with General Halleck. In regard to its being a rout of the enemy, I would say that some regiments in the rebel army went off in order. But the concurrent testimony given since of citizens then living in the neighborhood has satisfied me that my conjecture of that day was true—that they did go off in a rout. A Union man, who was in Corinth at the time they returned, says that he saw but one command come back in order; and that was Breckinridge's. They cut up their wagons; they destroyed their provisions, or at least large quantities of meal and flour; they left their wounded and their dead behind them. If they had gone off in order they would not have done that. It is a very strong necessity that compels a general to leave his dead and wounded behind him—particularly his wounded. I do not mean to say that they left all their wounded behind them. There were two days' fighting. The wounded of the first day, I suppose, they got off pretty generally. But the wounded of the second day's fight were not taken off. They threw away a great many of their arms. They burned some of their tents; others they left standing. Now I have every reason to believe that, within three or four days after that fight, they came out from Corinth, or their rear guard on this side of Corinth came back, and recovered large quantities of arms, and hauled off wagons and caissons that they had left behind, while we were lying in our camps.

By Mr. Gooch:

Question. Do you understand why the operations of our armies in the west have been suspended?

Answer. I have not the remotest idea of the reasons for the recent suspension of operations there.

Question. Have you any knowledge in your possession which would indicate that a suspension was necessary?

Answer. A suspension of two weeks' time, in that neighborhood, was necessary, in my opinion, in order to put the Memphis and Charleston railroad from Corinth to Memphis in running order.

Question. Is there any necessity for rebuilding those other roads in Tennessee which our army is now engaged in rebuilding?

Answer. I never could see the necessity for rebuilding any of the others, except the road from Purdy to Corinth. Purdy is near to Pittsburg Landing. Crump's Landing would also have furnished a place for the shipment of supplies to the army. That section of the road, I think, ought to have been repaired.

By Mr. Covode:

Question. How many days would it have taken to repair that road?

Answer. I think it took about two days, or two and a half.

By Mr. Gooch:

Question. Had it not been for the suspension of operations of our army in the west, would it have been possible for the rebels to have brought to Richmond any re-enforcement from their army there?

Answer. No, sir; I think not. At least I cannot see how it would have been possible for them to have done it.

By Mr. Chandler:

Question. You think they could not have done it?

Answer. I think not. I cannot pretend to any positive knowledge in regard to the matter; I can only give my opinion, from the best information I have got. But I am inclined to think that Beauregard sent what troops came from the west to the east, at least a portion of them, before Corinth was evacuated. It is my opinion now that Beauregard never intended to fight us at Corinth.

Question. The fight for Corinth was fought at Pittsburg Landing?

Answer. Entirely.

By Mr. Covode:

Question. What is the course of policy of our leading commanders in the west in regard to the protection of rebel property. What was it during the time you were out there?

Answer. All property was protected.

Question. Was it not all, or nearly all, rebel property?

Answer. Rebel property was protected in common with the property of Unionists.

Question. Was it not known to you all that it was nearly all rebel property that was protected?

Answer. It was very seldom that we did not know the character of the man whose property we came upon.

By Mr. Chandler:

Question. Were there many Union men to be found after you got into Tennessee?

Answer. I have reason to believe that there were. I think there are a great many more Union men there than many suppose; a great many more than will show themselves to be such, particularly in Tennessee; but they are overawed and cowed; they have long since been disarmed, and I think have to-day reached that point when they never will take up arms even to defend themselves.

By Mr. Covode:

Question. Was there any distinction made, that you were aware of, between the protection of the property of Unionists and the property of rebels?

Answer. I never made any distinction, and I know of no instance where any distinction of that kind was made. Under the orders that we all had, our duty was to protect all property. Now, if you ask me if that was consistent with my feelings, I will say very promptly that it was not.

Question. You did not give those orders then in accordance with your own judgment, or because you believed them to be right?

Answer. I gave those orders simply because they were in conformity with orders that I had received. I would have made my soldiers comfortable upon the property of anybody, Union man or secessionist.

Question. Have your soldiers not suffered very much when you could have made them comfortable by taking rebel property that was within your reach?

Answer. Yes, sir; they have; I know it, for I have seen it.

Question. Has not that policy been very discouraging to your command?

Answer. I have no doubt of it. I never want to command a column again through a country under those circumstances.

Question. In your judgment, will a continuance of the policy we have pursued ever subdue the rebellion?

Answer. Never, on earth. I understand, reasoning from general principles, that there are but two principles upon which you can sustain a government by the people—one is that of love, and when you cannot get their love then you must make them fear you.

By Mr. Julian:

Question. Has that policy tended to make the people out there Unionists?

Answer. A certain class of citizens it may have conciliated to some extent. But those conciliated by it are Union people, were in the beginning and are yet, and would have been under all circumstances. It conciliates no secessionist. The secessionist whose property is protected by our troops is a secessionist still. He stands in his porch, or at his door, sees our column advance, expresses his gratitude perhaps to the officer commanding for what he has done; his property is safe; not a blade of grass upon his premises has been touched. But the moment the column is gone, he is as much of a secessionist as ever, and laughs at your clemency. There is no question about that.

I recollect an instance that occurred out there in Tennessee. I went up to the gate of a secessonist, the owner of a beautiful property between Somerville and Memphis. In order to prevent his property from being injured, as his house was full of women and children, I had the negroes bring all the tubs and barrels he had on his premises out to the gate and fill them with water, and keep them filled for my troops when they passed. That man was sitting in his porch, and alongside of him were two women, the wives of rebel officers then in the army. I knew them to be such, and I knew him to be a secessionist.

Can anybody doubt what my feelings would have prompted me to have done under the circumstances? It was to have said to my troops, "boys, here are plenty of blackberries; yonder is an orchard full of ripening plums; you can see them on the trees from this distance; now help yourselves." It was to tell the boys, "come, here is a cool, shady place—a nice, grassy lawn—lie down and rest yourselves." It was to say, "yonder is a well of good, pure, cool water—draw it and help yourselves; fill your canteens with water fresh from the bucket and not from those tubs."

I recollect that just about that place a poor soldier went and squatted down in the fence corner to get out of the hot sunshine; as I passed him he made a remark, intended, I have no doubt, for me to hear, but said in such a way that, if I noticed it, he could say that he did not notice that I was there. Said he, "boys, isn't this a damned nice business to protect secesh property as we go along, and we can't get a plum to eat off those trees." I paid no attention to it, but rode along; but you must not think I did not feel it.

As a general rule I endeavor to make my soldiers comfortable, even when I am not comfortable myself; I see that their tents are pitched before I pitch mine. I see that they have their rations issued to them before I get anything for myself to eat. In that way I get their respect; in that way I look for their respect, and I never look for it that I do not get it.

During the last march I made, from Purdy to Memphis, I foraged on the enemy. I subsisted my cattle upon their corn-cribs, &c., giving the rebels vouchers for what I took. My quartermaster invariably gave a voucher to this effect—stating what property had been taken, and its value as near as he could get at it. Then he appended this condition to it, that it was to be paid for whenever Mr. So-and-so gave satisfactory proof to the United States government that he was a loyal man. In that way I got along on that march.

By Mr. Covode:

Question. Could you generally have subsisted your army in the west by pursuing that policy?

Answer. In some places you could not. There were some districts that were absolutely stripped. In other districts you could have done it. Whether you could have subsisted your whole army in that country is a different question; I do not think you could. That was the very region of country that the rebels had subsisted their great army in for so long a time; and when they left it, they endeavored to leave it as barren as possible before us.

Question. Are our commanders in Memphis, and at other points in the west, at this time, taking care of rebel property and returning their slaves?

Answer. I think not. We endeavored to execute General Halleck's order as far as possible.

Question. Did not that require you to do all that?

Answer. We never construed it in that way. I will tell you how I managed it. A man's negro came into my camp. The soldiers will smuggle them in, and there is no help for it. A negro makes his appearance inside the camp, but how he gets in the Lord only knows. In a very short time, in all human probability, you find some fellow looking around for his negro; for his bright mulatto Jim, or his black boy Sam, or Jake. He will want you to go and look him up for him. We will not do that. Then he wants a pass to go around and find him. Unless it is not a place where secrecy is a matter of no importance, we tell him he cannot have it. If he comes in and says he saw his negro in the camp of a certain regiment, I will send an order to the colonel of that regiment to turn that negro out of the camp, to put him outside of our lines. I then inform Mr. So-and-so: "Your negro is not in my camp; he is outside of our lines; if you can catch him you can do so." Where the negro belongs to a Union man, I have no hesitation at all about the matter. If I am satisfied he is a Union man, I issue a peremptory order to the colonel of the regiment in whose camp the negro is, to give him up to his master. But where I have the slightest ground of belief that he is a secessionist, I do not trouble myself to give him up.

Question. Has it not cost our government a vast amount of money in Memphis and about there, feeding and protecting and taking care of rebels?

Answer. I cannot say that it has. I am free to say that I do not think many of them have been fed by us.

By Mr. Julian:

Question. When you come to rebel property in abundance, and our troops need it, what do you do?

Answer. Well, I take it.

Question. You say the practice is the other way?

Answer. The practice is to take forage with you. But I seize the forage, giving the voucher I have already mentioned. My quartermaster takes it, and gives a voucher to pay when the party makes himself satisfactorily known to the government as a Union man.

By Mr. Covode:

Question. Would not our prospects of putting down the rebellion be better if we were to raise an army and take it down there with the understanding that it was not to be used to protect the property of rebels or to return their negroes to them?

Answer. I do not believe we can raise another army soon except upon such a principle. Our best friends there are the negroes. They might be made very valuable to us, not only to do our work, but as a means for obtaining information; and I cannot understand the military policy of refusing the proffered friendship and good will of all that people.

By Mr. Chandler:

Question. That has never been used in that army, as I understand it?

Answer. It has never been used. The labor of that class of people has never been used. How far the generals have acted upon information to be obtained from them I cannot say.

Question. Our own men have dug the ditches and built the intrenchments there?

Answer. Yes, sir. The rebels pursue a different policy. They had 4,000 negroes at Fort Pillow, and those negroes built all those miles of intrenchments; and when they evacuated that place, I have every reason to believe that they took the most of those negroes along with them.

Question. Suppose we had used negroes to have dug the intrenchments in front of Corinth, instead of using our own soldiers, what, in your judgment, would have been the difference in mortality among our troops?

Answer. That can only be a matter of conjecture.

Question. I want your opinion merely?

Answer. My conjecture is that it would have saved a great many valuable lives; I cannot approximate to the number. And another thing is certain: our troops would have been at all times fresh for battle.

By Mr. Gooch:

Question. Is it or not your opinion that the use of negroes for all such purposes as you indicate would greatly increase the efficiency of our forces in that country?

Answer. Undoubtedly. By that I mean this, more or less; it is possible to organize the negroes in such a way, making them part of a brigade or a division for instance, and giving them proper instruction and keeping them in proper order and in a certain state of discipline, charged with certain duties, as to relieve our soldiers in a great measure from those very duties that in most instances are most onerous.

Question. Have you ever felt authorized to use negroes for the purposes you have indicated?

Answer. I have never felt myself authorized to do it; in fact, I could not do it, for I have never yet, so far as I can recollect, been so situated as to feel myself authorized to issue rations to them. I would have had to have fed them as a matter of course, and I have had no authority at any time to issue rations to them.

Question. Then all that is required to accomplish this object is to authorize the commanders in the field to receive within their lines such negroes as choose to come, and to use them for such purposes as they could be used for to relieve our own soldiers and promote their efficiency?

Answer. Had I been President of the United States I would have issued that order a year ago.

Question. Would you carry the matter to the extent of arming the negroes, or would you merely use them in the capacity you have indicated?

Answer. It would be unjust and cruel to require the negro to form part of our army and do the labor of the army, and yet not give him the means of defending himself.

Question. Then you would arm him?

Answer. I would arm him. I am looking at this question not as a politician, but as a soldier.

Question. In other words, in order to put down this rebellion, you would make use of all legitimate instrumentalities which you found within your reach?

Answer. Yes, sir; and thank God for sending them to me.

Question. And you regard it proper and right to use every man, whoever he may be, who offers his services?

Answer. He would be an idiot who would not. I look at this matter as a soldier. It is to me precisely as if, in the midst of a battle, when the battle was going against me, God Almighty should stretch out his right hand with a brand in it, and say to me, "Take and use this brand, and I will help you," and I should turn my back upon it. It is a most astonishing thing to me that men should hesitate about the matter.

Question. What would be the effect upon the army of the adoption of this policy?

Answer. There are certain men in the army who at first would give play to their prejudices; and, in view of the prejudices of our soldiers, I would never, unless it was in a moment of extreme peril, ask a regiment of negroes to take their place in line of battle and fight side by side with our soldiers. When I propose to arm the negro, I propose it as a matter of humanity. I would require no man to labor for me under such circumstances and not give him the means to defend himself. I do not propose to put the negro upon an equality with the soldier. I propose to make him follow our army in a subordinate capacity. I propose to make him follow our army as a laborer, believing that it frequently happens that labor, such as the negro can perform, is of just as much importance to be done as it is for the soldier to fight in battle. For instance, I pass the house of a well-to-do secessionist to-day—one that I know to be a secessionist. I stop at his door and ask him if he has got any good cooks; if he has, I would take them, for I should need their services. To every company in each regiment I would give at least two good negro cooks, to every regiment I would give at least a company of negroes as laborers, and to every brigade of soldiers I would add a regiment of negroes for laborers.

By Mr. Chandler:

Question. And have them armed?

Answer. Of course I would.

By Mr. Gooch:

Question. And in that way you deem you would greatly promote the efficiency of the army?

Answer. Yes, sir; and as an incentive to the negroes—though it is my opinion that the great mass of the negroes do not need any incentive to join us—I would say, "Here, I will feed you, clothe you, protect you, and give you the means of self-protection. Now, follow my army, labor for us, and when this war is over you shall be free."

Question. What would be the effect upon the army by the adoption of that policy?

Answer. It would be good; there is no doubt about it.

Question. Both soldiers and officers, in your opinion, would be gratified and pleased with it?

Answer. Why, sir, do you not suppose that the poor soldier laboring in the trenches would be gratified if he could find a substitute ready and willing to take his place? Human nature furnishes the answer to that question.

By Mr. Julian:

Question. And all of the negroes thus employed in our army would be withdrawn from the plantations of the rebels?

Answer. Yes, sir; and that, I should say, was the reason above all others why that should be done. Permit me to explain my idea about that. To-day I am marching my column past the house of a secessionist. I go to the gate or the door and ask the folks about the house, and in all human probability I will find that the man's wife and children and his negroes have been left behind to take care of the property. I ask where is the man of the house. I am told that he is gone. I ask where has he gone. They do not know. Go to the negroes privately and ask them, and they will tell you that he is hiding in the woods, or else he is in the rebel army. Suppose that the man is in the rebel army. Do you not see the difference between the position of that soldier in the rebel army and the farmer who is a soldier in our army? Many of our soldiers are farmers. Take two soldiers in the opposite armies who are farmers. The rebel farmer soldier has his field hands at work on his farm at home; they plant it and cultivate it for him, and when the harvest comes they gather it and put it in his granaries. It is not so with our northern farmer soldier. When he is away in the army his farm to a great extent, if not altogether, goes untended and unsown; or if he has any harvest it goes unreaped, unless his neighbors, through charity, do it for him. Is not the inference inevitable? He must be blind who does not see it. In the one instance the man is away, but his farming goes on as well as if he were at home, and his harvest is gathered and stowed away. And do we take it under our present policy? No, sir; it is there in his barns, and we protect it for him, unless we happen to be marching as I was upon my last march, when I had permission to take it if I needed it.

Now, is it not military policy to strike at a man's operations as well as at himself? I would take every negro from every secessionists' farm, if for no other purpose than to prevent him from being able to work his farm, for just so far do I deprive that southern army of food. I would do it more particularly this year than ever. You may stop by the fences, as you go through the country, and you will see in almost every wheat fieldand cornfield last year's cotton-stalks. They have this year, in obedience to orders from headquarters, put corn and wheat in the fields where last year they planted cotton.

To sum it all up: I do not want to set our soldiers to murdering people; all the ordinary amenities of war should be observed; but for God's sake do let our armies make war.

Question. You do not want our armies to go through the enemy's country like organized peace societies?

Answer. No, sir; I do not; nor like knight-errants, each general travelling, with his train following him, in search of some enemy to fight him, and doing it upon the pure principles of the chivalry of olden times.

Mr. Julian. Northern chivalry.

The Witness. That is well said.

By Mr. Chandler:

Question. They have no such chivalry.

Answer. Just imagine for a moment a southern army let loose in Indiana or Ohio. Suppose that Beauregard's army had got into Indiana; what would he have spared? They make war; they are bold, and are powerful simply because they are bold. When they want soldiers they do not hesitate; they conscript them. Yet we hesitate. This is a moment of desperate emergency; and yet you and your friends here will not pass a drafting law. You should have upon your statute book a law which will bring every militiaman from Pennsylvania, New York, New England, Ohio, Indiana, Michigan, &c., and bring them here in a week if necessary. You need not tell me the impressed man will not fight. I know they will fight. They have shot at me often enough for me to know that.

By Mr. Julian:

Question. If, in place of acting according to General Halleck's order No. 3, we had received the negroes that came to our lines, and got all the information we could of them, what would have been the effect upon the progress of our cause, do you suppose?

Answer. It would have been a great deal owing to the locality. A general ought to exercise discretion in regard to negroes; he ought to have discretion in regard to them. There are places where it would have been impolicy for him to have pursued that course. Of that he must be the judge.

Question. I mean if we had availed ourselves of all the information we could have obtained of them in regard to the movements and plans of the enemy, would it not have been of essential service to us?

Answer. There is no doubt of it. In making war I would regard that man as crazy who would refuse information, I do not care from what source it comes.

Question. Have you ever found any information they have given to be unreliable and untrustworthy?

Answer You must take a negro's statement with allowance, from the very nature of the man. He is an extravagant creature, prone to exaggeration. When he says that he saw 7,000 of the enemy pass through a certain place the day before I would divide his estimate by two, and that would be nearer correct. I would not doubt that he had seen the enemy; I would only doubt the correctness of his estimate of their numbers. If he said that he had passed through a camp of secessionists the day before, I would believe him.

Question. Is he trustworthy as to his loyalty?

Answer. There is no question about that. The last march I made, to Memphis, was an ovation. At every plantation the negroes would come and just line the fences as we passed; and the evidences of their feeling were unmistakable. They only waited for a little encouragement to have gone with us. And that is the very trouble about the matter; too many of them would come. I could have taken three times as many negroes with with me into Memphis as I marched white men in there. I propose to use the negro purely as a military instrument.

By Mr. Gooch:

Question. You mean that you would use that number of negroes that could be used to advantage?

Answer. That is what I mean. I would not cumber my army with them.

CAPTURE OF NEW ORLEANS.

WASHINGTON, *February* 2, 1863.

Major General B. F. BUTLER sworn and examined.

By the chairman:

Question. Will you please give the committee a concise account of your administration of the department of the Gulf?

Answer. I left Fortress Monroe on the 24th of February last, on the steamer Mississippi. After being run aground by the carelessness of the captain, and stopping at Port Royal to refit, I got to Ship island on the 23d of March. I had under my command 13,700 troops, all New England regiments but three, and from every State in New England except Rhode Island. Those three other regiments were western regiments, from Indiana, Michigan, and Wisconsin. On the 15th of April we left Ship island with 8,000 troops—which were all we had transportation for—to attempt to get to New Orleans. Two of the transports were steamers, the rest were sailing vessels. We entered the Mississippi and remained there during the attempted bombardment of Forts Jackson and Philip, until the morning of the 24th of April. We had agreed with Admiral Farragut, before the bombardment commenced, that if the bombardment failed to reduce the forts and he could run by enough of his fleet to clear the river above of the rebel gunboats, which would otherwise shell us off the levee if we attempted to land, we would go out of the Southwest Pass, come round in the rear of Fort St. Philip, and wade through the marsh until we could get on to the hard land, and in the rear of both the forts, so as to cut them off entirely from any supplies, and if possible take Fort St. Philip by assault. On the morning of the 24th of April, when Farragut succeeded in getting by the forts, I put that plan into execution, and landed 3,000 men here, (pointing to the place on the map—west of Sable island, at the quarantine station.) We had to row seven miles before we struck where we could find good footing. Then I threw a body of men across the Mississippi and entirely hemmed in the forts. The night after that was done the garrison of Fort Jackson mutinied against their officers, turned their guns against them, and the majority of them surrendered to our pickets. Commodore Porter, who lay below with the mortar fleet, had the day before, the 27th, sent up a flag of truce, asking the fort to surrender. He did not learn that we had captured the men in the forts. The next morning the officers sent down word that they were willing—as well they might be—to accept the terms offered them the day before. The white flag was hoisted and they surrendered.

In the meantime, leaving General Williams in command, I had gone up the river to join Farragut and to take part, if necessary, in the correspondence between him and the authorities of New Orleans. In that correspondence I advised that the city should be bombarded unless the forts about it were surrendered. The forts were the exterior defences, and, I thought, should be surrendered with the city. That was the origin of the notice to them to leave the city in forty-eight hours. Before that time expired the forts on the river surrendered, as well as the forts at the entrance of Lake Pontchartrain—Forts Pike and Wood. At that time my steamers were all around in the rear of Fort St. Philip. Some of the men had got across on the levee, and I had to get my steamers back again into the river so as to transport my troops up to the city, so that it took us until the 1st of May to get up. I had one steamer that would carry from 1,000 to 1,500 men, and another that would carry something like 500 men. I could get up to New Orleans only about 2,000 men at a time. As soon as I got up that number I landed and took possession of the city, and posted guards in and around it. Owing to an accident to these same steamers, it was a fortnight before I got any more men up there. So that I really lay for a fortnight in New Orleans—with guards posted in a city seven miles long and two and a half miles wide—having, within the city, only 250 men, as a reserve, whom I could call into line on a sudden occasion. The enemy thought I had a great many more men than that, for my men were very busy moving about in the daytime; and it so happened, too, that the papers all said that we landed 10,000 or 15,000 troops. We had the advantage of bragging a little on our side. The men were marched about pretty lively, so that they might learn the streets, and thus appeared to be a great many, more especially as I had those parts of four or five different corps, so that it looked like a great many regiments. We never had any trouble after the first day in the city. I found, when we got there, that the people were in a state of absolute starvation. There were not twenty days' provisions in the city, and they were wholly dependent upon the Red river and Mobile for their supply. I went into consultation with the city council. We fitted out boats to go to Mobile, where they had large supplies of provisions, and from which place, before we took New Orleans, provisions were got by means of the Jackson railway. The city council agreed that they would run the boat, and even, and fairly, and honestly, to bring in provisions. At the same time they agreed to go up the Red river and purchase provisions there. Two boat loads of provisions did come down from the Red river, and then Governor Moore stopped the further trade, and said we should have no more provisions from that part of the country. Representations were made to him by the leading citizens of New Orleans that my army had provisions enough, but the citizens were starving, but without effect. I found before long that this committee that had brought these provisions over from

Mobile were very careful, in their distribution, to distribute the provisions only to the families of confederate soldiers. So that I was really in the condition simply of having the Union citizens starving, while the provisions belonging to the city were fed out to the families of confederate soldiers. There was a "free market," but it was established and managed for the purpose of supplying only the families of confederate soldiers. When I found that out I shut up the "free market" and took charge of the distribution myself. In the meantime I found, in one of the warehouses in the city, some 2,000 tierces of beef which had belonged to the confederate army, and distributed that amongst the poor. I organized a relief association, and levied an assessment of $350,000, as a relief fund, on the cotton factors who had, by a published card, advised the planters not to bring in their cotton, as they said, for the purpose of forcing foreign intervention. And upon another set of men who had subscribed a million and a quarter of dollars for the defence of the city I assessed them 25 per cent. on that.

Among the earliest things which claimed attention was the quarantine and state of the health of the city. I organized a thousand men, to be employed at a dollar a day, to clean the streets; to be paid out of this "relief fund" thus assessed, and allowed them to buy of our commissaries their rations at the government prices, which was making their employment a charity, at the same time we made them earn their living. Thereupon the city council, by way of getting up a quarrel between me and the poor men, said, "This is a poor, mean, Yankee piece of business. In the confederacy the laboring men got a dollar and a half a day." And thereupon voted an extra fifty cents a day to the laborers, subject to my approbation, hoping that I would veto it. But I answered them at once that I was very glad they had fifty cents a day extra to spare for the laborers, and that I would rather pay them a dollar and a half a day than a dollar. And the men were accordingly employed at a dollar and a half a day, for a time, and were employed from that time until I left.

In the meantime the need of the relief commission grew, until I was feeding, on an average, about 10,000 families a day, nearly 3½ persons to each family, making about 34,000 persons. About 1,200 of these families were Americans; of the rest, about 4,000 families were British subjects, and the remainder were French, Spanish, German and Italian, &c. So that, while foreign resident officers were quarrelling with us for our harsh treatment of their subjects, we were feeding 34,000 persons, of whom a little over 4,000 claimed to be American citizens. That feeding was continued as long as I was there; and that was in addition to employing about a thousand—sometimes a little more and sometimes a little less—every day in cleaning the streets and building up the levees, and putting the city to rights, generally. All the drainage of the city is done by means of canals, and we cleaned out between ten and eleven miles of canal, some of which had not been cleaned for twelve or fifteen years. The consequence was that we had comparatively no sickness in the city of New Orleans. I had a regiment, a thousand strong, in the city during the months of July and August, and it buried but one man. There was some swamp fever at Carrolton, nine miles above, where the rebels had made a fortification which it became necessary for us to occupy.

I established a very strict quarantine. I would not allow any vessel that came from an infected port to come up to the city under thirty days. If she had anything like a perishable cargo it was taken out and thoroughly overhauled and fumigated. This strictness created a great deal of ill feeling among the merchants. A New York merchant would start his steamer laden with flour from New York to Havana, and thence to New Orleans, taking a great number of passengers on board, with large freight, and if he had to lay at quarantine for thirty days, while flour was running down from $40 to $20 a barrel, he, of course, felt very cross about it—especially if another New York merchant, who did not touch at an infected port, was allowed to come up and make a large profit on his cargo. If an English or a French vessel was allowed to come, that would cause complaints from the ships of all other nations who were forced to remain at quarantine; each charging that favoritism had been shown to the other. But it was necessary, and I strictly adhered to it. That was illustrated by this: I did allow a small steamer from New York to come up; the captain stating that he touched at Nassau merely to take in coal, and was there but a short time. It turned out, however, that he did take passengers on board, one of whom had the yellow fever after he arrived at New Orleans. I immediately had the square shut up completely, allowed no one to enter or leave it, white-washed everything, cleaned the square up, fumigated it, and when the man died buried him, and pretty much everything he had ever looked at. This ended the matter; we did not have another case of yellow fever in New Orleans. That, however, demonstrated the fact that yellow fever is not indigenous there, but requires to be imported, and that it may be quarantined even after it has been brought into the river. It, perhaps, can be fully done only by military measures; but it was effectually done there, although they had everywhere on the coast—at Matamoras, Galveston, Sabine Pass, and at Pensacola, and I had five or six cases down at quarantine.

About the 5th of June I sent off the first troops I got from Ship island to take possession of Baton Rouge. I then learned that there was no other garrison, or fortifications, or guns, between there and Vicksburg. We went up and took Natchez with the gunboats, and it has been practically in our possession ever since. The mayor and people of Natchez behaved very well.

I learned that there was a garrison of 1,200 or 1,500 men at Vicksburg, and somewhere about the 5th of June I sent General Williams up there with somewhere in the neighborhood of 4,000 men, including two batteries of artillery, to co-operate with Commodore Farragut in taking Vicksburg. We heard of the retreat of Beauregard from Corinth soon after that expedition left. The next thing we knew about their movements, Villipigne's division and Breckinridge's division of the rebel army came to Vicksburg. That determined Farragut to run by the battery at Vicksburg and communicate with Davis above Vicksburg. He also wanted to get up there before Davis came down, so as to protect the other end of our cut-off that we had determined to make. He ran by and opened communication. We sent up to Halleck's army for re-enforcement, because we had heard that 30,000 men had gone off with Buell to Chattanooga, and we supposed that 10,000 or 15,000 would be enough to hold Memphis in that direction, and there would still be left a force that could be sent down to operate against us; especially was this desirable, as we had already heard that Villipigne and Breckinridge had come down to Vicksburg with 15,000 men. There was an awful mortality in the enemy's ranks there, and they never had at any time over 9,000 men there fit for duty.

Grant having sent down word that he could not send us men, that there was none left, that they had all gone forward, General Williams determined to land at Warrenton, about eight miles from Vicksburg, and fight his way up on the bluff, being aided as much as possible by the gunboats on the river. But in the meantime the malaria struck down our men, so that we brought of the force we sent to Vicksburg only a little over 1,000 well men. This prevented Williams's movement. When that force returned, Farragut ran down the river again past their batteries, and came down with us. On the way down we stopped at Port Hudson, and some men went on shore and examined, but found no fortifications there then. When we got to Baton Rouge we had a little less than 1,000 effective men of Williams's up-river force, and much less than that number went out to battalion drill and dress parade. Thereupon Breckinridge, with all the men he could spare, about 8,000 men, came down on the Jackson railroad to Camp Moore, above Ponchatoula, and marched across sixty miles and camped ten miles from Baton Rouge. More than one-half of all my effective force, after garrisoning Pensacola, Ship island, and the various forts, and Algiers, on the opposite side of the river from New Orleans, was up the river at Baton Rouge, after General Williams returned there. It was supposed by the rebels that if they could overcome my force there that I would not have enough left to man the lines at Carrolton, above New Orleans, and to guard the approaches from Lake Pontchartrain, and therefore a movement upon New Orleans would be practicable. Upon that theory they made the attack upon General Williams at Baton Rouge. But they were very badly repulsed, very badly beaten indeed. The death of General Williams put a good officer in command, but one with so little experience, and with his small force he did not dare pursue. I think if General Williams had lived he would have pursued the rebels, cut them off, and destroyed their entire force. I had issued an order that any confederate soldier who chose to desert and leave the rebel army might come into New Orleans and register his name. There had come into New Orleans up to this time something over 6,000 men, who had been soldiers in the confederate army, and registered themselves as paroled prisoners. So that I had in New Orleans nearly twice as many men who had been soldiers in the confederate army as I had of Union soldiers. I had asked for leave, which had been granted, to recruit my regiments. I recruited in Louisiana all of my old regiments up to the full standard, raised two new white regiments, and four companies of cavalry—all of men living in Louisiana. They fought bravely at Baton Rouge. Out of 460 men of the 14th Maine who were in line nearly 200 of them were recruits from Louisiana. They, of course, were healthy men, not having suffered the troubles either of Camp Parapet or Vicksburg. I ordered $8 a month to be paid out of the provost fund to the widows and mothers of quite a number of Louisiana soldiers that were killed under our flag, because I knew it would take a long time to get it from Washington, and I wanted to encourage others to enlist. The provost fund was made up of fines and forfeitures, sales of confiscated property, and two dollars charged for each pass, &c. I asked for liberty to raise five thousand native Louisianians, and raised nearly that number, including recruits in the old regiments. White recruiting began then to fall off, because of the high wages beginning to be paid for white labor on the plantations, in order to save the sugar crop where the negroes had left. I had written to Washington for re-enforcements, but they replied that they could not give me any, though they wrote that I must hold New Orleans at all hazards. I determined to do that, if for no other reason, because the rebels had offered a reward for my head, if they could catch me, and it would have been rather inconvenient to me to have lost it. White recruiting had come to an end, and I could get no re-enforcements from Washington.

Upon examining the records I found that Governor Moore, of Louisiana, had raised a regiment of free colored people, and organized it and officered it; and I found one of his commissions. I sent for a colored man as an officer of that regiment, and got some fifteen or sixteen of the officers together—black and mulatto, light and dark colored—and asked them what they meant by being organized under the rebels. They said they had been ordered out, and could not refuse; but that the rebels had never trusted them with arms. They had been drilled in company drill. I asked them if that organization could be resuscitated, provided they were supplied with arms. They said that it could. Very well, I said, then I will resuscitate that regiment of Louisiana militia. I thereupon issued an order, stating the precedent furnished by Governor Moore, and in a week from that time I had in that regiment a thousand men, reasonably drilled and well disciplined; better disciplined than any other regiment I had there, because the blacks had been always taught to do as they were told. It was composed altogether of free men; made free under some law.

There was a very large French and English population in Louisiana. I ascertained that neither French nor English law permitted French or English subjects to hold slaves in a foreign country. According to the French law, any French citizen who holds slaves in a foreign country forfeits his citizenship. According to the British law, any Englishman holding slaves in a foreign country forfeits £100.

I thereupon issued an order that every person should register himself; the loyal as loyal; French subjects as French subjects; English subjects as English subjects, &c., under their own hands, so that there could be no mistake in the books of the provost marshal. That was accordingly done.

I then said to those who claimed to be French and English subjects: "According to the law of the country to which you claim by this register to owe allegiance, all the negroes claimed by you as slaves are free, and being free I may enlist as many of them as I please." And I accordingly enlisted one regiment and part of another from men in that condition. We had a great many difficulties about it. But the English consul came very fairly up to the mark, and decided that the negroes claimed as slaves by those who had registered themselves as British subjects were all free. So that I never enlisted a slave. Indeed, it was a general order that no slave should be enlisted.

In the meantime I was informed from Washington that it would be very desirable to have congressional elections held in that portion of Louisiana which was under our control. The difficulty about that was that New Orleans was divided into two election districts. The lower district was composed of the lower part of the city of New Orleans, and all of the State below the city. The other district comprised the remainder of New Orleans, and all along the river above for 60 miles to Donaldsonville. I therefore sent an expedition under General Weitzel to Donaldsonville, and swept down through that country to Berwick bay; drove out the enemy, who were there in considerable force, and brought the whole of that region, from one end to the other, within the Union lines. I thus got under the control of the American soldiery nearly the entire two districts now represented by Mr. Flanders and Mr. Hahn. General Shepley, as military governor, then issued his proclamation for an election, in order that every man in those districts should be allowed to vote who had taken the oath, and had the other qualifications prescribed by the laws of Louisiana; and everybody did vote. There were seven candidates running in one district and two in the other.

In taking possession of that district, which had theretofore been in the possession of the enemy, we obtained possession of a region of country containing more sugar plantations and more slaves than any other portion of Louisiana. Some 15,000, perhaps 20,000, slaves came, by that one expedition, under our control; and as Congress had passed a law declaring that all slaves, held by rebels in regions that afterwards came into our possession, should be free, all those slaves became free. And I enlisted a third regiment and two batteries of heavy artillery from among these negroes thus made free. Two of these colored regiments were employed in guarding the Opelousas railroad, running from Algiers to Berwick bay; and when I left there they were still thus employed. For the other regiments I had enlisted I found this use: The planters there, while some claimed to be loyal and some disloyal, had come to the conclusion not to lay down any "ratoons" of sugar cane, as they are called; that is, pieces of cane are laid in the ground in order to preserve their eyes from injury by frost, and when the season comes they are planted and the new cane springs up from these eyes. They had come to the conclusion not to lay down any ratoons, and to preserve no seed for other crops, so that if the President's proclamation of September should be followed, as they feared, by one in January, declaring the slaves free, they would throw them upon us, and we would have nothing for them to do, and nothing for them to eat during the coming year from the crops. I therefore employed, for many weeks, the last regiment that I raised in laying down cane—cutting it down and laying it in the ground to protect the eyes from the frost. And I have no doubt that in that way I have made sufficient provision for the coming cane crop upon the plantations necessary to be worked by the government; and also in preserving sweet potatoes and corn for the next year's planting, to find employment and sustenance, if these 15,000 or 20,000 negroes should be thrown upon us, provided we went no further. I turned over to my successor, of soldiers, 17,800, including the black regiments, though I had but 13,700 to start with. The Jews, who have been, in my judgment, one half of the cause of this war, as they are among the principal supporters of it in the south, followed Weitzel's army over into La Fourche county, and attempted to buy up everything that was there for a nominal price, both from loyal and disloyal men. I had foreseen that state of things. Of course I knew, as early as any one, at least, when I was going to make a move, and where I was going to make it. And on the 18th of September, some month or so before I got ready to start the expedition under General Weitzel, I published an order that there should be no more selling of property by disloyal men, so that I could set aside all those sales which I knew would be attempted to those Jews. The army moved on the 26th or 27th of October, and these Jews followed the army and, whenever they could get by, they would go to the planters and buy sugar at $30 a hogshead, and so on. I then issued my order, No. 91, that all property in this newly acquired territory should be sequestered, not confiscated; should come under the power of the United States. Whenever it belonged to disloyal men it should be taken for the United States, and whenever it belonged to loyal men they might take the proceeds and keep it. I ordered that the whole of the property that could be should be gathered up and brought to the city of New Orleans; there to be sold at public auction, and an accurate account kept of each lot of property; the money to be subject to the claim of whoever it might concern. And I appointed a commission of the best men I could find in my army to administer that order. We got ready to do that about the middle of November; and from that time we received and sold something over $800,000 worth of sugar and cotton, and the money in the hands of the commission was turned over to General Banks when I left there. I also turned over to the commissary $160,000 for property we had captured; and into the quartermaster's department we turned over $36,000.

I have charged myself, in my accounts with the War Department, with $1,088,000, which I had received from taxation, assessments, fines, and forfeitures, and confiscated property in one way or another, in behalf of the United States. I sent home here to the treasury the sum of $345,000. When I came away I turned over to General Banks $160,000 and odd dollars. About $525,000 I expended in nine months, feeding of the poor and in the employment of labor. The rest I hold myself responsible for in various accounts and by vouchers, which I hope the government will allow, as the sums were expended in good faith.

I found, when I got to New Orleans last April, that the banks had apparently sent off all their specie. There had been $9,000,000 of specie in New Orleans, but I could not find half a million in the banks. I became very soon convinced that all of it had not been sent off. After a little examination I found that only about half of it had gone. I found one loyal cashier there, the cashier of the Bank of America. He went up into the Red River region under the name of Beef, and succeeded in obtaining and bringing down on a river steamer in barrels $625,000 in specie, belonging to the Bank of America. That was all we got back from without our lines that had been sent away. The rest of it was taken to Atlanta, Georgia. Mr. Memminger, the secretary of the treasury for the Confederate States, informed the bankers of New Orleans that the confederacy would not touch this specie; but just before I left he informed them that the confederacy had need of it, but would be responsible for it.

A negro would come in now and then and tell me that there was money buried in such a place; that a quantity was in the French consul's office, &c. I began looking about and making the bankers exceedingly uncomfortable. At last they sent a committee to me to learn if their specie was got back into their vaults in any way whether it would be safe. I told them it would be as safe as it ever was. Thereupon they brought out of their various hiding places about $4,000,000 of specie. And when I came away there was about $4,000,000 of specie in the bank vaults, and about $1,500,000 which was in the possession of the French and Dutch consuls, and which caused a great deal of correspondence between Mr. Johnson and myself, and the State Department.

I have spoken of my administration so far as regards aliens. They registered themselves under an order which I issued. The same order required all loyal citizens to register themselves; and it also required every man who claimed to be a subject of the Confederate States to register himself as an enemy of the United States, and to bring in, when he registered himself, a schedule of all his property. I waited, before I did that, until the 23d of September, till the expiration of the sixty days' notice given in the President's proclamation of the 23d of July. I required these rebels to bring in a list of their property and to register themselves over their own signatures in the books of the provost marshal as enemies of the United States, if they claimed so to be, and would not take the oath of allegiance. And some 4,000, out of a city of 160,000 inhabitants so registered themselves. I required every man and woman above the age of eighteen so to register themselves, in order to settle the rights of the United States in their property. All the rest, besides the 4,000, either took the oath of allegiance or claimed to be subject to some foreign flag. There was registered property to the amount of some millions of dollars, which I held under the law to be confiscated.

My object in doing this was to settle titles, because I had some experience in looking up confiscated titles. A large portion of the landed property of Massachusetts depends upon confiscation titles. As all property was against the revolution at that time, so all property in the South is now in favor of the rebellion. The act of Congress provides that the fact of a man having aided and abetted the rebellion, and not having returned at the time to his allegiance, shall be a good plea to bar any suit for the recovery of his property. And I supposed I might have occasion to sell the property of these rebels, and it would bring a great deal more money, and the title would be a great deal better, if I had under the former owner's own hand that he was an enemy of the United States at the time. This explains what is meant by a registered enemy—in the department of the Gulf—a man who, after the 23d of September, 1862, registered himself as a friend of the confederate government, and as an enemy of the United States, and when he did so he was obliged to hand in a list of all his property. It is fair to say that many men of large means did so.

After that I had no hesitation in taking the property of any man who had thus registered himself, and using it in any way or form for the benefit of the United States or my troops. Up to that time I never allowed my officers to occupy the houses or use the property of any others than officers in the rebel army. Afterwards, however, when I found a good house that belonged to a registered enemy, we had no hesitation in turning him out and using it, because we held that it was confiscated to the United States, and was United States property. And whenever any officer used a house in that way it saved to the government commutation for quarters.

There is one subject which it is due to myself I should say something about. I have heard something about "sugar speculations by the commanding general." I desire to make a statement upon that subject. On the 16th of May, or about that time, I was in New Orleans, and had twelve or fifteen transport ships which were under charter at so much a day, or so much a month—the United States to find them in ballast to get home again. Now, be it known, that there is not a stone in all that part of Louisiana which we occupied to throw at a dog; and it will not do to put mud into a transport vessel for ballast, because the earth would settle to the bottom, and the water come to the top, and wash about and make trouble. The only way to ballast these vessels was to send them to Ship island, where there was no wharf for a ship of any draft of water to load at when it got there; and the only means of giving her ballast was to wheel white sand into boats, take the boats alongside of a vessel, and then hoist the sand on board; and it became a question of importance to me how these vessels were to be ballasted.

In the meantime the guerrillas were going about all through the country advising the planters to destroy all their cotton and sugar, telling them it would be confiscated by the United States if they did not destroy it. To put a stop to that, I issued a general order saying that all such stories were lies; that if the people would bring their cotton and sugar into New Orleans it would have safe guard and be bought. But there was another misfortune. I had in all $75, and that would not go a great ways in buying cotton and sugar. I had no quartermaster at that time; he had not got down; and no quartermaster's funds, and the entire funds of the expedition, so far as I know, was the aforesaid $75. I went to a banker, who had known of me in happier times, and agreed to borrow of him $100,000, giving him drafts therefor, as I used it, on my private banker; and with that money I caused to be bought sugar, rosin, turpentine, &c., enough to ballast these vessels, and for a large vessel 200 tons of ballast would be required. To illustrate the advantage of this: Take the steamer Mississippi, for instance; I had her there with a swept hold; if I had sent her to Ship island for sand, it would have taken her thirty hours to get there—call it a day—which would be $1,500; then it would take ten days to put 250 tons of sand on board of her; that would be $15,000 more. It would have taken four days to have got the sand out of her after she had got at the wharf in New York, besides the expense of carting it away from the wharf, which would have cost a great deal. So that it would have cost at least the sum of $20,000 to get her home in ballast. Now, I gave five dollars a hogshead for the sugar; the quartermaster at New York complained that it took two days to unload that sugar, and that it cost more to unload it than they could get for it. He did not think that by not putting in sand I had saved some $1,200 freight, in addition to saving $20,000, which I would have had to pay.

By Mr. Odell:

Question. You chartered the vessels to deliver them back in New York?

Answer. Yes, sir; at so much a day or month, to be delivered in ballast in New York. I bought $60,000 worth of sugar, and tar and turpentine. At the same time I wrote to the War Department, stating exactly what I had done—stating that I had no right to use the money of the United States to make these purchases, and even if I had the right, I had no United States money to use. I wrote that I had used my own money, but that the government could take the property I had bought, and sell it for the benefit of the United States if they chose, provided they would answer my drafts here. If they did not choose to cover my drafts, and would inform my agent of that fact, he would take care of the property for myself and pay the drafts; for I had bought the sugar at two cents and a half per pound, when it was selling in New York at six cents; and tar at three dollars a barrel, when it was selling in New York at thirty-eight dollars. One would therefore suppose that I would be willing to take the property if the government did not want it. Being the agent of the government, however, and paid for my time, I had no right to do that.

The government let my drafts go to protest for non-acceptance, while the matter was getting settled, but finally concluded to assume the business and paid my drafts. They took the tar and turpentine for their own use; they had no occasion to sell that. The shipments of sugar that went to Boston alone paid to the government after all expenses the sum of $17,550 16, and the freight upon it was $12,436 32. So it paid a net profit to the government.

As this matter may be brought up some time hereafter, when things are not as fresh in the mind as they are now, I make this statement with your leave, for the purpose of placing these facts upon the record. I can say that I would have given, if I had been allowed the chance for the speculation, $100,000 for the profits.

Question. Did you consign this property to your private banker in Boston?

Answer. Yes, sir, of course, for I had nobody else to consign it to. I consigned it to my agent so that he could have the property to pay the drafts. The government, so far as they were concerned, let the drafts go to protest, and my friends had to raise the money to pay them.

Question. Was all the property bought and shipped through your agency not shipped on your account, and sold on account of the government?

Answer. All the property bought and shipped by me, or through my agency, was shipped not on my account, but for the government, if they chose to take it.

Question. And the government did take it?

Answer. Yes, sir. I had two views in purchasing it. One was to ballast the government transports; and the other was to let the people there know that if they brought their cotton and sugar to New Orleans they could sell it.

There was one difficulty I found then. Nobody in the port could trade at that time but me. They might buy and sell, but they could not send it out of the port, for it was not opened until the first of June. After the port was opened, this made the shipmasters grumble very much. What they wanted of me was to allow them lay days, say twenty, to go home in, five days to get ballast, &c., as the case might be, certify that I discharged them there, so they could wait until the port was open and make profit on their return cargoes. And one who was sensible enough to be discharged without lay days, actually, as I am informed, made $60,000 on his profits home.

After the opening of the port there was but one restriction upon trade in New Orleans, and that was that the trader should be a loyal citizen of the United States, and have taken the oath of allegiance. No one was allowed to teach or preach, or deal in New Orleans after the first day of June, if we knew it, who was not a loyal man.

And I would like to refer to another matter right here. I never shut up any church in New Orleans. I shut up the ministers, but kept the churches open and found chaplains for them. I see it has been commonly stated that General Banks had reopened the churches in New Orleans. He could not have done that, for they were not closed. I provided chaplains for the churches, and paid the choir and sexton, &c., out of the provost fund. And I shut up the ministers who were disloyal. One had been a private in the rebel army; another had preached against the government; and a third had expressly refused to take the oath of allegiance or use the form of prayer required by his church service.

Question. Then, on the 1st of June, you gave orders for trade?

Answer. Then came the proclamation opening the port.

Question. And on the opening of the port you threw trade open to every one?

Answer. Yes, sir.

Question. You gave no special permits to any one?

Answer. No, sir. Everybody who would pay $2 could get a permit.

Question. Did you give special permits to anybody to trade in the country?

Answer. No, sir; except to sutlers to carry supplies for the troops. I gave any loyal man a pass, whoever he was, to go into the country; and I sent an official letter to the commander at Mobile, being the nearest person in authority I could deal with, telling him I would allow neutral foreigners to exchange with him salt for cotton—a bag of salt for a bale of cotton, and pay the difference—

and that cotton should go to English or French subjects, and go out on neutral bottoms, if he chose. That was forwarded to Richmond, and they refused to do it.. Governor Pettis, of Mississippi, made a point upon it, and there was almost a rebellion between the State government of Mississippi and the confederate government, as I am informed; and just before I came away Governor Pettis said that he would send out the cotton at all hazards. My object in that was especially to keep the governments good natured in London and Paris. I wrote my action in that matter to Washington as long ago as the 19th of July last, but I have not yet got any answer to it.

Question. What regulations had you in reference to the towage of vessels up to New Orleans from below?

Answer. The only regulation was that government vessels should be first served. After that towage should be open to all.

Question. Did you, by any order, give special permits to special vessels?

Answer. No, sir. For the first month after we got there the only tow-boats there were government boats.

Question. Did those government boats do the towage?

Answer. Yes, sir.

Question. And the proceeds of that labor performed accrued to the government?

Answer. Yes, sir. The only wrong that ever took place about that was that different vessels would bribe the captains of the tow-boats to give them preference. I discharged one captain for taking a bribe. He was the only one I got at. There was one man, who had a cargo of ice, complained because I ordered up two transports loaded with government troops before I let the tow-boat take his vessel up. That was when I had only 250 extra men in New Orleans. Of course, I could not tell him then why I would not allow his vessel to be towed up first. But I have since told him, and now he is one of the best friends I have.

By the chairman:

Question. On what day did the knowledge of General Banks coming to New Orleans to supersede you get to New Orleans?

Answer. On the 23d of November, eleven days before General Banks left New York, it was known in New Orleans that I was to be superseded by him; and a bet of $100 to $10 was made in a secesh club room that within twenty days I would be relieved by General Banks. General Weitzel's scouts brought in the same news from the Teche; and a drunken broker, whom I had put on Ship island for three months, and who had served out his time there, came to General Shepley as early as that day and boasted of the fact of my being superseded; and five days before General Banks left New York I wrote here to Washington in consequence of the information I had got. On the 16th day of December, the day I turned the command over to General Banks, Jeff. Davis had come down to Jackson, only forty miles from Vicksburg, upon an expedition to strengthen the defences on the river to meet Banks's expedition. Yet after knowing all that, he, on the 23d, issued his proclamation that I should be treated as a felon, knowing that on the 16th I had turned over my command to General Banks.

Question. Have you any means of knowing the causes for your removal?

Answer. I have no knowledge. I have asked everybody I have seen in Washington, and nobody has been able to tell me.

By Mr. Gooch:

Question. What kind of soldiers do these black men make whom you took into your regiments?

Answer. I had two regiments of them guarding the railroad for six weeks before I came away; and they were as well disciplined, as well drilled, and as orderly as any soldiers I had in the department of the Gulf, and I had some there as good as any in the armies of the United States.

Question. Can any number of blacks fit for soldiers be obtained in that section of country?

Answer. Black men are like white men: they do not all want to fight. But a much larger proportion of black men will enlist for soldiers than of whites who have enlisted in any loyal State in the Union. They will enlist voluntarily; come forward of their own accord; for they take great pride in the position of soldier.

By the chairman:

Question. And their habits of submission to the whites will make them easier to discipline?

Answer. They are already disciplined. They have already learned to do exactly as they are told, and that is a thing we never can teach our white soldiers.

By Mr. Gooch:

Question. In your judgment, then, the best interests of the service require that black regiments shall be organized and taken into the service?

Answer. I have no doubt upon that subject any more than I have that the best interests of the service require that we should look for aid wherever we can get it. The black regiments will be efficient just in proportion to their intelligence, like white regiments; and, while the more intelligent white men make the best soldiers, the next class in intelligence, the next best, &c., when with the black man you strike the same degree of intelligence, the black men will make as good soldiers as the white.

By the chairman:

Question. Then you do not hold with that reputed maxim of Frederick the Great, that the more stupid the man the better the soldier?

Answer, No, sir; and I do not believe he ever said that. I want soldiers as intelligent as possible. When you ask me if black men will fight, I will give you this answer, which is a philosophical one: The very reason why they are now, and their ancestors were, slaves, is that they were captured in war, in hand-to-hand conflicts, and sold as slaves. They started into slavery in that way. They come from a fighting race, or they never would have been slaves.

INVASION OF NEW MEXICO.

WASHINGTON, *July* 15, 1862.

Colonel B. S. ROBERTS sworn and examined.

By Mr. Covode:

Question. What is your position and rank in the army?

Answer. I am a brevet lieutenant colonel in the regular army, and a major in the third regular cavalry.

Question. Where have you been in service latterly?

Answer. For the last two years in New Mexico.

Question. Were you in service in New Mexico at the time so many officers of the United States service there left and went over to the rebels?

Answer. Yes, sir.

Question. Are you aware of any conspiracy, or acts that would indicate the existence of a conspiracy, to turn over New Mexico to the rebels? If so, will you please give a statement of what you know in regard to that matter?

Answer. Colonel Loring, a well known secessionist, was sent to New Mexico, in the spring of 1860, to command that department Soon after Colonel Loring assumed the command an expedition was formed, consisting of the mounted rifles, now the third cavalry, against the Mescaloros Apache Indians. Six companies of the regiment, under the command of Colonel Crittenden, were assembled at Fort Staunton. A march was made in the direction of the Apaches, who were on the line of Texas, between Texas and New Mexico, but none were found. Previous to this the Apache Indians had been induced to leave the vicinity of Fort Staunton, upon representations made to them by Captain Claibourne, one of the leading rebels, that the small-pox was there, or in the neighborhood, and that if they did not leave they would have the small-pox. It appears to me that this was a pretence to get up a campaign, as Indians leaving a military post and refusing to return are regarded as showing evidences of hostility. Colonel Crittenden, who is one of the leading rebels, was in command of the expedition. I joined him, at Fort Staunton, with two companies of cavalry. While at Fort Staunton, Colonel Crittenden, having been drunk for a long time, was about leaving the post, and had his ambulance brought up for that purpose. He sent for me, as I would be left in command, and told me he was going to Fort Union. In the course of the conversation he said to me: "Colonel, we have known each other a long time, and I am going to tell you my plans. I am going to bring the regiment all here; I am going to bring the other companies from Fort Union, Fort Craig, and Fort Albuquerque, and I am going to march the regiment into Texas and deliver it over to the confederate States." This was about the 1st of May, 1861. He said: "Will you obey my orders, and march with me?" I told him that I considered him crazy, for he would be attempting what he could not succeed in doing, and I tried to dissuade him from his purpose. He said that all hell could not persuade him from it, and repeated the question to me again: "Will you march with me, and obey my orders?" I then told him that, as he had made known to me the object of the expedition, I would not obey his orders or march with him, but would resist any such attempt with all the force I could. In the course of the day he called to see me at my headquarters, and asked me if I would take a furlough. I told him I would. My object in doing so was to get away from the post for the purpose of defeating his object, by giving information of it to others. I went immediately to Santa Fé, and had a private interview with Colonel Loring, who commanded the department, and his adjutant general. I there became satisfied that they were in the conspiracy also. I was treated very rudely by them; told that I was neglecting my duty and had no business to come there, and was ordered immediately back. I, however, succeeded in giving notice to Captain Hatch, commanding at Albuquerque, and had him give notice to Captain Morris, commanding at Fort Craig, and to other officers in the Territory, of this conspiracy, for the purpose of putting them on their guard, and causing them to disobey the orders of the commanding officer of the department, or of Colonel Crittenden. Within a few days all the officers concerned in this conspiracy left the country, by the shortest route, for Texas, and abandoned the service of the United States.

Before leaving Fort Staunton for Santa Fé, I had notified my lieutenant of what I had learned, and told him all about it. I also sent for my orderly sergeant and prepared a plan for them to resist, if any attempt was made before I could succeed in preventing the movement. The plan was for them to seize the ordnance which was in the company quarters where my company was quartered, and resist any such order, if any attempt was made in my absence to carry this conspiracy into execution. My impression is that those officers left so hurriedly in consequence of their being convinced that they would be arrested and put in irons if they remained. They left the country as rapidly as they could get out of it. I was informed by a number of the soldiers and the sutler at Fort Staunton, the orderly sergeant of Captain Claiborn's company, and others in that company, that Captain Claiborn had made several harrangues to his company to persuade them to desert the service of the United States and go with him to Texas. And I have no doubt, from information received from others, that all the other officers who left had used their influence with all the soldiers in the country to persuade them into this conspiracy, by representing to them that there was no longer any Union, that it was dissolved, and they never would be paid by the government; but if they would go to Texas their payment would be guaranteed to them. They told them that they had promises of money for that purpose from Mr. Hartt, a man of great wealth at El Paso. But the men proved loyal, and not one went with the officers. The most of those officers, among them Colonel Loring, Colonel Crittenden, Captain Claiborn, Captain Wilcox, Lieutenant Jackson, Lieutenant McNeil, and a great number of other infantry officers, made their rendezvous at Fort Filmore, twenty miles from the Texas line, and near old El Paso. They there used great exertions to induce the command of Major Lynde to desert, by representing to them that they were under no obligations to serve this government longer; that the Union was dissolved; that they would never be paid if they remained; but they would guarantee their pay if they would go over to the confederate service. And, in my opinion, so many officers, far outnumbering the loyal officers who were at the post, demoralized the command of Major Lynde to such an extent that his surrender was consequent upon that state of demoralization, as he had no confidence that his men would fight. After the surrender of Major Lynde, the regular troops left in the department of New Mexico were mainly assembled at Fort Craig. All the regular troops in the Territory amounted, according to my recollection, to about 1,200 men. This force was wholly insufficient to hold the Territory against the invasion of the Territory under the rebel General Sibley, who commanded the Texans. We were without supplies, without money, without clothing, without means of transportation, without subsistence, and without any efficient sinew of war for offensive or defensive operations. Our condition, as I have been informed by General Canby, who is in command of that department, has been frequently represented by him to General Thomas, the adjutant general of the army of the United States; but during the year 1861, and the first four months of the year 1862, up to the time that I left, we had no relief in the shape of re-enforcements ordered by the department here in Washington, or of supplies or money. We were reduced to short rations as early as January last, and continued on short rations at Fort Craig, where the main body of the troops was as late as April of this year; and the troops in the field from Fort Craig were on short rations in the campaign against the Texans. No supplies of any kind, or subsistence, was received from the States, and the country produced nothing. The volunteers that came into the Territory and saved Fort Union, and enabled General Canby to hold Fort Craig, were brought in on General Canby's urgent and repeated representations to the governor of Colorado that the Territory would be lost unless he sent in volunteers and saved Fort Union. The arrival of those volunteers, in my estimation, saved New Mexico to the United States.

Question. Proceed and give your own connexion with the military operations in the Territory.

Answer. On the 8th day of August, 1861, I was assigned by general orders from General Canby to the command of that portion of New Mexico south of Albuquerque to Texas, and placed on duty according to my brevet rank of lieutenant colonel; and I continued in command of all the troops in the field in the southern district up to the 16th day of April, 1862, after the last battle was fought with the Texans at Peralta. Immediately upon being put in command of the southern district of New Mexico, I proceeded to fortify Fort Albuquerque, which, up to that time, was a mere defenceless post with adobe buildings. I was in command of all the troops in the field at the battle of Valverde, on the 21st of April, from $8\frac{1}{2}$ o'clock in the morning until a quarter before three in the afternoon, when General Canby arrived on the field with re-enforcements.

Question. What were the relative forces engaged in that battle?

Answer. I commenced the action in the morning with 220 regular cavalry, at the ford of the Rio Grande, against the whole of Greene's regiment of cavalry, on the opposite side, amounting to 800 men.

Question. With what success?

Answer. I forced him from the ford and drove him from his position a mile, and brought up my battery and planted it at the ford—it was McRae's battery—supported by two companies of regular infantry and two companies of New Mexican volunteers. With this force I fought the whole Texan army until half past eleven o'clock.

Question. What was the number of the Texan army?

Answer. During this time I was re-enforced twice, and at half past eleven o'clock it amounted to over 2,000 men. I succeeded, with McRae's battery, in silencing one of their batteries, destroying two guns and one caisson, and forcing the two batteries in other positions to withdraw. At half past eleven I was re-enforced by the whole of the regular infantry, 720 men, under command of Captain Selden. I threw this force immediately across the river at another crossing and, as soon as line of battle could be formed, charged the whole Texan force with the bayonet and drove them back from all their positions on to their baggage, repulsed a charge, led up two companies of lancers supported by two regiments of cavalry, killing great numbers. It was the most gallant repulse of the bayonet I ever saw in my life. The troops allowed them to come within fifteen paces of them before drawing a trigger, and then literally annihilated the leading company. After this repulse of the enemy and driving them from their positions, I changed the position of McRae's battery and crossed it over the river, continuing the artillery fire until General Canby came on the field at a quarter before three o'clock. The good service of McRae's battery had so annoyed the Texans for seven hours that they resolved to take it at all hazards, and making a demonstration to charge the dismounted cavalry on our extreme right, which drew off some of the supporting troops of the battery, an overwhelming charge was made upon the battery from the extreme right of the enemy, and after desperate fighting, in which one company of infantry lost twenty-two men killed at the guns, the horses all killed or wounded, Captain McRae, commanding the battery, killed, Lieutenant Mitchell, the next in rank, killed, Lieutenant Bell twice wounded, the overwhelming force of the enemy succeeded in capturing the battery. Under the direction of General Canby the force fell back in order, re-crossed the river, and fell into the fort. Previous to this, about one o'clock in the day, a train of the Texan army, which was yet on the sand-hills, was to a large extent destroyed; a herd of cattle stampeded, and driven off in great numbers, and great numbers of their mules captured. General Sibley having succeeded in getting between Fort Craig and its supplies, and having demanded the surrender of the fort, and fearing a failure to take it by siege or assault, proceeded on up the Rio Grande, and there being no troops to oppose him he marched through the country, and took possession of the capital at Santa Fé. In the attempt of his forces to march upon Fort Union from Sante Fé he was fought in the cañon Gloriata by the Colorado volunteers and some 300 or 400 regulars, with artillery and cavalry, and defeated on the 27th of March, and, according to my recollection of the dates, on the 29th of March his forces fell back into Santa Fé; and Colonel Slough fell back towards Fort Union on the pickets. On the 1st of April I moved the regular forces, except the wounded, from Fort Craig to make a junction with the Colorado volunteers, and the regulars serving with them, to attack General Sibley wherever he could be found in the Territory. I reached Albuquerque on the evening of the 8th of April, and made an immediate demonstration upon the city to discover their batteries. I made a feint of a real attack, intending to pass by under cover of the feint, reach the mountains, and join the other forces, under Colonel Ball. I lay before Albuquerque on the 9th, continuing these demonstrations, having set large bodies of men at work with spade and pick, as if throwing up intrenchments. Immediately after nightfall I withdrew all my forces, made a night march, reached the mountains, and in three days' forced march succeeded in joining my command to that of Colonel Ball's. The two columns on the 14th, immediately upon making this junction made forced marches, having heard that General Sibley was in full retreat, and fell upon his rear on the morning of the 15th of April, at Peralta, capturing a large train and a large number of prisoners, and killing a large number of his escort. Peralta was bombarded on the 15th by the combined batteries of our two commands, and at night the two commands advanced to a close investment of the place. During the night, under cover of the darkness, and during a sand-storm, which lasted all that twenty-four hours, General Sibley succeeded in withdrawing from Peralta and crossing the river. His rear was attacked, a large portion of his train captured, and some of his guns were taken. He continued his retreat, abandoning his guns and wagons, leaving his sick and wounded behind him, and his dead to be buried by us. After a close pursuit for 150 miles, he was obliged to break up his forces into small parties, take to the mountains, and reach Arizona in small parties, having left all along the line of his retreat his ambulances and the private and public stores of his entire command, burning his gun carriages, and concealing his guns in the changing sands of the plains, so that but few of them were discovered. That closed operations in New Mexico up to the time I left.

Question. What recognition from the government have you had for the services you have rendered in New Mexico?

Answer. My services have been recognized by General Canby, commanding the department of New Mexico, in several reports, an extract from one of which I herewith submit:

"HEADQUARTERS DEPARTMENT OF NEW MEXICO,
"*Fort Craig, New Mexico, March* 1, 1862.

"SIR: * * * * * * * *

"I desire to bring to your notice Colonel Roberts, 3d cavalry, for some time past the energetic and efficient commander of the troops at Fort Craig, and on the 21st the immediate commander of the troops at Valverde until half-past two o'clock. He was there, as he has always been, distinguished for coolness, gallantry, and efficiency.

"I have the honor to be, very respectfully, sir, your obedient servant,

"E. R. S. CANBY,
"*Commanding Department.*

"ADJUTANT GENERAL OF THE ARMY,
"*Washington, D. C.*"

I am informed by General Canby, in a letter dated Santa Fé, May 13, 1862, that, in addition to that brief recognition of my services, a special report of my services, and of other officers of the department, during the past twelve months, has been made. I also brought here from General Canby a letter to the adjutant general, in which he informed that officer that he had relieved me from duty in New Mexico, and had sent me as the bearer of triplicates of his reports and the flags which had been taken from the enemy in the different battles; assigning as a special reason for ordering me to report at Washington, that I had been in command of the troops in the field in New Mexico, and that, being mustered out as a volunteer colonel, he did not see fit to require me to serve there under those I had been commanding, and he recommended me in that letter to the consideration of the government for my services in that department. On reaching Washington, and delivering these letters and these trophies to the adjutant general, about the 20th of June, I was received by that officer in a very rude and discourteous manner. I was told that General Canby had no right to order me in on such a pretence, and that he should bring it immediately to the notice of the Secretary of War, and have me returned to New Mexico—or words to that effect. On the 25th of June General Thomas addressed to me the following order:

"WAR DEPARTMENT,
"*Adjutant General's Office, Washington, June 25*, 1862.

"SIR: The Secretary of War directs that you immediately join your regiment in New Mexico.

"I am, sir, very respectfully, your obedient servant,

"L. THOMAS,
"*Adjutant General.*

"Brevet Lieutenant Colonel B. S. ROBERTS,
"*Major 3d United States Cavalry, Washington, D. C.*"

He has in no manner expressed to me any acknowledgment of any services whatever I have rendered in New Mexico, nor has he spoken to me about the condition of the army there, although in the letter from General Canby it is mentioned particularly that I have a full knowledge of the condition of the military forces of New Mexico, and of all past operations, and requests that I may make them known. I have brought to the notice of General Thomas important matters requiring his attention, and that of the War Department, but I have not been able in any way or manner to represent the condition of affairs in New Mexico, its wants, or to get the acts of General Canby in any manner confirmed—acts which of necessity General Canby, without authority, was obliged to order.

General Canby appointed non-commissioned officers to act as officers, because there were companies there without a single commissioned officer to a company. They have been acting for five or six months as such officers; most of them have drawn no pay as soldiers for twenty months or two years. They have been at all the expense of officers in clothing themselves, in living, and in purchasing horses, but they can draw no pay as officers until the action of General Canby is recognized by the War Department. I have strongly urged General Thomas to have this recognition made, to have their acts as officers legalized, as some acknowledgment of their faithful, gallant, and meritorious services since they have been promoted. But he has done nothing either in this or in any other matter that I have brought to his attention.

Instead of acknowledging any of the services I have rendered in New Mexico, he has interfered with the President to persuade him to withdraw an order that he had given to promote me to a brevet brigadiership in the army, and I am undoubting in my belief that he has never brought to the notice of either the Secretary of War or the President the names of any of the officers who have been mentioned by General Canby for the consideration of the government for their meritorious services in New Mexico, and their gallant conduct in battles there.

Question. Can you account for this course of conduct towards you and the men who served with you so gallantly in the field?

Answer. It appears to me to be the determination of General Thomas not to acknowledge the services of the officers who saved the Territory of New Mexico, and the utter neglect of the adjutant general's department for the last year to communicate in any manner with the commanding officer of the department of New Mexico, or to answer his urgent appeals for re-enforcements, for money, and other supplies, in connexion with his repudiation of the services of all the army there, convinces me that he is not gratified at their loyalty and their success in saving that Territory to the Union.

Question. Were those troops that have been so treated the men who saved that Territory to us?

Answer. Yes, sir; and I want to say, for the credit of the rank and file of that army, that but one solitary man of them has deserted from the regular army in New Mexico during all these hardships and troubles, while all the officers I have mentioned, and many others, have deserted to the enemy.

Question. Can it be possible that these men, the rank and file as well as the officers, after rendering these important services, have gone without pay for nearly two years?

Answer. Yes, sir. It is now from twenty months to two years that the most of these soldiers have been without pay.

Question. How did the men live all that time without pay?

Answer. We had nothing for them but their clothing and parts of rations, and nothing else; but they served with the utmost willingness. Many of them made the campaign without drawers and some of them without socks. We reduced the rations at different times. It was first reduced to 16 ounces of flour, then to 12 ounces, and at one time there was no flour. The saving of the soldiers gave them about four ounces a day, but this was but a short time. At one time we were reduced to one day's rations of four ounces a day for all the men who were left to hold the post while we were driving the Texans out of the Territory, and yet I have never heard a complaint from a soldier there.

Question. How did it happen that there were so many disloyal officers in that particular division of the army?

Answer. By the withdrawal from the Territory of most of the loyal officers.

Question. How was that?

Answer. It so happened that most of the loyal officers belonging to the different commands in New Mexico were withdrawn from the Territory, and a large majority of those remaining were disloyal.

Question. If the rank and file had been as disloyal as the officers were, the Territory would have been lost?

Answer. Certainly it would, for there would have been no force there to have held it. At Fort Staunton, after the disloyal officers had all left, I found the men in bad humor, and I did not know what to think of it. I thought it might be because they had not been paid for a long time, and had been expecting it. Every paymaster in that country went off and carried off the funds with him. I formed my command—all of them—on parade. I told them it was a time when true and loyal men were called upon to make sacrifices; that the government was in trouble; that the paymasters in the country who had had the money to pay them had all gone over to the southern confederacy; that it might be a long time that they would be without pay before the paymasters could get funds to pay them in this time of trouble, and come there to pay them; but I told them it would be sure to come; that the government would be maintained; and I appealed to their manliness and gratitude, as they had been sustained by the government in its time of strength, to stand by it in its time of need; that it was the time for men to show their good qualities. After that I never heard a complaint of any kind from them, or knew a man to grumble or decline to do his duty because he had not been paid, fed, or clothed. I requested the non-commissioned officers, the most intelligent of them, to state to the men that though the officers of the army had deserted in so many instances, the example should not be followed by the men; that officers, although they were bound by a higher duty and higher obligations to serve the government, yet they had never taken the oath to serve the government for a specific period, and might have had an idea that they had a right to go when they pleased. The soldiers were, however, under an oath to serve five years honestly and faithfully, and no soldier could leave without violating his oath and having the reproach of deserter and perjurer follow him through life. The non-commissioned officers soon afterwards all assured me that the men were perfectly contented.

Question. What force is there in New Mexico at this time, as near as you can estimate?

Answer. My impression is that there are about 900 regulars of all arms, two regiments of Colorado volunteers, and probably 1,500 volunteers from California have now reached the Territory, as they were last heard from at Tucson.

Question. Do you know of anything that would indicate any fault or neglect on the part of the commanding general in New Mexico in representing to the government the state of things there, or did he report to Washington the condition of affairs there; and if so, with what success?

Answer. I have, at different times, received from the commanding general of that department a great number of letters, in which he informed me, while I was in the southern district, of his efforts to represent to the government at Washington the state of things in the Territory, and to get re-enforcements and supplies into the Territory. I had no money in the department, and yet was expected to fortify Fort Craig, subsist the army there, enroll volunteers, and defend the country, all without means. And in representing the impossibility of doing all those things, these communications with the general commanding were had. He has since told me, and that, too, but a very short time before I left New Mexico, that he never yet had heard from the War Department at Washington, or received any answer to the communications that he had made on these subjects. I will make one exception: When General McClellan entered upon the command of all our armies, and General Canby communicated to him the state of affairs in New Mexico, General McClellan, as General Canby informed me, immediately answered the letter, and told him that he was astonished to learn the state of things there, and that it would be repaired without any delay.

Question. To whom were the communications of the commanding general in New Mexico sent here?

Answer. His communications to the government are made through the adjutant general of the army.

Question. Have you any means of knowing whether his communications ever reached the Secretary of War or the President?

Answer. I have no means of knowing; but I have every reason to believe that they never have been brought to the attention of either of those officers.

Question. What reasons have you for entertaining that opinion?

Answer. I know that General Canby, in his reports, has recommended a large number of officers in New Mexico for meritorious services and gallant conduct to the Secretary of War and to the President for promotion, and not one promotion has yet been made.

Question. Were the vacancies, made by officers going over to the rebels, ever filled by appointments made here?

Answer. They were filled by appointments, but the officers so appointed had not joined up to the time I left. They have been permitted to remain all last winter and last fall at or near Fort Leavenworth. I met them about five hundred miles from Santa Fé, on their way to New Mexico, as I was coming in from that Territory about six weeks ago. But at that time the Texans had been all driven from New Mexico, and there was no enemy in the country.

Question. Are those officers who have thus failed to reach that Territory under the pay of the government before they reach there?

Answer. They are all entitled to pay, and I presume are under pay.

Question. And during all this time are those who rendered the service in New Mexico not paid according to the rank of the service they rendered?

Answer. No, sir. I was myself assigned to duty according to my brevet rank of lieutenant colonel. I had all of the time the command of a brigadier general, and exercised it in the field; and yet I have been refused my lieutenant colonel's pay, and I do not know of any officer who has been assigned to duty there according to his brevet rank who has not been without pay, except as they would accept drafts upon the treasurer at New York and other places east, there being no money in the Territory.

Question. Is there anything else that came under your observation that it would be important and proper for this committee to know? If so, please state it.

Answer. I can see that there has been great culpability on the part of some officers in the War Department in Washington in not sustaining General Canby in his great efforts to save New Mexico. He was forced to make appointments from the ranks of the best men, non-commissioned officers to act as commissioned officers, in consequence of the great number of officers who deserted and went over to the enemy. General Canby has made the strongest representations of the necessity and propriety of his action, and has urged, in the strongest terms, upon the War Department, the ratification of these acts. Yet they have done nothing; and since I have been in Washington, although I have repeatedly called at the Adjutant General's office for that purpose, I have not been able to get the acts of General Canby legalized. I can represent the hardships of some of the cases if the committee desire.

Question. State one or two of the most prominent, if you please.

Answer. One young man who had the courage to stand up at Fort Bliss and Franklin against the secessionists was thrown into prison there, and kept in confinement, and, I believe, in irons, for a very long time, and his life threatened. He succeeded in making his escape, and in reaching Fort Craig, having undergone great hardships, having been several days (three, I think) without anything to eat, and without water. He passed around the range of mountains known as the Sierra Blanca and came into Fort Craig. He gave the most important military information, and in consequence of his loyalty, and the services he had rendered, General Canby appointed him an acting lieutenant. He served in that capacity five or six months as I remember. He was my aide-de-camp at the battle of Valverde, and his conduct there was not only meritorious, but it was highly distinguished for zeal, daring, and efficiency. This young man came on to Washington in the hope of getting his appointment legalized by having it acted upon by the War Department, but he has not succeeded. He was in the service for six months and over at great expense, and rendered distinguished service, and yet he is on his board here and without pay. It is the general sentiment of the army in New Mexico that it has been ignored by the War Department at Washington. It was a common saying in the army there that it had been sold.

ACCOMACK EXPEDITION.

WASHINGTON, *January* 28, 1862.

Colonel HALBERT E. PAINE sworn and examined.

By Mr. Chandler:

Question. What is your rank and position in the army?

Answer. I am colonel commanding the 4th Wisconsin regiment.

Question. Where are you stationed?

Answer. At Baltimore now.

Question. Did you go down to Accomack with the expedition under General Lockwood?

Answer. I did.

Question. With your regiment?

Answer. Yes, sir. I did not start with him, but I was subsequently under him.

Question. Where did you first come upon the rebel camp?

Answer. The first rebel camp we got to, there were no rebels in the camp. The first place we got to occupied by the rebels that amounted to anything was at a place called Oak Hall, in Virginia.

Question. How long after you reached this deserted rebel camp was it before you commenced the pursuit of the rebels? Give us a narrative, as brief as possible, of your movement.

Answer. I landed with the 4th Wisconsin, Nimm's battery, and Richards's cavalry, opposite White Haven, Maryland, on the forenoon of the 5th of November, which was Tuesday. I marched that day to Princess Anne, a distance of about eight miles. The next day I marched to Snow Hill, where we remained one week, and then marched to Newtown. We reached Newtown, I think, on Wednesday evening. On Sunday, the 17th, we marched from Newtown to Oak Hall, and arrived there the same day. On the 20th we left Oak Hall and marched to Drummondtown, reaching there the next day. We left Drummondtown on the 26th, and camped the first night at Pungoteague, the next night at Franktown, and the third day we arrived at Eastville.

Question. What was the distance between Drummondtown and Eastville?

Answer. I think it was not far from thirty-six miles, so that our average day's march was only about twelve miles. But I will not be absolutely sure about that.

Question. Did you capture the arms of the rebels? Did they give them up to you, or did they simply disperse with their arms?

Answer. I will tell all I know about that. When we were at Oak Hall, one day, with General Lockwood's permission, I took a detachment from my regiment and Richards's cavalry and went down to what is called Chingoteague inlet; and during my absence a detachment of the 5th New York regiment, the 21st Indiana, with a section of Nimm's battery, were sent forward by General Lockwood to a lower point of the peninsula, and I saw no more of them until I reached Eastville some time after. It was in the lower country, not very far from the extreme point of the peninsula. They probably had more to do with this business of taking arms, capturing cannon and muskets, than we had.

Question. What do you know about the capturing of cannon and muskets, from what you heard among the officers?

Answer. I saw in the court-house yard at Drummondtown six or seven cannon, with caissons, that had been taken from the rebels; I think taken at Pungoteague Landing, from a fortification I afterwards saw there, and brought up to Drummondtown. I heard that there were some muskets in a jail at Drummondtown, but I never saw them, and was never able to learn the history of those muskets, whether they were captured, or whether they were found there in the jail.

Question. What was done with these cannon that were captured?

Answer. They were there the last I saw of them.

Question. Did you capture any shot or shell, any munitions of war, or any provisions?

Answer. We found at Oak Hall a small quantity of sweet potatoes and a small quantity of oats, which I think belonged to the rebel army encamped there before we arrived. But of that I am not certain.

Question. What was done with them?

Answer. We consumed the most of them. We took them from those who had them. I told them that if they were private property they would be paid for; but if not, they would be used as captured property belonging to our government. I think the conclusion of it was that they gave up any claim to the property. It did not amount to much.

Question. Do you know anything about the capture of fugitive slaves upon that expedition, and their being returned to rebel masters?

Answer. Not of my own knowledge. I have heard a great deal said about it.

Question. State what you heard among officers there.

Answer. We marched to Eastville, the southern limit of our march. We then returned, by slow marches, to Pungoteague Landing, to embark from that point to Baltimore. While we were lying there at Pungoteague, I went one day with Major Van Norstrand, the surgeon of our regiment, to call upon General Lockwood, who was quartered in a private house pretty near the landing. While the surgeon and I were there, he remarked to us that a fugitive slave had been found by his owner, somewhere in the neighborhood of that camp, who had come up from a town lower down, and I think he said he had caused him to be taken out and flogged.

Question. Who caused it to be done?

Answer. General Lockwood. Neither Major Van Norstrand nor myself made any response to that remark. I think we did not either of us look at him. After a moment's silence he remarked that "he only had the slave slightly tickled." I think he used the word "slightly;" I know he used the word "tickled." He said something more upon the subject; I said nothing. I know nothing else about that except what I heard from the officers of the regiment.

Question. Do you know whether any cavalry horses were given back to their owners after having been captured by our soldiers?

Answer. The officers of our regiment took a large number of horses which they supposed to belong to rebel cavalry officers, and I believe all of them were given up except one.

Question. By order of the general?

Answer. Yes, sir. I do not know but they all went into the hands of the rebel officers finally. They were taken from our possession.

Question. Can you tell whether any attempt was made to administer the oath of allegiance to these pretended owners before these horses were given up to them, or whether they took the oath?

Answer. I never heard of any attempt being made to administer the oath to them; it may be that that attempt was made, and it may be that the oath was administered. But I never heard of any such thing.

By the chairman:

Question. You said that all but one horse was given up. What was done with that?

Answer. I do not know that all were given to the rebels, but they were taken from us. There was one very fine horse taken by the adjutant of our regiment. He made application to the government, through General Dix, for leave to purchase that horse at its valuation, and finally consent was given by the government. He did intend to buy the horse, but finding it was foundered he would not take it.

By Mr. Chandler:

Question. Do you know what was done with those horses? Whether some of them went across the bay or not?

Answer. I do not. I know that some of them were taken home by their owners.

Question. Do you know anything about the return of arms and ammunition to the rebels after they had been captured?

Answer. The arms that my soldiers took we took in small numbers, generally one or two from a house. They would go into a house sometimes with permission and sometimes without permission, I think—not to my knowledge, however, without permission—and take them in small numbers, one or two in a place. I do not know that I recollect of any muskets being returned; I recollect that some small weapons, a pistol for example, was restored by order of General Lockwood.

By Mr. Julian:

Question. What do you know about the return of provisions captured from the rebels, returned under order of General Lockwood?

Answer. I think I never heard of any such thing; I do not now remember of having heard of it.

Question. About the flogging of slaves that came to your camps: what do you know, on the information of other officers besides General Lockwood, as to his ordering slaves to be flogged?

Answer. The rumor of that circumstance of which I have spoken ran through the camps. I heard of it from different sources.

Question. Were any arms laid down by the rebels?

Answer. I never knew anything about anything being laid down. But, as I said before, a part of the 21st Indiana and the 5th New York, with a section of Nimm's battery, went ahead of us. And what may have been done by them I do not know. There were some arms in the jail at Drummondtown, as I was told, which may have been surrendered by the rebels.

Question. Did any of the rebels in Northampton county return to their allegiance?

Answer. Not to my knowledge.

Question. Do you know anything about General Lockwood sending outside of Northampton county to get a loyal man to take the post office in that county?

Answer. One day while at headquarters, at the lowest point on the peninsula to which we marched, I heard one of his staff—I do not now recollect who—say that no man had yet taken the oath of allegiance. And I was then informed who had been appointed postmaster; but I cannot now recollect his name.

Question. There were very few loyal men, if any, in that region, then?

Answer. I do not know of more than two; I never heard of more than two men about Eastville that I thought were loyal men.

Question. Did the rebels in that county disperse by reason of General Dix's proclamation, or by reason of the military force brought against them?

Answer. I will tell the facts, and then you can judge for yourselves. I did not know what the object of the expedition was at all. I was ordered to White Haven, and to march to Snow Hill, and to be there with my force on a certain day and await orders. I was there awhile, and there received orders to report myself to General Lockwood, who would take command of the force which up to that time were with me. I did report myself to General Lockwood when he arrived, and he took command of the force. We marched, as I have already stated, to Newtown At Newtown was a detachment of the 21st Indiana, and during the day upon which we arrived there a part of the 5th New York—about 500 men—arrived there. Subsequently portions of the 17th Massachusetts, 6th Michigan, 2d Delaware, and Purnell's (Maryland) Legion, arrived; I think about half of each regiment. I did not know up to that time what the object of that expedition was; I do not know now. I do not know who planned it; whether by the President, the commander-in-chief, General Dix, or who it was.

General Lockwood sent me from Newtown to Oak Hall, on the 17th, with my own regiment, Nimm's battery, Richards's cavalry, and detachments of the

21st Indiana, the 5th New York, and the 6th Michigan, under my command. And it was on that day, on that march, that we expected to meet the rebels between Newtown and Oak Hall. We crossed the boundary line between Maryland and Virginia that day. We expected to meet the enemy during the day, and marched in such shape as to be ready for them. But we did not meet them. We found the roads obstructed near the boundary line by fallen trees; we found some intrenchments thrown up, but the enemy had fled, and we came to their camp which they had left. We were informed that they had left on Friday night. I was informed by a Dr. Watson, who was a Union man, that he had been forced into their service as one of their soldiers—impressed into their service; that he retreated with them; that they went down very rapidly from Oak Hall on Friday night to Drummondtown, and there dispersed.

Question. How long was that after the proclamation?

Answer. The proclamation was issued from Newtown, I think, some time between the 13th and the 17th. It might have been issued before the 13th.

Question. What was the date of this dispersion?

Answer. The Friday they dispersed was the 15th, I think.

Question. Did General Lockwood tell you, or state in your presence, that the line of policy under which the campaign was conducted was in accordance with orders from headquarters of the department, or headquarters of the army?

Answer. I cannot say that he ever in my presence made any discrimination as to the source of the authority or policy he was acting under, whether from the headquarters of the army or the headquarters of the department. I have an order which may throw some light on the subject.

Question. What is that order?

Answer. It is as follows:

"HEADQUARTERS PENINSULA BRIGADE,
"*Newtown, Md., November* 15, 1861.

"General Orders, No. 11.]

"In consideration of the importance attached to the present expedition by the commander of the army and the general commanding the department, and the proximity of the enemy, no officer or soldier will be allowed to remain out of camp at night, unless by the special permission of the general commanding this brigade; and any violation of this order will occasion the necessity of placing every one so violating it under arrest.

"By command:

"Brigadier General LOCKWOOD."

I was in General Lockwood's office at Eastville, and we fell into conversation respecting the policy of the expedition, its objects, &c., and his mode of conducting it.

Question. Will you state what General Lockwood said about it?

Answer. From what General Lockwood said to me, I inferred that it had come to his knowledge that criticisms had been made by some persons on his course there. He showed me his instructions from General Dix, and requested me to read them, and assured me that it had been his honest purpose to conform his duty there strictly in accordance with the instructions of the major general. I read the instructions, and I was satisfied from what I had observed of General Lockwood's conduct, and from the tenor of those instructions, that it was General Lockwood's honest purpose to execute the orders which he had received directly and literally.

Question. Have you a copy of the instructions under which General Lockwood acted?

Answer. I have not. When I started on that expedition I did not know what I was going for, or what superior officers were to go with me. I followed instructions in writing that General Dix gave me. General Lockwood informed me that he did not know he was to command that expedition until he left Baltimore, though he had thought for some time that he should command an expedition to the Eastern Shore of Maryland.

Question. I think that you have stated that on the march from Drummondtown to Eastville you averaged about 12 miles a day?

Answer. Yes, sir.

Question. How did it happen that you marched only that far in a day? What was the cause of your detention?

Answer. I do not know. The orders from General Lockwood were to consume three days in the march from Drummondtown to Eastville. The march from Oak Hall to Drummondtown was a longer march than 12 miles a day; but I cannot give the exact distance.

Question. Were the rebels in advance of you in making the march from Oak Hall to Drummondtown?

Answer. We arrived in their camp at Oak Hall on Sunday afternoon; they had left it the Friday evening before.

Question. How far in advance of you were they then?

Answer. When we reached Drummondtown I do not know where they were. I never heard where they were.

Question. I have been informed that the enemy were immediately before you, and that by a rapid march you could have captured them, with their baggage and ammunition.

Answer. We lay at Newtown from the 13th to the 17th. That was not very far from their camp at Oak Hall. They left Oak Hall before we left Newtown. I never heard of our being nearer to the rebels than the distance from Newtown to Oak Hall, which was not far from 20 miles.

Question. You do not know how far they may have been in advance of you?

Answer. I was told by Dr. Watson, a man in whose statements I place implicit confidence, that they went, and he went with them, from Oak Hall to Drummondtown, and that that was the last place they were together; there they scattered and dispersed.

WASHINGTON, *January* 28, 1862.

Captain W. P. MOORE sworn and examined.

By Mr. Julian:

Question. What is your rank and position in the army?

Answer. I am captain of company E, 4th Wisconsin regiment.

Question. Were you on the Accomack expedition, under General Lockwood?

Answer. I was.

Question. Will you state what you know about the flogging or returning of fugitive slaves, under the direction of General Lockwood, during that expedition?

Answer. I did not see anything of the sort myself; I only heard reports.

Question. Reports from whom?

Answer. From some officers of our regiment.

Question. What did they report to you?

Answer. They reported that while we were at Pungoteague, on our return from Eastville, General Lockwood had had some one of the Purnell Legion, or of the Delaware regiment—the Purnell Legion, I think—flog a slave for running away, and had him returned to his master.

Question. Flog a slave and return him?

Answer. Yes, sir.

Question. Is that all that was reported to you on that matter?

Answer. Yes, sir; I think so.

Question. What do you know about the return of cavalry horses to rebels after they had been captured?

Answer. I know there were a number of horses, from six to twelve, that I saw. The most of them were taken by our regiment. I did not see any orders for delivering them up; but I know they were delivered over to General Lockwood. What became of them after that I do not know, except by report.

Question. What was reported to have been done with them by General Lockwood?

Answer. The report was that some citizen was there and swore the horses were his, and that they were returned.

Question. Do you know whether they were returned?

Answer. I do not. I did see one little black mare that we had had in our regiment. I saw some citizen have it afterwards; who he was I do not know. It was said that she had been returned to him.

Question. Do you know anything about the capture of arms and ammunition that was returned afterwards to the rebels by order of General Lockwood?

Answer. No, sir; I do not.

Question. Were you at Drummondtown when General Lockwood arrived there?

Answer. I was.

Question. Did he make a speech there to the rebels?

Answer. He was reported to have so done. I did not hear the speech. I was down town that afternoon that he made the speech.

Question. You do not know what he said?

Answer. I do not, except by report.

Question. Did you hear General Lockwood say anything about his policy about the returning or flogging of fugitive slaves?

Answer. No, sir; I did not. I had no personal intercourse with him. All that I know about that came through orders—through our colonel.

Question. Do you know what those orders were?

Answer. They were orders to allow no negro to come within our lines; that was when I was officer of the day. I believe I was not ordered to catch them. I do not think I received any such orders as that. I know there were a number of persons in search of fugitives, who came into our camp to search for them.

Question. Do you know anything about the return of a number of fugitive slaves from Baltimore to Pungoteague, Virginia, or whether they were simply landed at the wharf, or whether their masters were sought after?

Answer. I do not. I know that a steamer came down, and it was reported to me that some slaves came in at the time.

Question. How many?

Answer. I do not know; I think four or five.

Question. Do you know what became of those slaves that came on that steamer?

Answer. I do not.

Question. Do you know anything about the laying down of arms by the rebels?

Answer. I never saw any that were laid down by the rebels that I know of. I saw a great many arms that were reported by different parties to have been found at different places.

Question. Did any of the rebels of Northampton county return to their allegiance after you went down there?

Answer. I think they did, some of them. I do not know that they took the oath. There was one man who reported himself to me as having been in the rebel army. He said he had been drafted in, and was glad of an opportunity to get out.

Question. Were there any loyal men at all in that region?

Answer. I talked with half a dozen men, I think, who talked as if they were loyal to some extent. They did not seem to be very enthusiastic in the matter.

Question. Did not the general have to look to the country outside of that county to find a postmaster?

Answer. There was a postmaster at Drummondtown at that time who was looked after. I do not know whether he found him or not.

Question. Do you know whether the line of policy under which General Lockwood acted was in accordance with orders from the headquarters of the department, or the headquarters of the army?

Answer. I think they were from the headquarters of the department—from General Dix; at least I saw the proclamation that General Dix issued, and heard the instructions that were given to Colonel Paine.

Question. What were the instructions to Colonel Paine?

Answer. They were that we were to be very careful in our intercourse with the citizens, and allow no slaves to come within our lines; they were very particular on that point, and to keep the soldiers very strictly within the lines, so as not to have them meddle with the citizens at all, as we were going there for a very particular purpose. We went down, in the first place, to protect the polls, to protect the loyal citizens in Somerset county, Maryland, from those in Virginia, who it was supposed would come over. Afterwards these same instructions, that we had applied down in Virginia, were read over to us again; I cannot remember the full particulars. I will state that I was informed by a man that I met there in Virginia—he reported himself as a citizen—that the rebel forces did not have much to fear from General Lockwood, because an agent of Smith had seen General Lockwood while he was at Newtown, and there was some kind of agreement or understanding between them that he would not harm the rebels.

Question. Smith was the rebel general?

Answer. Yes, sir. I think they called him Colonel Smith. He was commanding the force. This report I also got from some of the men who talked with the slaves there.

Question. What was the distance between Oak Hall and Drummondtown?

Answer. I think the distance by the most direct route was twenty miles; but one road was blocked up, and the way we marched made it about twenty-four miles.

Question. What was the distance between Drummondtown to Eastville?

Answer. We made three marches to get there; one, I think, of 15 or 18 miles, and two of 12 miles each. I think it is 36 or 38 miles.

Question. What time was consumed in the march from Oak Hall to Eastville?

Answer. We left Oak Hall, I think, on Thursday morning—the fifth New York went the night before—and marched that day to Drummondtown. We remained there until after the next Sunday. I think it was Monday or Tuesday that we started from Drummondtown to Eastville, and got to Eastville on the 28th of November.

Question. What I want to know is why you were so slow in passing between those points, being in pursuit of the rebels?

Answer. There was no reason for it at all, that I know.

Question. Could you not, in your opinion, have captured the rebels, with their ammunition and provisions, if you had made a quick march, such as was possible?

Answer. I think if we had started out from Snow Hill as soon as we could, we could have taken them without any doubt. But after we got to Newtown, on Friday night, the rebels left. I think they left the night after we got into Newtown, or the night after that.

Question. The rebels dispersed?

Answer. I do not know whether they dispersed or not; they left their fortifications—that was the rumor we got at the time. I think if we had marched on vigorously, we should have marched right upon them in their fortifications, and I have no doubt we would have taken them.

WASHINGTON, *January* 28, 1862.

Colonel GOVERNEUR K. WARREN sworn and examined.

By Mr. Julian:

Question. What is your rank and position in the army?

Answer. I am a captain of topographical engineers, and colonel of the fifth regiment New York volunteers.

Question. Were you in the Accomack expedition under General Lockwood?

Answer. Yes, sir.

Question. After you left Baltimore and reached Accomack county, where did you first come on a rebel camp?

Answer. We found no rebel camp.

Question. Found none?

Answer. No, sir; we found where a camp had been.

Question. Where was that?

Answer. I have not got my journal with me, and I do not recollect. We passed it the first day's march, before we arrived at Oak Hall.

Question. It was near Oak Hall?

Answer. It was nearly to Oak Hill—about two or three miles from there. We found an earthwork thrown up.

Question. How long were you occupied in pursuit of the retreating forces?

Answer. I do not think we made any march that might be considered a pursuit of the retreating forces. We got orders to march. The rumor had come that the rebels had disbanded, and we never saw anything more of them, except the ruins of camps, old field-works, and occasionally arms thrown away.

Question. You knew they were in advance of you?

Answer. We went prepared to clear the road of anything. We had information of the fact that they had all disbanded, and they must have preceded us three or four days.

Question. What is the distance between Oak Hall and Drummondtown?

Answer. I cannot give the exact distance. The whole thing consisted in a direct march, the same as I have made on the plains a hundred times.

Question. What is the distance between Oak Hall and Eastville, and how long were you on the march?

Answer. We left Newtown on Sunday morning, and I believe the whole command followed. We got to Oak Hall that Sunday evening. We remained there until Wednesday noon. On Wednesday noon Colonel McMillan, with his 500 men, and myself having 500 men and two field-pieces, left and arrived at the same place on Wednesday evening. The next day we marched 24 miles, to Drummodtown, and encamped at a mill. The next day we passed Pungoteague, and another earth-work at a place called Dr. Henderson's, about 16 miles from there, and remained and rested until the next day at 10 o'clock. Colonel McMillan went on, and I remained there. I got to Eastville on Sunday.

Question. Just a week from the time you started from Newtown?

Answer. Yes, sir; a week and 12 hours.

Question. Why did you stop at Oak Hall from Sunday evening until Wednesday?

Answer. I do not know all the reasons, but I suppose it was on account of the want of transportation and the want of provisions. We did not have transportation enough, when we started from Newtown, to take all our tents. We started with half our tents and a limited amount of provisions.

Question. You were in pursuit of the rebels during this time, or on an expedition for that purpose?

Answer. Yes, sir.

Question. If you had had the transportation you ought to have had, and had made a vigorous march, could you have captured them with their ammunition and provisions?

Answer. I think it is very doubtful if we could by going to Newtown first. It is my opinion that if we had landed at Pungoteague—however, I never thought much about that; I know that at the rate they fell back there was very little chance of our catching them.

Question. What do you know about General Lockwood flogging fugitive slaves and returning them to their claimants?

Answer. I do not know that he ever flogged any.

Question. Did any slaves come to your camp?

Answer. No, sir; not that I know of. The orders were strictly to keep them out of the camps, and there were none of them harbored there or lingering around the camp, to my knowledge. My camp was always separate from the rest after we left Eastville. It was not generally near the others. The only thing that might seem to have a bearing upon that subject was this: General Lockwood sent a Mr. Clark, of Northampton, one day to my camp with this order:

"DECEMBER 1, 1861.

"COLONEL: Mr. Clark, the bearer, informs me that a servant of his is in the zouave camp. Please give him every facility to recover him; and if found, send him to me with a file of troops. He has broken the law, and I will punish him.

"Very respectfully,

"H. H. LOCKWOOD,

"*Brigadier General Commanding.*

"To COLONEL *of 5th N. Y. Regiment.*"

There was no man that Mr. Clark could point out as his servant in the camp, although every facility was given him to look around. This is, if it could be called a search, the only one I have any knowledge of.

Question. Do you know anything about cavalry horses being captured and delivered back to the rebels by General Lockwood?

Answer. I do not know of any such thing. I have heard of such things, but I do not know anything about the merits of it.

Question. Did you hear of it from officers of your regiment?

Answer. No, sir.

Question. Do you know anything about the rebels themselves being captured and turned loose on taking the oath of allegiance?

Answer. No, sir.

Question. Were you at Drummondtown when General Lockwood arrived there?

Answer. No, sir; I do not know exactly where we were. I suppose we were at Eastville when he got to Drummondtown.

Question. Do you know anything about restoring arms and ammunition to the rebels after they had been captured?

Auswer. No, sir.

Question. Do you know anything about contrabands that came on board a vessel from Virginia to Baltimore that were said to have been delivered up?

Answer. Yes, sir.

Question. Were they landed at the wharf?

Answer. I will tell you what I know about that. I was ordered to return to Baltimore with the 17th Massachusetts regiment when it got orders to return home. I was not very well at the time, and General Lockwood ordered me home on that steamer, and my regiment returned afterwards under command of the lieutenant colonel. I know what he told me—that some three or four colored men secreted themselves on board when he lay at Pungoteague, and came to Baltimore, and he gave them up to the civil authorities.

Question. Who gave them up?

Answer. Lieutenant Colonel Duryea, of the 5th New York regiment.

Question. Were the claimants of those fugitives there demanding them?

Answer. Not that I know of; I presume they were not.

Question. Did General Lockwood cause inquiries to be made at Baltimore for the claimants?

Answer. General Lockwood has not been at Baltimore at all since then. He remained at Eastville, or at Pungoteague, or Drummondtown, somewhere there. He did not come up with any troops, and I do not know that he has ever been to Baltimore since.

Question. Were there any loyal people in Northampton county?

Answer. I should say that strictly there were none—none that I saw. They were of this class of people, opposed to taking up arms. All that I saw claimed to be opposed to taking up arms against the government; considered that the vote of Maryland had settled their policy, that their interests were one; but their sympathies and feelings in the rebellion were with the south.

Question. Did any of them return to their allegiance?

Answer. I think they did.

Question. Did they all take the oath?

Answer. It was not done when I was there. I saw a great deal of them. The citizens of Northampton county came very freely into the camp, and we had very free and frequent conversations with them.

Question. Can you tell whether the rebels dispersed on account of General Dix's proclamation, or on account of the military force you brought against them?

Answer. I think it was both combined—the proclamation backed by the military force.

Question. Was the line of policy that General Lockwood adopted in accordance with orders from the headquarters of the department, or the headquarters of the army?

Answer. That I do not know. I supposed he acted under instructions from General Dix; they were authorized, I believe, at the headquarters of the army. That, of course, is entirely outside of my knowledge.

Question. Did you ever see General Lockwood's instructions, under which he acted?

Answer. No, sir.

Question. You do not know what they were?

Answer. No, sir.

WASHINGTON, *January* 28, 1862.

Colonel G. K. WARREN sworn and examined.

By Mr. Chandler:

Question. Were you in the affair at Big Bethel, Virginia?

Answer. Yes, sir.

Question. What was your rank then?

Answer. I was lieutenant colonel of the 5th New York regiment—zouaves.

Question. Will you give us a brief account of what you know of that affair?

Answer. I was officer of the day the day before, and joined my regiment at 9 o'clock in the morning. I had been on the ground six days previously, and had reconnoitred it, though nobody there present knew that I had done so. When I arrived on the ground two companies of our regiment were deployed as skirmishers in advance, skirmishing along at least half a mile in front of the whole command. The rest of the regiment were drawn up in line of battle, and two other regiments were in the road just to the rear. Everything was halted then. I asked and obtained permission to join the reconnoitring party. This advanced party had discovered that there was an enemy there in position. I went forward with the two companies of skirmishers and ordered an advance. We advanced pretty close up to the swamp or creek in front of the position, and as we did so the enemy opened on us with artillery down the road, the balls going over our heads. We pushed up as rapidly as we could, until we got within 200 or 300 yards. When they saw us their fire was directed in the woods where we were, and it was pretty heavy. I ordered a halt, and went back to report. Our regiment was ordered up to support, and took position in front of the battery, but sheltered by the woods. Lieutenant Greble came up with guns and drove away the enemy's guns, which commanded the road; they were not protected. I stayed in front long enough to see that they had guns under cover of some work. I then went back and reported, or suggested, to Colonel Duryea that we better hold on to the position we had.

I went back and informed General Pierce of the state of things, and told him that he better send one regiment around on each flank to get across the creek, and as soon as they commenced firing on the flank we could go in on the front. He told me to convey that order to the colonels. The order was given and the movement was commenced. The 3d regiment had a chance to go under cover, by going off to the left about half a mile, and could have gone down across the swamp and got behind the battery, all the time being under cover of the woods. But the direction to do so was not specific. I supposed at the time that they had all the information they might have had, and I did not give specific instructions. I only told them to go. They went right across the field, and when they got pretty close up they had a pretty heavy fire from the battery. They fell back to a position towards where we were.

Question. Then if they had gone around they would have flanked the battery?

Answer. Yes, sir.

Question. That was the intended order?

Answer. Yes, sir. If Colonel Townsend had gone into the woods the enemy would have been compelled, judging from what I have since learned, to have left the ground at once, or run the risk of having everything captured. He would have been masked, and they would not know where he was until he had taken the battery in the rear. A portion of the regiment on the other flank did cross the creek, so I am informed, but they were not in a good position, but were brought pretty near as much in front of the battery as we were. After that I did not hear any further commands given. We remained in position under fire for two hours, pretty well sheltered by the woods.

Question. Your men firing during the time?

Answer. Some of the time, but not much. We remained there waiting orders. I was with my regiment, and did not see General Pierce. I supposed he was waiting for re-enforcements, as we had two regiments on the road coming up. They did come up, and finally took position in front, where they were directed, I believe. Then General Pierce called a meeting of the colonels about what should be done, and news of some sort came from General Butler by his aid. I am sorry to say they all determined that we had better retire. I opposed it myself.

Question. You think the battery might have been easily carried?

Answer. Yes, sir; I am certain of it. Then they went off the ground. I told General Pierce that if he was going to retire that he ought to make the same disposition as if he was going to advance. He detailed a regiment, as he says, to cover a retreat. From what I knew of the troops there, I urged him to stay himself in the rear. My own regiment was the first that was ordered off. He did not remain, and the regiment he ordered did not remain. They all went right off, one after the other—marched off as they did off parade. The men were as well under command as at any time. The 2d New York regiment brought off a gun.

While this charge was going on Lieutenant Greble was killed away up in front at his gun. His cannon was spiked by his men, as they could not draw it off, and the second New York drew it off, and ten men of the first New York regiment brought away his limber and the body after all that. And then Dr. Winslow and myself remained on the ground, I think, an hour and a half, and brought off the wounded we thought could live, every one of them; we had to draw them off in hand-carts. I thought at the time they abandoned the battery, about the time these re-enforcements came up, was a good time to have taken possession there. I think they left the works while we were on the ground. We saw no one. We went up all through the woods and were not fired at. I was dressed in this red zouave uniform. I went down with six or seven men about one o'clock in the day, and put Lieutenant Greble on the limber and went right down the road in plain sight. There was no general there at the fight at all.

Question. And the men were not well handled I suppose?

Answer. General Pierce, as I have learned since from the proceedings of the court-martial, was never mustered into the service of the United States, and really had no right to command the colonels there, and I think he felt it, though they did not know it.

Question. Are there any other material points that you think of?

Answer. I think the plan of the fight, which was got up beforehand, from the very beginning involved a failure, so much so that I was ready to state that it was planned for a failure, and must have been one except by great good luck.

Question. What were the particulars of the plan, as briefly as you can state them?

Answer. It was planned for a night attack with very new troops, some of them had never been taught even to load and fire. It was planned to proceed from two different points, distant from each other six or seven miles. The ground between was unknown, and then the map which General Butler furnished was a wrong map, made in 1819, and the roads were all laid down wrong. The specific points of instructions were that the troops at Newport News being some three miles nearer should start about an hour after the others. The true state of the case was that they were about four miles nearer, and that brought on the collision which took place, and which was inevitable. I think the two regiments, when they arrived on the ground in the early morning, finding things not at all as they had been instructed, were justified in firing on each other. I am satisfied of that.

WASHINGTON, *January* 28, 1862.

Colonel S. A. BEAN sworn and examined.

By Mr. Julian:

Question. What is your rank and position in the army?

Answer. I am lieutenant colonel of the 4th Wisconsin regiment.

Question. Were you in this Accomac expedition, under General Lockwood?

Answer. I was.

Question. Whereabouts did you first come upon the camp of the rebels after reaching that county, or a camp that had been occupied by the rebels?

Answer. We came on their camping ground at Oak Hall, about twelve miles south of the Maryland and Virginia line.

Question. How long were you in pursuit of the enemy?

Answer. I do not know that we were properly in pursuit of them at all.

Question. You thought you were, I presume?

Answer. No, sir; I do not know that we thought we were.

Question. You went down there after them, did you not?

Answer. Yes, sir; we went after them. We thought we were to have a battle; thought we would meet them when we were at Newtown, that is, near the border; but after we got to Oak Hall we knew they were all dispersed. But beyond that, we did not know what was the reason of our action at all.

Question. What did you do when you found their camp evacuated?

Answer. We were marched to their camp, and camped upon the same ground that they had, and waited there three or four days, and then went to Drummondtown.

Question. Were you at Drummondtown when General Lockwood arrived there?

Answer. Yes, sir.

Question. Did he make a speech to the people there?

Answer. Yes, sir; he accompanied the army previous to that. He took command of the army at Newtown. He made a speech to the people at Drummondtown.

Question. Did you hear the speech?

Answer. I did not. I heard numerous accounts of it.

Question. You do not know what he did say?

Answer. Not positively; I only know from hearsay.

Question. What was the purport of the speech as you learned from others?

Answer. I learned from others that the purport of the speech was to assure the people of the security of their slave property, and of his sympathy with them in holding slaves; that he was a slaveholder himself, and his father had been before him; and he advised them to punish their slaves very severely if they attempted to run away. That, I think, was the general purport of the speech as I heard from others.

Question. Did you learn that he avowed any policy in regard to returning fugitives? Was there anything said about that in that speech?

Answer. No, sir; I do not recollect that there was anything said about that.

Question. What was the distance between Oak Hall and Drummondtown?

Answer. About twenty or twenty-one miles.

Question. How far from Drummondtown to Eastville?

Answer. About thirty-five miles.

Question. How much time did you consume between Oak Hall and Eastville?

Answer. We were twelve days from the time we started to the end of our journey.

Question. Where did you tarry?

Answer. We tarried at Oak Hall four days.

Question. Why did you tarry there so long; and why did you consume so much time in marching between those places?

Answer. I do not know.

Question. Was there any military necessity that you know of?

Answer. No, sir; I do not think there was.

Question. Do you know where the rebels were that you were hunting? How near them were you at any time in that march?

Answer. We arrived at Oak Hall on Sunday. They broke up their camp the Friday night before, as I understood from parties on the ground, and we supposed that they were just south of us trying to escape. We did not know positively that they were.

Question. Your march was in the direction of the rebels, as you supposed?

Answer. Yes, sir.

Question. What is your opinion about whether you could have overtaken them or not if you had made a quick, rapid movement, as you might have done, instead of occupying twelve days?

Answer. It was said that the rebels had dispersed; that they had gone to their several homes. We could never have overtaken them that way; but we understood, from popular rumor and reports of responsible persons, that there was a large body of troops there who had been in the regular service who had fled south, gone beyond Eastville, and were trying to escape over to the main land. I suppose if we had made a rapid march, we might have overtaken them.

By Mr. Chandler:

Question. What was the number of that body of rebels?

Answer. About six hundred, according to our information.

Question. What do you know about General Lockwood's flogging slaves?

Answer. Nothing positively; nothing except what I have heard said.

Question. Did you hear it from officers?

Answer. Yes, sir.

By Mr. Julian:

Question. From officers who professed to know?

Answer. Who professed that General Lockwood told them he had done it.

Question. Did they mention any particular cases he had mentioned?

Answer. There were two officers who told me that General Lockwood told them that he had caused runaways to be flogged.

Question. Do you know anything about the capture of some cavalry horses from the enemy?

Answer. Yes, sir.

Question. How many were there, and what was done with them?

Answer. There were a good number of horses taken. I took some myself—three horses—in connexion with other officers under my direction. They were all returned but one.

Question. To their owners?

Answer. Yes, sir.

Question. Under whose orders?

Answer. The general's.

By Mr. Chandler:

Question. Had you satisfactory evidence that they had been used by the rebels?

Answer. Yes, sir.

Question. And their owners were rebels?

Answer. Well, sir, that point was the point of dispute. I took one horse which was reported to me as belonging to Captain Henderson, at Drummondtown, who was captain of a cavalry company there. Afterwards his brother, a Dr. Henderson, appeared and claimed him. He brought before me a certificate from the general, guaranteeing the possession of the horse to him, and I refused to deliver the horse upon the certificate without further explanation. So I took Dr. Henderson and his certificate to the general, and asked him about it. The general told me that the doctor claimed the horse as his. I told the general I knew the doctor claimed the horse, but I also knew the horse had been used by his brother, a captain in the rebel service, and with the doctor's consent. The doctor said it was not with his consent. I asked him if he did not know that his brother took the horse. He said "Yes." I asked him if he ever demanded the horse of his brother, and he said "No." I asked if his brother and his horse had not been frequently at his house. He acknowledged that he could have taken him at any time. I then asked him if it was not with his consent that his brother had taken his horse. He said he supposed it was. But the general afterwards gave him up.

Question. How many horses, in all, were captured?

Answer. I could not say exactly; quite a number.

Question. Did you understand, from information from others, that they were all delivered back?

Answer. Not absolutely all. There were some of the horses for whom no claimants appeared. I took no horses for whom claimants appeared.

Question. Most of them were delivered up?

Answer. Yes, sir; all but a very few.

Question. Were there any loyal people down there?

Answer. In Accomac county there were. In Northampton county there were none that I found. My sources of information were quite numerous.

Question. Did any people take the oath of allegiance to the government?

Answer. None that I heard of.

Question. Do you know whether any of these horses were taken over the bay to the Virginia side?

Answer. No, sir; I do not know that, of course. I should have stated, perhaps, in connexion with that affair about Henderson, that I was informed by his own slaves that his brother was in a regiment in the rebel service.

Question. Did you capture any arms and ammunition?

Answer. Personally, I did not take any arms. My soldiers did.

Question. That is what I mean. What was done with them?

Answer. There were a few muskets taken; that is all. A few were found in the woods. I sent out a company one time, having received some information, and they found a few muskets—five muskets—and some ammunition buried in the woods.

Question. What was done with them?

Answer. They were handed over to the general.

Question. What did he do with them?

Answer. I do not know. I presume, of course, he kept them. They were army muskets.

Question. Were you at Baltimore when some contrabands were brought on a steamboat there?

Answer. No, sir. There were some contrabands brought to Pungoteague while I was there. They did not come from Baltimore.

Question. How many were there?

Answer. There were five, I believe.

Question. Do you know what became of them?

Answer. Returned to their owners, I think.

Question. Rebel owners?

Answer. Yes, sir. These went to Baltimore, and came back. I did not see them until they came back.

By Mr. Julian:

Question. Do you know anything about General Lockwood, hunting for a postmaster, having to go outside of Northampton county to find a postmaster who was loyal?

Answer. Nothing except rumor; that was the rumor.

Question. Do you know whether the rebels dispersed by reason of General Dix's proclamation, or of your presence there with a military force?

Answer. It is a difficult thing to tell the motives in their minds for dispersing. I know they dispersed at the time they received the proclamation. I know that soldiers who were in the army there say that they dispersed on account of exaggerated reports that they received of our forces.

Question. Do you know what General Lockwood's instructions were?

Answer. I heard of them, but I did not see them.

Question. Do you remember the substance of them?

Answer. I do not; I cannot tell.

By Mr. Chandler:

Question. Did you capture an amount of provisions, (bacon, &c.,) at any point where you were, that was supposed to have belonged to the rebel army?

Answer. No, sir; we took nothing of that kind. We made no captures of that sort.

Question. Do you know anything about compensating the rebel owners of property for what was taken by our army?

Answer. Property that was reported to have been stolen. I know that soldiers took things, and the most abundant compensation was made for everything that was taken, or claimed to have been taken.

Question. Large compensation?

Answer. Yes, sir; according to the general's order.

Question. In every instance?

Answer. Yes, sir.

Question. Even where they were known to be rebels?

Answer. Yes, sir. I did not learn that any distinction at all was made between rebels and others.

Question. As a rule, the property of rebels was always given up, or paid for by the commanding general of your division?

Answer. Yes, sir.

WASHINGTON, *January* 28, 1862.

Major EDWARD BACON sworn and examined.

By Mr. Chandler:

Question. What is your rank and position in the army?

Answer. Major of the 6th Michigan.

Question. Were you connected with the expedition to Accomac county, Virginia, under General Lockwood?

Answer. Yes, sir.

Question. When did you first come to where a rebel camp had been?

Answer. On Sunday, November 17; at least, I think that is the time.

Question. After finding this camp that the enemy had left, how long did you wait before you went in pursuit of the enemy?

Answer. Until November 21.

Question. Four days?

Answer. Yes, sir.

Question. Do you know of any reason for that long delay?

Answer. I am not familiar with the nice points of the quartermaster's department; but I know of no reason. I know it was unnecessary.

Question. Had you pressed on with the expedition, is it your opinion that you might have overtaken and captured the enemy?

Answer. Yes, sir. I could have killed enough of them to have given every one of my men a scalp, if they had let me.

Question. You know of no reason for the delay?

Answer. Nothing but mercy and leniency.

Question. It was a peace-principle expedition?

Answer. That is it.

Question. Can you tell me the distance between Oak Hall and Drummondtown?

Answer. It was variously stated at twenty-one or twenty-two miles.

Question. Do you know the distance from Drummondtown to Eastville?

Answer. It is thirty-five miles.

Question. Then the distance from Oak Hall to Eastville is fifty-six or fifty-seven miles?

Answer. Just about that.

Question. What time did you occupy in making the march from Oak Hall to Eastville?

Answer. We left Oak Hall November 21, and reached Eastville November 28. We arrived at Oak Hall, from Newtown, on the 17th.

Question. So that, in point of fact, you were some twelve days in getting from Newtown to Eastville?

Answer. Yes, sir.

Question. Do you know anything about the rendition of fugitive slaves, or the flogging of any fugitives by order of General Lockwood?

Answer. I know it circumstantially, but not from my own sight.

Question. State what you know.

Answer. At Drummondtown one slave having attempted to escape, or having escaped, I could not state which, the sentence against him was, to be whipped with fifteen lashes. The blows were inflicted by one Massey, or Macy, who was put in jailer as a Union man, the old jailer being supposed to be a secessionist. One or two of my men boarded there.

Question. That was done by order of the commanding general?

Answer. That was the statement.

Question. Was the owner of this slave reputed to be a secessionist?

Answer. On that point I could not state. He seemed to be possessed of the same idea that all seemed to have, that their bondage was at an end when the northern army came near them.

By Mr. Gooch:

Question. He ran away and came to your lines?

Answer. That was the substance of the report, as stated. I know that is what the negroes believed all about us, and supposed so at first.

By Mr. Chandler:

Question. Supposed they would be protected when they came within our lines?

Answer. Yes, sir.

Question. Do you know anything about any cavalry horses being taken and given back?

Answer. I know quite a number of horses were captured that had been used by the enemy, and those horses were given back to the people on various grounds. There was some sort of investigation. Men came and claimed their horses, and the general heard their statements, and they usually received back their horses. Many of the horses, however, were not given back, but were kept by the general, or under his control in some way.

Question. As a rule, were they given up or retained?

Answer. They were taken away from their captors, but what disposition was made of them, after they left our possession, I could not tell. But I have no doubt, from statements made to me, that the most of them were given back to citizens. Those persons to whom they were given back generally represented themselves to be Union men, or the horses were claimed by Union men, or some claimed a share or interest, or that the secessionist who had used him did not really own him, or that the Union men had been compelled to let them be used. There was every possible dodge resorted to to get back their horses.

Question. Horses that were known to have been in the service of the enemy?

Answer. Yes, sir.

Question. Do you know of any of these horses having been sent across the Chesapeake to the other side, after having been given up?

Answer. No, sir.

Question. Do you know whether any of these rebels who professed to lay down their arms were required to take the oath of allegiance?

Answer. I do not know that any of them were. There was an offer—as I understood it, being frequently in the general's quarters, and hearing the statement—that they might take the oath of allegiance; and some few did voluntarily take it.

Question. Do you know whether any of those men to whom horses were given back took the oath of allegiance before they received back their horses?

Answer. It was not required. Whether they did take it or not I do not know. When I say it was not required, I mean that that was the universal understanding of the matter; inasmuch as, by the proclamation under which we went out, if they laid down their arms, they were to be protected in their property.

Question. They were not required to take any oath of allegiance?

Answer. Nothing was stated about the oath there. It was the common understanding that no oath was required.

Question. Do you know anything about the capture of arms or ammunition?

Answer. Yes, sir; we captured both arms and ammunition in considerable quantities, but a very inferior quality of arms, (flint-lock muskets, old swords, and the like,) the better quality having disappeared. These arms were universally found concealed. There may have been some exceptions that I do not know of. Most all were concealed, either in houses or buried in the ground or in the woods. We found scarcely any arms that would be really dangerous, except some cannon.

Question. The cannon you took possession of and kept, I suppose?

Answer. They were at Drummondtown when I last saw them.

Question. Do you know anything about the capture of ammunition in any considerable quantities?

Answer. No, sir; nor of arms in any considerable quantity. We brought in a small number of arms at a time, which were found concealed.

Question. Did you capture any considerable amount of forage or provisions that belonged to the rebels?

Answer. No, sir; not that I know of.

Question. How were the people in that region? Were there many Union people there?

Answer. No, sir.

Question. Mostly secessionists?

Answer. Yes, sir.

Question. When forage, or property of any sort, kind, or description, was taken from these rebels, were they remunerated for it?

Answer. I know that we usually took fodder to sleep on rather than sleep on the ground; and if we had horses to feed, and there was no feed provided by the quartermaster, we usually took fodder. It was cornstalks and corn leaves. They did not have hay in that country. Sometimes we found straw, and took a sufficient quantity for our use. That was strictly forbidden; but the orders became a dead letter.

By Mr. Julian:

Question. Did you pay for it?

Answer. I understood that they were well paid for it every time.

Question. Do you know anything about any slaves having been returned from Baltimore to Pungoteague, Virginia?

Answer. I saw a small steamboat arrive, and it was generally understood that there were four or five runaway slaves on the boat, who had gone up with the 5th (Zouave) New York regiment, and were brought back.

Question. Do you know anything about a speech that General Lockwood made on that expedition to the people at Drummondtown?

Answer. I heard a portion of it.

Question. What was the character of that speech?

Answer. I viewed it something in this form: "Will your negroes be taken away from you? No. If any slaves come inside of the lines, you may search for them. I am not a slave-catcher; but you shall have every opportunity to get your negroes back. If necessary, I will have the men brought out of the tents, the tents struck, and the men formed in a hollow square, and you may then go through and search for your slaves." He proceeded further in reviewing General Dix's proclamation; said that every word of General Dix's proclamation should be carried out; that they should be protected in their property. He advised them to meet on a certain day in the magisterial districts, and vote to annex themselves to Maryland; follow Western Virginia as an example. Speaking of himself, he said he was a slaveholder, and that they should be protected in their right to their slaves.

Question. Can you tell whether any arms were laid by down by bodies of rebels?

Answer. I know of none.

Question. They dispersed without their arms?

Answer. They concealed their arms systematically.

Question. Do you know whether any returned to their allegiance, or took the oath of allegiance?

Answer. I do not know of anything of the kind. I heard that a few did take the oath of allegiance.

Question. None, of your own personal knowledge?

Answer. No, sir; it was the general understanding that a few took it.

Question. Do you know whether the general went out of Northampton county to find a loyal man to keep the post office in Northampton county?

Answer. I do not know. I heard such a report, but I do not know anything on that point.

Question. Do you know whether the rebels dispersed on account of General Dix's proclamation, or on account of your force?

Answer. On account of our force, and the proclamation assuring them protection in their property.

Question. What was their manner towards you when you were among them? Did they act like loyal citizens?

Answer. No, sir; only waiting a chance to rise again.

Question. Then, in your opinion, the pacification was not a very important matter, so far as this government was concerned?

Answer. Worth nothing except while one or two small garrisons are there.

The people are weak and cowardly; inferior to their own slaves, the majority of them, and may be held down by a small number of troops.

Question. Did General Lockwood state that his line of conduct was in accordance with instructions had from headquarters?

Answer. He referred to some instructions for his conduct.

Question. Did you ever see those instructions?

Answer. I saw a lengthy paper in his hands, but did not read it.

By Mr. Gooch:

Question. Did you hear it read?

Answer. I heard a few lines read, that was all.

By Mr. Chandler:

Question. You took no prisoners of war?

Answer. One of my captains took a rebel ceptain, (Captain Fletcher,) who was a prisoner when I came away. There were two or three other rebel officers that my men captured, who were handed over to General Lockwood. Others were let go. The general made this distinction: that those who had been made to serve by compulsion he would let go, but the volunteers—the regulars, as they were called by the secessionists—ought to be arrested if the officers could be found.

By Mr. Gooch:

Question. Do you know whether this Captain Fletcher was subsequently released?

Answer. I do not know what became of him. There were two or three others brought in by this same captain of mine. He seemed to have a peculiar faculty for hunting them up.

By Mr. Chandler:

Question. On the whole, you had rather a peaceable expedition?

Answer. We did not see any blood let, or a blow struck. The object was to bring about a good feeling towards our government by an exhibition of good will towards them.

Question. Did you see any exhibition of good feeling towards our government?

Answer. Not the least of it.

Question. What was your opinion about the sympathies of General Lockwood—that they were with our troops or with the rebels?

Answer. He is just as good a Union man as a man who has been brought up a slaveholder can possibly be.

WASHINGTON, *February* 12, 1862.

Captain JOHN H. KNIGHT sworn and examined.

By the chairman:

Question. What is your position in the army?

Answer. I am assistant adjutant general of General Lockwood's brigade, with the rank of captain.

Question. You accompanied him to Accomac, through the campaign there?

Answer. I did.

Question. Will you tell us what you think material to be stated in regard to that campaign?

Answer. We went into Accomac county, Virginia, and found that the forces which had been in arms there against the government had dispersed, and gone we did not know where; to their homes we supposed. We proceeded to take military occupation of the two counties, and General Lockwood administered the affairs down there.

Question. Did he take any military stores?

Answer. He took all the military stores that he heard of.

Question. What amount of arms did he get down there?

Answer. I think there were some 600 or 700 old muskets.

Question. Did he take any cannon?

Answer. Yes, sir; he took some eight or nine pieces of artillery; took several pieces of cannon that had no carriages—old iron pieces; found some of them buried.

Question. What kind of muskets did he take?

Answer. They were common muskets. Some of them were Springfield muskets altered to flint-lock. They were all either flint-locks, or altered from flint-locks.

Question. What did he do with the arms he took?

Answer. He has them in store yet, under guard; the artillery he uses down at the inlets. He has guards at every inlet along the coast, and uses these pieces of artillery there; has them on board of some vessels he took, which belonged to persons some of whom had run off.

Question. The papers have accused him of dealing a little too fairly with the secessionists there; I do not know upon what authority.

Answer. I do not think there is any foundation at all for that. Now, in regard to horses and negroes, (and I suppose when that is explained all is explained:) When we went down there we found three kinds of horses, which had been used in the rebel service. One kind was those which had been bought by the rebel government; another kind was those which had been used by the officers, and the third kind was those which had been used by the privates who had gone into the ranks and taken their own horses from the plough, and were to be paid for their use. He wrote to General Dix, asking him what he should do in regard to these horses. Before he received an answer he seized the horses belonging to the rebel government and those owned by the rebel officers, and kept them; those belonging to privates he seized, but let the owners have them upon giving a written pledge that they would return the horses when called for. Those persons came to him and claimed that they had submitted to the government, had laid down their arms, and intended to be obedient, &c., and wanted their horses. The general allowed them to take them upon giving written pledges for all the horses, which pledges he now has on file.

By Mr. Odell:

Question. Let them have their horses on parole?

Answer. Yes, sir; the privates. Those belonging to the rebel government, and the horses of the officers he has now. General Dix wrote to him, approving what he had done.

By the chairman:

Question. General Dix approved upon being informed that he had allowed the privates' horses to be taken on parole?

Answer. Yes, sir.

Question. The officers' horses he confiscated?

Answer. Yes, sir; he has them yet. I will say that a great many of these men, as we found afterwards, had been pressed into the rebel service; some of them who are known to have been loyal all the time. When they were pressed into the rebel service they refused to take the oath of allegiance to the rebel government, and had made arrangements to desert as soon as we had advanced into that county.

Question. Did General Lockwood require them to take the oath?

Answer. I do not think he did. Some of them he made take the oath, where he had evidence of their disloyalty. I know I have great packages of the forms of the oath of allegiance in my office—thousands of them. But he did not, as a general rule, require the oath of allegiance of those persons who came and got their property. It did not occur to him, I suppose. Now, in regard to the negroes: When he learned that the negroes had worked on the rebel embankments there, he wrote to General Dix to know what he should do about them. General Dix wrote back to him, sending him a copy of the confiscation act of Congress, passed at the last session. General Dix told him he could do nothing with this property; that it had to be condemned by a court; but, still, that General Lockwood had done right in holding on to the other property. In regard to the negroes, General Dix did not know what to advise him; to take his own course. Now, General Lockwood, for fear that he would some day be called upon to produce these negroes, had inventories made—one for Accomac and one for Northampton county—of all the negroes who had worked on the embankments, so that he should know where to put his hand on them if called upon for them. It is impossible for the negroes to get away, for he has guards there, so that they cannot be run off. He obtained from the negroes a knowledge of a great many facts connected with that matter, the tools they worked with, and all that. A great many of these negroes were used by persons who had hired them of their masters and mistresses. We took from the slaves themselves their own statements. A knowledge of the matter got circulated around among the slaves, and they would come in and inform us of what they had done, and we took notes of it, under General Lockwood's order.

Question. Did he punish any of them because of their leaving their masters and coming into the lines?

Answer. I never heard of such a thing. The only case of the kind I know of was one that the general told me about just as I left there. It had occurred at Pungoteague. In accordance with instructions from General Dix, General Lockwood had issued an order strictly forbidding the negroes coming within the lines of his camp. When we went down there the negroes flocked to the camp by hundreds. They were a great nuisance there. Their masters were coming to the camps, complaining that their slaves had been secreted there. The colonels of the regiments said they had carried out their orders. But there was one negro man who had troubled him both at Drummondtown and at Eastville—all the way down. He had driven him away three or four times, and told him he could not do anything for him. When he got to Pungoteague he found him there, on board one of the boats, where he had secreted himself, trying to get off. The general told Lieutenant Lammot to take the boy out and whip him in the presence of the negroes there. General Lockwood told me, just before I left, about it, and said that he was sorry he had done it, for he expected it would be misrepresented, and he would have difficulty about it. When I heard of it I addressed Lieutenant Lammot a letter, and received this one in reply:

"HEADQUARTERS,
"*Drummondtown, Va., February* 6, 1862.

"CAPTAIN: In reply to your letter of the 5th instant, in reference to the whipping of a fugitive slave by order of General Lockwood, I will state the facts as they came under my own observation:

"General Lockwood had frequently forbidden slaves from coming within the lines, and, I believe, this one in particular had been repeatedly driven off. But on the arrrival of the general at Pungoteague, the owner of this slave came to him and complained that our troops had secreted, within their lines, a negro boy belonging to him, and upon search this one was discovered. Whereupon General Lockwood directed him to be whipped, and desired me to see it done, not only as a punishment to the negro for his persistent disobedience of orders, but to deter, by this example, other negroes from doing the same thing, and thus bring upon our troops the undeserved name of 'negro stealers.'

"I saw the boy taken out and twenty-one lashes administered with a small apple switch over his waistcoat, his coat having been removed for the purpose. The punishment was anything but severe, and such as might be taken by any school-boy without a whimper. But it had the desired effect of relieving General Lockwood from the annoyance to which he had been subjected on this account.

"This, I believe, is the full statement of the facts as they occurred and came to my own knowledge.

"I am, very respectfully, your obedient servant,

"C. E. LAMMOT,

"1*st Lieutenant and Aide-de-Camp.*

"Captain JOHN H. KNIGHT,

"*Assistant Adjutant General, Peninsula Brigade.*"

This is the only instance, and I never heard of this before General Lockwood told me about it.

Question. This was done at General Lockwood's instance?

Answer. Yes, sir. General Lockwood issued strict orders forbidding the slaves coming into camp. He issued orders for the capture of rebel property. I have one here in which he orders the taking of a carriage and horses, some ladies having waved a rebel flag from the carriage and hurrahed for Jeff. Davis He would allow no one to hurrah for Jeff. Davis in the presence of his troops. There was one man, a very respectable person, who was shot by one of the guards in the hips for persisting in shouting for Jeff. Davis. He stated to General Dix that he had taken inventories of the property of persons who had gone off to the other side, (many of them are not in arms and some are,) for the purpose of being able to obtain it in case a general confiscation act is passed. He has taken inventories, I suppose, of more than $50,000 worth of property.

By Mr. Odell:

Question. That is, in view of a confiscation act being passed by Congress, so that he can put his hand on the property?

Answer. Yes, sir. In reference to the whipping of this negro, he did it in a moment of passion, when he was annoyed almost to death by these negroes coming into his lines, when he had positive instructions from General Dix forbidding their being allowed to come within our lines. I never heard of it until the morning before I left, except from the papers, and I had treated it as an idle rumor. I did so because there is no more loyal man living than General Lockwood. Since he has been there it has been his constant effort to crush out all disloyalty.

By the chairman:

Question. What is the condition of things there now among the people in regard to their loyalty?

Answer. I think it is a very happy condition. At the election which took place there on the 25th of January, the Union triumph was so complete that it shows a healthy tone of sentiment existing there. At the election held for a rebel congressman some time before we went down there, there were but about 600 votes cast in the two counties; while at the election on the 25th of January there were over 1,200 votes cast, being more than two-thirds of all the voters in the counties.

Question. Was that in Wise's old district?

Answer. Yes, sir. Our troops are now quartered on Wise's property there. The men who have been elected there now are men who have been Union men all through the troubles there; who had been persecuted, threatened at the polls, their lives threatened, and public meetings held in regard to them.

Question. You observed that many of these men were coerced into the rebel service?

Answer. Yes, sir.

Question. How was that done when a majority were Union men?

Answer. The majority were not Union men formerly, nor one-third of them. In Northampton county I believe the vote originally was every man for secession; not a vote for the Union cause. In Accomac county the majority voted against secession.

Question. Is there anything else that you deem material to be stated?

Answer. I do not know that I could state anything else in this connexion. I simply wanted to let you know how matters have been conducted down there. General Dix announced to me that his plan was one of conciliation, to win these people back to their allegiance; and General Lockwood has endeavored to conciliate them in every manner that he could and not violate the laws, and so far as his duty to the government would permit him to do so?

By Mr. Odell:

Question. Do you think the people there would remain loyal if our troops should be taken away?

Answer. General Lockwood has written to General Dix and General McClellan that he has more troops there than is necessary, and that he can be spared for a more active field. He says that Colonel Wallace, with two regiments of home guards, can protect the telegraph lines there, and asks that he may be assigned to a more active field. I think that General Lockwood is a man that should be placed in a more active field. He is a graduate of West Point, and has been in the military all his life, and has shown considerable ability in his writings upon the subject. About the telegraph: He was about issuing an order when I left, making the offence subject to the penalty of death for cutting the wire—proceeding upon Halleck's plan with bridge-burners in the west. He has so posted the troops to protect the line so that there will be a soldier at every three hundred yards; and the troops for that purpose, and to guard the inlets, are all that are needed there now.

WASHINGTON, *February* 13, 1862.

Colonel JAMES W. MCMILLAN sworn and examined.

By the chairman:

Question. What is your rank and position in the army, and where are you stationed?

Answer. I am colonel of the 21st Indiana volunteers, and am stationed at Baltimore, under command of General Dix.

Question. What do you know in regard to the campaign into Accomac county, Virginia, under General Lockwood?

Answer. I know that in the forepart of November—about the 13th—we started. I had been told by General Dix that there would be a campaign set on foot. I was the ranking officer, and had orders to proceed to Newtown and report to General Lockwood.

Question. You were there under General Lockwood?

Answer. Yes, sir; I reported to him there on his arrival.

Question. General Lockwood has been accused of some unmilitary conduct—something in regard to his dealings with secessionists and appropriating public property he had taken, &c. These accusations have gone forth. I want you to state what you know about his administration as regards those matters.

Answer. I know of nothing he has done in conflict with the rules and regulations governing the army of the United States; and having been in command of the advance after we left Newtown, or rather Drummondtown, I took possession of a great deal of property.

Question. What kind of property?

Answer. I took cannon, muskets, swords, horses, &c.—property that belonged to the confederates. The horses that had been sold to the confederate government were turned over to the quartermaster, and I understood were held as confiscated to the government of the United States. The horses that had been in the service of the southern confederacy, that had been owned by the persons claiming them, or having them in possession at the time, and who were to have been compensated for the use of them, were not confiscated, but were returned to their owners. But all the horses we could find that had been sold to the southern confederacy, whether paid for or not, were held as confiscated to the United States, and were turned over to the quartermaster.

Question. What was done with the cannon and the muskets you took?

Answer. The cannon I sent to Drummondtown from Pungoteague. I captured seven there and sent them up to Drummondtown. The muskets were of a very worthless character, but they were put in the jail at Drummondtown, and the keys delivered to the quartermaster. When I left there they were still in the jail, in the possession of the quartermaster of the brigade.

Question. How long were you there?

Answer. I was there until the 4th or 5th of December. I was in advance, and went down as far as I could go—down to Cape Charles light-house, or as near to it as we could get.

Question. Do you know anything in the administration of that department inconsistent with an officerlike course on the part of General Lockwood?

Answer. Nothing, except his making a speech. I do not think that is exactly consistent with the duty of an officer. The making a speech is about the only thing I know of that I consider inconsistent with the duty of an officer.

Question. What portion of the people there seem to be loyal, and what portion opposed to us?

Answer. When I came away it was with the impression that they would all become loyal, and I so reported to General Dix. They are clannish there. They are not very well informed, and they go in clans upon any subject. I found there, I think, a very strong disposition, upon the part of quite a number of the citizens, to become loyal to the government, and they all told me so. If they could be assured and satisfied that they would be protected, they would submit to the Constitution and laws of the United States. They believed that that portion of Virginia would, in any event, be attached to Maryland, and wherever Maryland went they must go. The probability was, they argued, that even if the rebellion was successful, the Potomac river and the Chesapeake bay would be the dividing line, and they would be under the northern government.

Question. Do you know of General Lockwood holding any improper inter course with the rebels, or with persons who were secessionists?

Answer. No, sir; and I do not think, from his conversation with me, that he would have done any such thing. I believe he is as strictly loyal as any person can be, and he manifested a desire to be a little more harsh with those people than his instructions would warrant.

Question. How about the slaves of secessionists coming into your camps? What was done with them?

Answer. We were ordered to prohibit slaves from coming about our camps. That order was given by General Lockwood, and I understood that it was in accordance with his instructions from General Dix. When I went on in advance, he furnished me a copy of General Dix's instructions to be governed by. I did not have any particular instructions from General Lockwood. The orders were to prohibit the slaves coming about our camps.

Question. You do not know of his returning any of them to secessionists?

Answer. No, sir. I heard a report that he had one whipped and driven out of the camp.

Question. What do you know about that?

Answer. Personally I do not know anything about it. I was in the advance, and it was done by some troops in rear of me.

By Mr. Julian:

Question. What kind of a speech was that that General Lockwood made?

Answer. I did not hear the speech; I was not there. I only spoke in disapproval of it, because I think speech-making is not the duty of an officer.

By Mr. Odell:

Question. In speaking of the unofficerlike conduct of making that speech, you merely referred to the fact of making the speech, and not to the character of the speech?

Answer. That was all.

By the chairman:

Question. Is there anything more you desire to state as illustrating or throwing light upon that campaign?

Answer. Nothing more than I think the campaign was as successful as it was possible for it to have been under the circumstances. And I believe any expression or charge against General Lockwood's loyalty is unjust. I may have an opinion as to his capacity as an officer, but I think it is unjust to make any charge against his loyalty. Being intrusted with the advance, I probably became more fully acquainted with his opinions than any other officer in his command.

WASHINGTON, *February* 13, 1862.

Captain HOBART sworn and examined.

By the chairman:

Question. What is your rank and position in the army?

Answer. I am captain of company K, of the 4th regiment of Wisconsin volunteers.

Question. Were you under General Lockwood in the Accomac expedition?

Answer. I was. I went down there, and proceeded to Princess Anne and Snow Hill, and to Newtown, where General Lockwood joined us. I was there and around about him during the entire campaign, until I returned to Baltimore. I was present at the time he delivered his speech that has been referred to. It was delivered on the court-house steps at Drummondtown.

Question. What was the occasion of his making that speech?

Answer. It was in consequence of the desire of the people of Accomac county to know what they should do in the *interim*, having no local government of their own. It was made on the day the county court was to have sat. General Lockwood had forbidden any court to be held, as its organization was responsive to the confederate government. There was a very large turnout by the people of the county there, and they desired to hear from General Lockwood what was to be their destiny—what was to be their government during this *interim*. I was near him and heard his speech, which was very short, and in substance very similar to a speech made by the colonel of my regiment at Snow Hill, in response to the desire of the people there to be informed upon the same subject.

Question. That speech of General Lockwood has been violently criticised. Can you give us an idea of it?

Answer. The speech was very short; the whole of it was merely an elaboration of General Dix's proclamation that he held in hand and commented upon. I judged from his manner that he was not much given to speech-making. He took up the several points in General Dix's proclamation, and elaborated upon them very briefly. He stated to the people that, in the absence of any government in Accomac, he felt it his duty to protect them in their persons and in their rights until they could take the initiative and form some government for their own protection. There was a sensitive feeling among the planters there as to what should become of their slaves in the absence of all law officers. He told them that, until they could form a government under and responsive to the government and Constitution of the United States, he felt bound, with his military power, to protect them in their persons and property. He recommended an immediate movement on their part—I think the next Saturday, for notice could not be given to the people before—to take steps at once to reform their government, to take the oath of allegiance, and proceed to construct a local government. Until that time, he said he should feel it to be his duty to protect them in their persons and property. He made use of one or two expressions which probably have given rise to much that has been said. I heard those expressions. There were very few soldiers present, but a large number of the citizens of the county. He assured them that he did not come among them as an enemy to their institutions; he came there to represent the Constitution and government of the United States. Said he, "It must be obeyed, and it shall be obeyed. I will march those troops I have here from one end to the other of the peninsula, and I shall command obedience, and you must yield. But I do not come here as an enemy to your institutions; I have no cause to be an enemy to them. I am myself a slaveholder, and my father before me held slaves." That was about the substance of his speech. But from that there was a feeling excited in the camp that they were under a slaveholder, and they did not want to be under a slaveholder, &c. That was really the only point in the speech to which there was any exception taken. It was very brief; not more than twice as long as what I have said here about it.

Question. What was his treatment of the soldiers?

Answer. Well, sir, I know considerable about that. When he arrived at Newtown, and took charge of the army, he enforced strict military discipline. Our officers had gone off to hotels, some to boarding-houses. He ordered them all to camp, to remain with their soldiers. He issued an order prohibiting the sale of liquor to officers or soldiers. He went around and saw that his orders were enforced. He was very strict and somewhat severe in carrying out these orders; and in passing over the peninsula he took great pains to prevent the soldiers from preying upon the farmers, seizing their chickens, &c. He was so severe that it created some dissatisfaction. But I do not hesitate to state, under oath, before this committee, that the severity of his discipline was one of the chief causes of our gaining the affection of the people of that country. They had expected, as I know from intercourse with them, that we were come down there to lay their country desolate, and to rob them of all they possessed. That was what they had been told. And I think the course of the general had much to do with winning back the feelings of this people. As to their loyalty, I had occasion to see many of the people of Northampton and Accomac, and I am satisfied that, setting aside a few of the leading men, the middle classes of the people there are now loyal, and desire to remain so.

By Mr. Odell:

Question. Did your officers and men come to appreciate the rigor of General Lockwood, with reference to forbidding the sale of liquor and prohibiting absence from camp, as being what was proper and right?

Answer. I think they did. I think they became satisfied that was the way to keep the regiments under good discipline; that the officers should be with them constantly, sharing with the men all their privations and perils. There is one point that has been mooted in this matter in reference to the taking of horses. I know all about that matter. I saw it all, and was in among it all, and although I took no horses whatever, I will give my impression about it. In going through the peninsula a disposition sprang up among some of our officers to possess themselves of fine horses. I think, in many instances, it proceeded from a desire simply to get hold of contraband property—of property that belonged to the confederates. I have good reason to believe that negroes were employed and sent out over the country to find out where there were fine horses that had been impressed into the confederate service. And when such horses were discovered they were taken and brought into our camps. In nearly every instance they were brought in by the staff officers of the regiments; and at one time it created quite a feeling on the part of captains as to whether they had not the same right to forage the country to find blooded horses as the staff officers of their regiments. General Lockwood adopted the rule which has been referred to by Colonel McMillan in his testimony here. In all instances where he found that these horses had not been actually transferred to the confederate government, he permitted them to be taken by their owners; and I know that the order of General Lockwood, as carried out in these two counties, making that distinction clearly, and returning to the owners who were loyal, who had not contributed to the confederate army, these horses, had a very salutary effect upon the people there.

Question. As far as you know, did he return any horses to disloyal citizens?

Answer. Not that I know of. I will say one thing in relation to those horses. The horses of Accomac and Northampton counties, when Smith, the rebel commander, organized his force there, were all pressed into his service.

Colonel McMillan, (previously examined:) As I myself took all the horses that were taken by authority, I will state that I took possession of all that I could find that had been in the confederate service, except those that had been pressed into service. There were two classes of horses in the confederate service besides those that had been pressed into the service: One class was those that had been bought by the confederate authorities. The other class was those that had been taken by their owners when they went, and for the services of which they were to be paid. General Lockwood allowed the owners of the second class to take their horses. But those that had been sold to the confederate government, whether paid for or not, were not returned. Many of them had been sold, not paid for, and then returned by the confederates to their owners to reimburse them to that extent. But in every case of that kind they were taken and turned over to the quartermaster, and held as confiscated to the government. And I think that General Lockwood, under his instructions, could not have done otherwise than he did in regard to that class of property.

The chairman: Do you know whether any horses were returned to disloyal men?

Colonel McMillan: That is a question of considerable nicety. I think they were all disloyal when we arrived there; but they laid down their arms in obedience to the proclamation, with a determination to be loyal. When I say all were disloyal, of course there were a few exceptions. But the most of them were disloyal; that is, they had become identified with the southern confederacy; they supposed it was a reality, and was likely to succeed. General Lockwood delivered horses to them, to some even who had been in the militia of the confederacy, not in the regular army. But those persons had expressed their determination to be loyal to the government of the United States.

Mr. Odell: Have they kept faith?

Colonel McMillan: Yes, sir.

Mr. Odell: And are now loyal?

Colonel McMillan: That is my opinion. They have since voted almost unanimously for officers holding authority under the government of the United States.

Mr. Julian: Do you think they would continue loyal if our army should be taken away?

Colonel McMillan: Yes, sir; I think if the southern confederacy should be a success, there would be little disposition to go with it, if it was practicable. If it should be a failure, there would never be any uneasiness or dissatisfaction among them. That is the conviction I had when I came away from there. When I left I think they were convinced that under no circumstances could they be a portion of the southern confederacy; that they were geographically a portion of Maryland, and Maryland would be held at all events.

The witness, (Captain Hobart:) I will simply make one remark. I have the same opinion the colonel has expressed in reference to a large portion of Northampton county, where all, or nearly all, the horses were taken. I think that in their feelings and prejudices they are with the main State across the bay. But still I think they did not wait until we arrived with our forces before they abandoned that idea. The means of communication had been cut off for a long time, and they knew hardly anything until we arrived there as to what was going on. They all yielded, laid down their arms, and professed to be willing to be obedient to the government of the United States.

Mr. Odell: Did not these horses that were returned belong to farmers who had left their farms when they were pressed into the rebel service, as a general thing?

Witness: Yes, sir.

Mr. Odell, (to Colonel McMillan:) Do you not know that those horses were delivered on parole, on written pledge or receipt that they should be returned when called for.

Colonel McMillan: Certainly. At the time they were delivered up by General Lockwood it was with the understanding that if the government should claim them as confiscated they should be returned.

Mr. Odell: And the horses are now under parole in that way?

Colonel McMillan: Unless the thing has been decided, they are.

Mr. Odell: So far as General Lockwood is concerned, the horses are under parole, are they not?

Colonel McMillan: So I understand.

WASHINGTON, *February* 13, 1862.

Major F. A. BOARDMAN sworn and examined.

By Mr. Odell:

Question. What is your rank and position in the army?

Answer. I am major of the 4th Wisconsin regiment.

Question. Were you under General Lockwood on his Accomack expedition?

Answer. Yes, sir.

Question. Do you know anything about the delivery of horses back to parties claiming to own them?

Answer. Yes, sir.

Question. State what you know about that.

Answer. The horses were at General Lockwood's headquarters. The owners came after them, and the general allowed them to take them conditionally—that is, subject to the order of the government in case they were confiscated; then they were to be restored to him.

Question. On his demand?

Answer. Yes, sir.

Question. Were all the horses, so far as you know, delivered up in this way?

Answer. I believe so, with the exception of those belonging to men who have escaped and crossed over into Virginia.

Question. And those he confiscated?

Answer. Those were confiscated, I understood.

Question. As a general thing, did the horses thus delivered belong to farmers?

Answer. They were generally hired—that is, they took them whether the owners were willing or not, and agreed to pay for their services so much a week. I concur with what Captain Hobart has testified to in every respect. As to the flogging the negro, General Lockwood told me about that. There was but one negro flogged. The general told me the negro had been hanging about the camp for some time; our regiment was about embarking for Baltimore, and the negro would not be driven away. Therefore the general had one of the Delaware or Maryland soldiers take him out and give him a brushing, some fifteen or twenty blows with a switch—nothing to hurt him at all. He said he did it for the purpose of having the negro go among the others and tell them he had been flogged, and that would prevent them coming around our camps, and among us. We had strict orders to prevent them coming about the camp. General Lockwood desired me to make this explanation in case I heard anybody refer to the matter. He said he had heard that it had been reported about the camp, and had created some feeling against him among the officers and men. He said it was entirely from a misunderstanding of the case.

By Mr. Julian:

Question. Was the owner a loyal man?

Answer. I do not know anything about the owner of the slave. I know there was a man came to the camp who had lost a negro. He was a loyal man by the name of Dr. Irby. He finally found his negro before we left.

Question. Did he get him by the help of the army?

Answer. I think not. I think that he was found by some men he had out after him.

Colonel McMillan, (previously examined:) There is one other thing I may state in regard to catching negroes. I refused to have anything to do with it in any way, shape, or form. The owners requested me to arrest them and put them in jail. I told them they had taken their negroes to build fortifications, and had then got scared and run off home faster than the negroes could; they had taken part against the United States, and I would not condescend to arrest their negroes under any circumstances. I spoke rather sharp to them sometimes. On one or two occasions I was told they reported the matter to General Lockwood; but he never referred to it at all in any conversation with me. I refused to send an escort with men who came to my camp while I was at Pungoteague to search it. I refused either to go myself or send an officer to hunt for negroes in the camp. I told them they could go and look, and the men would not disturb them. But they refused to go to the camp and reported the matter to General Lockwood, who, however, paid no attention to it.

By Mr. Odell:

Question. (To Major Boardman.) Have you anything else to state about the matter?

Answer. No, sir; there is nothing I think of.

Question. What is your opinion of the loyalty of the people there, and the influence of our army among them?

Answer. I think it was very beneficial. I think the expedition was entirely successful in every way.

Question. Is that indicated by the result of the election last month?

Answer. I think so.

By Mr. Julian:

Question. How long were you in making your march during that expedition?

Answer. The 4th Wisconsin left Baltimore the first Monday of November, and returned to Baltimore the first Sunday in December.

Question. I mean how long was it from the time you landed down there until you finished your expedition?

Answer. About a month.

Question. What was the distance you marched?

Answer. I cannot tell.

Colonel McMillan: It was about seventy miles from Newtown to Eastville; and I went some eighteen or twenty miles further.

By Mr. Julian:

Question. (To Major Boardman.) Why were you so long in making that march, being after the rebels?

Answer. The first portion of the expedition sent down was not sufficient for the purpose. The rebels would have fought us with that small force; and General Dix sent force enough to make them lay down their arms without having any fight, and to accomplish his ends peaceably. It was the other portions of the regiments coming down that detained us longer than we would have been detained otherwise.

Question. You waited for them?

Answer. Yes, sir.

Question. It has been reported that General Lockwood paid exorbitant prices for everything he got from the rebels.

Answer. Not to my knowledge; I do not know anything about that.

Colonel McMillan: All that I got was about 130 bushels of sweet potatoes, for part of which I paid thirty cents a bushel, and for the rest twenty-five cents a bushel; and we got some beef at six cents a pound.

BATTLE OF WINCHESTER.

WASHINGTON, *May* 22, 1862.

Colonel JOHN S. MASON sworn and examined.

By Mr. Gooch:

Question. What is your rank and position in the army?

Answer. I am a captain in the regular army, and colonel of the 4th regiment of Ohio volunteers.

Question. Were you at the battle of Winchester, in March last?

Answer. Yes, sir.

Question. Will you give us a concise account of that battle?

Answer. To do so, it may be well for me to state some matters that preceded the battle itself.

Question. Please do so, in your own way.

Answer. On the morning of the Monday preceding the battle, March 17, I was directed by General Shields to make a reconnoissance in the direction of Strasburg. He placed at my disposal a squadron of cavalry and two companies of my own regiment, the 4th Ohio, with instructions to examine the by-roads, and to ascertain what force the enemy had in front of us, and look at the enemy in front. I went out the main road, examining those to the right and left. When we arrived at the town of Newtown, a distance probably of six or seven miles, we encountered the pickets of the enemy and drove them through the town. That was about 2 o'clock in the afternoon. I then turned off to the left, on to the Front Royal road, and examined that from there back to Winchester. I reported to General Shields the result of the reconnoissance.

General Williams was present at the time I made my report, and suggested that it would be well to make a reconnoissance in the direction of Strasburg, and see what there was then in our front, before General Banks's column should leave us. He said that he could support me with about 6,000 men. Arrangements were immediately made to carry that suggestion into effect. I was ordered to be in readiness to march the next morning at 4 o'clock, on the Front Royal road. My instructions were to proceed down the Front Royal road, taking some cavalry with me, and leaving some men on the way to communicate with General Shields's column, and to try to get in the rear of the enemy, whilst General Shields, with the main division, moved down the regular Strasburg route. He furnished me with a squadron of cavalry, two sections of artillery, two regiments of infantry, and my own two companies of infantry I had had the day before. We moved down until we came to the last road turning to the right before reaching Front Royal. I turned to the right, and in going into the town of Middletown—about 13 miles from Winchester, on the main road, though I had come by a somewhat circuitous route—we encountered the enemy's pickets, and drove them before us until they arrived at Cedar Creek bridge, which they had covered with combustibles, ready for burning. They burned the bridge before we could approach them. They then opened upon us with a battery of artillery from the opposite bank of the creek, to which we replied for some little time. There was very little effect on either side, the distance was so great.

As one of my regiments had by that time marched some 27 or 28 miles, and was a great deal fatigued, and as it was near sunset, within a few minutes of it, I concluded to wait until morning, and then cross the creek under cover of our batteries. Shortly afterwards, probably within three-quarters of an hour, General Shields arrived with his whole division. After examining the ground, he concluded to wait until morning before going forward.

The next morning we moved forward without opposition, the small force in our front having left, until we arrived at Strasburg. At Strasburg the enemy opened upon us from a battery which they had planted upon a hill in front of us. General Shields sent for Colonel Kimball, Colonel Tyler, Colonel Sullivan, and myself to come forward. He stated that he was under the impression that Jackson's whole force was in front of us, and he should make his dispositions for battle immediately. He placed his batteries on a hill on our right, supported by the three brigades of infantry in the rear leaving me on the extreme left, and near the turnpike, with his cavalry force, (I suppose the cavalry numbered from 300 to 350,) and the same in fantry force I had the day before—two regiments and my own two companies.

I was ordered, as soon as our artillery opened, to move forward on the main road with the cavalry, supported by a regiment of infantry. We moved forward about a mile and a quarter, when, upon arriving on the crest of a hill, we were fired upon by our own batteries. Fortunately, the fire, though well directed, caused only the loss of a few horses. The force of the enemy in my front was principally cavalry. They had, I thought at that time, two guns; they may have had three. As we approached them on one hill they would fall back to the next and open fire on us again. General Shields came up in person, bringing up his division, and pursued the enemy a distance of perhaps five miles, throwing out a regiment of infantry as skirmishers in front, followed by a section of artillery. He continued the pursuit until about 5 o'clock in the afternoon of Wednesday. He then returned to Strasburg with his whole force, leaving a strong picket on the hills towards the enemy.

On Thursday morning General Shields ordered the whole command to return to Winchester, giving me, with the same force I had taken out, the rear guard. We arrived in Winchester about dark on Thursday evening without seeing any of the enemy. It was reported to me that there were a few of the enemy's cavalry on the route, but I did not see them; they did not annoy us at all; there was not a gun fired.

The general had had his headquarters in the town of Winchester; but when he returned from Strasburg he moved back about two miles beyond the town, a little to the left of the Martinsburg road. His whole command was encamped in that vicinity—from there to about four miles out. His nearest camp was probably about two miles from town, except the two companies I had had near his headquarters when in town.

All was quiet on Friday. In conversation with General Shields and others on Friday we all came to the conclusion that our reconnoissance had been successful; that there was no enemy on that front; that Jackson was off a long distance, and that all we would have to do, until we had got things in readiness for an advance, would be to picket well in front.

On Saturday there was considerable firing during the early part of the day; but for a good while I do not think anybody but those engaged really knew what it was. Some thought it was some of General Williams's men who were discharging their guns, firing at targets, or something of the kind. About four o'clock in the evening, however, General Shields passed through the town with his whole division, and I joined him as he passed through town. He moved out to the front. When he got out about a mile and a half the enemy opened upon us with artillery. I was not close up at the time, and therefore cannot give an accurate account of what transpired. When I arrived on the ground General Shields had just been wounded, and was being taken into a house on the side road. Dr. McAbee, who was with me, dismounted, and went into the house with him.

I asked who was in command, and found that for the time being I was the senior officer present. One of our batteries had gone into position on a side hill, and was firing. I ordered it to cease firing, as any further firing was useless. Before I had made any further dispositions, the general's aids came forward, and gave some orders in reference to the batteries ceasing firing and the encamping the first brigade on the ground for the night, throwing out a strong picket to the front. That was Colonel Kimball's brigade. The brigades of Colonels Sullivan, Tyler, and my own, with the two companies of my regiment, were ordered. I do not think Colonel Tyler had got up through town at all. He had been ordered out, but had not got forward. Colonel Sullivan's brigade, I think, had just got through town. Colonel Tyler went back to his old camp, and Colonel Sullivan's force encamped on the outskirts of the town. General Shields was carried into town in a carriage.

On Sunday morning, just about eight o'clock, after breakfast, I called on General Shields, and he directed me to go to the front, and take my adjutant and orderly with me, and make a reconnoissance from different points of the field, with reference to the force and disposition of the enemy, &c., and to report to him. When I got out I found that Colonel Kimball had thrown forward the 8th Ohio, deploying them as skirmishers in front, and that he had two of his regiments, with a battery of artillery, posted near him, and about a mile and a half from town. We examined the ground to the front for some distance, and became satisfied that there was no force there greater than the force that had made the attack the night before, which we all supposed was Jackson's rear guard, under Ashby, which we had pursued towards Strasburg. Colonel Carroll had deployed six of his companies, of the 8th Ohio, on the left, near the wood, where he encountered quite a force of infantry and cavalry, and, I believe, two pieces of artillery. I was not close enough to perceive the full effect of the fire. They had quite a heavy little skirmish there, which lasted probably fifteen or twenty minutes. Colonel Carroll sent back for re-enforcements, and Colonel Kimball ordered up the 14th Indiana, under Colonel Harrow, to support him.

About this time, which was about ten o'clock—a little after, perhaps—Colonel Sullivan's brigade appeared on the field, and was thrown to the left of the road, in support of Colonel Carroll. The apparent intention of the enemy at that time was to turn our left, and Colonel Kimball threw the most of the force he had on the left.

In the mean time Colonel Kimball and myself rode forward and examined the ground to his right and left. He remarked that he would hold the hills on the right and in advance. General Shields had directed him to press the enemy in front and pursue them. But Colonel Kimball concluded that if they were in any force in front we better hold on any good ground we had. There was a succession of rolling ground, high points and knobs, one of them very high, but all commanding positions, overlooking the valley, to our front and left. We threw forward a battery on one of the advanced hills, and kept up an artillery fire from that position nearly the whole morning up till two o'clock.

About twelve o'clock I went into town and reported to General Shields that we could discover nothing more than we had seen during the day previous; that up to that time the enemy certainly were not in any force, and that we thought it was nothing but Ashby. And it afterwards turned out that up to that hour there was no other force there.

General Shields directed me to return to the field and continue my observations. I immediately went back, and found that during my absence the enemy had been very heavily re-enforced, and that there was an evident intention on their part to endeavor to turn our right. I rode up to Colonel Kimball, who was then on the advanced hill to the right that I have spoken of, and had been playing a battery of artillery for some time, to which the enemy were replying. The battery was supported by the fourteenth Indiana, four companies of the eighth Ohio, and, if I mistake not, the sixty-seventh Ohio. I omitted to state that early in the morning I remarked that it would be well to throw some troops over to our right. There was a wood there, near where the main fight afterwards occurred. Colonel Kimball replied that he had already sent the eighty-fourth Pennsylvania over there, and they were holding the wood. That was early in the morning, probably between nine and ten o'clock. He also remarked, when I asked him to ride forward and look at the ground to the front, that now he had his flanks sufficiently protected he could look well to the front. About four o'clock, I should think it was, Major Armstrong, of General Shields's staff, came laughingly up to me, and said: "Perhaps Colonel Kimball will say to me, as McClellan did to Lander, that I am too suggestive. I remarked to him," said he, "that he better occupy that hill on our right." Said I, "he better occupy it, or they will open a battery upon us." Even while I was speaking, the enemy did open a battery upon us from that hill. I understood that Colonel Kimball was at that time making dispositions to occupy the hill. The enemy came up to that position in considerable force, and planted a battery there to reply to the one we had on this advanced hill. Colonel Kimball remarked at once that he must take that battery. He sent myself, my adjutant, Lieutenant Greene, and Lieutenant Blinn, of the fourteenth Indiana, I think, to bring up Tyler's brigade. Tyler's brigade, in the mean time, had advanced along the road, and was held in reserve. When Tyler arrived he was thrown immediately over to the right, behind a skirt of woods, passing through a little valley up on the hill, being ordered to move forward and take the position the enemy occupied. As soon as Tyler became engaged, Colonel Kimball at once sent forward the fourteenth Indiana, which was supporting our battery on the hill in front, the eighth Ohio, and the sixty-seventh Ohio. In the mean time he had signalled to Colonel Sullivan, who was on the field to the left, to send over some regiments. The next regiment that arrived was the thirteenth Indiana, which was thrown right in on the left to support Colonel Tyler. That was followed by the sixty-seventh Ohio and a portion of the fifth Ohio. The eighty-fourth Pennsylvania had come up early in the engagement from the rear, and was still on that flank. The sixty-seventh Ohio scarcely got under fire. The others came up in the order named, if I remember rightly. The musketry fire lasted about two hours.

During that time I was by the side of Colonel Kimball on horseback, and I think that he made every direction with reference to the dispositions of troops that was made. Of course he did not give any instructions to the troops after they had passed into the wood on the hill towards the stone wall, for then each commanding officer manœuvred his own troops. The re-enforcements of Tyler were led into the field by my adjutant, Lieutenant Greene; that is, they were led by him to their position. It happened in this way: After the fight became pretty heavy, quite a number of men attempted to leave the field, stragglers running back, Colonel Kimball asked me and my adjutant, Lieutenant Greene, to ride forward and try to turn these men back. My adjutant went off in one direction, and I went in another. The direction I took brought me up among the wounded and the surgeons. I turned back quite a number of stragglers, and forced quite a number of men who were able to walk. Lieutenant Greene went off a little further to my left, and came across quite a number who had taken advantage of the confusion to go to the rear. After he had got back into the woods, he found a regiment coming in, and showed them the road into the woods. He continued showing the other regiments to their position as they came up. The firing ceased about dark, after it had become so dark that we could not distinguish friend from foe. I then left the field, and rode into town and reported to General Shields the result of the fight. Shortly afterwards Colonel Kimball came in and reported to the general. General Shields directed me to picket strongly in front, and to pursue at daylight.

By Mr. Gooch:

Question. Did you hear the report from Colonel Kimball to General Shields?

Answer. Yes, sir.

Question. Can yon tell us whether Colonel Kimball acted that day on his own responsibility, or in pursuance of orders received from General Shields ?

Answer. I was satisfied at the time that he acted on his own responsibility ; and I have always held that opinion.

Question. How far distant from the field of battle was the house in which General Shields lay wounded ?

Answer. It was fully four miles.

Question. At what time did you leave General Shields in the afternoon ?

Answer. I think it was between one and two o'clock.

Question. Were you and he then both of the opinion that it was only Ashby's force that was in front of you ?

Answer. I was of that opinion ; and the general remarked at the time that he thought there was only Ashby's force there. He also said that Kimball wanted re-enforcements, but Kimball wanted more troops than were necessary for the force opposed to him.

Question. When you then left General Shields did you immediately return to the field ?

Answer. Yes, sir.

Question. And you found that the battle had already commenced with this superior force of the enemy ?

Answer. Yes, sir; that is, we were then making dispositions for the battle. The firing of the artillery had become heavier, but no infantry had then become engaged, though they had been sent forward to the woods.

Question. Do you know at what time the first news reached General Shields that there was a greater force of the enemy there than Ashby's ?

Answer. He did not know it at the time I left him in the afternoon, between one and two o'clock ; I can say that. But I cannot say when he received positive information upon that point. Colonel Kimball had reported to him that he thought the force in front of him was stronger than Ashby's force. But when I left General Shields I certainly was under the impression, and I know General Shields was also, that the force there was nothing but Ashby's.

Question. The forces on the field during the day were directed by Colonel Kimball ?

Answer. That is my belief.

Question. And the next morning the pursuit of the enemy was commenced ?

Answer. Yes, sir.

Question. By order of General Shields ?

Answer. Yes, sir ; General Shields directed the pursuit. He directed me during the night to collect the re-enforcements that were coming in, and have them rendezvous at a certain point, at the edge of town, to wait his orders, and just after daylight he gave me an order to move forward and report to Colonel Kimball, who was in pursuit.

Question. Do you know at what time General Banks left Winchester ?

Answer. I know from hearsay that it was between twelve and one o'clock on Sunday, the day of the battle.

Question. And at that time it was believed that there was only Ashby's force opposed to you ?

Answer. Yes, sir.

Question. Do you know when General Banks returned ?

Answer. I think it was about daylight on Monday morning.

Question. Do you know how far he had gone ?

Answer. I understood that he went as far as Harper's Ferry.

Question. And there heard of your engagement at Winchester ?

Answer. Yes, sir, and that caused his return ; and his troops were ordered back in consequence of that attack.

Question. He then assumed command?

Answer. Yes, sir, on his return. He made his appearance on the field between nine and ten o'clock on Monday, I think. The first intimation I had that General Banks had returned was just after daylight on Monday morning; I had ridden down towards the depot, as I was expecting Donelly's brigade, of Williams's division. I met Colonel Donelly coming in, and asked him where his brigade was. And as I rode back to report to General Shields, I saw General Banks and his staff at his own quarters, apparently just arrived. I rode on up to where General Shields was, and a moment or two afterwards General Banks came in—just about daylight on Monday morning.

Question. Then, if I understand you, you are satisfied that General Shields did not suppose that Jackson was present with his force until after you left him on Sunday, at about two o'clock?

Answer. I am satisfied that was his impression. It was my impression. We were talking freely about the matter. I do not think he thought there was any other force there than Ashby's. I know General Banks had that impression, and that was the reason he left Winchester on Sunday.

Question. Then the truth about that battle is, that it was not the result of any strategy or skill on the part of General Shields, by which he succeeded in getting the enemy into a position where he could successfully give him battle; but the good planning, if there was any, was on the part of the enemy, and the victory to our troops was the result solely of the good fighting on the part of our men?

Answer. I am of the opinion that the strategy was on the part of the enemy, and that the victory was due solely to the good fighting of our men. I do not believe that very many of our command expected a fight with Jackson within two weeks at any rate.

WASHINGTON, *May* 22, 1862.

Dr. H. M. McABEE sworn and examined.

By Mr. Gooch:

Question. What is your rank and position in the army?

Answer. I am surgeon of the 4th Ohio volunteers, with the rank of major.

Question. Were you present at the battle of Winchester?

Answer. I was with General Shields during the battle. I was not present on the battle-field.

Question. Will you state to the committee what you know in relation to that battle—what came under your own observation?

Answer. My relation to General Shields and the command at the time was simply this: On the evening of Saturday, when General Shields was wounded, I was called to dress his wound, and found him prostrated with the shock to his nervous system. He said his arm would be dressed soon, and he would then take his horse. We attempted to put him in an upright posture to dress his arm, and he fainted. He then said he would have an open carriage brought, which was ordered. But upon attempting to sit up again to have his arm dressed, he again fainted. We abandoned that, and proposed to send for an ambulance in which to take him to town. At first he declined to be taken in the ambulance, but finally consented, and was thus taken to town.

I remained with him all that night. The next morning all his staff went to the field, and he asked me to act as an aid to him that day. He and

I were alone in his room nearly all day of Sunday, except occasionally when for a few minutes some of the messengers would be there. I received the messages from the field, and opened them and read them for him. And I wrote almost all the messages he dictated during that day and the night following. I think he regarded himself to be in command of his division, but not in active command on the field. And I think that is the light he intended his orders or messages to be taken. That is, he did not propose to make the dispositions of the forces in the field. His messages were mainly addressed to Colonel Kimball, in the shape of suggestions or general instructions as to how this or that should be done; not as orders for the specific movements of this or that body of troops.

He was under the impression until a late hour of the afternoon, until three o'clock, I think, that he was being trifled with by Ashby's command. He issued a great many messages to Colonel Kimball, but none of them in the shape of specific orders; rather as suggestions, he relying on Colonel Kimball's discretion as to whether it was advisable to adopt them or not, when they should be received upon the field.

Question. How long did you remain with General Shields at that time?

Answer. I remained with him from the time he was wounded, on Saturday afternoon, until about 10 o'clock on Monday morning.

Question. There have been statements that there was a great scarcity of surgeons and medical attendants at that time, and that there was great suffering on the part of our wounded for that reason. What was the fact in relation to that?

Answer. I know something about that. About noon, or a little after noon, on Sunday, when our wounded were beginning to be brought in, application was made to General Shields to have me detailed in charge of the hospitals in Winchester. He had asked me in the morning to remain and act as his aid during the day. He declined to release me, detaining me with him for his own purposes. Another detail was therefore made. Messages were received at his rooms several times during the evening and night of Sunday, complaining that there was a want of surgical aid.

After the work of the day was mainly over, at the suggestion of an officer who came in I requested General Shields to allow me to go out for two or three hours and assist in dressing the wounded. It was granted me, and I was out about two hours and a half, coming in again about 11 o'clock at night.

I am satisfied that there was not a sufficient number of surgeons there to take care of the wounded; and no arrangements had been made, not even so much as a single bunk or bed prepared previous to the engagement. There was not even any understanding, I think, until the day was somewhat advanced, as to where the wounded should be carried.

Question. Why did you not remain and assist in taking care of the wounded?

Answer. I was under General Shields's particular orders.

Question. Was his wound of such a character as to require the constant attendance of a physician?

Answer. No, sir. I think not.

Question. Could you not get leave, after you had been there and seen how he was, to go out and assist in dressing the wounds of the soldiers?

Answer. I did not feel at liberty to make such an application, after a similar application had been made by the medical director and refused. The officers of General Shields's staff were all absent, and I was alone with him almost all the day.

Question. I mean at night, after the battle was over, could you not have remained out during the night to assist in dressing the wounds of the soldiers?

Answer. I think I could.

Question. Why did you not do so?

Answer. I considered myself as obeying his orders to remain with him. My duties during the day, and the night after the battle, and the Monday morning following, were not mainly in connexion with my position in the army. They were services for which I had no commission, and for which I was entitled to no credit, and for which I, of course, received none

Question. Did not General Shields have his staff after the battle was over?

Answer. Not long; they went to bed directly after they returned.

Question. His staff came in from the field?

Answer. Yes, sir; but retired soon after. And during the night I remained in his room, as I had done during the day, receiving the messages to him and writing his orders.

Question. How many officers were on his staff?

Answer. Three or four

Question. Did they all come in and retire to bed?

Answer. Yes, sir.

Question. And left you to perform their duties, when you should have been attending to the wounded soldiers; is not that the fact?

Answer. That is, I suppose, the fact.

By the chairman:

Question. You have observed that General Shields supposed, up to 3 o'clock in the afternoon of Sunday, that it was Ashby's cavalry who were trifling with him?

Answer. Yes, sir.

Question. At what time did he become aware that Jackson was there in force?

Answer. I think somewhere along between 3 and 4 o'clock in the afternoon.

Question. What did he do when he ascertained that fact?

Answer. He could send no more forces on the field, for they were all there then.

Question. Did he assume the command then?

Answer. Not in any other sense than he had done before.

WASHINGTON, *May* 22, 1862.

Colonel WILLIAM HARRON sworn and examined.

By Mr. Gooch:

What is your rank and position in the army?

Answer. I am colonel of the 14th Indiana volunteers.

Question. Were you at the battle of Winchester?

Answer. Yes, sir.

Question. Will you give the committee a short statement of what fell under your own observation at that time?

Answer. Towards 5 or 6 o'clock, on the day previous, Saturday, I was ordered to get my regiment out and move as rapidly as I could to the front.

Question. By whom was that order issued?

Answer. By Colonel Kimball, acting as brigadier general. I moved them about two miles to the front, and was there ordered to halt. I saw nothing of the skirmish that took place that afternoon; I was off to the left of where it occurred.

Question. Tell the committee what occurred the next day.

Answer. We remained in that position until the next morning. About 10 o'clock I received an order from Colonel Kimball, through an aide-de-camp, to move forward rapidly down the turnpike. I proceeded down the turnpike about one mile. The order was to put myself in position to support, if necessary, Colonel Carroll, whose regiment had been sent forward as skirmishers. No point was indicated to me where to rest. About the time I halted my regiment, still upon the left of the road, I received a further order from Colonel Kimball, through his acting adjutant, to move yet further front, the report being that Carroll was being hardly pressed. I then moved forward until I reached Kernstown, and formed my men upon the left of the road, across a meadow, and remained there two hours. During this time the enemy had opened a battery upon our extreme left, and fired upon us very vigorously, but injured only one or two men. Colonel Carroll fell back with his line of skirmishers to my extreme left, leaving between Colonel Sullivan's command, in my rear, and myself an open space about sufficient, by prolonging his line, for one regiment. At this moment I received an order from Colonel Kimball to look well to the left, as he was fearful that the enemy were trying to turn our flank. I moved my regiment back, connecting with Colonel Carroll with my left, and then rode forward to him, telling him what order I had received. He said to me, "I am looking out carefully for that." We remained there for some time; I cannot say how long. I did not take much note of time then. The next order I received was from Colonel Kimball to move my regiment across the road to the right, and form it on the immediate left of the battery at which he was stationed on a hill. I did so, remaining there considerable time, perhaps a half or three-quarters of an hour; when from our extreme right a very rapid and vigorous fire of artillery was opened upon us, and from some concealed men immediately in our front. While waiting, in that position, for what might transpire, Colonel Tyler's brigade, upon our extreme right, commenced a fire upon the enemy's extreme left. As soon as his fire demonstrated that the engagement was becoming general, Colonel Kimball turned to me and ordered me to move as rapidly as possible to the support of Colonel Tyler, pointing out with his hand the direction I was to take, and telling me to fall in as nearly on his left as I could. I then moved forward until we rose a hill and entered the fight, to the left of the 5th Ohio, about 25 minutes after the fight had commenced. From that time, as the fight was continued, I think the men were at no time stationary. The enemy started as soon as we commenced the attack upon them; they commenced falling back, and continued that backward movement, rallying themselves, from time to time, and firing upon us; so that my men, at no time, were entirely stationary. Sometimes they were moving very slowly, until they reached the stone wall. At that time they opened a concealed and very destructive fire upon our regiment. The 84th Pennsylvania, in the mean time, had become engaged, as also the 67th Ohio. Colonel Murray having been killed at that time, the 84th Pennsylvania became a great deal disorganized.

Whilst this was progressing the 13th Indiana moved up on our extreme left, coming to the left of the stone wall. They received three or four fires from the enemy before they returned any. They delivered their first fire upon them from their front rank, at about 100 yards distance. Upon the delivery of the second fire, from the rear rank of that battalion, the enemy commenced a rapid retreat, and from that time, for 15 or 20 minutes, it was a complete rout.

That is about as correct a history as I can give of the matter.

Question. Whom did you understand to be in command of our forces on the Sunday of the battle?

Answer. Colonel Kimball, I supposed.

Question. Did you receive any orders at any time from any one else?

Answer. No, sir, none; except it was through some one authorized by him to give them.

Question. Did you receive any orders from General Shields?

Answer. No, sir; I received none directly from him. All that I received came through Colonel Kimball or some of his aids.

Question. Do you know whether any orders came from General Shields through Colonel Kimball?

Answer. No, sir; I do not. In truth, I did not see General Shields from the time he came on the field on Saturday until some time after the battle of Sunday. The order to myself to enter into the contest with my own regiment was given to me by Colonel Kimball in person. I had command of his own regiment, of which I was the lieutenant colonel, commanding the regiment at the time. He took great pride in his regiment, and kept it under his own personal observation.

WASHINGTON, *May* 22, 1862.

General J. C. SULLIVAN sworn and examined.

By Mr. Gooch:

Question What is your rank and position in the army?

Answer. I am a brigadier general of volunteers.

Question. From what State?

Answer. From the State of Indiana.

Question. Have you received a military education, and what service have you had?

Answer. I received an education in the naval service, and have had seven years' service in the navy of the United States.

Question. Were you present at the battle of Winchester, in March last?

Answer. Yes, sir.

Question. Will you give to the committee a short statement in regard to that battle?

Answer. From Saturday afternoon?

Question. Yes, sir.

Answer. I was in command of a brigade. On Saturday afternoon I heard firing to the front, but could obtain no information as to the cause of that firing. About 5 o'clock I was told that the enemy were driving in our pickets; that they had been fighting all day. I immediately called my aids and told them that, if that was so, in a short time it would be necessary for us to move. I directed them to go to our regiments and get them in readiness to move. At that moment an aid of General Shields rode up and said that the General wanted my brigade to move forward at that time. We were out two miles on the Martinsburg side of Winchester. I formed my brigade, and rode up to General Shields's headquarters for orders. When I arrived there I was told that the general had gone out to the front where the fighting was. A moment afterwards another aid rode up and told me that the general wanted my brigade to move rapidly to the front. In moving my brigade through the town I perceived the shells of the enemy exploding within the city limits. Shortly afterwards I was told that the general was wounded, and was told to halt my brigade where it was, just this side of the city; and I was told to picket the town and the roads leading into it on each side.

I called on the general just after dark, and was there told that he considered that the attack was made by only Ashby's cavalry; that he did not suppose that Jackson's force was near there.

The next morning early the general sent for me, and told me that the enemy was gone; that there was no danger of Jackson's fighting again; that he knew him, and Jackson was afraid of him, and that I could go out and pick out a camp.

In riding to the front with the assistant adjutant general I selected a nice piece of ground, but thought I would ride to the top of a hill and see if I could not throw a regiment over it. At that moment the enemy opened fire upon us with artillery. The fight lasted until about 3 o'clock, I should think, when the musketry fire commenced. I saw none of General Shields's aids at all; and if he had been in command he ought to have sent orders to me by his own aids. Colonel Kimball's aids came to me, but none of General Shields's aids came to me. During the afternoon Colonel Kimball requested assistance from me—the request coming as from himself—and I sent him four regiments.

At night after the battle I received an order from General Shields—I had only 500 men at the time—to attack the enemy the next morning with the force I had. I started at daylight to do it, and pursued them for some time.

We all considered there that Colonel Kimball was in command during the battle of Sunday; that was our understanding.

Question. Did you understand that Colonel Kimball directed the movements of our troops during the battle of Sunday?

Answer. Entirely.

Question. That was your opinion?

Answer. Yes, sir. It was impossible for anybody else to have done it. It required some one to be on the ground, to see its conformation, the position of the troops and the movements of the enemy, to be enabled to direct our troops properly.

Question. You consider that it would have been impossible for any man several miles distant from the battle-field to have directed the operations of the day?

Answer. Yes, sir; I think so.

Question. In regard to that battle, do you think it was brought about by any strategy or skill of any of our generals, in getting the enemy into a position where they could be beaten; or was the strategy on the part of the enemy, and the victory the result of good fighting on the part of our troops?

Answer. I believed that the fighting of our troops gained the victory; that there was no strategy on our part at all. I had orders to drill my troops; to commence Sunday morning, before the fighting commenced. I was to drill my troops and get them ready for the fight to come off at some future time.

Question. Drill them preparatory to action when?

Answer. At some future time—we did not know when. The general is very fond of underrating the troops. Some movements had been made in skirmishing that I was not aware of. The general wanted the men drilled to move in certain ways in skirmishing, and had ordered me to commence the drill on that Sunday; I objected, because my men had been on picket all night and were very much fatigued.

Question. That order had reference to no immediate engagement?

Answer. No, sir. I was to take my brigade and occupy the front on Sunday, and commence drilling.

MONITOR AND MERRIMACK.

IN THE SENATE OF THE UNITED STATES,
March, 11, 1862.

On motion by Mr. WILSON, of Massachusetts,

Resolved, That the select committee on the conduct of the war be directed to inquire into the late engagement between the rebel steamers and the vessels of the United States, near Fortress Monroe, with all the circumstances that led to such destruction of the property of the United States, and that they be authorized to send for persons and papers.

Attest: J. W. FORNEY, *Secretary*.

WASHINGTON, *March* 19, 1862.

Captain GUSTAVUS V. FOX sworn and examined.

By the chairman:

Question. We have been directed to inquire into the late engagement with the rebel iron-clad ship Merrimack, at Fortress Monroe. (The resolution of the Senate was then read to the witness.) Will you please state what you know about that engagement and the causes of the disaster to our shipping there.

Answer. The Cumberland and Congress were attacked by the rebel vessel Merrimack, which was invulnerable. She fired into the one and destroyed it, and ran into the other and sunk it.

Question. The Cumberland and Congress were sailing vessels?

Answer. Yes, sir; Commodore Goldsborough told me that his instructions about these vessels had not been followed out. He had directed that they never should be left without a steam-tug with which to manage them. The Merrimack attacked them when it was slack water, and had them completely at her mercy. But she got a very good pounding herself before she destroyed them.

The shaft of the Roanoke was broken about the 5th of November, and it was believed that it could be repaired in about two months. That was the report made to us. But upon inquiry it was found that every forge in the country capable of doing the work was employed. There being a large number of contracts out for steamers, every one of which must have a shaft, every available forge in the country was running to the utmost of its capacity. Finally we found one establishment that agreed to forge the shaft, but refused to turn and finish it, which, of itself, is as important and difficult a matter as the forging. The government had no adequate means to turn such an enormous piece of forging. They undertook it, however, with such means as they had at the New York navy yard, and it is now about finished—although it broke every piece of machinery they had which was put upon it, and special machinery had to be made for it.

The Roanoke was left at Fortress Monroe at the request of Commodore Goldsborough, and the sailing vessels were kept there at the request of the military authorities. A week before this affair happened the Congress was ordered away from there, but for some reason she was suffered to remain there for a time. The department, as well as the country, knew that the

Merrimack was coming out. But my feeling was that we could manage her, and I have no doubt we should have done it, had not the Minnesota got aground. But for that the Merrimack, having but three guns on each side, could not have disabled her before the Minnesota could have got alongside of her.

Question. Which was the fastest?

Answer. The Minnesota could sail two miles to the Merrimack's one.

By Mr. Wright:

Question. What would you have done if you could have got up alongside of the Merrimack?

Answer. Run into her and destroyed her; her iron plating would not have protected her against that.

Question. You think her greater speed would have enabled her to do that?

Answer. Yes, sir; and it would have crushed her, broken her in two. She is a large vessel, and her frame can be broken in almost any part by a vessel of the size and weight of the Minnesota running into her end on. It is well known that even our common wooden steamers have run into the docks and piers of New York city, and penetrated them to the distance of ten or twelve feet, though they were built of heavy timbers and filled with stone, broken granite, &c. But the Minnesota, having to pass over a shoal place to reach the Merrimack, ran aground; and she was the only vessel there able to cope with the Merrimack.

By the chairman:

Question. The Minnesota was a vessel of the same size as the Merrimack before the latter was cut down?

Answer. Yes, sir; the Minnesota, Roanoke, and Merrimack, were of the same class.

By Mr. Wright:

Question. The Minnesota was not plated with iron?

Answer. No, sir; and for that reason she would not do in a contest with the Merrimack hour by hour. But she is sufficiently protected to stand the hammering of the Merrimack until she got alongside of her. The proof of that is that the Merrimack fired at her all day and put twelve shots right through her, and did not destroy her.

By the chairman:

Question. What is the calibre of the guns of the Merrimack?

Answer. She has three 9-inch guns on a side, and has a rifled gun at each end, which is said by them to be a 100-pounder.

Question. What is the calibre of the guns of the Minnesota?

Answer. She has 9-inch guns, the same as the Merrimack, with a pivot 10-inch gun. The gun of the Monitor is 11-inch calibre. This matter of iron-clad vessels was brought up by the department a year ago, and Congress was asked for an appropriation of $50,000 in July to test the different kinds of plating, which was refused. We went to the President and he held a meeting at General Scott's office, and we were authorized to go ahead, without waiting for Congress, and make these iron plates. But when we came to call for proposals, which we did without authority from Congress, we ran against this difficulty—that there was a limit to the making of these vessels. There is no preparation for making the plates in this country, except by forging them, which is altogether too slow and tedious for the necessity. There is but one rolling mill in the country that can make the plates by rolling, and that is the one that made the plates for the Monitor. You can plate vessels with railroad iron, as the Merrimack has been plated, and you might make a half a dozen Monitors, but then you run aground. All nations have become satisfied of the value of these iron-plated vessels, and the agents we sent abroad six months ago found that all the establishments there were engaged to their utmost, and consequently they found difficulty in obtaining any plates at all.

Question. Is it possible to take this Merrimack by boarding?

Answer. No, sir. She has a sloping roof of 45 degrees, covered with tallow as thickly as it can be put on. You could not climb up her sides, which are on the slope some 15 or 16 feet, I should think, the only flat portion being in the centre. There is no possibility of boarding her, or of heaving shot and shell down her smoke stack, as has been proposed. There is no way of taking her except by running her down, except it be by a fight between her and the Monitor, which would be like a contest between knights in the tournaments of olden times, where each was incased in armor, and the result depended mainly upon the quality of the armor.

By Mr. Wright:

Question. What is the comparative speed of the Merrimack and the Monitor?

Answer. The Monitor is a little the fastest; not much, but still enough to enable her to keep clear of the Merrimack. There is no way for those two but to lie close to each other and fire under this armor. The captain of the Monitor thinks he did put a shot into her right under the water's edge. As she retreated she sagged down aft, showing that she had got a leak. But as she steamed off she showed that she had her machinery all right. My impression is that she is now shifting her guns for the heaviest guns in the southern confederacy.

By the chairman:

Question. Did it ever occur to the Navy and the War Departments, before this Merrimack was prepared, to see whether it was not well enough to take Norfolk, shipping and all?

Answer. The matter of taking Norfolk has been talked over a great deal. The movement of General Butler taking Newport News was in reference to the ultimate possession of Norfolk. The President at that time was very much in favor of it, and it was believed that it could be done without any difficulty. I think there is a memorandum here from General Butler, dated some time in the latter part of May, when he was down there, setting forth the feasibility of capturing Norfolk.

Question. How came that to fall through?

Answer. That I could not say. The matter was presented to General Scott. I can give you my impression about it.

Question. Do so, if you please.

Answer. My impression is that the panic in regard to Washington that occurred after the battle of Bull Run blocked this enterprise as it seemed to block every other enterprise that was proposed elsewhere. General Butler had at one time got as high as 11,000 men down there, and they were still sending troops to him until this panic here, when they were all taken from him except some 4,000 or 5,000 men.

Question. The ghost of Bull Run was in the way.

Answer. Yes, sir; and it also put off DuPont's expedition two or three months. We could get no soldiers after that for any of our expeditions.

Question. If I understand you in regard to the condition of the Roanoke, she had her shaft broken, and the Navy Department set about repairing it with as much expedition as they could?

Answer. It was done by telegraph the same day we heard of it.

Question. And the difficulty was finding an establishment not already engaged that was competent to undertake the work?

Answer. Yes, sir; it was estimated that two months would be all that would be necessary for the work under ordinary circumstances. Orders were at once given to contract for the shaft, but we found great difficulty in getting anybody to take hold of it. We went to parties and begged them to undertake the job; and every one refused but one establishment, who said they would forge the shaft but would not turn it. Now, turning requires as much time, if not as difficult a job, as forging it. Having no one in the whole country to do that, we had to take it to the New York yard, where there was no adequate machinery to do such an enormous piece of work. After the making of some machinery for the purpose, the work was commenced, and it is now about completed.

Question. You were at Fortress Monroe during the action?

Answer. I was there the second day.

Question. What is your opinion in regard to the ability of this Monitor to cope with the Merrimack?

Answer. Well, sir, it was an uneven fight, but the Monitor has proved herself a little the superior. But then you must consider that the Merrimack had got a tremendous pounding the day before from the Cumberland. The Cumberland dismounted one of her guns, injured two others, and shook her plates all over her. The Monitor fought under very great disadvantages. She had been three days coming from New York, and the pipe that brought fresh air down into her hold was not high enough to keep the sea out, and had to be closed, so that they were almost suffocated. They had but little sleep, and got there at half-past ten at night, and at once went to work to prepare for action, and went into the action the next morning at eight o'clock with a vessel entirely novel to everybody on board. They had had but very little drill, and were not well acquainted with each other, and deserve very great praise for going right into the midst of the rebel vessels and attacking them as they did. When the rebel vessels moved down upon the Minnesota, on Sunday morning, as she was lying there helpless, this little thing pushed right off in the midst of them, when she soon disappeared in the smoke. The next that was seen, everything was running away from her, except the Merrimack.

Question. What is the size of the Monitor compared to that of the Merrimack?

Answer. In tonnage she is about one-fifth the size of the Merrimack. She will be handled the next time with a great deal more rapidity than she was this time. But the Merrimack has got warning of the customer she has to deal with, and they will resort to every means they have to render themselves more formidable. The engines of the Monitor are now being increased so that with them they can get a knot and a half more speed out of her. Even now she can be handled more easily than the Merrimack.

By Mr. Chandler:

Question. Why did not she follow the Merrimack?

Answer. She was disabled herself, and it was not known to what extent. The pilot-house is only a log-cabin of iron logs twelve inches thick. The man who was steering and the captain were standing in the pilot-house, looking out, and one of the rifle shots struck right in front of his eyes. It broke one of the 12-inch logs of iron, and threw down the plate, and disabled the captain. It was feared his eyes were gone entirely. The more vulnerable part of the vessel being apparently very much injured, they hauled off to see what the damage was. The Merrimack hauled off too, and went off up to Norfolk. My impression is that but for that unfortunate shot, disabling the captain, in whom the crew had great confidence, he would have demolished the Merrimack entirely. She was evidently leaking very badly when she went off, while the Monitor, except the damage to that pilot-house, was entirely uninjured.

By the chairman:

Question. What is this pilot-house?

Answer. It is a square house of iron logs twelve inches through. One of the logs was broke, the plate was thrown out of place, and they did not know but what the next shot might knock the whole thing off, and then it would be gone. I told Mr. Ericsson that he ought to make it round, but he thought it was strong enough to resist any shot. They are now building an inclined wood-work of heavy timber around it and covering it with iron. That was probably completed day before yesterday. Mr. Ericsson was told about making it round, but he said no balls could break it, and it did not break but one piece. We have ordered Mr. Ericsson to go ahead and build six more as soon as he possibly can, and they will be great improvements upon this one, and carry 15-inch guns.

Question. It was said that cast-iron instead of wrought-iron shot were used, for fear the latter would burst the guns.

Answer. That is true. The wrought-iron shot weighs 185 pounds, and the cast-iron shot about 169 pounds, and as those shot did not break on the Merrimack there was no advantage in using the wrought-iron shot.

Question. They did not break?

Answer. No, sir; they glanced off.

Question. We understood that upon the trial the cast-iron shot broke?

Answer. So it will when fired against a perpendicular wall. These 11-inch guns are shell guns, and 85 or 86 of the wrought-iron shot make the weight of the gun. It is not safe to fire from a gun a shot of more than one one hundred and fiftieth part of the weight of the gun; if the gun should burst in there we would lose the vessel, and it is too great a risk to undertake. The officer in command of her now, one of the most excellent officers in the navy, told me down there that at the last pinch he thought he should put in a wrought-iron shot. But Captain Dahlgren yesterday received a letter from him in which he wrote that, upon thinking the matter over, he had concluded that it was too great a risk to do so. Captain Dahlgren has sent him down a brown shot, which weighs no more than a cast-iron shot, and will not crumble; the two have been tested with a steam trip-hammer, and while the cast-iron shot at one blow was broken all to flinders, nine blows of the trip-hammer only crushed the brown shot. These guns are intended to fire shell mostly, and are not constructed for solid shot—though solid shot are fired from them sometimes when occasion demands it; but when we do so we are not sure but the gun will give away at any moment, and that would probably blow the tower off.

Question. You say you were expecting the Merrimack there some time before she came out?

Answer. When Commodore Goldsborough came back I heard him remark to Captain Van Brunt, "I only got your letter a day or two ago, in which you write that you were sick and tired of waiting for the Merrimack, and hoped she would come out."

Question. They thought they were able to cope with her?

Answer. I have no doubt we could have done so, but for the fact that she took us at a disadvantage when the tide was low, and we had no steam-tugs ready. The Secretary of the Navy has written down to Commodore Goldsborough to inquire what directions he had given, and what had been neglected on the part of the officers he had left behind. All I know is that the commodore remarked to me that he had given orders that those vessels at Newport News should never be left without a tug to manage them, should the Merrimack come out.

Question. They were left without those tugs?

Answer. So I understand.

Question. Who was in fault in that?

Answer. The senior officer down there, in the absence of Commodore Goldsborough, is Captain Marston, of the Roanoke.

By Mr. Chandler:

Question. Have you ever ascertained the force of the enemy at Norfolk?

Answer. I was told at Old Point that they had 15,000 men at Norfolk, and it was believed 18,000 men on the York peninsula.

By the chairman:

Question. Do you think of anything else material that you desire to state?

Answer. I do not know that there is, except that I do not think we have been sufficiently alive to the power of these iron-clad vessels. And I think that both ourselves and the country at large have got a lesson that we have needed. I am willing to take my share of it. I do not know how we should have got it but for this affair—as it terminated. If we had been successful we should have slept in fancied security for the next twenty-five years, but for some such disaster hereafter.

Question. Is the Merrimack a sea-going vessel?

Answer. No, sir. It is utterly impossible for her to go to sea.

Question. What is your opinion of the European iron-clad vessels? Are they sea-going vessels?

Answer. It has been denied that the Warrior is a sea-going vessel. But I see that Lord Paget, one of the admiralty, has stated in Parliament that the reports of her commander speak of her in the highest terms of praise, saying that she behaved perfectly in the most terrific weather. They are laying down a large number of these vessels, and are laying down vessels very similar to this one of ours; that is, vessels with cupolas, circular towers.

Question. Is this vessel, the Monitor, different from their ships?

Answer. Entirely.

Question. She is a new invention?

Answer. Yes, sir; she is a perfect mechanism throughout.

Question. Did you say they were building the like of her in Europe?

Answer. This revolving tower is nothing new. It has been experimented upon in England for a year and a half, and was found to answer admirably; but it was believed by them that it could not be turned at sea. But there is nothing in the experiments abroad, that I have seen, that indicates a vessel similar to Ericsson's. His vessel, as against cannon now used, is absolutely invulnerable.

By Mr. Chandler:

Question. What would be the effect of one of these fifteen-inch solid shot upon her?

Answer. It would probably knock her all to pieces; that is what we will come to at last; we will probably go on until we have guns that will throw shot of a ton weight, until we shall have guns so large that no vessel can be built that will be protected against the shot. A fifteen-inch solid shot would knock the tower of the Monitor all to pieces. This one hundred-pound bolt that struck the tower went four and a half inches into the solid iron, and left the head of it sticking in there.

By the chairman:

Question. Did the bolt break?

Answer. Yes, sir; all except the head, which was left sticking in. If it had been a steel bolt it would, probably, have gone right through.

By Mr. Chandler:

Question. It was a rifled shot?

Answer. Yes, sir; they all have a brass fuse in the end. We found the one belonging to this shot. The Monitor was struck twenty-three times, and this was the greatest indentation that was made.

Question. What is the reason you cannot mount one of these 15-inch guns in the tower?

Answer. It can be done. We have a fifteen-inch gun at Hampton Roads, which could be fitted in there if the tower had been made in New York especially for it, but the tower now would have to be all taken apart to get it in. They are going to make all the others for fifteen-inch guns, and have the towers twelve inches thick; this one is seven inches.

By the chairman:

Question. How long do they suppose it will take to get these vessels out?

Answer. It will take four months to get the first one out, but if we can get rid of this Merrimack with this little Monitor, they would have no hesitation in taking the Monitor right into Charleston.

Question. Have we any more iron-clad vessels?

Answer. We have another nearly ready; it will be ready in about ten days.

Question. Where is that? In Boston?

Answer. No, sir; in Mystic, Connecticut.

By Mr. Chandler:

Question. Those now being built are different from this Monitor?

Answer. Yes, sir. The one at Mystic is more like an ordinary vessel, plated with iron, with masts, to go to sea with a crew. It is not invulnerable as the Monitor is.

By Mr. Wright:

Question. What is the cost of the Monitor?

Answer. She cost the government $275,000, and the builders say they have lost $25,000 on her. These vessels can be stopped from going into a harbor by stretching ropes or seines across, for the propeller would suck them right in, and get them all wound around it, and would have to go into dock to get cleared of them. I suggested to Mr. Ericsson to enclose his propeller entirely in an iron netting with large meshes, which would prevent any such thing as that.

PROTECTING REBEL PROPERTY.

In the House of Representatives, *June* 16, 1862.

On motion of Mr Wilson the following preamble and resolution were adopted:

Whereas a communication, dated Front Royal, Virginia, June 7, 1862, was published in the New York Tribune of June 14th instant, containing the following statements and charges, viz:

"During the week our men suffered severely. I never before knew what it was to be without shelter for days and nights in a terrible storm, without food and without the means to procure it. Men and horses were completely exhausted. Although the storm is now over, the sun shining, and everything presenting a cheerful appearance, we are even yet unable to procure the necessaries of life for man and beast, while there is plenty here belonging to the rebels in arms, carefully guarded by our own men, but no one permitted to take a particle. I do know where there is a commissary store belonging to the rebels, very near our late camping ground, with corn, bacon, &c., which our commissaries were not permitted to touch, but which was carefully guarded by our own soldiers, while our own division was in great danger of mutiny by reason of starvation. Rebel corn can be procured here in abundance, and also bacon, flour, &c. Yet our orders are that it shall not be touched. Now, if I were in my own sweet home, and would read of such warfare here in this hot-bed of treason, I would not believe it. But I am here and see it for myself, and I affirm that it is true. Nor is this all. I believe that the 160 rebel prisoners confined here are now better fed and cared for than our own brave soldiers. Almost every rebel house in Front Royal is guarded by our soldiers, while the inmates freely express their contempt for our government, and some of them demand nothing less than gold and silver, and enormous prices, for their bread and meat. In a word, everything that can be done for the benefit and comfort of our enemies seems to be done, while our own soldiers must put up with what they get, which is about half rations, little or no shelter, and forced marches through storm and mud, day and night." Therefore be it—

Resolved, That the select committee on the conduct of the war be instructed to make inquiry of and concerning the truth of said statements and charges, and report to this House as soon as practicable the result of such inquiry, with such recommendations in the premises as in the judgment of the committee the public interests may require. And if said allegations be true, that the committee report to this House the name of the commanding officer of such troops.

Attest:

EM. ETHERIDGE, *Clerk*.

WASHINGTON, *July* 21, 1862.

B. H. MORSE sworn and examined.

By Mr. Gooch:

Question. What is your rank and position in the army?

Answer. I have no rank, though I am called major. I have been in the government employ since the first day of April last, in the valley along the Manassas Gap railroad. My business has been the collecting of and sending in to the government abandoned rebel property all through upon the line of railroad commencing at Manassas.

Question. State what you have been doing?

Answer. I have been collecting abandoned rebel property. In the first place I collected all the property that could be got hold of, that was left there by the rebels when they evacuated that place.

Question. Under whose orders have you been acting?

Answer. In the first place I was acting under the orders of Colonel Baker, the special agent of the War Department; and after he got through I acted under the order of Captain Ferguson, quartermaster.

Question. Under whose orders was Captain Ferguson acting?

Answer. Under Quartermaster General Meigs. I have taken this ground, as I have been upon that line of railroad, under instructions, wherever I found a farm that was abandoned, or the property simply left in the hands of an overseer; or, as was the case in many instances, a negro would be left upon the place, and all the property would be left in his charge, while the owner was in the southern army, my instructions have been to take that property and send it in to the government; horses, cattle, sheep, hogs, grain, personal property. In most cases, where we find property in that situation, if it is left long it is all taken away and scattered, so that we can get nothing. If we could get at it in a short time after the army has left we could sometimes get pretty large amounts. A Captain Fletcher, who lives very near Upperville, was killed at the battle of Front Royal. I visited his place, after consulting with General Geary, and found 65 head of cattle there and 800 bushels of wheat, and various things, all amounting to some $3,000 or $4,000. And I was about to visit the place of John A. Washington, who was killed in battle some time ago. His wife is dead, and his property is left in the hands of an overseer there. But I received a summons from General McDowell to report myself at Manassas, at his headquarters there. I reported to him immediately, the day before yesterday. He took the ground that all property that was left in the hands of an overseer, no matter whether a white man or a negro, the government should not touch; and that if they called for a guard they were to have the property protected. He requested me to desist from any further operations until I had seen him further about it, in the course of two or three days; so that my operations now in that neighborhood have ceased. I have a drove of cattle coming in from there, which I took, and which will, probably, be in to-night. I think, 108 head. I have been very careful, and endeavored not to touch any property unless it was in such a situation that there could be no question about it.

Question. You mean the property of rebels?

Answer. Yes, sir, abandoned rebel property; the property of those who are voluntarily in arms; those who have accepted office under the southern confederacy, or who have been fighting against us.

Question. Have you been acting under these instructions: that, wherever you found that parties had left their property and gone into the rebel service as officers, and have left their property in charge of overseers, you have taken it for the use of the government?

Answer. Yes, sir.

Question. Do you keep an account of the property taken?

Answer. Yes, sir; and if any of the parties require receipts—that is, the heirs of the property, for instance—I give receipts in the usual manner, to be accounted for after the close of the war, if they prove their loyalty.

Question. And your instructions from General McDowell prohibited your pursuing that course any further until further orders?

Answer. He stopped me; but the quartermaster under whom I act thinks I ought to go on and perform my duty the same as I have done. There is a very large amount of property in that section. It is a rich country, and there is any quantity of grain there.

By Mr. Covode:

Question. Is there enough there to feed our army?

Answer. There is enough there to feed any number of men; and it is a great temptation to the enemy to come back there and possess themselves of that property, if for no other purpose; and I am satisfied they will attempt to do so, if they are short of food where they are. The secessionists who live there are very sanguine that will be done, I can assure you. The Union people who live in Front Royal, and in that vicinity, are moving their families away from there because they do not dare to live there now. Three families came down on the train that I came down on yesterday; they dare not stay there any longer.

The residents there say that Jackson will very soon be back there, within a very few days, surely; and that, too, seems to be the opinion of the officers and soldiers with whom I have talked.

By Mr. Odell:

Question. That he will come back?
Answer. Yes, sir.

By Mr. Gooch:

Question. Do you think of anything else you can communicate to us in connexion with your operations, except what you have already stated?
Answer. I can only state what I have seen through the lines. There is very great dissatisfaction among the Union people, and among our officers and men, with the course pursued by General McDowell in that section of country?
Question. In what respect?
Answer. They say that he presses very hard upon the Union portion of the community, not fearing to tax them to any extent as he passes through, while he protects the property of rabid secessionists there. That is the general speech of the people there. There seems to be but one opinion about it.
Question. Do you know, of your own knowledge, in relation to it, whether that be true or not?
Answer. I do not know except what people have told me, because I have not come in direct connexion with General McDowell, except in regard to my own matters.
Question. Do you know of the property of General Ashby being protected there, day and night?
Answer. I stayed at that house three nights ago. That property has now all been taken away and scattered. There were but four head of cattle there, which I took possession of, or left directions that it should be done.

By Mr. Gooch:

Question. Do you know where that property has been taken?
Answer. By the soldiers and people who have been along there.
Question. By our soldiers or theirs?
Answer. By our soldiers, who happen to get at it. This very property which General McDowell pretends to protect as he passes through, after his army is gone, is taken by irresponsible persons, who step in and take it, and use it as they think proper.
Question. What do you mean by "irresponsible persons?"
Answer. I mean persons who have no business to take it. Our own soldiers do it as well as Jackson's soldiers.
Question. Jackson forages for his army as he goes along?
Answer. Yes, sir. I know he does, because he took a large amount of property during his late raid up there.

By Mr. Covode:

Question. He has no heavy trains with him; does not haul his supplies with him?
Answer No, sir.
Question. Were you there at the time that General Geary fell back?
Answer. Yes, sir.
Question. What do you know about the amount of property destroyed on that retreat?
Answer. The amount that was destroyed was by the 104th New York regiment at Broad Run. I did know something near what was destroyed there. The value of the property was less than $3,000.

Question. Do you know anything about new cases of arms or guns being destroyed?

Answer. I was told at the time that there was something like twenty guns destroyed there that had been condemned.

Question. Was there any occasion, so far as you could see, for the destruction of that property?

Answer. There was no occasion, in my opinion. General Geary himself told me that the train was there long enough for them to have loaded everything on the train, and he felt very bad that that was not done. His own regiment had everything prepared, and they saved everything on that retreat. This other regiment came in there, and was not under his command over ten hours.

Question. Was there any occasion for a retreat at all?

Answer. That I do not know. I supposed it was done under orders. I sent teams myself from Manassas up to Gainesville to get all the baggage of the 12th Pennsylvania cavalry, who were stationed all along there, and bring the property down for fear there might be something left.

WASHINGTON, *July* 2, 1862.

Captain FREDERICK MYERS sworn and examined.

By Mr. Gooch:

Question. What is your position and rank in the army?

Answer. I am in the quartermaster's department, with the rank of captain.

Question. Under whom have you been serving of late?

Answer. Since the 16th of April last I have been serving under General McDowell, as chief quartermaster of the department of the Rappahannock.

Question. Do you know the course of policy pursued by General McDowell in relation to the property of rebels in that department?

Answer. Yes, sir; in a great measure, since I have been with him.

Question. Will you state to the committee what it has been, so far as you know?

Answer. His instructions to me have been always to take what property the government required, giving receipts to the proprietor, to the effect that such property had been taken; and to allow no person to take it except regularly authorized agents of the quartermaster's and commissary's departments.

Question. Wherever you have found rebel property which was needed for the army, in such quantities that you could take a portion of it, and still leave the owners enough to provide for their present subsistence, has that property been taken?

Answer. Yes, sir; and at times we have exceeded that. On one occasion, I now recollect, I was forced to give orders to take the property, where we were not leaving enough to feed the family there; but I promised that if I could I would return a portion to them. It was 100 barrels of corn; and the man begged me not to take it; but I had to take it.

Question. Have you known of any instance where corn, or grain of any kind, in large quantities, has been guarded for a time by our troops, and then left in the possession of the rebels?

Answer. No, sir. I know of but two cases where there was any large quantity, and that has been taken. I mean by large quantities, 3,000 or 4,000 bushels.

Question. I mean where there has been any considerable quantity, more than enough for the subsistence of the family?

Answer. No, sir; I do not. I know of no protection, except to growing crops that we might want ourselves. In such cases, and for that purpose, we have tried to save the fences. The understanding was with General McDowell and myself, and, I believe, with his officers, that we might need those growing crops ourselves, and that we better save them. The grass and clover we did not view as growing crops, and we used them wherever we found them; and the fences around the fields also, when we required them.

Question. How long were you at Fredericksburg?

Answer. I thing we arrived there on the evening of the 22d of April, and we left there about the 23d or 24th of May.

Question. Who was the military governor of Fredericksburg?

Answer. General Patrick.

Question. Was he military governor all the time you were there?

Answer. I will not be certain. That information does not come in my office exactly. I think that when we expected to move on Richmond, the order was for General Doubleday to relieve General Patrick. That, I think, was either the day we left there, or the day previous. Whether or not he did relieve General Patrick, I do not know.

Question. Do you know what was done in pursuance of that order?

Answer. I do not.

Question. Do you know whether General Doubleday ever took up his quarters in Fredericksburg?

Answer. I do not.

Question. Do you know whether or not General Patrick, after General Doubleday had been ordered to relieve him, resumed his position of military governor there?

Answer. Not unless he has done so since he went back there again. He went back, I think, a week or ten days ago.

Question. Do you know whether General Doubleday ever acted as military governor of Fredericksburg?

Answer. I do not know it personally. I heard that he was left behind as governor.

Question. You do not know how long he may have acted as such military governor?

Answer. No, sir; I do not. The understanding was that he was to be military governor when General Patrick should leave; and when General Patrick did leave it was supposed that General Doubleday was military governor.

Question. During your service under General McDowell did you observe any disposition or desire on his part to protect rebel property for the sake of leaving it again in the possession of rebels?

Answer. No, sir; I never saw anything of that kind.

Question. Do you know what his orders have been in relation to restraining the soldiers under his command from committing depredations?

Answer. I could not tell you the wording of the order; it was an order in which he said they would be severely dealt with for anything of the kind.

Question. Are those orders any more stringent than are necessary for the wholesome police regulation and discipline of the army?

Answer. No, sir. I always supposed those orders were for the purpose of promoting and preserving the discipline of the army, and that the proper men in each department would take whatever was necessary.

Question. Will you state what you know with reference to what passed between General McDowell and a Mr. Morse—a man said to have been acting as an agent for the government in collecting rebel property?

Answer. It was reported to me that Mr. Morse was taking rebel property of all kinds. I saw him, or his agent, with a large flock of sheep; and it was reported to the chief commissary, Captain Sanderson, that some of those sheep had been disposed of. I asked who this Mr. Morse was, and was told that he was an officer in the employ of the government, in the quartermaster's department. I asked him to report to me personally, and he said that he was acting under orders of Captain Ferguson, quartermaster. He showed me his orders, and I took them in to General McDowell; General McDowell read them, and told me to direct Mr. Morse not to take any more property until he could communicate with the Secretary of War, as he wished to know the operations of all officers in his department, and the authority by which they were there. He directed him to remain there until he could telegraph to the Secretary of War about it. It was that same day that General McDowell got hurt, and I have heard nothing more on the subject.

Question. Did you consider that the course pursued by this Mr. Morse was irregular?

Answer. In some cases I did. In the case of taking property and selling it on the road—I considered that irregular. In one case where a horse was stolen, taken out of a plough, it was taken to him, and, instead of its being turned over to the government, I found it in the hands of a restaurant keeper.

Question. Had it been sold to him?

Answer. I do not know whether it had been sold to him or not. I did not make any inquiries about that. It was in the hands of a restaurant keeper, who at first refused to give it up, but was directed to do so. I thought it was very irregular for property to be taken in the name of the government and then be sold to private individuals.

Question. Who is Captain Ferguson?

Answer. He is depot quartermaster at Alexandria. These things that were sold did not belong to my department, but to the commissary department. What was done with them I do not know.

WASHINGTON, *July* 15, 1862.

Colonel HERMAN HAUPT sworn and examined.

By Mr. Covode:

Question. What connexion have you had with the army?

Answer. I am a colonel on the staff of General McDowell, and chief of construction and transportation.

Question. When did your connexion with the army commence, and what services have you rendered?

Answer. I was telegraphed about the 20th of April to come to Washington, and was requested by the Secretary of War to see General McDowell, and undertake the reconstruction of the railroad between Aquia Creek and Fredericksburg, in order to facilitate some forward movements upon Richmond. I repaired to Aquia Creek, where I had an interview with General McDowell, and learned the position of affairs. I found that it was impossible for General McDowell to advance until the road between Aquia Creek and Fredericksburg was reconstructed, and the bridges on the road rebuilt. All the bridges between Fredericksburg and Aquia Creek had been burned; three miles of track had been torn up and the rails transported below Fredericksburg; the cross-ties placed together in piles and burned, and the wharf and buildings at Aquia Creek burned to the water's edge.

I commenced operations as soon as possible—within two or three days; I set men at work in the woods to cut cross-ties, transported rails from Alexandria; worked night and day, using lanterns at night, and in three days reconstructed the three miles of road, and in about two weeks completed the whole of the road and rebuilt the bridges from Aquia Creek to Falmouth, opposite Fredericksburg, so as to enable transportation to be commenced.

During all this time General McDowell was daily upon the work, urging it forward with all possible expedition, and inquiring continually of me whether he could in any way facilitate my operations; whether there was anything which I needed that it was in his power to supply.

About the time of the completion of the road to Fredericksburg the greater part of General McDowell's army was concentrated at Falmouth. At that time, or about that time, Yorktown was evacuated, and arrangements had been made by General McDowell, as was understood, with the permission of the President and the Secretary of War, to commence immediately a movement upon Richmond direct from Fredericksburg.

Question. What force had General McDowell at Fredericksburg at that time, with which to move on Richmond?

Answer. His force exceeded somewhat 40,000, after General Shields's division had joined him.

Question. Were you present at any interview between the President and General McDowell, about that time?

Answer. About the 28th of May I was present at General McDowell's headquarters; the President, the Secretary of War, and I think the Secretary of the Treasury, were there. In my presence General McDowell remarked to the President that Shields's division had joined him in very bad condition, out of shoes, clothing, and ammunition; that he would like very much to move on Saturday, but that he could not possibly be ready on that day; that Monday was a little too late. He wished very much to move on Sunday, but knowing the President's objections to these Sunday movements, he would prefer to ask his advice in regard to it. The President said to him that he should make "a good ready," and start on Monday morning.

On Saturday night the bridge across the Massaponax river, six miles below Fredericksburg, which had been prepared for burning by the rebels for about two weeks, was set on fire, they being apparently informed of our intended movements; and the rebels retreated, as was understood, to a distance of about twenty-five miles below Fredericksburg. Anticipating this movement, we had prepared a bridge ready to be loaded upon cars, which would be thrown across a stream in a single day, or less than a day, by means of which we expected to advance to a distance of twenty-five miles. Then by forced marches the whole of the corps of General McDowell was to be taken to Richmond, where he would be able to act in concert with General McClellan.

But on the Sunday after the visit of the President I received a message requesting me to go immediately to headquarters. I complied at once. I found General McDowell there very much depressed. He had just received orders to take his whole force to Front Royal. He had replied to the President that it would be impossible to accomplish the object proposed, the capture of Jackson, and by attempting that he would lose an exceedingly favorable opportunity, perhaps the most favorable opportunity they ever would have, of securing the early fall of Richmond. But, nevertheless, he would, of course, obey orders, unless those orders were countermanded, or something to that effect. The orders were not countermanded, and the movement towards Front Royal was commenced immediately.

I was requested by General McDowell to accompany him. I replied that I could not immediately do so, without leaving the transportation in great confusion; that I must first regulate the transportation, which would require a day or two, and then I would be with him.

I joined him at Manassas, two or three days afterwards. I learned from him that the bridges had been burned, and a portion of the track torn up on the Manassas Gap railroad. I sent for the construction corps, started the same night for Rectortown, constructed two bridges the next day, Friday, five more on Saturday, and reached Front Royal about Sunday noon, having reconstructed the track on the mountains on Sunday morning.

During this time General McDowell had been using every exertion to forward his troops by forced marches, and succeeded in reaching Front Royal, as I understood from him, one hour before the time fixed by the President for him to be there. When I reached Front Royal there appeared to be an engagement going on; frequent discharges of artillery were heard; and General McDowell was about moving out with his forces, expecting a general engagement. He requested me to hurry on the supplies and re-enforcements. I returned immediately on an engine, and on the same afternoon I put 5,000 troops into Front Royal; but they were not needed, as Jackson had escaped.

Question. Had you any conversation with General McDowell as to army movements, and as to what was his policy?

Answer. I had frequent conversations with him on the subject; and he was always a very decided advocate of vigorous and prompt action.

Question. Did General McDowell ever express any unwillingness to act under, or in concert with, General McClellan?

Answer. He always expressed a perfect willingness and a desire to act in concert with him. He frequently said that he was willing to act in any capacity whatever, provided something could be accomplished. His great desire appeared to be to move forward and act in concert with General McClellan to secure the fall of Richmond. That seemed to be his great desire, to press forward and hurry the fall of Richmond.

Question. Did you hear General McDowell say anything with regard to his movement up to Front Royal; that he had, for instance, so much further to move than Jackson had to retreat that there was no chance to overtake him?

Answer. Yes, sir. He said it would be impossible for him to overtake Jackson, as he (General McDowell) had nearly three times as far to advance as Jackson had to retreat, and consequently there would be no possibility of overtaking him at that point. And again that it would be very difficult for General Frémont and himself to effect a junction at the place and time designated. He felt confident that Jackson would escape before he could, by any possibility, get there.

Question. What, in your judgment, would have been the result of an advance by General McDowell upon Richmond, at the time he had made his arrangements for such an advance?

Answer. I have no doubt that Richmond would have been taken within a very few days. General McClellan's army at that time was probably 50,000 stronger than it is at present, being now wasted by casualty and disease. General McDowell's force was 40,000 strong, and in a very few days, probably in three or four days, he could have been in front of Richmond; and the two armies, acting in concert with each other, would have either caused Richmond to capitulate, or the rebels would have retreated, as on other occasions. We would have obtained possession of the city in either case.

Question. What do you know about the protection of rebel property by order of General McDowell; what was his policy in regard to that?

Answer. I am able to speak confidently upon that subject, because I have had frequent conversations with him about it. The instructions given by him to his officers have been to take not only the property of rebels, but any property that was necessary for the supply of the army; but that in all cases it should be done by proper authority. He never would permit individuals to straggle over the country and plunder on their own account, robbing farm houses and insulting citizens. He has extended protection to those who were defenceless. Where quiet citizens have remained at home, attending to the cultivation of their land, and pursuing their legitimate business, not in arms against the government in any way, if they have asked protection he has generally allowed a sentinel to be placed in their houses; one man, not a number of men; one man staying there during the whole time, not being relieved, so that the number required for this service was very small.

Question. Do you know of his seizing any rebel property?

Answer. A large amount of corn was taken along the line of the road between Aquia Creek and Fredericksburg; grain of different kinds. At Fredericksburg we took possession of a foundry and machine shop, which was converted into a repair shop for the use of the road and the repair of engines and cars. A track was laid to it, and it was used for that purpose. He has never hesitated, that I am aware of, to take any property which was necessary for the use of the army. He gave orders to his troops that they should not tear down fences, and expose growing crops of grain to destruction. The reason assigned for that was that we would probably need that grain ourselves; and if we starved the people completely out, we would probably have to support them. In taking grain from the inhabitants of the country, General McDowell directed that enough for their support should always be left, and also enough for seed. But in very many cases, after grain to that extent had been taken, leaving sufficient for the support of the families, individuals belonging to the army have robbed the people of everything that remained, leaving them without a particle of food. This occurred in numerous instances that came under my own observation.

WASHINGTON, *June* 20, 1862.

General ABNER DOUBLEDAY recalled and examined.

By the chairman:

Question. Will you state, in your own way, as briefly as you can conveniently do so, the course of conduct of our generals and officers in regard to the protection of the property of rebels, and their treatment of rebels, so far as our armies have gone, to the extent that the same has come to your knowledge?

Answer. Upon my arrival in Fredericksburg, to report to General McDowell for duty——

Question. What time was that?

Answer. About the 23d of May, I should think——I received a long lecture on the necessity of doing my best to conciliate these secessionists; the people about there, who were said to be all secessionists. The general told me with a great deal of pride and satisfaction, apparently, that he had succeeded in guarding and protecting their property for a long distance around there.

Question. The property of these rebels?

Answer. Yes, sir; he said that there had been some little disorder, or that some fences had been taken down by General Shields's brigade. I understood him to say that he would have Shields's brigade rebuild them, if he was going to stay there. At that time he supposed he was about leaving for Richmond. He said that he had sent men to repair all around the neighborhood every fence that had been taken down. He said he thought the leading rebels were not quite as bitter now as they had been; that they acknowledged that he guarded their property better than it had been guarded by their own troops; that there was better discipline among our troops, and better guards around their property. He then directed me to remain as military governor of Fredericksburg, and to guard the railroad, while he went on to Richmond with his troops. He directed me to go over and see General Patrick, who was then the military governor of Fredericksburg, and get from him such orders and directions as he had received, in order that I might be posted as to the state of affairs before entering upon the discharge of my duties. I went over to see General Patrick, but found that he was absent.

Being over there, and my baggage and tents not having arrived, and as I had to reside in the city of Fredericksburg, my duties being there, I inquired if there was any house belonging to a noted secessionist who was absent, fighting in the rebel army, that I could take for a temporary residence. The residence of a Dr. Carmichael was pointed out to me as fulfilling those conditions. He was at Richmond, and his son was in the rebel army. They had apparently abandoned the place. I went to the house, and found that a woman, an interloper, had moved in the house the day before. She said she had come there to take care of the property for Dr. Carmichael. I told her that I was coming in there to stay a few days, and I thought it would be more pleasant for her to move elsewhere. I told her to lock up everything particularly valuable in one room, and take the key of that room with her. She sent for her son, an Episcopal minister there, named Randolph. He came and talked to us ; his manner was very offensive ; he gave us to understand that he was a rampant secessionist. He attempted to argue with some members of my staff about our injustice, or something to that effect, in bringing on this war. But they set him adrift very soon ; they gave him some answers that did not please him. The next thing I knew I found that this position of military governor of Fredericksburg was taken away from me. I then left the house, upon finding that I was not to stay there, and crossed the river to the north bank. After I had left the house, I received a note from General McDowell, which I considered a very insulting one—or rather it was from General King, but written by order of General McDowell—directing me to immediately leave that residence, and give it up to Mr. Randolph, this secession minister. I mention this as an instance of the power these secessionists seem to exercise there. I understood that he represented us as having pillaged the house, carrying off bedding, &c. I directed my men not to take anything away from the house, except some secession arms and ammunition which I considered it dangerous to leave there. In my interview with General Patrick to receive instructions, or rather to obtain information—I will use that expression—in regard to my duties as military governor there, he informed me that there were some six or seven of the principal men there who were very bitter secessionists ; that one of them in particular, named Brandon, who lived out between the pickets of the two armies, and who had been protected by us, had written several very insulting letters to him. He stated that when our troops first came there these leading men were very violent indeed in their secession talk and language ; but he thought they had begun to be a little afraid now, and had latterly quieted down somewhat in their expressions.

Question. Do you know anything about the detailing of our soldiers to guard the premises of any of these secessionists ?

Answer. The soldiers, in many cases, have been utterly worn out with the duty of guarding the premises of secessionists. I will mention one case which will illustrate this matter. Two soldiers went up to a residence where there is a pump or well of water, and asked for a drink. A young woman came out, and, pointing to the canal full of dirty ditch water, told them they might drink that ; and abused and insulted them very grossly, calling them contemptible Yankees, and such names. The soldiers went off without making any reply. But a guard was immediately detailed and sent to the house to guard the premises.

Question. By whose order was that guard detailed ?

Answer. By order of General Patrick, who was carrying out the orders of General McDowell in the premises. The soldiers complain that while they are doing this duty of guarding secession houses and property the secession women insult them, drawing up their dresses as they pass them ; and that they are obliged to listen to treasonable language, and the abuse of the Yankees and their institutions.

Question. Is there any attempt to provide for the army, by foraging on the enemy, or these secession people there ?

Answer. I do not know how that is. I captured very heavy amounts of forage, which were concealed in places in town ; forage belonging to the confederate army, which I thought might have been taken before, had there not been such extreme delicacy about entering secession residences. I would mention also, that although the secessionists whose farms are guarded are apparently satisfied, yet, as you cannot guard everybody's farm without consuming the entire army for that purpose, those whose farms are not guarded are loud in their complaints, and the demands for sentinels to guard the houses of these secessionists, in almost every case, come, not in the form of a request, but in the form of exceedingly insulting demands.

Question. Is any regard paid to these insulting demands to have guards detailed for that purpose ?

Answer. I did not pay any regard to them. I have understood, however, that they have been attended to just the same as the others. Among several who came to me with such requests, a woman came to me, stating that her husband and sons were in the rebel army, and demanded that I should immediately send up a guard to protect herself and property, not that any outrage had been committed there, but because there might be. I know that is the usual form in which they come ; that of insolent and insulting demands.

Question. In your opinion, as a military man, could not the expenses of this war be greatly diminished by treating these rebels as enemies, and foraging our armies upon them as far as possible ?

Answer. Immensely diminished. I do not believe we can keep up the war without doing that. I heard of immense flocks of sheep, belonging to secessionists of the most violent character, within easy reach, which are not touched, while we are paying for cattle from Pennsylvania and elsewhere, perhaps, to go down from Washington along the Potomac river. We are guarding their property for them, very carefully guarding it, while they are in the rebel army fighting us.

Question. You say that we are extensively guarding the property of rebels, while they are in the rebel army fighting against us ?

Answer. Yes, sir. And one of those secessionists—a classmate of Henry A. Wise in college, a wealthy man, one of the leading men there—told me that we might guard every rod of their property, and still they would guard us just the same. It was stated to me that some of the market gardening belonging to them which we had been guarding had been sent to their friends in the rebel army at Richmond. We had kept a sharp watch over it, to keep our soldiers from touching it, and that is the way they had disposed of it.

By Mr. Covode:

Question. How did they treat your men while on guard ? Did they give them anything to eat while guarding their property ?

Answer. In consequence of my having entered this secession house, all my men were taken away from me and placed under the command of another general. The men made very bitter complaints of their treatment by these secessionists; but being outside of my command, I cannot tell about that. The men complained that the secessionists looked upon them as so many hogs that had been put in the houses for a time; that the women would draw up their dresses contemptuously as they passed them, and make insulting remarks in their presence; and their food would be put out to them as though they were some unclean animals that must be borne with for a time. Those are the complaints of the soldiers; but they were soldiers who were beyond my jurisdiction.

Question. You have no reason to suspect those statements of the soldiers to be untrue?

Answer. No, sir.

By Mr. Gooch:

Question. What, in your judgment as a military man, should be the course to be pursued by a general marching through the portions of country you have marched through with General McDowell, with reference to the treatment of the people there, and with reference to the disposition made of any property they might have which would be useful to our army?

Answer. Our course should be, in the first place, to encourage Union men and develop the Union element in the country. I have found in every place where I have been about a certain proportionate number of prominent violent secessionists, whom our army have been protecting and conciliating, instead of punishing. I am satisfied that if such men as those should be punished, the Union element would immediately develop itself. But the Union men are now paralyzed by the power, wealth, and influence of these secessionists, and their threats of future vengeance. I would not have these secessionists received and treated as friends—dined and wined, and having all requests coming through them; and have the power of this government pass through their hands from us to the Union men. Whatever authority was to be given should be given to the Union men. I would mete out to these men the same measure they mete out to our men. They carry off our men to Richmond, tying them to the backs of horses and mules, and carrying them off in that way. For every Union man they treated in that way I would take one or more of the most violent secessionists of the neighborhood, and hold them as hostages. That course would protect Union men. And if the property of Union men was destroyed by these secessionists, I would destroy their property, or hold it responsible for the loss. The Union men are continually haunted with the fear that as we do not put our foot down firmly and remain there, but simply put it down and withdraw it after a little while—they fear that the moment they develop their Union sentiments they will become marked, and be liable to seizure the moment we retire, and their property be left in the hands of their and our enemies. I would prevent marauding by the soldiers, by sending out mounted patrols on all the roads.

Question. Where you found grain and forage of any kind, what would you do?

Answer. I would take it without any hesitation. And instead of driving down, at a heavy expense, herds of cattle from Washington, I would take he cattle, and horses, and sheep there, and give the owners certificates. If hey are loyal men, they would get their pay; if they are disloyal men, they ught not to be paid—or I would attach some condition, such as if they ecome loyal by a certain time, and then continue loyal, they should be aid.

By Mr. Chandler:

Question. Are there sheep left there now?

Answer. Yes, sir.

Question. I supposed the rebels had taken all such things foraging for their army.

Answer. We came upon Fredericksburg so suddenly that there were immense quantities of such things that they could not take off.

By Mr. Gooch:

Question. Do you find it to be true that the leading rebel men have been the men who have been received with favor by our officers in command, and preference given to them over men who are Union men?

Answer. I think so. I think they have been courted for the purpose of conciliation and keeping the country quiet. I find that the Union men have not been regarded; that very little attention has been paid to them; that they have been treated as people of very little earthly consequence; while the others have been sent for and dined and wined and treated as people of high consideration.

Question. What has been the effect of that course of conduct?

Answer. The effect has been utterly to dishearten the Union men. They say they will have to abandon all their property and leave their homes if this thing is to go on.

By Mr. Julian:

Question. Has that course conciliated the rebels?

Answer. Not in the slightest degree. As I have before stated, one of them said to me that we might guard every atom of their property, and still they would hate us just the same. They have their sons and brothers in the rebel army, and are all fully committed to this rebellion. If we conquer them, they sink into insignificance; if they succeed, they rise into prominence and importance.

By Mr. Gooch:

Question. Your opinion is that this rebellion must be conquered and not coaxed down?

Answer. We must whip them; that is the only thing for us to do.

WASHINGTON, *June* 20, 1862.

Captain E. P. HALSTED sworn and examined.

By the chairman:

Question. What is your rank and position in the army?

Answer. I am a captain, and assistant adjutant general on General Dou bleday's staff.

Question. What facts have come under your observation touching th manner in which rebel property is protected by soldiers of our army d tailed for that purpose?

Answer. One particular instance, which General Doubleday has omitted t state, is this: Seven men of the 76th New York regiment were posted som six or seven miles down the river from Fredericksburg, away from the mai body of the army, to guard the houses of four secessionists there, when, i case of any accident, they were liable to be cut off and captured. In regar to the protection of the property of secessionists there generally, I kno from observation, and from information received from reliable sources, th all that General Doubleday has stated is true. And, furthermore, I am i formed by Major Livingston, of the 76th New York regiment, who has be military governor down there for a time, that, for two weeks after General McDowell commanded the town by his guns, the cars were running on the railroad from Fredericksburg every night, as soon as their operations were covered by the darkness, carrying off all the property they could get out of town, in the way of grain, &c. I speak of this, as it might lead to further investigation on your part. And I think Major Livingston might afford you very reliable evidence on the subject. And for two weeks before the troops were sent to the other side of the river to prevent any property from being taken away, the markets were guarded very sedulously by our soldiers, and their produce was sent off to Richmond.

Question. Sent to Richmond?

Answer. Yes, sir; sent to Richmond. This information I have from the nilitary governor; of course, I do not know it myself personally.

Question. Where is that military governor?

Answer. He is down there yet. He has recently removed from town, and s now doing duty with his regiment.

Question. By whose permission did you understand this to be done?

Answer. I did not understand that it was done by any person's order, ex-ept so far as the guarding of secession property, and the conciliatory policy owards the rebels, have allowed it to be done. It has rather been permitted han ordered.

Question. Did General McDowell know that these things were going on?

Answer. I could not say that he did. When the secession mail was cap-ured by Major Livingston, it was some five miles from town, with a woman nd a man in a carriage driving it. One woman, whose husband is in the ebel army, had a pair of Yankee-made boots which she was taking to her usband. Those letters, which the Secretary of War has now, were con-ealed under this woman's clothes. She was brought back and searched, nd the letters taken from her.

Question. Do you know what were the contents of those letters?

Answer. I read only a few of them. I glanced over some of them. I do ot recollect the contents of them well enough to state them, or much of iem. As far as I read them, they all concurred in this: that they had not een insulted or abused by any of our troops; that the conducts in town ad been very kind to them.

Question. How far out are our troops ever detailed to guard rebel prop-ty?

Answer. I do not know of any case where they are further out than in at case I have already spoken of—some six or seven miles down the river.

Question. Has the detailing of men to guard rebel property been carried to such an extent as to impede the operation of our forces there and to eaken our army any?

Answer. Yes, sir. I think every detail for such guard has a tendency to eaken the army. And since the general has been there, whenever parties ve asked for a guard, they have said invariably that they were allowed a iard by General McDowell, in every instance; and there have been a great any instances of their demanding a guard. They come as though they emed it their right, and demand it.

Question. In your judgment, could not the expense of our army be im-nsely reduced if we were to treat the rebels as enemies, and forage upon em?

Answer. Yes, sir; I think it could be. I am told that there are, between Rappahannock and Potomac rivers, thousands of bushels of grain stored, d there are herds of cattle and sheep. And up to the time that Major vingston and General Doubleday were in command of the town, there has n in the town a large quantity of grain, the most of which General Doubleday seized. He did not believe in the policy of allowing it to be shoved off to Richmond to support the rebel army. Now they may go anywhere from the south bank of the Rappahannock and take all their produce to Richmond; and I understand they do it now.

There are one or two circumstances I would speak of in regard to those captured letters. One of them, written by a lady to a friend in Richmond, I think, speaks of a General G. who came to her house to eat strawberries and cream; they discussed times less perilous than the present, and soon they found their hearts heaving deep sighs. She expressed the hope that he would be the next military governor. We took it that the reference was to General Gibbon, who, a few nights since, sent two of his staff to the town to escort the Reverend Mr. Lacy to his tent, on the north side of the river, to dine with. This Reverend Mr. Lacy, I understand, is the brother of the Major Lacy who was captured the day that General McCall gave up the command there and left for Richmond. I refer to that to show the feeling of some of our military officers, and as, perhaps, explaining this mild, conciliatory policy.

Question. Is this Lacy a secessionist?

Answer. Yes, sir, notoriously so, and one of the most influential and bitter men in town.

By Mr. Odell:

Question. Do you refer to the minister?

Answer. Yes, sir, and to the other man also. The other man was one o the most zealous secessionists. Whenever there was a town meeting held before the ordinance of secession was passed, Major Lacy was present, ex horting the people to go for secession, so I am told there. He owns a ver large estate where General McDowell has his headquarters; and on th morning of the same day that Major Lacy was arrested, application wa made to General Doubleday for permission to arrest him; stating that ther was information that he was about 10 miles out from town at his farn house. The application, in writing, was sent to General McCall by an ai of General Doubleday, and it was refused, with the statement that l thought it was not worth while.

A day or two days before the arrest of Major Lacy, General McCall r leased six prisoners, I think, in all; four of whom, we learned afterwards fro a captain of the 4th Pennsylvania cavalry, were at that time with the regiment again, (as he understood from one of his scouts)—the 9th Virgin cavalry.

By the chairman:

Question. Released six prisoners to go back into the rebel ranks?

Answer. He gave them liberty to go back into their own country agai and being soldiers of that regiment, they went back to their regiment aga That is the milk and water policy of conducting this war.

Question. Is there anything more you think of connected with the tre ment of the rebels?

Answer. I do not think of anything further. General Doubleday's sta ment was very full.

By Mr. Odell:

Question. When you speak of forage, &c., in Virginia, to what extent country do you refer?

Answer. We have information extending—

Question. We do not want your information. What do you know?

Answer. I know nothing about it, except this fact.

Question. Do you know this fact, that General McDowell has fed his army, since he started, upon the rebel grain and forage in the valley?

By Mr. Gooch:

Question. Is that so? Do you know whether he has or has not?
Answer. I know that he has not entirely.

By Mr. Odell:

Question. Do you not know that he has to a great extent?
Answer. I do not.
Question. Do you know that he has to any extent?
Answer. I do.
Question. Do you know of his taking possession of large quantities of grain and forage, and giving the owners receipts for it, for the foraging and feeding of his army?
Answer. I do not know that it is so; it may be so.
Question. Have you heard it was so?
Answer. I heard that he did capture a large quantity of grain when he first went there. I heard that from the 4th Pennsylvania cavalry.

By Mr. Gooch:

Question. Tell us all you know about that, either from your own observation or from what you have heard from others?
Answer. Of course I know only what I have heard. I do not know it to any great extent.

By the chairman:

Question. We want the general idea of how the thing is conducted?
Answer. Captain McRae, of the Freeborn, lying there at Fredericksburg, told me that he had information of large quantities of grain, as I have already stated, between the Rappahannock and Potomac rivers.

By Mr. Gooch:

Question. Do you know anything—I do not mean from actual knowledge merely—as to what has been the course pursued by General McDowell in reference to that matter? Whether, where he has found abundance of grain and forage, he has guarded it and left it in the possession of the rebels, or whether he has seized it for the use of his own army?
Answer. I have understood generally that he has not taken it for the support of his army, but it has been guarded and then left.
Question. Where it was in large quantities?
Answer. In considerably large quantities.

By Mr. Julian:

Question. How have you learned that?
Answer. From different individuals; officers of the army.

By Mr. Gooch:

Question. Can you tell us who can give us information upon that point?
Answer. I heard it spoken of by Colonel Lord, of the 35th New York, for one, and I have heard Major Livingston speak generally of these things.

By the chairman:

Question. Major Livingston was provost marshal there?
Answer. He was provost marshal and military governor there. I do not think of any others at this time. I do not know of a single foraging party being sent out to forage, or anything of that kind.

WASHINGTON, *June* 21, 1862.

Major JAMES H. TRIMBLE sworn and examined:

By Mr. Covode:

Question. Where do you reside when you are at home?

Answer. In Westmoreland county, Pennsylvania.

Question. What is your position in the army?

Answer. Major of the 4th Pennsylvania cavalry.

Question. I understand you have been down in the neighborhood of the Rappahannock, at Fredericksburg.

Answer. Yes, sir; I have. I came up from there, getting here last night.

Question. Will you state what you and your command have been engaged in there?

Answer. I have been engaged in scouring the country around between here and there, and out beyond there.

Question. How far have you advanced beyond Fredericksburg?

Answer. I do not rightly know. I think that at the time that Lieutenant Martin captured this Major Lacy, he was out some eighteen or twenty miles south and west of the city of Fredericksburg.

Question. Who is Lieutenant Martin?

Answer. He is first lieutenant of company C, of the 4th Pennsylvania cavalry; a company that I raised myself.

Question. What force had Lieutenant Martin with him at the time he made this dash and captured Major Lacy?

Answer. When I send out scouts on such expeditions we generally take men out of two or three different companies. He had with him some of company C, a part of a company that your son, George Covode, brought into the regiment, and a part of company A.

Question. Has your command (the 4th Pennsylvania cavalry) been made use of to guard rebel property?

Answer. Yes, sir; where we are encamped, or were encamped when I came away, we were guarding a corn-crib of about 3,000 bushels of ears of corn. We had a guard right around it. It was right about the centre of our encampment. And we had to guard that man's strawberry patch; he was very much afraid that our boys would get over into it and destroy it. And I had to guard his spring-house. And finally, about dark, he called upon me for a guard for his house. Our horses were suffering, and I did not like the idea of guarding that corn-crib when we needed the forage so much. I had pushed about 300 head of horses through there for forty-eight hours without a bite. I lost a splendid horse.

Question. When there was feed in plenty in the neighborhood?

Answer. Yes, sir; but under General McDowell's orders we could not take it; we must pay for everything that we take. We were bound to protect property as we passed through. Our orders were very severe. I pastured some horses once.

Question. Is there not a great unwillingness on the part of the soldiers in our army to be used for that purpose?

Answer. It is near about played out, I judge. The men have got tired of passing through the enemy's country and having to protect their property, and then be insulted by the women there; they are tired of it.

Question. Does this protecting their property do any good? Does it gain their good will?

Answer. Not a particle; I do not see that it does a particle of good. Right above where we were there were some negroes cutting some wheat the other day, and some of the boys went up to get a little for their horses—

a handful of wheat to give them a bite. Soon word was sent down, and I had to send up a lot of men and arrest them and bring them back. We have no hay; what little feed we get down there for our horses is oats.

Question. There is plenty of good pasture there?

Answer. There are lots of good pasture—splendid pastures—there.

Question. And yet you have lost horses from starvation?

Answer. Yes, sir; they gave out on account of our work.

By Mr. Julian:

Question. You could get forage by paying for it?

Answer. Yes, sir; but we have not the money to pay as we go along, and there are numbers of them who will not sell to us at any rate. I have given orders on the quartermaster's department for forage, where they would let us have it; I have also turned my horses into a clover field, and given orders on the quartermaster to pay for it.

Question. Did you not have to put men there to guard your horses?

Answer. Yes, sir; there would be a corner cut off for me, and I had to place men there to guard the horses.

By Mr. Odell:

Question. Did you make a bargain to give them so much for that?

Answer. Yes, sir; I told them what I would give them—about what I thought it was worth.

By Mr. Gooch:

Question. You fix your own price?

Answer. Yes, sir; what I think it is worth.

Question. You took what you pleased?

Answer. No, sir, I did not.

Question. Who limits you? You are not allowed as you go along to feed your horses in the fields and pastures wherever you please?

Answer. No, sir.

Question. Are your orders such that you must let your horses starve to death instead of doing that?

Answer. Our orders are to protect the property as we pass through.

Question. So stringent that you cannot put your horses into the fields?

Answer. Yes, sir. If we obey them strictly.

By Mr. Covode:

Question. Have you not had to take the property of professed Union men because the secessionists would not sell you any of their property?

Answer. I do not know as I have, because in that section of country I do not know many Union men. On the other side of the Occoquan—about five miles on the south side of that creek—I met with a man whom I took to be a Union man, by the name of Joy. I think probably he is a Union man. He has given us the privilege and not asked us a *haet*—given to my men as far as he was able.

Question. You know this of your own knowledge, and you have yourself had to give orders to our troops to go and guard this property?

Answer. Yes, sir.

Question. Day and night?

Answer. Yes, sir.

Question. If it were not for these restrictions thrown around the property of the rebels, could you not forage on the enemy, and support the army?

Answer. Yes, sir. We could keep our stock and everything in first-rate plight.

Question. In your judgment, does the present mode of warfare in that country tend to gain us the day?

Answer. I never was an abolitionist, but still I think we must take other measures if we would quell this rebellion.

Question. What do you mean—to use the negroes?

Answer. Yes, sir. I would arm the negroes; give them arms, and let them assist us.

Question. What do you know of organized guerilla parties of farmers there?

Answer. I do not know much about them. I have the names here of some three men who were said to have been in the rebel army, and who came home here a short time ago. They are now officers of a guerilla party of farmers, of about 120 men. These men live in what is called the "Maple Bottom Flats." I cannot tell just exactly where that is. There is a railroad station on the railroad that runs up to Manassas called Lee Station, and this guerilla party is made up of farmers in the section of country around there. These three men are named John A. King, Mortrivel Cornell, and William Lin. This William Lin is said to be the ringleader. There is a man by the name of John Finch, who lives in that neighborhood. He has a very nice farm there. He has had to leave his farm, and has lost all his stock. And on last Saturday, I think it was, he was then leaving there with a little two-horse wagon, into which he had put his family and some few little things, and was coming up to the city here. Yesterday I gave these names to one of the captains of Colonel Biddle's command down here at Aquia creek, and told him I thought it would be well to send out a squad of infantry into this neighborhood, as it would not be far, and have them watch the manœuvres of those men; watch them both day and night.

Question. As far as you observed, is not the whole white population of the country there turning guerillas—none of them at work?

Answer. I cannot say that I have seen any whites at work there, without it was some woman working in some little garden-patch. On the Rappahannock all the work is done by slaves. I did not see any white men at work there at all.

Question. Were they cutting their wheat there before it was ripe?

Answer. It did not look to me to be near ripe. They were cutting it and letting it lay in swathes.

Question. What do you think was their reason for cutting it so early?

Answer. I think it was because they want to make use of it.

Question. Could you not seize that wheat now if you were allowed to do so?

Answer. Yes, sir; I could.

By Mr. Gooch:

Question. You say you are guarding a corn-crib which has about 3,000 bushels in it?

Answer. Yes, sir; it is a large, common log-house.

Question. And you say that at the same time your horses were suffering for want of feed?

Answer. We have not feed enough. We have to draw rations (oats) now from Fredericksburg, and we do not get as much as we should have. Twelve pounds of oats, with no hay at all, is not enough to do horses for twenty-four hours.

Question. What do you understand to be the intention in relation to that corn-crib? Are you to leave it in possession of the rebel owners?

Answer. Of course.

Question. You do not understand that it is ever to be taken for the use of our army?

Answer. No, sir.

Question. You understand that it is not to be taken?

Answer. Yes, sir; that it is to be left there.

Question. Have you ever known of any instances where any corn-cribs, or any kind of provender, of any description, in large quantities, have been guarded and left?

Answer. No more than what we have done ourselves.

Question. Have you guarded any such property for a while, and then left it when you passed on?

Answer. Yes, sir.

Question. In large quantities?

Answer. Yes, sir.

Question. Do your instructions go to the extent of guarding this property, and leaving it in possession of the rebels, when we need it for the use of our own troops?

Answer. Yes, sir; that is our instructions; to guard it and leave it. As long as we are there, we are bound to guard it and protect it all.

Question. Your instructions extend to this extent: that you are not allowed to pasture or feed your horses in the fields?

Answer. Yes, sir; that is our instructions. I would take it in this way: that, according to orders, we must protect all property as we pass along. I look at it in this way: that if we turn our horses into a pasture field, we are trespassing, not protecting it.

Question. You are disobeying orders?

Answer. Yes, sir.

Question. And you understand that to extend throughout the whole army?

Answer. As far as our command, at any rate.

Question. Have you known of any instance where, by orders of superior officers, property has been taken, such as grain, &c.?

Answer. No, sir; we have not.

Question. You have known no such instance?

Answer. I think we sent out a squad while on patrol duty in this city here, pretty early in the spring.

Question. I refer to General McDowell's command.

Answer. No, sir; we have never taken anything in that way.

By Mr. Odell:

Question. I understood you to say that in some instances you go into a field and forage your horses, and pay as you choose for it?

Answer. Yes, sir.

Question. How do you reconcile that with your positive orders not to do it?

Answer. I did that because my horses had given out; and I was obliged to do it.

Question. Were you censured for it?

Answer. I have had no report of it, at any rate.

By Mr. Covode:

Question. Have you bargained with parties for permission to do so?

Answer. I turned my horses into one field without bargaining.

By Mr. Odell:

Question. Do you not feel competent to do that whenever necessity requires it?

Answer. I do not know; we have to obey orders.

Question. Do you not do it when necessity requires it?
Answer. I never did it, except in that one field.

By Mr. Gooch:

Question. When you are passing by the corn of a secessionist, and you are actually in need of that corn for your horses, do you feel that you violate your orders to take it?
Answer. Yes, sir.

By Mr. Covode:

Question. When you set our soldiers to guard their strawberry patches, do they ever give them any?
Answer. I never heard the boys say they ever got any. And they know very well that they dare not go and take any themselves; because if they should, and it should be reported, they would be punished. That is our orders; we are to punish them severely if they touch a *haet*. They must protect what they are placed over to guard. If they do not do it, we punish them severely.

WASHINGTON, *June* 30, 1862.

General IRVIN McDOWELL re-examined.

By Mr. Gooch:

The following preamble and resolution were read to the witness:

"HOUSE OF REPRESENTATIVES, *June* 16, 1862.

"On motion of Mr. Wilson, the following preamble and resolution were adopted:

"Whereas a communication, dated Front Royal, Virginia, June 7, 1862, was published in the New York Tribune of June 14, instant, containing the following statements and charges, viz:

"'During the week our men suffered severely. I never before knew what it was to be without shelter for days and nights in a terrible storm without food, and without the means to procure it. Men and horses were completely exhausted. Although the storm is now over, the sun shining, and everything presenting a cheerful appearance, we are even yet unable to procure the necessaries of life for man and beast, while there is plenty here belonging to the rebels in arms carefully guarded by our own men, but no one permitted to take a particle. I do know where there is a commissary store belonging to the rebels, very near our late camping ground, with corn, bacon, &c., which our commissaries were not permitted to touch, but which was carefully guarded by our own soldiers, while our own division was in great danger of mutiny by reason of starvation! Rebel corn can be procured here in abundance, and also bacon, flour, &c.; yet our orders are that it shall not be touched. Now, if I were in my own sweet home, and would read of such warfare here in this hotbed of treason, I would not believe it. But I am here, and see it for myself, and I affirm that it is true. Nor is this all. I believe that the 160 rebel prisoners confined here are now better fed and cared for than our own brave soldiers. Almost every rebel house in Front Royal is guarded by our soldiers, while the inmates freely express their contempt for our government, and some of them demand nothing less than gold and silver, and enormous prices, for their bread and meat. In a word, everything that can be done for the benefit and comfort of our enemies seems to be done, while our own soldiers must put up with what they get, which is about half rations, little or no shelter, and forced marches through storm and mud, day and night.'

"Therefore be it—

"*Resolved*, That the select committee on the conduct of the war be instructed to make inquiries of and concerning the truth of said statements and charges, and report to this house, as soon as practicable, the result of such inquiry, with such recommendations in the premises as, in the judgment of the committee, the public interests may require. And if said allegations be true, that the committee report to this house the name of the commanding officer of such troops."

By Mr. Gooch:

Question. Are the statements embodied in that preamble true or false?

Answer. Some of them are true, and some of them are false. It is true that the men had little shelter after a forced march, and were very much exposed. It is not true that they were without food, or without the means to procure it. It is true that the men and horses were very much exhausted. It is not true that they were unable to procure the necessaries of life for man and beast. I do not know whether the writer of that knew where there was a commissary store of the rebels. If he did, he knew more than I did. I should think that is hardly likely to be true. I do not believe it is true. It certainly is not true, if the one he says he knew was carefully guarded by our own soldiers. I put no guard over a rebel commissary at all. He says, "Rebel corn can be procured in abundance, and also bacon, flour, &c.; yet our orders are that it shall not be touched." I will answer that soon. He says, "I believe that the 160 rebel prisoners confined here are now better fed and cared for than our own brave soldiers." I think that is very likely. They were in a house, to begin with, and the citizens of the place gave them things from their own houses.

Here is a report of the chief of the commissary department, in answer to an inquiry as to whether or not the troops at Front Royal were at any time without supplies from the government:

"*Received June* 28, 1862, *from Manassas.*

"12.30 *p. m.*

"COLONEL: At no time that I am aware of were the troops short of subsistence at Front Royal. A wagon train and a railroad train arrived the very day their requisitions ran out, and Hartsuff's and Ricketts's brigades, and Shields's division, were immediately supplied, through their commissaries, by me in person, acting for Captain Willard, then acting as post commissary. Bayard's brigade may have suffered, but from causes beyond our control.

"Bayard's brigade was not at Front Royal, but had gone over to Strasburg, and were swallowed up in General Frémont's army.

"I am under the impression the salt did not arrive with the other subsistence, but came up next day. At Fredericksburg, the provost marshal, Colonel Gates, under direction of General Patrick, seized and turned to the commissary about 500 bushels of corn meal, and 1,500 barrels of flour, for all of which the proper certificates of indebtedness were tendered. At Front Royal, to prevent speculation, I seized 367 barrels and 19 sacks of flour stored in Mr. Weston's mill, of which I issued to the citizens (they paying for the same to the miller or his agent) 34 barrels; the balance I turned over to General Ricketts, who returned it to the owner. I have no official intelligence, nor do I know of any other seizures, except by marauders in this department.

"Respectfully,

"JAMES S. SANDERSON,
Captain, and Chief Commissary.

"Colonel E. SCHRIVER, *Chief of Staff.*"

I have answered generally as to this, that the troops were at no time without their full supply of subsistence, brought there by railroad or wagon trains from Manassas to Front Royal. I did prevent the men from robbing houses. I will read my order on that subject, which, perhaps, may have been one of the causes of this resolution:

"HEADQUARTERS DEPARTMENT RAPPAHANNOCK,
"*Front Royal, Virginia, June* 3, 1862.

"General Orders No. 18.]

"There has been, recently, so much irregularity on the subject of levying contributions, and so much misconception on the part of many commanders and their officers as to their powers and duties in this respect, that it has become necessary to call the attention of all concerned to the subject, to the end that the gross abuses which have been committed may cease.

"Paragraph 491, Army Regulations:

"'When the wants of the army absolutely require it, and in other cases, under special instructions from the War Department, the general commanding may levy contributions, in money or kind, in the enemy's country occupied by troops. No other commander can levy such contributions without written authority from the general commanding in chief.'

"This paragraph applies to domestic as well as to foreign enemies.

"No other commander than the general-in-chief of an army can levy contributions without written authority from such general-in-chief. Yet not only do other commanders, but corporals and privates even undertake to assume the power, without authority from any one. Such conduct is simply pillage, theft, or robbery.

"When, in the judgment of the major general commanding, the wants of the army under his command require it, he will exercise, as he has already most freely done, this extraordinary power, and will prescribe fully by whom, when, in what way, to what extent, and in what measure those contributions shall be levied. The allowances of the government to the army, issued through the quartermaster and subsistence departments, are to be obtained by commanders, by requisitions on the proper officers of those departments; and if they have not the supplies to meet those requisitions, they will apply to their superiors in the department, and the articles will be furnished, if on hand, if the requisitions be approved, or means will be taken to obtain them.

"No one has the right to take private property for public uses, except those whom the major general commanding may authorize. Those who take for private uses will be tried by a military commission for stealing.

"Commanders are especially enjoined to protect growing crops, and not suffer them to be trodden down, save in cases of manifest necessity.

"No one has a right to enter private houses, and thus disturb non-combatants—women and children.

"The above, without in any way wishing to seem even to interfere or suggest to others the course to be pursued in respect to the subject here in question, will apply to the troops of the department of the Rappahannock, whether within or beyond the department limits.

"By command of General McDowell.

"SAM'L BRECK, *Assistant Adjutant General.*"

The system which I pursued was to take flour, corn, or whatever was necessary, and take it by the officers of the quartermaster's and commissary departments, and issue it. But as a matter of economy in the use of supplies, and as a measure of discipline, I would not permit men with arms in their hands to go and take whatever they might deem necessary from houses along the roads. Troops that are allowed to do that soon become utterly worthless.

It may seem hard to put men to guard property, but otherwise you must pursue a course which will seem to be harder still. General Pope tells me that out west they pursue a much simpler plan. They put men out on a march as patrols, with orders to shoot every man who attempts to enter a private house.

Generally, therefore, in regard to the letter embraced in this preamble, it is not true that the troops suffered for the want of the ordinary supplies of the government. It is true they suffered from the exposure to rains and by forced marches. That is a kind of suffering incidental to the service they performed; not from my own orders simply, but from what was required by my superiors. That forced march was made without my wish and against my judgment. But I carried out my orders as well as I could. It rained and stormed all the while. The men went without their knapsacks, so that they might move the faster; and they suffered accordingly. But they did not suffer for want of food, unless it was through the neglect of their officers, for the food was there.

The statement that I protected property is true I did it on principle. And I think you can accomplish nothing in any military department without you act on that principle. As a question of economy in the use of these very supplies, as a question of discipline among the men themselves, you cannot allow them to do as they please, and to plunder as they go through a country.

Question. What were your orders and instructions to your quartermasters and commissaries in relation to supplies in the possession of rebels, where they were found in abundance—where a man was found to have more than was needed for the necessary subsistence of his family and those dependent upon him for the time being?

Answer. I gave orders at Fredericksburg under which we took largely of flour and corn.

By Mr. Julian:

Question. Belonging to rebels?

Answer. I did not ask to whom it belonged, but took it wherever I found it. I always found that whenever the men wanted to take anything from a house, the owner was sure to be a rabid secessionist. I did not make a test of administering the oath of allegiance, because I thought a scoundrel might take it and a conscientious man might not. But I took what was necessary for the service and gave a receipt for it, stating that the person from whom the property was taken would be entitled to payment at the end of this rebellion, provided he could prove that he had been a faithful and loyal citizen of the United States from that time forth. I made but two or three payments all the time. I paid one man, a very old man, who had some grain which we took; and I paid a poor man, a blacksmith, whose only means of subsistence was the work of his shop. I needed the shop and everything he had in it to shoe my horses. I took possession of his premises and all the coal which he had, for which I paid him five dollars. There was another case of a woman at Front Royal. I did not ask whether she was a rebel or not, or whether she had rebel kindred in the army of the confederates. She was a widow woman, and had in her house some of our wounded soldiers, and had shown every attention to them. That woman I paid for what things I took from her. We took some bacon from her, and, I think, some corn and flour. I also gave her a safeguard—the second safeguard I have given on the other side of the river. The other safeguard was given to a northern man in possession of a mine on the other side of the Rappahannock, who had suffered a great deal from guerilla parties, and who also was suffering from some of our troops, for our troops strayed all over the country. I tried to protect the growing crops. I tried to have the wheat protected until it arrived at maturity; for whether we want it or not, or whether it was for them, it was a thing that was desirable to be had.

Question. What do you mean by "if it was for them?"

Answer. In that country the men are mostly gone; there are none but women, children, and negroes left behind. They must be fed. I fed a great many hundreds of women and children there, who had nothing to eat and came to me for assistance. I used to ask the negroes how they expected to live. They would say that their masters had left them a little bacon and corn. The next day, perhaps, I would find that the soldiers had been there and taken what little bacon and corn had been left, under the general idea that they were entitled to take what they pleased. If these people do not get something to eat from their growing crops, we will have to feed them. Therefore I looked upon it as a matter of principle that I should do what I could to protect growing crops. I did not protect clover or pasturage; that was used abundantly and freely.

Question. Did you in any cases protect large quantities of corn and other articles of subsistence by our soldiers when our army was in the vicinity, and then, when our army left, leave those articles in the possession of the enemy?

Answer. I know of no such case as that, except what I have just seen in the letter of Captain Sanderson. I directed him to seize the flour in the mill there. He writes that he did seize it, and turned it over to General Ricketts, who returned it to the owner. This is the first I knew of that.

By Mr. Gooch:

Question. Will you state to the committee exactly the course of conduct pursued by you with reference to rebel property and the protection of the rebels themselves in your late department of the Rappahannock?

Answer. As to the rebels themselves, or their families that I found in the country, (the non-combatants—the women and children,) I gave them all the protection I could. As to the property that I found there which was necessary for the army, I caused it to be taken by the quartermaster or commissary and issued to the troops; causing it to be accounted for as property belonging to the government, or which the government had seized for its own use, requiring a statement or receipt to be given; which, I am very free to say, I do not think was invariably done, though I tried to have it done. The statement or receipt was given to the possessor of the property, stating that he would be entitled to be paid for it at the close of this rebellion, provided that he shall show from that time forth he has behaved himself as a loyal citizen of the United States. I have paid but three persons, I believe, anything for what I have taken from them—the cases I have already referred to. [After a pause:] I am not certain but there was another case, that of the only Union man said to be in Fredericksburg—a Mr. Clark, a northern man, who has since left and gone north. He was, perhaps, paid for some supplies. I have taken a great many barrels of flour, and thousands of bushels of corn, a great deal of pasturage, a great deal of lumber, a large machine-shop, a foundery, quantities of forage, long and short; corn meal, beef cattle, &c.; and have taken, or authorized to be taken, a quantity of horses by General Shields, and whatever other supplies he might need or find necessary on his trip up the Valley. That is what I have positively done. What I have forbidden to be done can be seen from my order, which I have read here.

Question. Have you in any instances caused to be protected large quantities of corn and grain of any kind, and left it in the possession of disloyal citizens?

Answer. I am not aware of anything of the kind. I could with great difficulty answer that question. I had a command which extended over a great many square miles. I gave general orders, and what was done under those general orders, I, of course, cannot tell. What may have been done in one portion of the department under those general orders, I do not, of course, know until the case is brought to my attention. It may be that this case is the one that may have caused your inquiry. It is the case of property down the Rappahannock, below Fredericksburg, of some property that was guarded there, belonging to a Mrs. Grey. I had taken from her abundantly of corn; reduced her stock of corn to as low a point as she could bear. I did not see it myself. I sent down General Van Rensselaer to make examination of two cases down there, alleged to be cases of great hardship—cases of women. I have taken all but what is called the reserve corn—that which is necessary to carry the family through until the next crop can be made available. I gave orders that the reserve corn should not be touched. I have taken a great many barrels of corn from the place of Mrs. Grey. She was living on the place with a large family, taking care of the place herself. I quartered a regiment of cavalry on her place, almost around the house itself. They took abundantly from her; but this reserve corn I ordered should not be touched, because so much corn had been taken from her. I did take more at last, and then representations came up to me that if more was taken they would be left in a state of starvation; and I sent General Van Rensselaer down to examine into the matter.

Question. Your directions were to leave that only which was necessary for the subsistence of the family?

Answer. Yes, sir; that which was necessary to subsist them until they could use their next crop. In that part of the country the farms are very large; there are many negroes and many children upon them. The white men, perhaps, have gone off with the rebel army, leaving the farms under the care of negroes. The men have left, while the women and children—the helpless portion of the family—are left behind. There may have been quite a large quantity of corn left for the use of non-combatants in such cases.

Question. The intention was to leave only enough to subsist them?

Answer. That is all. It was done upon reports of officers that I sent there to examine. Without knowing that that was the case you refer to, that may be the case, and there may be other cases. The principle I went on was to take whatever I could, without leaving the people to starve, except in the last extremity.

Question. That is, you would not take all unless it was necessary for the subsistence of the troops?

Answer. Yes, sir. When the question was whether the people should starve or my troops should starve, then I would take it for my troops.

Question. I now desire to call your attention to an order made by you, which was read in the Senate the other day by Mr. Wade. The order is as follows:

"HEADQUARTERS DEPARTMENT OF THE RAPPAHANNOCK,
" *Opposite Fredericksburg, Va., May* 26, 1862.

" Special Order No. 68.]

" Colonel Meredith, commanding the 56th Pennsylvania volunteers, will furnish from his regiment a guard for the house and property of Mr. L. J. Huffman, who lives near Bell Plain. Colonel Meredith will see that no more corn is taken from Mr. Huffman, and that no more fencing is disturbed. The guard will be so placed as to make this sure, even if it should be necessary to place a sentinel over every panel of fence.

"By command of Major General McDowell.

"SAMUEL BRECK,
"*Assistant Adjutant General.*

"Colonel S. A. MEREDITH,
"*Commanding 56th Pennsylvania Volunteers.*"

Have you any statement or explanation which you desire to make in reference to that matter ?

Answer. This Mr. Huffman lives at Bell Plain, a few miles south of Aquia creek. Bell Plain was chosen by me as a temporary landing and depot for my supplies, which were required for the troops at Fredericksburg, until such time as the railroad from Aquia creek to Fredericksburg should be completed and could be used for the bringing up of supplies. When we first came to Bell Plain we found that a house at that place had been destroyed by the rebels. In a field close by were several grain-houses full of corn in the ear, and there was a large field of clover which had been put in by drilling; it was a beautiful field of clover. I seized upon all his corn for the government, and turned my beef cattle into his clover field, and took the remains of his house to build a wharf—and camped my troops upon his place. Some time afterwards, I cannot tell how long, while going from Aquia creek to Fredericksburg in company with Mr. Seward, Mr. Stanton, and Mr. Chase, the owner of this property came to see me, and asked me if he could get any compensation for the damage my troops had caused him, and also if he could have any protection in putting in and taking care of his growing crops for the next season. He said that I had taken all his corn except a little he had at his house for family use, and that the troops were committing a great many depredations upon the enclosures immediately around his house. There was a second house there ; there had been another, but it had been burned down.

I told him that as to compensation, I could make him none. He said that he had taken no part in this war, and that he had refused to give supplies to the other side. The proof of that was that he had these supplies when I got there. He said that he had not gone away as most of his neighbors had done, but had remained on his farm to take care of it, and to see if he could raise something of a crop for the coming year. I told him that I would take no more corn from him; would not take what was left, and that I would, so far as I could, protect him in his efforts to raise a crop; that I would give him the usual receipt for the property I had taken, but I could make him no payments.

I gave him an order at that time, which he carried to the commanding officer at Bell Plain. Subsequently the commanding officer at Bell Plain was changed, and another regiment went there. Mr. Huffman came to Fredericksburg and complained to me that my order had not been complied with; that the soldiers were still depredating upon his premises, burning his fences, so that his crops were in the commons. He asked if I could give him some protection. His house was close by the wayside, on the road used for bringing supplies from Bell Plain to Fredericksburg, and the road was constantly being passed over by trains, teamsters, bodies of troops, and stragglers, and he was very much exposed.

Having taken from him all that I thought he could spare, and he having suffered much damage at our hands, I reiterated the order, or rather I gave directions to my staff officer to reiterate the order, in pretty strong terms, to the commanding officer at Bell Plain, directing that the man should be no further molested, but that he should be protected in his efforts to put in his crop; that his fences should be spared, and that a guard should be detailed to see that this was done. The terms of the order I did not see when it was made out, nor were my directions to the staff-officer given to him in the terms which he used.

Question. Your directions were merely that a stringent order should be issued to that effect?

Answer. That is all. It is very seldom that a commanding officer sees to details of that kind. Mr. Wade said, in his remarks in the Senate, that the man was as rank a traitor as there is on the face of the earth. I never knew anything about the man being a traitor. I should judge that if he was a traitor he was a very mild one, from the fact that he was one of the very few persons who remained in that part of the country, trying to cultivate his farm. He certainly was a heavy sufferer from our presence. That form of expression—"a sentinel to every panel of fence"—was merely this young man's way of expressing the idea that the order must be complied with, must be carried out, in some form or manner.

REBEL BARBARITIES.

IN THE SENATE OF THE UNITED SATES, *April* 1, 1862.

On motion by Mr. SUMNER,

Resolved, That the select committee on the conduct of the war be directed to collect the evidence with regard to the barbarous treatment by the rebels, at Manassas, of the remains of officers and soldiers of the United States killed in battle there; and that said select committee also inquire into the fact whether Indian savages have been employed by the rebels in their military service, and how such warfare has been conducted by said savages against the government of the United States.

Attest:

J. W. FORNEY, *Secretary.*

Mr. Wade, from the joint committee on the conduct of the present war, begs leave respectfully to submit a report, in part, as follows:

On the first day of April the Senate of the United States adopted the following resolution; which was referred to the committee on the conduct of the war:

> *Resolved,* That the select committee on the conduct of the war be directed to collect the evidence with regard to the barbarous treatment by the rebels, at Manassas, of the remains of officers and soldiers of the United States killed in battle there; and that the said select committee also inquire into the fact whether the Indian savages have been employed by the rebels, in their military service, against the government of the United States, and how such warfare has been conducted by said savages.

In pursuance of the instructions contained in this resolution, your committee have the honor to report that they examined a number of witnesses, whose testimony is herewith submitted.

Mr. Nathaniel F. Parker, who was captured at Falling Waters, Virginia, testifies that he was kept in close confinement, denied exercise, and, with a number of others, huddled up in a room; that their food, generally scant, was always bad, and sometimes nauseous; that the wounded had neither medical attention nor humane treatment, and that many of these latter died from sheer neglect; that five of the prisoners were shot by the sentries outside, and that he saw one man, Tibbetts, of the New York twenty-seventh regiment, shot as he was passing his window on the 8th of November, and that he died of the wound on the 12th. The perpetrator of this foul murder was subsequently promoted by the rebel government.

Dr. J. M. Homiston, surgeon of the 14th New York or Brooklyn regiment, captured at Bull Run, testifies that when he solicited permission to remain on the field and to attend to wounded men, some of whom were in a helpless and painful condition and suffering for water, he was brutally refused. They offered him neither water nor anything in the shape of food. He and his companions stood in the streets of Manassas, surrounded by a threatening and boisterous crowd, and were afterwards thrust into an old building, and left, without sustenance or covering, to sleep on the bare floor. It was only when faint and exhausted, in response to their earnest petitions, they having been without food for twenty-four hours, that some cold bacon was grudgingly given to them. When, at last, they were permitted to go to the relief of our wounded, the secession surgeon would not allow them to perform operations, but intrusted the wounded to his young assistants, "some of them with no more knowledge of what they attempted to do than an apothecary's clerk." And further, "that these inexperienced surgeons performed operations upon our men in a most horrible manner; some of them were absolutely frightful." "When," he adds, "I asked Doctor Darby to allow me to amputate the leg of Corporal Prescott, of our regiment, and said that the man must die if it were not done, he told me that I should be allowed to do it." While Doctor Homiston was waiting, he says a secessionist came through the room and said, "they are operating upon one of the Yankee's legs up stairs." "I went up and found that they had cut off Prescott's leg. The assistants were pulling on the flesh at each side, trying to get flap enough to cover the bone. They had sawed off the bone without leaving any of the flesh to form the flaps to cover it; and with all the force they could use they could not get flap enough to cover the bone. They were then obliged to saw off about an inch more of the bone, and even then, when they came to put in the sutures (the stitches) they could not approximate the edges within less than an inch and a half of each other; of course, as soon as there was any swelling, the stitches tore out and the bone stuck through again. Dr. Swalm tried afterwards to remedy it by performing another operation, but Prescott had become so debilitated that he did not survive." Corporal Prescott was a young man of high position, and had received a very liberal education.

The same witness describes the sufferings of the wounded after the battle as inconceivably horrible; with bad food, no covering, no water. They were lying upon the floor as thickly as they could be laid. "There was not a particle of light in the house to enable us to move among them." Deaf to all his appeals, they continued to refuse water to these suffering men, and he was only enabled to procure it by setting cups under the eaves to catch the rain that was falling, and in this way he spent the night catching the water and conveying it to the wounded to drink. As there was no light, he was obliged to crawl on his hands and knees to avoid stepping on their wounded limbs; and, he adds, "it is not a wonder that next morning we found that several had died during the night." The young surgeons, who seemed to delight in hacking and butchering these brave defenders of our country's flag, were not, it would seem, permitted to perform any operations upon the rebel wounded. "Some of our wounded," says this witness, "were left lying upon the battle-field until Tuesday night and Wednesday morning. When brought in, their wounds were completely alive with larvæ deposited there by the flies, having laid out through all the rain-storm of Monday, and the hot, sultry sunshine of Tuesday." The dead laid upon the field unburied for five days; and this included men not only of his own, the 14th regiment, but of other regiments. This witness testifies that the rebel dead were carried off and interred decently. In answer to a question whether the confederates themselves were not also destitute of medicine, he replied, "they could not have been, for they took all ours, even to our surgical instruments." He received none of the attention from the surgeons on the other side, "which," to use his own language, "I should have shown to them had our position been reversed."

The testimony of William F. Swalm, assistant surgeon of the 14th New York regiment, who was taken prisoner at Sudley's church, confirms the statement of Dr. Homiston in regard to the brutal operations on Corporal Prescott. He also states that after he himself had been removed to Richmond, when seated one day with his feet on the window-sill, the sentry outside called to him to take them in, and on looking out he saw the sentry with his musket cocked and pointed at him, and withdrew in time to save his life. He gives evidence of the careless, heartless, and cruel manner in which the surgeons operated upon our men. Previous to leaving for Richmond, and ten or twelve days after the battle, he saw some of the Union soldiers unburied on the field, and entirely naked. Walking around were a great many women, gloating over the horrid sight.

The case of Dr. Ferguson, of one of the New York regiments, is mentioned by Dr. Swalm. "When getting into his ambulance to look after his own wounded he was fired upon by the rebels. When he told them who he was, they said they would take a parting shot at him, which they did, wounding him in the leg. He had his boots on, and his spurs on his boots, and as they drove along his spurs would catch in the tail-board of the ambulance, causing him to shriek with agony." An officer rode up, and, placing his pistol to his head, threatened to shoot him if he continued to scream. This was on Sunday, the day of the battle.

One of the most important witnesses was General James B. Ricketts, well known in Washington and throughout the country, lately promoted for his daring and self-sacrificing courage. After having been wounded in the battle of Bull Run, he was captured, and as he lay helpless on his back, a party of rebels passing him cried out, "knock out his brains, the d——d Yankee." He met General Beauregard, an old acquaintance, only a year his senior at the United States Military Academy, where both were educated. He had met the rebel general in the south a number of times. By this head of the rebel army, on the day after the battle, he was told that his (General Ricketts's) treatment would depend upon the treatment extended to the rebel privateers. His first lieutenant, Ramsey, who was killed, was stripped of every article of his clothing but his socks, and left naked on the field. He testified that those of our wounded who died in Richmond were buried in the negro burying-ground among the negroes, and were put into the earth in the most unfeeling manner. The statement of other witnesses as to how the prisoners were treated is fully confirmed by General Ricketts. He himself, while in prison, subsisted mainly upon what he purchased with his own money, the money brought to him by his wife. "We had," he says, "what they called bacon soup—soup made of boiled bacon, the bacon being a little rancid—which you could not possibly eat; and that for a man whose system was being drained by a wound is no diet at all." In reply to a question whether he had heard anything about our prisoners being shot by the rebel sentries, he answered: "Yes, a number of our men were shot. In one instance two were shot; one was killed, and the other wounded, by a man who rested his gun on the window-sill while he capped it."

General Ricketts, in reference to his having been held as one of the hostages for the privateers, states: "I considered it bad treatment to be selected as a hostage for a privateer, when I was so lame that I could not walk, and while my wounds were still open and unhealed. At this time General Winder came to see me. He had been an officer in my regiment; I had known him for twenty-odd years. It was on the 9th of November that he came to see me. He saw that my wounds were still unhealed; he saw my condition; but that very day he received an order to select hostages for the privateers, and, notwithstanding he knew my condition, the next day, Sunday, the 10th of November, I was selected as one of the hostages." "I heard," he continues, "of a great many of our prisoners who had been bayonetted and shot. I saw three of them—two that had been bayonetted and one of them shot. One was named Louis Francis, of the New York 14th. He had received fourteen bayonet wounds—one through his privates—and he had one wound very much like mine, on the knee, in consequence of which his leg was amputated after twelve weeks had passed; and I would state here that in regard to his case, when it was determined to amputate his leg, I heard Dr. Peachy, the rebel surgeon, remark to one of his young assistants, 'I won't be greedy; you may do it;' and the young man did it. I saw a number in my room, many of whom had been badly amputated. The flaps over the stump were drawn too tight, and some of the bones protruded. A man by the name of Prescott (the same referred to in the testimony of Surgeon Homiston) was amputated twice, and was then, I think, moved to Richmond before the taps were healed—Prescott died under this treatment. I heard a rebel doctor on the steps below my room say, 'that he wished he could take out the hearts of the d——d Yankees as easily as he could take off their legs.' Some of the southern gentlemen treated me very handsomely. Wade Hampton, who was opposed to my battery, came to see me and behaved like a generous enemy."

It appears, as a part of the history of this rebellion, that General Ricketts was visited by his wife, who, having first heard that he was killed in battle, afterwards that he was alive but wounded, travelled under great difficulties to Manassas to see her husband. He says: "She had almost to fight her way through, but succeeded finally in reaching me on the fourth day after the battle. There were eight persons in the Lewis House, at Manassas, in the room where I lay, and my wife, for two weeks, slept in that room on the floor by my side, without a bed. When we got to Richmond, there were six of us in a room, among them Colonel Wilcox, who remained with us until he was taken to Charleston. There we were all in one room. There was no door to it. It was much as it would be here if you should take off the doors of this committee room, and then fill the passage with wounded soldiers. In the hot summer months the stench from their wounds, and from the utensils they used, was fearful. There was no privacy at all, because there being no door the room could not be closed. We were there as a common show. Colonel Wilcox and myself were objects of interest, and were gazed upon as if we were a couple of savages. The people would come in there and say all sorts of things to us and about us, until I was obliged to tell them that I was a prisoner and had nothing to say. On our way to Richmond, when we reached Gordonsville, many women crowded around the cars, and asked my wife if she cooked? if she washed? how she got there? Finally, Mrs. Ricketts appealed to the officer in charge, and told him that it was not the intention that we should be subjected to this treatment, and if it was continued she would make it known to the authorities. General Johnston took my wife's carriage and horses at Manassas, kept them, and has them yet for aught I know. When I got to Richmond I spoke to several gentlemen about this, and so did Mrs. Ricketts. They said, of course, the carriage and horses should be returned, but they never were. "There is one debt," says this gallant soldier, "that I desire very much to pay, and nothing troubles me so much now as the fact that my wounds prevent me from entering upon active service at once."

The case of Louis Francis, who was terribly wounded and maltreated, and lost a leg, is referred to by General Ricketts; but the testimony of Francis himself is startling. He was a private in the New York 14th regiment. He says: "I was attacked by two rebel soldiers, and wounded in the right knee with the bayonet. As I lay on the sod they kept bayonetting me until I received fourteen wounds. One then left me, the other remaining over me, when a Union soldier coming up, shot him in the breast, and he fell dead. I lay on the ground until 10 o'clock next day. I was then removed in a wagon to a building; my wounds examined and partially dressed. On the Saturday following we were carried to Manassas, and from there to the general hospital at Richmond. My leg having partially mortified, I consented that it should be amputated, which operation was performed by a young man. I insisted that they should allow Dr. Swalm to be present, for I wanted one Union man there if I died under the operation. The stitches and the band slipped from neglect, and the bone protruded; and about two weeks after another operation was performed, at which time another piece of the thigh bone was sawed off. Six weeks after the amputation, and before it healed, I was removed to the tobacco factory."

Two operations were subsequently performed on Francis—one at Fortress Monroe, and one at Brooklyn, New York—after his release from captivity.

Revolting as these disclosures are, it was when the committee came to examine witnesses in reference to the treatment of our heroic dead, that the fiendish spirit of the rebel leaders was most prominently exhibited. Daniel Bixby, jr., of Washington, testifies that he went out in company with Mr. G. A. Smart, of Cambridge, Massachusetts, who went to search for the body of his brother, who fell at Blackburn's Ford in the action of the 18th of July. They found the grave. The clothes were identified as those of his brother on account of some peculiarity in the make, for they had been made by his mother; and, in order to identify them, other clothes made by her were taken, that they might compare them. "We found no head in the grave, and no bones of any kind—nothing but the clothes and portions of the flesh. We found the remains of three other bodies all together. The clothes were there; some flesh was left, but no bones." The witness also states that Mrs. Pierce Butler, who lives near the place, said that she had seen the rebels boiling portions of the bodies of our dead in order to obtain their bones as relics. They could not wait for them to decay. She said that she had seen drumsticks made of "Yankee shinbones," as they called them. Mrs. Bulter also stated that she had seen a skull that one of the New Orleans artillery had, which, he said, he was going to send home and have mounted, and that he intended to drink a brandy punch out of it the day he was married.

Frederick Scholes, of the city of Brooklyn, New York, testified that he proceeded to the battle-field of Bull Run on the fourth of this month (April) to find the place where he supposed his brother's body was buried. Mr. Scholes, who is a man of unquestioned character, by his testimony fully confirms the statements of other witnesses. He met a free negro, named Simon or Simons, who stated that it was a common thing for the rebel soldiers to exhibit the bones of the Yankees. "I found," he says, "in the bushes in the neighborhood, a part of a zouave uniform, with the sleeve sticking out of the grave, and a portion of the pantaloons. Attempting to pull it up, I saw the two ends of the grave were still unopened, but the middle had been prised up, pulling up the extremities of the uniform at some places, the sleeves of the shirt in another, and a portion of the pantaloons. Dr. Swalm (one of the surgeons, whose testimony has already been referred to) pointed out the trenches where the secessionists had buried their own dead, and, on examination, it appeared that their remains had not been disturbed at all. Mr. Scholes met a free negro, named Hampton, who resided near the place, and when he told him the manner in which these bodies had been dug up, he said he knew it had been done, and added that the rebels had commenced digging bodies two or three days after they were buried, for the purpose, at first, of obtaining the buttons off their uniforms, and that afterwards they disinterred them to get their bones. He said they had taken rails and pushed the ends down in the centre under the middle of the bodies, and pried them up. The information of the negroes of Benjamin Franklin Lewis corroborated fully the statement of this man, Hampton. They said that a good many of the bodies had been stripped naked on the field before they were buried, and that some were buried naked. I went to Mr. Lewis's house and spoke to him of the manner in which these bodies had been disinterred. He admitted that it was infamous, and condemned principally the Louisiana Tigers, of General Wheat's division. He admitted that our wounded had been very badly treated." In confirmation of the testimony of Dr. Swalm and Dr. Homiston, this witness avers that Mr. Lewis mentioned a number of instances of men who had been murdered by bad surgical treatment. Mr. Lewis was afraid that a pestilence would break out in consequence of the dead being left unburied, and stated that he had gone and warned the neighborhood and had the dead buried, sending his own men to assist in doing so. "On Sunday morning (yesterday) I went out in search of my brother's grave. We found the trench, and dug for the bodies below. They were eighteen inches to two feet below the surface, and had been hustled in in any way. In one end of the trench we found, not more than two or three inches below the surface, the thigh bone of a man which had evidently been dug up after the burial. At the other end of the trench we found the shinbone of a man, which had been struck by a musket ball and split. The bodies at the ends had been pried up. While digging there, a party of soldiers came along and showed us a part of a shinbone, five or six inches long, which had the end sawed off. They said that they had found it among many other pieces in one of the cabins the rebels had deserted. From the appearance of it, pieces had been sawed off to make finger-rings. As soon as the negroes noticed this, they said that the rebels had had rings made of the bones of our dead, and that they had them for sale in their camps. When Dr. Swalm saw the bone he said it was a part of the shinbone of a man. The soldiers represented that there were lots of these bones scattered through the rebel huts sawed into rings," &c. Mr. Lewis and his negroes all spoke of Colonel James Cameron's body, and knew that "it had been stripped, and also where it had been buried." Mr. Scholes, in answer to a question of one of the committee, described the different treatment extended to the Union soldiers and the rebel dead. The latter had little head-boards placed at the head of their respective graves and marked; none of them had the appearance of having been disturbed.

The evidence of that distinguished and patriotic citizen, Hon. William Sprague, governor of the State of Rhode Island, confirms and fortifies some of the most revolting statements of former witnesses. His object in visiting the battle-field was to recover the bodies of Colonel Slocum and Major Ballou, of the Rhode Island regiment. He took out with him several of his own men to identify the graves. On reaching the place, he states that "we commenced digging for the bodies of Colonel Slocum and Major Ballou at the spot pointed out to us by these men who had been in the action. While digging, some negro women came up and asked whom we were looking for, and at the same time said that 'Colonel Slogun' had been dug up by the rebels, by some men of a Georgia regiment, his head cut off, and his body taken to a ravine thirty or forty yards below, and there burned. We stopped digging and went to the spot designated, where we found coals and ashes and bones mingled together. A little distance from there we found a shirt (still buttoned at the neck) and a blanket with large quantities of hair upon it, everything indicating the burning of a body there. We returned and dug down at the spot indicated as the grave of Major Ballou, but found no body there; but at the place pointed out as the grave where Colonel Slocum was buried we found a box, which, upon being raised and opened, was found to contain the body of Colonel Slocum. The soldiers who had buried the two bodies were satisfied that the grave had been opened, the body taken out, beheaded, and burned, was that of Major Ballou, because it was not in the spot where Colonel Slocum was buried, but rather to the right of it. They at once said that the rebels had made a mistake, and had taken the body of Major Ballou for that of Colonel Slocum. The shirt found near the place where the body was burned I recognized as one belonging to Major Ballou, as I had been very intimate with him. We gathered up the ashes containing the portion of his remains that were left, and put them in a coffin together with his shirt and the blanket with the hair left upon it. After we had done this we went to that portion of the field where the battle had first commenced, and began to dig for the remains of Captain Tower. We brought a soldier with us to designate the place where he was buried. He had been wounded in the battle, and had seen from the window of the house where the captain was interred. On opening the ditch or trench we found it filled with soldiers, all buried with their faces downward. On taking up some four or five we discovered the remains of Captain Tower, mingled with those of the men. We took them, placed them in a coffin, and brought them home."

In reply to a question of a member of the committee as to whether he was satisfied that they were buried intentionally with their faces downward, Governor Sprague's answer was, "Undoubtedly! Beyond all controversy!" and that "it was done as a mark of indignity." In answer to another question as to what their object could have been, especially in regard to the body of Colonel Slocum, he replied: "Sheer brutality, and nothing else. They did it on account of his courage and chivalry in forcing his regiment fearlessly and bravely upon them. He destroyed about one-half of that Georgia regiment, which was made up of their best citizens." When the inquiry was put whether he thought these barbarities were committed by that regiment, he responded, "by that same regiment, as I was told." While their own dead were buried with marble head and foot stones, and names upon them, ours were buried, as I have stated, in trenches. This eminent witness concludes his testimony as follows: "I have published an order to my second regiment, to which these officers were attached, that I shall not be satisfied with what they shall do unless they give an account of one rebel killed for each one of their own number."

The members of your committee might content themselves by leaving this testimony to the Senate and the people without a word of comment; but when the enemies of a just and generous government are attempting to excite the sympathy of disloyal men in our own country, and to solicit the aid of foreign governments by the grossest misrepresentations of the objects of the war, and of the conduct of the officers and soldiers of the republic, this, the most startling evidence of their insincerity and inhumanity, deserves some notice at our hands. History will be examined in vain for a parallel to this rebellion against a good government. Long prepared for by ambitious men, who were made doubly confident of success by the aid and counsel of former administrations, and by the belief that their plans were unobserved by a magnanimous people, they precipitated the war (at a moment when the general administration had just been changed) under circumstances of astounding perfidy. Without a single reasonable ground of complaint, and in the face of repeated manifestations of moderation and peace on the part of the President and his friends, they took up arms and declared that they would never surrender until their rebellion had been recognized, or the institutions established by our fathers had been destroyed. The people of the loyal States, at last convinced that they could preserve their liberties only by an appeal to the God of battles, rushed to the standard of the republic, in response to the call of the Chief Magistrate.

Every step of this monstrous treason has been marked by violence and crime. No transgression has been too great, no wrong too startling for its leaders. They disregarded the sanctity of the oaths they had taken to support the Constitution; they repudiated all their obligations to the people of the free States; they deceived and betrayed their own fellow-citizens, and crowded their armies with forced levies; they drove from their midst all who would not yield to their despotism, or filled their prisons with men who would not enlist under their flag. They have now crowned the rebellion by the perpetration of deeds scarcely known even to savage warfare. The investigations of your committee have established this fact beyond controversy. The witnesses called before us were men of undoubted veracity and character. Some of them occupy high positions in the army, and others high positions in civil life. Differing in political sentiments, their evidence presents a remarkable concurrence of opinion and of judgment. Our fellow-countrymen, heretofore sufficiently impressed by the generosity and forbearance of the government of the United States, and by the barbarous character of the crusade against it, will be shocked by the statements of these unimpeached and unimpeachable witnesses; and foreign nations must, with one accord, however they have hesitated heretofore, consign to lasting odium the authors of crimes which, in all their details, exceed the worst excesses of the Sepoys of India.

Inhumanity to the living has been the leading trait of the rebel leaders; but it was reserved for your committee to disclose as a concerted system their insults to the wounded, and their mutilation and desecration of the gallant dead. Our soldiers, taken prisoners in honorable battle, have been subjected to the most shameful treatment. All the considerations that inspire chivalric emotion and generous consideration for brave men have been disregarded. It is almost beyond belief that the men fighting in such a cause as ours, and sustained by a government which, in the midst of violence and treachery, has given repeated evidences of its indulgence, should have been subjected to treatment never before resorted to by one foreign nation in a conflict with another.

All the courtesies of professional and civil life seem to have been discarded. General Beauregard himself, who, on a very recent occasion, boasted that he had been controlled by humane feelings after the battle of Bull Run, coolly proposed to hold General Ricketts as a hostage for one of the murderous privateers, and the rebel surgeons disdained intercourse and communication with our own surgeons taken in honorable battle.

The outrages upon the dead will revive the recollections of the cruelties to which savage tribes subject their prisoners. They were buried in many cases naked, with their faces downward; they were left to decay in the open air; their bones were carried off as trophies, sometimes, as the testimony proves, to be used as personal adornments, and one witness deliberately avers that the head of one of our most gallant officers was cut off by a secessionist to be turned into a drinking cup on the occasion of his marriage. Monstrous as this revelation may appear to be, your committee have been informed that during the last two weeks the skull of a Union soldier has been exhibited in the office of the Sergeant-at-arms of the House of Representatives, which had been converted to such a purpose, and which had been found on the person of one of the rebel prisoners taken in a recent conflict. The testimony of Governor Sprague, of Rhode Island, is most interesting. It confirms the worst reports against the rebel soldiers, and conclusively proves that the body of one of the bravest officers in the volunteer service was burned. He does not hesitate to add that this hyena desecration of the honored corpse was because the rebels believed it to be the body of Colonel Slocum, against whom they were infuriated for having displayed so much courage and chivalry in forcing his regiment fearlessly and bravely upon them.

These disclosures establishing, as they incontestably do, the consistent inhumanity of the rebel leaders, will be read with sorrow and indignation by the people of the loyal States. They should inspire these people to renewed exertions to protect our country from the restoration to power of such men. They should, and we believe they will, arouse the disgust and horror of foreign nations against this unholy rebellion. Let it be ours to furnish, nevertheless, a continued contrast to such barbarities and crimes. Let us persevere in the good work of maintaining the authority of the Constitution, and of refusing to imitate the monstrous practices we have been called upon to investigate.

Your committee beg to say, in conclusion, that they have not yet been enabled to gather testimony in regard to the additional inquiry suggested by the resolution of the Senate, whether Indian savages have been employed by the rebels in military service against the government of the United States, and how such warfare has been conducted by said savages, but that they have taken proper steps to attend to this important duty.

B. F. WADE, *Chairman.*

WASHINGTON, *February* 18, 1862.

NATHANIEL F PALMER sworn and examined.

[See Bull Run testimony.]

By Mr. Covode:

Question. How were you treated while you were a prisoner in Richmond?

Answer. Our fare was pretty rough; we were kept closely confined, and had no exercise except what we could get all huddled up in a room. Our food was bread and beef only; nothing else. Sometimes they would take the water the beef was boiled in and put a little corn meal in it to thicken it, and give us that for soup.

Question. Did you have any coffee?

Answer. No, sir; no coffee or tea, or anything of that kind. I believe some of the wounded had a little coffee at first, but not long.

Question. How were the wounded treated there—the wounded prisoners?

Answer. I suppose they were treated about as well as they could be. Their statement was that they had no medicines; but what facilities they had for taking care of them was perhaps as good as could be had. But a great many of them died who could have been saved if they had been at home where they could have had proper treatment.

Question. Were there any men shot or abused there while in prison?

Answer. Yes, sir; five were shot.

Question. Under what circumstances?

Answer. One was shot, I was told, as he was hanging his blanket out of the window to air. Three others were shot while looking out of the window, and one was shot in the room where I was. He had been to the sink, near the window, where we all had to go to get water to drink, and was coming back to his bed. As he came back, the light being in the middle of the room, he was just in range between the window and the light; and as he was on his way back, when he was about ten feet from the window, he was shot, the bullet going in his back and coming out of his breast and lodging in another man's arm.

Question. Who was he?

Answer. His name was Tibbetts, of the New York 27th regiment. He was shot in the evening of the 8th of November and died on the 12th. I do not remember exactly when the others were shot, because they were not in our room.

Question. Did you find out why he was shot?

Answer. No, sir; only that the fellow could say he had killed a Yankee.

Question. What did they do with the man who shot him?

Answer. He was taken and put in the jail or guard-house for four or five days, and then they took him out and promoted him—made a corporal of him.

WASHINGTON, *April* 2, 1862.

Dr. JAMES B. GREELEY sworn and examined.

By the chairman:

Question. This committee have been directed by the Senate to collect evidence with regard to the barbarous practices of the rebels in disturbing the graves of our dead at Bull Run, &c.; will you please state to the committee, in your own way, what you know about that matter?

Answer. I, with others, accompanied Governor Sprague, of Rhode Island, to the battle-field of Bull Run, to endeavor to recover the bodies of Colonel Slocum, Major Ballou, Captain Tower, and others.

Question. About what time was that?

Answer. I think it was the 20th of March; either the 19th or 20th. We took with us, as a guide, a Mr. Richardson, I forget his first name, who assisted at the burial of Colonel Slocum and Major Ballou, to identify the spot where they were buried. We arrived at the place of burial on the 21st, I think. The hospital in which Colonel Slocum died had been burned, and we passed it. As we were passing I saw a negro girl at a spring; I questioned her about the way to the battle-field, and she directed us. We made some mistake, which we very soon discovered, when we turned back. Some of our party had been left behind, and when we returned we met Major Anthony, who commanded the escort. He informed us that they had commenced digging at a grave, and, while digging, this colored girl came down where they were and asked them what they were digging for. Said she, "if you are digging for the body of Colonel Sloke—," she hesitated about the name, saying two or three times, "Colonel Sloke, Sloke." One of the party said "Colonel Slocum." "Yes, sir," said she, "that is the name; you won't find him; the Georgia regiment men dug him up some weeks ago, and first cut off his head and then burned his body in the little hollow there," pointing it out to us. She told us that his shirts were down in a place that she pointed out, and that his coffin had been left in the stream, and afterwards used to bury a colored pauper in. We went to the place she had pointed out to us, and found where there had been a fire, evidently for the purpose of burning the body, as she stated. In raking over the ashes we found a femur, or thigh bone, partly burned, some of the vertebræ, or back bone, and portions of the pelvis bones. We also found, in a stream near by, two shirts, both of them still buttoned together at the neck, partially torn open in the centre, and with the wrists unbuttoned.

Question. How did they get the shirts off without unbuttoning at the neck?

Answer. The head had been cut off. We called the attention of every person present to that fact. We supposed that this body thus burned was that of Colonel Slocum. But when we found these shirts, Governor Sprague said Colonel Slocum never wore such a shirt as that. One of the shirts was a silk shirt, and the other was a striped shirt of some kind, I think. We had proceeded with the full conviction that the body thus burned had been that of Colonel Slocum; and when Governor Sprague said those shirts were not those of Major Ballou, we could not believe it possible, and went back to the graves to examine them. Before we had arrived there, Mr. Richardson had described to us the relative position of the graves of Colonel Slocum and Major Ballou. While we were down examining the ashes, men were engaged in digging out one of the graves—the upper grave; and when we returned there they had dug down nearly a foot, and had discovered nothing. Mr. Richardson was positive the coffins had not been buried more than two feet beneath the surface. It was very hard digging, and having discovered nothing after digging down a foot, I suggested taking a sabre and running it down, by which we could very easily discover if there was a coffin there. I took a sabre myself and thrust it in the ground at least two feet, but could discover nothing. We then thrust it in the place where Mr. Richardson said the other officer was buried, and we struck a coffin not more than two feet below the surface. The coffin was taken out, and the top taken off, when Colonel Slocum's friends recognized him at once, by his uniform, and also by his countenance, his moustache, &c. Major Ballou's body was not found in the grave. We then went to a house on the battle-field which had been used as a hospital, in the yard of which Captain Tower had been buried. We exhumed there at least seven bodies, which had been buried in their garments, apparently just as they fell. They were buried with their faces downward. Among them we found the body of Captain Tower. His orderly was positive that when Captain Tower died he had on a very fine pair of boots; they were not on his body when we found him.

Question. Did you make any further search to ascertain whether there had been any further mutilation of the bodies or barbarities practised upon the dead?

Answer. No, sir. We made inquiries of the inhabitants there, and they all corroborated the girl's story. There was a lad there, about fourteen years of age, I should judge, and he was questioned very closely about it. Colonel Sayles was with us, and was very skeptical about the burning of this body. He questioned the boy very closely, but the boy stood the examination very well. The boy said that it was the 21st Georgia regiment who came there, and he saw the body burned. He said they put the fire out afterwards, because it made such a horrible stench. He said that he knew, several days before, that they were going to do it. After they did it, it was talked of a great deal in the neighborhood, and they all condemned it.

By Mr. Wright:

Question. What could have been the object of digging up this body, after it had been buried several months, and then burning it?

Answer. I could think of no object.

By the chairman:

Question. You spoke of seven or eight bodies being buried with their faces downward. What did you consider the significance of that?

Answer. I did not know. My impression was that it was intended as a mark of indignity; it seemed so to me. Every one we exhumed was found buried with the face downward, no matter in what position they lay. Sometimes they would lie crosswise of each other, four or five packed in together, sometimes with their legs sticking out of the ground, and all with their faces downward.

Question. Did you make any inquiries of the inhabitants to ascertain any further than you have already stated?

Answer. Yes, sir.

Question. State it, if you please.

Answer. They spoke of this burning of Major Ballou's body particularly, and several of them said they knew of the fact, supposing, however, that it was Colonel Slocum's body. One man told me that the Georgia regiment was very bitter against Colonel Slocum, because his regiment had been instrumental in cutting them up very badly. I examined the remains in the ashes very carefully. We brought them all home, and I examined them through my own hands. I examined especially for teeth, for I knew if the head had been there, the teeth would have been the last to have been destroyed. I found the femur, or thigh-bone, which must have been that of a man over thirty years of age. The angle at the neck of it indicated a man at least thirty years of age. The body was proved to be that of a man by the pelvis-bone that was found; but we found no portion of the skull.

Question. You have stated that you found that the shirts were buttoned at the neck?

Answer. Yes, sir.

Question. The wristbands, however, were not buttoned?

Answer. Yes, sir.

Question. What inference did you draw from that?

Answer. The shirts could not have been taken off from the body without the head had been taken off, unless they had been unbuttoned.

Question. You understood that the head had been taken off?

Answer. Yes, sir.

By Mr. Chandler:

Question. Did you hear anything said about the skulls of our dead being used for drinking-cups, &c.?

Answer. The negro girl and the young boy I have referred to said that the Georgia regiment carried the skull of what they considered Colonel Slocum home with them.

Question. You are satisfied that it was Major Ballou's body they had thus treated?

Answer. Yes, sir; and another reason was that we knew Major Ballou had lost a limb.

WASHINGTON, *April* 2, 1862.

Reverend FREDERIC DENISON sworn and examined.

By the chairman:

Question. Have you heard the testimony of Dr. Greeley just given to the committee?

Answer. I have.

Question. Will you state whether you were with him during the examination he has referred to, and whether you concur in what he has stated?

Answer. So far as he has stated any matters of which I was a witness, I concur entirely. I accompanied Governor Sprague as a member of his staff; we left here on Wednesday, the 19th of March, and returned here on Sunday morning following. It was on the 21st of March that we went on the battle-field.

Question. If there is anything in addition to what he has stated that you deem of importance you will please state it.

Answer. I would state, in addition to what he has stated in regard to the grave of Major Ballou, that I accompanied the governor up through some pine woods to a house where resided an old gentleman of the name of Newman, a man I should judge to be sixty years of age. The colored girl had told us her story, the lad had told us the same story, and we wanted to learn what we could from others. This old gentleman seemed to be a man highly esteemed by all who knew him, and we went to him and asked him what he knew about the matter. He stated that the Georgia regiment, as he had understood, had suffered severely from the Rhode Island soldiers in the battle of Bull Run, and that through revenge they had exhumed this body, beheaded it and burned it. He said he was not present when it was done, and had not seen it, but that every one who had talked about it had said it was so. But he said that three or four days after it was done he went down there, and saw the fire and the bones, and the coffin, and that the coffin had been afterwards used to bury a colored pauper in. I asked him to go to the spot and show it to me, and he did so; went with me directly to the spot and pointed it out to me, and also showed me where the coffin lay when he saw it last, before it was used for the purpose of burying the negro pauper in.

Question. Did you understand what they did with the head after they cut it off the body?

Answer. This Mr. Newman, or else the colored woman, I cannot recollect which, said it was understood that the head was carried off south. They were not witnesses of the fact. I guess they heard it was so. I looked particularly among the ashes, but saw nothing that to my eye looked like any portion of the skull. In regard to the place where Captain Tower was buried, which was up on the battle-field, I counted eight bodies, as they were laid bare. They were buried in a pit, or a kind of a square hole, into which they had been thrown, with the earth thrown in perhaps two feet deep over them. On top we found an unexploded shell, which I brought with me. What it meant I cannot say—whether a matter of accident or a mark of indignity. It hardly seemed to me that it could be a mere accident.

Question. Did you observe whether they had been buried with their faces down?

Answer. Yes, sir; all of them.

Question. Did you make examination of other graves?

Answer. We opened no graves except those containing the bodies of the dead for whom we were seeking. There was another pit, not far from the one from which we took Captain Tower. We did not open it, not knowing positively that it contained any of our dead, though we suspected it contained the body of Lieutenant Prescott. Mr. Newman spoke a great deal of this matter of exhuming, beheading, and burning the body of Major Ballou. He called it Colonel Slocum, as that was what he had all along understood. He was very emphatic in his declarations that it could not have been done by Virginians. He seemed to think it a very barbaric thing, and wished to exculpate Virginians.

Question. Do you think of anything further that you desire to state?

Answer. In the pit from which we took the body of Captain Tower I counted eight bodies. There may have been more there. We began at one end, and uncovered until we came to the body of Captain Tower, and then opened it no further. There was one body lying right across the feet of the others, and to all appearance must have been trodden down very compactly, as there seemed to be hardly room for a body there. There seemed to have been no attempt to bury the bodies in any orderly, decent, or respectful manner. In regard to the mistaking of the body of Major Ballou for that of Colonel Slocum by the Georgians, it resulted from this, I have no doubt: Colonel Slocum was buried in an oblong box—a square box; Major Ballou was buried in a coffin, or a box which was coffin-shaped; and it is supposed (of course we know nothing about that) that they exhumed both coffins, and supposing the superior officer was in the coffin, and not in the box, which was the one they meant to take, they took the body of Major Ballou. Rumor accordingly stated that they had taken the body of Colonel Slocum. But his body we found. It was the body of Major Ballou that they took.

WASHINGTON, *April* 3, 1862.

General JAMES B. RICKETTS sworn and examined.

[See Bull Run testimony.]

By the chairman:

Question. Did you observe any barbarous treatment on the part of the enemy towards our prisoners and wounded soldiers?

Answer. On the field?

Question. On the field or elsewhere.

Answer. A party of rebels passed by where I was lying, and called out, "Knock out his brains, the damned Yankee," referring to me. I said nothing to them. When we were taken to this house there was a general want of everything for our men. Of course I was on my back and could not see much.

By Mr. Odell:

Question. The house to which you were taken was what is known as the Lewis House?

Answer. Yes, sir; I was taken there in a blanket, and on the way I met General Beauregard. Some one asked who that was, and the reply was that it was Captain Ricketts. When General Beauregard heard my name he jumped off his horse and spoke to me. He was an old acquaintance, but a year my senior at the Military Academy. I had been a great deal at the south—in New Orleans, Texas, and other places—and had been thrown a number of times in his company. He told me my treatment would depend upon the treatment that their privateers should receive.

Question. He told you that at that early period?

Answer. Yes, sir. I was much struck with what he said. I asked him where we were to be taken, and what they were going to do with us. He said: "Your treatment will depend upon that of the privateers," and then directed me to be taken to the Lewis House.

By the chairman:

Question. How long were you a prisoner in the hands of the rebels?

Answer. I was two weeks at the Lewis House, and then I was in Richmond up to the 18th of December.

Question. It has been said that the rebels mutilated our dead and killed our wounded prisoners. Do you know anything about that?

Answer. I know this: that Lieutenant Ramsay, my first lieutenant, who was killed at my battery, was entirely stripped. The first one of the rebels who asked my name was a Lieutenant Colonel Harman. He was a lieutenant in the Mexican war, where I had known him very well. As soon as he heard my name he asked me if I knew him; and when he mentioned his name, of course I knew him. He said to the men with him, "Respect the captain's person; he is an old friend of mine; don't take anything from him." And I had nothing taken from me, on account of Harman, I suppose.

Question. But your lieutenant was stripped?

Answer. Yes, sir.

Question. What do you mean by that—stripped of his clothing?

Answer. Yes, sir; he had nothing left on him but his socks, so one of our surgeons who saw him told me.

By Mr. Chandler:

Question. Do you know anything about their method of burying our dead?

Answer. I know nothing except about their manner of burial in Richmond. I could from my room overlook the place where they buried our dead. I know they were buried in the negro burying-ground among the negroes. They had no funeral service over them, but they were just taken out and put in the ground in the most unfeeling manner. At the Lewis House there was a great want of everything in the way of supplies, medicines, bandages, &c.

By the chairman:

Question. That may have been the case with their own men as well as ours

Answer. Yes, sir.

Question. What was their general treatment of prisoners in Richmond?

Answer. The general treatment of the prisoners there, I thought, was very bad, indeed. We were very much crowded. Our diet was very meagre, indeed. I subsisted mainly upon what I purchased with my own money, which my wife brought me. That is the way I got along, and I assisted the others all I could. For instance, we had at times what they called bacon soup, soup made from boiled bacon, the bacon being a little rancid, which you could not possibly eat, and the bacon was served with the soup; and that for a man whose system is being drained by a wound is no diet at all. Then we had some thin beef soup, so thin that we were induced to ask one of the assistants how it happened to be so, and we were told that it was first served to their own people in the hospitals, and afterwards it was watered for us. They stopped giving us tea and coffee, and we had to buy them for ourselves. We had to buy our butter and eggs, and everything of that sort, beyond the mere prison fare that they gave us.

Question. It has been said that they shot some of our prisoners while looking out of the windows?

Answer. I was not in the prison. I was too lame to be taken to the tobacco factory. I was in the hospital all the time.

Question. Did you hear anything about that while you were there?

Answer. Yes, sir; there were a number of our men shot. On one occasion there were two shot, one was killed and the other wounded, by a man on the outside, who rested his gun on the window-sill while he capped it; while drawing back the hammer, in this position, it escaped from his fingers, came down upon the cap, and the gun went off.

Question. That was an accident, was it?

Answer. Well, sir, it was a very singular accident. If I should point a gun towards you, instead of towards the ceiling, when I went to put a cap on, and it should go off, it would, to say the least, be regarded as a very unpardonable accident.

By Mr. Chandler:

Question. You thought it was intentional?

Answer. Yes, sir; I did think so.

By Mr. Gooch:

Question. Do yon know whether that man received any punishment?

Answer. The man was taken up, but he made some explanation and was let go again. I considered it very bad treatment, also, to be selected as a hostage for the privateers, when I was so lame I could not walk; while my wounds were still open and unhealed. General Winder came to see me. He had been an officer in my regiment, and I had known him for twenty-odd years. He came to see me on the 9th of November; he saw my wounds, that they were still unhealed; he saw my condition. He that very day received an order to select hostages for the privateers; and, notwithstanding he knew what my condition was, the next day, on Sunday, the 10th of November, I was selected as one of the hostages. I heard of a great many of our prisoners who had been bayonetted and shot. I saw three of them, two of them had been bayonetted and one of them had been shot. One of them was named Lewis Francis, of the New York 14th. He had received fourteen bayonet wounds, one through his privates, by which he lost one of his testicles. And he had one wound, very much like mine, on the knee, in consequence of which his leg was amputated after some twelve weeks had passed. And I would state here that, in regard to his case, when it was determined to amputate his leg, I heard Dr. Peachy, the surgeon, remark to one of his young assistants, "I won't be greedy, you may do it;" and the young man did it.

Mr. Odell: I would state here that he has just had his leg amputated the second time in consequence of the faulty manner in which it was done the first time.

The witness: It is surprising how that man lived through it all, old as he was. I should take him to be over forty years of age.

Mr. Odell: He is over fifty years of age; fifty-three or four, I should think.

The witness: I did not think he was as old as that. That only renders his recovery the more surprising. I saw him, and my wife was with him, down where he was, doing what she could for him; she gave him some of my clothes. Then there was a man named Briggs, of a Michigan regiment, who has a scar on his hand now from a bayonet wound. He says he saw the rebels coming, bayonetting our men and pillaging their pockets. He had a little portmonnaie, with about eight dollars in it. He put it inside his shirt, and let it fall down his back, and laid down on it. He was wounded, shot below the knee somewhere. When they came to him they asked for his money, and commenced thrusting a bayonet at him. He caught it in his hand, and as they withdrew it his hand was cut by it.

By Mr. Chandler:

Question. Did this man who received so many bayonet wounds receive them after he was a prisoner?

Answer. He was not wounded at all at first. That was their method of taking him prisoner, piercing him as much as possible. He was in their power entirely; there was no necessity for their doing any such thing, as there was one man against several.

Question. Instead of demanding his surrender they bayonetted him?

Answer. Yes, sir; it was entirely wanton on their part.

By Mr. Julian:

Question. And they supposed they had killed him?

Answer. Yes, sir. Another man was shot through the body, and he fell, and they supposed he was killed. Many of those men came into my room, and I saw them there and talked with them; and many of our men were badly amputated; the laps over the stump were drawn too tight, and soon the bones protruded. A man by the name of Prescott was amputated twice, and was then moved to Richmond before the laps were healed. He died from lockjaw after he reached Richmond, and always said that it was the railroad that killed him.

By Mr. Odell:

Question. Do you know anything more about the treatment of our prisoners?

Answer. I heard a doctor on the steps below my room say that he wished he could take out the hearts of the damned Yankees as easily as he could take off their legs. Those little things show exactly the state of feeling on their part.

By Mr. Gooch:

Question. What was their treatment of you, personally?

Answer. I had no particular consideration shown me personally, excepting from some persons whom I knew. I had a great many acquaintances in Richmond, and a great many among those in the field, for I had been a great deal in the south. I had met many at Newport, a great many from South Carolina. Those Charleston gentlemen treated me very handsomely. Wade Hampton, who was opposed to my battery, came to see me, and behaved towards me as a generous enemy should. He brought me a couple of bottles of ale, riding seven miles to bring it to me.

By Mr. Odell:

Question. The papers have criticised their treatment of your lady, alleging that they evinced a lack of respect towards the sex.

Answer. My wife, in the first place, joined me while I was at the Lewis House, on the field of battle. The first rumor she had heard was that I was killed. When she heard that I was alive, but wounded, she started with her carriage and horses to come to me. She almost had to fight her way out there, but succeeded finally in reaching me on the fourth day after the battle. There were eight persons in the Lewis house in the room where I lay, and my wife for two weeks slept in that room on the floor by my side without a bed. When we got to Richmond there were six of us in a room, among them Colonel Wilcox, who remained with us until he was taken to Charleston. There we were, all in that one room. There was no door to it. It was very much as it would be here if you should take away the door of this committee room, and then fill up the passage with wounded soldiers. And in the hot summer months the stench from their wounds and from the utensils they used was fearful. There was no privacy at all, because there being no door the room could not be closed. The hospital was an unfinished building, one half the windows being out of it; and there we were, a common show. There was a general interest to see Colonel Wilcox and myself, as though they expected to see a couple of savages.

Question. Did not the officers of the southern army protect you from that sort of indignity?

Answer. They made some attempt to do it.

Question. But they did not use the means they might have used?

Answer. No, sir; and the people would come in there and say all sorts of things to us and about us. In fact, people that I knew would come in and commence discussions, until I was obliged to tell them that I was a prisoner, and had nothing to say. When we went down to Richmond in the cars from Manassas, wherever we stopped crowds of people would gather around and stare at us. At Gordonsville, particularly, crowds of women came around there to see the prisoners and the Yankee woman. They would ask my wife if she cooked, if she washed, and how she got there. Finally, Mrs. Ricketts appealed to the officer in charge, and told him that it was not the intention that we should be subjected to this treatment, and that if it was continued she would make it known to the authorities. He then said he would stop it. General Johnston took my wife's carriage and horses away from her at Manassas, and kept them, and has them yet, for aught I know. When we got down to Richmond I spoke to several gentlemen about it, and so did Mrs. Ricketts. They said that of course the carriage and horses would be returned. But they never were. Instead of that, when I was exchanged, and we were about to leave, they refused Mrs. Ricketts a transportation ticket to Norfolk, obliging her to purchase it. Dr. Gibson, who was in charge of the hospital, when he heard of it, said that such a thing was very extraordinary in General Winder, and that he would speak to him about it. I said that it made no difference, though I thought as General Johnston had taken her carriage and horses and left her on foot, it would be nothing more than fair to give her a ticket to Norfolk. Our prisoners were treated very badly there, and I am surprised that some of them lived through it, like that man Lewis Francis.

Mr. Odell. He is recovering, and though he has lost one leg, he is very anxious to get back into the field again.

The witness. I must say that I have a debt that I desire very much to pay, and nothing troubles me so much now as the fact that my wounds prevent me from entering upon active service again at once.

WASHINGTON, *April* 7, 1862.

FREDERICK SCHOLES sworn and examined.

By Mr. Odell:

Question. Where is your residence?

Answer. City of Brooklyn, New York.

Question. What do you know in relation to the burial of our dead at Bull Run, and the treatment of those of our soldiers who fell there?

Answer. I proceeded to the battle field of Bull Run on Friday last, the 4th of this month. We passed across the battle field, and proceeded to the place where I supposed my brother's body was buried, which was on a knoll on Chinn's farm. We found a trench there where bodies had evidently been buried. I then proceeded to a stone house on Young's branch. The owner of that house told me that on the Tuesday after the battle he saw two men sitting by a stone fence, both of them wounded. One of them opened his waistcoat and showed him a gash down the whole of his breast, and begged him for some water. The other one was also badly wounded, and he wanted some water. He could not tell me how the men were dressed, as he was very much excited from what he had passed through. He told me about the number buried, and pointed out the locality of several bodies buried in the yard of his house and in the vicinity. We then proceeded over to the house of a free negro, named Simon or Simons, and had a long conversation with him. He said he was a sutler, or rather kept a little store, and supplied the rebel soldiers with eatables. He said the rebel soldiers would come in his store with bones in their hands, which they showed to him, and said they were bones of Yankees which they had dug up. He said it was a common thing for the soldiers to exhibit the bones of "the Yankees." From there we proceeded to the portion of the battle-field where Ricketts's battery was. Near there I found a part of what I supposed, from the description I had heard, to be the uniform of one of Ricketts's men. The ball had gone through the left breast. On examining it I found a piece of the shirt sleeve, and there was still some flesh in the sleeve. I found portions of the uniforms of the Ellsworth Zouaves in the same state. In the bushes in the neighborhood I found a part of a Zouave uniform with a sleeve sticking out of the grave, and a portion of the pantaloons sticking out. On attempting to pull it up I found that the two ends of the grave were still unopened, but the middle had been pried up, pulling up the extremities of the uniform in some places, and pulling up the sleeves of the shirts and a portion of the pantaloons. There were portions of flesh, as I found, remaining there. I found likewise the remains of one of the 14th New York regiment in the same condition, the grave having been pried open. There were pieces of the backbone and some of the ribs sticking up in the middle of the grave, where the centre had been pried up, the two ends of the grave being unopened. Back in the bushes we found some appearances of where bodies had been buried and washed out by the rains. But those I have been speaking of had evidently been dug up. Doctor Swalm, who was with me, pointed out the trenches where the secessionists had buried their own dead, almost immediately adjoining where our dead had been buried. Their remains had not been disturbed at all. After examining there I went over to the house of a free negro named Hampton, as I understood he had assisted in burying some of our dead. He told me he had buried the bodies on the Chinn farm, in the trenches that we first found. He had been notified by a man named Benjamin Franklin Lewis to proceed over there and bury the bodies there. They were buried on the Tuesday after the battle. I spoke to him about the manner in which these bodies had been dug up. He said he knew it had been done, and said it was most shameful. He said the rebels had commenced digging up the bodies two or three days after they were buried for the purpose, at first, of obtaining the buttons on their uniforms; afterwards they dug them up as they decayed to get their bones. I asked him how they had dug up the bodies. He said they had taken rails and pushed the ends down in the centre under the middle of the bodies and then pried them up in that way. He said that Lewis's men also knew about it. I went over where some of Lewis's negro men were and inquired of them. Their information corroborated fully the statement of this man Hampton. They also stated that a great many of the bodies had been stripped naked on the field before they were buried, and some were buried naked; others were buried with their clothes on. They said that numbers of them had been dug up through the winter, and even shortly after they had been buried. I went to Mr. Lewis's house, and after waiting some time he came in. I spoke to him about the manner in which the bodies had been dug up. He said that their whole army should not be blamed for that. He admitted it was infamous, but said a few men had done it who could not be controlled.

Question. Did he say what soldiers they were who had treated the bodies of our dead in this way?

Answer. He condemned principally the New Orleans Tigers, of General Wheat's division; the Louisiana Tigers, I believe they were called. He said they were the men who had done the principal part of it. He said that after the battle the men went over the field and robbed all indiscriminately, both friend and foe. He said they had all along been the cause of a great deal of trouble, and that two or three of them had been shot during the winter for mutiny. He said that the most of them had deserted their cause and were over on our side now. He said our wounded had been very badly treated; and Doctor Swalm told me about the unnecessary amputations that had been performed by the rebel surgeons. He said that limbs had been taken off unnecessarily and in a very bad manner; that, after the confederates had taken possession of the hospital, they would not allow our surgeons to use the knife at all, but used it themselves, and that some of the men had died in consequence of their bad treatment, and from want of the necessary nourishment. He mentioned a number of instances of men who had been actually murdered by bad treatment. I spoke to Mr. Lewis about that, and he admitted that it was so. He spoke of doctors on their own side who had spoken about the manner in which the wounded had been cut and neglected and treated badly after the battle. He said that he had become afraid that a pestilence would break out there in the neighborhood, in consequence of the dead being left unburied. And accordingly, on the Tuesday following the battle, finding the dead still unburied, he had gone out and warned out the neighborhood and had them buried, sending his own men to assist in doing so. On Sunday morning (yesterday) I collected a party of men and went to the trench where I supposed my brother might have been buried, and dug down to the bodies. We found them covered by some eighteen inches to two feet of earth, just tumbled in any way, some on their sides and some on their backs. I found one body entirely naked. Upon digging at one end of the trench we found, not more than two inches below the surface, the thigh-bone of a man that had evidently been dug up after burial; and in digging at the other end of the trench, in throwing out the first shovelful of earth, we found the detached shin-bone of a man, which had been struck by a musket ball and split; a part of the thigh-bone was still attached to it. The bodies at the ends had been pried up, the clothing at each end of the body still in the ground, where the middle of the body had been pried up. The other bodies were perfect. While we were digging there a party of soldiers came up and showed us a part of a shin-bone five or six inches long, which had the end sawed off. They said they had found it among many other pieces in one of the cabins that the rebels had deserted. From the appearance of it, pieces had been sawed off, out of which to make finger-rings. As soon as the negroes saw it, they said that the rebels had had rings made of the bones of our dead that they had dug up; that they had had them for sale in their camps. As soon as Doctor Swalm saw the piece of bone the soldier had, he said that it was a part of a shin-bone of a man; and I compared it with the detached shin-bone we had dug up—the one split by a musket ball—and they corresponded exactly. The soldiers said there were lots of these bones scattered all through the rebel huts, sawed into rings, &c. One of the men said he had been looking for the body of his lieutenant, and had found where it had been left in the bushes unburied. He had found the bones and portions of the clothing scattered around by the hogs. They had buried the remains that they gathered up on Sunday last, together with other remains that they had collected Mr. Lewis and the negroes all spoke of Colonel Cameron's body, and knew about its being stripped, and where it had been buried. They said that General Johnston, I think, had sent around and collected some of the things taken from the body; among others, a locket, and had endeavored to find his coat. Some of the things had been found. He knew exactly where Colonel Cameron's body had been buried. All the negroes and those in the neighborhood seemed to know all about it. I talked in the presence of the ladies in Mr. Lewis's house of the manner in which our dead had been treated. Some of them denied it; it seemed to be well understood in the neighborhood that these things had been done.

By Mr. Covode:

Question. Did you find your brother's remains?

Answer. I do not know that they were in either of the trenches that we examined, unless it was the body that was naked and could not be recognized. I am not certain that he is dead. I know that he was wounded.

By Mr. Odell:

Question. Did you see any difference in the manner in which the confederates had buried our dead and their own?

Answer. I saw where one of their dead had been buried in a box, and afterwards his remains taken up and removed. A portion of the box was still there. I saw a number of the graves of the confederate soldiers that had little head-boards placed at the head and marked. None of them have any appearance of having been disturbed. I noticed in one of the graves where the body had been pried up a shoe with some of the remains still in it.

WASHINGTON, *April* 7, 1862.

Dr. J. M. HOMISTON sworn and examined.

By Mr. Odell:

Question. Where is your residence?

Answer. No. 83 Sands street, Brooklyn.

Question. What is your position in the army?

Answer. Surgeon.

Question. What position did you occupy at the battle of Bull Run?

Answer. I was the surgeon of the 14th New York (Brooklyn) regiment.

Question. Were you present during that engagement?

Answer. Yes, sir.

Question. Were you taken prisoner there?

Answer. I was.

Question. We have been directed to inquire into the treatment our wounded and dead received from the enemy there after the battle. Will you, in your own way, give us a statement of what you observed there?

Answer. The place where we first commenced attending to our wounded, whether through accident or some other cause, was fired into and became such a dangerous place that we had to stop bringing the wounded there. I believe there have been some reports about the hospitals being fired into. I have never been able to satisfy myself whether that was done intentionally or not. I was made prisoner on the field, and immediately taken inside the enemy's lines. I told them that my wish was to attend to the wounded men, there were so many of them wounded and crippled; that I had remained voluntarily with them for that purpose; I asked as a privilege that I should be permitted to attend to them. Two of the surgeons there permitted me to go to wash and attend to the wounded; I did so until just at dark, when a guard came up and said that I must accompany them. I told them that it was my wish to remain on the field; that I desired to remain all night with the wounded men, as there were so many who needed attention, and some of them in a very helpless and painful condition and suffering for water. I protested against being sent away from the field at that time. They became very rude and talked in a very ugly way, and insisted on my going with them. They marched me with a party of prisoners, mostly privates, to Manassas; they did not offer us even water, let alone anything in the shape of food; we stood in the streets of Manassas about an hour with a guard around us; a crowd collected about us, hooting and threatening in a very boisterous way what they would do with us. We were finally put into an old building and left to sleep on the floor there without anything in the shape of food being given to us. In the morning those of us who were surgeons were brought up before the medical director, as he was called, who took our names and then sent us back to the battle-field; there were three of us in that party; we told them we were already faint and exhausted, having been without food for twenty-four hours. They gave us some cold bacon and sent us back to the battle-field. When we reached the battle-field they took us to the Lewis house, as it is called; they had commenced bringing the wounded in there, mostly their own. They finally allowed us to have an ambulance, and we commenced picking up our wounded and bringing them in ourselves, a guard all the while accompanying us; we were then ordered to report ourselves to a secession surgeon, a Dr. Darby, of South Carolina. He said he had been sent there by General Beauregard to take charge of the wounded. He would not allow us to perform operations upon our own men, but had them performed by his assistants, young men, some of them with no nore knowledge of what they attempted to do than an apothecary's clerk. They performed the operations upon our men in a most horrible manner; some of them were absolutely frightful. I asked Dr. Darby to allow me to amputate the leg of Corporal Prescott, of our regiment. I told him the man must die if it was not done. He told me that it should be done, and that I should be allowed to do it. I told him that there were some things I would like to have; that I had not the proper instruments to perform the operation. He said he would furnish me with the instruments, and told me to sit down and wait a few moments; while I was sitting there, with another of our surgeons, one of their men came through and said, "They are operating on one of the Yankee's legs up stairs." I turned to the doctor, who was sitting there with me, and said, "I am sure that is Prescott they are operating upon." I went up stairs and found that they had cut off Prescott's leg, and the assistants were pulling on the flesh on each side, trying to get flap enough to cover the bone. They had sawed off the bone without leaving any of the flesh to form the flaps to cover it. With all the force they could use they could not get flap enough to cover the bone. They were obliged to saw off about an inch more of the bone, and even then, when they came to put in the sutures, the stitches, they could not approximate the edges within less than an inch and a half of each other; of course as soon as there was any swelling the stitches tore out and the bone stuck through again. Dr. Swalm tried afterwards to remedy it by performing another operation; but Prescott had become so debilitated that he did not survive.

Question. What kind of a man was Prescott? What was his character and standing?

Answer. He was a very fine young man, and had received a very liberal education. It was almost impossible for us to get anything for our wounded men there to eat; they paid no attention to us whatever. We suffered very much on acccount of the want of any kind of food for our men. They would not even bring water to us. On the Monday night after the battle all the wounded in that old house were lying there on the floor. They kept bringing in the wounded until they were lying upon the floor rs thickly as they could be laid. There was not a particle of light of any kind in the house to enable us to move about among the wounded. They were suffering very much for water; but with all the persuasion I could use they would not bring us any water, and the guard stationed about the house prevented us from going after any. Fortunately, I might say, it rained that night, and through the open windows the rain beat in and run down the floor among the wounded, wetting and chilling them; still I was enabled, by setting some cups under the eaves, to catch a little water for our poor soldiers to drink, and in that way I spent all the night, catching water from the eaves of the house and carrying it to our wounded to drink. As there was no light in the house, being perfectly dark, I was obliged to crawl on my hands and knees to avoid stepping on their wounded limbs. It is not a matter of wonder that the next morning we found that several had died there during the night. They seemed to be perfectly indifferent to the sufferings of our men—entirely so. There was occasionally a man here and there, who seemed to have no connexion with the army at all, who appeared desirous to extend some kindly assistance to our wounded; but those connected in any way with their army seemed to try to do everything to show their perfect indifference.

Question. Did these young men—these assistants you speak of—perform any operations upon their wounded?

Answer. I think not much; there were other surgeons there attending to their wounded; in fact, a great many of their wounded were taken away from there, those who could be moved with safety, so that we had not the chance of knowing so much what their treatment was. Dr. Swalm could tell you more of what their treatment was while he was in their general hospital in Richmond. Many of our men were left lying upon the field until Tuesday night and Wednesday.

Question. Our wounded men?

Answer. Yes, sir; some of them lay there upon the field until the Wednesday after the battle. Men were brought in Tuesday night and Wednesday morning with their wounds completely alive with larvæ deposited there by flies. They had lain out there through all the rain-storm of Monday, and the hot, sultry sunshine of Tuesday, and their wounds were completely alive with larvæ when they were brought in on Tuesday night and Wednesday. Our dead lay upon the field unburied, to my own knowledge, for five days, and I understood that many of them were left there much longer. But I can speak knowingly up to the time I left, that our dead were left unburied for five days. I was sent away with Colonel Wood to Charlottesville, Virginia, by permission of General Beauregard.

By Mr. Covode:

Question. You mean that some of the dead were not buried for that length of time?

Answer. Yes, sir; our men.

By Mr. Odell:

Question. You mean your own regiment?

Answer. Yes, sir; the 14th regiment. I do not think any of them were buried at the end of five days after the battle.

Question. Were any other of our dead of other regiments left unburied?

Answer. Yes, sir; a great many were not buried at the end of that time. There were some that died Monday night in the Lewis house that were taken out and buried on the premises there the next morning.

Question. Do you know anything about the manner in which they were buried?

Answer. I could see from the house how they buried two or three of them; they dug a hole and put them in just as they had died and were carried out of the house, and then covered them up as they were.

By Mr. Covode:

Question. How deep did they bury them?

Answer. Those who were buried about the house were buried in holes not dug over three feet deep. They buried those because their own safety required it.

By Mr. Odell:

Question. Did they bury their own dead at once after the battle?

Answer. Some were buried down about Manassas, generally; if there were any friends there, their dead were taken away from the field and buried elsewhere.

By Mr. Gooch:

Question. Were they destitute themselves of medical supplies that they refused to assist you?

Answer. They could not have been destitute, for they took all our supplies. Even if they had had none of their own they could not have been destitute. They even took our instruments away from us at last. They allowed us to keep them for the time being, but gave us to understand that they belonged to them. There were many individual instances of kindness extended to our wounded. I know of one instance where one of our officers made himself known to one of their officers as a free-mason, and that officer interested himself in procuring permission from General Beauregard to send this officer to a private house, with one of our surgeons detailed to attend to him. I was not a mason then, but I have become one since I returned. As an instance of the manner in which the surgeons of our army were treated there, I will state that though I was left on the field with only the clothes I had on, I received none of the attentions from those of the profession on their side which I should have deemed it my duty to have shown them had our positions been reversed. I had but one shirt (the one I had on when I was taken prisoner) for a month; and I used to wash that in the morning and go without it during the day that I might have something clean to sleep in at night. The one pair of socks I had on when I was captured I would wash myself until they were completely worn out, when I wore my boots without socks, my feet and ancles becoming so chafed that it was exceedingly painful for me to walk. Yet not one of their surgeons ever offered me any article of clothing to enable me to keep myself clean and decent, though I had to go this way for a month. It was not until some time after I got to Charlottesville that I had the opportunity of purchasing some of these articles with my own money, and while purchasing them a crowd collected about the store, making threats against "the damned Yankee," though I had a parole from Beauregard himself. And when I came out I should probably have been killed, for one ruffian there attacked me with a large bowie knife, when I had forced my way nearly through the crowd, and I had but the bundle in my hand to ward off his blows, when an officer seeing my situation came to my aid and drove him off after he had made several passes at me, and enabled me to reach my room in safety. For the first three days after the battle we suffered the most for the want of food. Even Captain Ricketts and Colonel Wilcox, who were in the house, had not enough to eat; and had it not been for Mr. Lewis, who owned the house, we should have suffered more than we did. On several occasions he rode six or seven miles from where he was living to this house and brought us food, which was about all we had to eat.

WASHINGTON, *April* 7, 1862.

Dr. WILLIAM F. SWALM sworn and examined.

By Mr. Odell:

Question. Where is your residence?

Answer. No. 28 East Warren street, Brooklyn.

Question. What is your position in the army?

Answer. Assistant surgeon of the 14th regiment, New York State militia.

Question. Were you at the battle of Bull Run?

Answer. I was.

Question. Were you made prisoner there?

Answer. Yes, sir; at Sudley church.

Question. Will you state what you know in reference to the treatment of those of our soldiers who were taken prisoners?

Answer. I was there attending to the wounded when some cavalry rode up and took myself and eight or nine other surgeons prisoners. We remained there until Monday afternoon at 5 o'clock, when we were removed from the church and taken to Manassas. There were some 300 wounded men in the church and on the ground outside. When we got to Manassas we were told that it was unintentional the taking us there and keeping us from the wounded. On Tuesday morning we were ordered to be taken back. On the way back I was detailed to the old Lewis house, and I attended to the wounded there in conjunction with Dr. Norval, of the 79th New York. On Wednesday morning I was told by a captain, as I judged from the uniform he wore, there were two of our men alive, but wounded, still on the field. He pointed up towards the Henry house, and told me that I had better go and get them down. I asked him if I was allowed to do so. He said I was, and gave me a guard of two men. I went up there, and there I saw the most of our men buried. I was there surrounded by some civilians, who were very insulting, until a chaplain came to my rescue and told me that I must go to Manassas again. I was then placed behind a cavalry soldier and taken to Manassas, where I was taken before General Beauregard again. I arrived there at, perhaps, 12 o'clock on Wednesday. He kept me there until, perhaps, 5 o'clock in the afternoon, and then gave me a pass to go and attend to the wounded again. On my way back I was fortunate enough to get into a wagon. It turned off towards the other Lewis house, and I went in there, and saw Dr. Homiston. On Thursday Dr. Homiston was sent off with Colonel Wood, and I did not see him again until I saw him in Richmond. The rebels removed all their wounded, and left me alone entirely with several of our wounded—Captain Ricketts, Captain Withington, and others. The food we had was very scanty, consisting principally of hard crackers, and hardly enough of them to subsist upon. There was a Major Creecy there, who was a relative of Mrs. Ricketts or some of her family, and through him we got something for our wounded men. He was stationed behind the last house on the field. It was in that house that the operations on Prescott and others were performed.

The time arrived for us to go to Manassas and from there to Richmond. We went on—Captain and Mrs. Ricketts, Dr. Lewis, and myself. Corporal Prescott, Colonel Wilcox, and others had gone on previously. Upon arriving at Manasses we remained there until evening, and then proceeded to Richmond—being twenty-four hours on the way. There was one death occurred on the way while in the cars from inattention, and was thrown from the cars while they were in motion. It is true they said they would see the body buried. We arrived in Richmond at ten o'clock at night, under charge of a second lieutenant, who took us before Adjutant General Cooper. General Cooper told us to go where we pleased, and to report ourselves to him on Monday at 9 o'clock. We left, and could not get into any of the hotels, they were so crowded. I found my way down to a tobacco warehouse at the foot of Main street. I went in there and made arrangements to remain there altogether, and attended to the wounded there on Sunday. On Monday morning, after some little trouble, I managed to get to see General Cooper, who told me to come again on Tuesday. I did not, however, go there again on Tuesday, but went to the prison and remained there. During my sojourn in the prison there, I was sitting one day leaning back with my feet upon the window sill, when the sentry outside called out to me to take them in; I got up and looked out of the window, and saw the sentry with his musket cocked and pointed towards me. Being cautioned by some one there to get out of the way lest I should be shot, I left the window. The commissary and quartermaster—one person, Mr. Warner, acting as both—who used to feed our men, did as well as he could; but the quality of the soup given their men and that given ours was very different. The soup was made of good enough meat, generally, but they put no vegetables in it. After from the first to the third week they stopped giving us coffee altogether. After some four or five days I was removed from the tobacco warehouse, by order of General Winder, to the general hospital, which was in charge of Dr. Gibson, surgeon general. The nurses there were sisters of charity. The left portion of the building, as you entered it, was set apart for our wounded, the right for theirs, and the main body of the building was used as as an operating room. I noticed that they used to bring in for their wounded nice biscuit, game, soft-boiled eggs, toast with eggs upon it, &c. This was done by the sisters of charity. I asked them to bring in some for our men, and was told that they had none. Of course, seeing what I did, I knew how much to believe of that. As to the way in which their operations were performed, I would mention the instance of Captain McQuade, of the 38th New York. He received a wound in the lower part of the left leg, which rendered amputation necessary. The operation was performed in Richmond, by a surgeon of the name of Peachy, I think. The flap was a very good one, but, in consequence of inattention, the inside flap entirely mortified, so that they had to cut it completely off, leaving the bone protruding from one and a half to two inches. Inflammation set in, and extended up the limb, and in this condition he was taken down to the tobacco warehouse at mid-day, his face exposed to the hot sun, and the result was, what might have been look for, his death.

Question. How long were you on the battle field after the battle?

Answer. I was at the Lewis house from fourteen to eighteen days. One afternoon Captain Withington and myself concluded we would take a walk over the battle field. This was some ten or twelve days after the battle. As we walked around I saw some of our men still unburied, and some of them entirely naked—shoes, stockings, everything they had had on stripped from them, and their bodies left exposed, naked, on the field. Yet I saw a great many women, ladies I suppose they would call themselves—walking about the field at that time, apparently entirely unmoved. I should judge that I saw ten or twelve of the 14th regiment unburied, many of the 71st regiment, and a number of others whose regiments I did not recognize.

Question. You spoke of going on the field at one time to get two wounded men of the 14th regiment; did you find them?

Answer. No, sir; as I have stated, I was surrounded by some civilians, and not allowed to go up there.

Question. Do you know anything of the manner in which they buried our dead?

Answer. At the time I went up for the two wounded men, on the Wednesday morning after the battle, I saw them digging some trenches, and saw some two or three buried. They paid no attention as to how they put them in, but put them in face downwards or in any other way, just as it happened. They buried a number in a ravine that had been washed out by the rains—throwing the bodies into the ravine, and covering them up with earth. In going over the battle field lately I noticed where some of the graves had been opened by pushing rails down under the bodies and prying them up. Many of the negroes said they had seen the soldiers doing that.

Question. What was their object?

Answer. As I was informed, it was to make drinking cups of the tops of the skulls and rings of the bones, sawing pieces off for that purpose

Question. You sum it all up as very inhuman treatment.

Answer. Yes, sir; I do. I will tell you how Doctor Ferguson, of New York, was treated. He was taking his ambulance for the wounded when he was fired into. He took of his green sash, to show his calling, and his hankerchief, as a sort of flag of truce, and waved them. A party rode up to him, and asked him who he was. He told them that he was a surgeon of the New York State militia. They said they would take a parting shot at him, any way. They fired at him, and shot him in the leg. He was taken prisoner, and laid in the ambulance. He had his boots on, and his spurs on his boots; and as they drove along his spurs would catch in the tail-board, causing him such agony that he screamed out. One of their officers rode up to him, and placed his pistol at his head, and threatened if he screamed again he would shoot him.

By Mr. Gooch:

Question. When was this?

Answer. On Sunday, the day of the battle.

WASHINGTON, *April* 11, 1862.

Governor WILLIAM SPRAGUE sworn and examined.

By Mr. Odell:

Question. What is your present position?

Answer. I am governor of the State of Rhode Island.

Question. You have recently visited the battle field of Bull Run?

Answer. Yes, sir.

Question. For the purpose of recovering the bodies of some of your soldiers who fell there last July?

Answer. Yes, sir.

Question. Will you state, in your own way, what you saw and learned there, in reference to the treatment of our wounded and dead by the rebels after the battle of Bull Run?

Answer. As to the officers?

Question. Generally, in regard to all. We have been instructed by the Senate to investigate the statements made public, concerning the cruel and barbarous treatment of our wounded and dead.

Answer. In that part of the field where I was our wounded were taken to two different places; one was a storehouse at the point where the engagement first took place; the other was about three-quarters of a mile in the rear of the battle field. Colonel Slocum and Major Ballou were taken to a position at the rear. When the retreat commenced we had in this hospital, as it was termed, several wounded rebel officers; and there were also several of our men there, who were promised, if they would stay with them, that they should be released. They did remain. When I went out there a few days since I took three men with me to designate the places where these officers had been buried. On reaching the place we commenced digging for the bodies of Colonel Slocum and Major Ballou at the spot which was pointed out to us by those soldiers. While we were digging there some negro women came up and asked who we were looking for; and, at the same time, said that "Colonel Slogan" had been dug up by the rebels, some men of a Georgia regiment, his head cut off, and his body taken to a ravine some thirty or forty yards below, and there burned. We stopped digging and went to the place thus designated, where we found coals, ashes, and bones mingled together. A little distance from there we found a shirt and a blanket with large quantities of hair upon it. Everything there indicated the buring of a body there. We then returned and dug down at the spot indicated as the grave of Major Ballou, but found no body there. But at the spot designated as the place where Colonel Slocum was burned we found a box, which, upon having raised and opened, was found to contain the body of Colonel Slocum. The soldiers who had buried the bodies of Colonel Slocum and Major Ballou were satified that the grave that had been opened and the body taken out, beheaded, and burned, was that of Major Ballou, because it was not in the spot where Colonel Slocum was buried, but rather to the right of it. They at once said that the rebels had made a mistake, and taken the body of Major Ballou for that of Colonel Slocum. The shirt we found near the place where the body was burned I recognized as one belonging to Major Ballou, as I had been very intimate with him. We gathered up the ashes containing the portions of his remains that were left and put them in a coffin, together with his shirt, and the blanket and the hair found upon it, and some hair also that was brought to us by a civilian who had expostulated with the rebels against this barbarity.

Question. What was the name of that civilian?

Answer. I do not know.

Question. He was a resident there?

Answer. Yes, sir; he resided near Sudley church. After we had done this we went to that portion of the field where the battle had first commenced, and began to dig there for the remains of Captain Tower. We had brought a soldier with us to designate the place where he was buried, who had been wounded at the battle, and had seen from the window of the house in which he was placed the spot where Captain Tower was buried. On opening the ditch, or trench, where he was buried, we found it filled with bodies of soldiers, all buried with their faces downwards. After taking up some four or five of them, we discovered the remains of Captain Tower, mingled with those of the men, and took them and placed them in a coffin and brought them home.

By Mr. Gooch:

Question. The position of these bodies was such that you were satisfied that they were buried intentionally with their faces downwards?

Answer. Undoubtedly; beyond all controversy.

By Mr. Chandler:

Question. Did you consider that that was done as a mark of indignity?

Answer. Yes, sir; as an indignity.

Question. What could have been their object in doing these things, especially what they did with what they considered the body of Colonel Slocum?

Answer. Sheer brutality; nothing else. They did it on accout of his courage and chivalry in forcing his regiment fearlessly and bravely upon them, and destroying about one-half of that Georgia regiment, which was made up of their best citizens.

Question. Were these barbarities perpetrated by that regiment?

Answer. By that same regiment, as I was told. We saw where their own dead were buried with marble head and foot stones, and the names upon them, while ours were buried, as I have stated, in trenches. I have published an order to my second regiment, to which these officers were attached, that I shall not be satisfied with what they shall do, unless they give an account of at least one rebel killed for each one of their own number.

WASHINGTON, *April* 11, 1862.

DANIEL BIXBY, jr., sworn and examined.

By Mr. Covode:

Question. Where do you reside?

Answer. I reside in this city.

Question. Have you been recently on a visit to Manassas and Bull Run?

Answer. I have.

Question. Will you state to the committee, in your own way, what you saw and learned in relation to the condition of our dead there?

Answer. I went out in company with Mr. G. A. Smart, of Cambridge, Massachusetts, who went to look for the body of his brother, who fell at Blackburn's Ford, in the action of the 18th of July. We took with us one who was there at the time, to point out where his brother fell. We found a grave there, which was opened. The clothes there found were identified as those of the brother of Mr. Smart, and were recognized from some peculiarities in the make; they were made by the mother. Other clothes of the same make, and with the same peculiarities, were taken with us, with which to compare those we might find in the grave. They were compared, and found to correspond exactly, We found no head in the grave, and no bones of any kind; nothing but the clothes and portions of the flesh of the body. We also saw the remains of three other bodies together that had not been buried at all, as we concluded from their appearance. The clothes were there, which we examined by cutting them open, and found some remains of flesh in them, but no bones. A Mrs. Pierce Butler, who lived near there, said that she had seen the rebels boiling portions of the bodies of our dead in order to obtain their bones as relics, the rebels not waiting for them to decay, so that they could take their bones from them. She said she had seen drum sticks made of "Yankee shin-bones," as the rebels call them.

By Mr. Odell:

Question. Are there any bones in a man's body long enough to make drumsticks?

Answer. The lower leg bone, the shin-bone, was used for that.

By Mr. Covode:

Question. Did you see more than the one grave opened?

Answer. No, sir; that was the only grave we examined.

Question. You were satisfied from examination of the remains that the bones had all been taken away?

Answer. Yes, sir; we examined the clothes thoroughly and found but one small piece of bone, perhaps as large as your little finger; that was all.

Question. Did the body appear to have been taken up after it had been burried?

Answer. We could not tell positively about that, but we thought it probable that it had been.

Question. How deep was it burried?

Answer. Two feet, perhaps; just covered over fairly. Mrs. Butler also said she had seen a skull that one of the New Orleans artillery had, which he said he was going to send home and have mounted, and was going to drink a brandy punch out of it the day he was married. I understood Mrs. Butler to say that the rebels had a force of some 90,000 men at Manassas, Centreville, and Bull Run, until the middle of February, when they began to leave. The artillery and infantry that were stationed near where she lived she said went away on the Friday before our troops went out there. But on Friday night they sent back a regiment of cavalry to do picket duty, and on Saturday morning they went away, and on Saturday afternoon our pickets and scouts came up there.

Question. On Saturday afternoon?

Answer. I will not be certain whether it was Saturday or Sunday afternoon. They came up in the afternoon of the day the enemy left in the morning.

Question. Had you any converation with any other parties relative to this matter?

Answer. No, sir; we saw none beside our own party, except Mr. Butler and his family.

BROOKLYN, NEW YORK, *April* 16, 1862.

LEWIS FRANCIS, being sworn, testified that he resides in Hamilton street, near Park avenue, in the city of Brooklyn; was at the battle of Bull Run as a private in the 14th regiment New York volunteers. As I was loading my musket I was attacked by two rebel soldiers and wounded in the right knee joint with a bayonet, when I fell. As I lay on the ground they kept bayonetting me until I received fourteen wounds; one of them then left, the other remaining over me, when a Union soldier coming up shot him in the breast, and he fell dead. I lay on the ground until about 10 o'clock the next day. I was then removed in a wagon to a building used as a temporary hospital. My wounds were then examined and partially dressed. On the Saturday following we were removed to the Manassas depot, and from there we were removed to the general hospital at Richmond. In October, my leg having partially mortified, I consented that it should be amputated, which operation was performed by a young man. I insisted that they should allow Dr. Swalm to be present. I wanted one Union man to be present if I died under the operation. The stiches and the band slipped from neglect, and the bone protruded, and about two weeks after another operation had to be performed, at which time another piece of the thigh bone was sawed off. About six weeks after the amputation, and before it healed, I was removed from the general hospital to the tobacco factory. On my removal from the prison to Fortress Monroe another operation was performed, when five pieces of bone were removed. I remained five weeks at this hospital, when I was removed to Washington and spent a week in the hospital at that place, when I was removed to Brooklyn, where an operation was performed by Dr. Lewis Bauer, who removed two splinters of bone and sawed off another piece of the thigh bone. Whilst at Manassas I recived for food but a small amount of boiled rice and hard bread. At Richmond, whilst in the general hospital, I was well fed; at the tobacco factory I had a small amount of sour bread and tough fresh beef. I should have perished for want, but a lady named Van Lew sent her slave every other day with food, and supplied me with clothing until January, when the officer in charge of the prison prevented her from sending me any more provisions. After they had removed me from the general hospital to the tobacco factory, they returned and removed the bed from under me, and removed all the pillows and bed clothing, and laid me on a blanket on a cot, with another blanket to cover me. At this time I was covered with bed sores, having lain in bed from July up to this time, December.

WASHINGTON, *April* 23, 1862.

Hon. SIMON CAMERON sworn and examined.

By the chairman:

Question. We have been directed by the Senate to inquire into the barbarous manner in which the wounded and dead of our army have been treated by the rebels. Will you state to the committee what you know in regard to their treatment of your brother, who was killed in the battle of Bull Run?

Answer. After my brother fell in that engagement, I am informed that his body was carried off by some of his men from the battle-field and placed, as was supposed, in a secure place, so that it could be recovered by his friends after the battle was over. There were eight men who took charge of the body and carried it back off the field, four of whom were killed. The body was placed in an ambulance and left there. When they returned, as I understand, they found that the body had been thrown out of the ambulance upon the ground, and his pockets rifled of his watch, purse, portraits, &c. The blanket that had been left over the body was taken away, and, as we have learned since, the body was thrown into a hole or ditch with several other bodies, and there covered up with earth.

The morning after I heard of his death, Mr. Magraw, of Pennsylvania, formerly State treasurer, called upon me and told me that he had some acquaintances among the rebels out there, and offered to go out and get the body of my brother. I told him that I thought it would be of no use for him to go out there. He went, however, and instead of being able to obtain the body, by order of Generals Johnston and Beauregard he was made prisoner and sent to Richmond, where he was kept four or five months.

By Mr. Chandler:

Question. The rebels knew the body to be that of Colonel Cameron, your brother?

Answer. Yes, sir.

By the chairman:

Question. And they knew these messengers went out there solely for the purpose of obtaining the body?

Answer. Yes, sir. They had no other object in going.

Question. And they took them prisoners of war and sent them to Richmond and kept them there?

Answer. Yes, sir; and part of the time close prisoners. The body of my brother, when lately recovered, was recognized by means of a truss which he wore.

WASHINGTON, *April* 24, 1862.

JOHN KANE sworn and examined.

By Mr. Gooch:

Question. Were you present at the battle of Bull Run?

Answer. Yes, sir.

Question. What position did you occupy there?

Answer. I was sergeant in the 10th company of the 79th regiment, and acting orderly to Colonel Cameron.

Question. Were you near him when he was killed?

Answer. Yes, sir; not more than 15 or 20 yards from him.

Question. Will you state the circumstances of his death, and what was done with his body afterwards?

Answer. He was standing conversing with a lieutenant of the 10th company in relation to taking off the wounded, when he received a bullet in his left breast and fell while in the act of speaking. He endeavored to say something after he was shot, but the blood gushed out of his mouth and nose, and he fell, dying almost instantly. As soon as it was ascertained that he was dead, some eight men placed his body across their muskets, and carried it back off the field, and placed it in an ambulance of the second Maine regiment. The surgeon at first objected to our placing a dead man in the ambulance, saying it was needed for the wounded. But when we told him it was the body of Colonel Cameron, the brother of the Secretary of War, he said we could put it in there.

At that time General McDowell rode up and told me to order our men, who were scattering, to rally on the hill and try to form a square and prepare to repel some cavalry who were coming. I replied that I was in charge of Colonel Cameron's body, and wanted to take it back to Washington. He then told me to pass the order to the first officer of the regiment I met, when I could return. I mounted Colonel Cameron's horse and rode back, until I saw the major of the regiment, to whom I gave the orders of General McDowell. General McDowell coming along there, I informed him that I had given his orders to the major of the regiment, when I got permission to return to where I had left the body of Colonel Cameron.

When I got back I met the surgeon of the regiment, who informed me that the hospital had been taken possession of by the enemy, and several prisoners taken; and that if I went where we had left the ambulance with the body of Colonel Cameron I would also be taken prisoner. I replied that it would not much matter if I were, and that I should try to find the body. When I reached where the ambulance was I found that some ten or fifteen of the rebel cavalry—black horse cavalry, as I understood—had been there, thrown all the bodies out of the ambulance, and driven it off for their own wounded. One of the surgeons then told me that I had better make the best of my way to Washington, for if I remained there I should be taken prisoner. I accordingly returned.

I afterwards went out with a flag of truce from Colonel McCunn's headquarters to endeavor to get the body. I saw a Lieutenant Barbour, who was the senior officer of the post at Fall's Church, to whom I gave my papers. We were obliged to wait there until he communicated with Colonel Stewart. Towards evening the messenger returned and said that we could not have permission to go to Centreville, but they would forward the papers to headquarters, and would give me an answer the next day. The next day we returned, and were informed that we could not have the permission we asked, because the papers were addressed "to whom it may concern;" that it did not concern them, and if they were not officially addressed they would not recognize any papers sent to them. I asked Lieutenant Barbour to see that some mark was put upon the grave of Colonel Cameron so that it could be found, and he promised that he would do so.

When Centreville was evacuated in March last, I accompanied a party down there to obtain the body of Colonel Cameron, but we could find nothing to indicate where the grave was. We asked one man living there—Mr. Lewis, I believe—who we understood knew where the grave was, but he denied having any knowledge of it, which I have reason to believe was false. I took the party to where Colonel Cameron fell, and also to where the ambulance was that his body was placed in. We met a slave, who said he knew where the body was, because he had heard his mistress—a widow Donn—say it was his body; and he had seen a locket, with a picture in it, and some papers that had been taken from his body. The negro said the body had remained on the field from Sunday till Thursday before it was buried, and that he had noted the place where it was buried particularly, as he had understood that a reward would be paid for finding the body.

We went to the place pointed out by the negro and opened the grave; we found several bodies there; they had to all appearance been thrown in in any way, just as they came to them; in endeavoring to remove the remains of Colonel Cameron without separating them any, which we did by inserting a board under the lower part of the body and pushing it gradually and carefully up towards the head, we had to take off one of his arms and the skull of another body that was lying on it; we recognized the body from the clothing on it; from a shirt that I had myself bought for him in Washington, and from a truss that we found on the body; several officers with us, who knew Colonel Cameron, also recognized the body; we placed the remains in a rough box coffin that we made there and brought them away with us; the other bodies in the same grave or ditch appeared to be bodies of private soldiers.

Question. Had anything been taken from the body?

Answer. Yes, sir; we found his pockets turned inside out, and his watch, ring, purse, locket, boots and spurs had been taken away; he had over $80 in his purse, for on the morning of the battle I had taken out of his valise and given to him four twenty dollar pieces and some smaller gold pieces; at the time he fell I took his revolvers and keys, and brought them back with me.

Question. Did you make any inquiry as to the rifling of the body?

Answer. Yes, sir; and I was told that the body was rifled by some of the black horse cavalry, and that some of the articles had been shown by one of Stewart's cavalry.

Question. From whom did you learn that fact?

Answer. This negro said his mistress had told him so; and I heard others speak of it; Lieutenant Barbour said he had heard something of it from his own men.

Question. Who buried the body of Colonel Cameron?

Answer. This negro said that he and two other negroes had buried the bodies there; the other two negroes have been carried away, but this one managed to remain some way; an order was given by some one that each resident should see that the bodies near their houses were buried; that is the way these negroes came to bury them; they dug the hole and put in it all the bodies they found anywhere near.

Question. Did you ask this negro who had rifled Colonel Cameron's body?

Answer. Yes, sir; he said he did not know, except that he had heard his mistress say that it was done by one of the black horse cavalry when they took it out of the ambulance in which we had left it; the negro said the pockets were turned inside out when he came across the body at the time they buried it.

WASHINGTON, *May* 7, 1862.

JOSEPH A. KIRBY sworn and examined.

By Mr. Covode:

Question. Where do you reside?

Answer. In Wilmore, Cambria county, Pennsylvania.

Question. What has been your occupation?

Answer. I have been engaged in telegraphing for the Pennsylvania railroad company in the office of Colonel Scott, at Pittsburg.

Question. Did Colonel Scott make you an offer to come to Washington, to engage in telegraphing here?

Answer. He telegraphed for me, and I met him at the Continental Hotel, in Philadelphia, on my way home in June last.

Question. Have you been a newspaper correspondent?

Answer. Yes, sir; for the Pittsburg Chronicle.

Question. From what places?

Answer. All through the south. I corresponded on as far as Montgomery, Alabama, until communication with the north was cut off after the fall of Fort Sumter.

Question. Did you go to Pensacola?

Answer. Yes, sir; but I was at Montgomery when the order was sent to Beauregard to commence firing upon Fort Sumter.

Question. How did you get your information of the attack?

Answer. I roomed in the Exchange Hotel, in Montgomery, right opposite the room of the confederate postmaster general, Reagan; and a young man who was with him told me that that day the ball would open at Fort Sumter. That was the first information I had of it. I waited until the next morning, and then we heard the news at Montgomery. As I supposed that the next attack would be upon Fort Pickens, that evening at four o'clock I took the boat to Mobile, and from there went to Pensacola, where I arrived at twelve o'clock on Saturday. I was within sight of Fort Pickens, and spent Sunday and two days thereafter in the rebel camp. I walked through all their fortifications—every one of them—was in Fort Barrancas, saw where preparations were being made for new batteries, and then returned to Pensacola, nine miles from the navy yard. The telegraph office was close by the hotel where I stopped, and by going near I could tell by the sound of the instrument, being an old telegraphic operator myself, what was passing over the line, and I heard some conversation which led me to believe that an attack was to be made on Fort Pickens. Cooper, from Montgomery, telegraphed to Bragg that Fort Sumter had surrendered, and asked when he was going to make the attack. Bragg did not himself send word; but one of the officers at Pensacola telegraphed to a friend in Macon, Georgia, that they were to land on Santa Rosa island in a few days. That night I disguised myself as a fisherman, and got a boat with a negro man to row it, and went over to Fort Pickens, in an open boat, and gave Colonel Brown, Captain Clitz, and Lieutenant Slemmer information of the intended attack. I had intended to return to Pensacola again, and go home through the rebel lines up through Virginia; but Captain Clitz told me it would be dangerous for me to do so. He said the information I had given him was important, and wanted to know what he could do for me. He offered to send me home. Colonel Brown did send me home, and I returned to New York in company with Lieutenant Slemmer.

Question. You say you took a negro along to row you over to Fort Pickens?

Answer. Yes, sir; but he did not know who I was until we had got into the middle of the bay. I came to New York, and then met Colonel Scott by appointment in Philadelphia. I then went on to Pittsburg, to see my friends, intending to come on to Washington to accept an appointment in the telegraph department here. But while on my way here I heard of the battle of Bull Run, and that spoiled all my plans about coming here.

I then went direct to Harper's Ferry, and offered my services to General Banks as a spy, and was making arrangements to enter the rebel lines and go on to Manassas, or to Richmond, or wherever else it was thought necessary. One evening two of us went across the river, and we got rather too far into the rebel lines. My companion laid down to rest himself, while I went on ahead alone. In a short time I met three rebel scouts, who, when they saw me, fired upon me, but did not hit me. I ran and got to the river, but could not cross, and they came up and captured me. I pretended to be very glad when I discovered they were the confederate scouts, and told them I was a Baltimorean, and was on my way south. They asked me why I ran when I saw them. I said I supposed they were federal scouts, which seemed to satisfy them, as they knew the federal soldiers were close by. They took me before General Beauregard, at Manassas, who asked me two or three questions. I remained there a few days. I was on the battle-ground at Bull Run on the Sunday two weeks after the battle. On the Tuesday after, I was sent to Fredericksburg, and from there went on to Richmond.

Question. What did you notice on the battle-ground at Bull Run, in regard to the treatment of our dead by the rebels who were there?

Answer. There were a captain of the rebel army, and two or three privates, teamsters, along with me. They all admitted that bodies of federal soldiers had been burned on the same pile with dead horses; they all admitted that. Some of them thought it was very hard, very wrong. And I saw at least ten bodies that were not more than half buried, and I did not go over all the battle-field. I saw arms and legs and heads sticking up out of the ground; they had only a little earth thrown over them, and a little brush thrown over that. The stench from the decaying bodies was very bad.

Question. Did you see where any bodies of our soldiers had been burned?

Answer. I saw piles of ashes and bones, but I could not tell what the bones were.

Question. You heard them say that they had burned the bodies of our soldiers?

Answer. Yes, sir; I heard them talking about it while I was there.

Question. You say you went to Richmond?

Answer. Yes, sir. I had an opportunity to escape, while I was at Fredericksburg, but I did not. I told them I was a Marylander and a secessionist, and by talking to them made them believe I was a secessionist. But when they got me to Richmond, they put me in one of their tobacco warehouses, with some Union men who had been brought from Western Virginia. However, they let me out when I had been there about five weeks, as I offered to do soldier's duty, and I went to work on some fortifications near the James river, and acted as a guard to some free negroes they had at work on the fortifications. The guns were not mounted then. I was there a little over three weeks, when I was taken sick and was relieved. I went to a private house on Main street, in Richmond, to board, and was there two or three weeks without any money or medical attendance or care whatever.

As soon as I got well enough to be able to go out, I walked to Petersburg, as I could not leave the city by railroad without a pass. At Petersburg I got on the train and went to Norfolk, intending to try and escape from there. I was there two nights and one day, but found I could not get away, as so strict a watch was kept in consequence of so many negroes escaping. I then returned to Richmond and worked in the laboratory there until the 10th of January. Being out of money, I enlisted in the third Maryland battery as a substitute, receiving $180 in confederate money, which was as good as any other there. I joined that battery because I expected it would be sent to join the army of the Potomac; and I intended, after finding out all I could about the fortifications at Manassas and Centreville, to make my way to the Union lines. But after Zollicoffer's defeat we were sent to East Tennessee to replace the artillery he had lost. I do not recollect how long I was at Knoxville. I was sent on one expedition up to Clinton, on Clinch river; then on another expedition to Kingston, on Holston river; and then I was sent by General E. Kirby Smith to Cumberland Gap with a pay-roll, to get certain men there to sign it, and then to return with it. When I arrived at Cumberland Gap, one evening I could see from a hill there the camp fires of the Union troops, and I made up my mind to escape there. The next morning a regiment passed down the valley to drill, and I mixed in with the soldiers and passed the inner pickets with them. When they became engaged in their drill I walked off, and after some time I reached General Carter's camp. I gave him information of every regiment in East Tennessee, the number of men, the name of the commanding officer, and the number and situation of the guns at Cumberland Gap. I was sent home at the expense of the United States government, and came on here about five days ago to get some employment from the government.

Question. What means of information had you concerning the strength of the rebels at Centreville and Manassas?

Answer. There were three young men in our company who had belonged to Calhoun's battery, of South Carolina; they were at Manassas and were discharged, and then joined our company in January. They told me that there were not more than 40,000 men at Manassas in December, and after that. All admitted that there were not more than that.

By Mr. Chandler:

Question. Does that include their troops at Centreville?

Answer. Yes, sir; that includes all except those at Aquia creek and those under Jackson over the ridge.

By Mr. Covode:

Question. That includes Manassas, Centreville, and all around there?

Answer. Yes, sir; it included what they called the army of the Potomac proper—not the Aquia army or the Shenandoah army. Having seen and talked with hundreds of persons who had been there, I was satisfied all the time that there were not more than 40,000 or 50,000 men there. That seemed to be the understanding of all with whom I talked upon the subject.

Question. What knowledge had you of the armament at Manassas and Centreville—of the number of cannon there?

Answer. I knew nothing except what I was told, that they had excellent fortifications at Centreville, much better than they had at Manassas.

Question. Did you hear anything about their wooden guns?

Answer. I knew that they had wooden guns at Munson's Hill; that they had been using wooden guns and stovepipes all along. I got that information from men who had been there. I knew an aide-de-camp who had been in the army that had retreated before Patterson at Winchester. He told me about them. They fully expected an attack at Manassas. I am confident of that from what they told me.

By Mr. Chandler:

Question. Do you mean that they expected an attack upon Manassas last fall?

Answer. Yes, sir.

By Mr. Covode:

Question. You think your sources of information, that there were not more than forty thousand troops at Manassas and Centreville, are perfectly reliable?

Answer. I have no doubt of it. I talked with a great many who had been there, and that appeared to be the general impression of them all. I thought you folks here knew all the time that there were only about forty thousand men there.

Question. What treatment did the Union men receive from the rebel army where you have been, in Tennessee, &c.?

Answer. When General Carter made an advance on Big Creek Gap, Leadbetter's brigade, consisting of about three thousand five hundred men, went there. We were to go up to Clinch river and meet General Carter's force, while General E. Kirby Smith was to bring up a force and get in his rear. The horses for the cavalry and artillery of our army were supplied almost altogether from the Union men along the route. We never gave them any receipts for them. We took every wagon and every horse from every Union man we came across, and all the corn and hay they had—everything that we wanted.

Question. Did the rebel army ever plunder their houses?

Answer. I went with one of the quartermasters who was a captain, and he, with two others, went into the house of a man who had been obliged to leave for Kentucky on account of his Union sentiments. I was ordered, and did so, to go into a field and tell a negro who was ploughing there to bring down the four mules he had and hitch them up in a wagon; and we went into the smoke-house and took every bit of bacon the woman had. She said it was all she had to keep her alive. We took her two negroes and blankets off the bed in the house and carried them off. There was no receipt, or order, or paper of any kind given her to show that this property had been appropriated by the rebels, and no report was made of it through the proper authorities. I helped to carry the meat and put it into the wagon. The woman was crying and the children were crying as we were doing this. When I came across the mountains into General Carter's camp, I inquired for the man. He was a captain in the Union army. I told him what had been done.

I was on two of these expeditions. On one we went to the house of an old man who had his wife with him. She was an old lady of sixty years of age; he was, I should think, seventy-five years of age. They had one negro boy to cut wood, bring water, and do everything of that kind for them. He offered us dinner. A commissioned officer who was with us asked him if he was a Union man. He said he was, and that he could not deny it. The only thing he regretted was that he had not died before Tennessee went out of the Union. The officer said he was a damned old fool, and without saying another word to him, he turned around and took his wagon, two horses, and his negro away from him, so that the old folks had no means to help them get along.

Question. Are the officers and the masses of the army informed as to the results of the battles that have been fought?

Answer. I held a position as gunner in the battery to which I belonged, and when I left I did not believe that Manassas had been evacuated.

Question. How long ago was that?

Answer. About four weeks ago. We had heard that Columbus had been evacuated by Beauregard, but were told that he brought away with him all his supplies, every gun, and without the loss of a man. We did not know anything of the troops leaving Pensacola. They claimed a victory for a while at Pea Ridge, and then afterwards said nothing about it. The battle at Winchester they told us was a drawn battle. The men are kept in complete ignorance of everything that is going on, especially in the army. They never know how badly they have been whipped.

Question. Did you know anything about the condition of affairs at Winchester when Patterson was before it with his army?

Answer. Only from what I heard from one of the aides-de-camp of one of the rebel generals who was there.

Question. Did they admit that Patterson could have taken Winchester?

Answer. Yes, sir; and they expected he would take it when he advanced within a few miles of it. The people there had pulled down all the secession flags, and the Union people had got Union flags to raise as soon as our troops should come, and were very much disappointed when Patterson turned away and left.

Question. Did you find many Union men in the secession army?

Answer. Yes, sir; there are a great many of them, particularly among the

Virginians, Tennesseeans, and North Carolinians. I do not recollect of seeing any from other States whom I thought to be Union men, except some few foreigners from New Orleans. They have so many Union men in the secession army in East Tennessee that they are afraid to give them arms of any kind in some places, except squirrel rifles, and they even took them away, and gave them axes and picks to clear away the woods, &c., so that they could get a range for their cannon.

Question. You found a great many Union men in East Tennessee?

Answer. Yes, sir. I found very few secessionists in East Tennessee. It was a very rare thing to find a secessionist there. I was intimate with Parson Brownlow's family, and was one of the guard set over his house for a time. I knew Mr. Maynard's family, and was acquainted with his brother. I am acquainted with the whole country all through East Tennessee, and also all about Richmond, Virginia, and from there out to East Tennessee. We were over a week going from Richmond to East Tennessee. The Union men threw the train we were on off the track in Southwestern Virginia, near East Tennessee. That is rather a common occurrence there. The secession troops never pass through that country without loading their guns before they get to Southwestern Virginia and into East Tennessee.

Question. What is the feeling in the southern army in regard to our commanders? Are there any of them that they fear more than others, or do they appear to know much about them?

Answer. From what I have heard the officers and men in the army say, I am of the opinion that they would all be very sorry to hear that General McClellan had resigned, or left the army. They admire him very much; but they were very much rejoiced when they learned that Secretary Cameron had resigned.

Question. Why would they dislike to have General McClellan resign?

Answer. It is principally on the negro question. They would fear that some one else would take his place who would work more against him. They regard him as the best friend they could have as a general, and think they could get along better with him than any other general. They are very much afraid of General Frémont.

Question. On account of his fighting qualities, or on account of his opinions on the negro question?

Answer. On account of the negro question.

Question. It would appear from that that they are more alarmed about the negroes than about the fighting?

Answer. Yes, sir. They are very much afraid, all through the south, that the federal government will make some use of the negroes; that the negroes will be interfered with and they be ruined; and they admit that would have been done before this time but for General McClellan.

Question. It is on account of the negro question that they feel so much interest about who commands our armies?

Answer. Yes, sir.

WASHINGTON, *March* 26, 1863.

Mr. S. A. PANCOAST sworn and examined.

By Mr. Gooch:

Question. Where is your present residence, and where has your residence been?

Answer. In Hampshire county, Virginia. I am a New Jerseyman by birth, but have lived in Hampshire county for the last fifteen years.

Question. What has been your occupation or employment?

Answer. Manufacturer of iron.

Question. Have you been arrested by the rebels at any time; and if so, when?

Answer. I was first arrested and taken to Winchester, Virginia, before the rebel General Carson. I was kept there three or four days, and then told by him that there was no evidence against me, and I was released. Before I left I asked him if it would be considered wrong for me to go north and get some groceries, salt, sugar, &c., as we should suffer very much there on account of the blockade during the fall and winter. He said no, that that must be winked at. I then came on here and saw the President of the United States, and he gave me a letter to General Scott, who gave me a permit to take over those things. I then went home, and saw General Carson, Colonel McDonald, and all the confederate officers within fifty miles of me, and got, in writing, their permit to go on and buy these groceries, and the confederate army should not take them from me when I brought them on. I came on here again. By that time General Scott had resigned, and General McClellan had taken his place. I got General McClellan's name to my paper, and went home again.

The night I got home—the 10th of November, 1861—I was arrested, and carried to Winchester on the charge of having carrier pigeons with me. I had four little tumblers and a pair of ruff-necked pigeons, which my little son had got in Baltimore. I was for a week kept there on parole. The provost marshal was acquainted with me, and resigned his situation because Jackson demanded that I should be put in prison. I was put in the guard-house, and remained there ten days, suffering every indignity that could be put upon me. I applied for a writ of *habeas corpus*, and was taken to Richmond the next night. The lawyer whom I had employed said that there was no charge against me; it was not what I had done, but what I might do; that it was in my power to injure them, and therefore I was sent to Richmond. In Richmond I was kept in the Main Street prison for three months, with the officers of the north. When they were released I was put in prison with the citizen prisoners. There were from 500 to 700 citizens, with some soldiers there. For a week or two we had no privy there, except by going down three flights of stairs. I have seen old men of seventy or eighty years of age stand from 7 o'clock in the morning until 12 o'clock the next day before they had an opportunity of going down stairs. Fifty cents and a dollar was frequently paid by those who had money for the privilege of going down. That was the cause of our greatest suffering there.

While in the Libby prison we had soup and beef once or twice a week. When the soup was brought into the room I have seen them pick the maggots out of it before they ate it. If they did not eat that, they would have to go without. After the battle of Williamsburg they picked out eight or ten of us—the worst Union men there—and carried us to Salisbury, North Carolina, where we remained about ten months. When we got there we were put into a small building, and kept there, without being allowed the privilege of going out for any purpose; and there, again, our greatest sufferings were caused by the difficulty of attending to the calls of nature. We had a box in the room, which we were compelled to use until the stench became awful We suffered very much during the warm weather. We were often compelled to lie so thick on the floor that one could not turn over without all turning over. After a while they allowed us a yard containing five or six acres, where we were allowed to go in the day-time. At five o'clock we were compelled to return to the prison, which was then closed, and we remained in a close room until eight or nine o'clock the next morning. We could cook only in the yard: there was no chance to do so in the prison. On our way from Richmond to Salisbury we were hurried off one morning because we had shown very great anxiety for McClellan to come to Richmond after the battle of Williamsburg, and we talked pretty loudly and freely about it. We started on the 15th of May, and arrived at Salisbury on the 17th of May, being fifty-three hours on the road. We were seated on benches without backs, (among us old men seventy to eighty years of age,) and compelled to sit there for all those fifty-three hours, for the guard had positive orders to shoot any of us who should stand up. I think that ride sent a great many old men to their graves; they never recovered from it. With the exception of the chills and fever of the country, we got along a great deal better than we did in Richmond. The deaths were not near so frequent. After Mr. Wood, superintendent of the Old Capitol prison here, returned from his visit to Salisbury, we were made to suffer very much, because we acknowledged that we were Union men. We were kept in close confinement from five o'clock in the evening until eight or nine o'clock the next morning, without any fire, all through the cold weather of the fall. From that exposure I was taken with the inflammatory rheumatism, and suffered very much; and at last a surgeon who was very kind to me had me placed in a building out in the yard; but this was not done until they said there was no hope of my living long. For six or eight weeks I could not get up, or dress or undress myself without assistance. At Richmond we had a loaf of bread a day, and it was always good; but at Salisbury the bread was always sour; but, with the exception of the bread, our food at Salisbury was better than at Richmond. We had a small allowance, however—from seven to fourteen ounces of food for the twenty-four hours. If we got fourteen ounces we thought we were doing very well indeed. While in prison in Richmond a lot of "Louisiana Tigers," sentenced to confinement with ball and chain, were put in the prison with us, and they abused us most shamefully. And at Salisbury, where we had a yard, the guard around the fence would strike and punch at us with their bayonets if we got near enough the fence for them to reach us. This they would do every chance they could get. And while in the prison the guard below would, at times, discharge their muskets up at the floor under our feet, and the balls would pass up among us. This was done several times. Since the 1st of August, a year ago, until we came away, we have buried 167 of our Union prisoners.

Question. What caused the deaths of those men?

Answer. Mostly want of suitable provisions. There was nothing for them when they were sick that was fitted for them. I think the most of them died from want of proper food. We had a surgeon there, but he had not much medicine to give us. And when a father was taken out to be buried it was seldom that the son, if he had one there, was allowed to go to his funeral. We were abused the most by the refugees placed over us from Maryland and Washington. When we were taken to Salisbury from Richmond they told us that we need not take anything with us, and they would not allow us to do it; and when we got to Salisbury we were compelled to sleep on the bare floor all the time we were there, except some few of us who had ticks furnished to sleep on.

Question. How many prisoners were kept in the prison at Salisbury?

Answer. Generally from 200 to 300. The clerk once told me that out of 400 names on the prison book mine was the only one that had no charge against it.

Question. When were you discharged?

Answer. We left on the 5th of March, 1863.

WASHINGTON, *March* 26, 1863.

JAMES M. SEEDS sworn and examined.

By Mr. Gooch:

Question. Where do you reside?

Answer. In Cincinnati.

Question. When and where were you arrested by the rebels?

Answer. I was arrested on the 6th of November, 1861, at Columbia, South Carolina. When I was first arrested they took of the money I had on my person $635. A few minutes after I was searched we started on the cars for Richmond. I was arrested on suspicion of being General Rosecrans going through the country, and was searched for important papers which it was supposed I had upon me. The next morning after we started, after we had passed Salisbury, North Carolina, I jumped off the train and made my escape, and took what is called the Western Extension train, and went as far as that went, 74 miles, and then took the stage. I took the stage at Morganton, Buncombe county, North Carolina. An extra train followed right on after me, and I was again arrested just on the other side of the Blue Ridge. I was taken out of the stage by a mob, and it was with great difficulty that some men, who were friendly toward me, saved my life. I was then tied with my hands behind me, and made to walk 17 miles to a town called Marion. There I again came very near being hung. I was there searched very closely and thoroughly, by pulling off my clothes and boots and searching them all, and $620 more was taken from me, partly paper and partly gold. I was then put in the county jail, in an iron cage, and locked up there that night with three thieves and two negroes. The next morning I was taken out, again tied with a rope, and put in a two-horse barouche and taken back to Morganton. There three dollars of stage-fare was paid back to me, and then they took that from me. That night I was made to walk six miles with my hands tied behind me, down to what is called the head of the road. I was treated very well there. The men working on the road there took the rope off me and gave me a comfortable bed. I found them all Union men. My arrest and re-arrest had been made by Georgia men—some men of a Georgia regiment. I was then taken to Salisbury, North Carolina, where, for the third time, I came near being hung. At Salisbury I was put in irons and taken to Richmond. On the way, above Raleigh, a mob wanted to take me out of the cars and hang me, but they did not do it. I arrived in Richmond on the night of the 12th of November, 1861, and was put in a building, called by them "No. 7," with some federal prisoners of war. The next morning, still handcuffed, I was taken out of that building and put in the Henrico county jail. A few days afterwards I had an examination before James Lyons, and there they swore that, from all the evidence they could get, they believed me to be General Rosecrans. Lyons himself told me that I ought to have been hung; that they never ought to have brought me there. After that examination I was taken back to the county jail. Lyons reported to their secretary of war that he believed me to be a spy, and recommended the government to hold me as such until he could get evidence enough to hang me. Some time in February I sued out a writ of *habeas corpus*, employing as my lawyers Messrs. Nance & Williams, a legal firm there. The suit was brought before Judge Meredith, I think. He said that, according to the evidence, he would have to discharge me from prison. A man named Patrick Henry Elliott was the lawyer for the government, and had put in the plea that the government should hold me as a spy. When the judge made this remark, and he found that I was about to be discharged, Elliott said he thought the secretary of war would discharge me if my attorneys would go before him. My attorneys were to meet Mr. Elliott, and did go before the secretary of war. Mr. Nance came to the county jail afterwards, and told me that the secretary of war did make out my discharge for release from prison, and that General Winder put in objections to my being discharged upon the ground of being a Union man; and stated that when I was arrested there was a letter found on me, written by a clergyman in Kentucky to a clergyman in Columbia, South Carolina, recommending me as a good and reliable Union man. That is what Mr. Nance told me was done at the war office. The secretary of war then said that he would hold me three or four days longer, and give General Winder a chance to produce that letter. Mr. Nance came to see me about it, and I told him that there was no such paper about me, and never had been. On the 18th of March I, with others, broke out of the county jail at Richmond and tried to make our escape. But I was recaptured on the Pamunkey river, and taken back and put in the county jail again, and there heavily ironed. They did not iron me quite so heavily as they did some, but more heavily than they did others. We were confined in jail with negroes, thieves, and all kinds of criminals. We were fed pretty well. But there were, at times, from eighteen to twenty negroes there, and never less than four or five. On the morning of the 15th of May we were hurried off to Salisbury, North Carolina, on the cars, as Mr. Pancoast has described, without the privilege of getting up from the seat under penalty of being shot, and without anything to eat until along in the afternoon of the 16th of May. While we were at Raleigh I got a man named Kaschmier, one of the police, to allow me to send out and get some cakes. That evening they gave each of us half a loaf of bread, and a slice of meat, both raw and fat. That is all they gave us from the time we left Richmond until we got to Salisbury. And as near as I can recollect, we were fifty-three hours on the road. When we left Richmond they lied to me, and took from me my cot bed and cover, and said they were not going to take us off, but were going to move us up in town; that they were going to burn the tobacco warehouses there, and were afraid we would be smothered to death by the smoke if we remained in the jail. When we reached Salisbury we were put in this little building described by Mr. Pancoast, and allowed no privileges of going out. One day while we were in that building a sentinel commenced raising a fuss with one of the prisoners, and ordered him to shut his mouth, and at the same time fired at him; the charge, (a ball and three buckshot) passed over his head and went into a joist above. He seized another gun to fire at him, but was stopped.

I think we were ten days in that building and were then moved into what was called the yard, with some brick houses about it, where our privileges were much greater. At that time our provisions were about a half a pound of pork and perhaps a pound of sour bread a day. This yard was afterwards enlarged to about 100 yards square. Some time in June there were 135 civilian prisoners brought there, and the yard was then enlarged to take them in. There was nothing transpired, other than sickness and death, until after the prisoners of war were carried off. Then they were very severe on us for a while; but by giving a written parole that we would not violate any of the regulations of the prison, we were allowed to go back into this yard again. After being there a while Mr. Wood, of the Old Capitol prison here, came on as a commissioner on the part of the United States government to intercede for our exchange. They had hoped to get some of us for the rebel army. After Mr. Wood and all the officers of the federal army went away, we were treated very severely, for we had declared ourselves to be Union men. They cursed us and called us all the names they could think of, and our rations were not much more than two-thirds of what they had been at first. Our rations had been decreasing gradually from the start; still, I think they were about as much as their private soldiers got, as far as I could judge. They furnished me no bed from the time I went into that prison until I came out. When I left Richmond I had some spreads which had cost me about $750. When I went out they told me they were contraband, and took them away from me; and as far as I know they served all the prisoners in the same manner. I had on an oil-cloth cape, and they raised that up to see if I had any blankets hid under it. One night, while a Mr. Allen Leonard was sitting at the prison window in Salisbury, singing Union songs, they shot at us, and the ball passed in the window over our heads, and up through the ceiling and floor above us, and missed the feet of one of the prisoners, as he was lying on the floor, by only about four or five inches. Captain Waters, the commander there, was very abusive to the Union prisoners. When I was retaken after my escape from the Richmond jail, they took $75 from me, giving me a receipt for only $65. They explained that by saying that it would cost $10 to fix the lock of the jail. Out of all the money they took from me I received about $315 in confederate money. The money they took from me was gold and silver and some paper, mostly Louisiana paper, some North and South Carolina paper. After they had kept my money for some time, they sent me word that there was $21 or $22 of the gold that was counterfeit.

By Mr. Odell:

Question. Did they have the means of treating you better in the way of food, &c., than they did?

Answer. I think they had. At the Libby prison the meat was bad while the bread was good. I do not know as they could have furnished us more, but they could have furnished us better food. At Salisbury we got more provisions than at Richmond.

HEADQUARTERS ARMY OF THE SOUTHWEST,
Camp near Batesville, Arkansas, May 21, 1862.

SIR: The absence from my immediate command of those men and officers who are best acquainted with the facts in regard to the employment of Indian savages has delayed my reply to your communication of April 2, 1861, until this time.

I have the honor to now lay before the committee the statements and affidavits enclosed, from which it will appear that large forces of Indian savages were engaged against this army at the battle of Pea Ridge, and that the warfare was conducted by said savages with all the barbarity their merciless and cowardly natures are capable of.

Very respectfully, your obedient servant,

S. R. CURTIS, *Major General.*

Hon. B. F. WADE,
Chairman of Committee on Conduct of the Present War.

HEADQUARTERS ARMY OF THE SOUTHWEST,
Forsyth, Missouri, April 12, 1862.

SIR: In compliance with your request, conforming to the wish of the joint committee of Congress "to inquire into the fact whether Indian savages have been employed by the rebels in their military service, and how such warfare has been conducted by such savages against the government of the United States," I hereby certify upon honor that I was present at the engagement near Leetown, Arkansas, on the 7th of March ultimo, when the main charge of the enemy's cavalry was made upon our line; that there were Indians among the forces making said charge; and that from personal inspection of the bodies of the men of the 3d Iowa cavalry, who fell upon that part of the field, I discovered that eight of the men of that regiment had been scalped. I also saw bodies of the same men, which had been wounded in parts not vital by bullets, and also pierced through the heart and neck with knives—fully satisfying me that the men had first fallen from the gun-shot wounds received, and afterwards brutally murdered.

The men of the 3d Iowa cavalry, who were taken prisoners by the enemy, and who have since returned, all state that there were great numbers of Indians with them on the retreat as far as Elm Springs. Their affidavits will be furnished to you as soon as possible.

Respectfully submitted.

JOHN W. NOBLE,
Regimental Adjutant 3d Iowa Cavalry.

Major General SAMUEL R. CURTIS, *Commanding.*

UNITED STATES OF AMERICA,
Southwestern District of Missouri:

I, Daniel Bradbury, on my oath, say that I am orderly sergeant of company A, 3d Iowa cavalry, and that I was present at the battle of Pea Ridge, near Leetown, Arkansas, on the 7th of March, 1862, and I then and there saw about three hundred (300) Indians scattered over the battle-field, without commanders, doing as they pleased. On the 8th of March I saw what I would judge to be about thousand (3,000) Indians marching in good order towards the battle-field, under the command of Albert Pike.

DANIEL BRADBURY,
First Sergeant Company A, 3d Iowa Cavalry.

Subscribed and sworn to before me this the 30th day of April, 1862.

GLENN LOWE,
Adjutant 3d Iowa Cavalry.

UNITED STATES OF AMERICA,
Southwestern District of Missouri:

I, John H. Lawson, on my oath, say that I am a private in company D, 3d Iowa cavalry, and that I was present at the battle of Pea Ridge, near Leetown, Arkansas, on the 7th of March, 1862, and I then and there saw, as near as I could judge, about one hundred and fifty (150) Indians scattered; they were afterwards formed into companies and marched out of my sight in good order. On the 8th of March I saw about two thousand (2,000) Indians, said to be under the command of Albert Pike and Martin Green, marching towards the battle-ground in good order. These were all mounted—armed with shot-guns, rifles, and large knives.

JOHN H. LAWSON.

Subscribed and sworn to before me this the 30th day of April, 1862.

GLENN LOWE,
Adjutant 3d Iowa Cavalry.

HEADQUARTERS THIRD IOWA CAVALRY,
Jacksonport, Arkansas, May 11, 1862.

GENERAL: On the morning of the 7th of March I was on the battle-field of Pea Ridge. While my command was engaging the enemy near Leetown, I saw in the rebel army a large number of Indians, estimated by me at one thousand.

After the battle I attended in person to the burial of the dead of my command. Of twenty-five men killed on the field of my regiment, eight were scalped, and the bodies of others were horribly mutilated, being fired into with musket-balls, and pierced through the body and neck with long knives. These atrocities I believe to have been committed by Indians belonging to the rebel army.

Very respectfully, your obedient servant,

CYRUS BUSSEY, *Colonel.*

Major General S. R. CURTIS,
Commanding Army of the Southwest.

WOUNDED FROM FRONT ROYAL, VIRGINIA.

IN THE HOUSE OF REPRESENTATIVES,
June 16, 1862.

On motion of Mr. Shellabarger,

Resolved, That "the committee upon the conduct of the war" be directed to inquire and report to this house whether our soldiers who were wounded at the battle of Port Republic upon the 8th and 9th instant were subjected to any unnecessary neglect, either by refusal by any officer or surgeon to permit them to receive surgical attendance or medical supplies from other than their own brigade or division, or from any other cause. Also, whether they were subjected to any such neglect by being left upon the cars, or otherwise, after their arrival in this city; and if any such neglect occurred, that they ascertain and report the cause thereof.

Attest:

EM. ETHERIDGE, *Clerk*.

WAR DEPARTMENT,
Washington City, D. C., June 18, 1862—12½.

SIR: In answer to your note of this date, just received, I transmit a communication from the surgeon general, which is all the information in possession of this department in relation to the alleged neglect of our soldiers wounded in the action of Port Republic.

Your obedient servant,

EDWIN M. STANTON,
Secretary of War.

Hon. B. F. WADE.

MEDICAL DIRECTOR'S OFFICE,
Military District of Washington, June 15, 1862.

GENERAL: I have the honor to invite your attention to the conduct of Surgeon David S. Hays, 110th Pennsylvania volunteers. He stated to me that he arrived here last night, between 8 and 9 o'clock, in charge of about four hundred sick and wounded men from Front Royal. He did not report his arrival at this office until after 9 o'clock this morning. Ambulances were at once sent to convey the men to hospitals; and I also sent my assistant, Dr. Sheldon, 78th New York, to superintend their removal, which he did well. As this is the second time that men have been neglected in this way by the medical officer in charge, I respectfully request that efficient measures may be taken to prevent its repetition. The conduct of Surgeon Hays is, I think, highly culpable, and without excuse. It is, I feel assured, only necessary to bring the facts to your notice to have him dealt with as he deserves.

I am, general, very respectfully, your obedient servant,

JONA. LETTERMAN,
Assistant Surgeon U. S. A., Medical Director.

Brigadier General W. A. HAMMOND,
Surgeon General U. S. A., Washington, D. C.

[Indorsement.]

SURGEON GENERAL'S OFFICE, *June* 16, 1862.

Respectfully transmitted to the Secretary of War. Surgeon Hays has exhibited a total want of comprehension of his duties, if not the grossest inhumanity. Whilst the men were being removed to the hospitals he absented himself, leaving the whole duty of taking care of these wounded soldiers to the medical officers having charge of the ambulances.

I therefore respectfully recommend that severe and summary punishment be awarded to Surgeon Hays. This is the second time within a short period that surgeons bringing sick and wounded to this city have neglected them. An example would be highly beneficial.

WILLIAM A. HAMMOND,
Surgeon General.

Referred to the adjutant general, with instructions to dismiss Surgeon Hays for neglect of duty.

EDWIN M. STANTON,
Secretary of War.

SURGEON GENERAL'S OFFICE,
Washington City, D. C., June 22, 1862.

DEAR SIR: I enclose you for the committee all the telegrams received at and sent from this office relative to the sick brought by Dr. Hays. I also enclose a copy of an order I had issued to Brigade Surgeon Cox for not having hospitals and stores.

The watchmen will report to-morrow. *They both say positively that Dr. Hays never came to the office till Sunday morning.*

Yours, truly,

WILLIAM A. HAMMOND.

Hon. Mr. ODELL, M. C., *Willards' Hotel.*

[Received June 13, 1862.]

FRONT ROYAL, *June* 13—11.20.

SIR: One hundred and eighty (180) wounded of Shields's division have just arrived here. We are without hospitals or other means for their comfort. I desire your orders with regard to them.

Respectfully,

ABRAM L. COX, *Brigade Surgeon.*

WM. A. HAMMOND, M. D., *Surgeon General.*

[Received June 13, 1862.]

FRONT ROYAL, *June* 13—3.50 *p. m.*

SIR: I arrived here this morning with two hundred and eighty (280) sick and wounded from Shields's division in charge. I reported to senior medical officer at this place, but General Ricketts, first brigade, second division, refuses to allow him to act. I am, therefore, without any medicines or dressings, which Dr. Cox is not permitted to furnish. Please telegraph me what disposition I shall make of them.

I am, sir, your obedient servant,

D. S. HAYS, *Surgeon in Charge.*

Surgeon General HAMMOND, *U. S. A.*

SURGEON GENERAL'S OFFICE,
Washington City, D. C., June 13, 1862.

Send your sick on to this city. Telegraph when they leave. You will be ordered to report in person to the surgeon general.

WILLIAM A. HAMMOND,
Surgeon General.

Dr. A. L. COX,
Brigade Surgeon, U. S. V., Front Royal, Va.

[Received June 14, 1862.]

MANASSAS, *June* 14, 1862—4.14 *p. m.*

The train will arrive at Washington by 8 or 9 o'clock p. m.

D. S. HAYS, *Surgeon in Charge.*

Surgeon General HAMMOND.

[Extract.]

SURGEON GENERAL'S OFFICE,
Washington City, D. C., June 13, 1862.

SIR: * * * * * And that Brigade Surgeon A. L. Cox, United States volunteers, be directed to report to the surgeon general in this city, to account for his neglect in not having provided proper hospitals and other accommodations for the sick and wounded at Front Royal. * *

I am, very respectfully, your obedient servant,

WILLIAM A. HAMMOND,
Surgeon General.

Brigadier General L. THOMAS,
Adjutant General United States Army.

WASHINGTON, *June* 20, 1862.

Dr. DAVID S. HAYS sworn and examined.

By Mr. Gooch:

Question. What has been your position and rank in the army?

Answer. Surgeon of the 110th regiment of Pennsylvania volunteers.

Question. Will you state, as concisely as possible, the history of your connexion with the sick and wounded who came to this city under your charge from Front Royal?

Answer. After the battle of Winchester, on the 23d of March, I was in charge of a hospital in that place, and I retreated with General Banks's column at the time they left. I belonged to General Shields's division, and Dr. King, at Williamsport, relieved me, and directed me to rejoin my regiment as soon as I could. The rebels were then in Winchester, and I rode to Frederick on horseback, and there got into the cars and came to Washington, and went from here to Alexandria, and from there to Manassas. I was ordered from there to Front Royal. When I got to Front Royal I learned of this fight on Monday. I got on my horse, and, with two other surgeons, rode to Luray, where we arrived about 2 o'clock in the day. Our medical director was not there. There were a number of surgeons there, and there were several hospitals opened. Several of us went to a hospital on the hill, where there were quite a number of wounded who had just been brought in. We were there with them that day, and the most of the night, dressing their wounds. The next morning (Wednesday morning) our medical director, Dr. Bryant, placed me in charge of a hospital there. I had not then received any orders from him, and was going on to join my regiment, but he stopped me and put me in charge of a hospital there. There were no supplies or anything there. I sent to the provost marshal, and had attendants sent down, and also a steward, and proceeded to organize the hospital as soon as I could. I drew rations and had them cooked, and proceeded to dress the wounds and take the names and regiments of the wounded. About 9 o'clock that night I received orders from Dr. Bryant to have my wounded ready, with two days' rations, to leave for Front Royal, there to report to the senior medical officer. I was up at work the most of that night. I again drew rations for two days for the wounded. It took us the most of the night to dress their wounds, and arrange all the other matters. We had to send around to the houses there to get kettles, &c., to cook the rations in. And I got some sheets from houses there to make bandages and dressings for the wounded men. Our orders were to be ready by 9 o'clock the next morning to proceed to Front Royal, but we could not get the wagons ready until about noon. We started about noon on Thursday, and drove fourteen miles, and encamped in a clover field for the night. We had the rations in the wagons; and each surgeon also received orders to have rations prepared for his own men. I received an order to have rations prepared for the men in my own hospital.

I then rode on, leaving three surgeons with the wounded, to report and provide hospital accommodations at Front Royal. I rode on about four miles, and as it was then getting dark, and as we were told that the rebels had fired upon our prisoners, we stopped at a house some five or six miles from Front Royal.

The next morning I rode into town and reported to General Ricketts. He told me that Dr. Cox, his brigade surgeon, was the senior medical officer there, but he was sick. I then went to the provost marshal to get hospital accommodations. With his assistance I obtained one hospital. I found Dr. Cox a short time afterwards, and reported to him. He directed me to prepare hospitals for the wounded, and I went to work and got three churches, into which I had the straw from the wagons carried, and then the sick taken in. It took some time to make these preparations. I then drew rations again, and as there were no accommodations for cooking there, I had to get camp-kettles and do the best I could.

Dr. Cox in the mean time had received orders from General Ricketts to join his brigade, and I had then to continue in charge. I had no dressings there, and there were none in town, as Dr. Magruder had broken up the hospitals there. I sent around to the houses, and got some sheets to make bandages of. About dusk, Dr. Mosely, a brigade surgeon, sent me in some assistants.

As soon as I had reported to Dr. Cox, he telegraphed to the surgeon general to learn what should be done with the wounded. That was in the morning, some time before 12 o'clock. No answer coming, about 3 o'clock that evening I telegraphed again. The next morning Dr. Cox received a despatch from the surgeon general, directing that the wounded should be brought to this city.

By Mr. Covode:

Question. How many wounded had you there?

Answer. Before we went to Front Royal I made out the list in my hospital, and one of the surgeons in charge of another hospital made out his list. But the other surgeons had not time to do so. When I got to Front Royal I set my steward to find that out, and he made it out to be 325 sick and wounded.

Question. How many surgeons had you along to take care of them?

Answer. There were four assistant surgeons besides myself.

Question. Was that enough to dress and take care of that number of sick and wounded men?

Answer. No, sir; I do not think it was. On Saturday morning, about eight o'clock, Dr. Cox received a despatch from the surgeon general directing him to have the men brought to this city, and to report to his office.

By Mr. Gooch:

Question. Have you that despatch?

Answer. Yes, sir; here it is:

"Send your sick to this city. Telegraph when you leave. You will be ordered to report in person to the surgeon general."

That is signed "Wm. A. Hammond."

As soon as Dr. Cox handed me that despatch, which was a short time after he received it, I immediately sent a despatch to the surgeon general's office, stating that we would leave about 11 o'clock that morning for Washington city. I then went to work to have the men put on the cars. They could furnish us, I think, with only seven cars. There were a few mattresses and some straw. The worst cases I put upon the mattresses. I got them all loaded, and started the train at about twenty minutes past 11 o'clock.

We came on to Manassas, and I got off the train there and immediately went to the telegraph office, and telegraphed to the surgeon general that the train would reach this city between 8 and 9 o'clock that night. We were at Manassas about an hour, I suppose. I had dinner cooked and served there, and then started on again.

A short time after we started the train stopped, and one of the assistants came to me and reported that two cars with sick had been attached to the train at Manassas, and that two of them had died. I had known nothing about that before; no one had reported to me that those two cars were to be attached to the train. I sent my assistant to see about it, and it was reported to me that the two had died of fever.

At a station between Manassas and Alexandria I went into the telegraph office to telegraph to the superintendent that we wished to cross Long Bridge. The conductor said he would attend to that himself.

We then came on to Alexandria, and I immediately went to the superintendent's office. They asked me there if it was known in Washington that I was coming. I told them that I had telegraphed twice to the surgeon general, and I supposed they knew we were coming.

It was after dark when we started from Alexandria, and when we got across Long Bridge I suppose it was between 9 and 10 o'clock. I expected to find ambulances and surgeons in attendance, but there were none when we got here. We waited for some time, and could not tell whether the cars were going to run down to the depot or not. I inquired of the conductor, but he could not tell. I told my assistant surgeons that I would go down and see if I could find out anything about it, and would be back in a short time. Dr. Stidger and myself then walked down to Willards'. Colonel Lewis and Captain Marshall, quartermaster, were with us. When we got there I asked what time it was, and found it was very near 10 o'clock. Supper was over at the hotel, but Colonel Lewis and Captain Marshall asked us to take some tea with them. Dr. Stidger and myself went in and took some tea. It was raining when I came out. Some one told me that I should find the surgeon general's office in the War Department. I drove around to the War Department and went into the hall. There was a man there sleeping on the floor, and I proceeded to wake him up. During the noise I made for that purpose some one came down the stairs. I told him I wanted to find the surgeon general's office, and he directed me to the place. I drove around there and went in, and found a watchman sitting there. I inquired if the surgeon general was in. He said he was not. I asked if any of his clerks were in, and he said there was no one there. I then asked if he would take a note to his house if I would write one. He said he did not know where he lived, and that there were some despatches waiting for him there then. Not finding any preparations made, and no one about, I concluded that it was not the intention to do anything with the men I had brought in before morning. I then got into a carriage and drove out to the train again.

By Mr. Covode:

Question. At what time was that?

Answer. I do not know the time. When I got back there I found that the citizens had been there and had got suppers for the men. They told me that all had had their suppers. Some of them—I do not know how many—had been taken from the cars and carried into some churches, and into a house just opposite the cars. I told Dr. Stidger that we better stay there until morning. "No," said he, "they are pretty comfortable now. The citizens will have them taken over to the churches, and you had better go and get some sleep, and report as soon as you can in the morning." I then went down to the hotel and went to bed. That was about 4 o'clock in the morning, for when I went in I inquired of the man there what time it was, and he said it was about 4 o'clock. I do not know how long I slept, but as soon as I got my breakfast I went around to the surgeon general's office. I am not quite certain, but I think he was not in when I first got there. However, when I saw him I reported to him. I gave him my order, in the first place, to take my wounded to Front Royal and report to the senior medical officer there, and I also gave him General Ricketts's letter. I told him I could not have got along at all had it not been for Dr. Mosely, who sent me some assistants, the night I got to Front Royal, to dress the wounds of the men. The surgeon general remarked: "Dr. Mosely, and you, too, deserve credit for the way you have acted;" and he told me to call around again the next morning, as he wanted to see me about Dr. Cox not receiving the wounded men when they got to Front Royal.

He then sent me to the medical director's office, and I went there and reported to him. I then told him that I had got in the night before, but had not found any ambulances or surgeons in attendance, and had gone to the surgeon general's office, but had not been able to find him. He told me that he had not received any despatches. He made out orders for ambulances to be sent over there, and I went over immediately to the cars again. I found that nearly all the men had been taken out of the cars and carried into the churches and some houses there, and the citizens were engaged in preparing breakfast for them. I asked for some bandages and some warm water, and proceeded to dress the stumps of some of those who had had limbs amputated. I suppose it was a half an hour or so after I got there before the ambulances arrived. The medical director came over there and told me to set my medical assistants at work to move the men, but to leave the worst cases in the churches. I set my assistants at work. A surgeon came there and took charge. After all had been got off but four of the worst cases, I told the assistant medical director that I would then go down and get my dinner, leaving my assistant surgeons there, and if they needed me for anything they could let me know. I then went down to the hotel. The next morning I went around and reported again to the surgeon general. Said he, "I am going to have you dismissed." I asked him upon what grounds he was going to have it done. He just handed me the charges and told me to look them over. I glanced at them, and asked him if he would not bring charges against me, and allow me an opportunity to defend myself. "No," said he, "that is too tedious a process." He then told me that he was going to send the charges right over to the Secretary of War, and I could go and see him about it. I then went up to the War Department, and went into the Secretary's office. The Secretary took up the paper and proceeded to read it to me. I told him I had glanced over it, and asked him to allow me to make some explanations. He asked me if I did go to bed. I told him I had towards morning, and was proceeding to explain, when he told me he would not hear me; not to interrupt him. He then immediately wrote an order to the adjutant general to strike me from the rolls. That is about as near as I can state the circumstances of the case.

By Mr. Gooch :

Question. You say you arrived here between nine and ten o'clock, Saturday night, with your train?

Answer. Yes, sir.

Question. And it stopped this side of Long Bridge, on the Island?

Answer. Yes, sir.

Question. And you left the sick and wounded in the train, and went with Dr. Stidger to find the surgeon general?

Answer. Yes, sir.

Question. And you went to Willards' Hotel and got supper there?

Answer. No, sir; supper was over. I got some tea there.

Question. How long were you there?

Answer. Not long, because I wished to get away as soon as I could.

Question. About how long? Fix some outside limit to the time you were probably there.

Answer. I went into Willards' Hotel, and went into the wash-room and washed my face and hands, and then immediately went in to tea. It was a very short time I was there.

Question. Was it a half an hour, or an hour, or two hours that you were there?

Answer. I was not there over half an hour.

Question. And you went from there to the War Department?

Answer. Yes, sir; it was there I was directed to go. I think it was Dr. Stidger who told me that the surgeon general's office was in the War Department?

Question. You found a man in the War Department who told you where the office of the surgeon general was?

Answer. Yes, sir.

Question. You went to the surgeon general's office and found a messenger or a watchman there?

Answer. Yes, sir.

Question. What information did you obtain from him?

Answer. I asked him if the surgeon general was in, and he said he was not. I asked if any of his clerks were there, and he said not. I then asked if I should write a note or a despatch would he take it to the surgeon general's house. He said he did not know where he lived, and that there were some despatches there waiting for him then. When I found that there were no ambulances there to receive the wounded and sick, and that I could find no one, I concluded that they did not intend to do anything until morning.

Question. You made no further effort to find the surgeon general that night?

Answer. No, sir; I went immediately from his office back to the train again.

Question. At what time did you get back to the train?

Answer. I do not know. I went immediately out there. I cannot tell exactly what time it was, but it was in the morning when I came in again.

Question. I want to know how long a time you think it was from the time you left Willards' till you got back to the train?

Answer. I should suppose it was an hour and a half or two hours.

Question. That would make it about one o'clock when you got back there?

Answer. Yes, sir; I should think it was something like that.

Question. How long did you remain there?

Answer. I was not there a great while. I went from car to car and saw Dr. Stidger and some citizens there, and then I came back to the hotel.

Question. Did you look after your sick and wounded when we went over to the cars that time?

Answer. I went to the cars and was told that a number of them had been taken from the cars and carried into the churches and some houses there. When I went back to the train that night I went back to see what could be done, and I was then told that they would be made as comfortable as possible there till morning, and I concluded that, as they were comfortable there, and had had some supper, I would wait until morning, as I was almost entirely broken down and prostrated.

Question. When you went back to the train did you see your assistant surgeons and the people moving any of them?

Answer. I did not see them moving any, but was told they were doing so.

Question. Did you go into any of the houses, or into any of the places into which they were being carried, to see to any of them?

Answer. No, sir; I did not. I stated to Dr. Stidger that I proposed staying there all night. But he said I had better go back to the hotel and get some rest, and he would remain there.

Question. Did Dr. Stidger remain there?

Answer. Yes, sir; so I was told.

Question. Did the other assistant surgeons remain there?

Answer. When I went back there I was told they were in the churches. I did not see them.

Question. Dr. Stidger went to the hotel with you the first time that you went there?

Answer. Yes, sir; and when I started out to find the surgeon general I told him he had better go to the train, while I went to look up the surgeon general.

Question. And you found him at the train when you went back?

Answer. Yes, sir.

Question. You saw no other of the assistant surgeons there?

Answer. No, sir; I did not see them.

Question. You were told there that the men were being moved into the churches and houses?

Answer. Yes, sir; and that they would see that they were comfortable.

Question. Who told you that, besides Dr. Stidger?

Answer. I cannot recollect who they were; they were citizens there, and strangers to me.

Question. Did you have any persons very badly wounded or dangerously sick on that train?

Answer. There was one there badly wounded, and another there who had had his leg amputated. There was one man who had been shot through the leg, who died in the morning. I was of the opinion that he died of gangrene, and that was also the opinion of Dr. Stidger.

Question. Did any die on your way down here, except the two who died near Manassas?

Answer. That was all that was reported to me.

Question. You had charge of the whole of these men?

Answer. I presume I took it because I ranked the other surgeons there. But our orders were all alike.

Question. Were you present during the time of the removal of these men on Sunday?

Answer. Yes, sir; I stayed there until about two o'clock; I think it was after two o'clock when I left there. The assistant surgeons were divided around to the different hospitals, to see to and direct the loading of the ambulances. I went to all the hospitals, and at the one I left last they reported to me that they had got them all moved. The medical director told me to leave the worst cases there; not to remove them. There were two wounded men and two typhoid cases that I concluded to leave there. The assistant medical director was there, and assisting. I said to him that they were all removed from the churches, and I would go down to the hotel, and he could send for me if he wanted me. Dr. Stidger, Dr. King, and myself then went to the hotel. It was not earlier than two o'clock.

Question. When did your duties in connexion with this train cease?

Answer. I presumed they ceased as soon as I delivered them into the hands of the authorities here.

Question. At what time did you consider that to be?

Answer. As soon as the gentleman reported there I reported to him, and supposed that he then took charge. The man did not come there for some time after I went out in the morning.

Question. About what time did he get there?

Answer. I should think that it was about eleven o'clock. The medical director was there before that time, I believe; and I supposed that they then took charge of the men in the train.

Question. When he got there did he assume charge of the men, or did you still retain the charge?

Answer. I presumed he did. He had some attendants there whom I supposed he brought with him, and had them carry out the wounded. I was assisting, myself.

Question. Did you understand that he had the control from that time?

Answer. Yes, sir?

Question. Did you return again after you went to the hotel, at two o'clock.

Answer. No, sir.

Question. You considered your duties ended then?

Answer. Yes, sir.

Question. And that the sick and wounded men had been passed over to the proper authorities here?

Answer. Yes, sir.

Question. Do any of the persons at the hotel know at what time you returned there in the morning?

Answer. There is one person there who, I think, does.

Question. Who went with you there?

Answer. I returned alone about four o'clock Sunday morning. Colonel Lewis had engaged a room for me.

Question. You had a room at the hotel when you went there?

Answer. Yes, sir.

Question. From whom did you learn that your conduct was disapproved?

Answer. On Sunday morning, when I reported to the surgeon general, he asked me why Dr. Cox had not received these men at Front Royal. I handed him the letter of General Ricketts, which he said he would keep. I also handed him my orders to take the men to Front Royal, and told him that Dr. Mosely had assisted me greatly. He then said, "Dr. Mosely and you, too, deserve credit for what you have done." And I heard nothing more until the next morning about ten o'clock. I had been directed by the surgeon general to call at his office on Monday morning to tell him about Dr. Cox. I do not think he was there when I first went in. I found him there about ten o'clock. Dr. Stidger went with me. The surgeon general had a paper in his hand. Said he, "I am going to have you dismissed from the service." It astonished me, and I asked him on what grounds. He commenced to read the paper, and then handed it to me. I glanced over it, and then asked if he would not bring charges against me in the usual manner, and allow me an opportunity to defend myself. He said that was too tedious a process. That was the first intimation I had of any such thing.

Question. And you followed the letter over to the office of the Secretary of War?

Answer. The surgeon general said, "You can see the Secretary; I am going to send this to him." I went over to the War Department and saw one of the Assistant Secretaries first. He had a paper there, which he commenced to read. As I supposed it was the one relating to me, I told him what it was, and said that I would like to explain the matter. He said he would take it in to the Secretary, and I followed him into the Secretary's office. The Secretary took the paper and commenced reading it. I told him I had read a portion of it at the surgeon general's office. He asked me if it was correct. I told him I could explain it if he would allow me. He asked me if I went to bed on Saturday night. I told him I did go to bed, but I did not go to bed that night, but late in the morning. I then told him I would explain if he would let me have a little time. He told me not to interrupt him, and immediately wrote an order to the adjutant general to strike me from the list.

Question. Did your assistant surgeons stay with the wounded during Saturday night?

Answer. I know that Dr. Stidger did.

Question. Do you know whether the other assistant surgeons stayed with them that night?

Answer. I do not.

By Mr. Odell:

Question. Have you heard that they did not remain there?

Answer. I heard to-day, for the first time, that two of them, I think, went into one of the houses there.

By Mr. Gooch:

Question. When you went back to the train you saw none of the assistant surgeons but Dr. Stidger?

Answer. He was the only one I saw.

Question. Did you leave any directions with Dr. Stidger?

Answer. Yes, sir. But in the first place, before I left the train the first time to hunt up the surgeon general, I told the other assistants to remain there. When I got back I said to Dr. Stidger that we better remain there all night. He said, "No; you go and get some sleep, and report as early as possible in the morning, and I will stay here and take the direction." I told him to do so, and to take the worst cases to a house there. The men had all had their suppers. That is often done by surgeons. I supposed when I gave Dr. Stidger charge there that that was enough.

Question. When you went back again did you not deem it your duty, before you left for the night, to see that the men were properly cared for, and that the assistant surgeons were there on the ground?

Answer. Dr. Stidger is a very competent surgeon, and I supposed when I gave him these instructions that he would assume the whole charge, which he did.

Question. You and the other surgeons had had substantially the same duties to perform?

Answer. Yes, sir; about the same.

Question. And their labors had been as arduous as yours had been?

Answer. I do not think they had. I was the one who made the arrangements for the hospitals at Front Royal, and had the superintendence of the whole matter. I gave them instructions. I was running from place to place in Front

Royal all the time, and I did all the business connected with the train. I gave directions for the whole thing.

Question. Do you know whether Dr. Stidger stayed there all night?

Answer. I am confident that he did. He told me that he did, and some of the attendants remarked to me that he had stayed there.

Question. Two of the assistant surgeons went to bed?

Answer. Yes, sir; at least I have been told so lately?

Question. And the third one you do not know anything about?

Answer. No, sir. But when I gave them directions first to remain there, I supposed they would do so. Dr. Stidger told me he would take charge there.

Question. Who were those three other assistant surgeons?

Answer. Dr. McCune, assistant surgeon of the 14th Indiana; Dr. Redlick, assistant surgeon of the 84th Pennsylvania, and Dr. Barrow, assistant surgeon of the 29th Ohio.

Question. Were not these sick and wounded men in such a condition that they needed the attendance of every one of the surgeons there?

Answer. I do not think so. There were quite a number of men put on who were sick, but the majority of them, I believe, were convalescent. My impression was, when I left that night, that they were all very comfortable, and that they would be properly cared for. I had every confidence in Dr. Stidger.

Question. Was it, or not, your opinion that those men needed the attendance of all the surgeons there that night?

Answer. I did not think so. If there had been that number of men badly wounded, four or five surgeons would not have been enough. But the majority of the wounds were slight ones.

Question. Were there not enough of badly wounded men there to require the attendance of all the surgeons there?

Answer. No, sir; I do not think they required it that night.

Question. Is it not necessary that the surgeon should be there on the ground to see that the attendants perform their duty?

Answer. It is presumed that when you have attendants appointed that they come there with instructions, and that they carry them out. Besides that, I left Doctor Stidger in charge over the whole matter. The cooks, nurses, and stewards were there with their directions.

By Mr. Odell:

Question. You say that you arrived in this city with the train between 9 and 10 o'clock at night?

Answer. Yes, sir.

Question. Did you make any provision for these men to have their supper before you left the train to find the surgeon general?

Answer. Not the first time; I did not.

Question. Then you went and got your own supper, and went to looking around?

Answer. I got some tea; I had no intention to take supper when I went there.

Question. And you got back to the train after some two or three hours, more or less?

Answer. I do not recollect how long it was.

Question. You had no idea, when you left the first time, that these men would be cared for by the people on the Island?

Answer. There were some citizens there while we were there. We came there and waited some time before I left.

Question. Had you any idea that they would take care of these sick and wounded men?

Answer. Yes, sir. There was a Mr. Lloyd there, I think. He said that there was a church there that he would get the key of, and also that there was a hall below that they would open. I said, "Very well, do so; I will go down." Before I left the first time there were ladies there with coffee, &c., for the men. We had got dinner for them at Manassas, at perhaps one or two o'clock.

Question. Did it not occur to you that it would be proper for you to go to see the surgeon general at his residence?

Answer. This is just the impression I had about the matter: When I found no ambulances there—supposing, of course, that they had got my telegraphic despatches—I thought that, as it was so late, they would not be removed to the hospitals that night. We talked with one another about it there. There were some gentlemen there, and we asked whether the cars would run on down to the depot. The conductor told me they would not. By that time the citizens had got there, and I started down to report to the surgeon general. At the hotel I told Doctor Stidger to go out to the train and superintend the whole matter there. When I did not find the surgeon general at his office, or any one there to attend to this matter—believing that they knew from my despatches that we were coming—I supposed it was the intention to let the men remain there all night. We all concluded so out there when I got back there. It was then that Doctor Stidger told me that I had better go to bed and get some sleep, and he would stay there and take charge of them. I never yet have neglected men placed in my care. I can get the testimony of all the surgeons in my division to that fact.

By Mr. Gooch:

Question. Have you made any publication in the newspapers in regard to your case?

Answer. I have authorized one to be made—but one.

Question. Have you a copy of that statement with you?

Answer. Yes, sir; here it is, [handing it to Mr. Gooch.]

Mr. Gooch proceeded to read it as follows:

"THE CASE OF DR. HAYS AND THE SICK AND WOUNDED SOLDIERS.—Doctor Hays makes the following statement in relation to the charges against him of neglecting the sick and wounded soldiers under his care:

"On Tuesday, the 10th instant, I rode to Luray, Virginia, from Front Royal, a distance of twenty-five miles, reaching Luray about 2 o'clock in the afternoon. The wounded from the battle at Port Republic were then being brought in, and I immediately entered upon the most arduous labors of attending to the necessities of the wounded. Through that afternoon, and the night following, my labors were almost incessant. My labors of Wednesday were equally fatiguing with those of Tuesday night, having the entire duty of establishing a hospital thrown upon me. In the midst of this care and anxiety I received orders to have all the wounded under my care, that could be transported, ready, with two days' rations each, at 9 o'clock the following morning, to be transported to Front Royal. This order was received by me about 9 o'clock on Wednesday night, and the time allotted me in which to make these preparations allowed me but little rest or sleep.

"After preparing the train, rations, and what few hospital stores could be obtained, the labor of loading these wounded men into the wagons can be better imagined than described. The train was not ready to start until noon on Thursday, and that day we drove over the most wretched roads a distance of fourteen miles. We stopped for the night in a clover field, where rations were cooked and distributed. We reached Front Royal on Friday, about noon, with 325 sick and wounded soldiers. Here they were unloaded from the wagons. Hospitals were prepared, rations cooked, and the wounds of all dressed."

Question. You have said that you did not stop with your wounded men that

Thursday night, but you rode on some five or six miles towards Front Royal, in advance of them, and slept in a house there that night?

Answer. Yes, sir. My medical director told me to ride on and report in Front Royal, and get things ready there as soon as I could.

Question. You did not go into Front Royal that night?

Answer. No, sir; but I got in there the next morning before the wagons got in.

Question. Why did you not go in that night?

Answer. That was my intention, and I started on for that purpose, but some persons told me that day, as they were bringing prisoners from Luray, they were fired on by some parties.

Question. And that was the reason you stopped in that house over night?

Answer. Yes, sir; and also because, as we came up towards the house about dark, we saw several people standing on the porch of the house—a number of men whom I supposed might be confederate soldiers. They came out and went down by the side of the house. It startled us somewhat, and I said to the other doctor who was with me that we would ride up and see. He rode down to see where they came out at, but we could not see them. We went to the house, and the man there told us that they were some of our men.

Question. Did you stay at that house that night?

Answer. Yes, sir.

Question. Did you consider it safe to remain over night in a house from which you had seen leave what you supposed might be confederate soldiers, then to ride on and take your chances?

Answer. I told them at the house that some of our men were back a piece and would be coming on. I told them this to produce an effect on them, should the men I saw be confederate soldiers, who might otherwise come back that night. They were in citizen's clothes, and I suppose may have been farmers about there. But I was frightened and uneasy about it all that night, and went into town the next morning as early as I could.

Question. What time did you get into Front Royal?

Answer. I started pretty early, and suppose that I got in there about eight o'clock in the morning.

Question. What time did you start?

Answer. We rode very slowly; my horse had pretty nearly given out.

Question. Well, what time did you start?

Answer. Between six and seven o'clock.

Question. How long did you get into the town ahead of your soldiers?

Answer. I cannot tell you the time exactly, but I will tell you what I did; I went to the provost marshal's office and was told that he was out. I then inquired for General Ricketts's headquarters, and was directed to them. But I was directed wrongly the first time and rode to the wrong place. I was then directed correctly, and rode out to General Rricketts's headquarters, about a mile out of town, and reported to him that I had some sick and wounded soldiers there.

Question. Can you not tell us the time the soldiers got in without going over all that?

Answer. I suppose the first wagons got in about 11 o'clock.

Question. How long after you had got in there?

Answer. Some two or three hours after I got in. I had time enough to make all the arrangements I could make.

By Mr. Odell:

Question. What were your orders?

Answer. To leave the men at Front Royal and then to return to my regiment as soon as possible.

Question. By whose authority did you bring the men on here?

Answer. Nothing more than this: Dr Cox telegraphed to the surgeon general and got the despatch which has been read here. He then wrote me a note to act upon that despatch in his place, as he was required at headquarters.

Mr. Gooch resumed the reading of the published statement of Dr. Hays, as follows:

"My orders were to report to the senior medical officer at Front Royal, leave the sick and wounded at the hospitals there, and rejoin my regiment as soon as possible. I reported to Brigade Surgeon Cox, and he declined receiving the sick and wounded, having received orders from General Ricketts requiring his services at the headquarters of his brigade. After reporting to Surgeon Cox, perhaps my duty required me to return to my command—humanity demanded that I should remain and care for the wounded, and remain I did.

"Immediately on arriving at Front Royal I reported to Surgeon Cox, and he telegraphed to the surgeon general at Washington. I also, on the same day, (Friday,) telegraphed to the surgeon general for orders. On Saturday, about 8 o'clock, Surgeon Cox received a reply from the surgeon general, when I immediately telegraphed to the surgeon general at Washington, stating the hour when the train would leave Front Royal for Washington. We left Front Royal about twenty minutes after eleven a. m. At Manassas we gave the men their dinner; and here I again telegraphed the surgeon general, saying the train would arrive at Washington with the sick and wounded that evening between eight and nine o'clock. At Alexandria we were delayed about one hour waiting for an engine, and did not reach Washington until between nine and ten o'clock Saturday night.

"Here, to my utter astonishment, I found neither ambulance nor wagon, surgeon or attendants in waiting. In fact, not the slightest evidence of preparation for our arrival had been made.

"A stranger in a strange city, I made all the haste possible to find the office of the surgeon general. That I found closed, and was unable to ascertain the locality of his residence. After making every search in my power for some one in authority to take charge of the sick and wounded, I returned to the train."

By Mr. Gooch:

Question. Did you make any effort to find the residence of the surgeon general?

Answer. I inquired of the watchman at the office if he could take a message from me to the house of the surgeon general; he said he did not know where the surgeon general lived, and that there were some despatches there waiting for him then.

Mr. Gooch concluded the reading of the published statement, as follows:

"Here I found the kind people of the neighborhood in attendance, doing all in their power to make the poor fellows under my charge comfortable as possible under the circumstances. Many were then being taken to the churches and houses that had been so generously opened for them. They were made as comfortable as it was in my power that night to make them. My assistant surgeons urged me to get to bed and get some rest, and report as early as possible in the morning. They said (and I knew it) there was no use in my remaining longer, and about four o'clock in the morning I went to bed. Before the surgeon general was at his office in the morning I was there to make my report and receive my orders. Immediately upon making my report and receiving my orders (which to me appeared strange when considering that the surgeon general was telegraphed of their coming—my orders from the surgeon general were to find and report to the medical director, and he would send ambulances,) I returned to my charge and found them exceedingly comfortable and cheerful.

"This morning (Monday) charges were preferred against me by the medical director and surgeon general, (without notifying me of the fact,) alleging gross neglect of duty, and the Secretary of War ordered my name to be struck from the rolls, without allowing me to make either argument or defence. Under these circumstances, with these facts existing, I ask my friends, I ask the public, if I am not being sacrificed in order to shield some one in a position much higher than I from charges of gross negligence? Am I not made the scape-goat of other men's sins? Who are the men in lucrative offices who should have prepared most bountifully for the reception of these sick and wounded soldiers? Ask the sick men, the wounded men themselves, if I neglected them. Ask the assistant surgeons and attendants. They know if I shirked my work or shunned any responsibility; and let them and the world say if the man who watched over these poor fellows, day and night, for almost a week, ought to be disgraced because somebody failed to provide for their comfort here.

"D. S. HAYS,

"*Surgeon* 110*th Regiment Pennsylvania Volunteers.*"

Question. Were there any private houses open for these soldiers when you got back to the train?

Answer. Yes, sir; there was one below the church.

Question. Do you know of any others?

Answer. No, sir; only that one.

WASHINGTON, *June* 21, 1862.

Dr. DAVID S. HAYS recalled and examined.

By Mr. Gooch:

Question. We understand that you desire to make some additions to your statements of yesterday before this committee.

Answer. I wish to state in regard to the treatment of wounded men: When men's wounds have been once properly dressed, they do not require the attendance of a surgeon all the time. Such I have found to be the practice since I have been in the service. The principal surgeon gives this instructions to his assistant surgeons, and also to the attendants. After the wounds have been once dressed, all that is necessary to be done is to keep the wounds wet, moist, apply cold water to them every half hour or hour, until the time comes to dress them again. The great labor is usually the first treatment—in amputating and dressing the wounds the first time. After that the labor required is slight compared with the first dressing.

The night we arrived here from Front Royal, when I left the train, Dr. Stidger, one of my assistant surgeons, told me that he would take charge and see that the men were all comfortable. And there was really no necessity for my remaining there. And more than that, a physician needs sleep and rest as well as other persons.

I can prove by all the surgeons, our medical directors, and officers, with whom I have been connected since I have been in the division, that I have never neglected my duty, never shirked it. And I can prove by the surgeon general of Pennsylvania, who was in our division on the 23d of March, that I worked very hard there, and was commended for it.

I really think, too, that the night I left these men they were more comfortable than they could have been in any hospital in town—at least the majority of them. Dr. Stidger said that he would take charge and see they were carried to the houses and churches. The usual custom among surgeons is for the surgeon in charge to give directions to the others, and if those directions are not executed, the surgeon in charge is not responsible. If I give directions and they are not carried out I have my redress.

By Mr. Odell:

Question. What redress?

Answer. I can bring charges against those who fail to carry out my directions.

Question. What good does that do the wounded men who have been neglected?

Answer. It does not do the wounded men any good, that is true; but I can have those punished who have not followed my directions.

Dr. Fais, the brigade surgeon of General Kimball's brigade, left town this morning. Before he did so, he gave me this letter, which I should like to have read to the committee.

The letter was read, as follows:

"WASHINGTON CITY, D. C., *June* 20, 1862.

"This is to certify that I am personally acquainted and have been an associate with Dr. D. S. Hays, of the 110th Pennsylvania regiment United States volunteers, under command of Generals Kelley, Lander, and Shields, embracing a period of eight months, and that during the above time I have invariably found Surgeon Hays ready and willing to perform all the duties assigned to him. I furthermore declare that during the above acquaintance with Dr. Hays he has at all times manifested a laudable ambition to excel in promptness and compliance with all orders from his superiors.

"On Tuesday, June 10, in company with Surgeon Hoop, of the 84th Pennsylvania regiment, and Surgeon Hays, I was ordered to attend the wounded brought from the battle-field of Port Republic, and I am happy to state that Dr. Hays, among other surgeons, did not leave the hospital until the wounded were cared for; that he labored incessantly the greater part of the night; and that on the following morning he was at his post awaiting orders. Prior to his leaving Luray for this city he remarked to me that 'he was worn out; that he preferred I would accompany the sick; but that he was willing to undergo any fatigue or any privation that would benefit our men.' With such feelings he gathered up his wounded and took up his march to Front Royal.

"That Dr. Hays has discharged his duties faithfully and cheerfully, in camp and on detailed duty, is a fact so apparent and plain to the whole medical corps of Shields's division, that it would be absurd to intimate that he has been or that he could be guilty of dereliction.

* * * * * * * * *

"JAS. H. FAIS,

"*Brig. Surg. 1st Brig. com'd by Gen. N. Kimball, Shields's Division.*"

The witness: Here is another letter, from the surgeon general of the State of Pennsylvania, which I would like to have read.

The letter was read, as follows:

"WILLARDS' HOTEL, *June* 21, 1862.

"SIR: Having since last November frequent opportunities of judging of your professional skill and actions as a medical officer of Pennsylvania volunteers, I cheerfully testify to my high appreciation of the manner in which your duties have been performed. After the battle at Winchester, March 23, 1862, I personally witnessed your untiring devotion to your duties in the Union Hotel hospital, and on my return to Pennsylvania I repeatedly spoke of them in terms of praise.

"The charge recently made against you of "gross neglect of your wounded and inhumanity" has surprised me and all who know your energetic habits, and,

I trust may be entirely disproved before a court of inquiry, as, I doubt not, they will.

"Very respectfully, your obedient servant,

"HENRY H. SMITH,
"*Surgeon General of Pennsylvania.*

"Surgeon D. S. HAYS,
"*110th Regiment Pennsylvania Volunteers.*"

The witness: I can prove by the surgeons in General Shields's division now, and by the wounded men themselves, how I labored for them, and, positively, I never had the slightest idea that I neglected my duty during that journey until the subject was mentioned to me by the surgeon general.

By Mr. Gooch:

Question. How many attendants had you for these men?

Answer. I had seven attendants for the forty-four that were in my own hospital.

Question. How many had the others?

Answer. That I do not know; I had no charge of the other hospitals. There was a surgeon appointed for each hospital. After the train was loaded I superintended the whole thing.

Question. Did you have especial charge of your own forty-four men, and each of the others have charge of the men from his hospital?

Answer. I had charge of my own men at Luray. All our orders read alike.

Question. No matter about the orders. Did you have special charge of the forty-four men from your own hospital?

Answer. Yes, sir; and I presume I had the oversight of all the others.

Question. But they were not your special charge?

Answer. I presume I had the oversight merely from the fact that I ranked them.

Question. Did you continue to take charge of your own men from your hospital, and each of the other surgeons of the men from his hospital?

Answer. I paid attention to the men of my own hospital on the train.

Question. You acted as their surgeon?

Answer. Yes, sir.

Question. The other surgeons did not interfere with them at all?

Answer. They attended to mine as to their own. But I kept my own attendants and nurses with my own wounded.

Question. Did you know the men were to be removed from the cars into the houses before you left them that night?

Answer. Yes, sir. When we first got there we stayed around there and waited to see if we could get any information. A short time after I got off the car a gentleman came up and said that there was a church there for them.

Question. You knew they were to be removed?

Answer. Yes, sir.

Question. When you went back there how many of your assistant surgeons did you see there?

Answer. I saw only Dr. Stidger.

Question. Did he tell you where the others were?

Answer. No, sir.

Question. Did you know that they had gone to bed?

Answer. I did not know it at that time. I was informed yesterday, for the first time, by Dr. Burrows, that he himself and Dr. Redlick, of the 84th Pennsylvania, went to bed. I am not certain whether he said the other one had gone to bed or not.

Question. What do you say about these assistant surgeons going to bed and leaving their wounded?

Answer. I say that they disobeyed my orders.

Question. Did you give them orders to remain there?

Answer. Yes, sir; before I left the first time I gave them orders to remain there till I returned.

Question. Did you give those orders to each of those assistant surgeons?

Answer. They were all standing together when I gave the orders.

Question. You gave the orders to all of them?

Answer. Yes, sir.

Question. And each man knew what your orders were?

Answer. Yes, sir.

Question. And those surgeons who went to bed disobeyed your orders?

Answer. Yes, sir.

Question. Did you not consider it necessary that there should be surgeons in attendance when those 300 or 400 wounded and sick men were being removed from the cars to the churches and houses?

Answer. Yes, sir; and I supposed they were.

Question. When you went back did you go around and see the men?

Answer. I went to some of the cars.

Question. You did not go through all the cars?

Answer. No, sir; I went through some of them.

Question. You saw but Dr. Stidger, and you inquired for none of the other assistant surgeons?

Answer. The first time I came I inquired where the three assistant surgeons were.

Question. What were you told?

Answer. Dr. Stidger told me that he had not seen them yet. I think he said they were then probably at the houses and churches. I know that was my impression, and that they were supervising the carrying in of the wounded.

Question. You did not look around to see that they were there?

Answer. No, sir; because Dr. Stidger said he would take charge and see that the men were properly cared for. It has been supposed that those men who died were my men. That is not so. A great portion of my men were only slightly wounded. Where men are badly wounded, the dressing requires a great deal of time and a number of attendants; but after that is once done, nothing is required but for the attendants to keep the wounds moist. The greater part of my men were but slightly wounded, and a great many of them walked from the hospitals to the cars and sat up.

Question. Still there were men who were so badly wounded or so sick that they died on the road and here?

Answer. No, sir; they were not my cases; I knew nothing about them.

By Mr. Odell:

Question. Did they not become your cases when you took charge of them?

Answer. They were not reported to me. The person who attached those cars to the train should have reported to me. I knew nothing about it until it was reported to me that two men had died in the cars. There was one who died the next morning of hospital gangrene. He was shot in the leg.

Question. Would it not have been well for that man to have had surgical attendance the night before?

Answer. Yes, sir; and I supposed he had. But surgeons will testify that when gangrene once attacks a limb it is usually fatal. But my principal duties were to superintend the arrangements, and my assistants were to attend to the wounded; and the men themselves have told me that they never were better treated than they were on that trip. A number of them met me on the street yesterday, and stopped me, and told me that that night their accommodations were good, and that they got better suppers that night than they had had before since they had been in the service. I had had almost nothing to eat since early in the morning of that day. The men had their dinners at Manassas about two o'clock that day. Wherever I have been the post surgeons would give directions to the surgeons of the hospitals; the post surgeon would supervise, and the others would carry out his directions. That I considered to be my duty in this case.

WASHINGTON, *June* 21, 1862.

Major JOHN C. JOHNSON sworn and examined.

By Mr. Gooch:

Question. What is your rank and position in the army?

Answer. I am major of the 110th regiment of Pennsylvania volunteers.

Question. Do you know Dr. D. S. Hays?

Answer. Yes, sir; very well.

Question. Did you come to this city with him when he brought some wounded men from Front Royal?

Answer. No, sir.

Question. Then you know nothing about that matter?

Answer. No, sir. I only knew him while acting surgeon of our regiment. I always found him a good and attentive surgeon—faithfully looking after the wants of the men. He was considered one of the best surgeons in all the Pennsylvania regiments. He was never absent from his post; he was always there rendering all the assistance he could. After the battle of Winchester, the 23d of last March, he was detailed from his command, and placed in charge of the Union Hotel hospital.

Question. Is that his general reputation in the regiment?

Answer. As a good surgeon.

Question. That is his general reputation?

Answer. Yes, sir.

WASHINGTON, *June* 21, 1862.

Lieutenant HENRY C. SPILMAN sworn and examined.

By Mr. Gooch:

Question. What is your rank and position in the army?

Answer. I am a lieutenant and adjutant of the 110th Pennsylvania volunteers.

Question. Do you know Surgeon D. S. Hays?

Answer. Yes, sir.

Question. Do you know his reputation in the regiment as a surgeon?

Answer. I do.

Question. Will you please state what it is?

Answer. He has been connected with us for several months past. I have always considered him a first rate surgeon?

Question. Is that his general reputation in the regiment?

Answer. Yes, sir.

Question. How long has he been with you?

Answer. He has been with us some seven months.

Question. Did you come to this city with him when he brought some wounded men here from front Royal?

Answer. No, sir.

WASHINGTON, *June* 21, 1862.

Captain S. L. HEWITT sworn and examined.

By Mr. Gooch:

Question. What is your rank and position in the army?

Answer. I am captain of company D, 110th regiment of Pennsylvania volunteers.

Question. Do you know Surgeon D. S. Hays?

Answer. Yes, sir; I do. I have known him for a long time; I knew him before he entered the army.

Question. What is his reputation and character in your regiment as a surgeon?

Answer. It is very good—excellent.

Question. You did not come to Washington with him when he came here in charge of the sick and wounded from Front Royal?

Answer. No, sir. In regard to his reputation, I have always thought he had a reputation beyond that of many other surgeons. After the battle of Winchester he was the head of the hospitals there. He not only had his own regiment to attend to, but a half a dozen others to see to at the same time. Among the men of our regiment his reputation is very good; and we all are very sorry, and regret, exceedingly, the misfortune that has happened to him.

By Mr. Covode:

Question. Do you know why he was transferred from his regiment to the hospital in Winchester?

Answer. I do not know. I thought it was because he was a more thorough-going surgeon than the others.

Question. Have you not often heard it remarked that he was one of the best surgeons in your regiments, and that it was for that reason that he was placed at the head of the hospital?

Answer. I do not remember hearing that remark exactly. I thought so myself, I know. The men of our regiment, the 110th, thought he was more competent than other surgeons. Of course, they had more dependence upon and more confidence in him than in any other surgeons.

WASHINGTON, *June* 21, 1862.

Colonel E. S. SANFORD sworn and examined.

By Mr. Gooch:

Question. Will you state your position here in connexion with the telegraph?

Answer. I am military supervisor of army intelligence.

Question. Do all telegraphic communications sent from officers in the field, and from the army generally, come to you?

Answer. They come to the War Department office; they are under my supervision.

Question. Do you recollect receiving, a week ago to-day, a telegraphic despatch from Surgeon D. S. Hays?

Answer. Yes, sir.

Question. How many did you receive?

Answer. I think there were two.

Question. Can you state the time when you received them?

Answer. One was received in the morning. I cannot say at what hour it was received, because that message does not happen to have been "timed," as it is termed; that is, it did not have the time of its reception marked upon it. But, judging from its position in the message book, it was, undoubtedly, early in the morning.

Question. Do you recollect the purport of that despatch?

Answer. In general terms, it stated that he would leave Front Royal at 11 o'clock.

Question. With a train of sick and wounded soldiers for this city?

Answer. Yes, sir.

Question. Did he state at what time he would probably arrive here?

Answer. Not in that message.

Question. At what time was the second despatch received?

Answer. At 4.14 p. m.

Question. What was the purport of that despatch?

Answer. It was dated at Manassas, and received here at 4.14 p. m. It stated that they had arrived at that place, and that the train would probably arrive at Washington between 8 and 9 o'clock that evening.

Question. To whom were those messages directed?

Answer. To Surgeon General Hammond.

Question. What was done with them?

Answer. They are supposed to have been treated as all other messages are, sent out immediately.

Question. Sent immediately to the surgeon general's office?

Answer. Yes, sir; it is supposed so. It is perhaps proper that I should explain more fully than I have done my position there. Formerly I had nothing to do with the practical part of telegraphing, that is, my position did not require that I should have anything to do with the practical operation of the telegraph, simply to have a supervision of all messages and intelligence. But since Colonel Slager, the superintendent of military telegraphs, has been sick, I have filled his place. For that reason I have given no instructions in regard to the practical part of the business at all, nor did I look over it very closely, but left it with the assistant superintendent, Mr. Eckert. But since this affair, and seeing some comments in the newspapers about telegraphic despatches not being delivered, I asked if these messages had been received. They turned to their books and said they had been received. I asked what was done with them, and they said they were sent off. I asked if there was any difficulty about finding the place, and if any answer came back, and they said no, from which I inferred that they were promptly delivered.

Question. In the usual course of things, how long after these despatches reached the War Department would they reach the surgeon general's office?

Answer. Not over from ten minutes to half an hour.

Question. Have you any knowledge as to the time when they did reach there?

Answer. No positive knowledge.

Question. What is the best information you have upon that point?

Answer. They have not been able to find yet or fix positively upon the orderly who delivered them. They are tracing that matter out this morning, and I presume they will be able to ascertain soon. There are changes occasionally made in the orderlies. Instead of having a regular set of orderlies, they are taken from a regiment, and do not remain permanently, but when the regiment leaves they go with it, and they have to get a new set of orderlies.

Question. These messages have been received at the surgeon general's office some time, have they not?

Answer. We have no knowledge of that; we have received no information about that.

Question. You only know the time at which they reached your office, and that in the usual course of business in the office they would have been received at the surgeon general's office in from ten to thirty minutes after they were received at your office?

Answer. Yes, sir.

Question. Would or would not the surgeon general have known, upon reading the first despatch from Front Royal, if it was delivered to him, that that train would probably reach this city that evening?

Answer. I cannot say whether he would have known it. I should have known it, and so would anybody familiar with railroad matters. I should have presumed that from the distance.

WASHINGTON, *June* 20, 1862.

Dr. S. S. BURROWS sworn and examined.

By Mr. Gooch:

Question. What is your position in the army?

Answer. I am assistant surgeon of the 29th Ohio volunteers.

Question. Did you come from Front Royal, Virginia, last week with Dr. Hays and his train of sick and wounded soldiers?

Answer. Yes, sir.

Question. At what time did you reach the city of Washington?

Answer. It would be a matter of a little uncertainty for me to state just the time. I judge it was between 9 and 10 o'clock at night.

Question. What happened after you got here; what was done?

Answer. We were left on Maryland avenue, on the Island. The cars were switched off there. I saw Dr. Hays and the other surgeons. There were five of us. We looked about and inquired to find who was to take charge of the wounded there. We expected to find some one there to whom to report. After making inquiries, and finding out that the cars were to be left there over night, and after waiting some considerable time, Dr. Hays and Dr. Stidger went off together to see if they could find the officials. I remained there with Dr. McCune and Dr. Redlick. We went through the cars and saw the sick and wounded. The citizens came in about that time, and commenced feeding them. They had some food; not enough for them, however. But the citizens came in, and they were furnished with a plenty to eat and drink. Some cases were taken to private houses. After the shower, I do not know exactly at what time that was—after we had seen to the soldiers all around, and had seen that they had plenty to eat and drink—Dr. McCune, Dr. Redlick, and myself went into a house near by and stopped there over night. I saw nothing more of Dr. Hays after he left and went off to search for some one to report to.

Question. When did you next see him?

Answer. It was the next morning, a couple of hours, or three hours, after I was there. I was there again early in the morning.

Question. How many of the men stayed in the cars that night?

Answer. I could not state how many.

Question. What proportion of them?

Answer. The most of them, unless they were taken out after I left. I saw some of them removed.

Question. How many did you see removed from the cars that night?

Answer. I do not know of but two, really. There was a captain who was taken to A. Lamon's house, and another person whose name I do not know.

Question. Did any surgeon see him after he was taken to the house?

Answer. The next morning I went to all the houses.

Question. I mean, did any of the surgeons see him that night?

Answer. I do not know that they did.

Question. Did you assist in the removal of either of those two men?

Answer. No, sir.

Question. You had nothing to do with the removal of any of the wounded men from the cars?

Answer. Nothing more than I asked this man Lamon if the captain could stay with him, and he said he could; and as the captain had a special attendant with him, I instructed him to take him there.

Question. Did the other surgeons go with you into the house where you stopped over night?

Answer. Yes, sir; two of them.

Question. Where did Dr. Stidger go?

Answer. Dr. Stidger, I supposed, went with Dr. Hays.

Question. You left all the sick and wounded men in the cars except the two you have mentioned?

Answer. If there were any others who went out they went out without my knowledge.

Question. You left in a short time after the train arrived?

Answer. No, sir; I should judge it was between 11 and 12 o'clock. We went around to the different cars; that is, we did not all go into the same cars; some went in one car, and some in another.

Question. After you had gone through the cars then you left them?

Answer. Yes, sir.

Question. Did you know at that time that any preparations were being made to take these sick and wounded men into the churches?

Answer. No, sir; not at that time.

Question. No arrangements had been made for that?

Answer. Not when I left.

Question. What time in the morning did you get back to the train?

Answer. I do not know just what time it was; soon after sunrise—before breakfast.

Question. Give us the hour as near as you can?

Answer. I should judge it was 6 o'clock.

Question. Did the other surgeons go back with you?

Answer. No, sir.

Question. At what time did they get back?

Answer. A short time after; I do not know exactly when.

Question. Then the fact was that neither of you three surgeons saw anything of these men from the time you left them at 11 o'clock until 6 or 7 o'clock the next morning?

Answer. Not so far as I know.

Question. Do you think that is the proper way to treat wounded and sick men?

Answer. We were expecting Dr. Hays back, and that they were to be reported to the authorities here.

Question. Did you think you were doing your duty as a surgeon, to leave these men in the cars in that way, not knowing whether Dr. Hays would find anybody, or would come back?

Answer. I thought I had done all I could do for them; all that I thought I was able to do under the circumstances.

By Mr. Odell:

Question. Would not your services have been required if Dr. Hays had succeeded in getting orders to have the men removed? You say he left for that purpose.

Answer. I did not know whether they were or were not to be removed that night. I supposed that the officials here knew about it. I did not know what arrangements were to be made.

WASHINGTON, *June* 21, 1862.

Surgeon General WILLIAM A. HAMMOND sworn and examined.

By Mr. Gooch:

Question. What is your position?

Answer. I am surgeon general of the army of the United States.

Question. Will you state to the committee whether or not any telegraphic despatches were received from Surgeon D. S. Hays last Saturday; and if so, what was their character, and at what time were they received by you, or at your office?

Answer. Perhaps I better state all the despatches I received, in order to give the committee a proper understanding of the whole matter.

Question. You will please do so.

Answer. On Friday afternoon or Saturday morning—I think it was Saturday, though it might have been Friday—I received a despatch from Brigade Surgeon Cox, at Front Royal, stating that he had received information that a number of sick and wounded of General Shields's division would reach Front Royal in a short time; that he had no hospitals or supplies for them, and asking what he should do with them. I telegraphed to him to send them to Washington, and that he would be ordered to report himself under arrest here for not having supplies and hospitals; and I immediately applied to the adjutant general to issue that order. He has not yet reported himself, and this morning I applied again to have a despatch sent to him to know why he had not reported himself under that order.

I received a telegram from Surgeon Cox, I think it was, that the men would be sent to Washington Saturday morning, and that I should be notified by telegraph of the time they would arrive here. I heard nothing more about them until Sunday morning. Some fifteen minutes after I got there a despatch was handed to me. I have every reason to believe that Dr. Hays has stated correctly as to the time he sent that despatch. There was a storm that evening, and I suppose that delayed it. At least I did not get it until the next morning. A few minutes after I received it Dr. Hays reported himself, and came into my office. He stated that he had arrived the night before, and had tried to find me and the medical director, and had not succeeded. He had to report that the men were now at the depot, and asked what he should do with them. I ordered him to go to the medical director and get ambulances, and have them removed. They were sent in a short time, for the horses are generally kept harnessed, and ready to move at a moment's notice. Dr. Hays represented his action to me in such a light, his energy, &c., that I was so well satisfied, that I complimented him for his activity in the matter. I know that he excused himself for not having reported to me the evening before, by saying that he could not find me; but I did not think of that at the time. When we went to Dr. Letterman's office he stated the matter to him. On Sunday afternoon I received a letter from Dr. Letterman to the effect that Surgeon Hays had neglected his duty; had not reported the evening before, as he should have done, but had gone to the hotel, and gone to bed, leaving the men there, and recommended that some action be taken in regard to the matter, as that was the second time such a thing had occurred. I took Dr. Letterman's letter, indorsed upon it a summary of its contents, to the Secretary of War, and requested that he would inflict severe punishment upon Dr. Hays, and have this course of conduct stopped.

Dr. Hays soon after came in and I handed him the letter to read. He read it and begged me not to send it. Said I, "You don't deny anything that is stated there?" Said he, "No; I admit that I went to Willard's, but I came to this office and tried to find you and I could not do it." Said I, "You don't expect me to sleep in my office all night. It is utterly useless for you to tell me that you could not find me in the city of Washington. They know at Willard's where I live, and also where Dr. Letterman lives." There are also watchmen in my office who know where I live, for I have frequently received despatches from the office after office hours. I told Dr. Hays that I should have to send that letter over to the Secretary. He begged that I would not, but did not deny anything that was in it, only asserted that he had tried to find me the evening before and could not. He followed my messenger out and I know nothing more of what happened, except from hearsay. I have seen the order to-day, officially published, directing that Dr. Hays be dropped from the army list.

Question. Did you read to him the letter you had received from Dr. Letterman and your comments upon it?

Answer. I gave it to him to read.

Question. Did you receive more than one despatch from Surgeon Hays while he was in charge of that train?

Answer. I think I received altogether three despatches in regard to those men. I received one from Dr. Cox informing me that the men were coming to Front Royal, one from Dr. Cox or Dr. Hays, I do not know which, informing me that the men had arrived at Front Royal and would leave for Washington, of which I would be advised. After that I received nothing until Sunday morning.

Question. Did you not receive a despatch stating, in substance, that they would leave Front Royal for this city at 11 o'clock on Saturday morning?

Answer. No, sir; I have not seen any such despatch.

Question. Where was the despatch dated that you received on Sunday morning?

Answer. It was dated at Front Royal, I think. I received none on Saturday stating when they would leave. The one I received on Sunday morning stated either that they would leave there at a certain time or that they would reach Washington at a certain time?

Question. Was that despatch dated at Front Royal or Manassas?

Answer. It was dated at Front Royal, I think. It may have been dated at Manassas. The despatch is at my office. I know this, that if that despatch had been received in time, the ambulances would have been there to receive the men. The despatch either stated when they would leave (when by a simple calculation I could have told at what time they would have been likely to arrive) or it stated when they would arrive. If the despatch had been received in time all would have been right. The fault I found with Dr. Hays was this: that when he arrived here and found that no preparations had been made to receive his men, he was bound to suppose either that his despatch had not been received, or that something had occurred to prevent his men being attended to, and it was his duty to find out what it was.

Question. We have testimony here that there were two despatches from Dr. Hays received at the War Department on Saturday, one early in the morning and the other in the evening. The first one was dated at Front Royal and stated that the train would leave there at 11 o'clock, for Washington, with these men. The other was dated at Manassas, and stated that the train would arrive at Washington between 8 and 9 o'clock that evening. The first one was received in the early part of the day, the time not fixed. The other was received between 4 and half past 4 o'clock in the afternoon. Have you received both of those despatches?

Answer. No, sir; I think not. If they had both been received I think I should certainly have seen them, and have recollected them. No, sir; I am certain I did not receive the first one; I never saw it. The only despatch I ever saw relating to the train arriving at all at any definite period, was the one I saw on Sunday morning. When that reached Washington I do not know. It did not reach my office, however, certainly, before I left there, which was 4 o'clock in the evening.

Question. Did you return to your office again after leaving it Saturday evening at 4 o'clock?

Answer. No, sir, I did not. I never return to my office after that time unless there is some pressing business to attend to there, because I am on a board of examination from 5 until 11 o'clock. I stayed at my office until 4 o'clock on Saturday; that is my rule. I take my dinner at 4 o'clock, and at 5 o'clock I go to this board of examination.

Question. What instructions are left with the persons who remain at the office after you leave?

Answer. I have never given him any definite instructions. He has been acting under the instructions that have always prevailed there I presume. I know that despatches have come to my house after I left.

Question. Does the watchman, who remains there, know where you live?

Answer. I presume he does. I have never asked him the question. The messengers of the office know where I live, because I have sent things up to my house by them.

Question. Does the man who was there last Saturday night know where you live?

Answer. I do not know whether he does or does not. But the fact that messages which are taken to my office after I leave come to my house would lead me to suppose that he does know, because he must tell the man who brings the messages where I live.

Question. Then you received no communication whatever stating when that train would leave Front Royal for Washington?

Answer. I saw no communication whatever that that train left Front Royal for Washington, until I saw the one that was handed to me on Sunday morning.

Question. You saw no communication, and had no knowledge of the fact on Saturday?

Answer. No, sir. The rule of the office is invariable, that whenever a despatch comes announcing the coming of troops that are sick or wounded it is sent over to the medical director at once, and he makes the necessary preparations. Now, last night I received a despatch from Dr. Bryant, who was the one who had been derelict before—the case referred to as the first case—Dr. Hays being the second. Yesterday afternoon he telegraphed to me that he was coming, and that he would let me know when the sick would arrive. He telegraphed again as to when they would arrive, and I got the despatch at 2 o'clock in the morning. In the first despatch he telegraphed me that they would leave Front Royal, and asked that arrangements be made to have them properly cared for at Manassas and Alexandria, which was done, and those men were properly taken care of. Even if the despatches had not been received at all, or even if they had been received and I had been grossly negligent; if I had received the despatches and had known perfectly well what had been done, and had not care enough to send the ambulances down there for them—all that would not excuse Dr. Hays. It was his business to have arrangements made, if he found none there.

Question. You deem that Dr. Hays was negligent in not finding you or some person to take charge of those men that night?

Answer. Yes, sir; I do.

Question. That is, you think he should have done that?

Answer. Yes, sir; that is the point precisely.

Question. He says he went to the war office, found out where your office was; then went to your office and found that you were not there, and that there was no one there to give him information. His own statement is that he then concluded that it was not proposed that the men should be removed to the hospitals that night. He then returned to the train, and after remaining there some time he went back to the hotel and went to bed.

Answer. I do not know whether that is so or not. He did not tell me that he even asked for me at the office. He never intimated the slightest thing of the kind to me. I think it was told to me by some one who came there as his counsel. But I did not want then to ascertain any more in regard to it, as I knew this thing would probably come up here.

Question. Did he give you a statement of what he did do?

Answer. No, sir; except that he had tried to find me and Dr. Letterman and could not.

Question. He did not give you any particulars of what he had done?

Answer. No, sir; only generalities; and I told him it was utterly useless for him to tell me that he could not find either me or Dr. Letterman, for they knew at Willard's where we lived. Dr. Letterman's office is at General Wadsworth's headquarters; he is on his staff, and could have been found at any time by applying there.

Question. This might be true, might it not: You were known to him as the proper officer to whom to report; you were the surgeon general; you were his superior, and the officer to whom he would most naturally report.

Answer. Yes, sir.

Question. And, therefore, he hunted for you. In trying to find you he went naturally, in the first place, to the War Department, and was told that your office was not there, and was directed to where it was. He went from the War Department to your office, and there he saw a watchman, as he says, and inquired for you, and was told you were not in. He asked the watchman whether he could take a message to you from him, and the watchman told him he did not know where you lived, and that there were despatches then in the office waiting for you.

Answer. I do not know about that; I have not inquired of the watchman. The counsel of Dr. Hays, who came to see me, told me something about that, but I did not care to ask the watchman anything about it, as I understood the matter was to be investigated here.

By Mr. Covode:

Question. Would not the prompt delivery of Dr. Hays's despatch to you have prevented all this difficulty?

Answer. Yes, sir; it would. But the fact of its not being delivered does not relieve Dr. Hays.

Question. Suppose that Dr. Hays, after making these inquiries and failing to find you, concluded that it was the intention not to have the men removed until morning; what was then his duty as a surgeon?

Answer. I can hardly conceive that any surgeon could entertain the idea that the men would be left there.

Question. I am assuming that he did conclude that you would take no steps in the matter that night?

Answer. Then his duty as a surgeon and an officer was to remain with those men until he could find what was to be done with them. He was the commanding officer of those men, and it was his duty to stay with them. He could not delegate that authority to any other person.

Question. What was the duty of the assistant surgeons with him?

Answer. To remain there if he required them to do so. He was the responsible man. He could dispense with their services if he chose, but they could not dispense with his. He could say to them, "You can go home; I will stay here."

Question. How many surgeons in reality ought to have attended upon that train of between 300 and 400 sick and wounded men that night?

Answer. There ought to have been at least a half a dozen surgeons. I would say that those men were not properly cared for at Front Royal, owing to a point between General Ricketts and his brigade surgeon. The facts of the case, as they are respresented to me in official circles, are as follows: I recollect now that the first despatch I received from Dr. Hays stated that the men had arrived at Front Royal, and that General Ricketts refused to allow his brigade surgeon to attend to them; that there were stores there that he could not get. This brigade surgeon was Dr. Cox. Dr. Cox was the one who was not allowed to attend to these men, by order of General Ricketts, on the ground that they belonged to General Shields's division, and did not belong to his brigade, and his medical stores should not be used for them. That is stated officially from Dr. Hays. And I also have a letter from the assistant adjutant general to General Ricketts's brigade, to Dr. Cox, inquiring by what authority he was attending to the sick and wounded of General Shields's division. Those papers I laid before the Secretary of War, with the request that he would have the conduct of General Ricketts investigated, because I considered it an outrage.

By Mr. Odell:

Question. Is that General Ricketts the one who was in command of a battery at the battle of Bull Run, and who was wounded and taken prisoner there?

Answer. Yes, sir; the same officer; and that accounts, as I afterwards learned, for Dr. Cox not having hospitals and stores provided for these men. He said he had no hospitals and stores for them. It turns out that he had stores, but General Ricketts had ordered him not to use them for that purpose. Dr. Cox has been ordered to report himself here, but he has not yet come. This morning I again telegraphed for him to come here immediately; and if he does not come I shall apply to the Secretary of War to have him dismissed the service. Dr. Hays also told me another thing, which I have no reason at all to doubt: that a number of sick men were put on board of his train (some twenty or more) at Catlett's station, I believe, with whom there was no surgeon, nurses, or anything of the kind, and that two of them died on the road. But these are faults of the commanding officer. It is his duty to send a surgeon with sick or wounded men whether they request it or not.

Question. Do you know anything more about those men than Dr. Hays told you?

Answer. No, sir; they sent no report—nothing whatever about them.

Question. How shall we ascertain about that matter?

Answer. I do not know. The men were too sick, the most of them, to answer any questions. I do not know where they came from. I presume it might, perhaps, be ascertained by following up the railroad conductors. The fact is, the whole organization of that part of the army is more deplorable than that of any other portion of the army.

Question. Is there any reason why that should be so?

Answer. I do not know. I would not like to give my personal opinion in regard to it.

Question. How should that difficulty be remedied?

Answer. I know no other remedy than changing the commanding officer.

Question. To whom do you refer now?

Answer. I refer to General Shields.

By Mr. Covode:

Question. Do you know whether the despatch that was delivered to you on Sunday morning had laid in your office over night, or was it brought over to the office on Sunday morning?

Answer. I do not know. I was informed on the day of Dr. Hays's dismissal, or early in the morning the day after, that I would probably be called before this committee, and I made no inquiries whatever about the matter. I will say this: that Dr. Edwards, one of my assistants, remains in the office every evening until 6 o'clock, and opens all the despatches that come there from the time I leave until he leaves himself. If any despatch had come there before he left he would have opened it.

Question. Do you recollect whether any other despatches were handed you on Sunday morning at the same time this one you refer to was handed to you?

Answer. That was the only one I have any recollection of. If there was any other it was some unimportant one, of no particular consequence.

Question. From the despatches you had received previously, were you led to believe that that train of sick and wounded would come in that night?

Answer. No, sir.

WASHINGTON, *June* 23, 1862.

JOSEPH H. HILTON sworn and examined.

By Mr. Gooch:

Question. What is your position?

Answer. I am a watchman in the surgeon general's and paymaster general's departments.

Question. Where were you between the hours of six and twelve o'clock a week ago last Saturday night?

Answer. I cannot say about six o'clock.

Question. Well, between eight and twelve o'clock?

Answer. I was in the building occupied by the surgeon general's and paymaster general's departments.

Question. Did any person come to the office that night in search of the surgeon general, to your knowledge?

Answer. Not to my knowledge.

Question. Where were you?

Answer. At the office, at the door where I am regularly stationed all night. We receive all the despatches that come there. If there are any for the surgeon general, and he is in, I give them to him. If he is not in, I leave them in his room.

Question. And they remain there all night?

Answer. Yes, sir.

Question. You had no orders to send them to his house?

Answer. No, sir; not until yesterday.

Question. Did any despatches come for him that night?

Answer. There may have been some for him but how many I cannot say.

Question. Are you sure you received any for him that night?

Answer. I will not be sure about that; but they come every night, and I think some came that night.

Question. You have no distinct recollection of receiving any for him that night?

Answer. No, sir.

Question. If any person had come there that night and inquired for the surgeon general would you now recollect it?

Answer. Yes, sir; particularly if he had inquired for the surgeon general and stated what his business was; for I then should have directed him to Dr. Wood, or some other surgeon who could have told him where to find the surgeon general; I did not know where the surgeon general lived until last Thursday.

Question. Do you recollect distinctly whether you told any person that night, who was inquiring if you could send a message to the surgeon general, that you did not know where he lived, and that there were then some messages there waiting for him?

Answer. No, sir; I am satisfied about that.

Question. Was there any time that night that you were absent?

Answer. No, sir; I was in the office all night, and until eight o'clock on Sunday morning.

Question. You know a surgeon by his dress?

Answer. Well, sir, I cannot say that I do.

Question. You would know an officer—a man with straps on his shoulders?

Answer. Yes, sir.

Question. Would you have remembered it if any man with shoulder-straps had come to that door that night?

Answer. Yes, sir; I think I would.

Question. Were there any other persons there to whom any one would make a communication but yourself?

Answer. Nobody but Mr. Kelly, my associate watchman.

Question. Have you ever seen Surgeon Hays at any time to know him?

Answer. I would not know him if he were standing here now.

By Mr. Covode:

Question. At which door are you stationed?

Answer. At the main entrance door of the surgeon general's and paymaster general's offices.

Question. On which floor?

Answer. On the lower floor, at the main entrance. I take all messages that come there.

Question. Was there not a portion of that time that you were absent from the door up stairs, on the surgeon general and paymaster general's floor?

Answer. I never go up stairs without closing the main entrance door and locking it.

Question. How do you get despatches into the surgeon general's room?

Answer. I have the key of his room, which I keep down stairs, hanging on a nail there. When I have a despatch for him I lock the street door, to keep anybody from coming in, and then take down the key of the surgeon general's room, and go up stairs and unlock the door, and go in and lay the despatch upon the table, when there is nobody there to receive it from me.

Question. Why do you lock the street door when you go up stairs if you have another watchman on duty with you?

Answer. Well, sir, that has always been my custom.

Question. Was it you that handed the despatches to the surgeon general the next morning?

Answer. No, sir; I never hand them to him, except at night, when he is there. His messenger hands them to him in the morning. The day watchman relieves me at 6 o'clock in the morning. When despatches come in during the night I distribute them around through the building, placing them in the proper rooms for the surgeon general, the paymaster general, and paymasters who have offices in the building, and in the morning the messenger puts them where they belong.

Question. Do you know of despatches coming to the surgeon general sometimes marked "important," and others not so marked?

Answer. I have never seen one marked "important;" not since I have been in the building.

By Mr. Gooch:

Question. What persons came to the office inquiring for the surgeon general, on the Thursday evening before, when you were on duty there? I understand that you are on duty there on alternate nights?

Answer. Yes, sir. I could not tell what persons were there on Thursday night. A great many persons call every evening and inquire for the surgeon general, and the paymaster general, and different paymasters there. Who came there that evening I could not tell.

Question. I mean between the hours of 8 and 12 o'clock.

Answer. I could not tell. There may have been a dozen called there, and there may have been not more than two or three.

Question. Did any officer call there on Thursday evening and inquire for the surgeon general?

Answer. As far as my recollection serves me, I do not think there was. But I cannot tell.

Question. How certain can you be about that?

Answer. I cannot be certain.

Question. How certain can you be?

Answer. They may have come, and I might have seen them and given them an answer; and they might not have come.

Question. Did any person come there a week ago last Thursday night, between the hours of 8 and 12 o'clock, and inquire for the surgeon general, and you tell them that you did not know where he lived?

Answer. That might have been, for I did not know then where he lived.

Question. Did any person come there and ask you if you could send a message to him, and you told him that you did not know where he lived?

Answer. No, sir. I am positive about that, because nobody ever asked me that.

Question. On that Thursday night did you tell anybody that there were despatches then up stairs for the surgeon general?

Answer. No, sir. No such question was ever put to me by any gentleman, in any shape or form, either that night or any other.

Question. Was there any person there on last Monday evening, between the hours of eight and twelve o'clock, inquiring for the surgeon general, and who asked you whether or not you could send a message or despatch to him?

Answer. No, sir; that has never been asked of me.

Question. Do you know whether there was any message came there that night for the surgeon general?

Answer. Despatches came that night and I distributed them.

Question. Who brought them?

Answer. Orderlies generally bring them; soldiers on horseback.

By Mr. Covode:

Question. Have you any recollection at what time the assistant surgeon general left the office on Saturday evening?

Answer. I could not tell. The doctors are generally coming in and going out all the time continually, and I cannot keep the run of them.

WASHINGTON, *June* 23, 1862.

WILLIAM KELLY sworn and examined.

By Mr. Gooch:

Question. What is your occupation?

Answer. I have been occupying the position of night watchman in the building where the surgeon general's office is for the last fourteen years.

Question. Where were you one week ago last Saturday night, between the hours of eight and twelve o'clock.

Answer. I go on that duty about half past three o'clock in the afternoon, from that to four o'clock, every second day in the year; and I never leave there, summer or winter, until the next morning. I bring my supper with me, or have it brought to me.

Question. Were you on duty that night?

Answer. Yes, sir; that evening and night all through.

Question. Do you know whether anybody came to that building that night, between the hours of eight and twelve o'clock, and inquired for the surgeon general?

Answer. No person, to my knowledge or recollection, on that evening.

Question. Down to as late as twelve o'clock?

Answer. Yes, sir; or through the night, as far as I can recollect or know. I am very glad that it has happened, as I am called before you on this occasion, that I recollect what happened that night.

Question. Why do you particularly recollect about that night?

Answer. Because it was not so long ago, and the gentleman called upon me the next morning.

Question. What gentleman?

Answer. Dr. Hays.

Question. Why did he call upon you?

Answer. Every fourth Sunday I am on duty a part of the day. I went home that morning, got a clean shirt and a bowl of coffee, and came back to the building about eight o'clock. I was sitting at the door, as I usually do in warm weather. My partner had gone a few minutes before. This gentleman, dressed in uniform, came to the door as I was sitting there. I took him to be an officer in the army of some grade. The first thing he said was to ask if the surgeon general had come into his office. That is what made me think that, perhaps, he had been there before. I told him he had not come in. The next thing he said was "I have just arrived in the cars"—I forget whether he said "this morning" or "last night." But what he said was that he had arrived in the cars with between 400 and 500, I think, wounded soldiers in his charge, and he could not remove them from the cars until he saw the surgeon general. I said, "I am sorry I cannot inform you where his residence is, but there is a man up stairs who can give you better information than I can." That was a laborer up stairs. He went up stairs, to the best of my knowledge, and soon came down, as if in a hurry, and went right across the street from where I was sitting. He was but a very few minutes gone when he and the surgeon general returned together. They both seemed to be in a hurry.

Question. Had you ever seen that surgeon, Dr. Hays, before that Sunday morning?

Answer. Not to my knowledge.

Question. Was he there in the night time during the night previous?

Answer. Not at all, to my knowledge or recollection.

Question. Could he have been there without your knowing it?

Answer. I believe not at all.

Question. Do you and your partner keep on the watch there, both of you, all night?

Answer. Yes, sir. And I have had another man there with me all the time for these 14 years.

Question. Then you say you are confident that this Surgeon Hays was not there during that night?

Answer. To the best of my knowledge and recollection he was not there that night.

Question. Was there any other person in charge there that night except you and your partner?

Answer. There is no other man in charge of that building at the present time on those nights but me and my partner. Some time ago we had two substitutes, but they have been withdrawn to the War Department.

By Mr. Covode:

Question. Did you say that you did not know where the surgeon general lived?

Answer. I told this gentleman that I did not know at that time where he lived.

Question. Did you tell him there were despatches there then for the surgeon general?

Answer. I told him nothing of the kind. He did not ask me that question. It runs in my mind that he said something to me about despatches, or a despatch; but I did not take much notice of that.

Question. What is the laborer's name that Dr. Hays went up stairs to see?

Answer. His name is James Palmer.

WASHINGTON, *June* 23, 1862.

Dr. JONATHAN LETTERMAN sworn and examined.

By Mr. Gooch:

Question. What is your position in connexion with the army?

Answer. I am assistant surgeon in the army, and medical director of this district.

Question. Have you any knowledge of the case of Surgeon Hays, who came from Front Royal to this city with a train of sick and wounded men last Saturday night a week ago; if you have, will you state to the committee all that you know about the matter?

Answer. When I went to my office on Sunday morning, as I entered one door Dr. Hays came in the other. He told me that he had a number—I forget now the exact number he stated, but it was a large number—of sick and wounded men on Maryland avenue, in some cars there. He told me that he had got in here between 9 and 10 o'clock the evening before; that there were no ambulances there, and the men had not been taken away. I asked him why he had not come to my office and let me know about it. He said he did not know where it was. I then sent ambulances over there and had the men removed. I had received no telegraphic despatches from him, and knew nothing about the matter before that Sunday morning.

Question. Is that all you know about the matter?

Answer. That is all, except some little outside matters; those are all the material facts that I know in the case. That is the statement Dr. Hays himself gave me Sunday morning, when I asked him why he had not been there before to let me know about it.

Question. Do telegraphic despatches coming from surgeons in charge of trains of sick and wounded come directly to you, or do they come to the surgeon general?

Answer. Sometimes they come to the surgeon general and sometimes to me.

Question. More usually how is it?

Answer. They come more generally to me, I think. I do not know how many exactly the surgeon general gets; but what he gets he sends to me.

Question. At the time you saw Dr. Hays and had this conversation with him, to which you refer, did he not state to you that he went to the office of the surgeon general the night before?

Answer. Yes, sir; he did, and said he could not find him.

Question. Did he give you the particulars?

Answer. No, sir; that is the substance of what he said in regard to the matter.

Question. Did he tell you that he went to the office of the surgeon general and there saw a watchman who told him that he did not know where the surgeon general lived?

Answer. No, sir; I do not think he did.

Question. And that he could not find any way of communicating with the surgeon general that night?

Answer. I think not. My conversation with him was very brief, because as soon as I learned the men were over there I immediately commenced to write orders for the ambulances to go down and remove them.

Question. You addressed a letter to the surgeon general on this subject?

Answer. Yes, sir.

Question. On what information did you base that letter?

Answer. On what Dr. Hays himself told me.

Question. Do you know what Dr. Hays did that night, what care he took of the men, or anything about that?

Answer. No, sir; I know nothing about that.

Question. You had no information upon that point?

Answer. No, sir.

Question. Would he have been derelict in his duty if he had come to this city, had gone to the surgeon general's office, had inquired for the surgeon general, and been told he was not there, and had then inquired where the surgeon general lived, and been told by the watchman there that he did not know; and had then inquired if a message could be sent to the surgeon general, and had been told that he, the watchman, did not know where he lived, and that there were messages there for the surgeon general then; and had then gone back to the train?

Answer. I think he would. I think he should have inquired of the military commander, and had him take such steps as were necessary. It is a military rule to report to the military commander, when you come to a place where a military commander is. That is a rule of the service. I do not know whether Dr. Hays understood it or not.

Question. You think he should have reported that night to the surgeon general, or to the military commander, or to some person who should receive the report?

Answer. Yes, sir.

Question. You think Surgeon Hays was derelict on that point?

Answer. Yes, sir.

Question. And it was on account of that fact that you addressed that letter to the surgeon general?

Answer. Yes, sir.

Question. You know nothing of his course during the night?

Answer. No, sir. The only conversation I had with him was just what I have stated to you.

Question. Suppose he had concluded that it was not possible for him to make his report that night to any person who was authorized to receive it, what was then his duty as a surgeon?

Answer. To remain with his men.

By Mr. Covode:

Question. Did not Dr. Hays come to you and complain that he had got here with these men, and there were no ambulances there, nor anybody to receive them?

Answer. He made no complaint of that kind on Sunday morning. On Monday morning he came to my office and said something of the kind.

Qnestion. Was that before or after you wrote that letter to the surgeon general?

Answer. Afterwards.

Question. What time on Monday morning was that?

Answer. I do not recollect; it was some time in the forepart of the day.

By Mr. Gooch:

Question. Was it before or after ten o'clock in the morning?

Answer. Indeed, I cannot say; we have so much to do there.

By Mr. Covode:

Question. Had Dr. Hays at that time received notice of your letter?

Answer. I think he had.

Question. And he made that complaint in justification of himself?

Answer. Yes, sir.

Question. Do you not know that Surgeon Hays was in communication with the surgeon general before he came here, and that the surgeon general had given him all the directions which he had, which were to bring the sick and wounded to Washington, and to report to him? That the surgeon general was the one that Dr. Hays was in communication with, and the only one?

Answer. I have an indistinct recollection of a despatch sent by the surgeon general up to my office. I have looked for that despatch and cannot find it, and therefore I think it must have been sent somewhere else.

Question. Did you direct the surgeon general to order Dr. Hays at Front Royal to bring the sick and wounded to Washington, or did the surgeon general do that on his own responsibility?

Answer. I never gave any such order.

Question. Then it appears that Dr. Hays, having had all his correspondence with the surgeon general, reported to him?

Answer. Yes, sir; that is very natural. I received no despatches.

Question. Dr. Hays did not come to you until he was sent there by the surgeon general?

Answer. I did not see him until Sunday morning.

By Mr. Gooch:

Question. When did you first learn that these men were coming from Front Royal to Washington?

Answer. I am not certain. I do not think I heard anything of it until Sunday morning.

Question. Are you pretty clear on that point, that you had no intimation that this train of cars with these men were coming here until Sunday morning?

Answer. I had some intimation about the train coming, but I think it was from some other person that the despatch came.

Question. Had you any expectation of the train arriving here that night?

Answer. Indeed, I cannot tell. I went up to the office after 9 o'clock on Saturday night, and there were no despatches at all there then.

Question. Were you expecting the arrival of any train in this city at that time?

Answer. I think not. I very frequently go to the office at that hour of the night.

Question. If you recollect going to the office that night, do you not know whether you were expecting any train here?

Answer. I recollected it, because Dr. Hays came to methe next morning, and told me that he had come the night before; and I wondered why he did not come to my office the night before. My assistants were there until after 11 o'clock.

Question. Do you recollect whether you were expecting any train that night?

Answer. I think I did; but I do not recollect whether it was Dr. Hays's train or not.

Question. Does anybody sleep in your office?

Answer. Yes, sir.

Question. What are your instructions to him?

Answer. That if any person calls for me with business of importance, he shall come and wake me up at any time of the night.

By Mr. Covode:

Question. You always leave a man there who knows where you live?

Answer. Yes, sir.

Question. Would you think you were doing your whole duty to leave a man in charge of your business at your office who did not know where you live?

Answer. No, sir; I should not. As soon as I took the quarters I now occupy, I took my orderly down there and showed him where I lived?

Question. So that he could go over and find you at any hour of the night?

Answer. Yes, sir; and he has done so at different times.

Question. If any other person here in position knew of a train of sick and wounded coming in here, in charge of any surgeon, would it not have been the duty of that person to make provision for receiving them, and look after them in some way.

Answer. I think so.

Question. If you had ordered that train loaded with sick and wounded to be brought to Washington immediately, would you not have felt that it was your duty to look after them, and not be away from your office for 10 or 15 hours?

Answer. Yes, sir; I think it would.

By Mr. Gooch:

Question. Did you have any communication with anybody in relation to the conduct of Surgeon Hays before writing that letter to the surgeon general?

Answer. No, sir.

Question. You did it upon your own motion, and not at the instigation of any body else?

Answer. Yes, sir; upon my own motion.

Question. Had you heard any outside clamor raised in relation to the treatment which these men had received?

Answer. No, sir; I did not know what treatment the men had received.

Question. You had then heard no complaints about it?

Answer. No, sir.

Question. Your letter was based upon what Dr. Hays himself stated to you?

Answer. Yes, sir. The same thing had occurred once before with a brigade surgeon. I did not think it right, and that it should be stopped and go no further.

WASHINGTON, *June* 23, 1862.

Dr. FRANCIS SALTER sworn and examined.

By Mr. Gooch:

Question. What is your rank and position in the service?

Answer. I am a surgeon of volunteers, of the 7th Ohio regiment, and am now in charge of the hospital in Hagerstown.

Question. What was your position prior to that?

Answer. I have been acting brigade surgeon of the 3d brigade, General Shields's division.

Question. Has Dr. Hays been under you?

Answer. Yes, sir.

Question. What do you know in relation to him?

Answer. I am free to say that he has always performed his duties as well as possible; always seemed exceedingly anxious to perform all his duties at all times. I have never known him to be absent from his post at any time; he was always there ready for orders.

Question. Is there anything else which you would wish to state?

Answer. I would be willing to answer any questions you may think proper to ask me. I only desire to show that Dr. Hays has never been in the habit of neglecting his duties. His habit has been just the reverse.

Question. Do you know anything about the particulars of this case where Dr. Hays is charged with being derelict in the performance of his duty?

Answer. I have heard, indirectly, about it. I think I am acquainted with the circumstances.

Question. You know nothing about it of your own knowledge?

Answer. No, sir.

Question. If a surgeon should come to this city with 300 or 400 sick and wounded persons in his charge, and find himself unable to report to the authorities here so as to have them taken charge of, because he arrived here in the night, between 9 and 10 o'clock, what would then be his duty?

Answer. To see the men provided for and made as comfortable as possible.

Question. What do you mean by "seeing the men provided for?"

Answer. To have them placed in as comfortable circumstances as possible in the then existing state of facts.

Question. There being that number of sick and wounded men upon a train of cars, either having to remain in the cars all night, or be removed that night to buildings temporarily provided for them, would or would it not be the duty of the surgeon in charge to be present, and superintend their removal, and look after them during the night?

Answer. During the most part of the night it would.

Question. At what time do you think it would be proper for him to leave?

Answer. I think he could leave, temporarily, with instructions to others to take his place.

Question. What do you mean by leaving temporarily?

Answer. I should think an absence during the night of three hours would be temporary.

Question. Would it be his duty, before he left, to see to it that all his assistant surgeons were properly at work and taking charge of the men in his care?

Answer. It would be his duty to have his assistants ordered and instructed properly as to what course they should pursue.

Question. And to see to it that they were doing that duty before he left?

Answer. To have orders given to them.

Question. Suppose that he should leave his men for the purpose of going away and reporting, and finding that he would not be able to give them over to the authorities here that night, he should come back to the train, would it then be his duty to see to it that his assistants were on the ground and doing their duty?

Answer. Yes, sir; I think so.

Question. Would anything excuse his leaving, under those circumstances, without seeing to that, unless it was a case of absolute prostration?

Answer. It would be his duty to remain there, unless his own health prevented his doing so.

Question. You mean by that, unless he was physically unable to remain?

Answer. Yes, sir. I would ask how many assistant surgeons were under Dr. Hays's command at that time?

Question. There were four of them.

Answer. I think, then, that for three or four hours he might leave, having such a staff under his command, provided they were at their posts and doing their duty.

Question. And it was his duty to see that they were there?

Answer. To issue orders to them to be at their posts.

By Dr. Hays, (who was present:)

Question. If I saw one of the assistants there, and supposed the others to be in the churches, as I had ordered them to be there, would I be justified in leaving?

Answer. I think an order issued to one for the whole would be sufficient.

By Mr. Gooch:

Question. Do you mean that, not finding the authorities here, and having to go back to the train again, it would be sufficient for him to issue his orders to one of the assistant surgeons, or should he see them all?

Answer. I think he might issue his orders to all through one.

Question. Would he be justified in going away without knowing whether the rest of the assistant surgeons were there or absent, asleep somewhere?

Answer. No, sir; unless he had evidence satisfactory to him of their being there. If one of the assistant surgeons informed him that the rest were there, I think that might satisfy him.

Question. If you had come back to the train under such circumstances, you having charge of a train of sick and wounded men, would you have felt that it was your duty to have given some personal supervision to the matter, to see what was being done for these men?

Answer. Yes, sir; I should.

WASHINGTON, *June* 23, 1862.

Dr. LEWIS A. EDWARDS sworn and examined.

By Mr. Gooch:

Question. What is your rank and position in the service?

Answer. I am a surgeon in the United States army, now on duty in the surgeon general's office. I am at present the senior surgeon. Dr. Wood was the senior surgeon before he was commissioned as assistant surgeon general. I ranked next to him.

Question. At what time did you leave the office a week ago last Saturday evening?

Answer. I cannot recollect very distinctly. I am hardly ever away from there before 5 or half past 5 o'clock, and sometimes I remain there until 7 o'clock.

Question. What despatches, if any, were received that day from Dr. Hays, who was coming in with a train of sick and wounded men from Front Royal?

Answer. That I cannot say. I was absent during the morning of that day. I had been to Annapolis, and I came into this city between 12 and 1 o'clock, and went to the office and remained there until about half past 5 o'clock. Up to that time I do not recollect of any despatch arriving from Dr. Hays. Whenever a despatch in relation to the transportation of sick and wounded, and their accommodation in this city, arrives, it is sent immediately to the medical director that he may make arrangements for them.

Question. To whom does it come—to your office?

Answer. To the surgeon general. If he is not there, I open it and act upon it.

Question. You think you remained there that day until half past 5 o'clock?

Answer. Yes, sir.

Question. The surgeon general leaves at 4 o'clock?

Answer. Yes, sir.

Question. If a despatch arrives after the surgeon general has left, you would open it if you were there?

Answer. Yes, sir.

Question. Do you think any arrived while you were there that day?

Answer. I do not think any did.

Question. You think you would have recollected it, if any had arrived?

Answer. There are so many despatches arriving, and that being a mere matter of routine, and one that would have been referred to the proper office, if one had arrived, I should not, perhaps, have recollected about it.

Question. If one had come what would have been done with it?

Answer. I should have sent it to the medical director, at the military headquarters of this district.

Question. Have you any recollection, one way or the other, as to whether a despatch did or did not arrive that day, between the time the surgeon general left and the time that you left that office?

Answer. I have no recollection at all of any coming of any kind, or from any source. If one had come from Dr. Hays, or from any one in reference to the sick, I might perhaps recollect it, because the next morning I saw the train on Maryland avenue, with sick persons in it, and I might, perhaps, have connected the two circumstances together, as relating the one to the other.

Question. What is your conclusion in relation to the matter? What is your belief?

Answer. My belief is that no despatch was received.

Question. That is between the time the surgeon general left, and the time of your leaving?

Answer: Yes, sir; there might have been one come in the morning before I arrived. But if one had come it would have been immediately sent to the medical director's office, and I would not charge my mind with it. Upon every letter and despatch that comes into the office is noted the day it is received.

Question. Do you keep a letter book?

Answer. We note the time on the original letter or message itself.

By Mr. Covode:

Question. As that was Saturday, might you not have left a little earlier than usual—say at 5 o'clock?

Answer. No, sir; it does not make any difference about my leaving, whether it be Saturday, Monday, or any other day. I might have left a little earlier than half past five, but I think not. I came over from Baltimore that morning, went immediately to the office, then over to the War Department and back to the office again, and remained there; sending word to my family that I had arrived, and would be at home to dinner. I think it was about half past five when I went home.

By Mr. Gooch :

Question. You have now made arrangements to have all despatches received after office hours sent directly to the surgeon general ?

Answer. All despatches received at the war office for the surgeon general after office hours are now sent to the surgeon general's residence. The medical director is the one who has charge of that matter; our duties are merely administrative.

By Mr. Covode :

Question. Did you know of that train being on its way here ?

Answer. No, sir; I did not hear anything of it until Sunday morning.

WASHINGTON, *June* 23, 1862.

JAMES PALMER sworn and examined.

By Mr. Gooch :

Question. What is your business ?

Answer. I am a laborer in the surgeon general's office.

Question. Do you know Surgeon Hays ?

Answer. I know him now when I see him.

Question. When did you first see him ?

Answer. I saw him for the first time last Sunday morning, a week ago; I did not know him then.

Question. Do you remember of seeing him a week ago last Sunday morning ?

Answer. Yes, sir.

Question. Did you have any conversation with him, or he with you ?

Answer. I was sweeping out the hall, and he came in and asked if the surgeon general was in, and I said no. He asked when he would be in, and I said that he was generally in about half past 9 o'clock. He then remarked that he had some sick and wounded soldiers here. I told him that he better see the medical director. He said he was ordered to report to the surgeon general, and I said nothing more to him. In a few minutes more he called my attention again, and asked me to give him the medical director's residence, and I did so. He then passed out of the building, and in a few minutes more he came back with General Hammond. General Hammond was in rather earlier that morning than he usually is; I suppose that Dr. Hays met him.

Question. Is that all you know about it ?

Answer. Yes, sir.

By Mr. Covode :

Question. At what time was it that you saw Dr. Hays that morning ?

Answer. It was some time between the hours of 7 and 9 o'clock. I could not say exactly what time.

By Mr. Gooch :

Question. Was it before 9 o'clock ?

Answer. Yes, sir; but I was busy, and I did not look at the clock.

WASHINGTON, *June* 24, 1862.

WILLIAM COOPER sworn and examined.

By Mr. Covode:

Question. Where do you reside?

Answer. I reside in this city, on what is called the Island here; a few doors east of the Island chapel.

Question. What is your occupation?

Answer. I have no occupation at present; I have been a police magistrate, but I am not in commission now.

Question. What information can you give us in regard to the case of Dr. Hays, in connexion with a train of sick and wounded soldiers that was brought in here on Saturday week last?

Answer. My evidence as to Dr. Hays himself, begins at a late period of the night.

Question. Just tell us what you know about it.

Answer. I saw Dr. Hays there, not knowing, however, who he was then. From his appearance, and his attention to the sick and wounded, I presumed that he belonged to the medical fraternity; but whether he was principal or secondary there, I did not know. He was very attentive, however; I saw him very busily engaged. Once or twice I entered into a little conversation with him, which was interrupted by his going to see some patient.

Question. What time of the night was that?

Answer. I cannot say; but it was long after midnight. I did not look at the time of night at all then, because I was very busily engaged, in conjunction with my family, in trying to do the best I could for the soldiers, and I did not look at my watch, or make any inquiry as to the time of night, until this circumstance took place. My sister and myself, and one of my next neighbors, a lady, got into conversation together. I think one of the soldiers was there forming a part of the group. A conversation ensued in which the word "to-morrow" was used. I jocularly remarked, "what do you mean by 'to-morrow?' It is time you ought to be thinking of going to church"—or something to that effect. "This is Sunday, recollect;" and at the instant, I pulled out my watch and looked at it; and at the same time this lady friend of mine said: "I think you ought;" that is, ought to think about going to church. I pulled out my watch at that time and looked at it; but whether it was twenty minutes past one o'clock, or twenty minutes before two o'clock, I cannot recollect; but it was considerably after one o'clock. Some minutes after that, I saw Dr. Hays—who, by the way, I did not know as Dr. Hays at the time—give a powder to one of the nurses, a youth there, whom I observed to be very handy, and it struck my attention—and the youth unfolded the paper, and poured the contents of it into a spoon that he had borrowed of one of my family, mixed it with a little water, and then gave it to a patient that was lying upon the floor of Island chapel. I was on the east side of the church when this conversation took place, at the time I pulled out my watch, and it was some time after that conversation that I saw Dr. Hays give this powder to the nurse, who administered it to a patient who was lying on the floor on the west side of the chapel. At that time it must have been very near two o'clock, if not quite.

Question. Did you see Dr. Hays at any time after that?

Answer. Not that I remember. I did not go to Potomac Hall, where some of the patients were.

Question. What was the condition of the sick and wounded at that time; had they been removed and all cared for?

Answer. As well as circumstances would possibly permit, I thought.

Question. Into what building had they been removed?

Answer. Into Potomac Hall, at the corner of South D and 11th streets, and into Island chapel, at the corner of South D and 10th streets, which is near my house. And the next day I know there were some in Grace church, which is about a square and a half east of my house; but whether they were removed there during the night or not, I have no means of knowing.

Question. Did you notice whether there was a large number of those sick and wounded who were able to walk?

Answer. There were a great many of them who were able to limp about. My attention was taken up with those in Island chapel, and I did not go into Potomac Hall at all. And during the night, I know, before I went into Island chapel at all, as I was standing in my porch, I saw several men in couplets with their hands locked together and a patient sitting up on their hands apparently unable to walk, and they were carrying them from the cars into the church.

It was a stormy night, and several females of my family, and my son, and others went over to give bread and other things to the poor fellows in the cars, and they came home dripping wet. I remained at home getting things ready to be carried over there, making tea, getting water ready, and all that sort of thing.

Question. Do you think that everything was done that night that could well be done for the relief of the suffering soldiers before Dr. Hays left?

Answer. I have not the slightest doubt that everything was done before he left that we were able to do. It was quite bedtime before the cars arrived; indeed it was after my bedtime, before anything was done to take the soldiers out of the cars; for we all thought that ambulances would come and take them away; and though my usual time of going to bed is about nine o'clock, yet having some curiosity to see whether the ambulances would come, I sat in a rocking chair near the front window of my house, waiting for them. I had dropped off asleep in my chair, when my daughter, who is married, came in and woke me up, and said, "There are a number of poor sick men here, and I think it is a shame that they are not removed;" and she said something about opening Island chapel for them. And then a number more of us got together, and got some bread and butter, and made some tea for the soldiers, which, of course, took some time.

Question. You and others attended to the providing of their wants as much as possible?

Answer. We did so to the best of our ability, and on Sunday it was rumored there, and generally believed, that another train would be in in the course of the day, with a parcel more of sick soldiers, and about 3 or 4 o'clock in the afternoon; and I had a hundred and odd loaves of bread piled up in my kitchen and about 200 pounds of ice; and I went over to Island chapel and to Grace church and told them that if they wanted any bread or anything of the kind, to send over to my house and get it. But no train arrived, and after keeping the bread until Tuesday, I sent it back. The ice, of course, all melted away.

Question. Have you any knowledge of the number that were carried into the churches?

Answer. I have no idea.

Question. Was there a considerable number?

Answer. Yes, sir; I went into Island chapel, but I did not go much about the church, because there were a great many females there—my own family numbered pretty sharply; I should think there were seven or eight of them—and they were all going around doing as much as they could; and I acted pretty much as their lackey?

Question. You are certain that you saw Dr. Hays bestowing attentions upon those men continuously up to 2 o'clock?

Answer. I did; and when I read the order, No. 66, I had no more idea that the doctor I had seen there was the surgeon in charge, there referred to, than that I was; and I said, "served him right." But when I came to find out who that surgeon was, I said it was essentially wrong.

Question. That is, you approved of the act of dismissing Dr. Hays until you learned it was the same man you had seen attending the wounded men there?

Answer. Yes, sir. And I had no idea that this gentleman, [pointing to Dr. Hays,] whom I had conversed with, and whom I had seen going about among the patients, and exerting himself to the best of his ability, as I thought—I had no idea that he was the surgeon in charge, but thought he was only secondary; and therefore when I read the order, which I did on Tuesday morning, at a friend's house, I said, "Served him right." I agreed with the order then, and so did my family. But my sister says, "How can that be? That gentleman I talked with was Dr. Hays—at least, they called him Dr. Hays." Says I, "What kind of a man was he?" She described him. But I thought it could not be Dr. Hays, for I knew that very often, in describing persons in that way, people mistake one person for another; and it was not until yesterday that I was positively convinced, of my own knowledge, that the surgeon I saw there that night was Dr. Hays.

Question. And you are certain now that this Dr. Hays (pointing to him) is the identical man who was attending to the soldiers that night.

Answer. This is the identical man.

Question. Did he say anything about having sent any despatches here about his coming here?

Answer. Yes, sir.

Question. When did he tell you that?

Answer. That night, at Island chapel.

Question. What did he tell you?

Answer. He told me that he had telegraphed, I think at Front Royal, that he was coming on with about 300 sick and wounded, and asked what he should do with them, or something of that import; and he said he received for answer, to come on. I think those were the words he said he received in reply, or something equivalent to that; that is, to bring them to Washington. He told me that when he arrived at Manassas he had there telegraphed that he had arrived at that point, and that he would be in Washington at a certain time. I do not recollect that he told me what that time was.

Question. Did he tell you to whom he directed those telegrams?

Answer. Not particularly, I think. He said "to the authorities," I think. He may have said "to headquarters."

Question. Did the doctor complain that night that no attention had been paid to his telegrams?

Answer. Yes, sir. He appeared to be very much hurt, indeed, to think that the men had been so neglected. And he said that the more neglected he thought the men had been, the more deserving of credit he thought the citizens there were for what they had done. I will not state positively that I did not see Dr. Hays after 2 o'clock in the morning. I might have seen him, and I might not; I could not state about that.

WASHINGTON, *June* 24, 1862.

ANSELM HATCH sworn and examined.

By Mr. Covode:

Question. Where do you reside?

Answer. I live in this city, on the Island, on 9th street and south D.

Question. Were you there a week ago last Saturday night, when a train of sick and wounded were brought into the city?

Answer. I was there between half past 10 and 11 o'clock, when I went over from the city.

Question. What did you see done there that night?

Answer. I saw citizens giving them refreshments, and taking them from the cars into the churches and their houses; I had several of them at my house, and one of them slept in my bed, while I sat up and slept in a chair.

Question. How were those sick and wounded provided for? Were they taken from the cars that night?

Answer. I saw a great many taken from the cars. They seemed to have every attention possible paid to them.

Question. Where were they taken to?

Answer. Some were taken into private houses, and some into churches. Potomac Hall was the first one I recollect hearing mentioned. I had four or five of them with me.

Question. Were there many of the citizens there attending to them?

Answer. Yes, sir. A great many were around there: pretty nearly everybody was out there.

Question. Did you see any surgeons there that night?

Answer. I heard that there were some there, but I did not see them. A Mr. Woodruff, who was along in care of the wounded, and who stayed over at my house, was up and around there until about 3 o'clock, I heard him say at one time that he would go and see the surgeons, and I understood from him that they were about. I paid but little attention to what was being done, except what little I was able to do myself.

Question. You did not see Dr. Hays or any of the other surgeons?

Answer. No, sir; I did not see any of them.

Question. You only know that the sick and wounded were cared for by the citizens and made as comfortable as possible?

Answer. Yes, sir.

By Mr. Gooch:

Question. You did not see a surgeon that night?

Answer. No, sir. I did not go over to the cars that night.

Question. None of them went to your house to see the sick and wounded there?

Answer. No, sir. There was no one there that required the attendance of a surgeon.

By Mr. Covode:

Question. Were there many there who could walk about?

Answer. A great many of them got out of the cars and walked about. Those at my house walked over there.

WASHINGTON, *June* 24, 1862.

HAMILTON K. GRAY sworn and examined.

By Mr. Gooch:

Question. Do you live in this city?

Answer. I do.

Question. What is your business?

Answer. I am at present bookkeeper for Mr. Ryan, grocer, on the corner of D and 9th streets.

Question. Did you see the train of sick and wounded soldiers that came into this city a week ago last Saturday night; and if so, about what time did you first see any of the soldiers? Go on, and tell us all you know about it.

Answer. I did not see the train when it first came in. I got to the train about 11 o'clock, as well as I can recollect, and I was told that there were some 300 and odd soldiers there. I immediately went to the assistance of the soldiers, and seeing no surgeons around, I inquired of the soldiers where the surgeons were, several of them said that Dr. Hays had gone to the surgeon general's office to procure ambulances to have them removed to the hospitals. After assisting the soldiers as much as I could—all in my power—I met a surgeon, who I afterwards learned was Dr. Hays. A friend of mine also came up to me at the same time and told me that Potomac Hall had been procured for the accommodation of the soldiers. I informed Dr. Hays of that fact, and he seemed to be very glad to know that we had procured a place, and he set to work to have the soldiers removed; all that could be removed. He seemed to be doing all he could for the relief of the soldiers. He complained very much that there were no ambulances there to remove them to the hospitals. He did not state anything that had transpired while he was away looking for the surgeon general, but he told me that he had telegraphed three times, once on his way down here, informing the authorities here that he was on the way here with soldiers, sick and wounded; yet they were not provided with ambulances when they arrived here. I saw him at times until a very late hour in the morning; and all the time he was doing his utmost for the relief of the soldiers.

Question. What was the latest hour at which you can fix the time positively that you saw Dr. Hays?

Answer. The latest specific hour that I can fix positively was half past twelve. I told some of the soldiers the time of night then. How long I remained there after that I cannot say.

Question. You saw the doctor there as late as what hour?

Answer. I am certain I saw him there as late as half past twelve o'clock; how much later I cannot say.

Question. And at that time he was assisting in removing the soldiers and doing all he could for their comfort?

Answer. Yes, sir.

Question. Did you see any of his assistants?

Answer. I saw only one.

Question. Do you know his name?

Answer. I do not know him. I do not know as I should know him if I saw him again. I recollect seeing one, and he said something to Dr. Hays about going to take some rest.

Question. You saw no surgeon there after you got there until you saw Dr. Hays?

Answer. None at all. When I got there Dr. Hays was off looking for the surgeon general, as some of the soldiers told me. In conversation with the soldiers they all spoke in the highest terms of their surgeons. Some person was complaining, I remember, of the soldiers being neglected by the surgeons, and one young man who was wounded emphatically contradicted it, and said the surgeons had done all they could for them.

Question. You say you heard some complaints of the surgeons?

Answer. Yes, sir; among the citizens.

Question. Not among the soldiers?

Answer. None at all among the soldiers.

Question. Some of the citizens were complaining?

Answer. Yes, sir. There are always some persons who take great delight in finding fault.

Question. They were complaining that the surgeons had not done their duty?

Answer. Yes, sir.

Question. And it was then that this young man said they had been taken good care of?

Answer. Yes, sir. The only complaint I heard from the soldiers was from one of them about having been carried twenty or thirty miles over a rough pike road, shaking them almost to pieces.

Question. These men were in a bad condition?

Answer. Yes, sir.

Question. They suffered more there than they would if they had been taken in ambulances to the hospitals?

Answer. Yes, sir.

Question. And they would have suffered very much more than they did if it had not been for the attention of the citizens?

Answer. No doubt of it. They were very hungry. Every man seemed as if he had not had anything to eat for two or three days, although some of the men who were themselves very much exhausted would not taste anything until we had served the wounded. I am sorry I took no more note of the time, but I did not think of the time then.

Question. Were the most of them taken out of the cars?

Answer. Yes, sir. There were some of the wounded left in the cars who begged not to be removed. They were in freight cars—very close cars. We placed them where they could get air, and they seemed to be very comfortable and very well satisfied. The next morning I went there, and they seemed to be a great deal refreshed. One of the soldiers told me that he thought that, if it had not been for the assistance they had received from the citizens of the island, many of those who were low of typhoid fever and of exhaustion would have died. In several cases we had to take them to the churches almost by main force. They were so much exhausted that they seemed to have lost all energy whatever.

Question. You mean you had to carry them to the churches?

Answer. Yes, sir. In some instances I saw some soldiers carrying other soldiers on their backs.

Question. Those that were able to do so?

Answer. Yes, sir; they helped each other as much as they could.

Question. There were five surgeons with that train. You saw two of them. Do you know what became of the other three?

Answer. No, sir; unless they were in private houses attending to the soldiers there.

Question. You had no knowledge of them?

Answer. No, sir; none but the one I saw with Dr. Hays. I talked some with Dr. Hays myself; and I also saw him there the next day.

Question. How late did you remain there that night?

Answer. I have no idea; it was very late when I left. I left when I found that nothing more could be done for them. The most of them seemed to be asleep and well cared for; and I knew that they must need rest. I would state, in addition to what I have already stated, that when I first got to the cars there were a great number of soldiers who were outside of the cars, and were able to move about without assistance from others.

WASHINGTON, *June* 24, 1862.

GEORGE H. MORSE sworn and examined.

By Mr. Gooch:

Question. What is your occupation?

Answer. I am a clerk at Willard's Hotel, in this city.

Question. At what hours were you on duty there?

Answer. From about 10 o'clock at night until half past 6 o'clock in the morning.

Question. Did Surgeon Hays come to your hotel and take tea on Saturday night, a week ago?

Answer. About ten minutes past 10 o'clock, Colonel Lewis and another officer—a quartermaster, I believe—came in and registered his name, and also the name of Dr. Hays. He said that Dr. Hays would be there after awhile. I think it was between half past 10 and a quarter to 11 o'clock that Dr. Hays came in, and I sent his baggage up to his room. He went into the dining-room and took tea; he was not there over ten minutes, I think, when he came out and asked me if I knew where the surgeon general lived. I told him that I did not know. He said he had come here with a train of sick and wounded soldiers; that he had telegraphed twice, and expected to find ambulances and the necessary conveyances to take them to the hospitals; but when he got here he found nothing there at all. He said that he was a stranger here and did not know where to find anybody. He inquired of several where the surgeon general lived, but could not find out. When he came out of the dining-room it had commenced to rain, and he requested me to send up to his room for his rubber coat. I did so and he put it on and went out, saying that he would go and try to find the surgeon general. I did not see Dr. Hays again until he came in very late in the morning. As he came in I looked at the clock, and saw that it was in the vicinity of 4 o'clock. The exact time I cannot state.

By Mr. Covode:

Question. Are you quite certain it was after 3 o'clock?

Answer. I am.

By Mr. Gooch:

Question. What office were you sitting in?

Answer. At the office of the hotel, behind the counter.

Question. Who else came in about that time?

Answer. No one that I have any recollection of.

Question. Did any other person come in after 2 o'clock?

Answer. There are persons coming in after 2 o'clock every night.

Question. Do you recollect of any coming in that night?

Answer. Not particularly. The reason why I recollect about Dr. Hays is that I knew the object he went out for.

Question. Had you any conversation with him at that time?

Answer. Not that I recollect.

Question. Did you ask whether he had found the surgeon general?

Answer. I did not.

Question. Did he say anything to you?

Answer. I think he went right to his room and said nothing; that is my impression. I may be mistaken.

Question You are sure he did not tell you whether he had found the surgeon general.

Answer. I did not think to ask him that.

Question. Are you perfectly sure that you looked at the clock?

Answer. I am.

Question. When was your attention first called to this matter, and that you would be wanted to testify here?

Answer. I did not know it until yesterday.

Question. Who saw you then about it?

Answer. Dr. Hays.

Question. What conversation passed between you and him?

Answer. No conversation, except that he had been before this committee, and they had sent him down to get me to testify as to the time he had come in that night.

Question. What else passed between you?

Answer. No other conversation.

Question. Nothing more?

Answer. Nothing that I recollect of.

Question. He did not ask you whether you remembered the time that he came in?

Answer. No, sir.

Question. No one has asked you whether you remembered the time?

Answer Mr Chadwick, one of the proprietors of the hotel, asked me; and Mr. Odell, of this committee, asked me night before last.

Question What did you tell Mr. Odell?

Answer. I told him the same, I think, that I have told you here, very nearly.

Question. Was that before you had the conversation with Dr. Hays?

Answer. Yes, sir; it was night before last. I did not know anything about coming here until I saw Dr. Hays yesterday evening.

By Mr. Covode:

Question. Who first broached the subject with regard to your knowing where the surgeon general lived? Was it you to Dr. Hays, or Dr. Hays to you?

Answer. Dr. Hays asked me if I knew where he lived.

Question. I mean when he asked you to come here?

Answer. He did not say anything to me then about the surgeon general.

Question. Did you say anything to him?

Answer. No, sir. All he said was that you wanted me here to testify about the time he came in.

By Mr. Gooch:

Question. Who was the first person who spoke to you about the time he came in that night?

Answer. I could not tell who was the first, because several about the hotel have asked me. I did not know I was to be called upon to testify until yesterday.

Question. Did anybody ask you before Mr. Odell did?

Answer. I think so.

Question. Who?

Answer. I think Mr. Chadwick asked me. He is one of the proprietors of the hotel.

Question. When did he ask you?
Answer. I could not state.
Question. Did he ask you within two or three days after the occurrence? It was a week afterwards that Mr. Odell asked you.
Answer. My impression is that Mr. Chadwick asked me. He did not ask me until after Dr. Hays was dismissed.
Question. Dr. Hays was dismissed on the Monday morning afterwards. You say you never had any conversation at all with Dr. Hays at the time?
Answer. To the best of my recollection I never spoke to Dr. Hays after that night until he came to me yesterday.
Question. Did he ask you then if you remembered at what time he came in that night?
Answer. He did not. He merely said you wanted me here to testify as to the time he came in.
Question. Do you know a Mr. Rider?
Answer. I do.
Question. Did he ever ask you about this matter?
Answer. He never did?
Question. He never said anything to you about it?
Answer. All that he ever said to me was this: I was sitting out in front of the hotel some days ago, and Mr. Rider came out there and sat down. I did not know who he was then. I do not recollect what was said. I had heard before that Mr. Rider had Dr. Hays's case in charge; and, from something that he said, I thought that he was the man. I asked if he had Dr. Hays's case in charge, and he said that he had. I said that I hoped that he would be able to clear him, as I thought it was a very unjust case anyway.
Question. What else was said?
Answer. Nothing more.
Question. Did he ask about what time Doctor Hays came in that night?
Answer. He did not.
Question. Did you tell him?
Answer. I did not. I did not say anything more to him.
Question. Did you not tell Mr. Rider anything at all about your knowing about this case?
Answer. I did not. To the best of my recollection, I said nothing more to him.

By Mr. Covode:

Question. Have you heard any other person connected with the hotel say that they knew where the surgeon general lived?
Answer. I have heard Mr. Chadwick and one or two of the clerks say that they did not know where he lived.
Question. Have you ever heard any of the others say they did know where he lived?
Answer. I have not.

WASHINGTON, *June* 25, 1862.

WILLIAM KIERNAN sworn and examined.

By Mr. Covode:

Question. Where do you live?
Answer. On 4½ street, between D street and Virginia avenue in this city.
Question. What is your business?

Answer. I am a hackman. I own hacks.
Question. Were you on the stand, at Willard's, on Saturday night week?
Answer. That is the night the wounded soldiers came here.
Question. Yes, sir.
Answer. Yes, sir; I was on the stand.
Question. Have you any recollection of seeing Doctor Hays—this gentleman (pointing to him) that night, and taking him to the War Department, and anywhere else? If so state to us about it.
Answer. Yes, sir. I drove him down to the cars on Maryland avenue first. He remained there some time. I could not state how long it was. He wanted to go to the surgeon general's office, and I did not know where it was. He told me to drive him to the War Department, and I drove him there. He then told me to drive him from there to the corner of F and 15th streets, and I drove him there. He got out and went to the door, and a man came to the door, and talked with him some 5 or 6 minutes.
Question. Do you know where the surgeon general's office is?
Answer. I did not know until then. It is a large building right on the corner of F and 15th streets.
Question. Did you see the man he was talking to?
Answer. Yes, sir.
Question. Where was he?
Answer. He was standing at the door when I saw him in the vestibule. I was standing out at the hack, on the curbing.
Question. You are certain that the Doctor got out of the hack and went to the door and talked to him?
Answer. Yes, sir.
Question. Did you drive Dr. Hays back to the cars after that again?
Answer. No, sir; I did not drive him back to the cars. I drove him to Willard's.
Question. What time of night was that as near as you can tell?
Answer. I could not say exactly what time it was. It was late, I know.

By Mr. Odell:

Question. Was it one o'clock?
Answer. Yes, sir; it was after one o'clock.
Question. Was it two o'clock?
Answer. I cannot say. If it was not not two o'clock it was mighty near it.
Question. Was it four o'clock?
Answer. It was not four o'clock.
Question. What time did you put up that night?
Answer. I did not put up that night at all. I stayed out all night.
Question. You put up some time?
Answer. I put up in the morning.
Question. At what time?
Answer. About six o'clock.

By Mr. Covode:

Question. Did you get off your hack and go into the War Department yourself?
Answer. No, sir; the doctor went in.
Question. Did you get off your hack at the surgeon general's office?
Answer. Yes, sir.
Question. You did not go in there?
Answer. No, sir.

By Mr. Gooch:

Question. The doctor engaged you at Willards'?

Answer: Yes, sir.

Question. You stand there?

Answer. Yes, sir.

Question. At what time did he engage you first?

Answer. I do not know what time.

Question. As near as may be?

Answer. I judge it was somewhere between 10 and 12 o'clock.

Question. Who went with you when you drove down to the cars?

Answer. There was another gentleman who went with the doctor to the cars.

Question. How long did you remain at the cars?

Answer. I do not know how long.

Question. State as near as you can.

Answer. I suppose we stopped there near an hour.

Question. Then where did you go?

Answer. I think I drove right up to the War Department.

Question. And from there to the surgeon general's office?

Answer. Yes, sir.

Question. And from there around to Willard's?

Answer. Yes, sir.

Question. And the doctor then got out and went into Willard's?

Answer. Yes, sir.

Question. Did you see him after he went into the hotel at that time?

Answer. No, sir; I did not see him after that.

Question. You left him there?

Answer. Yes, sir.

Question. You think that was as late as one o'clock?

Answer. Yes, sir; I do. I know it was that late.

Question. You know it was as late as one o'clock?

Answer. Yes, sir.

Question. Did the doctor hire you by the hour?

Answer. Yes, sir.

Question. How much did he give you for the hour?

Answer. A dollar and a half.

Question. How much money did he pay you?

Answer. He gave me three dollars. I did not charge him by the hour, for I did not know the time when we started. He asked me what his bill was when he got out, and I told him three dollars.

Question. Was that more than a dollar and a half an hour?

Answer. No. sir. It would have come to more than that if I had known the time.

Question. You charged him three dollars for all the time that he used your hack?

Answer. Yes, sir.

[Dr. Hays, who was present, was here asked how he reconciled the statement of this witness, that he drove him first to the cars, and then to the surgeon general's office, with his own statement that he went first to the surgeon general's office and then to the cars. The doctor said this witness was mistaken.]

The witness: When this gentleman first engaged me, he asked me if I knew where the office of the surgeon general was, and I told him that I did not. He then went into the hotel to inquire, and came out and told me to drive him to the cars, and I drove him down.

Question. Is there any possibility of your being mistaken as to the route you went that night?

Answer. No, sir; I think I could go the same route over again.

By Mr. Odell:

Question. What number do you drive?

Answer. No. 321.

Question. Who do you drive for?

Answer. For myself.

Subsequently Dr. Hays, having left the committee-room, returned and said that he desired to state that since hearing the testimony of the last witness, he had reflected upon it and had become satisfied that the witness was correct, and he himself had been mistaken. He stated that he had honestly told the committee what he believed to be the truth, and until he heard the statement of the hackman, he had religiously believed that he went first to the surgeon general's office and then to the cars. In that, however, he was mistaken. Dr. Stidger did go in the hack with him to the cars, and then he went to the surgeon general's office, and from there he went to Willard's and went to bed.

After some conversation with some members of the committee—

Mr. Gooch asked this question:

Question. Did you have champagne at supper?

Answer. [By the Doctor.] Yes, sir; I took some with Colonel Lewis; but not much.

WASHINGTON, *July* 5, 1862.

Dr. S. B. STIDGER sworn and examined.

By Mr. Gooch:

Question. What is your position and rank in the army?

Answer. I am assistant surgeon of the 1st Virginia regiment of infantry.

Question. Did you come to Washington with Dr. Hays when he was in charge of a train of sick and wounded soldiers from Front Royal three weeks ago to-day?

Answer. Yes, sir.

Question. At what time did you arrive here?

Answer. I think it was between 9 and 10 o'clock at night—perhaps 10 o'clock.

Question. Go on and state what happened during the night.

Answer. After arriving here we waited some time expecting to be moved up to the depot. Not finding ambulances there, we supposed we were not yet at the end of our journey. After waiting for some time, we found one of the men connected with the train, and asked him how soon we should move up to the depot. He told me that he had unhitched the engine and had switched off the train. We concluded, then, to go up town and report, and see if we could ascertain the reason why no arrangements had been made to receive us—to report in person to the surgeon general. We had our hand-trunks with us going up, and stopped at Willard's and took supper, and then went back to the train. Dr. Hays had been complaining for some time that he was unwell, and I suggested to him that he better go back and make an effort to report. We learned at the hotel that the office was closed, and we could make no report there that night. We were told that by some person. I do not know whom. I suggested to the doctor that he better go and try to find out where the surgeon general lived, and I would remain there with the train until morning. We were then getting the wounded into churches and halls. They had been fed. I told the doctor that if he could find no person to whom to report, he better lay down and get some rest, as he had been complaining for some days, and I would remain with the train until morning. During the night a doctor who lives on the street where the train was, but whose name I do not recollect, came up and asked me how it was that we were left there. I told him that I did not know; that we were surprised that no arrangements had been made for our reception; that the doctor in charge had telegraphed on the way, and that we were in rather an unpleasant situation, as we had no medicines and nothing to dress the wounds with. The doctor said that he would furnish me with medicines, and I went to his office and got some brandy and some morphine. Some dressings were brought there by the citizens, and I commenced dressing the wounds of the men, and got through in the morning. In the morning Dr. Hays came down and said that he had reported.

Question. Did you remain with the men during the night?

Answer. Yes, sir.

Question. During the whole night?

Answer. Yes, sir.

Question. What other surgeons remained with you?

Answer. No others.

Question. How many surgeons had you on the train?

Answer. There were five, including Dr. Hays and myself.

Question. When did you last see the other three surgeons that night?

Answer. As well as I recollect, the last we saw of them was about the time that we left and went to the hotel.

Question. Did you see them after your return?

Answer. No, sir.

Question. They did not appear that night?

Answer. No, sir.

Question. They took no charge of the men during the night?

Answer. No, sir.

Question. You had between 300 and 400 sick and wounded men on that train?

Answer. Yes, sir.

Question. During the night were most of the men removed from the cars into the churches, &c.?

Answer. There were enough removed to allow those remaining to lie down comfortably in the cars.

Question. Many of them were removed during the night into halls and private houses?

Answer. Yes, sir.

Question. You and Dr. Hays left the cars to go up and report?

Answer. Yes, sir.

Question. And you went to Willard's Hotel and there took supper?

Answer. Yes, sir.

Question. Did you have a cooked supper?

Answer. It was ready when we went in.

Question. It was cooked to order?

Answer. No, sir; I think not. They were eating supper when we got there.

Question. Who were eating supper?

Answer The boarders, I presumed they were.

Question. Did you not have a champagne supper that night?

Answer. No, sir; I think not. We had some champagne the next morning, I think, ordered by Colonel Lewis.

Question. Did you not have a champagne supper that night?
Answer. I cannot be positive. I know we drank champagne with Colonel Lewis.
Question. You drank it that night, did you not?
Answer. Well, sir; I think we did.
Question. Then when you and Dr. Hays came up to report why did you not go to the surgeon general's office?
Answer. We were told, on inquiring about the surgeon general's office, that it was closed.
Question. Who told you that?
Answer. I cannot tell you that.
Question. Where were you told that it was closed?
Answer. At the hotel; that it was after office hours. As far as my own opinions were concerned, I thought we had reported when we sent our telegraphic despatches here. Our object in going was to ascertain, if possible, why there was nobody there to receive the men.
Question. You did not expect to ascertain that at Willard's Hotel, did you?
Answer. No, sir; but that was on the way, and we had our hand-trunks in our hands and stopped there.
Question. You went to Willard's Hotel and inquired of somebody, you do not know who, and was told that it was after office hours, and you made no further efforts to find the office, but went back to the train?
Answer. Yes, sir; we went back to the train.
Question. Doctor Hays went back to the train with you?
Answer. Yes, sir.
Question. And you advised him afterwards to go to the hotel and go to bed?
Answer. I told the doctor I would remain there until morning, and, if it was possible, he better find out where the surgeon general lived, and find out what was to be done with the sick.
Question. What time was that suggestion made?
Answer. I do not know exactly; it was about as soon as we got back.
Question. That was in the neighborhood of twelve o'clock at night?
Answer. I suppose so; somewhere in that neighborhood.
Question. And the doctor acted on that suggestion?
Answer. Yes, sir; at least he left me.
Question. You do not know whether he went to the surgeon general's office that night or not, but you know that he left you on the suggestion you say you made to him about twelve o'clock?
Answer. Yes, sir; I suppose it was about twelve o'clock, as near as I can judge.
Question. At what time did you next see the doctor?
Answer. It was in the morning. Really I do not know what time it was, perhaps 8 o'clock, or after; I will not be positive about the time; I was attending to the wounded in the lower hall. I do not know how long he had been there before I saw him.
Question. You remained there all the night through?
Answer. Yes, sir. After seeing to the men in the cars I went into the church.
Question. Those men needed care that night?
Answer. Yes, sir. Their wounds had not been regularly dressed for some time, except that some dressings were changed, as far as we had them, at Manassas.
Question. How many wounded men had you on that train?
Answer. I should think perhaps 200.
Question. And some of them were badly wounded?

Answer. Yes, sir.

Question. And one of the men died the next morning?

Answer. Yes, sir.

Question. Did any die during the night?

Answer. There was a car attached to the train, the first of which I knew was at Manassas Junction. I was passing along the train and heard some complaining, and supposing it was some of our men, I got into the car to see about it. The steward, in company with them, told me they were taking them to Washington city, and that they had brought them from Catlett's Station. I do not know whether they were attached to our train there or not. I think two of them died before we got in.

Question. Was there any surgeon with them?

Answer. No, sir.

Question. And you had these men added to your list to take care of?

Answer. No, sir. They were in charge of a steward.

Question. Do you know anything further about these men—where they came from?

Answer. Nothing more than what the steward told me, which I have told you. I think they belonged to a New York regiment.

Question. How many were there of those men?

Answer. I do not remember distinctly; but I think there were four.

Question. We had got the impression that there were two car loads.

Answer. That is not so; so far as I know.

Question. You say there were only four of them?

Answer. There were four sick men, and I think two others in company of them as stewards.

Question. Did you ride back to the cars from the hotel in a hack?

Answer. Yes, sir.

Question. What do you say in relation to those surgeons who left that train of sick and wounded men, while you were about? Were they not negligent of their duty? Did not their duty require them to remain and take care of them?

Answer. I thought so.

Question. You felt it your duty to remain and take care of them during the whole of the night, after you returned?

Answer. I did.

Question. And some other surgeon could have helped you to advantage?

Answer. Yes, sir.

By Mr. Odell:

Question. Were you the surgeon in command there?

Answer. No, sir; Dr. Hays was.

Question. Whose duty was it to direct those surgeons to remain?

Answer. It was the duty of Dr. Hays.

Question. They were subordinate, and subject to the orders of Dr. Hays?

Answer. Yes. sir.

By Mr. Gooch:

Question. Had they any right to leave without authority to do so?

Answer. I hardly know how to answer that question, whether they were under obligations to remain and act as nurses.

Question. Was there not work for surgeons as well as nurses?

Answer. I think so.

Question. And they were bound to stay and do their duty as surgeons?

Answer. I think so.

Question. When you were removing between 300 and 400 sick and wounded men in the night to new places, was it not necessary for surgeons to remain there with them?

Answer. Yes, sir. I think this about it: that if they had remained we would have got through our labors sooner, and then we would have been under no obligations to sit up as nurses.

Question. You mean this, do you not: that if those surgeons ha mained and done all they could for the men they might then, with propriety, have taken some rest?

Answer. Yes, sir.

Question. But not until then?

Answer. No, sir.

Question. And to have done that would probably have used up that night pretty thoroughly?

Answer. Pretty much, I think; it would, at least, have been late in the night when we got through. I think I got through the next morning, perhaps, at 8 or 9 o'clock. I was not through when Dr. Hays came down the next morning.

Question. That must have been 9 or 10 o'clock?

Answer. I presume it was 9 o'clock.

Question. Is there anything further in relation to this matter that you desire to state?

Answer. Nothing I now think of.

By Mr. Covode:

Question. When you left the cars that night, to go to Willard's, did you know that the other surgeons there were also going away?

Answer. I believe the doctor, in my presence, ordered them to remain there until he came back.

Question. He ordered them to remain?

Answer. I think so. If I recollect rightly now, he told them to remain there until we returned.

Question. You say you were at work, attending to the wounded, all night; that being the case, knowing that you had so much to do, why did you advise the doctor to go and lie down?

Answer. At the time I told him that I did not know that I could get any dressings, or any medicines, or that I would be able to do anything more for the men. The doctor had been complaining for some time, and I thought he might as well have some rest.

Question. Why did you not know whether you could get dressings or not?

Answer. We had nothing to make dressings of, and it was not until after the doctor had left that a physician, residing on the street there, asked me if I wanted anything. I told him that we lacked dressings and medicines, and he said that if I would accompany him to his office he would let me have some medicines. And some of the citizens then proposed to get something for dressings.

Question. Was that before or after Dr. Hays went away?

Answer. I think it must have been after; though I will not be positive whether it was before or after he left.

Question. Did you make any effort to find where the other surgeons were after you went back to the cars?

Answer. No, sir.

Question. When Doctor Hays went away was there anything there for him to do, any business for him to perform?

Answer. No, sir.

Question. Nothing that he could have gone right at?

Answer. No, sir ; I think his business was to make a report as soon as possible, and have arrangements made to get the men taken away. That was one object I had in view in having him leave. And I did not think there was anything to do there, more than I could attend to at that time.

Question. What is the custom in the service in such cases ? Is it the custom for the principal surgeon to attend to dressing the wounds and to the sick himself all the time, or does he give orders to others to attend to it ?

Answer. We have been in the habit of going ahead, each man doing what he could. Sometimes, however, I have known brigade surgeons to give orders; superintending, but not doing much themselves.

Question. Did you hear the doctor complain of his health before he came here ?

Answer. I heard him complain mostly on the way to Front Royal, when riding on horseback. I believe I heard him complain at one time when attending to the sick at Luray. He said he was suffering very much.

Question. Was it the knowledge of his condition that induced you to advise him to go and lie down ?

Answer. Yes, sir, and also because I did not think there was any necessity for his being there. I must confess that I had a very strong inclination myself to go.

Question. But you promised to remain there all night ?

Answer. Yes, sir, though I felt a very strong inclination to accompany him when he retired.

Question. Were the men sleeping, many of them, or were they waiting attention ?

Answer. I do not think that many of them were waiting attention ; some of them were; very few of them had been moved at that time.

Question. How did the men go away from the cars ? Had they to be carried, or could the most of them walk ?

Answer. There were very few that had to be carried, except those who had had amputations performed. There were very few taken away that had to be carried.

Question. Do you know of the doctor telegraphing from Manassas that he was coming ?

Answer. I only know that he told me that he had telegraphed.

Question. I noticed that you said some time since that you considered that he had reported by telegraph from there ?

Answer. Yes, sir ; I understood from him that he had reported.

Question. Where are those surgeons now, who went off and went to bed that night ?

Answer. I do not know where they are. I do not know that they went to bed.

Question. If it had not been for getting those medicines from the physician you mention, and the dressings from the citizens, that night you would have had nothing to do ?

Answer. No, sir. And the reason why we had no rations was that we were ordered to take two day's rations, and take our men to Front Royal.

By Mr. Gooch :

Question. You expected to leave your sick and wounded at Front Royal, and that was the reason that you had no medicines or dressings ?

Answer. Yes, sir.

By Mr. Covode :

Question. You think it was after the doctor left that you got the medicines and dressings as you have mentioned ?

Answer. Yes, sir. I think one of the editors of one of the morning papers here was there, and went with me to the doctor's office to get the medicines.

CONVALESCENT CAMP.

IN THE HOUSE OF REPRESENTATIVES,
December 4, 1862.

Mr. Patton submitted the following, which were adopted:

Whereas it is reported that many abuses exist in connexion with the administration of "Camp Convalescent," near Alexandria, and until they are corrected the health and lives of the thousands of our brave soldiers there stationed will continue to be endangered, therefore be it—

Resolved, that the joint committee on the conduct of the war be directed to inquire and report upon the foregoing, with such recommendations as they may deem requisite.

Attest: EM. ETHERIDGE, *Clerk.*

IN THE HOUSE OF REPRESENTATIVES,
December 5, 1862.

Mr. Noble submitted the following, which were adopted:

Whereas many soldiers of the volunteer forces of the government are now, and have for many months been, confined in "Camp Convalescent," unable for duty, and are entirely without money or means to procure such necessaries as would add to their comfort, they not having been paid their monthly dues from the government, in many instances, for a period of from three to nine months, therefore—

Resolved, that the committee on military affairs be, and are hereby, requested to inquire what legislation, if any, is necessary to enable such soldiers, so confined and separated from their respective regiments, to receive and be paid their regular monthly dues, and to report by bill or otherwise.

Attest: EM. ETHERIDGE, *Clerk.*

SIR: In reply to your communication, asking as to the condition of the convalescent camp, I beg leave to state that in order to give you a correct idea of the present condition of the camp it will be necessary to explain to you its history, and some of the difficulties attending the organization of so large a body of men, brought together from all divisions of the army, of all sorts of characters, and in such a variety of conditions. The camp was organized in August, 1862, and Colonel J. S. Belknap, of the 85th New York volunteers, placed in command.

General Slough, the military governor of Alexandria, was directed to organize a camp of convalescents, stragglers, and recruits, under the following regulations:

All officers absent from their regiments without a proper pass, approved by their division commander, will, if their regiments are stationed in or near Washington, be ordered to join them in arrest, and the fact will be duly reported to division commanders by the provost marshal.

Every officer absent from his regiment without a proper pass, *and whose regiment is not near Washington,* will be ordered by the officers of the provost guard to report in person to the provost marshal, who will direct him in writing either to proceed to join his regiment within twenty-four hours, or within the same period to proceed to Alexandria, and report to the military governor of that place for duty at the convalescent camp.

All recruits arriving, for regiments which are not near Washington, will be sent to the convalescent camp.

At the time of the organization of the army, after the second Bull Run, the army had just passed through Alexandria, and had left a large number of stragglers, hence the necessity of some place being selected to collect them and distribute them among their regiments. As the organization was intended only as a temporary convenience, no record was kept until September 17th.

The following abstract of the morning report shows the immediate expansion of the camp a result unexpected:

Abstract of morning reports of convalescent, stragglers, recruits, and paroled and exchanged prisoners' camps, showing number of officers and men at various times from organization of the camps to January 31, 1863; *also showing gain and loss of each month.*

Date.		Officers.	Enlisted men.		Aggregate.	Received.	Sent away.
			For duty.	Unfit for duty.			
1862.							
Sept.	17	15	1,143	2,542	3,700	3,700	....
	20	51	3,933	2,542	6,526	2,826	....
	25	63	7,740	2,542	10,345	4,569	840
	30	87	11,692	3,851	15,630	6,158	873
Oct.	5	94	9,937	3,950	13,981	2,783	4,432
	10	100	8,538	2,520	11,158	1,220	4,043
	15	100	7,168	3,498	10,766	2,466	2,858
	20	100	7,334	3,556	10,990	720	496
	25	50	6,932	3,815	10,797	1,248	1,441
	31	62	7,090	4,360	11,512	1,908	1,193
Nov.	5	48	2,370	5,084	7,502	1,258	5,268
	10	48	3,384	5,000	8,432	1,512	582
	15	62	3,865	9,412	12,339	3,990	83
	20	66	3,902	10,093	14,061	1,970	248
	25	67	3,822	11,038	14,927	1,579	713
	30	67	3,662	11,401	15,130	1,535	1,332
Dec.	5	49	4,158	9,043	13,250	2,357	4,237
	10	46	2,594	7,774	10,414	1,446	4,282
	15	38	2,683	8,667	11,388	1,937	963
	20	35	2,729	8,810	11,574	1,653	1,467
	25	35	2,995	11,252	14,282	3,917	1,209
	31	44	2,594	8,070	10,708	928	4,502
1863.							
Jan.	10	40	3,116	8,365	11,521	1,956	1,143
	20	71	2,172	7,435	9,678	1,179	3,022
	31	57	2,579	7,706	10,342	2,183	1,519

Recapitulation of gain and loss by months.

	Received.	Sent away.
September	17,343	1,713
October	10,345	14,463
November	11,844	8,226
December	12,238	16,660
January	5,318	5,684
Number of officers and men estimated by Colonel Belknap, commandant, to have been received and sent away prior to organization—September 17	20,000	20,000
Number estimated to have "passed through" the camps since organization, of whom no account was taken	5,000	5,000
Total	82,088	71,746

Whole number received	82,088
Whole number sent away	71,746
Whole number now in all the camps	10,342

That the growth was not anticipated by the quartermaster's department is shown by the fact that about the 1st of November Colonel Belknap, with the approval of General Slough, made requisitions for lumber to build barracks, naming three thousand as the number *likely* to require accommodation.

The quartermaster general objected to filling the requisition "until it was positively ascertained that barracks for so *large* a number would be required."

General Slough, foreseeing that the camp must become a permanent institution, made requisition for barracks, which were not begun until on or about the 15th day of December. The hospital department being much neglected, the attention of the commanding general was early called to the fact. Two inspectors of the medical department had at different times inspected the hospital and the camps, and reported that the surgeon in charge was incompetent.

After waiting some time for his removal, and for reforms in that department, he, on the 17th of October, again called attention to the condition of things, and begged that steps might be taken to improve that department. In the meantime the camp had been divided into four parts, to wit: convalescents, recruits, stragglers, and paroled and exchanged prisoners. On that day, numbering over eleven thousand men, not including guards and employés, this number was subsequently increased to over seventeen thousand.

The provost marshal general of the army, on the 29th day of October, was directed to send an officer from each corps, weekly, to convey to the regiments such as were fit for duty.

General Slough used every effort to get the number at the camp reduced.

As the provost marshal was constantly interrupted in sending off the troops, and as the surgeons in charge of hospitals either ignorantly or designedly sent many to the camp who should have been discharged, the number continued to increase until, at the end of November, it exceeded sixteen thousand.

About the 1st of December General Heintzelman took command of the defences of Washington.

As numerous complaints had been made as to the location of the camp, and as General Heintzelman was convinced that the camp was to be permanent, I was directed "to examine the country in the neighborhood of Alexandria with a view to a permanent location."

Dr. Taylor, of the army, who was then the medical director, accompanied me. I selected the ground about four miles from Alexandria and about three miles from the Long Bridge, and reported "that in view of the ground being high and sandy, well sheltered and connected with Washington and Alexandria by railroad, it was particularly suited for a permanent camp or hospital."

My report was approved by General Heintzelman, and an order was at once issued to remove the camp and make arrangements to build barracks. This was on the 26th of November.

It was now presumed that suitable provision was to be made for the comfort of the inmates of this much abused camp, but it appears that the surgeon general had reported against it, I have no doubt, under the impression that the evils (which had been greatly exaggerated) could not be remedied.

It appears, however, as the following letter of the assistant surgeon general shows, that the recommendation of the surgeon general had induced the Secretary of War to issue an order breaking up the camp.

SURGEON GENERAL'S OFFICE,
Washington, D. C., December 9, 1862.

SIR: Your letter of the 7th instant is received, calling attention to the condition of the convalescent camp, near Alexandria.

In reply I must beg leave to disclaim, on behalf of the medical department, all responsibility for the deplorable state of things existing in that camp.

I am aware that the unfortunate misnomer "convalescent" has created an impression that this establishment was an outgrowth from the hospital department. Such is not the case. It was not established by directions from this office, and its connexion herewith is as incidental as that of any other military post. It was ordered by the general commanding the army of the Potomac that the soldiers belonging to that army, returning to duty from the general hospitals in this District, should be sent there, to be thence distributed to the regiments, and in obedience to these orders all soldiers returned to duty from hospitals within this District were sent to this camp. Several inspections were made by medical inspectors, under orders from this office, from the report of the last of which, made by Medical Inspector Vollum, I quote "as points prominent, it would seem to any observer," viz: "Bad police, uncleanliness, bad ventilation, and demoralization resulting from the promiscuous herding together, upon a limited area, of herds of idle, undisciplined men."

Upon this report, made on the 22d ultimo, it was recommended by the surgeon general that this camp be broken up, and, in conformity with this recommendation, the Secretary of War has acted promptly in the case. It will be a work of some days, however, even to break up a camp of this magnitude.

In the meantime it is known positively, at this office, that nineteen medical officers are on the ground exerting every energy in the proper discharge of their duties. And that, on the 20th of November, medical supplies for three months were received at this camp.

The cause of the sad state of things now existing are, in my opinion, first, the great expansion of this establishment to a size much beyond its capabilities or accommodation; and, second, the ill-judged plan of sending men recently from hospitals to a camp crowded with undisciplined stragglers, and then, instead of hurrying their departure from this place to their regiments, allowing them there to remain until crowding and exposure prostrated them again upon a sick bed.

* * * * * * * * * *

Very respectfully, your obedient servant,

JAMES R. SMITH,
Acting Surgeon General.

Colonel J. H. PULESTON,
Military Agent of Pennsylvania, and
Chairman Executive Committee Pa. Relief Association.

The order was issued soon after the 1st of December, but contained no provision for the disposition of the convalescents, and the usual number continued to be sent from all parts of the country daily; instead of lessening the evil it was increased, and on representations of the facts to the Secretary of War, the same day the letter of the assistant surgeon general was written, the order was countermanded, and the following issued:

WAR DEPARTMENT,
Washington City, D. C., December 9, 1862.

Ordered, I. That the commanding general of the defences of Washington establish at once a convalescent camp in the neighborhood of Alexandria, Virginia.

II. That the quartermaster general cause to be erected immediately suitable barracks for the accommodation of 5,000 enlisted men, with the proper compliment of officers, at the camp selected by the commanding general, defences of Washington.

EDWIN M. STANTON,
Secretary of War.

At the date of the receipt of the above order Colonel Belknap was sick. He had for over two months been in command of the camp, and was completely broken down, and was advised by his surgeon to apply for sick leave.

The quartermaster's department informed General Heintzelman that it had no quartermaster they could assign for the superintendence of building the barracks. As it was necessary to commence the work at once, he directed two of his staff officers to take charge of it—Colonel McKelvy, his chief commissary, as commander, and Captain Joshua Norton, an assistant quartermaster, as superintendent of the building. That they faithfully performed this duty is evident from the fact that within a month most of the convalescents were quartered in barracks, and the balance provided with suitable shelter in the new camp.

Another marked feature of improvement was manifest in the medical department. Incompetent surgeons were sent away, and experienced surgeons detailed. Dr. Page, an army surgeon of ten years' service, was placed in charge; and competent boards organized to discharge the sick and disabled, or send to regiments such as were fit for duty.

This new order did not take the general supervision of the camp from General Slough. He had faithfully executed his trust, and, under the adverse circumstances, is entitled to great credit that the condition was no worse.

I am confident that 80,000 men, of the varied characters of those that circumstances over which the officers had no control have brought together, have not, during the war, suffered less from sickness or exposure than those in this camp.

The agent of the State of New York thus mentions its condition as early as October 25:

OFFICE OF THE NEW YORK STATE AGENT, 252 G STREET,
Washington, D. C., October 25, 1862.

DEAR SIR: Yours of the 22d was duly received, and your inquiry concerning the camp of convalescents near Alexandria carefully noted.

I am aware of the feeling that exists in Albany, as well as other parts of the State, in regard to this camp, not only from the enclosed telegraph of William Olcotts, but from the various letters I have received from your city and elsewhere. While this feeling has grown out of the many letters that have been published, written by visitors to this camp, and those who have labored ardently, and contributed largely to its relief, which letters stated only such things as have existed in the past to a greater or less extent, yet I am glad to be able to say they do not now exist.

The camp has been removed on to grounds that were thoroughly policed before occupancy. The tents are placed in single rows, giving the freest circulation of air, and the more feeble portion placed in one part of the camp, and loose boards furnished to floor some portion, or all of this part of the camp tents, and the balance with straw. Every man has been furnished with a good army blanket, and all whose uniform was not sound and comfortable with new.

The men all have new, or fair shirts, and the requisition was made three days ago for enough to give all their proper change. Socks had been furnished to all who had none, and duplicates for all ordered. Their food is the regular army ration, improved by more than the regular allowance of fresh meat and all the vegetables that can be procured from government relief association stores, but not as much as they need for their proper improvement.

An efficient post office department has been established, with ten men detailed to its duties. The records are the most complete of any camp bearing any comparison in difficulty, employing thirty clerks.

The entire labor, voluntary and official, has resulted in changing this camp from one of confusion, filth, demoralization, want, and much real suffering, to one of cleanliness, order, and comfort to the extent that can be created, so long as permanent barracks are not built, with the following exceptions, which are to be instituted soon, unless the entire camp is dispensed with, viz: To be removed to grounds where water is easier of access; substitute barracks for tents; build appropriate cook-houses, and give them a new physician in charge.

Colonel Belknap, of the 85th New York volunteers, is in command, and deserves much credit for his energy and executive ability. Great credit is due to the New York State Association committees and many voluntary laborers in the field. It affords me great satisfaction to be able to announce to the public that all the real cases of suffering have been relieved there, or removed to permanent hospitals for their relief, except some sick in regular hospital tents, who are to go into a convalescent hospital in Axexandria, who are able, and the balance to the Mansion House.

The general condition of patients in hospital is comfortable, although daily complaints are made, and many of them justly, but mostly through the inefficiency of attendants and ward doctors in making requisitions.

The surgeon general is doing what he can to improve the hospitals in this regard.

S. H. SWETTAND,
New York State Agent.

Hon. IRA HARRIS.

Sometime in January it appears, by proceedings of the Senate, that Senator Harlan visited the camp He thus understandingly describes its condition:

"Now, I might illustrate what I mean by referring to the convalescent camp across the river, mentioned by the senator from New Jersey, which I have visited in person. I know the facts have existed there that were mentioned by the senator last evening. Convalescent soldiers have been put into tents there without blankets without beds, and without necessary clothing. At the time I last visited that camp there were about eighteen thousand convalescent soldiers in it. Perhaps ninety-nine in every hundred of them were living more comfortably than the majority of them live at home, and yet there were some who were without overcoats, and without blankets, and without beds of any kind. But, on inquiring of the proper officer for the cause, I ascertained that these destitute men had come there on that very day, or the day preceding, without previous notice, so that it was not yet possible for them to draw the necessary supplies from the proper department. But they were not suffering on account of this destitution. Although they had no overcoats that belonged to them in person, and no blankets, they were using blankets borrowed from other soldiers who had more than enough. It was said, yesterday, that they were compelled to sleep on brush. Mr. President, this may appear to those who have never lived in the open air like a great cruelty. But, Mr. President, I have lived, for months together, in the open field, not as a soldier, but in a situation where I had to provide for myself and my associates, far beyond the settlements. I have had some experience on this subject, and I will say to the senator from New Jersey that I would very much prefer to sleep on a bed of brush than a bed of boards. It is very far from being an uncomfortable bed, if men know how to make it. Soft brush, covered with straw or blankets, makes an excellent couch, far more comfortable than we always find in city hotels, and on which men may repose more pleasantly than a majority of us at home—as comfortably as many of us do in our own dwellings. Some are doubtless not properly provided for, and suffer great hardships. These cases are comparatively few, and are temporary, and are generally corrected as speedily as circumstances will permit.

"It is the recitation of these extreme cases which, I think, does the service a great damage in the country. Benevolent gentlemen and ladies, without a knowledge of all the facts and circumstances, shed tears over the sufferings of our soldiers, and recite them to their neighbors, and create impressions which do great injustice to the officers in charge. It is said that there has been much suffering in that encampment. I have no doubt there has been; but it has been of this exceptional character. Men have been sent there from battle-fields who have lost their clothing and blankets during the engagement, or threw them away in flight. For the first day or the first night, before the officers have been able to draw suitable clothing and blankets from the quartermaster's department, they have been compelled to borrow or sleep with their brother soldiers; and in tents that have not been provided with board flooring, they have cut boughs or branches of trees, and in this way provided for themselves what was, in fact, a very comfortable place to sleep.

"In that encampment, when I visited it, I have found numbers of our government teams—four and six horse teams, mule teams—constantly employed in hauling wood to the doors of the tents occupied by these men. Besides this, the encampment is in the timber; they are surrounded with groves. Now, I cannot be made to believe that convalescent men—for these are not sick men, they are men who are able to take care of themselves—will be likely to suffer much for the want of stoves, when they can have wood for the cutting, and are surrounded by timber. There are cases of suffering, and very frequently these cases of suffering arise on account of the prodigality of the soldiers themselves. It is much more pleasant to praise our brave troops in the field than to speak of their faults; but we find men in civil life that have faults, and some of these men, unfortunately, find their way to the army. There are soldiers who, for a glass of grog, will sell their blankets or coats, and then come to the agent of a sanitary commission, or a State agency, and make most piteous appeals for assistance on account of their destitution. Why, sir, it is known to those who have investigated this subject personally, that they often sell their munitions; that they carry their cartridges to traders and sell them for spirits, tobacco, or other little luxuries they may desire. Not unfrequently these men have deserted from the army, and have been arrested here at the depot, and have been sent to the convalescent encampment to await the necessary means of transportation to their regiments. For the purpose of eluding the vigilance of the proper officers of the government, they throw away their blankets and their overcoats, swap off all their military garb, and secure citizen's dress of a far inferior character, and of course suffer during severe weather, if arrested and returned; and persons visiting this encampment and seeing these parties thus improperly clad, are melted into tears on account of their sufferings, when it has all been brought about by their own folly, prodigality, or crime, for which, if the articles of war were rigorously enforced, they would be shot. A careful examination of these cases of suffering will establish the fact that officers of the army, medical and otherwise, are not the inhuman characters we might be induced to believe from some remarks which have been dropped even in the Senate. There are bad and incompetent officers, doubtless, at many of these hospitals, but I believe a large majority of them do the very best it is possible for Christian, humane gentlemen to do under the circumstances by which they are surrounded. The physicians in charge of the hospitals connected with the armies in the field, of course, are not always able to procure the necessaries for the sick and wounded men, nor are the commissaries always able to do so for the well men. The casualties of war necessarily produce these difficulties; and I suppose that the troops, when they enter the service, do it with a tolerable comprehension of the hardships which they may be called upon occasionally to suffer. They expect it, and endure it without a murmur when they know it cannot be remedied. I have reason to believe, and do believe, that there is far less complaining among the soldiers themselves in the field than by friends at home."

Mr. Wilson, of Massachusetts, truly said, "That is a military camp under military rules and regulations."

There are surgeons there who have duties to perform. I do not mean to say that they are fully performed.

From seventy to eighty thousand men have passed through that camp within the last six months. On the 10th of this month there were about five thousand there; eight hundred of them from my own State. I have visited the camp repeatedly, and I know something about it. I think the camp has been very badly managed, and the surgeon general thinks so, too, for he had a report from one of his inspectors, Colonel Vollum, who reported against it, and recommended that certain action be taken to reform it, which action was referred to the Secretary of War. I called upon the Secretary of War with a copy of it, and he said that he would place it in the hands of General Heintzelman, under whom this camp is. This camp, however, is not a hospital. It has no resemblance to a hospital.

Mr. Ten Eyck replied: It has a hospital name.

Mr. Wilson, of Massachusetts. Yes, sir, just as a regiment has a hospital name; but it is a camp where the men who have been away on furlough, who have been in the hospitals, and have been pronounced convalescents, go, in order to be transferred from there to their regiments.

(Dr. Vollum might have recommended that competent surgeons be sent there. The surgeons in charge of general hospitals should have been instructed not to send to this camp fit subjects for discharge.)

About the time of this discussion it was stated in the Senate that many of the inmates of the camp were without blankets. The committee on the conduct of the war were instructed to inquire into the facts. I have never seen their report; but I do know that a portion of the committee visited the camp, and that not a single person was found who was not well supplied with clothing, and *every man had a blanket.*

It is well known to officers accustomed to duty in the field that although there is much less suffering in such a camp, there is more grumbling. Almost every school district at the north has had a representative in this camp; some from their own misfortunes, but many of them have been of the poorest material of our army—the most useless of all soldiers—stragglers.

I trust I do no injustice to the real convalescents in this camp; there are many there who have proved to be good soldiers in the field, who were good soldiers when in camp, and will continue to be of credit to their regiments and honor to their States.

I do not desire to cast censure on any of the officers. I have no doubt all have done what they thought advisable to relieve the suffering of the sick, wounded, and unfortunate, yet their office has been a thankless one.

I have neglected to mention one great difficulty in the organization of this camp, viz: the officers have not been permanently assigned to duty there; many have looked upon it as a kind of Botany bay, instead of making the comfort of the unfortunate soldier a pleasure and duty; many of them, however, have, and are now, serving faithfully, and are entitled to praise rather than censure.

Since the 1st of February the number in the camps has been lessened daily; on the 15th the number at the convalescent camp proper was only 5,300.

It has been recommended that a portion of the men not fit for duty in the field, but who, under the present system, are necessarily discharged, shall be organized into companies and regiments for garrison duty. I am confident that the services of one-third of those who are discharged will be of great value, if so organized.

I have the honor to be your obedient servant,

S. H. LATHROP,
Lieut. Col., Assist. Inspec. Gen., Department of Washington.

Hon. DANIEL W. GOOCH,
Committee on Conduct of War.

TRADE IN MILITARY DISTRICTS.

IN THE HOUSE OF REPRESENTATIVES,
January 12, 1863.

On motion of Mr. Alley,

Resolved, That the committee on the conduct of the war be directed to enquire what rules or restrictions, if any, are applied to trade in those sections of the country now under military occupation, and whether any officers in the service of the government are, or have been engaged in trade or speculation, or affording special privileges or facilities to other persons to do so, and to report the facts to this House.

Attest: EM. ETHERIDGE, *Clerk.*

WAR DEPARTMENT,
Washington City, January 29, 1863.

SIR: In accordance with the request contained in your letter of the 13th instant, I have the honor to enclose copies of all rules, regulations, and restrictions, issued by this department for the government of trade in those portions of the country now under military occupation. These rules, regulations, and restrictions are based upon regulations issued August 28, 1862, by the Secretary of the Treasury, concerning commercial intercourse with insurrectionary States or sections, and for the purpose of enforcing them.

I am, sir, very respectfully, your obedient servant,

EDWIN M. STANTON,
Secretary of War.

Honorable B. F. WADE,
Chairman of the Committee on the Conduct of the War.

WAR DEPARTMENT,
Adjutant General's Office, Washington, August 29, 1862.

General orders, No. 119.]

The following orders are published for the information and government of all concerned:

ORDER RESPECTING TRADE REGULATIONS.

WAR DEPARTMENT,
Washington City, D. C., August 28, 1862.

The attention of all officers and others connected with the army of the United States is called to the regulations of the Secretary of the Treasury concerning commercial intercourse with insurrectionary States, or sections, dated August 28, 1862.

I. Commandants of departments, districts, and posts, will render all such military aid as may become necessary in carrying out the provisions of said regulations and enforcing observance thereof to the extent directed by the Secretary of the Treasury, so far as can possibly be done without danger to the operations or safety of their respective commands.

II. There will be no interference with trade in, or shipments of, cotton, or other merchandise, conducted in pursuance of said regulations, within any territory occupied and controlled by the forces of the United States, unless absolutely necessary to the successful execution of military plans or movements therein. But in cases of the violation of the conditions of any clearance or permit granted under said regulations, and in cases of unlawful traffic, the guilty party or parties will be arrested and the facts promptly reported to the commandant of the department for orders.

III. No officer of the army, or other person connected therewith, will seize cotton, or other property of individuals, unless exposed to destruction by the enemy, or needed for military purposes, or for confiscation under the act of Congress; and in all such cases of seizure the same shall be promptly reported to the commandant of the department wherein they are made for his orders therein.

By order of the Secretary of War.

E. D. TOWNSEND,
Assistant Adjutant General.

Official: E. D. TOWNSEND,
Assistant Adjutant General.

TREASURY DEPARTMENT, *February* 3, 1863.

SIR: I have received your letter of the 13th ultimo, (covering copy of a resolution of the House of Representatives on the subject,) requesting me to furnish to the committee on the conduct of the war, "a copy of all rules, regulations, and restrictions issued by your" [Treasury] "department for the government of trade in those places indicated in the resolution"—(to wit: in those portions of the country now under military occupation)—"said copy designating all rules, &c., &c., which have been, but are not now, in force, as well as those in force at the present time."

In compliance with your request, I now transmit copies of all letters, circulars, rules, &c., &c., upon the subject, emanating from or approved by this department from 2d May, 1861, to 20th January, 1863, inclusive.

I also transmit an analytical chronological index of the same, which may facilitate the labors of the committee in investigating the subject.

With great respect,

S. P. CHASE,
Secretary of the Treasury.

Hon. B. F. WADE,
Chairman Committee on Conduct of the War, Senate.

LIST OF DOCUMENTS.

No.	Date.	Subject of document.
	1861.	
1	May 2	Circular to collectors, surveyors, and other officers of the customs, in pursuance of the proclamation of the President of April 19, 1861.
2	15	Circular letter, allowing supplies to go forward to certain cannel-coal mines in Western Virginia.
3	29	General letter of instructions to special agents, relative to exchanges, &c., announcing the policy that commerce should follow the flag.
4	30	Modification of restrictions promulgated May 2, 1861, on trade with Western Virginia.
5	June 4	Letter to sundry persons—committee of citizens of Paducah, Kentucky—concerning restrictions upon free trade with Kentucky.
6	12	Circular to officers of the customs in addition to instructions of May 2, 1861.
7	August 22	Circular instructions to collectors and other officers of the customs, superseding instructions of May 2 and June 12, and embracing proclamation of the President of August 16, 1861, in pursuance of accompanying act of Congress of July 13, 1861.
8	31	Circular prohibiting trade with Paducah, Kentucky.
9	September 3	Circular designating what communication with insurrectionary sections is in accordance with law.
10	10	Order restricting trade in Kentucky with points south of Louisville, &c.
11	10	Instructions to special agents concerning restrictions on trade in Kentucky, west of the Cumberland river.
12	21	Circular to officers of the customs, relating to unwarrantable seizures of property.
13	October 2	Permits for sutlers at Cairo, Illinois.
14	2	Order mitigating restrictions on trade with Paducah.
15	3	Authorizing shipments of products from Kentucky, west of the Cumberland.
16	November 5	Regulations of trade with Paducah, &c.
17	12	Circular to officers of the customs in regard to seizures.
18	14	Authorizing trade with blockading squadrons.
19	25	Restrictions on trade in pork with Louisville, Kentucky.
20	30	General regulations relative to securing and disposing of the property found or brought within the territory occupied by the United States forces in the disloyal States.
21	30	Instructions to agents appointed to Territory above described for purposes there alluded to.
22	30	Instructions to agents appointed to receive property alluded to in the foregoing regulations.
23	Dec. 13	Modification of restrictions of November 25, 1861, on trade in pork with Louisville, Kentucky.
	1862.	
24	January 15	Rules required to be observed by steamboats navigating the Ohio river.
25	27	Rules for steamers between Pittsburg and Cincinnati.
26	February 14	Instructions in duties of special agent to Nashville, Tennessee, relative to trade in cotton and other products.
27	27	Communication from the Secretary of the Treasury to the Secretary of War, requesting him to advise the generals in command of the act of Congress of July 13, 1861, so far as it directs how commercial intercourse with the insurrectionary sections shall be regulated and controlled.
28	28	The President's license for commercial intercourse.
29	March 4	Rules and regulations concerning internal commercial intercourse under act of Congress of July 13, 1861.
30	7	Communication from the Secretary of the Treasury to the Secretary of War, concerning interference with rules of March 4, 1862.
31	29	Circular to officers of the customs, modifying the rules and regulations of commercial intercourse of March 4, 1862.

List of documents—Continued.

No.	Date.	Subject of document.
	1862.	
32	April 4	Order restricting trade in Tennessee to persons authorized by Governor Johnson.
33	7	Rules governing shipments to or by sutlers, under act of Congress of March 19, 1862.
34	22	Order that the question of the detention and seizure of goods shall be decided by the surveyor of the last port to be passed on the route of transportation.
35	22	Rules for commercial intercourse adapted to trade in the west.
36	May 12	Proclamation of the President opening certain ports to trade.
37	12	Regulations relating to trade with ports opened by proclamation.
38	16	Appointment of acting collector, and general instructions regulating trade at New Orleans.
39	17	Modifications of the restrictions upon trade on the Mississippi.
40	23	Circular to collectors of Atlantic ports concerning clearances to ports opened by proclamation, enumerating articles contraband of war.
41	....	Form of permit issued to officers of the customs to grant clearances to ports under blockade.
42	June 5	Circular to collectors relative to sending supplies to the relief of Norfolk.
43	17	Rules for trade at Memphis, Tennessee.
44	23	Letter from the Secretary of the Treasury to the Secretary of War, embodying the *modus operandi* in the transmittal of supplies to places declared by the President to be under blockade.
45	27	Additional instructions to the acting collector at New Orleans.
46	July 1	Certificates of permission to trade to be granted to loyal parties.
47	10	Instructions to special agents to co-operate in establishing rules for reopening trade with places heretofore in insurrection.
48	18	Instructions to surveyors of customs (west) requiring steamers to take out regular clearances each trip, &c.
49	18	Instructions to surveyors in western districts relative to trading boats.
50	August 15	Modification of instructions of June 27, 1862, to the acting collector at New Orleans.
51	28	Regulations concerning internal and coastwise intercourse, to which are appended the accompanying orders of the Secretary of War and the Secretary of the Navy, also the act of Congress of July 13, 1861, and the supplemental act of May 20, 1862.
52	September 8	Special orders concerning trade on the Mississippi river below Memphis, promulgated by the Treasury Department in conjunction with the military commander.
53	22	Special instructions to the collector at Baltimore concerning restrictions on trade.
54	22	Order imposing additional restrictions on the trade with Kentucky and Tennessee, west of the Cumberland river and north of the Ohio.
55	24	Order restricting trade on the Baltimore and Ohio railroad.
56	25	Order restricting trade between Parkersburg and Point Pleasant, Western Virginia.
57	October 1	Further instructions to the acting collector at New Orleans relative to trade below the city.
58	1	Communication to the Secretary of State as to the effect of treasury regulations upon trade in, and exportation of cotton and other products of the insurrectionary sections, in connexion with a letter from William P. Mellen, special agent, (of September 26, 1862,) in relation to the cotton trade of the southwest, &c., and the reply of the Secretary of the Treasury of this date.
59	4	Rules governing trade in Tennessee, adopted by Major General Grant.
60	23	Additional rules restricting trade in the west and south.
61	November 3	Regulations restricting trade north of the Potomac.
62	8	Instructions relative to trade on the Kanawha river.

List of documents—Continued.

No.	Date.	Subject of document.
	1862.	
63	November 5	Restrictions on trade on the north side of the Ohio river.
64	25	Restrictions on trade in Maryland, and appointments of boards of trade.
65	December 2	Board of trade at Memphis dissolved.
66	12	Circular relating to trade below Memphis issued by Thos. H. Yeatman, esq., special agent.
67	12	Restrictions on trade on the north side of the Ohio river modified.
68	16	Trade below Helena, Arkansas, prohibited; no trade opened below Memphis.
69	22	Order suspending trade with points in Kentucky and Tennessee.
	1863.	
70	January 24	Modification of restriction upon trade in salt in Kentucky advised.
71	January	Conditions upon which trade with Helena, Arkansas, is opened.

No. 1.

Circular to collectors, surveyors, and other officers of the customs.

TREASURY DEPARTMENT, *May* 2, 1861.

On the 19th of April, 1861, the President of the United States, by proclamation, declared the ports of South Carolina, Georgia, Florida, Alabama, Louisiana, Mississippi, and Texas under blockade, and on the same month, by another proclamation, declared the ports of Virginia and North Carolina, also, under blockade, since which proclamation this department has received reliable information that attempts are frequently made to furnish arms and munitions of war, provisions, and other supplies to persons and parties in those States in open rebellion against the constitutional authorities of the Union.

It becomes my duty, therefore, to instruct you to cause a careful examination to be made of the manifests of all steam or other vessels departing from your port with cargoes whose ultimate destination you have satisfactory reason to believe is for any port or place under the control of such insurrectionary parties, and to compare the same with the cargo on board; and if any such manifest be found to embrace any articles of the description before mentioned, or any such articles be found to constitute part of the cargo, you will take all necessary and proper measures to prevent the departure of the vessel and to detain the same in your custody until all such articles shall be removed therefrom and for further proceedings, according to law.

You will also make a careful examination of all flatboats and other water craft without manifests, and of railroad cars and vehicles arriving at or leaving your port, laden with merchandise, the ultimate destination of which you have good reason to believe is for any port or place under insurrectionary control; and if arms, munitions of war, provisions of war, provisions or other supplies are found, having such destination, you will seize and detain the same, to await the proper legal proceedings for confiscation or forfeiture.

In carrying out these instructions, you will bear in mind that all persons or parties in armed insurrection against the Union, however such persons may be organized or named, are engaged in levying war against the United States, and that all persons furnishing to such insurgents arms, munitions of war, provisions, or other supplies, are giving them aid and comfort, and so guilty of treason within the terms of the second section of the third article of the Constitution;

and you will therefore use your utmost vigilance to prevent the prohibited shipments, and to detect and to bring to punishment all who are in any way engaged in furnishing to such insurgents any of the articles above described.

You will, however, on the other hand, be careful not to interrupt, vexatiously or beyond necessity, by unwarranted or protracted detentions and examinations, the regular and lawful commerce of your port.

You will report forthwith whether any, and if any, what, additional measures may be necessary, in your judgment, to carry into full effect the foregoing directions; and you will report to this department, from time to time, your action under these instructions.

S. P. CHASE,
Secretary of the Treasury.

N. B.—Among prohibited supplies are included coals, telegraphic instruments, wire, porous cups, platina, sulphuric acid, zinc, and all other telegraphic materials. S. P. C.

MEMORANDUM.—This circular of instructions was superseded by the circular published on the 22d day of August, 1861.

No. 2.

Circular letter to surveyors of the customs west, allowing supplies to go forward to certain coal mines in Western Virginia.

TREASURY DEPARTMENT, *May* 15, 1861.

SIR: You are hereby authorized to allow goods and provisions, comprising the necessaries of life, to pass through your port from Philadelphia for the use of the workmen in the Cannel coal mines of Western Virginia; and all coal shipped from thence to your port to go forward or land without interruption.

I am, &c.,

S. P. CHASE,
Secretary of the Treasury.

ENOCH T. CARSON, Esq., *Surveyor, Cincinnati, Ohio.*
CHAS. W. BATCHELOR, Esq., *Surveyor, Pittsburg, Pennsylvania.*

No. 3.

General letter of instructions to William P. Mellen, special agent, relative to exchanges, and announcing the policy that commerce should follow the flag.

TREASURY DEPARTMENT, *May* 29, 1861.

SIR: I have little doubt that the exchange of provisions and supplies, except munitions of war and other articles usually prohibited, would be more useful than injurious. The difficulty, however, is this: The States controlled by insurrectionists, especially by insurrectionists exercising the powers of government, can hardly be regarded otherwise than as hostile communities, with which the United States are, for the time being, at actual war. The rules applicable to the relations of war must be applied. If war existed between this country and England, no trade whatever would be permitted. American property shipped to England and English property shipped to the United States would be liable to seizure. So constant experience teaches us that property shipped to the insurrectionary States is liable to seizure and actually seized; and if the property of citizens in those States shipped to the United States is not seized, it is simply because the federal government desires to treat them, as far as practicable, not as enemies, but as citizens.

I see no way in which safe intercourse can be established between citizens of the loyal States and those under insurrectionary control. The question is not one of *revenue* nor one of *rights* in a state of peace, but a question of supplies to enemies, and is controlled by considerations belonging to a state of war. The best thing to be done, it seems to me, is to establish the power of the government in co-operation with the people of Kentucky and Western Virginia within those limits, and to let commerce follow the flag.

This policy opens Missouri, Kentucky, and Western Virginia to trade, and will extend southward as rapidly and as far as the authority of the federal government can be restored.

Continue your conversations with reflecting men, and let me know the result.

Yours, &c.,

S. P. CHASE,
Secretary of the Treasury.

WM. P. MELLEN, Esq.,
Special Agent, Cincinnati, Ohio.

No. 4.

Modification of the restrictions on trade with Western Virginia, promulgated May 2, 1861.

TREASURY DEPARTMENT, *May* 30, 1861.

SIR: It is the purpose of the government, whenever practicable, consistently with its effort to restore the supremacy of the Constitution and laws, to mitigate, in favor of all citizens of the United States who remain loyal to the Union, the rigorous measures found necessary to suppress the insurrection. With that view, the instructions of the 2d instant, prohibiting the transmission of supplies to the insurgents, will not be enforced against the citizens of Western Virginia, who have so signally manifested, by recent acts, their continued attachment to the Union.

You will, in future, be careful that provisions and other like commodities, intended for consumption in Western Virginia, shall be permitted to proceed to their destination without interruption, satisfying yourself, of course, in every case, that such is the *bona fide* destination of the articles.

The substance of the foregoing instructions was communicated to you by telegraph on the 29th instant.

I am, &c.,

S. P. CHASE,
Secretary of the Treasury.

ENOCH T. CARSON, Esq.,
Surveyor, &c., Cincinnati, Ohio.

Similar letters of instructions were sent to the collectors of the various western ports.

No. 5.

Concerning restrictions on free trade with Kentucky via Paducah.—Letter to committee of citizens of Paducah.

TREASURY DEPARTMENT, *June* 4, 1861.

GENTLEMEN: On the 24th ultimo, the following despatch was sent from this department to William Nolen, collector at your port:

"'*Bona fide*' trade between States not under insurrectionary control, of which States Kentucky is one, is under no restrictions, but the sending of supplies of any kind, directly or indirectly, for the aid and comfort of insurgents, in or through Kentucky or any other State, is strictly forbidden."

Instructions have been sent to the collectors of various western ports not to interfere with the shipments of supplies *bona fide* intended for consumption within any State acknowledging and fulfilling its federal obligations. If, therefore, any obstruction is opposed to the sending of provisions or other supplies, it must be because the officers of the government at the places from which the supplies would be forwarded have reason to believe that those supplies will reach insurgents in arms against the Union and its government.

Some *facts*, such as the petition of certain citizens of Paducah to the Kentucky legislature for the fortification of the place, the support of that application by the senator from the district, and the arming of parties of men, avowedly intending to join the conspirators in insurrection, afford *some* ground for that belief. If the belief be a mistaken one, it will be easy to remove it by such manifestations on the part of the people of the town and surrounding country as will leave no doubt of their loyal attachment to the Constitution, the Union, and the flag of our fathers.

If the collector at Paducah has executed, and will continue to execute, impartially and completely, the order heretofore sent him, prohibiting supplies to parties levying war against the United States, and their aiders and comforters, all obstructions in the way of complete restoration of commercial intercourse between Paducah and loyal towns and States will be removed.

It is the earnest wish of this department that every part of the country may enjoy, in the most ample degree, the benefit of the Constitution and the laws, faithfully upheld and honestly administered, for the protection of every right and every interest.

Yours, &c.,

S. P. CHASE,
Secretary of the Treasury.

Messrs. J. CAMPBELL, J. H. TERRELL, S. B. HUGHES, R. C. WOOLFOLK, R. ENDERS, H. ENDERS, *Paducah, Kentucky.*

No. 6.

Circular to collectors, surveyors, and other officers of the customs.

TREASURY DEPARTMENT, *June* 12, 1861.

SIR: Referring to the circular instructions of the 2d ultimo, prohibiting the transmission of munitions of war, provisions, or other supplies to parties in insurrection against the United States, you are now further instructed to exercise the utmost vigilance in arresting and detaining all merchandise, of whatever character, the ultimate destination of which you have satisfactory reason to believe is for insurgents against the United States, or for places under their control.

If you are satisfied, either from the nature of the articles or otherwise, that any merchandise, wherever destined in name, is in *fact* destined for persons or combinations in actual insurrection against the government of the United States, you will cause the same to be seized and proceeded against for forfeiture.

If, however, you are satisfied that any merchandise transmitted for States or places under insurrectionary control is *not* intended for actual insurgents, and has been shipped or forwarded without intent to afford aid or comfort to such insurgents, or otherwise to violate the law, you will simply detain such merchandise, and notify the shippers or forwarders, or their agents, of such detention, and state the cause thereof. If such shipper or forwarder, personally or by agent, shall satisfy you that the merchandise so arrested will not be sent to any place under insurrectionary control, but will be either returned whence it came or be disposed of in good faith for consumption within loyal States, you will restore possession of the same, and allow such disposition thereof to be made as the parties in interest may desire.

You will regard all States in which the authority of the United States is temporarily subverted as under insurrectionary control; but any portions of such States in which the laws of the Union and the authority of the federal government are acknowledged and respected, will be considered as exempt from any interruption of commerce or intercourse beyond such as may be necessary in order to prevent supplies going to insurgents, or to places under their control.

It is the intention of the department to leave the owners of all property perfectly free to control it in such manner as they see fit, without interference or detention by officers of the federal government, except for the purpose of preventing any use or disposal of such property for the aid and comfort of insurgents, or in commerce with States or places controlled by insurgents.

I am, &c., &c., &c.,

S. P. CHASE,
Secretary of the Treasury.

MEMORANDUM.—This general circular of instructions was superseded by the more comprehensive circular of August 22, 1861.

No. 7.

Circular instructions to collectors and other officers of the customs.

TREASURY DEPARTMENT, *August* 22, 1861.

The attention of collectors and other officers of the customs is called to the act of Congress entitled "An act further to provide for the collection of duties on imports, and for other purposes," approved July 13, 1861, and the proclamation of the President of the United States of August 16, 1861, made in pursuance thereof, both of which are annexed.

In view, therefore, of the act aforesaid, and the proclamation of the President of the United States, made in pursuance thereof, I hereby direct and instruct the officers of the customs to use all vigilance in preventing commercial intercourse with the inhabitants of States in insurrection, except in the special cases in which it may be allowed by license and permit as therein set forth. The instructions of May 2 and June 12, 1861, heretofore in force, will be regarded as superseded by the more comprehensive provisions of the act and proclamation. The collectors and other officers of the customs will report all seizures made under the proclamation to the proper district attorney, for such proceedings as the law and facts may justify in each case; and they will also, as soon as practicable, and as frequently afterward as may be convenient, report their views in relation to the commercial intercourse contemplated, and the permits proper to be granted or withheld.

In the forms accompanying the weekly returns required by circular of the 5th August, 1861, to be made to this department, collectors and other officers of the customs will be careful to state what permits are asked for the shipment of goods, by whom asked, and the grounds on which the applications are based.

The attention of the collectors and other officers is especially directed to fifth and subsequent sections of the act.

S. P. CHASE, *Secretary of the Treasury.*

By the President of the United States of America.

A Proclamation.

Whereas, on the 15th day of April, 1861, the President of the United States, in view of an insurrection against the laws, Constitution, and government of the United States, which had broken out within the States of South Carolina, Georgia, Alabama, Florida, Mississippi, Louisiana, and Texas, and in pursuance of the provisions of the act entitled "An act to provide for calling forth the militia to execute the laws of the Union, suppress insurrections, and repel invasions, and to repeal the act now in force for that purpose," approved February 28, 1795, did call forth the militia to suppress said insurrection and to cause the laws of the Union to be duly executed, and the insurgents have failed to disperse by the time directed by the President; and whereas such insurrection has since broken out and yet exists within the States of Virginia, North Carolina, Tennessee, and Arkansas; and whereas the insurgents in all the said States claim to act under the authority thereof, and such claim is not disclaimed or repudiated by the persons exercising the functions of government in such State or States, or in the part or parts thereof in which such combinations exist, nor has such insurrection been suppressed by said States:

Now, therefore, I, Abraham Lincoln, President of the United States, in pursuance of an act of Congress approved July 13, 1861, do hereby declare that the inhabitants of the said States of Georgia, South Carolina, Virginia, North Carolina, Tennessee, Alabama, Louisiana, Texas, Arkansas, Mississippi, and Florida, (except the inhabitants of that part of the State of Virginia lying west of the Alleghany mountains, and of such other parts of that State and the other States hereinbefore named as may maintain a loyal adhesion to the Union and the Constitution, or may be, from time to time, occupied and controlled by forces of the United States engaged in the dispersion of said insurgents,) are in a state of insurrection against the United States; and that all commercial intercourse between the same and the inhabitants thereof, with the exceptions aforesaid, and the citizens of other States and other parts of the United States, is unlawful, and will remain unlawful until such insurrection shall cease or has been suppressed; that all goods and chattels, wares and merchandise, coming from any of said States, with the exception aforesaid, into other parts of the United States, without the special license and permission of the President, through the Secretary of the Treasury, or proceeding to any of said States, with the exceptions aforesaid, by land or water, together with the vessel or vehicle conveying the same, or conveying persons to or from said States, with said exceptions, will be forfeited to the United States; and that from and after fifteen days from the issuing of this proclamation, all ships and vessels belonging in whole or in part to any citizen or inhabitant of any of said States, with said exceptions, found at sea or in any port of the United States, will be forfeited to the United States. And I hereby enjoin upon all district attorneys, marshals, and officers of the revenue and of the military and naval forces of the United States, to be vigilant in the execution of said act, and in the enforcement of the penalties and forfeitures imposed or declared by it; leaving any party who may think himself aggrieved thereby to his application to the Secretary of the Treasury for the remission of any penalty or forfeiture, which the said Secretary is authorized by law to grant, if, in his judgment, the special circumstances of any case shall require such remission.

In witness whereof, I have hereunto set my hand and caused the seal of [L. S.] the United States to be affixed. Done at the city of Washington, this 16th day of August, in the year of our Lord one thousand eight hundred and sixty-one, and of the independence of the United States of America the eighty-sixth.

ABRAHAM LINCOLN.

By the President:

WILLIAM H. SEWARD, *Secretary of State.*

An act further to provide for the collection of duties on imports, and for other purposes.

Be it enacted by the Senate and House of Representatives of the United States of America in Congress assembled, That whenever it shall, in the judgment of the President, by reason of unlawful combinations of persons in opposition to the laws of the United States, become impracticable to execute the revenue laws and collect the duties on imports by the ordinary means, in the ordinary way, at any port of entry in any collection district, he is authorized to cause such duties to be collected at any port of delivery in said district until such obstruction shall cease; and in such case the surveyors at said ports of delivery shall be clothed with all the powers and be subject to all the obligations of collectors at ports of entry; and the Secretary of the Treasury, with the approbation of the President, shall appoint such number of weighers, gaugers, measurers, inspectors, appraisers, and clerks as may be necessary, in his judgment, for the faithful execution of the revenue laws at said ports of delivery, and shall fix and establish the limits within which such ports of delivery are constituted ports of entry as aforesaid. And all the provisions of law regulating the issue of marine papers, the coasting trade, the warehousing of imports, and collection of duties shall apply to the ports of entry so constituted in the same manner as they do to ports of entry established by the laws now in force.

SEC. 2. *And be it further enacted,* That if, from the cause mentioned in the foregoing section, in the judgment of the President, the revenue from duties on imports cannot be effectually collected at any port of entry in any collection district, in the ordinary way and by the ordinary means, or by the course provided in the foregoing section, then and in that case he may direct that the custom-house for the district be established in any secure place within said district, either on land or on board any vessel in said district or at sea near the coast; and in such case the collector shall reside at such place, or on shipboard, as the case may be, and there detain all vessels and cargoes arriving within or approaching said district, until the duties imposed by law on said vessels and their cargoes are paid in cash: *Provided,* That if the owner or consignee of the cargo on board any vessel detained as aforesaid, or the master of said vessel, shall desire to enter a port of entry in any other district in the United States where no such obstructions to the execution of the laws exist, the master of such vessel may be permitted so to change the destination of the vessel and cargo in his manifest, whereupon the collector shall deliver him a written permit to proceed to the port so designated: *And provided further,* That the Secretary of the Treasury shall, with the approbation of the President, make proper regulations for the enforcement on shipboard of such provisions of the laws regulating the assessment and collection of duties as, in his judgment, may be necessary and practicable.

SEC. 3. *And be it further enacted,* That it shall be unlawful to take any vessel or cargo detained as aforesaid from the custody of the proper officers of the customs, unless by process of some court of the United States; and in case of any attempt otherwise to take such vessel or cargo by any force, or combination, or assemblage of persons, too great to be overcome by the officers of the customs, it shall and may be lawful for the President, or such person or persons as he shall have empowered for that purpose, to employ such part of the army and navy or militia of the United States, or such force of citizen volunteers as may be deemed necessary, for the purpose of preventing the removal of such vessel or cargo, and protecting the officers of the customs in retaining the custody thereof.

SEC. 4. *And be it further enacted,* That if, in the judgment of the President, from the cause mentioned in the first section of this act, the duties upon imports in any collection district cannot be effectually collected by the ordinary means and in the ordinary way, or in the mode and manner provided in the foregoing sections of this act, then and in that case the President is hereby empowered to close the port or ports of entry in said district, and in such case give notice thereof by proclamation; and thereupon all right of importation, warehousing, and other privileges incident to ports of entry shall cease and be discontinued at such port so closed until opened by order of the President on the cessation of such obstructions. And if, while said ports are so closed, any ship or vessel from beyond the United States, or having on board any articles subject to duties, shall enter or attempt to enter any such port, the same, together with its tackle, apparel, furniture, and cargo, shall be forfeited to the United States.

SEC. 5. *And be it further enacted,* That whenever the President, in pursuance of the provisions of the second section of the act entitled "An act to provide for calling forth the militia to execute the laws of the Union, suppress insurrections, and repel invasions, and to repeal the act now in force for that purpose," approved February 28, 1795, shall have called forth the militia to suppress combinations against the laws of the United States, and to cause the laws to be duly executed, and the insurgents shall have failed to disperse by the time directed by the President, and when said insurgents claim to act under the authority of any State or States, and such claim is not disclaimed or repudiated by the persons exercising the functions of government in such State or States, or in the part or parts thereof in which said combination exists, nor such insurrection suppressed by said State or States, then and in such case it may and shall be lawful for the President, by proclamation, to declare that the inhabitants of such State, or any section or part thereof, where such insurrection exists, are in a state of insurrection against the United States; and thereupon all commercial intercourse by and between the same and the citizens thereof and the citizens of the rest of the United States, shall cease and be unlawful so long as such condition of hostility shall continue. And all goods and chattels, wares and merchandise, coming from said State or section into the other parts of the United States, and all proceeding to such State or section, by land or water, shall, together with the vessel or vehicle conveying the same, or conveying persons to or from such State or section, be forfeited to the United States: *Provided, however,* That the President may, in his discretion, license and permit commercial intercourse with any such part of said State or section, the inhabitants which are so declared in a state of insurrection, in such articles, and for such time, and by such persons, as he, in his discretion, may think most conducive to the public interest; and such intercourse, so far as by him licensed, shall be conducted and carried on only in pursuance of rules and regulations prescribed by the Secretary of the Treasury. And the Secretary of the Treasury may appoint such officers, at places where officers of the customs are not now authorized by law, as may be needed to carry into effect such licenses, rules, and regulations; and officers of the customs and other officers shall receive for services under this section, and under said rules and regulations, such fees and compensation as are now allowed for similar service under other provisions of law.

SEC. 6. *And be it further enacted,* That from and after fifteen days after the issuing of the said proclamation, as provided in the last foregoing section of this act, any ship or vessel belonging in whole or in part to any citizen or inhabitant of said State or part of a State whose inhabitants are so declared in a state of insurrection, found at sea, or in any port of the rest of the United States, shall be forfeited to the United States.

SEC. 7. *And be it further enacted,* That in the execution of the provisions of this act, and of the other laws of the United States providing for the collection of duties on imports and tonnage, it may and shall be lawful for the President, in addition to the revenue cutters in service, to employ in aid thereof such other suitable vessels as may, in his judgment, be required.

SEC. 8. *And be it further enacted,* That the forfeitures and penalties incurred by virtue of this act may be mitigated or remitted, in pursuance of the authority vested in the Secretary of the Treasury by the act entitled "An act providing for mitigating or remitting the forfeitures, penalties, and disabilities accruing in certain cases therein mentioned," approved March third, seventeen hundred and ninety-seven, or in cases where special circumstances may seem to require it, according to regulations to be prescribed by the Secretary of the Treasury.

SEC. 9. *And be it further enacted,* That proceedings on seizures for forfeitures under this act may be pursued in the courts of the United States in any district into which the property so seized may be taken and proceedings instituted; and such courts shall have and entertain as full jurisdiction over the same as if the seizure was made in that district.

Approved July 13, 1861.

No. 8.

Circular to surveyors of the customs of western ports, restricting trade with Paducah.

TREASURY DEPARTMENT, *August* 31, 1861.

SIR: The following telegram was sent to you on the 26th instant:

"Permit no goods destined to Paducah to pass your port."

You are to be strictly governed by it.

I am, &c.,

S. P. CHASE,
Secretary of the Treasury.

TO SURVEYORS OF CUSTOMS at Cairo, Ills.; Evansville, Ind.; Louisville, Ky.

No. 9.

(All communication with insurgent districts, without special permit, is in violation of law.)

Treasury Department, *September* 3, 1861.

Sir: Instances of communication, by land and water, with the States controlled by the insurrectionists, are still frequently brought to the knowledge of this department.

It is to be distinctly understood that all communication, whether for commercial or other purposes, without special permit, is, and since the date of the President's proclamation of the 16th ultimo has been, in violation of law; but it is also to be understood that no permit of any collector, or other officer connected with this department, is of any validity as a sanction to such intercourse, except as expressly authorized by the license or permission of the President of the United States, through the Secretary of the Treasury.

All goods and chattels, wares and merchandise, going to or coming from a State under insurrectionary control, and every vessel or vehicle conveying property or persons, to or from such States, is forfeited to the United States, and must be seized and proceeded against as so forfeited.

Any circumstances requiring or justifying the mitigation or remission of any such forfeiture will be duly considered, on application to the Secretary of the Treasury, in whom, by act of Congress, the sole power of such mitigation or remission is vested.

I have the honor to be, with great respect, your obedient servant,

S. P. CHASE,
Secretary of the Treasury.

No. 10.

Trade in Kentucky, south of Louisville, restricted.

Treasury Department, *September* 10, 1861.

Sir: Information having been received that prohibited goods, arrested by inspectors in southern parts of Kentucky and reshipped for Louisville, are forcibly taken from the cars at Elizabethtown and transported by wagons into Tennessee, you are hereby instructed to give no permits for provisions or supplies to any point in Southern Kentucky where the execution of the law is thus obstructed, and none whatever for any description of goods or property where the quality, description, or other circumstances indicate an intention to take them to Tennessee or other State in insurrection.

I am, &c.,

S. P. CHASE,
Secretary of the Treasury.

C. B. Cotton, Esq.,
Surveyor, Louisville, Kentucky.

No. 11.

Instructions to special agents concerning restrictions on trade in Kentucky west of the Cumberland river.

TREASURY DEPARTMENT, *September* 10, 1861.

SIR: Reliable information having been received that the section of the State of Kentucky lying west of the Cumberland river is so far under insurrectionary influence that the laws of the United States and the orders of the government cannot be executed therein by the civil authorities:

Now, therefore, in pursuance of law, and of the proclamation of the President of August 16, 1861, you are hereby instructed to prevent, as far as possible, and so long as such insurrectionary condition shall continue, all commercial intercourse between the citizens of said section and of the States named in the said proclamation and citizens of other States and parts of States, except in cases of special permission, under such rules and regulations as may be established by this department; and you will use your utmost vigilance to prevent all goods and chattels, wares and merchandise, as well as arms, munitions of war, and other supplies, from being sent to *said section*, or to any of the States named in the said proclamation, no matter in what part of your district the same may be found or what may be the nominal destination thereof, except under special permission, as above stated.

In case of seizure under circumstances rendering the property liable to forfeiture, you will at once report the same to the district attorney of the United States, for his advice and action thereon.

In case of arrest and detention of goods, &c., the transmission of which is attended by circumstances rendering it probable that the ultimate destination thereof is for places under insurrectionary control, but not amounting to evidence of forfeiture, you will at once notify the owner or shipper of the detention, and allow him to dispose of the same as he may desire, upon satisfactory assurance from him that the goods, &c., shall not be sent to any of the places hereinbefore prohibited.

To obviate inconvenience and unnecessary trouble to loyal shippers and owners, the permits of any collector or surveyor of customs covering merchandise should be respected by every other officer, unless he may have information concerning the same not probably possessed by the officer granting the permit.

You will also cause careful examination to be made of all trunks, packages, and other articles used in the transportation of merchandise, letters, or other modes for conveying goods or communicating information to persons in insurrection; and in cases of detection, you will take possession thereof; and you will also retain the *person* so offending in custody; at once reporting the case to the district attorney of the United States.

You are referred to the acts of July 13, 1861, and August 6, 1861, as well as to the proclamation of the President of the 16th ultimo, as particularly bearing on the subjects above named. And you will from time to time report your proceedings to me, and suggest any additional measures which, in your opinion, may tend to subdue this rebellion.

I am, &c.,

S. P. CHASE,
Secretary of the Treasury.

WM. P. MELLEN, Esq.,
Special Agent, Cincinnati, Ohio, et al.

No. 12.

Circular to collectors and other officers of the customs, concerning unwarrantable seizures of property, &c.

Treasury Department, *September* 21, 1861.

In order to prevent seizures of property belonging to citizens of insurrectionary States not warranted by the acts of Congress relating to that subject, it is thought advisable to direct the special attention of the officers of the customs to the provisions of these acts.

The 5th section of the act of July 13 provides that all goods and chattels, wares and merchandise coming from or proceeding to a State or place declared by proclamation of the President to be in insurrection, together with the vessel or vehicle conveying the same, or conveying persons to or from such State or place, shall be forfeited to the United States.

This section obviously applies to all property in transit, or purchased or provided with a view to transit, between loyal and disloyal States, and especially to property forming the subject of commercial intercourse. Such property, wherever found, is liable to seizure, and the only redress of parties who think themselves aggrieved is by appeal to the Secretary of the Treasury, who is invested by law with full power of mitigation and remission.

The 1st section of the act approved August 6 declares "that if any person or persons, his, her, or their agent, attorney, or employé, shall purchase or acquire, sell, or give any property, of whatever kind or description, with intent to use or employ the same, or suffer the same to be used or employed, in aiding, abetting, or promoting such insurrection, * * * or any person or persons engaged therein; or if any person or persons, being the owners of any such property, shall knowingly use or employ, or consent to the use or employment, of the same, as aforesaid, all such property is hereby declared to be lawful subject of prize or capture wherever found."

No doubt can be entertained that this section was well considered, and that its operation was intended to be limited to property used in furtherance of the insurrection only.

Seizures under the act of July 13 should be made by the officers, or under the direction of officers, of the Treasury Department; and all district attorneys and marshals of the United States should afford all practicable counsel and aid in the execution of the law.

Seizures under the act of August 6 should be made by the marshal of the district in which such property may be found, under the general or particular direction of the district attorney or other superior authority. For such seizures there is no power of mitigation or remission in the Secretary of the Treasury; but the district attorney or other superior authority may direct the discontinuance of any proceeding in relation thereto, and the restoration of the property seized.

It will be seen from an inspection of these provisions of the acts of Congress that no property is confiscated or subjected to forfeiture except such as is in transit, or provided for transit, to or from insurrectionary States, or used for the promotion of the insurrection. The only exception to this rule of forfeiture is that, made by the 5th section, of ships belonging, in whole or in part, to citizens of a State in insurrection, which are declared to be forfeited after fifteen days from the date of proclamation, without reference to actual or intended use. Real estate, bonds, promissory notes, moneys in deposit, and the like, are, therefore, not subject to seizure or confiscation in the absence of evidence of such unlawful use. All officers, while vigilant in the prevention of the conveyance of property to or from insurrectionary States, or the use of it for insurrectionary purposes, are expected to be careful in avoiding unnecessary vexation and cost by seizures not warranted by law.

S. P. CHASE, *Secretary of the Treasury.*

No. 13.

Permits for sutlers at Cairo.

TREASURY DEPARTMENT, *October* 2, 1861.

SIR: I have received your letter of the 24th ultimo, informing me that, at the request of Generals Grant and McClernand, you have granted permits for sutlers' goods, upon the production of certificates from the proper officers showing the parties to be duly appointed, and upon their taking an oath, filed at your office, not to vend any of such goods except to those belonging to the United States army.

Your course is approved, and you will continue to exercise the most vigilant care to prevent any evasion of the law.

* * * * * * * * *

I am, &c.,

S. P. CHASE, *Secretary of the Treasury.*

D. ARTER, Esq., *Collector, Cairo, Illinois.*

No. 14.

Mitigation of restrictions on trade with Paducah.

TREASURY DEPARTMENT, *October* 2, 1861.

SIR: You are hereby authorized to allow the transit of small lots of goods to loyal citizens of the United States in Paducah, Kentucky, provided the consent of the military commandant at that place be previously obtained.

A telegram to this effect was sent in reply to your despatch of yesterday.

I am, &c.,

S. P. CHASE, *Secretary of the Treasury.*

A. L. ROBINSON, Esq.,
Surveyor, &c., Evansville, Indiana.

No. 15.

Authorizing shipment of products from Kentucky west of the Cumberland.

TREASURY DEPARTMENT, *October* 3, 1861.

SIR: * * * * * * * *

There is no objection to the shipment of tobacco or any other article from that region west of the Cumberland to loyal States, and you will be expected to exercise a sound discretion in permitting or preventing shipments thither.

It is not possible to determine all cases arising from the circumstances of a country *partially* in military occupation by our troops by a general rule.

Yours, &c.,

S. P. CHASE, *Secretary of the Treasury.*

WILLIAM P. MELLEN, Esq.,
Special Agent, Cincinnati, Ohio.

No. 16.

Regulations of trade with Paducah.

PADUCAH, *Kentucky, November* 5, 1861.

SIR: General Smith has assumed entire control as to what may pass out of his lines here, either for family use or purposes of trade in the neighborhood. * * * * * * * *

He has agreed that if the applicant will bring to him a bill of items of the articles he wants, not exceeding twenty-five dollars in value for family use, or seventy-five dollars for purposes of trade, with the certificate of one of the committee indorsed that it is proper to allow it to go, he will allow it to pass out. I hope to find, on my next visit here, that this arrangement has given general satisfaction. The *Jews* here are making a good deal of *fuss*, because the committee will not indorse them more freely for permits, under which they can continue their troublesome practices. * * *

If you purpose permitting exchanges of western staple products and unobjectionable merchandise for Tennessee cotton, tobacco, and turpentine, value for value, this place may be one good point for exchange. I think the permitting of such exchanges would be exceedingly advantageous to our side, provided the cotton, tobacco, and turpentine are *first delivered here*, and then the articles allowed to be given in exchange restricted, so as not to give them munitions of war, leather, men's shoes or boots, woollen blankets, and perhaps woollen goods generally, salt, lard oil, harness, and saddlery.

The reasons for permitting such exchanges, and particularly its effects in Tennessee, will readily occur to your mind. I am often questioned on the subject, and will be glad to have an expression of your views and intentions at your early convenience, that I may indicate them to persons inquiring.

* * * * * * * * * *

Respectfully, yours, &c.,

WM. P. MELLEN, *Special Agent.*

Hon. S. P. CHASE, *Secretary of the Treasury.*

Approval of foregoing arrangement and instructions of the Secretary of the Treasury.

TREASURY DEPARTMENT, *November* 12, 1861.

SIR: * * * Your arrangement with General Smith in relation to permits is satisfactory.

* * * * * * * * * *

You are authorized to allow exchanges to be made at Paducah, of western staple products and unobjectionable merchandise for Tennessee cotton, tobacco, and turpentine, value for value; provided the cotton, tobacco, and turpentine are first delivered at Paducah, and that no munitions of war, leather, boots or shoes, woollen blankets or goods, salt, lard oil, harness or saddlery, be allowed to be given in exchange.

The transactions under this permission must be guarded with the utmost vigilance, and every precaution taken to prevent any undue advantage being taken thereof.

* * * * * * * * * *

I am, &c.,

S. P. CHASE, *Secretary of the Treasury.*

WM. P. MELLEN, Esq., *Special Agent.*

No. 17.

Circular to collectors and other officers of the customs.

TREASURY DEPARTMENT, *November* 12, 1861.

The following regulations will be observed in regard to seizures of vessels made in pursuance of the 6th section of the act of July 13, 1861:

First. All such seizures must be made by the collector of customs, or other proper revenue officer, except in case of his absence or disability, or where immediate action is necessary, and no such officer is at hand to make the seizures.

Second. In all cases of seizure, the collector, or other officer acting in his stead, shall notify the proper district attorney, who will at once institute proceedings for the condemnation of the vessel. After the commencement of such proceedings, if it shall appear to the satisfaction of the district attorney instituting them that the vessel is owned in part by persons not citizens of any State or part of a State in insurrection against the United States, and not residing therein, and that she will not be employed in aiding the existing rebellion, or in violating any law of the United States, such vessel may be discharged on bail being given, according to the course of admiralty proceedings, for the share or shares owned by any person or persons residing in any such insurgent State or part of State; in which case the proceedings so instituted will be prosecuted, without delay, to condemnation and sale of such insurgent interest, and as to the remainder of the vessel, the forfeiture thereof will be remitted.

Third. Should there be any unusual delay in the commencement of such proceedings, or should there be any other circumstances rendering it proper, in the judgment of the collector, or other officer acting in his stead, that the vessel should be released from custody before the commencement of proceedings, the same may be done; provided the collector, or other officer acting in his stead, shall be satisfied that no such improper use, as before mentioned, is to be made of said vessel. And one or more of the owners residing in loyal States shall give a bond, with sufficient sureties, to the United States, in double the value of the share or shares thereof owned in any such insurgent State or part of a State, with the condition that the vessel shall be safely, and in good order, returned to the collector or other officer in whose custody she may be, within such time as he shall direct, and without any change in the ownership of said share or shares; and with the further condition that the vessel shall at all times be subject to any order or decree of the court in which any proceedings for her condemnation may be instituted, or of any appellate court to which the same may be removed; and with the further condition that any costs or other moneys which shall be awarded by either of said courts, in said proceedings, shall be paid; together with such other conditions as the collector or other officer shall deem just and expedient, in order to secure the objects contemplated by the act aforesaid. The execution of such bond and the discharge of the vessel shall not delay the institution or prosecution of proceedings for the condemnation of the insurgent interest, but the same shall be commenced and prosecuted, in all respects, so far as practicable, in the same manner as if the vessel still remained in the custody of the officer.

The district attorney will notify the collector, or other officer making the seizure in his stead, of the commencement of proceedings for the condemnation of the vessel, of the time of trial of the suit, of the result of the trial, and of the time of sale, (if a sale be ordered,) and the result thereof.

S. P. CHASE, *Secretary of the Treasury.*

No. 18.

Authority to trade with blockading squadron.

TREASURY DEPARTMENT, *November* 14, 1861.

SIR: Your letter of the 17th ultimo, transmitting an application from Messrs. Sprague, Soule & Co. and others, merchants of Boston, under date of the 15th ultimo, requesting permission to transmit a vessel to the blockading squadron with supplies, is received. I see no objection to allowing such a legitimate trade as is proposed, and you are hereby authorized to give clearances to vessels despatched by the parties referred to, requesting them to use steamers and to give bonds in double the value of the cargo, with sureties, to your satisfaction, that they will communicate only with the blockading vessels of the United States, touching at every port in our possession in the insurrectionary States. They will also submit a list of officers of said vessels to this department for approval.

I am, &c.,

S. P. CHASE,
Secretary of the Treasury.

J. Z. GOODRICH, Esq.,
Collector, Boston, Massachusetts.

No. 19.

Restrictions on trade in pork with Louisville.

LOUISVILLE, *Kentucky, November* 25, 1861.

SIR: * * * * * * * *

I have advised Surveyor Anthony, of New Albany, to grant permits for the shipment to this city of all hogs offered; but to require, as a condition precedent to granting the permit, that the party into whose possession they are to come *here* make an affidavit that neither the hogs nor the product thereof shall leave the city, by his knowledge or consent, without the permission of the surveyor; and also that he will support the Constitution of the United States. On the affidavit is to be indorsed the bond of the buyer here, without surety, to only dispose of the hogs and product in pursuance of the asseverations of the affidavit.

I am, &c.,

WM. P. MELLEN, *Special Agent.*

Hon. S. P. CHASE, *Secretary of the Treasury.*

This restriction was approved by the Secretary of the Treasury by letter to Mr. Mellen dated November 30, 1861; modified December 13, 1861.

No. 20.

General regulations relative to securing and disposing of the property found or brought within the territory now or hereafter occupied by the United States forces in the disloyal States.

TREASURY DEPARTMENT, *November* 30, 1861.

In order to the security and proper disposition of the productions of the soil and of all other property found within the limits of States or parts of

States declared to be in insurrection against the United States, and now occupied or to be hereafter occupied by the troops and authorities of the Union, the following regulations are established :

There shall be appointed by the Secretary of the Treasury, with the approbation of the President, agents to reside at such ports or places as are or may be occupied by the forces of the United States, whose duties shall be to secure and prepare for market the cotton and such other products and property as may be found or brought within the lines of the army or under the control of the federal authorities.

To enable such agents to fulfil the duties devolved upon them, the military and naval authorities, under proper instructions, will render such military protection and aid as may be required to carry out the intentions of this department.

All persons held to service for life under State laws, who may be found within such limits, may be employed by the agent, who will prepare lists embracing the names, sex, and condition of such persons, and, as near as may be, their respective ages, together with the name of any person claiming their services, which lists shall be in triplicate—one for the military commandant, one for the files of the agent, and one to be immediately forwarded to the Secretary of the Treasury.

The persons so listed will be organized for systematic labor in securing and preparing for market the cotton, rice, and other products found within the territory brought under federal control. Pay-rolls will be prepared, and a strict account of the labor daily performed by each person entered thereon, for which a proper compensation shall be allowed and paid to the laborers. The amount of such compensation will be fixed, in proportion to the service rendered, by the agent and approved by the military commandant and by the Secretary of the Treasury.

An inventory of all horses, mules, and other stock, vehicles of transportation, and other property, will be carefully made, and a copy transmitted to the Secretary of the Treasury, signed by such agent.

A record of all products taken possession of will be made, and those of each plantation kept distinct. When prepared for shipment, the packages from the several plantations will be plainly marked and numbered, so as to be easily distinguished.

An account of all provisions of whatsoever character found on each plantation will be taken, and such provisions will be used, so far as may be necessary, for the sustenance of the laborers thereon. Any deficiencies of subsistence will be supplied by the United States commissary, upon the requisition of the agent, to whom they will be charged, and for which he will account.

The cotton and other articles, when prepared for market, shall be shipped to New York, and, so far as practicable, by the returning government transports; and all shipments shall be consigned to the designated agent at New York, unless otherwise specially directed by the Secretary of the Treasury.

A carefully detailed account will be kept by the agent of all supplies furnished by the government and of all expenditures made.

Each agent will transmit a weekly report of his proceedings to the Secretary of the Treasury, and render his accounts in duplicate monthly for settlement.

All requisitions, bills of lading, and invoices will be countersigned by the military commander, or by such officer as he may designate for the purpose.

Each agent will so transact his business and keep his accounts that as little injury as possible may accrue to private citizens who now maintain or may within reasonable time resume the character of loyal citizens of the United States.

S. P. CHASE, *Secretary of the Treasury.*

No. 21.

Treasury Department, *November* 30, 1861.

Sir: With the approbation of the President of the United States, and by virtue of the authority vested in the Secretary of the Treasury by the act of July 13, 1861, I hereby appoint you a special agent to proceed to ——— to receive and take charge of all cotton, rice, or other products of the soil, and of all other property found or brought within the territory now or hereafter occupied by the United States forces in the State of ———.

For the purposes of this appointment, and to carry out the views of the government, the chief military and naval commandants at ——— will receive the necessary instructions from the Secretary of War and the Secretary of the Navy to afford you proper military protection, and to detail such aid as may be requisite in the fulfilment of these instructions, not incompatible with their military duties.

You will, on your arrival, forthwith make lists of all persons held to service for life within the military lines, or who may from time to time claim the protection of our forces, noting their names and sex, and as near as may be their respective ages, and the names of the persons to whom their services are alleged to have been due.

You will organize the persons thus listed, as may be found most convenient, for work in picking cotton, conveying it to the gin-houses, ginning, baling, and otherwise preparing it for market. If any rice plantations fall within your supervision you will take the necessary steps to gather into the storehouses all unhoused crops, and, if the proper machinery is at hand, have the rice hulled and prepared for market. If machinery and conveniences for preparing either product for market are not accessible, you will take proper measures to have it shipped in its rough state to New York. The length and character of the voyage would seem to require the shipment of rice in bags rather than in bulk.

You will also take an account of all other produce, whether native or foreign, and ship to New York such as is not perishable and not wanted for the troops. Whatever may be required for the troops you will deliver to the officer authorized to receive it, taking therefor his receipt, setting forth the quantity, character, and estimated value of the article so delivered.

You will cause complete pay-rolls to be prepared, on which you will enter the names of all the persons employed under your direction, and you will determine the compensation proper to be allowed, if approved by the commanding officer, and inform the laborers that the sum allowed will be paid to them as compensation for their own use and support.

It is presumed that the provisions upon the respective plantations, of which you will make an inventory, (as also of all stock, plantation tools, vehicles of transportation, horses, mules, &c.,) will be sufficient for the sustenance of the laborers and employés. For any deficiency you will make your requisitions at stated periods upon the government commissary, keeping a distinct account thereof, and charging, so far as practicable, to the product of each plantation whatever expenditure is incurred in securing, preparing, and shipping such product to market.

When such product is ready for shipment you will affix such shipping marks as may be necessary for identification, adopting the same mark for the whole production of a plantation, and varying the marks to accord with the various plantations or reputed owners.

Shipments must be made as rapidly as the cotton or other articles can be prepared and means of transportation afforded; and you will give such advices of each shipment to the agent in New York as will enable him to keep his accounts of advances and sales, with each mark or with each plantation, distinct from the others. You will be supplied from time to time with the necessary bagging and bale-rope for the cotton and bags for other shipments upon your requisition on the agent in New York. All such bags, bagging, rope, or other articles required, you will be careful to count, measure, or weigh, when received, and charge to each shipment the quantity delivered and used for the products shipped.

For all shipments you will make out invoices and bills of lading, in triplicate, forwarding one of each to the consignee, one to the Secretary of the Treasury, and retain one subject to the disposition of the military commandant of the port. All requisitions, bills of lading, and invoices must be countersigned by the commandant-in-chief, or such officer as he may detail for the purpose.

In order to economize freights, you will give preference in shipments to returning transports.

It is presumed that all clerical force required can be furnished by the military commandant, by detailing persons competent to perform such service, and you will procure, so far as the military commandant shall not be able to supply you, necessary stationery, blank books, &c.

You will keep a record of all your proceedings, and report to this department weekly, as much in detail as practicable, and will send duplicates of your requisitions to the Secretary of the Treasury.

With these general instructions, I confide in your activity, integrity, and practical knowledge of the duties assigned to you to carry out the views of this department with the utmost economy and vigor. Your first care should be to secure the maturing crop which being *sea-island* cotton must be picked as fast as the bolls open, otherwise it will fall and become damaged, if not entirely ruined; and in all your action you will endeavor so to transact your business and keep your accounts that no unnecessary injury may accrue to private citizens who now maintain or may within a reasonable time resume the character of loyal citizens of the United States.

With great respect,

S. P. CHASE,
Secretary of the Treasury.

No. 22.

TREASURY DEPARTMENT, *November* 30, 1861.

SIR: With the approbation of the President of the United States, and by virtue of the authority vested in the Secretary of the Treasury by the act of July 13, 1361, I hereby appoint you agent of this department to receive, on account of the United States, and to take charge of all consignments of cotton or other articles shipped to you by direction of this department. Until otherwise directed, you will be governed in the disposition of such cotton or other articles by these general instructions. You will keep an accurate account, by names and numbers, and such other distinctive marks as may be forwarded to you by the respective agents and shippers, of each consignment received, debiting such consignment with whatever expenses may be paid by you on its account, whether of freight, labor, storage, or commissions, and credit such consignment with the gross proceeds of sales when realized, and so keep your accounts that the net receipts arising from each shipment may be at once known, and thereby the aggregate net receipts arising from the products of each plantation and owner be distinctly set forth.

You are hereby authorized and directed to sell the cotton or other productions received by you at public auction, after due notice of time and place being given in two newspapers in Boston, three in New York, and two in Philadelphia, at least ten days prior to the sale, unless, from the perishable nature of the article, it is deemed expedient to dispose of it immediately after its receipt, in which case you will pursue such course as you deem best for the interest of all concerned.

It is suggested that large lots of cotton, if from the same plantation, bring in the foreign markets enhanced prices over small or promiscuous lots, and therefore the entire crop of a plantation should, in the absence of reasons to the contrary, be so offered.

You are expected to procure, upon the most economical terms, and forward to the respective agents, upon their requisitions, proper bags, bagging, bale-rope, twine, needles, or other articles required for the preparation of the cotton, rice, or other productions for market, and also blank bills of lading, blank books, and other stationery in reasonable and proper quantities for their use; and you will advise them from time to time of any deficiencies in making up the bales or other packages, or in their marks and numbers, or in the invoices sent, and offer such suggestions as, in your opinion, will tend to increase the market value of the articles to be forwarded, and give effect to the wishes and intentions of the government.

You will make a special deposit with the assistant treasurer at New York, to the credit of the Treasurer of the United States, of the gross proceeds of all sales, taking duplicate receipts therefor, which you will retain as your voucher for such payment. Your accounts must be rendered monthly, in duplicate, and transmitted to the Secretary of the Treasury.

You will report weekly your general transactions under this appointment, specifying any receipts or sales of articles, and the receipt and filling of any requisitions made upon you by the agents of the department.

A copy of the instructions to the agents is enclosed for your further information.

Before entering on the duties of your office, you will execute an official bond to the United States in the sum of $50,000, agreeably to the form accompanying these instructions, and take the oath of office and allegiance prescribed therein, following the directions as to the execution of the bond and other requisite acts noted at the foot of the form.

You will be allowed a compensation at the rate of twenty-five hundred dollars per annum.

Respectfully, yours,

S. P. CHASE,
Secretary of the Treasury.

No. 23.

Modification of the restrictions on trade in pork with Louisville, Kentucky, of November 25, 1861.

TREASURY DEPARTMENT, *December* 13, 1861.

SIR: In addition, (as to shipments of pork, to which your attention was called in my letter of the 30th ultimo,) it must be borne in mind that Louisville is a loyal city; and, unless you are satisfied that the supplies are intended for disloyal parties in that part of Kentucky held by the insurgents, or under insurrectionary control, or destined for States in rebellion against the government of the United States, or to give aid and comfort to the rebels, you will protect the merchants and traders of that city in their operations, and allow them the same facilities for the transaction of business as are enjoyed in other loyal cities.

I am, &c.,

S. P. CHASE, *Secretary of the Treasury.*

WM. P. MELLEN, Esq., *Special Agent, Cincinnati, Ohio.*

No. 24.

Rules required to be observed by steamboats navigating the Ohio river.

1. No boat shall receive on board any freight, baggage, or parcel, unless the same is accompanied with a permit of a duly authorized officer of the Treasury Department.

2. No boat shall put off or discharge any freight, baggage, or parcel, at any place different from that named in the permit as its place of destination.

3. All army supplies, shipped under military orders, are excepted from the above rules; but this exception does not extend to goods of sutlers, or others, designed for trade or sale at military posts.

4. No boat, running below Louisville, having taken freight on board at any point where there is a surveyor of customs, shall depart from such port before exhibiting a true manifest of its entire cargo to such surveyor, and obtaining from him written permission to proceed on the voyage; and, on arriving at the port ending the trip, such manifest shall be delivered to the surveyor thereof before discharging any part of its freight. In case there is no surveyor there, then such manifest shall be delivered to the surveyor of the last port passed on the trip where there is such an officer.

5. To prevent inconvenience to shippers at way points, and to enable boats to take all proper freights, baggage, and parcels, at such points, without violating the above rules, an "aid to the revenue" will be placed on all the boats desiring it, authorized to grant permits for the shipment of all such way-freights, baggage, and parcels, provided the boat will carry and accommodate such aid free of charge.

6. A fee of twenty cents, for the permit, will be charged on each shipment made for purposes of trade. But family supplies, goods of families moving, and articles sent to soldiers by their friends, shall be exempt from such charge.

7. All boats violating the above rules will be proceeded against pursuant to law, and no permits will be granted for the shipment of any freight, baggage, or parcel on board any boat having violated any of the above rules.

By order of the Treasury Department.

WILLIAM P. MELLEN,
Special Agent.

Dated January 15, 1862.

The foregoing rules were approved by the Secretary of the Treasury by letter dated January 18, 1862.

No. 25.

Rules for the steamers on the Ohio river between Pittsburg and Cincinnati.

CINCINNATI, *Ohio, January* 27, 1862.

All steamboats navigating the Ohio river, between Pittsburg and Cincinnati, are required to observe the following rules:

1. [Same as promulgated by Mr. W. P. Mellen, January 15, 1862.]
2. [Same as promulgated by Mr. W. P. Mellen, January 15, 1862.]
3. [Same as promulgated by Mr. W. P. Mellen, January 15, 1862.]
4. [Corresponds with the sixth rule of Mr. Mellen of January 15.]
5. Boats clearing for points below Cincinnati will report a manifest of their cargoes to Enoch T. Carson, esq., surveyor of that port, and be governed by his instructions.
6. Every steamboat, clearing at the port of Pittsburg, must take out, at the custom-house, a regular "clearance" for each trip, for which a charge will be made of fifty cents. To this rule there are no exceptions.
7. [Corresponds with rule of William P. Mellen, special agent, of January 15, 1862.]

THO. HEATON,
Special Agent Treasury Department.

No. 26.

Instructions in duties of special agent to Nashville, Tennessee, relative to trade in cotton and other products.

TREASURY DEPARTMENT, *February* 14, 1862.

SIR: With the approbation of the President of the United States, and by virtue of the authority vested in the Secretary of the Treasury by the act of July 13, 1861, I hereby appoint you a special agent to proceed to Tennessee, with the forces of the United States, to receive and take charge of all cotton, tobacco, and other products or property, which it may become proper to seize, as forfeited or abandoned to the United States, and to discharge all such other duties for the protection of the interests of the United States as may be assigned to you.

For the purposes of this appointment, and to carry out the views of the government, the proper military and naval commandants of the United States forces in the west will receive the necessary instructions from the Secretary of War and Secretary of the Navy to afford you proper military protection, and to detail such aid as may be requisite in the fulfilment of these instructions, not incompatible with their military duties. In the disposition of the property so seized or abandoned you will necessarily be governed, to some extent, by the character of the product or property so taken possession of, and must exercise a sound judgment and discretion in relation thereto.

Cotton taken possession of must be prepared for market in the manner usual in that locality, if the surrounding circumstances will permit with safety; if, however, you shall deem it necessary to security to make immediate shipments, you will promptly do so, and send such cotton, distinctly marked, to Hiram Barney, collector of customs at New York, forthwith, advising him of the quantity and character of such shipments. If, from any cause, such shipments cannot be made to Mr. Barney direct, you will forward it to Mr. Barney, *to the care of* Charles B. Cotton, surveyor of customs at Louisville, or Enoch T. Carson, surveyor of customs at Cincinnati, as the most direct or certain conveyance may dictate, advising both Mr. Barney and Mr. Cotton (or Mr. Carson, as the case may be,) thereof, instructing the latter to receive and forward the same to Mr. Barney, collector of customs at New York.

If, under proper authority—viz., the permits of the surveyor of the customs at Cincinnati, Louisville, or Paducah, or the permits of other surveyors, countersigned and permitted by the surveyors above named—parties present themselves to you for the purpose of purchasing cotton or other property in your possession as the property of the United States, you are authorized to sell such property at prices governed by its value in the loyal States, less the cost of transportation and other necessary charges, receiving in payment therefor only lawful money of the United States, which moneys, as well as others coming into your possession as the property of the government, you will promptly deposit, or cause to be deposited, in the designated depositary at Louisville or Cincinnati, as may be most convenient, to the credit of William P. Mellen, special agent.

It may become necessary, to the prompt security of cotton and other articles, that you should command bale-rope and bagging, and other supplies for like purposes, and you are therefore authorized to make requisitions upon the surveyors at Louisville or Cincinnati, dependent upon the latter source of supply, for such quantities as may be deemed essential, taking great care to restrict such requisitions to the smallest amounts. You will require invoices to be sent to you of quantities and values, which you will verify by examination of the articles by weight, measure, or count, when received.

No shipments from Tennessee must be allowed without your previous assent and a permit granted by you, for which permit you will exact a fee equal to one-half of one per cent. on all articles not purchased of you. For such as are sold by you you will grant the permit without charge. No permit to be granted until all dues to the United States are previously paid.

For all shipments you will make out invoices and bills of lading in triplicate, forwarding one to the consignee, one to the Secretary of the Treasury, and retain one, subject to the disposition of the military commandant of the United States forces in Kentucky.

All permits, whether granted for individuals or merchandise, and all requisitions, bills of lading, or invoices, whether coming from or going to Tennessee, must be countersigned by the commandant of the department, or such officer as he may detail for the purpose.

It is presumed that all clerical force required can be furnished by the military commandant by detailing persons competent to perform such service; and you will procure, so far as the military commandant shall not be able to supply you, necessary stationery, blank books, &c.

You will keep a record of all your proceedings, and report to this department weekly, as much in detail as practicable, and will send duplicates of your requisitions to the Secretary of the Treasury.

With these general instructions, I confide in your activity, integrity, and practical knowledge of the duties assigned to you, to carry out the views of this department with the utmost economy and vigor.

In all your action you will endeavor so to transact your business and keep your accounts that no unnecessary injury may accrue to private citizens who now maintain or may within a reasonable time resume the character of loyal citizens of the United States.

Your compensation will be five dollars ($5) per day and your necessary expenses, of which you will keep an accurate account.

Very respectfully,

S. P. CHASE,
Secretary of the Treasury.

ALLEN A. HALL, Esq., *Special Agent.*

No. 27.

Communication from the Secretary of the Treasury to the Secretary of War, requesting him to advise the generals in command of the act of Congress of July 13, 1861, *so far as it directs how commercial intercourse with the insurrectionary sections shall be regulated and controlled.*

TREASURY DEPARTMENT,
February 27, 1862.

SIR: I beg leave to call your attention to the fifth section of the act of Congress of July 13, 1861, "further to provide for the collection of duties on imports and for other purposes."

Under the act the President, on the 16th day of August, 1861, issued his proclamation declaring the inhabitants of the States of Georgia, South Carolina, Virginia, North Carolina, Tennessee, Louisiana, Alabama, Texas, Arkansas, Mississippi, and Florida, (except the inhabitants of that part of the State of Virginia lying west of the Alleghany mountains,) to be in a state of insurrection. All commercial intercourse, therefore, between the inhabitants of the insurrectionary region and the citizens of the loyal States is and must remain unlawful, until, by proclamation, the President shall declare the conditions of hostility to have ceased; and all goods and merchandise, and all vessels or vehicles conveying the same, or conveying persons to or from the insurrectionary district, are forfeited to the United States. The only exception from the law is that of intercourse permitted by the President, and conducted in pursuance of rules and regulations prescribed by the Secretary of the Treasury.

A few permits, authorizing such intercourse, have been granted, with the sanction of the President, and it is contemplated to establish regulations in accordance with which it may be carried on hereafter.

If you think it useful, will you be pleased to advise the generals commanding in the insurrectionary region of the existence of this law, and of its provisions, in order that mistakes prejudicial to private and public interests may be avoided as far as practicable.

With great respect,

S. P. CHASE, *Secretary of the Treasury.*

Hon. EDWIN M. STANTON, *Secretary of War.*

MEMORANDUM.—Rules and regulations, concerning internal intercourse, framed under act of July 13, 1861, were adopted and promulgated on the 4th of March, 1862. It came to the knowledge of the Secretary of the Treasury that orders (or permits under sanction) of the military, in some sections, militated against the regulations of the Treasury Department, another communication was accordingly sent to the Secretary of War on the 7th of March, 1862, on the above subject, *q. v.*

No. 28.

License for commercial intercourse.—By the President of the United States.

Considering that the existing circumstances of the country allow a partial restoration of commercial intercourse between the inhabitants of those parts of the United States heretofore declared to be in insurrection and the citizens of the loyal States of the Union, and exercising the authority and discretion confided to me by the act of Congress, approved July 13, 1861, entitled "An act further to provide for the collection of duties on imports, and for other purposes," I hereby license and permit such commercial intercourse, in all cases within the rules and regulations which have been or may be prescribed by the Secretary of the Treasury for the conducting and carrying on of the same on the inland waters and ways of the United States.

ABRAHAM LINCOLN.

WASHINGTON, *February* 28, 1862.

No. 29.

Rules and regulations concerning internal commercial intercourse under act of Congress, July 13, 1861.

By virtue of the authority confided to the Secretary of the Treasury by the act of Congress approved July 13, 1861, entitled "An act further to provide for the collection of duties on imports, and for other purposes," and in pursuance of the license of the President of the United States, permitting commercial intercourse in certain cases under said act, the following rules and regulations are hereby prescribed by the Secretary of the Treasury for conducting commercial intercourse between the inhabitants of those parts of the United States heretofore declared by the President to be in insurrection and the citizens of the loyal States of the Union; which rules and regulations are to remain in force so long as the condition of hostilities shall continue, unless sooner modified or revoked:

TREASURY DEPARTMENT, *March* 4, 1862.

First. All licenses shall be issued by the Secretary of the Treasury, and all applications therefor must be made in writing to him, stating specifically the purposes for which the license is desired; and if for general or special trade, setting forth the character and aggregate value of the merchandise to be transported, the destination thereof, and the proposed route of transportation, and also the character of the merchandise, if any, desired in exchange, with the proposed route of transit thereof and its destination.

Second. Before the delivery of any license the party therein permitted to trade shall execute a bond to the United States, with sufficient sureties, in the penal sum of at least twice the amount of the trade so licensed, which bond shall be subject to such approval and conditioned in such terms as shall be specified in the license.

Third. All transportation to be made by virtue of any license shall be made under permits, to be issued by such duly authorized officers of the Treasury Department as shall be designated in the license, which permits shall specify the number and kind of packages, with the marks thereon, and in general terms the character thereof.

Fourth. When application is made for a transportation permit, the applicant shall file with the officer authorized by the license to grant such permits a copy of the license under which application is made, which copy shall be compared with the original and certified by such officer, and also correct invoices in duplicate, signed by the consignor, showing the actual values of the merchandise at the place of purchase, and also a statement in duplicate of the route of transit and destination of the merchandise to be transported and the consignee thereof. The applicant shall also make and file with such officer an affidavit that the values are correctly stated in the invoices, and that the packages contain nothing except as stated therein, and that the merchandise so permitted to be transported shall not, nor shall any part thereof, be disposed of by him or by his authority or connivance in violation of the terms of the license.

Fifth. All transportation shall be permitted, and all exchanges supervised, either at Cincinnati, Louisville, Paducah, St. Louis, or such other place as may hereafter be specified by the Secretary of the Treasury. Transportation permits shall be granted by the surveyor of the port whence the transit commenced, or by other officers named in the license for that purpose, and all exchanges shall be supervised by such officer as may be designated for that purpose in the license, and the amount of such permit shall at the date of its issue be indorsed upon the original license.

Sixth. All packages whatsoever, before being permitted to go into any part of the United States heretofore declared by the President to be in insurrection, shall be examined by a duly authorized officer, which examination shall be certified and approved by such officer as shall be specified in the license.

Seventh. For each permit granted under the provisions of these rules and regulations there shall be charged and collected one-half of one per cent. upon the value of the merchandise, so permitted, at the place of purchase, which shall be collected by the officer granting the permit before delivery thereof.

Eighth. All officers acting under these rules shall keep an accurate record of all their transactions under the several licenses granted by the Secretary of the Treasury, and shall make weekly reports to him in relation thereto, as much in detail as practicable, transmitting with such reports a list of all permits granted, and one of the duplicate invoices and statements, upon which shall be indorsed the date of the authority under which such permit was granted. Weekly returns shall be made of all fees and emoluments received.

Ninth. All licenses and permits shall be liable to modification or revocation by the Secretary of the Treasury.

S. P. CHASE,
Secretary of the Treasury.

MEMORANDUM.—These rules and regulations were *modified* by the general circular of March 29.

No. 30.

Communication from the Secretary of the Treasury to the Secretary of War, concerning rules, of March 4, 1862.

TREASURY DEPARTMENT, *March* 7, 1862.

SIR: I enclose copies of rules and regulations concerning internal intercourse, framed under the act of July 13, 1861.

Great dissatisfaction exists on the Ohio river on account of the preference given to the Saint Louis trade by the orders of General Halleck. Will you be good enough to telegraph both General Halleck and General Buell that the law does not authorize commercial intercourse except upon the license of the President, under the rules and regulations established by the Secretary of the Treasury?

I should be very glad to remit this trade to the charge of military officers, and to be relieved from all duties connected with it; but the law is imperative, and until repealed, must be complied with.

* * * * * * * * * *

With great respect,

S. P. CHASE, *Secretary of the Treasury.*

Hon. E. M. STANTON, *Secretary of War.*

No. 31.

Circular to officers of the customs modifying the rules and regulations for internal commercial intercourse, of March 4, 1862.

TREASURY DEPARTMENT, *March* 29, 1862.

SIR: It is desirable to remove, as far as may properly be done, the restrictions upon commercial intercourse between the loyal States and those States and parts of States heretofore declared, by proclamation of the President, to be in insurrection, and which may resume and maintain a loyal adhesion to the Union and the Constitution, or may be occupied and controlled by the forces of the United States engaged in the dispersion of the insurgents.

The rules and regulations governing internal commerce, heretofore prescribed by the Secretary of the Treasury, are therefore hereby so far modified as to authorize the respective surveyors of the customs at the ports of Pittsburg, Wheeling, Cincinnati, Madison, Louisville, New Albany, Evansville, Paducah, Cairo, and St. Louis, to issue permits for the transportation of merchandise and for the exchange of the same for money or products of such States and parts of States, upon application being made to them respectively, if satisfied of the loyalty and good faith of the applicant, and upon the filing of an affidavit, properly executed, that the permit so applied for shall not, if granted, be used so as to give, in any way, any aid, comfort, information or encouragement to persons in insurrection against the government of the United States, or under insurrectionary control and direction.

You will hereafter cease collecting any percentage or fees for permitting the transit and exchange of merchandise between the citizens of loyal States and loyal citizens of insurrectionary sections of the country occupied or controlled by the forces of the United States, other than the usual charge of twenty cents for such permit so granted, and you will make no charge for permits for merchandise forwarded from any place in a loyal State to another in the same or other like State, nor exercise any supervision over the trade between such States, except such as may be necessary to prevent supplies of any description being furnished to insurgents.

It is furthermore directed that *no* permits be granted for any articles forbidden by the military authorities to be transported into the territory occupied by the forces of the United States. Parties, therefore, desiring licenses and permits for commercial trade, under the rules and regulations as herein modified, will hereafter make their application direct to the proper surveyor and not to the Secretary of the Treasury.

I am, &c., &c., &c.,

S. P. CHASE, *Secretary of the Treasury.*

(See regulations of August 28, 1862.)

No. 32.

Trade in Tennessee to be restricted to persons authorized by Governor Johnson.

TREASURY DEPARTMENT, *April* 4, 1862.

SIR: I this day send you the following telegram:

"Your suggestions are approved. Let permits to trade in Tennessee be restricted to persons authorized by Governor Johnson, or committees appointed by him, to receive and dispose of the goods. As he is military governor of

Tennessee, the sole authority to appoint such committees belongs, necessarily, to him, though he will probably confer with Mr. Hall."

I am, &c.,

S. P. CHASE, *Secretary of the Treasury.*

WM. P. MELLEN, Esq.,
Special Agent, Cincinnati, Ohio.

(Copy of the above sent to Governor Johnson.)

No. 33.

Rules governing shipments to or by sutlers, under the act of Congress of March 19, 1862.

1st. All surveyors, before granting permits to ship merchandise to or for sutlers, shall require the exhibition of the original certificate of appointment of such sutler, pursuant to the act of Congress of March 19, 1862, and that a copy thereof be filed with him.

2d. The date of permitting each shipment, and the value thereof, shall be indorsed on such original certificate, and a corresponding record thereof shall be kept by the surveyor granting the permit.

3d. Not more than three thousand dollars worth of goods shall be permitted to be shipped by, to, or for, any one sutler per month.

4th. The sutler or his agent shall deposit duplicate invoices of the goods to be shipped with the officer granting the permit.

5th. The invoices shall show truly the goods to be shipped, their value, and the number and description of packages containing them.

6th. The application for permission to ship shall be in writing, and shall state that nothing shall be shipped under it except as allowed by the above act of Congress; the route of transportation and the destination of the goods; that they belong in good faith to the sutler by or to whom they are to be shipped, and shall not be disposed of by him, or with his knowledge, connivance or assent, except to the officers and soldiers of his regiment, and to them only in such quantities as may be proper for their individual use or consumption; and every such application shall be sworn to.

7th. Surveyors, before granting permits, may require *bond* with *surety* in such cases as they think necessary, to prevent a violation of the law, in a penalty equal to the value of the goods permitted, and conditioned that there shall be no violation of the terms of the application and affidavit by the shipment thereof.

8th. All shipments by or for sutlers shall be subject to the same rules and regulations as shipments of other persons for purposes of trade.

WILLIAM P. MELLEN,
Special Agent Treasury Department.

Dated April 7, 1862.

These rules were approved by the Secretary of the Treasury in letters of the 30th of April and 19th May, 1862, and were adopted by the special agents throughout the western districts.

No. 34.

The question of detention and seizure of goods to be decided by the surveyor of the last port to be passed on the route of transportation.

TREASURY DEPARTMENT, *April* 22, 1862.

SIR: * * * * * * * *

You will allow all goods now detained by you, because unaccompanied by a permit, to be sent forward immediately, and you will not in future detain any articles on that account. The question of detention and seizure of goods *en route* from eastern cities to points in States heretofore declared by proclamation to be in insurrection against the government of the United States will be decided by the surveyor of the last port to be passed on the route of transportation; and you will receive the certificate to that effect of any collector or surveyor of customs as sufficient evidence of the loyalty of the shipper. You will continue to issue permits for goods shipped from Pittsburg and from eastern ports, as heretofore, when requested so to do.

I am, &c.,

S. P. CHASE, *Secretary of the Treasury.*

CHAS. W. BATCHELOR,
Surveyor, &c., Pittsburg, Pa.

No. 35.

Rules for commercial intercourse adapted to trade in the west.

The following rules were approved by the Treasury Department April 20, 1862, and were adopted and published by the special agents of the department in the western district on the 22d April, 1862:

Whereas commercial intercourse has been duly authorized between the loyal States and those States and parts of States heretofore declared to be in insurrection which may resume and maintain a loyal adhesion to the Union and Constitution of the United States or may be occupied and controlled by the forces of the United States engaged in the dispersion of the insurgents, which intercourse is to be governed by such rules and regulations as are or may be prescribed by the Secretary of the Treasury:

Now, therefore, the said intercourse and all transportation connected therewith shall be subject to the following rules and regulations:

1. All applications for permits to ship, transport, and trade shall be accompanied by the original invoices of the merchandise to be shipped, which invoices shall state the number and description of the packages containing the same, duplicates of which shall be filed with the officer granting the permit.

2. All steamboats navigating the western and southwestern rivers below Louisville are required to observe the following rules, viz: [MEMORANDUM.—The rules referred to were the seven rules adopted and published by William P. Mellen, special agent, on the 15th day of January, 1862, *q. v.*]

3. All applications for permits to ship or trade under the above-named authority shall state the character and value of the merchandise to be shipped, the consignee and destination thereof, the number and kind of packages with the marks thereon.

4. All applicants for permits to ship and trade shall make and file with the officer granting the permit an affidavit that the values of all merchandise are correctly stated in the invoices, true copies of which shall be annexed to the affidavit, and that the packages contain nothing except as stated in the invoices; that the merchandise so permitted to be transported shall not, nor shall any

part thereof, be disposed of by him or by his authority, connivance, or assent, in violation of the terms of the permit; and that neither the permit so granted, nor the merchandise shipped under it, shall be so used as in any way to give any aid, comfort, information, or encouragement to persons in insurrection against the United States; and, furthermore, that the applicant is loyal to the government of the United States, and will, in all things, so deport himself.

5. No permit shall be granted to ship merchandise to States or parts of States heretofore declared to be in insurrection except for delivery to such persons residing or doing business therein as shall be recommended therefor by an officer of the government duly authorized to make such recommendation; and no permit shall be granted for the shipment of merchandise from such States or parts of States except by persons with similar recommendation.

6. Surveyors, before granting permits, may require bond with surety in such cases as they think necessary, to prevent a violation of the law, in a penalty equal to the value of the merchandise permitted, and conditioned that there shall be no violation of the terms or spirit of the permit, nor of the asseverations of the affidavit above provided for.

7. No permit shall be granted to ship intoxicating drinks, or anything else forbidden by the military authorities, into the territory occupied by the forces of the United States or heretofore under insurrectionary control, except upon the written permission of the commandant of the department in which such territory is embraced, or of some person duly authorized by him to grant such permission. This rule does not apply to ale, beer, and Catawba wine.

8. To facilitate trade and guard against improper transportation, "aids to the revenue" shall be appointed, from time to time, on boats desiring it, and engaged in the trade of the west and southwest, which aids shall have carriage and be reasonably compensated by the respective boats upon which they are appointed, and they may grant permits for the shipment of way-freights on their boats, subject to the approval of the surveyor of the first port to be passed on the trip where there is such an officer; and no permits will be granted for transportation into States and parts of States heretofore declared to be in insurrection, except on boats carrying such aids to the revenue.

By order of the Secretary of the Treasury.

WM. D. GALLAGHER,
Special Agent Treasury Department.

ST. LOUIS, *April* 22, 1862.

MEMORANDUM.—The foregoing rules and regulations were essentially modified by the special agents on the 17th May, 1862, as per copy of rules for "trade on the Mississippi," (received from Mr. Gallagher in a letter of same date,) *q. v.*

No. 36.

PORTS OPENED TO TRADE.

By the President of the United States of America.—A proclamation.

Whereas, by my proclamation of the nineteenth day of April, one thousand eight hundred and sixty-one, it was declared that the ports of certain States, including those of Beaufort, in the State of North Carolina; Port Royal, in the State of South Carolina; and New Orleans, in the State of Louisiana, were, for reasons therein set forth, intended to be placed under blockade; and whereas the said ports of Beaufort, Port Royal, and New Orleans have since been blockaded; but as the blockade of the same ports may now be safely relaxed with advantage to the interests of commerce: Now, therefore, be it known that

I, Abraham Lincoln, President of the United States, pursuant to the authority in me vested by the fifth section of the act of Congress approved on the 13th of July last, entitled "An act further to provide for the collection of duties on imports, and for other purposes," do hereby declare that the blockade of the said ports of Beaufort, Port Royal, and New Orleans shall so far cease and determine from and after the 1st day of June next that commercial intercourse with those ports, except as to persons and things and information contraband of war, may from that time be carried on, subject to the laws of the United States and to the limitations, and in pursuance of the regulations which are prescribed by the Secretary of the Treasury in his order of this date, which is appended to this proclamation.

In witness whereof, I have hereunto set my hand and caused the seal of the United States to be affixed.

Done at the city of Washington this twelfth day of May, in the year of our Lord one thousand eight hundred and sixty-two, and of the independence of the United States the eighty-sixth.

[L. S.]

ABRAHAM LINCOLN.

By the President:

WILLIAM H. SEWARD,
Secretary of State.

No. 37.

Regulations relating to trade with the ports opened by proclamation.

TREASURY DEPARTMENT, *May* 12, 1862.

1. To vessels clearing from foreign ports, and destined to ports opened by proclamation of the President of the United States of this date, viz: Beaufort, in North Carolina; Port Royal, in South Carolina; and New Orleans, in Louisiana, licenses will be granted by consuls of the United States, upon satisfactory evidence that the vessels so licensed will convey no persons, property, or information contraband of war either to or from the said ports, which licenses shall be exhibited to the collector of the port to which said vessels may be respectively bound, immediately on arrival, and, if required, to any officer in charge of the blockade; and on leaving either of said ports every vessel will be required to have a clearance from the collector of the customs, according to law, showing no violation of the conditions of the license. Any violation of said conditions will involve the forfeiture and condemnation of the vessel and cargo, and the exclusion of all parties concerned from any further privilege of entering the United States during the war for any purpose whatever.

2. To vessels of the United States clearing coastwise for the ports aforesaid licenses can only be obtained from the Treasury Department.

3. In all other respects the existing blockade remains in full force and effect, as hitherto established and maintained, nor is it relaxed by the proclamation, except in regard to the ports to which the relaxation is by that instrument expressly applied.

S. P. CHASE,
Secretary of the Treasury.

part thereof, be disposed of by him or by his authority, connivance, or assent, in violation of the terms of the permit; and that neither the permit so granted, nor the merchandise shipped under it, shall be so used as in any way to give any aid, comfort, information, or encouragement to persons in insurrection against the United States; and, furthermore, that the applicant is loyal to the government of the United States, and will, in all things, so deport himself.

5. No permit shall be granted to ship merchandise to States or parts of States heretofore declared to be in insurrection except for delivery to such persons residing or doing business therein as shall be recommended therefor by an officer of the government duly authorized to make such recommendation; and no permit shall be granted for the shipment of merchandise from such States or parts of States except by persons with similar recommendation.

6. Surveyors, before granting permits, may require bond with surety in such cases as they think necessary, to prevent a violation of the law, in a penalty equal to the value of the merchandise permitted, and conditioned that there shall be no violation of the terms or spirit of the permit, nor of the asseverations of the affidavit above provided for.

7. No permit shall be granted to ship intoxicating drinks, or anything else forbidden by the military authorities, into the territory occupied by the forces of the United States or heretofore under insurrectionary control, except upon the written permission of the commandant of the department in which such territory is embraced, or of some person duly authorized by him to grant such permission. This rule does not apply to ale, beer, and Catawba wine.

8. To facilitate trade and guard against improper transportation, "aids to the revenue" shall be appointed, from time to time, on boats desiring it, and engaged in the trade of the west and southwest, which aids shall have carriage and be reasonably compensated by the respective boats upon which they are appointed, and they may grant permits for the shipment of way-freights on their boats, subject to the approval of the surveyor of the first port to be passed on the trip where there is such an officer; and no permits will be granted for transportation into States and parts of States heretofore declared to be in insurrection, except on boats carrying such aids to the revenue.

By order of the Secretary of the Treasury.

WM. D. GALLAGHER,
Special Agent Treasury Department.

ST. LOUIS, *April* 22, 1862.

MEMORANDUM.—The foregoing rules and regulations were essentially modified by the special agents on the 17th May, 1862, as per copy of rules for "trade on the Mississippi," (received from Mr. Gallagher in a letter of same date,) *q. v.*

No. 36.

PORTS OPENED TO TRADE.

By the President of the United States of America.—A proclamation.

Whereas, by my proclamation of the nineteenth day of April, one thousand eight hundred and sixty-one, it was declared that the ports of certain States, including those of Beaufort, in the State of North Carolina; Port Royal, in the State of South Carolina; and New Orleans, in the State of Louisiana, were, for reasons therein set forth, intended to be placed under blockade; and whereas the said ports of Beaufort, Port Royal, and New Orleans have since been blockaded; but as the blockade of the same ports may now be safely relaxed with advantage to the interests of commerce: Now, therefore, be it known that customs, and you will be careful to enforce the provisions of law as well as the regulations of the Treasury Department. If there shall be any violation of law or regulation by any vessel arriving at or within your port, such as conveying persons, property, or merchandise, contraband of war, or failure to exhibit her license and manifest to you immediately on arrival, or of any other violation of law sufficient to forfeit the vessel or cargo, you will forthwith seize the vessel and cargo and report the facts to the proper law officer, in order that proceedings may be instituted with a view to her condemnation and forfeiture. If proper law officers, appointed by the government, shall not have reached your port, or if no court of the United States, having jurisdiction of the matter, shall have been organized at the time of seizure, you will send the vessel and cargo, under safe custody, to the care of the collector of customs at New York, or any other loyal port, reporting to him all the facts in the case, in order that he may take the proper steps for the condemnation and forfeiture. The officer in command of the squadron will furnish you the means to carry out the above instructions. All moneys collected by you, you will keep in some safe and proper place, and for their full security you will, if necessary, call upon the commanding general for such aid as may be required. You will render your accounts in accordance with your instructions from the commissioner of customs.

I am, &c.,

S. P. CHASE,
Secretary of the Treasury.

GEO S. DENISON, Esq.,
Special Agent and Acting Collector, District of New Orleans.

No. 39.

Modification of the restrictions upon trade on the Mississippi.

ST. LOUIS, MISSOURI, *May* 17, 1862.

The Secretary of the Treasury having directed that the restrictions heretofore placed upon the trade and transportation of the interior shall be removed as fast as may be done with safety, notice is hereby given that, on and after the 24th instant, the regulations governing the commerce of the upper Mississippi and its tributaries will be so far modified as that—

1st. All merchandise, other than munitions of war, may, without permits, pass from the loyal States into the city of St. Louis; into all that part of the State of Missouri lying immediately on the Missouri river, and all north of that river; and into all the States of the northwest, and also the territories thereof; and all the custom-house supervision over this trade is abolished, except such as may be deemed necessary to prevent supplies of any description being furnished to insurgents.

2d. Merchandise destined for any place in that part of the State of Missouri lying south of the Missouri river must still be covered by custom-house permits before it can go forward, but the charge heretofore collected for the same is hereby discontinued.

3d. All the duties heretofore devolved upon surveyors and other officers of the customs, except such as are abolished by these modifications, those officers are expected still diligently and faithfully to perform, to the end that this desirable removal of certain restrictions upon trade may not operate to the prejudice of the government, or in any manner strengthen the hands of those who are in rebellion against its authority.

4th. The regulations established for conducting the commerce of the loyal States with the States and places recovered from the insurrectionary forces by soldiers of the United States engaged in suppressing the rebellion remain unchanged.

W. D. GALLAGHER,
Special Agent Treasury Department.

No. 40.

Circular to collectors of Atlantic ports concerning clearances to ports opened by proclamation, enumerating articles contraband of war.

TREASURY DEPARTMENT, *May* 23, 1862.

SIR: In pursuance of the provisions of the proclamation of the President, modifying the blockade of the ports of Beaufort, Port Royal, and New Orleans, and the regulations of the Secretary of the Treasury relating to trade with those ports, no articles contraband of war will be permitted to enter at either of said ports, and you will accordingly refuse clearances to vessels bound for those ports, or either of them, with any such articles on board.

Until further instructed you will regard as contraband of war the following articles, viz: Cannons, mortars, fire-arms, pistols, bombs, grenades, fire-locks, flints, matches, powder, saltpetre, balls, bullets, pikes, swords, sulphur, helmets or boarding caps, sword-belts, saddles and bridles, (always excepting the quantity of said articles which may be necessary for the defence of the ships, or those who compose the crew,) cartridge-bag material, percussion and other caps, clothing adapted for uniforms, resin, sail-cloth of all kinds, hemp and cordage, masts, ship timber, tar and pitch, ardent spirits, military persons in the service of the enemy, despatches of the enemy, and articles of like character with those specially enumerated.

You will also refuse clearances to all vessels which, whatever the ostensible destination, are believed by you, on satisfactory grounds, to be intended for ports or places in possession or under control of insurgents against the United States, or that there is imminent danger that the goods, wares, or merchandise, of whatever description, laden on such vessels, will fall into the possession or under the control of such insurgents. And in all cases where, in your judgment, there is ground for apprehension that any goods, wares, or merchandise shipped at your port will be used in any way for the aid of the insurgents or the insurrection, you will require substantial security to be given that such goods, wares, or merchandise shall not be transported to any place under insurrectionary control, and shall not in any way be used to give aid or comfort to such insurgents.

You will be specially careful, upon applications for clearances, to require bonds, with sufficient sureties, conditioned for fulfilling faithfully all the conditions imposed by law or departmental regulations, from shippers of the following articles to the ports opened, or to any other ports from which they may easily be, and are probably intended to be, reshipped in aid of the existing insurrection, namely: Liquors of all kinds, coals, iron, lead, copper, tin, brass, telegraph instruments, wire, porous cups, platina, sulphuric acid, zinc, and all other telegraphic materials, marine engines, screw propellers, paddle wheels, cylinders, cranks, shafts, boilers, tubes for boilers, fire-bars, and every article, or any other component part of an engine or boiler, or any article whatever which is, can, or may become applicable for the manufacture of marine machinery, or for the armor of vessels.

I am, &c., &c.,

S. P. CHASE,
Secretary of the Treasury.

No. 41.

Form of permit issued to officers of the customs to grant clearances to ports under blockade.

TREASURY DEPARTMENT, ——— —, 186 .

SIR: The War Department having certified that the shipment proposed to be made by ———— to ————, consisting of the following articles, viz: ————, is required for military purposes, and having requested that the transportation of the same may be permitted, you are hereby authorized to grant a clearance for the same, subject to the condition that all parties interested in the proposed shipment shall have first taken the prescribed oath of allegiance, and that the vessel and all her cargo are to be forfeited to the United States if any other goods are found on board of her than those specified above, on examination by the custom-house officers, or by the military or naval authorities, after clearing for ———.

You will insert the above condition in the clearance, and you will also require a suitable bond, that none of the articles so conveyed shall be used with the consent or knowledge of the shippers, or their agents, to give aid or comfort to the insurgents.

I am, very respectfully,

Per order. ——— ———,

Assistant Secretary of the Treasury.

——— ———, Esq., *Collector, &c., &c.*

No. 42.

Circular to certain collectors relative to sending supplies for the relief of Norfolk.

TREASURY DEPARTMENT, *June* 5, 1862.

SIR: The Secretary of War has just sent me a telegram from General Dix, representing that much suffering exists in Norfolk, and asking that some shipments of provisions may be made to that place for the relief of the inhabitants.

As Norfolk is a blockaded port, this can only be done as a military measure, and at the request of the Secretary of War.

I have therefore verbally advised the Secretary, through his chief clerk, that I would refer the matter to the several collectors of Baltimore, Philadelphia, New York, and Boston, with instructions to confer with any reliable and loyal persons who may be disposed to make a shipment, consisting exclusively of provisions and clothing, and materials for clothing; and in case any such person is found, to request him to forward at once a statement of the articles proposed to be shipped, with a request for a clearance, to this department. On receipt of the statement, and a request, it will be submitted to the Secretary of War, and the clearance authorized, on his statement of the military necessity and request, in the usual way.

It is not best to authorize more than one, or, at most, two shipments from each port, until further instructions as to the character and urgency of the necessity.

I am, &c., &c.,

S. P. CHASE,

Secretary of the Treasury.

J. Z. GOODRICH, Esq., *Collector, &c., Boston.*
HIRAM BARNEY, Esq., *Collector, &c., New York.*
WILLIAM B. THOMAS, Esq., *Collector, &c., Philadelphia.*
HENRY W. HOFFMAN, Esq., *Collector, &c., Baltimore.*

No. 43.

Rules for trade at Memphis.

A "local board of trade" was appointed for Memphis by W. D. Gallagher, esq., special agent, consisting of Messrs. B. D. Nabers and C. P. Ware, to which W. P. Mellen, esq., special agent, added Mr. Ruel Hough. June 17, 1862.

The following rules were established at the same time:

1. The military commander of the post details a squad of men to be at the landing at all times, and on the arrival of every boat to see that no merchandise is taken from the landing, except upon permits first obtained from the board of trade.
2. The board of trade grant permission to receive and sell goods to such persons only as take the usual oath as to disposing of them; and the oath of allegiance is made a part of the affidavit.
3. The military pickets around the city are allowed to pass out of the city only such persons with merchandise as have the permit of the board covering the merchandise.
4. The board permit persons in and out of the city to purchase family supplies in such quantities as may be necessary for individual use, without question as to loyalty; but no goods can be sold for purposes of trade in or out of the city, except by and to persons having the permit to trade, and this will only be given upon the affidavit above named.

* * * * * * * * * * * * * *

WILLIAM P. MELLEN,
Special Agent.

MEMORANDUM.—The foregoing regulations were approved by the Secretary of the Treasury, July 8, 1862.

No. 44.

Letter to the Secretary of War, embodying the "modus operandi" in the transmittal of supplies to places declared by the President to be under blockade.

TREASURY DEPARTMENT, *June* 23, 1862.

SIR: I have the honor to return the letter of George Bent, addressed to this department, requesting permission to ship a cargo of provisions and other articles to St. Augustine, Florida, from New York, to which you say you have no objection.

Since the port of St. Augustin is under blockade, and wholly within the control of the naval and military authorities, and, by the proclamation of the President, all commercial intercourse is forbidden at that point, I do not feel authorized to grant permission for the shipment of articles thither, unless the War or Navy Department shall certify that they are needed for military or naval purposes, and request their transmission.

Whether, under the head of military or naval purposes, may be properly included the furnishing of such supplies or provisions, clothing, and the like, to the inhabitants, as may be justly thought necessary to insure their tranquility and, mediately, the success of military operations, is a question for your determination, not for mine.

My jurisdiction in the premises extends no further than to the granting of clearances for whatever cargoes you, in the exercise of your discretion, may see fit to certify to be needed as above stated, and to request clearances for.

Without such certificate and request, I apprehend foreign powers and prize courts might regard and, perhaps, justly, coastwise clearances, as annulling the blockade.

I am, &c., &c.,

S. P. CHASE,
Secretary of the Treasury.

Hon. EDWIN M. STANTON, *Secretary of War.*

No. 45.

Additional instructions to the acting collector at New Orleans.

TREASURY DEPARTMENT,
June 27, 1862.

SIR:

* * * * * * * * * * *

Until otherwise directed you will permit *no* shipments by sea from any point on the Mississippi river or tributaries, except New Orleans, at which place all goods will be laden on board under the inspection of the officers of the customs.

* * * * * * * * * *

I am, &c.,

S. P. CHASE,
Secretary of the Treasury.

GEORGE S. DENISON, Esq.,
Acting Collector, &c., New Orleans, La.

No. 46.

Certificates of permission to trade to be granted to loyal parties.

TREASURY DEPARTMENT,
July 1, 1862.

SIR: Referring you to the modifications of the system of issuing permits for trade with those sections of the country heretofore declared under insurrectionary control, under the rules and regulations governing internal commercial intercourse, adopted on the 29th of March last, you are hereby directed, when applied to by parties desiring to make shipments of goods to those sections, to furnish, if satisfied of their loyalty, and of the good faith of the proposed transaction, certificates to that effect, which will be regarded as sufficient evidence on those points by the surveyors of customs at the internal ports, to whom application for permits may be made by the shippers, unless such surveyors shall be satisfied of disloyal intent on grounds not publicly known.

I am, &c.,

S. P. CHASE,
Secretary of the Treasury.

TO COLLECTORS *of Atlantic Ports.*

No. 47.

Instructions to special agents of the Treasury Department in view of opening trade on the Mississippi river, &c.—Mode of procedure.

TREASURY DEPARTMENT,
July 10, 1862.

SIR: Whenever any section of the country bordering on the Mississippi river, or its affluents, heretofore declared to be under insurrectionary control, shall come into the possession of the United States forces, such arrangements should be made for the resumption of trade therewith, under the general regulations now in force governing internal commercial intercourse, as will allow all persons desiring to participate in such trade equal opportunities for so doing.

It is suggested that when, in the opinion of any one of the special agents of this department, it is proper to reopen trade with any such section, he will promptly communicate the fact to the other agents of the department having co-operative supervision, and, if they shall concur in his views, they will fix upon a day after which shipments of goods may be made thence, giving public notice thereof, and advising forthwith this department.

Should they disagree they will submit the facts to the Secretary of the Treasury for his consideration.

Very respectfully,

S. P. CHASE,
Secretary of the Treasury.

No. 48.

Instructions to surveyors of customs at Pittsburg and Wheeling, requiring steamers to take out clearances each trip, &c.

PITTSBURG, *July* 18, 1862.

SIR: Hereafter, and till otherwise advised, you will require all boats clearing at this port for points and places below Cincinnati, to take out regular clearances for each trip; and you will also require permits to be taken out at your office for each shipment of goods to points and places on both sides of the river, below Louisville.

For clearances you will charge twenty-five cents, and for the permits twenty cents each.

Very respectfully,

THOMAS HEATON,
Special Agent, Treasury Department.

To ——— ———.

The foregoing instructions were approved by the Secretary of the Treasury, July 25, 1862, with the following construction:

"*Provided,* that the boatmen and shippers shall not be required to take out clearances or permits at any other point for the same trip or shipment."

No. 49.

Instructions to surveyors in western districts, relative to trading boats.

LOUISVILLE, KY., *July* 18, 1862.

SIR: I am satisfied that "trading boats," that have been permitted to go down the Mississippi river, are guilty of gross violations of the regulations of the Secretary of the Treasury, and of conveying aid and comfort to rebels, and that there is no way in which transportation of merchandise by such craft can be permitted with safety to the public interests.

You will, therefore, please grant no permit to any trading boat, whatsoever, to go down the Mississippi river, no matter what pretences or circumstances they may present to you, either for purposes of trade by the way or of transportation to a point named.

In all cases of permitting barges or flatboats, loaded with produce for a destination on the Mississippi, named, you will require bond, in the full value of the cargo, that no part thereof shall be landed or delivered at any place other than that named in the permit, as the final destination thereof.

WILLIAM P. MELLEN,
Special Agent, Treasury Department.

The foregoing letter of instructions was sent to all the surveyors in the districts involved, and the same was approved by the Secretary of the Treasury in letter to Mr. Mellen, dated July 29, 1862.

No. 50.

Modification of the instructions to the acting collector of customs at New Orleans, of June 27, 1862.

TREASURY DEPARTMENT, *August* 15, 1862.

SIR: It is represented that strict compliance with the instructions of June 27th last, directing you to permit no shipments by sea, from any point on the Mississippi river or tributaries, except New Orleans, works injustice to owners of produce lying below New Orleans, in consequence of the trouble and expense of transporting it to that point for clearance.

You are therefore authorized, when applied to for clearance by parties under such circumstances, and when satisfied of the good faith of the proposed transaction, to detail an inspector to visit the point and supervise the shipment, and issue a clearance on his certificate; provided that all expense attending such special shipments shall be borne by the parties making the same.

I am, &c.,

S. P. CHASE, *Secretary of the Treasury.*

GEORGE S. DENISON, Esq.
Special Agent and Acting Collector, New Orleans, La.

No. 51.

[Act of Congress July 13, 1861, and an act supplementary thereto, May 20, 1862.]

Regulations concerning internal and coastwise intercourse, to which are appended the accompanying orders of the Secretary of War and the Secretary of the Navy.

TREASURY DEPARTMENT, *August* 28, 1862.

In pursuance of law, and by virtue of the authority conferred upon the Secretary of the Treasury by the act of Congress approved July 13, 1861, entitled, "An act further to provide for the collection of duties on imports, and for other purposes," and an act supplementary thereto, approved May 20, 1862, and for the purpose of preventing the conveyance of arms, munitions of war, and other supplies to persons in insurrection against the United States, the following regulations concerning commercial intercourse with insurrectionary States and sections are prescribed.

S. P. CHASE,
Secretary of the Treasury.

I. No goods, wares, or merchandise, whatever may be the ostensible destination thereof, shall be transported to any place now under the control of insurgents; nor to any place on the south side of the Potomac river; nor to any place on the north side of the Potomac, and south of the Washington and Annapolis railroad; nor to any place on the eastern shore of the Chesapeake; nor to any place on the south side of the Ohio river below Wheeling, except Louisville; nor to any place on the west side of the Mississippi river below the mouth of the Des Moines, except St Louis without a permit of a duly authorized officer of the Treasury Department. And the special agents of this department may temporarily extend these restrictions to such other places in their respective districts, and make such local rules to be observed therein, as may from time to time become necessary, promptly reporting their action to the Secretary of the Treasury for his sanction or disapproval.

II. All transportation of coin or bullion to any State or section heretofore declared to be in insurrection is absolutely prohibited, except for military purposes and under military orders, or under the special license of the Secretary of the Treasury. And no payment of gold or silver shall be made for cotton or other merchandise within any such State or section. And all cotton or other merchandise purchased or paid for therein, directly or indirectly, in gold or silver, shall be forfeited to the United States.

III. No clearance or permit whatsoever will be granted for any shipment to any port, place, or section affected by the existing blockade, except for military purposes, and upon the certificate and request of the Department of War or the Department of the Navy.

IV. All applications for permits to transport or trade under these regulations shall state the character and value of the merchandise to be transported, the consignee and destination thereof, with the route of transportation and the number and description of the packages, with the marks thereon.

V. Every applicant for such permits shall present with his application the original invoices of the goods, wares, and merchandise to be transported, and shall make and file with the officer granting the permit an affidavit that the quantities, descriptions, and values are correctly stated in said invoices, true copies of which shall be annexed to and filed with the affidavit; and that the packages contain nothing except as stated in the invoices; that the merchandise so permitted shall not, nor shall any part thereof, be disposed of by him or by his authority, connivance, or assent, in violation of the terms of the permit, and that neither the permit so granted, nor the merchandise to be transported shall be so used or disposed of by him or by his authority, connivance or assent, as in any way to give aid, comfort, information, or encouragement to persons in insurrection against the United States. And furthermore, that the applicant is loyal to the government of the United States and will in all things so deport himself.

VI. No permit shall be granted to ship goods, wares, or merchandise *to* States or parts of States heretofore declared to be in insurrection, or to places under insurrectionary control, or occupied by the military forces of the United States, except to persons residing or doing business therein whose loyalty and good faith shall be certified by an officer of the government or other person duly authorized to make such certificate, or by a duly appointed board of trade therein, by whose approval and permission only the same shall be unladed or disposed of. And no permit shall be granted to ship merchandise *from* any such State or part of State in violation of any order restricting shipments therefrom, made for military purposes by the commandant of the *department* from which such shipment is to be made.

VII. Collectors or surveyors of customs, before granting clearances or permits, may require bond, with reasonable surety, in such cases as they shall think necessary, to protect the public interests, conditioned that there shall be no violation of the terms or spirit of the clearance or permit, or of the averments of the affidavit upon which the same is granted.

VIII. No permit shall be granted to ship intoxicating drinks, or other things prohibited by the military authorities, into territory occupied by the military forces of the United States, except upon the written request of the commandant of the *department* in which such territory is embraced, or of some person duly authorized by him to make such request.

IX. In order to defray the expenses under these regulations, a fee of twenty cents will be charged for each permit granted; and shipments permited to and from States heretofore declared to be in insurrection shall, in addition thereto, be charged with the following fees, viz: Five cents on each one hundred dollars over three hundred dollars on all shipments *to* such States or sections; fifty cents on each one thousand pounds of cotton, and twenty-five cents on each one thousand pounds of sugar permitted *from* such State.

X. No vessel, boat, or vehicle used for transportation upon or south of the Potomac river, or north of the Potomac and south of the Washington and Annapolis railroad, or to the eastern shore of the Chesapeake, or southwardly on or from the Ohio river below Wheeling, or westwardly or southwardly on or from the Mississippi river below the mouth of the Des Moines, shall receive on board any goods, wares or merchandise destined to any place, commercial intercourse with which now is or hereafter may be restricted as aforesaid, unless the same be accompanied with a permit of a duly authorized officer of the Treasury Department, except as hereinafter provided in regulation number XIV.

XI. No vessel, boat, or other vehicle used for transportation from eastern cities, or elsewhere in the loyal States, shall carry goods, wares, or merchandise into any place, section, or State restricted as aforesaid, without the permit of the duly authorized officer of the customs, applications for which permit may be made to such authorized officer near the point of destination as may suit the convenience of the shipper.

XII. No vessel, boat, or other vehicle used for transportation shall put off any goods, wares, or merchandise at any place other than that named in the permit as the place of destination.

XIII. Before any boat or vessel running on any of the western waters south of Louisville or St Louis, or other waters within or adjacent to any State or section, commercial intercourse with which now is or may hereafter be restricted as aforesaid, shall depart from any port where there is a collector or surveyor of customs, there shall be exhibited to the collector or surveyor, or such other officer as may be authorized to act in his stead, a true manifest of its entire cargo and a clearance obtained to proceed on its voyage; and when freights are received on board at a place where there is no collector or surveyor, as hereinafter provided in regulation XIV, then the same exhibit shall be made and clearance obtained at the first port to be passed where there is such an officer, and such vessel or boat shall be reported and the manifest of its cargo exhibited to the collector or surveyor of every port to be passed on the trip where there is such an officer; but no new clearance shall be necessary unless additional freights shall have been taken on board after the last clearance. Immediately on arriving at the port of final destination, and before discharging any part of its cargo, the manifest shall be exhibited to the surveyor of such port, or other officer authorized to act in his stead, whose approval for landing the cargo shall be indorsed on the manifest before any part thereof shall be discharged; and the clearance and shipping permits of all such vessels and boats shall be exhibited to the officer in command of any naval vessel or military post whenever such officer may require it.

XIV. To facilitate trade and guard against improper transportation, "aids to the revenue" will be appointed from time to time on cars, vessels, and boats, when desired by owners, agents, or masters thereof, which aids will have free carriage on the respective cars, vessels, and boats on which they are placed, and will allow proper way freights to be taken on board without permit, keeping a statement thereof, and reporting the same to the collector or surveyor of the first port to be passed on the trip where there is such an officer, from whom a permit therefor must be obtained, or the goods returned under his direction. No permit will be granted for transportation into any insurrectionary State or district, except on cars, vessels, and boats carrying such aids.

XV. All vessels, boats, and other vehicles used for transportation, violating any of the above regulations, and all goods, wares, and merchandise shipped or transported in violation thereof, will be forfeited to the United States. If any false statement be made or deception practiced in obtaining a permit, such permit and all others connected therewith or affected thereby will be absolutely void, and all merchandise shipped thereunder shall be forfeited to the United States. In all cases of forfeiture, as aforesaid, immediate seizure will be made and proceedings instituted promptly for condemnation. The attention of all officers of the government, common carriers, shippers, consignees, owners, masters, agents, drivers, and other persons connected with the transportation of merchandise or trading therein, is particularly directed to the acts of July 13, 1861, and May 20, 1862, above referred to.

XVI. All army supplies transported under military orders are excepted from the above regulations. But this exception does not extend to sutlers' goods or others designed for sale at military posts or camps.

XVII. When any officer of the customs shall find in his district any goods, wares, or merchandise, which, in his opinion, are in danger of being transported to insurgents, he may, if he thinks it expedient, require the owner or holder thereof to give reasonable security that they shall not be transported to any place under insurrectionary control, and shall not in any way be used to give aid or encouragement to the insurgents.

If the required security be not given, such officer shall promptly state the facts to the United States marshal for the district within which such goods are situated, or, if beyond the jurisdiction of a United States marshal, then to the commandant of the nearest military post, whose duty it shall be to take possession thereof, and hold them for safe-keeping, reporting the facts promptly to the Secretary of the Treasury, and awaiting instructions.

XVIII. Where ports heretofore blockaded have been opened by the proclamation of the President, licenses will be granted, by United States consuls, on application by the proper parties, to vessels clearing from foreign ports to the ports so opened, upon satisfactory evidence that the vessel so licensed will convey no person, property, or information contraband of war, either to or from said ports, which license shall be shown to the collector of the port to which the vessel is bound, and, if required, to any officer in charge of the blockade. And on leaving any port so opened, the vessel must have a clearance from the collector, according to law, showing no violation of the conditions of the license. Any violation of the conditions will involve the forfeiture and condemnation of the vessel and cargo, and the exclusion of all parties concerned from entering the United States for any purpose during the war.

XIX. United States vessels clearing from domestic ports to any of the ports so opened will apply to the custom-house officers of the proper ports, in the usual manner, for licenses or clearances under the regulations heretofore established.

WAR DEPARTMENT,
Washington City, August 28, 1862.

The attention of all officers and others connected with the army of the United States is called to the regulations of the Secretary of the Treasury concerning commercial intercourse with insurrectionary States or sections, dated August 28, 1862.

I. Commandants of departments, districts, and posts, will render all such military aid as may become necessary in carrying out the provisions of said regulations and enforcing observance thereof to the extent directed by the Secretary of the Treasury, so far as can possibly be done, without danger to the operations or safety of their respective commands.

II. There will be no interference with trade or shipments of cotton or other merchandise conducted in pursuance of said regulations within any territory occupied and controlled by the forces of the United States, unless absolutely necessary to the successful execution of military plans or movements therein. But in cases of the violations of the conditions of any clearance or permit granted under such regulations, and in cases of unlawful traffic, the guilty party or parties will be arrested and the facts promptly reported to the commandant of the department for orders.

III. No officer of the army or other person connected therewith will seize cotton or other property of individuals unless exposed to destruction by the enemy, or needed for military purposes, or for confiscation under the act of Congress, and in all such cases of seizure the same shall be promptly reported to the commandant of the department wherein they are made for his orders therein.

EDWIN M. STANTON,
Secretary of War.

NAVY DEPARTMENT, *August* 28, 1862.

The attention of naval officers is called to the regulations of the Secretary of the Treasury concerning commercial intercourse with insurrectionary States or sections, dated August 28, 1862.

I. Commanders of naval vessels will render such aid as may be necessary in carrying out the provisions of said regulations, and enforcing observance thereof to the extent directed by the Secretary of the Treasury, so far as can possibly be done, without danger to the operations or safety of their respective commands.

II. There will be no interference with trade in or shipments of cotton or other merchandise conducted in pursuance of said regulations within any of the waters controlled by the naval forces of the United States, unless absolutely necessary to the successful execution of military or naval plans or movements. But in cases of the violation of the conditions of any clearance or permit granted under said regulations, and in cases of unlawful traffic, the guilty party or parties will be arrested and the facts promptly reported.

III. No officer of the navy will seize cotton or other property of individuals within the territory opened to traffic, and subject to the regulations of the Secretary of the Treasury, unless the same is exposed to destruction by the enemy or needed for naval purposes, or for confiscation under the act of Congress; and in all such cases the fact, with all attendant circumstances, shall be promptly reported to the department.

GIDEON WELLES, *Secretary.*

AN ACT further to provide for the collection of duties on imports, and for other purposes.

Be it enacted by the Senate and House of Representatives of the United States of America in Congress assembled, That whenever it shall, in the judgment of the President, by reason of unlawful combinations of persons in opposition to the laws of the United States, become impracticable to execute the revenue laws and collect the duties on imports by the ordinary means, in the ordinary way, at any port of entry in any collection district, he is authorized to cause such duties to be collected at any port of delivery in said district until such obstruction shall cease; and in such case the surveyors at said ports of delivery shall be clothed with all the powers and be subject to all the obligations of collectors at ports of entry; and the Secretary of the Treasury, with the approbation of the President, shall appoint such number of weighers, gaugers, measurers, inspectors, appraisers, and clerks as may be necessary, in his judgment, for the faithful execution of the revenue laws at said ports of delivery, and shall fix and establish the limits within which such ports of delivery are constituted ports of entry, as aforesaid; and all the provisions of law regulating the issue of marine papers, the coasting trade, the warehousing of imports, and collection of duties, shall apply to the ports of entry so constituted in the same manner as they do to ports of entry established by the laws now in force.

SEC. 2. *And be it further enacted,* That if, from the cause mentioned in the foregoing section, in the judgment of the President, the revenue from duties on imports cannot be effectually collected at any port of entry in any collection district, in the ordinary way and by the ordinary means, or by the course provided in the foregoing section, then and in that case he may direct that the custom-house for the district be established in any secure place within said district, either on land or on board any vessel in said district or at sea near the coast; and in such case the collector shall reside at such place, or on shipboard, as the case may be, and there detain all vessels and cargoes arriving within or approaching said district, until the duties imposed by law on said vessels and their cargoes are paid in cash: *Provided,* That if the owner or consignee of the cargo on board any vessel detained as aforesaid, or the master of said vessel shall desire to enter a port of entry in any other district of the United States where no such obstructions to the execution of the laws exist, the master of such vessel may be permitted so to change the destination of the vessel and cargo in his manifest, whereupon the collector shall deliver him a written permit to proceed to the port so designated: *And provided, further,* That the Secretary of the Treasury shall, with the approbation of the President, make proper regulations for the enforcement on shipboard of such provisions of the laws regulating the assessment and collection of duties as in his judgment may be necessary and practicable.

SEC. 3. *And be it further enacted*, That it shall be unlawful to take any vessel or cargo detained as aforesaid from the custody of the proper officers of the customs unless by process of some court of the United States; and in case of any attempt otherwise to take such vessel or cargo by any force, or combination, or assemblage of persons, too great to be overcome by the officers of the customs, it shall and may be lawful for the President, or such person or persons as he shall have empowered for that purpose, to employ such part of the army or navy or militia of the United States, or such force of citizen volunteers as may be deemed necessary, for the purpose of preventing the removal of such vessel or cargo, and protecting the officers of the customs in retaining the custody thereof.

SEC. 4. *And be it further enacted*, That if, in the judgment of the President, from the cause mentioned in the first section of this act, the duties upon imports in any collection district cannot be effectually collected by the ordinary means and in the ordinary way, or in the mode and manner provided in the foregoing section of this act, then and in that case the President is hereby empowered to close the port or ports of entry in said district, and in such case give notice thereof by proclamation; and thereupon all right of importation, warehousing, and other privileges incident to ports of entry, shall cease and be discontinued at such ports so closed, until opened by the order of the President on the cessation of such obstructions; and if, while said ports are so closed, any ship or vessel from beyond the United States, or having on board any articles subject to duties, shall enter or attempt to enter any such port, the same, together with its tackle, apparel, furniture, and cargo, shall be forfeited to the United States.

SEC. 5. *And be it further enacted*, That whenever the President, in pursuance of the provisions of the second section of the act entitled "An act to provide for calling forth the militia to execute the laws of the Union, suppress insurrections, and repel invasions, and to repeal the act now in force for that purpose," approved February twenty-eight, seventeen hundred and ninety-five, shall have called forth the militia to suppress combinations against the laws of the United States, and to cause the laws to be duly executed, and the insurgents shall have failed to disperse by the time directed by the President, and when said insurgents claim to act under the authority of any State or States, and such claim is not disclaimed or repudiated by the person exercising the functions of government in such State or States, or in the part or parts thereof in which said combination exists, nor such insurrection suppressed by said State or States, then and in such case it may and shall be lawful for the President, by proclamation, to declare that the inhabitants of such State, or any section or part thereof, where such insurrection exists, are in a state of insurrection against the United States; and thereupon all commercial intercourse by and between the same and the citizens thereof and the citizens of the rest of the United States shall cease and be unlawful so long as such condition of hostility shall continue; and all goods and chattels, wares and merchandise, coming from said State or section into the other parts of the United States, and all proceeding to such State or section, by land or water, shall, together with the vessel or vehicle conveying the same, or conveying persons to or from such State or section, be forfeited to the United States: *Provided, however*, That the President may, in his discretion, license and permit commercial intercourse with any such part of said State or section, the inhabitants of which are so declared in a state of insurrection, in such articles, and for such time, and by such persons, as he, in his discretion, may think most conducive to the public interests; and such intercourse, so far as by him licensed, shall be conducted and carried on only in pursuance of rules and regulations prescribed by the Secretary of the Treasury. And the Secretary of the Treasury may appoint such officers, at places where officers of the customs are not now authorized by law, as may be needed to carry into effect such licenses, rules, and regulations; and officers of the customs and other officers shall receive for services under this section, and under said rules and regulations, such fees and compensation as are now allowed for similar service under other provisions of law.

SEC. 6. *And be it further enacted,* That, from and after fifteen days after the issuing of the said proclamation, as provided in the last foregoing section of this act, any ship or vessel belonging in whole or in part to any citizen or inhabitant of said States or part of a State whose inhabitants are so declared in a state of insurrection, found at sea, or in any port of the rest of the United States, shall be forfeited to the United States.

SEC. 7. *And be it further enacted,* That, in the execution of the provisions of this act, and of the other laws of the United States providing for the collection of duties on imports and tonnage, it may and shall be lawful for the President, in addition to the revenue cutters in service, to employ in aid thereof such other suitable vessels as may, in his judgment, be required.

SEC. 8. *And be it further enacted,* That the forfeitures and penalties incurred by virtue of this act may be mitigated or remitted, in pursuance of the authority vested in the Secretary of the Treasury by the act entitled "An act providing for mitigating or remitting the forfeitures, penalties, and disabilities accruing in certain cases therein mentioned," approved March third, seventeen hundred and ninety-seven, or in cases where special circumstances may seem to require it, according to regulations to be prescribed by the Secretary of the Treasury.

SEC. 9. *And be it further enacted,* That proceedings on seizures for forfeitures under this act may be pursued in the courts of the United States in any district into which the property so seized may be taken and proceedings instituted; and such courts shall have and entertain as full jurisdiction over the same as if the seizure was made in that district.

Approved July 13, 1861.

AN ACT supplementary to an act approved on the thirteenth July, eighteen hundred and sixty-one, entitled "An act to provide for the collection of duties on imports, and for other purposes."

Be it enacted by the Senate and House of Representatives of the United States of America in Congress assembled, That the Secretary of the Treasury, in addition to the powers conferred upon him by the act of the thirteenth July, eighteen hundred and sixty-one, be, and he is hereby, authorized to refuse a clearance to any vessel or other vehicle laden with goods, wares, or merchandise, destined for a foreign or domestic port, whenever he shall have satisfactory reason to believe that such goods, wares, or merchandise, or any part thereof, whatever may be their ostensible destination, are intended for ports or places in possession or under control of insurgents against the United States; and if any vessel or other vehicle for which a clearance or permit shall have been refused by the Secretary of the Treasury, or by his order, as aforesaid, shall depart or attempt to depart for a foreign or domestic port without being duly cleared or permitted, such vessel or other vehicle with her tackle, apparel, furniture, and cargo, shall be forfeited to the United States.

SEC. 2. *And be it further enacted,* That whenever a permit or clearance is granted, for either a foreign or domestic port, it shall be lawful for the collector of the customs granting the same, if he shall deem it necessary, under the circumstances of the case, to require a bond to be executed by the master or the owner of the vessel, in a penalty equal to the value of the cargo, and with sureties to the satisfaction of such collector, that the said cargo shall be delivered at the destination for which it is cleared or permitted, and that no part thereof shall be used in affording aid or comfort to any person or parties in insurrection against the authority of the United States.

SEC. 3. *And be it further enacted,* That the Secretary of the Treasury be, and he is hereby, further empowered to prohibit and prevent the transportation in any vessel or upon any railroad, turnpike, or other road or means of transportation within the United States, of any goods, wares, or merchandise, of whatever character, and whatever may be the ostensible destination of the same, in all cases where there shall be satisfactory reasons to believe that such goods, wares, or merchandise are intended for any place in the possession or under the control of insurgents against the United States; or that there is imminent danger that such goods, wares, or merchandise will fall into the possession or under the control of such insurgents; and he is further authorized, in all cases where he shall deem it expedient so to do, to require reasonable security to be given that goods, wares, or merchandise shall not be transported to any place under insurrectionary control, and shall not, in any way, be used to give aid or comfort to such insurgents; and he may establish all such general or special regulations as may be necessary or proper to carry into effect the purposes of this act; and if any goods, wares, or merchandise shall be transported in violation of this act, or of any regulation of the Secretary of the Treasury, established in pursuance thereof, or if any attempt shall be made so to transport them, all goods, wares, or merchandise so transported or attempted to be transported shall be forfeited to the United States.

SEC. 4. *And be it further enacted,* That the proceedings for the penalties and forfeitures accruing under this act may be pursued, and the same may be mitigated or remitted by the Secretary of the Treasury in the modes prescribed by the eighth and ninth sections of the act of July thirteenth, eighteen hundred and sixty-one, for which this act is supplementary.

SEC. 5. *And be it further enacted,* That the proceeds of all penalties and forfeitures incurred under this act, or the act to which this is supplementary, shall be distributed in the manner provided by the ninety-first section of the act of March second, seventeen hundred and ninety-nine, entitled "An act to regulate the collection of duties on imports and tonnage."

Approved May 20, 1862.

No. 52.

Special order concerning trade on the Mississippi river, below Memphis, promulgated by the Treasury Department, in conjunction with the military commander.

HEADQUARTERS FIFTH DIVISION,
Memphis, Tennessee, September 8, 1862.

Until trade shall be regularly opened with ports and places on the Mississippi river below Memphis, all commercial intercourse between this city and Helena, and with intermediate points, will be under *joint military and civil jurisdiction,* and be governed by the following regulations, the object being, while guarding against the conveyance of supplies, of whatever description, to individuals or bands in armed or other hostility to the government of the United States, not to deny their usual family and plantation supplies to persons who have refused or declined to engage in or otherwise promote the existing rebellion.

I. All permits shall be issued by the board of trade in Memphis, and no merchandise, which is not so permitted, shall be received on board of any steamboat or other vessel or vehicle engaged in the business of common carriers, except army supplies, moving under military authority.

II. Merchandise needed for family and plantation supply, (not including arms and ammunition,) will be permitted by the board of trade to persons residing on either side of the Mississippi river, between Memphis and Helena, or at Helena and its neighborhood, who have not taken any active part in the rebellion themselves, or directly or indirectly, by connivance or assent, aided or encouraged those who have. Such supplies, however, must go forward from time to time, in limited quantities; and before the delivery of the first the recipient will be required to appear in person at either Memphis or Helena, and make affidavit, before a proper officer, that no part of the supplies so delivered shall be sold, or otherwise disposed of, to other parties, or used in any manner or for any purpose whatever, except for the consumption of his or her plantation laborers.

III. For the purpose of guarding against the abuse of this privilege, and of detecting attempts to evade or violate its terms, a list of persons of the character above described, residing or having their plantations within the district of country named, and who have remained at their usual places of residence, attending to their legitimate business, will be prepared at as early a period as practicable for the use of the board of trade. This list will, at all times, be subject to revision, that proper names which, at first, may be omitted, may be added to it, and improper ones, enrolled through misrepresentation, be erased.

IV. For the present, and until otherwise provided, all this special transportation will be committed to a single steamboat, to be selected by the board of trade, the master of which shall execute bond, with a reasonable security, that he will not deliver any package of merchandise, or any part thereof, at any place other than that for which it shall have been duly permitted. And such boat shall carry, and reasonably remunerate, a revenue aid, to be appointed subject to the approval of the Secretary of the Treasury, whose scope of duties shall be the same as those of similar officers on boats engaged in the St. Louis and Memphis trade.

V. The bar of this boat, and of all other boats running upon the waters within the district prescribed, shall carry among its stores no intoxicating liquors for sale or barter along the coast, and shall be immediately closed upon arriving at any port or place where the drinking saloons have been closed by either civil or military authority.

VI. All lots of cotton, horses, mules, or wagons shipped north from the lower Mississippi must be accompanied by the bills of sale, witnessed by at least two witnesses, and duly receipted at the time of delivery to the purchaser.

VII. These regulations are at all times subject to change or revocation by the authority that establishes them.

W. T. SHERMAN,
Major General, Commanding 5th Division.

W. D. GALLAGHER,
Special Agent Treasury Department.

No. 53.

Special instructions to collector at Baltimore concerning restrictions on trade.

TREASURY DEPARTMENT,
September 22, 1862.

SIR: All special permits addressed to you, authorizing shipments of goods to places in those sections heretofore declared to be in insurrection, are hereby revoked. Parties holding them will be referred by you to this department.

In your action under the regulations concerning internal and coastwise intercourse, promulgated August 28, 1862, you will pay strict attention to the boundary lines therein described, and you will grant no permit or clearance for shipments of goods to the sections specified until all parties interested or concerned in the proposed shipment shall have taken the prescribed oath of allegiance to the government of the United States. This you will regard as applying to *each individual* member of the firm from whom the goods may be bought, or proposing to make the shipment, whether as principals or agents, and the owner, master, or agent of the means of transportation proposed to be used, as well as the consignee or prospective recipient of the goods proposed to be shipped.

In granting permits or clearances for shipments to the eastern shore of Maryland, you will exercise the greatest vigilance to prevent, either by the frequency of permission or by the great quantity desired at any one shipment, a larger amount of goods or supplies reaching any one person than is reasonably presumed to be sufficient for home consumption.

Very respectfully,

S. P. CHASE,
Secretary of the Treasury.

HENRY W. HOFFMAN, Esq.,
Collector, &c., Baltimore, Maryland.

No. 54.

Order imposing additional restrictions on the trade with Kentucky and Tennessee west of the Cumberland river.

CINCINNATI, *Ohio, September* 22, 1862.

SIR: The present condition of the country bordering on the Tennessee and Cumberland rivers and on the line of the Mobile and Ohio railroad renders it necessary to suspend all permits to trade there at present. You will, therefore, grant no permits, whatever, for any shipment of merchandise to points or places upon either of said rivers or down said railroad below Columbus, until notified of a relaxation of this rule.

You will allow no salt to leave your place for Tennessee or any part of Kentucky in the valley of the Cumberland river, or west thereof, for sale, nor more to any one person than is absolutely necessary for his own use. All other merchandise that can be used by the rebels you will restrict to very small quantities at any one time.

Very respectfully,

THO. HEATON,
Special Agent Treasury Department.

The foregoing instructions were sent to surveyors in the districts under supervision of Thomas Heaton, special agent, and William P. Mellen, special agent. They were approved by the Secretary of the Treasury by letter to Mr. Heaton, dated October 4, 1862.

No. 55.

Order restricting trade on the Baltimore and Ohio railroad.

CINCINNATI, *Ohio, September* 24, 1862.

SIR: In accordance with the spirit and letter of the regulations promulgated by the Secretary of the Treasury on the 28th of August ultimo, you will not allow any goods, wares, or mechandise to be shipped over the Baltimore and Ohio railroad unless accompanied by a permit issued from your office; and you will, in every respect, conform your action to the requirements of the regulations referred to; anything contained in previous orders or instructions to the contrary notwithstanding.

Very respectfully, your obedient servant,

THO. HEATON,
Special Agent Treasury Department.

THOMAS HORNBROOK, Esq.,
Surveyor of Customs, Wheeling, Virginia.

Approved by the Secretary of the Treasury October 4, 1862.

No. 56.

Order restricting trade between Parkersburg and Point Pleasant, in Western Virginia.

WHEELING, *Virginia, September* 25, 1862.

SIR: As the section of country between Parkersburg and Point Pleasant, in Western Virginia, is at present under insurrectionary control, you will allow no goods, wares, or merchandise to leave your city destined for that section, which are intended for sale; but family supplies in such limited quantities as you may regard necessary for personal use and consumption may be permitted.

Very respectfully,

THO. HEATON,
Special Agent Treasury Department.

THOMAS HORNBROOK, Esq.,
Surveyor of Customs, Wheeling, Virginia.

Approved by the Secretary of the Treasury October 4, 1862.

No. 57.

Further instructions to the acting collector at New Orleans, relative to trade below the city.

TREASURY DEPARTMENT, *October* 1, 1862.

SIR: * * * * * * * * * * *

You are now further authorized to permit the *unlading* of vessels, on arrival at points below the city, on such vessels being duly entered at New Orleans, exercising the same care as in case of shipments *from* the points in question, and detailing an inspector to supervise the discharge of the cargo, in each case; provided, that all extra expense consequent upon the unlading at such points shall be borne by the parties interested.

I am, &c.,

S. P. CHASE,
Secretary of the Treasury.

GEO. S. DENISON, Esq.,
Special Agent and Acting Collector, New Orleans, La.

No. 58.

Communication to the Secretary of State as to the effect of Treasury regulations upon trade in and exportation of cotton and other products of the insurrectionary sections, to which is annexed letter from Wm. P. Mellen, special agent, of September 26, 1862, *in relation to the cotton trade of the southwest, &c., and the reply of the Secretary of the Treasury of October* 1, 1862.

TREASURY DEPARTMENT, *October* 1, 1862.

SIR: I have carefully reviewed the regulations concerning internal and coastwise intercourse, to which Mr. Stuart refers, in his "*private memorandum*," to which you have invited my attention.

There is nothing in those regulations which conflicts with a very free export of cotton from all places in which it is grown, through ports of the United States; unless it be found in regulation II, which forbids the transportation of coin and bullion into insurrectionary districts and payments for cotton and other merchandise within them, in gold or silver.

This regulation was adopted upon considerations of policy, affecting mainly citizens of the United States. If abrogated as to subjects of other powers, it must, of course, be abrogated altogether. It can, at most, occasion but a slight inconvenience to purchasers, whether American or foreign; for they can easily convert gold or silver designed for the purchase of cotton into United States notes or the notes of banks of the United States, or can deposit it with any bank or firm in any city of the United States and make their own bills on such deposits. With these notes or bills purchases may be made to any extent that military exigencies will permit.

If you are of opinion, however, that any implication has arisen from the acts of our generals or from assurances of your own, which would make the enforcement of this order a ground for the imputation by foreign powers of any willingness, however slight, to disappoint expectations reasonably excited, it shall be suspended.

To show you how entirely unfounded every suspicion that any disposition exists in any branch of the government to abridge, beyond actual necessity, the freedom of purchasing cotton or other products of the rebel States, I enclose a copy of a letter from Mr. Mellen, one of the special agents of this department, with a copy of my reply. It is my wish to have just as much cotton, rice, sugar, and tobacco brought out of the insurrectionary States as possible, without too serious injury to the general interests of our own and other countries, by increasing the resources of the rebels, and thus prolonging the war.

The regulations and action of this Department are inspired by this wish; but the interests involved in the suppression of the rebellion are, of course, paramount to the temporary advantages to flow from an increase, necessarily limited until the war shall be ended, of the supply of the products referred to.

With great respect, &c., &c.,

S. P. CHASE,
Secretary of the Treasury.

Hon. WILLIAM H. SEWARD, *Secretary of State.*

Cotton trade in the Southwest.

[Letter from Special Agent William P. Mellen, Esq.]

CINCINNATI, *Ohio, September* 26, 1862.

SIR: Mr. Gallagher and I do not understand alike as to our duties of inquiring into the *antecedents* of cotton offered for shipment at any port with which commerce is opened.

I do not understand that I am to investigate the *morals* of transactions connected with any lot of cotton previous to its shipment from any port where our official duties are exercised, nor how it got there even, nor whence it came from, nor who raised or owned it, except, possibly, as far as may be necessary to learn whether it is liable to confiscation; and, if even this inquiry be made, it is doubtful whether much, if any, of the cotton we get, if the title be followed back to the original owner, will escape liability under the confiscation act.

As strong a case as I know of *against my construction* of my official duty, occurred here a short time ago, viz: Five negroes, formerly slaves in Western Tennessee, who had performed valuable service in a regiment of sappers and miners, came here with a letter from the colonel of the regiment certifying the fact, and brought with them, under his certificate of approval, a few bales of cotton formerly belonging to their masters. It had been shipped from Columbus, *via* Cairo, in conformity with the regulations of the Treasury Department. Was it my official duty to have inquired into the history of that cotton, or how they had earned or paid for it, or by what means they had become possessed of it?

It is charged, and possibly true, that negroes and military men about Helena and elsewhere become possessed of considerable lots of cotton improperly. But it seems to me that the official duty of those supervising the commerce of the country does not require them to ascertain whether the negroes take the money back to their masters or how military officers become possessed of it. This is the business of magistrates, or others, it seems to me.

My understanding is, that when cotton is offered for shipment, in a regular way, if the shipment is proper we have no further official duty.

I hope for your immediate instructions on the subject.

I am, very respectfully, your obedient servant,

WILLIAM P. MELLEN,
Special Agent.

Hon. S. P. CHASE, *Secretary of the Treasury.*

Foregoing letter of Mr. Mellen was replied to by the Secretary on the 1st of October, 1862, *q. v.*

Morals of cotton transactions anterior to regular shipment not a proper question for officers of the Treasury Department to determine.

[Reply to letter of William P. Mellen, of September 26, 1862.]

TREASURY DEPARTMENT, *October* 1, 1862.

SIR: I have received your letter of the 26th ultimo, wherein you state that Mr. Gallagher and yourself do not understand alike your duties in regard to the "inquiring into the antecedents of cotton offered for shipment at any port with which commerce is open," and ask for instructions from this department on the subject.

I concur, generally, in the opinion held by you, and approve your action.

All cotton, or other produce, arriving under proper authority at ports open to commerce, will be treated alike, and it is not competent for any officer of this department to inquire into or decide upon the morals of transactions connected with it previous to its shipment from any port within the limits of their official duties.

It is, of course, not within my wishes to countenance any evasion of the confiscation act, or within my power to exempt any property from its operation. It is only to caution the officers of the department against unnecessarry interruption of commerce, and unnecessary interference with private business. To warrant any action against cotton, or other products, as confiscated, there must be clear and satisfactory evidence of liability.

Should any cases arise involving the detention or seizure of cotton, or other produce, so arriving, they will be promptly reported to this department.

I am, &c., &c.,

S. P. CHASE, *Secretary of the Treasury.*

WILLIAM P. MELLEN, Esq.,
Special Agent, Cincinnati, Ohio.

No. 59.

Rules governing trade in Tennessee, adopted by Major General Grant, upon the suggestion of Wm. P. Mellen, esq., special agent Treasury Department, October 4, 1862.

1st. All district and post commanders are to observe the order of the War Department of August 28, 1862, and not to interfere with any shipment or transportation of cotton or other merchandise moving under regulations of the Treasury Department.

2d. Under Section VIII of treasury regulations, the commandants of the posts at Memphis, Jackson, Corinth, and Bolivar, are authorized to recommend parties in their respective districts for permits to ship liquors, &c., for general purposes.

3d. All post commanders may recommend persons within their commands to receive liquors, &c., for their individual use.

4th. All packages for soldiers or officers within any post command, to be forwarded to the commandant thereof for delivery.

5th. No military goods or other thing intended for sale to officers and soldiers of the army are to be permitted to go into any military post except under permits to sutlers.

* * * * * * * * * *

WILLIAM P. MELLEN,
Special Agent.

The foregoing rules were approved by the Secretary of the Treasury, by letter dated October 13, 1862.

No. 60.

Additional rules restricting trade in the west and south.

The following rules or instructions were addressed to all the surveyors in the western collection districts on the 23d October, 1862, adopted by all the special agents, and were approved by the Secretary of the Treasury, by letter to William P. Mellen, esq., dated October 28, 1862.

CINCINNATI, *Ohio, October* 23, 1862.

SIR: On and after the first day of November next you will please observe the following rules in addition to those now in force as to shipments from your port, viz:

1st. The restrictions upon internal commerce, under the regulations of the Secretary of the Treasury of August 28, 1862, are extended so as to embrace all the counties on the north side of the Ohio river, bordering thereon, below Evansville. All shipments of merchandise to any place in the counties named must be subject to permits under the same regulations as if made to places on the south side of the Ohio river.

2d. No goods shall be permitted to go to Ford's Ferry or Cave in Rock, nor to the vicinity of those places, for sale there, except upon the recommendation of John Mitchell.

3d. No goods shall be permitted to go to any place on the south side of the Ohio river, below Henderson, except upon the satisfactory evidence that the person to whom they are permitted to go is a reliable friend of the government of the United States.

4th. No goods shall be permitted to go to any place in the valley of the Cumberland river, nor to any place in Kentucky or Tennessee west of the river, for sale, except to Smithland, Paducah, Columbus, and Hickman, except as follows, viz: permits may be granted for snipments for purposes of sale to Maysfield, Kentucky, upon the recommendation of the surveyor of Paducah, and subject to his supervision upon arrival thereof at Paducah; to Jackson, Tennessee, and Trenton, Tennessee, upon the recommendation of the respective commandants of those posts, whose *personal signatures* to such recommendation shall in all cases be required before permit can be granted.

5th. Shipments of boots, shoes, leather, salt, hats, caps, ready-made clothing, woollen goods, blankets, tanner's oil, lard oil, or other material that can be used for lubricating purposes, to any place or section where there has recently been or is in danger of being a rebel raid or robbery must be restricted to such small quantities as are necessary for the *immediate use* of the loyal people of the neighborhood to which the shipment is to be made, and in no case amounting in the aggregate to over three hundred dollars ($300.)

6th. All shipments to military posts of military goods, or other things intended for sale to the soldiers and officers, may duly be permitted upon the certificate of the respective commanders thereof that such shipment is desired by them.

* * * * * * * * *

WILLIAM P. MELLEN,
Special Agent Treasury Department.

No. 61.

Regulations restricting trade north of the Potomac.

PHILADELPHIA, *Pa., November* 3, 1862.

SIR: After the receipt hereof you will please to observe the following rule, in addition to those now in force, as to shipments and transportation from your port:

The restrictions upon internal commerce, under the regulations of the Secretary of the Treasury of August 28, 1862, are extended so as to embrace all the counties in Maryland on the north side of the Potomac, bordering thereon, west of Baltimore, and all that portion of the counties of Adams and Franklin, in Pennsylvania, south of the parallel of Gettysburg.

All transportation of merchandise to any place in the districts thus restricted must be subject to permits under the same regulations as if made to places in Maryland, south of the Washington and Annapolis railroad. Packages sent to officers and soldiers of the army by their friends are excepted from this restriction.

Shipments of boots, shoes, leather, tanner's oil, salt, hats, caps, ready-made clothing, woollen goods, and blankets, to any place within the districts above named should be carefully guarded, and restricted in quantities to the supply of the neighborhoods to which they are sent for the necessary and immediate use thereof.

I am, very respectfully, your obedient servant,

WM. P. MELLEN,
Special Agent Treasury Department.

The foregoing rules were sent to the various collectors immediately interested in this trade—Baltimore, New York, and Philadelphia.

The same were approved by the Secretary of the Treasury, by letter of the 5th November, 1862, to William P. Mellen, esq.

No. 62.

Instructions relative to trade on the Kanawha river.

GALLIPOLIS, *Ohio, November* 8, 1862.

SIR: You will require every steamboat departing from this port for Charleston, Virginia, on the Kanawha river, or points above that place, to exhibit to you a true manifest of its cargo, and obtain a clearance before proceeding on its voyage.

Very respectfully, your obedient servant,

THOMAS HEATON,
Special Agent Treasury Department.

WILLIAM NASH, Esq.,
Aid to the Revenue, Gallipolis, Ohio.

The above instructions were approved by the Secretary of the Treasury, by letter to Thomas Heaton, esq., dated November 15, 1862.

No. 63.

Restrictions on trade on the north side of the Ohio river.

TREASURY DEPARTMENT, *November* 5, 1862.

SIR: * * * * * * * *

You are hereby authorized to apply such restrictions on trade with points on the Ohio side of the river as are now imposed on trade with places on the opposite side, making such exceptions as you think proper, and sending, for my approval, such specific instructions as you may issue on the subject under this letter.

I am, &c., &c.,

S. P. CHASE,
Secretary of the Treasury.

THOMAS HEATON, Esq.,
Special Agent, Cincinnati, Ohio.

MEMORANDUM.—These restrictions were modified by Mr. Heaton December 12, 1862, *q. v.* The above letter was in reply to suggestions of Mr. Heaton in letter not on file.

No. 64.

Restrictions on trade in Maryland.

The several portions of Maryland, lying on the Chesapeake bay, were divided into *eleven* districts, for which "boards of trade" were appointed, and to each of which the following letter of appointment and instructions was delivered:

BALTIMORE, *Maryland, November* 25, 1862.

GENTLEMEN: You have been appointed, by direction of the Secretary of the Treasury, a "board of trade," for all that part of ——— county, Maryland, lying south of the parallel of ———, and north of the parallel of ———.

You are appointed for the purpose of supervising the trade of the district named, in such a manner as will prevent supplies going thence to rebels, causing no more inconvenience to loyal citizens, in so doing, than may be necessary to insure the desired end.

On and after the 15th day of December next, no permit will be granted by any officer of the customs to ship merchandise to any place in said district, except on presentation to him of your certificate, or that of a similar board in an adjoining district, that he has taken the oath herewith enclosed, (usual;) and that you are satisfied that no part of the goods to be permitted will be so disposed of as to give aid and comfort to the enemy.

A memorandum of the articles wanted must be presented to you, stating the estimated quantities and values thereof. You must write across the face of this memorandum, "Approved," and sign your names to it, and attach it to your certificate. You must date your approval, indorsed on the memorandum and the certificate of the same day, that frauds may not be practiced by attaching certificates and memorandums that do not belong together.

It does not follow that, *because* a man takes the oath, he shall be entitled, as a matter of course, to your certificate; this is left to your sound discretion; you should be satisfied, by his daily conduct, that he is a loyal man, and will act in good faith.

You should be careful, also, to restrict the amounts which you certify for, so that there may be at no time within your district more goods than are required for the proper use and consumption of the people thereof.

You will please notify the people of your district, as soon and as generally as you can, of your appointment and its object; and that, after the date named, they will not be permitted to take merchandise there without your certificate as above.

(Printed blanks for affidavits and certificates will be found at the custom-house in Baltimore. If you will send for them by some of your neighbors, who are coming up here, you can get what you need.)

As your office is without compensation, you can charge twenty-five cents for each affidavit.

All officers of the customs are informed of your appointment and of the purpose of it, and will be governed in their action by your certificates.

You will please to communicate with me, from time to time, as to any matters connected with your duties. You will address me at Washington city, in care of Hon. S. P. Chase, Secretary of the Treasury.

Very respectfully,

WM. P. MELLEN,
Special Agent Treasury Department.

To ——— ———.

MEMORANDUM.—The foregoing boards of trade, each consisted of two persons.

The collectors of customs of Baltimore, Philadelphia, and New York were notified of the above rules, and of the appointment of the several Boards of Trade, and their respective districts.

The restrictions, thus arranged by Mr. Mellen, were approved by the Secretary of the Treasury on the 5th December, 1862.

No. 65.

Board of Trade at Memphis dissolved.

NOTICE.

The Board of Trade for the city of Memphis is hereby dissolved. All commercial matters heretofore transacted by that board will receive attention, until the surveyor of the port is duly commissioned, by

THOS. H. YEATMAN,
Special Agent Treasury Department.

MEMPHIS, *Tennessee, December* 2, 1862.

The foregoing notice of dissolution of Board of Trade of Memphis was approved by the Secretary of the Treasury on the 16th day of December, 1862.

No. 66.

Circular relating to trade below Memphis, issued by Thomas H. Yeatman, esq., special agent.

SPECIAL AGENCY, TREASURY DEPARTMENT,
Memphis, Tennessee, December 12, 1862.

In pursuance of instructions and regulations by the honorable Secretary of the United States Treasury, August 28, 1862, referring to certain acts of Congress approved July 13, 1861, and May 20, 1862, authorizing "special agents of the department to temporarily extend restrictions to places in their respective districts, and make such local rules to be observed therein as may from time to time become necessary, promptly reporting their action to the Secretary of the Treasury for his sanction or disapproval."

Now, in accordance with the authority and with the consent of the military and naval commanding officers, clearances will be granted for steamboats to pass down the Mississippi river, as far as within ten miles of the mouth of White river, with permitted goods, not of a contraband character, and intended only for family supplies; the delivery thereof to be supervised by the revenue aid, and receipted for on oath by the parties receiving the same, that they will not be used directly or indirectly for any other purpose, and receive in exchange cotton.

In all cases it will be distinctly understood, by parties making such an adventure, that no reclamation will be acknowledged, by the government of the United States, for any loss of boat or cargo by persons in insurrection; and, furthermore, boats making the trip will be required to give bond in double the amount of their value for their return to Helena or Memphis; and an additional bond of twenty thousand dollars that no goods, of any kind whatever, shall be landed from said boat which are not fully set forth on her manifest and bills permitted by the proper authorities. Aids and other loyal citizens will report the name of any persons or boats paying out gold, or other articles of contraband, in exchange for cotton.

THOS. H. YEATMAN,
Special Agent Treasury Department.

No. 67.

Restrictions on trade on the north side of the Ohio river modified.

PITTSBURG, *Penn., December* 12, 1862.

SIR: The order in regard to restrictions on trade to places on the north side of the Ohio river is so far modified as not to require permits for shipments to such places of general merchandise, and imposing restrictions only on shipments of powder, lead, shot, percussion-caps, or other munitions of war, and also on quinine, chloroform, quicksilver, and morphine.

Very respectfully, &c.,

THO. HEATON, *Special Agent.*

Hon. S. P. CHASE,
Secretary of the Treasury.

MEMORANDUM.—The foregoing notice of restrictions, &c., was approved by the Secretary of the Treasury December 19, 1862.

No. 68.

Trade below Helena, Arkansas, prohibited; no trade opened below Memphis.

TREASURY DEPARTMENT, *December* 16, 1862.

SIR: I have received your letter of the 4th instant, informing me that, with the consent of certain military officers, you are permitting family supplies to go below Helena, to be exchanged for cotton.

Your action in the premises is not approved. No trade has been opened below Memphis with the sanction of this department; and no new sections can be opened to trade except upon the agreement of all the special agents exercising concurrent jurisdiction, or, should they fail to agree, by direction of the Secretary of the Treasury. You will therefore grant no permission for any section of country not thus regularly opened to trade.

Respectfully,

S. P. CHASE,
Secretary of the Treasury.

THOS. H. YEATMAN, Esq.,
Special Agent, Memphis, Tennessee.

No. 69.

Order suspending trade with points in Kentucky and Tennessee.

CINCINNATI, *Ohio, December* 22, 1862.

SIR: Until further notice you will not permit any goods to points on the Mobile and Ohio railroad south of Columbus, Kentucky; nor up the Cumberland river above Smithland.

Very respectfully,

DAVID G. BARNITZ,
Special Agent Treasury Department.

WARREN THORNBERRY, Esq.,
Surveyor, Paducah, Kentucky.

Letters of same tenor sent to the other surveyors.

The foregoing order was approved by the Secretary of the Treasury on the 16th December, 1862.

No. 70.

Modification of restrictions upon trade in salt, in Kentucky, directed.

TREASURY DEPARTMENT, *January* 24, 1863.

SIR: It is represented to the department that the restrictions at present imposed upon shipments of salt into Kentucky are onerous and unnecessary.

You will therefore, as soon as practicable after the receipt of this letter, confer with Special Agent Barnitz, and ascertain and report to the department, as early as possible, whether the restrictions now in relation to shipments of salt into Ken tucky may be removed, and that article placed upon the same footing as other merchandise; and to what extent they may, with safety, be removed or modified. Also, whether such removal or modification could apply to the whole State or only certain portions or sections thereof, which you will please designate.

Very respectfully,

GEO. HARRINGTON,
Acting Secretary of the Treasury.

THO. HEATON, Esq.,
Special Agent, Cincinnati, Ohio.

No. 71.

Conditions upon which trade with Helena, Arkansas, is opened.

The only places on the Mississippi, between Memphis and Cairo, to which merchandise can be permitted to go, for sale, are Columbus, Hickman, and New Madrid. Permits to all other places can only be granted for strictly family supplies, upon the personal application of the party who is to use them, and upon his affidavit that they are for his own use, and shall not be sold or otherwise disposed of to other parties, and that he is loyal to the government of the United States, and will in all things so deport himself.

It is agreed that trade with Helena, Arkansas, shall be opened from the 1st of January, 1863, subject to the following conditions, viz:

1. Permits may be granted to ship merchandise to that place only upon the recommendation of the Board of Trade, to be at once appointed there by the special agent of the Treasury Department at Memphis.

2. Persons residing on or near the river, between Memphis and Helena, may have permits for strictly family supplies for their own use; but all applications for such permits must be made in person by the party who is to use them to the surveyor at Memphis or Board of Trade at Helena, and the permits granted must be subject to compliance with any military orders pertaining to the place of destination.

The foregoing rules were submitted by David G. Barnitz, esq., special agent of the Treasury Department, on the 12th day of January, 1863, after having been agreed upon by the several special agents having co-ordinate supervision over the trade on the western rivers, and were approved by the Secretary of the Treasury, by letter to Mr. Barnitz, dated January 20, 1363.

COMMUNICATING COUNTERSIGN TO THE ENEMY.

IN THE HOUSE OF REPRESENTATIVES,
February 11, 1862.

Mr. F. A. CONKLING submitted the following, which were adopted:

Whereas, it is asserted, on authority worthy the notice of this House, that the countersign of the army was in possession of the rebel pickets, on the west side of the Potomac, before it had been communicated to our men, on the day the Pensacola ran the gauntlet of the river batteries; and whereas it is also asserted that information of the movement of the national army and fleets is frequently communicated in advance to the enemy, under circumstances which justify a suspicion of treachery on the part of persons in the civil or military service; therefore—

Resolved, That the joint committee on the conduct of the war be requested, at their earliest convenience, to investigate these charges and report such action in the premises as the circumstances shall warrant.

Attest: EM. ETHERIDGE, *Clerk*.

WASHINGTON, *March* 4, 1862.

Lieutenant Colonel FRANK S. FISKE sworn and examined.

By the chairman:

Question. What is your rank and position in the army?

Answer. I am Lieutenant Colonel of the 2d New Hampshire regiment.

Question. Where are you stationed?

Answer. In General Hooker's division, below Matawoman creek, near Budd's Ferry.

Question. Please state what you know about the enemy obtaining possession of our countersign on any occasion?

Answer. I was told by a staff officer, whose name I do not now remember, I think about the 8th of February, that the afternoon previous, our pickets had reported to the officer of the picket that the enemy had cried out the countersign to them across the river before they had received it.

Question. What time is this countersign given out?

Answer. The orders were that the brigade officer of the day should report to brigade headquarters at four o'clock in the afternoon and receive the countersign. The pickets reported to their officers that they had received the countersign from the enemy before that time.

Question. So the enemy announced the countersign about the time it was given out?

Answer. Yes, sir; a little before.

Question. What other information did they have?

Answer. Lieutenant Ellis, the signal officer there, told me that he heard the enemy give the countersign. He was in my tent the next morning, and said it was the subject of general conversation among the officers there. He said he heard the enemy give it.

Question. What was the countersign on that occasion?

Answer. "Chippeway."

Question. What did the enemy say in regard to it?

Answer. This was the day when the Pensacola was expected down. That is another fact. That was one reason why some supposed it might have been taken from the telegraph wire. The information was telegraphed down to our division that the Pensacola would come down that night, what they cried out was: "The Pensacola is coming down to-night, isn't she? Damn her, we are ready for her. We have got your countersign—Chippeway."

Question. And both particulars were correct?

Answer. Yes, sir.

Question. What is the mode of giving out these countersigns?

Answer. The mode now is, as I understand it, that one of the staff of the brigadier general reports at division headquarters at about two o'clock in the afternoon, and receives the countersign, and from him it is given to the brigade officer of the day, and he gives it to the regimental officers of the guard.

Question. From whom does it come at first?

Answer. When I was with my regiment, alone, at the station, I used to receive a list of countersigns for the succeeding week, one for each day; for instance, for Monday, so and so; Tuesday, so and so, and so on through the week.

Question. Have you any theory to explain the way the enemy obtained possession of that information, or have you any suspicion of any person who might have given it?

Answer. None whatever. I have always supposed that it came down the river on the other side. It was impossible for them to get it from our side, because there was no means of crossing there in the daytime, certainly, and no one would shout out that information to them, because they would be heard by us. And I think we watched so closely that no signals could have been made.

Question. Where were the enemy situated as from you?

Answer. Directly opposite from us. In a still day, particularly if the weather is a little heavy, the sentinels frequently converse across the river.

Question. How wide is the river there?

Answer. From a mile to a mile and a quarter or a mile and a half.

Question. When did you come up from down there?

Answer. Last Saturday.

Question. What is the condition of the army there now?

Answer. I think it is in a very good condition, indeed. We have only one man sick. There are nine in the hospital who are somewhat ailing, but not so sick as to need to be taken out of their quarters. But they are in the hospital, because the hospital is empty, and they might as well be there as in their quarters.

Question. Have you any evidence to show whether the enemy have left on the other side?

Answer. I went up in a balloon the other day, and I concluded that they had left and that they had returned. Their pickets along the shore were nearly trebled during last week, and their encampments have reappeared; some of them in the same places as before, and some in different localities. They used to be constantly firing from their batteries, but they have never done any injury at all. We were calculating the other day the number of shots they must have fired, and we made it out that they had fired from 8,000 to 10,000 shots since they have been there, and no person has been injured, and no vessel has been injured seriously.

Question. Are the ranges of the shots too long?

Answer. The officer of the gunboats said he thought that they changed their companies too often; before one could learn how to manage the guns it was changed. Another reason was that the quaility of their powder was unequal.

Question. Is there any difficulty in taking those batteries and clearing the river?

Answer. There would be no difficulty at all if we could land. But we could not land near there without being exposed to a very destructive fire of canister. There is a little promontory there, a semicircle running out so that they could fire up and down. They have some very good guns there. If we could once land a force there I should think, from the topography of the country, they could be driven out.

Question. Could you not land out of reach of their canister?

Answer. There are a great many marshes and ravines over there. There would be some difficulty in landing. If they have, as is supposed, 30,000 or 40,000 men there, it would be difficult to land up at Freestone Point, or near there, and get down to the batteries before they could send a large force down there to meet us.

Question. The truth is if you could drive out their army from the country there, their batteries fall of course?

Answer. Yes, sir. I think if we could have sent over a regiment when their pickets were not so numerous as now, if you could have landed a regiment in the night, you could have taken the batteries very easily. It might have been a sharp struggle, but the result could not be doubtful.

Question. Do you know why that has not been attempted?

Answer. I do not know.

Question. Where are those batteries located to which you refer?

Answer. There is one at Cockpit Point, a short distance below Powell creek; another on Shipping Point just below Quantico creek; and there are two batteries on the same promontory below, which are called the Evansport batteries, I think.

PAYMASTERS, &c.

WASHINGTON, *January* 2, 1862.

General B. F. LARNED sworn and examined.

By the chairman:

Question. What is your position?

Answer. I am now paymaster general of the army.

By Mr. Odell:

Question. We wanted to find from you to what extent paymasters are required in the service as it has developed itself during the last four or six months. We thought the best information we could get would be from you.

Answer. I long since requested the President and Secretary of War to appoint no more paymasters, for I thought I had enough. As the army is situated now I have just about enough, but none to spare. They have to work very hard to meet all the demands upon them, particularly as the troops are scattering.

Question. Our inquiry is in reference to paymasters ranking as majors?

Answer. I think I have enough now to accomplish the whole payment of the army. I do not think I have too many.

Question. Do you know how many you have now?

Answer. I think about one hundred and twenty-one additional paymasters, and twenty-seven regulars. The law would give the President power to appoint three hundred.

Question. That is one to every two regiments?

Answer. Yes, sir.

Question. Are the whole of these one hundred and forty-eight men now on duty?

Answer. Yes, sir.

Question. Have you any data from which you can give, or can you give from memory, how they are divided up?

Answer. I have six on the Pacific slope; I have about thirty in Missouri and Leavenworth; I have some ten in Kentucky; about the same number in Illinois; and about the same number in Western Virginia; and between fifty and sixty here, including those belonging to the expeditions.

Question. That does not embrace them all?

Answer. I give these numbers from recollection only, not undertaking to be specific.

Question. Can you not give us from your office a statement as to where these one hundred and forty-eight paymasters are posted?

Answer. I could in a little while.

Question. Could you do it in a day or two?

Answer. Yes, sir. We want more paymasters out west, and I am only trying to get through this payment, which is a very heavy one, in order to send more out west.

Question. From the force you have here?

Answer. Yes, sir.

Question. In your judgment how much can one paymaster do in the army as it is situated upon the Potomac?

Answer. He can pay four regiments; that is double what the law allows. The States are constantly calling upon me to send paymasters to the regiments they are organizing, and have organized. I have a call from Massachusetts for them, a call from Vermont, from Wisconsin, from Michigan; hence I have to send paymasters from here in all directions to meet these demands. And sometimes it embarrasses me a great deal, because they are hard at work here.

Question. Your department is so organized that these men can be detailed to be sent anywhere?

Answer. Yes, sir.

Question. Does each paymaster have a clerk?

Answer. Yes, sir.

Question. What is his salary?

Answer. They get $700 a year, and 75 cents a day for subsistence.

Question. Do they have mileage?

Answer. No, sir; they have their actual expenses when they travel under orders.

Question. What is the pay of paymasters?

Answer. I suppose you might put them down at an average of $2,500.

Question. That is exclusive of mileage?

Answer. Yes, sir. They get mileage when they travel, as any other officer.

Question. Ten cents a mile?

Answer. Yes, sir.

Question. Anything for subsistence?

Answer. No, sir; except their pay.

Question. The clerks get subsistence as well as their pay?

Answer. Yes, sir; seventy five cents a day. The salary of a paymaster's clerk is small—is considerably less than the lowest class of clerks in this city. And it is very difficult ordinarily to get that class of men for paymaster's clerks which we really need. We want intelligent men—men of great integrity, for we must trust them.

Question. And men of some clerkly abilities, too, I suppose?

Answer. Yes, sir. Some clerks are a great deal better than the paymasters themselves. In many cases they are dependent upon their clerks.

Question. Now, in brief, what are the duties of these paymasters? What papers do they have to prepare?

Answer. Whenever the muster-rolls of the regiments come in, they are placed in the paymasters' hands. They have then to take blank pay-rolls and draw off the names, and make up calculations of the amounts due to the men in the regiments—each company by itself—and they then go and pay them.

Question. Do they make duplicate pay-rolls?

Answer. Yes, sir; everything is in duplicate. He keeps one pay-roll for himself, and sends one to my office for examination.

Question. That has to be done for every regiment in duplicate?

Answer. Yes, sir.

Question. And that is done by himself or his clerk?

Answer. Yes, sir.

By the chairman:

Question. And that is done every payment that is made?

Answer. Yes, sir.

Question. How often is that?

Answer. The whole of the troops are paid every two months. But in the mean time a large number of these paymasters are in their offices every day paying, hard at work. For instance, we have particular officers designated so as to keep the accounts together. We have a paymaster who is assigned to paying resigned officers. He is paying from twenty to forty and fifty officers a day, being kept at work until 5 o'clock.

Question. He is connected with your office?

Answer. He is an additional paymaster, and we assign this matter to him in order to keep his accounts together.

Question. His duties are discharged in your paymaster's department?

Answer. Not necessarily.

By Mr. Gooch:

Question. Does he have any regiments to pay besides?

Answer. No, sir; he has no time for that. Another paymaster is assigned to paying discharged men, which amount sometimes to seventy and eighty a day; and you may judge that that is as much as one man can do.

By Mr. Odell:

Question. And then there is another who pays the accounts of prisoners?

Answer. Yes, sir.

By the chairman:

Question. You say you have none now out of employ?

Answer. No, sir. There is one man about getting his bonds whom I am exceedingly anxious to send away. He has not yet furnished his bonds. The President appointed this man—a sort of secret appointment, as I afterwards learned—and ordered him to report to the Secretary of State.

Question. We are thus minute in our inquiries, because we are told all around that we had more paymasters than were needed—a great supernumerary number of paymasters, and that many of them could be dispensed with.

Answer. That is a mistake.

By Mr. Odell:

Question. If there are 160 of them, it is not a mistake, is it, by your testimony here?

Answer. That would be but one to six.

Question. I do not speak with reference to how many it would be. You say you have enough, and if there are 160 additional paymasters, that is forty more than you say you are using.

Answer. That is my mistake. I had got the impression that I had counted up these officers and found that there were 121 of them; but taking the new rolls, I think I have more. But I do not think I have 160.

By the chairman:

Question. But, more or less, you employ them all—every man?

Answer. Yes, sir.

Question. And, of course, it is your judgment that you could not dispense with any without injury to the service?

Answer. I think not.

By Mr. Gooch:

Question. How many regiments can one paymaster pay?

Answer. There is a great difference in paymasters. One will pay six regiments while another will pay two.

Question. I mean a competent man.

Answer. They all pretend to be competent. They are very slow, timid, fearful that they are going to make mistakes, and will take a week to do what others would do in two days.

Question. Then such men are not fit for the service?

Answer. They are not the best, that is certain; but they all think they are competent.

Question. How many men are employed in paying discharged soldiers, officers, &c.?

Answer. I am speaking of those around here, for I cannot judge of other points. Perhaps you may say there are five here, constantly engaged, with as much as they can do.

WASHINGTON, *January* 2, 1862.

E. H. BROOKS sworn and examined. (Paymaster General Larned being present during the examination.)

By the chairman:

Question. What position do you hold?

Answer. I am chief clerk in the paymaster general's department.

Question. Have you heard the testimony of General Larned?

Answer. I have.

Question. Do you concur in it all?

Answer. Yes, sir.

By Mr. Gooch:

Question. How long will it take a paymaster to pay a regiment?

Answer. If he is a good one he can do it in three days.

Question. Do all that is necessary to be done?

Answer. Yes, sir. However, that depends upon where the regiment is situated. In General Hooker's division, it will take the paymaster six days to go down there, pay a regiment, and come back.

By Mr. Odell:

Question. Suppose it takes him six days, what has he then to do?

Answer. In the first place, he has copies of all the allotment rolls to send or take to the person designated to receive them. By this last law, where he has to draw a check for every man, he must double his work.

General Larned: Certainly. Where a man could before pay a regiment in three days, under this allotment law he cannot do it now in less than ten days.

The witness: He must use up eight check-books in paying off one regiment.

Question. If the soldiers make the allotments, how is that?

Answer. Some of the regiments come in with the allotment rolls full; others have only two or three to a company.

By Mr. Julian:

Question. What is a paymaster doing after he pays the regiment?

Answer. He has just as much as he can do, after paying his regiments, going around to pay the sick in the hospitals, &c., to make up and close his accounts in the two months.

Question. How long do paymasters work?

Answer. Some of them say they work all night. Others, as I see, work as long as I do, and I leave the office at 5 o'clock.

By the chairman:

Question. You do not expect a decrease of the labor in the future?

Answer. No, sir. The further the troops are sent from Washington the more labor there will be. The labor increases every payment. To make the present payment, some of the paymasters go up as far as Cumberland—go up to General Banks's column. We take a four-horse wagon and go up there, and go from regiment to regiment to pay the men, and it will take a week—some of them ten days—to get through their payments.

Question. Do you concur with the paymaster general in saying that you have enough paymasters now?

Answer. I think we could do the work with what we have.

Question. Do you think you could spare any without injury to the service?

Answer. No, sir; I do not, because you are increasing the work every payment. But as they become more familiar with their duties they can, of course, do more. There are certain paymasters who, this last payment, paid six regiments, while others could hardly get through three.

General Larned: We could very well exchange some of them; but that is not in our power.

The witness: We are about making a payment at Annapolis for this expedition that is about getting off. We expect to make that payment by the end of this week, though we only got the rolls on Wednesday. But that is done by extraordinary work, and a detail for the duty. We sent off, yesterday, some eight paymasters to go to that expedition and pay it off before it sailed.

Question. We make this inquiry because we had it from what we considered very good authority that there was quite an expense to the government, in this matter of paymasters, that might be dispensed with without injury to the service.

Answer. I don't see it.

Question. Of course you are the one to see it, if it is so.

Answer. If there are any particular persons, we can now find out what work they are doing. Every man that is here is charged with all the work he does. Away from here we cannot tell exactly now; but we can after the accounts come in. But here we can tell, after each payment, what each man has done.

Question. We had no reference to any one in particular, but as a general thing. We supposed that perhaps the President had been forced, by the pressure upon him, to make more appointments than there is any necessity for.

Answer. A great deal of this comes from men who are disposed to brag of what they have done. Some of them come in and say: "I have paid five or six regiments, while such a person has not done anything." Now, they do not know that, for they do not know what that person has done.

By Mr. Odell:

Question. Who appoints the paymaster's clerk?

Answer. The paymaster himself. And I will remark here that the expenses of a paymaster's clerk are just as much as the expenses of a paymaster himself.

By Mr. Johnson:

Question. How many regiments are there to be paid off at Annapolis?

Answer. About seventeen regiments.

By Mr. Odell:

Question. You sent so many paymasters there in order to pay them off rapidly, I suppose?

Answer. Yes, sir; we expect to pay them off in forty-eight hours.

Question. Are these men detailed on special duty, or are they subject to the orders of the paymaster general to go to and fro as he may order?

Answer. They are subject to the orders of the paymaster general to go where he chooses to send them.

Question. Are there paymasters who go with expeditions, and belong to those expeditions especially?

Answer. There were three sent with General Sherman's expedition who will go back again, I suppose.

Question. They came back from there?

Answer. They have to come back for their money as a matter of course.

General Larned: You refer to using up the time between the payments. There is one thing to be taken into consideration. We do not get the rolls and get the money from the Treasury Department to make this payment at the end of December. We shall not accomplish it until within a day or two of the next month, on the 28th of February. We have to wait to get our money. And we are going to be exceedingly embarrassed now by the stoppage of specie payments by the government and by the banks. We cannot get the specie to make our change. What we are going to do I cannot imagine. It is going to embarrass us exceedingly, unless the men agree, after receiving the even amounts which we can pay them, to club together for the balances and put them in the hands of the captain or some one else.

Mr. Odell: I suppose the paymaster could arrange for that by taking a little change.

General Larned: We cannot get it; the treasury will not give it, and the banks will not give it. And I think it will come to compelling Congress to use small bills.

The witness: Each regiment, at the lowest calculation, takes $1,500 in small change.

Mr. Odell: They can manage that by four or five men clubbing together to make an even amount.

General Larned: They dislike very much to do that.

By Mr. Gooch:

Question. (To witness.) Do your paymasters average four regiments?

Answer. I think they do. I only speak of the army here. I cannot tell exactly how it is in other places.

WASHINGTON, *January* 21, 1862.

Captain WILLIAM WILSON sworn and examined,

By Mr. Covode:

Question. What is your rank and position in the army?

Answer. I am brigade commissary of subsistence, with the rank of captain.

Question. In what division?

Answer. In the fifth division, commanded by General Blenker.

Question. You have opportunities of knowing what is the condition of that division as regards sobriety, &c.? Go on and state what you know about it.

Answer. I would state this: that I think there must be in that division not less than fifteen, and probably as many as twenty-five, establishments where they sell liquor, lager beer especially, and they all have whiskey that they sell privately at the same stands. But lager beer is the principal article they deal in; that they deal out in great abundance. It is all over the division. I do not think there is a tent in the division but what has more or less of it. All the sutlers keep it, and the stands are crowded all the while.

Question. To what extent do they drink—so as to make them unfit for service?

Answer. I think if you were to pass through the division any day you will find from one hundred to five hundred men unfit for duty.

Question. In consequence of drinking?

Answer. Yes, sir.

Question. Officers and men?

Answer. They are about all alike. They all drink, and drink in great abundance. I have occasion very frequently to go to officers to get papers signed, and documents certified, in connexion with my post, and I frequently have to wait an hour or two hours, perhaps longer. I have, of course, to go to the inferior officers to get my papers presented, and it takes them a considerable time before they can approach their superior officers, and very frequently I am detained as much as two or three hours to get my papers to transact my business with the brigade.

Question. Is this dissipation in the army general, or is it confined to particular divisions?

Answer. I have been a great deal through other divisions, but I have seen nothing like that existing in any of the divisions but ours. A great many men from other regiments and divisions come into ours to get liquor. The nineteenth Indiana regiment is situated about a half a mile from where I am, and I know a great many men in that regiment. In fact, I know nearly all of them; for I was in Camp Morton, at Indianapolis, before I came away, and I know that many of them come over to our camp and get liquor, and go home intoxicated.

Question. They cannot get it in their own division?

Answer. No, sir. There are men from other regiments who come there. There are a great many troops scattered around there, and when the men get furloughs they come into our division and get what they want.

By Mr. Julian:

Question. Is there much drunkenness in the nineteenth Indiana regiment?

Answer. I do not think they have any intoxicating liquor in that regiment. I know the man who is the sutler there, and I am satisfied that he is a strictly temperance man, and keeps nothing of the kind.

By Mr. Covode:

Question. Do all the officers in your division keep liquor?

Answer. They all keep their wines and brandies; all of them.

Question. That is, in General Blenker's division?

Answer. Yes, sir.

Question. Do they sell liquor?

Answer. They sell it a little on the private; they keep it and do sell it.

By the chairman:

Question. Do the sutlers make arrangements to go snacks in the profits?

Answer. It is the presumption that the officers are all connected with the sutlers, and make a division of the profits. That is only a presumption, however, of those who have observed these things.

By Mr. Covode:

Question. Do you state that the number of men thus rendered unfit for service in this division amount to 500 a day?

Answer. I think it is safe to say that you can go there any day in the week and find, on an average, 500 men in that division who you would say were unfit for duty; enough to put the whole division to flight on the field of battle.

Question. Do you see any remedy for this thing?

Answer. I know of no remedy in the world that you can devise, except to cut off liquor from officers and all; or to break up the division, separate the brigades and put them in other divisions with good commanders. There are three brigades, in that division. If you were to separate them, and put them in other divisions with good commanders, good sober officers, I think they would make very good soldiers.

By the chairman:

Question. Who know these facts besides yourself?

Answer. There are two other commissaries there who are Americans, and have been appointed as I have been. The soldiers are all Germans. I do not think there are 100 Americans in the whole division. J. B. Salisbury and L. G. Hewling are the other commissaries. They know about these matters. Mr. Salisbury is a son-in-law of General Jesup.

By Mr. Odell:

Question. Who is your general?

Answer. General Bowlin is the general of my brigade. He is a German, and acts as brigadier general of the third brigade.

Question. General Blenker is in charge of the division?

Answer. Yes, sir.

Question. Who are the brigadier generals?

Answer. General Bowlin is one; the other two I cannot give the names of. The other commissaries can give them, as they serve under them. The brigadier general of the second brigade, as I am told, is a sober man, and would gladly see this thing stopped entirely. I do not know that fact myself, but Mr. Salisbury, the commissary of that brigade, tells me so.

WASHINGTON, *January* 29, 1862.

Captain THORNTON SMITH sworn and examined.

By the chairman:

Question. What is your rank and position in the army.

Answer. I am quartermaster of the Excelsior brigade, with the rank of captain; appointed by the War Department.

Question. What do you know with regard to the administration of affairs under General Sickles?

Answer. Previous to my taking charge of the brigade I was told by the acting quartermaster who had been assigned to that duty by General Sickles that I would have a great deal of trouble with that brigade; that the general and other officers had been in the habit of getting everything they wanted from the quartermaster's department without requisitions. I told him I should have no trouble at all in that respect, for they could not have them without requisitions; that I was going into that department with sureties entered against me that would make me responsible. The first day after I got there one of the general's orderlies came down for supplies without a requisition; I told him I should not furnish them without a requisition. That was the last of that line, and requisitions always came afterwards. When I began to look around to find the property that had been captured there from the rebels, I found that the horse the general was riding, a very fine white horse, had been taken from a man of the name of Cox, and never turned over to the quartermaster's department, as should have been done. And Doctor Brown, surgeon of the 1st regiment, had got a horse captured on the same expedition, which he has sold, and has appropriated the proceeds to his own use. And the colonel of the first regiment I think beyond a doubt, sold me a horse for $125 that he traded two government horses for to an Indiana cavalryman, whose name I do not know. That is the way the horse was obtained. I paid him $125 for the horse. Lieutenant Colonel Potter, of the 2d regiment, captured a horse down in Maryland, and sold him to Captain Bradley, of his own regiment, and the proceeds, I presume, he appropriated. It has never been returned to the department, and I believe, to the best of my knoweledge, that four-fifths of all the property captured in lower Maryland has been appropriated by General Sickles and his officers to their own private uses.

Question. What amount of property has been captured there?

Answer. I think there was one instance of a store out of which $1,000 worth of property was taken and distributed among the officers, sutlers, &c. Every man who could get his hand on it took it.

Question. Do you now hold the position of quartermaster there?

Answer. I do not. I was relieved from duty there because General Sickles had a man of his own choice from New York city that he wished to be quartermaster. I was told when I was assigned there that I could not stay; that he would have no man in his brigade that was not pliable enough to be used for his own purposes.

Question. Who told you that?

Answer. A member of the brigade.

Question. Were you acting in the capacity of quartermaster there when this property was captured?

Answer. I was not. There was a person named Gerard ——— who acted as quartermaster at that time.

Question. Do you know whether any property that was captured has been returned to the owners?

Answer. Some of it has been, but a very small part of it.

Question. From whom was this property taken?

Answer. It was taken from various men. There was one by the name of Cox, who owns the horse that General Sickles now rides.

Question. Was he a secessionist?

Answer. There appears to be no evidence to that effect. He still lives there in Maryland.

Question. How was the property captured—in battle?

Answer. No, sir; he went there and took it. A farmer will not stand out in the face of a parcel of officers who ride up and demand these things.

Question. They took this property from the citizens, without capturing it in battle, or anything of that sort?

Answer. Certainly. There have been no battles there. There is one case which I have handed over to General Meigs, of the quartermaster's department, and also a copy to the military committee of the Senate, of which Mr. Wilson is chairman. It is the case of a bill of three hundred and odd dollars, of citizens within three miles of that place, against General Sickles and Colonel White, for keeping horses and boarding them, they telling him that the bill would be paid by the quartermaster. That bill has been sworn to, and was presented to me for payment, and there is no place where the brigade has been but what the officers have left their individual bills in that way. That has been the case all through that section of the country, until the presence of the brigade is dreaded, from the fact that they take what they want, and their individual bills are not paid. Any of them will sign a voucher for anything to be paid for by the government. I know of one instance where I went to get a voucher signed for sixteen cords of wood where the first brigade was located, which I considered was the amount of fuel burned. The fences I considered damages which should not go into the fuel account. The colonel of the regiment, who had not paid his individual bill, altered it from 16 to 71 cords for the destroying of the fences, and I do not know but what it may have been to remunerate the man for his board, which the colonel never paid for.

Question. What do the people say or do when this property is taken from them? Do they make complaints about it?

Answer. They make complaints, but what redress have they? The War Department does not recognize or assume the individual bills of officers. They will pay whatever belongs to the government to pay—whatever is taken for government supplies. But if an officer or a soldier goes to a citizen there and compels him to board him and feed his horse, and then goes away without paying him, the citizen has no redress as against the government.

Question. Have they entered no complaints here at the War Department against this mode of proceeding?

Answer. I know that this man from whom I have sent a communication here has been working with General McClellan and the War Department for the last four months, and he never has received a dollar. He lives at Good Hope, where the brigade was encamped, I think, from June up to the first of November.

Question. Do you know any more instances of delinquency on the part of General Sickles or any of his officers?

Answer. In this second regiment, Colonel White, who has been in command of the brigade during General Sickles's absence—and he has been absent a month—has had charges preferred against him for drunkenness, and various charges of that kind. The lieutenant colonel has had the same charge preferred against him. Three of the captains are under arrest upon various charges, and the result is that that regiment is entirely demoralized from the fact that there is hardly an officer in it that has not been involved in one way or another; and when you come to ascertain what the brigade is made of, what its officers are, you find that the lieutenant colonel of the second regiment was one of those engaged in the slaver Wanderer; another colonel was one of those in the Lopez expedition and in the Walker Nicaragua expedition. That class of men are all through that brigade as officers. So that their high moral character will not sustain them very far.

Question. Do slaves come into the camp there?

Answer. There have some come in. What have come in have been generally kept and secreted. There are slaves there now. General Sickles has, I think, six at his headquarters that he uses for his help. They were captured over in Virginia. A special order came from General McClellan, through General Hooker, to return them to the government; but they have never been returned.

Question. To return them to the government?

Answer. Yes, sir; to send them up to Washington.

Question. Are any of these slaves ever returned to their masters?

Answer. Not that I know of. I have not seen any that have been returned.

WASHINGTON, *April* 10, 1862.

General DANIEL E. SICKLES sworn and examined.

By the chairman:

Question. What is your rank and position in the army, and where are you stationed?

Answer. I have commanded a brigade on the Lower Potomac, in the division of General Hooker, of the army of the Potomac.

Question. How long have you been stationed there?

Answer. I have been stationed in Maryland since September last; I have been upon the Lower Potomac since the 28th of October last. On Monday, the 6th instant, I was relieved from my command.

Question. We have been directed by the House of Representatives to inquire into the treatment of contrabands coming within your lines. What has been the custom of dealing with them in your division, so far as you know and have observed?

Answer. I will, if you please, state my own practice first, when not acting under orders from superior authority. My own practice has been, when contrabands came into my lines from Virginia, crossing the river, to examine them and obtain what information that was practicable. When I found them intelligent and well behaved I have retained them in camp, sometimes in the quartermaster's department, sometimes in charge of suitable persons near my headquarters, that they might be employed as scouts and guides.

When those belonging to, or said to belong to, persons in our own neighborhood, or anywhere about Maryland, came into our lines, they have been subject to a general order issued in September last; an order having reference chiefly to the police of the camp, and the exclusion of persons not employed in the army; under that order they have been excluded from the camps. Sometimes they would make their way back again, and when no objection has been made they have been employed, in a few instances, by officers as servants.

At first there were several applications made by persons claiming them as their slaves, and when they were identified by their description, application has been made that they should be surrendered through the action of officers of my command, which has been declined. But orders have been sent to the commanding officers of the several camps that, if such described persons were within the lines, they should, under the operation of the general order to which I have already adverted, be excluded from the camps, and let whoever might have a claim to them assert that claim before the civil tribunals of Maryland.

That is, as succinctly as I can state it, the course I have pursued in my own command in reference to those two classes of cases, and I think we have had no contrabands within my lines except those from Virginia and those from Maryland.

Question. From whence did that general order emanate to which you have referred?

Answer. I will now proceed and state the orders upon the subject of contrabands that have come from the headquarters of the army of the Potomac, and those that have come from the headquarters of that division. I have received no orders recently from the headquarters of the army of the Potomac. In September and October last, and perhaps as late as November, in two or three instances orders came from the headquarters of the army of the Potomac, directing that such and such persons, naming them, claiming to have slaves within one of my camps, the camp being generally named, should be permitted to search the camp and reclaim their slaves. I addressed a communication in regard to the most important case that occurred, five or six persons being claimed, stating that such steps would be likely to lead to disorder and mischief in the camps; because in several instances the sympathies of the men have been excited by seeing slaves, reclaimed under such circumstances, very harshly treated. I recommended to the headquarters of the army of the Potomac the other practice, which I have just described as the one pursued by myself; that I should be permitted to send the descriptions of the persons to the camps with instructions that, as in the case of all other camp followers not claiming to belong to the army, they should be put outside of the lines, thus relieving the military authorities of any action in the premises, any identification with the surrender. That course was acquiesced in, and I was authorized to pursue that course in the future.

By Mr. Wright:

Question. Was that communication sent to General McClellan?

Answer. Yes, sir; through his adjutant general.

By the chairman:

Question. How late was that order?

Answer. I think it must have been in October. I will now pass to the action at the division headquarters in the division to which I was assigned in October—the latter part of October, I think—since which time I have had no direct correspondence with the headquarters of the army of the Potomac upon the subject. When I was assigned to the division of course my own relation was to the division commander alone. The practice of the division has been to give to Maryland claimants—Maryland owners—letters, partaking something of the nature of safeguards and something of the nature of orders, to the commanding officers of brigades and regiments. I have one in my pocket now, which will indicate the nature of the practice. The purport of the last was this, and they are all pretty much alike: Orders would be given to John Doe and Richard Roe to visit any of the camps in the division, with direction to the commanding officers of the several camps to permit those persons to pass freely through the camps to search for their slaves, with leave, upon their identifying them, to take them away, and with instructions that if any officer or man interfered he should be reported to division headquarters. These orders were not promulgated through the regular military channel, but were placed in the hands of those persons themselves, and they bore them to the different camps.

Question. From whom did they emanate?

Answer. From the division commander, General Hooker. My attention was called to it in the first instance by the commanding officer of the first regiment in my brigade. I had no official knowledge of the matter before. It was late in February or early in March that my attention was first formally called to an order of that kind. I gave directions that if any such orders again came to camp the persons bearing it should be sent to me before any steps were taken under it. Some two weeks ago, as I was visiting my camps for the purpose, I think, of inspecting the 3d regiment in the bayonet exercise, as I was approaching the camp of the 2d regiment I heard a couple of pistol shots, and, upon looking towards the quarter in which they were fired, I saw a number of persons mounted, and one of them firing towards the woods. I sent an officer to learn what it meant; and, observing that a large collection of soldiers had gathered together in the camp, I put spurs to my horse and hastened up to see what was the cause of the excitement. As soon as I entered the camp the commanding officer present, in response to my inquiry, informed me that a party of men were in the camp hunting for negroes, while another party were waiting outside, and that there was great excitement in camp in consequence. He reported to me immediately, before I got the reply from the officer I had sent for information, that the firing was from some of the party outside upon some negroes who had left the camp, gone outside of the lines, and flew towards the woods, and that the soldiers were very much exasperated, as I could myself see. I asked by what authority these men were admitted within the lines, and an order from General Hooker was produced, permitting nine of them to enter the camp for that purpose. There were a great many more than nine present. I should think there were some fifteen or twenty there, all mounted, but only nine had been admitted within the lines. Three or four of them were passing up and down the company streets, while the others had dismounted and were examining the company quarters. I immediately directed the commanding officer to give orders to the officer of the day to expel these men from the camp, and not again permit them to enter it; and, upon his calling my attention to the peremptory nature of the order, and the responsibility which would be imposed upon him, I relieved him from that responsibility and told him to report that what he did was done by my orders, so that, of course, whatever responsibility was to be taken about it would fall upon myself. The order was immediately obeyed, and the men were put outside of the lines; and I gave directions that if they should return upon that or any similar mission to say that by my directions they could not be admitted. I have heard nothing further since that occurrence.

Question. How long ago was that?

Answer. I should say that it was about a couple of weeks since—some time in the latter part of March. Then there was another order, the last one in reference to contrabands. It was a portion of the order for our embarcation. I was directed on Sunday evening last to embark my command on board transports and there wait marching orders. On Sunday evening I got three regiments on board. On Monday, while waiting transports for the other two regiments, I received an order relieving me from my command of that brigade. What has been subsequent to that I do not know. The part of the order for embarcation to which I refer is as follows:

"Under no circumstances will officers or men having slaves, owned in the secession States, permit them to embark with the troops, but will direct that they be left at the depots, where they will be protected. It is in violation of the laws of the land to use them for private purposes. Nor will those having slaves owned in Maryland, for that is pillage. Commanders of brigades will see that every part of this order is rigidly observed."

Under that order I directed the quartermaster of my brigade, Captain Austin, as part of the duty of embarking the troops which was confided to his superintendence, to be present at the wharf and to see that no negroes embarked on board the vessels except the private servants of officers; and in case others should attempt to go on board to detain them, subject to such orders as might emanate from me or through me; either emanating from myself, or emanating from superior authority, and communicated from me.

Question. Who signed that order which you have read?

Answer. It was from General Hooker, signed "William H. Lawrence, A. D. C." After my brigade had commenced to embark, Mr. Posey, Mr. Mason, and several other persons, residing in that vicinity—men of known sympathy with the enemy, one or two of whom, Posey in particular, had been under arrest—came down and asked permission to go on board the vessels and search for negroes. I declined to give the permission. They then asked permission to reclaim such as might be in the quartermaster's department, stating that they had been sent there for that purpose. But they showed no written authority to that effect. They were among the persons whom I had seen at the camp of the 2d regiment, and ordered to be expelled from the camp. I declined to give that permission to them, and referred them to General Hooker. I told them that I had no orders upon that subject, and could not take any action of my own authority. The following morning I was relieved from command, and of course know nothing of what steps may have been taken since in the matter. Captain Austin, I think, is still at Liverpool Point; at least, my orders were for him to remain there and see to the embarcation of the two remaining regiments, and the care of the public property, and then to follow the troops. Perhaps, in order to give you fully everything that bears upon the subject, I ought not to pass over some steps and some correspondence that took place in December last, I think, upon this subject. I had a regiment encamped lower down on the peninsula, part of the time at Port Tobacco and part of the time at Pope's Creek—the fifth regiment of my command—under Colonel Graham. I received several applications from citizens requesting me to issue orders to that regiment to permit them to go in the camp and search for and take their negroes. That neighborhood was a very strong secession neighborhood. It was the principal point where communication was carried on between Maryland and Virginia, by way of Matthias Point. And the object of stationing the regiment there was to intercept that communication and break it off. A number of persons who owned boats there, and were engaged in ferrying across, were arrested by my orders and sent to Washington. And a number of negroes, employed by their masters in that business, were taken by me and detained. Two of those negroes, belonging to Henry Ferguson, I was directed by General Hooker to return to him. This Ferguson was himself in Virginia when I took possession of the negroes, had abandoned his place in Maryland and been in Virginia for some months. And these negroes, who were very intelligent, had been, according to their own testimony and the testimony of neighbors there, employed in ferrying persons and goods over into Virginia from Ferguson's Point, which was still further down the peninsula. I remonstrated against the order to give these men up, in a written communication, in which I set forth the facts I have stated here, and the grounds upon which they had been taken; that they had been employed by their master in acts of disloyalty, and I thought they should not be returned. First, because, if they were, I thought they would be so employed again to our detriment; and, second, that if they were to be regarded as property, I considered that they were confiscated as property, having been used in aid of the rebellion. I requested that my communication should be forwarded to the headquarters of the army of the Potomac to be considered there.

In reply, I was informed by General Hooker that his own instructions from the headquarters of the army of the Potomac left him no discretion in the premises, but the men must be immediately surrendered to their owner. The owner, Mr. Ferguson, had called for them, and I had told him that I could not act in the case at that moment, because I had addressed a communication which I hoped would be forwarded to the headquarters of the army of the Potomac, and until action was had upon it I should not proceed. I received General Hooker's answer, stating that his instructions left him no discretion. I sent for the negroes, and told them I could protect them no longer. I gave them a small gratuity, and told them to go their way. They returned home, as I afterwards understood, and again came to my camp some ten or twelve days ago. They stated, and their statement was corroborated by other information that I had from different sources, that Mr. Ferguson and several other slaveholders in that neighborhood were sending their slaves over into Virginia to work upon the military works of the enemy on the Rappahannock and at Richmond. I told my quartermaster to receive those men and take care of them, and I suppose they are still with him. Other applications were made to me by citizens in the neighborhood of Port Tobacco, requesting me to interfere and direct the surrender of contrabands who were in the camps, that had been, as I had been informed, taken possession of lest they might be similarly employed with those I have mentioned. But I declined to interfere, for the reasons I have given, and also because one of the residents of that neighborhood, a Mr. Samuel Cox, had obtained possession of one of his negroes from that camp, not through any order of mine, but through the action of one of the officers present on duty in the camp, and had subjected him to very brutal treatment, from which, as it was stated from very respectable authority, he had died. Those circumstances produced a great deal of excitement and feeling in the 5th regiment, which was located in the neighborhood, and it was not safe for any of these claimants to go into the camps for their negroes.

Question. Do you recollect the name of the contraband said to be abused in that way by Cox?

Answer. I do not recollect the name. The matter has been referred to several times in the newspapers. He belonged to this Samuel Cox, who was in Virginia when I was first ordered into the lower part of Maryland. I have been ordered down there twice. When I was myself in command, I was ordered down by General McClellan to make a very thorough reconnoissance in person of all the lower part of Maryland. That was in September last. At that time I was informed that Cox commanded a company of cavalry there, and that a portion of his company had gone with him over into Virginia.

Question. He was a secessionist?

Answer. Yes, sir, openly and avowedly one. At that time it was expected that Maryland would take part in the secession movement. The election had not taken place in Maryland, and especially that part of the State was in a very unsettled condition, and was there placed under military occupation. It was before the arrest of the secession legislature, all of the members of which from that part of the State were afterwards arrested. Cox and a number of other persons were looked after, and if we could have found them we should have arrested them and sent them up here. This negro in question was one of those who had been employed by him for similar disloyal purposes as those of Ferguson's. I did not hear anything of the circumstances of the surrender of this man to Cox until it was reported to me in connexion with the barbarous treatment he received, and its fatal consequences. I made inquiries of some of the neighbors, who were reputed to be Union men, as to the truth of the occurrence, and they denied it; they said it was not true; that one of Cox's men had died. They described him to be a bad fellow, the one who had died, and said that perhaps he may have been flogged; but they denied that it was done by Cox himself; for they insisted that Cox was not there. They said that the excitement about it they thought had proceeded to a great extent from false statements. My course about it, however, was predicated upon the fact that the men believed that it had occurred. I received a sharp communication from General Hooker, stating that a number of citizens in that part of Maryland had complained to him that the officers of the 5th regiment would not permit them to come within their camp and reclaim their runaways; and expressing his surprise that any of the officers of his command should be so derelict in their duty as to refuse them this privilege. I replied in writing, and stated that this duty was an extremely disagreeable one; that it was very odious to that regiment; that the men and officers were from eastern States, some of them from New England, some from New Jersey, and some from New York; and that the practice, if persisted in, would lead to very serious and unpleasant events in the regiment. And stating also that under these circumstances I had declined to issue any orders to the regiment, with the view to either a surrender of negroes or to permit the owners to go within the camps; and that if any further orders were issued upon the subject the responsibility must be assumed by higher authority than myself. And there the matter remained from that time.

What few loyal people there were about Port Tobacco united in a written communication to me, speaking in the highest terms of the conduct of this regiment; the protection it had afforded to them; the order that had been observed about the camp; and assuming that I had authority in the matter to order the regiment back there—this was after it had been called away—requesting me to send the regiment back. I had no authority to do so, as I had recalled the regiment back to Liverpool Point in pursuance to orders from division headquarters, and there it ended.

Question. Do you remember the name of the officer who surrendered this man to Cox?

Answer. He was a lieutenant. This man, as I understood, was employed as a private servant; his capture, or the possession taken of him, had not been reported to headquarters. I had no official cognizance of the fact that he was in the camp. That officer resigned soon afterwards; he is not now in the service. Colonel Graham, at the time, was under arrest and was in Washington.

Colonel Graham had shortly previous to that time crossed over into Virginia and scoured out Matthias Point pretty thoroughly, and had destroyed a house there which was occupied by the enemy's pickets—some of his men had done so. It was a house which the flotilla had shelled several times, but had failed to set it on fire. It was a house used by the enemy for two purposes—for the protection of their pickets, and for purposes of signalling. Signalling was going on all the time from the Maryland shore. The destruction of this house was contrary to the orders from the headquarters of the army of the Potomac. In his official report, Colonel Graham failed to state that it had been occupied by the enemy for military purposes, and that was what led to his arrest. He was in Washington for some days, and upon his explanation of the matter he was relieved from arrest and returned to duty. It was in his absence that this lieutenant allowed this man to be taken.

Question. It was stated in the papers that this negro man had given you information as to where military stores had been secreted by the enemy?

Answer. I have always found these contrabands very willing to tell all they knew, and sometimes they told what they thought they knew, but what they did not know. I could not learn that this man had ever furnished any information to any officers of the 5th regiment. But it is very likely that when I first went down in the lower part of Maryland and took the 1st regiment down, he may have been one of the persons who communicated information to the colonel of that regiment. His instructions were to look after arms. A great many arms had been buried by the secessionists to escape seizure, which, it was supposed, were intended to be carried over into Virginia as rapidly as opportunity presented. Many of these arms had been furnished by the State of Maryland soon after the John Brown affair; and that part of the State was very thoroughly armed. Those arms were used afterwards in the organizations got up in aid of the rebellion. Some companies were organized there with a view to service in the State in case Maryland seceded. When that proved abortive, as many as possible were got over into Virginia to swell the Maryland contingent there. We searched very faithfully for these arms, and we found a great many. Nearly all the information we got in reference to them we got from negroes. The Union men there had no knowledge upon the subject, or were under so much terror that they were afraid to communicate.

Question. You speak of some higher authority in this matter; do you refer to General McClellan?

Answer. The authority to which I was immediately subject of course would be my immediate commander, General Hooker; when, however, occasion would justify it, in a matter of any grave importance, it would be proper for me always to apply through him, in an open letter, to the headquarters of the army of the Potomac, which would be the chief authority which I could address upon the subject.

Question. Did you ever make these practices known to the headquarters here, to General McClellan, in any communication?

Answer. No, sir.

Question. You spoke of the barbarous treatment these men had received sometimes when they had been surrendered; what can you state about that more than you have already stated?

Answer. Lieutenant Colonel Benedict reported to me one or two instances that had come under his notice, where the Maryland owners had obtained possession of their slaves, and would immediately set to work flogging them in view of the troops; and the result would be that the soldiers would go out and rescue the negro, and in some instances would thrash the masters. That, of course, would lead to a great deal of excitement, and the result was that it was impossible to send any communication of the kind to any of the camps of that regiment. One or two such instances of that kind had occurred there. It was a regiment of excellent soldiers, but they were resolute, desperate men; they were all firemen of New York city—the 2d regiment of Fire Zouaves—and they came to the conclusion—without any efforts on the part of the officers, for I think, even if they had been disposed to exert their authority, they could not have changed it—they came to the conclusion that they would not permit any man to come within their lines upon a similar mission. It was because I had understood from officers and others that this was the sentiment of the troops that I was led, at an early day, to study the question very carefully, in order to ascertain as nearly as I could the exact limitations of my duty, and I came to this conclusion, and it has governed my own action ever since: I came to the conclusion that the rendition of fugitive slaves was strictly a civil proceeding. I have always regarded it as a matter of constitutional obligation, as a civil proceeding, and to be faithfully obeyed within that limit as a judicial proceeding; but that the civil authority could take no steps in aid of it, except in one contingency, and that was in aid of civil process, when in the hands of the United States marshal. I had determined in my own mind that whenever the question should arise, so that I could present it in a proper form, I would take that ground, await orders through the proper military channel directing me to place an indicated amount of force at the disposal of the United States marshal; such an order I would not have felt at liberty to disregard; but in no other case, or under any other circumstances, would I carry out such orders.

Question. You spoke of some orders of General Hooker directing that certain men, who were disloyal, should be permitted to go into their camp and search for their men.

Answer. Some of them were disloyal.

Question. Was any inquiry made as to that matter?

Answer. No, sir; not that I know of. I know that Posey was under arrest in Washington for some time, for using his house as a signal station for the enemy.

Question. Could not these men obtain all the information they desired for the enemy, if they were allowed to go into your camps in that way?

Answer. Yes, sir; that was the reason I assigned to Colonel Toler, and others, in reference to these persons, that I believed them to be dangerous as spies.

Question. One would suppose that General Hooker must have known that he could not have prevented information in regard to our condition getting to the enemy while these things were being allowed?

Answer. The probability is, that the enemy were never at a loss to know the exact number of the troops that we had there. The population surrounding us was so hostile, and the means of communicating by signal lights across the river into Virginia, along such an extended peninsula, were so numerous, that I suppose they were always pretty well informed; and of course the permission to persons to go in and come out of our lines so frequently would be dangerous, if we, for instance, should have just received marching orders, as we recently had orders to proceed down the Potomac, to Fortress Monroe, or anywhere else, or if we were about starting an expedition, a reconnoissance, or what not. We were always advised to take the utmost precaution to prevent the enemy obtaining information; and the permission to disloyal persons to come in and go out of our lines was liable to very dangerous abuse in that point of view.

Question. Congress some time ago enacted an additional article of war, making it a penal offence for officers to surrender fugitive slaves—an offence for which, upon conviction, they were to be deprived of their offices. Has that order been communicated to your command ?

Answer. No, sir.

Question. It never has been ?

Answer. No, sir. I know of it unofficially, only, from having seen it in the newspapers. To receive it formally I would receive it through division headquarters.

Question. It would come that way officially?

Answer. Yes, sir.

Question. And it never has come ?

Answer. No, sir.

By Mr. Julian :

Question. It is known in the army ?

Answer. Yes, sir, unofficially, as a newspaper fact; as we read the proceedings of Congress. The regular official way is to communicate such matters in a general order. We have never been officially notified of any such article.

By the chairman :

Question. Is it not customary to communicate to the army an order so important as that, one affecting so vitally the action of the officers of the army ?

Answer. Yes, sir; promptly. The announcement in the public journals that Congress had passed that article of war was very gratifying to my command at least, for it relieved us from very great embarrassment—relieved us from carrying out an order which ran counter to the feeling of our troops, whose feelings were always keenly aroused whenever any of these scenes occurred. It was rumored on board the transports where I had put three regiments that these persons were to be sent on board on Monday with permission to search the transports for their people. But my officers were of the opinion that if they came they would be thrown into the river, and that no possible exertion of the officers could prevent it. I mention that only as a fact to indicate the feeling of the soldiers. I have never seen an instance in which my men failed to obey orders. Perhaps, if they had been ordered to allow these men to search they would obey orders. But it was the opinion of the officers that most serious consequences would follow. At all events, both for prudential reasons as well as for the execution of what I regarded to be my duty, the men were not permitted to go on board.

By Mr. Julian :

Question. I was told yesterday that you knew some officers who have openly declared that they would not execute this new article of war. Is that so ?

Answer. Yes, sir; I know of one who has said so. But I would rather not be interrogated on that point, because all that was said upon the subject was said unofficially, was said at dinner table sociably, and it was said by a person that I dislike, too; and whose behavior at the table was such that I had to tell him he was impertinent.

Question. What was his rank ?

Answer. That of brigadier general. We had quite a discussion on the subject, and it led to some unpleasant words.

By the chairman:

Question. Was he a West Pointer?

Answer. He was reported to be; I do not know myself that he was.

By Mr. Julian:

Question. Will you look at this, and state whether it is a correct copy of orders from your division headquarters? [Handing witness a written paper.]

Answer. [Examining the paper.] Yes, sir; I believe it to be a correct copy.

The paper was read, as follows:

"HEADQUARTERS HOOKER'S DIVISION,
"*Camp Baker, Lower Potomac, Maryland, March* 26, 1862.

"*To the brigade and regimental commanders of this division:*

"Messrs. Nally, Gray, Dummington, Dent, Adams, Speake, Price, Posey, and Cobey, citizens of Maryland, have negroes supposed to be with some of the regiments of this division. The brigadier general commanding directs that they be permitted to visit all the camps of his command in search of their property, and if found that they be allowed to take possession of the same, without any interference whatever.

"Should any obstacle be thrown in their way by any officer or soldier in the division, they will be at once reported by the regimental commander to these headquarters.

"By command of Brigadier General Hooker.

"JOS. DICKINSON,
"*Assistant Adjutant General.*"

The witness: This is the order that the men had whom I ordered out of camp at the time they fired upon the negroes there. Several of these men were well-known secessionists. It was my action on this particular order, I think, that deprived me of my command—at least, I presumed so. And one of the chaplains of my brigade applied to me for official copies of some of these orders, which I directed my adjutant to give him; at which General Hooker was very indignant. Notwithstanding the action of the Senate upon my nomination as brigadier general, I was still in command, as the senior colonel of the brigade, and expected to continue as senior colonel commanding the brigade. But I was relieved from my command on Monday last by General Hooker. It was the impression of my officers that I was relieved in consequence of my action on this order. Of course, however, that is mere conjecture. The reason assigned by General Hooker was that my nomination as brigadier general had not been confirmed. That would have been a sufficient reason to relieve me from the command of the brigade if another brigadier general had been appointed to take command of it. But until then I was entitled to continue in command of it, as senior colonel.

Question. Do you know the document of which this purports to be a copy? [Handing witness a paper.]

Answer. [Examining it.] Yes, sir; this is the official report of Major Toler to my adjutant of the occurrences to which I have referred.

The paper was read, as follows:

"HEADQUARTERS 2D REGIMENT EXCELSIOR BRIGADE,
"*Camp Hall, March* 27, 1862.

"LIEUTENANT: In compliance with verbal directions from Brigadier General D. E. Sickles to report as to the occurrence at this camp on the afternoon of the 26th instant, I beg leave to submit the following:

"At about 3.30 o'clock p. m., March 26th, 1862, admission within our lines was demanded by a party of horsemen, (civilians,) numbering perhaps fifteen.

They presented the lieutenant commanding the guard with an order of entrance from Brigadier General Hooker, commanding division, [copy appended,] the order stating that *nine* men should be admitted. I ordered that the balance of the party should remain without the lines, which was done. Upon the appearance of the others, there was visible dissatisfaction and considerable murmuring among the soldiers—to so great an extent that I almost feared for the safety of the slave owners. At this time General Sickles opportunely arrived, and instructed me to order them outside the camp, which I did, amidst the loud cheers of our soldiers.

"It is proper to add that before entering our lines, and when within seventy-five or one hundred yards of our camp, one of their number discharged two pistol shots at a negro, who was running past them, with an evident intention of taking his life. This justly enraged our men.

"All of which is respectfully submitted.

"Your obedient servant,

"JOHN TOLER,

"Major Commanding 2d Regiment Excelsior Brigade.

"Lieutenant J. L. Palmer,

"Aide-de-Camp and Acting Assistant Adjutant General."

Question. That is a correct copy?

Answer. Yes, sir. I directed Major Toler to report to me officially what had occurred, and my adjutant would be the channel through which he would do it.

By the chairman:

Question. Have you been able to obtain valuable information from these contrabands who have come into your camp?

Answer. The most valuable and reliable information of the enemy's movements in our vicinity that we have been able to get we have derived from negroes who have come into our lines. They have been frequently employed by me as scouts, sometimes singly and sometimes in parties of two or three. Sometimes they have been sent as guides with our troops when it was not deemed proper to hazard them unattended; and they have uniformly, whether employed as scouts or guides, proved faithful. In many instances they have proved to be persons of remarkable intelligence. I left several of them at my camp, whose services for the government in the past, and whose means of usefulness in the future, if we are to operate upon the line of the Rappahannock, in my judgment, entitle them to the particular care of the military authorities. Similar services, if rendered by white men, would, according to the usages of the army, be very liberally rewarded pecuniarily.

By Mr. Covode:

Question. Were these colored men, who rendered you these services, slaves or free?

Answer. All of them slaves, I presume. I will mention one instance particularly, where a colored man named Jim, the slave of a Colonel Tayloe who commands the cavalry outposts in the rebel service on the line of the Potomac from Evansport to Mathias Point, is a man of remarkable intelligence. He was sent on a number of scouting expeditions, both for the army and the navy, for the Potomac flotilla and for myself. And one duty that he performed was attended with so much danger, and was performed with so much fidelity and ability, that I recommended that he should be allowed one hundred dollars for it. My recommendation was complied with, and he received that sum. That is but one of twenty services that he has rendered the government, all of more or less magnitude. That man is in Washington now. I recommended him to Lieutenant Commanding Samuel McGaw of the flotilla to bring up here with him.

By Mr. Julian:

Question. Do you know of any instance where they have been treacherous to the Union cause?

Answer. No, sir; not one. They exhibit the greatest alacrity and pleasure in showing us in any way in their power. They will submit to any privation, perform any duty, incur any danger. I know an instance in which four of them recently carried a boat from the Rappahannock river, passing through the enemy's pickets successfully, to the Potomac and crossed over to my camp and reported themselves there. They gave us information of the position of the enemy's force, which was communicated to headquarters; a service upon which it would be difficult to fix a price. These services rendered by these men are known to the soldiers, and contribute, I presume, largely to the sympathy which they feel for them, and to the strong, I may say the irrepressible disinclination they feel when called upon to witness their surrender.

WASHINGTON, *April* 15, 1862.

Lieutenant JOSEPH L. PALMER, jr., sworn and examined.

By Mr. Covode:

Question. What has been your position in the army?

Answer. First lieutenant of company A 2d regiment of the Excelsior brigade. I have been detached as aide-de-camp to General Sickles, and acting as his assistant adjutant general.

Question. What do you know in relation to parties owning slaves coming into your camps after them; by whose orders has it been done, and what has been General Sickles's position in relation to that matter?

Answer. On three or four occasions within my knowledge owners of slaves have come into our camps. How often besides I do not know. General Sickles has uniformly received them courteously, but has been very unwilling to deliver up the slaves that they claimed.

Question. Were these claimants loyal slaveholders or rebels?

Answer. The best means of information that we had was very prejudicial to them as Union men in many cases, particularly in the cases of claimants living at Port Tobacco and in that vicinity. The slaves they claimed we always found to be very good and faithful men. We used them many times as guides and scouts. Colonel Graham, of the 5th regiment, which was down at Port Tobacco, used them to great advantage, and placed great confidence in them, when he went on his expedition across the river to Mathias Point.

Question. They were reliable?

Answer. Yes, sir; very reliable. One morning two persons appeared and claimed some slaves that had come to our headquarters and had served us there. They had a letter from General Hooker, the terms of which were, I think, to the effect that if General Sickles was satisfied that these negroes belonged to the persons who claimed them they should be delivered up to the claimants. The letter also stated that there was sufficient evidence that these persons were good and loyal citizens. Now, General Sickles, and, I think, every officer in the 5th regiment and at headquarters, and we were nearest to Port Tobacco where these persons lived, had ample evidence that these persons had not been good Union men. The general doubted their sincerity very much. However, there was the order, and he did not know what to do. He put them off finally, and told them to come the next Sunday. In the meantime, he sent for these negroes, who had become quite famous with us as scouts, and told them that he could protect them no longer; that they must leave the camp. He gave them some money and some clothes, and told them they better go home, which they did. One of them came back about a week afterwards, and another one came back some two or three weeks after that. When the troops left Liverpool Point they were still in camp. What has become of them I do not know. I think they have been put in charge of the division quartermaster there, as was the case with most of the other contrabands.

On another occasion Captain Brunn, of the 1st regiment, was called upon to deliver up a man whom he had been employing as his servant, I think. However, I will not be positive about that. I know that the captain knew of his whereabouts, and he was called upon to deliver him up. There was some correspondence grew out of that case between Lieutenant Colonel Farnham and headquarters. What was done in the matter I do not know. Whether he was delivered up or not is more than I can tell. But I do know that General Sickles never himself gave up any, although he never positively refused.

Sometimes, and more often than otherwise, orders would be sent directly to the commanding officers of regiments, not through headquarters, the usual channel of communicating orders—orders would be sent through the slaveholders directly to the regiments. That was the case with the 1st regiment; and the first we heard of it was from Lieutenant Colonel Farnham asking for instructions.

There was one case in the 5th regiment where a man named Cox claimed some slaves. He was very badly treated by the soldiers. He came there with an order from division headquarters for two or three slaves. He pointed out who they were, and undertook to take them away; but the soldiers pounced upon him and beat him severely, injuring him considerably. The officers interfered, and saw him safely out of the camp, but not until he had been considerably injured. He went away without his slaves. I do not know whether he got them afterwards or not.

The first correspondence that arose on the subject was early in December last or late in November; I think it was early in December. That was in relation to some contrabands in the 5th regiment. General Hooker instructed General Sickles to deliver them over to their owners, and to instruct the officers of the 5th regiment to aid the owners in every possible way in recovering their property. At the same time the letter rather animadverted upon the seeming unwillingness of the officers to perform such a plain duty without being ordered to do so. The general protested against it in a letter to General Hooker, and there the matter was dropped; we had no more correspondence upon that subject until recently, for a long time. We would occasionally hear through the officers of the various regiments, of orders being received by them through residents of Maryland, to allow them to enter their camps and search for slaves. But no such orders came direct to the headquarters of the brigade after this correspondence had taken place.

Question. Do you know whether General Sickles was opposed to being employed to catch and return slaves?

Answer. I know that was the spirit in which he wrote to General Hooker on the subject.

Question. What was the feeling among the troops in reference to that matter.

Answer. With our people, there was a feeling of indignation against it, from the lowest to the highest; it was the universal feeling. Some of the officers would turn away, saying to those claimants: "you can take your property if you will, but I will have nothing to do with it," and then walk into their tents and pay no more attention to them. Sometimes they would allow their men to treat these people very roughly, until they were obliged to interpose to prevent their being seriously injured.

Question. What recent transactions have taken place there?

Answer. There have been some there entirely unexpected. An order was sent from General Hooker directly to the commanding officer of the 2d regiment. Neither General Sickles, or myself, nor any officer at headquarters knew a word about it until the general returned. He told me at table, in the evening, that as he was passing near the camp of the second regiment he saw that there was a disturbance there, and that the major of the regiment came to him in great haste, and with considerable excitement, and told him that some parties had come there with an order from General Hooker, that they should be allowed to search the camp and take away their slaves; that the men were terribly excited, and he feared some evil consequence. The general ordered the men to be put out of the camp at once. I think there was no further excitement on that subject. I will remark that General Hooker visited General Sickles the following morning, paid him a friendly visit; partly official and partly unofficial. But that subject was not mentioned at all; not a word was dropped about it on either side.

The only other circumstance bearing upon the subject of General Sickles's conduct in regard to this contraband question, that I now think of, was a little passage of words that took place between General Sickles and General Negley one day at dinner. General Hooker, General Sickles, General Negley, and several other officers were at dinner together. I was not present myself, but the affair was detailed to me by Lieutenant Hart, who was present. It became generally known throughout the camp that such an affair had taken place, in relation to this contraband matter.

WASHINGTON, *February* 11, 1862.

Dr. BENJ. LIPPINCOTT sworn and examined.

By the chairman:

Question. Are you a physician?

Answer. I have been. I have not practiced for some time. I am now located in Washington. My home is in Philadelphia.

Question. Have you visited the prisons, or the places in Alexandria where soldiers are confined for minor offences? If so, tell us what you saw there.

Answer. I was there between 12 and 2 o'clock last Sunday—day before yesterday.

Question. Did you visit the places of confinement there?

Answer. Yes, sir; in company with Dr. Seltzer, Quartermaster Jones, and two or three visitors from Philadelphia. We were taken into the slave pen by Dr. Seltzer—the place where soldiers are imprisoned. I walked around the pen. I should say it was some 40 or 50 feet square. It is enclosed by a high wall, with a little shed along on one side of it; the rest of it with no roof at all, but all open to the weather. The shed was simply a roof on one side that afforded no shelter, for it was so narrow that the slightest storm would strike the wall inside and under the shed. I thought it was a horrible place to keep men in, and spoke to the doctor about it. I asked him how he got along with the men—if he did not have a plenty of cases of pneumonia after they got out.

Question. What was the doctor doing there?

Answer. He was the surgeon of the regiment. He said it was a disgraceful place. He showed me where he had had a cellar entrance filled up, where one man who had been put in there intoxicated had fallen down and broken his back. The privy there had been open when the men were put in there, and he had had that covered over. He told me of the depth of the filth that had been in the pen. He said that at one time there was some two or three inches of mud, and some two inches of snow and slush on top of that, during that severe spell of weather, and one of the prisoners who had been put in there during the bad weather had been found dead in the morning. He had laid down in the slush there during the night and been frozen to death. I saw in an adjoining room a man some 50 years of age, who had been exposed in that pen over night. He was suffering from pneumonia, and looked to me as if he must die.

Question. How many men were in there when you saw it?

Answer. There were some four or five in the pen. As I went up to the grating in the door they begged me, for God's sake, to use some kind of influence to have them let out, as they were nearly frozen to death. They had no covering at all, no blankets, and no place to sit or lay down upon, except the brick pavement.

Question. What were they put in there for; what had they done?

Answer. One said he was put in there because he was a little late in getting out of town; he said his pass had expired about a half an hour. He was a member of one of the Pennsylvania regiments. A soldier of one of the Massachusetts regiments said he was put in there for being intoxicated. Another man there, between 45 and 50 years of age, who looked like a very good fellow, said he had gone in to church Sunday morning. He had stopped to warm himself where there was some soldier who had no bayonet on his gun. He asked why he did not put his bayonet on and be in full rig. The soldier took umbrage at that and arrested him. He showed him the pass he had to come in town, but the soldier said he did not care for his pass; he must go to the prison, and he was put in there.

Question. Who ordered these men to prison?

Answer. I talked with Colonel McLane, who has a regiment there. The colonel said he had deputed one of his captains as provost marshal of the town; but General Montgomery has the control and ordering of those things. Dr. Seltzer said he had plead with General Montgomery to take the jail in town for this purpose, but he could not succeed.

Question. Why did he not remonstrate?

Answer. He said he had, but he could not do anything at all. He expressed himself that General Montgomery favored the secessionists considerably, and seemed to have a great deal of charity for them. General Montgomery was away at one time on leave of absence for some sickness or indisposition of some kind. While he was away Colonel McLane was in command. Colonel McLane said that during that time he had taken, for some use of the army, a house that belonged to a son-in-law of Reverdy Johnson. But when the general came back he had ordered the house to be given up, and had rented a house of a man then in Alexandria. That man immediately turned around and rented this house belonging to Reverdy Johnson's son-in-law for some $200 or $300 less than he got from the government for his own house, thus speculating upon the government in that way. The owner of the house the government had hired, which the colonel was occupying, had gone off to the south with the rebels; and the colonel thought they better have occupied the house rent free than to have paid money for it. He said Reverdy Johnston had talked with General Montgomery, and got him to order his son-in-law's house to be given up. He told me furthermore of some minister of the gospel there who had given General Montgomery a special invitation to attend his church. General Montgomery did attend, by special invitation. The minister in the service refused to repeat that part containing the prayer for the President of the United States; yet

General Montgomery sat there and heard and saw it all, and made no opposition to it. Colonel McLane said he had been anxious for some time to have the man arrested, but he could get no authority to do so. But on Sunday, while I was there, the man was arrested in his pulpit. As soon as the prayer was ended and he commenced the litany, he was arrested and taken out of the pulpit. The gentleman who reported the case to the colonel, while I was there, said it grew out of an order from Secretary Seward.

Question. Do you suppose this slave pen is still used there as a prison?

Answer. I judge it is; it was on Sunday last. The colonel said that while he was in command there, during General Montgomery's absence, people would come to him with complaints; secessionists would come with complaints regarding their houses, &c.; and when he would not do as they wanted they would ask when General Montgomery would be back again, saying that if they could see him he would assist them. And I was told that the general had given passes to these secessionists, who had never taken the oath of allegiance to the government. Some rebels who had been taken prisoners were brought in there, and allowed to be fed by the secessionists of the city. And eventually the thing went so far that the secessionists used to invite them out to dinner, and they went out as invited guests to dinner, with a guard deputed to go with them and to escort them back to jail.

By Mr. Covode:

Question. Do you know anything about any effort being made to get the bank building there for some purpose connected with the army?

Answer. The managers of the bank there are all secessionists; not a loyal man connected with it. The mother bank is in Richmond, and the greater part of the stock is owned in Richmond. The colonel said that he had been unable to get the general to agree to allow him to take that bank building as a hospital.

Question. Do you know anything about General Montgomery affording protection to the property of rebels?

Answer. They all told me there that the secessionists could do anything with General Montgomery, if they could get at him.

WASHINGTON, *February* 12, 1862.

Colonel GEORGE P. MCLEAN sworn and examined, (Dr. Seltzer and Quartermaster Jones being present.)

By the chairman:

Question. What is your rank and position in the army?

Answer. Colonel of the 88th Pennsylvania volunteers.

Question. Where stationed?

Answer. At Alexandria.

Question. Will you state in regard to the place where your prisoners are kept?

Answer. They are generally, and I believe always, put in the slave pen in Alexandria.

Question. Is that a fit place for men to be put in during the winter season?

Answer. In my opinion it is not, and I have so expressed myself frequently. It is not a proper place from the fact that the prisoners there are exposed to the inclemency of the weather. The men coming in from the various camps generally come in without blankets, and very frequently without overcoats; and they are put in there without any covering, and have nothing to lie upon except the brick pavement. My opinion is that it is a very unfit place to put the men in.

Question. Would it endanger the life or health of a man to remain there over night during this inclement season?

Answer. I think it would endanger, or have a tendency to endanger, his life.

Question. Who is responsible for placing prisoners in such a place as that?

Answer. I could not say exactly who is responsible. I should judge that it was probably within the power of the commanding general to order it otherwise.

Question. Have you remonstrated with him about it—reported the state and condition of it to him?

Answer. I have had inspectors appointed regularly to visit the various quarters on Sunday morning, who have reported to me, and I have referred the report to the commanding general.

By Mr. Odell:

Question. In this report was this slave pen spoken of?

Answer. Yes, sir, and condemned.

By the chairman:

Question. Have these facts come to the knowledge of the commanding general?

Answer. Yes, sir; they are within his knowledge. He may possibly imagine that he has no other place to put prisoners in, and I do not really know that he has any other place to put them in. But I am free to say that I think it is the privilege of the commanding officer to take other quarters. I do not know that he has ever given instructions to do so.

Question. Who is this commanding officer you refer to?

Answer. The commanding general there is General Montgomery.

Question. Has he not power, as a military commander, either to get other and better quarters, or to repair those now being used?

Answer. I so understand it.

Question. What do you know of any particular injury resulting to men by reason of being imprisoned there?

Answer. I do not know anything positively myself, from the fact that it has never been my duty to be there. I have sent others to inspect it. I have visited the quarters as commanding officer of the regiment, and on one occasion the surgeon called upon me and I went with him, and saw perhaps some forty odd men there suffering very much. They were cold and shivering, and I released some of them, seeing they were perfectly sober, with instructions to them to go out to their camps. I thought it was nothing more than proper and right to do, assuming that it was right, as there were orders from the commanding general that all prisoners should be released the next day at guard mounting. Some of them had been there over night, and should have been released in the morning. I saw that it was not a proper place for men to be in. But, of course, it is not a very pleasant thing to blame and find fault with the officer over me, and I have never assumed anything but my own duties.

Question. Is the place clean and neat, or is it filthy and loathsome?

Answer. It is very dirty at times, as the snow and rain beat in.

Question. For what offences are men put in there?

Answer. For drunkenness, and for being in the city without passes. The commanding officers of the various camps have instructed their officers and men not to visit Alexandria without a pass, and they have called upon us to assist them in carrying out these orders; and General Montgomery has also issued an order that all soldiers shall leave Alexandria at 4 o'clock in the afternoon, and if they are found there without a pass they are arrested, and there is no other place to put them in but the slave pen. And if they are found drunk, with or without a pass, they are arrested by our guards and placed in there.

Question. These are what you consider as trivial offences in the army, but not of a serious character?

Answer. They are of that character that never can be avoided.

By Mr. Covode:

Question. Did you ever exert yourself with the general to get a better place to keep them in?

Answer. It would not be a proper thing for me to urge my commanding officer. I have sent him the reports. We have placed the matter before him in the shape of reports, containing the opinions of inspectors.

By the chairman:

Question. And of course they condemned that place?

Answer. Yes, sir. I might remark that I endeavored on one occasion to secure the jail for that purpose, and I received a censure from my commanding officer, and, very likely, properly, too. I had no right, perhaps, to move in the mattter when there was an officer who was my senior.

By Mr. Odell:

Question. What was his objection to the use of the jail for that purpose?

Answer. I do not know that he gave an objection; only gave me to understand that he was the commanding officer.

Question. What objection is there to taking the jail for that purpose, as a temporary jail for that purpose?

Answer. I do not know that I have ever heard any objection.

Question. Does any suggest itself to your mind?

Answer. None. It might be presumed that drunken, crazy men might destroy the building; but that might be prevented by proper guards.

Question. Is any man any more drunk and crazy with military clothes on than without?

Answer. No, sir.

By the chairman:

Question. Would the jail, in your judgment, be a proper place for this purpose?

Answer. That is my opinion, and my attempt was to secure it.

By Mr. Odell:

Question. What number would the jail accommodate?

Answer. I suppose it would accommodate some 200.

Question. Would it meet the wants of that department?

Answer. Yes, sir. I spoke to the mayor of the city about it, and I got reprimanded, and made up my mind, of course, that perhaps I was in error.

Question. Did the mayor object to it?

Answer. No, sir; he did not.

Question. Did he accord with you as to the propriety of using the jail?

Answer. He said that he was perfectly willing himself; that he had no objection.

By the chairman:

Question. Is there anything more you think of that is material?

Answer. There are little matters that perhaps it would be better for me not to say anything about.

By Mr. Odell:

Question. How long are these men kept there by your regulations?

Answer. They are put in there any time during the day, and released the next morning at nine o'clock.

By the chairman:

Question. Those little things you speak of may throw light upon the subject we are investigating.

Answer. I might state some things that would reflect on my commanding officer. I do not care to do that. Perhaps he did not mean any injury to the men.

Question. It may be improper for an officer to speak against his superior under ordinary circumstances; but we are here for the purpose of inquiring into the conduct of any one; no matter how high or low he may be, he is under our jurisdiction.

Answer. When I spoke to the general in regard to the slave pen, he decided that it was a very suitable place, and said the men were better provided for there than our men on picket were.

By Mr. Gooch:

Question. Did you inform him that you thought it was not a a suitable place?

Answer. Yes, sir.

Question. And that was the reply you received?

Answer. Yes, sir.

Question. How long ago did you call his attention to it?

Answer. I have done so frequently. It has been a subject of conversation. I cannot remember precisely when the last time was. It was last week, I think, one day, that the general was talking to me about it, trying to convince me that it was a suitable place; but I was not convinced.

By Mr. Covode:

Question. Have you given any passes?

Answer. In regard to giving passes, when passes were issued, of course, it was the commanding officer who gave them.

Question. Do you know that he has given passes to parties who have refused to take the oath of allegiance?

Answer. Yes, sir.

Question. How do you know that?

Answer. I was temporarily in command while the general was away on sick leave, and a number of written passes came to me to be renewed which I positively refused.

Question. Why did you refuse them?

Answer. I had passes with the obligation attached to them to be signed, and I supposed it was my duty to carry out those orders, and I positively refused to give passes to any one unless he would sign the obligation. There are a number of persons there who are strong secessionists who have passes.

By the chairman:

Question. Who gave them?

Answer. General Montgomery, of course; that he does not deny.

By Mr. Covode:

Question. Gave them to parties who did not take or sign the obligation?

Answer. Yes, sir. They came in to me when I was temporarily in command, and I refused positively to renew them. Gentlemen would bring others in and introduce them and recommend them as good citizens and ask for passes for them. My question was, "Are you a loyal citizen? will you sign the obligation? if so, I will be pleased to give you a pass." A great many refused, and I told them that stripped me of any privilege or right to give them passes. Those passes, I told them, were in my hands with the obligation attached to them to be signed; and it was only in compliance with that regulation that I could issue a pass; that I was there to carry out orders, not to make them Of course I was not much thought of by that class of people there.

Question. Is it a common thing there to issue passes to persons who do not sign the obligation?

Answer. An order has recently been issued from Washington to prevent the general from giving passes anywhere, whether through the lines or anywhere else.

Question. Did they get passes by which they went to Baltimore and obtained goods to take through our lines?

Answer. I do not know as to which way they went. The passes gave them the privilege of crossing the ferry over the Potomac from Alexandria to the city of Washington, &c.

By Mr. Odell:

Question. Were any passes given by which these parties could pass through our lines into the enemy's country?

Answer. Not positively.

Question. Do you know anything about any other slave pen in Alexandria than the one used?

Answer. No, sir.

WASHINGTON, *February* 12, 1862.

Doctor J. H. SELTZER sworn and examined, (Colonel McLane and Quartermaster Jones present.)

By the chairman:

Question. What is your position in the army?

Answer. I am surgeon of the 88th Pennsylvania regiment.

Question. Where are you stationed?

Answer. At Alexandria.

Question. What do you know about the manner in which prisoners for minor offences are punished there; how are they confined, and where?

Answer. I presume you want a plain, undisguised, unvarnished statement of the whole affair.

Question. We want it exactly as it is.

Answer. I have called the attention of the authorities to this matter of confining soldiers in that slave pen. I have visited it daily, and seen as high as 150 or 200 (between 200 and 300) men confined in that pen. They are men who have come in from their camps, and are probably from five to ten minutes behind their time; not having a watch, they cannot tell what the time is, or they may have taken a glass of liquor too much, and our soldiers arrest them and take them to that slave pen. You know what a drunken man is; he feels unpleasant at the idea of going to a slave pen rather than to a guard-house. I have heard them say that if they were put in the guard-house they, at least, had a comfortable place to lie on. They are generally pretty roughly handled when taken to this slave pen, as drunken men usually are, and then they are confined there. I have called the attention of those in authority to these matters. There have been at times three and a half inches of snow, dirt, filth, and such truck, on the pavement, and they had to lie there without any covering at all; and I have seen as many as one hundred men in there when the thermometer was at twenty-one degrees. The men were wet, were brought in there wet, and they were forced to lie down there, as there was no other place for them to lie down, except right on the bricks. The place was not fit to put dumb brutes in, let alone the freemen of the north.

Question. Did you not remonstrate against it?

Answer.. I did.

Question. To whom?

Answer. I remonstrated with General Montgomery. I made a report to the colonel, and handed the report to General Montgomery; and I took the general himself out there, and showed him the place. I said to him, "General, when Providence endows us with good qualities and better comforts than our neighbor is possessed of, should it not prompt us to endeavor to ameliorate the condition of our fellow men?" He said, "That is very true, and it is very patriotic in us to come out here to-day." Now, I cannot lie down on my bed at night and rest with any peace when I have seen my fellow men who lived alongside of me, and who had come out here to fight for his country, forced to remain in such a place as that, when the secessionist or disloyal man, upon being arrested, is sent to the provost marshal, and furnished with a room and fire.

Question. Is that so?

Answer. Yes, sir; there is no mistake about that.

Question. What is the effect of this confinement upon the health of the inmates?

Answer. It produces pleurisy and pneumonia. Let any man reflect a moment. If any one of you should go to his room to-night, even if there is a fire in it, and lay down on the floor and remain there over night, you will wake up in the morning with a chill. And some of these men have been brought up with all the comforts of life about them; and yet I saw a man in that slave pen the night before last as bare as he came into this world. Out of pity to him I told them to put him inside. One man was found dead there a few days ago; frozen to death. I have expostulated until I thought the authorities would not listen, and then I said I would appeal to the country, to the public press.

Question. Do you know anything about the jail that has been spoken of?

Answer. No, sir; I have not been inside of that. Yesterday I went through the different camps to find out the condition of the guard-houses in the camps and every one I saw was comfortable. A gentleman of the sanitary commission was down there yesterday to investigate the matter, and I went around with him. I asked the soldiers why they objected so much to being in that slave pen. They all said that the idea of freemen being put in a slave pen was, of itself, horrible; and then, if they were put in a guard-house they would have some comforts; they could get there blankets to lie upon; and then there was not so much feeling about it. This slave pen is in such a condition that a man broke his back there, and another man, of our regiment, broke his thigh, which has disabled him for life.

Question. How did that happen?

Answer. There was an open place in the cellar-way down which the man fell; and by almost fighting I have succeeded in having it closed up. The men put in there, having nothing to sit upon, would pull up the bricks of the pavement to make a seat to sit on; and then they would have some drunken men in there who would get into a fight, and the loose bricks would fly, and, most generally, some one will be disabled for life.

Question. You have made this known to the commanding general?

Answer. I have taken him there in person and pointed it out to him.

Question. What did he say about it?

Answer. He said, "What are we to do? I have no power to do anything; I can't do anything." Said I, "General, take the responsibility, as Jackson did, and do it."

Question. Do you know anything about the giving of passes?

Answer. I have seen passes in the hands of the rankest, open-avowed secessionists in Alexandria, with General Montgomery's signature, to pass anywhere.

Question. Has he obliged them to sign the obligations?

Answer. There was no obligation signed to those passes. I have myself seen the general give passes, when I was present, to ladies who defiantly told him they would not take the oath of allegiance. I remember a gentleman coming in who had a pass for himself and family, who is an open and avowed secessionist. He lived next door to the colonel's headquarters. He wanted the colonel to renew the pass, and the colonel told him he would not do it unless he took the oath of loyalty; and that he said he would not do, and walked out. His pass had expired while the general was away.

Question. How long have persons been confined in this slave pen?

Answer. Some have been there for ten days at a time. I have known them to be in there for three days without a bed or a fire, and they got nothing but a little water that the parties standing outside, out of compassion, passed in. On one occasion I appealed to the colonel to go out with me and look at it, and when we got out there I said to the colonel, "I know you have a commander over you, but, colonel, just take the responsibility, and let these men go home;" and he did release some forty of them that afternoon.

Question. Were they confined there during the months of December and January?

Answer. They were put in there in January, while the weather was so cold that it was freezing. A secessionist can get more out of General Montgomery than a Union man can. If a secessionist is arrested and taken before him, he is released in half an hour. I will tell you a case in point. There was a man arrested for declaring open and avowed secessionist doctrines, and General Montgomery released him, and allowed him to go to Mayor McKensie and stay all night.

Colonel McLane: I will take occasion to say, for fear there might be some censure cast upon me, that I have endeavored to stop this matter with what I conceived to be my duty as an officer there. There were privileges granted to secessionists. A number of them were selling rum, and demoralizing our army. I gave instructions to my guard to arrest all such men, and to arrest, of course, the soldiers there collected. My guards returned to me, and told me that they could not carry out my order. I asked them why they could not do so, and they said that the proprietor of the house, who is a secessionist, showed them a permit from General Montgomery that he should not be interfered with; and, if necessary, they were entitled to call on the guards for protection; and following that I received an order from General Montgomery that I should not hereafter issue any orders to my officers or men, or interfere with the police arrangements of the city of Alexandria. Of course my hands were then tied. If I had had the right, I should have made a different arrangement. I only state this in justification to myself, lest I might be censured.

The chairman: Did he know why you had issued your order—that it was to prevent drunkenness and the selling of liquor by secessionists?

Colonel McLane: He told me himself that he desired it to be done, and I supposed I was but carrying out his orders; but after we would seize their liquors, and send them to the mayor, they would go to him and get permission to get them back.

The greatest evil of all, in my opinion, is the influence there of a man who, I am free to say, is a traitor. I refer to the assistant adjutant general—J. R. Freeze. I have been on the eve of asking to be relieved. I did not enter the service for dollars and cents. I left a business that paid me more than the government pays me. But having been connected with the military for some years, I felt that I might, perhaps, be able to render some service to my country. This adjutant has interfered with me in the discharge of my duties time and time again. He has even come in and sat down in my quarters and issued a regimental order. I told him I was colonel of my regiment, and demanded the right to issue my own orders, as I was responsible for what my regiment did. There was a lady there by the name of Burns, who had been pleading with tears in her eyes to get possession of her house, which was being occupied by the wife of a rebel officer. I believe that General Montgomery had consented that she should have her property. This Freeze interfered, and, having entire control over the general, prevented it. While I was there, one day she saw Freeze, who insulted her. As she was returning to her home, one of the sentinels, who had been frequently kindly treated by her as he passed her door on his beat, seeing she was in trouble, asked her what the matter was. She said she had just been to see Captain Freeze, to see if there was any possibility of her getting her house. They owed her $114 rent then. The last thing her husband had done in Alexandria was to vote for the Union, and he had done all he could for that. The sentinel said, "Why don't you go to my colonel?" At that time, fortunately, I was temporarily in command there. She came to me and related her story, and I gave notice to this wife of the rebel officer to vacate the premises in forty-eight hours, or suffer the consequences. The father of this lady, who was also in the house, went to Freeze about it. Freeze wrote to me saying that Mr. Lovejoy—the father of this rebel officer's wife—should not be interfered with, either by military or civil authority. I ordered the one who brought me the note to say to Mr. Freeze that I was then in command; that he had about as much to do with the matter as a boy in the street; that I had issued my order, and should see that it was carried out. He called in the evening himself, and told me that it was as much as my commission was worth to do that thing. I told him my commission did not come from him, and that if any one interfered with me he should be shot. The result of it was that I handed the house over to Mrs. Burns.

The chairman: You have said that General Montgomery was under the influence of this man Freeze. Explain that.

Colonel McLane: I have always had the kindest feelings towards General Montgomery, and I desire to believe that the general means to do what is right. But I am not of the opinion that this Freeze desires to do what is right. General Montgomery is old, and he is easily persuaded. This Freeze has no military knowledge whatever, but he is there as his assistant adjutant general, and whatever Freeze proposes is carried out. I have had to submit as well as all the rest. And my hands are now so tied that I dare not give an order to my own officers and men; and I will not for all the money in the United States be held in that position long. I conceive that it is my right as commanding officer of my regiment to issue orders to my own command. My reason for having hesitated to speak of this was because I did entertain kind feelings towards General Montgomery, and I do not want to believe that he is not a loyal citizen. But I have seen very strange things there.

The chairman: What strange things have you seen?

Colonel McLean: I have seen privileges granted to secessionists that I think they ought not to enjoy, giving them passes, &c. We have had rebel prisoners there, and the secessionists there have been allowed to visit them, and entertain them sumptuously. That came to my knowledge when I was temporarily in command, and I issued an order at once that these things should not be permitted. Secessionists were inviting out the rebel prisoners to their residences, and entertaining them at dinners, while our guards were sent to escort them. I issued an order to stop that, and not only that, but that the rebel prisoners should have the same rations as our men did, and why they should be sumptuously entertained more than our soldiers is more than I could understand, and I determined that it should not be while I was in command, and I would not allow them to visit them; they were not on exhibition, and we were capable of taking charge of our prisoners. The result of it was that some ladies called upon me, and asked me if they could go and see the prisoners. I asked if they were relatives, and they said they were not. I then told them I could not allow it. They then asked me when General Montgomery would be back. I told them that he would be back before long, as his leave of absence would expire in a few days. Seeing an order to send prisoners to Washington, I took occasion, before General Montgomery returned, to send to Washington every prisoner in Alexandria. I am free to say that things have occurred in Alexandria since I have been there that, under my oath, with my disposition to do my duty as a soldier, my conscience would not allow me to do. This Freeze has been there so long that he has become familiar with the secessionists, and I am satisfied that he ought not to be there. He has no military knowledge, in the first place; never was a soldier, and had no experience, and I do not know why the government should be paying a man there who can perform nothing.

The witness, (Dr. Seltzer:) If this committee will send to the sanitary board they will be able to obtain an elaborate report of their investigations in this matter.

By the chairman:

Question. When were the sanitary board down there?

Answer. Dr. Parrish left there this morning, and said that he would write out a report on this slave pen.

WASHINGTON, *February* 12, 1862.

Lieutenant D. D. JONES sworn and examined.

By the chairman:

Question. What is your position?

Answer. I am quartermaster of the 88th Pennsylvania regiment.

Question. You are stationed at Alexandria?

Answer. Yes, sir.

Question. What do you know about the manner in which soldiers are imprisoned there?

Answer. I can say that I concur fully in the testimony of Colonel McLane and Dr. Seltzer.

Question. You are knowing to the facts, and concur in what they have stated?

Answer. Yes, sir.

Question. Do you know anything about passes having been granted to secessionists, or to those who would not take the oath of allegiance?

Answer. I have seen such passes granted at different times by General Montgomery's aid to persons who would not sign the obligation. I saw, what I term very loosely conducted, in the office of General Montgomery, men receiving passes there without any obligation being signed by them, and others who simply stood back and touched the pen without looking at it, under the pretence that they could not write; persons, too, who were doing such a business as to naturally require them to have some education, and at least to know how to sign their names. They would hold the pen while the aid made the mark, and turn their backs to it the while. That I have seen myself. When the colonel was in command I frequently saw them bring in passes that had no obligation signed, and ask the colonel to renew them, they having expired. This he positively refused to do, unless they would sign the obligation. They endeavored to persuade the colonel to do it, using, as an argument, the fact that General Montgomery had not asked it of them. They were secessionists, and known to be such by the Union people there. You asked the colonel if he knew anything about any other slave pen there. I would remark that there is a slave pen further on in the same street. I was in General Montgomery's headquarters when a captain reported to him the existence of such a slave pen, and he has visited it. It belongs to a secessionist, and has many comforts in it. He reported that to General Montgomery about two weeks ago.

Question. Why did he not take that?

Answer. I do not know.

Question. Do you know anything about the jail there?

Answer. I know that there is a jail there, and that the colonel has on more than one occasion spoken to the mayor about using it; to which the mayor consented.

Question. Do you know any objection to using the jail?

Answer. No, sir; General Montgomery remonstrated about the colonel interfering in reference to the jail. There was an article in the paper some two weeks ago about this slave pen being used to confine soldiers in. General Montgomery spoke about officers interfering with his command, and said, "There is an article in the paper saying that Colonel McLane is using his efforts to get possession of the jail for the confinement of these prisoners. I don't see what he has got to do with that." Those are the words he used.

Colonel McLane: The general put me under arrest for interfering with his duties.

The chairman: In what particular?

Colonel McLane: There was a lady called on me and said that she was a Union lady and that she had two sons who were selling waffles up at the corner of King and Royal streets, and she desired to have them allowed to remain there. She said they were driving them off. I was going out at that time in company with the quartermaster. I turned around to one of my men and asked him to go out and see that this lady was not imposed upon. During my absence my adjutant issued an order that these boys should be allowed this privilege. It appeared that the general had previously issued orders that they should not be allowed to sell waffles there. But that I knew nothing at all about. This was one of the charges against me. Another charge was that I had not issued an order to my surgeon to vaccinate the men of my regiment. Now, in fact, I had issued that order; now, I knew that it was a matter of spite on the part of some one, for there was no foundation for the charges, and the general voluntarily withdrew them. I told him that if I had committed any breach of discipline I wanted to be tried and punished; that I did not want to be excused myself any more than I would excuse any of my men. He concluded that I had not and withdrew the charges.

INDEX TO PART III.

WESTERN DEPARTMENT, OR MISSOURI.

MISCELLANEOUS.

www.ingramcontent.com/pod-product-compliance
Lightning Source LLC
LaVergne TN
LVHW021052110826
845150LV00001B/58